Black Writers of America

Black Writers of America

A Comprehensive Anthology

Richard Barksdale
University of Illinois

Keneth Kinnamon
University of Illinois

The Macmillan Company

NEW YORK

Macmillan Publishing Co., Inc.
866 Third Avenue, New York, New York 10022

Collier-Macmillan Canada, Ltd.

Library of Congress catalog card number: 70–163234

PRINTING   1314   YEAR   3456789

ISBN   0-02-306080-8

Acknowledgments

Copyrighted works, listed in the order of appearance, are printed by permission of the following.

Part IV—Reconstruction and Reaction: 1865–1915

W. E. B. Du Bois, "In Black." Reprinted with the permission of the National Association for the Advancement of Colored People. W. E. B. Du Bois, from *The Autobiography of W. E. B. Du Bois*. Reprinted by permission of International Publishers Co., Inc. Copyright © 1968.

William Stanley Braithwaite, "Rhapsody," "Scintilla," "The Watchers," "Sandy Star." Reprinted by permission of Coward, McCann and Geoghegan, Inc. from *Selected Poems* by William Stanley Braithwaite. Copyright 1948 by William Stanley Braithwaite.

"No Mo Cane on Dis Brazis," "Po Laz'us," "Another Man Done Gone," "Shorty George," "John Hardy." Collected, adapted, and arranged by John A. Lomax and Alan Lomax. TRO-© Copyright 1947 Ludlow Music, Inc., New York, New York. Used by permission.

Part V—Renaissance and Radicalism: 1915–1945

James Weldon Johnson, from *The Book of American Negro Poetry*. Excerpted from *Preface* by James Weldon Johnson to *The Book of American Negro Poetry* edited by James Weldon Johnson, copyright 1922 by Harcourt Brace Jovanovich, Inc.;

copyright 1950 by Mrs. Grace Johnson. Reprinted by permission of the publisher. James Weldon Johnson, "Sence You Went Away." From *Saint Peter Relates an Incident* by James Weldon Johnson. Copyright 1913 by G. Recoidi & Company, renewed 1941 by Mrs. James Weldon Johnson. All rights reserved. Reprinted by permission of The Viking Press, Inc. James Weldon Johnson, "Fifty Years (1863–1913)," "O Black and Unknown Bards," "The White Witch," "Fragment." From *Saint Peter Relates an Incident* by James Weldon Johnson. Copyright 1917 by James Weldon Johnson. All rights reserved. Reprinted by permission of The Viking Press, Inc. James Weldon Johnson, "Go Down Death—A Funeral Sermon." From *God's Trombones* by James Weldon Johnson. Copyright 1927 by The Viking Press, Inc., renewed 1955 by Grace Nail Johnson. Reprinted by permission of The Viking Press, Inc.

Claude McKay, "Spring in New Hampshire," "My Mother," "Flame-Heart," "The Tropics in New York," "If We Must Die," "The Lynching," "Like a Strong Tree," "Tiger," "The Desolate City," "America," "Harlem Shadows," "The Harlem Dancer," "The White House," "St. Isaac's Church, Petrograd," "Flower of Love," "A Memory of

June," "Memorial." Reprinted by permission of Twayne Publishers, Inc. Claude McKay, from *Home to Harlem*. From pp. 10–16 in *Home to Harlem* by Claude McKay. Copyright 1928 by Harper & Brothers; renewed 1956 by Hope McKay Virtue. Reprinted by permission of the publishers.

Jean Toomer, from *Cane*. Permission of Liveright, Publisher. Copyright (R) 1951 by Jean Toomer. Jean Toomer, "Blue Meridian." Reprinted from *The New Caravan*, edited by Alfred Kreymborg, Lewis Mumford, and Paul Rosenfeld. By permission of W. W. Norton & Company, Inc. Copyright 1936 by W. W. Norton & Company, Inc. Copyright renewed 1964 by Lewis Mumford.

Langston Hughes, "The Negro Speaks of Rivers," "Mother to Son." Copyright 1926 by Alfred A. Knopf, Inc. and renewed 1954 by Langston Hughes. Reprinted from *Selected Poems,* by Langston Hughes, by permission of the publisher. Langston Hughes, "Jazzonia." Copyright 1926 by Alfred A. Knopf, Inc. and renewed by Langston Hughes. Reprinted from *The Weary Blues,* by Langston Hughes. Reprinted by permission of Alfred A. Knopf, Inc. Langston Hughes, "Dream Variation," "I, Too," "The Weary Blues," "Cross." Copyright 1926 by Alfred A. Knopf, Inc. and renewed 1954 by Langston Hughes. Reprinted from *Selected Poems,* by Langston Hughes, by permission of the publisher. Langston Hughes, "Bound No'th Blues." Copyright 1927 by Alfred A. Knopf, Inc. and renewed 1955 by Langston Hughes. Reprinted from *Selected Poems,* by Langston Hughes, by permission of the publisher. Langston Hughes, "Brass Spittoons." Reprinted by permission of Harold Ober Associates Incorporated. Copyright © 1927 by Langston Hughes. Langston Hughes, "Song for a Dark Girl." Copyright 1926 by Alfred A. Knopf, Inc. and renewed 1955 by Langston Hughes. Reprinted from *Selected Poems,* by Langston Hughes, by permission of the publisher. Langston Hughes, "Sylvester's Dying Bed." Copyright 1942 by Alfred A. Knopf, Inc. Reprinted from *Selected Poems,* by Langston Hughes, by permission of the publisher. Langston Hughes, "Ballad of the Landlord," "Dream Boogie." Reprinted by permission of Harold Ober Associates Incorporated. Copyright © 1951 by Langston Hughes. Langston Hughes, "I've Known Rivers," "Harlem Literati." From *The Big Sea* by Langston Hughes. Copyright 1940 by Langston Hughes. Reprinted by permission of Hill and Wang, Inc. Langston Hughes, "Dear Dr. Butts." Reprinted by permission of Harold Ober Associates Incorporated. Copyright © 1953 by Langston Hughes.

Countee Cullen, "Yet Do I Marvel," "A Brown Girl Dead," "Incident," "Heritage," "For John Keats, Apostle of Beauty," "For Paul Laurence Dunbar," "She of the Dancing Feet Sings," "To John Keats, Poet. At Springtime." From *On These I Stand* by Countee Cullen. Copyright 1925 by Harper & Row, renewed 1953 by Ida M. Cullen. Countee Cullen, "From the Dark Tower," "Threnody for a Brown Girl," "Variations on a Theme," "A Song of Sour Grapes." From *On These I Stand* by Countee

Cullen. Copyright 1927 by Harper & Row, renewed 1955 by Ida M. Cullen. Countee Cullen, "That Bright Chimeric Beast," "Little Sonnet to Little Friends," "Therefore, Adieu," "Nothing Endures," "Black Majesty." From *On These I Stand* by Countee Cullen. Copyright 1929 by Harper & Row, renewed 1957 by Ida M. Cullen. Countee Cullen, "Magnets." From *On These I Stand* by Countee Cullen. Copyright 1935 by Harper & Row, renewed 1963 by Ida M. Cullen. Countee Cullen, "A Negro Mother's Lullaby." From *On These I Stand* by Countee Cullen. Copyright 1947 by Harper & Row, Publishers, Inc. Reprinted by permission of Harper & Row, Publishers, Inc.

Richard Wright, "The Ethics of Living Jim Crow." From *Uncle Tom's Children* (1938) by Richard Wright. Copyright 1937 by Richard Wright. Reprinted by permission of Harper & Row, Publishers, Inc. Richard Wright, "Big Boy Leaves Home." From *Uncle Tom's Children* (1938) by Richard Wright. Copyright 1936 by Richard Wright. Reprinted by permission of Harper & Row, Publishers, Inc.

Marcus Garvey, "Speech Delivered at Liberty Hall N.Y.C. During Second International Convention of Negroes, August 1921," "Speech Delivered at Madison Square Garden, March 1924." Reprinted by permission of Amy Jacques Garvey.

Walter White, "I Investigate Lynchings." Reprinted by permission of Mrs. Walter White and *The American Mercury.*

Rudolph Fisher, "The City of Refuge." Reprinted by permission of *The Atlantic Monthly.*

Eric Walrond, "Subjection." From *Tropic Death* by Eric Walrond. Permission of Liveright, Publishers. Copyright (R) 1954 by Eric Walrond.

Zora Neale Hurston, "The Gilded Six-Bits." Reprinted by permission of Scholastic Magazines, Inc., from *Story,* copyright 1933 by Story Magazine, Inc.

Chester Himes, "Salute to the Passing." Reprinted with permission of the National Urban League, Inc., from *Opportunity: Journal of Negro Life.*

Angelina Grimké, "A Mona Lisa," "Grass Fingers." From *Caroling Dusk* edited by Countee Cullen. Copyright 1927 by Harper & Row, renewed 1955 by Ida M. Cullen. Reprinted by permission of Harper & Row, Publishers, Inc.

Anne Spencer, "Lines to a Nasturtium," "Letter to My Sister." Reprinted by permission of Anne Spencer.

Arna Bontemps, "A Black Man Talks of Reaping," "Reconnaissance," "Nocturne at Bethesda," "Southern Mansion." Reprinted by permission of Harold Ober Associates Incorporated. Copyright 1963 by Arna Bontemps.

Margaret Walker, "For My People." Reprinted from *For My People* by Margaret Walker. Copyright © 1942 by Yale University Press.

Willis Richardson, "The Broken Banjo." Reprinted by permission of Willis Richardson.

Part VI—The Present Generation: 1945–1970

Etheridge Knight, "Sweethearts in a Mulberry Tree."

From *Poems from Prison* by Etheridge Knight © 1968. Reprinted by permission of Broadside Press.

Sonia Sanchez, "Poem at Thirty." From *Homecoming* by Sonia Sanchez © 1969. Reprinted by permission of Broadside Press.

Melvin B. Tolson, "Dark Symphony." Reprinted by permission of Dodd, Mead & Company, Inc. from *Rendezvous with America* by Melvin B. Tolson. Copyright 1944 by Dodd, Mead & Company, Inc. Melvin B. Tolson, from *Harlem Gallery*. Reprinted by permission of Twayne Publishers, Inc.

Robert Hayden, "Frederick Douglass," "Runagate Runagate," "Homage to the Empress of the Blues," "A Ballad of Remembrance," "Tour 5," "Mourning Poem for the Queen of Sunday," "Middle Passage." From *Selected Poems* by Robert Hayden. Copyright © 1966 by Robert Hayden. Reprinted by permission of October House Inc.

Ralph Ellison, "Richard Wright's Blues." Copyright 1945 by Ralph Ellison. Reprinted from *Shadow and Act,* by Ralph Ellison, by permission of Random House, Inc. Ralph Ellison, "And Hickman Arrives.' Reprinted by permission of The World Publishing Company from *The Noble Savage 1* (1960). Copyright © 1960 by Meridian Books, Inc.

Don L. Lee, "Gwendolyn Brooks." From *Don't Cry, Scream* by Don L. Lee. Copyright © 1969. Reprinted by permission of Broadside Press.

Gwendolyn Brooks, "The Mother,' "Of De Witt Williams on His Way to Lincoln Cemetery," "Piano After War," "Mentors." From *Selected Poems* (1963) by Gwendolyn Brooks. Copyright 1945 by Gwendolyn Brooks Blakely. Gwendolyn Brooks, "'Do Not Be Afraid of No,'" "The Children of the Poor." From *Selected Poems* (1963) by Gwendolyn Brooks. Copyright 1949 by Gwendolyn Brooks Blakely. Gwendolyn Brooks, "We Real Cool." From *Selected Poems* (1963) by Gwendolyn Brooks. Copyright © 1959 by Gwendolyn Brooks. Gwendolyn Brooks, "The Chicago *Defender* Sends a Man to Little Rock." From *Selected Poems* (1963) by Gwendolyn Brooks. Copyright © 1960 by Gwendolyn Brooks. Gwendolyn Brooks, "Riders to the Blood-Red Wrath." From *Selected Poems* (1963) by Gwendolyn Brooks. Copyright © 1963 by Gwendolyn Brooks Blakely. Gwendolyn Brooks, "Way-Out Morgan." From *In the Mecca* (1968) by Gwendolyn Brooks. Copyright © 1968 by Gwendolyn Brooks Blakely. Gwendolyn Brooks, "The Wall." From *In the Mecca* (1968) by Gwendolyn Brooks. Copyright © 1967 by Gwendolyn Brooks Blakely. Gwendolyn Brooks, "Loam Norton." From *In the Mecca* (1968) by Gwendolyn Brooks. Copyright © 1968 by Gwendolyn Brooks Blakely. All reprinted by permission of Harper & Row, Publishers, Inc.

James Baldwin, "Everybody's Protest Novel." From *Notes of a Native Son* by James Baldwin. Reprinted by permission of the Beacon Press, copyright © 1949, 1955 by James Baldwin. James Baldwin, "Sonny's Blues." From *Going to Meet the Man* by James Baldwin. Copyright © 1965 James Baldwin. Used by permission of the publisher, The Dial Press.

Imamu Amiri Baraka (LeRoi Jones), "Preface to a Twenty Volume Suicide Note." Copyright © 1961 by LeRoi Jones. Reprinted by permission of Corinth Books. Imamu Amiri Baraka, "*An Agony. As Now.*" Copyright © 1964 by LeRoi Jones. Reprinted by permission of The Sterling Lord Agency. Imamu Amiri Baraka, "A Poem for Black Hearts," "leroy," "Black People!" From *Black Magic Poetry 1961–1967,* copyright © 1969, by LeRoi Jones, reprinted by permission of the publisher, The Bobbs-Merrill Company, Inc. Imamu Amiri Baraka, "The Last Days of the American Empire (Including Some Instructions for Black People)." From *Home: Social Essays by LeRoi Jones.* Reprinted by permission of William Morrow and Company, Inc. Copyright © 1964, 1966 by LeRoi Jones. Imamu Amiri Baraka, "Nationalism Vs. PimpArt." Originally published in the *New York Times,* November 16, 1969, with slight modifications, under the title "To Survive the Reign of the Beasts." Copyright © 1969 by the New York Times Company. Reprinted by permission.

Ann Petry, "Like a Winding Sheet." Reprinted with permission of Crisis Publishing Company, Inc.

William Demby, "The Table of Wishes Come True." Reprinted by permission of Curtis Brown, Ltd. Copyright © 1951 by William Demby.

Paule Marshall, "Barbados." Copyright © 1961 by Paule Marshall.

Ernest J. Gaines, "The Sky Is Gray." Reprinted from *Bloodline* by Ernest J. Gaines. Copyright © 1963, 1964, 1968 by Ernest J. Gaines and used by permission of the publisher, The Dial Press, Inc.

William Melvin Kelley, "The Dentist's Wife." Copyright © 1968 by William Melvin Kelley. Originally appeared in *Playboy* magazine. Reprinted by permission of William Morris Agency, Inc.

Don L. Lee, "Two Poems." From *Black Pride* by Don L. Lee © 1968. Reprinted by permission of Broadside Press.

Sonia Sanchez, "The Final Solution." From *Homecoming* by Sonia Sanchez © 1969. Reprinted by permission of Broadside Press.

Don L. Lee, "Black Sketches," "Nigerian Unity." From *Don't Cry, Scream* by Don L. Lee © 1969. Reprinted by permission of Broadside Press.

Sonia Sanchez, "Black Lovers." From *We a BaddDDD People* by Sonia Sanchez © 1970. Reprinted by permission of Broadside Press.

Etheridge Knight, "The Violent Space," "To Make a Poem in Prison." From *Poems from Prison* by Etheridge Knight © 1968. Reprinted by permission of Broadside Press.

Owen Dodson, "Sorrow Is the Only Faithful One." Reprinted with the permission of Farrar, Straus and Giroux, Inc. from *Powerful Long Ladder* by Owen Dodson, copyright 1946 by Owen Dodson. Owen Dodson, "Yardbird's Skull." Reprinted by permission of Farrar, Straus and Giroux, Inc. and the author.

Dudley Randall, "Booker T. and W. E. B.," "Legacy: My South," "Perspectives." Reprinted by permission of Broadside Press.

Samuel Allen, "A Moment Please," "To Satch," "Nat Turner." Reprinted by permission of Samuel Allen.

Margaret Danner, "Far from Africa: Four Poems." Reprinted by permission of Margaret Danner.

Mari E. Evans, "When in Rome," "Black Jam for Dr. Negro." Reprinted by permission of Mari E. Evans.

Etheridge Knight, "The Idea of Ancestry," "2 Poems for Black Relocation Centers." Reprinted by permission of Broadside Press.

Don L. Lee, "Assassination," "A Poem Looking for a Reader." Reprinted by permission of Broadside Press.

Sonia Sanchez, "Small Comment." From *Homecoming* by Sonia Sanchez © 1969. Reprinted by permission of Broadside Press.

Nikki Giovanni, "For Saundra." Reprinted by permission of Broadside Press.

Carlton W. Molette II and Barbara Molette, "Rosalee Pritchett." Reprinted by permission of Carlton and Barbara Molette. Copyright © 1970 by Carlton and Barbara Molette. *Caution:* Professionals and amateurs are hereby warned that "Rosalee Pritchett," being fully protected by copyright, is subject to a royalty. All rights, including professional, amateur, motion picture, lecturing, public reading, radio and television, and the rights of translation into foreign languages, are strictly reserved. Particular emphasis is laid on the question of readings, permission for which must be secured in writing. No amateur performance of the play may be given without obtaining in advance the written permission of the authors. All inquiries should be addressed to Carlton and Barbara Molette, 3775 Village Dr., S.W., Atlanta, Georgia 30331. "Rosalee Pritchett" was first produced by the Spelman College Department of Drama and the Morehouse-Spelman Players in Atlanta, Georgia, on March 23, 1970. The play was directed by Carlton Molette; designed by Luis Maza; costumes and make-up by Barbara Molette; with Glenda Stevens in the title role. The play was produced in New York (on a double bill with "Perry's Mission" by Clarence Young III) by the Negro Ensemble Company at the St. Marks Playhouse on January 12, 1971. "Rosalee Pritchett" was directed by Shauneille Perry; setting by Edward Burbridge; lighting by Ernest Baxter; costumes by Monica Myrie; photography by Bert Andrews; with the following cast: Rosalee (Rose) Pritchett, Frances Foster; Doretha Ellen (Dorry) Sanders, Roxie Roker; Maybelle (Belle) Johnson, Esther Rolle; Dolly Mae (Doll) Anderson, Clarice Taylor; Robert Barron, Adolph Caesar; Augustin (Gus) Lowe; Arthur French; Donald King, William Jay; Wilbur Wittmer, David Downing; Thelma Franklin, Anita Wilson.

Nathan Hare, "The Challenge of a Black Scholar." Reprinted by permission of Nathan Hare.

Martin Luther King, Jr., from *Stride Toward Freedom*. "The Day of Days, December 5" and "Where Do We Go from Here" from *Stride Toward Freedom* by Martin Luther King, Jr. Copyright © 1958 by Martin Luther King, Jr. Reprinted by permission of Harper & Row, Publishers, Inc. Martin Luther King, Jr., "Letter from Birmingham Jail"—April 16, 1963—from *Why We Can't Wait* by Martin Luther King, Jr. Copyright © 1963 by Martin Luther King, Jr. Reprinted by permission of Harper & Row, Publishers, Inc. Martin Luther King, Jr., "I Have a Dream." Reprinted by permission of Joan Daves. Copyright © 1963 by Martin Luther King, Jr.

Malcolm X, from *The Autobiography of Malcolm X*. Reprinted by permission of Grove Press, Inc. Copyright © 1964 by Alex Haley and Malcolm X. Copyright © 1965 by Alex Haley and Betty Shabazz.

Eldridge Cleaver, "To All Black Women, From All Black Men." From *Soul on Ice* by Eldridge Cleaver. Copyright © 1968 by Eldridge Cleaver. Used with permission of McGraw-Hill Book Company and Jonathan Cape Ltd.

To Our Wives and Children

To Our Wives and Families

Preface

This book is a comprehensive collection of Afro-American literature from the eighteenth-century beginnings to the present time. Recognizing the limitations of a narrowly esthetic approach to a body of writing of great social import, we have provided generous selections of auto-biographies, essays, speeches, letters, political pamphlets, histories, journals, and folk literature as well as poems, plays, and stories. Our criteria for inclusion were both artistic and social; indeed, facile or rigid separation of the two seems to us misguided. For this reason, our anthology serves as an introduction not only to the literature of Black people in America, but to their intellectual and social history as well.

The introductions to the six chronological periods examine the literature and relate it closely to the life and circumstances out of which it grew. Headnotes provide critical assessments as well as biographical facts. The extensive suggestions for further reading to be found at the end of each headnote, together with the Bibliography at the end of the book, will enable the reader, whether freshman or mature scholar, to pursue his individual interests.

The scope and diversity of the selections make this anthology suitable to a variety of approaches. It is inclusive enough to satisfy the needs of a two-semester survey course, but its selections from nineteen major Black writers alone could constitute a semester's or a quarter's work. Organization by topic, theme, or genre is also feasible.

Wherever feasible we have presented complete works rather than fragments. The very few exceptions to this practice include extracts from novels by Claude McKay and Ralph Ellison. However, both of these can be considered complete works in themselves, the selection from Ellison having been separately published, indeed, while the whole work was in progress. In any case, the teacher may wish to supplement our text with longer works by Douglass, Du Bois, Wright, Ellison, and others.

It is also important to state here the editorial policy that we have followed in this anthology. Whenever an author uses a spelling or employs a grammatical construction at variance with current practice, we have not changed that author's spelling or grammar. Our purpose has been to preserve each author's text in its original version except when there were obvious typographical errors.

Finally, we wish to acknowledge our indebtedness to the many people who helped, directly or indirectly, to give this work the proper direction and impetus. First, we are grateful to Scott Bridge, who implemented the idea for an anthology of this scope and dimension. We have found particularly helpful the pioneering scholarship of Benjamin Brawley, Alain Locke, Vernon Loggins, Sterling Brown, Saunders Redding, Hugh Gloster, Robert Bone, and Jean Wagner. For advice and help of various kinds, we are grateful to the following colleagues at the University of Illinois: D. Alexander Boyd, Archie Green, and Robert McColley. To Mrs. Gaynelle Barksdale, Librarian of Trevor Arnett Library of Atlanta University, and to Mrs. Lillian Lewis, Supervisor of the Negro Collection of Trevor Arnett Library, go our thanks for assistance. Lyle Glazier of the State University of New York, Buffalo, made helpful suggestions. We also thank Miss Willie Jackson, Miss JoAnne Bayneum, and Mrs. Elsie H. Jones for assistance with selected materials. Last, we wish to thank our wives, Mildred Barksdale and Paquita Kinnamon, for their patient understanding and encouragement during the many months in which this book has been in preparation.

R. B.
K. K.

Contents

Religion

Folk Literature

Part III The Black Man in the Civil War: 1861–1865

The Black Man in Battle

Part V Renaissance and Radicalism: 1915–1945 467

The Major Writers

Oratory and Essays

Fiction

Poetry

Drama

Folk Literature

Part VI The Present Generation: Since 1945

The Major Writers

Fiction

Poetry

Drama

Essay

Racial Spokesmen

Folk Literature

PART I

The Eighteenth-Century Beginnings

Black people have been present in the Western Hemisphere for more than four and a half centuries, virtually as long as white people have. After Spain permitted Blacks to enter the New World in 1501, most of the major expeditions of the conquistadors included them. The most famous of these early Black explorers, Estevanico, penetrated deep into what is now the southwestern states of Arizona and New Mexico. Shortly afterward, Spain's great rival, Portugal, introduced the first few Black slaves into Brazil, a number that swelled to more than half the population of that colony by the end of the eighteenth century. In French America, Blacks helped to explore and settle the Mississippi River Valley in the seventeenth and eighteenth centuries. One of these was Jean Baptiste Point du Sable, who established in 1779 a trading post on the southern shore of Lake Michigan, a settlement that eventually became the city of Chicago.

Thus the famous "twenty Negars" brought by a Dutch vessel to Jamestown in 1619 (quite literally "before the *Mayflower*")—the first Black people in the first British colony on the mainland of North America —were part of a larger Black presence that by the end of the seventeenth century could be found in the Canadian forests, in the Mississippi River Valley, in the West Indies, in Mexico and Central America, and in all the colonies of South America, as well as on the Atlantic Seaboard of North

1

America. However diverse in culture, language, or condition, these Black people shared two common characteristics: African origin and subordination to white people.

The circumstance of slavery is crucial to an understanding of early Afro-American literature in two ways. First, slavery had the negative effect of divesting Africans of a substantial portion of their own culture. Though the extent of survivals of African culture in the New World is a matter of considerable scholarly dispute, it is clear that whatever literature survived the traumatic experiences of enslavement, the middle passage on crowded slave ships, and the brutal oppression and forced labor in America was oral in nature, not written. Indeed, the African literary tradition was mainly oral. When Afro-Americans began to write in the eighteenth century, their language and literary models were English, not African, even though the two most important of these writers, Phillis Wheatley and Olaudah Equiano, were African by birth.

Not only did the agents of slavery attempt, often quite systematically, to obliterate the sense of culture and personality out of which literature usually grows, but slavery by its very nature as an economic institution largely denied Blacks the opportunity and the occasion to create written literature. The vast majority of both slaves and free Blacks in colonial and revolutionary America were illiterate, prevented by custom and by expediency (later by law) from learning even the barest rudiments. The old Greco-Roman tradition of the erudite slave was never followed in British America. After all, the rationale went, Blacks were to supply physical labor under the system of slavery; their white masters would contribute whatever mental exertion was required. With education monopolized by whites, it is not surprising that Black literature in the early period is sparse. The wonder, rather, is that anything got written at all.

Two related cultural developments in the British colonies help to explain the remarkable emergence of the earliest voices of Black literature in English. These were the religious fervor of the Great Awakening and related movements, especially American Wesleyanism, that swept the land in the middle third of the eighteenth century and the revolutionary ferment in colonial political life that quickly followed. Both of the two early Black poets of note, Jupiter Hammon and Phillis Wheatley, were deeply influenced by evangelical Methodism, their first published poems being "An Evening Thought: Salvation by Christ with Penetential Cries" and "On the Death of the Rev. Mr. George Whitefield," respectively. In the case of the two most significant early writers of prose, Olaudah Equiano and Benjamin Banneker, the impulse to creativity came partly from the radical implications of the American Revolution, particularly those pertaining to liberty and equality. For the first century and a half of Afro-American literature, these two themes—the appeal of Christianity and the quest for liberty and equality—were paramount, and the latter is still central today. In this light the first Black writers acquire a prophetic quality. Their work can be viewed both as an intrinsic part of the general American literary experience and as the pioneering efforts of a specifically Black literary tradition.

The animating spirit of the American Revolution was hostile to slavery. The rights of life and liberty and the concept of equality were chiefly designed by and for whites, it is true, but many revolutionary leaders recognized their incompatibility with the institution of Black chattel slavery. One of the specific grievances of some of the rebellious colonists against King George III was his support of the international slave trade, by which, in the words of Thomas Jefferson, "He has waged cruel war against human nature itself, violating its most sacred rights of life and liberty in the persons of a distant people who never offended him, captivating and carrying them into slavery in another hemisphere, or to incur miserable death in their transportation thither." Convinced of the inherent inferiority of Black people and unwilling to suppress the internal slave trade, Jefferson nevertheless consistently opposed slavery, though, it must be added, he could never bring himself to make the financial sacrifice of manumitting his own slaves.

That other great architect of early American institutions, Benjamin Franklin, likewise opposed slavery. In the humanitarian tradition of his contemporaries John Woolman and Anthony Benezet, Franklin was the first president of the first abolition society in America, organized in Philadelphia in 1775. He supported both the abolition of slavery and the rehabilitation of its victims. At the end of his long life, he petitioned the first American Congress in 1790 "to use all justifiable endeavors to loosen the bonds of slavery, and promote a general enjoyment of the blessings of freedom." On another occasion he suggested that "attention to emancipated blacks" be made public policy as well as a major goal of private philanthropy. In addition to such giants as Franklin and Jefferson, other leaders of late eighteenth-century American thought and action spoke out against slavery: Samuel Hopkins, Ezra Stiles, Jeremy Belknap, Thomas Paine, Benjamin Rush, George Mason, John Jay, Alexander Hamilton, St. George Tucker, William Cushing, Gouverneur Morris, Roger Sherman, James Wilson, Noah Webster, Theodore Dwight.

Nor was the opposition to slavery merely verbal. At the outbreak of the Revolution, slavery existed in all thirteen colonies. Twenty-five years later, all the states, including even Georgia and South Carolina, had legally abolished the international slave trade, and the federal government followed in 1807. By the beginning of the nineteenth century, slavery in most Northern states was on the way out, persisting a few years longer in New York and New Jersey. In 1787 the Continental Congress prohibited slavery in the area of the Northwest Ordinance. There had been considerable antislavery sentiment, as well, just below the Mason-Dixon line in Maryland, Delaware, and Virginia.

Why, then, did the forces of reaction and inhumanity come to prevail in the first half of the nineteenth century? The collapse of the revolutionary spirit in the early republic, its tragic failure to resolve the paradox of racism and slavery in the young "democracy," is an exceedingly complex subject. Externally, it can be viewed as a series of moral compromises by temporizing politicians whose commitment to abstract justice was not firm enough to resist sectional and economic interests. The War of Independence itself was by no means a social revolution in the modern sense, for in the deliberations of the Constitutional Convention the forces of property and wealth largely defeated the radical threat and consolidated their political power. The result was a Constitution that recognized the institution of slavery, though hypocritically refusing to use the word. For purposes of taxation and representation, slaves were considered three fifths of a person. Under pressure of threats of disunion by South Carolina and Georgia, the international slave trade was granted a twenty-year lease on life in Article I, Section 9. Even the question of the return of fugitive slaves, which was to prove so catalytic in the mid-nineteenth century, was decided in favor of the South by Article IV, Section 2. As John Hope Franklin has observed, "When the delegates to the Constitutional Convention returned to their homes in September, 1787, they could look back on three months of political and economic wire-pulling that was to check effectively the trend toward social upheaval. Perhaps in no area had there been greater success than in the matter of checking the anti-slavery movement." Those who advocated repression of Blacks rather than liberation felt confirmed in their policy during the next few years by the successful revolution of the "Black Jacobins" of St. Domingue, who proudly proclaimed the new republic of Haiti on January 1, 1804. Liberty and independence were all very well for whites, but that Blacks should have them was unthinkable. Moreover, the invention of the cotton gin in 1793 proved to be the most decisive event of the Industrial Revolution as far as Blacks were concerned, for by stimulating the rapid development of cotton as the staple Southern crop, it greatly increased the economic incentive for maintaining the institution of slavery.

Underlying the betrayal of Black hopes of participation in the fruits of the American Revolution was white racism, that whole complex of attitudes and motivations—psychosexual as well as economic—that Winthrop D. Jordan has recently explored at length for the period 1550–1812 in *White Over Black*.* Indeed, white racism, in its myriad forms, has been the constant factor in American history with which Black writers and Black people have had to contend, though often it has been disguised under such evasive euphemisms as "the peculiar institution" or "the Negro problem" or "law and order."

---

* The practice in this book is to use italics for the title of any work separately published, whether novel, play, long poem, newspaper, speech, or pamphlet. Titles for the following are quoted in the text and are merely roman in the selection titles: unpublished works and works published in a magazine, newspaper, anthology, or collection.

The Major Writers

Olaudah Equiano (1745–1797)

Few men in the eighteenth century lived a life more varied and adventurous than that of Olaudah Equiano (or Ekwuano), known in later life as Gustavus Vassa (or Vasa). An Ibo, Equiano was born east of the Niger in what is now south-central Nigeria. His account of Ibo life and culture in the first chapter of his autobiography, *The Interesting Narrative of the Life of Olaudah Equiano, or Gustavus Vassa, the African* (1789), is invaluable as one of the first descriptions of an African society by an African. Many of the customs and beliefs recorded by Equiano still prevail among the Ibo people. His story of his kidnapping at the age of eleven, his overland travel to the coast, his being sold into slavery to strange white creatures (or spirits), and the horrors of his transportation to Barbados in the filthy hold of a slave ship, told in the second chapter, recapitulates not only a personal experience but that of millions of his fellow West Africans over a period of four centuries.

From Barbados, Equiano was taken to Virginia, where he was bought by a British naval officer engaged in international commerce. During the Seven Years' War, he served with his master in the waters of the Maritime Provinces of Canada, where he met "the good and gallant General Wolfe," who once saved him from "a flogging for fighting with a young gentleman." After returning to England, he next served in the Mediterranean under Admiral Boscawen, and later, in 1761, he participated in a naval campaign off the coast of France. "I longed to engage in new adventures, and see fresh wonders," Equiano wrote enthusiastically of this period of his life. Expecting to be freed for his good service in the war, he was instead sold by his master to the captain of a ship bound for the West Indies.

In Montserrat he was sold to Robert King of Philadelphia, a Quaker merchant engaged in the rum and sugar trade. During his three years in the West Indies, Equiano became thoroughly familiar with the atrocious general conditions of slave life in these islands, which he denounces so vigorously in the fifth chapter of the *Narrative*. His own situation was much more favorable, however, and after further adventures and voyages to Georgia and South Carolina, he was able to purchase his freedom from King on July 11, 1766, after which he worked for wages as a seaman on one of his former master's ships.

Before he finally settled down in England in 1777, Equiano's further experiences included a shipwreck and a fire at sea, lessons on the French horn, voyages to Turkey, Italy, Portugal, Spain, and elsewhere, an expedition to the Arctic, conversion to Methodism (an event that he recorded poetically), and a stay of six months in Central America among the Miskito Indians. All the while he seems to have harbored the hope of returning to Africa some day, for in 1779 he petitioned unsuccessfully to the Bishop of London to be appointed a missionary to that continent, and eight years later he was named "Commissary of Provisions and Stores for the Black Poor Going to Sierra Leone." When he complained of white mismanagement and dishonesty in the preparations for this colonization venture, he was dismissed from his position, but his fears were realized when the expedition failed. Equiano himself never fulfilled his dream of returning to Africa.

After the publication of the *Narrative* in 1789, Equiano traveled for several years in England and Northern Ireland selling his immensely popular book. Little is known of his last years, but he married an Englishwoman in 1792, had at least one child (born in 1793), and died in London on March 31, 1797.

During the last twenty years of his life, Equiano's chief interest was the cause of abolition, to which the *Narrative* was his greatest contribution. He maintained friendships with such white abolitionists as Granville Sharp, James Edward Oglethorpe, Thomas Hardy, and Peter Peckard, as well as with another expatriated West African, Ottobah Cugoano, author of *Thoughts and Sentiments on the Evil of Slavery* (1787). In 1783 he appealed to Sharp concerning the *Zong* case, in which more than 130 slaves were thrown from a British ship into the sea in order to collect on cargo insurance. In 1788, as he notes in the last chapter of his autobiography, he petitioned Queen Charlotte herself on behalf of "millions of my African countrymen, who groan under the lash of tyranny in the West Indies." One of his friends, Thomas Digges, said that Equiano "was a principal instrument in bringing about the motion for a repeal of the Slave-act," though repeal was not finally achieved until long after his death.

Equiano's *Narrative* is the first great Black autobiography, a genre to which Frederick Douglass, Booker T. Washington, W. E. B. Du Bois, James Weldon Johnson, Richard Wright, Claude Brown, and others were to contribute significantly. Equiano has been compared to John Bunyan, Daniel Defoe, and Jonathan Swift, but perhaps a more apposite comparison is to Benjamin Franklin as an autobiographer. Like Franklin, Equiano wrote vivid, flowing narrative in a plain style, enlivened by a sharp eye for detail, a comic and sometimes ironic self-awareness, and an insatiable curiosity. But Equiano is above all himself—resourceful, adaptable, perceptive, ambitious, but never forgetful of his enslaved brothers or his African identity. In the third chapter of his *Narrative,* he recalls his then naïve attraction to books: "I had often seen my master and Dick [a young white American friend and shipmate] employed in reading; and I had a great curiosity to talk to the books as I thought they did, and so to learn how all things had a beginning. For that purpose I have often taken up a book, and have talked to it, and then put my ears to it, when alone, in hopes it would answer me; and I have been very much concerned when I found it remained silent." Not only did Olaudah Equiano learn to read, to make books speak to him, but he learned to write a book that would speak to others, a book whose voice, while very much his own, was the collective voice of eighteenth-century Black people in contact with whites.

The Interesting Narrative of the Life of Olaudah Equiano, or Gustavus Vassa, the African went through nine editions before the author's death and ten editions afterward, as well as two abridged versions. Of the recent editions, the most easily available is in *Great Slave Narratives* (1969), edited by Arna Bontemps.

The foremost authority on Equiano is Paul Edwards, whose introductions to his abridged edition of the *Narrative* (1967) and his two-volume facsimile reprint of the first edition (1969) are essential reading for the serious student. G. I. Jones provides useful ethnographic information in his introduction to selections from Equiano in *Africa Remembered: Narratives by West Africans from the Era of the Slave Trade* (1967), edited by Philip D. Curtin. In *The Negro Author* (1931), Vernon Loggins gives a highly favorable assessment of the *Narrative* as literature, though he overemphasizes Equiano's naïveté. See also Marion L. Starkey, *Striving to Make It My Home: The Story of Americans from Africa* (1964).

from *The Interesting Narrative of the Life of Olaudah Equiano, or Gustavus Vassa, the African*

Chapter 1

The author's account of his country, and their manners and customs—Administration of justice—Embrenche—Marriage ceremony, and public entertainments—Mode of living—Dress—Manufactures—Buildings—Commerce—Agriculture—War and religion—Superstition of the natives—Funeral ceremonies of the priests or magicians—Curious mode of discovering poison—Some hints concerning the origin of the author's countrymen, with the opinions of different writers on that subject.

I believe it is difficult for those who publish their own memoirs to escape the imputation of vanity; nor is this the only disadvantage under which they labor: it is also their misfortune that what is uncommon is rarely, if ever, believed, and what is obvious we are apt to turn from with disgust, and to charge the writer with impertinence. People generally think those memoirs only worthy to be read or remembered which abound in great or striking events, those, in short, which in a high degree excite either admiration or pity; all others they consign to contempt and oblivion. It is therefore, I confess, not a little hazardous in a private and obscure individual, and a stranger too, thus to solicit the indulgent attention of the public, especially when I own I offer here the history of neither a saint, a hero, nor a tyrant. I believe there are few events in my life which have not happened to many; it is true the incidents of it are numerous, and, did I consider myself an European, I might say my sufferings were great; but when I compare my lot with that of most of my countrymen, I regard myself as a *particular favorite of heaven*, and acknowledge the mercies of Providence in every occurrence of my life. If, then, the following narrative does not appear sufficiently interesting to engage general attention, let my motive be some excuse for its publication. I am not so foolishly vain as to expect from it either immortality or literary reputation. If it affords any satisfaction to my numerous friends, at whose request it has been written, or in the smallest degree promotes the interests of humanity, the ends for which it was undertaken will be fully attained, and every wish of my heart gratified. Let it therefore be remembered, that, in wishing to avoid censure, I do not aspire to praise.

That part of Africa, known by the name of Guinea, to which the trade for slaves is carried on, extends along the coast above 3400 miles, from Senegal to Angola, and includes a variety of kingdoms. Of these the most considerable is the kingdom of Benin, both as to extent and wealth, the richness and cultivation of the soil, the power of its king, and the number and warlike disposition of the inhabitants. It is situated nearly under the line, and extends along the coast about 170 miles, but runs back into the interior part of Africa to a distance hitherto, I believe, unexplored by any traveller, and seems only terminated at length by the empire of Abyssinia, near 1500 miles from its beginning. This kingdom is divided into many provinces or districts, in one of the most remote and fertile of which, I was born, in the year 1745, situated in a charming fruitful vale, named Essaka. The distance of this province from the capital of Benin and the sea coast must be very considerable, for I had never heard of white men or Europeans, nor of the sea; and our subjection to the king of Benin was little more than nominal, for every transaction of the government, as far as my slender observation extended, was conducted by the chief or elders of the place. The manners and government of a people who have little commerce with other countries are generally very simple, and the history of what passes in one family or village may serve as a specimen of the whole nation. My father was one of those elders or chiefs I have spoken of, and was styled Embrenche, a term, as I remember, importing the highest distinction, and signifying in our language a *mark* of grandeur. This mark is conferred on the person

entitled to it, by cutting the skin across at the top of the forehead, and drawing it down to the eyebrows; and while it is in this situation applying a warm hand, and rubbing it until it shrinks up into a thick *weal* across the lower part of the forehead. Most of the judges and senators were thus marked; my father had long borne it; I had seen it conferred on one of my brothers, and I also was *destined* to receive it by my parents. Those Embrenche, or chief men, decided disputes and punished crimes, for which purpose they always assembled together. The proceedings were generally short, and in most cases the law of retaliation prevailed. I remember a man was brought before my father, and the other judges, for kidnapping a boy; and, although he was the son of a chief or senator, he was condemned to make recompense by a man or woman slave. Adultery, however, was sometimes punished with slavery or death, a punishment which I believe is inflicted on it throughout most of the nations of Africa,[1] so sacred among them is the honor of the marriage bed, and so jealous are they of the fidelity of their wives. Of this I recollect an instance—a woman was convicted before the judges of adultery, and delivered over, as the custom was, to her husband, to be punished. Accordingly he determined to put her to death; but it being found, just before her execution, that she had an infant at her breast, and no woman being prevailed on to perform the part of a nurse, she was spared on account of the child. The men, however, do not preserve the same constancy to their wives which they expect from them; for they indulge in a plurality, though seldom in more than two. Their mode of marriage is thus—both parties are usually betrothed when young by their parents (though I have known the males to betroth themselves). On this occasion a feast is prepared, and the bride and bridegroom stand up in the midst of all their friends, who are assembled for the purpose, while he declares she is henceforth to be looked upon as his wife, and that no other person is to pay any addresses to her. This is also immediately proclaimed in the vicinity, on which the bride retires from the assembly. Some time after, she is brought home to her husband, and then another feast is made, to which the relations of both parties are invited; her parents then deliver her to the bridegroom, accompanied with a number of blessings, and at the same time they tie round her waist a cotton

[1] See Benezet's "Account of Guinea," throughout.

string of the thickness of a goosequill, which none but married women are permitted to wear; she is now considered as completely his wife; and at this time the dowry is given to the new married pair, which generally consists of portions of land, slaves, and cattle, household goods, and implements of husbandry. These are offered by the friends of both parties; besides which the parents of the bridegroom present gifts to those of the bride, whose property she is looked upon before marriage; but after it she is esteemed the sole property of her husband. The ceremony being now ended, the festival begins, which is celebrated with bonfires and loud acclamations of joy, accompanied with music and dancing.

We are almost a nation of dancers, musicians, and poets. Thus every great event, such as a triumphant return from battle or other cause of public rejoicing, is celebrated in public dances, which are accompanied with songs and music suited to the occasion. The assembly is separated into four divisions, which dance either apart or in succession, and each with a character peculiar to itself. The first division contains the married men, who in their dances frequently exhibit feats of arms and the representation of a battle. To these succeed the married women, who dance in the second division. The young men occupy the third, and the maidens the fourth. Each represents some interesting scene of real life, such as a great achievement, domestic employment, a pathetic story, or some rural sport; and as the subject is generally founded on some recent event, it is therefore ever new. This gives our dances a spirit and variety which I have scarcely seen elsewhere.[2] We have many musical instruments, particularly drums of different kinds, a piece of music which resembles a guitar, and another much like a stickado. These last are chiefly used by betrothed virgins, who play on them on all grand festivals.

As our manners are simple, our luxuries are few. The dress of both sexes is nearly the same. It generally consists of a long piece of calico, or muslin, wrapped loosely round the body, somewhat in the form of a highland plaid. This is usually dyed blue, which is our favorite color. It is extracted from a berry, and is brighter and richer than any I have seen in Europe. Besides this, our women of distinction wear golden ornaments, which they dispose with some profusion on their arms and legs. When our women are not employed with the men in tillage, their usual occupation is spinning and weaving cotton, which they afterwards dye, and make into garments. They also manufacture earthen vessels, of which we have many kinds. Among the rest, tobacco pipes, made after the same fashion, and used in the same manner, as those in Turkey.[3]

Our manner of living is entirely plain; for as yet the natives are unacquainted with those refinements in cookery which debauch the taste; bullocks, goats, and poultry supply the greatest part of their food. (These constitute likewise the principal wealth of the country, and the chief articles of its commerce.) The flesh is usually stewed in a pan; to make it savory we sometimes use pepper, and other spices, and we have salt made of wood ashes. Our vegetables are mostly plantains, eadas, yams, beans, and Indian corn. The head of the family usually eats alone; his wives and slaves have also their separate tables. Before we taste food we always wash our hands; indeed, our cleanliness on all occasions is extreme, but on this it is an indispensable ceremony. After washing, libation is made, by pouring out a small portion of the drink on the floor, and tossing a small quantity of the food in a certain place, for the spirits of departed relations, which the natives suppose to preside over their conduct and guard them from evil. They are totally unacquainted with strong or spirituous liquors; and their principal beverage is palm wine. This is got from a tree of that name, by tapping it at the top and fastening a large gourd to it; and sometimes one tree will yield three or four gallons in a night. When just drawn it is of a most delicious sweetness; but in a few days it acquires a tartish and more spirituous flavor, though I never saw anyone intoxicated by it. The same tree also produces nuts and oil. Our principal luxury is in perfumes: one sort of these is an odoriferous wood of delicious fragrance, the other a kind of earth, a small portion of which thrown into the fire diffuses a most powerful odor.[4] We beat this wood into powder, and mix it with palm oil,

---

[2] When I was in Smyrna I have frequently seen the Greeks dance after this manner.

[3] The bowl is earthen, curiously figured, to which a long reed is fixed as a tube. This tube is sometimes so long as to be borne by one, and frequently out of grandeur, two boys.

[4] When I was in Smyrna I saw the same kind of earth, and brought some of it with me to England; it resembles musk in strength, but is more delicious in scent, and is not unlike the smell of a rose.

with which both men and women perfume themselves.

In our buildings we study convenience rather than ornament. Each master of a family has a large square piece of ground, surrounded with a moat or fence, or enclosed with a wall made of red earth tempered, which, when dry, is as hard as brick. Within this are his houses to accommodate his family and slaves, which, if numerous, frequently present the appearance of a village. In the middle, stands the principal building, appropriated to the sole use of the master and consisting of two apartments; in one of which he sits in the day with his family, the other is left apart for the reception of his friends. He has besides these a distinct apartment in which he sleeps, together with his male children. On each side are the apartments of his wives, who have also their separate day and night houses. The habitations of the slaves and their families are distributed throughout the rest of the enclosure. These houses never exceed one story in height; they are always built of wood, or stakes driven into the ground, crossed with wattles, and neatly plastered within and without. The roof is thatched with reeds. Our day houses are left open at the sides; but those in which we sleep are always covered, and plastered in the inside, with a composition mixed with cow-dung, to keep off the different insects, which annoy us during the night. The walls and floors also of these are generally covered with mats. Our beds consist of a platform, raised three or four feet from the ground, on which are laid skins, and different parts of a spongy tree, called plantain. Our covering is calico or muslin, the same as our dress. The usual seats are a few logs of wood; but we have benches, which are generally perfumed to accommodate strangers: these compose the greater part of our household furniture. Houses so constructed and furnished require but little skill to erect them. Every man is a sufficient architect for the purpose. The whole neighborhood afford their unanimous assistance in building them, and in return receive and expect no other recompense than a feast.

As we live in a country where nature is prodigal of her favors, our wants are few and easily supplied; of course we have few manufactures. They consist for the most part of calicoes, earthen ware, ornaments, and instruments of war and husbandry. But these make no part of our commerce, the principal articles of which, as I have observed, are provisions. In such a state, money is of little use; however, we have some small pieces of coin, if I may call them such. They are made something like an anchor, but I do not remember either their value or denomination. We have also markets, at which I have been frequently with my mother. These are sometimes visited by stout mahogany-colored men from the south-west of us: we call them *Oye-Eboe*, which term signifies red men living at a distance. They generally bring us fire-arms, gun-powder, hats, beads, and dried fish. The last we esteemed a great rarity, as our waters were only brooks and springs. These articles they barter with us for odoriferous woods and earth, and our salt of wood ashes. They always carry slaves through our land; but the strictest account is exacted of their manner of procuring them before they are suffered to pass. Sometimes, indeed, we sold slaves to them, but they were only prisoners of war, or such among us as had been convicted of kidnapping, or adultery, and some other crimes, which we esteemed heinous. This practice of kidnapping induces me to think, that, notwithstanding all our strictness, their principal business among us was to trepan our people. I remember too, they carried great sacks along with them, which not long after, I had an opportunity of fatally seeing applied to that infamous purpose.

Our land is uncommonly rich and fruitful, and produces all kinds of vegetables in great abundance. We have plenty of Indian corn, and vast quantities of cotton and tobacco. Our pine-apples grow without culture; they are about the size of the largest sugar-loaf, and finely flavored. We have also spices of different kinds, particularly pepper, and a variety of delicious fruits which I have never seen in Europe, together with gums of various kinds, and honey in abundance. All our industry is exerted to improve these blessings of nature. Agriculture is our chief employment; and everyone, even the children and women, are engaged in it. Thus we are all habituated to labor from our earliest years. Everyone contributes something to the common stock; and, as we are unacquainted with idleness, we have no beggars. The benefits of such a mode of living are obvious. The West India planters prefer the slaves of Benin or Eboe to those of any other part of Guinea, for their hardiness, intelligence, integrity, and zeal. Those benefits are felt by us in the general healthiness of the people, and in their vigor and activity; I might have added, too, in their comeliness. Deformity is indeed unknown amongst us, I mean that of shape. Numbers of the natives of Eboe now in London might be brought in support of this assertion: for, in regard to complexion, ideas of beauty are wholly relative. I remember while in Africa to have seen three Negro children who were tawny, and another quite white, who were universally regarded by myself, and the natives in general, as far as related to their complexions, as deformed. Our women, too, were, in my eye at least, uncommonly graceful, alert, and modest to a degree of bashfulness; nor do I remember to have heard of an instance of incontinence amongst them before marriage. They are also remarkably cheerful. Indeed, cheerfulness and affability are two of the leading characteristics of our nation.

Our tillage is exercised in a large plain or common, some hour's walk from our dwellings, and all the neighbors resort thither in a body. They use no beasts of husbandry; and their only instruments are hoes, axes, shovels, and beaks, or pointed iron, to dig with. Sometimes we are visited by locusts, which come in large clouds, so as to darken the air, and destroy our harvest. This, however, happens rarely, but when it does, a famine is produced by it. I remember an instance or two wherein this happened. This common is often the theatre of war; and therefore when our people go out to till their land, they not only go in a body, but generally take their arms with them for fear of a surprise; and when they apprehend an invasion, they guard the avenues to their dwellings, by driving sticks into the ground, which are so sharp at one end as to pierce the foot, and are generally dipt in poison. From what I can recollect of these battles, they appear to have been irruptions of one little state or district on the other, to obtain prisoners or booty. Perhaps they were incited to this by those traders who brought the European goods I mentioned, amongst us. Such a mode of obtaining slaves in Africa is common; and I believe more are procured this way, and by kidnapping, than any other.[5] When a trader wants slaves, he applies to a chief for them, and tempts him with his wares. It is not extraordinary, if on this occasion he yields to the temptation with as little firmness, and accepts the price of his fellow creature's liberty, with as little reluctance as the enlightened merchant. Accordingly he falls on his neighbors,

[5] See Benezet's "Account of Africa," throughout.

and a desperate battle ensues. If he prevails and takes prisoners, he gratifies his avarice by selling them; but, if his party be vanquished, and he falls into the hands of the enemy, he is put to death; for, as he has been known to foment their quarrels, it is thought dangerous to let him survive, and no ransom can save him, though all other prisoners may be redeemed. We have fire-arms, bows and arrows, broad two-edged swords and javelins; we have shields also which cover a man from head to foot. All are taught the use of these weapons; even our women are warriors, and march boldly out to fight along with the men. Our whole district is a kind of militia: on a certain signal given, such as the firing of a gun at night, they all rise in arms and rush upon their enemy. It is perhaps something remarkable, that when our people march to the field a red flag or banner is borne before them. I was once a witness to a battle in our common. We had been all at work in it one day as usual, when our people were suddenly attacked. I climbed a tree at some distance, from which I beheld the fight. There were many women as well as men on both sides; among others my mother was there, and armed with a broad sword. After fighting for a considerable time with great fury, and many had been killed, our people obtained the victory, and took their enemy's Chief a prisoner. He was carried off in great triumph, and, though he offered a large ransom for his life, he was put to death. A virgin of note among our enemies had been slain in the battle, and her arm was exposed in our market-place, where our trophies were always exhibited. The spoils were divided according to the merit of the warriors. Those prisoners which were not sold or redeemed, we kept as slaves; but how different was their condition from that of the slaves in the West Indies! With us, they do no more work than other members of the community, even their master; their food, clothing, and lodging were nearly the same as theirs (except that they were not permitted to eat with those who were free-born); and there was scarce any other difference between them, than a superior degree of importance which the head of a family possesses in our state, and that authority which, as such, he exercises over every part of his household. Some of these slaves have even slaves under them as their own property, and for their own use.

As to religion, the natives believe that there is one Creator of all things, and that he lives in the

sun, and is girted round with a belt; that he may never eat or drink, but, according to some, he smokes a pipe, which is our own favorite luxury. They believe he governs events, especially our deaths or captivity; but, as for the doctrine of eternity, I do not remember to have ever heard of it; some, however, believe in the transmigration of souls in a certain degree. Those spirits which were not transmigrated, such as their dear friends or relations, they believe always attend them, and guard them from the bad spirits or their foes. For this reason they always, before eating, as I have observed, put some small portion of the meat, and pour some of their drink, on the ground for them; and they often make oblations of the blood of beasts or fowls at their graves. I was very fond of my mother, and almost constantly with her. When she went to make these oblations at her mother's tomb, which was a kind of small solitary thatched house, I sometimes attended her. There she made her libations, and spent most of the night in cries and lamentations. I have been often extremely terrified on these occasions. The loneliness of the place, the darkness of the night, and the ceremony of libation, naturally awful and gloomy, were heightened by my mother's lamentations; and these concurring with the doleful cries of birds, by which these places were frequented, gave an inexpressible terror to the scene.

We compute the year, from the day on which the sun crosses the line, and on its setting that evening, there is a general shout throughout the land; at least, I can speak from my own knowledge, throughout our vicinity. The people at the same time make a great noise with rattles, not unlike the basket rattles used by children here, though much larger, and hold up their hands to heaven for a blessing. It is then the greatest offerings are made; and those children whom our wise men foretell will be fortunate are then presented to different people. I remember many used to come to see me, and I was carried about to others for that purpose. They have many offerings, particularly at full moons; generally two, at harvest, before the fruits are taken out of the ground; and when any young animals are killed, sometimes they offer up part of them as a sacrifice. These offerings, when made by one of the heads of a family, serve for the whole. I remember we often had them at my father's and my uncle's, and their families have been

present. Some of our offerings are eaten with bitter herbs. We had a saying among us to anyone of a cross temper, "That if they were to be eaten, they should be eaten with bitter herbs."

We practised circumcision like the Jews, and made offerings and feasts on that occasion, in the same manner as they did. Like them also, our children were named from some event, some circumstance, or fancied foreboding, at the time of their birth. I was named *Olaudah*, which in our language signifies vicissitude, or fortunate; also, one favored, and having a loud voice and well spoken. I remember we never polluted the name of the object of our adoration; on the contrary, it was always mentioned with the greatest reverence; and we were totally unacquainted with swearing, and all those terms of abuse and reproach which find their way so readily and copiously into the language of more civilized people. The only expressions of that kind I remember were, "May you rot, or may you swell, or may a beast take you."

I have before remarked that the natives of this part of Africa are extremely cleanly. This necessary habit of decency was with us a part of religion, and therefore we had many purifications and washings; indeed almost as many, and used on the same occasions, if my recollection does not fail me, as the Jews. Those that touched the dead at any time were obliged to wash and purify themselves before they could enter a dwelling-house. Every woman, too, at certain times was forbidden to come into a dwelling-house, or touch any person, or anything we eat. I was so fond of my mother I could not keep from her, or avoid touching her at some of those periods, in consequence of which I was obliged to be kept out with her, in a little house made for that purpose, till offering was made, and then we were purified.

Though we had no places of public worship, we had priests and magicians, or wise men. I do not remember whether they had different offices, or whether they were united in the same persons, but they were held in great reverence by the people. They calculated our time, and foretold events, as their name imported, for we called them *Ah-affoe-way-cah*, which signifies calculators or yearly men, our year being called *Ah-affoe*. They wore their beards, and when they died, they were succeeded by their sons. Most of their implements and things of value were interred along with them. Pipes and tobacco were also put into the grave with the corpse, which was always perfumed and ornamented, and animals were offered in sacrifice to them. None accompanied their funerals, but those of the same profession or tribe. They buried them after sunset, and always returned from the grave by a different way from that which they went.

These magicians were also our doctors or physicians. They practised bleeding by cupping, and were very successful in healing wounds and expelling poisons. They had likewise some extraordinary method of discovering jealousy, theft, poisoning, the success of which, no doubt, they derived from the unbounded influence over the credulity and superstition of the people. I do not remember what those methods were, except that as to poisoning. I recollect an instance or two, which I hope it will not be deemed impertinent here to insert, as it may serve as a kind of specimen of the rest, as is still used by the Negroes in the West Indies. A young woman had been poisoned, but it was not known by whom; the doctors ordered the corpse to be taken up by some persons, and carried to the grave. As soon as the bearers had raised it on their shoulders, they seemed seized with some[6] sudden impulse, and ran to and fro, unable to stop themselves. At last, after having passed through a number of thorns and prickly bushes unhurt, the corpse fell from them close to a house, and defaced it in the fall; and the owner being taken up, he immediately confessed the poisoning.[7]

The natives are extremely cautious about poi-

[6] See also Lieutenant Matthew's Voyage, p. 123.

[7] An instance of this kind happened at Montserrat, in the West Indies, in the year 1763. I then belonged to the *Charming Sally*, Capt. Doran. The chief mate, Mr. Mansfield, and some of the crew being one day on shore, were present at the burying of a poisoned Negro girl. Though they had often heard of the circumstance of the running in such cases, and had even seen it, they imagined it to be a trick of the corpse bearers. The mate therefore desired two of the sailors to take up the coffin, and carry it to the grave. The sailors, who were all of the same opinion, readily obeyed, but they had scarcely raised it to their shoulders before they began to run furiously about, quite unable to direct themselves, till at last, without intention, they came to the hut of him who had poisoned the girl. The coffin then immediately fell from their shoulders against the hut, and damaged part of the wall. The owner of the hut was taken into custody on this, and confessed the poisoning. I give this story as it was related by the mate and crew on their return to the ship. The credit which is due to it, I leave with the reader.

son. When they buy any eatables, the seller kisses it all round before the buyer, to shew him it is not poisoned; and the same is done when any meat or drink is presented, particularly to a stranger. We have serpents of different kinds, some of which are esteemed ominous when they appear in our houses, and these we never molest. I remember two of those ominous snakes, each of which was as thick as the calf of a man's leg, and in color resembling a dolphin in the water, crept at different times into my mother's night house, where I always lay with her, and coiled themselves into folds, and each time they crowed like a cock. I was desired by some of our wise men to touch these, that I might be interested in the good omens, which I did, for they were quite harmless, and would tamely suffer themselves to be handled; and then they were put into a large earthen pan, and set on one side of the highway. Some of our snakes, however, were poisonous; one of them crossed the road one day as I was standing on it, and passed between my feet without offering to touch me, to the great surprise of many who saw it; and these incidents were accounted by the wise men, and likewise by my mother and the rest of the people, as remarkable omens in my favor.

Such is the imperfect sketch my memory has furnished me with, of the manners and customs of a people among whom I first drew my breath. And here I cannot forbear suggesting what has long struck me very forcibly, namely, the strong analogy which even by this sketch, imperfect as it is, appears to prevail in the manners and customs of my countrymen and those of the Jews, before they reached the land of promise, and particularly the patriarchs while they were yet in that pastoral state which is described in Genesis—an analogy, which alone would induce me to think that the one people had sprung from the other. Indeed, this is the opinion of Dr. Gill, who, in his commentary on Genesis, very ably deduces the pedigree of the Africans from Afer and Afra, the descendents of Abraham by Keturah his wife and concubine (for both these titles are applied to her). It is also conformable to the sentiments of Dr. John Clarke, formerly Dean of Sarum, in his truth of the Christian religion; both these authors concur in ascribing to us this original. The reasonings of those gentlemen are still further confirmed by the scripture chronology; and if any further corroboration were required, this resemblance in so many respects, is a strong evidence in support of the opinion. Like the Israelites in their primitive state, our government was conducted by our chiefs or judges, our wise men and elders; and the head of a family with us enjoyed a similar authority over his household, with that which is ascribed to Abraham and the other patriarchs. The law of retaliation obtained almost universally with us as with them: and even their religion appeared to have shed upon us a ray of its glory, though broken and spent in its passage, or eclipsed by the cloud with which time, tradition, and ignorance might have enveloped it; for we had our circumcision (a rule, I believe, peculiar to that people), we had also our sacrifices and burnt-offerings, our washings and purifications, and on the same occasions as they did.

As to the difference of color between the Eboan Africans and the modern Jews, I shall not presume to account for it. It is a subject which has engaged the pens of men of both genius and learning, and is far above my strength. The most able and Reverend Mr. T. Clarkson, however, in his much admired essay on the Slavery and Commerce of the Human Species, has ascertained the cause in a manner that at once solves every objection on that account, and, on my mind at least, has produced the fullest conviction. I shall therefore refer to that performance for the theory,[8] contenting myself with extracting a fact as related by Dr. Mitchel.[9] "The Spaniards, who have inhabited America, under the torrid zone, for any time, are become as dark colored as our native Indians of Virginia; of which *I myself have been a witness.*" There is also another instance[10] of a Portuguese settlement at Mitomba, a river in Sierra Leone, where the inhabitants are bred from a mixture of the first Portuguese discoverers with the natives, and are now become in their complexion, and in the woolly quality of their hair, *perfect Negroes*, retaining however a smattering of the Portuguese language.

These instances, and a great many more which might be adduced, while they show how the complexions of the same persons vary in different climates, it is hoped may tend also to remove the prejudice that some conceive against the natives of Africa on account of their color. Surely the minds of the Spaniards did not change with

[8] Pages 178 to 216.
[9] Philos. Trans. No. 476, Sec. 4, cited by Mr. Clarkson, p. 205.
[10] Same page.

their complexions! Are there not causes enough to which the apparent inferiority of an African may be ascribed, without limiting the goodness of God, and supposing he forebore to stamp understanding on certainly his own image, because "carved in ebony." Might it not naturally be ascribed to their situation? When they come among Europeans, they are ignorant of their language, religion, manners, and customs. Are any pains taken to teach them these? Are they treated as men? Does not slavery itself depress the mind, and extinguish all its fire and every noble sentiment? But, above all, what advantages do not a refined people possess, over those who are rude and uncultivated? Let the polished and haughty European recollect that his ancestors were once, like the Africans, uncivilized, and even barbarous. Did Nature make *them* inferior to their sons? and should *they too* have been made slaves? Every rational mind answers, No. Let such reflections as these melt the pride of their superiority into sympathy for the wants and miseries of their sable brethren, and compel them to acknowledge that understanding is not confined to feature or color. If, when they look round the world, they feel exultation, let it be tempered with benevolence to others, and gratitude to God, "who hath made of one blood all nations of men for to dwell on all the face of the earth";[11] "and whose wisdom is not our wisdom, neither are our ways his ways."

Chapter 2

The author's birth and parentage—His being kidnapped with his sister—Their separation—Surprise at meeting again—Are finally separated—Account of the different places and incidents the author met with till his arrival on the coast—The effect the sight of a slave-ship had on him—He sails for the West Indies—Horrors of a slave-ship—Arrives at Barbadoes, where the cargo is sold and dispersed.

I hope the reader will not think I have trespassed on his patience in introducing myself to him, with some account of the manners and customs of my country. They had been implanted in me with great care, and made an impression on my mind, which time could not erase, and which all the adversity and variety of fortune I have since experienced, served only to rivet and record: for, whether the love of one's country be

[11] Acts 17:26.

real or imaginary, or a lesson of reason, or an instinct of nature, I still look back with pleasure on the first scenes of my life, though that pleasure has been for the most part mingled with sorrow.

I have already acquainted the reader with the time and place of my birth. My father, besides many slaves, had a numerous family, of which seven lived to grow up, including myself and sister, who was the only daughter. As I was the youngest of the sons, I became, of course, the greatest favorite with my mother, and was always with her; and she used to take particular pains to form my mind. I was trained up from my earliest years in the art of war: my daily exercise was shooting and throwing javelins, and my mother adorned me with emblems, after the manner of our greatest warriors. In this way I grew up till I had turned the age of eleven, when an end was put to my happiness in the following manner: Generally, when the grown people in the neighborhood were gone far in the fields to labor, the children assembled together in some of the neighboring premises to play; and commonly some of us used to get up a tree to look out for any assailant, or kidnapper, that might come upon us—for they sometimes took those opportunities of our parents' absence, to attack and carry off as many as they could seize. One day as I was watching at the top of a tree in our yard, I saw one of those people come into the yard of our next neighbor but one, to kidnap, there being many stout young people in it. Immediately on this I gave the alarm of the rogue, and he was surrounded by the stoutest of them, who entangled him with cords, so that he could not escape, till some of the grown people came and secured him. But, alas! ere long it was my fate to be thus attacked, and to be carried off, when none of the grown people were nigh. One day, when all our people were gone out to their works as usual, and only I and my dear sister were left to mind the house, two men and a woman got over our walls, and in a moment seized us both, and, without giving us time to cry out, or make resistance, they stopped our mouths, and ran off with us into the nearest wood. Here they tied our hands, and continued to carry us as far as they could, till night came on, when we reached a small house, where the robbers halted for refreshment, and spent the night. We were then unbound, but were unable to take any food; and, being quite overpowered by fatigue and grief, our only relief was some sleep, which allayed our misfortune for a

short time. The next morning we left the house, and continued travelling all the day. For a long time we had kept the woods, but at last we came into a road which I believed I knew. I had now some hopes of being delivered; for we had advanced but a little way before I discovered some people at a distance, on which I began to cry out for their assistance; but my cries had no other effect than to make them tie me faster and stop my mouth, and then they put me into a large sack. They also stopped my sister's mouth, and tied her hands; and in this manner we proceeded till we were out of sight of these people. When we went to rest the following night, they offered us some victuals, but we refused it; and the only comfort we had was in being in one another's arms all that night, and bathing each other with our tears. But alas! we were soon deprived of even the small comfort of weeping together. The next day proved a day of greater sorrow than I had yet experienced; for my sister and I were then separated, while we lay clasped in each other's arms. It was in vain that we besought them not to part us; she was torn from me, and immediately carried away, while I was left in a state of distraction not to be described. I cried and grieved continually; and for several days did not eat anything but what they forced into my mouth. At length, after many days' travelling, during which I had often changed masters, I got into the hands of a chieftain, in a very pleasant country. This man had two wives and some children, and they all used me extremely well, and did all they could do to comfort me; particularly the first wife, who was something like my mother. Although I was a great many days' journey from my father's house, yet these people spoke exactly the same language with us. This first master of mine, as I may call him, was a smith, and my principal employment was working his bellows, which were the same kind as I had seen in my vicinity. They were in some respects not unlike the stoves here in gentlemen's kitchens, and were covered over with leather; and in the middle of that leather a stick was fixed, and a person stood up, and worked it in the same manner as is done to pump water out of a cask with a hand pump. I believe it was gold he worked, for it was of a lovely bright yellow color, and was worn by the women on their wrists and ankles. I was there I suppose about a month, and they at last used to trust me some little distance from the house. This liberty I used in embracing every opportunity to inquire the way to my own home; and I also sometimes, for the same purpose, went with the maidens, in the cool of the evenings, to bring pitchers of water from the springs for the use of the house. I had also remarked where the sun rose in the morning, and set in the evening, as I had travelled along; and I had observed that my father's house was towards the rising of the sun. I therefore determined to seize the first opportunity of making my escape, and to shape my course for that quarter; for I was quite oppressed and weighed down by grief after my mother and friends; and my love of liberty, ever great, was strengthened by the mortifying circumstance of not daring to eat with the free-born children, although I was mostly their companion. While I was projecting my escape one day, an unlucky event happened, which quite disconcerted my plan, and put an end to my hopes. I used to be sometimes employed in assisting an elderly slave to cook and take care of the poultry; and one morning, while I was feeding some chickens, I happened to toss a small pebble at one of them, which hit it on the middle, and directly killed it. The old slave, having soon after missed the chicken, inquired after it; and on my relating the accident (for I told her the truth, for my mother would never suffer me to tell a lie), she flew into a violent passion, and threatened that I should suffer for it; and, my master being out, she immediately went and told her mistress what I had done. This alarmed me very much, and I expected an instant flogging, which to me was uncommonly dreadful, for I had seldom been beaten at home. I therefore resolved to fly; and accordingly I ran into a thicket that was hard by, and hid myself in the bushes. Soon afterwards my mistress and the slave returned, and, not seeing me, they searched all the house, but not finding me, and I not making answer when they called to me, they thought I had run away, and the whole neighborhood was raised in the pursuit of me. In that part of the country, as in ours, the houses and villages were skirted with woods, or shrubberies, and the bushes were so thick that a man could readily conceal himself in them, so as to elude the strictest search. The neighbors continued the whole day looking for me, and several times many of them came within a few yards of the place where I lay hid. I expected every moment, when I heard a rustling among the tree, to be found out, and punished by my master; but they never discovered me, though they were often so near that I even heard their conjectures as they were looking about for me; and I now learned from them that any attempts to return home would be hopeless. Most of them supposed I had fled towards home; but the distance was so great, and the way so intricate, that they thought I could never reach it, and that I should be lost in the woods. When I heard this I was seized with a violent panic, and abandoned myself to despair. Night, too, began to approach, and aggravated all my fears. I had before entertained hopes of getting home, and had determined when it should be dark to make the attempt; but I was now convinced it was fruitless, and began to consider that, if possibly I could escape all other animals, I could not those of the human kind; and that, not knowing the way, I must perish in the woods. Thus was I like the hunted deer—

> Every leaf and every whisp'ring breath,
> Convey'd a foe, and every foe a death.

I heard frequent rustlings among the leaves, and being pretty sure they were snakes, I expected every instant to be stung by them. This increased my anguish, and the horror of my situation became now quite insupportable. I at length quitted the thicket, very faint and hungry, for I had not eaten or drank anything all the day, and crept to my master's kitchen, from whence I set out at first, which was an open shed, and laid myself down in the ashes with an anxious wish for death, to relieve me from all my pains. I was scarcely awake in the morning, when the old woman slave, who was the first up, came to light the fire, and saw me in the fireplace. She was very much surprised to see me, and could scarcely believe her own eyes. She now promised to intercede for me, and went for her master, who soon after came, and, having slightly reprimanded me, ordered me to be taken care of, and not ill treated.

Soon after this, my master's only daughter, and child by his first wife, sickened and died, which affected him so much that for sometime he was almost frantic, and really would have killed himself, had he not been watched and prevented. However, in a short time afterwards he recovered, and I was again sold. I was now carried to the left of the sun's rising, through many dreary wastes and dismal woods, amidst the hideous roarings of wild beasts. The people I was sold to used to carry me very often, when I was tired, either on their shoulders or on their backs. I saw many convenient well-built sheds along the road, at proper distances, to accommodate the merchants and travellers, who lay in those buildings along with their wives, who often accompany them; and they always go well armed.

From the time I left my own nation, I always found somebody that understood me till I came to the sea coast. The languages of different nations did not totally differ, nor were they so copious as those of the Europeans, particularly the English. They were therefore, easily learned; and, while I was journeying thus through Africa, I acquired two or three different tongues. In this manner I had been travelling for a considerable time, when, one evening, to my great surprise, whom should I see brought to the house where I was but my dear sister! As soon as she saw me, she gave a loud shriek, and ran into my arms—I was quite overpowered; neither of us could speak, but, for a considerable time, clung to each other in mutual embraces, unable to do anything but weep. Our meeting affected all who saw us; and, indeed, I must acknowledge, in honor of those sable destroyers of human rights, that I never met with any ill treatment, or saw any offered to their slaves, except tying them, when necessary, to keep them from running away. When these people knew we were brother and sister, they indulged us to be together; and the man, to whom I supposed we belonged, lay with us, he in the middle, while she and I held one another by the hands across his breast all night; and thus for a while we forgot our misfortunes, in the joy of being together; but even this small comfort was soon to have an end; for scarcely had the fatal morning appeared when she was again torn from me forever! I was now more miserable, if possible, than before. The small relief which her presence gave me from pain, was gone, and the wretchedness of my situation was redoubled by my anxiety after her fate, and my apprehensions lest her sufferings should be greater than mine, when I could not be with her to alleviate them. Yes, thou dear partner of all my childish sports! thou sharer of my joys and sorrows! happy should I have ever esteemed myself to encounter every misery for you and to procure your freedom by the sacrifice of my own. Though you were early forced from my arms, your image has been always riveted in my heart, from which neither time nor fortune have been able to remove it; so that, while the thoughts of

your sufferings have damped my prosperity, they have mingled with adversity and increased its bitterness. To that Heaven which protects the weak from the strong, I commit the care of your innocence and virtues, if they have not already received their full reward, and if your youth and delicacy have not long since fallen victims to the violence of the African trader, the pestilential stench of a Guinea ship, the seasoning in the European colonies, or the lash and lust of a brutal and unrelenting overseer.

I did not long remain after my sister. I was again sold, and carried through a number of places, till after travelling a considerable time, I came to a town called Tinmah, in the most beautiful country I had yet seen in Africa. It was extremely rich, and there were many rivulets which flowed through it, and supplied a large pond in the centre of the town, where the people washed. Here I first saw and tasted cocoanuts, which I thought superior to any nuts I had ever tasted before; and the trees, which were loaded, were also interspersed among the houses, which had commodious shades adjoining, and were in the same manner as ours, the insides being neatly plastered and whitewashed. Here I also saw and tasted for the first time, sugar-cane. Their money consisted of little white shells, the size of the finger nail. I was sold here for one hundred and seventy-two of them, by a merchant who lived and brought me there. I had been about two or three days at his house, when a wealthy widow, a neighbor of his, came there one evening, and brought with her an only son, a young gentleman about my own age and size. Here they saw me; and, having taken a fancy to me, I was bought of the merchant, and went home with them. Her house and premises were situated close to one of those rivulets I have mentioned, and were the finest I ever saw in Africa: they were very extensive, and she had a number of slaves to attend her. The next day I was washed and perfumed, and when meal time came, I was led into the presence of my mistress, and ate and drank before her with her son. This filled me with astonishment; and I could scarce help expressing my surprise that the young gentleman should suffer me, who was bound, to eat with him who was free; and not only so, but that he would not at any time either eat or drink till I had taken first, because I was the eldest, which was agreeable to our custom. Indeed, every thing here, and all their treatment of me, made me forget that I was a slave. The language of these people resembled ours so nearly, that we understood each other perfectly. They had also the very same customs as we. There were likewise slaves daily to attend us, while my young master and I, with other boys, sported with our darts and bows and arrows, as I had been used to do at home. In this resemblance to my former happy state, I passed about two months; and I now began to think I was to be adopted into the family, and was beginning to be reconciled to my situation, and to forget by degrees my misfortunes, when all at once the delusion vanished; for, without the least previous knowledge, one morning early, while my dear master and companion was still asleep, I was awakened out of my reverie to fresh sorrow, and hurried away even amongst the uncircumcised.

Thus, at the very moment I dreamed of the greatest happiness, I found myself most miserable; and it seemed as if fortune wished to give me this taste of joy only to render the reverse more poignant. The change I now experienced was as painful as it was sudden and unexpected. It was a change indeed, from a state of bliss to a scene which is inexpressible by me, as it discovered to me an element I had never before beheld, and till then had no idea of, and wherein such instances of hardship and cruelty continually occurred, as I can never reflect on but with horror.

All the nations and people I had hitherto passed through, resembled our own in their manners, customs, and language; but I came at length to a country, the inhabitants of which differed from us in all those particulars. I was very much struck with this difference, especially when I came among a people who did not circumcise, and ate without washing their hands. They cooked also in iron pots, and had European cutlasses and cross bows, which were unknown to us, and fought with their fists among themselves. Their women were not so modest as ours, for they ate, and drank, and slept with their men. But above all, I was amazed to see no sacrifices or offerings among them. In some of those places the people ornamented themselves with scars, and likewise filed their teeth very sharp. They wanted sometimes to ornament me in the same manner, but I would not suffer them; hoping that I might some time be among a people who did not thus disfigure themselves, as I thought they did. At last I came to the banks of a large river which was covered with canoes, in which the people appeared to live with their household utensils, and provisions of all kinds. I was beyond measure astonished at this, as I had never before seen any water larger than a pond or a rivulet; and my surprise was mingled with no small fear when I was put into one of these canoes, and we began to paddle and move along the river. We continued going on thus till night, and when we came to land, and made fires on the banks, each family by themselves; some dragged their canoes on shore, others stayed and cooked in theirs, and laid in them all night. Those on the land had mats, of which they made tents, some in the shape of little houses; in these we slept; and after the morning meal, we embarked again and proceeded as before. I was often very much astonished to see some of the women, as well as the men, jump into the water, dive to the bottom, come up again, and swim about. Thus I continued to travel, sometimes by land, sometimes by water, through different countries and various nations, till, at the end of six or seven months after I had been kidnapped, I arrived at the sea coast. It would be tedious and uninteresting to relate all the incidents which befell me during this journey, and which I have not yet forgotten; of the various hands I passed through, and the manners and customs of all the different people among whom I lived—I shall therefore only observe, that in all the places where I was, the soil was exceedingly rich; the pumpkins, eadas, plantains, yams, &c. &c., were in great abundance, and of incredible size. There were also vast quantities of different gums, though not used for any purpose, and everywhere a great deal of tobacco. The cotton even grew quite wild, and there was plenty of red-wood. I saw no mechanics whatever in all the way, except such as I have mentioned. The chief employment in all these countries was agriculture, and both the males and females, as with us, were brought up to it, and trained in the arts of war.

The first object which saluted my eyes when I arrived on the coast, was the sea, and a slave ship, which was then riding at anchor, and waiting for its cargo. These filled me with astonishment, which was soon converted into terror, when I was carried on board. I was immediately handled, and tossed up to see if I were sound, by some of the crew; and I was now persuaded that I had gotten into a world of bad spirits, and that they were going to kill me. Their complexions, too, differing so much from ours, their long hair, and the language they spoke (which was very different from any I had ever heard), united to confirm me in this belief. Indeed, such were the horrors of my views and fears at the moment, that, if ten thousand worlds had been my own, I would have freely parted with them all to have exchanged my condition with that of the meanest slave in my own country. When I looked round the ship too, and saw a large furnace of copper boiling, and a multitude of black people of every description chained together, every one of their countenances expressing dejection and sorrow, I no longer doubted of my fate; and, quite overpowered with horror and anguish, I fell motionless on the deck and fainted. When I recovered a little, I found some black people about me, who I believed were some of those who had brought me on board, and had been receiving their pay; they talked to me in order to cheer me, but all in vain. I asked them if we were not to be eaten by those white men with horrible looks, red faces, and long hair. They told me I was not, and one of the crew brought me a small portion of spirituous liquor in a wine glass; but, being afraid of him, I would not take it out of his hand. One of the blacks, therefore, took it from him and gave it to me, and I took a little down my palate, which, instead of reviving me, as they thought it would, threw me into the greatest consternation at the strange feeling it produced, having never tasted any such liquor before. Soon after this, the blacks who brought me on board went off, and left me abandoned to despair.

I now saw myself deprived of all chance of returning to my native country, or even the least glimpse of hope of gaining the shore, which I now considered as friendly; and I even wished for my former slavery in preference to my present situation, which was filled with horrors of every kind, still heightened by my ignorance of what I was to undergo. I was not long suffered to indulge my grief; I was soon put down under the decks, and there I received such a salutation in my nostrils as I had never experienced in my life: so that, with the loathsomeness of the stench, and crying together, I became so sick and low that I was not able to eat, nor had I the least desire to taste anything. I now wished for the last friend, death, to relieve me; but soon, to my grief, two of the white men offered me eatables; and, on my refusing to eat, one of them held me fast by the hands, and laid me across, I think, the windlass, and tied my feet, while the other flogged

me severely. I had never experienced anything of this kind before, and, although not being used to the water, I naturally feared that element the first time I saw it, yet, nevertheless, could I have got over the nettings, I would have jumped over the side, but I could not; and besides, the crew used to watch us very closely who were not chained down to the decks, lest we should leap into the water; and I have seen some of these poor African prisoners most severely cut, for attempting to do so, and hourly whipped for not eating. This indeed was often the case with myself. In a little time after, amongst the poor chained men, I found some of my own nation, which in a small degree gave ease to my mind. I inquired of these what was to be done with us? They gave me to understand, we were to be carried to these white people's country to work for them. I then was a little revived, and thought, if it were no worse than working, my situation was not so desperate; but still I feared I should be put to death, the white people looked and acted, as I thought, in so savage a manner; for I had never seen among any people such instances of brutal cruelty; and this not only shown towards us blacks, but also to some of the whites themselves. One white man in particular I saw, when we were permitted to be on deck, flogged so unmercifully with a large rope near the foremast, that he died in consequence of it; and they tossed him over the side as they would have done a brute. This made me fear these people the more; and I expected nothing less than to be treated in the same manner. I could not help expressing my fears and apprehensions to some of my countrymen; I asked them if these people had no country, but lived in this hollow place (the ship)? They told me they did not, but came from a distant one. "Then," said I, "how comes it in all our country we never heard of them?" They told me because they lived so very far off. I then asked where were their women? had they any like themselves? I was told they had. "And why," said I, "do we not see them?" They answered, because they were left behind. I asked how the vessel could go? They told me they could not tell; but that there was cloth put upon the masts by the help of the ropes I saw, and then the vessel went on; and the white men had some spell or magic they put in the water when they liked, in order to stop the vessel. I was exceedingly amazed at this account, and really thought they were spirits. I therefore wished much to be from amongst them, for I expected they would sacrifice me; but my wishes were vain—for we were so quartered that it was impossible for any of us to make our escape.

While we stayed on the coast I was mostly on deck; and one day, to my great astonishment, I saw one of these vessels coming in with the sails up. As soon as the whites saw it, they gave a great shout, at which we were amazed; and the more so, as the vessel appeared larger by approaching nearer. At last, she came to an anchor in my sight, and when the anchor was let go, I and my countrymen who saw it, were lost in astonishment to observe the vessel stop—and were now convinced it was done by magic. Soon after this the other ship got her boats out, and they came on board of us, and the people of both ships seemed very glad to see each other. Several of the strangers also shook hands with us black people, and made motions with their hands, signifying I suppose, we were to go to their country, but we did not understand them.

At last, when the ship we were in, had got in all her cargo, they made ready with many fearful noises, and we were all put under deck, so that we could not see how they managed the vessel. But this disappointment was the least of my sorrow. The stench of the hold while we were on the coast was so intolerably loathsome, that it was dangerous to remain there for any time, and some of us had been permitted to stay on the deck for the fresh air; but now that the whole ship's cargo were confined together, it became absolutely pestilential. The closeness of the place, and the heat of the climate, added to the number in the ship, which was so crowded that each had scarcely room to turn himself, almost suffocated us. This produced copious perspirations, so that the air soon became unfit for respiration, from a variety of loathsome smells, and brought on a sickness among the slaves, of which many died— thus falling victims to the improvident avarice, as I may call it, of their purchasers. This wretched situation was again aggravated by the galling of the chains, now become insupportable, and the filth of the necessary tubs, into which the children often fell, and were almost suffocated. The shrieks of the women, and the groans of the dying, rendered the whole a scene of horror almost inconceivable. Happily perhaps, for myself, I was soon reduced so low here that it was thought necessary to keep me almost always on deck; and from my extreme youth I was not put in fetters. In this situation I expected every hour

to share the fate of my companions, some of whom were almost daily brought upon deck at the point of death, which I began to hope would soon put an end to my miseries. Often did I think many of the inhabitants of the deep much more happy than myself. I envied them the freedom they enjoyed, and as often wished I could change my condition for theirs. Every circumstance I met with, served only to render my state more painful, and heightened my apprehensions, and my opinion of the cruelty of the whites.

One day they had taken a number of fishes; and when they had killed and satisfied themselves with as many as they thought fit, to our astonishment who were on deck, rather than give any of them to us to eat, as we expected, they tossed the remaining fish into the sea again, although we begged and prayed for some as well as we could, but in vain; and some of my countrymen, being pressed by hunger, took an opportunity, when they thought no one saw them, of trying to get a little privately; but they were discovered, and the attempt procured them some very severe floggings. One day, when we had a smooth sea and moderate wind, two of my wearied countrymen who were chained together (I was near them at the time), preferring death to such a life of misery, somehow made through the nettings and jumped into the sea; immediately, another quite dejected fellow, who, on account of his illness, was suffered to be out of irons, also followed their example; and I believe many more would very soon have done the same, if they had not been prevented by the ship's crew, who were instantly alarmed. Those of us that were the most active, were in a moment put down under the deck; and there was such a noise and confusion amongst the people of the ship as I never heard before, to stop her, and get the boat out to go after the slaves. However, two of the wretches were drowned, but they got the other, and afterwards flogged him unmercifully, for thus attempting to prefer death to slavery. In this manner we continued to undergo more hardships than I can now relate, hardships which are inseparable from this accursed trade. Many a time we were near suffocation from the want of fresh air, which we were often without for whole days together. This, and the stench of the necessary tubs, carried off many.

During our passage, I first saw flying fishes, which surprised me very much; they used frequently to fly across the ship, and many of them fell on the deck. I also now first saw the use of the quadrant; I had often with astonishment seen the mariners make observations with it, and I could not think what it meant. They at last took notice of my surprise; and one of them, willing to increase it, as well as to gratify my curiosity, made me one day look through it. The clouds appeared to me to be land, which disappeared as they passed along. This heightened my wonder; and I was now more persuaded than ever, that I was in another world, and that every thing about me was magic. At last, we came in sight of the island of Barbadoes, at which the whites on board gave a great shout, and made many signs of joy to us. We did not know what to think of this; but as the vessel drew nearer, we plainly saw the harbor, and other ships of different kinds and sizes, and we soon anchored amongst them, off Bridgetown. Many merchants and planters now came on board, though it was in the evening. They put us in separate parcels, and examined us attentively. They also made us jump, and pointed to the land, signifying we were to go there. We thought by this, we should be eaten by these ugly men, as they appeared to us; and, when soon after we were all put down under the deck again, there was much dread and trembling among us, and nothing but bitter cries to be heard all the night from these apprehensions, insomuch, that at last the white people got some old slaves from the land to pacify us. They told us we were not to be eaten, but to work, and were soon to go on land, where we should see many of our country people. This report eased us much. And sure enough, soon after we were landed, there came to us Africans of all languages.

We were conducted immediately to the merchant's yard, where we were all pent up together, like so many sheep in a fold, without regard to sex or age. As every object was new to me, everything I saw filled me with surprise. What struck me first, was, that the houses were built with bricks and stories, and in every other respect different from those I had seen in Africa; but I was still more astonished on seeing people on horseback. I did not know what this could mean; and, indeed, I thought these people were full of nothing but magical arts. While I was in this astonishment, one of my fellow prisoners spoke to a countryman of his, about the horses, who said they were the same kind they had in their country. I understood them, though they were from a distant part of Africa; and I thought it odd I had not seen any horses there; but afterwards, when I came to converse with different Africans, I found they had many horses amongst them, and much larger than those I then saw.

We were not many days in the merchant's custody, before we were sold after their usual manner, which is this: On a signal given (as the beat of a drum), the buyers rush at once into the yard where the slaves are confined, and make choice of that parcel they like best. The noise and clamor with which this is attended, and the eagerness visible in the countenances of the buyers, serve not a little to increase the apprehension of terrified Africans, who may well be supposed to consider them as the ministers of that destruction to which they think themselves devoted. In this manner, without scruple, are relations and friends separated, most of them never to see each other again. I remember, in the vessel in which I was brought over, in the men's apartment, there were several brothers, who, in the sale, were sold in different lots; and it was very moving on this occasion, to see and hear their cries at parting. O, ye nominal Christians! might not an African ask you—Learned you this from your God, who says unto you, Do unto all men as you would men should do unto you? Is it not enough that we are torn from our country and friends, to toil for your luxury and lust of gain? Must every tender feeling be likewise sacrificed to your avarice? Are the dearest friends and relations, now rendered more dear by their separation from their kindred, still to be parted from each other, and thus prevented from cheering the gloom of slavery, with the small comfort of being together, and mingling their sufferings and sorrows? Why are parents to lose their children, brothers their sisters, or husbands their wives? Surely, this is a new refinement in cruelty, which, while it has no advantage to atone for it, thus aggravates distress, and adds horrors even to the wretchedness of slavery.

Chapter 5

The author's reflections on his situation—Is deceived by a promise of being delivered—His despair at sailing for the West Indies—Arrives at Montserrat, where he is sold to Mr. King—Various interesting instances of oppression, cruelty, and extortion, which the author saw practised upon the slaves in the West Indies, during his captivity from the year 1763 to 1766—Address on it to the planters.

Thus, at the moment I expected all my toils to end, was I plunged, as I supposed, in a new slavery; in comparision of which, all my service hitherto had been perfect freedom; and whose horrors, always present to my mind, now rushed on it with tenfold aggravation. I wept very bitterly for some time, and began to think I must have done something to displease the Lord, that he thus punished me so severely. This filled me with painful reflections on my past conduct; I recollected that on the morning of our arrival at Deptford, I had rashly sworn that as soon as we reached London, I would spend the day in rambling and sport. My conscience smote me for this unguarded expression. I felt that the Lord was able to disappoint me in all things, and immediately considered my present situation as a judgment of Heaven, on account of my presumption in swearing. I therefore, with contrition of heart, acknowledged my trangression to God, and poured out my soul before him with unfeigned repentance, and with earnest supplications I besought him not to abandon me in my distress, nor cast me from his mercy forever. In a little time, my grief, spent with its own violence, began to subside, and after the first confusion of my thoughts was over, I reflected with more calmness on my present condition. I considered that trials and disappointments are sometimes for our good, and I thought God might perhaps have permitted this, in order to teach me wisdom and resignation; for he had hitherto shadowed me with the wings of his mercy, and by his invisible but powerful hand brought me the way I knew not. These reflections gave me a little comfort, and I rose at last from the deck with dejection and sorrow in my countenance, yet mixed with some faint hope that the Lord would appear for my deliverance.

Soon afterwards, as my new master was going on shore, he called me to him, and told me to behave myself well, and do the business of the ship the same as any of the rest of the boys, and that I should fare the better for it; but I made him no answer. I was then asked if I could swim, and I said, No. However, I was made to go under the deck, and was well watched. The next tide the ship got under way, and soon after arrived at the Mother Bank, Portsmouth, where she waited a few days for some of the West India convoy. While I was here I tried every means I could devise, amongst the people of the ship, to get me a boat from the shore, as there was none suffered to come alongside of the ship; and their own,

whenever it was used, was hoisted in again immediately. A sailor on board took a guinea from me on pretence of getting me a boat, and promised me, time after time, that it was hourly to come off. When he had the watch upon deck, I watched also, and looked long enough, but all in vain; I could never see either the boat or my guinea again. And what I thought was still the worst of all, the fellow gave information, as I afterwards found, all the while to the mates, of my intention to go off, if I could in any way do it; but, rogue-like, he never told them he had got a guinea from me to procure my escape. However, after we had sailed, and his trick was made known to the ship's crew, I had some satisfaction in seeing him detested and despised by them all, for his behavior to me. I was still in hopes that my old shipmates would not forget their promise to come for me at Portsmouth. And, indeed, at last, but not till the day before we sailed, some of them did come there, and sent me off some oranges, and other tokens of their regard. They also sent me word they would come off to me themselves the next day, or the day after; and a lady also, who lived in Gosport, wrote to me that she would come and take me out of the ship at the same time. This lady had been once very intimate with my former master. I used to sell and take care of a great deal of property for her, in different ships; and in return, she always showed great friendship for me, and used to tell my master that she would take me away to live with her. But, unfortunately for me, a disagreement soon afterwards took place between them; and she was succeeded in my master's good graces by another lady, who appeared sole mistress of the *Etna*, and mostly lodged on board. I was not so great a favorite with this lady as with the former; she had conceived a pique against me on some occasion when she was on board, and she did not fail to instigate my master to treat me in the manner he did.[12]

However, the next morning, the 30th of December, the wind being brisk and easterly, the *Eolus* frigate, which was to escort the convoy, made a signal for sailing. All the ships then got up their

---

[12] Thus was I sacrificed to the envy and resentment of this woman for knowing that the lady whom she had succeeded in my master's good graces, designed to take me into her service; which, had I once got on shore, she would not have been able to prevent. She felt her pride alarmed at the superiority of her rival, in being attended by a black servant. It was not less to prevent this, than to be revenged on me, that she caused the captain to treat me thus cruelly.

anchors; and, before any of my friends had an opportunity to come off to my relief, to my inexpressible anguish, our ship had got under way. What tumultuous emotions agitated my soul when the convoy got under sail, and I a prisoner on board, now without hope! I kept my swimming eyes upon the land in a state of unutterable grief; not knowing what to do, and despairing how to help myself. While my mind was in this situation, the fleet sailed on, and in one day's time I lost sight of the wished-for land. In the first expression of my grief I reproached my fate, and wished I had never been born. I was ready to curse the tide that bore us, the gale that wafted my prison, and even the ship that conducted us. And I called on death to relieve me from the horrors I felt and dreaded, that I might be in that place

Where slaves are free, and men oppress no more.
Fool that I was, inur'd so long to pain,
To trust to hope, or dream of joy again.

    .   .   .

Now dragg'd once more beyond the western main,
To groan beneath some dastard planter's chain;
Where my poor countrymen in bondage wait
The long enfranchisement of a ling'ring fate.
Hard ling'ring fate! while, ere the dawn of day,
Rous'd by the lash they go their cheerless way;
And as their souls with shame and anguish burn,
Salute with groans unwelcome morn's return;
And, chiding ev'ry hour the slow pac'd sun,
Pursue their toils till all his race is run.
No eye to mark their suff'rings with a tear,
No friend to comfort, and no hope to cheer;
Then, like the dull unpity'd brutes, repair
To stalls as wretched, and as coarse a fare;
Thank heaven one day of misery was o'er,
Then sink to sleep, and wish to wake no more.[13]

The turbulence of my emotions, however, naturally gave way to calmer thoughts, and I soon perceived what fate had decreed no mortal on earth could prevent. The convoy sailed on without any accident, with a pleasant gale and smooth sea, for six weeks, till February, when one morning the *Eolus* ran down a brig, one of the convoy, and she instantly went down, and was

[13] "The Dying Negro," a poem originally published in 1773. Perhaps it may not be deemed impertinent here to add, that this elegant and pathetic little poem was occasioned, as appears by the advertisement prefixed to it, by the following incident. "A black, who, a few days before had run away from his master, and got himself christened, with intent to marry a white woman, his fellow-servant, being taken and sent on board a ship in the Thames, took an opportunity of shooting himself through the head."

engulfed in the dark recesses of the ocean. The convoy was immediately thrown into great confusion till it was day-light; and the *Eolus* was illumined with lights, to prevent any further mischief. On the 13th of February, 1763, from the mast-head, we descried our destined island, Montserrat; and soon after I beheld those

Regions of sorrow, doleful shades, where peace
And rest can rarely dwell. Hope never comes
That comes to all, but torture without end
Still urges.

At the sight of this land of bondage, a fresh horror ran through all my frame, and chilled me to the heart. My former slavery now rose in dreadful review to my mind, and displayed nothing but misery, stripes, and chains; and, in the first paroxysm of my grief, I called upon God's thunder, and his avenging power, to direct the stroke of death to me, rather than permit me to become a slave, and be sold from lord to lord.

In this state of my mind our ship came to anchor, and soon after discharged her cargo. I now knew what it was to work hard; I was made to help unload and load the ship. And, to comfort me in my distress in that time, two of the sailors robbed me of all my money, and ran away from the ship. I had been so long used to a European climate, that at first I felt the scorching West India sun very painful, while the dashing surf would toss the boat and the people in it, frequently above high water mark. Sometimes our limbs were broken with this, or even attended with instant death, and I was day by day mangled and torn.

About the middle of May, when the ship was got ready to sail for England, I all the time believing that fate's blackest clouds were gathering over my head, and expecting their bursting would mix me with the dead, Captain Doran sent for me ashore one morning, and I was told by the messenger that my fate was then determined. With trembling steps and fluttering heart, I came to the captain, and found with him one Mr. Robert King, a Quaker, and the first merchant in the place. The captain then told me my former master had sent me there to be sold; but that he had desired him to get me the best master he could, as he told him I was a very deserving boy, which Captain Doran said he found to be true; and if he were to stay in the West Indies, he would be glad to keep me himself; but he could not venture to take me to London, for he was very sure that when I came there I would leave him. I at that instant burst out a crying, and begged much of him to take me to England with him, but all to no purpose. He told me he had got me the very best master in the whole island, with whom I should be as happy as if I were in England, and for that reason he chose to let him have me, though he could sell me to his own brother-in-law for a great deal more money than what he got from this gentleman. Mr. King, my new master, then made a reply, and said the reason he had bought me was on account of my good character; and as he had not the least doubt of my good behavior, I should be very well off with him. He also told me he did not live in the West Indies, but at Philadelphia, where he was going soon; and, as I understood something of the rules of arithmetic, when we got there he would put me to school, and fit me for a clerk. This conversation relieved my mind a little, and I left those gentlemen considerably more at ease in myself than when I came to them; and I was very thankful to Captain Doran, and even to my old master, for the character they had given me. A character which I afterwards found of infinite service to me. I went on board again, and took leave of all my ship-mates, and the next day the ship sailed. When she weighed anchor, I went to the waterside and looked at her with a very wishful and aching heart, and followed her with my eyes until she was totally out of sight. I was so bowed down with grief, that I could not hold up my head for many months; and if my new master had not been kind to me, I believe I should have died under it at last. And, indeed, I soon found that he fully deserved the good character which Captain Doran gave me of him, for he possessed a most amiable disposition and temper, and was very charitable and humane. If any of his slaves behaved amiss he did not beat or use them ill, but parted with them. This made them afraid of disobliging him; and as he treated his slaves better than any other man on the island, so he was better and more faithfully served by them in return. By this kind treatment I did at last endeavor to compose myself; and with fortitude, though moneyless, determined to face whatever fate had decreed for me. Mr. King soon asked me what I could do; and at the same time said he did not mean to treat me as a common slave. I told him I knew something of seamanship, and could shave and dress hair pretty well; and I could refine wines, which I had learned on shipboard, where I had often done it; and that I could write, and understood arithmetic tolerably well, as far as the Rule of Three. He then asked me if I knew anything of gauging; and, on my answering that I did not, he said one of his clerks should teach me to gauge.

Mr. King dealt in all manner of merchandise, and kept from one to six clerks. He loaded many vessels in a year; particularly to Philadelphia, where he was born; and was connected with a great mercantile house in that city. He had, besides, many vessels and droggers, of different sizes, which used to go about the island; and others, to collect rum, sugar, and other goods. I understood pulling and managing those boats very well. And this hard work, which was the first that he set me to, in the sugar seasons used to be my constant employment. I have rowed the boat, and slaved at the oars, from one hour to sixteen in the twenty-four, during which I had fifteen pence sterling per day to live on, though sometimes only ten pence. However, this was considerably more than was allowed to other slaves that used to work often with me, and belonged to other gentlemen on the island. Those poor souls had never more than nine pence per day, and seldom more than six pence, from their masters or owners, though they earned them three or four pistareens.[14] For it is a common practice in the West Indies for men to purchase slaves, though they have not plantations themselves, in order to let them out to planters and merchants at so much a piece by the day, and they give what allowance they choose out of this product of their daily work to their slaves, for subsistence; this allowance is often very scanty. My master often gave the owners of the slaves two and a half of these pieces per day, and found the poor fellows in victuals himself, because he thought their owners did not feed them well enough according to the work they did. The slaves used to like this very well; and, as they knew my master to be a man of feeling, they were always glad to work for him, in preference to any other gentleman; some of whom, after they had been paid for these poor people's labors, would not give them their allowance out of it. Many times have I even seen these unfortunate wretches beaten for asking for their pay; and often severely flogged by their owners if they did not bring them their daily or weekly money exactly to the time;

[14] These pistareens are of the value of a shilling.

though the poor creatures were obliged to wait on the gentlemen they had worked for, sometimes more than half the day before they could get their pay; and this generally on Sundays, when they wanted the time for themselves. In particular, I knew a countryman of mine who once did not bring the weekly money directly that it was earned; and, though he brought it the same day to his master, yet he was staked to the ground for his pretended negligence, and was just going to receive a hundred lashes, but for a gentleman who begged him off with fifty. This poor man was very industrious; and by his frugality, had saved so much money by working on ship-board, that he had got a white man to buy him a boat, unknown to his master. Some time after he had this little estate, the governor wanted a boat to bring his sugar from different parts of the island; and, knowing this to be a Negro man's boat, he seized upon it for himself, and would not pay the owner a farthing. The man, on this, went to his master, and complained to him of this act of the governor; but the only satisfaction he received was to be damned very heartily by his master, who asked him how dared any of his Negroes to have a boat. If the justly merited ruin of the governor's fortune could be any gratification to the poor man he had thus robbed, he was not without consolation. Extortion and rapine are poor providers; and some time after this the governor died in the King's Bench in England, as I was told, in great poverty. The last war favored this poor Negro man, and he found some means to escape from his Christian master. He came to England, where I saw him afterwards several times. Such treatment as this often drives these miserable wretches to despair, and they run away from their masters at the hazard of their lives. Many of them, in this place, unable to get their pay when they have earned it, and fearing to be flogged, as usual, if they return home without it, run away where they can for shelter, and a reward is often offered to bring them in dead or alive. My master used sometimes, in these cases, to agree with their owners, and to settle with them himself; and thereby he saved many of them a flogging.

Once, for a few days, I was let out to fit a vessel, and I had no victuals allowed me by either party; at last I told my master of this treatment, and he took me away from it. In many of the estates, on the different islands where I used to be sent for rum or sugar, they would not deliver it to me, or any other Negro; he was therefore obliged to send a white man along with me to those places; and then he used to pay him from six to ten pistareens a day. From being thus employed, during the time I served Mr. King, in going about the different estates on the island, I had all the opportunity I could wish for, to see the dreadful usage of the poor men; usage that reconciled me to my situation, and made me bless God for the hands into which I had fallen.

I had the good fortune to please my master in every department in which he employed me; and there was scarcely any part of his business, or household affairs, in which I was not occasionally engaged. I often supplied the place of a clerk, in receiving and delivering cargoes to the ships, in tending stores, and delivering goods. And besides this, I used to shave and dress my master when convenient, and take care of his horse; and when it was necessary, which was very often, I worked likewise on board of different vessels of his. By these means I became very useful to my master, and saved him, as he used to acknowledge, above a hundred pounds a year. Nor did he scruple to say I was of more advantage to him than any of his clerks; though their usual wages in the West Indies are from sixty to a hundred pounds current a year.

I have sometimes heard it asserted that a Negro cannot earn his master the first cost; but nothing can be further from the truth. I suppose nine-tenths of the mechanics throughout the West Indies are Negro slaves; and I well know the coopers among them earn two dollars a day, the carpenters the same, and oftentimes more; as also the masons, smiths, and fishermen, &c. And I have known many slaves whose masters would not take a thousand pounds current for them. But surely this assertion refutes itself; for, if it be true, why do the planters and merchants pay such a price for slaves? And, above all, why do those who make this assertion exclaim the most loudly against the abolition of the slave trade? So much are men blinded, and to such inconsistent arguments are they driven by mistaken interest! I grant, indeed, that slaves are sometimes, by half-feeding, half-clothing, over-working, and stripes, reduced so low, that they are turned out as unfit for service, and let to perish in the woods, or expire on the dung-hill.

My master was several times offered, by different gentlemen, one hundred guineas for me, but he always told them he would not sell me, to my great joy. And I used to double my diligence and care, for fear of getting into the hands of those men who did not allow a valuable slave the common support of life. Many of them even used to find fault with my master for feeding his slaves so well as he did, although I often went hungry, and an Englishman might think my fare very indifferent; but he used to tell them he always would do it, because the slaves thereby looked better and did more work.

While I was thus employed by my master, I was often a witness to cruelties of every kind, which were exercised on my unhappy fellow slaves. I used frequently to have different cargoes of new Negroes in my care for sale; and it was almost a constant practice with our clerks, and other whites, to commit violent depredations on the chastity of the female slaves; and these I was, though with reluctance, obliged to submit to at all times, being unable to help them. When we have had some of these slaves on board my master's vessels, to carry them to other islands, or to America, I have known our mates to commit these acts most shamefully, to the disgrace, not of Christians only, but of men. I have even known them to gratify their brutal passion with females not ten years old; and these abominations, some of them practised to such scandalous excess, that one of our captains discharged the mate and others on that account. And yet in Montserrat I have seen a Negro man staked to the ground, and cut most shockingly, and then his ears cut off bit by bit, because he had been connected with a white woman, who was a common prostitute. As if it were no crime in the whites to rob an innocent African girl of her virtue, but most heinous in a black man only to gratify a passion of nature, where the temptation was offered by one of a different color, though the most abandoned woman of her species.

One Mr. D—— told me that he had sold 41,000 Negroes, and that he once cut off a Negro man's leg for running away. I asked him if the man had died in the operation, how he, as a Christian, could answer for the horrid act before God? and he told me, answering was a thing of another world, what he thought and did were policy. I told him that the Christian doctrine taught us to do unto others as we would that others should do unto us. He then said that his scheme had the desired effect—it cured that man and some others of running away.

Another Negro man was half hanged, and then burnt, for attempting to poison a cruel overseer. Thus, by repeated cruelties, are the wretched first urged to despair, and then murdered, because they still retain so much of human nature about them as to wish to put an end to their misery, and retaliate on their tyrants! These overseers are indeed for the most part persons of the worst character of any denomination of men in the West Indies. Unfortunately, many humane gentlemen, but not residing on their estates, are obliged to leave the management of them in the hands of these human butchers, who cut and mangle the slaves in a shocking manner on the most trifling occasions, and altogether treat them in every respect like brutes. They pay no regard to the situation of pregnant women, nor the least attention to the lodging of the field Negroes. Their huts, which ought to be well covered, and the place dry where they take their little repose, are often open sheds, built in damp places; so that when the poor creatures return tired from the toils of the field, they contract many disorders, from being exposed to the damp air in this uncomfortable state, while they are heated, and their pores are open. This neglect certainly conspires with many others to cause a decrease in the births as well as in the lives of the grown Negroes. I can quote many instances of gentlemen who reside on their estates in the West Indies, and then the scene is quite changed; the Negroes are treated with lenity and proper care, by which their lives are prolonged, and their masters profited. To the honor of humanity, I knew several gentlemen who managed their estates in this manner, and they found that benevolence was their true interest. And, among many I could mention in several of the islands, I knew one in Montserrat[15] whose slaves looked remarkably well, and never needed any fresh supplies of Negroes; and there are many other estates, especially in Barbadoes, which, from such judicious treatment, need no fresh stock of Negroes at any time. I have the honor of knowing a most worthy and humane gentleman, who is a native of Barbadoes, and has estates there.[16] This gentleman has written a treatise on the usage of his own slaves. He allows them two hours of refreshment at mid-day, and many other indulgencies and comforts, particularly in their lodging; and, besides this, he raises more pro-

[15] Mr. Dubury, and many others, Montserrat.
[16] Sir Phillip Gibbes, Baronet, Barbadoes.

visions on his estate than they can destroy; so that by these attentions he saves the lives of his Negroes, and keeps them healthy, and as happy as the condition of slavery can admit. I myself, as shall appear in the sequel, managed an estate, where, by those attentions, the Negroes were uncommonly cheerful and healthy, and did more work by half than by the common mode of treatment they usually do. For want, therefore, of such care and attention to the poor Negroes, and otherwise oppressed as they are, it is no wonder that the decrease should require 20,000 new Negroes annually, to fill up the vacant places of the dead.

Even in Barbadoes, notwithstanding those humane exceptions which I have mentioned, and others I am acquainted with, which justly make it quoted as a place where slaves meet with the best treatment, and need fewest recruits of any in the West Indies, yet this island requires 1000 Negroes annually to keep up the original stock, which is only 80,000. So that the whole term of a Negro's life may be said to be there but sixteen years![17] And yet the climate here in every respect is the same as that from which they are taken, except in being more wholesome. Do the British colonies decrease in this manner? And yet what prodigious difference is there between an English and West India climate?

While I was in Montserrat I knew a Negro man, named Emanuel Sankey, who endeavored to escape from his miserable bondage, by concealing himself on board of a London ship, but fate did not favor the poor oppressed man; for, being discovered when the vessel was under sail, he was delivered up again to his master. This *Christian master* immediately pinned the wretch down to the ground at each wrist and ankle, and then took some sticks of sealing wax, and lighted them, and dropped it all over his back. There was another master who was noted for cruelty; and I believe he had not a slave but what had been cut, and had pieces fairly taken out of the flesh. And after they had been punished thus, he used to make them get into a long wooden box or case he had for that purpose, in which he shut them up during pleasure. It was just about the height and breadth of a man; and the poor wretches had no room, when in the case, to move.

It was very common in several of the islands, particularly in St. Kitts, for the slaves to be

[17] Benezet's Account of Guinea, p. 16.

branded with the initial letters of their master's name; and a load of heavy iron hooks hung about their necks. Indeed, on the most trifling occasions, they were loaded with chains; and often instruments of torture were added. The iron muzzle, thumb-screws, &c., are so well known as not to need a description, and were sometimes applied for the slightest faults. I have seen a Negro beaten till some of his bones were broken, for only letting a pot boil over. Is it surprising that usage like this should drive the poor creatures to despair, and make them seek a refuge in death from those evils which render their lives intolerable?—while,

> With shudd'ring horror pale, and eyes aghast,
> They view their lamentable lot, and find
> No rest!

This they frequently do. A Negro man, on board a vessel of my master, while I belonged to her, having been put in irons for some trifling misdemeanor, and kept in that state for some days, being weary of life, took an opportunity of jumping overboard into the sea; however, he was picked up without being drowned. Another, whose life was also a burden to him, resolved to starve himself to death, and refused to eat any victuals. This procured him a severe flogging; and he also, on the first occasion which offered, jumped overboard at Charleston, but was saved.

Nor is there any greater regard shown to the little property than there is to the persons and lives of the Negroes. I have already related an instance or two of particular oppression out of many which I have witnessed; but the following is frequent in all the islands. The wretched field slaves, after toiling all the day for an unfeeling owner, who gives them but little victuals, steal sometimes a few moments from rest or refreshment to gather some small portion of grass, according as their time will admit. This they commonly tie up in a parcel; either a bit's worth (six pence) or half a bit's worth, and bring it to town, or to the market, to sell. Nothing is more common than for the white people on this occasion to take the grass from them without paying for it; and not only so, but too often also, to my knowledge, our clerks, and many others, at the same time have committed acts of violence on the poor, wretched, and helpless females; whom I have seen for hours stand crying to no purpose, and get no redress or pay of any kind. Is not this one common and crying sin enough to bring down God's judgment on the islands? He tells us the oppressor and the oppressed are both in his hands; and if these are not the poor, the broken-hearted, the blind, the captive, the bruised, which our Saviour speaks of, who are they? One of these depredators once, in St. Eustatius, came on board of our vessel, and bought some fowls and pigs of me; and a whole day after his departure with the things, he returned again and wanted his money back. I refused to give it, and, not seeing my captain on board, he began the common pranks with me; and swore he would even break open my chest and take my money. I therefore expected, as my captain was absent, that he would be as good as his word. And was just proceeding to strike me, when fortunately a British seaman on board, whose heart had not been debauched by a West India climate, interposed and prevented him. But had the cruel man struck me I certainly should have defended myself at the hazard of my life; for what is life to a man thus oppressed? He went away, however, swearing, and threatened that whenever he caught me on shore, he would shoot me, and pay for me afterwards.

The small account in which the life of a Negro is held in the West Indies is so universally known that it might seem impertinent to quote the following extract, if some people had not been hardy enough of late to assert that Negroes are on the same footing in that respect as Europeans. By the 329th Act, page 125, of the Assembly of Barbadoes, it is enacted "That if any Negro, or other slave, under punishment by his master, or his order, for running away, or any other crime or misdemeanor towards his said master, unfortunately shall suffer in life or member, no person whatsoever shall be liable to a fine; but if any person shall, out of wantonness, or only of bloody-mindedness, or cruel intention, willfully kill a Negro, or other slave, of his own, he shall pay into the public treasury fifteen pounds sterling." And it is the same in most, if not all of the West India islands. Is not this one of the many acts of the islands which call loudly for redress? And do not the assembly which enacted it deserve the appellation of savages and brutes, rather than of Christians and men? It is an act at once unmerciful, unjust, and unwise; which for cruelty would disgrace an assembly of those who are called barbarians; and for its injustice and insanity would shock the morality and common sense of a Samaide or Hottentot.

Shocking as this and many other acts of the bloody West India code at first view appear, how is the iniquity of it heightened when we consider to whom it may be extended! Mr. James Tobin, a zealous laborer in the vineyard of slavery, gives an account of a French planter of his acquaintance, in the island of Martinique, who showed him many mulattoes working in the field like beasts of burden; and he told Mr. Tobin these were all the produce of his own loins! And I myself have known similar instances. Pray, reader, are these sons and daughters of the French planter less his children by being the progeny of black women? And what must be the virtue of those legislators, and the feelings of those fathers, who estimate the lives of their sons, however begotten, at no more than fifteen pounds; though they should be murdered, as the act says, out of wantonness and bloody-mindedness! But is not the slave trade entirely at war with the heart of man? And surely that which is begun by breaking down the barriers of virtue, involves in its continuance destruction to every principle, and buries all sentiment in ruin!

I have often seen slaves, particularly those who were meagre, in different islands, put into scales and weighed, and then sold from three pence to six pence or nine pence a pound. My master, however, whose humanity was shocked at this mode, used to sell such by the lump. And at or after a sale, it was not uncommon to see Negroes taken from their wives, wives taken from their husbands, and children from their parents, and sent off to other islands, and wherever else their merciless lords choose; and probably never more during life see each other! Oftentimes my heart has bled at these partings, when the friends of the departed have been at the waterside, and with sighs and tears, have kept their eyes fixed on the vessel, till it went out of sight.

A poor Creole Negro, I knew well, who, after having been often thus transported from island to island, at last resided in Montserrat. This man used to tell me many melancholy tales of himself. Generally, after he had done working for his master, he used to employ his few leisure moments to go a fishing. When he had caught any fish, his master would frequently take them from him without paying him; and at other times some other white people would serve him in the same manner. One day he said to me, very movingly, "Sometimes when a white man take away my fish, I go to my maser, and he get me my right;

and when my maser by strength take away my fishes, what me must do? I can't go to any body to be righted; then," said the poor man, looking up above, "I must look up to God Mighty, in the top, for right." This artless tale moved me much, and I could not help feeling the just cause Moses had in redressing his brother against the Egyptian. I exhorted the man to look up still to the God on the top, since there was no redress below. Though I little thought then that I myself should more than once experience such imposition, and need the same exhortation hereafter, in my own transactions in the islands, and that even this poor man and I should some time after suffer together in the same manner, as shall be related hereafter.

Nor was such usage as this confined to particular places or individuals, for in all the different islands in which I have been (and I have visited no less than fifteen) the treatment of the slaves was nearly the same; so nearly, indeed, that the history of an island, or even a plantation, with a few such exceptions as I have mentioned, might serve for a history of the whole. Such a tendency has the slave trade to debauch men's minds, and harden them to every feeling of humanity! For I will not suppose that the dealers in slaves are born worse than other men—No; such is the fatality of this mistaken avarice that it corrupts the milk of human kindness and turns it into gall. And, had the pursuits of those men been different, they might have been as generous, as tender-hearted and just, as they are unfeeling, rapacious, and cruel. Surely this traffic cannot be good, which spreads like a pestilence, and taints what it touches! which violates that first natural right of mankind, equality and independency, and gives one man a dominion over his fellows which God could never intend! For it raises the owner to a state as far above man as it depresses the slave below it; and, with all the presumption of human pride, sets a distinction between them, immeasurable in extent, and endless in duration! Yet how mistaken is the avarice even of the planters. Are slaves more useful by being thus humbled to the condition of brutes than they would be if suffered to enjoy the privileges of men? The freedom which diffuses health and prosperity throughout Britain answers you—No. When you make men slaves, you deprive them of half their virtue; you set them, in your own conduct, an example of fraud, rapine, and cruelty, and compel them to live with you in a state of war; and yet you complain that they are not honest or faithful! You stupify them with stripes, and think it necessary to keep them in a state of ignorance. And yet you assert that they are incapable of learning; that their minds are such a barren soil or moor that culture would be lost on them; and that they come from a climate where nature, though prodigal of her bounties in a degree unknown to yourselves, has left man alone scant and unfinished, and incapable of enjoying the treasures she has poured out for him! An assertion at once impious and absurd. Why do you use those instruments of torture? Are they fit to be applied by one rational being to another? And are ye not struck with shame and mortification, to see the partakers of your nature reduced so low? But, above all, are there no dangers attending this mode of treatment? Are you not hourly in dread of an insurrection? Nor would it be surprising; for when

> No peace is given
> To us enslav'd, but custody severe,
> And stripes and arbitrary punishment
> Inflicted—What peace can we return?
> But to our power, hostility and hate;
> Untam'd reluctance, and revenge, though slow.
> Yet ever plotting how the conqueror least
> May reap his conquest, and may least rejoice
> In doing what we most in suffering feel.

But by changing your conduct, and treating your slaves as men, every cause of fear would be banished. They would be faithful, honest, intelligent, and vigorous; and peace, prosperity, and happiness would attend you.

from Chapter 10

MISCELLANEOUS VERSES:

OR,

Reflections on the state of my mind during my first Convictions, of the necessity of believing the Truth, and experiencing the inestimable benefits of Christianity.

> Well may I say my life has been
> One scene of sorrow and of pain;
> From early days I griefs have known,
> And as I grew my griefs have grown:
>
> Dangers were always in my path;
> And fear of wrath, and sometimes death:
> While pale dejection in me reign'd,
> I often wept, by grief constrained.

When taken from my native land,
By an unjust and cruel band,
How did uncommon dread prevail!
My sighs no more I could conceal.

To ease my mind I often strove,
And tried my trouble to remove;
I sung, and utter'd sighs between—
Assay'd to stifle guilt with sin.

But O! not all that I could do
Would stop the current of my woe:
Conviction still my vileness shew'd;
How great my guilt—how lost to good.

"Prevented that I could not die,
Nor could to one sure refuge fly:
An orphan state I had to mourn—
Forsook by all, and left forlorn."

Those who beheld my downcast mien,
Could not guess at my woes unseen;
They by appearance could not know
The troubles that I waded through.

Lust, anger, blasphemy, and pride,
With legions of such ills beside,
"Troubled my thoughts," while doubts and fears,
Clouded and darken'd most my years.

"Sighs now no more would be confin'd—
They breath'd the trouble of my mind:"
I wish'd for death, but check the word,
And often pray'd unto the Lord.

Unhappy more than some on earth,
I thought the place that gave me birth—
Strange thoughts oppress'd—while I replied
"Why not in Ethiopia died?"

And why thus spar'd when nigh to hell?—
God only knew—I could not tell!
"A tott'ring fence a bowing wall,"
"I thought myself ere since the fall."

Oft times I mus'd, and nigh despair,
While birds melodious fill'd the air:
"Thrice happy songsters, ever free,"
How blest were they, compar'd to me!

Thus all things added to my pain,
While grief compell'd me to complain!
When sable clouds began to rise
My mind grew darker than the skies.

The English nation call'd to leave,
How did my breast with sorrows heave!
I long'd for rest—cried, "Help me Lord;
Some mitigation, Lord, afford!"

Yet on, dejected, still I went—
Heart-throbbing woes within me pent;
Nor land, nor sea, could comfort give,
Nor aught my anxious mind relieve.

Weary with troubles yet unknown
To all but God and self alone,
Numerous months for peace I strove,
Numerous foes I had to prove.

Inur'd to dangers, griefs, and woes,
Train'd up 'midst perils, death, and foes,
I said, "Must it thus ever be?
No quiet is permitted me."

Hard hap, and more than heavy lot!
I pray'd to God "Forget me not—
What thou ordain'st help me to bear;
But O! deliver from despair!"

Strivings and wrestling seem'd in vain;
Nothing I did could ease my pain:
Then gave I up my work and will,
Confess'd and owned my doom was hell!

Like some poor pris'ner at the bar,
Conscious of guilt, of sin and fear,
Arraign'd, and self-condemned, I stood—
"Lost in the world and in my blood!"

Yet here, 'midst blackest clouds confin'd,
A beam from Christ, the day star shin'd:
Surely, thought I, if Jesus please,
He can at once sign my release.

I, ignorant of his righteousness,
Set up my labors in its place;
"Forgot for why his blood was shed,
And pray'd and fasted in its stead."

He died for sinners—I am one!
Might not his blood for me atone?
Tho' I am nothing else but sin,
Yet surely he can make me clean!

Thus light came in, and I believed;
Myself forgot, and help receiv'd!
My Saviour then I know I found,
For, eas'd from guilt no more I groan'd.

O, happy hour, in which I ceas'd
To mourn, for then I found a rest!
My soul and Christ were now as one—
Thy light, O Jesus, in me shone!

Bless'd be thy name, for now I know
I and my works can nothing do;
"The Lord alone can ransom man—
For this the spotless Lamb was slain!"

When sacrifices, works, and pray'r,
Prov'd vain, and ineffectual were—
"Lo, then I come!" the Saviour cried,
And bleeding, bow'd his head, and died!

He died for all who ever saw
No help in them, nor by the law:
I this have seen: and gladly own
"Salvation is by Christ alone!"[18]

[18] Acts 4:12.

Chapter 12

Different transactions of the author's life, till the present time—His application to the late Bishop of London to be appointed a missionary to Africa—Some account of his share in the conduct of the late expedition to Sierra Leone—Petition to the Queen—Conclusion.

Such were the various scenes which I was a witness to, and the fortune I experienced until the year 1777. Since that period, my life has been more uniform, and the incidents of it fewer, than in any other equal number of years preceding; I therefore hasten to the conclusion of a narrative which I fear the reader may think already sufficiently tedious.

I had suffered so many impositions in my commercial transactions in different parts of the world, that I became heartily disgusted with the sea-faring life, and was determined not to return to it, at least for some time. I therefore once more engaged in service shortly after my return, and continued for the most part in this situation until 1784.

Soon after my arrival in London, I saw a remarkable circumstance relative to African complexion, which I thought so extraordinary that I beg leave just to mention it. A white Negro woman, that I had formerly seen in London and other parts, had married a white man, by whom she had three boys, and they were every one mulattoes, and yet they had fine light hair. In 1779, I served Governor Macnamara, who had been a considerable time on the coast of Africa. In the time of my service, I used to ask frequently other servants to join me in family prayer; but this only excited their mockery. However, the Governor, understanding that I was of a religious turn, wished to know what religion I was of; I told him I was a protestant of the church of England, agreeable to the thirty-nine articles of that church; and that whomsoever I found to preach according to that doctrine, those I would hear. A few days after this, we had some more discourse on the same subject; when he said he would, if I chose, as he thought I might be of service in converting my countrymen to the Gospel faith, get me sent out as missionary to Africa. I at first refused going, and told him how I had been served on a like occasion, by some white people, the last voyage I went to Jamaica, when I attempted (if it were the will of God) to

be the means of converting the Indian prince; and said I supposed they would serve me worse than Alexander, the coppersmith, did St. Paul, if I should attempt to go amongst them in Africa. He told me not to fear, for he would apply to the Bishop of London to get me ordained. On these terms I consented to the Governor's proposal, to go to Africa in hope of doing good, if possible, amongst my countrymen; so, in order to have me sent out properly, we immediately wrote the following letters to the late Bishop of London:

To the Right Reverend Father in God, ROBERT, *Lord Bishop of London:*

THE MEMORIAL OF GUSTAVUS VASSA

SHEWETH,

That your memorialist is a native of Africa, and has a knowledge of the manners and customs of the inhabitants of that country.

That your memorialist has resided in different parts of Europe for twenty-two years last past, and embraced the Christian faith in the year 1759.

That your memorialist is desirous of returning to Africa as a missionary, if encouraged by your Lordship, in hopes of being able to prevail upon his countrymen to become Christians; and your memorialist is the more induced to undertake the same, from the success that has attended the like undertakings when encouraged by the Portuguese through their different settlements on the Coast of Africa, and also by the Dutch; both governments encouraging the blacks, who, by their education are qualified to undertake the same, and are found more proper than European clergymen, unacquainted with the language and customs of the country.

Your memorialist's only motive for soliciting the office of a missionary is that he may be a means, under God, of reforming his countrymen and persuading them to embrace the Christian religion. Therefore your memorialist humbly prays your Lordship's encouragement and support in the undertaking.

GUSTAVUS VASSA

AT MR. GUTHRIE'S, TAYLOR,
NO. 17, HEDGE LANE.

MY LORD,

I have resided near seven years on the coast of Africa, for most part of the time as commanding officer. From the knowledge I have of the country and its inhabitants, I am inclined to think that the within plan will be attended with great success, if countenanced by your Lordship. I beg leave further to represent to your Lordship, that the like attempts, when encouraged by other governments, have met with uncommon success; and at this very time I know a very respectable character, a black priest, at Cape Coast Castle. I know the within named Gustavus Vassa, and believe him a moral good man.

I have the honor to be, my Lord,
Your Lordship's
Humble and obedient servant,
MATT. MACNAMARA

GROVE, 11TH MARCH, 1779.

This letter was also accompanied by the following from Doctor Wallace, who had resided in Africa for many years, and whose sentiments on the subject of an African mission were the same with Governor Macnamara's.

MARCH 13, 1779.

MY LORD,

I have resided near five years on Senegambia, on the coast of Africa, and have had the honor of filling very considerable employments in that province. I do approve of the within plan, and think the undertaking very laudable and proper, and that it deserves your Lordship's protection and encouragement, in which case it must be attended with the intended success.

I am, my Lord, your Lordship's
Humble and obedient servant,
THOMAS WALLACE

With these letters, I waited on the Bishop by the Governor's desire, and presented them to his Lordship. He received me with much condescension and politeness; but from some certain scruples of delicacy, and saying the Bishops were not of opinion of sending a new missionary to Africa, he declined to ordain me.

My sole motive for thus dwelling on this transaction, or inserting these papers, is the opinion which gentlemen of sense and education, who are acquainted with Africa, entertain of the probability of converting the inhabitants of it to the faith of Jesus Christ, if the attempt were countenanced by the Legislature.

Shortly after this I left the Governor, and served a nobleman in the Dorsetshire militia, with whom I was encamped at Coxheath for some time; but the operations there were too minute and uninteresting to make a detail of.

In the year 1783, I visited eight counties in Wales, from motives of curiosity. While I was in that part of the country, I was led to go down into a coal-pit in Shropshire, but my curiosity nearly cost me my life; for while I was in the pit

the coals fell in, and buried one poor man, who was not far from me: upon this, I got out as fast as I could, thinking the surface of the earth the safest part of it.

In the spring of 1784, I thought of visiting old ocean again. In consequence of this I embarked as steward on board a fine new ship called the *London*, commanded by Martin Hopkin, and sailed for New York. I admired this city very much; it is large and well built, and abounds with provisions of all kinds. While we lay here a circumstance happened which I thought extremely singular. One day a malefactor was to be executed on a gallows; but with a condition that if any woman, having nothing on but her shift, married the man under the gallows, his life was to be saved. This extraordinary privilege was claimed; a woman presented herself, and the marriage ceremony was performed.

Our ship having got laden, we returned to London in January 1785. When she was ready again for another voyage, the captain being an agreeable man, I sailed with him from hence in the spring, March 1785, for Philadelphia. On the 5th of April, we took our departure from the lands-end, with a pleasant gale; and about nine o'clock that night the moon shone bright, and the sea was smooth, while our ship was going free by the wind, at the rate of about four or five miles an hour. At this time another ship was going nearly as fast as we on the opposite point, meeting us right in the teeth; yet none on board observed either ship until we struck each other forcibly head and head, to the astonishment and consternation of both crews. She did us much damage, but I believe we did her more; for when we passed by each other, which we did very quickly, they called to us to bring to, and hoist out our boat, but we had enough to do to mind ourselves; and in about eight minutes we saw no more of her. We refitted as well as we could the next day, and proceeded on our voyage, and in May arrived at Philadelphia.

I was very glad to see this favorite old town once more; and my pleasure was much increased in seeing the worthy Quakers freeing and easing the burdens of many of my oppressed African brethren. It rejoiced my heart when one of these friendly people took me to see a free school they had erected for every denomination of black people, whose minds are cultivated here, and forwarded to virtue; and thus they are made useful members of the community. Does not the success of this practice say loudly to the planters, in the language of scripture—"Go ye and do likewise"?

In October 1785, I was accompanied by some of the Africans, and presented this address of thanks to the gentlemen called Friends or Quakers, in Grace Church Court, Lombard street:

GENTLEMEN,

By reading your book, entitled a Caution to Great Britain and her Colonies, concerning the calamitous state of the enslaved Negroes: We, part of the poor, oppressed, needy, and much degraded Negroes, desire to approach you with this address of thanks, with our inmost love and warmest acknowledgement; and with the deepest sense of your benevolence, unwearied labor, and kind interposition, towards breaking the yoke of slavery, and to administer a little comfort and ease to thousands and tens of thousands of very grievously afflicted, and too heavy burthened Negroes.

Gentlemen, could you, by perseverance, at last be enabled under God, to lighten in any degree the heavy burthen of the afflicted, no doubt it would in some measure, be the possible means, under God, of saving the souls of many of the oppressors; and if so, sure we are that the God, whose eyes are ever upon all his creatures, and always rewards every true act of virtue, and regards the prayers of the oppressed, will give to you and yours those blessings which it is not in our power to express or conceive, but which we, as a part of those captivated, oppressed, and afflicted people, most earnestly wish and pray for.

These gentlemen received us very kindly, with a promise to exert themselves on behalf of the oppressed Africans, and we parted.

While in town, I chanced once to be invited to a Quaker's wedding. The simple and yet expressive mode used at their solemnizations is worthy of note. The following is the true form of it:

After the company have met they have seasonable exhortations by several of the members; the bride and bridegroom stand up, and, taking each other by the hand in a solemn manner, the man audibly declares to this purpose: "Friends, in the fear of the Lord, and in the presence of this assembly, whom I desire to be my witnesses, I take this my friend, M——— N———, to be my wife; promising, through divine assistance, to be unto her a loving and faithful husband till death separate us," and the woman makes the like declaration. Then the two first sign their names to the record, and as many more witnesses as have a mind. I had the honor to subscribe mine to a register in Grace Church Court, Lombard street.

My hand is ever free—if any female Debonair wishes to obtain it, this mode I recommend.

We returned to London in August; and our ship not going immediately to sea, I shipped as a steward in an American ship, called the *Harmony,* Captain John Willet, and left London in March 1786, bound to Philadelphia. Eleven days after sailing, we carried our foremast away. We had a nine weeks' passage, which caused our trip not to succeed well, the market for our goods proving bad; and to make it worse, my commander began to play me the like tricks as others too often practise on free Negroes in the West Indies. But, I thank God, I found many friends here, who in some measure prevented him.

On my return to London in August, I was very agreeably surprised to find that the benevolence of government had adopted the plan of some philanthropic individuals, to send the Africans from hence to their native quarter; and that some vessels were then engaged to carry them to Sierra Leone, an act which redounded to the honor of all concerned in its promotion, and filled me with prayers and much rejoicing. There was then in the city a select committee of gentlemen for the black poor, to some of whom I had the honor of being known; and as soon as they heard of my arrival, they sent for me to the committee. When I came there, they informed me of the intention of government; and as they seemed to think me qualified to superintend part of the undertaking, they asked me to go with the black poor to Africa. I pointed out to them many objections to my going; and particularly I expressed some difficulties on the account of the slave dealers, as I would certainly oppose their traffic in human species, by every means in my power. However, these objections were over-ruled by the gentlemen of the committee, who prevailed on me to consent to go; and recommended me to the honorable commissioners of his Majesty's Navy, as a proper person to act as commissary for government in the intended expedition; and they accordingly appointed me, in November 1786, to that office, and gave me sufficient power to act for the government, in the capacity of commissary, having received my warrant and the following order:

BY THE PRINCIPAL OFFICERS AND COMMISSIONERS OF HIS
MAJESTY'S NAVY

Whereas you were directed, by our warrant, of the 4th of last month, to receive into your charge from Mr. Joseph Irwin, the surplus provisions remaining of what was provided for the voyage, as well as the provisions for the support of the black poor, after the landing at Sierra Leone, with the clothing, tools, and all other articles provided at government's expense; and as the provisions were laid in at the rate of two months for the voyage, and for four months after the landing, but the number embarked being so much less than we expected, whereby there may be a considerable surplus of provisions, clothing, &c. These are in addition to former orders, to direct and require you to appropriate or dispose of such surplus to the best advantage you can for the benefit of government, keeping and rendering to us a faithful account of what you do herein. And for your guidance in preventing any white persons going, who are not intended to have the indulgence of being carried thither, we send you herewith a list of those recommended by the Committee for the black poor, as proper persons to be permitted to embark, and acquaint you that you are not to suffer any others to go who do not produce a certificate from the Committee for the black poor, of their having their permission for it. For which this shall be your warrant. Dated at the Navy Office, Jan. 16, 1787.

> J. HINSLOW
> GEO. MARSH
> W. PALMER

TO MR. GUSTAVUS VASSA, COMMISSARY
OF PROVISIONS AND STORES FOR THE
BLACK POOR GOING TO SIERRA LEONE.

I proceeded immediately to the executing of my duty on board the vessels destined for the voyage, where I continued till the March following.

During my continuance in the employment of government, I was struck with the flagrant abuses committed by the agent, and endeavored to remedy them, but without effect. One instance, among many which I could produce, may serve as a specimen. Government had ordered to be provided all necessaries (slops, as they are called, included) for 750 persons; however, not being able to muster more than 426, I was ordered to send the superfluous slops, &c., to the king's stores at Portsmouth; but, when I demanded them for that purpose from the agent, it appeared they had never been bought, though paid for by government. But that was not all; government were not the only objects of peculation; these poor people suffered infinitely more; their accommodations were most wretched, many of them wanted beds, and many more clothing and other necessaries. For the truth of this, and much more, I do not seek credit from my own assertion.

I appeal to the testimony of Captain Thompson, of the *Nautilus,* who conveyed us, to whom I applied in February 1787, for a remedy, when I had remonstrated to the agent in vain, and even brought him to be a witness of the injustice and oppression I complained of. I appeal also to a letter written by these wretched people, so early as the beginning of the preceding January, and published in the *Morning Herald,* on the 4th of that month, signed by twenty of their chiefs.

I could not silently suffer government to be thus cheated and my countrymen plundered and oppressed, and even left destitute of the necessaries for almost their existence. I therefore informed the Commissioners of the Navy, of the agent's proceeding, but my dismission was soon after procured, by means of a gentleman in the city, whom the agent, conscious of his peculation, had deceived by letter, and who, moreover, empowered the same agent to receive on board, at the government expense, a number of persons as passengers, contrary to the orders I received. By this I suffered a considerable loss in my property; however, the commissioners were satisfied with my conduct, and wrote to Captain Thompson, expressing their approbation of it.

Thus provided, they proceeded on their voyage; and at last, worn out by treatment, perhaps not the most mild, and wasted by sickness, brought on by want of medicine, clothes, bedding, &c., they reached Sierra Leone, just at the commencement of the rains. At that season of the year, it is impossible to cultivate the lands; their provisions therefore were exhausted before they could derive any benefit from agriculture; and it is not surprising that many, especially the Lascars, whose constitutions are very tender, and who had been cooped up in ships from October to June, and accommodated in the manner I have mentioned, should be so wasted by their confinement as not to survive it.

Thus ended my part of the long talked of expedition to Sierra Leone; an expedition which, however unfortunate in the event, was humane and politic in its design, nor was its failure owing to government; everything was done on their part; but there was evidently sufficient mismanagement attending the conduct and execution of it to defeat its success.

I should not have been so ample in my account of this transaction, had not the share I bore in it been made the subject of partial animadversion, and even my dismission from my employment thought worthy of being made by some a matter of public triumph.[19] The motives which might influence any person to descend to a petty contest with an obscure African, and to seek gratification by his depression, perhaps it is not proper here to inquire into or relate, even if its detection were necessary to my vindication, but I thank Heaven it is not. I wish to stand by my own integrity, and not to shelter myself under the impropriety of another; and I trust the behavior of the Commissioners of the Navy to me entitle me to make this assertion; for after I had been dismissed, March 24, I drew up a memorial thus:

To the Right Honorable the Lord's Commissioners of his Majesty's Treasury.

The Memorial and Petition of GUSTAVUS VASSA, a black man, late Commissary to the black poor going to Africa.

HUMBLY SHEWETH,

That your Lordship's memorialist was, by the Honorable the Commissioners of his Majesty's Navy, on the 4th of December last, appointed to the above employment by warrant from that board;

That he accordingly proceeded to the execution of his duty on board of the *Vernon*, being one of the ships appointed to proceed to Africa with the above poor;

That your memorialist, to his great grief and astonishment, received a letter of dismission from the Honorable Commissioners of the Navy, by your Lordships orders:

That, conscious of having acted with the most perfect fidelity and the greatest assiduity in discharging the trust reposed in him, he is altogether at a loss to conceive the reasons of your Lordships having altered the favorable opinion you were pleased to conceive of him, sensible that your Lordships would not proceed to so severe a measure without some apparent good cause; he therefore has every reason to believe that his conduct has been grossly misrepresented to your Lordships, and he is the more confirmed in his opinion, because, by opposing measures of others concerned in the same expedition, which tended to defeat your Lordship's humane intentions, and to put the government to a very considerable additional expense, he created a number of enemies, whose misrepresentations, he has too much reason to believe, laid the foundation of his dismission. Unsupported by friends, and unaided by the advantages of a liberal education, he can only hope for redress from the justice of his cause, in addition to the mortification of having been removed from his employment, and the advantage which he reasonably might have expected to have derived therefrom. He has had the misfortune to have

[19] See the *Public Advertiser*, July 14, 1787.

sunk a considerable part of his little property in fitting himself out, and in other expenses arising out of his situation, an account of which he here annexes. Your memorialist will not trouble your Lordships with a vindication of any part of his conduct, because he knows not of what crimes he is accused; he, however, earnestly entreats that you will be pleased to direct an enquiry into his behavior during the time he acted in the public service; and, if it be found that his dismission arose from false representations, he is confident that in your Lordship's justice he shall find redress.

Your petitioner therefore humbly prays that your Lordships will take his case into consideration; and that you will be pleased to order payment of the above referred to account, amounting to 321.4s. and also the wages intended which is most humbly submitted.
LONDON, MAY 12, 1787.

The above petition was delivered into the hands of their Lordships, who were kind enough, in the space of some few months afterwards, without hearing, to order me 501. sterling—that is, 181. wages for the time (upwards of four months) I acted a faithful part in their service. Certainly the sum is more than a free Negro would have had in the western colonies!!!

From that period, to the present time, my life has passed in an even tenor, and a great part of my study and attention has been to assist in the cause of my much injured countrymen.

March the 21st, 1788, I had the honor of presenting the Queen with a petition in behalf of my African brethren, which was received most graciously by Her Majesty.[20]

To the Queen's most Excellent Majesty:

MADAM,

Your Majesty's well known benevolence and humanity emboldens me to approach your royal presence, trusting that the obscurity of my situation will not prevent your Majesty from attending to the sufferings for which I plead.

Yet I do not solicit your royal pity for my own distress; my sufferings, although numerous, are in a measure forgotten. I supplicate your Majesty's compassion for millions of my African countrymen, who groan under the lash of tyranny in the West Indies.

The oppression and cruelty exercised to the unhappy Negroes there, have at length reached the British Legislature, and they are now deliberating on its redress; even several persons of property in slaves in the West Indies, have petitioned Parliament against

[20] At the request of some of my most particular friends, I take the liberty of inserting it here.

its continuance, sensible that it is as impolitic as it is unjust—and what is inhuman must ever be unwise.

Your Majesty's reign has been hitherto distinguished by private acts of benevolence and bounty; surely the more extended the misery is, the greater claim it has to your Majesty's compassion, and the greater must be your Majesty's pleasure in administering to its relief.

I presume, therefore, gracious Queen, to implore your interposition with your royal consort, in favor of the wretched Africans; that, by your Majesty's benevolent influence, a period may now be put to their misery—and that they may be raised from the condition of brutes, to which they are at present degraded, to the rights and situation of freemen, and admitted to partake of the blessings of your Majesty's happy government; so shall your Majesty enjoy the heart-felt pleasure of procuring happiness to millions, and be rewarded in the grateful prayers of themselves, and of their posterity.

And may the all-bountiful Creator shower on your Majesty, and the Royal Family, every blessing that this world can afford, and every fulness of joy which divine revelation has promised us in the next.

I am your Majesty's
Most dutiful and devoted servant to command,
GUSTAVUS VASSA
The Oppressed Ethiopian
NO. 53, BALDWIN'S GARDENS.

The Negro consolidated act, made by the assembly of Jamaica last year, and the new act of amendment now in agitation there, contain a proof of the existence of those charges that have been made against the planters relative to the treatment of their slaves.

I hope to have the satisfaction of seeing the renovation of liberty and justice, resting on the British government, to vindicate the honor of our common nature. These are concerns which do not perhaps belong to any particular office; but, to speak more seriously, to every man of sentiment, actions like these are the just and sure foundation of future fame; a reversion, though remote, is coveted by some noble minds as a substantial good. It is upon these grounds that I hope and expect the attention of gentlemen in power. These are designs consonant to the elevation of their rank and the dignity of their stations; they are ends suitable to the nature of a free and generous government, and, connected with views of empire and dominion, suited to the benevolence and solid merit of the legislature. It is a pursuit of substantial greatness. May the time come—at least the speculation to me is pleasing—when the sable people shall gratefully commemorate the auspicious era of extensive freedom: then shall those persons[21] particularly be named with praise and honor who generously proposed and stood forth in the cause of humanity, liberty, and good policy, and brought to the ear of the legislature designs worthy of royal patronage and adoption. May Heaven make the British senators the dispersers of light, liberty, and science, to the uttermost parts of the earth: then will be glory to God in the highest, on earth peace, and good will to men. Glory, honor, peace, &c. to every soul of man that worketh good: to the Britons first (because to them the gospel is preached), and also to the nations. "Those that honor their Maker have mercy on the poor." It is "righteousness exalteth a nation, but sin is a reproach to any people; destruction shall be to the workers of iniquity, and the wicked shall fall by their own wickedness." May the blessings of the Lord be upon the heads of all those who commiserated the cases of the oppressed Negroes, and the fear of God prolong their days; and may their expectations be filled with gladness! "The liberal devise liberal things, and by liberal things shall stand" (Isaiah 32:8). They can say with pious Job, "Did not I weep for him that was in trouble? was not my soul grieved for the poor?" (Job 30:25).

As the inhuman traffic of slavery is to be taken into the consideration of the British legislature, I doubt not, if a system of commerce was established in Africa, the demand for manufactures will most rapidly augment, as the native inhabitants will sensibly adopt the British fashions, manners, customs, &c. In proportion to the civilization, so will be the consumption of British manufactures.

The wear and tear of a continent, nearly twice as large as Europe and rich in vegetable and mineral production, is much easier conceived than calculated.

A case in point. It cost the Aborigines of Britain little or nothing in clothing, &c. The difference between their forefathers and the present generation, in point of consumption, is literally infinite. The supposition is most obvious. It will be equally immense in Africa—The same cause, viz. civilization, will ever have the same effect.

[21] Granville Sharp, Esq., the Rev. Thomas Clarkson, the Rev. James Ramsay, our approved friends, men of virtue, are an honor to their country, ornamental to human nature, happy in themselves, and benefactors to mankind!

It is trading upon safe grounds. A commercial intercourse with Africa opens an inexhaustible source of wealth to the manufacturing interest of Great Britain;[22] and to all which the slave trade is an objection.

If I am not misinformed, the manufacturing interest is equal, if not superior, to the landed interest, as to the value, for reasons which will soon appear. The abolition of slavery, so diabolical, will give a most rapid extension of manufactures, which is totally and diametrically opposite to what some interested people assert.

The manufactures of this country must and will, in the nature and reason of things, have a full and constant employ, by supplying the African markets.

Population, the bowels and surface of Africa, abound in valuable and useful returns; the hidden treasures of centuries will be brought to light and into circulation. Industry, enterprise, and mining will have their full scope, proportionably as they civilize. In a word, it lays open an endless field of commerce to the British manufacturers and merchant adventurer. The manufacturing interest and the general interests are synonymous. The abolition of slavery would be in reality an universal good.

Tortures, murder, and every other imaginable barbarity and iniquity, are practised upon the poor slaves with impunity. I hope the slave trade will be abolished. I pray it may be an event at hand. The great body of manufacturers, uniting in the cause, will considerably facilitate and expedite it; and as I have already stated, it is most substantially their interest and advantage, and as such the nation's at large (except those persons concerned in the manufacturing neck yokes, collars, chains, handcuffs, leg bolts, drags, thumbscrews, iron muzzles, and coffins; cats, scourges, and other instruments of torture used in the slave trade). In a short time one sentiment will alone prevail, from motives of interest as well as justice and humanity. Europe contains one hundred and twenty millions of inhabitants. Query: How many millions doth Africa contain? Supposing the Africans, collectively and individually, to expend £5 a head in raiment and furniture yearly when civilized, &c., an immensity beyond the reach of imagination!

This I conceive to be a theory founded upon facts, and therefore an infallible one. If the blacks were permitted to remain in their own country, they would double themselves every fifteen years. In proportion to such increase will be the demand for manufactures. Cotton and indigo grow spontaneously in most parts of Africa; a consideration this of no small consequence to the manufacturing towns of Great Britain. It opens a most immense, glorious, and happy prospect—the clothing, &c., of a continent ten thousand miles in circumference, and immensely rich in productions of every denomination in return for manufactures.

Since the first publication of my Narrative, I have been in a great variety of scenes in many parts of Great Britain, Ireland, and Scotland, an account of which might not improperly be added here;[23] but this would swell the volume too much, I shall only observe in general, that in May 1791, I sailed from Liverpool to Dublin, where I was very kindly received, and from thence to Cork, and then travelled over many counties in Ireland. I was everywhere exceedingly well treated, by persons of all ranks. I found the people extremely hospitable, particularly in Belfast, where I took my passage on board of a vessel for Clyde, on the 29th of January, and arrived at Greenock on the 30th. Soon after I returned to London, where I found persons of note from Holland and Germany, who requested me to go there; and I was glad to hear that an edition of my Narrative had been printed in both places, also in New York. I remained in London till I heard the debate in the House of Commons on the slave trade, April the 2d and 3d. I then went to Soham in

---

[22] "In the ship Trusty, lately for the new Settlement of Sierra Leone, in Africa, were 1,300 pair of shoes (an article hitherto scarcely known to be exported to that country) with several others equally new, as articles of export. Thus will it not become the interest, as well as the duty, of every artificer, mechanic, and tradesman, publicly to enter their protest against this traffic of the human species? What a striking—what a beautiful contrast is here presented to view, when compared with the cargo of a slave ship! Every feeling heart indeed sensibly participates of the joy, and with a degree of rapture reads of barrels of *flour* instead of *gunpowder*—*biscuits and bread* instead of *horse beans*—*implements of husbandry* instead of *guns* for destruction, rapine, and murder—and various articles of *usefulness* are the pleasing substitutes for the *torturing thumbscrew*, and the *galling chain*, &c."

[23] Viz. Some curious adventures beneath the earth in a river in Manchester, and a most astonishing one under the Peak of Derbyshire—and in September 1792, I went 90 fathoms down St. Anthony's Colliery, at Newcastle, under the river Tyne, some hundreds of yards on Durham side.

Cambridgeshire, and was married on the 7th of April to Miss Cullen, daughter of James and Ann Cullen, late of Ely.[24]

I have only therefore to request the reader's indulgence, and conclude. I am far from the vanity of thinking there is any merit in this narrative: I hope censure will be suspended, when it is considered that it was written by one who was as unwilling as unable to adorn the plainness of truth by the coloring of imagination. My life and fortune have been extremely checkered, and my adventures various. Nay even those I have related are considerably abridged. If any incident in this little work should appear uninteresting and

[24] See *Gentleman's Magazine* for April 1792, *Literary and Biographical Magazine,* and *British Review* for May 1792, and the *Edinburgh Historical Register* or *Monthly Intelligencer* for April 1792.

trifling to most readers, I can only say, as my excuse for mentioning it, that almost every event of my life made an impression on my mind, and influenced my conduct. I early accustomed myself to look at the hand of God in the minutest occurrence, and to learn from it a lesson of morality and religion; and in this light every circumstance I have related was to me of importance. After all, what makes any event important, unless by its observation we become better and wiser, and learn "to do justly, to love mercy, and to walk humbly before God"? To those who are possessed of this spirit, there is scarcely any book or incident so trifling that does not afford some profit, while to others the experience of ages seems of no use; and even to pour out to them the treasures of wisdom is throwing the jewels of instruction away.

Phillis Wheatley (1753?–1784)

The Black girl who became Phillis Wheatley was born free in Senegal on the African west coast in the early 1750's. When she was five or six years old, she was kidnapped by slavers, eventually transported in a slave ship to Boston, and sold in 1761 to John Wheatley, a well-to-do merchant-tailor. Her precocity encouraged the Wheatleys to educate her, and, within sixteen months after her arrival in the Wheatley household, the young slave girl had learned to speak and to write English. She then received, through informal tutorial sessions, a New England education, with considerable stress on the Bible and on the classics. As a consequence, the poetry that she wrote reflects a heavy emphasis on the religious as well as a deep knowledge of the classics. Her education also prepared her to write the kind of neoclassical poetry very much in vogue at that time. It should also be noted that her upbringing and training did not give her a deep sense of identification with her people. She wrote no poems of social or moral protest against slavery and apparently had little communication with the free Blacks of Boston until her unfortunate marriage in 1778.

Her earliest verses were written during her first years of adolescence, and her first published poem appeared when she was seventeen. It is entitled "On the Death of the Rev. Mr. George Whitefield. 1770." Another early poem was "The King's Most Excellent Majesty," written in 1768.

As the young poet grew into young womanhood, her physical frailness became a matter of serious concern to the Wheatleys, and in 1773 Phillis was manumitted from slavery and sent to London in the company of other members of the family. It was hoped that there she could receive the medical attention she needed. Interestingly enough, her arrival in London occurred at an auspicious moment in the Black man's history. In 1772, a few months before, Chief Justice Mansfield had passed down his famous ruling freeing all slaves in England, thus enabling Phillis and other Blacks to move about England in a slavery-free environment. There is no evidence, however, that this circumstance in any way affected her stay in London. Evidently, the young Black poet found London to be an exciting and exhilarating city. Not only was she introduced to the famous Mr. Benjamin Franklin of Philadelphia, but, under the auspices of the Countess of Huntingdon, she met the cream of London society and was hailed as the "Sable Muse." Also in London, in late 1773, when she was no more than twenty years old, Phillis Wheatley published her first volume of poetry entitled *Poems on Various Subjects, Religious and Moral, by Phillis Wheatley, Negro Servant to Mr. Wheatley of Boston.* This proved to be a very popular volume of poetry, not only during the author's short lifetime but on into the nineteenth century. There were several subsequent editions, the most interesting of which was published by Mrs. Margaretta Odell in 1834. Mrs. Odell, a descendant of the poet, added a memoir on the life and times of the young Phillis.

News of Mrs. Wheatley's illness forced Phillis to return to America in early 1774. When Mrs. Wheatley died in March of that year and the remaining Wheatleys died in quick succession in the late 1770's, Phillis became in truth a free woman. Ironically, this change radically altered her good fortune. Indeed, her survival time in total freedom from the Wheatley household was a scant and tragic six years—from 1778 to 1784. First, she married John Peters, a free Black, who proved to be both ambitious and irresponsible. Then, their three children died in infancy. Moreover, like most of Boston's free Blacks at this time, the Peters family was forced to live in squalor and poverty. Under these circumstances, Phillis' health, which had always been delicate, rapidly deteriorated; and in 1784 she died at the age of about thirty.

Her early death provides a commentary on the desperate marginality of life among Boston's free Blacks at that time. To a Phillis Wheatley, at one time a privileged servant who enjoyed an extremely benign master–servant relationship, freedom's uncertainties and insecurities were overwhelming. Certainly, had she been initially free in Boston, she would probably never have had the time, the opportunity, or the peace of mind to write poetry. For the state of freedom for the Black man in the 1780's—even in godly, liberty-loving Boston—was indeed precarious. As David Walker was to indicate later in his famous *Appeal*, "freedom" meant economic insecurity, social ostracism, and psychological oppression.

In the almost two hundred years since her death, Phillis Wheatley as poet has been subjected to both praise and censure. Many Blacks have been indignant at her failure to protest against slavery in her poetry. Other critics have been disenchanted with her rigid neoclassicism in theme, subject, and style and her obvious bent for pious sentimentalizing about Truth, Salvation, Mercy, and Goodness. In her defense, one can say that this young Black poet was a child of her times and was molded and directed by the kind of education she received. Certainly, during her short but productive poetic life, she used her gifts honestly and well, producing well-wrought poems that have withstood the test of time.

As indicated above, there have been several editions of Phillis Wheatley's poems, but the most valuable is the recent critical edition prepared by Julian Mason—*The Poems of Phillis Wheatley* (1966). There is also a very informative article by Robert C. Kuncio on "Some Unpublished Poems of Phillis Wheatley," in *The New England Quarterly*, XLIII (June 1970), 287–297. Good critical assessments of her poetry can be found in Vernon Loggins' *The Negro Author* (1931), in Benjamin Brawley's *The Negro in Literature and Art* (1929), and in Saunders Redding's *To Make a Poet Black* (1939). Shirley Graham's *The Story of Phillis Wheatley* (1949) is an excellent biographical treatment.

On the Death of the
Rev. Mr. George Whitefield. 1770

Hail, happy saint, on thine immortal throne,
Possest of glory, life, and bliss unknown;
We hear no more the music of thy tongue,
Thy wonted auditories cease to throng.
Thy sermons in unequalled accents flow'd,
And every bosom with devotion glowed;
Thou didst in strains of eloquence refin'd
Inflame the heart, and captivate the mind.
Unhappy we the setting sun deplore,
So glorious once, but ah! it shines no more.

Behold the prophet in his tow'ring flight!
He leaves the earth for heav'n's unmeasured height,
And worlds unknown receive him from our sight.
There Whitefield wings with rapid course his way,
And sails to Zion through vast seas of day.
Thy prayers, great saint, and thine incessant cries
Have pierced the bosom of thy native skies.
Thou moon has seen, and all the stars of light,
How he has wrestled with his God by night.
He pray'd that grace in ev'ry heart might dwell,
He long'd to see America excell;
He charg'd its youth that ev'ry grace divine
Should with full lustre in their conduct shine;

That Saviour, which his soul did first receive,
The greatest gift that ev'n a God can give,
He freely offer'd to the num'rous throng,
That on his lips with list'ning pleasure hung.

"Take him, ye wretched, for your only good,
"Take him, ye starving sinners, for your food;
"Ye thirsty, come to this life-giving stream,
"Ye preachers, take him for your joyful theme;
"Take him my dear Americans, he said,
"Be your complaints on his kind bosom laid:
"Take him, ye Africans, he longs for you,
"Impartial Saviour is his title due:
"Washed in the fountain of redeeming blood,
"You shall be sons, and kings, and priests to God."

Great Countess,[1] we Americans revere
Thy name, and mingle in thy grief sincere;
New England deeply feels, the Orphans mourn,
Their more than father will no more return.

But, though arrested by the hand of death,
Whitefield no more exerts his lab'ring breath,
Yet let us view him in th' eternal skies,
Let ev'ry heart to this bright vision rise;
While the tomb safe retains its sacred trust,
Till life divine re-animates his dust.

[1] [The Countess of Huntingdon, to whom Mr. Whitefield was Chaplain.—Editors' note]

On Virtue

O thou bright jewel in my aim I strive
To comprehend thee. Thine own words declare
Wisdom is higher than a fool can reach.
I cease to wonder, and no more attempt
Thine height t'explore, or fathom thy profound.
But, O my soul, sink not into despair,
Virtue is near thee, and with gentle hand
Would now embrace thee, hovers o'er thine
    head.
Fain would the heav'n-born soul with her
    converse,
Then seek, then court her for her promis'd bliss.

Auspicious queen, thy heaven'ly pinions
    spread,

And lead celestial Chastity along;
Lo! now her sacred retinue descends,
Array'd in glory from the orbs above.
Attend me, Virtue, thro my youthful years!
O leave me not to the false joys of time!
But guide my steps to endless life and bliss.
Greatness, or Goodness, say what shall I call
    thee,
To give an higher appellation still,
Teach me a better strain, a nobler lay,
O Thou, enthron'd with Cherubs in the realms
    of day!

To the University of Cambridge, in New England

While an intrinsic ardor prompts to write,
The muses promise to assist my pen;
'Twas not long since I left my native shore
The land of errors, and Egyptian gloom:
Father of mercy, 'twas thy gracious hand
Brought me in safety from those dark abodes.

Students, to you 'tis giv'n to scan the heights
Above, to traverse the ethereal space,
And mark the systems of revolving worlds.
Still more, ye sons of science ye receive
The blissful news by messengers from heav'n,
How Jesus' blood for your redemption flows.
See him with hands out-stretcht upon the cross;
Immense passion in his bosom glows;
He hears revilers, nor resents their scorn:

What matchless mercy in the Son of God!
When the whole human race by sin had fall'n,
He deigned to die that they might rise again,
And share with him in the sublimest skies,
Life without death, and glory without end.

Improve your privileges while they stay,
Ye pupils, and each hour redeem, that bears
Or good or bad report of you to heav'n.
Let sin, that baneful evil to the soul,
By you be shunn'd, nor once remit your guard;
Suppress the deadly serpent in its egg.
Ye blooming plants of human race divine,
An Ethiope tells you 'tis your greatest foe;
Its transient sweetness turns to endless pain,
And in immense perdition sinks the soul.

On Being Brought from Africa to America

'Twas mercy brought me from my pagan land,
Taught my benighted soul to understand
That there's a God, that there's a Saviour too:
Once I redemption neither sought nor knew.

Some view our sable race with scornful eye,
"Their colour is a diabolic die."
Remember, *Christians, Negroes,* black as *Cain,*
May be refin'd, and join th' angelic train.

An Hymn to the Morning

Attend my lays, ye ever honour'd nine,
Assist my labours, and my strains refine;
In smoothest numbers pour the notes along.
For bright Aurora now demands my song.

Aurora hail, and all the thousand dies,
Which deck thy progress through the vaulted
skies:
The morn awakes, and wide extends her rays,
On ev'ry leaf the gentle zephyr plays;
Harmonious lays the feather'd race resume,
Dart the bright eye, and shake the painted plume.

Ye shady groves, your verdant gloom display
To shield your poet from the burning day:
Calliope awake the sacred lyre,
While thy fair sisters fan the pleasing fire:
The bow'rs, the gales, the variegated skies
In all their pleasures in my bosom rise.

See in the east th' illustrious king of day!
His rising radiance drives the shades away—
But Oh! I feel his fervid beams too strong,
And scarce begun, concludes th' abortive
song.

A Farewell to America

I
Adieu, New-England's smiling meads,
  Adieu, th' flow'ry plain:
I leave thine op'ning charms, O spring,
  And tempt the roaring main.

II
In vain for me the flow'rets rise,
  And boast their gaudy pride,
While here beneath the northern skies
  I mourn for health deny'd.

III
Celestial maid of rosy hue,
  Oh let me feel thy reign!
I languish till thy face I view,
  Thy vanish'd joys regain.

IV
Susannah mourns, nor can I bear
  To see the crystal shower
Or mark the tender falling tear
  At sad departure's hour;

V
Not regarding can I see
  Her soul with grief opprest
But let no sighs, no groans for me
  Steal from her pensive breast.

VI
In vain the feather'd warblers sing
  In vain the garden blooms
And on the bosom of the spring
  Breathes out her sweet perfumes.

VII
While for Britannia's distant shore
  We weep the liquid plain,
And with astonish'd eyes explore
  The wide-extended main.

VIII
Lo! Health appears! celestial dame!
  Complacent and serene,
With Hebe's mantle o'er her frame,
  With soul-delighting mein.

IX
To mark the vale where London lies
  With misty vapors crown'd
Which cloud Aurora's thousand dyes,
  And veil her charms around.

X
Why, Phoebus, moves thy car so slow?
  So slow thy rising ray?
Give us the famous town to view,
  Thou glorious King of day!

XI
For thee, Britannia, I resign
  New-England's smiling fields;
To view again her charms divine,
  What joy the prospect yields!

XII
But thou! Temptation hence away,
  With all thy fatal train,
Nor once seduce my soul away,
  By thine enchanting strain.

XIII
Thrice happy they, whose heavenly shield
Secures their souls from harm,
And fell Temptation on the field
Of all its pow'r disarms.

To His Excellency General Washington

[The following LETTER and VERSES, were written by the famous Phillis Wheatley, The African Poetess, and presented to his Excellency Gen. Washington.]

SIR.
I Have taken the freedom to address your Excellency in the enclosed poem, and entreat your acceptance, though I am not insensible to its inaccuracies. Your being appointed by the Grand Continental Congress to be Generalissimo of the armies of North America, together with the fame of your virtues, excite sensations not easy to suppress. Your generosity, therefore, I presume, will pardon the attempt. Wishing your Excellency all possible success in the great cause you are so generously engaged in, I am

Your Excellency's most obedient humble servant,

PHILLIS WHEATLEY.
Providence, Oct. 26, 1775.
His Excellency Gen. Washington

Celestial choir! enthroned in realms of light,
Columbia's scenes of glorious toils I write
While freedom's cause her anxious breast alarms,
She flashes dreadful in refulgent arms.
See mother earth her offspring's fate bemoan,
And nations gaze at scenes before unknown!
See the bright beams of heaven's revolving light
Involved in sorrows and the veil of night!
    The goddess comes, she moves divinely fair,
Olive and laurel binds her golden hair:
Wherever shines this native of the skies,
Unnumbered charms and recent graces rise.
    Muse! bow propitious while my pen relates
How pour her armies through a thousand gates,
As when Eolus heaven's fair face deforms,
Enwrapped in tempest and a night of storms;
Astonished ocean feels the wild uproar,
The refluent surges beat the sounding shore;
Or thick as leaves in Autumn's golden reign,
Such, and so many, moves the warrior's train.
In bright array they seek the work of war,
Where high unfurl'd the ensign waves in air.
Shall I to Washington their praise recite?
Enough thou knowest them in the fields of fight.
Thee, first in peace and honours,—we demand
The grace and glory of thy martial band.
Fam'd for thy valour, for thy virtues more,
Hear every tongue thy guardian aid implore!
    One century scarce perform'd its destined round,
When Gallic powers Columbia's fury found;

And so may you, whoever dares disgrace
The land of freedom's heaven-defended race!
Fix'd are the eyes of nations on the scales,
For in their hopes Columbia's arm prevails.
Anon Britannia droops the pensive head,
While round increase the rising hills of dead.
Ah! cruel blindness to Columbia's state!
  Proceed, great chief, with virtue on thy side,
Thy every action let the goddess guide.
A crown, a mansion, and a throne that shine,
With gold unfading, WASHINGTON! be thine.

Note on Phillis Wheatley's Letter and Poem to George Washington

[General Washington's reply to Phillis Wheatley's poem was as follows.]

Cambridge, Mass.
February 28, 1776

Miss Phillis, Your favor of the 26th of October did not reach my hands, till the middle of December. Time enough, you will say, to have given an answer ere this. Granted. But a variety of important occurrences, continually interposing to distract the mind and withdraw the attention, I hope will apologize for the delay, and plead my excuse for the seeming but not real neglect. I thank you most sincerely for your polite notice of me, in the elegant lines you enclosed; and however undeserving I may be of such encomium and panegyric, the style and manner exhibit a striking proof of your poetical talents; in honor of which, and as a tribute justly due to you, I would have published the poem, had I not been apprehensive, that, while I only meant to give the world this new instance of your genius, I might have incurred the imputation of vanity. This, and nothing else, determined me not to give it place in the public prints.

If you should ever come to Cambridge, or near headquarters, I shall be happy to see a person so favored by the Muses, and to whom nature has been so liberal and beneficent in her dispensations. I am, with great respect,

Your obedient humble servant,

GEORGE WASHINGTON.

A Poet and an Intellectual

Jupiter Hammon (1720?–1800?)

Much about Jupiter Hammon's life and career is obscure. Only a few facts are known with any certainty. First, he was born a slave sometime around 1720 and remained a slave all of his life. Second, he belonged to the influential Lloyd family of Lloyd's Neck near Queen's Village on Long Island and found in this family the kind of benevolent understanding that encouraged him to write and publish poetry. Third, his "An Evening Thought," composed in December 1760 and published early in 1761, was the first poem published by a Black man in America. It is also known that he published "An Address to Miss Phillis Wheatly" in 1778, "A Poem for Children" in 1782, "An Evening's Improvement" in the mid-1780's, and composed an "Address to the Negroes of the State of New York" in 1786 that was later published in New York in 1806. But of the man Jupiter Hammon—his marriage and family, his reconciliation of fervent Christianity with chattel slavery, his attitudes and beliefs—little is known.

His poetry reflects a strong influence of Methodism and the Wesleyan Revival that swept America in the middle of the eighteenth century. This is particularly evident in the hymnal qualities of his verse. In fact, because all of his poetizing is on religious themes, some critics have speculated that Hammon may have been a preacher first and a poet only secondarily.

A strong religious bent is evident in the poem to Phillis Wheatley when, overwhelmed by religious fervor, the poet expresses joy that

> *God's tender mercy brought thee here;*
> *Tossed o'er the raging main*

Could it be that Jupiter Hammon, Black man of God and a slave, really did not know how far removed "God's tender mercy" was from a slave ship? Or could it be that he was so removed from worldly woe and attuned to anticipated heavenly joy that slavery, one of the world's major woes, no longer existed for him? Slavery was of this earth, and Jupiter Hammon longed for salvation on high. Indeed, in "An Evening Thought" the word "salvation" occurs in every stanza, giving some hint of the absorption in Christian otherworldliness that can render a man forgetful of his earthly state.

45

But his religious fervor seriously impaired his poetry. There is in Jupiter Hammon's verse none of the felicity of thought and verbal imagery found in Phillis Wheatley's poetry. Her subject matter is of broader range, and her classical training disciplined her to take a more balanced view of Man, God, and Nature.

Jupiter Hammon's last published work was his "Address to the Negroes of the State of New York." His brief comments on slavery in this address serve to confirm the view that, for him, slavery was an endurable and acceptable institution. Better to accept enslavement on earth and receive a Christian crown in the Hereafter than lose one's soul fighting against slavery. Thus he urged acceptance of the slavery system, although he did express regret that the Black veterans of the Revolutionary War were not rewarded for patriotic efforts with freedom from bondage.

In the final analysis, Jupiter Hammon's religion was an opiate that dulled him to the world's evil ways. Instead of giving him a revolutionary social vision, it filled him with penitential cries. And his poetry is esthetically anemic and almost stifling in its repetitive religiosity.

The last full-length study of Hammon's poetry appeared over a half century ago. This is Oscar Wegelin's *Jupiter Hammon: American Negro Poet* (1915). Since that time, the poet's work has received good critical treatment in Vernon Loggins' *The Negro Author* (1931) and in Saunders Redding's *To Make a Poet Black* (1939). William H. Robinson's edition of *Early Black American Poets* (1969) contains a good critical introduction to a generous sampling of Hammon's poems.

An Evening Thought: Salvation by Christ with Penetential Cries

Salvation comes by Christ alone,
  The only Son of God;
Redemption now to every one,
  That loves his holy Word.

    .   .   .

Dear Jesus, give thy Spirit now,
  Thy grace to every Nation,
That han't the Lord to whom we bow,
  The Author of Salvation.

Dear Jesus, unto Thee we cry,
  Give us the Preparation;
Turn not away thy tender Eye;
  We seek thy true Salvation.

    .   .   .

Lord, hear our penetential Cry:
  Salvation from above;
It is the Lord that doth supply,
  With his Redeeming Love.

Dear Jesus, by thy precious Blood,
  The World Redemption have:
Salvation now comes from the Lord,
  He being thy captive slave.

Dear Jesus, let the Nations cry,
  And all the People say,
Salvation comes from Christ on high,
  Haste on Tribunal Day.

We cry as Sinners to the Lord,
  Salvation to obtain;
It is firmly fixed, his holy Word,
  Ye shall not cry in vain.

    .   .   .

Lord, turn our dark benighted Souls;
  Give us a true Motion,
And let the Hearts of all the World,
  Make Christ their Salvation.

    .   .   .

Lord, unto whom now shall we go,
 Or seek a safe abode?
Thou hast the Word, Salvation Too:
 The only Son of God.

"Ho! every one that hunger hath,
 Or pineth after me,
Salvation be thy leading Staff,
 To set the Sinner free."

Dear Jesus, unto Thee we fly;
 Depart, depart from Sin,
Salvation doth at length supply,
 The glory of our King.

Come, ye Blessed of the Lord,
 Salvation greatly given;
O, turn your hearts, accept the Word,
 Your Souls are fit for Heaven.

Dear Jesus, we now turn to Thee,
 Salvation to obtain;
Our Hearts and Souls do meet again,
 To magnify thy Name.

Come, holy Spirit, Heavenly Dove,
 The Object of our Care;
Salvation doth increase our Love;
 Our Hearts hath felt thy fear.

Now Glory be to God on High,
 Salvation high and low;
And thus the Soul on Christ rely,
 To Heaven surely go.

Come, Blessed Jesus, Heavenly Dove,
 Accept Repentance here;
Salvation give, with tender Love;
 Let us with Angels share.

An Address to Miss Phillis Wheatly,
Ethiopian Poetess

An address to Miss Phillis Wheatly, Ethiopian Poetess, in Boston, who came from Africa at eight years of age, and soon became acquainted with the gospel of Jesus Christ.

1
O, come, you pious youth! adore
 The wisdom of thy God,
In bringing thee from distant shore,
 To learn His holy word,
2
Thou mightst been left behind,
 Amidst a dark abode;
God's tender mercy still combined,
 Thou hast the holy word.
3
Fair Wisdom's ways are paths of peace,
 And they that walk therein,
Shall reap the joys that never cease,
 And Christ shall be their King.
4
God's tender mercy brought thee here;
 Tossed o'er the raging main;
In Christian faith thou hast a share,
 Worth all the gold of Spain.
5
While thousands tossed by the sea,
 And others settled down,
God's tender mercy set thee free
 From dangers that come down.

6
That thou a pattern still might be,
 To youth of Boston town,
The blessed Jesus set thee free
 From every sinful wound.
7
The blessed Jesus, who came down,
 Unveiled his sacred face,
To cleanse the soul of every wound,
 And give repenting grace.
8
That we poor sinners may obtain
 The pardon of our sin,
Dear Blessed Jesus, now constrain,
 And bring us flocking in.
9
Come, you, Phillis, now aspire,
 And seek the living God,
So step by step thou mayst go higher,
 Till perfect in the word.
10
While thousands moved to distant shore,
 And others left behind,
The blessed Jesus still adore;
 Implant this in thy mind.
11
Thou hast left the heathen shore;
 Through mercy of the Lord,
Among the heathen live no more;
 Come magnify thy God.

12

I pray the living God may be,
  The shepherd of thy soul;
His tender mercies still are free,
  His mysteries to unfold.

13

Thou, Phillis, when thou hunger hast,
  Or pantest for thy God,
Jesus Christ is thy relief,
  Thou hast the holy word.

14

The bounteous mercies of the Lord
  Are hid beyond the sky,
And holy souls that have His word
  Shall taste them when they die.

15

These bounteous mercies are from God,
  The merits of His Son;
The humble soul that loves His word
  He chooses for his own.

16

Come, dear Phillis, be advised
  To drink Samaria's flood;
There nothing that shall suffice
  But Christ's redeeming blood.

17

While thousands muse with earthly toys,
  And range about the street,
Dear Phillis, seek for heaven's joys,
  Where we do hope to meet.

18

When God shall send his summons down,
  And number saints together,
Blessed angels chant (triumphant sound),
  Come live with me forever.

19

The humble soul shall fly to God,
  And leave the things of time,
Start forth as 'twere at the first word,
  To taste things more divine.

20

Behold! the soul shall waft away,
  Whene'er we come to die,
And leave its cottage made of clay,
  In twinkling of an eye.

21

Now glory be to the Most High,
  United praises given,
By all on earth, incessantly,
  And all the host of heaven.

Benjamin Banneker (1731–1806)

The myth of white superiority and Black inferiority infected some of the greatest minds of the eighteenth century. For example, the philosopher David Hume asserted that of all the Black slaves in Europe and its colonies, "none ever discovered any symptoms of ingenuity." In *Notes on Virginia,* Thomas Jefferson delivered the following opinion of Black intellectual capacity: "Comparing them by their faculties of memory, reason, and imagination, it appears to me, that in memory they are equal to the whites; in reason much inferior, as I think one could scarcely be found capable of tracing and comprehending the investigations of Euclid; and that in imagination they are dull, tasteless, and anomalous." With racism so deeply entrenched in the highest intellectual circles, as well as among the general white populace, the need for Black geniuses who could serve as living refutations of this nonsense was obvious. Of these, perhaps the most important was Benjamin Banneker, mathematician, naturalist, astronomer, inventor, poet, compiler of almanacs, and social critic.

As a child Benjamin was precocious; he learned to read from his grandmother and attended a rural school taught by a Quaker. His opportunities were meager enough, but he exploited them by cultivating his remarkable powers of observation and induction. By occupation a farmer, his chief interest was mathematics, in which he achieved an astonishing proficiency. In his twenties he constructed a faultless wooden clock with his pocket knife. One writer states: "It is probable that this was the first clock of which every portion was made in America; it is certain that it was as purely his own invention as if none had ever been before. He had seen a watch, but never a clock, such an article not being within fifty miles of him."

In 1772 Banneker's intellectual career received a new impetus from his friendship with the wealthy and educated Ellicott family, who had moved to Maryland from Pennsylvania in order to set up flour mills. Recognizing Banneker's genius, the family lent him tools and instruments. Later, George Ellicott gave him more mathematical instruments and books on astronomy, which quickly became his favorite study. For years he devoted himself to the science of the heavens, often sleeping all day in order to gaze at the stars all night. At the age of sixty he had developed his calculations far enough to write his first almanac, for the year 1792, a copy of which he presented, along with his famous letter, to Thomas Jefferson, then Secretary of State during the first administration of George Washington. Banneker continued to publish his annual almanacs to 1802.

Even before the letter to Jefferson, a signal honor had come to Banneker—appointment by President Washington to a commission headed by the French civil engineer Pierre Charles L'Enfant to lay out the city of Washington. Banneker made an important contribution to the design of the national capital, one of the great achievements of American urban planning. A contribution of much greater potential value to the young nation, his proposals for ensuring national and international peace, as outlined in "A Plan of Peace-Office for the United States," was unfortunately ignored.

The nation and the world have yet to realize the vision of universal peace and racial harmony expressed by the foremost Black intellectual of the eighteenth century. Yet at least this much is clear: after the example of Benjamin Banneker, no one with a trace of intellectual honesty could disagree with the verdict of James McHenry, a prominent white Marylander: "I consider this Negro as fresh proof that the powers of the mind are disconnected with the color of the skin, or, in other words, a striking contrast to Mr. Hume's doctrine, that 'the Negroes are naturally inferior to the whites, and unsusceptible of attainments in arts and sciences.' In every civilized country, we shall find thousands of whites liberally educated and who have enjoyed greater opportunities for instruction than this Negro, his inferiors in those intellectual acquirements and capacities that form the most characteristic features in the human race."

Shirley Graham's *Your Most Humble Servant* (1949) is a biography of Banneker. Chapters on Banneker appear in Benjamin Brawley's *Negro*

Builders and Heroes (1937) and Lerone Bennett, Jr.'s vividly written *Pioneers in Protest* (1968). A good scholarly article is Henry E. Baker, "Benjamin Banneker, The Negro Mathematician and Astronomer," *The Journal of Negro History,* III (1918), 99–118. Winthrop D. Jordan treats the exchange of correspondence between Banneker and Jefferson in the context of Jefferson's racial attitudes in *White Over Black: American Attitudes Toward the Negro, 1550–1812* (1968).

A Mathematical Problem in Verse*

A Cooper and Vintner sat down for a talk,
Both being so groggy, that neither could walk,
Says Cooper to Vintner, "I'm the first of my trade,
There's no kind of vessel, but what I have made,
And of any shape, Sir,—just what you will,—
And of any size, Sir,—from a ton to a gill!"
"Then," says the Vintner, "you're the man for me,—
Make me a vessel, if we can agree.
The top and the bottom diameter define,
To bear that proportion as fifteen to nine,
Thirty-five inches are just what I crave,
No more and no less, in the depth, will I have;
Just thirty-nine gallons this vessel must hold,—
Then I will reward you with silver or gold,—
Give me your promise, my honest old friend?"
"I'll make it tomorrow, that you may depend!"
So the next day the Cooper his work to discharge,
Soon made the new vessel, but made it too large;—
He took out some staves, which made it too small,
And then cursed the vessel, the Vintner and all.
He beat on his breast, "By the Powers!"—he swore,
He never would work at his trade any more.
Now my worthy friend, find out, if you can,
The vessel's dimensions and comfort the man!

Letter to Thomas Jefferson

Maryland, Baltimore County
Near Ellicotts' Lower Mills, August 19th, 1791

Thomas Jefferson, Secretary of State.

Sir:—I am fully sensible of the greatness of that freedom, which I take with you on the present occasion, a liberty which seemed to me scarcely allowable, when I reflected on that distinguished and dignified station in which you stand, and the almost general prejudice and prepossession which is so prevalent in the world against those of my complexion.

I suppose it is a truth too well attested to you, to need a proof here, that we are a race of beings who have long laboured under the abuse and

---

* Banneker included this untitled mathematical problem in verse in a letter he wrote to George Ellicott. According to George Washington Williams, "The greater diameter of Banneker's tub must be 24.746 inches; the less diameter, 14.8476 inches."

censure of the world, that we have long been considered rather as brutish than human, and scarcely capable of mental endowments.

Sir, I hope I may safely admit, in consequence of that report which hath reached me, that you are a man far less inflexible in sentiments of this nature than many others, that you are measurably friendly and well disposed towards us, and that you are willing and ready to lend your aid and assistance to our relief, from those many distresses and numerous calamities, to which we are reduced.

Now, sir, if this is founded in truth, I apprehend you will readily embrace every opportunity to eradicate that train of absurd and false ideas and opinions, which so generally prevails with respect to us, and that your sentiments are concurrent with mine, which are that one universal Father hath given Being to us all, and that he hath not only made us all of one flesh, but that he hath also without partiality afforded us all the same sensations, and endued us all with the same faculties, and that however variable we may be in society or religion, however diversified in situation or colour, we are all of the same family, and stand in the same relation to him.

Sir, if these are sentiments of which you are fully persuaded, I hope you cannot but acknowledge, that it is the indispensable duty of those who maintain for themselves the rights of human nature, and who profess the obligations of christianity, to extend their power and influence to the relief of every part of the human race, from whatever burden or oppression they may unjustly labour under, and this I apprehend a full conviction of the truth and obligation of these principles should lead all to.

Sir, I have long been convinced that if your love for yourselves and for those inesteemable laws, which preserve to you the rights of human nature, was found on sincerity, you could not but be solicitous that every individual of whatever rank or distinction, might with you equally enjoy the blessings thereof, neither could you rest satisfied, short of the most active diffusion of your exertions in order to their promotions from any state of degradation to which the unjustifiable cruelty and barbarism of men have reduced them.

Sir, I freely and cheerfully acknowledge that I am of the African race, and in that colour which is natural to them of the deepest dye, and it is under a sense of the most profound gratitude to the Supreme Ruler of the universe that I now confess to you that I am not under that state of tyrannical thraldom and inhuman captivity to which too many of my brethren are doomed; but that I have abundantly tasted of the fruition of those blessings which proceed from that free and unequalled liberty with which you are favoured and which, I hope you will willingly allow you have received from the immediate hand of that Being, from whom proceedeth every good and perfect gift.

Sir, suffer me to recall to your mind that time in which the arms and tyranny of the British Crown were exerted with every powerful effort in order to reduce you to a State of Servitude, look back I entreat you on the variety of dangers to which you were exposed; reflect on that time in which every human aid appeared unavailable, and in which even hope and fortitude wore the aspect of inability to the conflict and you cannot but be led to a serious and grateful sense of your miraculous and providential preservation; you cannot but acknowledge that the present freedom and tranquility which you enjoy you have mercifully received and that it is the pecular blessing of Heaven.

This sir, was a time in which you clearly saw into the injustice of a state of slavery and in which you had just apprehensions of the horrors of its condition, it was now, sir, that your abhorrence thereof was so excited, that you publickly held forth this true and valuable doctrine, which is worthy to be recorded and remembered in all succeeding ages. "We hold these truths to be self-evident, that all men are created equal, and that they are endowed by their creator with certain unalienable rights, that among these are life, liberty and the pursuit of happiness."

Here, sir, was a time in which your tender feelings for yourselves had engaged you thus to declare, you were then impressed with proper ideas of the great valuation of liberty and the free possession of those blessings to which you were entitled by nature; but, sir, how pitiable is it to reflect that although you were so fully convinced of the benevolence of the Father of mankind and of his equal and impartial distribution of those rights and privileges which he had conferred upon them, that you should at the same time counteract his mercies in detaining by fraud and violence so numerous a part of my brethren under groaning captivity and cruel oppression, that you should at the same time be found guilty of that most criminal act which you professedly detested in others with respect to yourselves.

Sir, I suppose that your knowledge of the situation of my brethren is too extensive to need a recital here; neither shall I presume to prescribe methods by which they may be relieved, otherwise than by recommending to you and all others to wean yourselves from those narrow prejudices which you have imbibed with respect to them and as Job proposed to his friends, "put your souls in their souls stead," thus shall your hearts be enlarged with kindness and benevolence towards them, and thus shall you need neither the direction of myself or others, in what manner to proceed herein.

And now, sir, although my sympathy and affection for my brethren hath caused my enlargement thus far, I ardently hope that your candour and generosity will plead with you in my behalf when I make known to you that it was not originally my design; but that having taken up my pen in order to direct to you as a present, a copy of an almanac, which I have calculated for the succeeding year, I was unexpectedly and unavoidably led thereto.

This calculation, sir, is the production of my arduous study in this my advanced stage of life; for having long had unbounded desires to become acquainted with the secrets of nature, I have had to gratify my curiosity herein through my own assiduous application to astronomical study, in which I need not to recount to you the many difficulties and disadvantages which I have had to encounter.

And although I had almost declined to make my calculation for the ensuing year, in consequence of that time which I had allotted therefor being taken up at the Federal Territory by the request of Mr. Andrew Ellicott, yet finding myself under several engagements to printers of this state, to whom I had communicated my design, on my return to my place of residence I industriously applied myself thereto which I hope I have accomplished with correctness and accuracy, a copy of which I have taken the liberty to direct to you and which I humbly request you will favorably receive. Although you may have the opportunity of perusing it after its publication yet I chose to send it to you in manuscript previous thereto that you might not only have an earlier inspection but that you might also view it in my own handwriting.

And now, sir, I shall conclude and subscribe myself, with the most profound respect, your most obedient humble servant,

B. BANNEKER

PART II

The Struggle Against Slavery and Racism: 1800–1860

As the nineteenth century began, more than a million Blacks lived in the United States, comprising almost twenty per cent of the total population. In the South, most Blacks were slaves, though some, especially in Baltimore, Charleston, and New Orleans, were nominally free. In the North, most Blacks were nominally free, though some were slaves. By 1860, the Black population of the United States had grown to 4,441,830, four million of whom were slaves. Between Gabriel Prosser's revolt in 1800 and the outbreak of the Civil War, both whites and Blacks struggled with the problems posed by the interaction of this Black presence with white racism. White proposals for solution—or evasion—of these problems comprise much of the American political history of this period. On the other hand, Black proposals for solution provide most of the themes for the Black literature written during these years.

In the first decade of the nineteenth century the major racial question was the international slave trade. Though illegal in all states in 1800, the trade continued to prosper because of the extremely lax enforcement of the bans. When three years later South Carolina went so far as to repeal its law against slave importation, the issue could no longer be evaded. In 1807 the federal government outlawed the importation of slaves, but the coastal trade was permitted under certain tonnage restrictions and the internal domestic trade was entirely unaffected by the legislation. Again, however, as in the case of the state prohibitions, the law proved ineffective because of lack of enforcement. As late as the Civil War, slaves from Africa were still crossing the Atlantic bound for Southern plantations.

The slave trade flourished in the first half of the nineteenth century because of westward expansion. From South Carolina and Georgia, cotton cultivation spread to Alabama, Mississippi, and Louisiana, and tobacco crossed the mountains from Virginia and North Carolina to Kentucky and Tennessee. Meanwhile, pioneers from New England and the Middle Atlantic states were moving into the free territory of the Northwest and forming the states of Ohio, Indiana, and Illinois. The rival economic systems and the competition for political power that developed led to sectional animosities. The first crisis—the "mere preamble," as John Quincy Adams called it—of what was destined to become a protracted struggle occurred when the Territory of Missouri, originally a part of the Louisiana Purchase, sought admission to the Union in 1819. Representative James Tallmadge of New York introduced an amendment to ban slavery from the new state, and the fight was on. In 1821 Missouri did enter as a slave state, but Maine entered as a free state to maintain the political balance of power between North and South. Most importantly, the enabling legislation provided that, except for Missouri, "in all that territory ceded by France . . . which lies north of thirty-six degrees and thirty minutes north latitude . . . slavery and involuntary servitude . . . shall be, and is hereby, forever prohibited."

During the 1820's and 1830's, the organized abolition movement emerged from its comatose state of the first years of the century. In 1821 Benjamin Lundy began a paper called *The Genius of Universal Emancipation*, and ten years later William Lloyd Garrison issued his ringing call for immediate abolition: "I am in earnest—I will not equivocate—I will not excuse—I will not retreat a single inch—AND I WILL BE HEARD." The voices of Lundy and Garrison and Theodore Weld and others, Black and white, were at first heard by only a few as they began the monumental task of organizing public sentiment against slavery.

One issue that did arouse considerable opposition was the expansion of slavery westward into Texas. Despite the abolition of slavery by Mexico in 1829, Anglo-Americans continued to settle with their slaves west of the Sabine. After a brief revolution against the Mexican regime in 1836, the Republic of Texas emerged as an independent slave power with close ties to the South. Almost immediately, Texas sought annexation, but the North managed to postpone this action until the presidential campaign of 1844, when the election of James Knox Polk of Tennessee on a proannexation platform ensured the addition of another slave state to the Union. Annexation led in 1846 to war with Mexico, which had not recognized Texas independence. The Mexican War was the most unpopular national conflict before the Vietnamese War, and resembled it in a number of ways. Abolitionists were of course outraged, but many other Northerners resented fighting a war in the interest of the slave power.

After the war, Northern antislavery sentiment was expressed in the Wilmot Proviso, which would have banned slavery in all the territory acquired from Mexico, but the measure failed. The political spectrum on the slavery question now ranged from abolitionists to proslavery imperialists. In an effort to reconcile these irreconcilable elements, the Compromise of 1850 admitted California as a free state and abolished the slave trade in the nation's capital, but also provided for the territories of New Mexico and Utah to "be received into the Union, with or without slavery, as their constitutions may provide at the time of their admission." The most malevolent part of the Compromise of 1850, however, was the stringent Fugitive Slave Act, the provisions of which jeopardized the liberty of every Black person in the Northern states, free as well as fugitive, and made criminals of those Northern whites who aided alleged fugitive slaves. So usually mild a man as Ralph Waldo Emerson recorded his bitter reaction to this legislation in his journal: "this is befriending in our own State, on our own farms, a man who has taken the risk of being shot, or burned alive, or cast into the sea, or starved to death, or suffocated in a wooden box, to get away from his driver: and this man who has run the gauntlet of a thousand miles for his freedom, the statute says, you men of Massachusetts shall hunt, and catch, and send back again to the dog-hutch he fled from. And this filthy enactment was made in the nineteenth century, by people who could read and write. I will not obey it, by God." And Frederick Douglass wrote grimly: "The only way to make the Fugitive Slave Law a dead letter is to make a half dozen or more dead kidnappers."

Thus the Compromise of 1850 really settled nothing. The publication in 1852 of Harriet Beecher Stowe's great novel, *Uncle Tom's Cabin,* greatly increased antislavery feeling, especially in resistance to the Fugitive Slave Act. This sentiment led to action and violence after the passage of the Kansas-Nebraska Act in 1854. Repealing the Missouri Compromise, this measure opened the territories named to settlement, the question of slavery to be left to the "popular sovereignty" of the squatters themselves. The result in "bleeding Kansas" was a small-scale civil war between proslavery settlers and free-soil men. John Brown was counted among the latter.

Another blow to antislavery and free-soil forces, some of whom had organized the Republican Party, was the Dred Scott decision of the Supreme Court in 1857. In denying the claim of freedom by Scott, who had lived with his master for years in the free state of Illinois and then in territory designated free by the Missouri Compromise, the Court based its decision in part on the belief imputed to the founding fathers that Blacks as a race "had no rights which the white man was bound to respect." From this decision the steps were short to John Brown at Harpers Ferry and to the firing on Fort Sumter. Political efforts to resolve the question of slavery had failed. Armed conflict was now the only recourse.

The fate of the Black slave was at the center of the American historical experience for over half a century. The destiny of the free Black was by comparison a peripheral matter, but he too found himself the victim of a repressive white racism not unlike that suffered by his brother in bondage. Three schools of thought existed among whites regarding the treatment of the free Black. A tiny minority of radical abolitionists would have extended to him egalitarian rights as "a man and a brother." Though pitifully few in number, these whites together with Blacks themselves kept alive the concept of human fraternity across racial lines in an era extremely inhospitable to such a notion. The other two schools of white thought were much more influential at the time. These were the advocates of colonization and the proponents of discrimination and repression. The latter carried the day.

Colonizationists wished to eliminate the Black man's problems by expelling him from the American scene, either by repatriation to Africa or by emigration to Mexico, Central or South America, Haiti, or elsewhere. Suggestions of this kind had been made since the early eighteenth century, but the campaign began in earnest in 1816 with the organization of the American Colonization Society. With the support of such public figures as John Randolph, James Madison, Francis Scott Key, Stephen Douglas, Henry Clay, Andrew Jackson, Daniel Webster, Roger Taney, and John Marshall, the Society rapidly gained adherents, especially after the establishment of the Liberian colony in 1822. At first the Society attracted some men of goodwill who acted out of a genuine humanitarian impulse, but the essential racism of the project had by 1831 become clear to the abolitionists, who attacked it unremittingly thereafter. The vast majority of free Blacks, especially in the North, had seen through the scheme from the very beginning. Only a month after the Society was formed, Richard Allen and James Forten led three thousand Philadelphia Blacks in a vehement denunciation of the organization and its philosophy. The chief beneficiaries of colonization, they recognized, would be the slaveholders, who would no longer need to fear the economic competition and the political danger represented by free Blacks. For all the propaganda on behalf of colonization, in the end less than fifteen thousand free Blacks left this country, and most of them went to Liberia as a condition of their emancipation.

The varieties of coercion inflicted upon the vast majority of free Blacks—almost half a million by 1860—who remained in the United States were limited only by the imagination of the white establishment. In general, their position in the national life deteriorated from 1800 to 1860 as white laws and customs regulated their existence ever more repressively.

Politically, only in the four northernmost New England states, where Blacks were only a minute percentage of the population, could they vote on a substantially equal basis with whites. In Rhode Island, Blacks were finally enfranchised in 1842. More often, however, the trend was in the opposite direction. The states of Connecticut, Pennsylvania, New Jersey, Maryland, Tennessee, North Carolina, and Indiana all disfranchised

Black voters who earlier had presumably enjoyed suffrage. In New York the constitutional convention of 1821 and subsequent legislation removed property qualifications from whites but not from Blacks, who were required to reside in the state three years as well as own property worth two hundred and fifty dollars. In all the states not mentioned above, the law denied the ballot to Black people at all times prior to the adoption of the Fifteenth Amendment. Even in those states where *de jure* Black suffrage obtained, community custom, pressure, or subterfuge often prevented the actual exercise of this most basic of democratic rights.

Another means of repression was legislation prohibiting or severely restricting the immigration of Blacks, as in the states of Ohio, Illinois, Indiana, and Iowa, and the territories of Michigan and Oregon. The alternative to exclusion, some Westerners threatened, was extermination. Although only rarely enforced, such legislation demonstrated clearly the negrophobia rampant on the frontier.

If a Black man sought to redress his grievances in the courts, he faced formidable obstacles. In the South and in several Northern states, his testimony was prohibited in cases involving whites. Nowhere did Black judges sit on the bench. Nowhere, with the sole exception of Massachusetts the year before the Civil War, did Black jurymen sit in the jury box. It was only logical that the system of racist "justice" developed under these conditions would culminate in such a decision as that handed down in the case of Dred Scott *v.* Sandford. As the folk tale pointed out, Ole Sis Goose had little chance in a courtroom filled with foxes.

Excluded from meaningful political participation and denied justice in the courts, free Blacks had to endure the further humiliation of social ostracism. In the North, almost all kinds of public transportation, entertainment, and accommodation were either segregated or denied to Blacks altogether. In the South, the very movement of free Blacks was restricted with ever increasing rigor as the sectional debate intensified. Passes were required in all Southern states, and white guardians or registration in some. In North Carolina, a free Black could travel only as far as the adjacent county. In ports on the Gulf, Black sailors were confined to their ships. Freedom of assembly was denied twenty-five years before the war. Everywhere in the South a free Black risked slipping into slavery under the flimsiest pretense. In a bewildering variety of legal and extralegal ways, free Blacks were constantly reminded of their inferior status. When the usual measures seemed inadequate, white racists could always resort to mob violence. Major anti-Black riots occurred in Cincinnati in 1829, in Philadelphia in 1834, 1835, 1842, and 1849, in New York City in 1834. The climax was reached in the terrible New York Draft Riots of 1863, in which hundreds of Blacks were slaughtered in the streets.

In the struggle against the handicaps imposed on him in every area of life, the free Black turned to education as his best weapon. But here too his efforts were hindered by white racism. In the South, public education was largely unknown, and in any case laws were passed making it a crime to teach free Blacks. In the Western states, where public education was established, Blacks were excluded before 1850, though some segregated schools were later set up. Only in the North did Blacks enjoy easy access to public education—segregated, of course. The only exception to the Jim Crow educational system occurred in 1855 when Boston and New Bedford desegregated their public schools.

Despite the hardships, many free Blacks did acquire some education, and a few became truly learned men. Private instruction was widespread, even in the South, where it was forbidden. Some wealthy Blacks from New Orleans were educated in France. James McCune Smith earned an M.D. degree from the University of Glasgow in 1837, and Alexander Crummell was graduated from Queen's College, Cambridge, in 1853. In this country, in 1826, Edward Jones was graduated from Amherst and John B. Russwurm from Bowdoin, and others followed in some of the nation's leading universities. Two Black institutions, Lincoln in Pennsylvania and Wilberforce in Ohio, were established in the decade before the Civil War. But for the most part, education for free Black people to 1860 was separate and unequal—or nonexistent.

The economic life of free Blacks from the turn of the century to the Civil War presents a picture of deteriorating conditions for the masses and improving opportunities for a fortunate few. During the entire period, Blacks were concentrated in the lowest-paid, least desirable unskilled jobs: agriculture, common labor, personal service, maritime work, and domestic occupations. For the first three decades of the century, a period of an expanding national economy, Blacks at least could feel some assurance that employment was available in the menial positions open to them. Beginning in the 1830's, however, Black economic security, even on its subsistence level, withered under the onslaught of competition from immigrant groups (particularly the Irish), the hostility of organized labor, and the omnipresent racism that led employers to believe that Blacks were fit only for the lowest jobs and white workers to believe that association with Blacks on the job was degrading. After fighting for his life against whites on the docks of Baltimore, Frederick Douglass escaped to New Bedford and attempted to find work as a calker, but, as he recalled in his *Narrative,* "such was the strength of prejudice against color, among the white calkers, that they refused to work with me, and of course I could get no employment."

There were many exceptions to the general economic degradation of free Blacks. Some, in the South as well as in the North, gained an adequate living as artisans or mechanics. Others took advantage of opportunities created by ghetto living conditions to become businessmen or professionals. A few—Paul Cuffe, Solomon Humphries, Jehu Jones, and James Forten among them—even acquired fortunes. Thomy Lafon of New Orleans accumulated half a million dollars. Much more typical, however, was the hod carrier or canal digger or washerwoman or cook: underpaid, overworked, and then displaced by Irish competition. As the lowest class in the "free" economy of young America, Black people were the most ruthlessly exploited.

At the outbreak of the Civil War, then, the situation of the free Black was desperate. Leon F. Litwack, one of the closest students of the subject, summarizes his findings in this way:

> *Discrimination still barred him from most polls, juries, schools, and workshops, as well as from many libraries, theaters, lyceums, museums, public conveyances, and literary societies. Although he himself was responsible for this exclusion, the white man effectively turned it against the Negro. Having excluded the Negro from profitable employments, the whites scorned his idleness and poverty; having taxed him in some states for the support of public education, they excluded his children from the schools or placed them in separate and inferior institutions and then deplored the ignorance of his race; having excluded him from various lecture halls and libraries, they pointed to his lack of culture and refinement; and, finally, having stripped him of his claims to citizenship and having deprived him of opportunities for political and economic advancement, the white concluded that the Negro had demonstrated an incapacity for improvement in this country and should be colonized in Africa.*

Litwack was referring to the Northern Black. The plight of the Southern free Black was much worse.

Inevitably, the literature created by Black people living in these circumstances was a literature of survival, of protest, a literature responsive in a very direct way to the most pressing problems of the race. The characteristic forms of Black literature in the first half of the nineteenth century were the oration, the public letter, and the autobiography, not the novel or play or poem. When the traditional belletristic forms were used, more often than not they also spoke to the immediate crisis of Blacks, as in the fiction and drama of William Wells Brown or the poetry of Frances Watkins Harper or James M. Whitfield.

The appeal of a basically utilitarian literature written to meet the exigencies of a specific historical occasion usually declines after the occasion has passed. That this is much less true of Black literature is due to the constant factors in Afro-American history—the Black presence and white racism. Because Black history in this country does repeat itself, one can hear in Eldridge Cleaver the accents of David Walker, or examine in Martin Luther King ideas similar to those of William Whipper. Only when racism loses its grip on the white American psyche and the nation solves its racial dilemma will early Black writing exchange its pressing contemporary relevance for a merely "historical" interest.

The two great concerns of Black writing before the Civil War were the institution of slavery and the destiny of free Blacks. An important body of writing dealt with religion; in a sense, this represented a turning away from the immediate problems of slavery and racism. But much religious literature, from the spirituals to the writings of Alexander Crummell, addressed itself simultaneously to the hope of an afterlife and the need to ameliorate the Black man's present condition.

Black writers were unanimously opposed to slavery, but differences existed as to the best means of fighting it. The most direct way was open rebellion. The nineteenth century began with Gabriel Prosser's revolt. Twenty-two years later, Denmark Vesey's well-planned conspiracy in Charleston, South Carolina, involved hundreds, perhaps thousands, of Black rebels. Neither Prosser nor Vesey left a literary record of his revolt, but *The Confessions of Nat Turner,* dictated by Turner to a white amanuensis, provides an unforgettable account of the Southampton insurrection, the most famous of slave uprisings. Other radical Blacks not themselves directly involved cheered on the slave revolts. Again and again in his famous *Appeal* of 1829, David Walker threatened slave-holders with violent retribution for their sins. Blacks may well be the agents of divine wrath: "Will he let the oppressors rest comfortably and happy always? Will he not cause the very children of the oppressors to rise up against them, and oftimes put them to death? 'God works in many ways his wonders to perform.'" In the 1840's, Henry Highland Garnet continued the militant tradition of Turner and Walker. Violent Black resistance to slavery achieved its greatest success, however, in 1862, when Lincoln at last reluctantly consented to use Black troops in the Union Army. Without the contribution of Black soldiers and laborers to the war effort—the final resort to violence—the South might never have been defeated.

By definition, rebellion is a collective act designed to alter radically the relation between a subordinate group and established authority. Much more common in antebellum America were acts of violence, subversion, or sabotage by individual slaves against particular masters or overseers. This form of resistance might result in severe punishment and even greater repression, or it might, on the other hand, actually change the power equation between Black and white. After young Frederick Douglass fought his overseer rather than submit to a whipping, he was never whipped again.

But for many a slave, especially in the Upper South, the surest solution to his slave status was to escape it. From the beginning of slavery in America, slaves had fled their masters. During the Revolution, many joined the British, lured by promises of freedom. The problem of the fugitive slave was so serious as to call for legislation during the colonial period, in the Constitution itself, and of course in the infamous Fugitive Slave Act of 1850. As the rigors of slavery and the spirit of abolition both intensified in the middle third of the nineteenth century, runaways increased in number. Thousands of them were aided in their flight north by the Underground Railroad, a highly organized and efficient network of Black and white abolitionists who provided food, shelter, clothing, money, transportation, encouragement, and at times armed defense against slavecatchers.

By its very nature, escape from slavery was a dangerous and dramatic endeavor. It stimulated a whole subgenre of Black autobiography—the fugitive slave narrative. Many of these were dictated to or ghostwritten by white abolitionists, because most fugitive slaves were by necessity illiterate. Some of the narratives, however, were written by the fugitives themselves, notably the *Narrative of the Life of Frederick Douglass, an American Slave,* one of the great American autobiographies. In addition to narrating the thrilling experience of escape itself, the fugitive slave narratives provide an invaluable source of information on the actuality of slavery from the slave's own perspective. In addition to Frederick Douglass' classic, some of the most memorable examples of this important type of Black literature are *A Narrative of the Uncommon Sufferings and Surprizing Deliverance of Briton Hamon, a Negro Man* (1760), *Recollections of Slavery* (1838), *Narrative of William W. Brown, a Fugitive Slave* (1847), *The Fugitive Blacksmith; or, Events in the Life of James W. C. Pennington* (1849), *Narrative of the Life and Adventures of Henry Bibb, Written by Himself* (1849), *The Life of Josiah Henson, Formerly a Slave, Now an Inhabitant of Canada, as Narrated by Himself* (1849), *Narrative of Henry Box Brown* (1849), *Twelve Years a Slave; Narrative of Solomon Northrup, a Citizen of New York, Kidnapped in Washington City in 1841, and Rescued in 1853, from a Cotton Plantation near the Red River in Louisiana* (1853), and *Running a Thousand Miles for Freedom; or, The Escape of William and Ellen Craft from Slavery* (1860).

Blacks could rebel against their masters or flee from them, but the permanent solution was obviously the total abolition of slavery from American life. Rebels and fugitives were often among the most effective of the Black abolitionists. However, the main weapons of the propagandists for freedom were not the sword and the knapsack, but the pen and the platform.

Before the turn of the century, free Blacks had lifted their voices against the condition of their slave brothers. The most forceful of the early antislavery tracts appeared in 1829—David Walker's *Appeal.* So disturbing was Walker's incendiary pamphlet to the Southern power structure that a price was placed on his head and he died under mysterious circumstances less than a year later. Walker's contemporary and fellow North Carolinian, the slave George Moses Horton, was at the same time expressing his protest in verse in *The Hope of Liberty.* Other Black poets devoted to the abolitionist cause included James M. Whitfield, Charles L. Reason, George B. Vashon, James Madison Bell, Frances E. W. Harper, and that versatile literary pioneer, William Wells Brown.

Not only did Black autobiographers, polemicists, and poets exercise their pens against slavery, but Black abolitionist lecturers ventured across the North carrying the message of freedom to town, hamlet, and cabin. Oratory, it should be remembered, was a major literary form in nineteenth-century America, and few orators excelled Frederick Douglass, William Wells Brown, Samuel Ringgold Ward, and Henry Highland Garnet. Douglass and Brown electrified audiences in Great Britain as well as America with their denunciations of slavery. The best Black oratory still retains considerable emotive power in printed form. We can only conjecture its impact on a crowded lecture hall in 1850, coming from the lips of men who were living refutations of the racism on which the system of slavery was based.

As we have seen, this racism affected free Blacks almost as much as it did slaves. Not content to be permanently relegated to a second-class status, free Blacks wrote and spoke in defense of their own human rights as well as against slavery. Most directed their efforts to attaining full equality within the American political, economic, and social system. Others, either as a temporary expedient or in despair at ever securing fair treatment from whites, embraced Black nationalism.

Whenever a bill abridging the civil rights of Black men was introduced into a state legislature in the North, whenever the race was traduced or reviled, whenever the social or religious rights of Black men were circumscribed, the resentment and opposition of articulate Black spokesmen could be expected. This was particularly true in Philadelphia, New York, and Massachusetts, the intellectual centers of Black America before the Civil War. Even before the turn of the century, Richard Allen and Absalom Jones, early Black church leaders, rebutted unjust aspersions against Black behavior during a terrible yellow fever epidemic in *A Narrative of the Proceedings of the Black People during the late Awful Calamity in Philadelphia; and a Refutation of Some Censures Thrown upon Them in Some Late Publications* (1794). The anonymously published *Letters from a Man of Colour, on a Late Bill before the Senate of Pennsylvania* (1813), probably by the important Philadelphian James Forten, was an effective protest against a measure, which eventually failed to pass, designed to prohibit immigration of Blacks into the state. Moreover, the pamphlet supported the concept of full civil equality for all people. Twenty-five years later, James Forten's son-in-law, Robert Purvis, spoke forcefully for the race in *Appeal of Forty Thousand Citizens Threatened with Disfranchisement to the People of Pennsylvania.*

In New York, Black leaders active in defense of civil rights included Peter Williams, Jr., Theodore S. Wright, Samuel E. Cornish, David Ruggles, and James McCune Smith. For over a year in 1859 and 1860, Thomas Hamilton of New York edited *The Anglo-African Magazine*, the first Black literary periodical. Although civil and social matters were not neglected, this journal's chief thrust was cultural as it challenged white dominance in intellectual and artistic pursuits.

In Massachusetts, two early racial leaders who contributed writings of interest were Paul Cuffe, the New Bedford sea captain and philanthropist, and Prince Hall of Boston, the founder of Black Masonry. More militant than these men was David Walker, who was concerned with the disabilities of free Blacks as well as slaves. Discrimination in education, Walker argued, was a particularly severe obstacle to racial progress.

To some Blacks, white racism seemed so firmly entrenched that efforts to ameliorate the condition of the race in this country seemed hopeless. Instead, they insisted, Blacks should establish their own nation, where they could develop their own institutions free of white domination. The first and apparently most logical site for such a colony was Africa, the ancestral home of Black people. Repatriated Blacks settled the adjacent colonies of Sierra Leone and Liberia on the continent's western coast. Sierra Leone was founded by the British in 1787 as a home for emancipated slaves. It was populated mainly from the West Indies, but the project also interested Paul Cuffe, who visited Freetown in his ship the *Traveller* in 1811. In the following year his *Brief Account of the Settlement and Present Situation of the Colony of Sierra Leone* was published. The War of 1812 postponed a repeat voyage until late in 1815, when he sailed with thirty-eight American Blacks, the first to be repatriated in Africa.

The success of Cuffe's voyage stimulated the formation of the American Colonization Society, whose chief project was Liberia. It has been pointed out that most Blacks rejected the Liberian experiment. Important exceptions were George Moses Horton, who hoped that his poetry would prove lucrative enough to buy his freedom and to finance his resettlement in Liberia, John B. Russwurm, and Alexander Crummell. Together with Samuel E. Cornish, Russwurm founded in 1827 the first Black newspaper in America, *Freedom's Journal*. These two pioneer journalists differed sharply over the question of colonization, however, and Cornish resigned from the paper when Russwurm began to favor the American Colonization Society. Settling in Liberia, Russwurm continued his journalistic career by starting the *Liberia Herald* in 1831. For many years he was one of Liberia's most important leaders. The brilliant Alexander Crummell, the most accomplished Black prose stylist in nineteenth-century America, labored for two decades, 1853 to 1873, in Christian ministerial and missionary work in Liberia and Sierra Leone. Prophetically, Crummell envisioned an Africa redeemed from her despoilers: "an uprising of her sons from intellectual sloth and spiritual inertness; a seeking and a stretching forth of her hands, for light, instruction, and spirituality, such as the world has never before seen . . . when the giant sins and the deadly evils which have ruined her, shall be effectively stayed; and when Ethiopia, from the Atlantic to the Indian Ocean, from the Mediterranean to the Cape, 'shall stretch out her hands unto God!'" The final African venture before the Civil War was an expedition to the Niger Valley to determine its suitability for settlement. The leader of the expedition, Martin R. Delany, published in 1861 the *Official Report of the Niger Valley Exploring Party,* and in the same year another member of the party, Robert Campbell, wrote *A Pilgrimage to My Motherland*.

Black nationalists also looked elsewhere for the site of a new Black nation. As the sectional polarization of the 1850's developed, the whole question of colonization was reopened. One proposal with considerable support among whites in the Republican party, including that of Abraham Lincoln, was the settlement of Blacks in Central America. Martin R. Delany supported this plan in his important work *The Condition, Elevation, Emigration, and Destiny of the Colored People of the United States, Politically Considered* (1852). The poet James M. Whitfield enthusiastically endorsed the proposals of Delany, to whom his book of verse *America, and Other Poems* (1853) is dedicated.

Central or South American colonization never materialized and Black settlements in Canada weakened after some favorable beginnings, but all Blacks could recognize in Haiti the feasibility of Black nationalism. Tributes to the valor of Toussaint L'Ouverture and other Haitian heroes are common in Black American literature, but the most extended eulogy is "Vincent Ogé," a long poem by George B. Vashon, an Oberlin graduate who taught in Port-au-Prince from 1847 to 1850. In prose, James Theodore Holley published in 1857 *A Vindication of the Capacity of the Negro Race for Self-Government and Civilized Progress, as Demonstrated by Historical Events of the Haitian Revolution, and the Subsequent Acts of That People since Their National Independence.* The title of this publication adequately indicates the role of Haiti in bolstering Black self-esteem at a difficult time in history.

A different expression of the Black nationalistic impulse was the development of social, educational, and religious institutions of, by, and for Black people. Rigidly separated from most areas of white life, free Blacks who wished to remain in this country had no other recourse. Fraternal and benevolent societies provided some economic protection as well as good fellowship. Black teachers, in schools and as private instructors, battled against illiteracy. By far the most important Black institution, however, was the church.

In Georgia and Virginia, Blacks began organizing separate Baptist churches, with or without white assistance, immediately after the American Revolution. The most important early Black church movement in the North began in 1787, when Richard Allen and Absalom Jones refused to submit to a recently instituted Jim Crow seating arrangement in the white St. George Methodist Episcopal Church of Philadelphia. Forming the Free African Society, incensed Philadelphia Blacks gathered funds to erect a church of their own. Out of this movement finally emerged the African Methodist Episcopal church, with Richard Allen as bishop and the most influential early Black religious leader.

The Black church began and has continued as not only a place of religious worship, but also as a social center and a forum for political discussion. As such, it has strengthened Black group cohesiveness and helped to formulate a sense of collective identity. Religion—specifically Christianity—has been criticized by some modern Black writers, notably Richard Wright and James Baldwin, because of its emphasis on individual piety, on the notion that the rewards of a glorious afterlife will compensate for the deprivation of this life, and on a high moral valuation on patient suffering of present ills. In this way, the argument goes, religion has been truly an opiate of the Black people, a tool of the white oppressor.

One cannot deny a core of validity to this line of reasoning, but important qualifications should be made. As Benjamin E. Mays has shown in *The Negro's God as Reflected in His Literature,* Black religion before the Civil War was not mainly otherworldly and compensatory in its emphasis; on the contrary, it concerned itself deeply with social problems, especially the overriding one of slavery. Some Black ministers such as William Douglass avoided social issues and at least one, Lemuel B. Haynes, confined his ministry to white congregations, but more typical were Henry Highland Garnet, Daniel A. Payne, Theodore S. Wright, and J. W. C. Pennington—all ministers of a church militant. And one cannot ignore the deeply felt religious fervor of Nat Turner, for whom Christianity brought not peace but a sword against oppression and injustice.

For the supreme expression of Black religion, of course, one should look to the spirituals, which W. E. B. Du Bois called "the most original and beautiful expression of human life and longing yet born on American soil." Many of the spirituals are undoubtedly consolatory, but consolation was a psychological necessity to most slaves in a desperate and hopeless situation. But in their very yearning for a better world than this where burdens could be eased, where they could enjoy comforts and luxuries denied them here, where they could be free at last, in this poignant yearning that permeates the spirituals, the slaves were expressing a powerful protest, even if implicit, against slavery. Duplicity was a basis tactic of survival for the slave, and when he sang of the delivery of Daniel and the Hebrew children, of Moses and Pharaoh, of stealing away to Jesus, he was referring to his own temporal condition as well as to Biblical themes. Thus in their richness of meaning, as well as in their emotional profundity and surpassing poetic quality, the spirituals are among the most impressive achievements of Afro-American—and American—literature and culture.

The Major Writers

Frederick Douglass (1817–1895)

If one were to make a fair and equitable reassessment of nineteenth-century American history, one would have to conclude that the legislative, moral, and political struggle over slavery and slavery's aftermath was the central issue in this young nation's first century. One would also have to conclude that, by a twist of irony, the person who occupied the pivotal position amid the swirling controversies and crises in the fight over slavery was an ex-slave and fugitive from that same slavery system. Fortunately for this country, he had escaped from the "dark night" of his imprisonment, not dulled, brutalized, and demoralized, but full of passion and strong of purpose. It soon became clear after his flight from Maryland to Massachusetts in 1838 that Frederick Douglass possessed intellectual gifts possessed by few other men. As one examines the life and times of this great man, it also becomes clear that the history of America would have been quite different had he not fled to freedom as a young man. First, the world would never have heard the splendid mixture of verbal eloquence, wisdom, passion, and anger that became the oratorical hallmark of Frederick Douglass. There were other antislavery orators but none who spoke with the glowing fervor of Frederick Douglass. Nor would the world have seen an American Black Zola emerge, his pen dipped in the fire of righteous indignation—pleading, urging, demanding, threatening, but never compromising. Other Black men were writing in support of the Black man's cause, but none wrote with the skill and effectiveness of Frederick Douglass. Finally, had not Frederick Douglass emerged to provide leadership and guidance in the fight against slavery, all might have gone awry. First, he effectively countered the Garrisonian approach to abolitionism with its emphasis on moral persuasion and Northern secession and the political ineffectiveness of the Constitution as a document of freedom. History has since proved the Garrisonians wrong and Douglass right on all counts. Second, Douglass early took a stand against colonization as a solution. Physical separation from the white man, in Douglass' view, would not benefit the Black man; neither Black colonization nor any other kind of Black separatism was to be preferred to integration of the Black man into the fabric of American society. Here again, history has proven

Douglass right, despite the occasional clamor of Black nationalist groups who desire some kind of separation from America.

Thus, Frederick Douglass, ex-slave, was the indispensable man in the events that culminated in freeing the young American nation of chattel slavery. Without the spadework of this Black man's antislavery campaigns and his fervent oratory and his energetic counsel and guidance, the cautious, political Lincoln would never have moved forward to his destiny as "The Great Emancipator." Similarly, the strength of Douglass lay behind the effort to pass the Fourteenth and Fifteenth Amendments to the Constitution and thus laid the groundwork for later legal attacks against economic and social segregation. In every sense, then, he was the "mover and shaker" of his century.

Douglass' story of action and involvement was told three times. First, in 1845, he published the *Narrative of the Life of Frederick Douglass, an American Slave*. It was published over the vehement objections of Garrison and the Boston abolitionists, who feared that Douglass' direct identification of himself as a fugitive slave would destroy his effectiveness as an antislavery campaigner and lecturer. Next, he published, in 1855, an enlarged autobiography entitled *My Bondage and My Freedom*. Then, in 1881, he produced what scholars of American autobiography have termed a classic—*The Life and Times of Frederick Douglass*. From any of the three accounts of his life, one inference is easily made. Douglass' life style was one of dynamic activity combined with a great capacity for incisive reflective thought. Behind his busyness were thoughtful strategies and preconceived philosophical positions. When, for instance, he went to see President Lincoln early in 1863, he not only knew what he himself was going to say but also had some answers in mind to reply to what Lincoln was going to say. Similarly, when he called on President Andrew Johnson during the dark days immediately following the close of the war, he was fully prepared to argue the case for the Negro franchise with a man who actually stood in awe of the Southern planter aristocracy and hence tended to take no action that might offend that aristocracy. And it was Frederick Douglass who led the participants in the Colored Man's Convention in 1843 to disavow the proposal by Henry Highland Garnet to arm the slaves and thus achieve a violent overthrow of the slave autocracy. So thoughtful and persuasive was Douglass' argument against Garnet's proposal that the Convention refused to endorse what has since gone down in history as a great and memorable speech.

Fortunately, Douglass never veered from his fundamental purpose, but he was always alert for new strategies and methods to achieve that purpose. For instance, a long talk with John Brown in Springfield, Massachusetts, in 1847 left Douglass convinced that the institution of slavery could be destroyed only by a superior physical force that would topple the slave plantation autocracy. The questions that then haunted him all during the 1850's were where such a physical force could be found and how it could be used with maximum advantage. Certainly, when he again "consulted" with John Brown in an abandoned stone quarry in Chambersburg, Pennsylvania, early in 1858, Douglass argued strenuously but futilely that the proposed attack on the Harpers Ferry arsenal with a small assault force would be suicidal and unwise. However, many years later, in a speech at Storer College in Harpers Ferry in 1881, he described John Brown's raid as the one event that cleared the crisis-ridden air of "words, votes, and compromises" and started the irrepressible conflict in earnest. In other words, Frederick Douglass was a man who had a rare sense of historical timing that told him when certain beliefs and positions had to be critically re-examined and modified. It was this faculty that kept him remarkably in tune with the fast-moving events of a calamitous period in American history.

Excerpts from Douglass' speeches and writings are included in literary anthologies not only because of his historical eminence but also because his writings illustrate an extraordinarily precise blending of content and style. What he wrote or spoke always had a mode of presentation that added depth to the meaning. Indeed, his speeches have a dramatic presence of their own that carries the reader away from the printed page to the emotional atmosphere of the actual occasion. His speech delivered before the Rochester Antislavery Sewing Society on July 5, 1852, and included herein is an excellent example. When Douglass asks the rhetorical question "What, to the American slave, is your 4th of July?" his answer is a series of seemingly carefully balanced phrases:

> *To him, your celebration is a sham; your boasted liberty, an unholy license; your national greatness, swelling vanity; your sounds of rejoicing are empty and heartless; your denunciations of tyrants, brass fronted impudence; your shouts of liberty and equality, hollow mockery; your prayers and hymns, your sermons and thanksgivings, with all your religious parade and solemnity, are, to him, mere bombast, fraud, deception, impiety, and hypocrisy—a thin veil to cover up crimes which would disgrace a nation of savages. There is not a nation on earth guilty of practices, more shocking and bloody, than are the people of these United States, at this very hour.*

This is oratory in the grand manner, but there is high drama here as well. The reader can see the ladies of the sewing society and their friends squirming in their collective guilt as they listened to the speech. The reader can also sense the dumb and inarticulate anger of the slave Douglass portrays as he witnesses the celebration of independence by a society that seemed to dedicate all of its power to keeping the Black man in slavery. In its fine blending of style with content, the speech is an indispensable piece of Americana.

Generally speaking, the writings of Frederick Douglass fall into three groups: the editorial essays written for his journals (*The North Star, Frederick Douglass' Paper,* and the *Douglass' Monthly*); his speeches and orations; and his autobiographical writings. All three groups are appropriately represented in Philip Foner's four-volume edition of *The*

Life and Writings of Frederick Douglass (1945). In addition, there are two very fine biographical treatments of Douglass. One is Shirley Graham's *There Once Was a Slave* (1947), and the second is Benjamin Quarles' *Frederick Douglass* (1948).

from *Narrative of the Life of*
Frederick Douglass, an American Slave

Chapter X

I left Master Thomas's house, and went to live with Mr. Covey, on the 1st of January, 1833. I was now, for the first time in my life, a field hand. In my new employment, I found myself even more awkward than a country boy appeared to be in a large city. I had been at my new home but one week before Mr. Covey gave me a very severe whipping, cutting my back, causing the blood to run, and raising ridges on my flesh as large as my little finger. The details of this affair are as follows: Mr. Covey sent me, very early in the morning of one of our coldest days in the month of January, to the woods, to get a load of wood. He gave me a team of unbroken oxen. He told me which was the in-hand ox, and which the off-hand one. He then tied the end of a large rope around the horns of the in-hand ox, and gave me the other end of it, and told me, if the oxen started to run, that I must hold on upon the rope. I had never driven oxen before, and of course I was very awkward. I, however, succeeded in getting to the edge of the woods with little difficulty; but I had got a very few rods into the woods, when the oxen took fright, and started full tilt, carrying the cart against trees, and over stumps, in the most frightful manner. I expected every moment that my brains would be dashed out against the trees. After running thus for a considerable distance, they finally upset the cart, dashing it with great force against a tree, and threw themselves into a dense thicket. How I escaped death, I do not know. There I was, entirely alone, in a thick wood, in a place new to me. My cart was upset and shattered, my oxen were entangled among the young trees, and there was none to help me. After a long spell of effort, I succeeded in getting my cart righted, my oxen disentangled, and again yoked to the cart. I now proceeded with my team to the place where I had,

the day before, been chopping wood, and loaded my cart pretty heavily, thinking in this way to tame my oxen. I then proceeded on my way home. I had now consumed one half of the day. I got out of the woods safely, and now felt out of danger. I stopped my oxen to open the woods gate; and just as I did so, before I could get hold of my ox-rope, the oxen again started, rushed through the gate, catching it between the wheel and the body of the cart, tearing it to pieces, and coming within a few inches of crushing me against the gate-post. Thus twice, in one short day, I escaped death by the merest chance. On my return, I told Mr. Covey what had happened, and how it happened. He ordered me to return to the woods again immediately. I did so, and he followed on after me. Just as I got into the woods, he came up and told me to stop my cart, and that he would teach me how to trifle away my time, and break gates. He then went to a large gum-tree, and with his axe cut three large switches, and, after trimming them up neatly with his pocket-knife, he ordered me to take off my clothes. I made him no answer, but stood with my clothes on. He repeated his order. I still made him no answer, nor did I move to strip myself. Upon this he rushed at me with the fierceness of a tiger, tore off my clothes, and lashed me till he had worn out his switches, cutting me so savagely as to leave the marks visible for a long time after. This whipping was the first of a number just like it, and for similar offences.

I lived with Mr. Covey one year. During the first six months, of that year, scarce a week passed without his whipping me. I was seldom free from a sore back. My awkwardness was almost always his excuse for whipping me. We were worked fully up to the point of endurance. Long before day we were up, our horses fed, and by the first approach of day we were off to the field with our hoes and ploughing teams. Mr. Covey gave us enough to eat, but scarce time to eat it. We were often less than five minutes taking our meals. We were often in the field from the first approach of day till its last lingering ray had left us; and at saving-fodder time, midnight often caught us in the field binding blades.

Covey would be out with us. The way he used to stand it, was this. He would spend the most of his afternoons in bed. He would then come out fresh in the evening, ready to urge us on with his words, example, and frequently with the whip. Mr. Covey was one of the few slaveholders who could and did work with his hands. He was a hard-working man. He knew by himself just what a man or a boy could do. There was no deceiving him. His work went on in his absence almost as well as in his presence; and he had the faculty of making us feel that he was ever present with us. This he did by surprising us. He seldom approached the spot where we were at work openly, if he could do it secretly. He always aimed at taking us by surprise. Such was his cunning, that we used to call him, among ourselves, "the snake." When we were at work in the cornfield, he would sometimes crawl on his hands and knees to avoid detection, and all at once he would rise nearly in our midst, and scream out, "Ha, ha! Come, come! Dash on, dash on!" This being his mode of attack, it was never safe to stop a single minute. His comings were like a thief in the night. He appeared to us as being ever at hand. He was under every tree, behind every stump, in every bush, and at every window, on the plantation. He would sometimes mount his horse, as if bound to St. Michael's, a distance of seven miles, and in half an hour afterwards you would see him coiled up in the corner of the wood-fence, watching every motion of the slaves. He would, for this purpose, leave his horse tied up in the woods. Again, he would sometimes walk up to us, and give us orders as though he was upon the point of starting on a long journey, turn his back upon us, and make as though he was going to the house to get ready; and, before he would get half way thither, he would turn short and crawl into a fence-corner, or behind some tree, and there watch us till the going down of the sun.

Mr. Covey's *forte* consisted in his power to deceive. His life was devoted to planning and perpetrating the grossest deceptions. Every thing he possessed in the shape of learning or religion, he made conform to his disposition to deceive. He seemed to think himself equal to deceiving the Almighty. He would make a short prayer in the morning, and a long prayer at night; and, strange as it may seem, few men would at times appear more devotional than he. The exercises of his family devotions were always commenced with singing; and, as he was a very poor singer himself, the duty of raising the hymn generally came upon me. He would read his hymn, and nod at me to commence. I would at times do so; at others, I would not. My noncompliance would almost always produce much confusion. To show himself independent of me, he would start and stagger through with his hymn in the most discordant manner. In this state of mind, he prayed with more than ordinary spirit. Poor man! such was his disposition, and success at deceiving, I do verily believe that he sometimes deceived himself into the solemn belief, that he was a sincere worshipper of the most high God; and this, too, at a time when he may be said to have been guilty of compelling his woman slave to commit the sin of adultery. The facts in the case are these: Mr. Covey was a poor man; he was just commencing in life; he was only able to buy one slave; and, shocking as is the fact, he bought her, as he said, for *a breeder*. This woman was named Caroline. Mr. Covey bought her from Mr. Thomas Lowe, about six miles from St. Michael's. She was a large, able-bodied woman, about twenty years old. She had already given birth to one child, which proved her to be just what he wanted. After buying her, he hired a married man of Mr. Samuel Harrison, to live with him one year; and him he used to fasten up with her every night! The result was, that, at the end of the year, the miserable woman gave birth to twins. At this result Mr. Covey seemed to be highly pleased, both with the man and the wretched woman. Such was his joy, and that of his wife, that nothing they could do for Caroline during her confinement was too good, or too hard, to be done. The children were regarded as being quite an addition to his wealth.

If at any one time of my life more than another, I was made to drink the bitterest dregs of slavery, that time was during the first six months of my stay with Mr. Covey. We were worked in all weathers. It was never too hot or too cold; it could never rain, blow, hail, or snow, too hard for us to work in the field. Work, work, work, was scarcely more the order of the day than of the night. The longest days were too short for him, and the shortest nights too long for him. I was somewhat unmanageable when I first went there, but a few months of this discipline tamed me. Mr. Covey succeeded in breaking me. I was broken in body, soul, and spirit. My natural elasticity was crushed, my intellect languished, the disposition to read departed, the cheerful spark that lingered about my eye died; the dark night of slavery closed in upon me; and behold a man transformed into a brute!

Sunday was my only leisure time. I spent this in a sort of beast-like stupor, between sleep and wake, under some large tree. At times I would rise up, a flash of energetic freedom would dart through my soul, accompanied with a faint beam of hope, that flickered for a moment, and then vanished. I sank down again, mourning over my wretched condition. I was sometimes prompted to take my life, and that of Covey, but was prevented by a combination of hope and fear. My sufferings on this plantation seem now like a dream rather than a stern reality.

Our house stood within a few rods of the Chesapeake Bay, whose broad bosom was ever white with sails from every quarter of the habitable globe. Those beautiful vessels, robed in purest white, so delightful to the eye of freemen, were to me so many shrouded ghosts, to terrify and torment me with thoughts of my wretched condition. I have often, in the deep stillness of a summer's Sabbath, stood all alone upon the lofty banks of that noble bay, and traced, with saddened heart and tearful eye, the countless number of sails moving off to the mighty ocean. The sight of these always affected me powerfully. My thoughts would compel utterance; and there, with no audience but the Almighty, I would pour out my soul's complaint, in my rude way, with an apostrophe to the moving multitude of ships:—

"You are loosed from your moorings, and are free; I am fast in my chains, and am a slave! You move merrily before the gentle gale, and I sadly before the bloody whip! You are freedom's swift-winged angels, that fly round the world; I am confined in bands of iron! O that I were free! O, that I were on one of your gallant decks, and under your protecting wing! Alas! betwixt me and you, the turbid waters roll. Go on, go on. O that I could also go! Could I but swim! If I could fly! O, why was I born a man, of whom to make a brute! The glad ship is gone; she hides in the dim distance. I am left in the hottest hell of unending slavery. O God, save me! God, deliver me! Let me be free! Is there any God? Why am I

a slave? I will run away. I will not stand it. Get caught, or get clear, I'll try it. I had as well die with ague as the fever. I have only one life to lose. I had as well be killed running as die standing. Only think of it; one hundred miles straight north, and I am free! Try it? Yes! God helping me, I will. It cannot be that I shall live and die a slave. I will take to the water. This very bay shall yet bear me into freedom. The steamboats steered in a north-east course from North Point. I will do the same; and when I get to the head of the bay, I will turn my canoe adrift, and walk straight through Delaware into Pennsylvania. When I get there, I shall not be required to have a pass; I can travel without being disturbed. Let but the first opportunity offer, and, come what will, I am off. Meanwhile, I will try to bear up under the yoke. I am not the only slave in the world. Why should I fret? I can bear as much as any of them. Besides, I am but a boy, and all boys are bound to some one. It may be that my misery in slavery will only increase my happiness when I get free. There is a better day coming."

Thus I used to think, and thus I used to speak to myself; goaded almost to madness at one moment, and at the next reconciling myself to my wretched lot.

I have already intimated that my condition was much worse, during the first six months of my stay at Mr. Covey's, than in the last six. The circumstances leading to the change in Mr. Covey's course toward me form an epoch in my humble history. You have seen how a man was made a slave; you shall see how a slave was made a man. On one of the hottest days of the month of August, 1833, Bill Smith, William Hughes, a slave named Eli, and myself, were engaged in fanning wheat. Hughes was clearing the fanned wheat from before the fan. Eli was turning, Smith was feeding, and I was carrying wheat to the fan. The work was simple, requiring strength rather than intellect; yet, to one entirely unused to such work, it came very hard. About three o'clock of that day, I broke down; my strength failed me; I was seized with a violent aching of the head, attended with extreme dizziness; I trembled in every limb. Finding what was coming, I nerved myself up, feeling it would never do to stop work. I stood as long as I could stagger to the hopper with grain. When I could stand no longer, I fell, and felt as if held down by an immense weight. The fan of course stopped; every one had his own work to do; and no one could do the work of the other, and have his own go on at the same time.

Mr. Covey was at the house, about one hundred yards from the treading-yard where we were fanning. On hearing the fan stop, he left immediately, and came to the spot where we were. He hastily inquired what the matter was. Bill answered that I was sick, and there was no one to bring wheat to the fan. I had by this time crawled away under the side of the post and rail-fence by which the yard was enclosed, hoping to find relief by getting out of the sun. He then asked where I was. He was told by one of the hands. He came to the spot, and, after looking at me awhile, asked me what was the matter. I told him as well as I could, for I scarce had strength to speak. He then gave me a savage kick in the side, and told me to get up. I tried to do so, but fell back in the attempt. He gave me another kick, and again told me to rise. I again tried, and succeeded in gaining my feet; but, stooping to get the tub with which I was feeding the fan, I again staggered and fell. While down in this situation, Mr. Covey took up the hickory slat with which Hughes had been striking off the half-bushel measure, and with it gave me a heavy blow upon the head, making a large wound, and the blood ran freely; and with this again told me to get up. I made no effort to comply, having now made up my mind to let him do his worst. In a short time after receiving this blow, my head grew better. Mr. Covey had now left me to my fate. At this moment I resolved, for the first time, to go to my master, enter a complaint and ask his protection. In order to do this, I must that afternoon walk seven miles; and this, under the circumstances, was truly a severe undertaking. I was exceedingly feeble; made so as much by the kicks and blows which I received, as by the severe fit of sickness to which I had been subjected. I, however, watched my chance, while Covey was looking in an opposite direction, and started for St. Michael's. I succeeded in getting a considerable distance on my way to the woods, when Covey discovered me, and called after me to come back, threatening what he would do if I did not come. I disregarded both his calls and his threats, and made my way to the woods as fast as my feeble state would allow; and thinking I might be overhauled by him if I kept the road, I walked through the woods, keeping far enough from the road to avoid detection, and near enough to prevent losing my

way. I had not gone far before my little strength again failed me. I could go no farther. I fell down, and lay for a considerable time. The blood was yet oozing from the wound on my head. For a time I thought I should bleed to death; and think now that I should have done so, but that the blood so matted my hair as to stop the wound. After lying there about three quarters of an hour, I nerved myself up again, and started on my way, through bogs and briers, barefooted and bareheaded, tearing my feet sometimes at nearly every step; and after a journey of about seven miles, occupying some five hours to perform it, I arrived at master's store. I then presented an appearance enough to affect any but a heart of iron. From the crown of my head to my feet, I was covered with blood. My hair was all clotted with dust and blood; my shirt was stiff with blood. My legs and feet were torn in sundry places with briers and thorns, and were also covered with blood. I suppose I looked like a man who had escaped a den of wild beasts, and barely escaped them. In this state I appeared before my master, humbly entreating him to interpose his authority for my protection. I told him all the circumstances as well as I could, and it seemed, as I spoke, at times to affect him. He would then walk the floor, and seek to justify Covey by saying he expected I deserved it. He asked me what I wanted. I told him, to let me get a new home; that as sure as I lived with Mr. Covey again, I should live with but to die with him; that Covey would surely kill me; he was in a fair way for it. Master Thomas ridiculed the idea that there was any danger of Mr. Covey's killing me, and said that he knew Mr. Covey; that he was a good man, and that he could not think of taking me from him; that, should he do so, he would lose the whole year's wages; that I belonged to Mr. Covey for one year, and that I must go back to him, come what might; and that I must not trouble him with any more stories, or that he would himself *get hold of me.* After threatening me thus, he gave me a very large dose of salts, telling me that I might remain in St. Michael's that night, (it being quite late,) but that I must be off back to Mr. Covey's early in the morning; and that if I did not, he would *get hold of me,* which meant that he would whip me. I remained all night, and, according to his orders, I started off to Covey's in the morning, (Saturday morning,) wearied in body and broken in spirit. I got no supper that night, or breakfast that morning. I reached Covey's about nine o'clock; and just as I was getting over the fence that divided Mrs. Kemp's fields from ours, out ran Covey with his cowskin, to give me another whipping. Before he could reach me, I succeeded in getting to the cornfield; and as the corn was very high, it afforded me the means of hiding. He seemed very angry, and searched for me a long time. My behavior was altogether unaccountable. He finally gave up the chase, thinking, I suppose, that I must come home for something to eat; he would give himself no further trouble in looking for me. I spent that day mostly in the woods, having the alternative before me,—to go home and be whipped to death, or stay in the woods and be starved to death. That night, I fell in with Sandy Jenkins, a slave with whom I was somewhat acquainted. Sandy had a free wife who lived about four miles from Mr. Covey's; and it being Saturday, he was on his way to see her. I told him my circumstances, and he very kindly invited me to go home with him. I went home with him, and talked this whole matter over, and got his advice as to what course it was best for me to pursue. I found Sandy an old adviser. He told me, with great solemnity, I must go back to Covey; but that before I went, I must go with him into another part of the woods, where there was a certain *root,* which, if I would take some of it with me, carrying it *always on my right side,* would render it impossible for Mr. Covey, or any other white man, to whip me. He said he had carried it for years; and since he had done so, he had never received a blow, and never expected to while he carried it. I at first rejected the idea, that the simple carrying of a root in my pocket would have any such effect as he had said, and was not disposed to take it; but Sandy impressed the necessity with much earnestness, telling me it could do no harm, if it did no good. To please him, I at length took the root, and, according to his direction, carried it upon my right side. This was Sunday morning. I immediately started for home; and upon entering the yard gate, out came Mr. Covey on his way to meeting. He spoke to me very kindly, bade me drive the pigs from a lot near by, and passed on towards the church. Now, this singular conduct of Mr. Covey really made me begin to think that there was something in the *root* which Sandy had given me; and had it been on any other day than Sunday, I could have attributed the conduct to no other cause than the influence of that root; and as it was, I was half inclined to think the *root* to be something more than I at first had taken it to be. All went well till Monday morning. On this morning, the virtue of the *root* was fully tested. Long before daylight, I was called to go and rub, curry, and feed, the horses. I obeyed, and was glad to obey. But whilst thus engaged, whilst in the act of throwing down some blades from the loft, Mr. Covey entered the stable with a long rope; and just as I was half out of the loft, he caught hold of my legs, and was about tying me. As soon as I found what he was up to, I gave a sudden spring, and as I did so, he holding to my legs, I was brought sprawling on the stable floor. Mr. Covey seemed now to think he had me, and could do what he pleased; but at this moment—from whence came the spirit I don't know —I resolved to fight; and, suiting my action to the resolution, I seized Covey hard by the throat; and as I did so, I rose. He held on to me, and I to him. My resistance was so entirely unexpected, that Covey seemed taken all aback. He trembled like a leaf. This gave me assurance, and I held him uneasy, causing the blood to run where I touched him with the ends of my fingers. Mr. Covey soon called out to Hughes for help. Hughes came, and, while Covey held me, attempted to tie my right hand. While he was in the act of doing so, I watched my chance, and gave him a heavy kick close under the ribs. This kick fairly sickened Hughes, so that he left me in the hands of Mr. Covey. This kick had the effect of not only weakening Hughes, but Covey also. When he saw Hughes bending over with pain, his courage quailed. He asked me if I meant to persist in my resistance. I told him I did, come what might; that he had used me like a brute for six months, and that I was determined to be used so no longer. With that, he strove to drag me to a stick that was lying just out of the stable door. He meant to knock me down. But just as he was leaning over to get the stick, I seized him with both hands by his collar, and brought him by a sudden snatch to the ground. By this time, Bill came. Covey called upon him for assistance. Bill wanted to know what he could do. Covey said, "Take hold of him, take hold of him!" Bill said his master hired him out to work, and not to help to whip me; so he left Covey and myself to fight our own battle out. We were at it for nearly two hours. Covey at length let me go, puffing and blowing at a great rate, saying that if I had not resisted, he would not have whipped me half so much. The truth was, that he had not whipped me at all. I considered him as getting entirely the worst end of the bargain; for he had drawn no blood from me, but I had from him. The whole six months afterwards, that I spent with Mr. Covey, he never laid the weight of his finger upon me in anger. He would occasionally say, he didn't want to get hold of me again. "No," thought I, "you need not; for you will come off worse than you did before."

This battle with Mr. Covey was the turning-point in my career as a slave. It rekindled the few expiring embers of freedom, and revived within me a sense of my own manhood. It recalled the departed self-confidence, and inspired me again with a determination to be free. The gratification afforded by the triumph was a full compensation for whatever else might follow, even death itself. He only can understand the deep satisfaction which I experienced, who has himself repelled by force the bloody arm of slavery. I felt as I never felt before. It was a glorious resurrection, from the tomb of slavery, to the heaven of freedom. My long-crushed spirit rose, cowardice departed, bold defiance took its place; and I now resolved that, however long I might remain a slave in form, the day had passed forever when I could be a slave in fact. I did not hesitate to let it be known of me, that the white man who expected to succeed in whipping, must also succeed in killing me.

From this time I was never again what might be called fairly whipped, though I remained a slave four years afterwards. I had several fights, but was never whipped.

It was for a long time a matter of surprise to me why Mr. Covey did not immediately have me taken by the constable to the whipping-post, and there regularly whipped for the crime of raising my hand against a white man in defence of myself. And the only explanation I can now think of does not entirely satisfy me; but such as it is, I will give it. Mr. Covey enjoyed the most unbounded reputation for being a first-rate overseer and negro-breaker. It was of considerable importance to him. That reputation was at stake; and had he sent me—a boy about sixteen years old—to the public whipping-post, his reputation would have been lost; so, to save his reputation, he suffered me to go unpunished.

My term of actual service to Mr. Edward Covey ended on Christmas day, 1833. The days between Christmas and New Year's day are allowed as holidays; and, accordingly, we were not required to perform any labor, more than to feed and take care of the stock. This time we regarded as our own, by the grace of our masters; and we therefore used or abused it nearly as we pleased. Those of us who had families at a distance, were generally allowed to spend the whole six days in their society. This time, however, was spent in various ways. The staid, sober, thinking and industrious ones of our number would employ themselves in making corn-brooms, mats, horse-collars, and baskets; and another class of us would spend the time in hunting opossums, hares, and coons. But by far the larger part engaged in such sports and merriments as playing ball, wrestling, running foot-races, fiddling, dancing, and drinking whisky; and this latter mode of spending the time was by far the most agreeable to the feelings of our masters. A slave who would work during the holidays was considered by our masters as scarcely deserving them. He was regarded as one who rejected the favor of his master. It was deemed a disgrace not to get drunk at Christmas; and he was regarded as lazy indeed, who had not provided himself with the necessary means, during the year, to get whisky enough to last him through Christmas.

From what I know of the effect of these holidays upon the slave, I believe them to be among the most effective means in the hands of the slaveholder in keeping down the spirit of insurrection. Were the slaveholders at once to abandon this practice, I have not the slightest doubt it would lead to an immediate insurrection among the slaves. These holidays serve as conductors, or safety-valves, to carry off the rebellious spirit of enslaved humanity. But for these, the slave would be forced up to the wildest desperation; and woe betide the slaveholder, the day he ventures to remove or hinder the operation of those conductors! I warn him that, in such an event, a spirit will go forth in their midst, more to be dreaded than the most appalling earthquake.

The holidays are part and parcel of the gross fraud, wrong, and inhumanity of slavery. They are professedly a custom established by the benevolence of the slaveholders; but I undertake to say, it is the result of selfishness, and one of the grossest frauds committed upon the downtrodden slave. They do not give the slaves this time because they would not like to have their work during its continuance, but because they know it would be unsafe to deprive them of it.

This will be seen by the fact, that the slave-holders like to have their slaves spend those days just in such a manner as to make them as glad of their ending as of their beginning. Their object seems to be, to disgust their slaves with freedom, by plunging them into the lowest depths of dissipation. For instance, the slaveholders not only like to see the slave drink of his own accord, but will adopt various plans to make him drunk. One plan is, to make bets on their slaves, as to who can drink the most whisky without getting drunk; and in this way they succeed in getting whole multitudes to drink to excess. Thus, when the slave asks for virtuous freedom, the cunning slaveholder, knowing his ignorance, cheats him with a dose of vicious dissipation, artfully labelled with the name of liberty. The most of us used to drink it down, and the result was just what might be supposed: many of us were led to think that there was little to choose between liberty and slavery. We felt, and very properly too, that we had almost as well be slaves to man as to rum. So, when the holidays ended, we staggered up from the filth of our wallowing, took a long breath, and marched to the field,— feeling, upon the whole, rather glad to go, from what our master had deceived us into a belief was freedom, back to the arms of slavery.

I have said that this mode of treatment is a part of the whole system of fraud and inhumanity of slavery. It is so. The mode here adopted to disgust the slave with freedom, by allowing him to see only the abuse of it, is carried out in other things. For instance, a slave loves molasses; he steals some. His master, in many cases, goes off to town, and buys a large quantity; he returns, takes his whip, and commands the slave to eat the molasses, until the poor fellow is made sick at the very mention of it. The same mode is sometimes adopted to make the slaves refrain from asking for more food than their regular allowance. A slave runs through his allowance, and applies for more. His master is enraged at him; but, not willing to send him off without food, gives him more than is necessary, and compels him to eat it within a given time. Then, if he complains that he cannot eat it, he is said to be satisfied neither full nor fasting, and is whipped for being hard to please! I have an abundance of such illustrations of the same principle, drawn from my own observation, but think the cases I have cited sufficient. The practice is a very common one.

On the first of January, 1834, I left Mr. Covey, and went to live with Mr. William Freeland, who lived about three miles from St. Michael's. I soon found Mr. Freeland a very different man from Mr. Covey. Though not rich, he was what could be called an educated southern gentleman. Mr. Covey, as I have shown, was a well-trained negro-breaker and slave-driver. The former (slaveholder though he was) seemed to possess some regard for honor, some reverence for justice, and some respect for humanity. The latter seemed totally insensible to all such sentiments. Mr. Freeland had many of the faults peculiar to slaveholders, such as being very passionate and fretful; but I must do him the justice to say, that he was exceedingly free from those degrading vices to which Mr. Covey was constantly addicted. The one was open and frank, and we always knew where to find him. The other was a most artful deceiver, and could be understood only by such as were skillful enough to detect his cunningly-devised frauds. Another advantage I gained in my new master was, he made no pretensions to, or profession of, religion; and this, in my opinion, was truly a great advantage. I assert most unhesitatingly, that the religion of the south is a mere covering for the most horrid crimes,—a justifier of the most appalling barbarity,—a sanctifier of the most hateful frauds,— and a dark shelter under which the darkest, foulest, grossest, and most infernal deeds of slaveholders find the strongest protection. Were I to be again reduced to the chains of slavery, next to that enslavement, I should regard being the slave of a religious master the greatest calamity that could befall me. For of all slaveholders with whom I have ever met, religious slaveholders are the worst. I have ever found them the meanest and basest, the most cruel and cowardly, of all others. It was my unhappy lot not only to belong to a religious slaveholder, but to live in a community of such religionists. Very near Mr. Freeland lived the Rev. Daniel Weeden, and in the same neighborhood lived the Rev. Rigby Hopkins. These were members and ministers in the Reformed Methodist Church. Mr. Weeden owned, among others, a woman slave, whose name I have forgotten. This woman's back, for weeks, was kept literally raw, made so by the lash of this merciless, *religious* wretch. He used to hire hands. His maxim was, Behave well or behave ill, it is the duty of a master occasionally to whip a slave, to remind him of his master's authority. Such was his theory, and such his practice.

Mr. Hopkins was even worse than Mr. Weeden. His chief boast was his ability to manage slaves. The peculiar feature of his government was that of whipping slaves in advance of deserving it. He always managed to have one or more of his slaves to whip every Monday morning. He did this to alarm their fears, and strike terror into those who escaped. His plan was to whip for the smallest offences, to prevent the commission of large ones. Mr. Hopkins could always find some excuse for whipping a slave. It would astonish one, unaccustomed to a slaveholding life, to see with what wonderful ease a slaveholder can find things, of which to make occasion to whip a slave. A mere look, word, or motion,—a mistake, accident, or want of power,—are all matters for which a slave may be whipped at any time. Does a slave look dissatisfied? It is said, he has the devil in him, and it must be whipped out. Does he speak loudly when spoken to by his master? Then he is getting high-minded, and should be taken down a button-hole lower. Does he forget to pull off his hat at the approach of a white person? Then he is wanting in reverence, and should be whipped for it. Does he ever venture to vindicate his conduct, when censured for it? Then he is guilty of impudence,—one of the greatest crimes of which a slave can be guilty. Does he ever venture to suggest a different mode of doing things from that pointed out by his master? He is indeed presumptuous, and getting above himself; and nothing less than a flogging will do for him. Does he, while ploughing, break a plough,—or, while hoeing, break a hoe? It is owing to his carelessness, and for it a slave must always be whipped. Mr. Hopkins could always find something of this sort to justify the use of the lash, and he seldom failed to embrace such opportunities. There was not a man in the whole county, with whom the slaves who had the getting their own home, would not prefer to live, rather than with this Rev. Mr. Hopkins. And yet there was not a man any where round, who made higher professions of religion, or was more active in revivals,—more attentive to the class, love-feast, prayer and preaching meetings, or more devotional in his family,— that prayed earlier, later, louder, and longer,— than this same reverend slave-driver, Rigby Hopkins.

But to return to Mr. Freeland, and to my experience while in his employment. He, like Mr.

Covey, gave us enough to eat; but, unlike Mr. Covey, he also gave us sufficient time to take our meals. He worked us hard, but always between sunrise and sunset. He required a good deal of work to be done, but gave us good tools with which to work. His farm was large, but he employed hands enough to work it, and with ease, compared with many of his neighbors. My treatment, while in his employment, was heavenly, compared with what I experienced at the hands of Mr. Edward Covey.

Mr. Freeland was himself the owner of but two slaves. Their names were Henry Harris and John Harris. The rest of his hands he hired. These consisted of myself, Sandy Jenkins,[1] and Handy Caldwell. Henry and John were quite intelligent, and in a very little while after I went there, I succeeded in creating in them a strong desire to learn how to read. This desire soon sprang up in the others also. They very soon mustered up some old spelling-books, and nothing would do but that I must keep a Sabbath school. I agreed to do so, and accordingly devoted my Sundays to teaching these my loved fellow-slaves how to read. Neither of them knew his letters when I went there. Some of the slaves of the neighboring farms found what was going on, and also availed themselves of this little opportunity to learn to read. It was understood, among all who came, that there must be as little display about it as possible. It was necessary to keep our religious masters at St. Michael's unacquainted with the fact, that, instead of spending the Sabbath in wrestling, boxing, and drinking whisky, we were trying to learn how to read the will of God; for they had much rather see us engaged in those degrading sports, than to see us behaving like intellectual, moral, and accountable beings. My blood boils as I think of the bloody manner in which Messrs. Wright Fairbanks and Garrison West, both class-leaders, in connection with many others, rushed in upon us with sticks and stones, and broke up our virtuous little Sabbath school, at St. Michael's —all calling themselves Christians! humble followers of the Lord Jesus Christ! But I am again digressing.

[1] This is the same man who gave me the roots to prevent my being whipped by Mr. Covey. He was "a clever soul." We used frequently to talk about the fight with Covey, and as often as we did so, he would claim my success as the result of the roots which he gave me. This superstition is very common among the more ignorant slaves. A slave seldom dies but that his death is attributed to trickery.

I held my Sabbath school at the house of a free colored man, whose name I deem it imprudent to mention; for should it be known, it might embarrass him greatly, though the crime of holding the school was committed ten years ago. I had at one time over forty scholars, and those of the right sort, ardently desiring to learn. They were of all ages, though mostly men and women. I look back to those Sundays with an amount of pleasure not to be expressed. They were great days to my soul. The work of instructing my dear fellow-slaves was the sweetest engagement with which I was ever blessed. We loved each other, and to leave them at the close of the Sabbath was a severe cross indeed. When I think that these precious souls are to-day shut up in the prison-house of slavery, my feelings overcome me, and I am almost ready to ask, "Does a righteous God govern the universe? and for what does he hold the thunders in his right hand, if not to smite the oppressor, and deliver the spoiled out of the hand of the spoiler?" These dear souls came not to Sabbath school because it was popular to do so, nor did I teach them because it was reputable to be thus engaged. Every moment they spent in that school, they were liable to be taken up, and given thirty-nine lashes. They came because they wished to learn. Their minds had been starved by their cruel masters. They had been shut up in mental darkness. I taught them, because it was the delight of my soul to be doing something that looked like bettering the condition of my race. I kept up my school nearly the whole year I lived with Mr. Freeland; and, beside my Sabbath school, I devoted three evenings in the week, during the winter, to teaching the slaves at home. And I have the happiness to know, that several of those who came to Sabbath school learned how to read; and that one, at least, is now free through my agency.

The year passed off smoothly. It seemed only about half as long as the year which preceded it. I went through it without receiving a single blow. I will give Mr. Freeland the credit of being the best master I ever had, *till I became my own master.* For the ease with which I passed the year, I was, however, somewhat indebted to the society of my fellow-slaves. They were noble souls; they not only possessed loving hearts, but brave ones. We were linked and interlinked with each other. I loved them with a love stronger than any thing I have experienced since. It is sometimes said that we slaves do not love and confide in each other. In answer to this assertion, I can say, I never loved any or confided in any people more than my fellow-slaves, and especially those with whom I lived at Mr. Freeland's. I believe we would have died for each other. We never undertook to do anything, of any importance, without a mutual consultation. We never moved separately. We were one; and as much so by our tempers and dispositions, as by the mutual hardships to which we were necessarily subjected by our condition as slaves.

At the close of the year 1834, Mr. Freeland again hired me of my master, for the year 1835. But, by this time, I began to want to live *upon free land* as well as *with Freeland;* and I was no longer content, therefore, to live with him or any other slaveholder. I began, with the commencement of the year, to prepare myself for a final struggle, which should decide my fate one way or the other. My tendency was upward. I was fast approaching manhood, and year after year had passed, and I was still a slave. These thoughts roused me— I must do something. I therefore resolved that 1835 should not pass without witnessing an attempt, on my part, to secure my liberty. But I was not willing to cherish this determination alone. My fellow-slaves were dear to me. I was anxious to have them participate with me in this, my life-giving determination. I therefore, though with great prudence, commenced early to ascertain their views and feelings in regard to their condition, and to imbue their minds with thoughts of freedom. I bent myself to devising ways and means for our escape, and meanwhile strove, on all fitting occasions, to impress them with the gross fraud and inhumanity of slavery. I went first to Henry, next to John, then to the others. I found, in them all, warm hearts and noble spirits. They were ready to hear, and ready to act when a feasible plan should be proposed. This was what I wanted. I talked to them of our want of manhood, if we submitted to our enslavement without at least one noble effort to be free. We met often, and consulted frequently, and told our hopes and fears, recounted the difficulties, real and imagined, which we should be called on to meet. At times we were almost disposed to give up, and try to content ourselves with our wretched lot; at others, we were firm and unbending in our determination to go. Whenever we suggested any plan, there was shrinking—the odds were fearful. Our path was beset with the greatest obstacles; and if we succeeded in gaining the end of it, our right to be free was yet questionable—we were yet liable to be returned to bondage. We could see no spot, this side of the ocean, where we could be free. We knew nothing about Canada. Our knowledge of the north did not extend farther than New York; and to go there, and be forever harassed with the frightful liability of being returned to slavery—with the certainty of being treated tenfold worse than before—the thought was truly a horrible one, and one which it was not easy to overcome. The case sometimes stood thus: At every gate through which we were to pass, we saw a watchman—at every ferry a guard—on every bridge a sentinel—and in every wood a patrol. We were hemmed in upon every side. Here were the difficulties, real or imagined—the good to be sought, and the evil to be shunned. On the one hand, there stood slavery, a stern reality, glaring frightfully upon us,—its robes already crimsoned with the blood of millions, and even now feasting itself greedily upon our own flesh. On the other hand, away back in the dim distance, under the flickering light of the north star, behind some craggy hill or snow-covered mountain, stood a doubtful freedom—half frozen—beckoning us to come and share its hospitality. This in itself was sometimes enough to stagger us; but when we permitted ourselves to survey the road, we were frequently appalled. Upon either side we saw grim death, assuming the most horrid shapes. Now it was starvation, causing us to eat our own flesh;—now we were contending with the waves, and were drowned;—now we were overtaken, and torn to pieces by the fangs of the terrible bloodhound. We were stung by scorpions, chased by wild beasts, bitten by snakes, and finally, after having nearly reached the desired spot,—after swimming rivers, encountering wild beasts, sleeping in the woods, suffering hunger and nakedness,—we were overtaken by our pursuers, and, in our resistance, we were shot dead upon the spot! I say, this picture sometimes appalled us, and made us

> rather bear those ills we had,
> Than fly to others, that we knew not of.

In coming to a fixed determination to run away, we did more than Patrick Henry, when he resolved upon liberty or death. With us it was a doubtful liberty at most, and almost certain death if we failed. For my part, I should prefer death to hopeless bondage.

Sandy, one of our number, gave up the notion, but still encouraged us. Our company then consisted of Henry Harris, John Harris, Henry Bailey, Charles Roberts, and myself. Henry Bailey was my uncle, and belonged to my master. Charles married my aunt: he belonged to my master's father-in-law, Mr. William Hamilton.

The plan we finally concluded upon was, to get a large canoe belonging to Mr. Hamilton, and upon the Saturday night previous to Easter holidays, paddle directly up the Chesapeake Bay. On our arrival at the head of the bay, a distance of seventy or eighty miles from where we lived, it was our purpose to turn our canoe adrift, and follow the guidance of the north star till we got beyond the limits of Maryland. Our reason for taking the water route was, that we were less liable to be suspected as runaways; we hoped to be regarded as fishermen; whereas, if we should take the land route, we should be subjected to interruptions of almost every kind. Any one having a white face, and being so disposed, could stop us, and subject us to examination.

The week before our intended start, I wrote several protections, one for each of us. As well as I can remember, they were in the following words, to wit:—

This is to certify that I, the undersigned, have given the bearer, my servant, full liberty to go to Baltimore, and spend the Easter holidays. Written with mine own hand, &c., 1835.

WILLIAM HAMILTON,
Near St. Michael's, in Talbot county, Maryland.

We were not going to Baltimore; but, in going up the bay, we went toward Baltimore, and these protections were only intended to protect us while on the bay.

As the time drew near for our departure, our anxiety became more and more intense. It was truly a matter of life and death with us. The strength of our determination was about to be fully tested. At this time, I was very active in explaining every difficulty, removing every doubt, dispelling every fear, and inspiring all with the firmness indispensable to success in our undertaking; assuring them that half was gained the instant we made the move; we had talked long enough; we were now ready to move; if not now, we never should be; and if we did not intend to move now, we had as well fold our arms, sit down, and acknowledge ourselves fit only to be slaves. This, none of us were prepared to acknowledge. Every man stood firm; and at our last meeting, we pledged ourselves afresh, in the most solemn manner, that, at the time appointed, we would certainly start in pursuit of freedom. This was in the middle of the week, at the end of which we were to be off. We went, as usual, to our several fields of labor, but with bosoms highly agitated with thoughts of our truly hazardous undertaking. We tried to conceal our feelings as much as possible; and I think we succeeded very well.

After a painful waiting, the Saturday morning, whose night was to witness our departure, came. I hailed it with joy, bring what of sadness it might. Friday night was a sleepless one for me. I probably felt more anxious than the rest, because I was, by common consent, at the head of the whole affair. The responsibility of success or failure lay heavily upon me. The glory of the one, and the confusion of the other, were alike mine. The first two hours of that morning were such as I never experienced before, and hope never to again. Early in the morning, we went, as usual, to the field. We were spreading manure; and all at once, while thus engaged, I was overwhelmed with an indescribable feeling, in the fulness of which I turned to Sandy, who was near by, and said, "We are betrayed!" "Well," said he, "that thought has this moment struck me." We said no more. I was never more certain of any thing.

The horn was blown as usual, and we went up from the field to the house for breakfast. I went for the form, more than for want of any thing to eat that morning. Just as I got to the house, in looking out at the lane gate, I saw four white men, with two colored men. The white men were on horseback, and the colored ones were walking behind, as if tied. I watched them a few moments till they got up to our lane gate. Here they halted, and tied the colored men to the gatepost. I was not yet certain as to what the matter was. In a few moments, in rode Mr. Hamilton, with a speed betokening great excitement. He came to the door, and inquired if Master William was in. He was told he was at the barn. Mr. Hamilton, without dismounting, rode up to the barn with extraordinary speed. In a few moments, he and Mr. Freeland returned to the house. By this time, the three constables rode up, and in great haste dismounted, tied their horses, and met Master William and Mr. Hamilton returning from the barn; and after talking awhile, they all walked up to the kitchen door. There was no one in the kitchen but myself and John. Henry and Sandy were up at the barn. Mr. Freeland put his head in at the door, and called me by name, saying, there were some gentlemen at the door who wished to see me. I stepped to the door, and inquired what they wanted. They at once seized me, and, without giving me any satisfaction, tied me—lashing my hands closely together. I insisted upon knowing what the matter was. They at length said, that they had learned I had been in a "scrape," and that I was to be examined before my master; and if their information proved false, I should not be hurt.

In a few moments, they succeeded in tying John. They then turned to Henry, who had by this time returned, and commanded him to cross his hands. "I won't!" said Henry, in a firm tone, indicating his readiness to meet the consequences of his refusal. "Won't you?" said Tom Graham, the constable. "No, I won't!" said Henry, in a still stronger tone. With this, two of the constables pulled out their shining pistols, and swore, by their Creator, that they would make him cross his hands or kill him. Each cocked his pistol, and, with fingers on the trigger, walked up to Henry, saying, at the same time, if he did not cross his hands, they would blow his damned heart out. "Shoot me, shoot me!" said Henry; "you can't kill me but once. Shoot, shoot,—and be damned! *I won't be tied!*" This he said in a tone of loud defiance; and at the same time, with a motion as quick as lightning, he with one single stroke dashed the pistols from the hand of each constable. As he did this, all hands fell upon him, and, after beating him some time, they finally overpowered him, and got him tied.

During the scuffle, I managed, I know not how, to get my pass out, and, without being discovered, put it into the fire. We were all now tied; and just as we were to leave for Easton jail, Betsy Freeland, mother of William Freeland, came to the door with her hands full of biscuits, and divided them between Henry and John. She then delivered herself of a speech, to the following effect:—addressing herself to me, she said, "*You devil! You yellow devil!* it was you that put it into the heads of Henry and John to run away. But for you, you long-legged mulatto devil! Henry nor John would never have thought of such a thing." I made no reply, and was immediately hurried off towards St. Michael's. Just a moment previous to the scuffle with Henry, Mr. Hamilton suggested the propriety of making a search for the protections which he had understood Frederick had written for himself and the rest. But, just at the moment he was about carrying his proposal into effect, his aid was needed in helping to tie Henry; and the excitement attending the scuffle caused them either to forget, or to deem it unsafe, under the circumstances, to search. So we were not yet convicted of the intention to run away.

When we got about half way to St. Michael's, while the constables having us in charge were looking ahead, Henry inquired of me what he should do with his pass. I told him to eat it with his biscuit, and own nothing; and we passed the word around, *"Own nothing;"* and *"Own nothing!"* said we all. Our confidence in each other was unshaken. We were resolved to succeed or fail together, after the calamity had befallen us as much as before. We were now prepared for any thing. We were to be dragged that morning fifteen miles behind horses, and then to be placed in the Easton jail. When we reached St. Michael's, we underwent a sort of examination. We all denied that we ever intended to run away. We did this more to bring out the evidence against us, than from any hope of getting clear of being sold; for, as I have said, we were ready for that. The fact was, we cared but little where we went, so we went together. Our greatest concern was about separation. We dreaded that more than any thing this side of death. We found the evidence against us to be the testimony of one person; our master would not tell who it was; but we came to a unanimous decision among ourselves as to who their informant was. We were sent off to the jail at Easton. When we got there, we were delivered up to the sheriff, Mr. Joseph Graham, and by him placed in jail. Henry, John, and myself, were placed in one room together— Charles, and Henry Bailey, in another. Their object in separating us was to hinder concert.

We had been in jail scarcely twenty minutes, when a swarm of slave traders, and agents for slave traders, flocked into jail to look at us, and to ascertain if we were for sale. Such a set of beings I never saw before! I felt myself surrounded by so many fiends from perdition. A band of pirates never looked more like their father, the devil. They laughed and grinned over us, saying, "Ah, my boys! we have got you, haven't we?" And after taunting us in various ways, they one by one went into an examination of us, with intent to ascertain our value. They would impudently ask us if we would not like

to have them for our masters. We would make them no answer, and leave them to find out as best they could. Then they would curse and swear at us, telling us that they could take the devil out of us in a very little while, if we were only in their hands.

While in jail, we found ourselves in much more comfortable quarters than we expected when we went there. We did not get much to eat, nor that which was very good; but we had a good clean room, from the windows of which we could see what was going on in the street, which was very much better than though we had been placed in one of the dark, damp cells. Upon the whole, we got along very well, so far as the jail and its keeper were concerned. Immediately after the holidays were over, contrary to all our expectations, Mr. Hamilton and Mr. Freeland came up to Easton, and took Charles, the two Henrys, and John, out of jail, and carried them home, leaving me alone. I regarded this separation as a final one. It caused me more pain than any thing else in the whole transaction. I was ready for any thing rather than separation. I supposed that they had consulted together, and had decided that, as I was the whole cause of the intention of the others to run away, it was hard to make the innocent suffer with the guilty; and that they had, therefore, concluded to take the other home, and sell me, as a warning to the others that remained. It is due to the noble Henry to say, he seemed almost as reluctant at leaving the prison as at leaving home to come to the prison. But we knew we should, in all probability, be separated, if we were sold; and since he was in their hands, he concluded to go peaceably home.

I was now left to my fate. I was all alone, and within the walls of a stone prison. But a few days before, and I was full of hope. I expected to have been safe in a land of freedom; but now I was covered with gloom, sunk down to the utmost despair. I thought the possibility of freedom was gone. I was kept in this way about one week, at the end of which, Captain Auld, my master, to my surprise and utter astonishment, came up, and took me out, with the intention of sending me, with a gentleman of his acquaintance, into Alabama. But, from some cause or other, he did not send me to Alabama, but concluded to send me back to Baltimore, to live again with his brother Hugh, and to learn a trade.

Thus, after an absence of three years and one month, I was once more permitted to return to my old home at Baltimore. My master sent me away, because there existed against me a very great prejudice in the community, and he feared I might be killed.

In a few weeks after I went to Baltimore, Master Hugh hired me to Mr. William Gardner, an extensive ship-builder, on Fell's Point. I was put there to learn how to calk. It, however, proved a very unfavorable place for the accomplishment of this object. Mr. Gardner was engaged that spring in building two large man-of-war brigs, professedly for the Mexican government. The vessels were to be launched in the July of that year, and in failure thereof, Mr. Gardner was to lose a considerable sum; so that when I entered, all was hurry. There was no time to learn any thing. Every man had to do that which he knew how to do. In entering the shipyard, my orders from Mr. Gardner were, to do whatever the carpenters commanded me to do. This was placing me at the beck and call of about seventy-five men. I was to regard all these as masters. Their word was to be my law. My situation was a most trying one. At times I needed a dozen pair of hands. I was called a dozen ways in the space of a single minute. Three of four voices would strike my ear at the same moment. It was—"Fred., come help me to cant this timber here."—"Fred., come carry this timber yonder."—"Fred., bring that roller here."—"Fred., go get a fresh can of water."—"Fred., come help me saw off the end of this timber."—"Fred., go quick, and get the crowbar."—"Fred., hold on the end of this fall."—"Fred., go to the blacksmith's shop and get a new punch."—"Hurra, Fred.! run and bring me a cold chisel."—"I say, Fred., bear a hand, and get up a fire as quick as lightning under that steam-box."—"Halloo, nigger! come, turn this grindstone."—"Come, come! move, move! and *bowse* this timber forward."—"I say, darky, blast your eyes, why don't you heat up some pitch?"—"Halloo! halloo! halloo!" (Three voices at the same time.) "Come here!—Go there!—Hold on where you are! Damn you, if you move, I'll knock your brains out!"

This was my school for eight months; and I might have remained there longer, but for a most horrid fight I had with four of the white apprentices, in which my left eye was nearly knocked out, and I was horribly mangled in other respects. The facts in the case were these: Until a very little while after I went there, white and black ship-carpenters worked side by side, and no one

seemed to see any impropriety in it. All hands seemed to be very well satisfied. Many of the black carpenters were freemen. Things seemed to be going on very well. All at once, the white carpenters knocked off, and said they would not work with free colored workmen. Their reason for this, as alleged, was, that if free colored carpenters were encouraged, they would soon take the trade into their own hands, and poor white men would be thrown out of employment. They therefore felt called upon at once to put a stop to it. And, taking advantage of Mr. Gardner's necessities, they broke off, swearing they would work no longer, unless he would discharge his black carpenters. Now, though this did not extend to me in form, it did reach me in fact. My fellow-apprentices very soon began to feel it degrading to them to work with me. They began to put on airs, and talk about the "niggers" taking the country, saying we all ought to be killed; and, being encouraged by the journeymen, they commenced making my condition as hard as they could, by hectoring me around, and sometimes striking me. I, of course, kept the vow I made after the fight with Mr. Covey, and struck back again, regardless of consequences; and while I kept them from combining, I succeeded very well; for I could whip the whole of them, taking them separately. They, however, at length combined, and came upon me, armed with sticks, stones, and heavy handspikes. One came in front with a half brick. There was one at each side of me, and one behind me. While I was attending to those in front, and on either side, the one behind ran up with the handspike, and struck me a heavy blow upon the head. It stunned me. I fell, and with this they all ran upon me, and fell to beating me with their fists. I let them lay on for a while, gathering strength. In an instant, I gave a sudden surge, and rose to my hands and knees. Just as I did that, one of the number gave me, with his heavy boot, a powerful kick in the left eye. My eyeball seemed to have burst. When they saw my eye closed, and badly swollen, they left me. With this I seized the handspike, and for a time pursued them. But here the carpenters interfered, and I thought I might as well give it up. It was impossible to stand my hand against so many. All this took place in sight of not less than fifty white ship-carpenters, and not one interposed a friendly word; but some cried, "Kill the damned nigger! Kill him! kill him! He struck a white person." I found my only chance for life was in flight. I succeeded in getting away without an additional blow, and barely so; for to strike a white man is death by Lynch law,—and that was the law in Mr. Gardner's ship-yard; nor is there much of any other out of Mr. Gardner's ship-yard.

I went directly home, and told the story of my wrongs to Master Hugh; and I am happy to say of him, irreligious as he was, his conduct was heavenly, compared with that of his brother Thomas under similar circumstances. He listened attentively to my narration of the circumstances leading to the savage outrage, and gave many proofs of his strong indignation at it. The heart of my once overkind mistress was again melted into pity. My puffed-out eye and blood-covered face moved her to tears. She took a chair by me, washed the blood from my face, and, with a mother's tenderness, bound up my head, covering the wounded eye with a lean piece of fresh beef. It was almost compensation for my suffering to witness, once more, a manifestation of kindness from this, my once affectionate old mistress. Master Hugh was very much enraged. He gave expression to his feelings by pouring out curses upon the heads of those who did the deed. As soon as I got a little the better of my bruises, he took me with him to Esquire Watson's, on Bond Street, to see what could be done about the matter. Mr. Watson inquired who saw the assault committed. Master Hugh told him it was done in Mr. Gardner's ship-yard, at midday, where there were a large company of men at work. "As to that," he said, "the deed was done, and there was no question as to who did it." His answer was, he could do nothing in the case, unless some white man would come forward and testify. He could issue no warrant on my word. If I had been killed in the presence of a thousand colored people, their testimony combined would have been insufficient to have arrested one of the murderers. Master Hugh, for once, was compelled to say this state of things was too bad. Of course, it was impossible to get any white man to volunteer his testimony in my behalf, and against the white young men. Even those who may have sympathized with me were not prepared to do this. It required a degree of courage unknown to them to do so; for just at that time, the slightest manifestation of humanity toward a colored person was denounced as abolitionism, and that name subjected its bearer to frightful liabilities. The watchwords of the bloody-minded in that region, and in those days, were, "Damn the abolitionists!" and "Damn the niggers!" There was nothing done, and probably nothing would have been done if I had been killed. Such was, and such remains, the state of things in the Christian city of Baltimore.

Master Hugh, finding he could get no redress, refused to let me go back again to Mr. Gardner. He kept me himself, and his wife dressed my wound till I was again restored to health. He then took me into the ship-yard of which he was foreman, in the employment of Mr. Walter Price. There I was immediately set to calking, and very soon learned the art of using my mallet and irons. In the course of one year from the time I left Mr. Gardner's, I was able to command the highest wages given to the most experienced calkers. I was now of some importance to my master. I was bringing him from six to seven dollars per week. I sometimes brought him nine dollars per week: my wages were a dollar and a half a day. After learning how to calk, I sought my own employment, made my own contracts, and collected the money which I earned. My pathway became much more smooth than before; my condition was now much more comfortable. When I could get no calking to do, I did nothing. During these leisure times, those old notions about freedom would steal over me again. When in Mr. Gardner's employment, I was kept in such a perpetual whirl of excitement, I could think of nothing, scarcely, but my life; and in thinking of my life, I almost forgot my liberty. I have observed this in my experience of slavery,—that whenever my condition was improved, instead of its increasing my contentment, it only increased my desire to be free, and set me to thinking of plans to gain my freedom. I have found that, to make a contented slave, it is necessary to make a thoughtless one. It is necessary to darken his moral and mental vision, and, as far as possible, to annihilate the power of reason. He must be able to detect no inconsistencies in slavery; he must be made to feel that slavery is right; and he can be brought to that only when he ceases to be a man.

I was now getting, as I have said, one dollar and fifty cents per day. I contracted for it; I earned it; it was paid to me; it was rightfully my own; yet, upon each returning Saturday night, I was compelled to deliver every cent of that money to Master Hugh. And why? Not because he earned it,—not because he had any hand in earning it,—

not because I owed it to him,—nor because he possessed the slightest shadow of a right to it; but solely because he had the power to compel me to give it up. The right of the grim-visaged pirate upon the high seas is exactly the same.

Chapter XI

I now come to that part of my life during which I planned, and finally succeeded in making, my escape from slavery. But before narrating any of the peculiar circumstances, I deem it proper to make known my intention not to state all the facts connected with the transaction. My reasons for pursuing this course may be understood from the following: First, were I to give a minute statement of all the facts, it is not only possible, but quite probable, that others would thereby be involved in the most embarrassing difficulties. Secondly, such a statement would most undoubtedly induce greater vigilance on the part of slaveholders than has existed heretofore among them; which would, of course, be the means of guarding a door whereby some dear brother bondman might escape his galling chains. I deeply regret the necessity that impels me to suppress any thing of importance connected with my experience in slavery. It would afford me great pleasure indeed, as well as materially add to the interest of my narrative, were I at liberty to gratify a curiosity, which I know exists in the minds of many, by an accurate statement of all the facts pertaining to my most fortunate escape. But I must deprive myself of this pleasure, and the curious of the gratification which such a statement would afford. I would allow myself to suffer under the greatest imputations which evil-minded men might suggest, rather than exculpate myself, and thereby run the hazard of closing the slightest avenue by which a brother slave might clear himself of the chains and fetters of slavery.

I have never approved of the very public manner in which some of our western friends have conducted what they call the *underground railroad,* but which I think, by their open declarations, has been made most emphatically the *upperground railroad.* I honor those good men and women for their noble daring, and applaud them for willingly subjecting themselves to bloody persecution, by openly avowing their participation in the escape of slaves. I, however, can see very little good resulting from such a course, either to themselves or the slaves escaping; while, upon the other hand, I see and feel assured that those open declarations are a positive evil to the slaves remaining, who are seeking to escape. They do nothing towards enlightening the slave, whilst they do much towards enlightening the master. They stimulate him to greater watchfulness, and enhance his power to capture his slave. We owe something to the slave south of the line as well as to those north of it; and in aiding the latter on their way to freedom, we should be careful to do nothing which would be likely to hinder the former from escaping from slavery. I would keep the merciless slaveholder profoundly ignorant of the means of flight adopted by the slave. I would leave him to imagine himself surrounded by myriads of invisible tormentors, ever ready to snatch from his infernal grasp his trembling prey. Let him be left to feel his way in the dark; let darkness commensurate with his crime hover over him; and let him feel that at every step he takes, in pursuit of the flying bondman, he is running the frightful risk of having his hot brains dashed out by an invisible agency. Let us render the tyrant no aid; let us not hold the light by which he can trace the footprints of our flying brother. But enough of this. I will now proceed to the statement of those facts, connected with my escape, for which I am alone responsible, and for which no one can be made to suffer but myself.

In the early part of the year 1838, I became quite restless. I could see no reason why I should, at the end of each week, pour the reward of my toil into the purse of my master. When I carried to him my weekly wages, he would, after counting the money, look me in the face with a robber-like fierceness, and ask, "Is this all?" He was satisfied with nothing less than the last cent. He would, however, when I made him six dollars, sometimes give me six cents, to encourage me. It had the opposite effect. I regarded it as a sort of admission of my right to the whole. The fact that he gave me any part of my wages was proof, to my mind, that he believed me entitled to the whole of them. I always felt worse for having received any thing; for I feared that the giving me a few cents would ease his conscience, and make him feel himself to be a pretty honorable sort of robber. My discontent grew upon me. I was ever on the look-out for means of escape; and, finding no direct means, I determined to try to hire my time, with a view of getting money with which to make my escape.

In the spring of 1838, when Master Thomas came to Baltimore to purchase his spring goods, I got an opportunity, and applied to him to allow me to hire my time. He unhesitatingly refused my request, and told me this was another stratagem by which to escape. He told me I could go nowhere but that he could get me; and that, in the event of my running away, he should spare no pains in his efforts to catch me. He exhorted me to content myself, and be obedient. He told me, if I would be happy, I must lay out no plans for the future. He said, if I behaved myself properly, he would take care of me. Indeed, he advised me to complete thoughtlessness of the future, and taught me to depend solely upon him for happiness. He seemed to see fully the pressing necessity of setting aside my intellectual nature, in order to contentment in slavery. But in spite of him, and even in spite of myself, I continued to think, and to think about the injustice of my enslavement, and the means of escape.

About two months after this, I applied to Master Hugh for the privilege of hiring my time. He was not acquainted with the fact that I had applied to Master Thomas, and had been refused. He too, at first, seemed disposed to refuse; but, after some reflection, he granted me the privilege, and proposed the following terms: I was to be allowed all my time, make all contracts with those for whom I worked, and find my own employment; and, in return for this liberty, I was to pay him three dollars at the end of each week; find myself in calking tools, and in board and clothing. My board was two dollars and a half per week. This, with the wear and tear of clothing and calking tools, made my regular expenses about six dollars per week. This amount I was compelled to make up, or relinquish the privilege of hiring my time. Rain or shine, work or no work, at the end of each week the money must be forthcoming, or I must give up my privilege. This arrangement, it will be perceived, was decidedly in my master's favor. It relieved him of all need of looking after me. His money was sure. He received all the benefits of slaveholding without its evils; while I endured all the evils of a slave, and suffered all the care and anxiety of a freeman. I found it a hard bargain. But, hard as it was, I thought it better than the old mode of getting along. It was a step towards freedom to be allowed to bear the responsibilities of a freeman, and I was determined to hold on upon it. I bent myself to the work of making money. I was ready to work at night as well as day, and by the most untiring perseverance and industry, I made enough to meet my expenses, and lay up a little money every week. I went on thus from May till August. Master Hugh then refused to allow me to hire my time longer. The ground for his refusal was a failure on my part, one Saturday night, to pay him for my week's time. This failure was occasioned by my attending a camp meeting about ten miles from Baltimore. During the week, I had entered into an engagement with a number of young friends to start from Baltimore to the camp ground early Saturday evening; and being detained by my employer, I was unable to get down to Master Hugh's without disappointing the company. I knew that Master Hugh was in no special need of the money that night. I therefore decided to go to camp meeting, and upon my return pay him the three dollars. I stayed at the camp meeting one day longer than I intended when I left. But as soon as I returned, I called upon him to pay him what he considered his due. I found him very angry; he could scarce restrain his wrath. He said he had a great mind to give me a severe whipping. He wished to know how I dared go out of the city without asking his permission. I told him I hired my time, and while I paid him the price which he asked for it, I did not know that I was bound to ask him when and where I should go. This reply troubled him; and, after reflecting a few moments, he turned to me, and said I should hire my time no longer; that the next thing he should know of, I would be running away. Upon the same plea, he told me to bring my tools and clothing home forthwith. I did so; but instead of seeking work, as I had been accustomed to do previously to hiring my time, I spent the whole week without the performance of a single stroke of work. I did this in retaliation. Saturday night, he called upon me as usual for my week's wages. I told him I had no wages; I had done no work that week. Here we were upon the point of coming to blows. He raved, and swore his determination to get hold of me. I did not allow myself a single word; but was resolved, if he laid the weight of his hand upon me, it should be blow for blow. He did not strike me, but told me that he would find me in constant employment in future. I thought the matter over during the next day, Sunday, and finally resolved upon the third day of September, as the day upon which I would make a second attempt to secure my freedom. I now had three weeks during which to prepare for my journey. Early on Monday morning, before Master Hugh had time to make any engagement for me, I went out and got employment of Mr. Butler, at his ship-yard near the drawbridge, upon what is called the City Block, thus making it unnecessary for him to seek employment for me. At the end of the week, I brought him between eight and nine dollars. He seemed very well pleased, and asked why I did not do the same the week before. He little knew what my plans were. My object in working steadily was to remove any suspicion he might entertain of my intent to run away; and in this I succeeded admirably. I suppose he thought I was never better satisfied with my condition than at the very time during which I was planning my escape. The second week passed, and again I carried him my full wages; and so well pleased was he, that he gave me twenty-five cents, (quite a large sum for a slaveholder to give a slave,) and bade me to make a good use of it. I told him I would.

Things went on without very smoothly indeed, but within there was trouble. It is impossible for me to describe my feelings as the time of my contemplated start drew near. I had a number of warm-hearted friends in Baltimore,—friends that I loved almost as I did my life,—and the thought of being separated from them forever was painful beyond expression. It is my opinion that thousands would escape from slavery, who now remain, but for the strong cords of affection that bind them to their friends. The thought of leaving my friends was decidedly the most painful thought with which I had to contend. The love of them was my tender point, and shook my decision more than all things else. Besides the pain of separation, the dread and apprehension of a failure exceeded what I had experienced at my first attempt. The appalling defeat I then sustained returned to torment me. I felt assured that, if I failed in this attempt, my case would be a hopeless one—it would seal my fate as a slave forever. I could not hope to get off with any thing less than the severest punishment, and being placed beyond the means of escape. It required no very vivid imagination to depict the most frightful scenes through which I should have to pass, in case I failed. The wretchedness of slavery, and the blessedness of freedom, were perpetually before me. It was life and death with me. But I remained firm, and, according to my resolution, on the third day of September, 1838, I left my chains, and succeeded in reaching New York without the slightest interruption of any kind. How I did so,—what means I adopted,—what direction I travelled, and by what mode of conveyance,—I must leave unexplained, for the reasons before mentioned.

I have been frequently asked how I felt when I found myself in a free State. I have never been able to answer the question with any satisfaction to myself. It was a moment of the highest excitement I ever experienced. I suppose I felt as one may imagine the unarmed mariner to feel when he is rescued by a friendly man-of-war from the pursuit of a pirate. In writing to a dear friend, immediately after my arrival at New York, I said I felt like one who had escaped a den of hungry lions. This state of mind, however, very soon subsided; and I was again seized with a feeling of great insecurity and loneliness. I was yet liable to be taken back, and subjected to all the tortures of slavery. This in itself was enough to damp the ardor of my enthusiasm. But the loneliness overcame me. There I was in the midst of thousands, and yet a perfect stranger; without home and without friends, in the midst of thousands of my own brethren—children of a common Father, and yet I dared not to unfold to any of them my sad condition. I was afraid to speak to any one for fear of speaking to the wrong one, and thereby falling into the hands of money-loving kidnappers, whose business it was to lie in wait for the panting fugitive, as the ferocious beasts of the forest lie in wait for their prey. The motto which I adopted when I started from slavery was this— "Trust no man!" I saw in every white man an enemy, and in almost every colored man cause for distrust. It was a most painful situation; and, to understand it, one must needs experience it, or imagine himself in similar circumstances. Let him be a fugitive slave in a strange land—a land given up to be the hunting-ground for slaveholders— whose inhabitants are legalized kidnappers— where he is every moment subjected to the terrible liability of being seized upon by his fellowmen, as the hideous crocodile seizes upon his prey!—I say, let him place himself in my situation—without home or friends—without money or credit— wanting shelter, and no one to give it—wanting bread, and no money to buy it,—and at the same time let him feel that he is pursued by merciless men-hunters, and in total darkness as to what to do, where to go, or where to stay,—perfectly helpless both as to the means of defence and means of escape,—in the midst of plenty, yet suffering the terrible gnawings of hunger,—in the midst of houses, yet having no home,— among fellow-men, yet feeling as if in the midst of wild beasts, whose greediness to swallow up the trembling and half-famished fugitive is only equalled by that with which the monsters of the deep swallow up the helpless fish upon which they subsist,—I say, let him be placed in this most trying situation,—the situation in which I was placed,—then, and not till then, will he fully appreciate the hardships of, and know how to sympathize with, the toil-worn and whip-scarred fugitive slave.

Thank Heaven, I remained but a short time in this distressed situation. I was relieved from it by the humane hand of Mr. DAVID RUGGLES, whose vigilance, kindness, and perseverance, I shall never forget. I am glad of an opportunity to express, as far as words can, the love and gratitude I bear him. Mr. Ruggles is now afflicted with blindness, and is himself in need of the same kind offices which he was once so forward in the performance of toward others. I had been in New York but a few days, when Mr. Ruggles sought me out, and very kindly took me to his boarding-house at the corner of Church and Lespenard Streets. Mr. Ruggles was then very deeply engaged in the memorable *Darg* case, as well as attending to a number of other fugitive slaves, devising ways and means for their successful escape; and, though watched and hemmed in on almost every side; he seemed to be more than a match for his enemies.

Very soon after I went to Mr. Ruggles, he wished to know of me where I wanted to go; as he deemed it unsafe for me to remain in New York. I told him I was a calker, and should like to go where I could get work. I thought of going to Canada; but he decided against it, and in favor of my going to New Bedford, thinking I should be able to get work there at my trade. At this time, Anna,[2] my intended wife, came on; for I wrote to her immediately after my arrival at New York, (notwithstanding my homeless, houseless, and helpless condition,) informing her of my successful flight, and wishing her to come on forthwith. In a few days after her arrival, Mr. Ruggles called in the Rev. J. W. C. Pennington, who, in the presence of Mr. Ruggles, Mrs. Michaels, and two or three others, performed the marriage ceremony, and gave us a certificate, of which the following is an exact copy:—

[2] She was free.

This may certify, that I joined together in holy matrimony Frederick Johnson[3] and Anna Murray, as man and wife, in the presence of Mr. David Ruggles and Mrs. Michaels.

JAMES W. C. PENNINGTON

New York, Sept. 15, 1838.

Upon receiving this certificate, and a five-dollar bill from Mr. Ruggles, I shouldered one part of our baggage, and Anna took up the other, and we set out forthwith to take passage on board of the steamboat John W. Richmond for Newport, on our way to New Bedford. Mr. Ruggles gave a me letter to a Mr. Shaw in Newport, and told me, in case my money did not serve me to New Bedford, to stop in Newport and obtain further assistance; but upon our arrival at Newport, we were so anxious to get to a place of safety, that, notwithstanding we lacked the necessary money to pay our fare, we decided to take seats in the stage, and promise to pay when we got to New Bedford. We were encouraged to do this by two excellent gentlemen, residents of New Bedford, whose names I afterward ascertained to be Joseph Ricketson and William C. Taber. They seemed at once to understand our circumstances, and gave us such assurance of their friendliness as put us fully at ease in their presence. It was good indeed to meet with such friends, at such a time. Upon reaching New Bedford, we were directed to the house of Mr. Nathan Johnson, by whom we were kindly received, and hospitably provided for. Both Mr. and Mrs. Johnson took a deep and lively interest in our welfare. They proved themselves quite worthy of the name of abolitionists. When the stage-driver found us unable to pay our fare, he held on upon our baggage as security for the debt. I had but to mention the fact to Mr. Johnson, and he forthwith advanced the money.

We now began to feel a degree of safety, and to prepare ourselves for the duties and responsibilities of a life of freedom. On the morning after our arrival at New Bedford, while at the breakfast-table, the question arose as to what name I should be called by. The name given me by my mother was, "Frederick Augustus Washington Bailey." I, however, had dispensed with the two middle names long before I left Maryland so that I was generally known by the name of "Frederick Bailey." I started from Baltimore bearing the

[3] I had changed my name from Frederick *Bailey* to that of *Johnson*.

name of "Stanley." When I got to New York, I again changed my name to "Frederick Johnson," and thought that would be the last change. But when I got to New Bedford, I found it necessary again to change my name. The reason of this necessity was, that there were so many Johnsons in New Bedford, it was already quite difficult to distinguish between them. I gave Mr. Johnson the privilege of choosing me a name, but told him he must not take from me the name of "Frederick." I must hold on to that, to preserve a sense of my identity. Mr. Johnson had just been reading the "Lady of the Lake," and at once suggested that my name be "Douglass." From that time until now I have been called "Frederick Douglass;" and as I am more widely known by that name than by either of the others, I shall continue to use it as my own.

I was quite disappointed at the general appearance of things in New Bedford. The impression which I had received respecting the character and condition of the people of the north, I found to be singularly erroneous. I had very strangely supposed, while in slavery, that few of the comforts, and scarcely any of the luxuries, of life were enjoyed at the north, compared with what were enjoyed by the slaveholders of the south. I probably came to this conclusion from the fact that northern people owned no slaves. I supposed that they were about upon a level with the non-slaveholding population of the south. I knew *they* were exceedingly poor, and I had been accustomed to regard their poverty as the necessary consequence of their being non-slaveholders. I had somehow imbibed the opinion that, in the absence of slaves, there could be no wealth, and very little refinement. And upon coming to the north, I expected to meet with a rough, hard-handed, and uncultivated population, living in the most Spartan-like simplicity, knowing nothing of the ease, luxury, pomp, and grandeur of southern slaveholders. Such being my conjectures, any one acquainted with the appearance of New Bedford may very readily infer how palpably I must have seen my mistake.

In the afternoon of the day when I reached New Bedford, I visited the wharves, to take a view of the shipping. Here I found myself surrounded with the strongest proofs of wealth. Lying at the wharves, and riding in the stream, I saw many ships of the finest model, in the best order, and of the largest size. Upon the right and left, I was walled in by granite warehouses of the widest dimensions, stowed to their utmost capacity with the necessaries and comforts of life. Added to this, almost every body seemed to be at work, but noiselessly so, compared with what I had been accustomed to in Baltimore. There were no loud songs heard from those engaged in loading and unloading ships. I heard no deep oaths or horrid curses on the laborer. I saw no whipping of men; but all seemed to go smoothly on. Every man appeared to understand his work, and went at it with a sober, yet cheerful earnestness, which betokened the deep interest which he felt in what he was doing, as well as a sense of his own dignity as a man. To me this looked exceedingly strange. From the wharves I strolled around and over the town, gazing with wonder and admiration at the splendid churches, beautiful dwellings, and finely-cultivated gardens; evincing an amount of wealth, comfort, taste, and refinement, such as I had never seen in any part of slaveholding Maryland.

Every thing looked clean, new, and beautiful. I saw few or no dilapidated houses, with poverty-stricken inmates; no half-naked children and bare-footed women, such as I had been accustomed to see in Hillsborough, Easton, St. Michael's, and Baltimore. The people looked more able, stronger, healthier, and happier, than those of Maryland. I was for once made glad by a view of extreme wealth, without being saddened by seeing extreme poverty. But the most astonishing as well as the most interesting thing to me was the condition of the colored people, a great many of whom, like myself, had escaped thither as a refuge from the hunters of men. I found many, who had not been seven years out of their chains, living in finer houses, and evidently enjoying more of the comforts of life, than the average of slaveholders in Maryland. I will venture to assert, that my friend Mr. Nathan Johnson (of whom I can say with a grateful heart, "I was hungry, and he gave me meat; I was thirsty, and he gave me drink; I was a stranger, and he took me in") lived in a neater house; dined at a better table; took, paid for, and read, more newspapers; better understood the moral, religious, and political character of the nation,— than nine tenths of the slaveholders in Talbot county Maryland. Yet Mr. Johnson was a working man. His hands were hardened by toil, and not his alone, but those also of Mrs. Johnson. I found the colored people much more spirited than I had supposed they would be. I found among them a determination to protect each other from the blood-thirsty kidnapper, at all hazards. Soon after my arrival, I was told of a circumstance which illustrated their spirit. A colored man and a fugitive slave were on unfriendly terms. The former was heard to threaten the latter with informing his master of his whereabouts. Straightway a meeting was called among the colored people, under the stereotyped notice, "Business of importance!" The betrayer was invited to attend. The people came at the appointed hour, and organized the meeting by appointing a very religious old gentleman as president, who, I believe, made a prayer, after which he addressed the meeting as follows: *"Friends, we have got him here, and I would recommend that you young men just take him outside the door, and kill him!"* With this, a number of them bolted at him; but they were intercepted by some more timid than themselves, and the betrayer escaped their vengeance, and has not been seen in New Bedford since. I believe there have been no more such threats, and should there be hereafter, I doubt not that death would be the consequence.

I found employment, the third day after my arrival, in stowing a sloop with a load of oil. It was new, dirty, and hard work for me; but I went at it with a glad heart and a willing hand. I was now my own master. It was a happy moment, the rapture of which can be understood only by those who have been slaves. It was the first work, the reward of which was to be entirely my own. There was no Master Hugh standing ready, the moment I earned the money, to rob me of it. I worked that day with a pleasure I had never before experienced. I was at work for myself and newly-married wife. It was to me the starting-point of a new existence. When I got through with that job, I went in pursuit of a job of calking; but such was the strength of prejudice against color, among the white calkers, that they refused to work with me, and of course I could get no employment.[4] Finding my trade of no immediate benefit, I threw off my calking habiliments, and prepared myself to do any kind of work I could get to do. Mr.

[4] I am told that colored persons can now get employment at calking in New Bedford—a result of anti-slavery effort.

Johnson kindly let me have his wood-horse and saw, and I very soon found myself a plenty of work. There was no work too hard—none too dirty. I was ready to saw wood, shovel coal, carry wood, sweep the chimney, or roll oil casks, —all of which I did for nearly three years in New Bedford, before I became known to the anti-slavery world.

In about four months after I went to New Bedford, there came a young man to me, and inquired if I did not wish to take the "Liberator." I told him I did; but, just having made my escape from slavery, I remarked that I was unable to pay for it then. I, however, finally became a subscriber to it. The paper came, and I read it from week to week with such feelings as it would be quite idle for me to attempt to describe. The paper became my meat and my drink. My soul was set all on fire. Its sympathy for my brethren in bonds—its scathing denunciations of slaveholders—its faithful exposure of slavery—and its powerful attacks upon the upholders of the institution—sent a thrill of joy through my soul, such as I had never felt before!

I had not long been a reader of the "Liberator," before I got a pretty correct idea of the principles, measures and spirit of the anti-slavery reform. I took right hold of the cause. I could do but little; but what I could, I did with a joyful heart, and never felt happier than when in an anti-slavery meeting. I seldom had much to say at the meetings, because what I wanted to say was said so much better by others. But, while attending an anti-slavery convention at Nantucket, on the 11th of August, 1841, I felt strongly moved to speak, and was at the same time much urged to do so by Mr. William C. Coffin, a gentleman who had heard me speak in the colored people's meeting at New Bedford. It was a severe cross, and I took it up reluctantly. The truth was, I felt myself a slave, and the idea of speaking to white people weighed me down. I spoke but a few moments, when I felt a degree of freedom, and said what I desired with considerable ease. From that time until now, I have been engaged in pleading the cause of my brethren—with what success, and with what devotion, I leave those acquainted with my labors to decide.

Oration, Delivered in Corinthian Hall, Rochester, July 5, 1852

Mr. President, Friends and Fellow Citizens:

He who could address this audience without a quailing sensation, has stronger nerves than I have. I do not remember ever to have appeared as a speaker before any assembly more shrinkingly, nor with greater distrust of my ability, than I do this day. A feeling has crept over me, quite unfavorable to the exercise of my limited powers of speech. The task before me is one which requires much previous thought and study for its proper performance. I know that apologies of this sort are generally considered flat and unmeaning. I trust, however, that mine will not be so considered. Should I seem at ease, my appearance would much misrepresent me. The little experience I have had in addressing public meetings, in country school houses, avails me nothing on the present occasion.

The papers and placards say, that I am to deliver a 4th July oration. This certainly, sounds large, and out of the common way, for me. It is true that I have often had the privilege to speak in this beautiful Hall, and to address many who now honor me with their presence. But neither their familiar faces, nor the perfect gage I think I have of Corinthian Hall, seems to free me from embarrassment.

That fact is, ladies and gentlemen, the distance between this platform and the slave plantation, from which I escaped, is considerable—and the difficulties to be overcome in getting from the latter to the former, are by no means slight. That I am here to-day, is, to me, a matter of astonishment as well as of gratitude. You will not, therefore, be surprised, if in what I have to say, I evince no elaborate preparation, nor grace my speech with any high sounding exordium. With little experience and with less learning, I have been able to throw my thoughts hastily and imperfectly together; and trusting to your patient and generous indulgence, I will proceed to lay them before you.

This, for the purpose of this celebration, is the 4th of July. It is the birthday of your National Independence, and of your political freedom.

This, to you, is what the Passover was to the emancipated people of God. It carries your minds back to the day, and the act of your great deliverance; and to the signs, and to the wonders, associated with that act, and that day. This celebration also marks the beginning of another year of your national life; and reminds you that the Republic of America is now 76 years old. I am glad, fellow-citizens, that your nation is so young. Seventy-six years, though a good old age for a man, is but a mere speck in the life of a nation. Three score years and ten is the allotted time for individual men; but nations number their years by thousands. According to this fact, you are, even now only in the beginning of your national career, still lingering in the period of childhood. I repeat, I am glad this is so. There is hope in the thought, and hope is much needed, under the dark clouds which lower above the horizon. The eye of the reformer is met with angry flashes, portending disastrous times; but his heart may well beat lighter at the thought that America is young, and that she is still in the impressible stage of her existence. May he not hope that high lessons of wisdom, of justice and of truth, will yet give direction to her destiny? Were the nation older, the patriot's heart might be sadder, and the reformer's brow heavier. Its future might be shrouded in gloom, and the hope of its prophets go out in sorrow. There is consolation in the thought, that America is young.— Great streams are not easily turned from channels, worn deep in the course of ages. They may sometimes rise in quiet and stately majesty, and inundate the land, refreshing and fertilizing the earth with their mysterious properties. They may also rise in wrath and fury, and bear away, on their angry waves, the accumulated wealth of years of toil and hardship. They, however, gradually flow back to the same old channel, and flow on as serenely as ever. But, while the river may not be turned aside, it may dry up, and leave nothing behind but the withered branch, and the unsightly rock, to howl in the abyss-sweeping wind, the sad tale of departed glory. As with rivers so with nations.

Fellow-citizens, I shall not presume to dwell at length on the associations that cluster about this day. The simple story of it is, that, 76 years ago, the people of this country were British subjects. The style and title of your "sovereign people" (in which you now glory) was not then born. You were under the British Crown. Your fathers esteemed the English Government as the home government; and England as the fatherland. This home government, you know, although a considerable distance from your home, did, in the exercise of its parental prerogatives, impose upon its colonial children, such restraints, burdens and limitations, as, in its mature judgment, it deemed wise, right and proper.

But, your fathers, who had not adopted the fashionable idea of this day, of the infallibility of government, and the absolute character of its acts, presumed to differ from the home government in respect to the wisdom and the justice of some of those burdens and restraints. They went so far in their excitement as to pronounce the measures of government unjust, unreasonable, and oppressive, and altogether such as ought not to be quietly submitted to. I scarcely need say, fellow-citizens, that my opinion of those measures fully accords with that of your fathers. Such a declaration of agreement on my part, would not be worth much to anybody. It would, certainly, prove nothing, as to what part I might have taken, had I lived during the great controversy of 1776. To say *now* that America was right, and England wrong, is exceedingly easy. Everybody can say it; the dastard, not less than the noble brave, can flippantly discant of the tyranny of England towards the American Colonies. It is fashionable to do so; but there was a time when, to pronounce against England, and in favor of the cause of the colonies, tried men's souls. They who did so were accounted in their day, plotters of mischief, agitators and rebels, dangerous men. To side with the right, against the wrong, with the weak against the strong, and with the oppressed against the oppressor! *here* lies the merit, and the one which, of all others, seems unfashionable in our day. The cause of liberty may be stabbed by the men who glory in the deeds of your fathers. But, to proceed.

Feeling themselves harshly and unjustly treated, by the home government, your fathers, like men of honesty, and men of spirit, earnestly sought redress. They petitioned and remonstrated; they did so in a decorous, respectful, and loyal manner. Their conduct was wholly unexceptionable. This, however, did not answer the purpose. They saw themselves treated with sovereign indifference, coldness and scorn. Yet they persevered. They were not the men to look back.

As the sheet anchor takes a firmer hold, when the ship is tossed by the storm, so did the cause of your fathers grow stronger, as it breasted the chilling blasts of kingly displeasure. The greatest and best of British statesmen admitted its justice, and the loftiest eloquence of the British Senate came to its support. But, with the blindness which seems to be the unvarying characteristic of tyrants, since Pharaoh and his hosts were drowned in the Red Sea, the British Government persisted in the exactions complained of.

The madness of this course, we believe, is admitted now, even by England; but we fear the lesson is wholly lost on our present rulers.

Oppression makes a wise man mad. Your fathers were wise men, and if they did not go mad, they became restive under this treatment. They felt themselves the victims of grievous wrongs, wholly incurable in their colonial capacity. With brave men there is always a remedy for oppression. Just here, the idea of a total separation of the colonies from the crown was born! It was a startling idea, much more so, than we, at this distance of time, regard it. The timid and the prudent (as has been intimated) of that day, were, of course, shocked and alarmed by it.

Such people lived then, had lived before, and will, probably, ever have a place on this planet; and their course, in respect to any great change, (no matter how great the good to be attained, or the wrong to be redressed by it,) may be calculated with as much precision as can be the course of the stars. They hate all changes, but silver, gold and copper change! Of this sort of change they are always strongly in favor.

These people were called tories in the days of your fathers; and the appellation, probably, conveyed the same idea that is meant by a more modern, though a somewhat less euphonious term, which we often find in our papers, applied to some of our old politicians.

Their opposition to the then dangerous thought was earnest and powerful; but, amid all their terror and affrighted vociferations against it, the alarming and revolutionary idea moved on, and the country with it.

On the 2d of July, 1776, the old Continental

Congress, to the dismay of the lovers of ease, and the worshippers of property, clothed that dreadful idea with all the authority of national sanction. They did so in the form of a resolution; and as we seldom hit upon resolutions, drawn up in our day, whose transparency is at all equal to this, it may refresh your minds and help my story if I read it.

Resolved, That these united colonies *are,* and of right, ought to be free and Independent States; that they are absolved from all allegiance to the British Crown; and that all political connection between them and the State of Great Britain *is,* and ought to be, dissolved.

Citizens, your fathers made good that resolution. They succeeded; and to-day you reap the fruits of their success. The freedom gained is yours; and you, therefore, may properly celebrate this anniversary. The 4th of July is the first great fact in your nation's history—the very ring-bolt in the chain of your yet undeveloped destiny.

Pride and patriotism, not less than gratitude, prompt you to celebrate and to hold it in perpetual remembrance. I have said that the Declaration of Independence is the RINGBOLT to the chain of your nation's destiny; so, indeed, I regard it. The principles contained in that instrument are saving principles. Stand by those principles, be true to them on all occasions, in all places, against all foes, and at whatever cost.

From the round top of your ship of state, dark and threatening clouds may be seen. Heavy billows, like mountains in the distance, disclose to the leeward huge forms of flinty rocks! That *bolt* drawn, that *chain* broken, and all is lost. *Cling to this day—cling to it,* and to its principles, with the grasp of a storm-tossed mariner to a spar at midnight.

The coming into being of a nation, in any circumstances, is an interesting event. But, besides general considerations, there were peculiar circumstances which make the advent of this republic an event of special attractiveness.

The whole scene, as I look back to it, was simple, dignified and sublime.

The population of the country, at the time, stood at the insignificant number of three millions. The country was poor in the munitions of war. The population was weak and scattered, and the country a wilderness unsubdued. There were then no means of concert and combination, such as exist now. Neither steam nor lightning had

then been reduced to order and discipline. From the Potomac to the Delaware was a journey of many days. Under these, and innumerable other disadvantages, your fathers declared for liberty and independence and triumphed.

Fellow Citizens, I am not wanting in respect for the fathers of this republic. The signers of the Declaration of Independence were brave men. They were great men too—great enough to give fame to a great age. It does not often happen to a nation to raise, at one time, such a number of truly great men. The point from which I am compelled to view them is not, certainly the most favorable; and yet I cannot contemplate their great deeds with less than admiration. They were statesmen, patriots and heroes, and for the good they did, and the principles they contended for, I will unite with you to honor their memory.

They loved their country better than their own private interests; and, though this is not the highest form of human excellence, all will concede that it is a rare virtue, and that when it is exhibited, it ought to command respect. He who will, intelligently, lay down his life for his country, is a man whom it is not in human nature to despise. Your fathers staked their lives, their fortunes, and their sacred honor, on the cause of their country. In their admiration of liberty, they lost sight of all other interests.

They were peace men; but they preferred revolution to peaceful submission to bondage. They were quiet men; but they did not shrink from agitating against oppression. They showed forbearance; but they knew its limits. They believed in order; but not in the order of tyranny. With them, nothing was "*settled*" that was not right. With them, justice, liberty and humanity were "*final;*" not slavery and oppression. You may well cherish the memory of such men. They were great in their day and generation. Their solid manhood stands out the more as we contrast it with these degenerate times.

How circumspect, exact and proportionate were all their movements! How unlike the politicians of an hour! Their statesmanship looked beyond the passing moment, and stretched away in strength into the distant future. They seized upon eternal principles, and set a glorious example in their defence. Mark them!

Fully appreciating the hardships to be encountered, firmly believing in the right of their cause, honorably inviting the scrutiny of an on-looking world, reverently appealing to heaven to attest their sincerity, soundly comprehending the solemn responsibility they were about to assume, wisely measuring the terrible odds against them, your fathers, the fathers of this republic, did, most deliberately, under the inspiration of a glorious patriotism, and with a sublime faith in the great principles of justice and freedom, lay deep, the corner-stone of the national superstructure, which has risen and still rises in grandeur around you.

Of this fundamental work, this day is the anniversary. Our eyes are met with demonstrations of joyous enthusiasm. Banners and pennants wave exultingly on the breeze. The din of business, too, is hushed. Even mammon seems to have quitted his grasp on this day. The ear-piercing fife and the stirring drum unite their accents with the ascending peal of a thousand church bells. Prayers are made, hymns are sung, and sermons are preached in honor of this day; while the quick martial tramp of a great and multitudinous nation, echoed back by all the hills, valleys and mountains of a vast continent, bespeak the occasion one of thrilling and universal interest—a nation's jubilee.

Friends and citizens, I need not enter further into the causes which led to this anniversary. Many of you understand them better than I do. You could instruct me in regard to them. That is a branch of knowledge in which you feel, perhaps, a much deeper interest than your speaker. The causes which led to the separation of the colonies from the British crown have never lacked for a tongue. They have all been taught in your common schools, narrated at your firesides, unfolded from your pulpits, and thundered from your legislative halls, and are as familiar to you as household words. They form the staple of your national poetry and eloquence.

I remember, also, that, as a people, Americans are remarkably familiar with all facts which make in their own favor. This is esteemed by some as a national trait—perhaps a national weakness. It is a fact, that whatever makes for the wealth or for the reputation of Americans, and can be had *cheap!* will be found by Americans. I shall not be charged with slandering Americans, if I say I think the American side of any question may be safely left in American hands.

I leave, therefore, the great deeds of your fathers to other gentlemen whose claim to have been regularly descended will be less likely to be disputed than mine!

The Present

My business, if I have any here to-day, is with the present. The accepted time with God and his cause is the ever-living now.

> Trust no future, however pleasant,
>   Let the dead past bury its dead;
> Act, act in the living present,
>   Heart within, and God overhead.

We have to do with the past only as we can make it useful to the present and to the future. To all inspiring motives, to noble deeds which can be gained from the past, we are welcome. But now is the time, the important time. Your fathers have lived, died, and have done their work, and have done much of it well. You live and must die, and you must do your work. You have no right to enjoy a child's share in the labor of your fathers, unless your children are to be blest by your labors. You have no right to wear out and waste the hard-earned fame of your fathers to cover your indolence. Sydney Smith tells us that men seldom eulogize the wisdom and virtues of their fathers, but to excuse some folly or wickedness of their own. This truth is not a doubtful one. There are illustrations of it near and remote, ancient and modern. It was fashionable, hundreds of years ago, for the children of Jacob to boast, we have "Abraham to our father," when they had long lost Abraham's faith and spirit. That people contented themselves under the shadow of Abraham's great name, while they repudiated the deeds which made his name great. Need I remind you that a similar thing is being done all over this country to-day? Need I tell you that the Jews are not the only people who built the tombs of the prophets, and garnished the sepulchres of the righteous? Washington could not die till he had broken the chains of his slaves. Yet his monument is built up by the price of human blood, and the traders in the bodies and souls of men, shout —"We have Washington to '*our father.*' "—Alas! that it should be so; yet so it is.

> The evil that men do, lives after them,
> The good is oft' interred with their bones.

Fellow-citizens, pardon me, allow me to ask, why am I called upon to speak here to-day? What have I, or those I represent, to do with your national independence? Are the great principles of political freedom and of natural justice, embodied in that Declaration of Independence, extended to us? and am I, therefore, called upon to bring our humble offering to the national altar, and to confess the benefits and express devout gratitude for the blessings resulting from your independence to us?

Would to God, both for your sakes and ours, that an affirmative answer could be truthfully returned to these questions! Then would my task be light, and my burden easy and delightful. For *who* is there so cold, that a nation's sympathy could not warm him? Who so obdurate and dead to the claims of gratitude, that would not thankfully acknowledge such priceless benefits? Who so stolid and selfish, that would not give his voice to swell the hallelujahs of a nation's jubilee, when the chains of servitude had been torn from his limbs? I am not that man. In a case like that, the dumb might eloquently speak, and the "lame man leap as an hart."

But, such is not the state of the case. I say it with a sad sense of the disparity between us. I am not included within the pale of this glorious anniversary! Your high independence only reveals the immeasurable distance between us. The blessings in which you, this day, rejoice, are not enjoyed in common.—The rich inheritance of justice, liberty, prosperity and independence, bequeathed by your fathers, is shared by you, not by me. The sunlight that brought life and healing to you, has brought stripes and death to me. This Fourth July is *yours, not mine. You* may rejoice, *I* must mourn. To drag a man in fetters into the grand illuminated temple of liberty, and call upon him to join you in joyous anthems, were inhuman mockery and sacrilegious irony. Do you mean, citizens, to mock me, by asking me to speak to-day? If so, there is a parallel to your conduct. And let me warn you that it is dangerous to copy the example of a nation whose crimes, towering up to heaven, were thrown down by the breath of the Almighty, burying that nation in irrecoverable ruin! I can to-day take up the plaintive lament of a peeled and woe-smitten people!

"By the rivers of Babylon, there we sat down. Yea! we wept when we remembered Zion. We hanged our harps upon the willows in the midst thereof. For there, they that carried us away captive, required of us a song; and they who wasted us required of us mirth, saying, Sing us one of the songs of Zion. How can we sing the Lord's song in a strange land? If I forget thee, O Jerusalem, let my right hand forget her cun-

ning. If I do not remember thee, let my tongue cleave to the roof of my mouth."

Fellow-citizens; above your national, tumultuous joy, I hear the mournful wail of millions! whose chains, heavy and grievous yesterday, are, to-day, rendered more intolerable by the jubilee shouts that reach them. If I do forget, if I do not faithfully remember those bleeding children of sorrow this day, "may my right hand forget her cunning, and may my tongue cleave to the roof of my mouth!" To forget them, to pass lightly over their wrongs, and to chime in with the popular theme, would be treason most scandalous and shocking, and would make me a reproach before God and the world. My subject, then, fellow-citizens, is AMERICAN SLAVERY. I shall see, this day, and its popular characteristics, from the slave's point of view. Standing, there, identified with the American bondman, making his wrongs mine, I do not hesitate to declare, with all my soul, that the character and conduct of this nation never looked blacker to me than on this 4th of July! Whether we turn to the declarations of the past, or to the professions of the present, the conduct of the nation seems equally hideous and revolting. America is false to the past, false to the present, and solemnly binds herself to be false to the future. Standing with God and the crushed and bleeding slave on this occasion, I will, in the name of humanity which is outraged, in the name of liberty which is fettered, in the name of the constitution and the Bible, which are disregarded and trampled upon, dare to call in question and to denounce, with all the emphasis I can command, everything that serves to perpetuate slavery—the great sin and shame of America! "I will not equivocate; I will not excuse;" I will use the severest language I can command; and yet not one word shall escape me that any man, whose judgment is not blinded by prejudice, or who is not at heart a slaveholder, shall not confess to be right and just.

But I fancy I hear some one of my audience say, it is just in this circumstance that you and your brother abolitionists fail to make a favorable impression on the public mind. Would you argue more, and denounce less, would you persuade more, and rebuke less, your cause would be much more likely to succeed. But, I submit, where all is plain there is nothing to be argued. What point in the anti-slavery creed would you have me argue? On what branch of the subject do the people of this country need light? Must I undertake to prove that the slave is a man? That point is conceded already. Nobody doubts it. The slave-holders themselves acknowledge it in the enactment of laws for their government. They acknowledge it when they punish disobedience on the part of the slave. There are seventy-two crimes in the State of Virginia, which, if committed by a black man, (no matter how ignorant he be,) subject him to the punishment of death; while only two of the same crimes will subject a white man to the like punishment.—What is this but the acknowledgement that the slave is a moral, intellectual and responsible being. The manhood of the slave is conceded. It is admitted in the fact that Southern statute books are covered with enactments forbidding, under severe fines and penalties, the teaching of the slave to read or to write.—When you can point to any such laws, in reference to the beasts of the field, then I may consent to argue the manhood of the slave. When the dogs in your streets, when the fowls of the air, when the cattle on your hills, when the fish of the sea, and the reptiles that crawl, shall be unable to distinguish the slave from a brute, *then* will I argue with you that the slave is a man!

For the present, it is enough to affirm the equal manhood of the negro race. Is it not astonishing that, while we are ploughing, planting and reaping, using all kinds of mechanical tools, erecting houses, constructing bridges, building ships, working in metals of brass, iron, copper, silver and gold; that, while we are reading, writing and cyphering, acting as clerks, merchants and secretaries, having among us lawyers, doctors, ministers, poets, authors, editors, orators and teachers; that, while we are engaged in all manner of enterprises common to other men, digging gold in California, capturing the whale in the Pacific, feeding sheep and cattle on the hill-side, living, moving, acting, thinking, planning, living in families as husbands, wives and children, and, above all, confessing and worshipping the Christian's God, and looking hopefully for life and immortality beyond the grave, we are called upon to prove that we are men!

Would you have me argue that man is entitled to liberty? that he is the rightful owner of his own body? You have already declared it. Must I argue the wrongfulness of slavery? Is that a question for Republicans? Is it to be settled by the rules of logic and argumentation, as a matter beset with great difficulty, involving a doubtful application of the principle of justice, hard to be understood?

How should I look to-day, in the presence of Americans, dividing, and subdividing a discourse, to show that men have a natural right to freedom? speaking of it relatively, and positively, negatively, and affirmatively. To do so, would be to make myself ridiculous, and to offer an insult to your understanding.—There is not a man beneath the canopy of heaven, that does not know that slavery is wrong *for him.*

What, am I to argue that it is wrong to make men brutes, to rob them of their liberty, to work them without wages, to keep them ignorant of their relations to their fellow men, to beat them with sticks, to flay their flesh with the lash, to load their limbs with irons, to hunt them with dogs, to sell them at auction, to sunder their families, to knock out their teeth, to burn their flesh, to starve them into obedience and submission to their masters? Must I argue that a system thus marked with blood, and stained with pollution, is *wrong?* No! I will not. I have better employment for my time and strength, than such arguments would imply.

What, then, remains to be argued? Is it that slavery is not divine; that God did not establish it; that our doctors of divinity are mistaken? There is blasphemy in the thought. That which is inhuman, cannot be divine! *Who* can reason on such a proposition? They that can, may; I cannot. The time for such argument is past.

At a time like this, scorching irony, not convincing argument, is needed. O! had I the ability, and could I reach the nation's ear, I would, to-day, pour out a fiery stream of biting ridicule, blasting reproach, withering sarcasm, and stern rebuke. For it is not light that is needed, but fire; it is not the gentle shower, but thunder. We need the storm, the whirlwind, and the earthquake. The feeling of the nation must be quickened; the conscience of the nation must be roused; the propriety of the nation must be startled; the hypocrisy of the nation must be exposed; and its crimes against God and man must be proclaimed and denounced.

What, to the American slave, is your 4th of July? I answer; a day that reveals to him, more than all other days in the year, the gross injustice and cruelty to which he is the constant victim. To him, your celebration is a sham; your boasted liberty, an unholy license; your national greatness, swelling vanity; your sounds of rejoicing are empty and heartless; your denunciations of tyrants, brass fronted impudence; your shouts of liberty and equality, hollow mockery; your prayers and hymns, your sermons and thanksgivings, with all your religious parade, and solemnity, are, to him, mere bombast, fraud, deception, impiety, and hypocrisy—a thin veil to cover up crimes which would disgrace a nation of savages. There is not a nation on the earth guilty of practices, more shocking and bloody, than are the people of these United States, at this very hour.

Go where you may; search where you will, roam through all the monarchies and despotisms of the old world, travel through South America, search out every abuse, and when you have found the last, lay your facts by the side of the every day practices of this nation, and you will say with me, that, for revolting barbarity and shameless hypocrisy, America reigns without a rival.

The Internal Slave Trade

Take the American slave-trade, which we are told by the papers, is especially prosperous just now. Ex-Senator Benton tells us that the price of men was never higher than now. He mentions the fact to show that slavery is in no danger. This trade is one of the peculiarities of American institutions. It is carried on in all the large towns and cities in one half of this confederacy; and millions are pocketed every year, by dealers in this horrid traffic. In several states, this trade is a chief source of wealth. It is called (in contradistinction to the foreign slave-trade) "*the internal slave-trade.*" It is, probably, called so, too, in order to divert from it the horror with which the foreign slave-trade is contemplated. That trade has long since been denounced by this government, as piracy. It has been denounced with burning words, from the high places of the nation, as an execrable traffic. To arrest it, to put an end to it, this nation keeps a squadron, at immense cost, on the coast of Africa. Everywhere, in this country, it is safe to speak of this foreign slave-trade, as a most inhuman traffic, opposed alike to the laws of God and of man. The duty to extirpate and destroy it, is admitted even by our DOCTORS OF DIVINITY. In order to put an end to it, some of these last have consented that their colored brethren (nominally free) should leave this country, and establish themselves on the western coast of Africa! It is, however, a notable fact, that, while so much execration is poured out by Americans, upon those engaged in the foreign slave-trade, the men engaged in the slave-trade between the states pass without condemnation, and their business is deemed honorable.

Behold the practical operation of this internal slave-trade, the American slave-trade, sustained by American politics and American religion. Here you will see men and women, reared like swine, for the market. You know what is a swine-drover? I will show you a man-drover. They inhabit all our Southern States. They perambulate the country, and crowd the highways of the nation, with droves of human stock. You will see one of these human flesh jobbers, armed with pistol, whip, and bowie-knife, driving a company of a hundred men, women, and children, from the Potomac to the slave market at New Orleans. These wretched people are to be sold singly, or in lots, to suit purchasers. They are food for the cotton-field, and the deadly sugar-mill. Mark the sad procession, as it moves wearily along, and the inhuman wretch who drives them. Hear his savage yells and his blood-chilling oaths, as he hurries on his affrighted captives! There, see the old man, with locks thinned and gray. Cast one glance, if you please, upon that young mother, whose shoulders are bare to the scorching sun, her briny tears falling on the brow of the babe in her arms. See, too, that girl of thirteen, weeping, *yes!* weeping, as she thinks of the mother from whom she has been torn! The drove moves tardily. Heat and sorrow have nearly consumed their strength; suddenly you hear a quick snap, like the discharge of a rifle; the fetters clank, and the chain rattles simultaneously; your ears are saluted with a scream, that seems to have torn its way to the centre of your soul! The crack you heard, was the sound of the slave-whip; the scream you heard, was from the woman you saw with the babe. Her speed had faltered under the weight of her child and her chains! that gash on her shoulder tells her to move on. Follow this drove to New Orleans. Attend the auction; see men examined like horses; see the forms of women rudely and brutally exposed to the shocking gaze of American slave-buyers. See this drove sold and separated for ever; and never forget the deep, sad sobs that arose from that scattered multitude. Tell me citizens, WHERE, under the sun, you can witness a spectacle more fiendish and shocking. Yet this is but a glance at the American slave-trade, as it exists, at this moment, in the ruling part of the United States.

I was born amid such sights and scenes. To me the American slave-trade is a terrible reality. When a child, my soul was often pierced with a sense of its horrors. I lived on Philpot Street, Fell's Point, Baltimore, and have watched from the wharves, the slave ships in the Basin, anchored from the shore, with their cargoes of human flesh, waiting for favorable winds to waft them down the Chesapeake. There was, at that time, a grand slave mart kept at the head of Pratt Street, by Austin Woldfolk. His agents were sent into every town and county in Maryland, announcing their arrival, through the papers, and on flaming "*hand-bills,*" headed CASH FOR NEGROES. These men were generally well dressed men, and very captivating in their manners. Ever ready to drink, to treat, and to gamble. The fate of many a slave has depended upon the turn of a single card; and many a child has been snatched from the arms of its mother, by bargains arranged in a state of brutal drunkenness.

The flesh-mongers gather up their victims by dozens, and drive them, chained, to the general depot at Baltimore. When a sufficient number have been collected here, a ship is chartered, for the purpose of conveying the forlorn crew to Mobile, or to New Orleans. From the slave prison to the ship, they are usually driven in the darkness of night; for since the anti-slavery agitation, a certain caution is observed.

In the deep still darkness of midnight, I have been often aroused by the dead heavy footsteps, and the pitious cries of the chained gangs that passed our door. The anguish of my boyish heart was intense; and I was often consoled, when speaking to my mistress in the morning, to hear her say that the custom was very wicked; that she hated to hear the rattle of the chains, and the heart-rending cries. I was glad to find one who sympathized with me in my horror.

Fellow-citizens, this murderous traffic is, to-day, in active operation in this boasted republic. In the solitude of my spirit, I see clouds of dust raised on the highways of the South; I see the bleeding footsteps; I hear the doleful wail of fettered humanity, on the way to the slave-markets, where the victims are to be sold like *horses, sheep,* and *swine,* knocked off to the highest bidder. There I see the tenderest ties ruthlessly broken, to gratify the lust, caprice and rapacity of the buyers and sellers of men. My soul sickens at the sight.

Is this the land your Fathers loved,
　The freedom which they toiled to win?
Is this the earth whereon they moved?
　Are these the graves they slumber in?

But a still more inhuman, disgraceful, and scandalous state of things remains to be presented.

By an act of the American Congress, not yet two years old, slavery has been nationalized in its most horrible and revolting form. By that act, Mason & Dixon's line has been obliterated; New York has become as Virginia; and the power to hold, hunt, and sell men, women and children, as slaves, remains no longer a mere state institution, but is now an institution of the whole United States. The power is co-extensive with the star-spangled banner, and American Christianity. Where these go, may also go the merciless slave-hunter. Where these are, man is not sacred. He is a bird for the sportsman's gun. By that most foul and fiendish of all human decrees, the liberty and person of every man are put in peril. Your broad republican domain is hunting ground for *men*. *Not* for thieves and robbers, enemies of society, merely, but for men guilty of no crime. Your law-makers have commanded all good citizens to engage in this hellish sport. Your President, your Secretary of State, your *lords, nobles,* and ecclesiastics, enforce, as a duty you owe to your free and glorious country, and to your God, that you do this accursed thing. Not fewer than forty Americans, have, within the past two years, been hunted down, and, without a moment's warning, hurried away in chains, and consigned to slavery, and excruciating torture. Some of these have had wives and children, dependent on them for bread; but of this, no account was made. The right of the hunter to his prey, stands superior to the right of marriage, and to *all* rights in this republic, the rights of God included! For black men there are neither law, justice, humanity, nor religion. The Fugitive Slave *Law* makes MERCY TO THEM, A CRIME; and bribes the judge who tries them. An American JUDGE GETS TEN DOLLARS FOR EVERY VICTIM HE CONSIGNS to slavery, and five, when he fails to do so. The oath of any two villains is sufficient, under this hell-black enactment, to send the most pious and exemplary black man into the remorseless jaws of slavery! His own testimony is nothing. He can bring no witnesses for himself. The minister of American justice is bound, by the law to hear but *one* side; and *that* side, is the side of the oppressor. Let this damning fact be perpetually told. Let it be thundered around the world, that, in tyrant-killing, king-hating, people-loving, democratic, Christian America, the seats of justice are filled with judges, who hold their offices under an open and palpable *bribe,* and are bound, in deciding in the case of a man's liberty, *to hear only his accusers!*

In glaring violation of justice, in shameless disregard of the forms of administering law, in cunning arrangement to entrap the defenceless, and in diabolical intent, this Fugitive Slave Law stands alone in the annals of tyrannical legislation. I doubt if there be another nation on the globe, having the brass and the baseness to put such a law on the statute-book. If any man in this assembly thinks differently from me in this matter, and feels able to disprove my statements, I will gladly confront him at any suitable time and place he may select.

Religious Liberty

I take this law to be one of the grossest infringements of Christian Liberty, and, if the churches and ministers of our country were not stupidly blind, or most wickedly indifferent, they, too, would so regard it.

At the very moment that they are thanking God for the enjoyment of civil and religious liberty, and for the right to worship God according to the dictates of their own consciences, they are utterly silent in respect to a law which robs religion of its chief significance, and makes it utterly worthless to a world lying in wickedness. Did this law concern the "*mint, anise* and *cummin*"—abridge the right to sing psalms, to partake of the sacrament, or to engage in any of the ceremonies of religion, it would be smitten by the thunder of a thousand pulpits. A general shout would go up from the church, demanding *repeal, repeal, instant repeal!*—And it would go hard with that politician who presumed to solicit the votes of the people without inscribing this motto on his banner. Further, if this demand were not complied with, another Scotland would be added to the history of religious liberty, and the stern old covenanters would be thrown into the shade. A John Knox would be seen at every church door, and heard from every pulpit, and Fillmore would have no more quarter than was shown by Knox, to the beautiful, but treacherous Queen

Mary of Scotland.—The fact that the church of our country, (with fractional exceptions,) does not esteem "the Fugitive Slave Law" as a declaration of war against religious liberty, implies that that church regards religion simply as a form of worship, an empty ceremony, and *not* a vital principle, requiring active benevolence, justice, love and good will towards man. It esteems sacrifice above mercy; psalm-singing above right doing; solemn meetings above practical righteousness. A worship that can be conducted by persons who refuse to give shelter to the houseless, to give bread to the hungry, clothing to the naked, and who enjoin obedience to a law forbidding these acts of mercy, is a curse, not a blessing to mankind. The Bible addresses all such persons as "scribes, pharisees, hypocrites, who pay tithe of *mint, anise,* and *cummin,* and have omitted the weightier matters of the law, judgment, mercy and faith."

The Church Responsible

But the church of this country is not only indifferent to the wrongs of the slave, it actually takes sides with the oppressors. It has made itself the bulwark of American slavery, and the shield of American slave-hunters. Many of its most eloquent Divines, who stand as the very lights of the church, have shamelessly given the sanction of religion, and the bible, to the whole slave system.—They have taught that man may, properly, be a slave; that the relation of master and slave is ordained of God; that to send back an escaped bondman to his master is clearly the duty of all the followers of the Lord Jesus Christ; and this horrible blasphemy is palmed off upon the world for christianity.

For my part, I would say, welcome infidelity! welcome atheism! welcome anything! in preference to the gospel, *as preached by those Divines!* They convert the very name of religion into an engine of tyranny, and barbarous cruelty, and serve to confirm more infidels, in this age, than all the infidel writings of Thomas Paine, Voltaire, and Bolingbroke, put together, have done. These ministers make religion a cold and flinty-hearted thing, having neither principles of right action, nor bowels of compassion. They strip the love of God of its beauty, and leave the throne of religion a huge, horrible, repulsive form. It is a religion for oppressors, tyrants, man-stealers, and *thugs*. It is not that *"pure and undefiled religion"* which is from above, and which is *"first pure, then peaceable, easy to be entreated,* full of mercy and good fruits, *without partiality, and without hypocrisy."* But a religion which favors the rich against the poor; which exalts the proud above the humble; which divides mankind into two classes, tyrants and slaves; which says to the man in chains, *stay there;* and to the oppressor, *oppress on;* it is a religion which may be professed and enjoyed by all the robbers and enslavers of mankind; it makes God a respecter of persons, denies his fatherhood of the race, and tramples in the dust the great truth of the brotherhood of man. All this we affirm to be true of the popular church, and the popular worship of our land and nation—a religion, a church and a worship which, on the authority of inspired wisdom, we pronounce to be an abomination in the sight of God. In the language of Isaiah, the American church might be well addressed, "Bring no more vain oblations; incense is an abomination unto me: the new moons and Sabbaths, the calling of assemblies, I cannot away with; it is iniquity, even the solemn meeting. Your new moons, and your appointed feasts my soul hateth. They are a trouble to me; I am weary to bear them; and when ye spread forth your hands I will hide mine eyes from you. Yea! when ye make many prayers, I will not hear. YOUR HANDS ARE FULL OF BLOOD; cease to do evil, learn to do well; seek judgment; relieve the oppressed; judge for the fatherless; plead for the widow."

The American church is guilty, when viewed in connection with what it is doing to uphold slavery; but it is superlatively guilty when viewed in connection with its ability to abolish slavery.

The sin of which it is guilty is one of omission as well as of commission. Albert Barnes but uttered what the common sense of every man at all observant of the actual state of the case will receive as truth, when he declared that "There is no power out of the church that could sustain slavery an hour, if it were not sustained in it."

Let the religious press, the pulpit, the sunday school, the conference meeting, the great ecclesiastical, missionary, bible and tract associations of the land array their immense powers against slavery, and slave-holding; and the whole system of crime and blood would be scattered to the winds, and that they do not do this involves

them in the most awful responsibility of which the mind can conceive.

In prosecuting the anti-slavery enterprise, we have been asked to spare the church, to spare the ministry; but *how,* we ask, could such a thing be done? We are met on the threshold of our efforts for the redemption of the slave, by the church and ministry of the country, in battle arrayed against us; and we are compelled to fight or flee. From *what* quarter, I beg to know, has proceeded a fire so deadly upon our ranks, during the last two years, as from the Northern pulpit? As the champions of oppressors, the chosen men of American theology have appeared—men, honored for their so called piety, and their real learning. The LORDS of Buffalo, the SPRINGS of New York, the LATHROPS of Auburn, the COXES and SPENCERS of Brooklyn, the GANNETS and SHARPS of Boston, the DEWEYS of Washington, and other great religious lights of the land, have, in utter denial of the authority of *Him,* by whom they professed to be called to the ministry, deliberately taught us, against the example of the Hebrews, and against the remonstrance of the Apostles, they teach *that we ought to obey man's law before the law of God.*

My spirit wearies of such blasphemy; and how such men can be supported, as the "standing types and representative of Jesus Christ," is a mystery which I leave others to penetrate. In speaking of the American church, however, let it be distinctly understood that I mean the *great mass* of the religious organizations of our land. There are exceptions, and I thank God that there are. Noble men may be found, scattered all over these Northern States, of whom Henry Ward Beecher, of Brooklyn, Samuel J. May, of Syracuse, and my esteemed friend[1] on the platform, are shining examples; and let me say further, that, upon these men lies the duty to inspire our ranks with high religious faith and zeal, and to cheer us on in the great mission of the slave's redemption from his chains.

Religion in England and Religion in America

One is struck with the difference between the attitude of the American church towards the anti-slavery movement, and that occupied by the churches in England towards a similar movement in that country. There, the church, true to

[1] Rev. R. R. Raymond.

its mission of ameliorating, elevating, and improving the condition of mankind, came forward promptly, bound up the wounds of the West Indian slave, and restored him to his liberty. There, the question of emancipation was a high religious question. It was demanded, in the name of humanity, and according to the law of the living God. The Sharps, the Clarksons, the Wilberforces, the Buxtons, the Burchells, and the Knibbs, were alike famous for their piety, and for their philanthropy. The anti-slavery movement *there,* was not an anti-church movement, for the reason that the church took its full share in prosecuting that movement: and the anti-slavery movement in this country will cease to be an anti-church movement, when the church of this country shall assume a favorable, instead of a hostile position towards that movement.

Americans! your republican politics, not less than your republican religion, are flagrantly inconsistent. You boast of your love of liberty, your superior civilization, and your pure christianity, while the whole political power of the nation, (as embodied in the two great political parties,) is solemnly pledged to support and perpetuate the enslavement of three millions of your countrymen. You hurl your anathemas at the crowned headed tyrants of Russia and Austria, and pride yourselves on your Democratic institutions, while you yourselves consent to be the mere *tools* and *body-guards* of the tyrants of Virginia and Carolina. You invite to your shores fugitives of oppression from abroad, honor them with banquets, greet them with ovations, cheer them, toast them, salute them, protect them, and pour out your money to them like water; but the fugitives from your own land, you advertise, hunt, arrest, shoot and kill. You glory in your refinement, and your universal education; yet you maintain a system as barbarous and dreadful, as ever stained the character of a nation—a system begun in avarice, supported in pride, and perpetuated in cruelty. You shed tears over fallen Hungary, and make the sad story of her wrongs the theme of your poets, statesmen and orators, till your gallant sons are ready to fly to arms to vindicate her cause against her oppressors; but, in regard to the ten thousand wrongs of the American slave, you would enforce the strictest silence, and would hail him as an enemy of the nation who dares to make those wrongs the subject of public discourse! You are all on fire at the mention of liberty for France or for Ireland;

but are as cold as an iceberg at the thought of liberty for the enslaved of America.—You discourse eloquently on the dignity of labor; yet, you sustain a system which, in its very essence, casts a stigma upon labor. You can bare your bosom to the storm of British artillery, to throw off a three-penny tax on tea; and yet wring the last hard earned farthing from the grasp of the black laborers of your country. You profess to believe "that, of one blood, God made all nations of men to dwell on the face of all the earth," and hath commanded all men, everywhere to love one another; yet you notoriously hate, (and glory in your hatred,) all men whose skins are not colored like your own. You declare, before the world, and are understood by the world to declare, that you "*hold these truths to be self evident, that all men are created equal; and are endowed by their Creator with certain inalienable rights; and that, among these are, life, liberty, and the pursuit of happiness;*" and yet, you hold securely, in a bondage, which according to your own Thomas Jefferson, "*is worse than ages of that which your fathers rose in rebellion to oppose,*" a *seventh part* of the inhabitants of your country.

Fellow-citizens! I will not enlarge further on your national inconsistencies. The existence of slavery in this country brands your republicanism as a sham, your humanity as a base pretence, and your christianity as a lie. It destroys your moral power abroad; it corrupts your politicians at home. It saps the foundation of religion; it makes your name a hissing, and a bye-word to a mocking earth. It is the antagonistic force in your government, the only thing that seriously disturbs and endangers your *Union.* It fetters your progress; it is the enemy of improvement, the deadly foe of education; it fosters pride; it breeds insolence; it promotes vice; it shelters crime; it is a curse to the earth that supports it; and yet, you cling to it, as if it were the sheet anchor of all your hopes. Oh! be warned! be warned! a horrible reptile is coiled up in your nation's bosom; the venomous creature is nursing at the tender breast of your youthful republic; *for the love of God, tear away,* and fling from you the hideous monster, and *let the weight of twenty millions, crush and destroy it forever!*

The Constitution

But it is answered in reply to all this, that precisely what I have now denounced is, in fact, guaranteed and sanctioned by the Constitution of the United States; that, the right to hold, and to hunt slaves is a part of that Constitution framed by the illustrious Fathers of this Republic.

Then, I dare to affirm, notwithstanding all I have said before, your fathers stooped, basely stooped.

> To palter with us in a double sense:
> And keep the word of promise to the ear,
> But break it to the heart.

And instead of being the honest men I have before declared them to be, they were the veriest imposters that ever practised on mankind. *This* is the inevitable conclusion, and from it there is no escape; but I differ from those who charge this baseness on the framers of the Constitution of the United States. *It is a slander upon their memory,* at least, so I believe. There is not time now to argue the constitutional question at length; nor have I the ability to discuss it as it ought to be discussed. The subject has been handled with masterly power by Lysander Spooner, Esq., by William Goodell, by Samuel E. Sewall, Esq., and last, though not least, by Gerritt Smith, Esq. These gentlemen have, as I think, fully and clearly vindicated the Constitution from any design to support slavery for an hour.

Fellow-citizens! there is no matter in respect to which, the people of the North have allowed themselves to be so ruinously imposed upon, as that of the pro-slavery character of the Constitution. In *that* instrument I hold there is neither warrant, license, nor sanction of the hateful thing; but interpreted, as it *ought* to be interpreted, the Constitution is a GLORIOUS LIBERTY DOCUMENT. Read its preamble, consider its purposes. Is slavery among them? Is it at the gateway? or is it in the temple? it is neither. While I do not intend to argue this question on the present occasion, let me ask, if it be not somewhat singular that, if the Constitution were intended to be, by its framers and adopters, a slaveholding instrument, why neither *slavery, slaveholding,* nor *slave* can anywhere be found in it. What would be thought of an instrument, drawn up, *legally* drawn up, for the purpose of entitling the city of Rochester to a track of land, in which no mention of land was made? Now, there are certain rules of interpretation, for the proper understanding of all legal instruments. These rules are well established. They are plain, common-sense rules, such as you and I, and all of us, can understand and apply, without having passed years in the study of law. I scout the idea that the question of the constitutionality, or unconstitutionality of slavery, is not a question for the people. I hold that every American citizen has a right to form an opinion of the constitution, and to propagate that opinion, and to use all honorable means to make his opinion the prevailing one. Without this right, the liberty of an American citizen would be as insecure as that of a Frenchman. Ex-Vice-President Dallas tells us that the constitution is an object to which no American mind can be too attentive, and no American heart too devoted. He further says, the constitution, in its words, is plain and intelligible, and is meant for the home-bred, unsophisticated understandings of our fellow-citizens. Senator Berrien tells us that the Constitution is the fundamental law, that which controls all others. The charter of our liberties, which every citizen has a personal interest in understanding thoroughly. The testimony of Senator Breese, Lewis Cass, and many others that might be named, who are everywhere esteemed as sound lawyers, so regard the constitution. I take it, therefore, that it is not presumption in a private citizen to form an opinion of that instrument.

Now, take the constitution according to its plain reading, and I defy the presentation of a single pro-slavery clause in it. On the other hand it will be found to contain principles and purposes, entirely hostile to the existence of slavery.

I have detained my audience entirely too long already. At some future period I will gladly avail myself of an opportunity to give this subject a full and fair discussion.

Allow me to say, in conclusion, notwithstanding the dark picture I have this day presented, of the state of the nation, I do not despair of this country. There are forces in operation, which must inevitably, work the downfall of slavery. *"The arm of the Lord is not shortened,"* and the doom of slavery is certain. I, therefore, leave off where I began, with *hope.* While drawing encouragement from "the Declaration of Independence," the great principles it contains, and the genius of American Institutions, my spirit is also cheered by the obvious tendencies of the age. Nations do not now stand in the same relation to each other that they did ages ago. No nation can now shut itself up, from the surrounding world, and trot round in the same old path of its fathers without interference. The time *was* when such could be done. Long established customs of hurtful character could formerly fence themselves in, and do their evil work with social impunity. Knowledge was then confined and enjoyed by the privileged few, and the multitude walked on in mental darkness. But a change has now come over the affairs of mankind. Walled cities and empires have become unfashionable. The arm of commerce has borne away the gates of the strong city. Intelligence is penetrating the darkest corners of the globe. It makes its pathway over and under the sea, as well as on the earth. Wind, steam, and lightning are its chartered agents. Oceans no longer divide, but link nations together. From Boston to London is now a holiday excursion. Space is comparatively annihilated.—Thoughts expressed on one side of the Atlantic, are distinctly heard on the other.

The far off and almost fabulous Pacific rolls in grandeur at our feet. The Celestial Empire, the mystery of ages, is being solved. The fiat of the Almighty, *"Let there be Light,"* has not yet spent its force. No abuse, no outrage whether in taste, sport or avarice, can now hide itself from the all-pervading light. The iron shoe, and crippled foot of China must be seen, in contrast with nature. *Africa must rise and put on her yet unwoven garment. "Ethiopia shall stretch out her hand unto God."* In the fervent aspirations of William Lloyd Garrison, I say, and let every heart join in saying it:

God speed the year of jubilee
  The wide world o'er!
When from their galling chains set free,
Th' oppress'd shall vilely bend the knee,
And wear the yoke of tyranny
  Like brutes no more.
That year will come, and freedom's reign,
To man his plundered rights again
  Restore.

God speed the day when human blood
  Shall cease to flow!
In every clime be understood,
The claims of human brotherhood,
And each return for evil, good,
  Not blow for blow;
That day will come all feuds to end,
And change into a faithful friend
  Each foe.

God speed the hour, the glorious hour,
  When none on earth
Shall exercise a lordly power,
Nor in a tyrant's presence cower;
But all to manhood's stature tower,
  By equal birth!
THAT HOUR WILL COME, to each, to all,
And from his prison-house, the thrall
  Go forth.

Until that year, day, hour, arrive,
With head, and heart, and hand I'll strive,
To break the rod, and rend the gyve,
The spoiler of his prey deprive—
  So witness Heaven!
And never from my chosen post,
Whate'er the peril or the cost,
  Be driven.

Alexander Crummell (1819–1898)

Alexander Crummell was born free in New York City on March 2, 1819. The facts that he enjoyed free status from birth and was of unmixed African blood made him slightly different from some of his contemporaries who became his close associates. For instance, both Henry Highland Garnet and Samuel Ringgold Ward were escaped slaves, and William Wells Brown and Frederick Douglass were not only escaped slaves but had a goodly mixture of white blood. So in his group Alexander Crummell was the one truly free Black man. But his freeborn status was of no value to him in racially prejudiced America, and, like John B. Russwurm and many other freeborn Blacks, Crummell had to seek refuge first in

England and then in Africa in order to enjoy the liberties of free movement and self-development.

Young Crummell's efforts to secure an education in America were typically frustrating. First, along with Garnet and Ira Aldridge and others who were to gain some historical renown, he attended the New York African Free School. Then, in an effort to improve his education, Crummell's parents made the fateful decision to send him, along with his friend Henry Garnet and two other boys, to a new academy for colored youths located in Canaan, New Hampshire. This venture nearly proved to be a total disaster. The godly and self-righteous citizens of this little New England community, determined that no school for Negroes would embellish its fair contours, assembled one hundred yoke of oxen to pull the school down and then drove the young Black scholars out of town by threatening to fire on them with the town cannon, which had been dragged from the village green. After this somewhat unsettling academic adventure, both Crummell and Garnet were able to enter and finish a good academic program at Oneida Institute in Oneida, New York. Both then elected to enter the ministry, Crummell desiring to take orders for the priesthood in the Episcopal Church and Garnet aspiring for a place in the Presbyterian Church.

Here again Alexander Crummell felt the sting of American racial prejudice against Blacks, be they freeborn or the illegitimate offspring of the white planter aristocracy. His admission application to the General Theology Seminary in New York was rejected for racial reasons. Then, after successfully completing his ministerial training at the Episcopal Seminary in Boston, he once again faced the indomitable proslavery racism of the power structure of the New York City Episcopal Diocese. Fortunately, certain friends of the young minister encouraged him to go to England and there advance the cause of Negro Episcopalianism.

The decision to go to England in the late 1840's changed the course of Alexander Crummell's life. Not only did he encounter in England an atmosphere quite sympathetic to the Black man's cause, but he was able to enroll in Queen's College at Cambridge. After receiving his divinity degree from that institution in 1853, he chose to go to Liberia rather than return to America. There he stayed for twenty years.

When Crummell finally returned to the United States in 1873, he found many changes in the status of the Black man. First, after a long and withering fight, Black men were free from chattel slavery. Then, too, the colonization issue, which had been an important and serious matter during the 1840's, had at least been temporarily settled; the Black man was going to stay in America. Furthermore, Crummell found that a Black Reconstruction was taking place in the South; Black men were in state offices and state legislatures; Black men were in Congress. Hoping that these events augured well for the Black man's future in America, Crummell chose to remain in the country of his birth and became rector of St. Luke's Church in Washington, D.C.

His hopes for a better America soon faded as he beheld the rapidly deteriorating condition of the Black man, particularly in the South following the Hayes-Tilden compromise of 1876. In response to the times, a new Alexander Crummell emerged. Whereas in Africa his essays and letters—collected in *The Future of Africa* (1862)—had a somewhat lofty tone reflecting a moral and philosophical approach to racial concerns, the quality of his written protest became more caustic and virulent during his years in Washington, D.C. He still continued to write with great stylistic finesse and polish, but he was more God's angry man than gentle cleric. For instance, there have been few speeches on the Black woman that match Alexander Crummell's "The Black Woman of the South" in passionate bitterness and angry protest. Speaking before the annual meeting of the Freedman's Aid Society in 1883, he catalogued the long list of abuses suffered by the Black woman, both during slavery and after slavery. Emancipation, he observed, had actually brought no end to her brutalization and degradation; in her fight for dignity and freedom she needed aid and assistance from her more fortunate Northern sisters. Hers had been the sustaining heroism of the dark days of slavery, but now she seemed to be ensnared by the hazards of freedom and economic dependence.

During this period, Crummell also wrote his very fine eulogy for his lifetime friend, Henry Highland Garnet, who died in Liberia in 1882. In this lovingly written personal memoir, Garnet—a fugitive slave in his youth and great-grandson of a Mandingo chieftain—is depicted as a leader who, in every crisis, stood tall "like a cedar of Lebanon." Crummell describes how the crippled, half-sick youthful Garnet led the other Black students at short-lived Noyes Academy in repelling white rioters with blasts from their one doublebarreled shotgun. He also recounts the resolute heroism of Garnet during the New York riots of 1863. His crippled leg now amputated and supporting himself on his crutch, Garnet refused to flee from the howling mob and by a miracle saved himself and his church from the destructive fury of the rioters.

Fortunately, sixteen of the speeches and essays that Crummell wrote after 1862 were collected and published in 1891 under the title *Africa and America*. In tone and literary style they represent some of the best writing by a Black man in America during the nineteenth century. Crummell's work and significance have been noted in every major historical study of the Black man in the nineteenth century. Probably the most touching and stirring comment is found in Du Bois' *Souls of Black Folk,* as Du Bois recounts how he—a man of the twentieth century—met and was so impressed by the dignity and learning of this Black man of the nineteenth century.

The Relations and Duties of Free Colored Men in America to Africa

A Letter to Charles B. Dunbar, 1861

HIGH SCHOOL, MT. VAUGHAN, CAPE PALMAS, LIBERIA, 1st Sept., 1860.

MY DEAR SIR,—It is now many months since I received a letter from you, just as you was about sailing from our shores for your home. In that note you requested me to address you a letter setting forth my views concerning Liberia, suggesting at the same time that such a letter might prove interesting to many of our old friends and school-mates in New York. I have not forgotten your request, although I have not heretofore complied with it. Though convinced of the need and possible usefulness of such a letter as you asked from me, I have shrunk from a compliance with your request. Not to mention other grounds of reluctance, let me say here that I have felt it a venturesome thing to address four hundred thousand men; albeit, it be indirectly through you. Neither my name, position, nor any personal qualities, give me authority thus to do. The only excuse I have is the depth and solemnity of all questions connected with Africa. I see that no one else of our race has done it; perhaps I may be pardoned for assuming so great a task.

I may add here that I address the "Free Colored Men of America," because I am identified with them; and not because I feel that *they,* especially, and above all the other sons of Africa, in distant lands, are called upon for zeal and interest in her behalf. It is the exaggeration of the relation of *American* black men to Africa, which has turned the hearts of many of her own children from her. Your duties, in this respect are no greater than those of our West Indian, Haytian, and eventually our Brazilian brethren. Whatever in this letter applies to our brethren in the United States, applies in an equal degree to them. But I am not the man to address them. I fear I *presume,* even in writing this letter to American black men, and have only just now concluded to do so by the encouragement I have received in two pleasant interviews with Mr. Campbell and Dr. Delany.

And even now it is with doubt and diffidence that I conclude to send you this communication.

My reluctancy has arisen chiefly from a consideration of the claim put forth by leading colored men in the United States, to the effect "that it is unjust to disturb their residence in the land of their birth, by a continual call to go to Africa." This claim is, in my opinion, a most just one. Three centuries residence in a country seems clearly to give any people a right to their nationality therein, without disturbance. Our brethren in America have other claims besides this; they have made large contributions to the clearing of their country; they have contributed by sweat and toil to the wealth thereof; and by their prowess and their blood, they have participated in the achievement of its liberties. But their master right lies in the fact that they are Christians; and one will have to find some new page and appendage to the Bible, to get the warrant for Christians to repel and expatriate Christians, on account of blood, or race, or color. In fact, it seems to me a most serious thing to wantonly trench upon rights, thus solemnly and providentially guaranteed a people, that is, by a constant, ceaseless, fretting iteration of a repelling sentiment.

Of course I do not intend anything akin to this in my letter. I need not insult the intellect and conscience of any colored man who thinks it his duty to labor for his race on American soil, by telling him that it is his duty to come to Africa. If he is educated up to the ideas of responsibility and obligation, he knows his duty better than I do. And, indeed, generally, it is best to leave individuals to themselves as to the *details* of obligation and responsibility.

"The primal duties shine aloft like stars;" and it is only when men *will* not see them, we are bound to repeat and re-utter them, until the souls of men are aroused, and they are moved to moral resolution and to noble actions. But as to the *mode, form* and *manner* of meeting their duties, let the common sense of every man decide it for himself.

My object in writing this letter is not to vex any of our brethren by the iteration of the falsehood that America is not their home; nor by the misty theory, "that they will all yet have to come to

Liberia." I do not even intend to invite any one to Liberia; glad as I would be to see around me many of the wise and sterling men I know in the U. States, who would be real acquisitions to this nation, and as much as I covet their society. I am not putting in a plea for Colonization. My object is quite different; in fact it is not a strict compliance with the terms of your letter, for I shall have but little to say about Liberia. But believing that *all* men hold some relation to the land of their Fathers, I wish to call the attention of the sons of Africa in America to their "RELATIONS AND DUTY TO THE LAND OF THEIR FATHERS."

And even on such a theme I know I must prepare myself for the rebuff from many—"Why talk to *us* of Fatherland? What have we to do with Africa? We are not Africans; we are Americans. You ask no peculiar interest on the part of Germans, Englishmen, the Scotch, the Irish, the Dutch, in the land of their fathers; why then do you ask it of us?"

Alas for us, as a race! so deeply harmed have we been by oppression, that we have lost the force of strong, native principles, and prime natural affections. Because exaggerated contempt has been poured upon us, we too become apt pupils in the school of scorn and contumely. Because repudiation of the black man has been for centuries the wont of civilized nations, black men themselves get shame at their origin and shrink from the terms which indicate it.

Sad as this is, it is not to be wondered at. "Oppression" not only "makes a wise man mad," it robs him also of his self-respect. And this is our loss; but having emerged from slavery, it is our duty to cast off its grave-clothes and resist its deadly influences.

Our ancestors were unfortunate, miserable, and benighted; but nothing more. Their history was a history, not of ignominy and disgrace, but of heathenism and benightedness. And even in that state they exhibited a nobleness of native character, they cherished such virtues, and manifested so much manliness and bravery, that the civilized world is now magnanimous enough to recognize such traits; and its greatest men are free to render their warm eulogies.[1]

When these colored men question the duty of

[1] For a most able and discriminating article upon this topic, see "WESTMINSTER REVIEW," January 7, 1842, Art., Dr. Arnold. Also, those humane and truthful Essays of Mr. HEAPS.—"FRIENDS IN COUNCIL," vol. 2.

interest in Africa because they are not Africans, I beg to remind them of the kindred duty of self-respect. And my reply to such queries as I have mentioned above is this: 1. That there is no need of asking the interest of Englishmen, Germans, Dutchmen and others in the land of their Fathers, because they have this interest, and are always proud to cherish it. And 2nd, I remark that the abject state of Africa is a most real and touching appeal to *any* heart for sympathy and aid. It is an appeal, however, which comes with a double force to every civilized man who has negro blood flowing in his veins.

Africa lies low and is wretched. She is the maimed and crippled arm of humanity. Her great powers are wasted. Dislocation and anguish have reached every joint. Her condition in every point calls for succor; moral, social, domestic, political, commercial, intellectual. Whence shall flow aid, mercy, advantage to her? Here arises the call of duty and obligation to colored men. Other people may, if they choose, forget the homes of their sires; for almost every European nation is now reaping the fruits of a thousand years civilization. Every one of them can spare thousands and even millions of their sons to build up civilization in Australia, Canada, New Zealand, South Africa, or Victoria. But Africa is the victim of her hetorogenous idolatries. Africa is wasting away beneath the accretions of civil and moral miseries. Darkness covers the land and gross darkness the people. Great social evils universally prevail. Confidence and security are destroyed. Licentiousness abounds everywhere. Molock rules and reigns throughout the whole Continent; and by the ordeal of Sassy-wood, Fetiches, human sacrifices and devil-worship is devouring men, women and little children. They have not the Gospel. They are living without God. The cross has never met their gaze; and its consolations have never entered their hearts, nor its everlasting truths cheered their deaths.

And all this only epitomizes the miseries of Africa, for it would take a volume to detail and enumerate them. But this is sufficient to convince any son of Africa that the land of our fathers is in great spiritual need, and that those of her sons who haply have ability to aid in her restoration, will show mercy to her, and perform an act of filial love and tenderness which is but their "reasonable service."

I have two objects in view in addressing you this letter: *one* relates to the temporal, material interests of adventurous, enterprising, colored men; and the *other* pertains to the best and most abiding interests of the million masses of heathen on this continent—I mean their evangelization.

First, I am to speak with reference to the temporal, and material interests of adventurous, enterprising and aspiring men in the United States of America. I wish to bring before such persons reasons why they should feel interest in Africa. These reasons are not, I am free to confess, directly and distinctively philanthropic; although I do, indeed, aim at human well-being through their force and influence. But I appeal now more especially to the hopes, desires, ambition, and aspirations of such men. I am referring to that sentiment of self-regard which prompts to noble exertions for support and superiority. I am aiming at that principle of SELF LOVE which spurs men on to self advantage and self aggrandizement; a principle which, in its normal state and in its due degree, to use the words of BUTLER, "is as just and morally good as any affection whatever." In fine, I address myself to all that class of sentiments in the human heart which creates a thirst for wealth, position, honor, and power. I desire the auxiliary aid of this class of persons, and this class of motives, for it is such influences and agencies which are calculated to advance the material growth of Africa. She needs skill, enterprise, energy, *worldly* talent, to raise her; and these applied here to her needs and circumstances, will prove the handmaid of Religion, and will serve the great purposes of civilization and enlightenment through all her borders.

There seems to me to be a natural call upon the children of Africa in foreign lands, to come and participate in the opening treasures of the land of their fathers. Though these treasures are the manifest gift of God to the negro race, yet that race reaps but the most partial measure of their good and advantage. It has always been thus in the past, and now as the resources of Africa are being more and more developed, the extent of *our* interest therein is becoming more and more diminutive. The slave-trade is interdicted throughout Christendom; the chief powers of earth have put a lien upon the system of slavery; interest and research in Africa have reached a state of intensity; mystery has been banished from some of her most secret quarters; sunlight, after ages of darkness, has burst in upon the charmed regions of her wealth and value; and yet the negro, on his native soil, is but "a

hewer of wood and drawer of water;" and the sons of Africa in foreign lands, inane and blinded, suffer the adventurous foreigner, with greed and glut, to jostle him aside, and to seize, with skill and effect, upon their own rightful inheritance.

For three centuries and upwards, the civilized nations of the earth have been engaged in African commerce. Traffic on the coast of Africa anticipated the discoveries of Columbus. From Africa the purest gold got its characteristic three hundred years ago. From Africa dyes of the greatest value have been carried to the great manufacturing marts of the world. From Africa palm oil is exported by thousands of tons; and now as the observant eye of commerce is becoming more and more fastened upon this continent, grain, gums, oils of divers kinds, valuable woods, copper and other ore, are being borne from the soil to meet the clamorous demands of distant marts.

The chief item of commerce in this continent has been the "slave trade." The coast of Africa has been more noted for this than for anything else. Ever since 1600, the civilized nations of the earth have been transporting in deadly holds, in poisonous and pestilential cabins, in "perfidious barks," millions of our race to foreign lands. This trade is now almost universally regarded as criminal; but in the light of commercial prudence and pecuniary advantage, the slave trade was as great a piece of folly as it was a crime; for almost beneath their eyes, yea, doubtless, often immediately in their sight, were lying treasures, rivaling far the market value of the flesh and blood they had been so eager to crowd beneath their hatches.

Africa is as rich in resources as India is; not as yet as valuable in products, because she is more unenlightened, and has a less skilful population. But so far as it respects mineral and vegetable capacity, there seems to me but little, if any, doubt that Africa more than rivals the most productive lands on the globe.

Let me set before you, though briefly, some of the valuable articles of West African trade. I must remind you, however, of three things; *first,* that the soil, the rocks, and the flora of Africa have not had the advantage of scientific scrutiny, and as a consequence but little is known as yet of her real worth and wealth in these respects. *Second,* that West African trade is only in a nascent state—that it comes from but a slight fringe of the coast, while the rich interior yields, as yet, but a reluctant hold upon the vast and various treasures it possesses. And *third,* that such is the mysterious secrecy American and English houses retain and *enjoin* upon this subject, that even approximation to the facts of the case is remote and distant.

The following Table is an attempt to classify valuable products and articles of present trade. Nearly every article mentioned has come under my own personal inspection; the exceptions are not over a dozen and a half.

Nuts.	Dyes and Dyewood.	Gums and Wax.	Animals.	Skins.	Grains.
Palm Nut.	Camwood.	Beeswax.	Oxen.	Bullock.	Rice.
Ground Nut.	Barwood.	Grove Tree.	Sheep.	Sheep.	Maize.
Cocoa Nut.	Indigo.	India Rubber.	Hogs.	Deer.	Millet.
Cold Nut.	Christmas nut.	Gutta Percha.	Goats.	Monkey.	
Castor Nut.	And divers other colors, blue, red, yellow, & brown.	Copal. Mastic. Senegal.	Fowls. Ducks. Pigeons.	Leopard. Gazelle. Squirrel. Raccoon. Lion.	

Fruits.	Vegetables.	Timber.	Minerals.	Special articles connected with trade & domestic use.	Fish.
Oranges.	Yams.	Teak.	Iron.	Sugar Cane.	Mackerel.
Lemons.	Cassada.	Ebony.	Copper.	Coffee.	Mango Perch.
Plantains.	Potatoes.	Lignum Vitæ.	Gold.	Cocoa.	Caualla.
Bananas.	Tan yah.	Mahogany.		Pepper.	Gripper.
Citrons.		Brimstone.		Cotton.	Herring.
Limes.		Rosewood.		Tobacco.	Mullet.
Guavas.		Walnut.			Chub.
Pine Apples.		Hickory.			Perch.
Papaw.		Oak.			Pike.
Mango Plums.		Cedar.			Trout.
Alligator Pear.		Unevah.			Cod.
Bread Nut.		Mangrove.			Skate.
Tamarind.					Eels.
					Oysters.

I can not dismiss these Tables without a few remarks relative to some few prominent items they enumerate; I mean the PALM NUT and OIL, COTTON, INDIAN CORN, and SUGAR CANE.

PALM OIL.—This article, more than any other West African product, shows the rapidity with which legitimate commerce has sprung up on the coast of Africa. A few years ago palm oil was an insignificant item in the coast trade.[2] *Now* it is an article which commands whole fleets of sailing vessels, seeks the auxiliary aid of steamers, and effects most powerfully the commerce of England, France, and the United States.

I copy several items pertaining to this export from a report of a former acquaintance and correspondent, the late Mr. Consul Campbell, of Lagos. The report, as will be seen, includes

several other items besides palm oil, and it refers exclusively to LAGOS.

I have no reliable information of the amount of oil exported at the present; but I do not think I shall be far from the point of accuracy, if I put it down at 60,000 tons, which, at the probable value of £45 per ton, equals £2,700,000.

COTTON.—Next to palm oil, cotton is now commanding more attention than any other article. The interesting fact with regard to this staple is that it excites as much interest in Africa as it does in England and America. There are few things in the history of trade more important, more interesting, morally as well as commercially, than the impetus which has recently been given to the growth of cotton.

In 185–, Mr. Consul Campbell made a statement of the probable amount of cotton exported from West Africa. I have to rely upon my memory for the items of that statement; and, if I mistake

[2] In 1808, the quantity imported into England was only 200 (two hundred) tons.

Shipped from Lagos During 1857.

		Value.
13,097 casks of Palm Oil,	4,942 tons,	£222,390
1,053 Elephant Tusks,	24,118 lbs.,	4,220
868 bales of Cotton,	114,848 lbs.,	3,490
		230,200
50,000 native Cotton Cloths,		25,000
Total value of exports from Lagos,		£255,200

Palm Oil—

From the Benin River,	2,650 tons,	
" Palma,	3,250 "	
" Badagry,	1,250 "	
" Porto Novo, Appi, Vista, &c.,	4,500 "	
" Whydah,	2,500 "	
" Ahguay and neighbor'g ports,	2,500 "	
	16,650 tons,	£732,600
150,000 country Cloths of native manufacture from above ports,		75,000
		£1,062,800

Of the above productions there was shipped from Lagos in the year—

	1856.	1857.	Increase.
Palm Oil,	3,884 tons.	4,942 tons.	1,058 tons.
Ivory,	16,057 lbs.	24,118 lbs.	8,061 lbs.
Cotton,	34,491 lbs.	114,844 lbs.	81,353 lbs.

Palm Oil from other ports—

	1856.	1857.	Increase.
Benin River,	2,500 tons.	2,650 tons.	150 tons.
Palma,	2,250 "	3,250 "	1,000 "
Badagry,	1,250 "	1,250 "	
Porto Novo, &c.,	4,000 "	4,500 "	500 "
Whydah,	2,500 "	2,500 "	
Ahguay, &c.,	1,800 "	2,500 "	700 "
	14,300 tons.	16,650 tons.	2,350 tons.
From Lagos,	3,884 "	4,942 "	1,058 "
Total shipment in 1857,		21,592 tons.	3,408 tons.

The export of Oil and Nuts from SIERRA LEONE, is as follows:

Palm Oil Exported from Sierra Leone During the Years

1850,	285,032 gallons,
1851,	212,577 "
1852,	307,988 "
1853,	181,438 "
1854,	304,406 "
1855,	364,414 "
1856,	463,140 "

Total, 2,118,985 gallons, equal to 6,835 tons.

Custom House, Sierra Leone, 18th February, 1857.

Port of Freetown, Sierra Leone.
Quantity of Palm-Nut Kernels Exported from the Colony,
as Follows, viz.:

1850,	4,096 bushels,
1851,	2,925 "
1852,	46,727 "
1853,	29,699 "
1854,	25,399½ "
1855,	65,388 "
1856,	90,282 "

Total, 264,516½ bushels, equal to 6,612 tons.
Customs, Sierra Leone, 30th January, 1857.

not, he stated that the people of Abbeokuta exported nigh 200,000 country cloths annually. These cloths are purchased for transportation to Brazil, where there are thousands of African slaves who still dress in the same style as when at their homes. He supposed that full 200,000 country cloths were manufactured for *home* use, which would make the probable number manufactured in Africa, 400,000. And he calculated 2½ lbs. as the average weight of each country cloth;—and 400,000 × 2½ = 1,000,000 lbs. of cotton *manufactured* by the natives of interior Africa, in *one* locality, that is Yoruba. Doubtless as much more is allowed to grow and run to waste, unused.

Now these facts, to a partial extent, were well known in Liberia, for our merchants are accustomed to purchasing "country cloths," as they are called, and selling them to foreign traders; but Consul Campbell's statements far exceed any realities we have ever thought of, and show that interior Africa is as great a field for the production of cotton, as America or India.

SUGAR CANE.—To what extent West Africa is to become a sugar-producing country it is difficult to conjecture. Many, doubtless, have grave doubts whether this will ever be the case; for my own part I have no misgivings upon the point, that is, its capability of becoming a great sugar-producing country. The natives grow it in all the country about Cape Palmas, and frequently bring cane to the American settlements for sale. With some small encouragement, and a little stimulus, it could easily be made a staple here. My opinions have been strengthened by some observations made in a recent missionary tour. I found cane but little inferior to that grown on the St. Paul's river, growing in nearly all the towns and villages through which I passed, forty, fifty, and sixty miles in the interior. On inquiry, I learned that it is grown by the natives in the interior, two hundred miles back. Dr. Livingstone, in his journal, states a like fact concerning the natives in South Africa.[3]

What a germ have we here for systematic labor, plodding industry, the proper direction of the acquisition principle, and thereby, of civilization and christianity, if only a company of right-minded men were settled on the Cavalla, prepared for the production of sugar, willing to stimulate national energy, and at the same time to uplift and enlighten the heathen!

MAIZE.—What is the case respecting sugar cane equally pertains to corn. It is grown plenteously and extensively in West Africa. On the Cavalla river it is planted with rice, and I am told that in the gathering season hundreds of bushels of corn are left by the natives untouched in their fields. In some cases American colonists have gone and gathered quantities of it without any payment. Here, then, with an enterprising settlement, corn could be obtained, as an export. The natives, if encouraged, might easily be made vast and extensive corn-growers. This has already taken place on the Gold Coast. Several cargoes of corn were exported thence in 1859, to England.

As with the palm oil, so with maize, sugar-cane, and cotton; civilized men could, with but little difficulty, increase the cultivation of these articles among the natives, and ship them to traders to their own advantage. And this process is the great secret of West African trade; the foreign merchant, by his goods, excites the cupidity of the simple native who at Fernandapo brings him barwood; at St. Paul Loando, bees-wax; at Congo, copal and gutta percha; at Accra, maize; at Calabar, black ebony wood; at Bonny

[3] Dr. Livingstone saw the cane growing in his tour through South Africa. It is more than probable that that cane is indigenous to both West and South Africa.

and Lagos, palm oil; at Bassa, (Liberia,) cam-wood; at Lagos, cotton; at Tantamquerry and Gambra, ground nuts and pepper; at Sierra Leone, nearly *all* kinds of African produce; at Elmina, Cape Coast, Accra, and Bassam, gold. By this multiform traffic, yet, be it remembered, in its infancy, and capable of being increased a thousand-fold, millions of dollars are being made, every year, on the coast of Africa.

Now all this flows into the coffers of white men. I mean nothing invidious by this. I state a fact, and am utterly unconscious of any unworthy or ungenerous feeling, in stating it. "The earth is the Lord's, and the fullness thereof;" and this "fullness" he has given to MAN, irrespective of race or color. The main condition of the obtain-ment of it is intelligence, forecast, skill, and enter-prise. If the black man—the black man, I mean, civilized and enlightened, has lying before him a golden heritage, and fails to seize upon and to appropriate it; Providence, none the less, intends it to be seized upon, and wills it to be used. And if the white man, with a keen eye, a cunning hand, and a wise practicalness, is enabled to appro-priate it with skill and effect, it is his; God gives it to him; and he has a right to seek and to search for a multiplication of it; and when he secures it, a right to the use of it,—responsible, however, both to God and man for the use of right means to the ends he has before him, and for the moral features of his traffic.

But while conceding that the white man has, in the main, fairly won the present trade of Africa; I can not but lament over non-participation therein; for the larger advantages of it, go to Europe and America, and help to swell the broad stream of their wealth, luxury, and refinement. And how deep and broad and mighty is that stream, as shown by two facts: 1st, That England, France, and the United States, expend annually more than a million and a half of dollars for the protection of trade on this coast.[4] And 2d, That the coast swarms with white men, using all possible means and contrivances *to open trade into the interior*. To this one single end, an immense amount of capital is spent by great mercantile houses, in England, France, and America. One single house in Liverpool, employs such a fleet of trading vessels, that it is necessitated to keep a resident physician at the mouth of one of our

great rivers for the benefit of their captains and sailors. "A single merchant now living, in the course of three or four years has spent more than $100,000 in exploring the rivers and creeks of Western Africa, merely to ascertain the extent of her commercial relations."[5] While I am writing these pages, I receive the information that one of the great Liverpool houses, has just sent out a small steamer to the Brights, to collect the oil for their trading vessels. Simultaneously with this intelligence, I am advised that a number of agents are employed by English capitalists to visit the towns from Lagos to Abbeokuta, and to leave with their chiefs, small bags of cotton seed for the growth of cotton. And but a few months ago we hailed in our roads a little fairy craft—the "Sunbeam," steamer sent out by "Laird and Company" for the Niger trade; and since then, I have heard of two of her trips, four hundred miles up that mighty river, bringing thence valuable cargoes from the factories which are now established three hundred miles up upon its banks.

And now perhaps you ask,—"How shall the children of Africa, sojourning in foreign lands, avail themselves of the treasures of this conti-nent?" I answer briefly,—"In the same way white men do." *They* have pointed out the way; let us follow in the same track and in the use of the like [legitimate] agencies by which trade is facilitated and money is made by them.

Perhaps this is too general; let me therefore attempt something more specific and distinctive.

First, then, I remark that if individuals are unable to enter upon a trading system, they can form associations. If *one* has not sufficient capital, four or six united can make a good beginning. If a few persons can not make the venture, then a company can be formed. It was in this way the first attempts at trading were made by the Dutch and the English, both in India and Africa. A few men associated themselves to-gether, and sent out their agent or agents, and started a factory. And from such humble begin-nings, in the 17th century, has arisen that magni-ficent Indian Empire, which has helped to swell the vast wealth, and the cumbrous capital of England, from whose arena have come forth such splendid and colossal characters, as Clive, and Wellington, and Metcalf, and the Laurences, and Havelock; and which has furnished the church of Christ a field on which to display the Apostolic

---

[4] I do not pretend to accuracy in this statement; the expenditure of Great Britain was, in 184–, £231,000.

[5] Wilson's "Western Africa," p. 521.

virtues and the primitive self-sacrifice of Middleton, and Heber, and Wilson, of Henry Martyn, of Fox and Ragland.

Without doubt God designs as great things as these for Africa, and among the means and agencies He will employ, commercial enterprise is most certainly one. To this end however, high souls and lofty resolves are necessary, as in any other vocation of life. Of course the timid, the over-cautious, the fearful; men in whose constitution FAITH is a needed quality, are not fitted for this service. If ever the epoch of negro civilization is brought about in Africa; whatever *external* influences may be brought to bear upon this end; whatever foreign agencies and aids, black men themselves are without doubt to be the chief instruments. But they are to be men of force and energy; men who will not suffer themselves to be outrivaled in enterprise and vigor; men who are prepared for pains, and want and suffering; men of such invincible courage that the spirit can not be tamed by transient failures, incidental misadventure, or even glaring miscalculations; men who can exaggerate the feeblest resources into potent agencies and fruitful capital. Moreover these men are to have strong moral proclivities, equal to the deep penetration and the unyielding tenacity of their minds. No greater curse could be entailed upon Africa than the sudden appearance upon her shores, of a mighty host of heartless black buccaneers [for such indeed they would prove themselves;]—men sharpened up by letters and training; filled with feverish greed; with hearts utterly alien from moral good and human well-being; and only regarding Africa as a convenient goldfield from which to extract emolument and treasure to carry off to foreign quarters.

Such men would only reproduce the worst evils of the last three sad centuries of Africa's history; and quickly and inevitably so soil their character, that the *just* imputation would be fastened upon them of that malignant lie which has recently been spread abroad through Europe and America against us; that is, of complicity with the slave trade.[6]

[6] Nothing can be more judicious than the following words of Commander Foote—"Let then the black man be judged fairly, and not presumed to have become all at once and by miracle, of a higher order than old historic nations, through many generations of whom the political organization of the world has been slowly developing itself. There will be among them men who are covetous, or men who are tyrannical, or men who would sacrifice public interests, or any

Happily for Africa, most the yearnings of her sons towards her are gentle, humane and generous. When the commercial one shall show itself, it will not differ, I feel assured, from all the others her children have showed. God grant that it may soon burst from many warm and ardent and energetic hearts, for the rescue of a continent!

SECOND. I proceed to show that the whole coast offers facilities for adventurous traders. There are few, if any localities but where they can set up their factories and commence business. If there are exceptions they are rare; and even then, not really such, but cases where at some previous time the natives have been so basely and knavishly treated, that they themselves have learned to practice the same upon some hapless, unsuspecting captain and his crew. As a general thing, however, native African chiefs court and invite the residence of a trader in their neighborhood; will give him protection; and will strive to secure his permanent stay. On our Liberian

others to their own; men who would now go into the slave trade if they could, or rob hen roosts, or intrigue for office, or pick pockets, rather than trouble their heads or their hands with more honorable occupations. It should be remembered by visitors that such things will be found in Liberia; *not because men are black, but because men are men.*" AFRICA AND THE AMERICAN FLAG, p. 206.

It is most encouraging to find ever and anon a writer who in speaking of colored men avoids the exaggeration of them either into demi-gods or monkeys. Even Commander Foote well nigh loses his balance, on the *same* page whence the above just sentence is taken. In the paragraph which immediately follows this extract, he gives expression to opinions sweepingly disparaging to the negro race, and not of *certain* historical accuracy. Commander Foote says— "*No negro has done anything to lighten or brighten the links of human policy.*" Such a broad assertion implies that the writer has cleared up all the mysteries of past history; but upon the point, that is, "the relation of Egypt to the negro race," though still a disputed question; yet, with such authorities on our side as Dr. Pitchard, Cardinal Wiseman and that ripe scholar, the late Alexander H. Everett, one would have supposed Commander Foote would have been a little less venturesome. Moreover, I beg to say that TOUISSANT L'OUVERTURE *is* an historical character. GOODWIN, in his lectures on colonial slavery says: "Can the West India Islands, since their first discovery by Columbus, boast a single name which deserves comparison with that of Touissant L'Ouverture?" Read Harriet Martineau's "Hour and the man;" Wordsworth's fine Sonnet addressed to "Touissant in prison;" and the noble Poem of John G. Whittier, on the same theme; and then compare the opinions of these high names with Commander Foote's broad assertions.

coast we see the proof of this in the many factories in existence at divers points. I have myself seen mere boys,—young Englishmen not of age,—who have come out to this country seeking their fortunes, living on the coast in native towns, without any civilized companionship, and carrying on a thriving trade. The chiefs have an interest in these men, and therefore make their residence safe and comfortable. The traders' presence and barter give the King or head-man importance, increase his wealth, augment his influence in the neighborhood, swell the population of his town, and thus make it the center or capital of the surrounding region. But even if it were not thus, the security of traders is insured by the felt power of the three great nations of the civilized world. Such, and so great is the naval force of England, France, and America, on this coast, that the coast may be regarded as protected. The native chiefs, for many hundred miles, have been taught to fear the destructive instruments of war they carry with them, and now a days but seldom give occasion for their use.

But aside from all this, I may remark here, 1st, that of all rude and uncivilized men, the native African is the mildest and most gentle; and 2nd, that no people in the world are so given to trade and barter as the negroes of the western coast of Africa.

THIRDLY. Let me refer to the means and facilities colored men have for an entrance upon African commerce. And 1st, I would point out the large amount of capital which is lying in their hands dead and unproductive. There is, as you are doubtless aware, no small amount of wealth possessed by the free colored population of the United States, both North and South. Notwithstanding the multitudinous difficulties which beset them in the pathway of improvement, our brethren have shown capacity, perseverance, oftentimes thrift and acquisitiveness. As a consequence they are, all over the Union, owners of houses, farms, homesteads, and divers other kinds of property; and stored away in safe quarters, they have large amounts of gold and silver; deep down in large stockings, in the corners of old chests, in dark and undiscoverable nooks and crannies; besides larger sums invested in banks, and locked up in the safes of city savings banks.

I have no statistics by me of the population and property of the colored people of Cincinnati, but I am told that their wealth exceeds that of the same class, in any other city in the American Union—that is, according to their numbers. Nashville, Tenn., Charleston, S. C., St. Louis, Mo., Mobile and New Orleans, stand in nearly the same category. Baltimore holds a respectable position. In the "Weekly Anglo-African," (September, 1859,) I find that the CHURCH PROPERTY of the colored population in Philadelphia is put down at $231,484. Doubtless their personal real estate must be worth millions. And the same must be true of New York city.

The greater portion of their wealth, however, is unproductive. As a people we have been victimized in a pecuniary point of view, as well as morally and politically; and as a consequence there is an almost universal dread of entrusting our monies in the hands of capitalists, and trading companies, and stock; though in the great cities large sums are put in savings banks. There are few, however, who have the courage to take shares in railroad and similar companies, and in many places it could not be done.

There is *one* most pregnant fact that will serve to show, somewhat, their monetary ability. "THE AFRICAN METHODIST EPISCOPAL CHURCH" is one of the denominations of the United States. It has its own organization; its own bishops; its conferences, its organ, or magazine; and these entirely *inter se*—absolutely disconnected with all the white denominations of America. This religious body is spread out in hamlet, village, town, and city, all through the eastern, northern, western, and (partly) the southern States. But *the* point to which I desire to direct your attention is the fact that they have built and now own some 300 church edifices, mostly brick; and in the large cities, such as New York, Philadelphia and Baltimore, they are large, imposing, capacious, and will seat some two or three thousand people. The free black people of the United States built these churches; the funds were gathered from their small and large congregations; and in some cases they have been known to collect, that is, in Philadelphia and Baltimore, at one collection, over $1,000. The aggregate value of their property can not be less than $5,000,000.

Now this, you will notice, is an exhibit of the corporate monied power of but *one* class of our brethren. I have said nothing about the Episcopal churches, of the Presbyterians, of the Baptists, nor of the divers sections of the Methodists. But this will suffice. You can easily see from the above, that there must be a large amount of pecuniary means in the hands of the free colored population of the American States.

2nd. I turn now to another of their facilities for engaging in African commerce. I refer to NAVIGATION. And here I might rest the case upon the fact that money will purchase vessels, and command seamen and navigators. But you already have *both*. Turn for a moment to New Bedford, Mass. It is now some twenty years since I visited that important seaport. Though but a boy, I kept my eyes open, especially upon the condition of our race there; and I retain still a vivid remembrance of the signs of industry and thrift among them, of the evidences of their unusual wealth, and of their large interest in shipping. I had the names of several parties mentioned to me who were owners of whale craft, and I made the acquaintance of some of them. Among these I remember well some youthful descendants of Paul Cuffee. The same state of things, I apprehend exists, though perhaps in a much less degree, in some places in Connecticut; on the Hudson, that is, at Albany and Newburgh, in the State of New York; on the Potomac; at St. Louis, on the Mississippi, and on the Red River. There are scores, if not hundreds of colored men who own schooners, and other small craft in those localities; pilots and engineers, captains and seamen, who, if once moved with a generous impulse to redeem the land of their fathers, could, in a brief time, form a vast commercial marine, equal to all the necessities of such a glorious project.

Let me dwell for a moment upon one suggestion, that is, the facilities for securing seamen, and the comparative ease of forming crews. Colored seamen, in large numbers, I apprehend, can easily be obtained. Even in the United States their numbers are legion; and we may proudly say that, in activity, dutifulness and skill, they are equal to any sailors on the globe. Nor would there be any great lack of the needed class just above the grade of sailors, that is, a class who would join intelligence and knowledge to practicalness. What a number of men, trained to a late boyhood in the colored schools, do we not know who have sailed for years out of New York as "stewards" in the great "liners"! How many of these are there not, who both at school and by experience, have attained a real scientific acquaintance with navigation. And how many of them, had they been white men, would long ere this, have risen to the posts of mates and captains! How many of such could you and I point out,

who were our school-mates, in the old "free school," in Mulberry street![7]

Here, then, you have the material and the designated agency for an almost boundless commercial staff, for the purposes of trade in West Africa. The facts I have adduced can not, I think, be disputed. And on the condition that this machinery is brought into operation, the influences and results are easily anticipated. It must follow, as a necessity, that the trade and commerce of Africa shall fall into the hands of black men. At an early day whole fleets of vessels, manned and officered by black men from the United States and Liberia, would outrival all the other agencies which are now being used for grasping West African commerce. Large and important houses would spring into existence among you, all through the states. Wealth would flow into your coffers, and affluence would soon exhibit itself amid all your associations. The reproach of penury and the consciousness of impotency in all your relations would rapidly depart. And as a people you would soon be able to make yourselves a felt element of society in all the relations of life, on the soil where you were born.

These are some of the *material* influences which would result from this movement. The moral and philanthropic results would be equally if not more notable. The kings and tradesmen of Africa, having the *demonstration* of negro capacity before them, would hail the presence of their black kinsmen from America,[8] and would be stimulated to a generous emulation. To the farthest interior, leagues and combinations would be formed with the men of commerce, and thus civilization, enlightenment and Christianity would

[7] In a most elaborate paper, entitled "THE NIGER TRADE," by Sir George Stephen (Simpkin, Marshall & Co., London, 1849), the author shows, most clearly, the need and the practicability of employing the agency of black men, for the purposes of African civilization. Sir George suggested the employment of them, in the [British] naval as well as merchant service; in all grades of office, from seamen and marines up to naval officers; and he points to the West India Colonies, and Hayti, remarking, "Hayti has a navy exceeding twenty in number, of which four are steamers; all are, of course, manned and officered by black or colored men." In this paper, Sir George quotes and emphasises the words of McQueen—"*It is by African hands and African exertions chiefly that the evil must be rooted out.*"

[8] Just this has been the experience of Dr. Delany, as I hear from valued friends there, at Lagos, and other places.

be carried to every state, and town, and village of interior Africa. The galling remembrances of the slave trade on the coast, and of slavery in America, would quicken the blood and the brain of both parties; and every wretch of a slave trader who might visit the coast, would have to atone for his temerity by submitting to the rigid code framed for piracy. And when *this* disturbing and destructive hindrance to African progress was once put down, noble cities, vast agricultural establishments, the seeds of universities, and ground-work of church organizations, would spring up all along the banks, and up the valley of the Niger.[9]

There is one certain commercial result—to return to my subject—that would surely grow out of this movement; I mean the flow of large amounts of capital from the monied men of America, that is, if black men showed skill, energy and practicability. Philanthropy would come forward with largess for colored men, thus developing the resources of Africa. Religion would open a large and generous hand in order to hasten the redemption of a continent, alien from Christ and His church. And capital would hasten forward, not only for its wonted reduplication, but also to exemplify the vitality and fruitfulness which it always scatters from golden hands in its open pathway. And when you consider the fact of kinship, on our part, with Africa, the less liability to fever, the incentive to gain, the magnificent objects before us, and the magnificent field on which to develop them, and the probable early power of intelligent black men to penetrate, scathless, any neighborhood where they might reside, you can see the likelihood of an early repossession of Africa, in trade, commerce, and moral power, by her now scattered children, in distant lands.

For the carrying out such a plan you have, I repeat myself, you have almost, if not quite, all the needed means and agencies, even now, at hand. You have, all through the states, men who can at once furnish the capital for the commencement of such a venture. You know I am not wont to exaggerate the wealth of colored men. In such matters I prefer fact to conjecture; for certainly among us on this subject, imagination has too often proved "a forward and delusive faculty." Yet I do know of some of our brethren in the

States who have become monied men,—not millionaires indeed, but men worth their thousands. Some of these men are more prominent individuals than others, and as their names are not unfrequently mentioned in such a connection as this, it may not seem invidious in a like mention on these pages. Some of these persons are acquaintances—a few, old friends of former years, but the most are personally unknown to me. There are Rev. Stephen Smith, William Whipper, Esq., of Philadelphia; Messrs. Knight & Smith, of Chicago, Ill.; Messrs. Cook & Moxly, of Buffalo, N. Y.; Youngs & Wilcox, of Cincinnati, &c., &c.

It is possible that in a few instances earnest prejudice against everything African may cause displeasure at this designation. Any one can see that I have intended nothing discourteous; and it should be remembered that commercial enterprise in Africa has no necessary connection with emigration, or colonization. How great soever the diversities of opinion upon these points, on *this* platform Douglass and Delany can stand beside the foremost citizens and merchants of Liberia. Hence those men whose feelings are the most averse to anything like colonization, can not object to the promotion of trade and the acquisition of wealth. Indeed, I have no doubt that there are thousands who would be glad of a safe investment in anything wherein there is probability of advantage. Moreover the fretted mind of our brethren needs distraction from griefs and the causes of grief. Just now, when darkness shrouds their Southron heavens, what could be more opportune, what more desirable than such a movement. The danger is that thousands of them, in their sorrows, may sit down, hopeless, careless, and

> Nurse despair
> And feed the dreadful appetite of death.

Your leading men should strive to occupy the vacant minds of their despairing brethren by the healthful stimulant of duty and enterprise.

Doubtless there are many persons in the States who will view the above suggestions in connection with the Liberian Republic, and in my opinion it will be wise and judicious for them so to do. I have nothing extravagant to say about Liberia. It is a theme upon which I never fall into ecstacies. I can not find in it as yet place or occasion for violent raptures. I get started a little, at times, from cool equanimity, when I read the wonderful tales

---

[9] The great hindrance to African evangelization at the present time is the slave trade. Missionaries feel this all along the coast, from Cape Palmas to Congo.

of travelers about the country, or the first letters of enthusiastic settlers. Liberia is a young country, hardly yet "in the gristle,"—laying, as I dare to affirm, good foundations, but with much pain, great trials, consuming anxieties, and with the price of great tribulation, and much mortality. But is not this the history of all young countries? Has not God married pain and suffering and death, to the fresh beginnings of all new nationalities? Would it not be marvelous, not to say miraculous, if it were true, that the history of *this* colony—for it is nothing more than a colony as yet—that it had been exempted from these trials? And what right have we to expect that God, in these days, will work miracles, especially for black men?[10]

I have never been disappointed in anything moral, social or political that I have met with in this land. I came to the country expecting all the peculiarities of struggling colonial life, with the added phase of imported habits, tinctured with the deterioration, the indifference, the unthriftiness, which are gendered by *any* servile system. "All work is badly done by people in despair," says Pliny the naturalist.[11] A forty days' passage through the deep sea can not effect such a regenerating influence as to alter character, and to implant hope, ambition, thrift, order, and perseverance, where they have never been cultivated.

These anticipations proved correct, save that I found a stronger and a more general disposition to labor than the sad history of our brethren warranted my looking for.[12] Many things gratified me from the first. Since then Liberia has grown much. Development shows itself on every side. The acquisition principle manifests itself, and in less than ten years large fortunes will be made; extensive farms spring up; ships be built on our rivers and sail to Europe and America. There is every sign, too, that the springs of trade will shortly, through our own direct influence, be started through all our native population, for 200 miles in the interior; and that this trade will be our own; and that it will originate a commerce excelling that of Sierra Leone. I believe verily that the great principles of industry, of thrift, and expansion are daily taking deeper root in the soil; and that ultimately they will outgrow and exclude all the weeds of lazy self-content, inflated and exaggerated vanity, unthrift, and extravagance. Of course we have here stupid obstructions, men who cling tenaciously to the "dead past;" a few millinered and epauleted gentry,

> Neat and trimly dressed,
> And fresh as bridegrooms,

who would civilize our heathen neighbors with powder and shot; and a few unthinking, unreasoning men; who verily believe that the foundations of all great states have been laid in barter and pelf. But these are by no means the *representative* men of the land. If they were, I should despair of any future for Liberia, and depart.

---

[10] "No new country can be founded unless under the greatest difficulties. It is the universal law of experience, that however in the late stages of their existence colonies may be prosperous, and to what state soever they may have advanced in the accumulation of wealth, their infant life must always be a life of difficulty and peril."—*Rt. Hon. W. E. Gladstone, Speech before Propagation Soc., Liverpool, 1858.*

[11] LORD BACON discourses most pertinently and powerfully to the same effect. See Art. 33 of "*Plantations,*" "Bacon's Essays and Wisdom of the Ancients." I regret I can not copy the whole of it here.

[12] The people of Liberia are not lazy, although I am sorry to say, *appearances* are sometimes against them. The case is this:—*Many new men do not know how to labor for* THEMSELVES! They come, at a mature age, when their habits are fixed, into a new school, the operations of which they are unacquainted with. They go into the "bush," and its formidableness overcomes, and crushes them; they sit down in despair and do nothing, and many perish. "Are not such men lazy?" asks some objector. I say no! and my reason for saying so is this: In the year 1856 there were scores of the class above described on the St. Paul's river, doing nothing. Some four or five farmers commenced the cultivation of sugar cane and the manufacture of sugar. This new effort required large numbers of laborers, and as soon as the need was known, the river was alive with men seeking labor. *Who* were these men? The hopeless, the despairing men, who could not see their way through the "bush," and could not improve their own farmsteads. I have seen scores of these men trudging through the rain and mud, in the rainy season, or paddling in fragile canoes, seeking the larger plantations, clamorous for labor; and I have seen the supply so great that a *dozen* men had to be refused at a time. Why was this? These men had been unaccustomed to self support. Placed under a proprietor, heart and limb were alive with an industrious impulse. Liberia needs CAPITAL-ISTS who can employ this large class of men. Mr. RUFFIN, of Virginia, will perhaps claim this as a proof that black men must have masters. Students of "Political Economy" will put it among the facts which show that where capital languishes, men die, both in body and soul.

We have another, a larger class than these; a class which comprises awakened old men, and generous and ardent youth; the minds, whose great object in life is not mere gain, or comfort; but who feel that they have a great work to accomplish for their children, for their race, and for God; who feel that they have been called to this mission, and who wish to spend themselves in the expansion and compacting of this youthful republic, to save bleeding, benighted Africa, and to help redeem the continent. I assure you that there is a school of this character in Liberia; men who feel obligated to philanthropy, who are burdened with a sense of duty; who have the keenest, most sensitive feeling of race, who love Africa, who are anxious for the welfare of the whole negro family, who labor with all their might for the advancement of industry and civilization, who would fain glorify God. When I look upon this class of men, and mark their ways, I feel that the country will yet attain standing and reach some distinction.[13]

It is these thoughts and observations, and some experiences, which lead me to think that those who look upon Liberia in connection with their commercial desires, are wise. I have no wish to discourage those who are looking to the banks of the Niger. God bless them, every way, if that is indeed their mission! But, as an individual, I have earnestly desired a non-sanguinary evangelization of West Africa. All empire, the world over, in rude countries, has been cemented by blood. In Western Africa the tribes, universally, save in Liberia, are strong, independent, warlike. Even British prowess, both at Sierra Leone, and on the Gold coast, succumbs, at

times, to their indomitable spirit. And thus you see that for the establishment of a strong black civilization in central Africa, a strong and a bloody hand must be used. Color is nothing, anywhere. Civilized *condition* differences men, all over the globe. Besides this, I have had a prejudice that *that* field God had given to the freed and cultivated men of Sierra Leone,—that they were better fitted to the evangelization of the Niger than we; that we, with our peculiarities, bred amid American institutions, might prove a disturbing element to the great work, for which, by blood, training, lingual capacity, and the sympathy of character and habits, they were peculiarly fitted; and that our governmental proclivities might jar with what seems a manifest providence, that is, that christianity is to be engrafted upon such strong states as Dahomey and Ashantee; whose fundamental *governmental* basis, it seems to me, it is not for the interests of civilization and of Africa to revolutionize or to disturb.

I would not pretend to argue these points, much less to dogmatise upon them; for the need of a civilizing element at Lagos, especially, at Abbeokuta, and on the Niger, is so great that I fear even to state the above impressions. And I stand ready to hail, at any time, any nucleus of freedom and enlightenment that may spring up anywhere on the coast of Africa.

In Liberia, we have the noblest opportunities and the greatest advantages. We have a rich and varied soil,—inferior, I verily believe, to but few, if any, on the globe. We have some of the proofs, and many of the indications of varied and vast mineral wealth of the richest qualities. We have a country finely watered in every section by multitudinous brooks and streams, and far-reaching rivers. We have a climate which needs but be educated and civilized and tempered by the plastic and curative processes of emigration, clearances and scientific farming, to be made as fine and as temperate as any land in the tropics can be.

On this soil have been laid the foundations of Republican Institutions. Our religion is Protestant, with its characteristic tendencies to freedom, progress and human well-being. We are reaching forward as far as a young and poor nation can, to a system of common schools. Civilization, that is, in its more simple forms, has displaced ancestral paganism in many sections of the land, has taken permanent foothold in our territory,

---

[13] I can not better illustrate the importance of such a class, as above mentioned, in Liberia, than by referring to a paragraph from a speech recently sent me by a friend: "If the founders of the American Republic had been formed by the same materials as the settlers of California, the genius and liberties of America would have been lost in anarchy or absorbed in an inevitable despotism. It was because, on however small a scale, they were senators and soldiers, impressed with a due sense of the heavy responsibility that rested upon them, and not mere money-getters, that they succeeded in laying the foundations of the greatest republic in the world. They never lost sight of the responsibility of the task they had undertaken,— they felt that they were going for a high position in the eyes of the world, and to set an example for all ages. Feeling this, the early settlers of New England accomplished their mission."

JOHN ROBERT GODLY, ESQ., before the "Canterbury Association," London.

and already extended its roots among our heathen kin. Our heathen population, moreover, in the immediate neighborhood of our settlements, is but small and sparse; thus saving our civilization from too strong an antagonism, and allowing it room, scope and opportunity for a hardy growth in its more early days. Active industry is now exhibiting unwonted vigor, and begins to tell upon commerce and the foreign market.

Now when you consider that all these elements, humble, as indeed they are, are our own; that we are the creature and dependent of no foreign government; you will agree with me, I think, that men who have families will act wisely in looking narrowly at our advantages, ere they place themselves in circumstances where the moral elements of life and society are more rude, and where the formation agency and influence will belong to some foreign power. That these elements are slow in growth and expansion is true; but this, it will be remembered, furnishes probability of their being sure and permanent.

I have heard the poverty of our particular locality contrasted with the richness of other parts of West Africa. Well, this may be the case; but I think there can be no doubt that there is no nobler, more commanding position in West Africa, than that of Liberia. We hold, I think, the key to the vast interior. You have heard it said, and seen it published, that we have no great rivers. But the St. Paul's, the Booma,[14] the St. John's, and the Cavalla rivers, stretch away into the far interior 300 and 400 miles, with great breadth, and with a vast volume of water. That they come from the same great water-shed from whence, on an opposite side the Niger drains its mighty waters, seems almost a certainty. And if so, the valley of the Niger, with its wondrous resources, and its teeming wealth, will, ultimately, be as available to us as any other people. At present, these rivers are not navigable any great distance, owing to falls and rapids. But black men in Africa must do what enterprising men do in all other new lands; they must BEND NATURE TO THEIR WANTS AND WISHES. Ship canals are needed twenty miles from the coast, around the rapids of the St. Paul's, and eighty miles from the coast around the falls of the

Cavalla; and ship canals must therefore be made. If we have not the *means,* we must go to work and acquire them. If we have not the *science* and the *skill,* we must form our schools and colleges, and put our sons in the way of learning them. And if we have not the men, that is, the *population,* for such a vast and laborious undertaking, we must lift up a loud voice, and call upon hopeful, vigorous, intelligent and energetic black men, all over the globe, "Ho to the rescue!" "Come over and help us!"

And these are just the great needs of Liberia:— men, learning, and wealth. And wealth, here, as an acquisition, requires the use of the same means, and is regulated by the same laws, as in any other land. It requires forecast, wakefulness, industry, thrift, probity, and tireless, sweatful toil, as well in tropical Africa, as in cold Holland. There is no royal road to the soil.

Nil nisi magno
Vita labore dedit mortalibus.

As to *learning,* we have no greater need than this, save religion; and there can be no excess of means, no superabundance of agencies, no delicacy or profundity of culture, unadapted to actual present needs of all this wide region of Liberia. We have our native population, and we have our emigrant youth and children—thousands upon thousands, all around us. And when I look at the quickness, the capacity, and the thirst of the nations for enlightenment, I can see no difference in the needs of one from the other; I regard them in the general, as our intellectual equals. If I anticipated for them a merely *secular* training, I should prefer a difference; but feeling, knowing that the Christian religion is to mould, and fashion, and leaven everything here in future times, I go for the highest culture that can be given the rising generation, and hail every facility for the furtherance of this end, which providence grants us. In the first passage of the heathen from barbarism it will doubtless be advisable to make much of their training, physical, and to be content with the Bible and moral instruction; but the ultimate aim should be, and most surely will be here, to open to them all the broad avenues of instruction and culture. The great cause of apprehension, just now is, that the means for supplying general education are but partial; and that the actual need created by our circumstances, for the attainment of good literary and scientific training can not be obtained.

---

[14] The BOOMA is a river at Cape Mt. Settlement. I heard that it is the greatest river in Liberia. I am just informed, as this paper leaves me, that an acquaintance has ascended it, some 90 miles, without any obstruction.

I come to population. We *need* immigration. We are poor in men and women. We do not number over 14,000 emigrant citizens. Numbers of these are crippled, I mean in soul more than body, ere they come here. The poverty of emigrants dwarfs the otherwise actual force of the country; and old age, in both sexes, and especially the fact that a large per centage of emigrants are helpless females with children, without husbands, brings out the sad truth that our real available man-force is but small. And yet the moral calls upon us in this new sphere, the intellectual demands, and the physical requirements, with the vastness of territory, and the largeness of providential circumstances around us, while they quicken imagination, fix also the conviction of helpless weakness; and in some men produce indifference or despair; in others, vexation and painful anxiousness. The population question is dwarfing the powers of our strong and earnest leaders. They can not lift themselves up to grand ideas, and large conceptions. In all their efforts they are "cribbed, cabined and confined."

We need this day for the great work before us, in a region of not less than 500,000 square miles; we need, I say, not less than 50,000 *civilized men*. We ought to be traveling onward through the land; and to appropriate and modify a remark of De Toqueville's—to be "peopling our vast wilderness at the average rate of at least five miles per annum." And for the work of civilization and enlightenment among our aboriginal population, we should have even now, a mental power and a moral force working through all our territory, fitted for just such a transformation as has been produced in New Zealand and the Sandwich Islands, in a period of twenty-five years. The tide of immigration, as it now sets in, promises us no such results. Our ratio of increase, with our present diverse disturbing influences, is but small. Unfortunately there is no general consciousness of our lack and need in this respect. I have had the fear that some of my fellow-citizens accustomed themselves to look upon Liberia as a "close corporation." The attempt to pass a "naturalization law," in the face of the fact that it takes YEARS to add a thousand living men to our population, chiefly caused that fear. But we, in common with you, are becoming awake to the conviction that, *as a race,* we have a great work to do. The zeal of England and of America, for Africa, is opening our eyes. Our own thoughtful

men begin to feel the binding tie which joins them in every interest and feeling, with the negro race, all over the globe. Your "Anglo-African Magazines," "Douglas' Journal," and patriotic addresses begin to tell upon us. And soon there will be a kindled eye, a quickened pulse, a beating heart, and large and generous emotions, for our bruised and wounded brethren everywhere. And when that day comes the people of Liberia will cry out:— "*We* have the largest advantages of all our race. We have the noblest field. Ours is the most signal providence; and our State offers the grandest possibilities of good, the finest opportunities of manly achievement. Why then suffer ourselves to be hindered in working out of 'manifest destinies' of beneficence to suffering Africa by the narrowness of our aims, or the fewness of our numbers and means? It is true we have a wide field to enter, and need more and mightier men to enter it. Let us therefore call our skillful and energetic brethren to come to us and share the suffering and the glory of saving Africa. Let us stand on the beach and on the hill-side, and beckon to them in ALL LANDS to come and participate in lofty duty—in painful but saving labor, and to aid in the restoration and enlightenment of a vast continent!"

I turn now to the *religious* aspect of this subject. In speaking of the religious needs of Africa, it is not necessary I should attempt a picture of her miserable condition, nor enter into the details of her wretchedness. Her very name is suggestive of uttermost spiritual need; of abounding moral desolation; of the deepest, darkest ignorance; of wild and sanguinary superstitions. This whole continent, with its million masses of heathen, presents one broad, almost unbroken, unmitigated view of moral desolation and spiritual ruin. And this fact creates the demand upon the Christian world for ministers and teachers, for the purpose of her evangelization. "The field is the world," and the church is to occupy it; and she will occupy it.

As members of the church of Christ, the sons of Africa in foreign lands are called upon to bear their part in the vast and sacred work of her evangelization. I might press this point on the grounds of piety, of compassion, or sympathy, but I choose a higher principle. For next to the grand ideas which pertain to the Infinite, His attributes and perfections, there is none loftier and grander than that of DUTY—

Stern daughter of the voice of God.

It is the duty of black men to feel and labor for the salvation of the mighty millions of their kin all through this continent. I know that there is a class of her children who repudiate any close and peculiar connection with Africa. They and their fathers have been absent from this soil for centuries. In the course of time their blood has been mingled somewhat with that of other peoples and races. They have been brought up and habituated to customs entirely diverse from those of their ancestors in this land. And while the race here are in barbarism, they, on the other hand, are civilized and enlightened.

But notwithstanding these pleas there are other great facts which grapple hold of these men, and bind them to this darkened, wretched negro race, by indissoluble bonds. There is the fact of kinship, which a lofty manhood and a proud generosity keeps them now, and ever will keep them from disclaiming. There are the strong currents of kindred blood which neither time nor circumstance can ever entirely wash out. There are the bitter memories of ancestral wrongs, of hereditary servitude, which can not be forgotten till "the last syllable of recorded time." There is the bitter pressure of legal proscription, and of inveterate caste, which will crowd closer and closer their ranks, deepening brotherhood and sympathy, and preserving, vital, the deep consciousness of distinctive race. There still remains the low imputation of negro inferiority, necessitating a protracted and an earnest battle, creative of a generous pride to vindicate the race, and inciting to noble endeavor to illustrate its virtues and its genius.

How then can these men ever forget Africa? How cut the links which bind them to the land of their fathers? I affirm therefore that it is the duty of black men, in foreign lands, to live and to labor for the evangelization of the land of their fathers: 1st, on the ground of humanity; 2d, because they themselves are negroes, or the descendants of negroes, and are measurably responsible to God for the salvation of their heathen kin; and 3dly, I press the consideration of duty on the ground that they are Christians. In the good providence of God they have been enabled to pass out of the spiritual benightedness of their fathers, into the high table lands and the divine atmosphere of Christian truth and Christian conviction.

Now I shall not attempt any *formal* argument in proof that black men [or, to use the new term,] Anglo-Africans are duty bound to extend the gospel in Africa; for I know enough of human nature to see that such an argument would look like the assumption that our brethren in the States were so ignorant that they did not know their duty as Christians. The very men who, perchance, would contest every other point in this letter, would charge me with insult, if I had just here put forth an *argument to prove* that Christianity requires *black* Christians to be missionaries as well as white ones. They would start up and exclaim: "Do you think that we read our Bibles and yet remain ignorant of the evangelizing spirit of the Bible? Do you think that we are such fools as to suppose that the precepts and commands of scripture have a *color* on them? And do you suppose that we are such ignorant creatures, that you must needs present an argument to prove to us that we should manifest a missionary heart as well as other Christians? We do not need your teachings, sir. We know something about Christianity as well as you."

I attempt no such argument. It is not to be supposed for a moment, that black Christians in New York, Philadelphia and Baltimore, do not know that there are no distinctions in Christian requirement, that her obligations are as weighty upon them as upon any portion of the church. I am only endeavoring to show that while that portion of the race that lives in America, owes duty in America, it has obligations which likewise pertain to Africa; that devotedness to the cause of the black man in the United States, does not necessarily exclude sympathy for Africa. Let me illustrate this. There is a phase of modern theological writing, which brings out most prominently the fact that our Lord Jesus Christ, though born of a Jewish mother, shows no where Jewish idiosyncracies. You look at the Lord Jesus, you read his life, you study his words, and no where can you discover nationality. Men of every clime and blood and nation turn to Him, and they find each and all in Him, the reflex of one common broad humanity.

The Apostle, St. Paul, more than any other mere man, reached the nearest to this grand and divine Catholicity of the Master. "I am debtor both to the Greeks and to the Barbarians: both to the wise and to the unwise. So, as much as in me is, I am ready to preach the Gospel to you that are at Rome also." Romans, Chapter i, 14, 15.

Nay, he went even beyond this. In his Epistle to the Thessalonians he speaks of his kinsmen the Jews, in a way which would lead one to suppose that he had become thoroughly de-nationalized. "For ye also have suffered like things of your own countrymen, even as they have of the Jews: Who both killed the Lord Jesus, and their own prophets, and have persecuted us; and they please not God, and are contrary to all men." 1 Thessalonians, ii, 14, 15. So thoroughly had the grace of God eliminated from the soul of St. Paul, that withering and malignant principle of caste, which burned more fiercely and intensely in the Jewish mind and blood, than in any other people that ever lived.

And yet, look at this same large-hearted, Catholic-minded Paul; what a patriot he is! what longings he has for his race! How he falls back upon their high and noble prerogatives! Yea, what zeal, what deep desire, what earnest self-sacrifice he cherishes for them! "What advantage hath the Jew?" he asks, "Or what profit is there of circumcision? Much every way: chiefly because that unto them were committed the oracles of God." Romans, iii, 1, 2. The Epistle to the Romans was written after that to the Thessalonians. And again, in the 9th chapter. He says,—"I say the truth in Christ, I lie not, my conscience also bearing me witness in the Holy Ghost, that I have great heaviness and continual sorrow in my heart. For I could wish that myself were accursed from Christ for my brethren, my kinsmen according to the flesh: who are Israelites, to whom pertaineth the adoption, and the glory, and the covenants, and the giving of the law, and the service of God and the promises; whose are the fathers, and of whom as concerning the flesh Christ came, who is over all, God blessed for ever. Amen."

To be Catholic minded then does not imply a lack of patriotism. Large, yea cosmopolitan views, do not necessarily demand a sacrifice of kinship, a disregard of race, nor a spirit of denationality.

Even so our brethren in the United States; however manfully they claim citizenship in the land of their birth; however valiantly, against all odds they stand beside their brethren in bonds; however nobly they may continue to battle for their rights; need not, nevertheless feel less for the hundreds of millions of their kin "without God and without hope in the world," "in bondage to sin and Satan;" nor yet to put forth less generous effort for their well-being and eternal salvation.

I turn from the point of *duty* to the question of your *ability* and *power* to take part in this great work. I do not know whether or not, colored men in the United States would generally acknowledge that they could as a people do something for Africa; I assume, however, as most probable, the affirmative. At the same time I must say that I do not think there is any deep conviction of either the awful needs of the case, or the solemn obligation connected with it.

I see however, that this very question of your ability is both questioned and denied in some quarters. I see in the "Spirit of Missions" [October, 1858,] a report of a speech of Rev. Dr. I. Leighton Wilson, secretary of the Presbyterian Board of Missions, which is of this tenor. He says—"To withdraw our Missionaries, is virtually to consign those people to perpetual and unmitigated heathenism. The speaker knew of no substitute for the present plan of Missionary operation. In the colonization scheme, he entertained the liveliest interest. The Liberian Republic offers a comfortable home for those in the United States who choose to go there, but it can never exert an influence which will reach the remote part of the continent. To study out the barbarous languages—prepare dictionaries—to give shape to a community emerging into the light of civilization—we never look to colored men as best adapted to this work. We were shut up to the conclusion that we must pursue this work in the manner already commenced."

I regret exceedingly that one who has done and suffered so much for Africa, as Dr. Wilson has, should have ventured such disparaging remarks concerning any of her children as the above.[15] For if he had put himself to the pains of inquiring into the capacity of the "colored men around him," he would never, I feel convinced, have thus spoken. I am no more disposed to exaggerate the learning or mental ability of our race than their wealth. Indeed, as a race, there is no place for exaggeration. As yet, we are but "parvenus" in the intellectual world. Our greatness lies in the future, as yet we have not secured. Nevertheless

[15] It is hardly necessary for me to tell you that Dr. Wilson has spent the flower of his years on this coast in self sacrifice for Africa; nor to add that it was *chiefly* through a rigorous and timely pamphlet of his that the British Squadron was not withdrawn from this coast in 1851.

American black men have done, and are now doing enough to challenge respect. And even that seems to be withheld by Dr. Wilson; possibly I may mistake him. But when American black men are ably editing literary journals, publishing respectable newspapers, issuing from the press volumes of sermons, writing scientific disquisitions, venturing abstruse "Theories of Comets," and sending forth profound "vital statistics," vexatious alike to opposing Statesmen and Divines; they so far vindicate their mental power and ability, as to make it manifest, that, under better circumstances, in a clear field, they could

> Move and act
> In all the correspondences of nature,

with force, and skill, and effect.

But Dr. Wilson knows nothing of this particular class of black men. He and hundreds like him know nothing of them. And this is one of the original signs of the deadly power of caste. It victimizes the white as well as the black man. Here is mind,—active struggling mind—developing itself under most interesting circumstances; rising above the depression of centuries; breaking away from ancestral benightedness and hereditary night; gradually gathering strength, and emerging into light; and at length securing respectability and attracting attention, and yet if this phenomenon, which excited the admiration of Dr. Channing, and arrested the attention of Lord Carlyle and Dr. Playfair, passing travelers, Dr. Wilson apparently knows nothing of, but actually speaks slightingly of.

Dr. Wilson rejects the idea of your being capable of exerting a remote and extensive influence. I beg to point out his error by a reference again to the "African Methodist Church," in the United States. I make this reference on the ground that in the church of God "there are diversities of gifts, but the same spirit;" and "there are differences of administrations, but the same Lord;" and "that the manifestation of the spirit is given to every man to profit withal;" and yet again, that in the great work of Christ for the salvation of the heathen, even *those very* "*members of the body* [of Christ] *which seem to be more feeble, are necessary.*"[16]

And, while fully agreeing to the affirmation more distinctly stated by Dr. Wilson than I have ever seen it expressed before, that, "the idea of gathering up colored men indiscriminately, and setting them down upon the shores of Africa, with the design or expectation that they will take the lead in diffusing a pure Christianity among the nations, deserves to be utterly rejected by every friend of Africa."[17] Still it seems to me that he commits an error similar to that of rejecting the light artillery of an army, because the "cavalry" is a stronger arm of it.

Doubtless *all* the religious societies of colored people in America are humble, that is as it respects literary and theological qualifications; and the African Methodist Church as much as any other. I do not think they themselves would make any pretensions. *But have they fitness for practical usefulness?* We can only determine this by facts. Now this denomination has been in existence since 1790. It has gathered into its fold tens of thousands of the sons of Africa on American soil.

The poor forsaken ones.

Men however of earnest mind, who would not sit in the "negro pew;" men, who but for this society must have been left to indifferentism or infidelity, have had their wounded hearts soothed by the visitations of this society, and their anxious passionate gaze turned from the trials of caste and slavery, to "the Lamb of God, who taketh away the sin of the world." They have built churches, established schools, founded a college, raised up a ministry of over four hundred men, meet in several conferences, and are governed by their own bishops. Here then is a spiritual machinery which has saved the United States the shame of hundred of thousands black heathen. Where is a purely missionary enterprise in the full tide of success, which has been administered by black men over a half century—stretching from Maine to Louisiana, from Maryland to California; it shows that black men "*can exert an influence which will reach the remote part of the continent*" of America; and why not do the same on the continent of Africa? Operating among negroes, most of whom a century ago were recently from Africa; it shows that American Christians, even *now,* "*can look to colored men as*" [at least, *humbly*] "*adapted to the work,*" that is "*to give shape to a community emerging into the light of civilization.*" The disproof of Dr. Wilson's assertion is right before his eyes.

---

[16] 1 Corinthians xii: 5, 6, 7,–22.

[17] Wilson's "Western Africa," p. 507.

Dr. Wilson's objection, that we are "not best adapted to study out the barbarous languages and prepare dictionaries," I regard as exceedingly unfair. There is not a missionary society in Christendom whose choice of missionaries is conditioned on this single qualification—their "ability to study barbarous languages and prepare dictionaries!" It strikes too as much against *white* missionaries *abroad* as against black men; for are they "BEST ADAPTED," in these respects, compared with such distinguished divines and scholars as Dr. Robinson, Dr. Goodrich, Dr. Turner? Besides how many dictionaries have the fishermen of Galilee transmitted to modern times? What evidence have we of an eminent scholarship among them like to this demanded of us? Or where is the proof that even the Holy Spirit regarded "the preparation of dictionaries," or a critical lingual capacity as *the* qualifications of missionaries?

We read the history of the church, and see the conquests of the faith in ancient times in Europe, Asia, and Africa. But how rare a thing is it, to find such pre-eminent scholarships as, for instance, that of Henry Martyn, Bishop Middleton, and David Tappan Stoddard, the accessories of the devoted missionary spirit, which has converted millions, and brought whole nations into the kingdom of Christ. St. Paul founded the churches of Asia and Greece. But where is the proof that even he was an eminent critical scholar? Christianity was revived and energized in England by Augustine in the 6th century, and then traveled onward with conquering power, until the time of the reformation; and since then the evangelization of England has been progressing with a resistless march to the present. But the first English dictionary we know of is that of Dr. Johnson.

If I do not mistake the spirit of the New Testament, it requires, I apprehend, in addition to devoted piety, good sterling qualities, and an "aptness to teach," as the ordinary gifts of ministers: [and what are missionaries but ministers?] It can not go below this standard; but it may rise above it to the fiery zeal and wasting labors of St. Paul; the effective eloquence of Xavier, and Swartz, and Brainerd; the fine abilities and practical learning of Carey and Medhurst.

If to ordinary gifts, missionaries are able to add these other eminent ones, so much the better fitted will they be to make skillful and effective workers in the Lord's vineyard!

But if not, then missionaries, that is, colored missionaries, to Africa, must be content to labor as effectively as they can, without them; relying for translations and the superior literary work of missions, upon the occasional white laborers who come from abroad. And with respect to the languages, they must do as two-thirds, not to say three-fourths, of the white missionaries do, that is, work for the heathen through the agency of interpreters. In Liberia, however, more than a *third,* not to say *half,* of the colored ministers, speak the respective native tongues in their vicinity, with ease; and of candidates for the ministry, in the different denominations, I feel well nigh confident that four-fifths of them speak one or two *native* tongues.

You have then humble QUALIFICATIONS fitted to make you, although not learned, yet useful and effective instruments in the salvation of our heathen kin. You can become preachers and teachers; and the more learned labor can be done by white brethren. As you have fitness, so likewise you have the OPPORTUNITY to enter upon this glorious and saving work. I wish to show here that if you love Africa, and really possess a missionary spirit, the way is open before you to enter at once among the crowded populations of this continent, and to set up the standard of the Cross. From the port of Lagos in almost direct line through a crowded population, and passing by cities containing tens of thousands of people, a highway is now open reaching to RABBA on the banks of the Niger. All through this country the colored churches of America can send their missionaries, build up Christian schools, and lay the foundation of Christian colleges and universities. North of us lies the wide and open field of the Mendians, which is the door to the mighty millions of interior Africa, back to Timbuctoo. Between these two fields of labor is the republic of Liberia. Our name, our reputation, and our flag, will insure you safety two hundred miles from the coast, among large, important, industrious, and active-minded natives. It was only the other day that I made a second visit to an interior station, in company with Dr. Delany, who had been my guest for a few weeks, and became, for the time, my fellow traveler. We were paddled up the CAVALLA, a fine, broad-flowing river, running through a rich and populous country, with banks rising twenty, thirty, fifty feet, almost perpendicularly from the water's level, its turning points opening ever and anon to our view grand mountain scenery in the distance, with visions of ravishing beauty now and then bursting upon our sight, navigable for sloops and schooners near eighty miles from the coast, and stretching out beyond the falls which here obstruct its passage, some three or four hundred miles in the interior. Everywhere, in every town, we were most cordially received, hospitably entertained, and my teachings eagerly listened to, by whole towns and villages, who invariably turned out, in a body to hear the preacher. In most of these towns I had gone preaching before; other missionaries had been there long and often before me; and hence you can see that it was interest that excited them, and not mere novelty.

Now here is a vast, open field, ready for the Gospel; but it is but *one* among scores, in the limited territory of Liberia. Saving that the Cavalla can be navigated a further distance inland, there are many other as good opportunities and facilities for the conveyance of the Gospel interiorward, as this.

Now, let me ask, what hinders the colored Christians of America from entering these large, inviting missionary fields, and founding the institutions of christianity here? Putting aside, altogether, the question of colonization, why can they not as a people, come forward to save their race from heathenism, and to give them both the present and the future consolations of religion?

Let me refer in particular, to the three classes of religionists among our brethren, with whom I am more especially acquainted: the Methodists, Presbyterians, and Episcopalians.

The colored Episcopalians are a "small folk," I know, but both of us being churchmen, will make my mention of them excusatory. With three or four of these congregations I am intimately acquainted, and I see no difficulty whatever in the way of their adopting some such plan as this: 1. Preparing, as a commencement, some two or three young men for the ministry, for the special purpose of becoming missionaries to Africa. This, of course, presupposes a regular, systematic effort on the part of the ministers of these churches to interest their people in Africa, and to train them in the *habit* of giving to missions. In this way one young heart and another would ever and anon come forward, anxious to devote itself to the evangelization of Africa. The young men might take theological lessons of the minister, and when prepared, might be placed under the Episcopal authority on this coast, and receive orders. 2. When about sending off the young men, if any pious mechanics, or farmers, or school-masters, desired to devote themselves to the work, the congregation might extend their interest to them as well as to the candidates for orders, and assure them of continued regard and future zeal and self-sacrifice in their behalf.[18] 3. A company thus formed, might be placed at the disposal of the mission, with the request, perhaps, that they might be located together, as one party; and the church from whence they came, or some two or three colored churches, might regard *that* station as their own,—supply it with school books, farming utensils, clothes for missionaries and converts, and provisions to a greater or less extent; might recruit ever and anon with new schoolmasters, or replace decayed or deceased missionaries,—or take charge of their children, [in America,] and prepare them for the work of their parents, in the future.

This is only an outline of what the few colored Episcopal churches in the United States could do.[19] Perhaps you say, "this is a large scheme!" I reply without hesitation, that from my knowledge of the wealth that has been concentered in it, ST. THOMAS' CHURCH, Philadelphia, could have done all this thirty years ago. The expense of a small mission, thus constituted, would not near equal the lavish expenditure of some city congregation of colored people, in balls, parties, fashionable rivalry, jewelry, pic-nics, and the department which is politely termed *cuisine*.

Without entering into details, I merely remark that from their numbers, and the increasing intelligence and learning of their ministers, the Presbyterians could do a larger work than the Episcopalians. They have so many *white* colleges and seminaries opened to them, so many obstacles have been removed out of the way of their aspiring young men, and so wide and warm and

---

[18] I regret that the theme before me forbids that I should speak of the almost absolute necessity, in any such scheme, of connecting *manual labor* with missionary effort. Indeed no man should become a *colonist* to Africa whose example is likely to encourage the heathen in their irregular, unsystematic, unplodding modes of labor.

[19] There are no less than *three* different fields into which effective laborers would likely be welcomed:— the church in Sierra Leone, in Liberia, and in the projected field in South Africa, where the "Cambridge and Oxford" mission intend to establish a colony.

hearty is the desire of all classes of white Presbyterians to build up their denomination among the free colored people, that the colored Presbyterian churches could contemplate grand saving schemes for Africa, and undertake at once a large and noble work.

But the "African Methodist Episcopal Church" of the United States has the machinery for a most comprehensive missionary service in Africa. They have a well-tried system; they have experience; they have a large body of ministers; and they have a corresponding body, already in existence, under complete organization; in Liberia,—I mean the "Liberian Episcopal Church." If my old friend, Bishop Daniel A. Payne, would only enter into this work with all that warmth of heart, that energy of purpose, and that burning Christian eloquence, which characterize him, what blessedness would he not impart to this land; what spiritual life would he not diffuse among all the churches of his charge, in America! His people could start a saving, systematized plan, by which health, power, life and energy would be constantly poured, like a living stream, into the corresponding body in this country, and so be diffused throughout the land, to the villages, the hamlets, and the huts of tens of thousands of our needy heathen kin!

I am not blind to difficulties. I know some of the trials of emigration. I have been called to some of the difficulties, not to say severities of missionary life. And therefore I shall be free, I trust, from the charge of flippancy. So likewise I am aware of the peculiar obstacles in the way of our brethren in the States. I, too, am an American black man. I have an acquaintance with obstructive idiosyncracies in them. If you think of hindrances and difficulties specially theirs, I know all about them.

But I say it deliberatively, that the difficulties in the way of our brethren doing a goodly work for Africa, are more subjective than objective. *One of these hindrances is a want of missionary zeal.* This is a marked characteristic of *American* black Christians. I say *American,* for from all I hear it does not characterize our West Indian brethren, and the infant church of Sierra Leone is already, in sixty years from its birth a mother of missions. *This* is our radical defect. *Our* religion is not diffusive, but rather introversive. It does not flow out, but rather inward. As a people we like religion, we like religious services. Our people like to go to Church, to prayer meetings, to revivals. But we go to get enjoyment. We like to be made happy by sermons, singing, and pious talk. All this is indeed correct so far as it goes; but it is only *one* side of religion. It shows only that phase of piety which may be termed the *"piety of self-satisfaction."* But if we are true disciples, we should not only seek a comforting piety, but we should also exhibit an effective and expansive one. We should let our godliness exhale like the odor of flowers. We should live for the good of our kind and strive for the salvation of the world.

Another of these hindrances is what the phrenologists term *"inhabitativeness,"*—the stolid inhabitativeness of our race. As a people, we cling with an almost deadly fixity to locality. I see this on both sides of the Atlantic. Messrs. Douglass and Watkins assail Messrs. Horace Greeley and Gerrit Smith for pointing out this peculiarity of character in our people. But without doubt they tell the truth of us. We are not "given to change." The death of a master, the break up of a family, may cast a few black men from the farm to the city, but they go no further. We lack speculation. Man has been called a creature,

Looking before and after. . . .

But not so we. We look where we stand, and but few beyond.

So here, on this side of the water. The colonization-ship brings a few hundred freed men to this west coast of Africa. They gather together in the city of Monrovia, or the town of Greenville, and there they sit, yea, and would sit forever, if it were not for some strong *external* influence which now and then scatters a few, and a precious few, here and there along the coast.

Here then you see, in this same people, on both sides of the waters, an exaggeration of the "home feeling," which is so exceedingly opposite to Anglo-Saxon influences that I wonder that we, who have been trained for centuries under them, have not ere this outgrown it. Sixteen years from the settlement of Plymouth, sixty families started from Boston and cut their way to Windsor, on the Connecticut.[20] We, in Liberia, have never yet had a *spontaneous* movement of old settlers in a body and with a purpose to a new location. The colored people of Rochester, N.Y., in 1853, I hear, were mostly fugitive slaves. The "Fugitive Slave Law" prompted them to emigrate to

[20] Bancroft's History of America, ch. ix.

Canada; but proximity determined their choice of a home rather than any large principle. We read in the Acts of the Apostles, that when those who at Stephen's death were persecuted, were scattered abroad, "they went everywhere preaching the word." So when our brethren felt constrained to leave the United States, it was meet, it seems to me, that *some* of them should have thought of Africa and her needs. On the other hand, if Liberians had been duly awake to the welfare of our race, we should have shown our brotherly feeling by inviting the wanderers to our shores.

These *two* hindrances, that is, a lack of missionary zeal and a tenacious hold on locality, will doubtless prevent active efforts for the regeneration of Africa. So, too, they will serve to check commercial enterprise. But as a people, we shall have to rise above these things. The colored churches of America will find, bye and bye, they can retain no spiritual vitality unless they rise above the range of selfish observation to broad, general, humane ideas and endeavors. Self-preservation, self-sustenation, are only single items in the large and comprehensive category of human duties and obligations.

> Unless above himself, he can erect himself,
> How poor a thing is man.

And this is equally true with regard to Liberian black Christians. Do not think that I pretend to say that we in Africa stand on such a high vantage ground that we can point invidiously at our brethren in America. I have no hesitation in saying, as my own opinion, that in both the respects referred to above, we are more blameworthy than you.

A *third* hindrance may be mentioned here. There will be a reluctance on the part of even some good and zealous Christians to engage in the propagation of the gospel in Africa on the ground "that its ultimate tendency must be to subserve the objectionable scheme of African colonization." But surely any one can see that such an objection is wicked. The gospel *must* be preached in all the world. The master commands it. The history of the church shows that it does not necessarily, if generally, carry colonization with it. But even if in this particular case, it does so, no Christian has a right to shrink from his duty. And that man must be demented who can not see God's beneficent providence in colonization,—that man blind who does not recognize

good and mercy in its work—civil and religious, on the coast of Africa! The duties of our present state are not to be determined by imaginary results or prospective issues. They always grow out of the positive commands of the Bible, or manifest human relations, and *both* fasten the duty upon us to care for the heathen in general, and for our heathen kin in particular.

I have no doubt, however, that every effort that is henceforth made to spread the gospel in Africa, will bring many from the impulse of emigration, to Africa. Up to a certain future, but I hope not distant point in American sentiment, there will be, I feel quite certain, a large exodus of the better, more cultivated, and hence more sensitive minds, partly to Africa, Hayti, Brazil, and the British colonies. Those who "having done all," still STAND, must bear with those who leave. Hayti *needs a* PROTESTANT, Anglo-African element of the stamp Mr. Holly will give her. Jamaica is blessed by the advent in her midst of such a strong-minded, open-eyed, energetic spirit, as my old school-mate and friend, SAMUEL R. WARD. And Liberia's wants in this respect are stronger than either of the above. You should learn willingly to give, even of your best, to save and regenerate and build up the RACE in distant quarters.[21] You should study to rise above the niggard spirit which grudgingly and pettishly yields its grasp upon a fellow laborer. You should claim with regard to this continent that "THIS IS OUR AFRICA," in all her gifts, and in her budding grace and glory. And you should remember too, with regard to emigrants, the words of that great man, "EDMUND BURKE." "The poorest being that crawls on earth, contending to save itself from injustice and oppression, is an object respectable in the eyes of God and man."

But it is time that I should draw to a close, for I have fallen into a too common fault,—I have made too long a "palaver." My letter has run out to a greater length than I intended. And now I shall weary you no longer.

For near three centuries the negro race in exile and servitude has been groveling in lowly places, in deep degradation. Circumstance and position alike have divorced us from the pursuits which

---

[21] The 2d article of the Constitution of African Civilization Society sets forth my views in better language than my own: "The Evangelization and Civilization of Africa and the descendants of African ancestors, *wherever dispersed.*"

give nobleness and grandeur to life. In our time of trial we have shown, it is true, a matchless patience, and a quenchless hope; the one prophetic of victory, and the other the germ of a high Christian character, now developing. These better qualities, however, have been disproportioned, and the life of the race in general has been alien from ennobling and aspiring effort.

But the days of passivity should now come to an end. The active, creative, and saving powers of the race should begin to show themselves. The power of the negro, if he has such power, to tell upon human interests, and to help shape human destinies, should at an early day make full demonstration of itself. We owe it to ourselves, to our race, and to our generous defenders and benefactors, both in Europe and America, to show that we are capable "of receiving the seed of present history into a kindly yet a vigorous soil, and [that we can] reproduce it, the same, and yet new, for a future period"[22] in all the homes of this traduced, yet vital and progressive race.

Surely the work herein suggested is fitted to just such ends, and is fully worthy the noblest faculties and the highest ambition. If I were aiming but to startle the fancy, to kindle the imagination, and thereby to incite to brave and gallant deeds, I know no theme equal to this in interest and commanding influence. And just this *is* the influence it is now exerting upon passionate and romantic minds, in England and the United States, in France and Germany, in Austria and Sardinia. These civilized States are sending out their adventurous travelers to question, on the spot, the mysterious spell which seems to shut out Africa from the world and its civilization. These enterprising spirits are entering every possible avenue to the heart of Africa, anxious to assure the inner tribes of the continent that the enlightened populations of Europe would fain salute them as brethren, and share with them the culture and enlightenment which, during the ages, have raised *them* from rudeness and degradation, if they can only induce them to throw aside the exclusiveness of paganism and the repulsiveness of barbarism.

But the enlightened sons of Africa in distant lands, are called to a far higher work than even this; a work which as much transcends mere civilization as the abiding interests of eternity outvie the transient concerns of time. To wrest a continent from ruin; to bless and animate millions of torpid and benighted souls; to destroy the power of the devil in his strongholds, and to usher therein light, knowledge, blessedness, inspiring hope, holy faith, and abiding glory, is, without doubt, a work which not only commands the powers of the noblest men, but is worthy the presence and the zeal of angels. It is just this work which now claims and calls for the interest and the activity of the sons of Africa. Its plainest statement and its simplest aspect, are sufficient, it seems to me, to move these men in every quarter of the world to profound sensibility, to deep resolve, to burning ardor. Such a grand and awful necessity, covering a vast continent, touching the best hopes, and the endless destiny of millions of men, ought, I think, to stir the souls of many a self-sacrificing spirit, and quicken him to lofty purposes and noble deeds. And when one considers that never before in human history has such a grand and noble work been laid out in the Divine Providence, before the negro race, and that it rises up before them in its full magnitude now, at the very time when they are best fitted for its needs and requirements, it seems difficult to doubt that many a generous and godly soul will hasten to find his proper place in this great work of God and man, whether it be by the personal and painful endeavors of a laborer in the field of duty, or by the generous benefactions and the cheering incitements which serve to sustain and stimulate distant and tried workers in their toils and trials. A benefaction of this kind seems to enlarge the very being of a man, extending it to distant places and to future times, inasmuch as unseen countries and after ages may feel the effects of his bounty, while he himself reaps the reward in the blessed society of all those who "having turned many to righteousness, shine as the stars forever and ever."[23]

[22] Dr. Arnold. Inaugural Lecture.

[23] Bp. Berkley: "Proposal for supplying churches."

The Struggle for Civil Rights

Theodore S. Wright (1797–1847)

Born to free parents in Providence, Rhode Island, and educated at the Free African School of New York, Theodore S. Wright prepared himself for the Presbyterian ministry at the Princeton Theological Seminary, entering in 1825 and becoming its first Black graduate in 1828. Succeeding Samuel E. Cornish soon afterward as minister of the First Colored Presbyterian Church of New York, Wright quickly became an important religious, social, intellectual, and political leader of Blacks in that city during the 1830's and 1840's when the abolition movement was gaining momentum.

As a clergyman, Wright influenced not only his own congregation, of which the young Henry Highland Garnet was a member, but the larger religious community as well. In 1834 he was an officer of the New York Temperance Society. In 1841 he helped to found the Union Missionary Society, which elected him its first treasurer. Five years later, this organization and three other groups merged in the American Missionary Association. For the year he was able to serve before his death, Wright was one of the five vice-presidents of this Association and a member of its twelve-man executive committee. He was also a member of the executive committee of the Evangelical Alliance. His denominational leadership was recognized in 1845 by his election to the office of moderator of the Third Presbytery of New York.

But Wright conceived his ministerial role to include more than strictly religious duties. His labors for the cause of abolition were many. Active in the 1830's in the New York State Antislavery Society, in the 1840's he expanded his activities by helping to establish the American and Foreign Antislavery Society and by staunchly supporting the Liberty Party. He was even more tireless on behalf of civil and human rights for free Blacks. Like his father before him, he fiercely opposed the efforts of the American Colonization Society to deport Black people. The hypocrisy and racism of white colonizationists were revealed by Wright in his sharply satirical "Prayer of a Colonizationist," which appeared in a pamphlet he coauthored with Samuel E. Cornish: "We thank thee, O God, for the success which has thus far attended the efforts which have been made to raise up and increase prejudice against the work of thy hand in the person of our colored brethren; carry it on to a full consumation; but if this cannot be granted, change, thou, then their color, and in all things pertaining to their form and visage let the work of thy Infinite Wisdom be so modified as to adapt itself to the prejudices of us, a happier and more favored portion of the race—that we may, thus, be persuaded to love them as brethren belonging to the great family thou hast made." Together with Cornish, David Ruggles, and others, he organized the New York Committee of Vigilance, which maintained the Underground Railroad and defended the rights of all Black residents of the city. Because of his clear recognition of—and experience with—white racism, Wright early saw the need of Black self-help. In 1833 he was vice-president of the Phoenix Society of New York, the purpose of which was "to promote the improvement of the colored people in morals, literature, and the mechanical arts." Three years later, the Phoenix High School was set up with Wright as its president. He supported other Black endeavors of various kinds: cooperative agriculture, the newspaper *The Colored American,* the convention movement.

Wright's letter to Rev. Archibald Alexander, a white professor of theology at Princeton, was published in *The Emancipator,* an abolitionist newspaper, on October 27, 1836, and is reprinted here. The letter fully explains the incident which occasioned it, but one may add that President James Carnahan of Princeton had tried to smooth over the outrage by denying that any violent act had taken place. This could not have surprised Wright, who was familiar with the white racism of the North, found even among many abolitionists. As he said in a speech delivered a year later: "It is an easy thing to ask about the vileness of slavery at the South, but to call the dark man a brother, heartily to embrace the doctrine advanced in the second article of the constitution, to treat all men according to their moral worth, to treat the man of color in all circumstances as a man and brother—that is the test."

Two important speeches by Wright are included in Carter G. Woodson's *Negro Orators and Their Orations* (1925). The fullest biographical account is Bella Gross, "Life and Times of Theodore S. Wright, 1797–1847," *The Negro History Bulletin,* III (June 1940), 133–138, 144. Briefer treatments are those by Vernon Loggins in *The Negro Author* (1931) and Wilhelmina S. Robinson in *Historical Negro Biographies* (1967), a volume in the *International Library of Negro Life and History.* See also Benjamin Quarles, *Black Abolitionists* (1969).

Letter to Rev. Archibald Alexander, D.D.

New York, October 11th, 1836
Rev. Archibald Alexander, D.D.
Rev. and dear Friend,—In addressing you on this occasion, I do not detain you by the formality of an apology for the liberty I have taken, lest I should betray a want of those feelings of confidence and respect towards you, which my former relations to you as pupil, and our existing relation as brethren in the holy ministry ought to inspire.

If any apology were in place, I would advert to my anxiety that there may be before your mind, a detail of the circumstances of that wanton abuse, which I received on the day after the Seminary closed, from a reckless young man, represented to me as belonging to the College, but who, I have just learned, was some time since dismissed from the Institution. A member of the Faculty of the College kindly intimated to me, that my assailant endeavored to find a palliation for his abuse in some alleged imprudence on my part, which in the sequel you will find to be a mere pretext.

In this matter I am blameless. I appeal to all who witnessed the occurrence, if I said or did aught indecorous, either as a man or as a Christian. You, no doubt, sir, recollect, that on Tuesday the 20th of last month, the "Literary Society of the Alumni of Nassau Hall" convened at the chapel of the Seminary for the purpose of hearing their annual address. Desirous of partaking of the intellectual repast which was very justly anticipated, I was induced to attend. Accordingly, when the time arrived for the exercises to commence, I repaired to the place of meeting. I found the chapel crowded to overflowing. I was favored to stand inside by the door. After occupying that position some time, benches were passed in and placed in one of the aisles. Like those near me, I availed myself of a seat on one of those benches, perhaps ten feet from the door. There I sat until the close of the exercises. The band had played; the President had announced the appointments for the evening, and the audience had arisen to withdraw; when I heard with surprise the ungentlemanly outcry, "Out with the nigger"—"Out with the nigger," but I had not the least idea that I was the victim, until seized by the collar by a young man *who kicked me two or three times in the most ruthless manner*—at the same time saying, "What do you do here? What do you do here? Don't let me see you here again." Just at this instant an individual, who I am informed is a member of the Seminary, laid hold of the infatuated young man and prevented his farther abuse. With an air of conscious self-importance, he exclaimed, as if he had effected some noble exploit, "My name, sir, is Ancrum; my name is Ancrum."

Happy am I to say, that at that critical moment I was not left to become recreant to the comforting, but self-denying doctrine of non-resistance, so effective in curbing that vindictive spirit which naturally rises when suddenly assailed. Thankful am I that I was kept from lifting so much as a finger in self-defense, but continued my way out of the house.

I have felt very solicitous since this unhappy occurrence, not merely that I have apprehended evil resulting to myself, but lest the affair should be so construed as to attach blame to some individual connected with the Theological Seminary, which I should most deeply regret. Permit me, sir, in the fulness of my soul to say, that I cherish feelings of profound respect and affection for my "Alma Mater," for the worthy professors and students. During the three years in which it was my privilege to sustain an immediate connection with the Seminary, and the eight subsequent years, throughout the whole of which I have enjoyed the immediate counsel and support of the beloved Professors, and a delightful intercourse with the students, I have been received and treated in accordance with the interesting relations which we sustained to each other. I always feel, when at Princeton, that I am in the midst of fathers and brethren, in the holy and responsible work to which we are devoted. Considerations like these induced me to visit the Seminary at the close of your last term, during which my soul was truly refreshed.

In reflecting upon this unfortunate occurrence, it is manifest, that in attempting to degrade me, the rash youth has degraded himself in the eyes of all, whose opinions are worth regarding. I covet not the heart or head of him who in open day, in such a place, on such an occasion, in the presence of such an audience, and after such an address, could perpetrate an act so glaringly inconsistent, so degrading, so mean.

Dear sir, I am every mindful of the fact, that with the lives of those who have been connected with our useful Institution, is identified its honor, and the glory of our Divine Master. Without apprehension as to the result, I am entirely willing to submit to the decision of the public, whether or not, throughout my "public life," I have maintained a deportment in consistency with my relation to the church and to society. Comparatively speaking, it is of small moment to me, what I am called to encounter. Let me be persecuted and frowned upon, because of my identity with a class despised and oppressed, or for my feeble efforts to roll away the mountain of obstacles which retard their moral and intellectual elevation. Let every epithet which vile and unprincipled men can devise be heaped upon me;—let me be assailed by the hand of ruthless and even beardless violence,—and I will smile, and be happy, so long as I may stand forth to the view of Infinite Excellence, and of pure minded men, clad in the robes of moral worth; so long as I am enabled to, "maintain a conscience void of offence toward God and toward man."

May the Lord bless you and yours, and continue your health and strength and usefulness.

Yours, in the bonds of the Gospel,
THEODORE S. WRIGHT,
Pastor of the First Colored Presbyterian Church,
New York

William Whipper (1801–1885)

Although William Whipper's philosophy of nonviolence was criticized by other Black leaders, they invariably praised his stature and integrity. Samuel E. Cornish, the editor of *The Colored American*, sharply disagreed with Whipper's thought, but he expressed admiration for "the ingenuity, the tact and the talent, with which he maintained his positions and carried out his principles." Frederick Douglass, writing on another issue twelve years later in his abolitionist newspaper *The North Star,* December 14, 1849, likewise respected the man but rejected his argument: "He is a gentleman of acknowledged ability, a profound thinker, an eloquent and forcible writer, and withal an earnest friend of liberty. . . . With abstractions, and theories, he is at home, and in these he can easily find objections to measures which we deem of immediate and practical importance." An abstract theoretician William Whipper certainly was, but he was also practical minded enough to become one of the wealthiest Black men of his time. Indeed, twenty-four years after his *North Star* editorial, Douglass commended Whipper's pragmatic sagacity in an "Address Before the Tennessee Colored Agricultural and Mechanical Association."

William Whipper was born to a Black servant woman in the house of a Pennsylvania lumber dealer who was the child's father. He was educated by a tutor employed to teach his younger half-brother. When the white boy went to college at Swarthmore, he brought home his lessons for William to study during vacations. Makeshift though it was, this education was remarkably effective judging by the skill with which Whipper handled ideas in his published writings.

After apprenticeship as a joiner, Whipper went into the lumber business for himself in Columbia, Pennsylvania. In partnership with another Black man, Stephen Smith, Whipper prospered greatly, buying railroad boxcars and adding freightage service to Philadelphia to his lumber concern. He also dealt in real estate. So successful did he become that he was able to contribute a thousand dollars annually to the abolitionist cause from 1847 to 1860. During the Civil War, he gave five thousand dollars more to the Union. After the war, he was named an officer of the Freedmen's Savings Bank in Philadelphia, and he resided there and in New Brunswick, New Jersey, in his later years.

Whipper's reform activities embraced not only abolitionism, but a variety of other causes, including peace and temperance. He first came to public notice in the Black convention movement of the early 1830's, being the only man to attend every national convention from 1831 to 1835. In 1832 he joined with James Forten and Robert Purvis in writing an eleven-page petition to the Pennsylvania legislature protesting efforts to restrict Black migration to the state. In 1834 he established a grocery store near Bethel Church in Philadelphia that stocked only goods produced by free labor. He was perhaps the most important leader of the Moral Reform Society, which began to dominate the convention movement in 1835. Consisting mostly of Black Philadelphians, the Moral Reformers urged the universal elevation of all mankind. Beginning in September 1838, Whipper edited their organ, *The National Reformer,* which lasted two or three years. From the 1830's to the 1850's, he wrote thoughtful essays, speeches, and letters for a number of periodicals: *The Liberator, The Emancipator, The Colored American, The Demosthenian Shield, The National Anti-Slavery Standard, The North Star, Douglass' Monthly, The Pennsylvania Freeman, National Enquirer, The Anglo-African,* and probably others as well. After the war, he was a member of an eleven-man delegation led by Frederick Douglass that met with President Andrew Johnson to state the case for Black enfranchisement. Considering this record of activity, William Still in 1871 could confidently ask the rhetorical question: "Who, indeed, amongst those familiar with the history of public matters connected with the colored people of this country, has not heard of William Whipper?"

Not the least valuable of Whipper's activities was his service as an agent for the Underground Railroad. His station at Columbia was strategically located on the east bank of the Susquehanna River. It was "the great depot," he recalled, "where the fugitives from Virginia and Maryland first landed." In his large house at the end of the bridge over the river, he received hundreds, giving food and shelter to as many as seventeen at a time. Some were sent to Philadelphia in Smith and Whipper railroad cars; others went to Pittsburgh by boat; others proceeded north to Canada; still others stayed in Columbia. In the five years following the passage of the Fugitive Slave Act in 1850, however, the Black population of Columbia dropped from 943 to 487 as Canada came increasingly to seem the only safe refuge. One fugitive employed in a Smith and Whipper lumberyard was shot to death when he refused to surrender to a slavecatcher, and twice arson was attempted against the firm. Indeed, so difficult did life become that Whipper himself was planning as early as 1853 to emigrate to Canada, and he was preparing to do so in 1861 when the outbreak of the Civil War induced him to remain.

One of the most interesting aspects of Whipper's intellectual development was a movement away from the strong integrationism of his youth. Raised as he was in a white household and then prospering in a predominantly white town, he was reluctant to recognize his Black identity. Believing that "all moral principles are universal in their nature, and application: and that they embrace 'all men' without distinction," Whipper rejected all "complexional" labels. At the convention of 1835, he advocated dropping words like "colored" and "African" from the names of lodges, organizations, and churches. In a letter to the editors of *The Colored American,* July 15, 1837, he objected to the name of the paper. "Oppressed Americans" he thought a suitable designation for Black people. In 1840 he joined Robert Purvis in informing David Ruggles that they refused to attend any convention that was "exclusive in character," i.e., all Black. One of the chief benefits of the abolition movement he found to be its power "in checking their [Blacks'] evil dispositions and inculcating moral principles."

But the inexorable march of events during the late 1840's and the 1850's forced Whipper from his integrationist, Garrisonian position toward a more nationalistic posture. "In our onslaught upon what we term separate institutions," he wrote in 1855, "we too frequently lose sight of the fact that to our church, association and school we are at this hour chiefly indebted for whatever of preparation we have made for the great battle of today." A year later he was defending the right of Black men to emigrate to Canada, asserting that their success there constituted "a more practical anti-slavery work than they were capable of performing in the States." Soon afterwards, he was defending African settlement in opposition to James McCune Smith, the prominent Black physician from New York, and Julia Griffiths, the white English abolitionist. By introducing cotton culture to Africa, he pointed out to the latter, American free Blacks could compete with the American South for the great British market, thus weakening the slave economy. In 1861 Whipper was listed as one of twenty-one vice-presidents of the nationalistic African Civilization Society. Thereafter he wrote little, but his case is an instructive example of the difficulty faced by a Black intellectual in maintaining his belief in integration during a period of social crisis.

"An Address on Non-resistance to Offensive Aggression," reprinted here, appeared in four consecutive issues of *The Colored American,* September 9, 16, 23, and 30, 1837. In addition to his many contributions to periodicals, two of Whipper's orations were separately published: *An Address Delivered in Wesley Church . . . Before The Colored Reading Society of Philadelphia, for Mental Improvement* (n.d.) and *Eulogy on William Wilberforce . . .* (1833).

No satisfactory biographical study has been made, but facts may be gleaned from William Still, *The Underground Rail Road* (1872), which reprints a letter by Whipper; William Wells Brown, *The Rising Son* (1874); Vernon Loggins, *The Negro Author* (1931); Benjamin Quarles, "Letters From Negro Leaders to Gerrit Smith," *The Journal of Negro History,* XXVII (October 1942), 450–451; Quarles, *Black Abolitionists* (1969); *A Documentary History of the Negro People in the United States* (1951), edited by Herbert Aptheker; Howard H. Bell, *A Survey of the*

Negro Convention Movement, 1830–1861 (1969) and his edition of the *Minutes of the Proceedings of the National Negro Conventions, 1830–1864* (1969); and Louis C. Jones, "A Leader Ahead of His Times," *American Heritage,* XIV (June 1963), 58, 83.

An Address on Non-Resistance to Offensive Aggression

Resolved, That the practice of non-resistance to physical aggression, is not only consistent with reason, but the surest method of obtaining a speedy triumph of the principles of universal peace.

Mr. President,—The above resolution presupposes that if there were no God, to guide, and govern, the destinies of man on this planet, no Bible to light his path through the wilds of sin, darkness and error, and no religion to give him a glorious, and lasting consolation, while traversing the gloomy vale of despondency, and to light up his soul anew, with fresh influence, from the fountain of Divine grace,—that mankind might enjoy an exalted state of civilization, peace, and quietude, in their social, civil, and international relations, far beyond that which christians now enjoy, who profess to be guided, guarded and protected by the great Author of all good, and the doctrines of the Prince of Peace.

But, sir, while I am assuming the position, that the cause of peace amongst mankind, may be promoted without the scriptures, I would not, for a single moment, sanction the often made assertion, that the doctrines of the holy scripture justify war—for they are in my humble opinion its greatest enemy. And I further believe, that as soon as they become fully understood, and practically adopted, wars, and strifes will cease. I believe that every argument urged in favor of what is termed a "just and necessary war," or physical self defence, is at enmity with the letter, and spirit of the scriptures, and when they emanate from its professed advocates should be repudiated, as inimical to the principles they profess, and a reproach to christianity itself. I have said this much in favor of the influence of the scriptures, on the subject of peace. It is neither my intention, nor my province, under the present resolution, to give proofs for my belief by quotations from holy writ. That portion of the discussion, I shall leave to the minister of the *altar,* and the learned and biblical theologian. Though I may make a few incidental quotations hereafter, I shall now pass on for a few brief moments to the resolution under consideration.

The resolution asserts, that the practice of non-resistance to physical aggression is consistent with reason. A very distinguished man asserts, "that reason is that distinguishing characteristic that separates man from the brute creation," and that this power was bestowed upon him by his Maker, that he might be capable of subduing all subordinate intelligences to his will." It is this power when exerted in its full force, that enables him to conquer the animals of the forest, and which makes him lord of creation. There is a right, and a wrong method of reasoning. The latter is governed by our animal impulses, and wicked desires, without regard to the end to be attained. The former fixes its premises, in great fundamental, and unalterable truths—surveys the magnitude of the objects, and the difficulties to be surmounted, and calls to its aid the resources of enlightened wisdom, as a landmark by which to conduct its operations.

It is self evident, that when the greatest difficulties surround us, we should summon our noblest powers. "Man is a being formed for action as well as contemplation;" "For this purpose there are interwoven in his constitution, powers, instincts, feelings and affections, which have a reference to his improvement in virtue, and which excite him to promote the happiness of others." When we behold them by their nobel sentiments, exhibiting sublime virtues and performing illustrious actions, we ascribe the same to the goodness of their hearts, their great reasoning powers and intellectual abilities. For were it not for these high human endowments, we should never behold men in seasons of calamity, displaying tranquillity and fortitude in the midst of difficulties and dangers, enduring poverty and distress with a noble heroism, suffering injuries and affronts with patience and serenity— stifling resentment when they have it in their power to inflict vengeance—displaying kindness and generosity towards enemies and slanderers— submitting to pain and disgrace in order to promote the prosperity of their friends and relatives, or the great interests of the human race.

Such acts may be considered by persons of influence and rank as the offspring of pusillanimity, because they themselves are either incapable of conceiving the purity of the motives from which they emanate, or are too deeply engulphed in the ruder passions of our nature, to allow them to bestow a just tribute to the efforts of enlightened reason.

It is happy for us to contemplate, that every age, both of the pagan and the christian world, has been blessed, that they always have fastened their attention on the noblest gifts of our nature, and that they now still shine as ornaments to the human race, connecting the interests of one generation with that of another. Rollin, in speaking of Aristides the Just, says "that an extraordinary greatness of soul made him superior to every passion. Interest, pleasure, ambition, resentment and jealousy were extinguished in him by the love of virtue and his country," and just in proportion as we cultivate our intellectual faculties, we shall strengthen our reasoning powers, and be prepared to become his imitators.

Our country and the world have become the munificent patron of many powerful, existing evils, that have spread their devastating influence over the best interests of the human race. One of which is the adopting of the savage custom of wars, and fighting as a redress for grievances, instead of some means more consistent with reason and civilization.

The great law of love forbids our doing aught against the interests of our fellow men. It is altogether inconsistent with reason and common sense, for persons when they deem themselves insulted, by the vulgar aspersions of others, to maltreat their bodies for the acts of their minds. Yet how frequently do we observe those that are blest by nature and education, (and if they would but aspire to acts that bear a parallel to

their dignified minds, they would shine as illustrious stars, in the created throngs) that degrade themselves by practising this barbarous custom, suited only to tyrants—because in this they may be justly ranked with the untutored savages or the animals of the forest, that are impelled only by instinct.

Another fatal error arises from the belief that the only method of maintaining peace, is always to be ready for war. The spirit of war can never be destroyed by all the butcheries and persecutions the human mind can invent. The history of all the "bloody tragedies," by which the earth has been drenched by human blood, cannot be justified in the conclusion, for it is the spirit of conquest that feeds it—Thomas Dick, after collecting the general statistics of those that have perished by the all desolating pestilence of war, says "it will not be overrating the destruction of human life, if we affirm that one tenth of the human race has been destroyed by the ravages of war,—and if this estimate be admitted, it will follow that more than fourteen thousand millions of beings have been slaughtered in war since the beginning of the world, which is about eighteen times the number of its present inhabitants." This calculation proceeds from a geographical estimate, "that since the Mosaic creation one hundred and forty-five thousand millions of beings have existed."

But, sir, it is not my intention to give a dissertation on the subject of national wars, although it appropriately belongs to my subject. I decline it only for the simple reason, that it would be inapplicable to us as a people, while we may be more profitably employed in inveighing against the same evil as practised by ourselves, although it exists under another form, but equally obnoxious to the principles of reason and christianity. My reason for referring to national wars, was to exhibit by plain demonstration, that the war principle, which is the production of human passions, has never been, nor can ever be, conquered by its own elements.—Hence, if we ever expect the word of prophecy to be fulfilled— "when the swords shall be turned into plough shares, and the spears into pruning hooks, and that the nations of the earth shall learn war no more," we must seek the destruction of the principle that animates, quickens, and feeds it, by the elevation of another more powerful, and omnipotent, and proservative; or mankind will continue, age after age, to march on in their mad career, until the mighty current of time will doubtless sweep thousands of millions more into endless perdition, beyond the reach of mercy, and the hope of future bliss. Thus the very bones, sinews, muscles, and immortal mind, that God, in his infinite mercy has bestowed on man, that he might work out his own glory, and extend the principles of "Righteousness, justice, peace on earth, and good will to their fellow men," are constantly employed in protracting the period when the glorious mellenium shall illumine our world, "and righteousness cover the earth as the water of the great deep."

Now let us solemnly ask ourselves, Is it reasonable, that for the real or supposed injuries that have been inflicted on mankind from the beginning to the present day, that the attempted redress of the same should have cost so much misery, pain, sweat, blood, and tears, and treasure? Most certainly not; since the very means used has measurably entailed the evil a thousand fold, on coming generations. If man's superiority over the brute creation consists only in his reasoning powers and rationality of mind, his various methods of practising violence towards his fellow creatures, has in many cases placed him on a level with, and sometimes below many species of the quadruped race. We search in vain amongst the animal race to find a parallell, for their cruelties to each other on their own species, that is faithfully recorded in the history of wars and bloodshed, that have devoured empires, desolated kingdoms, overthrown governments, and well nigh aimed at the total annihilation of the human race. There are many species of animals that are so amiable in their disposition to each other, that they might well be considered an eminent pattern for mankind in their present rude condition. The sheep, the ox, the horse, and many other animals exist in a state of comparative quietude, both among themselves, and the other races of animals when compared with man. And if it were possible for them to know the will of their Author, and enjoy that communion with the Creator of all worlds, all men and all animals, they might justly be entitled to a distinction above all other species of creation, that had made greater departures from the will of the divine government.

It is evidently necessary that man should at all times bear in mind his origin and his end. That it is not because he was born a ruler, and superior to all other orders of creation, that he continually

reigns above them—it is because he has made a right use of the powers that God has given him of rising in the scale of existence. The rich bequest of Heaven to man, was a natural body, a reasonable soul, and an immortal mind. With these he is rendered capable through the wisdom of Providence, of ascending to the throne of angels, or descending to the abyss of devils. Hence there seems to be a relation between man and the animal creation, that subsists, neither in their origin nor their end, but satisfactorily exhibits that man may exist in a state of purity, as far *superior* to theirs, as future happiness is to this world, and as far *inferior,* as we are distant from future misery.

There is scarcely a single fact more worthy of indelible record, than the utter inefficiency of human punishments, to cure human evils. The history of wars exhibits a hopeless, as well as a fatal lesson, to all such enterprises. All the associated powers of human governments, have been placed in requisition to quell and subdue the spirit of passion; without improving the condition of the human family. Human bodies have been lacerated with whips and scourges—prisons and penitentiaries have been erected for the immolation of human victims—the gibbet and halter have performed their office—while the increase of crime has kept pace with the genius of punishment, and the whole march of mind seems to have been employed in evading penal enactments, and inventing new methods of destroying the blessings of the social state, not recognized by human codes.

If mankind ever expect to enjoy a state of peace and quietude, they must at all times be ready to sacrifice on the altar of principle, the rude passions that animate them. This they can only perform by exerting their reasoning powers. If there be those that desire to overlook the offences of others, and rise above those inflictions that are the offspring of passion, they must seek for protection in something *higher* than human power. They must place their faith in Him who is able to protect them from danger, or they will soon fall a prey to the wicked artifices of their wicked enemies.

Human passion is the hallucination of a distempered mind. It renders the subject of it like a ship upon the ocean, without ballast, or cargo, always in danger of being wrecked by every breeze. Phrenologically speaking, a mind that is subject to the fluctuating whims of passion, is without the organ of order, "which is nature's first law." Our reasoning powers ought to be the helm that should guide us through the shoals and quicksands of life.

I am aware that there are those who consider the non-resistance wholly impracticable. But I trust that but few such can be found, that have adopted the injunction of the Messiah for their guide and future hope, for he commands us to "love our enemies, bless them that curse you, pray for them that despitefully use you, and persecute you." These words were peculiarly applicable at the period they were uttered, and had a direct reference to the wars and strifes that then convulsed the world, and they are equally applicable at this moment. If the christian church had at her beginning made herself the enemy of war, the evil would doubtless have been abolished throughout christendom. The christians of the present day do not seem to regard the principles of peace as binding, or they are unwilling to become subject to the Divine government. Human governments then, as well as now, were too feeble to stay the ravages of passion and crime, and hence there was an evident necessity for the imperious command, "Whomsoever shall smite thee on thy right cheek, turn unto him the other also."

And now, Mr. President, I rest my argument on the ground, that whatever is *scriptural* is *right,* and that whatever is right, is reasonable, and from this invulnerable position I mean not to stray, for the sake of any expediency whatever. The doctrine evidently taught by the scriptural quotation, evidently instructs us that resistance to physical aggression is wholly unnecessary as well as unrighteous, and subjects the transgressor to the penalty due from a wilful departure from the moral and Divine law. Therefore every act of disobedience to the commands of christian duty, in relation to our fellow men, may fairly be deemed unreasonable, as it is at enmity with our true interests and the welfare of human society. We are further instructed to turn away from the evil *one,* rather than waste our strength, influence and passions, in a conflict that must in the end prove very injurious to both.

But some one perhaps is ready to raise an objection against this method of brooking the insults of others; and believes it right to refer to the maxim "that self defence is the first law of nature." I will readily agree that it is the unbounded duty of every individual to defend himself against both the vulgar and false aspersions of a wicked world. But then I contend that his weapons should be his reasoning powers. That since a kind Providence has bestowed on him the power of speech, and the ability to reason, he degrades his Creator by engulphing himself in the turmoils of passion, and physical conflict. A mode of warfare practised by barbarous tribes in their native forests, and suited only to those animals that are alone endowed with the powers of instinct. Nor is it possible to suppose that men can pursue such a course, without first parting with their reason. We often see men, while under the reigning influence of passion, as fit subjects for the lunatic asylum, as any that are confined in the lunatic asylum on account of insanity.

In every possible and impartial view we take of the subject, we find that physical conflict militates against the interest of the parties in collision. If I, in conflict with mine enemy, overcome him by my superior physical powers, or my skill in battle, I neither wholly subdue him, or convince him of the justice of my cause. His spirit becomes still more enraged, and he will seek retaliation and conquest on some future occasion, that may seem to him more propitious. If I intimidate him I have made him a slave, while I reign a despot; and our relation will continue unnatural, as well as dangerous to each other, until our friendship has become fully restored. And what has been gained by this barbarous method of warfare, when both parties become losers thereby? Yet this single case illustrates the value of all personal conflicts.

But let us pursue this subject in a more dignified view, I mean as it respects the moral and Divine government. Is it possible that any christian man or woman, that will flog and maltreat their fellow beings, can be in *earnest,* when they with apparent devotion, ask their heavenly Father to "forgive their trespass as they forgive others?" Surely they must be asking God to punish them—or when they say "lead us not into temptation, but deliver us from evil," do they mean that they should run headlong into both, with all their infuriated madness? Certainly not. Who would not be more willing to apply to them insincerity of motive, and that they knew not what they were doing, rather than suppose that intelligent minds would be capable of such gross inconsistency. Would it not prove infinitely better in times of trials and difficulties, to leave the temper, and temptation behind, and pursue our course onward? But says the objector, there will be no safety nor security in this method, from the insults of the vulgar, and the brutal attacks of the assassin. I am inclined to believe to the contrary, and will be borne out in that belief by the evidences of those that have pursued this christian course of conduct.

A writer under the signature of Philopacificus, while "taking a solemn view of the custom of war," says, "There are two sets of professed christians in this country, which, as sects, are peculiar in their opinions respecting the lawfulness of war, and the right of repelling injury by violence." These are the Quakers and Shakers. They are remarkably pacific. Now we ask, does it appear from experience, that their forbearing spirit brings on them a greater portion of injury and insults, than what is experienced by people of other sects? Is not the reverse of this true in fact? There may indeed be some such instances of gross depravity as a person taking advantage of their pacific character, to do them an injury with the hope of impunity. But in general it is believed their pacific principles and spirit command the esteem, even of the vicious, and operate as a shield from insult and abuse.

The question may be brought home to every society. How seldom do children of a mild and forbearing temper experience insults or injury, compared with the waspish, who will sting if they are touched? The same inquiry may be made in respect to persons of these opposite descriptions of every age, and in every situation of life, and the result will prove favorable to the point in question.

When William Penn took the government of Pennsylvania, he distinctly avowed to the Indians, his forbearing and pacific principles, and his benevolent wishes for uninterrupted peace with them. On these principles the government was administered while it remained in the hands of the Quakers. This was an illustrious example of government on religious principles, worthy of imitation by all the nations of the earth.

I am happy to state, that there are various incidents related by travellers, both among the native Africans and Indians, where lives have been saved by the presentation of a pacific attitude, when they would have otherwise fallen a prey to savage barbarity.

It has been my purpose to exhibit reason as a great safeguard, at all times capable of dethroning passion and alleviating our condition in periods of the greatest trouble and difficulty, and of being a powerful handmaid in achieving a triumph of the principles of universal peace. I have also thus far treated the subject as a grand fundamental principle, universal in its nature, and binding alike on every member of the human family. But if there be a single class of people in these United States, on which these duties are more imperative and binding, than another, that class is the colored population of this country, both free and enslaved. Situated as we are, among a people that recognize the lawfulness of slavery, and more of whom sympathize with the oppressor than the oppressed, it requites us to pursue our course calmly onward, with much self-denial, patience and perseverance.

We must be prepared at all times, to meet the scoffs and scorns of the vulgar and indecent— the contemptible frowns of haughty tyrants, and the blighting mildew of a popular and sinful prejudice. If amidst these difficulties we can but possess our souls in patience, we shall finally triumph over our enemies. But among the various duties that devolve on us, not the least is that which relates to ourselves. We must learn on all occasions to rebuke the spirit of violence, both in sentiment and practice. God has said, "vengeance is mine, and I will repay it." The laws of the land guarantee the protection of our persons from personal violence, and whoever for any cause, inflicts a single blow on a fellow being, violates the laws of God and of his country, and has no just claim to being regarded as a christian or a good citizen.

As a people we have suffered much from the pestilential influence of mob violence, that has spread its devastating influence over our country. And it is to me no matter of astonishment that they continue to exist. They do but put in practice a common every day theory that pervades every neighborhood, and almost every family, viz: That it is right, under certain circumstances, to violate all law, both civil and national, and abuse, kick and cuff your fellow man, when they deem that he has offended or insulted the community in which he resides.

Whenever the passions of individuals rise above all laws, human and divine, then they are in the first stages of anarchy, and then every act prosecuted under the influence of this spirit, necessarily extends itself beyond the boundary of our laws. The act of the multitude is carried out on the principle of combination, which is the grand lever by which machinery as well as man is impelled in this fruitful age. There is no difference in principle between the acts of a few individuals, and those of a thousand, while actuated by the spirit of passion, dethroning reason, the laws of our country and the liberty of man. Hence every individual that either aids or abets an act of personal violence towards the humblest individual, is guilty of sustaining the detestible practice of mobocratic violence. Yet such is the general spirit that pervades our common country, and receives its sanction from places of high honor, and trust, that it is patriotism to disregard the laws. It is but reasonable to suppose that individuals, guided by like views and motives, will on some occasions concentrate their power, and carry on their operations on a large scale. Unless the hearts and reasoning powers of man become improved, it is impossible for the most sagacious mind to augur the consequences. The spirit of passion has become so implanted in human bosoms, that the laws of our country give countenance to the same, by exhibiting lenity for those who are under its influence.

This is doubtless a great error in legislation, because it not only pre-supposes the irrationality of man, but gives him a plea of innocence, in behalf of his idiotism. The only sure method of conquering these evils, is to commend a reform in ourselves, and then the spirit of passion will soon be destroyed in individuals, and communities, and governments, and then the ground work will be fully laid for a speedy triumph of the principles of universal peace.

The love of power is one of the greatest human infirmities, and with it comes the usurping influence of despotism, the mother of slavery. Show me any country or people where despotism reigns triumphant, and I will exhibit to your view the spirit of slavery, whether the same be incorporated in the government or not. It is this demon-like spirit of passion that sends forth its poignant influence over professedly civilized nations, as well as the more barbarous tribes. Its effect on human interest is the same, whether it emanates from the subjugator of Poland—the throne of Britain—the torrid zone of the South, or the genial clime of Pennsylvania; from the white, the red, or the black man—whether he be of European or African descent—or the native Indian that resides in the wilds of the forest, their combined action is at war with the principles of peace, and the liberty of the world.

How different is the exercise of this love of power, when exercised by man, or enforced by human governments, to the exercise of Him who holds all "power over the heavens, earth, and seas, and all that in them is." With God, all is order—with man, all confusion. The planets perform their annual revolutions—the tides ebb and flow—the seas obey His command—the whole government of universal worlds are sustained by His wisdom and power—each invariably performing the course marked out by their great Author, because they are impelled by His love. But with man, governments are impelled by the law of force; hence despotism becomes an ingredient in all human governments.

The power of reason is the noblest gift of Heaven to man, because it assimilates man to his Maker. And were he to improve his mind by cultivating his reasoning powers, his acts of life would bear the impress of the Deity, indelibly stamped upon them. If human governments bore any direct resemblance to the government of God, they would be mild in their operation, and the principles of universal peace would become implanted in every mind. Wars, fighting, and strifes would cease—there would be a signal triumph of truth over error—the principles of peace, justice, righteousness, and universal love would guide and direct mankind onward in that sublime path marked out by the great Prince of Peace.

And now my friends, let us cease to be guided by the influence of a wild and beguiling passion—the wicked and foolish fantasies of pride, folly and lustful ambition—the alluring and detestable examples of despotism and governments—the sickly sensibility of those who from false notions of honor, attempt to promote the ends of justice, by placing "righteousness under their feet," and are at all times ready to imbue their hands in a fellow creature's blood, for the purpose of satisfying their voracious appetites for crime, murder and revenge. I say from them let us turn away, for a terrible retaliation must shortly await them, even in this life. The moral power of this nation and the world is fast wakening from the sleep of ages, and wielding a swift besom, that will sweep from the face of the earth error and iniquity with the power of a whirlwind. But a few years ago and duelling was considered necessary to personal honor, and the professional christian, or the most upright citizen might barter away the lives and happiness of a nation with his guilty traffic in ardent spirits, with impunity. But now a regenerated public sentiment not only repudiates their conduct, but consigns them with "body and soul murderers." Though the right to be free has been deemed inalienable by this nation, from a period antecedent to the declaration of American Independence, yet a mental fog hovered over this nation on the subject of slavery that had well nigh sealed her doom, were it not that in the Providence of God a few noble spirits arose in the might of moral power to her rescue. They girded on the power of truth, for their shield, and the principles of peace for their buckler and thus boldly pierced through the incrustations of a false and fatal philosophy, and from the *incision,* sprang forth the light of glorious liberty, disseminating its delectable rays over the dark chasms of slavery, and lighting up the vision of a ruined world. And the effect has been to awaken the nation to her duty with regard to the rights of man—to render slaveholders despicable and guilty of robbery and murder—and in many places, those that profess christianity have been unchurched, denied the privilege of christian fellowship. And the same moral power is now awakening in the cause of peace, and will bring disgrace and dishonor on all who engage in wars and fighting.[1]

．　．　．

The period is fast approaching when the church, as at present constituted, must undergo one of the severest contests she has met with since her foundation, because in so many cases she has refused to sustain her own principles. The moral warfare that is now commenced will not cease if the issue should be a dissolution of both church and state. The time has already come when there are those who believe that intemperance, slavery, war and fighting are sinful, and it will soon arrive when those who practice either will have their rights to enjoy christian fellowship questioned.

And now, Mr. President, I shall give a few practical illustrations, and then I shall have done. It appears by history that there have been many faithful advocates of peace since the apostolic age, but none have ever given a more powerful impetus to the cause of peace, than the modern abolitionists. They have been beaten and stoned, mobbed and persecuted from city to city, and

never returned evil for evil, but submissively, as a sheep brought before the shearer, have they endured scoffings and scourges for the cause's sake, while they prayed for their persecuters. And how miraculously they have been preserved in the midst of a thousand dangers from without and within. Up to the present moment not the life of a single individual has been sacrificed on the altar of popular fury. Had they have set out in this glorious undertaking of freeing 2,500,000 human beings, with the war cry of "liberty or death," they would have been long since demolished, or a civil war would have ensued; thus would have dyed the national soil with human blood. And now let me ask you, was not their method of attacking the system of human slavery the most reasonable? And would not their policy have been correct, even if we were to lay aside their christian motives? Their weapons were reason and moral truth, and on them they desired to stand or fall, and so it will be in all causes that are sustained from just and christian principles, they will ultimately triumph. Now let us suppose for a single moment what would have been our case, if they had started on the principle, that "resistance to tyrants is obedience to God?"— what would have been our condition, together with that of the slave population? Why, we should have doubtless perished by the sword, or been praying for the destruction of our enemies, and probably engaged in the same bloody warfare.

And now we are indebted to the modern abolitionists more than to any other class of men for the instructions we have received from the dissemination of their principles, or we would not at this moment be associated here to advocate the cause of moral reform—of temperance, education, peace and universal liberty. Therefore let us, like them, obliterate from our minds the idea of revenge, and from our hearts all wicked intentions towards each other and the world, and we shall be able through the blessing of Almighty God, to do much to establish the principles of universal peace. Let us not think the world has no regard for our efforts—they are looking forward to them with intense interest and anxiety. The enemies of the abolitionists are exhibiting a regard for the power of their principles that they are unwilling to acknowledge although it is every where known over the country, that abolitionists "will not fight," yet they distrust their own strength so much, that they frequently muster a whole neighborhood of from

---

[1] [Two paragraphs are omitted here which repeat, with some slight verbal alterations, paragraphs thirty-one through thirty-three above.—Editors' note.]

50 to 300 men, with sticks, stones, rotten eggs and bowie knives, to mob and beat a single individual, probably in his "teens," whose heart's law is non-resistance. There is another way in which they do us honor—they admit the right of all people to fight for their liberty, but colored people and abolitionists—plainly inferring that they are too good for the performance of such unchristian acts—and lastly, while we endeavor to control our own passions and keep them in subjection, let us be mindful of the weakness of others; and for acts of wickedness committed against us, let us reciprocate in the spirit of kindness. If they continue their injustice towards us, let us always decide that their reasoning powers are defective, and that it is with men as the laws of mechanics—large bodies move slowly, while smaller ones are easily propelled with swift velocity. In every case of passion that presents itself, the subject is one of pity rather then derision, and in his cooler moments let us earnestly advise him to improve his understanding, by cultivating his intellectual powers, and thus exhibit his close alliance with God, who is the author of all wisdom, peace, justice, righteousness and truth. And in conclusion, let it always be our aim to live in a spirit of unity with each other, supporting one common cause, by spreading our influence for the good of mankind; with the hope that the period will ultimately arrive when the principles of universal peace will triumph throughout the world.

Robert Purvis (1810–1898)

Perhaps the most influential of that stalwart group of Black leaders in nineteenth-century Philadelphia, Robert Purvis was born in Charleston, South Carolina, on August 4, 1810, the son of a wealthy Englishman of antislavery sentiments and a free woman of color whose mother was a Moor kidnapped at the age of twelve from her native Morocco in about 1766, sold into slavery, emancipated at the age of nineteen, and finally married to a German Jew. With this lineage Purvis was light enough to pass easily, but he always proudly identified himself as a Black man.

When the Purvis family arrived in Philadelphia in 1819, the father established a school for Black children. Here his three sons were educated, and Robert later attended the then new Amherst College. Around 1830 Purvis met Benjamin Lundy and William Lloyd Garrison, whose abolitionist principles fired his young imagination. Hardly had he attained his majority before he began his long career of leadership in the struggle for civil rights and against slavery. His early financial independence, made possible by a large legacy from his father, allowed him to concentrate his time and energy on Black causes.

One of his earliest goals was expanded educational opportunity for Black people. In 1831 he supported the projected manual labor college for Black youth at New Haven, Connecticut, but the plan was not realized. A year and a half later, he led in the organization of the Philadelphia Library Company of Colored Persons, dedicated to "promoting among our rising youth, a proper cultivation for literary pursuits and the improvement of the faculties and powers of their minds." Such endeavors were necessary because of the exclusion of Black children from white educational institutions. When in 1853 his own children suffered this treatment in Byberry, near Philadelphia, where Purvis had lived for a decade as one of the town's wealthiest citizens, he angrily refused to pay his school tax, calling it an encroachment on his rights "as contemptibly mean as it is infamously despotic."

The white assault on Black civil rights was made in other areas as well. Retreating from its early racial liberalism, the Commonwealth of Pennsylvania in 1831 was considering legislation to restrict Black migration into the state, with especially severe measures directed against fugitive slaves. Together with James Forten—the venerable Black sailmaker and civic leader soon to become his father-in-law—and William Whipper of Columbia, Purvis presented a memorial to the Pennsylvania legislature protesting the proposals. Six years later, he drafted the *Appeal of Forty Thousand Citizens, Threatened with Disfranchisement, to the People of Pennsylvania,* reprinted here, in a losing attempt to prevent ratification of a new state constitution disfranchising Black men. Purvis suffered not only legislative repression but personal harassment, his wealth and status being no buffer against racism. As a country gentleman, he was fond of raising fine poultry. After winning the first prize of the Philadelphia Chicken Fanciers for three consecutive years, he was disbarred from further competition in 1853!

In addition to his work as a civil rights advocate, Purvis was a pioneer in the antislavery cause. In the early 1830's he was active both in Black groups like the convention movement and the Moral Reform Society and in such interracial efforts as the American Anti-Slavery Society, which he helped to found in December 1833. In 1837 he was among the organizers of the Pennsylvania Anti-Slavery Society, which he later served as president from 1845 to 1850. By deed and purse as well as word, Purvis advanced the abolitionist struggle. An early and major figure in the Underground Railroad, he engineered one of the most celebrated early fugitive slave rescues, that of Basil Dorsey in 1836. As president of the Philadelphia Vigilance Committee from 1838 to 1844 and on his own initiative thereafter, he aided hundreds of fugitives. His home in Byberry was a station on the Underground Railroad with a specially designed room accessible only by a concealed trap door. "To the cause of the slave's freedom," his friend and coworker William Still recalled, "he gave with all his heart his money, his time, his talents."

As the crisis deepened in the 1850's, Purvis intensified his attack on the state and federal governments. Long a thoroughgoing Garrisonian, he considered the Constitution a proslavery document. As a Black Philadelphian who had seen his efforts to protect Black rights defeated, he had good evidence for saying after the riot of 1849 that "No man is safe—his life—his property—and all that he holds dear, are in the hands of a mob, which may come upon him at any moment—at midnight or mid-day, and deprive him of his all." Challenging the power of the United States government to enforce its Fugitive Slave Law, he swore on October 17, 1850, that "should any wretch enter my dwelling, any pale-faced spectre among ye, to execute this law on me or mine, I'll seek his life, I'll shed his blood." After the Dred Scott decision, Purvis thought that "the only duty the colored man owes to [the] Constitution . . . is to denounce and repudiate it, and to do what he can by all proper means to bring it into contempt." This position was elaborated in two important speeches delivered to annual meetings of the American Anti-Slavery Society in 1857 and 1860. It was implicit also in his support of John Brown.

Purvis' distrust of the normal two-party political process—working within the system—extended into the postwar period. Like Frederick Douglass and John Mercer Langston, he turned down Andrew Johnson's offer of the position of Commissioner of the Freedmen's Bureau because he rightfully suspected the President's motives. In 1874 he supported a People's Party candidate for mayor of Philadelphia, and in 1883, disgusted with the Republicans, he participated in a political movement of Black Independents in Pennsylvania. In a speech of May 8, 1860, he had prophesied that "Slavery will be abolished in this land, and with it, that twin relic of barbarism, prejudice against color." His efforts constituted a major contribution to the ending of chattel slavery, but even his more than six decades of activity did not finally avail to extirpate "that twin relic of barbarism."

A scarce pamphlet entitled *Letters and Speeches* (n.d.) collects some of Purvis' contributions. Two of his eulogies are *A Tribute to the Memory of Thomas Shipley, The Philanthropist* (1836) and "Eulogy on the Life and Character of James Forten" (delivered in 1842 and published in abridged form in 1855 in William C. Nell's *The Colored Patriots of the American Revolution*). A number of his letters, speeches, and petitions are easily available in *The Mind of the Negro as Reflected in Letters Written During the Crisis 1800–1860* (1926), edited by Carter G. Woodson, and *A Documentary History of the Negro People in the United States* (1951), edited by Herbert Aptheker. One of his last literary tasks was coediting R. C. Smedley's posthumous *History of the Underground Railroad in Chester and the Neighboring Counties of Pennsylvania* (1883), to which he contributed a long autobiographical letter including a full account of the Dorsey rescue.

Early notices of Purvis' life and career may be found in William Wells Brown, *The Black Man* (1863) and *The Rising Son* (1874); Samuel J. May, *Some Recollections of Our Antislavery Conflict* (1869); and William Still, *The Underground Rail Road* (1872). For further details, see Wilbur H. Siebert, *The Underground Railroad from Slavery to Freedom* (1898); Vernon Loggins, *The Negro Author* (1931); Leon F. Litwack, *North of Slavery* (1961); and, especially, Benjamin Quarles, *Black Abolitionists* (1969).

Appeal of Forty Thousand Citizens, Threatened with Disfranchisement, to the People of Pennsylvania

FELLOW CITIZENS:—We appeal to you from the decision of the "Reform Convention," which has stripped us of a right peaceably enjoyed during forty-seven years under the Constitution of this commonwealth. We honor Pennsylvania and her noble institutions too much to part with our birthright, as her free citizens, without a struggle. To all her citizens the right of suffrage is valuable in proportion as she is free; but surely there are none who can so ill afford to spare it as ourselves.

Was it the intention of the people of this commonwealth that the Convention to which the Constitution was committed for revision and amendment, should tear up and cast away its first principles? Was it made the business of the Convention to deny "that all men are born equally free," by making political rights depend upon the skin in which a man is born? or to divide what our fathers bled to unite, to wit, TAXATION and REPRESENTATION? We will not allow ourselves for one moment to suppose, that the majority of the people of Pennsylvania are not too respectful of the rights and too liberal towards the feelings of others, as well as too much enlightened to their own interests, to deprive of the right of suffrage a single individual who may safely be trusted with it. And we cannot believe that you have found among those who bear the burdens of taxation any who have proved, by their abuse of the right, that it is not safe in their hands. This is a question, fellow citizens, in which we plead *your* cause as well as our own. It is the safeguard of the strongest that he lives under a government which is obliged to respect the voice of the weakest. When you have taken from an individual his right to vote, you have made the government, in regard to him, a mere despotism; and you have taken a step towards making it a despotism to all.—To your women and children, their inability to vote at the polls may be no evil, because they are united by consanguinity and affection with those who can do it. To foreigners and paupers the want of the right may be tolerable, because a little time or labor will make it theirs. They are candidates for the privilege, and hence substantially enjoy its benefits. But when a distinct class of the community, already sufficiently the objects of prejudice, are wholly, and for ever, disfranchised and excluded, to the remotest posterity, from the possibility of a voice in regard to the laws under which they are to live—it is the same thing as if their abode were transferred to the dominions of the Russian Autocrat, or of the Grand Turk. They have lost their check upon oppression, their wherewith to buy friends, their panoply of manhood; in short, they are thrown upon the mercy of a despotic majority. Like every other despot, this despot majority, will believe in the mildness of its own sway; but who will the more willingly submit to it for that?

To us our right under the Constitution has been more precious, and our deprivation of it will be the more grievous, because our expatriation has come to be a darling project with many of our fellow citizens. Our abhorrence of a scheme which comes to us in the guise of Christian benevolence, and asks us to suffer ourselves to be transplanted to a distant and barbarous land, *because we are a "nuisance" in this,* is not more deep and thorough than it is reasonable. We love our native country, much as it has wronged us; and in the peaceable exercise of our inalienable rights, we will cling to it. The immortal Franklin, and his fellow laborers in the cause of humanity, have bound us to our homes here with chains of gratitude. We are PENNSYLVANIANS, and we hope to see the day when Pennsylvania will have reason to be proud of us, as we believe she has now none to be ashamed. Will you starve our patriotism? Will you cast our hearts out of the treasury of the commonwealth? Do you count our enmity better than our friendship?

Fellow citizens, we entreat you, in the name of fair dealing, to look again at the just and noble charter of Pennsylvania freedom, which you are asked to narrow down to the lines of caste and color. The Constitution reads as follows:—

"*Art.* 3, §1. In elections by the citizens, every freeman of the age of twenty-one years, having resided in the State two years next before the election, and within that time paid a State or county tax, which shall have been assessed at least six months before the election, shall enjoy the rights of an elector," &c.

This clause guaranties the right of suffrage to us as fully as to any of our fellow citizens whatsoever, for

1. Such was the intention of the framers. In the original draft, reported by a committee of nine, the word "WHITE" stood before "FREEMAN." On motion of ALBERT GALLATIN it was stricken out, for the express purpose of including colored citizens within the pale of the elective franchise. (See *Minutes of the Convention, 1790.*)

2. We are CITIZENS. This, we believe, would never have been denied, had it not been for the scheme of expatriation to which we have already referred. But as our citizenship has been doubted by some who are not altogether unfriendly to us, we beg leave to submit some proofs, which we think you will not hastily set aside.

We were regarded as *citizens* by those who drew up the articles of confederation between the States, in 1778. The fourth of the said articles contains the following language:—"The free inhabitants of each of these States, paupers, vagabonds, and fugitives from justice excepted, shall be entitled to all privileges and immunities of free *citizens* in the several States." That we were not excluded under the phrase "paupers, vagabonds, and fugitives from justice," any more than our white countrymen, is plain from the debates that preceded the adoption of the article. For, on the 25th of June, 1778, "the delegates from South Carolina moved the following amendment *in behalf of their State.* In article fourth, between the words *free* inhabitants, insert *white.* Decided in the negative; ayes, two States; nays, eight States; one State divided." Such was the solemn decision of the revolutionary Congress, concurred in by the entire delegation from our own commonwealth. On the adoption of the present Constitution of the United States no change was made as to the rights of citizenship. This is explicitly proved by the Journal of Congress. Take, for example, the following resolution passed in the House of Representatives, Dec. 21, 1803:

On motion, *Resolved,* That the Committee appointed to enquire and report whether any further provisions are necessary for the more effectual protection of American seamen, do enquire into the expediency of granting protections to such American seamen, *citizens of the United States,* as *are free persons of color,* and that they report by bill, or otherwise.

Journ. H. Rep., 1st Sess., 8th Cong., p. 224.

Proofs might be multiplied. In almost every State we have been spoken of, either expressly or by implication, as *citizens.* In the very year before the adoption of the present Constitution, 1789, the "Pennsylvania Society for Promoting the Abolition of Slavery, &c.," put forth an address, signed by "BENJAMIN FRANKLIN, *President,*" in which they stated one of their objects to be, "to *qualify* those who have been restored to freedom, for the exercise and enjoyment of CIVIL LIBERTY." The Convention of 1790, by striking out the word "WHITE," fixed the same standard of *qualification* for all; and, in fact, granted and guarantied "civil liberty" to all who possessed that qualification. Are we now to be told, that the Convention did not intend to include colored men, and that BENJAMIN FRANKLIN did not know what he was about, forasmuch as it was impossible for a colored man to become a citizen of the commonwealth?

It may here be objected to us, that in point of fact we have lost by the recent decision of the Supreme Court, in the case of *Fogg* vs. *Hobbs,* whatever claim to the right of suffrage we may have had under the Constitution of 1790; and hence have no reason to oppose the amended Constitution. Not so. We hold our rights under the present Constitution none the cheaper for that decision. The section already cited gives us all that we ask—all that we can conceive it in the power of language to convey. Reject, fellow citizens, the partial, disfranchising Constitution offered you by the Reform Convention, and we shall confidently expect that the Supreme Court will do us the justice and itself the honor to retract its decision. Should it not, our appeal will still be open to the conscience and common sense of the people, who through their chief magistrate and a majority of two-thirds of both branches of the Legislature may make way to the bench of the Supreme Court, for expounders of the Constitution who will not do violence to its most sacred and fundamental principles.

We cannot forbear here to refer you to some points in the published opinion of the Court as delivered by Chief Justice Gibson, which we believe will go far to strip it of the weight and authority ordinarily conceded to the decision of the highest tribunal (save the elections) of this commonwealth.

1. The Court relies much on a decision *said to have been had* "ABOUT" forty-three years ago, the claim of which to a place in the repository of the Pennsylvania law is thus set forth by the Court itself:—

> About the year 1795, as I have it from James Gibson, Esq., of the Philadelphia bar, the very point before us was ruled by the High Court of Errors and Appeals, against the right of negro suffrage. Mr. Gibson declined an invitation to be concerned in the argument, and therefore has no memorandum of the cause to direct us to the record. I have had the office searched for it; but the papers had fallen into such disorder as to preclude a hope of its recovery. Most of them were imperfect, and many were lost or misplaced. *But Mr. Gibson's remembrance of the decision is perfect and entitled to full confidence.*

Now, suppressing doubt, and supposing such a decision actually to have emanated from the then highest tribunal of the commonwealth, does not the fact that it was so utterly forgotten as not to have regulated the polls within the memory of the present generation, nor to have been brought up against us in the Reform Convention, prove that it was virtually retracted? And if retracted, is it now to be revived to the overthrow of rights enjoyed without contradiction during the average life of man?

2. The Court argues that colored men are not *freemen,* and hence not entitled by the present Constitution to vote, because under laws prior to the Constitution there *might be* individuals who were not slaves, and yet were not *freemen!* The deduction is, that as the word "freeman" was, *before* the present Constitution, used in a restricted sense, it must have been used in the same sense *in* it. The correctness of this interpretation will be tested by substituting, in Art. 3, Sec. 1, for the word "freeman" the meaning which the Court chooses to have attached to it. This meaning appears from the passages cited by the Court to be, *an elector.*[1] Making the substitution,

[1] "Thus," says the Chief Justice, "till the instant when the phrase on which the question turns was penned, the term freeman had a peculiar and specific sense, being used like the term *citizen* which supplanted it, to denote one who had a voice in public affairs. The citizens were denominated freemen even in the Constitution of 1776—and under the present Constitution, the word, though dropped in the style, was used in the legislative acts convertibly with *electors,* so late as the year 1798 when it grew into disuse."

the article reads, "In elections by the citizens, every *elector,* of the age of twenty-one years, &c. &c., shall enjoy the right of an *elector,* &c."— a proposition which sheds a very faint light upon the question of the extent of the elective franchise, and from which it would appear that there may be electors who are *not* to enjoy the rights of electors. But taking the less restricted term *citizen,* which the Court also seems to think of the same force with "freeman," the article will read more sensibly, that "In elections by the citizens, every *citizen* of the age of twenty-one," who has paid taxes, &c. "shall enjoy the right of an elector." To what evidence does the Court refer to show that a *colored* man may not be a *citizen?* To none whatever. We have too much respect for old Pennsylvania to believe that such puerile absurdity can become her fixed and irreversible law.

3. Since the argument above referred to, such as it is, does not rest upon color, it is not less applicable to the descendants of Irish and German ancestors than to ourselves. If there ever have been within the commonwealth, men, or sets of men, who though personally free were not technically *freemen,* it is unconstitutional, according to the doctrine of the Court, for their descendants to exercise the right of suffrage, pay what taxes they may, till in "the discretion of the judges," their blood has "become so diluted in successive descents as to lose its distinctive character." Is this the doctrine of Pennsylvania freedom?

4. Lastly, the Court openly rests its decision on the authority of a *wrong,* which this commonwealth so long ago as 1780 solemnly acknowledged, and, to the extent of its power, for ever repealed. To support the same *wrong* in *other States,* the Constitution of *this,* when it uses the words "every freeman," must be understood to exclude every freeman of a certain color! The Court is of opinion that the people of this commonwealth had no power to confer the rights of citizenship upon one who, were he in another State, *might be* loaded by its laws with "countless disabilities." Now, since in some of the States men may be found in slavery who have not the slightest trace of African blood, it is difficult to see, on the doctrine of the Court, how the Constitution of Pennsylvania could confer the right of citizenship upon any person; and, indeed, how it could have allowed the emancipation of slaves of any color. To such vile dependence on its own ancient *wrongs,* and on the present *wrongs*

of other States, is Pennsylvania reduced by this decision!

Are we then presumptuous in the hope that this grave sentence will be as incapable of resurrection fifty years hence, as is that which the Chief Justice assures us was pronounced "*about the year 1795?*" No. The blessings of the broad and impartial charter of Pennsylvania rights can no more be wrested from us by legal subtilty, than the beams of our common sun or the breathing of our common air.

What have we done to forfeit the inestimable benefits of this charter? Why should tax-paying colored men, any more than other tax-payers, be deprived of the right of voting for their representatives? It was said in the Convention, that this government belongs to the *Whites*. We have already shown this to be false, as to the past. Those who established our present government designed it equally for all. It is for you to decide whether it shall be confined to the European complexion in future. Why should you exclude us from a fair participation in the benefits of the republic? Have we oppressed the whites? Have we used our right to the injury of any class? Have we disgraced it by receiving bribes? Where are the charges written down, and who will swear to them? We challenge investigation. We put it to the conscience of every Pennsylvanian, whether there is, or ever has been, in the commonwealth, either a political party or religious sect which has less deserved than ourselves to be thus disfranchised. As to the charge of idleness, we fling it back indignantly. Whose brows have sweat for our livelihood but our own? As to vice, if it disqualifies us for civil liberty, why not apply the same rule to the whites, so far as they are vicious? Will you punish the innocent for the crimes of the guilty? The execution of the laws is in the hands of the whites. If we are bad citizens let them apply the proper remedies. We do not ask the right of suffrage for the inmates of our jails and penitentiaries, but for those who honestly and industriously contribute to bear the burdens of the State. As to inferiority to the whites, if indeed we are guilty of it, either by nature or education, we trust our enjoyment of the rights of freemen will on that account be considered the less dangerous. If we are incompetent to fill the offices of State, it will be the fault of the whites only if we are suffered to disgrace them. We are in too feeble a minority to cherish a mischievous ambition. Fair protection is all that we aspire to.

We ask your attention, fellow citizens, to facts and testimonies which go to show that, considering the circumstances in which we have been placed, our country has no reason to be ashamed of us, and that those have the most occasion to blush to whom nature has given the power.

By the careful inquiry of a committee appointed by the "Pennsylvania Society for Promoting the Abolition of Slavery," it has been ascertained that the colored population of Philadelphia and its suburbs, numbering 18,768 souls, possess at the present time, of real and personal estate, not less than $1,350,000. They have paid for taxes during the last year $3,252.83, for house, water, and ground rent, $166,963.50. This committee estimate the income to the holders of real estate occupied by the colored people, to be $7\frac{1}{2}$ per cent. on a capital of about $2,000,000. Here is an addition to the wealth of their white brethren. But the rents and taxes are not all; to pay them, the colored people must be employed in labor, and here is another profit to the whites, for no man employs another unless he can make his labor profitable to himself. For a similar reason, a profit is made by all the whites who sell to colored people the necessaries or luxuries of life. Though the aggregate amount of the wealth derived by the whites from our people can only be conjectured, its importance is worthy of consideration by those who would make it less by lessening our motive to accumulate for ourselves.

Nor is the profit derived from us counterbalanced by the sums which we in any way draw from the public treasures. From a statement published by order of the Guardians of the Poor of Philadelphia, in 1830, it appears that out of 549 out-door poor relieved during the year, only 22 were persons of color, being about four per cent. of the whole number, while the ratio of our population to that of the city and suburbs exceeds $8\frac{1}{4}$ per cent. By a note appended to the printed report above referred to, it appears that the colored *paupers* admitted into the almshouse for the same period, did not exceed four per cent. of the whole. Thus it has been ascertained that they pay more than they receive in the support of their own poor. The various "mutual relief" societies of Philadelphia expend upwards of $7,000 annually, for the relief of their members when sick or disabled.

That we are not neglectful of our religious interests, nor of the education of our children, is shown by the fact that there are among us in Philadelphia, Pittsburg, York, West Chester, and Columbia, 22 churches, 48 clergymen, 26 day schools, 20 Sabbath schools, 125 Sabbath school teachers, 4 literary societies, 2 public libraries, consisting of about 800 volumes, besides 8,333 volumes in private libraries, 2 tract societies, 2 Bible societies, and 7 temperance societies.

In other parts of the State we are confident our condition will compare very favorably with that in Philadelphia, although we are not furnished with accurate statistics.

Our fathers shared with yours the trials and perils of the wilderness. Among the facts which illustrate this, it is well known that the founder of your capital, from whom it bears the name of Harrisburg, was rescued by a *colored man,* from a party of Indians, who had captured, and bound him to the stake for execution. In gratitude for this act, he *invited colored persons* to settle in his town, and offered them land on favorable terms. When our common country has been invaded by a foreign foe, colored men have hazarded their lives in its defence. Our fathers fought by the side of yours in the struggle which made us an independent republic. We offer the following testimonies.

Hon. Mr. Burgess, of Rhode Island, said on the floor of Congress, January 28th, 1828—

At the commencement of the revolutionary war, Rhode Island had a number of this description of people, (slaves). A regiment of them were enlisted into the continental service, and no *braver* men met the enemy in battle; but not one of them was permitted to be a soldier until he had first been made a *freeman.*

Said the Hon. Mr. Martindale, of New York, in Congress, January 22d, 1828—

Slaves, or negroes who had been slaves, were enlisted as soldiers in the war of the revolution; and I myself saw a battalion of them, as fine martial looking men as I ever saw, attached to the northern army, in the last war, on its march from Plattsburg to Sacketts Harbor.

Said the Hon. Charles Miner, of Pennsylvania, in Congress, February 7th, 1828—

The African race make excellent soldiers. Large numbers of them were with Perry, and aided to gain the brilliant victory on lake Erie. A whole battalion of them was distinguished for its soldierly appearance.

The Hon. Mr. Clarke, in the Convention which revised the Constitution of New York, in 1821, said, in regard to the right of suffrage of colored men—

In the war of the revolution these people helped to fight your battles by land and by sea. Some of your States were glad to turn out corps of colored men, and to stand shoulder to shoulder with them. In your late war they contributed largely towards some of your most splendid victories. On lakes Erie and Champlain, where your fleets triumphed over a foe superior in numbers and engines of death, they were manned in a large proportion with men of color. And in this very house, in the fall of 1814, a bill passed, receiving the approbation of all the branches of your government, authorizing the governor to accept the services of 2,000 free people of color.

On the 20th of March, 1779, it was recommended by Congress to the States of Georgia and South Carolina to raise 3,000 colored troops who were to be rewarded for their services by their freedom. The delegations from those States informed Congress that such a body of troops would be not only "formidable to the enemy," but would "lessen the danger of revolts and desertions" among the slaves themselves. (See *Secret Journal of the Old Congress,* Vol. I. pages 105–107.)

During the last war the free colored people were called to the defence of the country by GENERAL JACKSON, and received the following testimony to the value of their services, in which let it be remarked that they are addressed as *fellow citizens* with the *whites:*

SOLDIERS! When, on the banks of the Mobile, I called you to take up arms, inviting you to partake the perils and glory of your white fellow citizens, I expected much from you—for I was not ignorant that you possessed qualities most formidable to an invading enemy. I knew with what fortitude you could endure hunger and thirst, and all the fatigues of a campaign. I *knew well how you loved your native country,* and that you had, as well as ourselves, to defend what man holds most dear, his parents, relations, wife, children, and property. *You have done more than I expected.* In addition to the qualities which I previously knew you to possess, I find, moreover, among you a noble enthusiasm, which leads you to the performance of great things. SOLDIERS—the President of the United States shall hear how praiseworthy was your conduct in the hour of danger, and the representatives of the American people will, I doubt not, give you the praise which your deeds deserve. Your General anticipates them in applauding your noble ardor, &c.

By order, (*Signed*)   THOMAS BUTLER,
Aid-de-Camp

Are we to be thus looked to for help in the "hour of danger," but trampled under foot in the time of peace? In which of the battles of the revolution did not our fathers fight as bravely as yours, for American liberty? Was it that their children might be disfranchised and loaded with insult that they endured the famine of Valley Forge, and the horrors of the Jersey Prison Ship? Nay, among those from whom you are asked to wrench the birthright of CIVIL LIBERTY, are those who themselves shed their blood on the snows of Jersey, and faced British bayonets in the most desperate hour of the revolution.

In other hours of danger, too, colored men have shown themselves the friends of their white countrymen. When the yellow fever ravaged Philadelphia in 1793, and the whites fled, and there were not found enough of them in the city to bury their own dead, the colored people volunteered to do that painful and dangerous duty. They appointed two of their own number to superintend the sad work, who afterwards received the following testimonial:—

Having, during the prevalence of the late malignant disorder, had almost daily opportunities of seeing the conduct of Absalom Jones and Richard Allen, and the people employed by them to bury the dead, I with cheerfulness give this testimony of my approbation of their proceedings, as far as the same came under my notice. Their diligence, attention, and decency of deportment, afforded me at the time much satisfaction.

(*Signed*) MATTHEW CLARKSON, *Mayor*
Philadelphia, Jan. 23, 1794

It is notorious that many whites who were forsaken by their own relations and left to the mercy of this fell disease, were nursed *gratuitously* by the colored people. Does this speak an enmity which would abuse the privileges of civil liberty to the injury of the whites? We have the testimony of a committee of the Senate of this commonwealth, no longer ago than 1830, who were appointed to report upon the expediency of restricting the emigration of colored people into the commonwealth. The following extract from their report, signed by the Hon. Mr. Breck, chairman, testifies to our character:

On this subject your committee beg to remark, that by the last census our colored population amounted to about 36,000 of whom 30,000 inhabit the eastern district, and only 6,000 the western. And this number, so small compared with the white population, is scattered among 1,500,000 of our own color, making 1 colored to 42 whites. So few of these, it is believed

by your committee, need not at present be an object of uneasiness, and would not seem to require the enactment of any restrictive laws; MORE ESPECIALLY AS THEY ARE, FOR THE GREATER PART, INDUSTRIOUS, PEACEABLE, AND USEFUL PEOPLE.

Be it remembered, fellow citizens, that it is only for the "*industrious, peaceable, and useful*" part of the colored people that we plead. We would have the right of suffrage only as the reward of industry and worth. We care not how high the qualification be placed. All we ask is, that no man shall be excluded on account of his *color,* that the same rule shall be applied to all.

Are we to be disfranchised, lest the purity of the *white* blood should be sullied by an intermixture with ours? It seems to us that our white brethren might well enough reserve their fear, till we seek such alliance with them. We ask no social favors. We would not willingly darken the doors of those to whom the complexion and features, which our Maker has given us, are disagreeable. The territories of the commonwealth are sufficiently ample to afford us a home without doing violence to the delicate nerves of our white brethren, for centuries to come. Besides, we are not intruders here, nor were our ancestors. Surely you ought to bear as unrepiningly the evil consequences of your fathers' guilt, as we those of our fathers' misfortune. Proscription and disfranchisement are the last things in the world to alleviate these evil consequences. Nothing, as shameful experience has already proved, can so powerfully promote the evil which you profess to deprecate, as the degradation of our race by the oppressive rule of yours. Give us that fair and honorable ground which self-repect requires to stand on, and the dreaded amalgamation, if it take place at all, shall be by your own fault, as indeed it always has been. We dare not give full vent to the indignation we feel on this point, but we will not attempt wholly to conceal it. We ask a voice in the disposition of those public resources which we ourselves have helped to earn; we claim a right to be heard, according to our numbers, in regard to all those great public measures which involve our lives and fortunes, as well as those of our fellow citizens; we assert our right to vote at the polls as a shield against that strange species of benevolence which seeks legislative aid to banish us— and we are told that our white fellow citizens cannot submit to an *intermixture of the races!*

Then let the indentures, title-deeds, contracts, notes of hand, and all other evidences of bargain, in which colored men have been treated as *men,* be torn and scattered on the winds. Consistency is a jewel. Let no white man hereafter ask his colored neighbor's *consent* when he wants his property or his labor, lest he should endanger the Anglo-Saxon purity of his descendants? Why should not the same principle hold good between neighbor and neighbor, which is deemed necessary, as a fundamental principle, in the Constitution itself? Why should you be ashamed to act in private business, as the Reform Convention would have you act in the capacity of a commonwealth? But, no! we do not believe our fellow citizens, while with good faith they hold ourselves bound by their contracts with us, and while they feel bound to deal with us only by fair contract, will ratify the arbitrary principle of the Convention, howmuchsoever they may prefer the complexion in which their Maker has pleased to clothe themselves.

We would not misrepresent the motives of the Convention, but we are constrained to believe that they have laid our rights a sacrifice on the altar of slavery. We do not believe our disfranchisement would have been proposed, but for the desire which is felt by political aspirants to gain the favor of the slave-holding States. This is not the first time that northern statesmen have "bowed the knee to the dark spirit of slavery," but it is the first time that they have bowed so low! Is Pennsylvania, which abolished slavery in 1780, and enfranchised her tax-paying colored citizens in 1790, now, in 1838, to get upon her knees and repent of her humanity, to gratify those who disgrace the very name of American Liberty, by holding our brethren as goods and chattels? We freely acknowledge our brotherhood to the slave, and our interest in his welfare. Is this a crime for which we should be ignominiously punished? The very fact that we are deeply interested for our kindred in bonds, shows that we are the right sort of stuff to make good citizens of. Were we not so, we should better deserve a lodging in your penitentiaries than a franchise at your polls. Doubtless it will be well pleasing to the slaveholders of the South to see us degraded. They regard our freedom from chains as a dangerous example, much more our political freedom. They see in every thing which fortifies our rights, an obstacle to the recovery of their fugitive property. Will Pennsylvania go backwards towards slavery, for the better safety of southern slave property? Be assured the South will never be satisfied till the old "Keystone" has returned to the point from which she started in 1780. And since the number of colored men in the commonwealth is so inconsiderable, the safety of slavery *may* require still more. It may demand that a portion of the white tax-payers should be unmanned and turned into chattels—we mean those whose hands are hardened by daily toil. Fellow citizens, will you take the first step towards reimposing the chains which have now rusted for more than fifty years? Need we inform you that every colored man in Pennsylvania is exposed to be arrested as a fugitive from slavery? and that it depends not upon the verdict of a jury of his peers, but upon the decision of a judge on summary process, whether or not he shall be dragged into southern bondage? The Constitution of the United States provides that "no person shall be deprived of life, liberty, or property, without due process of law" —by which is certainly meant a TRIAL BY JURY. Yet the act of Congress of 1793, for the recovery of fugitive slaves, authorizes the claimant to seize his victim without a warrant from any magistrate, and allows him to drag him before "any magistrate of a county, city, or town corporate, where such seizure has been made," and upon proving, by "oral testimony or affidavit," to the satisfaction of such magistrate that the man is his slave, gives him a right to take him into everlasting bondage. Thus may a free-born citizen of Pennsylvania be arrested, tried without counsel, jury, or power to call witnesses, condemned by a single man, and carried across Mason and Dixon's line, within the compass of a single day. An act of this commonwealth, passed 1820, and enlarged and re-enacted in 1825, it is true, puts some restraint upon the power of the claimant under the act of Congress; but it still leaves the case to the decision of a single judge, without the privilege of a jury! What unspeakably aggravates our loss of the right of suffrage at this moment is, that, while the increased activity of the slave-catchers enhances our danger, the Reform Convention has refused to amend the Constitution so as to protect our liberty by a jury trial! We entreat you to make our case your own—imagine your own wives and children to be trembling at the approach of every stranger, lest their husbands and fathers should be dragged into a slavery worse than Algerine—worse than death! Fellow citizens, if there is one of us who has abused the right of suffrage, let him be tried and punished according to law. But in the name of humanity, in the name of justice, in the name of the God you profess to worship, who has no respect of persons, do not turn into gall and wormwood the friendship we bear to yourselves by ratifying a Constitution which tears from us a privilege dearly earned and inestimably prized. We lay hold of the principles which Pennsylvania asserted in the hour which tried men's souls—which BENJAMIN FRANKLIN and his eight colleagues, in the name of the commonwealth, pledged their lives, their fortunes, and their sacred honor to sustain. We take our stand upon that solemn declaration, that to protect inalienable rights "governments are instituted among men, deriving their JUST POWERS from the CONSENT of the governed," and proclaim that a government which tears away from us and our posterity the very power of CONSENT, is a tyrannical usurpation which we will never cease to oppose. We have seen with amazement and grief the apathy of white Penn-sylvanians while the "Reform Convention" has been perpetrating this outrage upon the good old principles of Pennsylvania freedom. But however others may forsake these principles, we promise to maintain them on *Pennsylvania soil,* to the last man. If this disfranchisement is designed to uproot us, it shall fail. Pennsylvania's fields, vallies, mountains, and rivers; her canals, rail-roads, forests, and mines; her domestic altars, and her public, religious and benevolent institutions; her Penn and Franklin, her Rush, Rawle, Wistar, and Vaux; her consecrated past and her brilliant future, are as dear to us as they can be to you. Firm upon our old Pennsylvania BILL OF RIGHTS, and trusting in a God of Truth and Justice, we lay our claim before you, with the warning that no amendments of the present Constitution can compensate for the loss of its foundation principle of equal rights, nor for the conversion into enemies of 40,000 friends.

In behalf of the Committee,
ROBERT PURVIS, *Chairman*

Black Abolitionists

David Walker (1785–1830)

The most radical of the early written protests against the Black man's condition in America was *David Walker's Appeal, in Four Articles; Together with a Preamble, to the Coloured Citizens of the World, but in Particular, and Very Expressly, to Those of the United States of America* (1829). Called by Lerone Bennett, Jr., "the Fanon of the Nineteenth Century," David Walker also strikingly anticipates Eldridge Cleaver and other recent Black militants in this country.

David Walker was born in Wilmington, North Carolina, to a slave father (who died before his son's birth) and a free mother. Because children followed the condition of their mother, he was legally "free," but he found his life in the South intolerable because of his own suffering and that of his brothers in chains: "If I remain in this bloody land, I will not live long. As true as God reigns, I will be avenged for the sorrow which my people have suffered. This is not the place for me—no, no. I must leave this part of the country. It will be a great trial for me to live on the same soil where so many men are in slavery; certainly I cannot remain where I must hear their chains continually, and where I must encounter the insults of their hypocritical enslavers. Go, I must."

He went to Boston, where he taught himself to read and write. As the proprietor of a store dealing in new and used clothing, he became a prominent figure in the small Black community of Boston—member of the Massachusetts General Colored Association, agent for Samuel E. Cornish's newspaper *Rights for All*, and subscriber to a freedom fund for the slave poet George Moses Horton, a fellow North Carolinian. Walker's most important contribution to the cause of freedom, however, was the publication in the fall of 1829 of his *Appeal*, at the time the most bitter and fiery condemnation of white racism that had ever been written. The changes made in the second and third editions, which quickly followed the first, were designed not to tone down the work, but to make it even more excoriating.

Throughout Walker's *Appeal*, the primary object of attack is white racism, as manifested in slavery, in denial of educational opportunities to Blacks, in the perversion of the Christian faith by its white professors, and in colonization schemes. A secondary target is Black acquiescence in the racist status quo. In making his case, Walker employs a title and

151

a structural framework that recall the Constitution of the United States. The "preamble" is followed by four "articles." By this device, he reminds his readers of the contradiction between American ideals as expressed in the Constitution and the American realities of slavery and racism. Much of the substance of the pamphlet is based on another contradiction, that between the Christian ethic of brotherly love and the inhuman treatment of Black people by white Christians.

The technique of Walker's *Appeal* relies on both political and religious persuasion. It also relies on covert and overt threats to white racists. These can take the form of prophecies of divine wrath or Black revolt: "The whites want slaves, and want us for their slaves, but some of them will curse the day they ever saw us. As true as the sun ever shone in its meridian splendor, my color will root some of them out of the very face of the earth." In other ways, too, Walker speaks with the accents of the Black revolutionaries of today. He is not only anti-racist white, but pro-Black, preaching Black pride, unity, and collective advancement. Education, for example, should be viewed not as a tool for individual accommodation to the system, but as a revolutionary group weapon. Walker's analysis of white character in its historical role prefigures that of *Soul on Ice:* "The whites have always been an unjust, jealous, unmerciful, avaricious and bloodthirsty set of beings, always seeking after power and authority."

In its own time, the *Appeal* had a tremendous impact, both on slaveholders and on abolitionists. The white South—especially in Georgia, Virginia, and North Carolina—was so alarmed that hysterical actions were taken. Not only were copies seized and destroyed, but persons with the pamphlet in their possession were arrested, arms were distributed to whites to put down anticipated slave uprisings, and appeals were made to Mayor Harrison Gray Otis of Boston for Walker's arrest. Repressive legislation was passed to require quarantines for vessels with Black sailors in Georgia ports, denying them shore leave, to provide the death penalty for the circulation of publications that incited slave revolt, to prohibit the employment of slaves in printing offices, and to prevent the teaching of slaves to read and write. When Nat Turner's insurrection took place fourteen months after the third edition of Walker's *Appeal,* the white South felt that its worst fears had been realized.

Even many abolitionists were shocked by the incendiary nature of the pamphlet. The gentle Quaker Benjamin Lundy declared: "A more bold, daring, inflammatory publication, perhaps, never issued from the press, in any country. I can do no less than set the broadest seal of condemnation upon it." The response of William Lloyd Garrison, who began his famous antislavery journal *The Liberator* in January 1831, was ambivalent. As a nonresistant pacifist he disagreed with Walker's call to violence, but he nevertheless admired the *Appeal* as "one of the most remarkable productions of the age."

On the other hand, many Blacks warmly and unequivocally endorsed the works's undeniable power and genuine moral fervor. They recognized that David Walker was the first Black writer to speak out without fear or restraint. And he apparently paid the price. In the furor that his work aroused, Southern slaveholders were said to have placed a reward on his head, and he was found dead, perhaps of poisoning, on June 28, 1830.

Herbert Aptheker's "*One Continual Cry*" (1965) reprints the *Appeal* and provides useful background information. Another recent edition (1965) is edited by Charles M. Wiltse. An important early edition (1848) by Henry Highland Garnet contains a sketch of Walker's life and character. Walker's other published work was an address to the Massachusetts General Colored Association appearing in *Freedom's Journal,* December 20, 1828.

For a good account of Walker and his *Appeal,* see Vernon Loggins, *The Negro Author* (1931). The chapter on Walker in Lerone Bennett, Jr.'s *Pioneers in Protest* (1968) is a valuable recent assessment. In *Black Abolitionists* (1969) Benjamin Quarles provides an excellent treatment of the movement of which Walker was an initiator. The varying receptions of the *Appeal* may be studied in Clement Eaton, "A Dangerous Pamphlet in the Old South," *The Journal of Southern History,* II (1936), 323–334, and in the pieces on Walker in Truman Nelson's *Documents of Upheaval* (1966), an edition of selections from William Lloyd Garrison's *The Liberator.*

from *David Walker's Appeal*

It will be recollected, that I, in the first edition of my "Appeal,"[1] promised to demonstrate in the course of which, viz. in the course of my Appeal, to the satisfaction of the most incredulous mind, that we Coloured People of these United States, are, the most wretched, degraded and abject set of beings that ever lived since the world began, down to the present day, and, that, the white Christians of America, who hold us in slavery, (or, more properly speaking, pretenders to Christianity,) treat us more cruel and barbarous than any Heathen nation did any people whom it had subjected, or reduced to the same condition, that the Americans (who are, notwithstanding, looking for the Millennial day) have us. All I ask is, for a candid and careful perusal of this the third and last edition of my Appeal, where the world may see that we, the Blacks or Coloured People, are treated more cruel by the white Christians of America, than devils themselves ever treated a set of men, women and children on this earth.

It is expected that all coloured men, women and children,[2] of every nation, language and tongue under heaven, will try to procure a copy of this Appeal and read it, or get some one to read it to them, for it is designed more particularly for them. Let them remember, that though our cruel oppressors and murderers, may (if possible) treat us more cruel, as Pharaoh did the children of Israel, yet the God of the Ethiopians, has been pleased to hear our moans in consequence of oppression; and the day of our redemption from abject wretchedness draweth near, when we shall be enabled, in the most extended sense of the word, to stretch forth our hands to the LORD Our GOD, but there must be a willingness on

[1] See my Preamble in first edition, first page. See also 2nd edition, Article 1, page 9.

[2] Who are not deceitful, abject, and servile to resist the cruelties and murders inflicted upon us by the white slave holders, our enemies by nature.

our part, for GOD to do these things for us, for we may be assured that he will not take us by the hairs of our head against our will and desire, and drag us from our very, mean, low and abject condition.

Preamble

My dearly beloved Brethren and Fellow Citizens:—Having travelled over a considerable portion of these United States, and having, in the course of my travels, taken the most accurate observations of things as they exist—the result of my observations has warranted the full and unshaken conviction, that we, (coloured people of these United States,) are the most degraded, wretched, and abject set of beings that ever lived since the world began; and I pray God that none like us ever may live again until time shall be no more. They tell us of the Israelites in Egypt, the Helots in Sparta, and of the Roman Slaves, which last were made up from almost every nation under heaven, whose sufferings under those ancient and heathen nations, were, in comparison with ours, under this enlightened and Christian nation, no more than a cypher—or, in other words, those nations of antiquity, had but little more among them than the name and form of slavery; while wretchedness and endless miseries were reserved, apparently in a phial, to be poured out upon our fathers, ourselves and our children, by *Christian* Americans!

These positions I shall endeavour, by the help of the Lord, to demonstrate in the course of this APPEAL, to the satisfaction of the most incredulous mind—and may God Almighty, who is the Father of our Lord Jesus Christ, open your hearts to understand and believe the truth.

The *causes,* my brethren, which produce our wretchedness and miseries, are so very numerous and aggravating, that I believe the pen only of a Josephus or a Plutarch, can well enumerate and explain them. Upon subjects, then, of such incomprehensible magnitude, so impenetrable, and so notorious, I shall be obliged to omit a large class of, and content myself with giving you an exposition of a few of those, which do indeed rage to such an alarming pitch, that they cannot but be a perpetual source of terror and dismay to every reflecting mind.

I am fully aware, in making this appeal to my much afflicted and suffering brethren, that I shall not only be assailed by those whose greatest earthly desires are, to keep us in abject ignorance and wretchedness, and who are of the firm conviction that Heaven has designed us and our children to be slaves and *beasts of burden* to them and their children. I say, I do not only expect to be held up to the public as an ignorant, impudent and restless disturber of the public peace, by such avaricious creatures, as well as a mover of insubordination—and perhaps put in prison or to death, for giving a superficial exposition of our miseries, and exposing tyrants. But I am persuaded, that many of my brethren, particularly those who are ignorantly in league with slaveholders or tyrants, who acquire their daily bread by the blood and sweat of their more ignorant brethren—and not a few of those too, who are too ignorant to see an inch beyond their noses, will rise up and call me cursed—Yea, the jealous ones among us will perhaps use more abject subtlety, by affirming that this work is not worth perusing, that we are well situated, and there is no use in trying to better our condition, for we cannot. I will ask one question here.—Can our condition be any worse?—Can it be more mean and abject? If there are any changes, will they not be for the better, though they may appear for the worst at first? Can they get us any lower? Where can they get us? They are afraid to treat us worse, for they know well, the day they do it they are gone. But against all accusations which may or can be preferred against me, I appeal to Heaven for my motive in writing—who knows that my object is, if possible, to awaken in the breasts of my afflicted, degraded and slumbering brethren, a spirit of inquiry and investigation respecting our miseries and wretchedness in this REPUBLICAN LAND OF LIBERTY!!!!!!

The sources from which our miseries are derived, and on which I shall comment, I shall not combine in one, but shall put them under distinct heads and expose them in their turn; in doing which, keeping truth on my side, and not departing from the strictest rules of morality, I shall endeavour to penetrate, search out, and lay them open for your inspection. If you cannot or will not profit by them, I shall have done *my* duty to you, my country and my God.

And as the inhuman system of *slavery,* is the *source* from which most of our miseries proceed, I shall begin with that *curse to nations,* which has spread terror and devastation through so many nations of antiquity, and which is raging to such a pitch at the present day in Spain and in Portugal. It had one tug in England, in France, and in the United States of America; yet the inhabitants thereof, do not learn wisdom, and erase it entirely from their dwellings and from all with whom they have to do. The fact is, the labour of slaves comes too cheap to the avaricious usurpers, and is (as they think) of such great utility to the country where it exists, that those who are actuated by sordid avarice only, overlook the evils, which will as sure as the Lord lives, follow after the good. In fact, they are so happy to keep in ignorance and degradation, and to receive the homage and the labour of the slaves, they forget that God rules in the armies of heaven and among the inhabitants of the earth, having his ears continually open to the cries, tears and groans of his oppressed people; and being a just and holy Being will at one day appear fully in behalf of the oppressed, and arrest the progress of the avaricious oppressors; for although the destruction of the oppressors God may not effect by the oppressed, yet the Lord our God will bring other destructions upon them—for not infrequently will he cause them to rise up one against another, to be split and divided, and to oppress each other, and sometimes to open hostilities with sword in hand.

Some may ask, what is the matter with this united and happy people?—Some say it is the cause of political usurpers, tyrants, oppressors, &c. But has not the Lord an oppressed and suffering people among them? Does the Lord condescend to hear their cries and see their tears in consequence of oppression? Will he let the oppressors rest comfortably and happy always? Will he not cause the very children of the oppressors to rise up against them, and ofttimes put them to death? "God works in many ways his wonders to perform."

I will not here speak of the destructions which the Lord brought upon Egypt, in consequence of the oppression and consequent groans of the oppressed—of the hundreds and thousands of Egyptians whom God hurled into the Red Sea for afflicting his people in their land—of the Lord's suffering people in Sparta or Lacedemon, the land of the truly famous Lycurgus—nor have I time to comment upon the cause which produced the fierceness with which Sylla usurped the title, and absolutely acted as dictator of the Roman people—the conspiracy of Cataline— the conspiracy against, and murder of Caesar

in the Senate house—the spirit with which Marc Antony made himself master of the commonwealth —his associating Octavius and Lipidus with himself in power—their dividing the provinces of Rome among themselves—their attack and defeat, on the plains of Phillippi, of the last defenders of their liberty, (Brutus and Cassius)— the tyranny of Tiberius, and from him to the final overthrow of Constantinople by the Turkish Sultan, Mahomed II. A.D. 1453.

I say, I shall not take up time to speak of the *causes* which produced so much wretchedness and massacre among those heathen nations, for I am aware that you know too well, that God is just, as well as merciful!—I shall call your attention a few moments to that *Christian* nation, the Spaniards—while I shall leave almost unnoticed, that avaricious and cruel people, the Portuguese, among whom all true hearted Christians and lovers of Jesus Christ, must evidently see the judgments of God displayed. To show the judgments of God upon the Spaniards, I shall occupy but a little time, leaving a plenty of room for the candid and unprejudiced to reflect.

All persons who are acquainted with history, and particularly the Bible, who are not blinded by the God of this world, and are not actuated solely by avarice—who are able to lay aside prejudice long enough to view candidly and impartially, things as they were, are, and probably will be—who are willing to admit that God made man to serve Him *alone,* and that man should have no other Lord or Lords but Himself —that God Almighty is the *sole proprietor* or *master* of the WHOLE human family, and will not on any consideration admit of a colleague, being unwilling to divide his glory with another— and who can dispense with prejudice long enough to admit that we are *men,* notwithstanding our *improminent noses* and *woolly heads,* and believe that we feel for our fathers, mothers, wives and children, as well as the whites do for theirs.— I say, all who are permitted to see and believe these things, can easily recognize the judgments of God among the Spaniards. Though others may lay the cause of the fierceness with which they cut each other's throats, to some other circumstances, yet they who believe that God is a God of justice, will believe that SLAVERY *is the principal cause.*

While the Spaniards are running about upon the field of battle cutting each other's throats, has not the Lord an afflicted and suffering people in the midst of them, whose cries and groans in consequence of oppression are continually pouring into the ears of the God of justice? Would they not cease to cut each other's throats, if they could? But how can they? The very support which they draw from government to aid them in perpetrating such enormities, does it not arise in a great degree from the wretched victims of oppression among them? And yet they are calling for PEACE!—PEACE!! Will any peace be given unto them? Their destruction may indeed be procrastinated awhile, but can it continue long, while they are oppressing the Lord's people? Has He not the hearts of all men in His hand? Will he suffer one part of his creatures to go on oppressing another like brutes always, with impunity? And yet, those avaricious wretches are calling for PEACE!!!! I declare, it does appear to me, as though some nations think God is asleep, or that he made the Africans for nothing else but to dig their mines and work their farms, or they cannot believe history, sacred or profane.

I ask every man who has a heart, and is blessed with the privilege of believing—Is not God a God of justice to *all* his creatures? Do you say he is? Then if he gives peace and tranquillity to tyrants, and permits them to keep our fathers, our mothers, ourselves and our children in eternal ignorance and wretchedness, to support them and their families, would he be to us a God of *justice*? I ask, O ye *Christians!!!* who hold us and our children in the most abject ignorance and degradation, that ever a people were afflicted with since the world began—I say, if God gives you peace and tranquillity, and suffers you thus to go on afflicting us, and our children, who have never given you the least provocation—would he be to us *a God of justice*? If you will allow that we are MEN, who feel for each other, does not the blood of our fathers and of us their children, cry aloud to the Lord of Sabaoth against you, for the cruelties and murders with which you have, and do continue to afflict us. But it is time for me to close my remarks on the suburbs, just to enter more fully into the interior of this system of cruelty and oppression.

Article I: Our Wretchedness in Consequence of Slavery

My beloved Brethren:—The Indians of North and of South America—the Greeks—the Irish,

subjected under the king of Great Britain—the Jews, that ancient people of the Lord—the inhabitants of the islands of the sea—in fine, all the inhabitants of the earth, (except however, the sons of Africa) are called *men,* and of course are, and ought to be free. But we, (coloured people) and our children are *brutes!!* and of course are, and *ought to be* SLAVES to the American people and their children forever!! to dig their mines and work their farms; and thus go on enriching them, from one generation to another with our *blood* and our *tears!!!!*

I promised in a preceding page to demonstrate to the satisfaction of the most incredulous, that we, (coloured people of these United States of America) are the *most wretched, degraded* and *abject* set of beings that *ever lived* since the world began, and that the white Americans having reduced us to the wretched state of *slavery,* treat us in that condition *more cruel* (they being an enlighted and Christian people,) than any heathen nation did any people whom it had reduced to our condition. These affirmations are so well confirmed in the minds of all unprejudiced men, who have taken the trouble to read histories, that they need no elucidation from me. But to put them beyond all doubt, I refer you in the first place to the children of Jacob, or of Israel in Egypt, under Pharaoh and his people. Some of my brethren do not know who Pharaoh and the Egyptians were—I know it to be a fact, that some of them take the Egyptians to have been a gang of *devils,* not knowing any better, and that they (Egyptians) having got possession of the Lord's people, treated them *nearly* as cruel as *Christian Americans* do us, at the present day. For the information of such, I would only mention that the Egyptians, were Africans or coloured people, such as we are—some of them yellow and others dark—a mixture of Ethiopians and the natives of Egypt—about the same as you see the coloured people of the United States at the present day.—I say, I call your attention then, to the children of Jacob, while I point out particularly to you his son Joseph, among the rest, in Egypt.

"And Pharaoh, said unto Joseph, thou shalt be over my house, and according unto thy word shall all my people be ruled: only in the throne will I be greater than thou."[3]

---

[3] See Genesis, chap. xli.

"And Pharaoh said unto Joseph, see, I have set thee over all the land of Egypt."[4]

"And Pharaoh said unto Joseph, I am Pharaoh, and without thee shall no man lift up his hand or foot in all the land of Egypt."[5]

Now I appeal to heaven and to earth, and particularly to the American people themselves, who cease not to declare that our condition is not *hard,* and that we are comparatively satisfied to rest in wretchedness and misery, under them and their children. Not, indeed, to show me a coloured President, a Governor, a Legislator, a Senator, a Mayor, or an Attorney at the Bar.— But to show me a man of colour, who holds the low office of a Constable, or one who sits in a Juror Box, even on a case of one of his wretched brethren, throughout this great Republic!!— But let us pass Joseph the son of Israel a little farther in review, as he existed with that heathen nation.

"And Pharaoh called Joseph's name Zaphnathpaaneah; and he gave him to wife Asenath the daughter of Potipherah priest of On. And Joseph went out over all the land of Egypt."[6]

Compare the above, with the American institutions. Do they not institute laws to prohibit us from marrying among the whites? I would wish, candidly, however, before the Lord, to be understood, that I would not give a *pinch of snuff* to be married to any white person I ever saw in all the days of my life. And I do say it, that the black man, or man of colour, who will leave his own colour (provided he can get one, who is good for any thing) and marry a white woman, to be a double slave to her, just because she is *white,* ought to be treated by her as he surely will be, viz: as a NIGER!!!! It is not, indeed, what I care about inter-marriages with the whites, which induced me to pass this subject in review; for the Lord knows, that there is a day coming when they will be glad enough to get into the company of the blacks, notwithstanding, we are, in this generation, levelled by them, almost on a level with the brute creation: and some of us they treat even worse than they do the brutes that perish. I only made this extract to show how much lower we are held, and how much more cruel we are treated by the Americans, than were the children of Jacob, by the Egyptians.—We will notice the sufferings of Israel some further, under

[4] Genesis, chap. xli, 44.
[5] Genesis, chap. xli, 44.
[6] Genesis, chap. xli, 45.

heathen Pharaoh, compared with ours under the *enlightened Christians of America.*

"And Pharaoh spake unto Joseph, saying, thy father and thy brethren are come unto thee:"

"The land of Egypt is before thee: in the best of the land make thy father and brethren to dwell; in the land of Goshen let them dwell: and if thou knowest any men of activity among them, then make them rulers over my cattle."[7]

I ask those people who treat us so *well,* Oh! I ask them, where is the most barren spot of land which they have given unto us? Israel had the most fertile land in all Egypt. Need I mention the very notorious fact, that I have known a poor man of colour, who laboured night and day, to acquire a little money, and having acquired it, he vested it in a small piece of land, and got him a house erected thereon, and having paid for the whole, he moved his family into it, where he was suffered to remain but nine months, when he was cheated out of his property by a white man, and driven out of door! And is not this the case generally? Can a man of colour buy a piece of land and keep it peaceably? Will not some white man try to get it from him, even if it is in a *mud hole?* I need not comment any farther on a subject, which all, both black and white, will readily admit. But I must, really, observe that in this very city, when a man of colour dies, if he owned any real estate it most generally falls into the hands of some white person. The wife and children of the deceased may weep and lament if they please, but the estate will be kept snug enough by its white possessor.

But to prove farther that the condition of the Israelites was better under the Egyptians than ours is under the whites. I call upon the professing Christians, I call upon the philanthropist, I call upon the very tyrant himself, to show me a page of history, either sacred or profane, on which a verse can be found, which maintains, that the Egyptians heaped the *insupportable insult* upon the children of Israel, by telling them that they were not of the *human family.* Can the whites deny this charge? Have they not, after having reduced us to the deplorable condition of slaves under their feet, held us up as descending originally from the tribes of *Monkeys* or *Orang-Outangs?* O! my God! I appeal to every man of feeling—is not this unsupportable? Is it not heaping the most gross insult upon our miseries,

[7] Genesis, chap. xlvii, 5, 6.

because they have got us under their feet and we cannot help ourselves? Oh! pity us we pray thee, Lord Jesus, Master.—Has Mr. Jefferson declared to the world, that we are inferior to the whites, both in the endowments of our bodies and of minds? It is indeed surprising, that a man of such great learning, combined with such excellent natural parts, should speak so of a set of men in chains. I do not know what to compare it to, unless, like putting one wild deer in an iron cage, where it will be secured, and hold another by the side of the same, then let it go, and expect the one in the cage to run as fast as the one at liberty. So far, my brethren, were the Egyptians from heaping these insults upon their slaves, that Pharaoh's daughter took Moses, a son of Israel for her own, as will appear by the following.

"And Pharaoh's daughter said unto her, [Moses' mother] take this child away, and nurse it for me, and I will pay thee thy wages. And the woman took the child [Moses] and nursed it.

"And the child grew, and she brought him unto Pharaoh's daughter and he became her son. And she called his name Moses: and she said because I drew him out of the water."[8]

In all probability, Moses would have become Prince Regent to the throne, and no doubt, in process of time but he would have been seated on the throne of Egypt. But he had rather suffer shame, with the people of God, than to enjoy pleasures with that wicked people for a season. O! that the coloured people were long since of Moses' excellent disposition, instead of courting favour with, and telling news and lies to our *natural enemies,* against each other—aiding them to keep their hellish chains of slavery upon us. Would we not long before this time, have been respectable men, instead of such wretched victims of oppression as we are? Would they be able to drag our mothers, our fathers, our wives, our children and ourselves, around the world in chains and hand-cuffs as they do, to dig up gold and silver for them and theirs? This question, my brethren, I leave for you to digest; and may God Almighty force it home to your hearts. Remember that unless you are united, keeping your tongues within your teeth, you will be afraid to trust your secrets to each other, and thus perpetuate our miseries under the *Christians!!!!!* Addition.—Remember, also to lay humble at the feet of our Lord and Master Jesus Christ, with

prayers and fastings. Let our enemies go on with their butcheries, and at once fill up their cup. Never make an attempt to gain our freedom or *natural right,* from under our cruel oppressors and murderers, until you see your way clear[9]— when that hour arrives and you move, be not afraid or dismayed; for be you assured that Jesus Christ the King of heaven and of earth who is the God of justice and of armies, will surely go before you. And those enemies who have for hundreds of years stolen our *rights,* and kept us ignorant of Him and His divine worship, he will remove. Millions of whom, are this day, so ignorant and avaricious, that they cannot conceive how God can have an attribute of justice, and show mercy to us because it pleased Him to make us black—which colour, Mr. Jefferson calls unfortunate!!!!!! As though we are not as thankful to our God, for having made us as it pleased himself, as they (the whites,) are for having made them white. They think because they hold us in their infernal chains of slavery, that we wish to be white, or of their color—but they are dreadfully deceived—we wish to be just as it pleased our Creator to have made us, and no avaricious and unmerciful wretches, have any business to make slaves of, or hold us in slavery. How would they like for us to make slaves of, and hold them in cruel slavery, and murder them as they do us?—But is Mr. Jefferson's assertions true? viz. "that it is unfortunate for us that our Creator has been pleased to make us *black*." We will not take his say so, for the fact. The world will have an opportunity to see whether it is unfortunate for us, that our Creator *has made us* darker than the *whites.*

Fear not the number and education of our *enemies,* against whom we shall have to contend for our lawful right; guaranteed to us by our

[9] It is not to be understood here, that I mean for us to wait until God shall take us by the hair of our heads and drag us out of abject wretchedness and slavery, nor do I mean to convey the idea for us to wait until our enemies shall make preparations, and call us to seize those preparations, take it away from them, and put every thing before us to death, in order to gain our freedom which God has given us. For you must remember that we are men as well as they. God has been pleased to give us two eyes, two hands, two feet, and some sense in our heads as well as they. They have no more right to hold us in slavery than we have to hold them, we have just as much right, in the sight of God, to hold them and their children in slavery and wretchedness, as they have to hold us, and no more.

[8] See Exodus, chap. ii, 9, 10.

Maker; for why should we be afraid, when God is, and will continue, (if we continue humble) to be on our side?

The man who would not fight under our Lord and Master Jesus Christ, in the glorious and heavenly cause of freedom and of God—to be delivered from the most wretched, abject and servile slavery, that ever a people was afflicted with since the foundation of the world, to the present day—ought to be kept with all of his children or family, in slavery, or in chains, to be butchered by his *cruel enemies.*

I saw a paragraph, a few years since, in a South Carolina paper, which, speaking of the barbarity of the Turks, it said: "The Turks are the most barbarous people in the world—they treat the Greeks more like *brutes* than human beings." And in the same paper was an advertisement, which said: "Eight well built Virginia and Maryland *Negro fellows* and four *wenches* will positively be *sold* this day, *to the highest bidder!*" And what astonished me still more was, to see in this same *humane* paper!! the cuts of three men, with clubs and budgets on their backs, and an advertisement offering a considerable sum of money for their apprehension and delivery. I declare, it is really so amusing to hear the Southerners and Westerners of this country talk about *barbarity,* that it is positively, enough to make a man *smile.*

The sufferings of the Helots among the Spartans, were somewhat severe, it is true, but to say that theirs, were as severe as ours among the Americans, I do most strenuously deny—for instance, can any man show me an article on a page of ancient history which specifies, that, the Spartans chained, and hand-cuffed the Helots, and dragged them from their wives and children, children from their parents, mothers from their suckling babes, wives from their husbands, driving them from one end of the country to the other? Notice the Spartans were heathens, who lived long before our Divine Master made his appearance in the flesh.

Can Christian Americans deny these barbarous cruelties? Have you not, Americans, having subjected us under you, added to these miseries, by insulting us in telling us to our face, because we are helpless, that we are not of the human family? I ask you, O! Americans, I ask you, in the name of the Lord, can you deny these charges? Some perhaps may deny, by saying, that they never thought or said that we were not men. But

do not actions speak louder than *words?*—have they not made provisions for the Greeks, and Irish? Nations who have never done the least thing for them, while *we,* who have enriched their country with our blood and tears—have dug up gold and silver for them and their children, from generation to generation, and are in more miseries than any other people under heaven, are not seen, but by comparatively, a handful of the American people? There are indeed, more ways to kill a dog, besides choking it to death with butter. Further—The Spartans or Lacedemonians, had some frivolous pretext, for enslaving the Helots, for they (Helots) while being free inhabitants of Sparta, stirred up an intestine commotion, and were, by the Spartans subdued, and made prisoners of war. Consequently they and their children were condemned to perpetual slavery.[10]

I have been for years troubling the pages of historians, to find out what our fathers have done to the *white Christians of America,* to merit such condign punishment as they have inflicted on them, and do continue to inflict on us their children. But I must aver, that my researches have hitherto been to no effect. I have therefore, come to the immoveable conclusion, that they (Americans) have, and do continue to punish us for nothing else, but for enriching them and their country. For I cannot conceive of any thing else. Nor will I ever believe otherwise, until the Lord shall convince me.

The world knows, that slavery as it existed among the Romans, (which was the primary cause of their destruction) was, comparatively speaking, no more than a *cypher,* when compared with ours under the Americans. Indeed I should not have noticed the Roman slaves, had not the very learned and penetrating Mr. Jefferson said, "when a master was murdered, all his slaves in the same house, or within hearing, were condemned to death."[11]—Here let me ask Mr. Jefferson, (but he is gone to answer at the bar of God, for the deeds done in his body while living,) I therefore ask the whole American people, had I not rather die, or be put to death, than to be a slave to any tyrant, who takes not only my own, but my wife and children's lives by the inches? Yea, would I meet death with avidity far! far!! in preference to such *servile submission*

[10] See Dr. Goldsmith's History of Greece—page 9. See also, Plutarch's Lives. The Helots subdued by Agis, king of *Sparta.*

[11] See his Notes on Virginia, page 210.

to the murderous hands of tyrants. Mr. Jefferson's very severe remarks on us have been so extensively argued upon by men whose attainments in literature, I shall never be able to reach, that I would not have meddled with it, were it not to solicit each of my brethren, who has the spirit of a man, to buy a copy of Mr. Jefferson's "Notes on Virginia," and put it in the hand of his son. For let no one of us suppose that the refutations which have been written by our white friends are enough—they are *whites*—we are *blacks*.

We, and the world wish to see the charges of Mr. Jefferson refuted by the blacks *themselves,* according to their chance; for we must remember that what the whites have written respecting this subject, is other men's labours, and did not emanate from the blacks. I know well, that there are some talents and learning among the coloured people of this country, which we have not a chance to develop, in consequence of oppression; but our oppression ought not to hinder us from acquiring all we can. For we will have a chance to develop them by and by. God will not suffer us, always to be oppressed. Our sufferings will come to an *end,* in spite of all the Americans this side of *eternity.* Then we will want all the learning and talents among ourselves, and perhaps more, to govern ourselves.—"Every dog must have its day," the American's is coming to an end.

But let us review Mr. Jefferson's remarks respecting us some further. Comparing our miserable fathers, with the learned philosophers of Greece, he says: "Yet notwithstanding these and other discouraging circumstances among the Romans, their slaves were often their rarest artists. They excelled too, in science, insomuch as to be usually employed as tutors to their master's children; Epictetus, Terence and Phaedrus, were slaves,—but they were of the race of whites. It is not their *condition* then, but *nature,* which has produced the distinction."[12] See this, my brethren!! Do you believe that this assertion is swallowed by millions of the whites? Do you know that Mr. Jefferson was one of as great characters as ever lived among the whites? See his writings for the world, and public labours for the United States of America. Do you believe that the assertions of such a man, will pass away into oblivion unobserved by this people and the world? If you do you are much mistaken—See how the American people treat us—have we

[12] See his Notes on Virginia, page 211.

souls in our bodies? Are we men who have any spirits at all? I know that there are many *swell-bellied* fellows among us, whose greatest object is to fill their stomachs. Such I do not mean— I am after those who know and feel, that we are MEN, as well as other people; to them, I say, that unless we try to refute Mr. Jefferson's arguments respecting us, we will only establish them.

But the slaves among the Romans. Every body who has read history, knows, that as soon as a slave among the Romans obtained his freedom, he could rise to the greatest eminence in the State, and there was no law instituted to hinder a slave from buying his freedom. Have not the Americans instituted laws to hinder us from obtaining our freedom? Do any deny this charge? Read the laws of Virginia, North Carolina, &c. Further: have not the Americans instituted laws to prohibit a man of colour from obtaining and holding any office whatever, under the government of the United States of America? Now, Mr. Jefferson tells us, that our condition is not so hard, as the slaves were under the Romans!!!!!!

It is time for me to bring this article to a close. But before I close it, I must observe to my brethren that at the close of the first Revolution in this country, with Great Britain, there were but thirteen States in the Union, now there are twenty-four, most of which are slave-holding States, and the whites are dragging us around in chains and in handcuffs, to their new States and Territories to work their mines and farms, to enrich them and their children—and millions of them believing firmly that we being a little darker than they, were made by our Creator to be an inheritance to them and their children for ever— the same as a parcel of *brutes.*

Are we MEN!!—I ask you, O my brethren! are we *MEN?* Did our Creator make us to be slaves to dust and ashes like ourselves? Are they not dying worms as well as we? Have they not to make their appearance before the tribunal of Heaven, to answer for the deeds done in the body, as well as we? Have we any other Master but Jesus Christ alone? Is he not their Master as well as ours?—What right then, have we to obey and call any other Master, but Himself? How we could be so *submissive* to a gang of men, whom we cannot tell whether they are *as good* as ourselves or not, I never could conceive. However, this is shut up with the Lord, and we cannot precisely tell—but I declare, we judge men by their works.

The whites have always been an unjust, jealous, unmerciful, avaricious and blood-thirsty set of beings, always seeking after power and authority. —We view them all over the confederacy of Greece, where they were first known to be any thing, (in consequence of education) we see them there, cutting each other's throats—trying to subject each other to wretchedness and misery— to effect which, they used all kinds of deceitful, unfair, and unmerciful means. We view them next in Rome, where the spirit of tyranny and deceit raged still higher. We view them in Gaul, Spain, and in Britain.—In fine, we view them all over Europe, together with what were scattered about in Asia and Africa, as heathens, and we see them acting more like devils than accountable men. But some may ask, did not the blacks of Africa, and the mulattoes of Asia, go on in the same way as did the whites of Europe. I answer, no— they never were half so avaricious, deceitful and unmerciful as the whites, according to their knowledge.

But we will leave the whites or Europeans as heathens, and take a view of them as Christians, in which capacity we see them as cruel, if not more so than ever. In fact, take them as a body, they are ten times more cruel, avaricious and unmerciful than ever they were; for while they were heathens, they were bad enough it is true, but it is positively a fact that they were not quite so audacious as to go and take vessel loads of men, women and children, and in cold blood, and through devilishness, throw them into the sea, and murder them in all kind of ways. While they were heathens, they were too ignorant for such barbarity. But being Christians, enlightened and sensible, they are completely prepared for such hellish cruelties.

Now suppose God were to give them more sense, what would they do? If it were possible, would they not *dethrone* Jehovah and seat themselves upon his throne? I therefore, in the name and fear of the Lord God of Heaven and of earth, divested of prejudice either on the side of my colour or that of the whites, advance my suspicion of them, whether they are *as good by nature* as we are or not. Their actions, since they were known as a people, have been the reverse, I do indeed suspect them, but this, as I before observed, is shut up with the Lord, we cannot exactly tell, it will be proved in succeeding generations.—The whites have had the essence of the gospel as it was preached by my master and his apostles—the Ethiopians have not, who are to have it in its meridian splendor—the Lord will give it to them to their satisfaction. I hope and pray my God, that they will make good use of it, that it may be well with them.[13]

[13] It is my solemn belief, that if ever the world becomes Christianized, (which must certainly take place before long) it will be through the means, under God of the *Blacks,* who are now held in wretchedness, and degradation, by the white *Christians* of the world, who before they learn to do justice to us before our Maker—and be reconciled to us, and reconcile us to them, and by that means have clear consciences before God and man.—Send out Missionaries to convert the Heathens, many of whom after they cease to worship gods, which neither see nor hear, become ten times more the children of Hell, than ever they were, why what is the reason? Why the reason is obvious, they must learn to do justice at home, before they go into distant lands, to display their charity, Christianity, and benevolence; when they learn to do justice, God will accept their offering, (no man may think that I am against Missionaries for I am not, my object is to see justice done at home, before we go to convert the heathens.)

Nat Turner (1800–1831)

When William Styron's misleading and historically inaccurate novel *The Confessions of Nat Turner* appeared in 1967, it received wide critical acclaim from the white literary establishment. In 1970 the novel brought its author the Howells Medal of the American Academy of Arts and Letters as the most distinguished work of fiction produced in the preceding five-year period. Nothing would more vividly illustrate the cultural estrangement between white and Black intellectuals, for the latter almost unanimously condemned the novel for its distorted presentation of its protagonist as a Black-hating, pusillanimous onanist motivated mainly by his fantasies of coition with white women.

In historical actuality, Nat Turner was a slave leader of unquestioned intelligence and courage, close to his people and the husband of a Black wife, motivated both by his intense desire for Black liberation and by his equally intense religious zeal. He was a child of the century, born the slave of Benjamin Turner of Southampton County, Virginia, on October 2, 1800—in the very week that the first great Afro-American revolutionary, Gabriel Prosser, was waiting for the gallows. Taught to read and write, probably by his parents, he was a precocious boy who developed a strong religious vocation. The examples of his father, who ran away rather than submit to slavery, and of his grandmother and mother, who encouraged his religious interests, helped to form the incipient prophet-revolutionary. Running away once himself, either from Benjamin Turner or from his second master, Putnam Moore, he was sold early in 1830 to Joseph Travis. His personal life was abstemious, even ascetic, befitting his role as visionary and rebel. His relationship with other Blacks was warm, for he had been nurtured in Blackness and enjoyed the respect and admiration of his people, but he was also, like many other prophets, in certain ways a private person, communing with his visions and his sense of destiny.

This destiny took the form of the Southampton slave rebellion, in which from sixty to eighty Blacks led by Turner killed from fifty-five to sixty-five whites in a period of less than forty-eight hours beginning on the evening of August 21, 1831. The details of the revolt, its quick suppression, and the eventual capture of the rebel leader are best told in Turner's own account, reprinted here, but some mention should be made of the aftermath of this momentous event in Afro-American history.

Was Nat Turner's rebellion a failure? The answer depends on whether one is considering the immediate or the long-range consequences. In a practical sense it did fail, for the rebels were unable to capture Jerusalem, the county seat of Southampton, where they could have seized enough arms and ammunition to continue the rebellion and expand it into a guerrilla war, using the nearby Dismal Swamp as a base of operations. Instead, almost all of the rebels were captured and punished. Turner himself was hanged on November 11, 1831, after which his corpse was skinned and grease was made of his flesh. Some one hundred Blacks who had taken no part in the revolt were slaughtered ruthlessly as the hysteria spread in Virginia. In other slave states, too, panic gripped the white population. All over the South, slaves and free Blacks were flogged or executed on the slightest suspicion of rebellious tendencies. Repressive legislation followed in an effort to strengthen the chains of slaves and to restrict even further the activities of free Blacks or, as in Mississippi and Tennessee, to expel them. Everywhere the screws were tightened.

In a larger sense, however, Nat Turner did not fail. If his revolt brought a wave of repression from slaveholders, it also energized

Blacks and white abolitionists. The resulting polarization between North and South was necessary, one can say in retrospect, to force the crisis that culminated in the Civil War and the end of chattel slavery. As a martyr to Black freedom, moreover, Turner set an example that has inspired his own and succeeding generations. Writing some fifty years after Turner's execution, George Washington Williams declared, "The image of Nat. Turner is carved on the fleshy tablets of four million hearts. His history has been kept from the Colored people at the South, but the women have handed the tradition to their children, and the 'Prophet Nat.' is still marching on." More recently, Lerone Bennett, Jr., and others have recognized in Turner "the prototype of twentieth century revolutionaries"—one of the greatest of all Black heroes.

The Confessions of Nat Turner, first published in Baltimore in 1831, was the joint effort of Turner and Thomas R. Gray, a white lawyer who served as amanuensis and commentator. Gray's hostility to the rebel leader produced distortions, most of which are easily recognizable, but enough of Turner comes through, even in diluted form, to suggest something of the awesome intensity and power of the man. Nevertheless, the reader should remember that with Nat Turner the sword was mightier than the pen.

The most authoritative account is *Nat Turner's Slave Rebellion* (1966) by Herbert Aptheker, whose *American Negro Slave Revolts* (1943) is also valuable. Two good brief treatments are Rayford W. Logan, "Nat Turner: Fiend or Martyr?" *Opportunity,* IX (November 1931), 337–339, and Lerone Bennett, Jr.'s chapter on Turner in *Pioneers in Protest* (1968). *William Styron's Nat Turner: Ten Black Writers Respond* (1968), edited by John Henrik Clarke, has much of interest. Of the early accounts, two are of special importance: Thomas Wentworth Higginson, "Nat Turner's Insurrection," *The Atlantic Monthly,* VIII (August 1861), 173–187, and William Wells Brown's memoir in *The Black Man* (1863). See also F. N. Boney, "The Blue Lizard: Another View of Nat Turner's Country on the Eve of Rebellion," *Phylon,* XXXI (1970), 351–358.

The Confessions of Nat Turner

DISTRICT OF COLUMBIA, TO WIT:

Be it remembered, That on this tenth day of November, Anno Domini, eighteen hundred and thirty-one, Thomas R. Gray of the said District, deposited in this office the title of a book, which is in the words as following:

"The Confessions of Nat Turner, the leader of the late insurrection in Southampton, Virginia, as fully and voluntarily made to Thomas R. Gray, in the prison where he was confined, and acknowledged by him to be such when read before the Court of Southampton; with the certificate, under seal, of the Court convened at Jerusalem, November 5, 1831, for his trial. Also, an authentic account of the whole insurrection, and with lists of the whites who were murdered, and of the negroes brought before the Court of Southampton, and there sentenced, &. the right whereof he claims as proprietor, in conformity with an Act of Congress, entitled "An act to amend the several acts respecting Copy Rights."

EDMUND J. LEE, Clerk of the District. In testimony that the above is a true copy, from the record of the District Court for the District of Columbia, I, Edmund J. Lee, the Clerk thereof, have hereunto set my hand and affixed the seal of my office, this 10th day of November, 1831.

[Seal.]

EDMUND J. LEE, C.D.C.

The late insurrection in Southampton has greatly excited the public mind, and led to a thousand idle, exaggerated and mischievous reports. It is the first instance in our history of an open rebellion of the slaves, and attended with such atrocious circumstances of cruelty and destruction, as could not fail to leave a deep impression, not only upon the minds of the community where this fearful tragedy was wrought, but throughout every portion of our country, in which this population is to be found. Public curiosity has been on the stretch to understand the origin and progress of this dreadful conspiracy, and the motives which influence its diabolical actors. The insurgent slaves had all been destroyed, or apprehended, tried and executed, (with the exception of the leader,) without revealing any thing at all satisfactory, as to the motives which governed them, or the means by which they expected to accomplish their object. Every thing connected with the sad affair was wrapt in mystery, until Nat Turner, the leader of this ferocious band, whose name has resounded throughout our widely extended empire, was captured. This " great Bandit " was taken by a single individual, in a cave near the residence of his late owner, on Sunday, the thirtieth of October, without attempting to make the slightest resistance, and on the following day safely lodged in the jail of the County. His captor was Benjamin Phipps, armed with a shot gun well charged. Nat's only weapon was a small light sword which he immediately surrendered, and begged that his life might be spared. Since his confinement, by permission of the Jailor, I have had ready access to him, and finding that he was willing to make a full and free confession of the origin, progress and consummation of the insurrectory movements of the slaves of which he was the contriver and head; I determined for the gratification of public curiosity to commit his statements to writing, and publish them, with little or no variation, from his own words. That this is a faithful record of his con-

fessions, the annexed certificate of the County Court of Southampton, will attest. They certainly bear one stamp of truth and sincerity. He makes no attempt (as all the other insurgents who were examined did,) to exculpate himself, but frankly acknowledges his full participation in all the guilt of the transaction. He was not only the contriver of the conspiracy, but gave the first blow towards its execution.

It will thus appear, that whilst every thing upon the surface of society wore a calm and peaceful aspect; whilst not one note of preparation was heard to warn the devoted inhabitants of woe and death, a gloomy fanatic was revolving in the recesses of his own dark, bewildered, and over-wrought mind, schemes of indiscriminate massacre to the whites. Schemes too fearfully executed as far as his fiendish band proceeded in their desolating march. No cry for mercy penetrated their flinty bosoms. No acts of remembered kindness made the least impression upon these remorseless murderers. Men, women and children, from hoary age to helpless infancy were involved in the same cruel fate. Never did a band of savages do their work of death more unsparingly. Apprehension for their own personal safety seems to have been the only principle of restraint in the whole course of their bloody proceedings. And it is not the least remarkable feature in this horrid transaction, that a band actuated by such hellish purposes, should have resisted so feebly, when met by the whites in arms. Desperation alone, one would think, might have led to greater efforts. More than twenty of them attacked Dr. Blunt's house on Tuesday morning, a little before day-break, defended by two men and three boys. They fled precipitately at the first fire; and their future plans of mischief, were entirely disconcerted and broken up. Escaping thence, each individual sought his own safety either in concealment, or by returning home, with the hope that his participation might escape detection, and all were shot down in the course of a few days, or captured and brought to trial and punishment. Nat has survived all his followers, and the gallows will speedily close his career. His own account of the conspiracy is submitted to the public, without comment. It reads an awful, and it is hoped, a useful lesson, as to the operations of a mind like his, endeavoring to grapple with things beyond its reach. How it first became bewildered and confounded, and finally corrupted and led to the conception and perpetration of the most atrocious and heart-rending deeds. It is calculated also to demonstrate the policy of our laws in restraint of this class of our population, and to induce all those entrusted with their execution, as well as our citizens generally, to see that they are strictly and rigidly enforced. Each particular community should look to its own safety, whilst the general guardians of the laws, keep a watchful eye over all. If Nat's statements can be relied on, the insurrection in this county was entirely local, and his designs confided but to a few, and these in his immediate vicinity. It was not instigated by motives of revenge or sudden anger, but the results of long deliberation, and a settled purpose of mind. The offspring of gloomy fanaticism, acting upon materials but too well prepared for such impressions. It will be long remembered in the annals of our country, and many a mother as she presses her infant darling to her bosom, will shudder at the recollection of Nat Turner, and his band of ferocious miscreants.

Believing the following narrative, by removing doubts and conjectures from the public mind which otherwise must have remained, would give general satisfaction, it is respectfully submitted to the public by their ob't serv't,

T. R. GRAY

Jerusalem, Southampton, Va. Nov. 5, 1831.

We the undersigned, members of the Court convened at Jerusalem, on Saturday, the 5th day of Nov. 1831, for the trial of Nat. *alias* Nat Turner, a negro slave, late the property of Putnam Moore, deceased, do hereby certify, that the confessions of Nat, to Thomas R. Gray, was read to him in our presence, and that Nat acknowledged the same to be full, free, and voluntary; and that furthermore, when called upon by the presiding Magistrate of the Court, to state if he had any thing to say, why sentence of death should not be passed upon him, replied he had nothing further than he had communicated to Mr. Gray. Given under our hands and seals at Jerusalem, this 5th day of November, 1831.

JEREMIAH COBB,	[Seal.]
THOMAS PRETLOW,	[Seal.]
JAMES W. PARKER,	[Seal.]
CARR BOWERS,	[Seal.]
SAMUEL B. HINES,	[Seal.]
ORRIS A. BROWNE,	[Seal.]

State of Virginia, Southampton County, to wit:

I, James Rochelle, Clerk of the County Court of Southampton in the State of Virginia, do hereby certify, that Jeremiah Cobb, Thomas Pretlow, James W. Parker, Carr Bowers, Samuel B. Hines, and Orris A. Browne, esqr's are acting Justices of the Peace, in and for the County aforesaid, and were members of the Court which convened at Jerusalem, on Saturday the 5th day of November, 1831, for the trial of Nat *alias* Nat Turner, a negro slave, late the property of Putnam Moore, deceased, who was tried and convicted, as an insurgent in the late insurrection in the county of Southampton aforesaid, and that full faith and credit are due, and ought to be given to their acts as Justices of the peace aforesaid.

[Seal.] In testimony whereof, I have hereunto set my hand and caused the seal of the Court aforesaid, to be affixed this 5th day of November, 1831.

JAMES ROCHELLE,
C. S. C. C.

Agreeable to his own appointment, on the evening he was committed to prison, with permission of the jailor, I visited NAT on Tuesday the 1st November, when, without being questioned at all, he commenced his narrative in the following words:—

SIR,—You have asked me to give a history of the motives which induced me to undertake the late insurrection, as you call it—To do so I must go back to the days of my infancy, and even before I was born. I was thirty-one years of age the 2nd of October last, and born the property of Benj. Turner, of this county. In my childhood a circumstance occurred which made an indelible impression on my mind, and laid the ground work of that enthusiasm, which has terminated so fatally to many, both white and black, and for which I am about to atone at the gallows. It is here necessary to relate this circumstance—trifling as it may seem, it was the commencement of that belief which has grown with time, and even now, sir, in this dungeon, helpless and forsaken as I am, I cannot divest myself of. Being at play with other children, when three or four years old, I was telling them something, which my mother overhearing, said it had happened before I was born—I stuck to my story, however, and related somethings which went, in her opinion, to confirm it—others being called on were greatly astonished, knowing that these things had happened, and caused them to say in my hearing, I surely would be a prophet, as the Lord had shewn me things that had happened before my birth. And my father and mother strengthened me in this my first impression, saying in my presence, I was intended for some great purpose, which they had always thought from certain marks on my head and breast—[a parcel of excrescences which I believe are not at all uncommon, particularly among negroes, as I have seen several with the same. In this case he has either cut them off or they have nearly disappeared]—My grandmother, who was very religious, and to whom I was much attached—my master, who belonged to the church, and other religious persons who visited the house, and whom I often saw at prayers, noticing the singularity of my manners, I suppose, and my uncommon intelligence for a child, remarked I had too much sense to be raised, and if I was, I would never be of any service to any one as a slave—To a mind like mine, restless, inquisitive and observant of every thing that was passing, it is easy to suppose that religion was the subject to which it would be directed, and although this subject principally occupied my thoughts—there was nothing that I saw or heard of to which my attention was not directed—The manner in which I learned to read and write, not only had great influence on my own mind, as I acquired it with the most perfect ease, so much so, that I have no recollection whatever of learning the alphabet—but to the astonishment of the family, one day, when a book was shewn to me to keep me from crying, I began spelling the names of different objects—this was a source of wonder to all in the neighborhood, particularly the blacks—and this learning was constantly improved at all opportunities—when I got large enough to go to work, while employed, I was reflecting on many things that would present themselves to my imagination, and whenever an opportunity occurred of looking at a book, when the school children were getting their lessons, I would find many things that the fertility of my own imagination had depicted to me before; all my time, not devoted to my master's service, was spent either in prayer, or in making experiments in casting different things in moulds made of earth, in attempting to make paper, gun-powder, and many other experiments, that although I could not perfect, yet convinced me of its practicability if I had the means.[1] I was not addicted to stealing in my youth, nor have ever been—Yet such was the confidence of the negroes in the neighborhood, even at this early period of my life, in my superior judgment, that they would often carry me with them when they were going on any roguery, to plan for them. Growing up among them, with this confidence in my superior judgment, and when this, in their opinions, was perfected by Divine inspiration, from the circumstances already alluded to in my infancy, and which belief was ever afterwards zealously inculcated by the austerity of my life and manners, which became the subject of remark by white and black.—Having soon discovered to be great, I must appear so, and therefore studiously avoided mixing in society, and wrapped myself in mystery, devoting my time to fasting and prayer—By this time, having arrived to man's estate,

[1] When questioned as to the manner of manufacturing those different articles, he was found well informed on the subject.

and hearing the scriptures commented on at meetings, I was struck with that particular passage which says: "Seek ye the kingdom of Heaven and all things shall be added unto you." I reflected much on this passage, and prayed daily for light on this subject—As I was praying one day at my plough, the spirit spoke to me, saying "Seek ye the kingdom of Heaven and all things shall be added unto you."

Question—what do you mean by the Spirit.

Ans. The Spirit that spoke to the prophets in former days—and I was greatly astonished, and for two years prayed continually, whenever my duty would permit—and then again I had the same revelation, which fully confirmed me in the impression that I was ordained for some great purpose in the hands of the Almighty. Several years rolled round, in which many events occurred to strengthen me in this my belief. At this time I reverted in my mind to the remarks made of me in my childhood, and the things that had been shewn me—and as it had been said of me in my childhood by those by whom I had been taught to pray, both white and black, and in whom I had the greatest confidence, that I had too much sense to be raised, and if I was, I would never be of any use to any one as a slave. Now finding I had arrived to man's estate, and was a slave, and these revelations being made known to me, I began to direct my attention to this great object, to fulfil the purpose for which, by this time, I felt assured I was intended. Knowing the influence I had obtained over the minds of my fellow servants, (not by the means of conjuring and such like tricks—for to them I always spoke of such things with contempt) but by the communion of the Spirit whose revelations I often communicated to them, and they believed and said my wisdom came from God. I now began to prepare them for my purpose, by telling them something was about to happen that would terminate in fulfilling the great promise that had been made to me—About this time I was placed under an overseer, from whom I ran away—and after remaining in the woods thirty days, I returned, to the astonishment of the negroes on the plantation, who thought I had made my escape to some other part of the country, as my father had done before. But the reason of my return was, that the Spirit appeared to me and said I had my wishes directed to the things of this world, and not to the kingdom of Heaven, and that I should return to the service of my earthly master—"For he who knoweth his Master's will, and doeth it not, shall be beaten with many stripes, and thus have I chastened you." And the negroes found fault, and murmured against me, saying that if they had my sense they would not serve any master in the world. And about this time I had a vision—and I saw white spirits and black spirits engaged in battle, and the sun was darkened—the thunder rolled in the Heavens, and blood flowed in streams—and I heard a voice saying, "Such is your luck, such you are called to see, and let it come rough or smooth, you must surely bear it." I now withdrew myself as much as my situation would permit, from the intercourse of my fellow servants, for the avowed purpose of serving the Spirit more fully—and it appeared to me, and reminded me of the things it had already shown me, and that it would then reveal to me the knowledge of the elements, the revolution of the planets, the operation of tides, and changes of the seasons. After this revelation in the year of 1825, and the knowledge of the elements being made known to me, I sought more than ever to obtain true holiness before the great day of judgment should appear, and then I began to receive the true knowledge of faith. And from the first steps of righteousness until the last, was I made perfect; and the Holy Ghost was with me, and said, "Behold me as I stand in the Heavens"—and I looked and saw the forms of men in different attitudes—and there were lights in the sky to which the children of darkness gave other names than what they really were—for they were the lights of the Savior's hands, stretched forth from east to west, even as they were extended on the cross on Calvary for the redemption of sinners. And I wondered greatly at these miracles, and prayed to be informed of a certainty of the meaning thereof—and shortly afterwards, while laboring in the field, I discovered drops of blood on the corn as though it were dew from heaven—and I communicated it to many, both white and black, in the neighborhood—and I then found on the leaves in the woods hieroglyphic characters, and numbers, with the forms of men in different attitudes, portrayed in blood, and representing the figures I had seen before in the heavens. And now the Holy Ghost had revealed itself to me, and made plain the miracles it had shown me—For as the blood of Christ had been shed on this earth, and had ascended to heaven for the salvation of sinners, and was now returning to earth again in the form of dew—and as the leaves on the trees bore the impression of the figures I had seen in the heavens, it was plain to me that the Savior was about to lay down the yoke he had borne for the sins of men, and the great day of judgment was at hand. About this time I told these things to a white man, (Etheldred T. Brantley) on whom it had a wonderful effect—and he ceased from his wickedness, and was attacked immediately with a cutaneous eruption, and blood oozed from the pores of his skin, and after praying and fasting nine days, he was healed, and the Spirit appeared to me again, and said, as the Savior had been baptised so should we be also—and when the white people would not let us be baptised by the church, we went down into the water together, in the sight of many who reviled us, and were baptised by the Spirit— After this I rejoiced greatly, and gave thanks to God. And on the 12th of May, 1828, I heard a loud noise in the heavens, and the Spirit instantly appeared to me

and said the Serpent was loosened, and Christ had laid down the yoke he had borne for the sins of men, and that I should take it on and fight against the Serpent, for the time was fast approaching when the first should be last and the last should be first.

Ques. Do you not find yourself mistaken now?

Ans. Was not Christ crucified? And by signs in the heavens that it would make known to me when I should commence the great work—and until the first sign appeared, I should conceal it from the knowledge of men—And on the appearance of the sign, (the eclipse of the sun last February) I should arise and prepare myself, and slay my enemies with their own weapons. And immediately on the sign appearing in the heavens, the seal was removed from my lips, and I communicated the great work laid out for me to do, to four in whom I had the greatest confidence, (Henry, Hark, Nelson, and Sam)—It was intended by us to have begun the work of death on the 4th July last— Many were the plans formed and rejected by us, and it affected my mind to such a degree, that I fell sick, and the time passed without our coming to any determination how to commence—Still forming new schemes and rejecting them, when the sign appeared again, which determined me not to wait longer.

Since the commencement of 1830, I had been living with Mr. Joseph Travis, who was to me a kind master, and placed the greatest confidence in me; in fact, I had no cause to complain of his treatment to me. On Saturday evening, the 20th of August, it was agreed between Henry, Hark and myself, to prepare a dinner the next day for the men we expected, and then to concert a plan, as we had not yet determined on any. Hark, on the following morning, brought a pig, and Henry brandy, and being joined by Sam, Nelson, Will and Jack, they prepared in the woods a dinner, where, about three o'clock, I joined them.

Q. Why were you so backward in joining them.

Ans. The same reason that had caused me not to mix with them for years before.

I saluted them on coming up, and asked Will how came he there, he answered, his life was worth no more than others, and his liberty as dear to him. I asked him if he thought to obtain it? He said he would, or lose his life. This was enough to put him in full confidence. Jack, I knew, was only a tool in the hands of Hark, it was quickly agreed we should commence at home (Mr. J. Travis') on that night, and until we had armed and equipped ourselves, and gathered sufficient force, neither age nor sex was to be spared, (which was invariably adhered to). We remained at the feast, until about two hours in the night, when we went to the house and found Austin; they all went to the cider press and drank, except myself. On returning to the house, Hark went to the door with an axe, for the purpose of breaking it open, as we knew we were strong enough to murder the family, if they were awaked by the noise; but reflecting that it might create an alarm in the neighborhood, we determined to enter the house secretly, and murder them whilst sleeping. Hark got a ladder and set it against the chimney, on which I ascended, and hoisting a window, entered and came down stairs, unbarred the door, and removed the guns from their places. It was then observed that I must spill the first blood. On which, armed with a hatchet, and accompanied by Will, I entered my master's chamber, it being dark, I could not give a death blow, the hatchet glanced from his head, he sprang from the bed and called his wife, it was his last word, Will laid him dead, with a blow of his axe, and Mrs. Travis shared the same fate, as she lay in bed. The murder of this family, five in number, was the work of a moment, not one of them awoke; there was a little infant sleeping in a cradle, that was forgotten, until we had left the house and gone some distance, when Henry and Will returned and killed it; we got here, four guns that would shoot, and several old muskets, with a pound or two of powder. We remained some time at the barn, where we paraded; I formed them in a line as soldiers, and after carrying them through all the manoeuvres I was master of marched them off to Mr. Salathiel Francis', about six hundred yards distant. Sam and Will went to the door and knocked. Mr. Francis asked who was there, Sam replied it was him, and he had a letter for him, on which he got up and came to the door; they immediately seized him, and dragging him out a little from the door, he was dispatched by repeated blows on the head; there was no other white person in the family. We started from there for Mrs. Reese's, maintaining the most perfect silence on our march, where finding the door unlocked, we entered, and murdered Mrs. Reese in her bed, while sleeping; her son awoke, but it was only to sleep the sleep of death, he had only time to say who is that, and he was no more. From Mrs. Reese's we went to Mrs. Turner's, a mile distant, which we reached about sunrise, on Monday morning. Henry, Austin, and Sam, went to the still, where, finding Mr. Peebles, Austin shot him, and the rest of us went to the house; as we approached, the family discovered us, and shut the door. Vain hope! Will, with one stroke of his axe, opened it, and we entered and found Mrs. Turner and Mrs. Newsome in the middle of a room, almost frightened to death. Will immediately killed Mrs. Turner, with one blow of his axe. I took Mrs. Newsome by the hand, and with the sword I had when I was apprehended, I struck her several blows over the head, but not being able to kill her, as the sword was dull. Will turning around and discovering it, despatched her also. A general destruction of property and search for money and ammunition, always succeeded the murders. By this time my company amounted to fifteen, and nine men mounted, who

started for Mrs. Whitehead's, (the other six were to go through a by way to Mr. Bryant's, and rejoin us at Mrs. Whitehead's) as we approached the house we discovered Mr. Richard Whitehead standing in the cotton patch, near the lane fence; we called him over into the lane, and Will, the executioner, was near at hand, with his fatal axe, to send him to an untimely grave. As we pushed on to the house, I discovered some one run round the garden, and thinking it was some of the white family, I pursued them, but finding it was a servant girl belonging to the house, I returned to commence the work of death, but they whom I left, had not been idle; all the family were already murdered, but Mrs. Whitehead and her daughter Margaret. As I came round to the door I saw Will pulling Mrs. Whitehead out of the house, and at the step he nearly severed her head from her body, with his broad axe. Miss Margaret, when I discovered her, had concealed herself in the corner, formed by the projection of cellar cap from the house; on my approach she fled, but was soon overtaken, and after repeated blows with a sword, I killed her by a blow on the head, with a fence rail. By this time, the six who had gone by Mr. Bryant's, rejoined us, and informed me they had done the work of death assigned them. We again divided, part going to Mr. Richard Porter's, and from thence to Nathaniel Francis', the others to Mr. Howell Harris', and Mr. T. Doyle's. On my reaching Mr. Porter's, he had escaped with his family. I understood there, that the alarm had already spread, and I immediately returned to bring up those sent to Mr. Doyle's, and Mr. Howell Harris'; the party I left going on to Mr. Francis', having told them I would join them in that neighborhood. I met these sent to Mr. Doyle's and Mr. Harris' returning, having met Mr. Doyle on the road and killed him; and learning from some who joined them, that Mr. Harris was from home, I immediately pursued the course taken by the party gone on before; but knowing they would complete the work of death and pillage, at Mr. Francis' before I could get there, I went to Mr. Peter Edwards', expecting to find them there, but they had been here also. I then went to Mr. John T. Barrow's, they had been here and murdered him. I pursued on their track to Capt. Newit Harris', where I found the greater part mounted, and ready to start; the men now amounting to about forty, shouted and hurraed as I rode up, some were in the yard, loading their guns, others drinking. They said Captain Harris and his family had escaped, the property in the house they destroyed, robbing him of money and other valuables. I ordered them to mount and march instantly, this was about nine or ten o'clock, Monday morning. I proceeded to Mr. Levi Waller's, two or three miles distant. I took my station in the rear, and as it was my object to carry terror and devastation wherever we went, I placed fifteen or twenty of the best armed and most relied on, in front, who generally approached the houses as fast as their horses could run; this was for two purposes, to prevent escape and strike terror to the inhabitants—on this account I never got to the houses, after leaving Mrs. Whitehead's, until the murders were committed, except in one case. I sometimes got in sight in time to see the work of death completed, viewed the mangled bodies as they lay, in silent satisfaction, and immediately started in quest of other victims—Having murdered Mrs. Waller and ten children, we started for Mr. William Williams'—having killed him and two little boys that were there; while engaged in this, Mrs. Williams fled and got some distance from the house, but she was pursued, overtaken, and compelled to get up behind one of the company, who brought her back, and after showing her the mangled body of her lifeless husband, she was told to get down and lay by his side, where she was shot dead. I then started for Mr. Jacob Williams, where the family were murdered—Here he found a young man named Drury, who had come on business with Mr. Williams—he was pursued, overtaken and shot. Mrs. Vaughan was the next place we visited—and after murdering the family here, I determined on starting for Jerusalem—Our number amounted now to fifty or sixty, all mounted and armed with guns, axes, swords and clubs—On reaching Mr. James W. Parker's gate, immediately on the road leading to Jerusalem, and about three miles distant, it was proposed to me to call there, but I objected, as I knew he was gone to Jerusalem, and my object was to reach there as soon as possible; but some of the men having relations at Mr. Parker's it was agreed that they might call and get his people. I remained at the gate on the road, with seven or eight; the others going across the field to the house, about half a mile off. After waiting some time for them, I became impatient, and started to the house for them, and on our return we were met by a party of white men, who had pursued our blood-stained track, and who had fired on those at the gate, and dispersed them, which I knew nothing of, not having been at that time rejoined by any of them—Immediately on discovering the whites, I ordered my men to halt and form, as they appeared to be alarmed—The white men, eighteen in number, approached us in about one hundred yards, when one of them fired, (this was against the positive orders of Captain Alexander P. Peete, who commanded, and who had directed the men to reserve their fire until within thirty paces)—And I discovered about half of them retreating, I then ordered my men to fire and rush on them; the few remaining stood their ground until we approached within fifty yards, when they fired and retreated. We pursued and overtook some of them who we thought we left dead; (they were not killed) after pursuing them about two hundred yards, and rising a little hill, I discovered they were met by another party, and had halted, and were reloading

their guns, (this was a small party from Jerusalem who knew the negroes were in the field, and had just tied their horses to await their return to the road, knowing that Mr. Parker and family were in Jerusalem, but knew nothing of the party that had gone in with Captain Peete; on hearing the firing they immediately rushed to the spot and arrived just in time to arrest the progress of these barbarous villains, and save the lives of their friends and fellow citizens). Thinking that those who retreated first, and the party who fired on us at fifty or sixty yards distant, had all fallen back to meet others with ammunition. As I saw them reloading their guns, and more coming up than I saw at first, and several of my bravest men being wounded, the others became panic-struck and squandered over the field; the white men pursued and fired on us several times. Hark had his horse shot under him, and I caught another for him as it was running by me; five or six of my men were wounded, but none left on the field; finding myself defeated here I instantly determined to go through a private way, and cross the Nottoway river at the Cypress Bridge, three miles below Jerusalem, and attack that place in the rear, as I expected they would look for me on the other road, and I had a great desire to get there to procure arms and ammunition. After going a short distance in this private way, accompanied by about twenty men, I overtook two or three who told me the others were dispersed in every direction. After trying in vain to collect a sufficient force to proceed to Jerusalem, I determined to return, as I was sure they would make back to their old neighborhood, where they would rejoin me, make new recruits, and come down again. On my way back, I called at Mrs. Thomas's, Mrs. Spencer's, and several other places, the white families having fled, we found no more victims to gratify our thirst for blood, we stopped at Maj. Ridley's quarter for the night, and being joined by four of his men, with the recruits made since my defeat, we mustered now about forty strong. After placing out sentinels, I laid down to sleep, but was quickly roused by a great racket; starting up, I found some mounted, and others in great confusion; one of the sentinels having given the alarm that we were about to be attacked, I ordered some to ride round and reconnoitre, and on their return the others being more alarmed, not knowing who they were, fled in different ways, so that I was reduced to about twenty again; with this I determined to attempt to recruit, and proceed on to rally in the neighborhood, I had left. Dr. Blunt's was the nearest house, which we reached just before day; on riding up the yard, Hark fired a gun. We expected Dr. Blunt and his family were at Maj. Ridley's, as I knew there was a company of men there; the gun was fired to ascertain if any of the family were at home; we were immediately fired upon and retreated, leaving several of my men. I do not know what became of them, as

I never saw them afterwards. Pursuing our course back and coming in sight of Captain Harris', where we had been the day before, we discovered a party of white men at the house, on which all deserted me but two, (Jacob and Nat), we concealed ourselves in the woods until near night, when I sent them in search of Henry, Sam, Nelson, and Hark, and directed them to rally all they could, at the place we had had our dinner the Sunday before, where they would find me, and I accordingly returned there as soon as it was dark and remained until Wednesday evening, when discovering white men riding around the place as though they were looking for some one, and none of my men joining me, I concluded Jacob and Nat had been taken, and compelled to betray me. On this I gave up all hope for the present; and on Thursday night after having supplied myself with provisions from Mr. Travis's, I scratched a hole under a pile of fence rails in a field, where I concealed myself for six weeks, never leaving my hiding place but for a few minutes in the dead of night to get water which was very near; thinking by this time I could venture out, I began to go about in the night and eaves drop the houses in the neighborhood; pursuing this course for about a fortnight and gathering little or no intelligence, afraid of speaking to any human being, and returning every morning to my cave before the dawn of day. I know not how long I might have led this life, if accident had not betrayed me, a dog in the neighborhood passing by my hiding place one night while I was out, was attracted by some meat I had in my cave, and crawled in and stole it, and was coming out just as I returned. A few nights after, two negroes having started to go hunting with the same dog, and passed that way, the dog came again to the place, and having just gone out to walk about, discovered me and barked, on which thinking myself discovered, I spoke to them to beg concealment. On making myself known they fled from me. Knowing then they would betray me, I immediately left my hiding place, and was pursued almost incessantly until I was taken a fortnight afterwards by Mr. Benjamin Phipps, in a little hole I had dug out with my sword, for the purpose of concealment, under the top of a fallen tree. On Mr. Phipps' discovering the place of my concealment, he cocked his gun and aimed at me. I requested him not to shoot and I would give up, upon which he demanded my sword. I delivered it to him, and he brought me to prison. During the time I was pursued, I had many hair breadth escapes, which your time will not permit you to relate. I am here loaded with chains, and willing to suffer that fate that awaits me.

I here proceeded to make some inquiries of him, after assuring him of the certain death that awaited him, and that concealment would only bring destruction on the innocent as well as guilty, of his own color, if he knew of any extensive or concerted plan. His answer was, I do not. When I questioned him as to the insurrection in North Carolina happening about the same time, he denied any knowledge of it; and when I looked him in the face as though I would search his inmost thoughts, he replied, "I see sir, you doubt my word; but can you not think the same ideas, and strange appearances about this time in the heaven's might prompt others, as well as myself, to this undertaking." I now had much conversation with and asked him many questions, having forborne to do so previously, except in the cases noted in parenthesis; but during his statement, I had, unnoticed by him, taken notes as to some particular circumstances, and having the advantage of his statement before me in writing, on the evening of the third day that I had been with him, I began a cross examination, and found his statement corroborated by every circumstance coming within my own knowledge or the confessions of others who had been either killed or executed, and whom he had not seen nor had any knowledge since 22d of August last, he expressed himself fully satisfied as to the impracticability of his attempt. It has been said he was ignorant and cowardly, and that his object was to murder and rob for the purpose of obtaining money to make his escape. It is notorious, that he was never known to have a dollar in his life; to swear an oath, or drink a drop of spirits. As to his ignorance, he certainly never had the advantages of education, but he can read and write, (it was taught him by his parents,) and for natural intelligence and quickness of apprehension, is surpassed by few men I have ever seen. As to his being a coward, his reason as given for not resisting Mr. Phipps, shews the decision of his character. When he saw Mr. Phipps present his gun, he said he knew it was impossible for him to escape as the woods were full of men; he therefore thought it was better to surrender, and trust to fortune for his escape. He is a complete fanatic, or plays his part most admirably. On other subjects he possesses an uncommon share of intelligence, with a mind capable of attaining any thing; but warped and perverted by the influence of early impressions. He is below the ordinary stature, though strong and active, having the true negro face, every feature of which is strongly marked. I shall not attempt to describe the effect of his narrative, as told and commented on by himself, in the condemned hole of the prison. The calm, deliberate composure with which he spoke of his late deeds and intentions, the expression of his fiend-like face when excited by enthusiasm, still bearing the stains of the blood of helpless innocence about him; clothed with rags and covered with chains; yet daring to raise his manacled hands to heaven, with a spirit soaring above the attributes of man; I looked on him and my blood curdled in my veins.

I will not shock the feelings of humanity, nor wound afresh the bosoms of the disconsolate sufferers in this unparalleled and inhuman massacre, by detailing the deeds of their fiend-like barbarity. There were two or three who were in the power of these wretches, had they known it, and who escaped in the most providential manner. There were two whom they thought they left dead on the field at Mr. Parker's, but who were only stunned by the blows of their guns, as they did not take time to re-load when they charged on them. The escape of a little girl who went to school at Mr. Waller's, and where the children were collecting for that purpose, excited general sympathy. As their teacher had not arrived, they were at play in the yard, and seeing the negroes approach, she ran up on a dirt chimney, (such as are common to log houses,) and remained there unnoticed during the massacre of the eleven that were killed at this place. She remained on her hiding place till just before the arrival of a party, who were in pursuit of the murderers, when she came down and fled to a swamp, where, a mere child as she was, with the horrors of the late scene before her, she lay concealed until the next day, when seeing a party go up to the house, she came up, and on being asked how she escaped, replied with the utmost simplicity, "The Lord helped her." She was taken up behind a gentleman of the party, and returned to the arms of her weeping mother. Miss Whitehead concealed herself between the bed and the mat that supported it, while they murdered her sister in the same room, without discovering her. She was afterwards carried off, and concealed for protection by a slave of the family, who gave evidence against several of them on their trial. Mrs. Nathaniel Francis, while concealed in a closet heard their blows, and the shrieks of the victims of these ruthless savages; they then entered the closet, where she was concealed, and went out without discovering her. While in this hiding place, she heard two of her women in a quarrel about the

division of her clothes. Mr. John T. Baron, discovering them approaching his house, told his wife to make her escape, and scorning to fly, fell fighting on his own threshold. After firing his rifle, he discharged his gun at them, and then broke it over the villain who first approached him, but he was overpowered, and slain. His bravery, however, saved from the hands of these monsters, his lovely and amiable wife, who will long lament a husband so deserving of her love. As directed by him, she attempted to escape through the garden, when she was caught and held by one of her servant girls, but another coming to her rescue, she fled to the woods, and concealed herself. Few indeed, were those who escaped their work of death. But fortunate for society, the hand of retributive justice has over-taken them; and not one that was known to be concerned has escaped.

The Commonwealth vs. *Nat Turner*	Charged with making insurrection, and plotting to take away the lives of divers free white persons,

&c. on the 22d of August, 1831.

The court composed of ———, having met for the trial of Nat Turner, the prisoner was brought in and arraigned, and upon his arraignment pleaded *Not guilty;* saying to his counsel, that he did not feel so.

On the part of the Commonwealth, Levi Waller was introduced, who being sworn, deposed as follows: (*agreeably to Nat's own Confession.*) Col. Trezvant[2] was then introduced, who being sworn, narrated Nat's Confession to him, as follows: (*his Confession as given to Mr. Gray.*) The prisoner introduced no evidence, and the case was submitted without argument to the court, who having found him guilty, Jeremiah Cobb, Esq. Chairman, pronounced the sentence of the court, in the following words: "Nat Turner! Stand up. Have you any thing to say why sentence of death should not be pronounced against you?"

Ans. "I have not. I have made a full confession to Mr. Gray, and I have nothing more to say."

"Attend then to the sentence of the Court. You have been arraigned and tried before this court, and convicted of one of the highest crimes in our criminal code. You have been convicted of plotting in cold blood, the indiscriminate destruction of men, of helpless women, and of infant children. The evidence before us leaves not a shadow of doubt, but that your hands were often imbrued in the blood of the innocent; and your own confession tells us that they were

[2] The committing Magistrate.

stained with the blood of a master; in your own language, 'too indulgent.' Could I stop here, your crime would be sufficiently aggravated. But the original contriver of a plan, deep and deadly, one that never can be effected, you managed so far to put it into execution, as to deprive us of many of our most valuable citizens; and this was done when they were asleep, and defenseless; under circumstances shocking to humanity. And while upon this part of the subject, I cannot but call your attention to the poor misguided wretches who have gone before you. They are not few in number—they were your bosom associates; and the blood of all cries aloud, and calls upon you, as the author of their misfortune. Yes! You forced them unprepared, from Time to Eternity. Borne down by this load of guilt, your only justification is, that you were led away by fanaticism. If this be true, from my soul I pity you; and while you have my sympathies, I am, nevertheless called upon to pass the sentence of the court. The time between this and your execution, will necessarily be very short; and your only hope must be in another world. The judgment of the court is, that you be taken hence to the jail from whence you came, thence to the place of execution, and on Friday next, between the hours of 10 A.M. and 2 P.M. be hung by the neck until you are dead! dead! dead! and may the Lord have mercy upon your soul."

A list of persons murdered in the Insurrection, on the 21st and 22nd of August, 1831.

Joseph Travers and wife and three children, Mrs. Elizabeth Turner, Hartwell Prebles, Sarah Newsome, Mrs. P. Reese and son William, Trajan Doyle, Henry Bryant and wife and child, and wife's mother, Mrs. Catharine Whitehead, son Richard and four daughters and grand-child, Salathiel Francis, Nathaniel Francis' overseer and two children, John T. Barrow, George Vaughan, Mrs. Levi Waller and ten children, William Williams, wife and two boys, Mrs. Caswell Worrell and child, Mrs. Rebecca Vaughan, Ann Eliza Vaughan, and son Arthur, Mrs. John K. Williams and child, Mrs. Jacob Williams and three children, and Edwin Drury—amounting to fifty-five.

A List of Negroes brought before the Court of Southampton, with their owners' names, and sentence.

Daniel,	Richard Porter,	Convicted.
Moses,	J. T. Barrow,	Do.[3]
Tom,	Caty Whitehead,	Discharged.
Jack and Andrew,	Caty Whitehead,	Convicted and transported.
Jacob,	Geo. H. Charlton,	Discharged without trial.
Isaac,	Do.	Convicted and transported.
Jack,	Everett Bryant,	Discharged.
Nathan,	Benj. Blunt's estate,	Convicted.
Nathan, Tom, and Davy, (boys,)	Nathaniel Francis,	Convicted and transported.
Davy,	Elizabeth Turner,	Convicted.
Curtis,	Thomas Ridley,	Do.
Stephen,	Do.	Do.
Hardy and Isham,	Benjamin Edwards,	Convicted and transported.
Sam,	Nathaniel Francis,	Convicted.
Hark,	Joseph Travis' estate,	Do.
Moses, (a boy,)	Do.	Do. and transported.
Davy,	Levi Waller,	Convicted.
Nelson,	Jacob Williams,	Do.
Nat,	Edmund Turner's estate,	Do.
Dred,	William Reese's estate,	Do.
Arnold, Artist, (free,)	Nathaniel Francis,	Do.
Sam,		Discharged.
Ferry and Archer,	J. W. Parker,	Acquitted.
Jim,	J. W. Parker,	Discharged without trial.
Bob,	William Vaughan,	Acquitted.
Davy,	Temperance Parker,	Do.
Daniel,	Joseph Parker,	
	Solomon D. Parker,	Discharged without trial.

[3] ["Ditto."—Editors' note]

Thomas Haithcock, (free,)		Sent on for further trial.
Joe,	John C. Turner,	Convicted.
Lucy,	John T. Barrow,	Do.
Matt,	Thomas Ridley,	Acquitted.
Jim,	Richard Porter,	Do.
Exum Artes, (free,)		Sent on for further trial.
Joe,	Richard P. Briggs,	Discharged without trial.
Bury Newsome, (free,)		Sent on for further trial.
Stephen,	James Bell,	Acquitted.
Jim and Isaac,	Samuel Champion,	Convicted and transported.
Preston,	Hannah Williamson,	Acquitted.
Frank,	Solomon D. Parker,	Convicted and transported.
Jack and Shadrach,	Nathaniel Simmons,	Acquitted.
Nelson,	Benj. Blunt's estate,	Do.
Sam,	Peter Edwards,	Convicted.
Archer,	Arthur G. Reese,	Acquitted.
Isham Turner, (free,)		Sent on for further trial.
Nat Turner,	Putnam Moore, deceased,	Convicted.

Henry Highland Garnet (1815–1882)

There were four events in the life of Henry Garnet of pivotal significance. The first was his escape from slavery in 1824. Fortunately, like Douglass, he was enslaved in Maryland and not in the deep South, thus making the flight to freedom a real possibility. In a sense, Garnet's fortunes were even better than Douglass', for he was able to escape at the approximate age of nine with his family, whereas Douglass did not escape until he was in his early twenties. Having a father and mother with him gave Garnet in his growing years in New York City a sense of stability and familial unity that so many fugitive slaves did not have. Many lived furtive, rootless, wandering lives, moving from city to city, in their search for some kind of economic freedom and social ease in a land that really did not want them.

The second formative and significant event in Garnet's life was his brief enrollment at Noyes Academy in Canaan, New Hampshire, following his initial period of schooling at the New African Free School in New York City. In late June 1835, the young Garnet, accompanied by his schoolmate, Alexander Crummell, and two other boys, journeyed from New York City to New Hampshire, traveling by boat from New York to New Bedford and thence by overland coach to New Hampshire. The trip was particularly hazardous and painful for Garnet because of a serious leg infection that he had contracted while working during a previous summer as a farm hand in New Jersey. Moreover, the townspeople of the several New England towns through which they had to travel greeted the four Negro youths with jeers and racial insults. Garnet received the main brunt of the abuse; because his injured leg prevented his taking a seat inside the coach, he was strapped on top and therefore was a visible target for racial abuse and insult. According to Alexander Crummell's account, the cross-country ride was an almost week-long nightmare of pain, fever, and discomfort for Garnet. However, he endured the pain and suffering in the expectation that his experiences at Noyes Academy would fully compensate for the physical inconvenience of the trip. Upon his arrival at the new Noyes Academy, he was quickly and violently disabused of any hopes he might have had for a happy and serene school term. On the morning of July 3, 1835, a committee of Canaan's citizens drew up a team of one hundred yoke of oxen and physically removed the academy building into a nearby creek. Then, the same committee of citizens gave the young students a departure deadline and harassed them with gunfire and other kinds of intimidation until they were able to escape from Canaan. It is recorded of this traumatic incident that Garnet was the so-called sergeant-at-arms who supervised whatever defense the young Black scholars were able to mount against the fury of Canaan's white citizens. It was he who loaded and fired the one doublebarreled shotgun, and it was he who supervised the barricading of the house in which they were temporarily quartered. Because of his weakened physical condition, the ordeal almost cost him his life. Within a few years after this episode, his ailing leg had to be amputated.

The third significant event in the life and career of Henry Highland Garnet occurred in 1843, after he had entered the ministry of the Presbyterian Church and after he had become the minister of a predominantly white congregation at Troy, New York. Specifically, the event was a speech that Garnet delivered at the National Negro Convention, held in Buffalo, New York, from August 15 through 19. Because the Convention's announced purpose was to consider and discuss "the moral and political condition" of Negroes as "American citizens" and because the Convention's unannounced purpose was to draft a program of political action to achieve the abolition of slavery, Garnet prepared a speech that he considered fitting for the occasion. His paper was entitled "An Address to the Slaves of the United States of America." To the horror of the "moral suasionists" present and to the dismay of the Garrisonians everywhere, Garnet sounded a clarion peal that the four million slaves be armed and seek freedom through force. He urged them to "commence the work of death" and "rather die freemen than live to be slaves." His forceful utterance and militant theme held his audience spellbound and completely overwhelmed those of the abolitionist party who abhorred radical political action as a means of abolishing slavery. Actually, Garnet's speech was a blueprint for a massive armed insurrection that the Convention could not endorse. It is significant, however, that the vote not to endorse won by only one vote, this slender margin of victory being largely attributable to the persuasive powers of Frederick Douglass, who in 1843 still stood with the Garrisonians for "moral suasion" and against political action in the fight against slavery.

For five years, Garnet's eloquent address was unpublished and ignored. Then, in 1848, with the financial support of John Brown, it was issued to the public in a single volume that also contained David Walker's *Appeal,* which had been initially published almost twenty years before. By 1848, the mood of the nation had changed; proslavery elements and antislavery elements continued to be sharply divided and a tough new Fugitive Slave Law was only two years away, but there were fewer persons who approached the cause of abolitionism with the same old-fashioned hymn-singing idealism. Ex-slave Frederick Douglass now knew what ex-slave Henry Garnet had long known—the nation would have to be drenched in blood before the Black slave could be set free.

The fourth significant event in the life of Henry Garnet occurred in 1865. By this time, he had become the well-known and famous minister of New York City's Shiloh Presbyterian Church. During the war that had raged for almost five years, his church had become a spiritual mecca and meeting place for many Black organizations and causes. It was here that Black New Yorkers had gathered to celebrate Emancipation in January 1863, and it was here that they assembled to mourn their losses following the race and draft riot of July 1863. And it was to Shiloh and Henry Garnet that Elizabeth Keckley of Mrs. Lincoln's White House staff made her appeal for funds to help Black war refugees in the nation's capital. Thus, when, in the waning months of the war, a Black minister was sought who could address the United States Congress, Henry Highland Garnet was quickly named as that person. The sermon that he gave in the hall of the House of Representatives on Sunday, February 12, 1865, was well wrought and delivered in that spectacular, persuasive, and appealing manner that had become the hallmark of his pulpit oratory. On the matter of slavery, he remained obdurately militant and unsparing in his assault on the social, moral, and spiritual evil of the "peculiar institution." Undoubtedly, the eloquence of his message was enhanced by his unusual pulpit appearance; few in his audience had ever before beheld a tall, one-legged man of God who was the great-grandson of a Mandingo chieftain and who, at times, waved his crutch for rhetorical emphasis.

Henry Highland Garnet lived to see victory for his cause and lived to see the Black slave freed from bondage. He also lived to see the quick demise of Black Reconstruction and the beginning of the period of disenchantment and racial oppression. By this time, he had grown tired of the struggle. America, for him, had been a bitter land, from the dark squalor of a Maryland slave cabin all the way to the well-appointed splendor of the halls of Congress. So, in 1881 he returned to Africa, the home of his fathers, and died there in 1882.

One of Garnet's important lectures, *The Past and the Present Condition, and the Destiny of the Colored Race* (1848), has been recently reprinted (1969). He also contributed to *The Liberator* and *Douglass' Monthly.* For commentary on his career, see James McCune Smith's introductory "Sketch of the Life and Labors of Rev. Henry Highland Garnet" in Garnet, *Memorial Discourse* (1865); Alexander Crummell's eulogy in *Africa and America* (1891); Vernon Loggins, *The Negro Author* (1931); and Lerone Bennett, Jr., *Pioneers in Protest* (1968).

An Address to the Slaves of the United States of America

Brethren and Fellow Citizens: Your brethren of the North, East, and West have been accustomed to meet together in National Conventions, to sympathize with each other, and to weep over your unhappy condition. In these meetings we have addressed all classes of the free, but we have never, until this time, sent a word of consolation and advice to you. We have been contented in sitting still and mourning over your sorrows, earnestly hoping that before this day your sacred liberties would have been restored. But, we have hoped in vain. Years have rolled on, and tens of thousands have been borne on streams of blood and tears to the shores of eternity. While you have been oppressed, we have also been partakers with you; nor can we be free while you are enslaved. We, therefore, write to you as being bound with you.

Many of you are bound to us, not only by the ties of a common humanity, but we are connected by the more tender relations of parents, wives, husbands, and sisters, and friends. As such we most affectionately address you.

Slavery has fixed a deep gulf between you and us, and while it shuts out from you the relief and consolation which your friends would willingly render, it afflicts and persecutes you with a fierceness which we might not expect to see in the fiends of hell. But still the Almighty Father of mercies has left to us a glimmering ray of hope, which shines out like a lone star in a cloudy sky. Mankind are becoming wiser, and better—the oppressor's power is fading, and you, every day, are becoming better informed, and more numerous. Your grievances, brethren, are many. We shall not attempt, in this short address, to present to the world all the dark catalogue of the nation's sins, which have been committed upon an innocent people. Nor is it indeed necessary, for you feel them from day to day, and all the civilized world looks upon them with amazement.

Two hundred and twenty-seven years ago the first of our injured race were brought to the shores of America. They came not with glad spirits to select their homes in the New World. They came not with their own consent, to find an unmolested enjoyment of the blessings of this fruitful soil. The first dealings they had with men calling themselves Christians exhibited to them the worst features of corrupt and sordid hearts: and convinced them that no cruelty is too great, no villainy and no robbery too abhorrent for even enlightened men to perform, when influenced by avarice and lust. Neither did they come flying upon the wings of liberty to a land of freedom. But they came with broken hearts, from their beloved native land, and were doomed to unrequited toil and deep degradation. Nor did the evil of their bondage end at their emancipation by death. Succeeding generations inherited their chains, and millions have come from eternity into time, and have returned again to the world of spirits, cursed and ruined by American slavery.

The propagators of the system, or their immediate successors, very soon discovered its growing evil, and its tremendous wickedness, and secret promises were made to destroy it. The gross inconsistency of a people holding slaves, who had themselves "ferried o'er the wave" for freedom's sake, was too apparent to be entirely overlooked. The voice of Freedom cried, "Emancipate your slaves." Humanity supplicated with tears for the deliverance of the children of Africa. Wisdom urged her solemn plea. The bleeding captive plead his innocence, and pointed to Christianity who stood weeping at the cross. Jehovah frowned upon the nefarious institution, and thunderbolts, red with vengeance, struggled to leap forth to blast the guilty wretches who maintained it. But all was vain. Slavery had stretched its dark wings of death over the land, the Church stood silently by—

the priests prophesied falsely, and the people loved to have it so. Its throne is established, and now it reigns triumphant.

Nearly three millions of your fellow-citizens are prohibited by law and public opinion (which in this country is stronger than law) from reading the Book of Life. Your intellect has been destroyed as much as possible, and every ray of light they have attempted to shut out from your minds. The oppressors themselves have become involved in the ruin. They have become weak, sensual, and rapacious—they have cursed you—they have cursed themselves—they have cursed the earth which they have trod.

The colonies threw the blame upon England. They said that the mother country entailed the evil upon them, and they would rid themselves of it if they could. The world thought they were sincere, and the philanthropic pitied them. But time soon tested their sincerity. In a few years the colonists grew strong, and severed themselves from the British Government. Their independence was declared, and they took their station among the sovereign powers of the earth. The declaration was a glorious document. Sages admired it, and the patriotic of every nation reverenced the God-like sentiments which it contained. When the power of Government returned to their hands, did they emancipate the slaves? No; they rather added new links to our chains. Were they ignorant of the principles of Liberty? Certainly they were not. The sentiments of their revolutionary orators fell in burning eloquence upon their hearts, and with one voice they cried, LIBERTY OR DEATH. Oh, what a sentence was that! It ran from soul to soul like electric fire, and nerved the arms of thousands to fight in the holy cause of Freedom. Among the diversity of opinions that are entertained in regard to physical resistance, there are but a few found to gainsay the stern declaration. We are among those who do not.

SLAVERY! How much misery is comprehended in that single word. What mind is there that does not shrink from its direful effects? Unless the image of God be obliterated from the soul, all men cherish the love of liberty. The nice discerning political economist does not regard the sacred right more than the untutored African who roams in the wilds of Congo. Nor has the one more right to the full enjoyment of his freedom than the other. In every man's mind the good seeds of liberty are planted, and he who brings his fellow down so low, as to make him contented with a condition of slavery, commits the highest crime against God and man. Brethren, your oppressors aim to do this. They endeavor to make you as much like brutes as possible. When they have blinded the eyes of your mind—when they have embittered the sweet waters of life—when they have shut out the light which shines from the word of God—then, and not till then, has American slavery done its perfect work.

TO SUCH DEGRADATION IT IS SINFUL IN THE EXTREME FOR YOU TO MAKE VOLUNTARY SUBMISSION. The divine commandments you are in duty bound to reverence and obey. If you do not obey them, you will surely meet with the displeasure of the Almighty. He requires you to love Him supremely, and your neighbor as yourself—to keep the Sabbath day holy—to search the Scriptures—and bring up your children with respect for His laws, and to worship no other God but Him. But slavery sets all these at nought, and hurls defiance in the face of Jehovah. The forlorn condition in which you are placed does not destroy your obligation to God. You are not certain of heaven, because you allow yourselves to remain in a state of slavery, where you cannot obey the commandments of the Sovereign of the universe. If the ignorance of slavery is a passport to heaven, then it is a blessing, and no curse, and you should rather desire its perpetuity than its abolition. God will not receive slavery, nor ignorance, nor any other state of mind, for love and obedience to Him. Your condition does not absolve you from your moral obligation. The diabolical injustice by which your liberties are cloven down, NEITHER GOD NOR ANGELS, OR JUST MEN, COMMAND YOU TO SUFFER FOR A SINGLE MOMENT. THEREFORE IT IS YOUR SOLEMN AND IMPERATIVE DUTY TO USE EVERY MEANS, BOTH MORAL, INTELLECTUAL, AND PHYSICAL, THAT PROMISES SUCCESS. If a band of heathen men should attempt to enslave a race of Christians, and to place their children under the influence of some false religion, surely Heaven would frown upon the men who would not resist such aggression, even to death. If, on the other hand, a band of Christians should attempt to enslave a race of heathen men, and to entail slavery upon them, and to keep them in heathenism in the midst of Christianity, the God of heaven would smile upon every effort which the injured might make to disenthral themselves.

Brethren, it is as wrong for your lordly oppressors to keep you in slavery as it was for the man thief to steal our ancestors from the coast of Africa. You should therefore now use the same manner of resistance as would have been just in our ancestors when the bloody foot-prints of the first remorseless soul-thief was placed upon the shores of our fatherland. The humblest peasant is as free in the sight of God as the proudest monarch that ever swayed a sceptre. Liberty is a spirit sent out from God, and like its great Author, is no respecter of persons.

Brethren, the time has come when you must act for yourselves. It is an old and true saying that, "if hereditary bondmen would be free, they must themselves strike the blow." You can plead your own cause, and do the work of emancipation better than any others. The nations of the Old World are moving in the great cause of universal freedom, and some of them at least will, ere long, do you justice. The combined powers of Europe have placed their broad seal of disapprobation upon the African slave-trade. But in the slaveholding parts of the United States the trade is as brisk as ever. They buy and sell you as though you were brute beasts. The North has done much—her opinion of slavery in the abstract is known. But in regard to the South, we adopt the opinion of the *New York Evangelist*—"We have advanced so far, that the cause apparently waits for a more effectual door to be thrown open than has been yet." We are about to point you to that more effectual door. Look around you, and behold the bosoms of your loving wives heaving with untold agonies! Here the cries of your poor children! Remember the stripes your fathers bore. Think of the torture and disgrace of your noble mothers. Think of your wretched sisters, loving virtue and purity, as they are driven into concubinage and are exposed to the unbridled lusts of incarnate devils. Think of the undying glory that hangs around the ancient name of Africa—and forget not that you are native-born American citizens, and as such you are justly entitled to all the rights that are granted to the freest. Think how many tears you have poured out upon the soil which you have cultivated with unrequited toil and enriched with your blood; and then go to your lordly enslavers and tell them plainly, that you *are determined to be free.* Appeal to their sense of justice, and tell them that they have no

more right to oppress you than you have to enslave them. Entreat them to remove the grievous burdens which they have imposed upon you, and to remunerate you for your labor. Promise them renewed diligence in the cultivation of the soil, if they will render to you an equivalent for your services. Point them to the increase of happiness and prosperity in the British West Indies since the Act of Emancipation. Tell them in language which they cannot misunderstand of the exceeding sinfulness of slavery, and of a future judgment, and of the righteous retributions of an indignant God. Inform them that all you desire is FREEDOM, and that nothing else will suffice. Do this, and forever after cease to toil for the heartless tyrants, who give you no other reward but stripes and abuse. If they then commence work of death, they, and not you, will be responsible for the consequences. You had far better all die—*die immediately,* than live slaves, and entail your wretchedness upon your posterity. If you would be free in this generation, here is your only hope. However much you and all of us may desire it, there is not much hope of redemption without the shedding of blood. If you must bleed, let it all come at once—rather *die freemen than live to be the slaves.* It is impossible, like the children of Israel, to make a grand exodus from the land of bondage. The Pharaohs are on both sides of the blood-red waters! You cannot move *en masse* to the dominions of the British Queen—nor can you pass through Florida and overrun Texas, and at last find peace in Mexico. The propagators of American slavery are spending their blood and treasure that they may plant the black flag in the heart of Mexico and riot in the halls of the Montezumas. In language of the Reverend Robert Hall, when addressing the volunteers of Bristol, who were rushing forth to repel the invasion of Napoleon, who threatened to lay waste the fair homes of England, "Religion is too much interested in your behalf not to shed over you her most gracious influences."

You will not be compelled to spend much time in order to become inured to hardships. From the first movement that you breathed the air of heaven, you have been accustomed to nothing else but hardships. The heroes of the American Revolution were never put upon harder fare than a peck of corn and few herrings per week. You have not become enervated by the luxuries of life. Your sternest energies have been beaten out upon the anvil of severe trial. Slavery has done this to make you subservient to its own purposes; but it has done more than this, it has prepared you for any emergency. If you receive good treatment, it is what you can hardly expect; if you meet with pain, sorrow, and even death, these are the common lot of the slaves.

Fellowmen! patient sufferers! behold your dearest rights crushed to the earth! See your sons murdered, and your wives, mothers and sisters doomed to prostitution. In the name of the merciful God, and by all that life is worth, let it no longer be a debatable question, whether it is better to choose *liberty* or *death*.

In 1822, Denmark Veazie, of South Carolina, formed a plan for the liberation of his fellowmen. In the whole history of human efforts to overthrow slavery, a more complicated and tremendous plan was never formed. He was betrayed by the treachery of his own people, and died a martyr to freedom. Many a brave hero fell, but history, faithful to her high trust, will transcribe his name on the same monument with Moses, Hampden, Tell, Bruce, and Wallace, Toussaint L'Ouverture, Lafayette, and Washington. That tremendous movement shook the whole empire of slavery. The guilty soul-thieves were overwhelmed with fear. It is a matter of fact that at this time, and in consequence of the threatened revolution, the slave States talked strongly of emancipation. But they blew but one blast of the trumpet of freedom, and then laid it aside. As these men became quiet, the slaveholders ceased to talk about emancipation: and now behold your condition to-day! Angels sigh over it, and humanity has long since exhausted her tears in weeping on your account!

The patriotic Nathaniel Turner followed Denmark Veazie. He was goaded to desperation by wrong and injustice. By despotism, his name has been recorded on the list of infamy, and future generations will remember him among the noble and brave.

Next arose the immortal Joseph Cinque, the hero of the Amistad. He was a native African, and by the help of God he emancipated a whole ship-load of his fellowmen on the high seas. And he now sings of liberty on the sunny hills of Africa and beneath his native palm-trees, where he hears the lion roar and feels himself as free as the king of the forest.

Next arose Madison Washington, that bright star of freedom, and took his station in the constellation of true heroism. He was a slave on board the brig *Creole,* of Richmond, bound to New Orleans, that great slave mart, with a hundred and four others. Nineteen struck for liberty or death. But one life was taken, and the whole were emancipated, and the vessel was carried into Nassau, New Providence.

Noble men! Those who have fallen in freedom's conflict, their memories will be cherished by the true-hearted and the God-fearing in all future generations; those who are living, their names are surrounded by a halo of glory.

Brethren, arise, arise! Strike for your lives and liberties. Now is the day and the hour. Let every slave throughout the land do this, and the days of slavery are numbered. You cannot be more oppressed than you have been—you cannot suffer greater cruelties than you have already. *Rather die freemen than live to be slaves.* Remember that you are FOUR MILLIONS!

It is in your power so to torment the God-cursed slaveholders that they will be glad to let you go free. If the scale was turned, and black men were the masters and white men the slaves, every destructive agent and element would be employed to lay the oppressor low. Danger and death would hang over their heads day and night. Yes, the tyrants would meet with plagues more terrible than those of Pharaoh. But you are a patient people. You act as though you were made for the special use of these devils. You act as though your daughters were born to pamper the lusts of your masters and overseers. And worse than all, you tamely submit while your lords tear your wives from your embraces and defile them before your eyes. In the name of God, we ask, are you men? Where is the blood of your fathers? Has it all run out of your veins? Awake, awake; millions of voices are calling you! Your dead fathers speak to you from their graves. Heaven, as with a voice of thunder, calls on you to arise from the dust.

Let your motto be resistance! *resistance!* RESISTANCE! No oppressed people have ever secured their liberty without resistance. What kind of resistance you had better make you must decide by the circumstances that surround you, and according to the suggestion of expediency. Brethren, adieu! Trust in the living God. Labor for the peace of the human race, and remember that you are FOUR MILLIONS!

William Wells Brown (1815–1884)

William Wells Brown was Black America's first man of letters. Not only did he write the first novel, the first play, and the first book of travel, but he ranged beyond purely belletristic literature to write history, temperance essays, essays in support of prison reform, and, of course, many essays and speeches in support of abolition and freedom. Like Douglass, he was born a slave, the child of a slaveholder father and a slave mother. In 1825, when he was ten years old, he was taken from Lexington, Kentucky, his birthplace, to St. Louis, Missouri, to work on the river steamboats. After various experiences working on the river (including a brief time in the employ of Elijah Lovejoy, the abolitionist editor of the *St. Louis Times*), Brown escaped from slavery in 1834 at the age of nineteen. Like Douglass, who escaped when he was twenty-one years old, Brown at this point was a vigorous young man with more than a half century of labor for a righteous cause ahead of him.

By the 1840's he had acquired enough education to become a spokesman and participant in the antislavery movement, and he quickly emerged as a writer of note. First he published his own slave narrative in 1847. Then, in 1848, he published a book of song-poems entitled *The Anti-Slavery Harp*. His writing and antislavery work brought him fame, and in 1849 Victor Hugo, as President of the Paris Peace Congress, invited him to Paris to address that body. Afterward, fearing the Fugitive Slave Law of 1850, Brown remained in England until 1854, when he was officially granted his freedom.

During his stay in London he published *Clotel; Or, The President's Daughter* (1853), the first novel by a Black American. The book was well received and quickly went through three editions. Undoubtedly, the enormous success of Mrs. Stowe's *Uncle Tom's Cabin* in 1852 favorably influenced the reception of Brown's novel. Although today *Clotel*, the story of a beautiful quadroon trapped in slavery's web, is generally dismissed as a typically nineteenth-century "blood and tears" romance, as a "first" the novel does have considerable historical significance. It also is of interest because of the revelation that Brown intended the heroine to be a fictional representation of one of Thomas Jefferson's real-life illegitimate slave children. In an American edition (1864), an anonymous Senator is substituted for Jefferson.

Brown's other literary "firsts" were a vivid description of his travels entitled *Three Years in Europe* (1852) and a five-act drama *The Escape or a Leap for Freedom* (1858) published in Boston. Nor did the onset of the Civil War slow his literary production. In 1863 he published *The Black Man: His Antecedents, His Genius, and His Achievements*. Then, following the war, the versatile Brown wrote the first history of the Black soldier in the Civil War. This work, entitled *The Negro in the American Rebellion,* was published in 1867. Just as *Clotel* is not now considered to be particularly good fiction, Brown's account of the Black soldier in the

Civil War is not considered to be very good history. But its publication was timely and the book was well received.

Finally, his full literary career came to a close with two additional major publications. In 1873, he wrote a postwar addendum to his 1863 history of *The Black Man.* This was entitled *The Rising Son; or the Antecedents and Advancement of the Colored Race.* Emancipation and the Black man's new political stature in the Reconstruction era made this new assessment necessary. Then, in 1880, Brown published his last work, *My Southern Home,* which many consider to be his best work. It is an autobiographical narrative recounting experiences and reassessing events and circumstances in a crowded life, but it is better than the *Narrative* of 1847, primarily because there is less emphasis on propaganda and more concern for literary craftsmanship.

William Wells Brown's literary career has received considerable critical attention. His work is commented on in Hugh Gloster's *Negro Voices in American Fiction* (1948), Saunders Redding's *To Make a Poet Black* (1939), Arthur Davis' very good introduction to *Clotel* (1970), and in Jean Yellin's *The Intricate Knot* (1971). W. Edward Farrison's *William Wells Brown: Author and Reformer* (1969) is a definitive biographical study of Black America's first man of letters.

from *Clotel*

Chapter XIX: Escape of Clotel

The fetters galled my weary soul—
  The soul that seemed but thrown away;
I spurned the tyrant's base control,
  Resolved at least the man to play.

No country has produced so much heroism in so short a time, connected with escapes from peril and oppression, as has occurred in the United States among fugitive slaves, many of whom show great shrewdness in their endeavours to escape from this land of bondage. A slave was one day seen passing on the high road from a border town in the interior of the state of Virginia to the Ohio river. The man had neither hat upon his head or coat upon his back. He was driving before him a very nice fat pig, and appeared to all who saw him to be a labourer employed on an adjoining farm. "No negro is permitted to go at large in the Slave States without a written pass from his or her master, except on business in the neighbourhood." "Where do you live, my boy?" asked a white man of the slave, as he passed a white house with green blinds. "Jist up de road, sir," was the answer. "That's a fine pig." "Yes, sir, marser like

dis choat berry much." And the negro drove on as if he was in great haste. In this way he and the pig travelled more than fifty miles before they reached the Ohio river. Once at the river they crossed over; the pig was sold; and nine days after the runaway slave passed over the Niagara river, and, for the first time in his life, breathed the air of freedom. A few weeks later, and on the same road, two slaves were seen passing; one was on horseback, the other was walking before him with his arms tightly bound, and a long rope leading from the man on foot to the one on horseback. "Oh, ho, that's a runaway rascal, I suppose," said a farmer, who met them on the road. "Yes, sir, he bin runaway, and I got him fast. Marser will tan his jacket for him nicely when he gets him." "You are a trustworthy fellow, I imagine," continued the farmer. "Oh yes, sir; marser puts a heap of confidence in dis nigger." And the slaves travelled on. When the one on foot was fatigued they would change positions, the other being tied and driven on foot. This they called "ride and tie." After a journey of more than two hundred miles they reached the Ohio river, turned the horse loose, told him to go home, and proceeded on their way to Canada. However they were not to have it all their own way. There are men in the Free States, and especially in the states adjacent to the Slave States, who make their living by catching the runaway slave, and returning him for the reward that may be offered. As the two slaves above mentioned were travelling on towards the land of freedom, led by the North Star, they were set upon by four of these slave-catchers, and one of them unfortunately captured. The other escaped. The captured fugitive was put under the torture, and compelled to reveal the name of his owner and his place of residence. Filled with delight, the kidnappers started back with their victim. Overjoyed with the prospect of receiving a large reward, they gave themselves up on the third night to pleasure. They put up at an inn. The negro was chained to the bed-post, in the same room with his captors. At dead of night, when all was still, the slave arose from the floor upon which he had been lying, looked around, and saw that the white men were fast asleep. The brandy punch has done its work. With palpitating heart and trembling limbs he viewed his position. The door was fast, but the warm weather had compelled them to leave the window open. If he could but get his chains off, he might escape through the window to the piazza, and reach the ground by one of the posts that supported the piazza. The sleeper's clothes hung upon chairs by the bedside; the slave thought of the padlock key, examined the pockets and found it. The chains were soon off, and the negro stealthily making his way to the window: he stopped and said to himself, "These men are villains, they are enemies to all who like me are trying to be free. Then why not I teach them a lesson?" He then undressed himself, took the clothes of one of the men, dressed himself in them, and escaped through the window, and, a moment more, he was on the high road to Canada. Fifteen days later, and the writer of this gave him a passage across Lake Erie, and saw him safe in her Britannic Majesty's dominions.

We have seen Clotel sold to Mr. French in Vicksburgh, her hair cut short, and everything done to make her realise her position as a servant. Then we have seen her re-sold, because her owners feared she would die through grief. As yet her new purchaser treated her with respectful gentleness, and sought to win her favour by flattery and presents, knowing that whatever he gave her he could take back again. But she dreaded every moment lest the scene should change, and trembled at the sound of every footfall. At every interview with her new master Clotel stoutly maintained that she had left a husband in Virginia, and would never think of taking another. The gold watch and chain, and other glittering presents which he purchased for her, were all laid aside by the quadroon, as if they were of no value to her. In the same house with her was another servant, a man, who had from time to time hired himself from his master. William was his name. He could feel for Clotel, for he, like her, had been separated from near and dear relatives, and often tried to console the poor woman. One day the quadroon observed to him that her hair was growing out again. "Yes," replied William, "you look a good deal like a man with your short hair." "Oh," rejoined she, "I have often been told that I would make a better looking man than a woman. If I had the money," continued she, "I would bid farewell to this place." In a moment more she feared that she had said too much, and smilingly remarked, "I am always talking nonsense." William was a tall, full-bodied negro, whose very countenance beamed with intelligence. Being a mechanic, he had, by his own industry, made more than what he paid his owner; this he laid aside, with the hope that some day he might get enough to purchase his freedom. He had in his chest one hundred and fifty dollars. His was a heart that felt for others, and he had again and again wiped the tears from his eyes as he heard the story of Clotel as related by herself. "If she can get free with a little money, why not give her what I have?" thought he, and then he resolved to do it. An hour later, he came into the quadroon's room, and laid the money in her lap, and said, "There, Miss Clotel, you said if you had the means you would leave this place; there is money enough to take you to England, where you will be free. You are much fairer than many of the white women of the South, and can easily pass for a free white lady." At first Clotel feared that it was a plan by which the negro wished to try her fidelity to her owner; but she was soon convinced by his earnest manner, and the deep feeling with which he spoke, that he was honest. "I will take the money only on one condition," said she; "and that is, that I effect your escape as well as my own." "How can that be done?" he inquired. "I will assume the disguise of a gentleman and you that of a servant, and we will take passage on a steamboat and go to Cincinnati, and thence to Canada." Here William put in several objections to the plan. He feared detection, and he well knew that, when a slave is once caught when attempting to escape, if returned is sure to be worse treated than before. However, Clotel satisfied him that the plan could be carried out if he would only play his part.

The resolution was taken, the clothes for her disguise procured, and before night everything was in readiness for their departure. That night Mr. Cooper, their master, was to attend a party, and this was their opportunity. William went to the wharf to look out for a boat, and had scarcely reached the landing ere he heard the puffing of a steamer. He returned and reported the fact. Clotel had already packed her trunk, and had only to dress and all was ready. In less than an hour they were on board the boat. Under the assumed name of "Mr. Johnson," Clotel went to the clerk's office and took a private state room for herself, and paid her own and servant's fare. Besides being attired in a neat suit of black, she had a white silk handkerchief tied round her chin, as if she was an invalid. A pair of green glasses covered her eyes; and fearing that she would be talked to too much and thus render her liable to be detected, she assumed to be very ill. On the other hand, William was playing his part well in the servant's hall; he was talking loudly of his master's wealth. Nothing appeared as good on the boat as in his master's fine mansion. "I don't like dees steamboats no how," said William; "I hope when marser goes on a journey agin he will take de carriage and de hosses." Mr. Johnson (for such was the name by which Clotel now went) remained in his room, to avoid, as far as possible, conversation with others. After a passage of seven days they arrived at Louisville, and put up at Gough's Hotel. Here they had to await the departure of another boat for the North. They were now in their most critical position. They were still in a slave state, and John C. Calhoun, a distinguished slave-owner, was a guest at this hotel. They feared, also, that trouble would attend their attempt to leave this place for the North, as all persons taking negroes with them have to give bail that such negroes are not runaway slaves. The law upon this point is very stringent: all steamboats and other public conveyances are liable to a fine for every slave that escapes by them, besides paying the full value for the slave. After a delay of four hours, Mr. Johnson and servant took passage on the steamer Rodolph, for Pittsburgh. It is usual, before the departure of the boats, for an officer to examine

every part of the vessel to see that no slave secretes himself on board. "Where are you going?" asked the officer of William, as he was doing his duty on this occasion. "I am going with marser," was the quick reply. "Who is your master?" "Mr. Johnson, sir, a gentleman in the cabin." "You must take him to the office and satisfy that captain that all is right, or you can't go on this boat." William informed his master what the officer had said. The boat was on the eve of going, and no time could be lost, yet they knew not what to do. At last they went to the office, and Mr. Johnson, addressing the captain, said, "I am informed that my boy can't go with me unless I give security that he belongs to me." "Yes," replied the captain, "that is the law." "A very strange law indeed," rejoined Mr. Johnson, "that one can't take his property with him." After a conversation of some minutes, and a plea on the part of Johnson that he did not wish to be delayed owing to his illness, they were permitted to take their passage without further trouble, and the boat was soon on its way up the river. The fugitives had now passed the Rubicon, and the next place at which they would land would be in a Free State. Clotel called William to her room, and said to him, "We are now free, you can go on your way to Canada, and I shall to go Virginia in search of my daughter." The announcement that she was going to risk her liberty in a Slave State was unwelcome news to William. With all the eloquence he could command he tried to persuade Clotel that she could not escape detection, and was only throwing her freedom away. But she had counted the cost, and made up her mind for the worst. In return for the money he had furnished, she had secured for him his liberty, and their engagement was at an end.

After a quick passage the fugitives arrived at Cincinnati, and there separated. William proceeded on his way to Canada, and Clotel again resumed her own apparel, and prepared to start in search of her child. As might have been expected, the escape of those two valuable slaves created no little sensation in Vicksburgh. Advertisements and messages were sent in every direction in which the fugitives were thought to have gone. It was soon, however, known that they had left the town as master and servant; and many were the communications which appeared in the newspapers, in which the writers thought, or pretended, that they had seen the slaves in their disguise. One was to the effect that they had gone off in a chaise; one as master, and the other as servant. But the most probable was an account given by a correspondent of one of the Southern newspapers, who happened to be a passenger in the same steamer in which the slaves escaped, and which we here give:—

One bright starlight night, in the month of December last, I found myself in the cabin of the steamer Rodolph, then lying in the port of Vicksburgh, and bound to Louisville. I had gone early on board, in order to select a good berth, and having got tired of reading the papers, amused myself with watching the appearance of the passengers as they dropped in, one after another, and I being a believer in physiognomy, formed my own opinion of their characters.

The second bell rang, and as I yawningly returned my watch to my pocket, my attention was attracted by the appearance of a young man who entered the cabin supported by his servant, a strapping negro.

The man was bundled up in a capacious overcoat; his face was bandaged with a white handkerchief, and its expression entirely hid by a pair of enormous spectacles.

There was something so mysterious and unusual about the young man as he sat restless in the corner, that curiosity led me to observe him more closely.

He appeared anxious to avoid notice, and before the steamer had fairly left the wharf, requested, in a low, womanly voice, to be shown his berth, as he was an invalid, and must retire early: his name he gave as Mr. Johnson. His servant was called, and he was put quietly to bed. I paced the deck until Tybee light grew dim in the distance, and then went to my berth.

I awoke in the morning with the sun shining in my face: we were then just passing St. Helena. It was a mild beautiful morning, and most of the passengers were on deck, enjoying the freshness of the air, and stimulating their appetites for breakfast. Mr. Johnson soon made his appearance, arrayed as on the night before, and took his seat quietly upon the guard of the boat.

From the better opportunity afforded by daylight, I found that he was a slight built, apparently handsome young man, with black hair and eyes, and of a darkness of complexion that betokened Spanish extraction. Any notice from others seemed painful to him; so to satisfy my curiosity, I questioned his servant, who was standing near, and gained the following information.

His master was an invalid—he had suffered for a long time under a complication of diseases, that had baffled the skill of the best physicians in Mississippi.

He was now suffering principally with the "rheumatism," and he was scarcely able to walk or help himself in any way. He came from Vicksburgh, and was now on his way to Philadelphia, at which place resided his uncle, a celebrated physician, and through whose means he hoped to be restored to perfect health.

This information, communicated in a bold, offhand manner, enlisted my sympathies for the sufferer, although it occurred to me that he walked rather too gingerly for a person afflicted with so many ailments.

After thanking Clotel for the great service she had done him in bringing him out of slavery, William bade her farewell. The prejudice that exists in the Free States against coloured persons on account of their colour, is attributable solely to the influence of slavery, and is but another form of slavery itself. And even the slave who escapes from the Southern plantations, is surprised when he reaches the North, at the amount and withering influence of this prejudice. William applied at the railway station for a ticket for the train going to Sandusky, and was told that if he went by that train he would have to ride in the luggage-van. "Why?" asked the astonished negro. "We don't send a Jim Crow carriage but once a day, and that went this morning." The "Jim Crow" carriage is the one in which the blacks have to ride. Slavery is a school in which its victims learn much shrewdness, and William had been an apt scholar. Without asking any more questions, the negro took his seat in one of the first-class carriages. He was soon seen and ordered out. Afraid to remain in the town longer, he resolved to go by that train; and consequently seated himself on a goods' box in the luggage-van. The train started at its proper time, and all went on well. Just before arriving at the end of the journey, the conductor called on William for his ticket. "I have none," was the reply. "Well, then, you can pay your fare to me," said the officer. "How much is it?" asked the black man. "Two dollars." "What do you charge those in the passenger-carriage?" "Two dollars." "And do you charge me the same as you do those who ride in the best carriages?" asked the negro. "Yes," was the answer. "I shan't pay it," returned the man. "You black scamp, do you think you can ride on this road without paying your fare?" "No, I don't want to ride for nothing; I only want to pay what's right." "Well, launch out two dollars, and that's right." "No, I shan't; I will pay what I ought, and won't pay any more." "Come, come, nigger, your fare and be done with it," said the conductor, in a manner that is never used except by Americans to blacks. "I won't pay you two dollars, and that enough," said William. "Well, as you have come all the way in the luggage-van, pay me a dollar and a half and you may go." "I shan't do any such thing." "Don't you mean to pay for riding?" "Yes, but I won't pay a dollar and a half for riding up here in the freight-van. If you had let me come in the carriage where others ride, I would have paid you two dollars." "Where were you raised? You seem to think yourself as good as white folks." "I want nothing more than my rights." "Well, give me a dollar, and I will let you off." "No, sir, I shan't do it." "What do you mean to do then—don't you wish to pay anything?" "Yes, sir, I want to pay you the full price." "What do you mean by full price?" "What do you charge per hundred-weight for goods?" inquired the negro with a degree of gravity that would have astonished Diogenes himself. "A quarter of a dollar per hundred," answered the conductor. "I weigh just one hundred and fifty pounds," returned William, "and will pay you three-eighths of a dollar." "Do you expect that you will pay only thirty-seven cents for your ride?" "This, sir, is your price. I came in a luggage-van, and I'll pay for luggage." After a vain effort to get the negro to pay more, the conductor took the thirty-seven cents, and noted in his cash-book, "Received for one hundred and fifty pounds of luggage, thirty-seven cents." This, reader, is no fiction; it actually occurred in the railway above described.

Thomas Corwin, a member of the American Congress, is one of the blackest white men in the United States. He was once on his way to Congress, and took passage in one of the Ohio river steamers. As he came just at the dinner hour, he immediately went into the dining saloon, and took his seat at the table. A gentleman with his whole party of five ladies at once left the table. "Where is the captain," cried the man in an angry tone. The captain soon appeared, and it was sometime before he could satisfy the old gent. that Governor Corwin was not a nigger. The newspapers often have notices of mistakes made by innkeepers and others who undertake to accommodate the public, one of which we give below.

On the 6th inst., the Hon. Daniel Webster and family entered Edgartown, on a visit for health and recreation. Arriving at the hotel, without alighting from the coach, the landlord was sent for to see if suitable accommodation could be had. That dignitary appearing, and surveying Mr. Webster, while the hon. senator addressed him, seemed woefully to mistake the dark features of the traveller as he sat back in the corner of the carriage, and to suppose him a *coloured man*, particularly as there were two coloured servants of Mr. W. outside. So he promptly declared that there was no room for him and his family, and he could not be accommodated there—at the same time suggesting that he might perhaps find accommodation at some of the huts "up back," to which he pointed. So deeply did the prejudice of looks possess him, that he appeared not to notice that the stranger introduced himself to him as Daniel Webster, or to be so ignorant as not to have heard of such a personage; and turning away, he expressed to the driver his astonishment that he should bring *black* people there for *him* to take in. It was not till he had been repeatedly assured and made to understand that the said Daniel Webster was a real live senator of the United States, that he perceived his awkward mistake and the distinguished honour which he and his house were so near missing.

In most of the Free States, the coloured people are disfranchised on account of their colour. The following scene, which we take from a newspaper in the state of Ohio, will give some idea of the extent to which this prejudice is carried.

The whole of Thursday last was occupied by the Court of Common Pleas for this county in trying to find out whether one Thomas West was of the VOTING COLOUR, as some had very *constitutional doubts* as to whether his colour was orthodox, and whether his hair was of the official crisp! Was it not a dignified business? Four profound judges, four acute lawyers, twelve grave jurors, and I don't know how many venerable witnesses, making in all about thirty men, perhaps all engaged in the profound, laborious, and illustrious business, of finding out whether a man who pays tax, works on the road, and is an industrious farmer, has been born according to the republican, Christian constitution of Ohio—so that he can vote! And they wisely, gravely, and "JUDGMATICALLY" decided that he should not vote! What wisdom—what research it must have required to evolve this truth! It was left for the Court of Common Pleas for Columbian county, Ohio, in the United States of North America, to find out what Solomon never dreamed of—the courts of all civilised, heathen, or Jewish countries, never contemplated. Lest the wisdom of our courts should be circumvented by some such men as might be named, who are so near being born constitutionally that they might be taken for white by sight, I would suggest that our court be invested with SMELLING powers, and that if a man don't exhale the constitutional smell, he shall not vote! This would be an additional security to our liberties.

William found, after all, that liberty in the so-called Free States was more a name than a reality; that prejudice followed the coloured man into every place that he might enter. The temples erected for the worship of the living God are no exception. The finest Baptist church in the city of Boston has the following paragraph in the deed that conveys its seats to pewholders:

And it is a further condition of these presents, that if the owner or owners of said pew shall determine hereafter to sell the same, it shall first be offered, in writing, to the standing committee of said society for the time being, at such price as might otherwise be obtained for it; and the said committee shall have the right, for ten days after such offer, to purchase said pew for said society, at that price, first deducting therefrom all taxes and assessments on said pew then remaining unpaid. And if the said committee shall not so complete such purchase within said ten days, then the pew may be sold by the owner or owners thereof (after payment of all such arrears) to any one respectable *white person,* but upon the same conditions as are contained in this instrument; and immediate notice of such sale shall be given in writing, by the vendor, to the treasurer of said society.

Such are the conditions upon which the Rowe Street Baptist Church, Boston, disposes of its seats. The writer of this is able to put that whole congregation, minister and all, to flight, by merely putting his coloured face in that church. We once visited a church in New York that had a place set apart for the sons of Ham. It was a dark, dismal looking place in one corner of the gallery, grated in front like a hen-coop, with a black border around it. It had two doors; over one was B. M. —black men; over the other B. W.—black women.

Visit of a Fugitive Slave to the Grave
of Wilberforce

On a beautiful morning in the month of June, while strolling about Trafalgar Square, I was attracted to the base of the Nelson column, where a crowd was standing gazing at the bas-relief representations of some of the great naval exploits of the man whose statue stands on the top of the pillar. The death-wound which the hero received on board the Victory, and his being carried from the ship's deck by his companions, is executed with great skill. Being no admirer of warlike heroes, I was on the point of turning away, when I perceived among the figures (which were as large as life) a full-blooded African, with as white a set of teeth as ever I had seen, and all the other peculiarities of feature that distinguish that race from the rest of the human family, with musket in hand and a dejected countenance, which told that he had been in the heat of the battle, and shared with the other soldiers the pain in the loss of their commander. However, as soon as I saw my sable brother, I felt more at home, and remained longer than I had intended. Here was the Negro, as black a man as was ever imported from the coast of Africa, represented in his proper place by the side of Lord Nelson, on one of England's proudest monuments. How different, thought I, was the position assigned to the colored man on similar monuments in the United States. Some years since, while standing under the shade of the monument erected to the memory of the brave Americans who fell at the storming of Fort Griswold, Connecticut, I felt a degree of pride as I beheld the names of two Africans who had fallen in the fight, yet I was grieved but not surprised to find their names colonized off, and a line drawn between them and the whites. This was in keeping with American historical injustice to its colored heroes.

The conspicuous place assigned to this representative of an injured race, by the side of one of England's greatest heroes, brought vividly before my eye the wrongs of Africa and the philanthropic man of Great Britain, who had labored so long and so successfully for the abolition of the slave trade, and the emancipation of the slaves of the West Indies; and I at once resolved to pay a visit to the grave of Wilberforce.

A half an hour after, I entered Westminster Abbey, at Poets' Corner, and proceeded in search of the patriot's tomb; I had, however, gone but a few steps, when I found myself in front of the tablet erected to the memory of Granville Sharpe, by the African Institution of London, in 1816; upon the marble was a long inscription, recapitulating many of the deeds of this benevolent man, and from which I copied the following:—"He aimed to rescue his native country from the guilt and inconsistency of employing the arm of freedom to rivet the fetters of bondage, and establish for the negro race, in the person of Somerset, the long-disputed rights of human nature. Having in this glorious cause triumphed over the combined resistance of interest, prejudice, and pride, he took his post among the foremost of the honorable band associated to deliver Africa from the rapacity of Europe, by the abolition of the slave-trade; nor was death permitted to interrupt his career of usefulness, till he had witnessed that act of the British Parliament by which the abolition was decreed." After viewing minutely the profile of this able defender of the negro's rights, which was finely chiselled on the tablet, I took a hasty glance at Shakspeare, on the one side, and Dryden on the other, and then passed on, and was soon in the north aisle, looking upon the mementoes placed in honor of genius. There stood a grand and expressive monument to Sir Isaac Newton, which was in every way worthy of the great man to whose memory it was erected. A short distance from that was a statue to Addison, representing the great writer clad in his morning gown, looking as if he had just left the study, after finishing some chosen article for the *Spectator*. The stately monument to the Earl of Chatham is the most attractive in this part of the Abbey. Fox, Pitt, Grattan, and many others, are here represented by monuments. I had to stop at the splendid marble erected to the memory of Sir Fowell Buxton, Bart. A long inscription enumerates his many good qualities, and concludes by saying:—"This monument is erected by his friends and fellow-laborers, at home and abroad, assisted by the grateful contributions of many thousands of the African race." A few steps further and I was standing over the ashes of Wilberforce. In no other place so small do so many great men lie together. The following is the inscription on the monument erected to the memory of this devoted friend of the oppressed and degraded negro race:—

To the memory of WILLIAM WILBERFORCE, born in Hull, August 24, 1759, died in London, July 29, 1833. For nearly half a century a member of the House of Commons, and for six parliaments during that period, one of the two representatives for Yorkshire. In an age and country fertile in great and good men, he was among the foremost of those who fixed the character of their times; because to high and various talents, to warm benevolence, and to universal candor, he added the abiding eloquence of a Christian life. Eminent as he

was in every department of public labor, and a leader in every work of charity, whether to relieve the temporal or the spiritual wants of his fellow men, his name will ever be specially identified with those exertions which, by the blessings of God, removed from England the guilt of the African slave-trade, and prepared the way for the abolition of slavery in every colony of the empire. In the prosecution of these objects, he relied not in vain on God; but, in the progress, he was called to endure great obloquy and great opposition. He outlived, however, all enmity, and, in the evening of his days, withdrew from public life and public observation, to the bosom of his family. Yet he died not unnoticed or forgotten by his country; the Peers and Commons of England, with the Lord Chancellor and the Speaker at their head, in solemn procession from their respective houses, carried him to his fitting place among the mighty dead around, here to repose, till, through the merits of Jesus Christ his only Redeemer and Saviour, whom in his life and in his writings he had desired to glorify, he shall rise in the resurrection of the just.

The monument is a fine one; his figure is seated on a pedestal, very ingeniously done, and truly expressive of his age, and the pleasure he seemed to derive from his own thoughts. Either the orator or the poet have said or sung the praises of most of the great men who lie buried in Westminster Abbey, in enchanting strains. The statues of heroes, princes, and statesmen are there to proclaim their power, worth, or brilliant genius, to posterity. But as time shall step between them and the future, none will be sought after with more enthusiasm or greater pleasure than that of Wilberforce. No man's philosophy was ever moulded in a nobler cast than his; it was founded in the school of Christianity, which was, that all men are by nature equal; that they are wisely and justly endowed by their Creator with certain rights which are irrefragable, and no matter how human pride and avarice may depress and debase, still God is the author of good to man; and of evil, man is the artificer to himself and to his species. Unlike Plato and Socrates, his mind was free from the gloom that surrounded theirs. Let the name, the worth, the zeal, and other excellent qualifications of this noble man, ever live in our hearts, let his deeds ever be the theme of our praise, and let us teach our children to honor and love the name of William Wilberforce.

W. Wells Brown

LONDON

Black Nationalists

John Browne Russwurm (1799–1851)

For many years, John Browne Russwurm was accorded the distinction of having been the first Black man to graduate from a standard four-year college in America. It is now known that this achievement belongs to one Edward Jones, whose graduation on August 23, 1826, from Amherst College preceded Russwurm's graduation from Bowdoin College on September 6, 1826, by exactly two weeks. Although history and time conspired to rob Russwurm of this particular honor, his somewhat abbreviated career was full of pioneering achievements in education, journalism, and politics.

There is no doubt that the circumstances of his birth and early training helped immeasurably. First, he was born free in Port Antonio, Jamaica, his mother being a Black woman and his father a well-to-do American merchant. Being born free in these circumstances in Jamaica was quite different from being born free in these circumstances in America. In America, white people were both deeply afraid of miscegenation and haunted by guilt. Few white men who fathered a child by a Black woman dared to openly acknowledge either the woman or the child. Indeed, to be silent and furtive about such matters became, in America, the "gentlemanly" thing to do. Such was not true in Jamaica. In Russwurm's case, his father accepted his responsibilities and not only gave the child his name but took him into the Russwurm family and exposed him to the best in experience and training. And when the elder Russwurm transferred his business interests to Quebec, young John went with him and there received sound academic training that served him well during his Bowdoin years. When the Russwurms later moved to Maine, the father married a young widow who also had children, but there is no evidence that this new situation in any way changed young John's status. In fact, when the elder Russwurm died unexpectedly, his widow continued to support and supervise her newly acquired stepson. It was under her auspices that he enrolled in Bowdoin in 1824.

The choice of Bowdoin was fortunate. Although chartered in 1794 and hence in 1824 only thirty years old, the college was beginning in the 1820's to emerge as one of the great small liberal arts colleges dotting New England. For instance, one year after young Russwurm's enrollment, three men of future eminence—Hawthorne, Longfellow, and Franklin Pierce—were graduated in the famous class of 1825. And Harriet Beecher Stowe, author of *Uncle Tom's Cabin,* was the wife of a Bowdoin professor and wrote her book while living there in the early 1850's. Finally, when the Civil War began in the 1860's, many Bowdoinites such as General O. O. Howard not only fought in the war, but, when it was over, sought to help the Black people by establishing such schools as Howard University and by working with the Freedmen's Bureau.

Young John Russwurm thus found the atmosphere at Bowdoin both inspiring and racially salutary. He was such a good scholar that he was chosen to be one of the commencement orators, which was a notable "first" both for Bowdoin and its first Black student. The subject of his speech was "The Condition and Prospects of Hayti," and, according to a report on this singular event in the Portland, Maine, *Eastern Argus,* Russwurm's remarks were well delivered and well received. The newspaper report was as follows in part:

The Commencement of the Bowdoin College took place on Wednesday last [September 6, 1826]. Thirty-one gentlemen received the degree of Bachelor of Arts, of whom twenty-four were selected to take parts in the exhibition . . . .

One circumstance was particularly interesting and we believe it was a perfect novelty in the history of our Colleges. Among the young gentlemen who received the honors of the College, and who had parts assigned to them, was a Mr. Russwurm, a person of African descent. He came on the stage under an evident feeling of embarrassment, but finding the sympathies of the audience in his favor, he recovered his courage as he proceeded. He pronounced his part in a full and manly tone of voice, accompanied with appropriate gestures, and it was received by the audience with hearty applause . . . . It is but just to add that Russwurm has conducted [himself] with great propriety during the whole course of his college life, and has always enjoyed the esteem of his classmates.

The *Eastern Argus* further highlighted the event by publishing excerpts from Russwurm's speech, which, it editorialized, was on a "happily selected" topic.

Following his graduation, Russwurm went to New York City and became involved in the abolition movement. It had been his announced intention to study medicine and then emigrate to Haiti, but, for some unknown reason, he was unable to follow his plan. It is probable that the cause of abolition presented a more stimulating challenge. In any event, in 1827 he joined with Samuel B. Cornish in launching *Freedom's Journal,* America's first Black newspaper. For two years, the two neophyte publishers struggled to produce a paper that would speak out against the iniquity of slavery. By 1829, however, their funds were exhausted, and Russwurm was convinced that no Black man, however distinguished his antecedents and academic background, could be free of racial harassment and intimidation in America. He therefore joined those who were advocating colonization and in 1829 emigrated to Liberia.

At the time of Russwurm's emigration, Liberia was still a raw pioneering outpost for the emigrating Americo-Liberians. It had been founded by Jehudi Ashmun for the American Colonization Society just seven years before Russwurm's arrival, and the small number of freedmen who had come there in search of sanctuary from American prejudice were constantly harassed by one or more of the twenty-eight indigenous tribes. Russwurm found himself in a political, military, and social situation far more hazardous than he might have found in Haiti. Nevertheless, he persevered and used his skills in helping to develop the young colony. At first, he served as superintendent of public schools as well as editor of the Liberia *Herald*. Then, after a group of Americo-Liberians established "The Independent African State of Maryland" in 1833 in the Cape Palmas district, Russwurm accepted the governorship of the new state and occupied this position until his death in 1851. During his tenure of office, Liberia declared its independence (1847), and, six years after his death, the independent state of Maryland was annexed by Liberia during the administration of its first Black governor, Joseph Jenkins Roberts, an ex-slave from Virginia.

It has been said that there were three kinds of leaders' among America's Black freedmen during the years before the Civil War. First, there were those like James Forten, Robert Purvis, and Frederick Douglass who remained in America to fight against the apparently ever-increasing encroachments of virulent racism. Then, there were others like Martin Delany, Henry Garnet, and James Whitfield who were tempted by the idea of colonization and flight from America but, for some reason, remained. Then, there were gifted and articulate men like Russwurm, George B. Vashon, and Alexander Crummell who left, fully convinced that America would never prove to be a just society for the Black man. Crummell and Vashon eventually returned to America, and each found work to do during the Black Reconstruction. Russwurm did not live long enough to see America freed of slavery, but he too helped in freedom's cause, although from far away. All three groups of men are part of the Black man's history in America, and were produced and molded by the challenge to fight against racism.

The Condition and Prospects of Hayti

The changes which take place in the affairs of this world show the instability of sublunary things. Empires rise, and fall, flourish, and decay. Knowledge follows revolutions and travels over the globe. Man alone, remains the same being, whether placed under the torrid suns of Africa, or in the more congenial temperate zone. A principle of liberty is implanted in his breast, and all efforts to stifle it are as fruitless as would be the attempt to extinguish the fires of Etna.

It is in the irresistible course of events that all men, who have been deprived of their liberty, shall recover this portion of their indefeasible inheritance. It is in vain to stem the current; degraded man will rise in his native majesty, and claim his rights. They may be withheld from him now, but the day will arrive, when they must be surrendered.

Among the many interesting events of the present day, and illustrative of this, the Revolution in Hayti holds a conspicuous place. The former political condition of Hayti we all doubtless know. After years of sanguinary struggle for freedom and a political existence, the Haytiens on the auspicious day of January first 1804 declared themselves a free and independent nation. Nothing can ever induce them to recede from this declaration. They know too well by their past misfortunes; by their wounds which are yet bleeding, that security can be expected only from within themselves. Rather would they devote themselves to death than return to their former condition.

Can we conceive of anything which can cheer the desponding spirit, can reanimate and stimulate it to put every thing to the hazard? Liberty can do this. Such were its effects upon the Haytiens—men who in slavery showed neither spirit nor genius: but when Liberty, when once Freedom struck their astonished ears, they became new creatures: stepped forth as men, and showed to the world, that though Slavery may benumb, it cannot entirely destroy our faculties. Such were Touissant L'Overture [*sic*], Desalines [*sic*] and Christophe!

The Haytiens have adopted the republican form of government: and so firmly is it established, that in no country are the rights and privileges of citizens and foreigners more respected, and crimes less frequent. They are a brave and generous people. If cruelties were inflicted during the Revolutionary war, it was owing to the policy pursued by the French commanders, which compelled them to use retaliatory measures.

For who shall expostulate with men who have been hunted with bloodhounds—who have been threatened with an Auto-da-fé—whose relations and friends have been hung on gibbets before their eyes—have been sunk by hundreds in the sea—and tell them they ought to exercise kindness towards such mortal enemies? Remind me not of moral duties, of meekness and generosity. Show me the man who has exercised them under these trials, and you point to one who is more than human. It is an undisputed fact, that more than sixteen thousand Haytiens perished in the modes above specified. The cruelties inflicted by the French on the children of Hayti have exceded the crimes of Cortez and Pizarro.

Thirty-two years of their Independence so gloriously achieved, have effected wonders. No longer are they the same people. They had faculties, yet were these faculties oppressed under the load of servitude and ignorance. With a countenance erect and fixed upon Heaven, they can now contemplate the works of Divine munificence. Restored to the dignity of man to society, they have acquired a new existence—their powers have been developed: a career of glory and happiness unfolds itself before them.

The Haytien Government has arisen in the neighborhood of European settlements. Do the public proceedings and details of its Government bespeak any inferiority? Their state papers are distinguished from those of many European Courts, only by their superior energy and non-exalted sentiments; and while the manners and politics of Boyer emulate those of his Republican neighbours: the court of Christophe had almost as much foppery; almost as many lords and ladies of the bed-chamber; and almost as great a proportion of stars, and ribbons, and gilded chariots, as those of his brother potentates in any part of the world.

(Placed by Divine Providence amid circumstances more favourable, than were their ancestors, the Haytiens can more easily than they, make rapid strides in the career of civilization—they can demonstrate that although the God of nature may have given them a darker complexion, still are men alike sensible to all the miseries of slavery, and to all the blessings of freedom.)

May we not indulge in the pleasing hope, that the Independence of Hayti has laid the foundation of an Empire that will take a rank with the nations of the earth—that a country, the local situation of which is favourable to trade and commercial enterprise—possessing a free and well regulated government, which encourages the useful and liberal arts: a country containing an enterprising and growing population, which is determined to live free, or die gloriously: will advance rapidly in all the arts of civilization.

We look forward with peculiar satisfaction to the period when like Tyre of old, her vessels shall extend the fame of her riches and glory, to the remotest borders of the globe;—to the time when Hayti treading in the footsteps of her sister republicks, shall, like them, exhibit a picture of rapid and unprecedented advance in population, wealth and intelligence.

Martin R. Delany (1812–1885)

Martin Delany was a man of so many talents and accomplishments that it is difficult to discuss him in the context of any one specific area of endeavor. In his lifetime he was a journalist, physician, lecturer, explorer, ethnologist, army officer, civil servant, trial justice, novelist, abolitionist, promoter and organizer of Black emigration projects, and a candidate for political office. Besides traveling extensively in his own country, he went to Europe, Africa, and Canada. Delany's crowded life schedule also allowed him time to marry and raise a family of seven children.

Born free in Charles Town, Virginia, Delany moved to Pennsylvania, where he received his early education, and finally to New York, where he went to the African Free School and was graduated from Oneida Institute. Before entering Harvard Medical School, he married and was well embarked on a career of journalism. From 1843 to 1847, he published his own newspaper, *The Mystery,* and with Frederick Douglass he edited the *North Star* from 1847 to 1849. It was during this period that his unpopular ideas nearly cost him his life. In 1848 he was seriously beaten by a mob in Ohio.

In the same year that he received his M.D. degree from Harvard (1852), he published one of his most significant works, *The Condition, Elevation, and Destiny of the Colored People of the United States, Politically Considered,* one of the few theoretical works dealing with the Negro question published prior to the Civil War. Delany's approach in the tract is factual and practical. He promotes the emigration of American Blacks to nonwhite areas of the world in order that they might have the opportunity to form their own states and determine their own destinies. In *The Condition,* his vision is foresighted, his tone secular and modern, and his plan anticipatory of the boldest of Black reactions to white America. Thus he defends the political wisdom of Black withdrawal from the United States:

> *Every people should be the originators of their own destiny, the projectors of their own schemes, and the creators of the events that lead to their destiny . . . .*

The abolitionists' reaction against his publication was very strong. They convincingly argued to Delany that his tract was a serious impediment to emancipation. Delany's response was sympathetic, and he stopped circulation.

Between 1852 and the Civil War, Martin Delany's activities mushroomed. He practiced medicine in Chicago, Canada, and Pennsylvania; in Philadelphia he figured prominently in putting down a cholera epidemic. During this period he traveled extensively, speaking against slavery and promoting the idea of Black emigration. He was a moving force in establishing the National Emigration Convention of Colored Men in 1854. Later, he organized an expedition to Nigeria to explore the feasibility of emigration. In 1861 he published his famous *Official Report of the Niger Valley Exploring Party*. On his trips to Africa, he is reported to have negotiated with several African kings.

Martin Delany was also famed as a scholar. Besides being a published ethnologist, he wrote botanical articles and was a member of the International Statistical Congress of the National [British] Association for the Promotion of the Social Science Congress, Glasgow, Scotland. During the congress of 1860, an interesting incident occurred. In his address, Henry Brougham, British statesman and a vigorous antislavery man, honored the presence of Martin Delany, the only Black man there. Delany rose, thanked the gentleman, and assured the assemblage of his dignity and pride with the closing words, "I am a man." His unexpected response was applauded by all except the American delegates, who withdrew from the proceedings.

In 1859 Delany published portions of his only novel, *Blake or The Huts of America*. According to Robert Bone in *The Negro Novel in America*, it is a remarkable work that deviates from the "formula" of abolitionist literature (the broken home, the violated octoroon, and so on) and treats slavery as an exploitative labor system.

In the Civil War, Delany won the distinction of being the first Black man to be commissioned with a field rank by President Lincoln. He received the rank of major and served the Union army as a surgeon. After the war, Delany was an employee of the Freedmen's Bureau, a justice of the peace in South Carolina, and a candidate for lieutenant governor in South Carolina. Before he died in Xenia, Ohio, in 1885, Delany wrote three more essays dealing with his reflections on the Civil War, international policy toward Africa, and the political destiny of the Black man in America. All of these essays were included in Frank Rollin's 1883 edition of *The Life and Public Services of Martin Delany*.

Inevitably, every work giving some account of the Black man's record in the nineteenth century mentions Martin R. Delany. Benjamin Quarles in his *The Negro and the Civil War* (1953) describes Delany's extensive involvement in many of the activities and events surrounding the war. His military significance is also very well documented in James M. McPherson's *The Negro's Civil War* (1965). His work as an abolitionist is discussed in Quarles' *Black Abolitionists* (1969). There is also a recent effort to provide up-to-date editions of Delany's own works. The University of Michigan Press has published a reprint of the *Official Report of the Niger Valley Exploring Party* (1969), and Beacon Press has released an edition of *Blake* that includes some additional material not in the version of the novel originally serialized in Volume I of the *Anglo-African* in 1859. Critical comment on Delany's one and only novel may be found in Hugh Gloster's *Negro Voices in American Fiction* (1948) and in Robert Bone's *The Negro Novel in America* (1965). There is also extensive mention of Delany's intellectual impact and significance in Harold Cruse's *Crisis of the Negro Intellectual* (1967). Victor Ullman's *Martin R. Delany: The Beginnings of Black Nationalism* (1971) is a recent full-scale biography.

from *The Condition, Elevation, and Destiny of the Colored People of the United States, Politically Considered*

Chapter II: Comparative Condition of the Colored People of the United States

The United States, untrue to her trust and unfaithful to her professed principles of republican equality, has also pursued a policy of political degradation to a large portion of her native born countrymen, and that class is the Colored People. Denied an equality not only of political, but of natural rights, in common with the rest of our fellow citizens, there is no species of degradation to which we are not subject.

Reduced to abject slavery is not enough, the very thought of which should awaken every sensibility of our common nature; but those of their descendants who are freemen even in the non-slaveholding States, occupy the very same position politically, religiously, civilly and socially, (with but few exceptions,) as the bondman occupies in the slave States.

In those States, the bondman is disfranchised, and for the most part so are we. He is denied all civil, religious, and social privileges, except such as he gets by mere sufferance, and so are we. They have no part nor lot in the government of the country, neither have we. They are ruled and governed without representation, existing as mere nonentities among the citizens, and excrescences on the body politic—a mere dreg in community, and so are we. Where then is our political superiority to the enslaved? none, neither are we superior in any other relation to society, except that we are defacto masters of ourselves and joint rulers of our own domestic household, while the bondman's self is claimed by another, and his relation to his family denied him. What the unfortunate classes are in Europe, such are we in the United States, which is folly to deny, insanity not to understand, blindness not to see, and surely now full time that our eyes were opened to these startling truths, which for ages have stared us full in the face.

It is time that we had become politicians, we mean, to understand the political economy and domestic policy of nations; that we had become as well as moral theorists, also the practical demonstrators of equal rights and self-government. Except we do, it is idle to talk about rights, it is mere chattering for the sake of being seen and heard—like the slave, saying something because his so called "master" said it, and saying just what he told him to say. Have we not now sufficient intelligence among us to understand our true position, to realise our actual condition, and determine for ourselves what is best to be done? If we have not now, we never shall have, and should at once cease prating about our equality, capacity, and all that.

Twenty years ago, when the writer was a youth, his young and yet uncultivated mind was aroused, and his tender heart made to leap with anxiety in anticipation of the promises then held out by the prime movers in the cause of our elevation.

In 1830 the most intelligent and leading spirits among the colored men in the United States, such as James Forten, Robert Douglass, I. Bowers, A. D. Shadd, John Peck, Joseph Cassey, and John B. Vashon of Pennsylvania; John T. Hilton, Nathaniel and Thomas Paul, and James G. Barbodoes of Massachusetts; Henry Sipkins, Thomas Hamilton, Thomas L. Jennings, Thomas Downing, Samuel E. Cornish, and others of New York; R. Cooley and others of Maryland, and representatives from other States which cannot now be recollected, the data not being at hand, assembled in the city of Philadelphia, in the capacity of a National Convention, to "devise ways and means for the bettering of our condition." These Conventions determined to assemble annually, much talent, ability, and energy of character being displayed; when in 1831 at a sitting of the Convention in September, from their previous pamphlet reports, much interest having been created throughout the country, they were favored by the presence of a number of whites, some of whom were able and distinguished men, such as Rev. R. R. Gurley, Arthur Tappan, Elliot Cresson, John Rankin, Simeon Jocelyn and others, among them William Lloyd Garrison, then quite a young man, all of whom were staunch and ardent Colonizationists, young Garrison at that time, doing his mightiest in his favorite work.

Among other great projects of interest brought before the convention at a previous sitting, was that of the expediency of a general emigration, as far as it was practicable, of the colored people to the British Provinces of North America. Another was that of raising sufficient means for the establishment and erection of a College for the proper education of the colored youth. These gentlemen long accustomed to observation and reflection on the condition of their people, saw at once, that there must necessarily be means used adequate to the end to be attained—that end being an unqualified equality with the ruling class of their fellow citizens. He saw that as a class, the colored people of the country were ignorant, degraded and oppressed, by far the greater portion of them being abject slaves in the South, the very condition of whom was almost enough, under the circumstances, to blast the remotest hope of success, and those who were freemen, whether in the South or North, occupied a subservient, servile, and menial position, considering it a favor to get into the service of the whites, and do their degrading offices. That the difference between the whites and themselves, consisted in the superior advantages of the one over the other, in point of attainments. That if a knowledge of the arts and sciences, the mechanical occupations, the industrial occupations, as farming, commerce, and all the various business enterprises, and learned professions were necessary for the superior position occupied by their rulers, it was also necessary for them. And very reasonably too, the first suggestion which occurred to them was, the advantages of a location, then the necessity of a qualification. They reasoned with themselves, that all distinctive differences made among men on account of their origin, is wicked, unrighteous, and cruel, and never shall receive countenance in any shape from us, therefore, the first acts of the measures entered into by them, was to protest, solemnly protest, against every unjust measure and policy in the country, having for its object the proscription of the colored people, whether state, national, municipal, social, civil, or religious.

But being far-sighted, reflecting, discerning men, they took a political view of the subject, and determined for the good of their people to be governed in their policy according to the facts as they presented themselves. In taking a glance at Europe, they discovered there, however unjustly, as we have shown in another part of this pamphlet, that there are and have been numerous classes proscribed and oppressed, and it was not for them to cut short their wise deliberations, and arrest their proceedings in contention, as to the cause, whether on account of language, the color of eyes, hair, skin, or their origin of country—because all this is contrary to reason, a contradiction to common sense, at war with nature herself and at variance with facts as they stare us every day in the face, among all nations, in every country—this being made the pretext as a matter of *policy* alone—a fact worthy of observation, that wherever the objects of oppression are the most easily distinguished by any peculiar or general characteristics, these people are the more easily oppressed, because the war of oppression is the more easily waged against them. This is the case with the modern Jews and many other people who have strongly-marked, peculiar, or distinguishing characteristics. This arises in this wise. The policy of all those who proscribe any people, induces them to select as the objects of proscription, those who differed as much as possible, in some particulars, from themselves. This is to ensure the greater success, because it engenders the greater prejudice, or in other words, elicits less interest on the part of the oppressing class, in their favor. This fact is well understood in national conflicts, as the soldier or civilian, who is distinguished by his dress, mustache, or any other peculiar appendage, would certainly prove himself a madman, if he did not take the precaution to change his dress, remove his mustache, and conceal as much as possible his peculiar characteristics, to give him access among the repelling party. This is mere policy, nature having nothing to do with it. Still, it is a fact, a great truth well worthy of remark, and as such we adduce it for the benefit of those of our readers, unaccustomed to an enquiry into the policy of nations.

In view of these truths, our fathers and leaders in our elevation, discovered that as a policy, we the colored people were selected as the subordinate class in this country, not on account of any actual or supposed inferiority on their part, but simply because, in view of all the circumstances of the case, they were the very best class that could be selected. They would have as readily had any other class as subordinates in the country, as the colored people, but the condition of society *at the time,* would not admit of it. In the struggle for American Independence, there were among those who performed the most distinguished parts, the most common-place peasantry of the Provinces. English, Danish, Irish, Scotch, and others, were among those whose names blazoned forth as heroes in the American Revolution. But a single reflection will convince us, that no course of policy could have induced the proscription of the parentage and relatives of such men as Benjamin Franklin the printer, Roger Sherman the cobbler, the tinkers, and others of the signers of the Declaration of Independence. But as they were determined to have a subservient class, it will readily be conceived, that according to the state of society at the time, the better policy on their part was, to select some class, who from their political position—however much they may have contributed their aid as we certainly did, in the general struggle for liberty by force of arms—who had the least claims upon them, or who had the *least chance,* or was the *least potent* in urging their claims. This class of course was the colored people and Indians.

The Indians who in the early settlement of the continent, before an African captive had ever been introduced thereon, were reduced to the most abject slavery, toiling day and night in the mines, under the relentless hands of heartless Spanish taskmasters, but being a race of people raised to the sports of fishing, the chase, and of war, were wholly unaccustomed to labor, and therefore sunk under the insupportable weight, two millions and a half having fallen victims to the cruelty of oppression and toil suddenly placed upon their shoulders. And it was only this that prevented their farther enslavement as a class, after the provinces were absolved from the British Crown. It is true that their general enslavement took place on the islands and in the mining districts of South America, where indeed, the Europeans continued to enslave them, until a comparatively recent period; still, the design, the feeling, and inclination from policy, was the same to do so here, in this section of the continent.

Nor was it until their influence became too great, by the political position occupied by their brethren in the new republic, that the German and Irish peasantry ceased to be sold as slaves for a term of years fixed by law, for the repayment of their passage-money, the descendants of these classes of people for a long time being held as inferiors, in the estimation of the ruling class, and it was not until they assumed the rights and privileges guaranteed to them by the established policy of the country, among the leading spirits of whom were their relatives, that the policy towards them was discovered to be a bad one, and accordingly changed. Nor was it, as is frequently very erroneously asserted, by colored as well as white persons, that it was on account of hatred to the African, or in other words, on account of hatred to his color, that the African was selected as the subject of oppression in this country. This is sheer nonsense; being based on policy and nothing else, as shown in another place. The Indians, who being the most foreign to the sympathies of the Europeans on this continent, were selected in the first place, who, being unable to withstand the hardships, gave way before them.

But the African race had long been known to Europeans, in all ages of the world's history, as a long-lived, hardy race, subject to toil and labor of various kinds, subsisting mainly by traffic, trade, and industry, and consequently being as foreign to the sympathies of the invaders of the continent as the Indians, they were selected, captured, brought here as a laboring class, and as a matter of policy held as such. Nor was the absurd idea of natural inferiority of the African ever dreamed of, until recently adduced by the slave-holders and their abettors, in justification of their policy. This, with contemptuous indignation, we fling back into their face, as a scorpion to a vulture. And so did our patriots and leaders in the cause of regeneration know better, and never for a moment yielded to the base doctrine. But they had discovered the great fact, that a cruel policy was pursued towards our people, and that they possessed distinctive characteristics which made them the objects of proscription. These characteristics being strongly marked in the colored people, as in the Indians, by color, character of hair and so on, made them the more easily distinguished from other Americans, and the policies more effectually urged against us. For this reason they introduced the subject of emigration to Canada, and a proper institution for the education of the youth.

At this important juncture of their proceedings, the afore named white gentlemen were introduced to the notice of the Convention, and after gaining permission to speak, expressed their gratification and surprise at the qualification and talent manifested by different members of the Convention, all expressing their determination to give the cause of the colored people more serious reflection. Mr. Garrison, the youngest of them all, and none the less honest on account of his youthfulness, being but 26 years of age at the time, (1831) expressed his determination to change his course of policy at once, and espouse the cause of the elevation of the colored people here in their own country. We are not at present well advised upon this point, it now having escaped our memory, but we are under the impression that Mr. Jocelyn also, at once changed his policy.

During the winter of 1832, Mr. Garrison issued his "Thoughts on African Colonization," and near about the same time or shortly after, issued the first number of the "Liberator," in both of which, his full convictions of the enormity of American slavery, and the wickedness of their policy towards the colored people, were fully expressed. At the sitting of the Convention in this year, a number, perhaps all of these gentlemen were present, and those who had denounced the Colonization scheme, and espoused the cause of the elevation of the colored people in this country, or the Anti-Slavery cause, as it was now termed, expressed themselves openly and without reserve.

Sensible of the high-handed injustice done to the colored people in the United States, and the mischief likely to emanate from the unchristian proceedings of the deceptious Colonization scheme, like all honest hearted penitents, with the ardor only known to new converts, they entreated the Convention, whatever they did, not to entertain for a moment, the idea of recommending emigration to their people, nor the establishment of separate institutions of learning. They earnestly contended, and doubtless honestly meaning what they said, that they (the whites) had been our oppressors and injurers, they had obstructed our progress to the high positions of civilization, and now, it was their bounden duty to make full amends for the injuries thus inflicted on an unoffending people. They exhorted the Convention to cease; as they had laid on the burden, they would also take it off; as they had obstructed our

pathway, they would remove the hindrance. In a word, as they had oppressed and trampled down the colored people, they would now elevate them. These suggestions and promises, good enough to be sure, after they were made, were accepted by the Convention—though some gentlemen were still in favor of the first project as the best policy, Mr. A. D. Shadd of West Chester, Pa., as we learn from himself, being one among that number —ran through the country like wild-fire, no one thinking, and if he thought, daring to speak above his breath of going any where out of certain prescribed limits, or of sending a child to school, if it should but have the name of "colored" attached to it, without the risk of being termed a "traitor" to the cause of his people, or an enemy to the Anti-Slavery cause.

At this important point in the history of our efforts, the colored men stopped suddenly, and with their hands thrust deep in their breeches-pockets, and their mouths gaping open, stood gazing with astonishment, wonder, and surprise, at the stupendous moral colossal statues of our Anti-Slavery friends and brethren, who in the heat and zeal of honest hearts, from a desire to make atonement for the many wrongs inflicted, promised a great deal more than they have ever been able half to fulfill, in thrice the period in which they expected it. And in this, we have no fault to find with our Anti-Slavery friends, and here wish it to be understood, that we are not laying any thing to their charge as blame, neither do we desire for a moment to reflect on them, because we heartily believe that all that they did at the time, they did with the purest and best of motives, and further believe that they now are, as they then were, the truest friends we have among the whites in this country. And hope, and desire, and request, that our people should always look upon *true* anti-slavery people, Abolitionists we mean, as their friends, until they have just cause for acting otherwise. It is true, that the Anti-Slavery, like all good causes, has produced some recreants, but the cause itself is no more to be blamed for that, than Christianity is for the malconduct of any professing hypocrite, nor the society of Friends, for the conduct of a broad-brimmed hat and shad-belly coated horse-thief, because he spoke *thee* and *thou* before stealing the horse. But what is our condition even amidst our Anti-Slavery friends? And here, as our sole intention is to contribute to the elevation of our people, we must be permitted to express our opinion freely, without being thought uncharitable.

In the first place, we should look at the objects for which the Anti-Slavery cause was commenced, and the promises or inducements it held out at the commencement. It should be borne in mind, that Anti-Slavery took its rise among *colored men,* just at the time they were introducing their greatest projects for their own elevation, and that our Anti-Slavery brethren were converts of the colored men, in behalf of their elevation. Of course, it would be expected that being baptized into the new doctrines, their faith would induce them to embrace the principles therein contained, with the strictest possible adherence.

The cause of dissatisfaction with our former condition, was, that we were proscribed, debarred, and shut out from every respectable position, occupying the places of inferiors and menials.

It was expected that Anti-Slavery, according to its professions, would extend to colored persons, as far as in the power of its adherents, those advantages nowhere else to be obtained among white men. That colored boys would get situations in their shops and stores, and every other advantage tending to elevate them as far as possible, would be extended to them. At least, it was expected, that in Anti-Slavery establishments, colored men would have the preference. Because, there was no other ostensible object in view, in the commencement of the Anti-Slavery enterprise, than the *elevation* of the *colored man,* by facilitating his efforts in attaining to equality with the white man. It was urged, and it was true, that the colored people were susceptible of all that the whites were, and all that was required was to give them a fair opportunity, and they would prove their capacity. That it was unjust, wicked, and cruel, the result of an unnatural prejudice, that debarred them from places of respectability, and that public opinion could and should be corrected upon this subject. That it was only necessary to make a sacrifice of feeling, and an innovation on the customs of society, to establish a different order of things,—that as Anti-Slavery men, they were willing to make these sacrifices, and determined to take the colored man by the hand, making common cause with him in affliction, and bear a part of the odium heaped upon him. That his cause was the cause of God—that "In as much as ye did it not unto the least of these my little ones, ye did it not unto me," and that as Anti-Slavery men, they would "do right if the heavens fell."

Thus, was the cause espoused, and thus did we expect much. But in all this, we were doomed to disappointment, sad, sad disappointment. Instead of realising what we had hoped for, we find ourselves occupying the very same position in relation to our Anti-Slavery friends, as we do in relation to the pro-slavery part of the community—a mere secondary, underling position, in all our relations to them, and any thing more than this, is not a matter of course affair—it comes not by established anti-slavery custom or right, but like that which emanates from the proslavery portion of the community, by mere sufferance.

It is true, that the "Liberator" office, in Boston, has got Elijah Smith, a colored youth, at the cases—the "Standard," in New York, a young colored man, and the "Freeman," in Philadelphia, William Still, another, in the publication office, as "packing clerk;" yet these are but three out of the hosts that fill these offices in their various departments, all occupying places that could have been, and as we once thought, would have been, easily enough, occupied by colored men. Indeed, we can have no other idea about anti-slavery in this country, than that the legitimate persons to fill any and every position about an anti-slavery establishment are colored persons. Nor will it do to argue in extenuation, that white men are as justly entitled to them as colored men; because white men do not from *necessity* become anti-slavery men in order to get situations; they being white men, may occupy any position they are capable of filling—in a word, their chances are endless, every avenue in the country being opened to them. They do not therefore become abolitionists, for the sake of employment—at least, it is not the song that anti-slavery sung, in the first love of the new faith, proclaimed by its disciples.

And if it be urged that colored men are incapable as yet to fill these positions, all that we have to say is, that the cause has fallen far short; almost equivalent to a failure, of a tithe, of what it promised to do in half the period of its existence, to this time, if it have not as yet, now a period of twenty years, raised up colored men enough, to fill the offices within its patronage. We think it is not unkind to say, if it had been half as faithful to itself, as it should have been—its professed principles we mean; it could have reared and tutored from childhood, colored men enough by this time, for its own especial purpose. These we know could have been easily obtained, because colored people in general, are favorable to the anti-slavery cause, and wherever there is an adverse manifestation, it arises from sheer ignorance; and we have now but comparatively few such among us. There is one thing certain, that no colored person, except such as would reject education altogether, would be adverse to putting their child with an anti-slavery person, for educational advantages. This then, could have been done. But it has not been done, and let the cause of it be whatever it may, and let whoever may be to blame, we are willing to let all that pass, and extend to our anti-slavery brethren the right-hand of fellowship, bidding them God-speed in the propagation of good and wholesome sentiments —for whether they are practically carried out or not, the professions are in themselves all right and good. Like Christianity, the principles are holy and of divine origin. And we believe, if ever a man started right, with pure and holy motives, Mr. Garrison did; and that, had he the power of making the cause what it should be, it would all be right, and there never would have been any cause for the remarks we have made, though in kindness, and with the purest of motives. We are nevertheless, still occupying a miserable position in the community, wherever we live; and what we most desire is, to draw the attention of our people to this fact, and point out what, in our opinion, we conceive to be a proper remedy.

Chapter III: American Colonization

When we speak of colonization, we wish distinctly to be understood, as speaking of the "American Colonization Society"—or that which is under its influence—commenced in Richmond, Virginia, in 1817, under the influence of Mr. Henry Clay of Ky., Judge Bushrod Washington of Va., and other Southern slaveholders, having for their express object, as their speeches and doings all justify us in asserting in good faith, the removal of the free colored people from the land of their birth, for the security of the slaves, as property to the slave propagandists.

This scheme had no sooner been propagated, than the old and leading colored men of Philadelphia, Pa., with Richard Allen, James Forten, and others at their head, true to their trust and the cause of their brethren, summoned the colored people together, and then and there, in language and with voices pointed and loud, protested against the scheme as an outrage, having no other object in view, than the benefit of the slave-holding interests of the country, and that as freemen, they would never prove recreant to the cause of their brethren in bondage, by leaving them without hope of redemption from their chains. This determination of the colored patriots of Philadelphia was published in full, authentically, and circulated throughout the length and breadth of the country by the papers of the day. The colored people every where received the news, and at once endorsed with heart and soul, the doings of the Anti-Colonization Meeting of colored freemen. From that time forth, the colored people generally have had no sympathy with the colonization scheme, nor confidence in its leaders, looking upon them all, as arrant hypocrites, seeking every opportunity to deceive them. In a word, the monster was crippled in its infancy, and has never as yet recovered from the stroke. It is true, that like its ancient sire, that was "more subtile than all the beasts of the field," it has inherited a large portion of his most prominent characteristic—an idiosyncrasy with the animal—that enables him to entwine himself into the greater part of the Church and other institutions of the country, which having once entered there, leaves his venom, which put such a spell on the conductors of those institutions, that it is only on condition that a colored person consents to go to the neighborhood of his kindred brother monster the boa, that he may find admission in the one or the other. We look upon the American Colonization Society as one of the most arrant enemies of the colored man, ever seeking to discomfit him, and envying him of every privilege that he may enjoy. We believe it to be anti-Christian in its character, and misanthropic in its pretended sympathies. Because if this were not the case, men could not be found professing morality and Christianity—as to our astonishment we have found them—who unhesitatingly say, "I know it is right"—that is in itself—"to do" so and so, "and I am willing and ready to do it, but only on condition, that you go to Africa." Indeed, a highly talented clergyman, informed us in November last (three months ago) in the city of Philadelphia, that he was present when the Rev. Doctor J. P. Durbin, late President of Dickinson College, called on Rev. Mr. P. of B., to consult him about going to Liberia, to take charge of the literary department of an University in contemplation, when the following conversation ensued: Mr. P.—"Doctor, I have as much and more than I can do here, in educating the youth of our own country, and preparing them for usefulness here at home." Dr. D.—"Yes, but do as you may, you can never be elevated here." Mr. P.—"Doctor, do you not believe that the religion of our blessed Redeemer Jesus Christ, has morality, humanity, philanthropy, and justice enough in it to elevate us, and enable us to obtain our rights in this our own country?" Dr. D.— "No, indeed, sir, I do not, and if you depend upon that, your hopes are vain!" Mr. P.—Turning to Doctor Durbin, looking him solemnly, though affectionately in the face, remarked—"Well, Doctor Durbin, we both profess to be ministers of Christ; but dearly as I love the cause of my Redeemer, if for a moment, I could entertain the opinion you do about Christianity, I would not serve him another hour!" We do not know, as we were not advised, that the Rev. doctor added in fine,—"Well, you may quit now, for all your serving him will not avail against the power of the god (hydra) of Colonization." Will any one doubt for a single moment, the justice of our strictures on colonization, after reading the conversation between the Rev. Dr. Durbin and the colored clergyman? Surely not. We can therefore make no account of it, but that of setting it down as being the worst enemy of the colored people.

Recently, there has been a strained effort in the city of New York on the part of the Rev. J. B. Pinney and others, of the leading white colonizationists, to get up a movement among some poor pitiable colored men—we say pitiable, for certainly the colored persons who are at this period capable of loaning themselves to the enemies of their race, against the best interest of all that we hold sacred to that race, are pitiable in the lowest extreme, far beneath the dignity of an enemy, and therefore, we pass them by with the simple remark, that this is the hobby that colonization is riding all over the country, as the "tremendous" access of colored people to their cause within the last twelve months. We should make another remark here perhaps, in justification of governor Pinney's New York allies—that is, report says, that in the short space of some three or five months, one of his confidants, benefited himself to the "reckoning" of from eleven to fifteen hundred dollars, or "such a matter," while others were benefited in sums "pretty considerable" but of a less "reckoning." Well, we do not know after all, that they may not have quite as good a right, to pocket part of the spoils of this "grab game," as any body else. However, they are of little consequence, as the ever watchful eye of those excellent gentlemen and faithful guardians of their people's rights—the *Committee of Thirteen,* consisting of Messrs. John J. Zuille, *Chairman,* T. Joiner White, Philip A. Bell, *Secretaries,* Robert Hamilton, George T. Downing, Jeremiah Powers, John T. Raymond, Wm. Burnett, James McCuen Smith, Ezekiel Dias, Junius C. Morel, Thomas Downing, and Wm. J. Wilson, have properly chastised this pet-slave of Mr. Pinney, and made it "know its place," by keeping within the bounds of its master's enclosure.

In expressing our honest conviction of the designedly injurious character of the Colonization Society, we should do violence to our own sense of individual justice, if we did not express the belief, that there are some honest hearted men, who not having seen things in the proper light, favor that scheme, simply as a means of elevating the colored people. Such persons, so soon as they become convinced of their error, immediately change their policy, and advocate the elevation of the colored people, anywhere and everywhere, in common with other men. Of such were the early abolitionists as before stated; and the great and good Dr. F. J. Lemoyne, Gerrit Smith, and Rev. Charles Avery, and a host of others, who were Colonizationists, before espousing the cause of our elevation, here at home, and nothing but an honorable sense of justice, induces us to make these exceptions, as there are many good persons within our knowledge, whom we believe to be well wishers of the colored people, who may favor colonization.[1] But the animal itself is the same "hydra-headed monster," let whomsoever may fancy to pet it. A serpent is a serpent, and none

[1] Benjamin Coates, Esq., a merchant of Philadelphia, we believe to be an honest hearted man, and real friend of the colored people, and a true, though as yet, rather undecided philanthropist. Mr. Coates, to our knowledge, has supported three or four papers published by colored men, for the elevation of colored people in the United States, and given, as he continues to do, considerable sums to their support. We have recently learned from himself, that, though he still advocates Colonization, simply as a means of elevating the colored race of the United States, that he has *left* the Colonization Society, and prefers seeing colored people located on this continent, to going to Liberia, or elsewhere off of it—though his zeal for the enlightenment of Africa, is unabated, as every good man's should be; and we are satisfied, that Mr. Coates is neither well understood, nor rightly appreciated by the friends of our cause. One thing we do know, that he left the Colonization Society, because he could not conscientiously subscribe to its measures.

the less a viper, because nestled in the bosom of an honest hearted man. This the colored people must bear in mind, and keep clear of the hideous thing, lest its venom may be tost upon them. But why deem any argument necessary to show the unrighteousness of colonization? Its very origin as before shown—the source from whence it sprung, being the offspring of slavery—is in itself, sufficient to blast it in the estimation of every colored person in the United States, who has sufficient intelligence to comprehend it.

We dismiss this part of the subject, and proceed to consider the mode and means of our elevation in the United States.

Chapter IV: Our Elevation in the United States

That very little comparatively as yet has been done, to attain a respectable position as a class in this country, will not be denied, and that the successful accomplishment of this end is also possible, must also be admitted; but in what manner, and by what means, has long been, and is even now, by the best thinking minds among the colored people themselves, a matter of difference of opinion.

We believe in the universal equality of man, and believe in that declaration of God's word, in which it is there positively said, that "God has made of one blood all the nations that dwell on the face of the earth." Now of "the nations that dwell on the face of the earth," that is, all the people—there are one thousand millions of souls, and of this vast number of human beings, two-thirds are colored, from black, tending in complexion to the olive or that of the Chinese, with all the intermediate and admixtures of black and white, with the various "crosses" as they are physiologically, but erroneously termed, to white. We are thus explicit in stating these points, because we are determined to be understood by all. We have then, two colored to one white person throughout the earth, and yet, singular as it may appear, according to the present geographical and political history of the world, the white race predominates over the colored; or in other words, wherever there is one white person, that one rules and governs two colored persons. This is a living undeniable truth, to which we call the especial attention of the colored reader in particular. Now there is a cause for this, as there is no effect without a cause, a comprehensible remediable cause.

We all believe in the justice of God, that he is impartial, "looking upon his children with an eye of care," dealing out to them all, the measure of his goodness; yet, how can we reconcile ourselves to the difference that exists between the colored and the white races, as they truthfully present themselves before our eyes? To solve this problem, is to know the remedy; and to know it, is but necessary, in order successfully to apply it. And we shall but take the colored people of the United States, as a fair sample of the colored races everywhere of the present age, as the arguments that apply to the one, will apply to the other, whether Christians, Mahomedans, or pagans.

The colored races are highly susceptible of religion; it is a constituent principle of their nature, and an excellent trait in their character. But unfortunately for them, they carry it too far. Their hope is largely developed, and consequently, they usually stand still—hope in God, and really expect Him to do that for them, which it is necessary they should do themselves. This is their great mistake, and arises from a misconception of the character and ways of Deity. We must know God, that is understand His nature and purposes, in order to serve Him; and to serve Him well, is but to know him rightly. To depend for assistance upon God, is a *duty* and right; but to know when, how, and in what manner to obtain it, is the key to this great Bulwark of Strength, and Depository of Aid.

God himself is perfect; perfect in all his works and ways. He has means for every end; and every means used must be adequate to the end to be gained. God's means are laws—fixed laws of nature, a part of His own being, and as immutable, as unchangeable as Himself. Nothing can be accomplished but through the medium of, and comformable to these laws.

They are *three*—and like God himself, represented in the three persons in the God-head—the *Spiritual, Moral* and *Physical* Laws.

That which is Spiritual, can only be accomplished through the medium of the Spiritual law; that which is Moral, through the medium of the Moral law; and that which is Physical, through the medium of the Physical law. Otherwise than this, it is useless to expect any thing. Does a person want a spiritual blessing, he must apply through the medium of the spiritual law—*pray* for it in order to obtain it. If they desire to do a moral good, they must apply through the medium of the moral law—exercise their sense and feeling of *right* and *justice,* in order to effect it. Do they want to attain a physical end, they can only do so through the medium of the physical law—go to *work* with muscles, hands, limbs, might and strength, and this, and nothing else will attain it.

The argument that man must pray for what he receives, is a mistake, and one that is doing the colored people especially, incalculable injury. That man must pray in order to get to Heaven, every Christian will admit—but a great truth we have yet got to learn, that he can live on earth whether he is religious or not, so that he conforms to the great law of God, regulating the things of earth; the great physical laws. It is only necessary, in order to convince our people of their error and palpable mistake in this matter, to call their attention to the fact, that there are no people more religious in this Country, than the colored people, and none so poor and miserable as they. That prosperity and wealth, smiles upon the efforts of wicked white men, whom we know to utter the name of God with curses, instead of praises. That among the slaves, there are thousands of them religious, continually raising their voices, sending up their prayers to God, invoking His aid in their behalf, asking for a speedy deliverance; but they are still in chains, although they have thrice suffered out their three score years and ten. That "God sendeth rain upon the just and unjust," should be sufficient to convince us that our success in life, does not depend upon our religious character, but that the physical laws governing all earthly and temporary affairs, benefit equally the just and the unjust. Any other doctrine than this, is downright delusion, unworthy of a free people, and only intended for slaves. That all men and women, should be moral, upright, good and religious—we mean *Christians*—we would not utter a word against, and could only wish that it were so; but, what we here desire to do is, to correct the long standing error among a large body of the colored people in this country, that the cause of our oppression and degradation, is the displeasure of God towards us, because of our unfaithfulness to Him. This is not true; because if God is just—and he is—there could be no justice in prospering white men with his fostering care, for more than two thousand years, in all their wickedness, while dealing out to the colored people, the measure of his displeasure, for not half the wickedness as that of the whites. Here then is our mistake, and let it forever henceforth be corrected. We are no longer slaves, believing any

interpretation that our oppressors may give the word of God, for the purpose of deluding us to the more easy subjugation; but freemen, comprising some of the first minds of intelligence and rudimental qualifications, in the country. What then is the remedy, for our degradation and oppression? This appears now to be the only remaining question—the means of successful elevation in this our own native land? This depends entirely upon the application of the means of Elevation.

Chapter V: Means of Elevation

Moral theories have long been resorted to by us, as a means of effecting the redemption of our brethren in bonds, and the elevation of the free colored people in this country. Experience has taught us, that speculations are not enough; that the *practical* application of principles adduced, the thing carried out, is the only true and proper course to pursue.

We have speculated and moralised much about equality—claiming to be as good as our neighbors, and every body else—all of which, may do very well in ethics—but not in politics. We live in society among men, conducted by men, governed by rules and regulations. However arbitrary, there are certain policies that regulate all well organized institutions and corporate bodies. We do not intend here to speak of the legal political relations of society, for those are treated on elsewhere. The business and social, or voluntary and mutual policies, are those that now claim our attention. Society regulates itself—being governed by mind, which like water, finds its own level. "Like seeks like," is a principle in the laws of matter, as well as of mind. There is such a thing as inferiority of things, and positions; at least society has made them so; and while we continue to live among men, we must agree to all *just* measures—

.   .   .

Chapter XXIII: Things as They Are

> And if thou boast TRUTH to utter,
> SPEAK, and leave the rest to God.

In presenting this work, we have but a single object in view, and that is, to inform the minds of the colored people at large, upon many things pertaining to their elevation, that but few among us are acquainted with. Unfortunately for us, as a body, we have been taught to believe, that we must have some person to think for us, instead of thinking for ourselves. So accustomed are we to submission and this kind of training, that it is with difficulty, even among the most intelligent of the colored people, an audience may be elicited for any purpose whatever, if the expounder is to be a colored person; and the introduction of any subject is treated with indifference, if not contempt, when the originator is a colored person. Indeed, the most ordinary white person, is almost revered, while the most qualified colored person is totally neglected. Nothing from them is appreciated.

We have been standing comparatively still for years, following in the footsteps of our friends, believing that what they promise us can be accomplished, just because they say so, although our own knowledge should long since, have satisfied us to the contrary. Because even were it possible, with the present hate and jealousy that the whites have towards us in this country, for us to gain equality of rights with them; we never could have an equality of the exercise and enjoyment of those rights—because, the great odds of numbers are against us. We might indeed, as some at present, have the right of the elective franchise —nay, it is not the elective franchise, because the *elective franchise* makes the enfranchised, *eligible* to any position attainable; but we may exercise the right of *voting* only, which to us, is but poor satisfaction; and we by no means care to cherish the privilege of voting somebody into office, to help to make laws to degrade us.

In religion—because they are both *translators* and *commentators,* we must believe nothing, however absurd, but what our oppressors tell us. In Politics, nothing but such as they promulge; in Anti-Slavery, nothing but what our white brethren and friends say we must; in the mode and manner of our elevation, we must do nothing, but that which may be laid down to be done by our white brethren from some quarter or other; and now, even on the subject of emigration, there are some colored people to be found, so lost to their own interest and self-respect, as to be gulled by slave owners and colonizationists, who are led to believe there is no other place in which they can become elevated, but Liberia, a government of American slave-holders, as we have shown—simply, because white men have told them so.

Upon the possibility, means, mode and manner, of our Elevation in the United States—Our Original Rights and Claims as Citizens—Our Determination not to be Driven from our Native Country—the Difficulties in the Way of our Elevation—Our Position in Relation to our Anti-Slavery Brethren—the Wicked Design and Injurious Tendency of the American Colonization Society—Objections to Liberia—Objections to Canada—Preferences to South America, &c., &c., all of which we have treated without reserve; expressing our mind freely, and with candor, as we are determined that as far as we can at present do so, the minds of our readers shall be enlightened. The custom of concealing information upon vital and important subjects, in which the interest of the people is involved, we do not agree with, nor favor in the least; we have therefore, laid this cursory treatise before our readers, with the hope that it may prove instrumental in directing the attention of our people in the right way, that leads to their Elevation. Go or stay—of course each is free to do as he pleases—one thing is certain; our Elevation is the work of our own hands. And Mexico, Central America, the West Indies, and South America, all present now, opportunities for the individual enterprise of our young men, who prefer to remain in the United States, in preference to going where they can enjoy real freedom, and equality of rights. Freedom of Religion, as well as of politics, being tolerated in all of these places.

Let our young men and women, prepare themselves for usefulness and business; that the men may enter into merchandise, trading, and other things of importance; the young women may become teachers of various kinds, and otherwise fill places of usefulness. Parents must turn their attention more to the education of their children. We mean, to educate them for useful practical business purposes. Educate them for the Store and the Counting House—to do every-day practical business. Consult the children's propensities, and direct their education according to their inclinations. It may be, that there is too great a desire on the part of parents, to give their children a professional education, before the body of the people, are ready for it. A people must be a business people, and have more to depend upon than mere help in people's houses and Hotels, before they are either able to support, or capable of properly appreciating the services of professional men among them. This has been one of our great mistakes—we have gone in advance of ourselves. We have commenced at the superstructure of the building, instead of the foundation—at the top instead of the bottom. We should first be mechanics and common tradesmen, and professions as a matter of course would grow out of the wealth made thereby. Young men and women, must now prepare for usefulness—the day of our Elevation is at hand—all the world now gazes at us—and Central and South America, and the West Indies, bid us come and be men and women, protected, secure, beloved and Free.

The branches of Education most desirable for the preparation of youth, for practical useful every-day life, are Arithmetic and good Penmanship, in order to be Accountants; and a good rudimental knowledge of Geography—which has ever been neglected, and under estimated—and of Political Economy; which without the knowledge of the first, no people can ever become adventurous—nor of the second, never will be an enterprising people. Geography, teaches a knowledge of the world, and Political Economy, a knowledge of the wealth of nations; or how to make money. These are not abstruse sciences, or learning not easily acquired or understood; but simply, common School Primer learning, that every body may get. And, although it is the very Key to prosperity and success in common life, but few know any thing about it. Unfortunately for our people, so soon as their children learn to read a Chapter in the New Testament, and scribble a miserable hand, they are pronounced to have "Learning enough;" and taken away from School, no use to themselves, nor community. This is apparent in our Public Meetings, and Official Church Meetings; of the great number of men present, there are but few capable of filling a Secretaryship. Some of the large cities may be an exception to this. Of the multitudes of Merchants, and Business men throughout this country, Europe, and the world, few are qualified, beyond the branches here laid down by us as necessary for business. What did John Jacob Astor, Stephen Girard, or do the millionaires and the greater part of the merchant princes, and mariners, know about Latin and Greek, and the Classics? Precious few of them know any thing. In proof of this, in 1841, during the Administration of President Tyler, when the mutiny was detected on board of the American Man of War Brig Somers, the names of the Mutineers, were recorded by young S—a Midshipman in Greek. Captain Alexander Slidell McKenzie, Commanding, was unable to read them; and in his despatches to the Government,

in justification of his policy in executing the criminals, said that he "discovered some curious characters which he was unable to read," &c.; showing thereby, that that high functionary, did not understand even the Greek Alphabet, which was only necessary, to have been able to read proper names written in Greek.

What we most need then, is a good business practical Education; because, the Classical and Professional education of so many of our young men, before their parents are able to support them, and community ready to patronize them, only serves to lull their energy, and cripple the otherwise, praiseworthy efforts they would make in life. A Classical education, is only suited to the wealthy, or those who have a prospect of gaining a livelihood by it. The writer does not wish to be understood, as underrating a Classical and Professional education; this is not his intention; he fully appreciates them, having had some such advantages himself; but he desires to give a proper guide, and put a check to the extravagant idea that is fast obtaining, among our people especially, that a Classical, or as it is termed, a "finished education," is necessary to prepare one for usefulness in life. Let us have an education, that shall practically develope our thinking faculties and manhood; and then, and not until then, shall we be able to vie with our oppressors, go where we may. We as heretofore, have been on the extreme; either no qualification at all, or a Collegiate education. We jumped too far; taking a leap from the deepest abyss to the highest summit; rising from the ridiculous to the sublime; without medium or intermission.

Let our young women have an education; let their minds be well informed; well stored with useful information and practical proficiency, rather than the light superficial acquirements, popularly and fashionably called accomplishments. We desire accomplishments, but they must be *useful*.

Our females must be qualified, because they are to be the mothers of our children. As mothers are the first nurses and instructors of children; from them children consequently, get their first impressions, which being always the most lasting, should be the most correct. Raise the mothers above the level of degradation, and the offspring is elevated with them. In a word, instead of our young men, transcribing in their blank books, recipes for *Cooking;* we desire to see them making the transfer of *Invoices of Merchandise.* Come to our aid then; the *morning* of our *Redemption* from degradation, adorns the horizon.

In our selection of individuals, it will be observed, that we have confined ourself entirely to those who occupy or have occupied positions among the whites, consequently having a more general bearing as useful contributors to society at large. While we do not pretend to give all such worthy cases, we gave such as we possessed information of, and desire it to be understood, that a large number of our most intelligent and worthy men and women, have not been named, because from their more private position in community, it was foreign to the object and design of this work. If we have said aught to offend, "take the will for the deed," and be assured, that it was given with the purest of motives, and best intention, from a true hearted man and brother; deeply lamenting the sad fate of his race in this country, and sincerely desiring the elevation of man, and submitted to the serious consideration of all, who favor the promotion of the cause of God and humanity.

Chapter XXIV: A Glance at Ourselves—Conclusion

> With broken hopes—sad devastation;
> A race *resigned* to DEGRADATION!

We have said much to our young men and women, about their vocation and calling; we have dwelt much upon the menial position of our people in this country. Upon this point we cannot say too much, because there is a seeming satisfaction and seeking after such positions manifested on their part, unknown to any other people. There appears to be, a want of a sense of propriety or *self-respect,* altogether inexplicable; because young men and women among us, many of whom have good trades and homes, adequate to their support, voluntarily leave them, and seek positions, such as servants, waiting maids, coachmen, nurses, cooks in gentlemens' kitchen, or such like occupations, when they can gain a livelihood at something more respectable, or elevating in character. And the worse part of the whole matter is, that they have become so accustomed to it, it has become so "fashionable," that it seems to have become second nature, and they really become offended, when it is spoken against.

Among the German, Irish, and other European peasantry who come to this country, it matters not what they were employed at before and after they come; just so soon as they can better their condition by keeping shops, cultivating the soil, the young men and women going to night-schools, qualifying themselves for usefulness, and learning trades—they do so. Their first and last care, object and aim is, to better their condition by raising themselves above the condition that necessity places them in. We do not say too much, when we say, as an evidence of the deep degradation of our race, in the United States, that there are those among us, the wives and daughters, some of the *first ladies,* (and who dare say they are not the "first," because they belong to the "first class" and associate where any body among us can?) whose husbands are industrious, able and willing to support them, who voluntarily leave home, and become chamber-maids, and stewardesses, upon vessels and steamboats, in all probability, to enable them to obtain some more fine or costly article of dress or furniture.

We have nothing to say against those whom *necessity* compels to do these things, those who can do no better; we have only to do with those who can, and will not, or do not do better. The whites are always in the advance, and we either standing still or retrograding; as that which does not go forward, must either stand in one place or go back. The father in all probability is a farmer, mechanic, or man of some independent business; and the wife, sons and daughters, are chamber-maids, on vessels, nurses and waiting-maids, or coachmen and cooks in families. This is retrogradation. The wife, sons, and daughters should be elevated above this condition as a necessary consequence.

If we did not love our race superior to others, we would not concern ourself about their degradation; for the greatest desire of our heart is, to see them stand on a level with the most elevated of mankind. No people are ever elevated above the condition of their *females;* hence, the condition of the *mother* determines the condition of the child. To know the position of a people, it is only necessary to know the *condition* of their *females;* and despite themselves, they cannot rise above their level. Then what is our condition? Our *best ladies* being washerwomen, chamber-maids, children's traveling nurses, and common house servants, and menials, we are all a degraded, miserable people, inferior to any other people as a whole, on the face of the globe.

These great truths, however unpleasant, must be brought before the minds of our people in its true and proper light, as we have been too delicate about them, and too long concealed them for fear of giving offence. It would have been infinitely better for our race, if these facts had been presented before us half a century ago—we would have been now proportionably benefited by it.

As an evidence of the degradation to which we have been reduced, we dare premise, that this chapter will give offence to many, very many, and why? Because they may say, "He dared to say that the occupation of a *servant* is a degradation." It is not necessarily degrading; it would not be, to one or a few people of a kind; but a *whole race of servants* are a degradation to that people.

Efforts made by men of qualifications for the toiling and degraded millions among the whites, neither gives offence to that class, nor is it taken unkindly by them; but received with manifestations of gratitude; to know that they are thought to be, equally worthy of, and entitled to stand on a level with the elevated classes; and they have only got to be informed of the way to raise themselves, to make the effort and do so as far as they can. But how different with us. Speak of our position in society, and it at once gives insult. Though we are servants; among ourselves we claim to be *ladies* and *gentlemen,* equal in standing, and as the popular expression goes, "Just as good as any body"—and so believing, we make no efforts to raise above the common level of menials; because the *best* being in that capacity, all are content with the position. We cannot at the same time, be domestic and lady; servant and gentleman. We must be the one or the other. Sad, sad indeed, is the thought, that hangs drooping in our mind, when contemplating the picture drawn before us. Young men and women, "we write these things unto you, because ye are strong," because the writer, a few years ago, gave unpardonable offence to many of the young people of Philadelphia and other places, because he dared tell them, that he thought too much of them, to be content with seeing them the servants of other people. Surely, she that could be the mistress, would not be the maid; neither would he that could be the master, be content with being the servant; then why be offended, when we point out to you, the way that leads from the menial to the mistress or the master. All this we seem to reject with fixed determination, repelling with anger, every effort on the part of our intelligent men and women to elevate us, with true Israelitish degradation, in reply to any suggestion or proposition that may be offered, "Who made thee a ruler and judge?"

The writer is no "Public Man," in the sense in which this is understood among our people, but simply an humble individual, endeavoring to seek a livelihood by a profession obtained entirely by his own efforts, without relatives and friends able to assist him; except such friends as he gained by the merit of his course and conduct, which he here gratefully acknowledges; and whatever he has accomplished, other young men may, by making corresponding efforts, also accomplish.

We have advised an emigration to Central and South America, and even to Mexico and the West Indies, to those who prefer either of the last named places, all of which are free countries, Brazil being the only real slave-holding State in South America—there being nominal slavery in Dutch Guiana, Peru, Buenos Ayres, Paraguay, and Uraguay, in all of which places colored people have equality in social, civil, political, and religious privileges; Brazil making it punishable with death to import slaves into the empire.

Our oppressors, when urging us to go to Africa, tell us that we are better adapted to the climate than they—that the physical condition of the constitution of colored people better endures the heat of warm climates than that of the whites; this we are willing to *admit,* without argument, without adducing the physiological reason why, that colored people can and do stand warm climates better than whites; and find an answer fully to the point in the fact, that they also stand *all other* climates, cold, temperate, and modified, that white people can stand; therefore, according to our oppressors' own showing, we are a *superior race,* being endowed with properties fitting us for *all parts* of the earth, while they are only adapted to *certain* parts. Of course, this proves our right and duty to live wherever we may *choose;* while the white race may only live where they *can.* We are content with the fact, and have ever claimed it. Upon this rock, they and we shall ever agree.

Of the West India Islands, Santa Cruz, belonging to Denmark; Porto Rico, and Cuba with its little adjuncts, belonging to Spain, are the only slave-holding Islands among them—three-fifths of the whole population of Cuba being colored people, who cannot and will not much longer endure the burden and the yoke. They only want intelligent leaders of their own color, when they are ready at any moment to charge to the conflict—to liberty or death. The remembrance of the noble mulatto, PLACIDO, the gentleman, scholar, poet, and intended Chief Engineer of the Army of Liberty and Freedom in Cuba; and the equally noble black, CHARLES BLAIR, who was to have been Commander-in-Chief, who were shamefully put to death in 1844, by that living monster, Captain General O'Donnell, is still fresh and indelible to the mind of every bondman of Cuba.

In our own country, the United States, there are *three million five hundred thousand slaves;* and we, the nominally free colored people, are *six hundred thousand* in number; estimating one-sixth to be men, we have *one hundred thousand* able bodied freemen, which will make a powerful auxiliary in any country to which we may become adopted—an ally not to be despised by any power on earth. We love our country, dearly love her, but she don't love us—she despises us, and bids us begone, driving us from her embraces; but we shall not go where she desires us; but when we do go, whatever love we have for her, we shall love the country none the less that receives us as her adopted children.

For the want of business habits and training, our energies have become paralyzed; our young men never think of business, any more than if they were so many bondmen, without the right to pursue any calling they may think most advisable. With our people in this country, dress and good appearances have been made the only test of gentleman and ladyship, and that vocation which offers the best opportunity to dress and appear well, has generally been preferred, however menial and degrading, by our young people, without even, in the majority of cases, an effort to do better; indeed, in many instances, refusing situations equally lucrative, and superior in position; but which would not allow as much display of dress and personal appearance. This, if we ever expect to rise, must be discarded from among us, and a high and respectable position assumed.

One of our great temporal curses is our consummate poverty. We are the poorest people, as a class, in the world of civilized mankind—abjectly, miserably poor, no one scarcely being able to assist the other. To this, of course, there are noble exceptions; but that which is common to, and the very process by which white men exist, and succeed in life, is unknown to colored men in general. In any and every considerable community may be found, some one of our white fellow-citizens, who is worth more than all the colored people in that community put together. We consequently have

little or no efficiency. We must have means to be practically efficient in all the undertakings of life; and to obtain them, it is necessary that we should be engaged in lucrative pursuits, trades, and general business transactions. In order to be thus engaged, it is necessary that we should occupy positions that afford the facilities for such pursuits. To compete now with the mighty odds of wealth, social and religious preferences, and political influences of this country, at this advanced stage of its national existence, we never may expect. A new country, and new beginning, is the only true, rational, politic remedy for our disadvantageous position; and that country we have already pointed out, with triple golden advantages, all things considered, to that of any country to which it has been the province of man to embark.

Every other than we, have at various periods of necessity, been a migratory people; and all when oppressed, shown a greater abhorrence of oppression, if not a greater love of liberty, than we. We cling to our oppressors as the objects of our love. It is true that our enslaved brethren are here, and we have been led to believe that it is necessary for us to remain, on that account. Is it true, that all should remain in degradation, because a part are degraded? We believe no such thing. We believe it to be the duty of the Free, to elevate themselves in the most speedy and effective manner possible; as the redemption of the bondman depends entirely upon the elevation of the freeman; therefore, to elevate the free colored people of America, anywhere upon this continent; forebodes the speedy redemption of the slaves. We shall hope to hear no more of so fallacious a doctrine—the necessity of the free remaining in degradation, for the sake of the oppressed. Let us apply, first, the lever to ourselves; and the force that elevates us to the position of manhood's considerations and honors, will cleft the manacle of every slave in the land.

When such great worth and talents—for want of a better sphere—of men like Rev. Jonathan Robinson, Robert Douglass, Frederick A. Hinton, and a hundred others that might be named, were permitted to expire in a barber-shop; and such living men as may be found in Boston, New York, Philadelphia, Baltimore, Richmond, Washington City, Charleston, (S. C.) New Orleans, Cincinnati, Louisville, St. Louis, Pittsburg, Buffalo, Rochester, Albany, Utica, Cleveland, Detroit, Milwaukie, Chicago, Columbus, Zanesville,

Wheeling, and a hundred other places, confining themselves to Barber-shops and waiterships in Hotels; certainly the necessity of such a course as we have pointed out, must be cordially acknowledged; appreciated by every brother and sister of oppression; and not rejected as heretofore, as though they preferred inferiority to equality. These minds must become "unfettered," and have "space to rise." This cannot be in their present positions. A continuance in any position, becomes what is termed "Second Nature;" it begets an *adaptation,* and *reconciliation* of *mind* to such condition. It changes the whole physiological condition of the system, and adapts man and woman to a higher or lower sphere in the pursuits of life. The offsprings of slaves and peasantry, have the general characteristics of their parents; and nothing but a different course of training and education, will change the character.

The slave may become a lover of his master, and learn to forgive him for continual deeds of maltreatment and abuse; just as the Spaniel would couch and fondle at the feet that kick him; because he has been taught to reverence them, and consequently, becomes adapted in body and mind to his condition. Even the shrubbery-loving Canary, and lofty-soaring Eagle, may be tamed to the cage, and learn to love it from habit of confinement. It has been so with us in our position among our oppressors; we have been so prone to such positions, that we have learned to love them. When reflecting upon this all important, and to us, all absorbing subject; we feel in the agony and anxiety of the moment, as though we could cry out in the language of a Prophet of old: "Oh that my head were waters, and mine eyes a fountain of tears, that I might weep day and night for the" degradation "of my people! Oh that I had in the wilderness a lodging place of way-faring men; that I might leave my people, and go from them!"

The Irishman and German in the United States, are very different persons to what they were when in Ireland and Germany, the countries of their nativity. There their spirits were depressed and downcast; but the instant they set their foot upon unrestricted soil; free to act and untrammeled to move; their physical condition undergoes a change, which in time becomes physiological which is transmitted to the offspring, who when born under such circumstances, is a decidedly different being to what it would have been, had it been born under different circumstances.

A child born under oppression, has all the elements of servility in its constitution; who when born under favorable circumstances, has to the contrary, all the elements of freedom and independence of feeling. Our children then, may not be expected, to maintain that position and manly bearing; born under the unfavorable circumstances with which we are surrounded in this country; that we so much desire. To use the language of the talented Mr. Whipper, "they cannot be raised in this country, without being stoop shouldered." Heaven's pathway stands unobstructed, which will lead us into a Paradise of bliss. Let us go on and possess the land, and the God of Israel will be our God.

The lessons of every school book, the pages of every history, and columns of every newspaper, are so replete with stimuli to nerve us on to manly aspirations, that those of our young people, who will now refuse to enter upon this great theatre of Polynesian adventure, and take their position on the stage of Central and South America, where a brilliant engagement, of certain and most triumphant success, in the drama of human equality awaits them; then, with the blood of *slaves,* write upon the lintel of every door in sterling Capitals, to be gazed and hissed at by every passer by—

> Doomed by the Creator
> To servility and degradation;
> The SERVANT of the *white man,*
> And despised of every nation!

The Fugitive Slave Narrative

Moses Roper (1816?–?)

Little is known of Moses Roper beyond his own account in *A Narrative of the Adventures and Escape of Moses Roper, from American Slavery* (1837). Born about 1816 on a plantation in Caswell County in north-central North Carolina, Roper was the very light-skinned son of a white man and a part-white, part-Indian, part-Black slave woman, owned by the father of the white man's fiancée. When Mrs. Roper later learned that Moses was the son of her husband by her own slave, in a jealous rage she attempted to murder the infant with a knife and a club. Soon afterward, the mother and child were sold, and a few years later they were separated.

During childhood and youth, Roper was sold frequently. Traveling with his masters and often attempting to escape, he experienced and witnessed the cruelties of slavery in a large section of the Southeast: North Carolina, South Carolina, Georgia, and Florida. After many abortive efforts, in July 1834 he finally successfully escaped to Savannah, Georgia, where he signed as a steward on a coastal merchant vessel bound for New York. After brief stays in Poughkeepsie and Albany, New York, in Sudbury and Ludlow, Vermont, in New Hampshire, and in Boston and Brookline, Massachusetts, Roper sailed for England on November 11, 1835.

Bringing to England letters of recommendation from American abolitionists bearing "unequivocal witness to his sobriety, intelligence, and honesty," Roper was aided by English friends in attaining an education designed to prepare him for missionary service in Africa. After the publication of his *Narrative* he attended University College, London, with the somewhat altered goal of propagating Christianity in the West Indies. Whether Roper went to Africa or the West Indies is not known. As late as October 9, 1839, he was still in England. Whatever destiny he finally found, his lasting contribution was the uncompromisingly vivid picture of American slavery he presented in his *Narrative*.

The first American edition (1838) of Roper's *Narrative*, from which the present selection is taken, was reprinted in 1969 with a brief introduction by Maxwell Whiteman. Other details are given by Vernon Loggins in *The Negro Author* (1931). Roper is mentioned several times by Charles H. Nichols in *Many Thousands Gone: The Ex-Slaves' Account of Their Bondage and Freedom* (1963).

from *A Narrative of the Adventures and Escape of Moses Roper, from American Slavery*

Having been in the habit of going over many slave states with my master, I had good opportunities of witnessing the harsh treatment which was adopted by masters towards their slaves. As I have never read or heard of any thing connected with slavery so cruel as what I have myself witnessed, it will be well to mention a case or two.

A large farmer, Colonel M'Quiller, in Cashaw county, South Carolina, was in the habit of driving nails into a hogshead so as to leave the point of the nail just protruding in the inside of the cask. Into this he used to put his slaves for punishment, and roll them down a very long and steep hill. I have heard from several slaves, (though I had no means of ascertaining the truth of the statement,) that in this way he killed six or seven of his slaves. This plan was first adopted by a Mr. Perry, who lived on the Catawba River, and has since been adopted by several planters. Another was that of a young lad, who had been hired by Mr. Bell, a member of a Methodist church, to hoe three quarters of an acre of cotton per day. Having been brought up as a domestic slave, he was not able to accomplish the task assigned to him. On the Saturday night, he left three or four rows to do on the Sunday; on the same night it rained very hard, by which the master could tell that he had done some of the rows on Sunday. On Monday his master took and tied him up to a tree in the field, and kept him there the whole of that day, and flogged him at intervals. At night, when he was taken down, he was so weak that he could not get home, having a mile to go. Two white men, who were employed by Mr. Bell, put him on a horse, took him home, and threw him down on the kitchen floor, while they proceeded to their supper. In a little time they heard some deep groans proceeding from the kitchen; they went to see him die; he had groaned his last. Thus, Mr. Bell flogged this poor boy even to death; for what? for breaking the Sabbath, when he (his master) had set him a task on Saturday which it was not possible for him to do, and which, if he did not do, no mercy would be extended towards him. So much for the regard of this Methodist for the observance of the Sabbath.

The general custom in this respect is, that if a man kills his own slave, no notice is taken of it by the civil functionaries; but if a man kills a slave belonging to another master, he is compelled to pay the worth of the slave. In this case, a jury met, returned a verdict of "Wilful murder" against this man, and ordered him to pay the value. Mr. Bell was unable to do this, but a Mr. Cunningham paid the debt, and took this Mr. Bell, with this recommendation for cruelty, to be his overseer.

It will be observed, that most of the cases here cited are those in respect to males. Many instances, however, in respect to females might be mentioned, but are too disgusting to appear in this narrative. The cases here brought forward are not rare, but the continued feature of slavery. But I must now follow up the narrative as regards myself in particular. I stayed with this master for several months, during which time we went on very well in general. In August, 1831, (this was my first acquaintance with any date,) I happened to hear a man mention this date, and, as it excited my curiosity, I asked what it meant; they told me it was the number of the year from the birth of Christ. On this date, August, 1831, some cows broke into a crib where the corn is kept, and ate a great deal. For this his slaves were tied up and received several floggings; but myself and another man, hearing the groans of those who were being flogged, stayed back in the field, and would not come up. Upon this I thought to escape punishment. On the Monday morning, however, I heard my master flogging the other man who was in the field. He could not see me, it being a field of Indian corn, which grows to a great height. Being afraid that he would catch me, and dreading a flogging more than many others, I determined to run for it, and after travelling forty miles I arrived at the estate of Mr. Crawford, in North Carolina, Mecklinburgh county. Having formerly heard people talk about the free states, I determined upon going thither, and if possible, in my way, to find out my poor mother, who was in slavery several hundred miles from Chester; but the hope of doing the latter was very faint, and, even if I did, it was not likely that she would know me, having been separated from her when between five and six years old.

The first night I slept in a barn upon Mr. Crawford's estate, and, having overslept myself, was awoke by Mr. Crawford's overseer, upon which I was dreadfully frightened. He asked me what I was doing there? I made no reply to him then, and he making sure that he had secured a runaway slave, did not press me for an answer. On the way to his house, however, I made up the following story, which I told him in the presence of his wife:—I said, that I had been bound to a very cruel master when I was a little boy, and that having been treated very badly, I wanted to get home to see my mother. This statement may appear to some to be a direct lie, but as I understood the word *bound,* I considered it to apply to my case, having been sold to him, and thereby bound to serve him; though still, I did rather hope that he would understand it, that I was bound, when a boy, till twenty-one years of age. Though I was white at that time, he would not believe my story, on account of my hair being curly and woolly, which led him to conclude I was possessed of enslaved blood. The overseer's wife, however, who seemed much interested in me, said she did not think I was of African origin, and that she had seen white men still darker than me. Her persuasion prevailed; and, after the overseer had given me as much buttermilk as I could drink, and something to eat, which was very acceptable, having had nothing for two days, I set off for Charlotte in North Carolina, the largest town in the county. I went on very quickly the whole of that day, fearful of being pursued. The trees were very thick on each side of the road, and only a few houses at the distance of two or three miles apart. As I proceeded, I turned round in all directions to see if I was pursued, and if I caught a glimpse of any one coming along the road, I immediately rushed into the thickest part of the wood, to elude the grasp of what I was afraid might be my master. I went on in this way the whole day; at night I came up with two wagons: they had been to market. The regular road wagons do not generally put up at inns, but encamp in the roads and fields. When I came to them, I told them the same story I had told Mr. Crawford's overseer, with the assurance that the statement would meet the same success. After they had heard me, they gave me something to eat, and also a lodging in the camp with them.

I then went on with them about five miles, and they agreed to take me with them as far as they went, if I would assist them. This I promised to do. In the morning, however, I was much frightened by one of the men putting several questions to me; we were then about three miles from Charlotte. When within a mile of that town, we stopped at a brook to water the horses. While stopping here, I saw the men whispering, and fancying I overheard them say they would put me in Charlotte jail when they got there, I made my escape into the woods, pretending to be looking after something till I got out of their sight. I then ran on as fast as I could, but did not go through the town of Charlotte, as had been my intention; being a large town, I was fearful it might prove fatal to my escape. Here I was at a loss how to get on, as houses were not very distant from each other for nearly two hundred miles.

While thinking what I should do, I observed some wagons before me, which I determined to keep behind, and never go nearer to them than a quarter of a mile; in this way I travelled till I got to Salisbury. If I happened to meet any person on the road, I was afraid they would take me up; I asked them how far the wagons had got on before me, to make them suppose I belonged to the wagons. At night I slept on the ground in the woods, some little distance from the wagons, but not near enough to be seen by the men belonging to them. All this time I had but little food, principally fruit, which I found on the road. On Thursday night, I got into Salisbury, having left Chester on the Monday morning preceding. After this, being afraid my master was in pursuit of me, I left the usual line of road, and took another direction, through Huntoville and Salem, principally through fields and woods. On my way to Caswell Court-house, a distance of nearly two hundred miles from Salisbury, I was stopped by a white man, to whom I told my old story, and again succeeded in my escape. I also came up with a small cart, driven by a poor man who had been moving into some of the western territories, and was going back to Virginia to move some more of his luggage. On this, I told him I was going the same way to Hilton, thirteen miles from Caswell Court-house. He took me up in his cart, and we went to the Red House, two miles from Hilton, the place where Mr. Mitchell took me from when six years old, to go to the southern states. This was a very providential circumstance, for it happened that at the time I had to pass through Caswell Court-house, a fair or election was going on, which caused the place to be much crowded with people, and rendered it more dangerous for me to pass through.

At the Red House I left the cart and wandered about a long time, not knowing which way to go to find my mother. After some time, I took the road leading over to Ikeo Creek. I shortly came up with a little girl about six years old, and asked her where she was going; she said to her mother's, pointing to a house on a hill about half a mile off. She had been to the overseer's house, and was returning to her mother. I then felt some emotions arising in my breast which I cannot describe, but will be fully explained in the sequel. I told her that I was very thirsty, and would go with her to get something to drink. On our way, I asked her several questions, such as her name, that of her mother: she said hers was Maria, and her mother's Nancy. I inquired if her mother had any more children? She said five besides herself, and that they had been told that one had been sold when a little boy. I then asked the name of this child? She said, it was Moses. These answers, as we approached the house, led me nearer and nearer to the finding out the object of my pursuit, and of recognising in the little girl the person of my own sister. At last I got to my mother's house! My mother was at home; I asked her if she knew me? She said, No. Her master was having a house built just by, and the men were digging a well; she supposed that I was one of the diggers. I told her I knew her very well, and thought that if she looked at me a little she would know me; but this had no effect. I then asked her if she had any sons? She said, Yes; but none so large as me. I then waited a few minutes, and narrated some circumstances to her attending my being sold into slavery, and how she grieved at my loss. Here the mother's feelings on that dire occasion, and which a mother only can know, rushed to her mind; she saw her own son before her, for whom she had so often wept; and in an instant we were clasped in each other's arms, amidst the ardent interchange of caresses and tears of joy. Ten years had elapsed since I had seen my dear mother. My own feelings, and the circumstances attending my coming home, have often brought to mind since, on a perusal of the 42d, 43d, 44th, and 45th chapters of Genesis. What could picture my feelings so well, as I once more beheld the mother who had brought me into the world and had nourished me, not with the anticipation of my being torn from her

maternal care when only six years old, to become the prey of a mercenary and blood-stained slave-holder,—I say, what picture so vivid in description of this part of my tale, as the 7th and 8th verses of the 42d chapter of Genesis, "And Joseph saw his brethren and he knew them, but made himself strange unto them. And Joseph knew his brethren, but they knew not him." After the first emotion of the mother on recognising her first-born had somewhat subsided, could the reader not fancy the little one, my sister, as she told her simple tale of meeting with me to her mother, how she would say, while the parent listened with intense interest, "The man asked me straitly of our state and of our kindred, saying, Is your father yet alive, and have ye another brother?" Or, when at last, I could no longer refrain from making myself known, I say I was ready to burst into a frenzy of joy. How applicable the 1st, 2d, and 3d verses of the 45th chapter, "Then Joseph could not refrain himself before all them that stood by him; and he wept aloud, and said unto his brethren, I am Joseph; doth my father still live?" Then when the mother knew her son, when the brothers and sisters owned their brother; "He kissed all his brethren and wept over them, and after that his brethren talked with him." 15th verse. At night, my mother's husband, a blacksmith, belonging to Mr. Jefferson, at the Red House, came home. He was surprised to see me with the family, not knowing who I was. He had been married to my mother when I was a babe, and had always been very fond of me. After the same tale had been told him, and the same emotions filled his soul, he again kissed the object of his early affection. The next morning I wanted to go on my journey, in order to make sure of my escape to the free states. But, as might be expected, my mother, father, brothers, and sisters, could ill part with their long lost one, and persuaded me to go into the woods in the daytime, and at night come home and sleep there. This I did for about a week. On the next Sunday night, I laid me down to sleep between my two brothers, on a pallet which my mother had prepared for me. About twelve o'clock I was suddenly awoke, and found my bed surrounded by twelve slave-holders with pistols in hand, who took me away (not allowing me to bid farewell to those I loved so dearly) to the Red House, where they confined me in a room the rest of the night, and in the morning lodged me in the jail of Caswell Court-house.

What was the scene at home, what sorrow

possessed their hearts, I am unable to describe, as I never after saw any of them more. I heard, however, that my mother, who was in the family-way when I went home, was soon after confined, and was very long before she recovered the effects of this disaster. I was told afterwards that some of those men who took me were professing Christians; but to me they did not seem to live up to what they professed. They did not seem, by their practices, at least, to recognise that God as their God, who hath said, "Thou shalt not deliver unto his master, the servant which is escaped from his master unto thee; he shall dwell with thee, even among you, in that place which he shall choose, in one of thy gates, where it liketh him best; thou shalt not oppress him." Deut. xxiii. 15, 16.

I was confined here in a dungeon under ground, the grating of which looked to the door of the jailer's house. His wife had a great antipathy to me. She was Mr. Roper's wife's cousin. My grandmother used to come to me nearly every day, and bring me something to eat, besides the regular jail allowance, by which my sufferings were somewhat decreased. Whenever the jailer went out, which he often did, his wife used to come to my dungeon and shut the wooden door over the grating, by which I was nearly suffocated, the place being very damp and noisome. My master did not hear of my being in jail for thirty-one days after I had been placed there. He immediately sent his son and son-in-law, Mr. Anderson, after me. They came in a horse and chaise, took me from the jail to a blacksmith's shop, and got an iron collar fitted round my neck, with a heavy chain attached, then tied up my hands, and fastened the other end of the chain on another horse, and put me on its back. Just before we started, my grandmother came to bid me farewell; I gave her my hand as well as I could, and she having given me two or three presents, we parted. I had felt enough, far too much, for the weak state I was in; but how shall I describe my feelings upon parting with the *last* relative that I *ever saw?* The reader must judge by what would be his own feelings under similar circumstances. We then went on for fifty miles; I was very weak, and could hardly sit on the horse. Having been in prison so long, I had lost the southern tan; and, as the people could not see my hair, having my hat on, they thought I was a white man, a criminal, and asked what crime I had committed. We arrived late at night at the house of Mr. Britton. I shall never forget the

journey that night. The thunder was one continued roar, and the lightning blazing all around. I expected every minute that my iron collar would attract it, and I should be knocked off the horse and dragged along the ground. This gentleman, a year or two before, had liberated his slaves, and sent them into Ohio, having joined the society of Friends, which society does not allow the holding of slaves. I was, therefore, treated very well there, and they gave me a hearty supper, which did me much good in my weak state.

They secured me in the night by locking me to the post of the bed on which they slept. The next morning we went on to Salisbury. At that place we stopped to water the horses; they chained me to a tree in the yard, by the side of their chaise. On my horse they had put the saddle bags which contained the provisions. As I was in the yard, a black man came and asked me what I had been doing; I told him that I had run away from my master; after which he told me several tales about the slaves, and among them, he mentioned the case of a Quaker, who was then in prison, waiting to be hung, for giving a free pass to a slave. I had been considering all the way how I could escape from my horse, and once had an idea of cutting his head off, but thought it too cruel, and at last thought of trying to get a rasp and cut the chain by which I was fastened to the horse. As they often let me get on nearly a quarter of a mile before them, I thought I should have a good opportunity of doing this without being seen. The black man procured me a rasp, and I put it into the saddle-bags which contained the provisions. We then went on our journey, and one of the sons asked me if I wanted any thing to eat; I answered, No, though very hungry at the time, as I was afraid of their going to the bags and discovering the rasp. However, they had not had their own meal at the inn, as I supposed, and went to the bags to supply themselves, where they discovered the rasp. Upon this, they fastened my horse beside the horse in their chaise, and kept a stricter watch over me. Nothing remarkable occurred, till we got within eight miles of Mr. Gooch's, where we stopped a short time; and, taking advantage of their absence, I broke a switch from some boughs above my head, lashed my horse, and set off at full speed. I had got about a quarter of a mile before they could get their horse loose from the chaise; one then rode the horse, and the other ran as fast as he could after me. When I caught sight of them, I turned off the main road into the woods, hoping to escape their sight; their horse, however, being much swifter than mine, they soon got within a short distance of me. I then came to a rail fence, which I found it very difficult to get over, but breaking several rails away, I effected my object. They then called upon me to stop, more than three times, and I not doing so, they fired after me, but the pistol only snapped. This is according to law; after three calls they may shoot a runaway slave. Soon after the one on the horse came up with me, and catching hold of the bridle of my horse, pushed the pistol to my side; the other soon came up, and breaking off several stout branches from the trees, they gave me about a hundred blows. They did this very near to a planter's house; the gentleman was not at home, but his wife came out, and begged them not to *kill* me *so near the house:* they took no notice of this, but kept on beating me. They then fastened me to the axle-tree of their chaise, one of them got into the chaise, the other took my horse, and they run me all the eight miles as fast as they could, the one on my horse going behind to guard me. In this way we came to my old master, Mr. Gooch. The first person I saw was himself; he unchained me from the chaise, and at first seemed to treat me very gently, asking me where I had been, &c. The first thing the sons did, was to show the rasp which I had got to cut my chain. My master gave me a hearty dinner, the best he ever did give me, but it was to keep me from dying before he had given me all the flogging he intended. After dinner he took me to a log-house, stripped me quite naked, fastened a rail up very high, tied my hands to the rail, fastened my feet together, put a rail between my feet, and stood on one end of it to hold it down; the two sons then gave me fifty lashes each, the eldest another fifty, and Mr. Gooch himself fifty more. While doing this, his wife came out and begged him not to kill me, the first act of sympathy I ever noticed in her. When I called for water, they brought a pail-full and threw it over my back, ploughed up by the lashes. After this, they took me to the blacksmith's shop, got two large bars of iron, which they bent round my feet, each bar weighing twenty pounds, and put a heavy log-chain on my neck. This was on Saturday. On the Monday, he chained me to the same female slave as before. As he had to go out that day, he did not give me the punishment which he intended to give me every day, but at night when he came home, he made us walk round his estate, and by

all the houses of the slaves, for them to taunt us. When we came home, he told us we must be up very early in the morning, and go to the fields before the other slaves. We were up at daybreak, but we could not get on fast, on account of the heavy irons on my feet. We walked about a mile in two hours, but knowing the punishment he was going to inflict on us, we made up our minds to escape into the woods, and secrete ourselves. This we did, and he not being able to find us, sent all his slaves, about forty, and his sons, to find us, which they could not do; and about twelve o'clock, when we thought they would give up looking for us at that time, we went on, and came to the banks of the Catawba. Here I got a stone, and prized the ring of the chain on her neck, and got it off; and as the chain round my neck was only passed through a ring, as soon as I had got hers off, I slipped the chain through my ring and got it off my own neck. We then went on by the banks of the river for some distance, and found a little canoe about two feet wide. I managed to get in, although the irons on my feet made it very dangerous, for if I had upset the canoe I could not swim. The female got in after me, and gave me the paddles, by which we got some distance down the river. The current being very strong, it drove us against a small island; we paddled round the island to the other side, and then made towards the opposite bank. Here again we were stopped by the current, and made up to a large rock in the river, between the island and the opposite shore. As the weather was very rough, we landed on the rock and secured the canoe, as it was not possible to get back to the island. It was a very dark night and rained tremendously, and as the water was rising rapidly towards the top of the rock, we gave all up for lost, and sometimes hoped, and sometimes feared to hope, that we should never see the morning. But Providence was moving in our favour; the rain ceased, the water reached the edge of the rock, then receded, and we were out of danger from this cause. We remained all night upon the rock, and in the morning reached the opposite shore, and then made our way through the woods, till we came to a field of Indian corn, where we plucked some of the green ears and ate them, having had nothing for two days and nights. We came to the estate of ———, where we met with a colored man who knew me, and having run away himself from a bad master, he gave us some food, and told us we might sleep in the barn that night. Being very fatigued, we overslept ourselves; the proprietor came to the barn, but as I was in one corner under some Indian corn tops, and she in another, he did not perceive us, and we did not leave the barn before night, (Wednesday.) We then went out, got something to eat, and stayed about the estate till Sunday. On that day, I met with some men, one of whom had had irons on his feet the same as me; he told me, that his master was going out to see his friends, and that he would try and get my feet loose. For this purpose I parted with this female, fearing, that if she were caught with me, she would be forced to tell who took my irons off. The man tried some time without effect; he then gave me a file and I tried myself, but was disappointed, on account of their thickness.

On the Monday, I went on towards Lancaster, and got within three miles of it that night, and went towards the plantation of Mr. Crockett, as I knew some of his slaves, and hoped to get some food given me. When I got there, however, the dogs smelt me out and barked; upon which Mr. Crockett came out, followed me with his rifle, and came up with me. He put me on a horse's back, which put me to extreme pain, from the great weight hanging from my feet. We reached Lancaster jail that night, and he lodged me there.

I was placed in the next dungeon to a man who was going to be hung. I shall never forget his cries and groans, as he prayed all night for the mercy of God. Mr. Gooch did not hear of me for several weeks; when he did, he sent his son-in-law, Mr. Anderson, after me. Mr. Gooch himself came within a mile of Lancaster, and waited until Mr. Anderson brought me. At this time I had but one of the irons on my feet, having got so thin round my ankles that I had slipped one off while in jail. His son-in-law tied my hands, and made me walk along till we came to Mr. Gooch. As soon as we arrived at M'Daniel's Ford, two miles above the ferry, on the Catawba River, they made me wade across, themselves going on horseback. The water was very deep, and having irons on one foot and round my neck, I could not keep a footing. They dragged me along by my chain, floating on the top of the water. It was as much as they could do to hold me by the chain, the current being very strong. They then took me home, flogged me, put extra irons on my neck and feet, and put me under the driver, with more work than ever I had before. He did not flog me so severely as before, but continued it every day. Among the instruments of torture employed, I here describe one:

This is a machine used for packing and pressing cotton. By it he hung me up by the hands at letter *a*, a horse moving round the screw *e*, and carrying it up and down, and pressing the block *c* into the box *d*, into which the cotton is put. At this time he hung me up for a quarter of an hour. I was carried up ten feet from the ground, when Mr. Gooch asked me if I was tired. He then let me rest for five minutes, then carried me round again, after which he let me down and put me into the box *d*, and shut me down in it for about ten minutes. After this torture, I stayed with him several months, and did my work very well. It was about the beginning of 1832 when he took off my irons, and being in dread of him, he having threatened me with more punishment, I attempted again to escape from him. At this time I got into North Carolina; but a reward having been offered for me, a Mr. Robinson caught me, and chained me to a chair, upon which he sat up with me all night, and next day proceeded home with me. This was Saturday, Mr. Gooch had gone to church, several miles from his house. When he came back, the first thing he did was to pour some tar on my head, then rubbed it all over my face, took a torch, with pitch on, and set it on fire. He put it out before it did me very great injury, but the pain which I endured was most excruciating, nearly all my hair having been burnt off. On Monday he put irons on me again, weighing nearly fifty pounds. He threatened me again on the Sunday with another flogging; and on the Monday morning, before daybreak, I got away again, with my irons on, and was about three hours going a distance of two miles. I had gone a good distance, when I met with a colored man, who got some wedges and took my irons off. However, I was caught again, and put into prison in Charlotte, where Mr. Gooch came, and took me back to Chester. He asked me how I got my irons off? They having been got off by a slave, I would not answer his question, for fear of getting the man punished. Upon this, he put the fingers of my left hand into a vice, and squeezed all my nails off. He then had my feet put on an anvil, and ordered a man to beat my toes, till he smashed some of my nails off. The marks of this treatment still remain upon me, my nails never having grown perfect since. He inflicted this punishment, in order to get out of me how I got my irons off, but never succeeded. After this he hardly knew what to do with me, the whole stock of his cruelties seemed to be exhausted. He chained me down in the log-house. Soon after this, he sent a female slave to see if I was safe. Mr. Gooch had not secured me as he thought, but had only run my chain through the ring, without locking it. This I observed; and while the slave was coming, I was employed in loosening the chain with the hand that was not wounded. As soon as I observed her coming, I drew the chain up tight, and she observing that I seemed fast, went away and told her master, who was in the field ordering the slaves. When she was gone, I drew the chain through the ring, escaped under the flooring of the log-house, and went on under his house, till I came out at the other side, and ran on; but being sore and weak, I had not got a mile before I was caught, and again carried back. He tied me up to a tree in the woods at night, and made his slaves flog me. I cannot say how many lashes I received, but it was the worst flogging I ever had, and the last which Mr. Gooch ever gave me.

There are several circumstances which occurred on this estate while I was there, relative to other slaves, which it may be interesting to mention. Hardly a day ever passed without some one being flogged. To one of his female slaves he had given a dose of castor oil and salts together, as much as she could take; he then got a box, about six feet by two and a half, and one and a half feet deep; he put this slave under the box, and made the men fetch as many stones as they could get, and put them on the top of it; under this she was made to stay all night. I believe, that if he had given this slave one, he had given her three thousand lashes. Mr. Gooch was a member of a Baptist church. His slaves, thinking him a very bad sample of what a professing Christian ought to be, would not join the connexion he belonged to, thinking they must be a very bad set of people; there were many of them members of the Methodist church. On Sunday, the slaves can only go to church at the will of their master, when he gives them a pass for the time they are to be out. If they are found by the patrole after the time to which their pass extends, they are severely flogged.

On Sunday nights, a slave, named Allen, used to come to Mr. Gooch's estate for the purpose of exhorting and praying with his brother slaves, by whose instrumentality many of them had been converted. One evening Mr. Gooch caught them all in a room, turned Allen out, and threatened his slaves with a hundred lashes each, if they ever brought him there again. At one time Mr. Gooch was ill and confined to his room; if any of the slaves had done any thing which he thought deserving a flogging, he would have them brought into his bed-room and flogged before his eyes.

With respect to food, he used to allow us one peck of Indian meal each, per week, which, after being sifted and the bran taken from it, would not be much more than half a peck. Meat we did not get for sometimes several weeks together; however, he was proverbial for giving his slaves more food than any other slave-holder. I stayed with Mr. Gooch a year and a half. During that time the scenes of cruelty I witnessed and experienced, are not at all fitted for these pages. There is much to excite disgust in what has been narrated, but hundreds of other cases might be mentioned. After this, Mr. Gooch, seeing that I was determined to get away from him, chained me, and sent me with another female slave, whom he had treated very cruelly, to Mr. Britton, son of the before-mentioned, a slave-dealer. We were to have gone to Georgia to be sold, but a bargain was struck before we arrived there. Mr. Britton had put chains on me to please Mr. Gooch; but having gone some little distance, we came up with a white man, who begged Mr. Britton to unchain me; he then took off my hand-cuffs. We then went on to Union Court-house, where we met a drove of slaves; the driver came to me, and ultimately bought me, and sent me to his drove; the girl was sold to a planter in the neighbourhood, as bad as Mr. Gooch. In court week, the negro traders and slaves encamp a little way out of the town. The traders here will often sleep with the best-looking female slaves among them, and they will often have many children in the year, which are said to be slave-holder's children, by which means, through his villany, he will make an immense profit of this intercourse, by selling the babe with its mother. They often keep an immense stock of slaves on hand. Many of them will be with the trader a year or more before they are sold. Mr. Marcus Rowland, the drover who bought me, then returned with his slaves to his brother's house, (Mr. John Rowland,) where he kept his drove, on his way to Virginia. He kept me as a kind of servant. I had to grease the faces of the blacks every morning with sweet oil, to make them shine before they are put up to sell. After he had been round several weeks and sold many slaves, he left me and some more at his brother's house, while he went on to Washington, about six hundred miles, to buy some more slaves, the drove having got very small. We were treated very well while there, having plenty to eat, and little work to do, in order to make us fat. I was brought up more as a domestic slave, as they generally prefer slaves of my colour for that purpose. When Mr. Rowland came back, having been absent about five months, he found all the slaves well, except one female, who had been grieving very much at being parted from her parents, and at last died of grief. He dressed us very nicely, and went on again. I travelled with him for a year, and had to look over the slaves, and see that they were dressed well, had plenty of food, and to oil their faces. During this time, we stopped once at White House Church, a Baptist association; a protracted camp meeting was holding there, on the plan of the revival meetings in this country. We got there at the time of the meeting, and sold two female slaves on the Sunday morning, at the time the meeting broke up, to a gentleman who had been attending the meeting the whole of the week. While I was with Mr. Rowland we were at many such meetings, and the members of the churches are by this means so well influenced towards their fellow creatures, at these meetings for the worship of God, that it becomes a fruitful season for the drover, who carries on immense traffic with the attendants at these places. This is common to Baptists and Methodists. At the end of the year he exchanged me to a farmer, Mr. David Goodley, for a female slave, in Greenville, about fourteen miles from Greenville Court-house. The gentleman was going to Missouri to settle, and on his way had to pass through Ohio, a free state. But having learnt, after he bought me, that I had before tried to get away to the free states, he was afraid to take me with him, and I was again exchanged to a Mr. Marvel Louis. He was in the habit of travelling a great deal, and took me as a domestic slave to wait on him. Mr. Louis boarded at the house of Mr. Clevelin, a very rich planter at Greenville, South Carolina. Mr. L. was paying his addresses to the daughter of this gentleman, but was surprised and routed in his approaches, by a Colonel Dorkin, of Union Court-house, who ultimately carried her off in triumph. After this Mr. Louis took to drinking, to drown his recollection of disappointed love. One day he went to Pendleton races, and I waited on the road for him; returning intoxicated, he was thrown from his horse into a brook, and was picked up by a gentleman and taken to an inn, and I went there to take care of him. Next day he went on to Punkintown with Mr. Warren R.

Davis, a member of Congress; I went with him. This was at the time of the agitation of the Union and Nullifying party, which was expected to end in a general war. The Nullifying party had a grand dinner on the occasion, after which they gave their slaves all the refuse, for the purpose of bribing them to fight on the side of their party. The scene on this occasion was most humorous, all the slaves scrambling after bare bones and crumbs, as if they had had nothing for months. When Mr. Louis had got over this fit of drunkenness, we returned to Greenville, where I had little to do, except in the warehouse. There was preaching in the Court-house on the Sunday; but scarcely had the sweet savour of the worship of God passed away, when, on Monday, a public auction was held for the sale of slaves, cattle, sugar, iron, &c., by Z. Davis, the high constable, and others.

Poetry

George Moses Horton (1797–1883)

Although he was born a slave in Northampton County, North Carolina, and remained at least nominally a slave until freed by Union soliders in 1865, George Moses Horton found the means and the time to become America's first Black professional poet. It is said that he taught himself to read and write by studying the alphabet from scraps of paper and by reading Methodist hymnbooks. In any event, by the 1820's, enjoying a kind of freedom of movement rarely accorded a slave, Horton had journeyed from Northampton County to Raleigh, North Carolina, and thence to the state university at Chapel Hill, where he worked as a janitor and engaged in the modestly lucrative practice of writing occasional poems for lovelorn students at the price of about twenty-five or fifty cents a poem. Somehow he also found time to compose a volume of poems published in Raleigh in 1829 under the title *The Hope of Liberty*.

The Hope of Liberty contained only three poems that treated the subject of slavery, but it was Horton's hope that the book's sales would bring him enough money to purchase his freedom and go to Liberia. Although it went through two subsequent editions under the title of *Poems by a Slave* in Philadelphia in 1837 and in Boston in 1838, Horton did not realize his desire until the Union Army freed him in 1865. The Boston edition was published in a volume containing a memoir of Phillis Wheatley and a selection of her poems; its full title was *Memoir and Poems of Phyllis Wheatley, A Native African and Slave: Also Poems by a Slave*.

In 1845 Horton published a second volume of poetry somewhat grandiosely entitled *The Poetical Works of George M. Horton, The Colored Bard of North Carolina*. Few copies of this book now exist; this is unfortunate, because it contains, in addition to the poems, a short prefatory autobiography entitled "The Life of George M. Horton, The Colored Bard of North Carolina." Where copies have been found, this last has proved to be an invaluable source of information for students of early Black American poetry.

In the meantime, between the publications of his volumes of poetry, Horton was publishing individual poems in Northern abolitionist periodicals—in Garrison's *Liberator* in Boston, in Frederick Douglass' *North Star* in Rochester, New York, and in the Lancaster, Pennsylvania, *Gazette*.

219

Horton's last volume of poetry, copies of which are also in very short supply, was *Naked Genius*. It was published in Raleigh in 1865, apparently just before Horton went to Philadelphia in the company of a Union cavalry officer, Captain Will Banks, who intended to introduce "the slave poet" to people in Philadelphia who could aid him in publishing more of his poems. To this end, a special ceremony was held at Banneker Institution in August 1866 "to receive Mr. George Horton of North Carolina." However, the effort was unsuccessful; George Moses Horton was not well received by Philadelphia, and, after *Naked Genius,* he published no more poetry. It is said that until his death in 1883 he made a somewhat precarious living writing short stories for Sunday school publications.

The tone of Horton's poetry is distinctly different from that of the other two slave poets, Phillis Wheatley and Jupiter Hammon. Except for the poems in which he bitterly pleads for his own freedom from slavery, Horton's poems are generally bright with good humor, and they occasionally sparkle with fanciful bits of imagery. His poetry has little of the heavy religiosity of Jupiter Hammon or the pious sentimentality of Phillis Wheatley. He writes of love, Nature, and life's small ironies with simplicity and homely wit. Because of his early self-instruction in hymn-book literature, however, the form and meter of his poems reflect a strong hymnal influence that at times is somewhat monotonous.

The earliest critical comment on Horton's poetry is Collier Cobb's *An American Man of Letters—George Moses Horton* (1886). Subsequent critical assessments can be found in Vernon Loggins' *The Negro Author* (1931), in Saunders Redding's *To Make a Poet Black* (1939), and in Richard Walser's *The Black Poet* (1967).

Slavery

When first my bosom glowed with hope,
  I gazed as from a mountain top
    On some delightful plain;
But oh! how transient was the scene—
It fled as though it had not been,
    And all my hopes were vain.

How oft this tantalyzing blaze
  Has led me through deception's maze;
    My friends became my foe—
Then like a plaintive dove I mourned;
To bitter all my sweets were turned,
    And tears began to flow.

Why was the dawning of my birth
Upon this vile, accursed earth,
    Which is but pain to me?
Oh! that my soul had winged its flight,
When I first saw the morning light,
    To worlds of liberty!

Come, melting Pity, from afar,
And break this vast, enormous bar
    Between a wretch and thee;
Purchase a few short days of time,
And bid a vassal rise sublime
    On wings of liberty.

Is it because my skin is black,
That thou should'st be so dull and slack,
    And scorn to set me free?
Then let me hasten to the grave,
The only refuge for the slave,
    Who mourns for liberty.

The wicked cease from troubling there;
No more I'd languish or despair—
    The weary there can rest!
Oppression's voice is heard no more,
Drudg'ry and pain and toil are o'er,
    Yes! there I shall be blest!

The Slave's Complaint

Am I sadly cast aside,
On misfortune's rugged tide?
Will the world my pains deride
    Forever?

Must I dwell in Slavery's night,
And all pleasure take its flight,
Far beyond my feeble sight,
    Forever?

Worst of all, must hope grow dim,
And withold her cheering beam?
Rather let me sleep and dream
    Forever!

Something still my heart surveys,
Groping through this dreary maze;
Is it Hope?—then burn and blaze
    Forever!

Leave me not a wretch confined,
Altogether lame and blind—
Unto gross despair consigned,
    Forever!

Heaven! in whom can I confide?
Canst thou not for all provide?
Condescend to be my guide
    Forever:

And when this transient life shall end,
Oh, may some kind, eternal friend,
Bid me from servitude ascend,
    Forever!

On Hearing of the Intention of a Gentleman to Purchase the Poet's Freedom

When on life's ocean first I spread my sail,
I then implored a mild auspicious gale;
And from the slippery strand I took my flight,
And sought the peaceful haven of delight.

Tyrannic storms arose upon my soul,
And dreadful did their mad'ning thunders roll;
The pensive muse was shaken from her sphere,
And hope, it vanished in the clouds of fear.

At length a golden sun broke through the
    gloom,
And from his smiles arose a sweet perfume—
A calm ensued, and birds began to sing,
And lo! the sacred muse resumed her wing.

With frantic joy she chaunted as she flew,
And kiss'd the clement hand that bore her
    through;
Her envious foes did from her sigh retreat,
Or prostrate fall beneath her burning feet.

'Twas like a proselyte, allied to Heaven—
Or rising spirits' boast of sins forgiven,
Whose shout dissolves the adamant away,
Whose melting voice the stubborn rocks obey.

'Twas like the salutation of the dove,
Borne on the zephyr through some lonesome
    grove,
When Spring returns, and Winter's chill is past,
And vegetation smiles above the blast.

'Twas like the evening of a nuptial pair,
When love pervades the hour of sad despair—
'Twas like fair Helen's sweet return to Troy,
When every Grecian bosom swell'd with joy.

The silent harp which on the osiers hung,
Was then attuned, and manumission sung;
Away by hope the clouds of fear were driven,
And music breathed my gratitude to Heaven.

Hard was the race to reach the distant goal,
The needle oft was shaken from the pole;
In such distress who could forbear to weep?
Toss'd by the headlong billows of the deep!

The tantalizing beams which shone so plain,
Which turned my former pleasures into pain—
Which falsely promised all the joys of fame,
Gave way, and to a more substantial flame.

Some philanthropic souls as from afar,
With pity strove to break the slavish bar;
To whom my floods of gratitude shall roll,
And yield with pleasure to their soft control.

And sure of Providence this work begun—
He shod my feet this rugged race to run;
And in despite of all the swelling tide,
Along the dismal path will prove my guide.

Thus on the dusky verge of deep despair,
Eternal Providence was with me there;
When pleasure seemed to fade on life's gay
    dawn,
And the last beam of hope was almost gone.

James M. Whitfield (1823–1878)

James Whitfield might be called the first Black barber in American history who also wrote and published poetry. Born in Exeter, New Hampshire, he eventually settled in Buffalo, New York, after a short stay in Boston. It was in Buffalo that he became first a barber and then one of Black America's most forceful and angry abolitionist poets.

His first published poetry was simply entitled *Poems* and was offered to the public in 1846, but his best-known work is *America, and Other Poems* published in 1853. The reception of this volume was so encouraging that Whitfield virtually ceased barbering and devoted himself to writing and speaking for the abolitionist cause.

America was dedicated to Martin Delany, and in 1854 Whitfield joined that highly energetic proponent of Black colonization in sponsoring the National Emigration Convention of Colored Men. Following the convention, which had no tangible results, Whitfield and Douglass engaged in a lively newspaper controversy over the merits of colonization. In order to further clarify his views, Whitfield initiated his procolonization *African-American Repository* in 1858.

Involvement in colonization plans and proposals did not keep Whitfield from continuing his work as a poet of protest and abolition. His poem "How Long" appeared in Julia Griffith's *Autographs for Freedom* in 1853, his "Self-Reliance," "Delusive Hope," and "Ode for the Fourth of July" in the *Liberator* in the same year, and his "Lines to Mr. and Mrs. J. T. Holly" in *Frederick Douglass' Paper* in 1856.

Critics find in the brooding melancholy and latent anger of Whitfield's poetry the influence of Byron, particularly in the poem entitled "The Misanthropist." Here he speaks of himself as one "estranged from sympathy / Buried in doubt, despair, and gloom." But more important in his poetry is the strong note of abolitionist protest. America was to Whitfield a "boasted land of liberty" and a "land of blood, and crime, and wrong."

Unlike Martin Delany, Whitfield never changed his mind about colonization. When he died in California in 1878, he was apparently on his way to explore colonization possibilities in Central America.

A representative selection of Whitfield's poetry can be found in William H. Robinson's *Early Black American Poets* (1969). His work receives some critical comment in Vernon Loggins' *The Negro Author* (1931) and in Sterling Brown's *Negro Poetry and Drama* (1969).

America

America, it is to thee,
Thou boasted land of liberty,—
It is to thee I raise my song,
Thou land of blood, and crime, and wrong.
It is to thee, my native land,
From which has issued many a band
To tear the black man from his soil,
And force him here to delve and toil;
Chained on your blood-bemoistened sod,
Cringing beneath a tyrant's rod,
Stripped of those rights which Nature's God
Bequeathed to all the human race,
Bound to a petty tyrant's nod,
Because he wears a paler face.
Was it for this that freedom's fires
Were kindled by your patriot sires?
Was it for this they shed their blood,
On hill and plain, on field and flood?
Was it for this that wealth and life
Were staked upon that desperate strife,
Which drenched this land for seven long years
With blood of men, and women's tears?
When black and white fought side by side,
    Upon the well-contested field,—
Turned back the fierce opposing tide,
    And made the proud invader yield—
When, wounded, side by side they lay,
    And heard with joy the proud hurrah
From their victorious comrades say
    That they had waged successful war,
The thought ne'er entered in their brains
That they endured those toils and pains,
To forge fresh fetters, heavier chains
For their own children, in whose veins
Should flow that patriotic blood,
So freely shed on field and flood.
Oh, no; they fought, as they believed,
    For the inherent rights of man;
But mark, how they have been deceived
    By slavery's accursed plan.
They never thought, when thus they shed
    Their heart's best blood, in freedom's cause,
That their own sons would live in dread,
    Under unjust, oppressive laws:

That those who quietly enjoyed
    The rights for which they fought and fell,
Could be the framers of a code,
    That would disgrace the fiends of hell!

Could they have looked, with prophet's ken,
    Down to the present evil time,
Seen free-born men, uncharged with crime,
    Consigned unto a slaver's pen—
Or thrust into a prison cell,
With thieves and murderers to dwell—
While that same flag whose stripes and stars
Had been their guide through freedom's wars
As proudly waved above the pen
    Of dealers in the souls of men!
Or could the shades of all the dead,
    Who fell beneath that starry flag,
Visit the scenes where they once bled,
    On hill and plain, on vale and crag,
By peaceful brook, or ocean's strand,
    By inland lake, or dark green wood,
Where'er the soil of this wide land
    Was moistened by their patriot blood,—
And then survey the country o'er,
    From north to south, from east to west,
And hear the agonizing cry
Ascending up to God on high,
From western wilds to ocean's shore,
    The fervent prayer of the oppressed;

.   .   .

The shriek of virgin purity,
Doomed to some libertine's embrace,
Should rouse the strongest sympathy
    Of each one of the human race;
And weak old age, oppressed with care,
    As he reviews the scene of strife,
Puts up to God a fervent prayer,
    To close his dark and troubled life:
The cry of fathers, mothers, wives,
    Severed from all their hearts hold dear,
And doomed to spend their wretched lives
    In gloom, and doubt, and hate, and fear;
And manhood, too, with soul of fire,
And arm of strength, and smothered ire,

Stands pondering with brow of gloom,
Upon his dark unhappy doom,
Whether to plunge in battle's strife,
And buy his freedom with his life,
And with stout heart and weapon strong,
Pay back the tyrant wrong for wrong;

     ·   ·   ·

Here Christian writhes in bondage still,
  Beneath his brother Christian's rod,
And pastors trample down at will,
  The image of the living God.

     ·   ·   ·

Almighty God! 'tis this they call
  The land of liberty and law;

Part of its sons in baser thrall
  Than Babylon and Egypt saw—
Worse scenes of rapine, lust and shame,
  Than Babylonian ever knew,
Are perpetrated in the name
  Of God, the holy, just, and true;
And darker doom than Egypt felt,
  May yet repay this nation's guilt.
Almighty God! thy aid impart,
And fire anew each faltering heart,
And strengthen every patriot's hand,
Who aims to save our native land.

     ·   ·   ·

Frances Watkins Harper (1825–1911)

Born free in Baltimore, Frances Watkins Harper became one of the best-known antislavery poets of the ante-bellum period. She received her education in Pennsylvania and Ohio, and, after a brief spell of teaching in Pennsylvania, she volunteered her services to the Antislavery Society as a lecturer. In 1852 she was assigned to work for the Society in Maine, where for several years she proved herself to be a very effective lecturer and poetic orator. Her marriage to Fenton Harper in Cincinnati in 1860 brought a brief interlude in lecturing activities, but after her husband's early death in 1864, Mrs. Harper went back to work for the Society, traveling from Maine to Louisiana in dedicated service to the cause of abolition and freedom.

Her literary career was launched in 1854 when she published *Poems on Miscellaneous Subjects* in Philadelphia. This volume of poems was immensely popular and went through twenty editions by 1874. In general, the subject matter is slavery, its abominable practices and abuses; many of these poems the author recited to great effect in her lectures. Some of the pieces are poor imitations of Longfellow and Whittier, but throughout most of the second half of the nineteenth century the public bought and read her book in spite of its mediocrity.

After the war, Mrs. Harper's literary activity increased. Her narrative *Moses, A Story of the Nile* went through three editions by 1870, and a volume entitled *Poems* was published in 1870 with a second edition in 1900. She also attempted writing some prose fiction, her efforts culminating in *Iola LeRoy* (1892), a novel about the trials and tribulations of an octoroon. Earlier, in 1859, Mrs. Harper had published a short story, "The Two Offers," the first published by a Black writer, but, beyond its historical significance and value as antislavery propaganda, it has little merit. In *Iola LeRoy*, Mrs. Harper presents the somewhat melodramatic story of a typically tragic octoroon who, after being revealed as Black rather than white, is sold into slavery and finally, after the Civil War, devotes her life to the service of her people. The general critical assessment is that Mrs. Harper was a much better poet than a writer of prose fiction.

Some of Mrs. Harper's letters appear in William Still's *The Underground Railroad* (1872), and her poetry is discussed by Saunders Redding in *To Make a Poet Black* (1939). Representative selections from her poetry can be found in William H. Robinson's *Early Black American Poets* (1969). Vernon Loggins' *The Negro Author* (1931) also contains a good analysis of Mrs. Harper's work.

The Slave Mother

Heard you that shriek? It rose
　So wildly in the air,
It seemed as if a burdened heart
　Was breaking in despair.

Saw you those hands so sadly clasped—
　The bowed and feeble head—
The shuddering of that fragile form—
　That look of grief and dread?

　　. 　.　 .

She is a mother, pale with fear,
　Her boy clings to her side,
And in her kirtle vainly tries
　His trembling form to hide.

He is not hers, although she bore
　For him a mother's pains;
He is not hers, although her blood
　Is coursing through his veins!

He is not hers, for cruel hands
　May rudely tear apart
The only wreath of household love
　That binds her breaking heart.

Bury Me in a Free Land

Make me a grave where'er you will,
In a lowly plain, or a lofty hill;
Make it among earth's humblest graves,
But not in a land where men are slaves.

I could not rest if around my grave
I heard the steps of a trembling slave;
His shadow above my silent tomb
Would make it a place of fearful gloom.

I could not rest if I heard the tread
Of a coffle gang to the shambles led,
And the mother's shriek of wild despair
Rise like a curse on the trembling air.

I could not sleep if I saw the lash
Drinking her blood at each fearful gash,
And I saw her babes torn from her breast,
Like trembling doves torn from their parent nest.

I'd shudder and start if I heard the bay
Of bloodhounds seizing their human prey,
And I heard the captive plead in vain
As they bound afresh his galling chain.

If I saw young girls from their mother's arms
Bartered and sold for their youthful charms,
My eye would flash with a mournful flame,
My death-paled cheek grow red with shame.

I would sleep, dear friends, where bloated might
Can rob no man of his dearest right;
My rest shall be calm in any grave
Where none can call his brother a slave.

I ask no monument, proud and high,
To arrest the gaze of the passers-by;
All that my yearning spirit craves,
Is bury me not in a land of slaves.

Religion

Lemuel B. Haynes (1753–1833)

In his *Sketches of the Life and Character of the Reverend Lemuel Haynes* (1839), Timothy Cooley, a fellow Congregational minister, describes his subject as follows:

> *Of illegitimate birth, and of no advantageous circumstances of family, rank, or station, he became one of the choicest instruments of Christ. His face betrayed his race and blood, and his life revealed his Lord.*

It is obvious that the Reverend Mr. Cooley's interests led him to stress Haynes' life of ministerial dedication, but from the standpoint of Black history the life of Lemuel Haynes is in many other respects unique. First, his father was an African of unmixed ancestry and his mother was white; the circumstance of illegitimacy was common enough for a Black person in colonial America in 1753, but the father was usually white and the mother Black. Second, after he was abandoned by his mother shortly after his birth in West Hartford, Connecticut, Lemuel Haynes was adopted by a white family—Deacon David Rose and family—and reared free and virtually white in Granville, New York. Thus, at the same time that the Black girl later named Phillis Wheatley, who had been born both free and legitimate, was being brought to Boston to be sold off a slave ship into the comforts of the Wheatley household, the Black boy named Lemuel Haynes, who was the illegitimate son of a slave, was enjoying freedom amid the comforts of the Rose household. Eventually, both grew up to become conservative, pious New Englanders in thought and manner, and both were briefly famous. But Phillis married a Black man and died early and in poverty, whereas Lemuel married a white woman and lived to become a renowned Congregational minister, the Black Jonathan Edwards of his time.

In 1776, the year of American independence, Haynes joined the Patriot Army and participated in the campaign against Fort Ticonderoga. In the meantime, he had been able to secure a good education in the classics and had read widely in theological and homiletical literature. After his military service, he prepared himself for the ministry and was ordained in 1785.

226

As a preacher of the Christian Gospel, Lemuel Haynes was undoubtedly gifted. Not only did he serve pastorates with great success in Torrington, Connecticut; Rutland, Vermont; and Granville, New York; but many of his sermons were published during his lifetime, and he was invited to preach at the famous Blue Church in New Haven, where Jonathan Edwards had once served. Presidents Dwight of Yale and Humphrey of Amherst sought him for consultation on matters of theology and Christian doctrine. His most famous published sermon was *Universal Salvation* (1795), but his sermon against Jeffersonian political principles—"The Nature and Importance of True Republicanism" (1801)—was another example of impressive oratory, on a religio-political theme.

Thus, Lemuel Haynes was a Black man who, because of his intellectual powers and gift for pulpit oratory, achieved a fame unique for his race in his time. However, there is no evidence that, as he preached the Christian gospel and learnedly propounded the complicated syllogisms of Puritan theology, he ever mentioned slavery or the dilemma of the Black freedman in his native New England. Apparently, his religion, like that of Jupiter Hammon, did not lead him toward this kind of social concern. On his death in Granville in 1833, the following words were written on his tombstone:

Here lies the dust of a poor hell-deserving sinner who ventured into eternity trusting wholly on the merits of Christ for salvation.

By 1833, the fires of antislavery feeling were ablaze in the North, and the tracks of the Underground Railroad criss-crossed all over New York and New England. Any man in the North who in that time was untouched by, or unaware of, the Black man's fight for freedom would probably be described by his contemporaries as a "poor hell-deserving sinner" and regard his journey into eternity as a venture filled with some uncertainty.

In addition to Timothy Cooley's early biography of Haynes, see Vernon Loggins, *The Negro Author* (1931).

Universal Salvation—A Very Ancient Doctrine

A Sermon delivered at Rutland, West Parish, Vt., in the Year 1805 by Lemuel Haynes, A.M.

And the serpent said unto the woman,
Ye shall not surely die.—Genesis iii., 4

The Holy Scriptures are a peculiar fund of instruction. They inform us of the origin of creation; of the primitive state of man; of the fall, or apostasy from God. It appears that he was placed in the Garden of Eden, with full liberty to regale himself with all the delicious fruits that were to be found except what grew on one tree—if he ate of that he should surely die, was the declaration of the most High. Happy were the human pair amid this delightful paradise, until a certain preacher, in his journey, came that way, and disturbed their peace and tranquillity by endeavoring to reverse the prohibition of the Almighty, as in our text—"Ye shall surely die."

She pluck'd, she ate;
Earth felt the wound; nature from her seat,
Sighing through all her works, gave signs of woe,
That all was lost.—MILTON

We may attend,
To the *character* of the preacher—to the *doctrine* inculcated—to the *hearer* addressed—to the *medium* or *instrument* of the preaching.

I. As to the preacher, I would observe, he has many names given him in the sacred writings, the most common is the Devil. That it was he that disturbed the felicity of our first parents is evident from 2 Cor. xi., 3, and many other passages of Scripture. He was once an angel of light, and knew better than to preach such doctrine; he did violence to his own reason.

But, to be a little more particular, let it be observed,

1. He is an *old* preacher. He lived about one thousand seven hundred years before Abraham—above two thousand four hundred and thirty years before Moses—four thousand and four years before Christ. It is now five thousand eight hundred and nine years since he commenced preaching. By this time he must have acquired great skill in the art.

2. He is a very *cunning,* artful preacher. When Elymas, the sorcerer, came to turn away people from the faith, he is said to be *full of all subtlety, and a child of the devil*—not only because he was an enemy of all righteousness, but on account of his carnal cunning and craftiness.

3. He is a very *laborious,* unwearied preacher. He has been in the ministry almost six thousand years, and yet his zeal is not in the least abated. The apostle Peter compares him to a roaring lion, *walking* about, seeking whom he may devour. When God inquired of this persevering preacher, Job ii., 2, "From whence comest thou?" he "answered the Lord, and said, From *going to and fro* in the earth, and from *walking up and down in it.*" He is far from being circumscribed within the narrow limits of parish, state, or continental lines; but his haunt and travel is very large and extensive.

4. He is a *heterogeneous* preacher, if I may so express myself. He makes use of a Bible when he holds forth, as in his sermon to our Savior, Matt. iv., 6. He mixes truth with error, in order to make it go well, or to carry his point.

5. He is a very *presumptuous* preacher. Notwithstanding God had declared in the most plain and positive terms, "Thou shalt surely die"—or, "In dying thou shalt die"—yet this audacious wretch has the impudence to confront omnipotence, and say, "Ye shall not surely die!"

6. He is a very *successful* preacher. He draws a great number after him. No preacher can command hearers like him.—He was successful with our first parents—with the old world. Noah once preached to those spirits that are now in the prison of hell, and told them from God that they should surely die; but this preacher came along and declared the contrary—"Ye shall not surely die." The greater part, it seems, believed him, and went to destruction. So it was with Sodom and Gomorrah—Lot preached to them; the substance of which was, "Up, get ye out of this place; for the Lord will *destroy* this city."—Gen. xix., 14. But this old declaimer told them, No danger! no danger! "Ye shall not surely die." To which they generally gave heed; and Lot seemed to them as one who *mocked*—they believed the Universal preacher, and were consumed—agreeably to the declaration of the apostle Jude, "Sodom and Gomorrah, and the cities about them, suffering the vengeance of eternal fire."

II. Let us attend to the doctrine inculcated by this preacher, "Ye shall not surely die." Bold assertion! without a single argument to support it. The death contained in the threatening was doubtless *eternal* death, as nothing but this would express God's feelings towards sin, or render an infinite atonement necessary. To suppose it to be spiritual death is to blend crime and punishment together. To suppose temporal death to be the curse of the law, then believers are not delivered from it, according to Galatians iii., 13. What Satan meant to preach was, that there is no hell; and that the wages of sin is not death, but eternal life.

III. We shall now take notice of the hearer addressed by the preacher. This we have in the text—"And the Serpent said unto the WOMAN, Ye shall not surely die." That Eve had not so much experience as Adam is evident; and so not equally able to withstand temptation. This doubtless was the reason why the tempter chose her, with whom he might hope to be successful. Doubtless he took a time when she was separated from her husband.

That this preacher has had the greatest success in the dark and ignorant parts of the earth, is evident; his kingdom is a kingdom of darkness. He is a great enemy to light. St. Paul gives us some account of him in his day—2 Tim. iii., 6. "For of this sort are they which creep into houses, and lead captive *silly* women, laden with sins, led away with divers lusts." The same apostle observes, Rom. xvi., 17, 18, "Now I beseech you, brethren, mark them which cause divisions and offenses contrary to the doctrine which ye have learned, and avoid them. For they that are such serve not our Lord Jesus Christ, but their own belly; and by good words and fair speeches deceive the hearts of the simple."

IV. The instrument or medium made use of by the preacher will now be considered. This we have in the text—"And the SERPENT said unto the woman, Ye shall not surely die." But how came the devil to preach through the serpent?

1. To save his own character, and the better to carry his point. Had the devil come to our first parents personally and unmasked, they would have more easily seen the deception.—The reality of a future punishment is at times so clearly impressed on the human mind, that even Satan is constrained to own that there is a hell, although at other times he denies it. He does not wish to have it known that he is a liar; therefore he conceals himself, that he can the better accomplish his designs and save his own character.

2. The devil is an enemy to all good, to all happiness and excellence. He is opposed to the felicity of the brutes. He took delight in tormenting the swine. The serpent, before he set up preaching universal salvation, was a cunning, beautiful, and happy creature; but now his glory is departed. "And the Lord said unto the serpent, Because thou hast done this thou art cursed above all cattle, and above every beast of the field; upon thy belly shalt thou go, and dust shalt thou eat all the days of thy life." There is therefore a kind of duplicate cunning in the matter—Satan gets the preacher and hearers also.

And is not this triumphant treachery,
And more than simple conquest in the foe!—YOUNG

3. Another reason why Satan employs instruments in his service is, because his empire is large, and he cannot be everywhere himself.

4. He has a large number at his command that love and approve of his work, delight in building up his kindgom, and stand ready to go at his call.

Inferences

1. The devil is not dead, but still lives, and is able to preach as well as ever, "Ye shall not surely die."

2. Universalism is no new-fangled scheme, but can boast of great antiquity.

3. See a reason why it ought to be rejected, because it is an ancient and devilish doctrine.

4. See one reason why it is that Satan is such a mortal enemy to the Bible, and to all who preach the gospel, because of that injunction, Mark xvi., 15, 16—"And he said unto them, Go ye into all the world and preach the gospel to every creature. He that believeth and is baptised shall be saved; but he that believeth not shall be *damned*."

5. See whence it was that Satan exerted himself so much to convince our first parents that there was no hell, because the denunciation of the Almighty was true, and he was afraid that Adam and Eve would continue in the belief of it. Was there no truth in future punishment, or was it only a temporary evil, Satan would not be so busy in trying to convince men that there is none. It is his nature and element to lie. "When he speaketh a lie he speaketh of his own, for he is a liar, and the father of it."—John viii., 44.

6. We infer that ministers should not be proud of their preaching. If they preach the true gospel, they only in substance repeat Christ's sermons. If they preach "Ye shall not surely die," they only make use of the devil's old notes that he delivered almost six thousand years ago.

7. It is probable that the doctrine of universal salvation will still prevail, since this preacher is yet alive, and not in the least superannuated; and every effort against him only enrages him more and more and excites him to new inventions and exertions to build up his cause.

To close the subject. As the author of the foregoing discourse has confined himself wholly to the character of Satan, he trusts no one will feel himself personally injured by this short sermon. But should any imbibe a degree of friendship for this aged divine, and think that I have not treated this universal preacher with that respect and veneration that he justly deserves, let them be so kind as to point it out, and I will most cheerfully retract; for it has ever been a maxim with me, "*Render unto all their dues*."

Folk Literature

Tales

How Buck Won His Freedom

Buck was the shrewdest slave on the big Washington plantation. He could steal things almost in front of his master's eyes without being detected. Finally, after having had his chickens and pigs stolen until he was sick, Master Henry Washington called Buck to him one day and said, "Buck, how do you manage to steal without getting caught?"

"Dat's easy, Massa," replied Buck, "dat's easy. Ah kin steal yo' clo'es right tonight, wid you a-guardin' 'em."

"No, no," said the master, "you may be a slick thief, but you can't do that. I will make a proposition with you: If you steal my suit of clothes tonight, I will give you your freedom, and if you fail to steal them, then you will stop stealing my chickens."

"Aw right, Massa, aw right," Buck agreed. "Dat's uh go."

That night about nine o'clock the master called his wife into the bedroom, got his Sunday suit of clothes, laid it out on the table, and told his wife about the proposition he had made with Buck. He got on one side of the table and had his wife get on the other side, and they waited. Pretty soon, through a window that was open, the master heard the mules and the horses in the stable lot running as if someone were after them.

"Here wife," said he, "you take this gun and keep an eye on this suit. I am going to see what's the matter with those animals."

Buck, who had been out to the horse lot and started the stampede to attract the master's attention, now approached the open window. He was a good mimic, and in tones that sounded like his master's he called out, "Ol' lady, ol' lady, ol' lady, you better hand me that suit. That damn thief might steal it while I'm gone."

The master's wife, thinking that it was her husband asking for his suit, took it from the table and handed it out the window to Buck. This is how Buck won his freedom.

Swapping Dreams

Master Jim Turner, an unusually good-natured master, had a fondness for telling long stories woven out of what he claimed to be his dreams, and especially did he like to "swap" dreams with Ike, a witty slave who was a house servant. Every morning he would set Ike to telling about what he had dreamed the night before. It always seemed, however, that the master could tell the best dream tale, and Ike had to admit that he was beaten most of the time.

One morning, when Ike entered the master's room to clean it, he found the master just preparing to get out of bed. "Ike," he said, "I certainly did have a strange dream last night."

"Sez yuh did, Massa, sez yuh did?" answered Ike. "Lemme hyeah it."

"All right," replied the master. "It was like this: I dreamed I went to Nigger Heaven last night, and saw there a lot of garbage, some old torn-down houses, a few old broken-down rotten

230

fences, the muddiest, sloppiest streets I ever saw, and a big bunch of ragged, dirty Negroes walking around."

"Umph, umph, Massa," said Ike, "yuh sho' musta et de same t'ing Ah did las' night, 'cause Ah dreamed Ah went up ter de white man's paradise, an' de streets wuz all ob gol' an' silvah, and dey wuz lots o' milk an' honey dere, an' putty pearly pearly gates, but dey wuzn't uh soul in de whole place."

Lias' Revelation

Lias Jones was a praying slave. Lias would pray any time, but no matter what he was doing at twelve o'clock noon, he would stop short, kneel and pray to God. The prayer Lias prayed at this hour was a special one. "Oh, Lawd," he would pray, "won't yuh please gib us ouah freedom? Lawd, won't yuh please gib us ouah freedom?"

Yet Lias was not discouraged. Without variation he continued at high noon every day to pray that God would give him and his slave brothers freedom. Finally, one day the master sent for Lias to help clean the big house. Lias at twelve o'clock was starting in on the parlor, but had not been in the room long enough to examine the furnishings. Just then the big gong that called the Negroes to dinner started sounding. Lias stopped, as was his custom, to pray for freedom. So he knelt down in the parlor and began to pray: "Oh, Lawd, cum an' gib us all ouah freedom. Oh, Lawd, cum an' gib us all ouah freedom." When Lias got up, it happened that he was standing just opposite a lifesize mirror in the parlor, which reflected his image in it.

Since the slaves had no looking-glasses, Lias had never seen one before, and now he was amazed to see a black man gazing at him from the glass. The only think he could think of in connection with the image was that God had come down in answer to his prayers; so he said, looking at the image in the mirror, "Ah decla', Gawd, Ah didn't know yuh wuz black. Ah thought yuh wuz uh white man. If yuh is black, Ah's gwine make yuh gib us ouah freedom."

The Fox and the Goose

One day a Fox was going down the road and saw a Goose. "Good-morning, Goose," he said; and the Goose flew up on a limb and said, "Good-morning, Fox."

Then the Fox said, "You ain't afraid of me, is you? Haven't you heard of the meeting up at the hall the other night?"

"No, Fox. What was that?"

"You haven't heard about all the animals meeting up at the hall! Why, they passed a law that no animal must hurt any other animal. Come down and let me tell you about it. The hawk mustn't catch the chicken, and the dog mustn't chase the rabbit, and the lion mustn't hurt the lamb. No animal must hurt any other animal."

"Is that so!"

"Yes, all live friendly together. Come down, and don't be afraid."

As the Goose was about to fly down, way off in the woods they heard a "Woo-wooh! woo-wooh!" and the Fox looked around.

"Come down, Goose," he said.

And the Dog got closer. "Woo-wooh!"

Then the Fox started to sneak off; and the Goose said, "Fox, you ain't scared of the dog, is you? Didn't all the animals pass a law at the meeting not to bother each other any more?"

"Yes," replied the Fox as he trotted away quickly, "the animals passed the law; but some of the animals round here ain't got much respec' for the law."

Tar Baby

Rabbit says to himself, "Gee, it's gittin' dry here; can't git any mo' water. Git a little in the mornin' but that ain't enough." So he goes along an' gits the gang to dig a well. So the Fox goes roun' an' calls all the animals together to dig this well. He gits Possum, Coon, Bear, an' all the animals an' they start to dig the well. So they come to Rabbit to help. Rabbit he sick. They say, "Come on, Brother Rabbit, help dig this well; we all need water." Rabbit say, "Oh the devil. I don't need no water; I kin drink dew." So he wouldn't go. So when the well was done Rabbit he was the first one to git some of the water. He went there at night an' git de water in jugs. The other animals see Rabbit's tracks from gittin' water in jugs. So all the animals git together an' see what they goin' to do about Brother Rabbit. So Bear say, "I tell you, I'll lay here an' watch for it. I'll ketch that Rabbit." So Bear watched but Rabbit was too fast for him. So Fox said, "I tell you, let's study a plan to git Brother Rabbit." So they all sit together an' study a plan. So they made a tar baby an' put it up by the well. So Brother Rabbit come along to git some water. He see the tar baby an' think it is Brother Bear. He say, "Can't git any water tonight; there's Brother Bear layin' for me." He looked some more, then he said, "No, that ain't Brother Bear, he's too little for Brother Bear." So he goes up to the tar baby an' say, "Whoo-oo-oo-oo." Tar Baby didn't move. So Rabbit got skeered. He sneaked up to it an' said, "Boo!" Tar Baby didn't move. Then Rabbit run all aroun' an' stood still to see did he move. But Tar Baby kept still. Then he moved his claw at him. Tar Baby stood still. Rabbit said, "That must be a chunk o' wood." He went up to see if it was a man. He said, "Hello, old man, hello, old man, what you doin' here?" The man didn't answer. He said again, "Hello, old man,

hello, old man, what you doin' here?" The man didn't answer. Rabbit said, "Don't you hear me talkin' to you? I'll slap you in the face." The man ain't said nothin'. So Rabbit hauled off sure enough an' his paw stuck. Rabbit said, "Turn me loose, turn me loose or I'll hit you with the other paw." The man ain't said nothin'. So Rabbit hauled off with his other paw an' that one stuck too. Rabbit said, "You better turn me loose, I'll kick you if you don't turn me loose." Tar Baby didn't say anything. "Bup!" Rabbit kicked Tar Baby an' his paw stuck. So he hit him with the other an' that one got stuck. Rabbit said, "I know the things got blowed up now; I know if I butt you I'll kill you." So all the animals were hidin' in the grass watchin' all this. They all ran out an' hollered, "Aha, we knowed we was gonna ketch you, we knowed we was gonna ketch you." So Rabbit said, "Oh, I'm so sick." So the animals said, "Whut we gonna do?" So they has a great meetin' to see what they gonna do. So someone said, "Throw him in the fire." But the others said, "No, that's too good; can't let him off that easy." So Rabbit pleaded an' pleaded, "Oh, please, please throw me in the fire." So someone said, "Hang him." They all said, "He's too light, he wouldn't break his own neck." So a resolution was drawn up to burn him up. So they all went to Brother Rabbit an' said, "Well, today you die. We gonna set you on fire." So Rabbit said, "Aw, you couldn't give me anything better." So they all say, "We better throw him in the briar patch." Rabbit cry out right away, "Oh, for God's sake, don't do dat. They tear me feet all up; they tear me behind all up; they tear me eyes out." So they pick him up an' throw him in the briar patch. Rabbit run off an' cry, "Whup-pee, my God, you couldn't throw me in a better place! There where my mammy born me, in the briar patch."

Big Sixteen and the Devil

It was slavery time, Zora, when Big Sixteen was a man. They called 'im Sixteen 'cause dat was de number of de shoe he wore. He was big and strong and Ole Massa looked to him to do everything.

One day Ole Massa said, "Big Sixteen, Ah b'lieve Ah want you to move dem sills Ah had hewed out down in de swamp."

"Yassuh, Massa."

Big Sixteen went down in de swamp and picked up dem 12 × 12's and brought 'em on up to de house and stack 'em. No one man ain't never toted a 12 × 12 befo' nor since.

So Ola Massa said one day, "Go fetch in de mules. Ah want to look 'em over."

Big Sixteen went on down to de pasture and caught dem mules by de bridle but they was contrary and balky and he tore de bridles to pieces pullin' on 'em, so he picked one of 'em up under each arm and brought 'em up to Ole Massa.

He says, "Big Sixteen, if you kin tote a pair of balky mules, you kin do anything. You kin ketch de Devil."

"Yassuh, Ah kin, if you git me a nine-pound hammer and a pick and shovel!"

Ole Massa got Sixteen de things he ast for and tole 'im to go ahead and bring him de Devil.

Big Sixteen went out in front of de house and went to diggin'. He was diggin' nearly a month befo' he got where he wanted. Then he took his hammer and went and knocked on de Devil's door. Devil answered de door hisself.

"Who dat out dere?"

"It's Big Sixteen."

"What you want?"

"Wanta have a word wid you for a minute."

Soon as de Devil poked his head out de door, Sixteen lammed him over de head wid dat hammer and picked 'im up and carried 'im back to Ole Massa.

Ole Massa looked at de dead Devil and hollered, "Take dat ugly thing 'way from here quick! Ah didn't think you'd ketch de Devil sho 'nuff."

So Sixteen picked up de Devil and throwed 'im back down de hole.

'Way after while, Big Sixteen died and went to Heben. But Peter looked at 'im and tole 'im to g'wan 'way from dere. He was too powerful. He might git outa order and there wouldn't be nobody to handle 'im. But he had to go somewhere so he went on to hell.

Soon as he got to de gate de Devil's children was playin' in de yard and they seen 'im and run to de house, says, "Mama, Mama! Dat man's out dere dat kilt papa!"

So she called 'im in de house and shet de door. When Sixteen got dere she handed 'im a li'l piece of fire and said, "You ain't comin' in here. Here, take dis hot coal and g'wan off and start you a hell uh yo' own."

So when you see a Jack O'Lantern in de woods at night you know it's Big Sixteen wid his piece of fire lookin' for a place to go.

Marster's Body and Soul

When ole man Shiger come to die, Ole Miss were so worry 'bout de condition er he soul till she send for all de niggers to hold a prayer-meetin' over him. You know ole man Shiger been a wicked ole man. He have a heap er niggers an' he been a sportin' man. He love to fight game chickens an' play cards an' race horses an' gamble, an' he have hound dog an' run fox, an' dat wha' he mind run on—dat an' livin'.

When all dem niggers git here, he had de niggers bring him out in a big armchair an' set him down wey he could look at 'em an' listen to dey prayer in he behalf. An' he pick out two ole niggers to lead in prayer. De fust one been ole man July, an' he say:

"Lord, dey ain't nothin' to all dis talk 'about Ole Marster guh die. He guh be here. Luh him live, Lord, for de peace er dy servants. Luh him live to breed dat mare an' raise one more colt like de one he done raise, for he got de greates' race horse in all de land. Listen to my voice, Lord, an' luh him live to take he game chickens an' keep on whippin' all de other chickens like he been doin'.

"Luh him live, my Lord, so dat dis community kin keep de best hound. Ole Marster's hound kin outrun all de hound er all de other white folks in de world. Lord, you know dey aint' no use for you to worry an' debil Ole Marster 'bout dyin' now. He nothin' but a youth."

You know ole man July was a hundred an' fifteen year ole an' Ole Marster ain't but eighty.

"Lord, hear my prayer. Put Ole Marster's mind at ease. Don't debil him no more. Put he mind at ease, Lord. Dey ain't nothin' de matter wid he body."

Ole Marster love to hear dat. He git 'side he self he so please.

"Lord, I done axe you—"

An' de sisters was hollerin':

"Hear him, Lord! Hear him! Amen!"

An' den Ole Miss call ole man Noae an' ole man Noae git up an' say:

"Lord, listen to my prayer. I ain't botherin' 'bout Old Marster's body. I guh axe you 'bout he soul. Help him, Lord. Take him up an' turn him round in de palm er you hand an' luh him git a glimpse into de life he been leadin'. Luh him see he self as all dese lyin' niggers sees him. Save he soul, Lord. Save he soul.

"Take him up, Lord, an' hold him over hell an' swinge he hind-part good. Make tenst like you guh drap him in. Lord, bring him to he senses. Lord, it ain't matter 'bout he body. Save he soul, Lord."

An' den all dem niggers got to hollerin' an' geein' answer:

"Save he soul, Lord! Save he soul! Swinge he hind-part, Lord! Swinge he hind-part good!"

An' Ole Marster call he overseer an' tell him to gee ole man July a quarter er liquor' an' a plug er tobacco, an' to take ole man Noae into de stable an' gee him twenty lashes.

An' ole man Shiger he die next day.

Songs

De Ole Nigger Driver

O, de ole nigger driver!
  O, gwine away!
Fust ting my mammy tell me,
  O, gwine away!
Tell me 'bout de nigger driver,
  O, gwine away!

Nigger driver second devil,
  O, gwine away!
Best ting for do he driver,
  O, gwine away!
Knock he down and spoil he labor,
  O, gwine away!

Sellin' Time

Goodbye, Goodbye,
If I nevah, nevah see you any mo.
Goodbye, Goodbye,
I will meet you on the utha sho.

Pray for me,
Pray for me,
If I nevah, nevah see you any mo.
Pray for me,
Pray for me,
I will meet you on the utha sho.

Be strong, Be strong,
If I nevah, nevah see you any mo.
Be strong, Be strong,
I will meet you on the utha sho.

Fare thee well,
Fare thee well,
If I nevah, nevah see you any mo.
Fare thee well,
Fare thee well,
I will meet you on the utha sho.

JUba

JUba dis and JUba dat an
JUba killed my YALlow cat, O JUba,
JUba, JUba, JUba, JUba, JUba.

Mistah Rabbit

"Mistah Rabbit, Mistah Rabbit, yo tale's
mighty white."
"Yes, bless God, been gittin outa sight."

Refrain:
Ev'y little soul gwine-a shine, shine,
Ev'y little soul gwine-a shine along.

"Mistah Rabbit, Mistah Rabbit, yo coat's
mighty gray."
"Yes, bless God, been out fo day."
"Mistah Rabbit, Mistah Rabbit, yo ears mighty
long."
"Yes, bless God, been put on wrong."

"Mistah Rabbit, Mistah Rabbit, yo ears mighty
thin."
"Yes, bless God, been splittin the wind."

Raise a Ruckus Tonight

My ol missus promise me,
When she die she set me free.
Lived so long her haid got ball,
Give up the notion of dyin atall.

Chorus:
Come along, little chillun, come along,
While the moon is shinin' bright.
Git on board, down the river float,
We gonna raise a ruckus tonight.

My ol missus say to me,
John, Ize gonna set you free.
But when dat haid got slick an ball,
Couldn't killed her wid a big green maul.

My ol missus nevah die,
Wid her nose all hooked and skin all dry.
But when ol miss she somehow gone,
She lef po John a-hillin up de corn.

Ol mosser likewise promise me,
When he die he set me free.
But ol mosser go an mak his will,
For to leave me plowin ol Beck still.

Way down yonder in Chittlin Switch,
Bullfrog jump fum ditch to ditch.
Bullfrog jump fum de bottom of de well,
Swore, my Lawd, he jumped fum Hell.

Who-zen John, Who-za

Old black bull come down de hollow,
He shake hi' tail, you hear him bellow;
When he bellow he jar de river,
He paw de yearth, he make it quiver.
Who-zen John, who-za.

Misse Got a Gold Chain

Misse got a gold chain round her neck,
Misse got a gold chain round her neck,
Misse got a gold chain round her neck;
De watch on toder end tick tick tick,
De watch on toder end tick tick tick,
De watch on toder end tick tick tick,
Jus de same as Sambo when he cut up stick:
Zip e duden duden, duden duden da.

Miss Lucy she hab a gold chain too,
Miss Lucy she hab a gold chain too,
Miss Lucy she hab a gold chain too;
No watch on de toder end ob dat, I know,
No watch on de toder end ob dat, I know,
No watch on de toder end ob dat, I know,
I reckon it's a picture ob her handsome beau:
Zip e duden duden, duden duden da.

Zip e Duden Duden

Who dat nigger in a door I spy?
Who dat nigger in a door I spy?
Who dat nigger in a door I spy?
Dat old Scip, by de white ob him eye:
   Zip e duden duden, duden duden da.

By de white ob him eye and he tick out lip,
By de white ob him eye and he tick out lip,
By de white ob him eye and he tick out lip,
Sambo know dat old black Scip:
   Zip e duden duden, duden duden da.

Juber

Juber up and Juber down,
Juber all around de town,
Juber dis, and Juber dat,
And Juber roun' the simmon vat.
   Hoe corn! hill tobacco!
   Get over double trouble, Juber boys, Juber.

Uncle Phil, he went to mill,
He suck de sow, he starve de pig,
Eat the simmon, gi' me de seed,
I told him I was not in need.
   Hoe corn! hill tobacco!
   Get over double trouble, Juber boys, Juber.

Aunt Kate? look on de high shelf,
Take down de husky dumplin,
I'll eat it wi' my simmon cake.
To cure the rotten belly-ache.
   Hoe corn! hill tobacco!
   Get over double trouble, Juber boys, Juber.

Raccoon went to simmon town,
To choose the rotten from de soun,
Dare he sot upon a sill,
Eating of a whip-poor-will.
   Hoe corn! hill tobacco!
   Get over double trouble, Juber boys, Juber.

The Stoker's Chant

The ebben tide ib floating past,
   Fire down below!
The arrival time ib coming fast,
   Fire down below!
Raccoon cry in de maple tree,
   Fire down below!
The wood ib on fire, and the fire ah see,
   Fire down below!
Oo a oo oh! fire down below!

Uncle Gabriel

Oh, my boys I'm bound to tell you;
   Oh! Oh!
Listen awhile, and I will tell you;
   Oh! Oh!
I'll tell you little 'bout Uncle Gabriel;
Oh, boys, I've just begun.
Hard times in old Virginny.

Oh, don't you know old Uncle Gabriel?
   Oh! Oh!
Oh, he was a darkey General,
   Oh! Oh!
He was the chief of the insurgents,
Way down in Southampton.
Hard times in old Virginny.

It was a little boy betrayed him,
Oh! Oh!
A little boy by the name of Daniel,
Oh! Oh!
Betrayed him at the Norfolk landing;
Oh, boys I'm getting done.
Hard times in old Virginny.

Says he, How d'ye do, my Uncle Gabriel?
Oh! Oh!
I am not your Uncle Gabriel,
Oh! Oh!
My name it is Jim McCullen;
Some they calls me Archy Mullin.
Hard times in old Virginny.

They took him down to the gallows,
Oh! Oh!
They drove him down with four grey horses,
Oh! Oh!
Brice's Ben, he drove the wagon,
Oh, boys, I am most done.
Hard times in old Virginny.

And there they hung him, and they swung him,
Oh! Oh!
And they swung him and they hung him,
Oh! Oh!
And that was the last of the darkey General;
Oh, boys I'm just done.
Hard times in old Virginny.

. . .

Gen'el Jackson

Gen'el Jackson, mighty man—
　Whaw, my kingdom, fire away;
He fight on sea, and he fight on land,
　Whaw, my kingdom, fire away.

Gen'el Jackson gain de day—
　Whaw, my kingdom, fire away,
He gain de day in Floraday,
　Whaw, my kingdom, fire away.

Gen'el Jackson fine de trail,
　Whaw, my kingdom, fire away,
He full um fote wid cotton bale,
　Whaw, my kingdom, fire away.

Mary, Don You Weep

Mary, don you weep an Marthie don you moan,
Mary, don you weep an Marthie don you moan;
Pharaoh's army got drown-ded,
　Oh Mary don you weep.

I thinks every day an I wish I could,
Stan on de rock whar Moses stood,
Oh Pharaoh's army got drown-ded,
　Oh Mary don you weep.

Gonna Shout

Gonna shout trouble over,
　When I get home.
Gonna shout trouble over,
　When I get home.

No mo prayin, no mo dyin,
　When I get home.
No mo prayin an no mo dyin,
　When I get home.

Meet my father,
　When I get home.
Meet my father,
　When I get home.

Meet my mother,
　When I get home.
Meet my mother,
　When I get home.

When-a Mah Blood Runs Chilly an Col

Oh, when-a mah blood runs chilly an col, Ize got to go,
Ize got to go,
Oh, when-a mah blood runs chilly an col, Ize got to go,
Way beyond the moon.

Refrain:
Do, Lord, do, Lord, do remember me,
Oh do, Lord, do, Lord, do remember me,
Oh do, Lord, do, Lord, do remember me,
Do, Lord, remember me.

Ef you cain't bear no crosses, you cain't wear no crown,
Ef you cain't bear no crosses, you cain't wear no crown,
Ef you cain't bear no crosses, you cain't wear no crown,
Way beyond the moon.

Ize gotta mother in de Beulah land, she's callin me,
She's callin me, she's callin me,
Ize gotta mother in de Beulah land, she's callin me,
Way beyond de sun.

Soon One Mawnin

Soon one mawnin death come creepin in mah room,
Soon one mawnin death come creepin in mah room,
Soon one mawnin death come creepin in mah room,
Oh mah Lawd, Oh mah Lawd, what shall ah do to be saved?

Death done been heah, took mah mother an gone,
Death done been heah, took mah mother an gone,
Death done been heah, took mah mother an gone,
Oh mah Lawd, Oh mah Lawd, what shall ah do to be saved?

Don't move mah pillow till mah Jesus come,
Don't move mah pillow till mah Jesus come,
Don't move mah pillow till mah Jesus come,
Oh mah Lawd, Oh mah Lawd, what shall ah do to be saved?

I'm so glad I got religion in time,
I'm so glad I got religion in time,
I'm so glad I got religion in time,
Oh mah Lawd, Oh mah Lawd, what shall ah do to be saved?

Motherless Child

Sometimes I feel like a motherless child,
Sometimes I feel like a motherless child,
Sometimes I feel like a motherless child,
A long ways from home,
A long ways from home.

Sometimes I feel like I'm almost gone,
Sometimes I feel like I'm almost gone,
Sometimes I feel like I'm almost gone,
A long ways from home,
A long ways from home.

Sometimes I feel like a feather in the air,
Sometimes I feel like a feather in the air,
Sometimes I feel like a feather in the air,
And I spread my wings and I fly,

I spread my wings and I fly.

Swing Low, Sweet Chariot

Swing low, sweet chariot,
Coming for to carry me home,
Swing low, sweet chariot,
Coming for to carry me home.

I looked over Jordan and what did I see
Coming for to carry me home,
A band of angels, coming after me,
Coming for to carry me home.

If you get there before I do,
Coming for to carry me home,
Tell all my friends I'm coming too,
Coming for to carry me home.

Swing low, sweet chariot,
Coming for to carry me home,
Swing low, sweet chariot,
Coming for to carry me home.

Nobody Knows da Trubble Ah See

Oh, nobody knows da trubble ah see,
Nobody knows but Jesus.
Nobody knows da trubble ah see,
Glory, Hallelujah!

Sometimes I'm up, sometimes I'm down,
Oh, yes, Lord!
Sometimes I'm almost to the groun',
Oh, yes, Lord!
Although you see me goin along, so,
Oh, yes, Lord!
I have my trubbles here below,
Oh, yes, Lord!

Nobody knows da trubble ah see,
Nobody knows my sorrow.
Nobody knows da trubble ah see,
Glory, Hallelujah!

One day when I was walkin along,
Oh, yes, Lord!
The elements open and his love came down,
Oh, yes, Lord!
I never shall forget dat day,
Oh, yes, Lord!
When Jesus wash my sins away,
Oh, yes, Lord!

Oh, nobody knows da trubble ah see,
Nobody knows my sorrow.
Nobody knows da trubble ah see,
Glory, Hallelujah!

Were You Dere?

Were you dere when dey crucified my Lord?
                    (Were you dere?)
Were you dere when dey crucified my Lord?
O sometimes it causes me to tremble! tremble! tremble!
Were you dere when dey crucified my Lord?

Were you dere when dey nail'd him to da cross?
                    (Were you dere?)
Were you dere when dey nail'd him to da cross?
O sometimes it causes me to tremble! tremble! tremble!
Were you dere when dey nail'd him to da cross?

Were you dere when dey pierced him in da side?
                    (Were you dere?)
Were you dere when dey pierced him in da side?
O sometimes it causes me to tremble! tremble! tremble!
Were you dere when dey pierced him in da side?

Were you dere when da sun refused to shine?
                    (Were you dere?)
Were you dere when da sun refused to shine?
O sometimes it causes me to tremble! tremble! tremble!
Were you dere when da sun refused to shine?

Do, Lawd

O do, Lawd, remember me!
  O do, Lawd, remember me!
O, do remember me, until de year roll round!
  Do, Lawd, remember me!

If you want to die like Jesus died,
  Lay in de grave.
You want to fold your arms and close your
    eyes,
  And die wid a free good will.

For death is a simple ting,
  And he go from door to door,
And he knock down some, and he cripple up
    some,
  And he leave some here to pray.

O do, Lawd, remember me!
  O do, Lawd, remember me!
My old fader's gone till de year roll round;
  Do, Lawd, remember me!

Dis Worl Mos Done

Brudder, keep your lamp trimmin' and a-burnin',
Keep your lamp trimmin' and a-burnin',
Keep your lamp trimmin' and a-burnin',
  For dis world mos done.
So keep your lamp, &c.

Shout Along, Chillen

Shout along, chillen!
Shout along, chillen!
  Hear the dying Lamb:
Oh! take your nets and follow me
For I died for you upon the tree!
  Shout along, chillen!
  Shout along, chillen!
    Hear the dying Lamb!

PART III

The Black Man in the Civil War: 1861–1865

In the great five-year war that ended slavery in the United States, America's Blacks were ultimately deeply involved in many ways—as soldiers, sailors, spies, scouts, nurses, teachers, recruiters, chaplains, medical officers, war correspondents, political prognosticators, and presidential advisors. Finally, there were the "contraband of war"—the more than five hundred thousand who crossed into the Union lines from slavery to freedom. The story of the Black man's participation in this searing conflict has been told by Black writers many times. Two years after the war ended, William Wells Brown published his *Negro in the American Rebellion* (1867). Twenty-one years later, George Washington Williams produced his *History of the Negro Troops in the War of the Rebellion* (1888), and in that same year Joseph T. Wilson added his *Black Phalanx*. Both Williams and Wilson had been soldiers in Negro regiments and hence gave accounts that reflected a participant's point of view. In the twentieth century, there have been several additional studies of the Black man's involvement in the Civil War. These include Herbert Aptheker's *Negro in the Civil War* (1938), Benjamin Quarles' *Negro in the Civil War* (1953) and his *Lincoln and the Negro* (1962), and Dudley Cornish's *The Sable Arm: Negro Troops in the Union Army, 1861–65* (1956). One of the most recent books is James McPherson's *The*

243

Negro's Civil War (1965). In addition to these separate studies, a full-length official record of the Black man's involvement in the war may be found in *War of the Rebellion: A Compilation of Official Records of the Union and Confederate Armies* (1880–1901). In this official record of 128 volumes, the role of the Black man as soldier, sailor, laborer, and freedman is clearly presented.

But beyond the official record there is another record, told in the memoirs, reminiscences, pamphlets, speeches, articles, and letters written, not only by some of the 488,000 free Blacks of the Northern states, but by newly escaped ex-slaves who had a story to tell. Such a one was Susie King Taylor, who, born into slavery in 1848, secretly taught herself to read and write while still a slave. When, in 1862, she escaped from slavery at Savannah by fleeing to Fort Pulaski, she become a teacher of freedmen and a laundress at the Union encampments on the Sea Islands off the coast of South Carolina. In 1902, she, too, told her story in *Reminiscences of My Life in Camp*. In addition to information provided by official records, histories, memoirs, and letters, much is revealed about the status of the Black man during the war in journals—Garrison's *Liberator* and Redpath's *Pine and Palm* in Boston, Robert Hamilton's *Anglo-African* in New York, and the *Christian Recorder,* the official weekly publication of the A.M.E. Church in Philadelphia. In these periodicals and in the minutes of the conventions and meetings of Black organizations, the story of the Black man's confrontation with the great issues of the war years is told. And there were crisis-laden issues that called for thoughtful comment and analysis, ranging all the way from whether the Union Army would accept Black volunteers to whether the nation's four million Blacks should be colonized in *Ile à Vache* or in Chiriqui or in Haiti or in Liberia.

Amid the turmoil and tension of war, there were, then, momentous issues that agitated and disturbed the Black man on the home front. First, there were the twin issues of slavery's legal abolition and the slaves' legal emancipation. When the war began in April 1861, it was the common expectation that both emancipation and abolition would be immediately decreed. In May 1861 Frederick Douglass analyzed the matter in his *Douglass' Monthly* as follows:

> *The very stomach of this rebellion is the Negro in the condition of a slave. Arrest that hoe in the hands of the Negro, and you smite rebellion in the very seat of its life. . . . The Negro is the key of the situation—the pivot upon which the whole rebellion turns . . . . Teach the rebels and traitors that the price they are to pay for the attempt to abolish this government must be the abolition of slavery. . . . Henceforth, let the war cry be down with the treason, and down with slavery, the cause of treason!*

Douglass' position received solid support from Black Americans everywhere. In the fall of 1861, Dr. James W. C. Pennington, a New York Presbyterian minister who had advanced from a slave's illiteracy when he escaped from bondage in the 1840's to a Doctor of Divinity degree from Heidelberg in 1851, circulated a petition that summarized the hopes of Black Americans:

To the Hon. the Senate and House of Representatives of the United States in Congress assembled:

The undersigned, Free Colored Citizens of these United States, believing that African Slavery as it now exists in the South, is the prime cause of the present crisis and that permanent peace cannot be restored until said cause is removed, most respectfully petition your honorable body to take such measures, or enact such a law as may, in your wisdom, seem best for the immediate abolition of African Slavery.

This petition got nowhere, for both the Congress and the Administration in 1861 were wedded to the idea that the war was being fought to save the Union and that the existence of slavery was an extraneous issue having nothing to do with the war. Indeed, Lincoln, the "Great Emancipator," moved with exasperating slowness even to the position he held in the spring of 1862—that the government would compensate any of the rebellious states for their slaves if the slaves were set free and slavery was gradually abolished. This became known as the "principle of compensated emancipation." Like Dr. Pennington's petition, it, too, had no result. In the meantime, the President moved with unaccustomed swiftness to rebuke General John C. Fremont and repudiate the latter's proclamation freeing all slaves in his command jurisdiction in Missouri. Accordingly, Black hopes for freedom were, like the Union's military status, at a new low in the summer of 1862. Everyone agreed with Trenton's Rev. J. P. Campbell, an officer in the A.M.E. Church, that "The President is not now, and never was, either an abolitionist, or an anti-slavery man!"

When President Lincoln finally did draw up an Emancipation Proclamation in September 1862, he presented it as a war measure and not in response to the clamor of protest raised by men such as Douglass, Pennington, and Campbell. In fact, at Secretary of State Seward's suggestion, he withheld issuing the proclamation until the Union forces won a long-sought victory at the Battle of Antietam. Admittedly, the issuance of the proclamation eased tensions considerably on the Black home front, and Emancipation Day, January 1, 1863, was a day of great jubilation throughout all Black communities in the North. But perceptive leaders were quick to point out that the proclamation document was exceedingly conservative, emancipating slaves only in the states in rebellion and excepting the slaves in the border states.

Even as the sounds of Emancipation "Jubilee" were being heard throughout the land, Black leaders were contending with another problem—the refusal of the War Department to accept Black volunteers in the army. The army's "white-only" policy was, like the government's initial policy on abolition and emancipation, strangely inconsistent and unrealistic. Undoubtedly, it stemmed from the assumption that the war between the states was "a white man's war," although, in the early

months of the conflict, in any given Union encampment on the Sea
Islands or in New Orleans or in Missouri, Black "contrabands" easily
outnumbered white troops. So even if the war were "lily white," the
encampments were not. Moreover, general officers in the field such as
Butler in New Orleans, Hunter on the Sea Islands, and Fremont in
Missouri quickly put the Black contrabands to work as laborers,
foragers, cooks, and, in some instances, spies. Thus, the "white-only"
policy of the War Department in Washington was in some respects very
early breached on the actual field of battle. Moreover, the Navy Department did not adhere to a "white-only" policy. As historian Benjamin
Quarles points out in *The Negro in the Civil War*, "Throughout its
history, the navy had never debarred free Negroes from enlisting, and
in September, 1861 it had adopted the policy of signing up former slaves.
Suffering during the entire course of the war from a shortage of men, the
navy encouraged the blacks to join the service." That is, the Navy
ignored the implications of Judge Taney's 1857 Dred Scott decision that
Blacks were chattels and not men, and therefore could not be citizen-
soldiers, while the Army remained white supremacist. The cautious
Lincoln, in his zeal not to antagonize the enemy further, fully supported
the War Department's policy—at least until military expediency dictated otherwise.

Inevitably, the War Department's policy excited the Black man's
wrath. Frederick Douglass wrote in his *Douglass' Monthly* in September
1861:

> *What a spectacle of blind, unreasoning prejudice and pusillanimity
> is this! The national edifice is on fire. Every man who can carry a
> bucket of water, or remove a brick, is wanted; but those who have
> the care of the building, having a profound respect for the feeling of
> the national burglars who set the building on fire, are determined
> that the flames shall only be extinguished by Indo-Caucasian hands,
> and to have the building burnt rather than save it by means of any
> other. Such is the pride, the stupid prejudice and folly that rules the
> hour.*

Similarly, J. Madison Bell, a poet and former associate of John Brown,
urged that the contrabands be given arms to fight their former masters:

> *Shall we arm them? Yes, arm them! Give to each man
> A rifle, a musket, a cutlass or sword;
>   Then on to the charge! let them war in the van,
> Where each may confront with his merciless lord,
> And purge from their race, in the eyes of the brave,
> The stigma and scorn now attending the slave.*

By mid-1862 military expediency and the counsel of some of the Union's
general officers brought a change in policy. In July 1862 Congress empowered the President to "employ as many persons of African descent
as he may deem necessary and proper for the suppression of this
rebellion." Congress also repealed a 1792 law barring Blacks from
enrolling in state militias and authorized the enlistment of Blacks in the

Army. But the President used his newly granted powers with characteristic caution, this despite the fact that Union military units had suffered a series of defeats that lowered Union morale and in turn discouraged white enlistments. First, a Black regiment, the First South Carolina Volunteers, was formed under Massachusetts abolitionist Thomas Wentworth Higginson. Then, when there were no discernible disastrous aftereffects in this experiment with Black troops, a second Black regiment was formed of contrabands gathered on South Carolina's Sea Islands. When these two regiments in March 1863 captured and occupied Jacksonville, Florida, the President, the War Department, and the white North were finally convinced that the Black soldier, armed and trained, might be the one ingredient needed for victory. To this end, in May 1863, the War Department established a Bureau of Colored Troops to raise Black regiments everywhere they could be mustered up. And *L'Union,* the French-English Negro newspaper in New Orleans, tried to help:

> *To Arms! It is our duty. The nation counts on the devotion and courage of its sons. We will not remain deaf to its call; we will not remain indifferent spectators, like strangers who attach no value to the land .... He who defends his fatherland is the real citizen, and this time we are fighting for the rights of our race. ...*

The official record of the Union Army indicates that not only did the Black men flock to the colors, but they fought hard and well at all times. It is true that in April 1864 the contingent holding the Fort Pillow outpost on the Mississippi River was overrun by a superior force of Confederates under the command of the infamous Nathan Bedford Forrest, and three hundred Black troops were massacred after they had surrendered. But this incident merely fired Black soliders to fight better. For instance, in the battle for Petersburg in the Virginia sector, Black troops stormed the breastworks crying "Remember Fort Pillow!" And when some of the troopers in the heat of the battle could not remember the name of the fort, they yelled, "Remember what you done to us, way back, down dar!"

Thus, as in the fight for abolition and emancipation, the Black man won a hard-fought battle for the right to enlist in the Union Army. By war's end, 178,985 Black men had enlisted; Black regiments had participated in 449 engagements and 39 major battles. Their casualties numbered 37,300, but seventeen soldiers and four sailors won the Medal of Honor. And at war's end there were about a hundred Black commissioned officers (excluding chaplains and the eight Black surgeons who held the rank of major). When Richmond finally fell in April 1865, the first Union troops to enter the city were troops of the Fifth Massachusetts Cavalry (Black), followed by troops of the XXVth Army Corps, comprised of thirty-two Black regiments. Thus, within two years after Lincoln had hesitatingly proclaimed that all slaves in the states in rebellion were free, Black soldiers had fully validated that proclamation on the field of battle.

Inevitably, all did not go well with the Black soldier. The most agonizing issue was inequality in pay and the long delay in remedying it. For some reason, the Black enlisted man initially received $9.50 less per month than the white enlisted man. The white soldier's pay was $13.00 per month plus a $3.50 allowance for clothing. The Black soldier's pay was $10.00 per month less a $3.00 allowance for clothing. The official explanation for the salary inequity was that the Black soldier was being paid laborer's wages and not soldier's wages, but the discerning could see white supremacy at work in the War Department. The complaints from the Black soldier were many, particularly from those who were members of the famed Massachusetts 54th and 55th. One soldier in the 54th wrote to his sister:

> When we enlisted we were to get $13.00 per month, clothing and rations, and treatment the same as white soldiers; and now they want to cheat us out of what is justly due us, by paying us off with $10 per month, and taking three dollars out of that for clothing. . . . Why are we not worth as much as white soliders? We do the same work they do, and do what they cannot.

On the home front many prominent Blacks supported the soldier in his fight for equal pay. Said Rev. J. P. Campbell:

> We ask for equal pay and bounty, not because we set a greater value upon money than we do upon human liberty, compared with which money is mere trash; but we contend for equal pay and bounty upon the principle, that if we receive equal pay and bounty when we go into war, we hope to receive equal rights and privileges when we come out of the war.

Many of the Black soldiers had received no pay at all. Consequently, several Black units were on the verge of mutiny by the middle of 1864; several soldiers of the 14th Rhode Island Heavy Artillery refused to report for duty until they were paid $16.00 per month. They were charged with insubordination and jailed; the families of many suffered severe privations for want of funds. Two months before the settlement was finally made, the *Christian Recorder,* official organ of the A.M.E. Church, called down God's wrath on those in power who had created this confusion:

> We ask that Congress will remember the words of the Lord God: "Thou shalt not muzzle the ox that treadeth the corn." Will Congress violate that plain and positive language of the eternal Jehovah? We are frank to say, that God will not let us and our armies succeed, until those who have it in their power to do right, do it.

Fortunately, Congress heeded the word of the Lord. In June 1864 the Black soldier received full and equal compensation.

Many other issues agitated the Black home front during the war. Prejudice and discrimination were rampant in every Northern city and state. Philadelphia, for instance, with the largest and most prosperous Black community (22,185), did not get rid of segregated street cars until 1867. Black soldiers on furlough were often harassed, chased, and beaten by white hooligans. And, in July 1863, the infamous draft riot occurred in New York City that, after four days of wanton lawlessness, left hundreds of Blacks dead or maimed and over three thousand homeless and destitute. The principal instigators of the violence were Irish immigrants who were being forced to submit to military draft or risk deportation back to Ireland. Urged by politicians and ward bosses, they vented their anger on the Black population in a fury of arson, lynching, and ruthless destruction of property owned or occupied by Blacks. The reaction of Black New Yorkers to this calamity was summarized in August 1863 by Dr. James Pennington in a speech at Poughkeepsie, New York:

> *Let the greedy foreigner know that a part of this country* BELONGS TO US; *and that we assert the right to live and labor here; that in New York and other cities, we claim the right to buy, hire, occupy and use houses and tenements, for legal considerations; to pass and repass on the streets, lanes, avenues, and all public ways. Our fathers have fought for this country, and helped to free it from the British yoke. We are now fighting to free it from the combined conspiracy of Jeff Davis and Co.; we are doing so with the distinct understanding, that* WE ARE TO HAVE ALL OUR RIGHT AS MEN AND AS CITIZENS, *and, that there are to be no side issues, no* RESERVATIONS, *either political, civil, or religious. In this struggle we know nothing but God, Manhood and American Nationality, full and unimpaired. . . .*

Although these issues severely agitated the Black home front, they were, in a sense, insignificant compared to the colonization controversy that raged unabated during the early years of the war period. Interestingly, the leading proponent of colonization was Abraham Lincoln, who, even as late as August 1863 would have denied Dr. Pennington's claim that the Black man belonged in America or that he deserved "American Nationality, full and unimpaired." Rather, the President believed that the differences between the Black and the white were so deep and abiding that in no way could they inhabit the same land in mutual peace and understanding. That some Black leaders held the same position is not surprising in view of the prejudice and discrimination that oppressed the free Blacks throughout the North. In the 1850's, for instance, Henry Highland Garnet, Alexander Crummell, Martin Delany, and James T. Holley had all advocated emigration to Haiti or to Africa. Neither Garnet nor Crummell could forget how as young men they were both driven out of a preparatory school in New Hampshire by rioting whites. Joining the emigrationists were other prominent Blacks such as J. Willis Menard, a college graduate and later the first Black to hold a "white collar" position in the Federal Government, and William Wells Brown, the distinguished author and lecturer. At least in the initial stages of the movement, the great Frederick Douglass lent his support. The periodical of the emigrationists was *The Pine and Palm,* published both in New York and Boston under the general sponsorship of James Redpath, a white, English-born liberal who had received substantial funds from the Haitian government to support colonization in that country. In one issue of *Pine and Palm* in 1861, Menard wrote:

> *We need have no hope in the present conflict, for the atmosphere of North America is interwoven and vocal with the blasting breath of Negro prejudice. It is the first lesson taught by white parents to their children, that the Negro is a low, debased animal, not fit for their association nor their equal. . . .*

And, being a poet, Menard closed his article with a quatrain:

> *Ho! children of the dusky brow!*
> *Why will ye wear the chain?*
> *A fairer home is awaiting you*
> *In isles beyond the main!*

However, Menard himself never moved to Haiti. After serving the Federal Government in Washington during the war years, he spent the balance of his life actively involved in Reconstruction politics in Louisiana and Florida.

Evidently, Frederick Douglass' position on colonization was ambivalent from the outset. In 1860 he wrote:

> *If we go anywhere, let us go to Hayti. Let us go where we are still within hearing distance of the wails of our brothers and sisters in bonds. Let us not go to Africa, where those who hate and enslave us want us to go. . . .*

By mid-1861, Douglass had changed his mind. By that time it had become his opinion that what had been an "overture of benevolence" from the Haitian Government had "hardened into a grand scheme of public policy . . . the grand solution of the destiny of the colored people in America." He objected to the implications in colonization that "the prejudice of the whites is invincible and that the cause of human freedom and equality is hopeless for the black man in this country." In the final analysis, he concluded, "all schemes of wholesale emigration tend to awaken and keep alive and confirm the popular prejudices of the whites against us."

Many prominent Blacks stood with Douglass on this issue. One, James McCune Smith, a physician trained at the University of Glasgow, addressed an open letter to emigrationist Henry Highland Garnet as follows:

> *Your duty to our people is to tell them to aim higher. In advising them to go to Hayti, you direct them to sink lower. . . . Our people want to stay, and will stay, at home: we are in for the fight, and will fight it out here. Shake yourself free from these migrating phantasms, and join us. . . .*

The most resolute of the Black opponents to colonization resided in the Boston area. John Rock, a lawyer and justice of the peace in Suffolk County, responded as follows to a speech that Lincoln made to Congress recommending colonization for the nation's Blacks:

*Why is it that the white people of this country desire to get rid of us?
Does anyone pretend to deny that this is our country? or that much
of the wealth and prosperity found here is the result of the labor of
our hands? or that our blood and bones have not crimsoned and
whitened every battlefield from Maine to Louisiana? Why this desire
to get rid of us? Can it be possible that because the nation has robbed
us for nearly two and a half centuries, and finding that she can no
longer do it and preserve her character among nations, now, out of
hatred, wishes to banish, because she cannot continue to rob us? . . .*

*This nation has wronged us, and for this reason many hate us.
The Spanish proverb is, "Desde que te erre nunca bien te quise"—
Since I have wronged you, I have never liked you. This is true not
only of Spaniards and Americans, but of every other class of
people. . . . The more intelligent portion of the colored people will
remain here; not because we prefer being oppressed here to being
freemen in other countries, but we will remain because we believe
our future prospects are better here than elsewhere. . . .*

The most succinct rejection of the colonization concept, however, was
propounded by a group of Boston leaders in April 1862. Fired by the
revolutionary spirit of Crispus Attucks, Salem Poor, and Peter Salem and
moved by the pious patriotism of Phillis Wheatley, these gentlemen
issued four resolutions:

Resolved: *That when we wish to leave the United States we can
find and pay for that territory which shall suit us best.*

Resolved: *That when we are ready to leave, we shall be able to
pay our own expenses of travel.*

Resolved: *That we don't want to go now.*

Resolved: *That if anybody else wants us to go, they must compel us.*

By the middle of 1863, because of the pressures of the mounting war
effort and the increased involvement of Blacks, colonization ceased to be
a vital issue for Black Americans. Indeed, on May 5, 1863, the movement
was dealt a fatal blow at a meeting at Zion Church in New York City.
On this occasion, several families who were able to escape from the
economic quagmire of the Haitian experience were welcomed home,
and then the meeting closed with everyone resolving that

*We view with contempt, as our fathers nobly did, the old Hag, "The
American Colonization Society," its pet daughter, "The African
Civilization Society," also its deformed child, "The Haytian
Emigration Movement," and their efforts to remove the colored man
from the United States.*

With that the matter of colonization should have been buried and
forgotten but for the persistence of President Lincoln. Virtually until his
assassination in April 1865, the "Great Emancipator" continued to be an
active racial separatist, believing that the differences between Black man
and white man would forever militate against their living together in a
state of equality. After 1863, and after the significant build-up of Black
troops in the Union Army, the President's position became increasingly

repugnant to Black leaders. Frederick Douglass assailed him for "his inconsistencies, his pride of race and blood, his contempt for Negroes, and his canting hypocrisy." And to the President's specific proposal that Black Americans be colonized in Chiriqui in Central America, where digging coal would provide them with a source of income, A. P. Smith of Saddle River, New Jersey, published this response:

> *But say, good Mr. President, why we, why anybody should swelter, digging coal, if there be any in Central America? . . . But, say you: "Coal land is the best thing I know of to begin an enterprise." Astounding discovery! Worthy to be recorded in golden letters, like the Lunar Cycle in the temple of Minerva. "Coal land, sir!" Pardon, Mr. President, if my African risibilities get the better of me, if I do show my ivories, whenever I read that sentence! Coal land, sir! If you please, sir, give McClellan some, give Halleck some, and by all means, save a little strip for yourself.*

History records that although Congress actually gave the President an appropriation of $600,000 to finance the colonization experiment, in both the Chiriqui venture and the *Ile à Vache* venture the Chief Executive was victimized by unscrupulous promoters and adventurers. Thus, in the end, his program for colonization proved to be an embarrassing failure. In the aftermath of these historical events, one is forced to speculate about Lincoln's motives. In her book *Behind the Scenes*, Elizabeth Keckley, who as Mrs. Lincoln's seamstress and confidante was an intimate of the White House, presents the President as a man of warm humanity who loved goats and was bedeviled by poor Union generalship and Mrs. Lincoln's waspish ways, in that order. Nowhere in her book does he emerge as a fiery racial separatist, and, as an ex-slave, Mrs. Keckley presumably would have quickly recognized the type. On the other hand, Abraham Lincoln was not Charles Sumner with roots in liberty-loving Massachusetts and not Thaddeus Stevens with roots in quakerish Pennsylvania. Rather, he had come out of a poverty-stricken frontier background in middle America where white men feared Indians and hated Blacks—a land where the escaping slave was both an economic threat and a social encumbrance in a severely restricted labor market and social order. It was also a land where the "border-state mentality" prevailed, producing a strong sympathy for the property rights of slaveholders. Thus, here could possibly be the source of Lincoln's belief in racial separatism. If so, one might wonder what he felt as, at war's end, he watched contingents of Black troops marching as proud conquerors through the debris-cluttered streets of fallen Richmond. Perhaps he might have emerged from the experience with new insight and a new vision of an America that could accommodate both Black and white with liberty and equality for all. But no one will ever know, for soon thereafter he was dead.

These, then, were some of the issues that seared and agitated the Black home front during the Civil War. As we have seen, many Black writers responded to these issues in pamphlets, histories, periodicals, and speeches. Hence what happened and what was said and what was written are all meaningful parts of the Black literary experience. The Civil War period was a time when many Black Americans fought and lived and many fought and died. Many fought with weapons on the field of battle; many others fought with pen and printer's ink on the home front. In the selections that follow, an attempt is made to tell the story of both groups, for together they wrote a new chapter in the history of Black America.

The Black Man in Battle

William Wells Brown[*]

from *The Negro in the American*
Rebellion: His Heroism and His Fidelity

The Battle of Port Hudson

On the 26th of May, 1863, the wing of the army under Major-Gen. Banks was brought before the rifle-pits and heavy guns of Port Hudson. Night fell—the lovely Southern night—with its silvery moonshine on the gleaming waters of the Mississippi, that passed directly by the intrenched town. The glistening stars appeared suspended in the upper air as globes of liquid light, while the fresh soft breeze was bearing such sweet scents from the odoriferous trees and plants, that a poet might have fancied angelic spirits were abroad, making the atmosphere luminous with their pure presence, and every breeze fragrant with their luscious breath. The deep-red sun that rose on the next morning indicated that the day would be warm; and, as it advanced, the heat became intense. The earth had been long parched, and the hitherto green verdure had begun to turn yellow. Clouds of dust followed every step and movement of the troops. The air was filled with dust: clouds gathered, frowned upon the earth, and hastened away.

The weatherwise watched the red masses of the morning, and still hoped for a shower to cool the air, and lay the dust, before the work of death commenced; but none came, and the very atmosphere seemed as if it were from an overheated oven. The laying-aside of all unnecessary articles or accoutrements, and the preparation that showed itself on every side, told all present that the conflict was near at hand. Gen. Dwight, whose

antecedents with regard to the rights of the negro, and his ability to fight, were not of the most favorable character, was the officer in command over the colored brigade; and busy Rumor, that knows everything, had whispered it about that the valor of the black man was to be put to the severest test that day.

The black forces consisted of the First Louisiana, under Lieut-Col. Bassett, and the Third Louisiana, under Col. Nelson. The line-officers of the Third were white; and the regiment was composed mostly of freedmen, many of whose backs still bore the marks of the lash, and whose brave, stout hearts beat high at the thought that the hour had come when they were to meet their proud and unfeeling oppressors. The First was the noted regiment called "The Native Guard," which Gen. Butler found when he entered New Orleans, and which so promptly offered its services to aid in crushing the Rebellion. The line-officers of this regiment were all colored, taken from amongst the most wealthy and influential of the free colored people of New Orleans. It was said that not one of them was worth less than twenty-five thousand dollars. The brave, the enthusiastic, and the patriotic, found full scope for the development of their powers in this regiment, of which all were well educated; some were fine scholars. One of the most efficient officers was Capt. André Callioux, a man whose identity with his race could not be mistaken; for he prided himself on being the blackest man in the Crescent City. Whether in the drawing-room or on the parade,

[*] For headnote see p. 180.

254

he was ever the centre of attraction. Finely educated, polished in his manners, a splendid horseman, a good boxer, bold, athletic, and daring, he never lacked admirers. His men were ready at any time to follow him to the cannon's mouth; and he was as ready to lead them. This regiment petitioned their commander to allow them to occupy the post of danger in the battle, and it was granted.

As the moment of attack drew near, the greatest suppressed excitement existed; but all were eager for the fight. Capt. Callioux walked proudly up and down the line, and smilingly greeted the familiar faces of his company. Officers and privates of the white regiments looked on as they saw these men at the front, and asked each other what they thought would be the result. Would these blacks stand fire? Was not the test by which they were to be tried too severe? Col. Nelson being called to act as brigadier-general, Lieut-Col. Finnegas took his place. The enemy in his stronghold felt his power, and bade defiance to the expected attack. At last the welcome word was given, and our men started. The enemy opened a blistering fire of shell, canister, grape, and musketry. The first shell thrown by the enemy killed and wounded a number of the blacks; but on they went. "Charge" was the word.

> "Charge!" Trump and drum awoke:
> Onward the bondmen broke;
> Bayonet and sabre-stroke
> Vainly opposed their rush.

At every pace, the column was thinned by the falling dead and wounded. The blacks closed up steadily as their comrades fell, and advanced within fifty paces of where the rebels were working a masked battery, situated on a bluff where the guns could sweep the whole field over which the troops must charge. This battery was on the left of the charging line. Another battery of three or four guns commanded the front, and six heavy pieces raked the right of the line as it formed, and enfiladed its flank and rear as it charged on the bluff. It was ascertained that a bayou ran under the bluff where the guns lay,—a bayou deeper than a man could ford. This charge was repulsed with severe loss. Lieut-Col. Finnegas was then ordered to charge, and in a well-dressed steady line his men went on the double-quick down over the field of death. No matter how gallantly the men behaved, no matter how bravely they were led, it was not in the course of things that this

gallant brigade should take these works by charge. Yet charge after charge was ordered and carried out under all these disasters with Spartan firmness. Six charges in all were made. Col. Nelson reported to Gen. Dwight the fearful odds he had to contend with. Says Gen. Dwight, in reply, "Tell Col. Nelson I shall consider that he has accomplished nothing unless he take those guns." Humanity will never forgive Gen. Dwight for this last order; for he certainly saw that he was only throwing away the lives of his men. But what were his men? "Only niggers." Thus the last charge was made under the spur of desperation.

The ground was already strewn with the dead and wounded, and many of the brave officers had fallen early in the engagement. Among them was the gallant and highly cultivated Anselmo. He was a standard-bearer, and hugged the stars and stripes to his heart as he fell forward upon them pierced by five balls. Two corporals near by struggled between themselves as to who should have the honor of again raising those bloodstained emblems to the breeze. Each was eager for the honor; and during the struggle a missile from the enemy wounded one of them, and the other corporal shouldered the dear old flag in triumph, and bore it through the charge in the front of the advancing lines.

> "Now," the flag-sergeant cried,
> "Though death and hell betide,
> Let the whole nation see
> If we are fit to be
> Free in this land, or bound
> Down, like the whining hound,—
> Bound with red stripes and pain
> In our old chains again."
> Oh! what a shout there went
> From the black regiment!

Shells from the rebel guns cut down trees three feet in diameter, and they fell, at one time burying a whole company beneath their branches. Thus they charged bravely on certain destruction, till the ground was slippery with the gore of the slaughtered, and cumbered with the bodies of the maimed. The last charge was made about one o'clock. At this juncture, Capt. Callioux was seen with his left arm dangling by his side,—for a ball had broken it above the elbow,—while his right hand held his unsheathed sword gleaming in the rays of the sun; and his hoarse, faint voice was heard cheering on his men. A moment more, and the brave and generous Callioux was struck by a shell, and fell far in advance of his company. The fall of this officer so exasperated his men, that they appeared to be filled with new enthusiasm; and they rushed forward with a recklessness that probably has never been surpassed. Seeing it to be a hopeless effort, the taking of these batteries, order was given to change the programme; and the troops were called off. But had they accomplished any thing more than the loss of many of their brave men? Yes: they had. The self-forgetfulness, the undaunted heroism, and the great endurance of the negro, as exhibited that day, created a new chapter in American history for the colored man.

Many Persians were slain at the battle of Thermopylæ; but history records only the fall of Leonidas and his four hundred companions. So in the future, when we shall have passed away from the stage, and rising generations shall speak of the conflict at Port Hudson, and the celebrated charge of the negro brigade, they will forget all others in their admiration for André Callioux and his colored associates. Gen. Banks, in his report of the battle of Port Hudson, says, "Whatever doubt may have existed heretofore as to the efficiency of organizations of this character, the history of this day proves conclusively to those who were in a condition to observe the conduct of these regiments, that the Government will find in this class of troops effective supporters and defenders. The severe test to which they were subjected, and the determined manner in which they encountered the enemy, leaves upon my mind no doubt of their ultimate success."

Hon. B. F. Flanders paid them the following tribute:—

"The unanimous report of all those who were in the recent battle at Port Hudson, in regard to the negroes, is, that they fought like devils. They have completely conquered the prejudice of the army against them. Never before was there such an extraordinary revolution of sentiment as that of this army in respect to the negroes as soldiers."

This change was indeed needed; for only a few days previous to the battle, while the regiments were at Baton Rouge, the line-officers of the New-England troops, either through jealousy or hatred to the colored men on account of their complexion, demanded that the latter, as officers, should be dismissed. And, to the disgrace of these white officers, the colored men, through the mean treatment of their superiors in office, the taunts and jeers of their white assailants, were compelled to throw up their commissions. The colored soldiers were deeply pained at seeing the officers of their own color and choice taken from them; for they were much attached to their commanders, some of whom were special favorites with the whole regiment. Among these were First Lieut. Joseph Howard of Company I, and Second Lieut. Joseph G. Parker, of Company C. These gentlemen were both possessed of ample wealth, and had entered the army, not as a matter of speculation, as too many have done, but from a love of military life. Lieut. Howard was a man of more than ordinary ability in military tactics; and a braver or more daring officer could not be found in the Valley of the Mississippi. He was well educated, speaking the English, French, and Spanish languages fluently, and was considered a scholar of rare literary attainments. He, with his friend Parker, felt sorely the humiliation attending their dismissal from the army, and seldom showed themselves on the streets of their native city, to which they had returned. When the news reached New Orleans of the heroic charge made by the First Louisiana Regiment, at Port Hudson, on the 27th of May, Howard at once called on Parker; and they were so fired with the intelligence, that they determined to proceed to Port Hudson, and to join their old regiment as *privates*. That night they took passage, and the following day found them with their former friends in arms. The regiment was still in position close to the enemy's works, and the appearance of the two lieutenants was hailed with demonstrations of joy. Instead of being placed as privates in the ranks, they were both immediately assigned the command of a company each, not from any compliment to them, but from sheer necessity, because the *white officers* of these companies, feeling that the colored soldiers were put in the front of the battle owing to their complexion, were not willing to risk their lives, and had thrown up their commissions.

On the 5th of June, these two officers were put to the test, and nobly did they maintain their former reputation for bravery. Capt. Howard leading the way, they charged upon the rebel's rifle-pits, drove them out, and took possession, and held them for three hours, in the face of a raking fire of artillery. Several times the blacks were so completely hidden from view by the smoke of their own guns and the enemy's heavy cannon, that they could not be seen. It was at this time, that Capt. Howard exhibited his splendid powers as a commander. The negroes never hesitated. Amid the roar of artillery, and the rattling of musketry, the groans of the wounded, and the ghastly appearance of the dead, the heroic and intrepid Howard was the same. He never said to his men, "Go," but always, "Follow me." At last, when many of their men were killed, and the severe fire of the enemy's artillery seemed to mow down every thing before it, these brave men were compelled to fall back from the pits which they had so triumphantly taken. At nightfall, Gen. Banks paid the negro officers a high compliment, shaking the hand of Capt. Howard, and congratulating him on his return, and telling his aides that this man was worthy of a more elevated position.

Although the First Louisiana had done well, its great triumph was reserved for the 14th of June, when Capt. Howard and his associates in arms won for themselves immortal renown. Never, in the palmy days of Napoleon, Wellington, or any other general, was more true heroism shown. The effect of the battle of the 27th of May, is thus described in "The New-York Herald," June 6:—

"The First Regiment Louisiana Native Guard, Col. Nelson, were in this charge. *They went on the advance, and, when they came out, six hundred out of nine hundred men could not be accounted for. It is said on every side that they fought with the desperation of tigers.* One negro was observed with a rebel soldier in his grasp, tearing the flesh from his face with his teeth, other weapons having failed him. There are other incidents connected with the conduct of this regiment *that have raised them very much in my opinion as soldiers. After firing one volley, they did not deign to load again, but went in with bayonets; and, wherever they had a chance, it was all up with the rebels.*"

From "The New-York Tribune," June 8:—

"Nobly done, First Regiment of Louisiana Native Guard! though you failed to carry the rebel works against overwhelming numbers, you did not charge and fight and fall in vain. That heap of six hundred corpses, lying there dark and grim and silent before and within the rebel works, is a better proclamation of freedom than even President Lincoln's. A race ready to die thus was never yet retained in bondage, and never can be. Even the Wood copperheads, who will not fight themselves, and try to keep others out of the Union ranks, will not dare to mob negro regiments if this is their style of fighting.

"Thus passes one regiment of blacks to death and everlasting fame."

Humanity should not forget, that, at the surrender of Port Hudson, not a single colored man could be found alive, although thirty-five were known to have been taken prisoners during the siege. All had been murdered.

George Washington Williams (1849–1891)

Before turning to historical scholarship at the age of twenty-six, George Washington Williams had already achieved military and religious distinction. When he died in England two months before his forty-second birthday, he had added law and politics to his sphere of endeavor. Out of the crowded activity of this brief life, his most durable contributions to Black culture are two great historical works, *History of the Negro Race in America from 1619 to 1880* and *A History of the Negro Troops in the War of the Rebellion 1861–1865.*

Born in Bedford Springs, Pennsylvania, the young Williams moved with his parents to Newcastle in the same state and then to Massachusetts. His early education consisted of two years of tutorial instruction and four years of formal schooling. In 1863, while still a boy, he ran away from home and enlisted in the Union Army, lying about his age and giving an assumed name. Rising quickly to the rank of sergeant major, he was seriously wounded and mustered out, but after convalescing he re-enlisted and served with General N. J. Jackson in Texas until the end of the war. Having fought to liberate enslaved Blacks, Williams immediately joined the Mexican forces of Benito Juarez in the struggle against French imperialism. Rapidly winning the rank of lieutenant colonel, he served until the execution of Maximilian in June 1867, when he returned to the United States for service in the cavalry against the Comanches. Shortly after his nineteenth birthday he left the military life, "convinced as a Christian," William J. Simmons observed, "that killing people in time of peace as a profession was not the noblest life a man could live."

For the next five and a half years Williams prepared himself for the Baptist ministry at the Newton Theological Seminary in Massachusetts, delivering a graduation speech in 1874 on "The Early Church in Africa." His first call was to the Twelfth Street Baptist Church in Boston, then in its thirty-fourth year. During his pastorate he wrote an eighty-page history of the church, but unfortunately no copy of this work has survived. In 1875 he resigned and went to Washington to establish a Black magazine, *The Commoner,* but the enterprise soon failed despite the backing of Frederick Douglass and other prominent Washingtonians. After two months in the Washington Post Office, he accepted the pastorate of the Union Baptist Church of Cincinnati, serving until the end of 1877. Here, too, he investigated the history of the church that he served.

More importantly, at this time he began to expand his historical interests to encompass the entire story of his people. After delivering a Fourth of July oration in 1876 on the American Black, he dedicated himself to serious historical research. For a period of six years he carried out his labors, examining over twelve thousand books and thousands of pamphlets and newspapers, as well as consulting and corresponding with dozens of scholars, librarians, and government officials. The result of this massive effort was the publication in 1883 of the *History of the Negro Race in America* in two volumes totaling more than eleven hundred pages. The work was vividly written, copiously documented, and factually reliable. His notion of his role as historian is clearly stated in the preface:

> *Not as the blind panegyrist of my race, nor as the partisan apologist, but from a love for "the truth of history," I have striven to record the truth, the whole truth, and nothing but the truth. I have not striven to revive sectional animosities or race prejudices. I have avoided comment so far as it was consistent with a clear exposition of the truth. My whole aim has been to write a thoroughly trustworthy history; and what I have written, if it have no other merit, is reliable.*

So well did he perform his task that his work stood for sixty-four years—until the publication of John Hope Franklin's *From Slavery to Freedom*—as the standard authority on its subject.

What makes Williams' achievement all the more remarkable is that during the years of research and writing he was energetically pursuing other careers as well. Simmons points out that in 1878 "he was appointed internal revenue storekeeper by the Secretary of the Treasury, and served also in the Auditor's office as secretary of the four million dollar fund to build the Cincinnati Southern railroad." Next he took up the study of law, being admitted to practice in Ohio in 1881 and in Massachusetts two years later. Meanwhile he was elected to the state legislature of Ohio in 1879. Somehow he also found time to be active in the Grand Army of the Republic and the Young Men's Christian Association, and to practice occasional journalism and oratory.

Even before the publication of *History of the Negro Race in America,* Williams was planning a history of Black participation in the Civil War. While traveling in Europe and the Near East in 1884 he worked when he could. In the following year he was appointed Minister to Haiti by President Arthur, but the appointment was revoked by the new President, the racist Grover Cleveland, before Williams took office. With more time now available he completed *A History of the Negro Troops,* which appeared in 1888. In this volume Williams does full justice to the drama of his subject, but without surrendering his historian's sense of evidence. As he explained in the preface:

> The part enacted by the Negro soldier in the war of the Rebellion is the romance of North American history. It was midnight and noonday without a space between; from the Egyptian darkness of bondage to the lurid glare of civil war; from clanking chains to clashing arms; from passive submission to the cruel curse of slavery to the brilliant aggressiveness of a free solider; from a chattel to a person; from the shame of degradation to the glory of military exaltation; and from deep obscurity to fame and martial immortality. No one in this era of fraternity and Christian civilization will grudge the Negro soldier these simple annals of his trials and triumphs in a holy struggle for human liberty. Whatever praise is bestowed upon his noble acts will be sincerely appreciated, whether from former foes or comrades in arms. For by withholding just praise they are not enriched, nor by giving are they thereby impoverished.

Furthermore, he asserted, the reader will not

> find reason for complaint at the spirit of the historian. I have spoken plainly, it is true, but I have not extenuated nor set down aught in malice. My language is not plainer than the truth, my philippic is not more cruel than the crimes exposed, my rhetoric is not more fiery than the trials through which these black troops passed, nor my conclusions without warrant of truth or justification of evidence.

In his last three years Williams turned his attention to Africa, especially the Congo. His denunciation of Belgian imperialism in this unhappy region was scathing. One can only speculate what further contributions Williams might have made had he not died suddenly on August 4, 1891, in Blackpool, England, on his return journey to the United States from the Congo. In addition to his historical writing, journalism, and oratory, Simmons noted in 1887 that "he writes poetry with grace and unction and . . . has written three novels and a tragedy . . .," but unfortunately these were never published.

Both of Williams' histories have been recently reprinted. Of his numerous speeches, two were published as pamphlets: *1862—Emancipation Day—1884; The Negro as a Political Problem* and *Memorial Day; The Ethics of the War,* both appearing in 1884. Two pamphlets concerning the Congo are *Report upon the Congo State and Country to the President of the Republic of the United States* (n.d.) and *An Open Letter to . . . Leopold II* (1890).

An early but still indispensable account is the chapter on Williams in William J. Simmons, *Men of Mark: Eminent, Progressive and Rising* (1887). John Hope Franklin's "George Washington Williams, Historian," *The Journal of Negro History,* XXXI (January 1946), 60–90, is a characteristically excellent article by Williams' most distinguished successor. For an understanding of Williams' place in Black historiography, see either Ernest Kaiser, "The History of Negro History," *Negro Digest,* XVII (February 1968), 10–15, 64–80, or Benjamin Quarles, "Black History's Early Advocates," *Negro Digest,* XIX (February 1970), 4–9.

from *A History of the Negro Troops in the War of the Rebellion 1861–1865*

The Assault on Fort Wagner

General Quincy A. Gillmore, an excellent engineer officer, had carefully matured his plans for the proposed assault upon Fort Wagner. It was intended to open a preliminary bombardment at daylight on the 18th, and having by heavy ordnance tranquillized Wagner, to effect its reduction by the bayonet. But a tempest came on suddenly and delayed the cruel ingenuity of war. The thunder roared, the lightning flashed, and the rain fell in torrents. The military operations were suspended in the presence of Nature's awful spectacle. About eleven o'clock aides-de-camp and mounted couriers sped in different directions, and the force on land and its naval support upon the sea began to exhibit signs of preparation for the impending conflict. The pale face and steady look of officers as they transmitted their weighty orders told the nature of their mission here and there on the island. At 12.30 P.M. a flash of fire leaped from the mouths of batteries that were ranged in semicircle for a mile across the island, and the bombardment was formally opened. The naval vessels came into action also, within a few hundred yards of the fortress, and the enemy replied promptly from Wagner, Sumter, and Cumming's Point. A storm of fire and whirring

missiles was kept up all the afternoon. The enemy did not serve all his guns in Wagner, but the two operated were fought with admirable skill and daring. The infantry support clung to the bomb-proofs all the afternoon, for the commanding officer evidently knew what the Union troops would attempt at nightfall. At least one hundred great guns were engaged in an attempt to batter down this rebel fortress, and the work of destruction went on all the afternoon. Great clouds of sand were thrown into the air by the tons of metal that struck inside. A shot cut the halyards on the flag-staff, and the rebel banner went fluttering to the earth like a stricken bird.

Some of the Union officers thought the garrison was about to capitulate, but Sumter fired a shot over the fort, as much as to say, "I protest." Out from their bombs rushed a squad of men, and, with the rebel yell, hauled their colors to their place again.

As the day wore away it seemed certain, from the Union stand-point, that the garrison must yield or perish. Through a field-glass Wagner seemed little less than an unrecognizable mass of ruins, a mere heap of sand. It seemed as if the approaches to the bomb-proofs were choked with sand, and that most of the heavy guns were disabled and the fort practically dismantled. Its reduction seemed now near at hand, and the bombardment had facilitated the work of the infantry who were to consummate its reduction by a dash at the point of the bayonet. Towards evening the breaching siege guns and monitors slacked their fire. Soon the beach was filled with life. Couriers dashed in every direction, and the troops were now being disposed for an assault. At 6 P.M. the Fifty-fourth Regiment reached General Geo. C. Strong's headquarters, about the middle of the island, wet and weary, hungry and thirsty; but there was no time for rest or refreshments. Onward the Negro regiment marched several hundred yards farther, and proudly took its place at the head of the assaulting column. General Strong and Colonel Shaw addressed it briefly, and with burning words of eloquent patriotic sentiment urged the men to valorous conduct in the approaching assault. Both officers were inspired; the siren of martial glory was sedulously luring them to the bloody and inhospitable trenches of Wagner. There was a tremor in Colonel Shaw's voice and an impressiveness in his manner. He was young and beautiful, wealthy and refined, and his heroic words soon flowered into action—bravest of the brave, leader of men! The random shot and shell that screamed through the ranks gave the troops little annoyance. The first brigade consisted of the Fifty-fourth Massachusetts, Colonel Robert Gould Shaw; the Sixth Connecticut, Colonel Chatfield; the Forty-eighth New York, Colonel Barton; the Third New Hampshire, Colonel Jackson; the Seventy-sixth Pennsylvania, Colonel Strawbridge; and the Ninth Maine, Colonel Emory. After about thirty minutes' halt, General Strong gave the order for the charge, and the column advanced quickly to its perilous work. The ramparts of Wagner flashed with small-arms, and all the large shotted guns roared with defiance. Sumter and Cumming's Point delivered a destructive cross-fire, while the howitzers in the bastions raked the ditch; but the gallant Negro regiment swept across it and gained the parapet. Here the flag of this regiment was planted; here General Strong fell mortally wounded; and here the brave, beautiful, and heroic Colonel Shaw was saluted by death and kissed by immortality. The regiment lost heavily, but held its ground under the most discouraging circumstances. The men had actually gained the inside of the fort, where they bravely contended with a desperate and determined enemy. The contest endured for about an hour, when the regiment, shattered and

torn, with nearly all of its officers dead or wounded, was withdrawn under the command[1] of Captain Luis F. Emilio. He formed a new line of battle about seven hundred yards from the fort, and awaited orders for another charge. He despatched a courier to the commanding officer of the second brigade that had gone to the front, stating that he was in supporting position, and was ready and willing to do what he could. Word came that the enemy was quiet and that the Fifty-fourth was not needed. Captain Emilio then occupied the rifle-pits flanking the Union artillery which he found unoccupied, and being out of musket range, organized his men as best he could. The national colors of the regiment which he had brought back from the scene of the battle he sent to the rear with the wounded color-sergeant, William H. Carney, as they could not serve as a rallying point in the deep darkness. The following extracts from a letter written by a late sergeant of the Fifty-fourth to Captain Luis F. Emilio gives personal observations during this action that are not without their value:

"Regarding the assault on Fort Wagner, I recollect distinctly that when our column had charged the fort, passed the half-filled moat, and mounted to the parapet, many of the men clambered over and some entered by the large embrasure in which one of the big guns was mounted, the firing substantially ceased there by the beach, and the rebel musketry firing steadily grew hotter on our left. An officer of our regiment called out, 'Spike that gun.' Whether this was done I do not know, for we fired our rifles and fought as hard as we could to return the fire on our right.

"But the rebel fire grew hotter on our right, and a field-piece every few seconds seemed to sweep along our rapidly thinning ranks. Men all around me would fall and roll down the scarp into the ditch. Just at the very hottest moment of the struggle a battalion or regiment charged up to the moat and halted, and did not attempt to cross it and join us, but from their position commenced to fire upon us. I was one of the men who shouted from where I stood, 'Don't fire on us! We are the Fifty-fourth!' I have heard it was a Maine

[1] Several histories of the war have given Lieutenant Higginson the honor of leading the regiment from the parapets of Wagner. This is an error. Lieutenant Higginson was not in this action, but on detail at the other end of the island. *Captain Luis F. Emilio* was the officer who commanded at the close of the battle.— G. W. W.

regiment. This is God's living truth! Immediately after I heard an order, 'Retreat!' Some twelve or fifteen of us slid down from our position on the parapet of the fort.

"The men-of-war seemed to have turned their guns on the fort, and the fire of the Confederates on the right seemed to increase in power. The line of retreat seemed lit with infernal fire; the hissing bullets and bursting shells seemed angry demons.

"I was with Hooker's division, cooking for Colonel B. C. Tilghman, of the Twenty-sixth Pennsylvania Regiment, in the battle of Fredericksburg, when General Burnside commanded. I traversed the Hazel Dell Marr, the Stone House, when all the enemy's artillery was turned upon it; but hot as the fire was there, it did not compare to the terrific fire which blazed along the narrow approach to Wagner.

"I care not who the man is who denies the fact, our regiment did charge the fort and drove the rebels from their guns. Many of our men will join me in saying that in the early stages of the fight we had possession of the sea end of Battery Wagner. Indeed, most of the colored prisoners taken there were captured inside the battery.

"When we reached the Gatling Battery drawn up to repel the counter-attack, I remember you were the only commissioned officer present, and you placed us indiscriminately—that is, without any regard to companies—in line, and prepared to renew the charge. The commanding officer, whom I do not know, ordered us to the flanking rifle-pits, and we there awaited the expected counter-charge the enemy did not make."

Captain Emilio, who was an intelligent and experienced officer, thought that in all probability the enemy would make a counter-assault, having driven the Negro troops from the fort, and in forming a new line of battle, he was preparing for such a contingency. Fortunately for the Union forces no counter-assault was delivered, although a desultory firing was maintained nearly all night. Some time after midnight General Thomas G. Stevenson called upon Captain Emilio, where he held the front line, and personally thanked him for the dispositions he had made, and promised to relieve his gallant but weary command. Accordingly, the Tenth Connecticut relieved the Fifty-fourth Massachusetts at two o'clock the next morning, July 19th. Captain Emilio had rallied the stragglers of other regiments on the front line, and now that he was relieved he sent these men to the rear by detachments to join their regiments. With the remnant of the Fifty-fourth he went into bivouac for the night a short distance to the rear, where also some officers and men of this regiment had been swept by the tide of battle, which unfortunately had gone the wrong way that night. On the following morning Captain Emilio, still being in command of the regiment, led it to an old camp formerly occupied by the command near the south end of Morris Island.

The appalling list of casualties shows how bravely this Negro regiment had done its duty, and the unusually large number of men missing proves that the regiment had fought its way into the fort, and if properly supported, Wagner would have been captured. Colonel Shaw led about six hundred enlisted men and twenty-two officers into this action. Of the enlisted men thirty-one were killed, one hundred and thirty-five wounded, and ninety-two missing. Of the twenty-two officers participating three were killed and eleven were wounded. Nearly half of the enlisted men were killed, wounded, or missing, while more than one-half of the officers were either killed or wounded.

From a purely military stand-point the assault upon Fort Wagner was a failure, but it furnished the severest test of Negro valor and soldiership. It was a mournful satisfaction to the advocates of Negro soldiers to point the doubting, sneering, stay-at-home Negro-haters to the murderous trenches of Wagner. The Negro soldier had seen his red-letter day, and his title to patriotic courage was written in his own blood. Pleased with the splendid behavior of the regiment in particular and the special courage of several enlisted men, General Gillmore awarded a medal to the following soldiers of the Fifty-fourth: Sergeant Robert J. Simmons, Company B; Sergeant William H. Carney, Company C; Corporal Henry F. Peal, Company F; and Private George Wilson, Company A.

Two Black Soldiers Comment

Corporal John A. Cravat (1831–1897)

John A. Cravat's beginnings were somewhat unusual even for his times. His father, the son of a white indentured servant in the Philadelphia area, fell in love with a free woman of color and, to escape his mother's wrathful disapproval, fled with his beloved to Woonsocket, Rhode Island. There, in what was then a somewhat enlightened refuge for abolitionists and racial liberals, the runaway lovers were married and there their son John was born.

Few details are known of John Cravat's early years. One can assume from the style and manner of his letters that he had some schooling; his spelling is sometimes more "phonetic" than accurate, but, for his time and circumstances, John Cravat was a literate man. Certainly, his situation might have been worse had he grown up in Connecticut, where, following the assault of a mob on Prudence Crandall's school for colored in Canterbury in 1832, schooling for Blacks was outlawed. One can also assume that John Cravat was a strong abolitionist. The mere fact that he enlisted as soon as the Union Army ranks were open to Blacks is indicative of his devotion to the cause.

Sometime in 1847 John Cravat married Sarah B. Eldridge. Where they met and courted is not known, but her family came from Salem, New Jersey, a town lying close to the "free" side of the Delaware River. Many of the towns in this section of New Jersey were spotted with inhabitants whose immediate ancestors had escaped from the Delaware side of the river. The Cravats settled in Woonsocket, and by 1861—the year Fort Sumter was fired on—they had three children. The oldest was twelve-year-old Eldridge; the middle child was Clara, aged seven; and the youngest was Minnie, aged one.

It was not until the spring of 1863 that the Department of the Army actively began to recruit Blacks for all-Black combat units. When the 14th Rhode Island Heavy Artillery Regiment was organized in the late summer of 1863, John Cravat was one of the first to volunteer. His enlistment at the age of thirty-two reflected his idealism and enthusiasm for the Union cause. Moreover, he had heard stories of how well Rhode Island's Black citizens had fought in the Continental Army's one all-Black regiment to repel the British in the Battle of Rhode Island in 1778. Then the cause had been freedom from British rule; now the cause was freedom for four million Black people enslaved in the South. But however noble the cause, John Cravat's enlistment posed some practical and stressful economic problems for his young family. The Cravats, like other free Blacks in Northern communities, lived on the fringe of a white economy. The removal or forced absence of the breadwinner merely intensified the normal economic pressures. The recruitment officers sought to alleviate worry on this account by promising each volunteer a monthly wage of $16.00 per month and a matching monthly "bounty" of $16.00 to each volunteer's family.

Given this kind of assurance for the economic welfare of his family, John Cravat was mustered into the service on August 3, 1863. His entire twenty months of service, with the exception of a training period on Dutch Island near Newport, were spent in or around Fort Jackson, approximately thirty miles below New Orleans, and at Fort Esperanza on Matagorda Island near Corpus Christi, Texas. Although his particular unit—Company A, 1st Battalion—was involved in few hazardous combat missions, John Cravat's letters to Sarah reflect the tensions and loneliness of a soldier's existence and provide extensive comment on the unhealthy conditions of the Fort Jackson encampment. A large number of his comrades, for instance, were "shot down," not by Confederate or rebel bullets, but by disease and fever.

Undoubtedly, the one singular event of John Cravat's military career was his "confrontation" with the military power structure over his salary and his subsequent court-martial and consignment to the New Orleans Police Jail when he and seventeen other members of the 14th Rhode Island refused to report for duty. The confrontation occurred in late April 1864 when, after receiving no pay for eight months, he was given back pay at the rate of $7.00 per month, rather than at the promised rate of $16.00. Bitterly disappointed, he refused to accept any of his back pay and, after his court-martial, began to make plans to get out of the service. Fortunately, the vexatious question of salaries for Black troops was settled by June 1864, and John Cravat was returned to duty and eventually given all of his back pay at the agreed-upon rate. The official history of John Cravat's regiment—*The History of the 14th Rhode Island Heavy Artillery* (1891)—does not mention the salary-protest court-martials, and it is thus assumed that the charges were officially dismissed after the fact. In any event, John Cravat received an honorable discharge from the service in April 1865 and was happily reunited with his family.

The excerpts from his correspondence that follow describe the involvement of his unit in a near riot with the New Orleans police, his reaction to his court-martial, and his joy over the news that New Orleans had officially been declared a "free city."

Four Letters

Letter from Pfc. John A. Cravat to Mrs. Sarah B. Cravat

Fort Esperanza
Matagorda Island, Texas
January 10, 1864

Dear Wife,

I take this opportunity to write you these few lines to let you know I am well and safe and hope you and the family are well also. I wrote from New Orleans all about our trip to that plase. I will now commence at the latter plase. We arrived thear the 29th and remained there 5 days. The first 2 days I remained on bord of ship, for I felt afraid to go ashore, but the boys struck out by degres and got back safe. So, on a Friday I stole off and went for my self for I wanted to see the great City of New Orleans myself. We went all over the City and returned to the Ship. . . . Jest after we got to the bote the Police come down to the bote and kicked up a fuss with some of the boys that was standing on the dock. The Police fired a pistol. That was a nuff—the boys started for them and for one hour things was hot. Our boys beat one so bad that he died. It seems as tho a Friday nite there was a Ball and some of our boys was there and the Police made a rush to arrest them, and in the attempt one of the Police got a hole in him that left the wind all out. So a Saterday afternoon, they came to the bote for revenge but got saddely disipinted and drove off. They tried to shoot our Major, and if they had New Orleans today would lay in ashes. . . .

This island is about 30 miles long. There are 3 white regiments, one contraband regiment, and our own battalion here, in all about 5,000 men. This Fort Esperanza is a large one with 8 big guns. The white soldiers flock around us to bye our hard bread. They have not had any for 3 or 4 days.

I am sorry for one thing. This is I come away without my Pistol. I want you to send it to me as Soon as you can for now is the time I need it. I want you to get me 3 more boxes of cattreges like the one you have got. Take the Pistol and go on Broad Street above Charlie Corey's Shop to a gun store and get me 3 boxes of the same size as those you have got now and send them by Express. 3 boxes will cost $1.50. . . . Kiss the chil-dren for me. Give my love to Mother and all my frends. Write soon and let me know how you and money matters are. . . .

Your affecnet and
ever loving husben

JOHN A. CRAVAT

Letter from Corporal John A. Cravat to Mrs. Sarah B. Cravat

Fort Esperanza
Pass Cavallo, Texas
February 10, 1864

Dear Wife,

. . . I am absent bodily but my mind is with you and the children, day and nite. I sometimes wish I did not think of home so much for it makes me mellencolly. My three years cannot run out any too soon for me. . . . We think that we will be home befor long for if the government does not give us 13 dollers a month, we will com home. I hear that the 54, 55 Mass. has come home, and if they have we will. My Dear, I am on gard today but not as gard but as Coprel of the gard. I put on my stripes Jan. 17th. By this I get rid of so mutch hard work and my gard duty. Today, insted of walking my beat two hours every four, I merely take out my relief and place them on their post once every four hours. We thought two weeks ago that we were going to have a fite. The long roll was beat about half past four P.M. and it was laffebill to see us for the first time turn out for a fight. We were jest getting ready for dress parade when the messenger came. The roll was beat and to some it was the first time they had ever heard it. Some was anxious for a fite and some was not. Some fell into line with dress coats on, some with blouses. . . . Off we started for the scene of action with our littel major at our head, laughing and talking as tho we were going a fishing. Three miles from camp we halted, took a look for the enemy till most dark. Seeing nothing of him, we fell back a littel and laid on our guns all nite but did not sleep. . . .

I see in the Patriot an article about New Orleans that I must speak of for it is a lie. It says that we became riotous because we were kept on shipboard. The truth is this—the Police became riotous because we were not kept on shipboard and dared to come ashore and walk the streets of New Orleans like men. . . . The first thing they done was to fire their pistols at us. Then the ball opened and the 1st Bat., 14th Reg. came off the victors. The truth is they hate free blacks and all connected with them. They tried their best to shoot our officers and if they had we would have tried to burn the city. They say they don't want to see any more free long booted neggers there again. . . .

I will say nothing more at present, but ascribe myself your most affecnet husben for life and may God bless you and the children is my prayer.

> COPREAL JOHN A. CRAVAT
> Fort Esperanza
> Pass Cavallo, Texas

Letter from Pvt. John A. Cravat to Mrs. Sarah B. Cravat, from the Police Jail in New Orleans

> New Orleans
> April 29th, 1864

Dear Wife,

. . . You will see by my letter that I am today in New Orleans. I and 17 others arrived hear yesterday as Prisoners. Sergeants John A. Jenkins, Gor E. Wilson, Milven Graham, Corps John B. Lane, Howard Edwards, and a lot more of Co. A men for sticking up for their rights have bin Court Martialed and on our road somewhere to serve our sentences. I want you to strike at every point for my Discharge. . . . I want you to go see some of the white gentlemen of the city and see if we can't get out of the service. We have been in the service 8 months yesterday and have not received any monthly pay and will not receive the . . . sum of seven dollars a month and there have not been any provisions made by congress where colored soldiers can get the same pay as white soldiers. This has been the biggest humbug I ever had anything to do with and it ought to be brought before the Publick. My company is at Aranzo

Pass 65 miles from Mattagorder Island. I will never serve another day in my company, and if I must stay my three years, I will put the time in in the gard house. Cap. Fry is a liar and a raskell. Moses Brown is another. If you succeed and want to send any papers to the Major, send them to Texas as before. I am harty and hope it will not be long before we meet.

God bless you and the children.

> J. A. CRAVAT

Letter from Pfc. John A. Cravat to Mrs. Sarah B. Cravat, from the New Orleans Police Jail

> New Orleans
> May 16, 1864

Dear Wife,

I take the opportunity this Monday morning to write you a few lines to let you know I am well and hope this will find you and the Children, with Granmother and all the rest, well. I have bin here two weeks last friday and I am even glad I am here for today I stan in a free state. Yes the City of N.O. is a free City. Who would of thought this five or six months ago that the State of Lousiana could boast of having thrown off the yoak of bondage. I Send you the N.O. Papers with the Emancipation Reports. . . .

Oh Wife—now one knows the felen of a husben and a farther's hart tourren away from his family, as I have bin . . . and detaend nine months without compensation. There is but one thing I can due and that is I Sett here and wish my Self home. . . .

Kiss the children for me. God bless them. Write soon and I ma get it. I want you to take Susan Lane, and she will show you ware Henry Proctor lives. I want to know if it is my cousen. There is a Thomas Proctor in this City. I have sent him a letter, and am wayting his answer. Nothing more at present but remain your Moust affecnet husben

> JOHN A. CRAVAT   Police Jail
> New Orleans, La.

An "Old" Sergeant*

Dat's All What I Has to Say Now

A Statement by a Black Sergeant in a Lousiana Regiment

I has been a-thinkin' I was old man; for, on de plantation, I was put down wid de old hands, and I quinsicontly feeled myself dat I was a old man. But since I has come here to de Yankees, and been made a soldier for de United States, an' got dese beautiful clothes on, I feels like one young man; and I doesn't call myself a old man nebber no more. An' I feels dis ebenin' dat, if de rebs came down here to dis old Fort Hudson, dat I could jus fight um as brave as any man what is in the Sebenth Regiment. Sometimes I has mighty feelins in dis ole heart of mine, when I considers how dese ere ossifers come all de way from de North to fight in de cause what we is fighten fur. How many ossifers has died, and how many white soldiers has died, in dis great and glorious war what we is in! And now I feels dat, fore I would turn coward away from dese ossifers, I feels dat I could drink my own blood, and be pierced through wid five thousand bullets. I feels sometimes as doe I ought to tank Massa Linkern for dis blessin' what we has; but again I comes to de solemn conclusion dat I ought to tank de Lord, Massa Linkern, and all dese ossifers. 'Fore I would be a slave 'gain, I would fight till de last drop of blood was gone. I has 'cluded to fight for my liberty, and for dis eddication what we is now to receive in dis beautiful new house what we has. Aldo I hasn't got any eddication nor no booklearnin', I has rose up dis blessed ebenin' to do my best afore dis congregation. Dat's all what I has to say now.

* The author is unknown.

A Black Orator Speaks

Henry Highland Garnet*

A Memorial Discourse Delivered in the Hall of the House of Representatives, February 12, 1865

MATTHEW XXIII. 4: For they bind heavy burdens, and grievous to be borne, and lay them on men's shoulders, but they themselves will not move them with one of their fingers.

In this chapter, of which my text is a sentence, the Lord Jesus addressed his disciples, and the multitude that hung spell-bound upon the words that fell from his lips. He admonished them to beware of the religion of the Scribes and Pharisees, which was distinguished for great professions, while it succeeded in urging them to do but a little, or nothing that accorded with the law of righteousness.

In theory they were right; but their practices were inconsistent and wrong. They were learned in the law of Moses, and in the traditions of their fathers, but the principles of righteousness failed to affect their hearts. They knew their duty, but did it not. The demands which they made upon others proved that they themselves knew what things men ought to do. In condemning others they pronounced themselves guilty. They demanded that others should be just, merciful, pure, peaceable, and righteous. But they were unjust, impure, unmerciful—they hated and wronged a portion of their fellow-men, and waged continual war against the government of God.

On other men's shoulders they bound heavy and grievous burdens of duties and obligations. The people groaned beneath the loads which were

imposed upon them, and in bitterness of spirit cried out, and filled the land with lamentations. But with their eyes closed, and their hearts hardened, they heeded not, neither did they care. They regarded it to be but little less than intolerable insult to be asked to bear a small portion of the burdens which they were swift to bind on the shoulders of their fellow-men. With loud voice, and proud and defiant mien, they said these burdens are for them, and not for us. Behold how patiently they bear them. Their shoulders are broad, and adapted to the condition to which we have doomed them. But as for us, it is irksome, even to adjust their burdens, though we see them stagger beneath them.

Such was their conduct in the Church and in the State. We have modern Scribes and Pharisees, who are faithful to their prototypes of ancient times.

With sincere respect and reverence for the instruction, and the warning given by our Lord, and in humble dependence upon him for his assistance, I shall speak this morning of the Scribes and Pharisees of our times who rule the State. In discharging this duty, I shall keep my eyes upon the picture which is painted so faithfully and life-like by the hand of the Saviour.

Allow me to describe them. They are intelligent and well-informed, and can never say, either before an earthly tribunal or at the bar of God, "*We knew not of ourselves what was right.*" They are

* For headnote see p. 173.

268

acquainted with the principles of the law of nations. They are proficient in the knowledge of Constitutional law. They are teachers of common law, and frame and execute statute law. They acknowledge that there is a just and impartial God, and are not altogether unacquainted with the law of Christian love and kindness. They claim for themselves the broadest freedom. Boastfully they tell us that they have received from the court of heaven the MAGNA CHARTA of human rights that was handed down through the clouds, and amid the lightnings of Sinai, and given again by the Son of God on the Mount of Beatitudes, while the glory of the Father shone around him. They tell us that from the Declaration of Independence and the Constitution they have obtained a guaranty of their political freedom, and from the Bible they derive their claim to all the blessings of religious liberty. With just pride they tell us that they are descended from the Pilgrims, who threw themselves upon the bosom of the treacherous sea, and braved storms and tempests, that they might find in a strange land, and among savages, free homes, where they might build their altars that should blaze with acceptable sacrifice unto God. Yes! they boast that their fathers heroically turned away from the precious light of Eastern civilization, and taking their lamps with oil in their vessels, joyfully went forth to illuminate this land, that then dwelt in the darkness of the valley of the shadow of death. With hearts strengthened by faith they spread out their standard to the winds of heaven, near Plymouth rock; and whether it was stiffened in the sleet and frosts of winter, or floated on the breeze of summer, it ever bore the motto, "*Freedom to worship God.*"

But others, their fellow-men, equal before the Almighty, and made by him of the same blood, and glowing with immortality, they doom to life-long servitude and chains. Yes, they stand in the most sacred places on earth, and beneath the gaze of the piercing eye of Jehovah, the universal Father of all men, and declare, "*that the best possible condition of the negro is slavery.*"[1]

> Thus man devotes his brother and destroys;
> And more than all, and most to be deplored,
> As human nature's broadest, foulest blot,
> Chains him, and tasks him, and exacts his sweat
> With stripes, that Mercy with bleeding heart,
> Weeps to see inflicted on a beast.

[1] Speech of FERNANDO WOOD, of New York, in Congress, 1864.

In the name of the TRIUNE GOD I denounce the sentiment as unrighteous beyond measure, and the holy and the just of the whole earth say in regard to it, Anathema-maranatha.

What is slavery? Too well do I know what it is. I will present to you a bird's-eye view of it; and it shall be no fancy picture, but one that is sketched by painful experience. I was born among the cherished institutions of slavery. My earliest recollections of parents, friends, and the home of my childhood are clouded with its wrongs. The first sight that met my eyes was a Christian mother enslaved by professed Christians, but, thank God, now a saint in heaven. The first sounds that startled my ear, and sent a shudder through my soul, were the cracking of the whip, and the clanking of chains. These sad memories mar the beauties of my native shores, and darken all the slave-land, which, but for the reign of despotism, had been a paradise. But those shores are fairer now. The mists have left my native valleys, and the clouds have rolled away from the hills, and Maryland, the unhonored grave of my fathers, is now the free home of their liberated and happier children.

Let us view this demon, which the people have worshipped as a God. Come forth, thou grim monster, that thou mayest be critically examined! There he stands. Behold him, one and all. Its work is to chattelize man; to hold property in human beings. Great God! I would as soon attempt to enslave GABRIEL or MICHAEL as to enslave a man made in the image of God, and for whom Christ died. Slavery is snatching man from the high place to which he was lifted by the hand of God, and dragging him down to the level of the brute creation, where he is made to be the companion of the horse and the fellow of the ox.

It tears the crown of glory from his head, and as far as possible obliterates the image of God that is in him. Slavery preys upon man, and man only. A brute cannot be made a slave. Why? Because a brute has not reason, faith, nor an undying spirit, nor conscience. It does not look forward to the future with joy or fear, nor reflect upon the past with satisfaction or regret. But who in this vast assembly, who in all this broad land, will say that the poorest and most unhappy brother in chains and servitude has not every one of these high endowments? Who denies it? Is there one? If so, let him speak. There is not one; no, not one.

But slavery attempts to make a man a brute. It treats him as a beast. Its terrible work is not finished until the ruined victim of its lusts, and pride, and avarice, and hatred, is reduced so low that with tearful eyes and feeble voice he faintly cries, "*I am happy and contented—I love this condition.*"

> Proud Nimrod first the bloody chase began,
> A mighty hunter he; his prey was man.

The caged lion may cease to roar, and try no longer the strength of the bars of his prison, and lie with his head between his mighty paws and snuff the polluted air as though he heeded not. But is he contented? Does he not instinctively long for the freedom of the forest and the plain? Yes, he is a lion still. Our poor and forlorn brother whom thou hast labelled "*slave,*" is also a man. He may be unfortunate, weak, helpless, and despised, and hated, nevertheless he is a man. His God and thine has stamped on his forehead his title to his inalienable rights in characters that can be read by every intelligent being. Pitiless storms of outrage may have beaten upon his defenceless head, and he may have descended through ages of oppression, yet he is a man. God made him such, and his brother cannot unmake him. Woe, woe to him who attempts to commit the accursed crime.

Slavery commenced its dreadful work in kidnapping unoffending men in a foreign and distant land, and in piracy on the seas. The plunderers were not the followers of Mahomet, nor the devotees of Hindooism, nor benighted pagans, nor idolaters, but people called Christians, and thus the ruthless traders in the souls and bodies of men fastened upon Christianity a crime and stain at the sight of which it shudders and shrieks.

It is guilty of the most heinous iniquities ever perpetrated upon helpless women and innocent children. Go to the shores of the land of my forefathers, poor bleeding Africa, which, although she has been bereaved, and robbed for centuries, is nevertheless beloved by all her worthy descendants wherever dispersed. Behold a single scene that there meets your eyes. Turn not away neither from shame, pity, nor indifference, but look and see the beginning of this cherished and petted institution. Behold a hundred youthful mothers seated on the ground, dropping their tears upon the hot sands, and filling the air with their lamentations.

Why do they weep? Ah, Lord God, thou knowest! Their babes have been torn from their bosoms and cast upon the plains to die of hunger, or to be devoured by hyenas or jackals. The little innocents would die on the "Middle Passage," or suffocate between the decks of the floating slave-pen, freighted and packed with unparalleled human woe, and the slavers in mercy have cast them out to perish on their native shores. Such is the beginning, and no less wicked is the end of that system which the Scribes and Pharisees in the Church and the State pronounce to be just, humane, benevolent and Christian. If such are the deeds of mercy wrought by angels, then tell me what works of inquity there remain for devils to do?

This commerce in human beings has been carried on until three hundred thousand have been dragged from their native land in a single year. While this foreign trade has been pursued, who can calculate the enormities and extent of the domestic traffic which has flourished in every slave State, while the whole country has been open to the hunters of men.

It is the highly concentrated essence of all conceivable wickedness. Theft, robbery, pollution, unbridled passion, incest, cruelty, cold-blooded murder, blasphemy, and defiance of the laws of God. It teaches children to disregard parental authority. It tears down the marriage altar, and tramples its sacred ashes under its feet. It creates and nourishes polygamy. It feeds and pampers its hateful handmaid, prejudice.

It has divided our national councils. It has engendered deadly strife between brethren. It has wasted the treasure of the Commonwealth, and the lives of thousands of brave men, and driven troops of helpless women and children into yawning tombs. It has caused the bloodiest civil war recorded in the book of time. It has shorn this nation of its locks of strength that was rising as a young lion in the Western world. It has offered us as a sacrifice to the jealousy and cupidity of tyrants, despots, and adventurers of foreign countries. It has opened a door through which a usurper, a perjured, but a powerful prince, might stealthily enter and build an empire on the golden borders of our southwestern frontier, and which is but a stepping-stone to further and unlimited conquests on this continent. It has desolated the fairest portions of our land, "until the wolf long since driven back by the march of civilization returns after the lapse of a hundred years and howls amidst its ruins."

It seals up the Bible, and mutilates its sacred truths, and flies into the face of the Almighty, and impiously asks, "*Who art thou that I should obey thee?*" Such are the outlines of this fearful national sin; and yet the condition to which it reduces man, it is affirmed, is the best that can possibly be devised for him.

When inconsistencies similar in character, and no more glaring, passed beneath the eye of the Son of God, no wonder he broke forth in language of vehement denunciation. Ye Scribes, Pharisees, and hypocrites! Ye blind guides! Ye compass sea and land to make one proselyte, and when he is made ye make him twofold more the child of hell than yourselves. Ye are like unto whited sepulchres, which indeed appear beautiful without, but within are full of dead men's bones, and all uncleanness!

Let us here take up the golden rule, and adopt the self-application mode of reasoning to those who hold these erroneous views. Come, gird up thy loins and answer like a man, if thou canst. Is slavery, as it is seen in its origin, continuance, and end the best possible condition for thee? Oh, no! Wilt thou bear that burden on thy shoulders, which thou wouldest lay upon thy fellow-man? No. Wilt thou bear a part of it, or remove a little of its weight with one of thy fingers? The sharp and indignant answer is no, no! Then how, and when, and where, shall we apply to thee the golden rule, which says, "*Therefore all things that ye would that others should do to you, do ye even so unto them, for this is the law and the prophets.*"

Let us have the testimony of the wise and great of ancient and modern times:

Sages who wrote and warriors who bled.

PLATO declared that "Slavery is a system of complete injustice."

SOCRATES wrote that "Slavery is a system of outrage and robbery."

CYRUS said, "To fight in order not to be a slave is noble."

If Cyrus had lived in our land a few years ago he would have been arrested for using incendiary language, and for inciting servile insurrection, and the royal fanatic would have been hanged on a gallows higher than Haman. But every man is fanatical when his soul is warmed by the generous fires of liberty. Is it then truly noble to fight in order not to be a slave? The Chief Magistrate of the nation, and our rulers, and all truly patriotic men think so; and so think legions of black men, who for a season were scorned and rejected, but who came quickly and cheerfully when they were

at last invited, bearing a heavy burden of proscriptions upon their shoulders, and having faith in God, and in their generous fellow-countrymen, they went forth to fight a double battle. The foes of their country were before them, while the enemies of freedom and of their race surrounded them.

AUGUSTINE, CONSTANTINE, IGNATIUS, POLYCARP, MAXIMUS, and the most illustrious lights of the ancient church denounced the sin of slaveholding.

THOMAS JEFFERSON said at a period of his life, when his judgment was matured, and his experience was ripe, "There is preparing, I hope, under the auspices of heaven, a way for a total emancipation."

The sainted WASHINGTON said, near the close of his mortal career, and when the light of eternity was beaming upon him, "It is among my first wishes to see some plan adopted by which slavery in this country shall be abolished by law. I know of but one way by which this can be done, and that is by legislative action, and so far as my vote can go, it shall not be wanting."

The other day, when the light of Liberty streamed through this marble pile, and the hearts of the noble band of patriotic statesmen leaped for joy, and this our national capital shook from foundation to dome with the shouts of a ransomed people, then methinks the spirits of Washington, Jefferson, the Jays, the Adamses, and Franklin, and Lafayette, and Giddings, and Lovejoy, and those of all the mighty, and glorious dead, remembered by history, because they were faithful to truth, justice, and liberty, were hovering over the august assembly. Though unseen by mortal eyes, doubtless they joined the angelic choir, and said, Amen.

POPE LEO X. testifies, "That not only does the Christian religion, but nature herself, cry out against a state of slavery."

PATRICK HENRY said, "We should transmit to posterity our abhorrence of slavery." So also thought the Thirty-Eighth Congress.

LAFAYETTE proclaimed these words: "Slavery is a dark spot on the face of the nation." God be praised, that stain will soon be wiped out.

JONATHAN EDWARDS declared "that to hold a man in slavery is to be every day guilty of robbery, or of man stealing."

Rev. Dr. WILLIAM ELLERY CHANNING, in a *Letter on the Annexation of Texas* in 1837, writes as follows:

"The evil of slavery speaks for itself. To state is to condemn the institution. The choice which every freeman makes of death for his child and for every thing he loves in preference to slavery, shows what it is. The single consideration that by slavery one human being is placed powerless and defenceless in the hands of another to be driven to whatever labor that other may impose, to suffer whatever punishment he may inflict, to live as his tool, the instrument of his pleasure, this is all that is needed to satisfy such as know the human heart and its unfitness for irresponsible power, that of all conditions slavery is the most hostile to the dignity, self-respect, improvement, rights, and happiness of human beings. . . . Every principle of our government and religion condemns slavery. The spirit of our age condemns it. The decree of the civilized world has gone out against it. . . . Is there an age in which a free and Christian people shall deliberately resolve to extend and perpetuate the evil? In so doing we cut ourselves off from the communion of nations; we sink below the civilization of our age; we invite the scorn, indignation, and abhorrence of the world."

MOSES, the greatest of all lawgivers and legislators, said, while his face was yet radiant with the light of Sinai: "Whoso stealeth a man, and selleth him, or if he be found in his hand, he shall surely be put to death." The destroying angel has gone forth through this land to execute the fearful penalties of God's broken law.

The Representatives of the nation have bowed with reverence to the Divine edict, and laid the axe at the root of the tree, and thus saved succeeding generations from the guilt of oppression, and from the wrath of God.

Statesmen, Jurists, and Philosophers, most renowned for learning, and most profound in every department of science and literature, have testified against slavery. While oratory has brought its costliest, golden treasures, and laid them on the altar of God and of freedom, it has aimed its fiercest lightning and loudest thunder at the strongholds of tyranny, injustice, and despotism.

From the days of Balak to those of Isaiah and Jeremiah, up to the times of Paul, and through every age of the Christian Church, the sons of thunder have denounced the abominable thing. The heroes who stood in the shining ranks of the hosts of the friends of human progress, from Cicero to Chatham, and Burke, Sharp, Wilberforce, and Thomas Clarkson, and Curran, assaulted the citadel of despotism. The orators and statesmen of our own land, whether they belong to the past, or to the present age, will live and shine in the annals of history, in proportion as they have dedicated their genius and talents to the defence of Justice and man's God-given rights.

All the poets who live in sacred and profane history have charmed the world with their most enchanting strains, when they have tuned their lyres to the praise of Liberty. When the Muses can no longer decorate her altars with their garlands, then they hang their harps upon the willows and weep.

From Moses to Terence and Homer, from thence to Milton and Cowper, Thomson and Thomas Campbell, and on to the days of our own bards, our Bryants, Longfellows, Whittiers, Morrises, and Bokers, all have presented their best gifts to the interests and rights of man.

Every good principle, and every great and noble power, have been made the subjects of the inspired verse, and the songs of poets. But who of them has attempted to immortalize slavery? You will search in vain the annals of the world to find an instance. Should any attempt the sacrilegious work, his genius would fall to the earth as if smitten by the lightning of heaven. Should he lift his hand to write a line in its praise, or defence, the ink would freeze on the point of his pen.

Could we array in one line, representatives of all the families of men, beginning with those lowest in the scale of being, and should we put to them the question, Is it right and desirable that you should be reduced to the condition of slaves, to be registered with chattels, to have your persons, and your lives, and the products of your labor, subjected to the will and the interests of others? Is it right and just that the persons of your wives and children should be at the disposal of others, and be yielded to them for the purpose of pampering their lusts and greed of gain? Is it right to lay heavy burdens on other men's shoulders which you would not remove with one of your fingers? From the rude savage and barbarian the negative response would come, increasing in power and significance as it rolled up the line. And when those should reply, whose minds and hearts are illuminated with the highest civilization and with the spirit of Christianity, the answer deep-toned and prolonged would thunder forth, no, no!

With all the moral attributes of God on our side, cheered as we are by the voices of universal human nature,—in view of the best interests of the present and future generations—animated with the noble desire to furnish the nations of the earth with a worthy example, let the verdict of death which has been brought in against slavery, by the THIRTY-EIGHTH CONGRESS, be affirmed and executed by the people. Let the gigantic monster perish. Yes, perish now, and perish forever!

> Down let the shrine of Moloch sink,
>   And leave no traces where it stood;
> No longer let its idol drink,
>   His daily cup of human blood.
> But rear another altar there,
>   To truth, and love, and mercy given,
> And freedom's gift and freedom's prayer,
>   Shall call an answer down from heaven.

It is often asked when and where will the demands of the reformers of this and coming ages end? It is a fair question, and I will answer.

When all unjust and heavy burdens shall be removed from every man in the land. When all invidious and proscriptive distinctions shall be blotted out from our laws, whether they be constitutional, statute, or municipal laws. When emancipation shall be followed by enfranchisement, and all men holding allegiance to the government shall enjoy every right of American citizenship. When our brave and gallant soldiers shall have justice done unto them. When the men who endure the sufferings and perils of the battle-field in the defence of their country, and in order to keep our rulers in their places, shall enjoy the well-earned privilege of voting for them. When in the army and navy, and in every legitimate and honorable occupation, promotion shall smile upon merit without the slightest regard to the complexion of a man's face. When there shall be no more class-legislation, and no more trouble concerning the black man and his rights, than there is in regard to other American citizens. When, in every respect, he shall be equal before the law, and shall be left to make his own way in the social walks of life.

We ask, and only ask, that when our poor frail barks are launched on life's ocean—

> Bound on a voyage of awful length
> And dangers little known,

that, in common with others, we may be furnished with rudder, helm, and sails, and charts, and compass. Give us good pilots to conduct us to the open seas; lift no false lights along the dangerous coasts, and if it shall please God to send us propitious winds, or fearful gales, we shall survive or perish as our energies or neglect shall determine. We ask no special favors, but we plead for justice. While we scorn unmanly dependence; in the name of God, the universal Father, we demand the right to live, and labor, and to enjoy the fruits of our toil. The good work which God has assigned for the ages to come, will be finished, when our national literature shall be so purified as to reflect a faithful and a just light upon the character and social habits of our race, and the brush, and pencil, and chisel, and Lyre of Art, shall refuse to lend their aid to scoff at the afflictions of the poor, or to caricature, or ridicule a long-suffering people. When caste and prejudice in Christian churches shall be utterly destroyed, and shall be regarded as totally unworthy of Christians, and at variance with the principles of the gospel. When the blessings of the Christian religion, and of sound, religious education, shall be freely offered to all, then, and not till then, shall the effectual labors of God's people and God's instruments cease.

If slavery has been destroyed merely from *necessity,* let every class be enfranchised at the dictation of *justice.* Then we shall have a Constitution that shall be reverenced by all: rulers who shall be honored, and revered, and a Union that shall be sincerely loved by a brave and patriotic people, and which can never be severed.

Great sacrifices have been made by the people; yet, greater still are demanded ere atonement can be made for our national sins. Eternal justice holds heavy mortgages against us, and will require the payment of the last farthing. We have involved ourselves in the sin of unrighteous gain, stimulated by luxury, and pride, and the love of power and oppression; and prosperity, and peace can be purchased only by blood, and with tears of repentance. We have paid some of the fearful installments, but there are other heavy obligations to be met.

The great day of the nation's judgment has come, and who shall be able to stand? Even we, whose ancestors have suffered the afflictions which are inseparable from a condition of slavery, for the period of two centuries and a half, now pity our land and weep with those who weep.

Upon the total and complete destruction of this accursed sin depends the safety and perpetuity of our Republic and its excellent institutions.

Let slavery die. It has had a long and fair trial. God himself has pleaded against it. The enlightened nations of the earth have condemned it. Its death warrant is signed by God and man. Do not commute its sentence. Give it no respite, but let it be ignominiously executed.

Honorable Senators and Representatives! illustrious rulers of this great nation! I cannot refrain this day from invoking upon you, in God's name, the blessings of millions who were ready to perish, but to whom a new and better life has been opened by your humanity, justice, and patriotism. You have said, "Let the Constitution of the country be so amended that slavery and involuntary servitude shall no longer exist in the United States, except in punishment for crime." Surely, an act so sublime could not escape Divine notice; and doubtless the deed has been recorded in the archives of heaven. Volumes may be appropriated to your praise and renown in the history of the world. Genius and art may perpetuate the glorious act on canvass and in marble, but certain and more lasting monuments in commemoration of your decision are already erected in the hearts and memories of a grateful people.

The nation has begun its exodus from worse than Egyptian bondage; and I beseech you that you say to the people, "*that they go forward.*" With the assurance of God's favor in all things done in obedience to his righteous will, and guided by day and by night by the pillars of cloud and fire, let us not pause until we have reached the other and safe side of the stormy and crimson sea. Let freemen and patriots mete out complete and equal justice to all men, and thus prove to mankind the superiority of our Democratic, Republican Government.

Favored men, and honored of God as his instruments, speedily finish the work which he has given you to do. *Emancipate, Enfranchise, Educate, and give the blessings of the gospel to every American citizen.*

Hear ye not how, from all high points of Time,—
    From peak to peak adown the mighty chain
That links the ages—echoing sublime

A Voice Almighty—leaps one grand refrain,
Wakening the generations with a shout,
And trumpet-call of thunder—Come yet out!

Out from old forms and dead idolatries;
    From fading myths and superstitious dreams:
From Pharisaic rituals and lies,
    And all the bondage of the life that seems!
Out—on the pilgrim path, of heroes trod,
Over earth's wastes, to reach forth after God!

The Lord hath bowed his heaven, and come down!
    Now, in this latter century of time,
Once more his tent is pitched on Sinai's crown!
    Once more in clouds must Faith to meet him climb!
Once more his thunder crashes on our doubt
And fear and sin—"My people! come ye out!"

From false ambitions and base luxuries;
    From puny aims and indolent self-ends;
From cant of faith, and shams of liberties,
    And mist of ill that Truth's pure day-beam bends:
Out, from all darkness of the Egypt-land,
Into my sun-blaze on the desert sand!

                .   .   .

Show us our Aaron, with his rod in flower!
    Our Miriam, with her timbrel-soul in tune!
And call some Joshua, in the Spirit's power,
    To poise our sun of strength at point of noon!
God of our fathers! over sand and sea,
Still keep our struggling footsteps close to thee![2]

Then before us a path of prosperity will open, and upon us will descend the mercies and favors of God. Then shall the people of other countries, who are standing tip-toe on the shores of every ocean, earnestly looking to see the end of this amazing conflict, behold a Republic that is sufficiently strong to outlive the ruin and desolations of civil war, having the magnanimity to do justice to the poorest and weakest of her citizens. Thus shall we give to the world the form of a model Republic, founded on the principles of justice, and humanity, and Christianity, in which the burdens of war and the blessings of peace are equally borne and enjoyed by all.

[2] Atlantic Monthly, 1862.

Two Black Women Serve and Observe

Charlotte Forten Grimké (1838–1914)

Charlotte Forten, like her grandfather James Forten, lived with the comforting illusion that if the Black man could once prove his ability to learn, assimilate, and articulate in effective competition with the white man, then America would accept him as a full-fledged citizen and accord him all of a citizen's privileges and prerogatives. Grandfather James Forten, born free in Philadelphia in 1766, lived long, worked hard, and became a millionaire sailmaker. He gave his time and money to the cause of abolition, supported just and worthy issues, and paid his taxes. As a youth, he had even run away from home to serve his country as a drummer boy in the Continental Navy during the Revolutionary War. Despite all of this, this man of probity and wisdom lived the life of a segregated Black man in his native Philadelphia. He broke no laws and defied no covenants, but because he was Black, he never enjoyed the full rights of citizenship. However, until his death in 1842 he retained a hearty idealistic faith in the promise of America.

This faith he transmitted through his son James, Jr., and his son-in-law Robert Purvis to his granddaughter Charlotte. Believing that if she as a Black woman learned, achieved, and excelled, America would accept her, Charlotte left Philadelphia in 1854, at the age of sixteen, to attend school in Salem, Massachusetts. Her *Journal,* which she began during her school years in Salem, was meant to be the record of the implementation of her dream of faith. Achieve she did, both as a student and as a teacher in Salem, and the good people of this somewhat conservative New England seaport town applauded her efforts. But, by her achievements no miracles were wrought and no laws were rewritten. Federal marshals were still charged to drag fugitive slaves back into slavery just as they had dragged Anthony Burns back to slavery from Boston during her first year in Massachusetts.

So Charlotte Forten needed a larger arena to prove that not only could a particular Black girl learn and achieve, but all Black people could learn and achieve. They could shed the handicaps imposed on mind and body by slavery and could master concepts and ideas and the language needed to express them. Port Royal and the Sea Islands of

South Carolina afforded her the opportunity she wanted. Here, following the capture of the Sea Islands by the Union Navy, were living thousands of illiterate, poor, ill-clad, and ill-housed ex-slaves. They had served on the numerous large plantations, and now, abandoned by their masters, they were free. They were different in every way from slaves who lived in more accessible areas. The normal isolation of slavery was bad enough, but the slaves of the Sea Islands suffered an even greater isolation. So their culture was closer to that of Africa as a remembered motherland than to that of America. They spoke a patois that puzzled the invading Federals and defied interpretation. And they were hostile, insecure, and fearful.

Into such a challenging situation Charlotte came to teach in 1862. If these freedmen could learn to read, write, think, analyze, speculate, and dream, then there was hope that America would ultimately accept them or their sons and daughters as full-fledged citizens. Her *Journal* records that her efforts to teach them were ultimately successful. There were many almost overwhelming problems, of course, but when Charlotte Forten ended her mission in May 1864, she returned to Philadelphia with the firm belief that education could be the catalytic agent that could change an ex-slave into a citizen.

In 1878, in her fortieth year, Charlotte Forten married the Rev. Francis Grimké, a distinguished member of a distinguished family. In a sense, his life was proof of her faith in America's promise, for Francis Grimké had come out of slavery to achieve at Lincoln, Harvard, and Princeton. He was a polished, scholarly cleric, far removed from the nightmare of slavery. He bore no mark of the chain, and this, Charlotte Forten Grimké believed, was the metamorphosis wrought by educational achievement. When she died in 1914, she probably still retained her deep faith in America's promise and education's rewards. America's cities then held no sprawling Black ghettoes filled with human rubble to disabuse her of her hopes.

The excerpts from her *Journal* that follow describe her experiences during her stay on St. Helena, one of South Carolina's Sea Islands. During the two years that she served here as a teacher, there were many privations and many wartime aggravations, but the lines of her *Journal* pulse with happy optimism and *joie de vivre*. She also emerges as a person of considerable intellectual breadth, obviously well acquainted with poetry and philosophy and always eager for more knowledge, and possessing a gift for writing. Her style is lilting and her descriptive imagery at times quite effective. These effects, along with her candor, combine to make the *Journal* a remarkable piece of writing for a young Black girl who lived on the fringe of a slave culture.

Charlotte Forten's *Journal* was first published, in abridged form, in 1953, with a full introduction and helpful notes by Ray Allen Billington. Polly Longsworth's *I, Charlotte Forten, Black and Free* (1970) is "based upon Billington's book." Edmund Wilson treats Forten in *Patriotic Gore: Studies in the Literature of the American Civil War* (1962), and Willie Lee Rose tells the full story of the Sea Islands of South Carolina during the Civil War in *Rehearsal for Reconstruction: The Port Royal Experiment* (1964).

from *Journal of Charlotte Forten*

From Salem to St. Helena Island

June 22, 1862–November 29, 1862

Salem, June 22, 1862. More penitent than ever I come to thee again, old Journal, long neglected friend. More than two years have elapsed since I last talked to thee.—two years full of changes. A little while ago a friend read to me Miss Mullock's "Life for a Life." The Journal letters, which I liked so much,—were at first addressed to an unknown friend. So shall mine be. What name shall I give to thee, oh *ami inconnu?* It will be safer to give merely an initial—A. And so, dear A. I will tell you a little of my life for the past two years. When I wrote to you last,—on a bright, lovely New Year's Day, I was here in old Salem, and in this very house. What a busy winter that was for me, I was assisting my dear Miss S[hepard] with one of her classes, and at the same time studying, and reciting at the Normal, Latin, French and a little Algebra. Besides I was taking German lessons. Now was I not busy, dear A? Yet it seems to me I was never so happy. I enjoyed life perfectly, and all the winter was strong and well. But when Spring came my health gave way. First my eyesight failed me, and the German which I liked better than anything else, which it was a real luxury to study had to be given up, and then all my other studies. My health continuing to fail, I was obliged to stop teaching, and go away. Went to Bridgewater, and in the Kingman's delightful home grew gradually stronger. Then went to the Water Cure at Worcester, where the excellent Dr. R[ogers] did me a world of good— spiritually as well as physically. To me he seems one of the best and noblest types of manhood I ever saw. In my heart I shall thank him always. Early in September, came back from W[orcester] and recommenced teaching, feeling quite well. But late in October had a violent attack of lung fever, which brought me very, very near the grave, and entirely unfitted me for further work. My physician's commands were positive that I sh'ld not attempt spending the winter in S[alem], and I was obliged to return to P[hiladelphia]. A weary winter I had there, unable to work, and having but little congenial society, and suffering the many deprivations which all of our unhappy race

must suffer in the so-called "City of Brotherly Love." What a mockery that name is! But over those weary months it is better to draw the veil, and forget. In May I went to Byberry to see poor R[obert Purvis, Jr.] . . . ill with lung disease. And all the beautiful summer I stayed there trying to nurse and amuse him as well as I cl'd. It was so sad to see one so young, so full of energy and ambition, doomed to lead a life of inaction, and the weariness which ill health brings. R[obert] seemed to improve as the summer advanced, and in the Fall I left him, to take charge of Aunt M[argaretta]'s school in the city. A small school— but the children were mostly bright and interesting; and I was thankful to have anything to do. . . .

In March, poor R[obert] died. When I saw him lying so cold and still, and witnessed the agony of the loving hearts around him, I wished, dear A., that I cl'd have been taken instead of him. He had everything to live for, and I so very little. It seems hard; yet we *know* it must be right. . . . Week before last I had a letter from Mary S[hepard] asking me to come on and take charge of S. C.'s [?] classes during the summer, as she was obliged to go away. How gladly I accepted, you, dear A., may imagine. I had been *longing* so for a breath of N[ew] E[ngland] air; for a glimpse of the sea, for a walk over our good old hills. . . . We left P[hiladelphia] on Tuesday, the 10th; stopped a little while in N[ew] Y[ork]. . . . Then took the evening boat, and reached here Wed[nesday] morn. Mrs. I[ves] gave us a most cordial welcome; and we immediately felt quite at home. . . .

Sunday, July 6. Let me see? How did I spend last week? In teaching, as usual, until Friday, on which, being the "glorious Fourth," we had no school, and I went to Framingham to the Grove Meeting. The day was lovely, and I had a delightful time. Greatly to my disappointment Mr. Phillips was not there. But it was better that he sh'ld not attempt speaking in the open air.—His throat was troubling him so much. Mr. G[arrison] and all his children were there looking as well and happy as possible. He and Mr. Heywood and Miss Anthony made the best speeches. One cannot listen to Mr. H[eywood] without feeling that he is a "born orator." . . . Met some old friends at Framingham. Dr. and Mrs. Rogers were there from W[orcester]. How glad I was to see the Dr.

again. But it grieved me to see him looking so far from well. He has been quite ill since Feb[ruary], with pleurisy. He is certainly one of the most thoroughly good men in the world. . . . After the meeting spent a day or two in Boston. Had a lovely walk on the Common, Saturday morning. How fresh and beautiful the grass and trees looked. . . . On my way home, stopped at Williams and Everett's and saw a magnificent bust of Milton in marble. Saw a picture of "Rahl of the Rhine," which was really startling in its *lifelikeness*. The legend runs this wise.—Rahl and two wild companions were in the habit of meeting to drink together. And one night they took a vow that they w'ld continue to meet on that same night of every year, even although two of them sh'ld be dead. And the vow was kept. The painting, which is a large and very fine one, represents Rahl as raising a glass of wine, and at the same moment the four ghostly hands of his two dead companions are stretched out and clutch the other two glasses, while Rahl stands transfixed with fear and horror. There is something very life-like and striking about this picture. One cannot look at it without a shudder.—In the afternoon . . . spent a little time at the Atheneum. My attention was particularly attracted by a magnificent bust of John Brown, (in marble,) and by a landscape— I think it must have been a part of the German Alps—by a German artist. I thought it one of the most beautiful pictures I ever saw, but you know, dear A., that there never was a greater ignoramus than I about matters of Art. Still I do believe no one could have helped liking this picture. It was so lovely—Grand mountains, *real* mountains, rising above the clouds in the background, a lovely valley with a clear stream flowing through it at the foot of the mts. Near the stream was a party of gipsies in bright, picturesque costumes, preparing their meal. Over all bent a sky, blue and beautiful as an Italian sky. It was a most *enjoyable* picture, and one to be easily recalled. Had but little time to devote to others. . . . To-day —Sunday—had the great happiness of hearing Mr. Phillips. . . . Music Hall was crowded. The heat was so intense that I c'ld scarcely breathe. I thought, before the lecture commenced, that I sh'ld certainly have to go out. But after Mr. P[hillips] commenced speaking I forgot everything else. It was a grand, glorious speech, such as he alone can make. I wish the poor, miserable President whom he so justly criticized c'ld have heard it. It grieved me to see him looking so pale

and weary. And his throat troubles him much. I cannot bear to think of his health failing. Yet something I fear it is. Oh dear A. let us pray to the good All-Father to spare this noble soul to see the result of his life-long labors—the freedom of the slave. . . . Ah, friend of mine, I must not forget to tell you about a little adventure I met with to-day. I was boarding with Mrs. R[?] a very good anti-slavery woman, and kind and pleasant as can be. Well, when I appeared at the dinner-table to-day, it seems that a *gentleman* took umbrage at sitting at the same table with one whose skin chanced to be "not colored like his own," and rose and left the table. Poor man! he feared contamination. But the charming part of the affair is that I, with eyes intent upon my dinner, and mind entirely engrossed (by Mr. Phillips' glorious words, which were still sounding in my soul), did not notice this person's presence nor disappearance. So his proceedings were quite lost upon me, and I sh'ld have been in a state of blissful ignorance as to his very existence had not the hostess afterward spoken to me about it, expressing the wish, good woman—that my "feelings were not hurt." I told her the truth, and begged her to set her mind perfectly at ease, for even had I have noticed the simpleton's behavior it w'ld not have troubled me. I felt too thorough a contempt for such people to allow myself to be wounded by them. This wise gentleman was an *officer in the navy,* I understand. An honor to his country's service—isn't he? But he is not alone, I know full well. The name of his kindred is Legion,—but I defy and despise them all. I hope as I grow older I get a little more philosophy. Such things do not wound me so deeply as of yore. But they create a bitterness of feeling, which is far from desirable. "When, when will these outrages cease?" often my soul cries out—"How long, oh Lord, how long?"—You w'ld have pitied me during the last part of my ride back to S[alem] this afternoon. The first part of the ride—from B[oston] to L[ynn] in the horse cars, w'ld have been quite pleasant but for the heat. One has a good opprtunity of seeing the surrounding country—traveling in this way. At L[ynn] we met the stage, or rather omnibus. We packed in;—thirty outside; the inside crowded to suffocation with odorous Irish and their screaming babies;—the heat intense. Altogether it was quite unbearable. The driver refused to move with such a load. Nobody was willing to get off. And I think we must have been detained at L[ynn] an hour, till at last an open wagon drove up, and taking off part of the load, we started for S[alem]. We were altogether about three hours going from B[oston] to S[alem]. . . .

Wednesday, Aug. 6. Spent the day at Nahant. Had a glorious time. . . . Returning, how much we enjoyed the beautiful drive from N[ahant] to L[ynn] a narrow strip of land with the sea on either hand, and sea glowing in the sunset. It was very beautiful. Soon after I reached home . . . came . . . the kindest note from Whittier, in answer to one I had written asking what day we sh'ld come. (His sister had urgently invited us to come before I left N[ew] E[ngland].) We are to go on Saturday. My mind is filled with pleasant anticipations. Good night.—

Saturday, Aug. 9. Another "day to be marked with a white stone. Mary [Shepard] and I started early. . . . We changed cars at L[ynn] then proceeded to Amesbury. Did not see Whittier at the station. Drove to the house; met with a warm welcome from his sister. She looks very frail. Just as we entered the door of the house a lady came in behind us, whom we found afterward to be Lucy Larcom—a pleasant, motherly, unassuming kind of person, really quite lovable. W[hittier] was in one of his most delightful genial moods. His sister as lovely, childlike—I had almost said as Angelic as ever. The day was showery, and we c'ld not take any walks, but I enjoyed myself perfectly in the house. W[hittier] told us some amusing anecdotes of how he was pestered by people coming to see him—people who were utter strangers. Sometimes, he said they brought their carpet-bags. "Oh, Mr. W[hittier], not their carpet-bags!" we exclaimed. "Yes, actually" he replied, smiling quite grimly, "and they all have the same speeches to make 'Mr. W[hittier] we have read y[ou]r writings and admired them very much, and had such a great desire to see you'." He said he was thankful to live in such a quiet little place as Amesbury, where nobody said anything to him about his writings, and where he was not thought of as a writer. He said sometimes he had tracked these lion-hunters, and found that the same people went to Emerson and Longfellow and others. Emerson did not care so much for them. He rather enjoyed studying character in all its different phases. He (W[hittier]) and his sister told us a comical story about a "Mrs. Hanaford's husband," this Mrs. H[anaford] it seems, being one of the most persistent lion-hunters. The conversation turned on many topics, and was most enjoyable throughout. Miss W[hittier] showed us

photographs of her friends. Among them was one of a Mrs. Howell of Phila[delphia] (whom gossip once said W[hittier] w'ld marry) a face faultless in outline and coloring—exquisitely beautiful, yet lacking a little in depth of expression. Miss W[hittier] says it does not do her justice. That she is more beautiful than her picture. Then she must look like an angel. The picture of Helen W[hittier] the lovely, gifted girl who died in Italy, charmed me. A face at once most gentle and yet most spirited, beautiful, noble, and lighted up by the soul within. A cherished and only child, she died at seventeen. Miss W[hittier] showed us the picture of an Italian girl, in which she found a striking likeness to me. Everybody else agreed that there was a resemblance. But I utterly failed to see it: *I* thought the Italian girl very pretty, and I know myself to be the very opposite. We left the poet's home with regret. Such a quiet lovely home. It made my heart ache to see his sister looking so frail, knowing what these two are to each other. I was glad to find that she was going away for a while with Lucy Larcom, she is such a motherly person—one by whom it must be a real happiness to be taken care of. W[hittier] advised me to apply to the Port-Royal Com[mission] in Boston. He is very desirous that I sh'ld go. I shall certainly take his advice. . . .

Boston.—Monday, Aug. 11. Left S[alem] . . . this morn. Farewell, farewell again old town! I know not when I shall see thee again. S[allie] and I . . . walked from B[oston] to Bunker Hill. Charmed our eyes with Warren's statue; exhausted ourselves with ascending the Mon[ument] were refreshed again by the magnificent view from the top, descended, went to the Public Library and the Atheneum. Saw nothing new at the latter, but some old pictures of which one never wearies. . . .

Wednesday, Aug. 13. Had gone to see some members of the P[ort] R[oyal] Com[mission] and finding them all out of town, felt somewhat discouraged, when I rec'd the kindest letter from Whittier, advising me again to apply to the Com[mission] and giving me the names of several friends of his to whom to apply, also his permission to use his name as a reference. How very kind he is. I shall go and see those whom he mentions at once.

Watertown.—Sunday, Aug. 16. Have not yet succeeded in seeing any of the Com[mission] through I have traversed this hilly city enough; but I don't despair for I have seen Dr. Howe.

Was disappointed in his appearance. He is not the benevolent looking genial person I expected to see. At first he even seemed cold and hard, but no wonder, he was being so persecuted with some tiresome people. When I stated my business to him, and showed him W[hittier]'s letter he was as kind and cordial as c'ld be, and entered with much interest into my wishes. He is not a member of the Com[mission] but recommended me to go to a Dr. Peck, who has been Superintendent of the schools at P[ort] R[oyal] and who has great influence with the Com[mission]. . . . I have been to Roxbury to see Dr. P[eck] but he was not at home will probably be on Tuesday. So I determined instead of going to W[orcester] to come to Watertown and stay . . . till Monday. Had a delightful ride out in the horse cars, through old Cambridge, past Longfellow's home, and Lowell's, the Colleges, and Mt. Auburn. . . .

Sunday, Aug. 17. My twenty-fifth birthday. Tisn't a very pleasant thought that I have lived a quarter of a century, and am so very, very ignorant. Ten years ago, I hoped for a different fate at twenty-five. But why complain? The accomplishments, the society, the delights of travel which I have dreamed of and longed for all my life, I am now convinced can never be mine. If I can go to Port Royal, I will try to forget all these desires. I will pray that God in his goodness will make me noble enough to find my highest happiness in doing my duty. . . . Went to church this morning to hear Mr. Wiess—author of "The Horrors of San Domingo," in the Atlantic. It was a beautiful earnest sermon, and I enjoyed it, but was rather disappointed that it was not on the times, as I had hoped it w'ld be. *That* is the subject which he usually chooses, I am told. It was a pleasant little church and the altar adorned with the loveliest flowers. . . .

Monday, Aug. 18. Walked from W[atertown] to Mt. Auburn. It was a delightful walk through the quiet, beautiful country. Spent nearly all day at Mt. A[uburn]. It was very lovely there. The beautiful chapel with its noble statues, the grand view from the Observatory, the stately monuments, the exquisite flowers—I enjoyed all perfectly. Such flowers! Geranium, heliotrope, mignonette, and everything else that is fragrant and beautiful in profusion. I sat down and *luxuriated*. The whole cemetery is like a flower garden. One or two of the monuments I liked particularly. On one—over a child's grave—was carved a cross and anchor, and, twining around them, a morning-

glory vine also exquisitely carved. The inscription was—"Here in Faith and Hope, we placed our Morning Glory." On another simple white headstone, with no name upon it, were the words—"All I loved lies here." It was over the grave of a grown person. There was something very touching in those few, simple words.—

Worcester, Tuesday, Aug. 19. Saw Dr. P[eck] this morning. He was very kind, and assures me that he thinks there will be no difficulty about my going. He will speak to the Com[mission] about it, and let me know in a few days. It was very interesting to hear his account of his experiences at Port Royal. He seems deeply interested in the people there. I hope I can go. . . .

Wednesday, Sept. 3. Have been anxious and disappointed at not hearing from Dr. P[eck]. . . . The Com[mission] meets to-day, and then he will write immediately and let me know the final decision. Last week I heard from home that there was no doubt of my being able to go from the Phila[delphia] Com[mission]. Mr. McK[im] had spoken to them about it. So if I cannot go from B[oston] I am sure of going from P[hiladelphia]; but I w'ld rather go under Boston auspices. . . .

Monday, Sept. 8. No further news from B[oston]. I am determined to go to-morrow and see for myself what the trouble is. . . .

Phila. Sunday, Sept. 14. Back again in old abominable P[hiladelphia] . . . Went from W[orcester] to B[oston] on Tuesday afternoon. I got little satisfaction from the B[oston] Com[mission]. "They were not sending women at present" etc. Dr. R[ogers] promised to do all he c'ld for me, but I am resolved to apply to the Com[mission] here. . . . Remained in Boston till Friday afternoon. Had the happiness of getting a glimpse of Wendell P[hillips] before I left. W'ld not stop him to shake hands with him, and have been sorry ever since that I did not. It w'ld have been *such* a satisfaction to me, and I may never see him again. Too late now. Came to N[ew] Y[ork] on the Sound, and had a very rough night of it. On Sat[urday] Henry [Forten] went with me to Central Park. A delightful place it is. T'will be a perfect fairy-land when the trees are grown. H[enry] came to P[hiladelphia] with me. We got here between ten and eleven. Everybody was in bed but Aunt M[argaretta] who was astonished to see me. All well. . . .

Monday, Sept. 15. Through Mr. McK[im]'s kindness have seen the Com[mission]. They are perfectly willing for me to go. The only difficulty is that it may not be quite safe. They will write to Port Royal at once, and inquire about my going. I shall wait anxiously for a reply. . . .

Wednesday, Oct. 21. To-day rec'd a note from Mr. McK[im] asking me if I c[ou]ld possibly be ready to sail for Port Royal perhaps to-morrow. I was astonished, stupefied, and, at first thought it impossible, but on seeing Mr. McK[im] I found there was an excellent opportunity for me to go. An old Quaker gentleman is going there to keep store, accompanied by his daughter, and he is willing to take charge of me. It will probably be the only opportunity that I shall have of going this winter, so at any cost I *will* go. And so now to work. In greatest haste. . . .

At Sea. Oct. 27. Monday. Let me see. Where am I? What do I want to write? I am in a state of utter bewilderment. It was on Wed[nesday] I rec'd the note. On Thursday I said "good bye" to the friends that are so dear, and the city that is so hateful, and went to N[ew] Y[ork]. . . . The next morn did not hurry myself, having heard that the steamer "United States" w'ld not sail till twelve. . . . I went to "Lovejoy's" to meet the Hunns and found there a card from Mr. H[unn] bidding me hasten to the steamer, as it was advertised to sail at nine. It was then between ten and eleven. After hurrying down and wearying ourselves, found when I got on board that it was not to sail till twelve. But I did not go ashore again. It was too bad, for I had no time to get several things that I wanted much, among them "Les Miserables," which my dear brother H[enry] had kindly given me the money for. He had not had time to get it in P[hiladelphia].

Enjoyed the sail down the harbor perfectly. The shipping is a noble sight. Had no symptoms of sea-sickness until eve when, being seated at the table an inexpressibly singular sensation caused me to make a hasty retreat to the aft deck, where, by keeping perfectly still sitting on a coil of ropes spent a very comfortable eve. and had a pleasant conversation with one of the passengers. Did not get out of sight of land until after dark. I regretted that.

Went below for the night into the close ladies' cabin with many misgivings which proved not unfounded. Was terribly sea-sick that night and all the next morning. Did not reappear on deck till noon of the next day—Saturday. What an experience! Of all doleful, dismal, desperate experiences sea-sickness is certainly the dolefulest, dismalest, and desperate-est!

T'was rather a miserable afternoon. Was half sick all the time and scarcely dared to move. There was highly pleasant talk going on around me, to which I c'ld listen in silence—that was all. My companion Lizzie Hunn was sick all the time. Poor girl, she c'ld take no pleasure in anything.

When night came, we both determined that we w'ldn't go below and have a repetition of the agonies of the night before. We heroically resolved to pass the night on deck. A nice little nook was found for us "amidships," and there enveloped in shawls and seated in arm chairs we were made as comfortable as possible, and passed the night without being sick. Two of the passengers— young men from Hilton Head, who were very gentlemanly and attentive, entertained us for some time with some fine singing; then they retired, and we passed the rest of the night in the society of Old Ocean alone. How wild and strange it seemed there on the deck in the dark night, only the dim outlines of sea and sky to be seen, only the roaring of the waves to be heard. I enjoyed it much. The thought that we were far, far, away from land was a pleasant one to me.

The next day—Sunday—was emphatically a *dismal* day. It rained nearly all the time so that we c'ld not be on deck much of the time. As soon as we established ourselves nicely outside down came the rain and we were driven into the close cabin, which was almost unendurable to me. Tried to read a little in the French Bible which H[enry] gave me, but in vain. The day was mostly spent in the interesting occupation of preventing sea-sickness by keeping perfectly quiet and watching the rain drops.

Before night a storm came on. And a terrible storm it was. The steward arranged mattresses and blankets for us in the covered passage way "amidships," and we lay down, but not to rest. It was a veritable grand storm at sea. The vessel rocked and plunged, the planks creaked and groaned, the sea broke upon the bows with thunderous roars, and within one w'ld have thought that all the crockery in the establishment was going to pieces. Such a noise I never heard in my life. Such roaring and plunging, and creaking. Afterward we were told that one of the chains of the vessel broke, and indeed for a time she seemed to be at the mercy of the waves. Some one near us—one of the waiters, I think, was dreadfully frightened, and commenced praying and moaning most piteously, crying "Oh Jesus, dear Jesus," in most lamentable tones, till I began to think we must really be in danger. Then the water came into the ladies cabin, below. One lady who had a baby with her woke up in the night and c'ld not find the child. It had been rolled away from her by the tossing of the ship, the lamps were out, and after some time, and much terror on the part of the poor woman the baby was found by one of the waiters under the berth. She was very quiet, and did not seem at all alarmed at her involuntary journey. Despite all the alarm and distress and anxiety we c'ld not help being amused at this little episode. During all the storm, however, I felt no fear; and now that the danger has passed, I feel really glad that I have at last experienced a "veritable storm at sea." The most astonishing thing was that I had two or three most refreshing sleeps in the very height of the storm.

This morning the sea was still very rough, but I struggled up, and dressed with great difficulty, and with the aid of one of the waiters made my way on deck. The sky was still very much overcast, the great, white capped waves were rising to a great height and breaking against the sides of the vessel. It was a grand sight, and I enjoyed it greatly. It has quite cleared off now, and the day is most lovely. I am feeling well and *luxuriating* in the glorious beauty of sea and sky. But my poor companion is still quite sick, and while I write, sits before me on a coil of ropes, enveloped in shawls, and looking the picture of dolefulness and despair.

How grand, how glorious the sea is, to-day! It far more than realizes my highest expectations of it. The sky too is beautiful—a deep, delicious blue, with soft, white, fleecy clouds floating over it. We have seen several sails today, in the distance, but still no land, whereat I am rejoiced.

There's not much to be said about the passengers on board. There are about a dozen beside ourselves, none of whom seem to me especially interesting, except perhaps our friend from Hilton Head, Mr. B[?]. He is very intelligent, and I sh'ld think even a talented young man. He has read and admires all my favorite authors, and I enjoy talking with them [him] about them. I have rarely found a *man* with so keen and delicate an appreciation of the beautiful, both in Nature and Art. There are no soldiers on board but one officer who stalks about the boat looking well pleased with himself and evidently trying to look quite grand, but *sans* success, for he was rather insignificant despite his good figure, fierce moustaches, and epaulettes.

Of the three ladies on board two go South to join their husbands, and the third accompanies hers. The first two are quite talkative, the latter very quiet. I believe that is all that can be said of them. There is a sea captain here whom I like very much. He is a Cape Cod man; has been to sea ever since he was nine years old. Has visited many lands, and I enjoy hearing him talk about them. The other gentlemen do not interest me, so I shall let them pass.

Have only been able to go to the table twice. Then there was no difficulty as I feared there might be. People were as kind and polite as possible. Indeed I have had not the least trouble since I have been on board. The waiters are as obliging and attentive as they can be, and bring us our meals out on deck every day.—

Afternoon.—I have just beheld the most glorious sight I ever saw in my life. . . . I staggered to the bow of the ship (which still rolls and pitches terribly) and there saw the sea in all its glory and grandeur. Oh, how beautiful those great waves were as they broke upon the sides of the vessel, into the foam and spray, pure and white as new fallen snow. People talk of the monotony of the sea. I have not found it monotonous for a moment, since I have been well. To me there is "infinite variety," constant enjoyment in it.

I have tried to read, but in vain; there is so much to take off one's attention, besides reading makes my head dizzy. One of the most beautiful sights I have yet seen is the phosphorescence in the water at night—the long line of light in the wake of the steamer, and the stars, and sometimes balls of fire that rise so magically out of the water. It is most strange and beautiful. Had it not been for the storm we should have reached Port Royal to-day. But we shall not get there till to-morrow.

Tuesday, A. M. Oct. 28.   How very, very lovely it was last night. Saw at last what I have so longed to see—the ocean in the moonlight. There was a beautiful young moon. Our ship rode gently along over a smooth sea leaving a path of silver behind it. There was something inexpressibly sweet and soothing and solemn in that soft moonlight. We sat on deck a long time, and the friends from H[ilton] H[ead], both of whom have very fine voices, sang beautifully. They were kind enough to change state rooms with us, and we slept up stairs very quietly.

Early this morn Mr. H[unn] came to our door to tell us that we were in sight of the blockading fleet in Charleston harbor. Of course we sprang

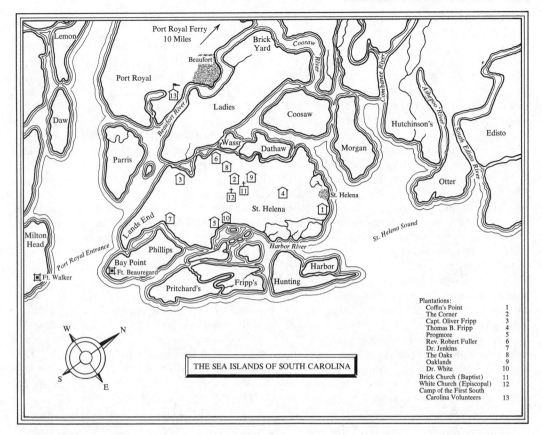

Plantations:

Coffin's Point	1
The Corner	2
Capt. Oliver Fripp	3
Thomas B. Fripp	4
Progmore	5
Rev. Robert Fuller	6
Dr. Jenkins	7
The Oaks	8
Oaklands	9
Dr. White	10
Brick Church (Baptist)	11
White Church (Episcopal)	12
Camp of the First South Carolina Volunteers	13

THE SEA ISLANDS OF SOUTH CAROLINA

to the window eagerly, and saw the masts of the ships looking like a grove of trees in the distance. We were not near enough to see the city. It was hard to realize that we were even so near that barbarous place.—

Later—We were again in sight of land. Have passed Edisto and several other islands, and can now see Hilton Head. Shall reach it about one. Tis nearly eleven now. The S[outh] C[arolina] shore is flat and low;—a long line of trees. It does not look very inviting. We are told that the oranges will be ripe when we get to Beaufort, and that in every way this is just the loveliest season to be there, which is very encouraging.

We approach Hilton Head. Our ship has been boarded by Health Officer and Provost Marshal. We shall soon reach the landing. All is hurry and confusion on board. I must lay thee aside, friend journal, and use my eyes for seeing all there is to be seen. When we reach our place of destination, I will give to thee, oh faithful friend, the result of my observations. So *au revoir*.—

Tuesday Night. T'was a strange sight as our boat approached the landing at Hilton Head. On the wharf was a motley assemblage,—soldiers, officers, and "contrabands" of every hue and size. They were mostly black, however, and certainly the most dismal specimens I ever saw. H[ilton] H[ead] looks like a very desolate place; just a long low, sandy point running out into the sea with no visible dwellings upon it but the soldiers' white roofed tents.

Thence, after an hour's delay, during which we signed a paper, which was virtually taking the oath of allegiance, we left the "United States," most rocking of rockety propellers,—and took a steamboat for Beaufort. On board the boat was General Saxton to whom we were introduced. I like his face exceedingly. And his manners were very courteous and affablè. He looks like a thoroughly *good* man.—From H[ilton] H[ead] to B[eaufort] the same low long line of sandy shore bordered by trees. Almost the only object of interest to me were the remains of an old Huguenot Fort, built many, many years ago.

Arrived at B[eaufort] we found that we had yet not reached our home. Went to Mr. French's, and saw there Reuben T[omlinson], whom I was very glad to meet, and Mrs. Gage, who seemed to be in a rather dismal state of mind. B[eaufort] looks like a pleasant place. The houses are large and quite handsome, built in the usual Southern style with verandahs around them, and beautiful trees. One magnolia tree in Mr. F[rench's] yard is splendid,—quite as large as some of our large shade trees, and, with the most beautiful foliage, a dark rich glossy green.

Went into the Commissary's Office to wait for the boat which was to take us to St. Helena's Island which is about six miles from B[eaufort]. T'is here that Miss Towne has her school, in which I am to teach, and that Mr. Hunn will have his store. While waiting in the Office we saw several military gentlemen [sic], *not* very creditable specimens, I sh'ld say. The little Commissary himself . . . is a perfect little popinjay, and he and a Colonel somebody who didn't look any too sensible, talked in a very smart manner, evidently for our special benefit. The word "nigger" was plentifully used, whereupon I set them down at once as *not* gentlemen [sic]. Then they talked a great deal about rebel attacks and yellow fever, and other alarming things, with significant nods and looks at each other. We saw through them at once, and were not at all alarmed by any of their representations. But if they are a fair example of army officers, I sh'ld pray to see as little of them as possible.

To my great joy found that we were to be rowed by a crew of negro boatmen. Young Mr. F[rench] whom I like—accompanied us, while Mr. H[unn] went with a flat to get our baggage. The row was delightful. It was just at sunset—a grand Southern sunset; and the gorgeous clouds of crimson and gold were reflected in the waters below, which were smooth and calm as a mirror. Then, as we glided along, the rich sonorous tones of the boatmen broke upon the evening stillness. Their singing impressed me much. It was so sweet and strange and solemn, "Roll, Jordan, Roll" was grand and another

> *Jesus make de blind to see*
> *Jesus make de deaf to hear*
> *"   "   " cripple walk*
> *Walk in, dear Jesus,*

and the refrain

> *No man can hender me.*

It was very, very impressive. I want to hear these men sing Whittier's "Song of the Negro Boat-

men." I am going to see if it can't be brought about in some way.

It was nearly dark when we reached St. Helena's, where we found Miss T[owne]'s carriage awaiting us, and then we three and our driver, had a long drive along the lonely roads in the dark night. How easy it w'ld have been for a band of guerillas—had any chanced that way—to seize and hang us. But we feared nothing of the kind. We were in a jubilant state of mind and sang "John Brown" with a will as we drove through the pines and palmettos. Arrived at the Superintendent's house we were kindly greeted by him and the ladies and shown into a lofty *ceilinged* parlor where a cheerful wood fire glowed in the grate, and we soon began to feel quite at home in the very heart of Rebeldom; only that I do not at all realize yet that we are in S[outh] C[arolina]. It is all a strange wild dream, from which I am constantly expecting to awake. But I can write no more now. I am tired, and still feel the motion of the ship in my poor head. Good night, dear A!

Wednesday, Oct. 29. A lovely day, but rather cool, I sh'ld think, for the "sunny South." The ship still seals [sic] in my head, and everything is most unreal, yet I went to drive. We drove to Oaklands, our future home. It is very pleasantly situated, but the house is in rather a dilapidated condition, as are most of the houses here, and the [sic] yard and garden have a neglected look, when it is cleaned up, and the house made habitable I think it will be quite a pleasant place. There are some lovely roses growing there and quantities of ivy creeping along the ground, even under the house, in wild luxuriance.—The negroes on the place are very kind and polite. I think I shall get on amicably with them.

After walking about and talking with them, and plucking some roses and ivy to send home, we left Oaklands and drove to the school. It is kept by Miss Murray and Miss Towne in the little Baptist Church, which is beautifully situated in a grove of live oaks. Never saw anything more beautiful than these trees. It is strange that we do not hear of them at the North. They are the first objects that attract one's attention here. They are large, noble trees with small glossy green leaves. Their great beauty consists in the long bearded moss with which every branch is heavily draped. This moss is singularly beautiful, and gives a solemn almost funereal aspect to the trees.

We went into the school, and heard the children read and spell. The teachers tell us that they have made great improvement in a very short time, and I noticed with pleasure how bright, how eager to learn many of them seem. The singing delighted me most. They sang beautifully in their rich, sweet clear tones, and with that peculiar swaying motion which I had noticed before in the older people, and which seems to make their singing all the more effective. Besides several other tunes they sang "Marching Along" with much spirit, and then one of their own hymns "Down in the Lonesome Valley," which is sweetly solemn and most beautiful. Dear children! born in slavery, but free at last! May God preserve to you all the blessings of freedom, and may you be in every possible way fitted to enjoy them. My heart goes out to you. I shall be glad to do all that I can to help you.—

As we drove homeward I noticed that the trees are just beginning to turn; some beautiful scarlet berries were growing along the roadside; and everywhere the beautiful live oak with its moss drapery. The palmettos disappoint me much. Most of them have a very jagged appearance, and are yet stiff and ungraceful. The country is very level—as flat as that in eastern Penn[sylvania]. There are plenty of woods, but I think they have not the grandeur of our Northern woods. The cotton fields disappoint me too. They have a very straggling look, and the pods are small, not at all the great snowballs that I had imagined. Altogether the country w'ld be rather desolate looking were it not for my beautiful and evergreen live oaks.

Friday, Oct. 31. Miss T[owne] went to B[eaufort] to-day, and I taught for her. I enjoyed it much. The children are well-behaved and eager to learn. It will be a happiness to teach them.

I like Miss Murray so much. She is of English parentage, born in the Provinces. She is one of the most whole-souled warm-hearted women I ever met. I felt drawn to her from the first (before I knew she was English) and of course I like her none the less for that.

Miss Towne also is a delightful person. "A charming lady" Gen. Saxton calls her and my heart echoes the words. She is housekeeper, physician, everything, here. The most indispensable person on the place, and the people are devoted to her. . . . And indeed she is quite a remarkable young lady. She is one of the earliest comers, and has done much good in teaching and superintending the negroes. She is quite young; not more than twenty-two or three I sh'ld think, and is superintendent of two plantations. I like

her energy and decision of character. Her appearance too is very interesting.

Mr. S[oule] the Superintendent is a very kind, agreeable person. I like him.

Sunday, Nov. 2. Drove to church to-day,—to the same little Baptist Church that the school is held in. The people came in slowly. They have no way of telling the time. About eleven they had all assembled; the church was full. Old and young were there assembled in their Sunday dresses. Clean gowns on, clean head handkerchiefs, bright colored, of course, I noticed that some had even reached the dignity of straw hats, with bright feathers.

The services were very interesting. The minister, Mr. P[hillips] is an earnest N[ew] E[ngland] man. The singing was very beautiful. I sat there in a kind of trance and listened to it, and while I listened looked through the open windows into the beautiful grove of oaks with their moss drapery. "Ah wld that my tongue c'ld utter

The thoughts that arise in me."

But it cannot. The sermon was quite good. But I enjoyed nothing so much as the singing—the wonderful, beautiful singing. There can be no doubt that these people have a great deal of musical talent. It was a beautiful sight,—their enthusiasm. After the service two couples were married. Then the meeting was out. The various groups under the trees forming a very pretty picture.

We drove to the Episcopal Church afterwards where the aristocracy of Rebeldom used to worship. The building is much smaller than the others, but there is a fine organ there on which Miss W[?] played while some of the young Superintendents sang very finely, and then we came home.

It is all like a dream still, and will be for a long time, I suppose; a strange wild dream. When we get settled in our own house and I have fairly entered into teaching, perhaps I shall begin to realize it all. What we are to do for furniture I know not. Our sole possessions now consist of two bureaus and a bedstead. Mr. H[unn] had not time to get the mattresses in N[ew] York. So I suppose we must use blanket substitutes till we can do better. I am determined not to be discouraged at anything. I have never felt more hopeful, more cheerful than I do now—

Oaklands, Tuesday, Nov. 4. Came to our new home to-day. Felt sorry to leave the friends who have been so kind to us, but as they are only three miles distant hope to see them occasionally. But nobody here has much time for visiting.

Our house looks rather desolate; the only furniture consisting of two bureaus, three small pine tables and two chairs, one of which has a broken back. L[izzie Hunn] and I have manufactured a tolerable drugget out of some woolen stuff, red and black plaid, which will give our "parlor" a somewhat more comfortable look. I have already hung up my lovely Evangeline, and two or three other prints, and gathered some beautiful roses. This has been a busy day. A few more such and we hope that our home will begin to look homelike. I am tired, dear A. Good night, and God be with you.

Wednesday, Nov. 5. Had my first regular teaching experience, and to you and you only friend beloved, will I acknowledge that it was *not* a very pleasant one. Part of my scholars are very tiny,— babies, I call them—and it is hard to keep them quiet and interested while I am hearing the larger ones. They are too young even for the alphabet, it seems to me. I think I must write home and ask somebody to send me picture-books and toys to amuse them with. I fancied Miss T[owne] looked annoyed when, at one time the little ones were unusually restless. Perhaps it was only my fancy. Dear Miss M[urray] was kind and considerate as usual. She is very lovable. Well I *must* not be discouraged. Perhaps things will go on better tomorrow.

I am sure I enjoyed the walk to school. Through those lovely woods, just brightening to scarlet now: Met the ladies about halfway, and they gave me a drive to the church.

Lizzie H[unn] tells me that the store has been crowded all day. Her father hasn't had time to arrange his goods. I foresee that his store, to which people from all the neighboring plantations come,—will be a source of considerable interest and amusement.

We've established our household on—as we hope—a firm basis. We have *Rose* for our little maid-of-all-work, *Amaretta* for cook, washer, and ironer, and *Cupid,* yes Cupid himself, for clerk, oysterman and future coachman. I must also inform you dear A., that we have made ourselves a bed, whereon we hope to rest to-night, for rest *I* certainly did not last night, despite innumerable blankets designed to conceal and render inactive the bones of the bed. But said bones did so protrude that sleep was almost an impossibility to our poor little body.

Everything is still very, very strange. I am not at all home-sick. But it does seem *so* long since I saw some who are very dear, and I believe I am quite sick for want of a letter. But patience! patience! *That* is a luxury which cannot possibly be enjoyed before the last of next week.

Thursday, Nov. 6. Rained all day so that I c'ldn't go to school. Attended store part of the day. T'was crowded nearly all the time. It was quite amusing to see how eager the people are to buy. The bright handerchiefs—imitation—Madras —are an especial attraction. I think they were very quiet and orderly considering how crowded the place was.

This afternoon made another bed; and this eve. finished a very long letter to father, the first part of which was begun last month. I wish I c'ld see them all. It w[ou]ld be such a happiness. . . .

Cut out a dress to-day for an old woman— Venus,—who thanked and blessed me enough. Poor old soul. It was a pleasure to hear her say what a happy year this has been for her. "Nobody to whip me nor dribe me, and plenty to eat. Nebber had such a happy year in my life before." Promised to make a little dress for her great-grandchild—only a few weeks old. It shall be a bright pink calico, such as will delight the little free baby's eyes, when it shall be old enough to appreciate it.

Friday, Nov. 7. Had a lovely walk to school. The trees,—a few of them—are thinning beautifully now, but they have not in general the brilliant hues of the Northern woods. The mocking birds were singing sweetly this morn. I think my "babies" were rather more manageable to-day, but they were certainly troublesome enough.

This afternoon L[izzie] and I went round to the "quarters." Some of the people are really quite interesting, and all were pleasant and seemed glad to see us. One poor woman has a very sick child. The poor little thing is only a few months old, and is suffering dreadfully with whooping cough. It is pitiful to hear it moan. If our good doctor Miss T[owne] were only here. But she does not come to-day. . . .

Saturday, Nov. 8. Spent part of the morn. in the store which was more crowded than ever. So much gold and silver I've not seen for many months. These people must have been hoarding it up for a long time. They are rather unreasonable, and expect one to wait on a dozen at once. But it is not strange.

Miss T[owne] came this afternoon, and gave

medicine to Tilla's baby, which seems, I think, a little better; and to all the other children. Every one of them has the whooping cough.

I've put my books and a vase of lovely roses and oleanders on our little table. The fire burns brightly, and the little room looks quite cheerful and homelike. Have done some sewing and reading.

Monday, Nov. 10. We taught—or rather commenced teaching the children "John Brown," which they entered into eagerly. I felt to the full significance of that song being sung here in S[outh] C[arolina] by little negro children, by those whom he—the glorious old man—died to save. Miss T[owne] told them about him.

A poor mulatto man is in one of our people's houses, a man from the North, who assisted Mr. Phillips (a nephew of Wendell P.) when he was here, in teaching school; he seems to be quite an intelligent man. He is suffering from fever. I shall be glad to take as good care of him as I can. It is so sad to be ill, helpless and poor, and so far away from home. . . .

Thursday, Nov. 13. Was there ever a lovelier road than that through which part of my way to school lies? Oh, I wish you were here to go with me, *cher ami.* It is lined with woods on both sides. On the one tall stately pines, on the other the noble live oaks with their graceful moss drapery. And the road is carpeted with those brown odorous pine leaves that I love so well. It is perfectly lovely. I forgot that I was almost ill to day, while sauntering along, listening to the birds, and breathing the soft delicious air. Of the last part of the walk, through sun and sand, the less said the better.

Talked to the children a little while to-day about the noble Toussaint [L'Ouverture]. They listened very attentively. It is well that they sh'ld know what one of their own color c'ld do for his race. I long to inspire them with courage and ambition (of a noble sort,) and high purpose.

It is noticeable how very few mulattoes there are here. Indeed in our school, with one or two exceptions, the children are all black. A little mulatto child strayed into the school house yesterday—a pretty little thing, with large beautiful black eyes and lovely long lashes. But so dirty! I longed to seize and thoroughly cleanse her. The mother is a good-looking woman, but quite black. "Thereby," I doubt not, "hangs a tale."

This eve. Harry, one of the men on the place, came in for a lesson. He is most eager to learn, and is really a scholar to be proud of. He learns rapidly.

I gave him his first lesson in writing to-night, and his progress was wonderful. He held the pen almost perfectly right the first time. He will very soon learn to write, I think. I must inquire if there are not more of the grown people who w'ld like to take lessons at night. Whenever I am well enough it will be a real happiness to me to teach them.

Finished translating into French Adelaide Proctor's poem "A Woman's Question," which I like so much. It was an experiment, and I assure you, *mon ami,* tis a queer translation. But it was good practice in French. Shall finish this eve. by copying some of my Journal for dear Mary S[hepard].

Sunday, Nov. 16. Felt too tired to go to church to-day. Some of the grown people came in this morn. I read them the Sermon on the Mount. And then they sang some of their own beautiful hymns; among them "Down in the Lonesome Valley" which I like best of all. I want to hear it every day. This afternoon some of the children came in and sang a long time. Then I commenced teaching them the 23rd Psalm, which Miss M[urray] is teaching the children in school. Ours here are too ill with whooping cough to attend school.

I have enjoyed this day very much. For my own special benefit, have read and re-read my dear Mrs. E[lizabeth Barrett] Browning. Can anything be more exquisite than those Sonnets from the Portuguese. Is *any* man, even Browning himself, worthy of such homage from such a soul? yes, yes *he* is, I do believe. But few others are.

This eve. finished my Journal for Mary S[hepard]. Tis so voluminous, so badly written, and so stupid that I am ashamed to send it. But I suppose almost anything from this region w'ld be interesting to people at the N[orth] so it might as well go.—

Monday, Nov. 17. Had a dreadfully wearying day in school, of which the less said the better. Afterward drove with the ladies to "The Corner," a collection of negro houses, whither Miss T[owne] went on a doctoring expedition. The people there are very pleasant. Saw a little baby, just borne [sic] today—and another—old Venus' great grand-child for whom I made the little pink frock. These people are very gratiful [sic]. The least kindness that you do them they insist on repaying in some way. We have had a quantity of eggs and potatoes brought us despite our remonstrances. Today one of the women gave me some Tanias. Tania is a queer looking root. After it is boiled it looks like a potato, but is much larger. I don't like the taste.

Tuesday, Nov. 18. After school went to The Corner again. Stopped at old Susy's house to see some sick children. Old Susy is a character. Miss T[owne] asked her if she wanted her old master to come back again. Most emphatically she answered. "No *indeed,* missus, no indeed dey treat we too bad. Dey tuk ebery one of my chilen away from me. When we sick and c'ldnt work dey tuk away all our food from us; gib us nutten to eat. Dey's orful hard Missis." When Miss T[owne] told her that some of the people said they wanted their old masters to come back, a look of supreme contempt came to old Susy's withered face. "Dat's 'cause dey's got no sense den, missus," she said indignantly. Susy has any quantity of children and grandchildren, and she thanks God that she can now have some of them with her in her old age.

To-night gave Cupid a lesson in the alphabet. He is not a brilliant scholar, but he tries hard to learn, and so I am sure will succeed in time. A man from another plantation came in for a lesson. L[izzie] attended to him while I had Cupid. He knows his letters, and seems very bright.

Wednesday, Nov. 19. A steamer is in! Miss T[owne] had letters from Phila[delphia] to-day. The mail is not yet all distributed. If I don't get any I shall be *perfectly* desperate. But I surely will get some to-morrow. To-night had another pupil —Robert—brighter than Harry [Cupid]—not so bright as Harry. He will do well I think.—

Thursday, Nov. 20. . . . Wrote to-night to . . . [John Greenleaf] Whittier asking him to write a little Christmas hymn for our children to sing. I hope he will do it. . . .

Saturday, Nov. 22. Had the loveliest walk this afternoon to Mr. R[uggle]'s our nearest neighbor's. The path lay partly through beautiful woods principally pines and live oaks. The air was delicious, the sunlight bright, the brown pine leaves odorous as usual, and I noticed some maple [gum] leaves that had turned a rich dark, almost copper color. Plucked some for my dear Miss M[urray] whom I heard express a wish for some a day or two ago.

Found that Miss R[uggles] was not at home. They have a pleasant little place, rather more civilized looking than ours. Returning, just at sunset saw a beautiful sight. In some parts of the wood the branches of the live oak formed a perfect ceiling overhead and from them depended long sprays of that exquisite moss lighted up by the sun's last rays. I c'ld think only of some fairy palace, at first, then the sight suggested the Mammoth cave as I had seen it once in an excellent Panorama. Those sprays of moss, glowing in the sunlight, were perfect stalactites, as I saw them illuminated. If they lacked the sparkling crystals they quite made up for the loss in airy grace and lightness. I wanted you my dearest A.,—and several dear friends of mine who like you have a most keen and delicate perception of the beautiful —to look upon that scene with me. And since that c'ld not be, I longed to be an artist that I might make a sketch and send it to you.

Sunday, Nov. 23. Attended church to-day. T'was even a pleasanter experience than before. Saw several new arrivals there—old ones returned, rather—among them Mr. S[amuel] Phillips, a nephew of *the* Phillips. He has not the glorious beauty of the illustrious relative, but still has somewhat the Phillips style of face. He is not at all handsome; has bright red hair, but a pleasant face, and an air *distingue.*

After the sermon an old negro prayed a touching and most effective prayer. Then the minister read Gen. Saxton's Proclamation for Thanksgiving—which is grand—the very best and noblest that c'ld have been penned. I like and admire the Gen. more than ever now.

Six couples were married to-day. Some of the dresses were unique. Am sure one must have worn a cast-off dress of her mistress's. It looked like white silk covered with lace. The lace sleeves, and other trimmings were in rather a decayed state and the white cotton gloves were well ventilated. But the bride looked none the less happy for that. Only one had the slightest claim to good looks. And she was a demure little thing with a neat, plain silk dress on. T'was amusing to see some of the headdresses. One, of tattered flowers and ribbons, was very ridiculous. But no matter for that. I am *truly* glad that the poor creatures are trying to live right and virtuous lives. As usual we had some fine singing. It was very pleasant to be at church again. For two Sundays past I had not been, not feeling well.

This eve. our boys and girls with others from across the creek came in and sang a long time for us. Of course we had the old favorites "Down in the Lonesome Valley," and "Roll, Jordan, Roll," and "No man can hender me," and beside those several shouting tunes that we had not heard before; they are very wild and strange. It was impossible for me to understand many of the words although I asked them to repeat them for me. I only know that one had something about "De Nell Am Ringing." I think that was the refrain; and of another, some of the words were "Christ build the church widout no hammer nor nail." "Jehovah Halleluhiah," which is a grand thing, and "Hold the light," an especial favorite of mine —they sang with great spirit. The leader of the singing was Prince, a large black boy, from Mr. R[uggle]'s place. He was full of the shouting spirit, and c'ld not possibly keep still. It was amusing to see his gymnastic performances. They were quite in the Ethiopian Methodists' style. He has really a very fine bass voice. I enjoyed their singing so much, and sh'ld have enjoyed it so much more if some dear ones who are far away c'ld have listened it to [sic] with me. How delighted they would have been.

The effect of the singing has been to make me feel a little sad and lonely to-night. A yearning for congenial companionship *will* sometimes come over me in the few leisure moments I have in the house. T'is well they are so few. Kindness, most invariable,—for which I am most grateful—I meet with constantly but congeniality I find not at all in this house. But silence, foolish murmurer. He who knows all things knows that it was for no selfish motive that I came here, far from the few who are so dear to me. Therefore let me not be selfish now. Let the work to which I have solemnly pledged myself fill up my whole existence to the exclusion of all vain longings.

Tuesday, Nov. 25. . . . Miss M[urray] is teaching the children in school "Sound the Loud Timbrel." They like the words so much that I think they will soon learn them.

Saw the [Anti-Slavery] Standard to-night. Twas welcome as the face of an old friend. Read also a few numbers of "Salem Chapel," which is as intensely interesting and exciting as ever. This eve. gave Harry and Rob[ert] their lesson.

Yesterday had some visitors in school—Miss T[?] and her brother, and a Miss Merrick from Syracuse. I liked the latter's face. She looks like an earnest worker. . . .

Wednesday, Nov. 26. Miss T[owne] was not at school, and Miss M[urray] and I had sole charge. After school told the children a little about the sun, stars etc., and then Miss M[urray] taught them some verses of "Sound the Loud Timbrel" which she wants them to learn for the New Year. Had a lovely walk in the woods gathering leaves and berries wherewith to decorate the church to-morrow.

Thursday, Nov. 27. Thanksgiving Day. This, according to Gen. Saxton's noble Proclamation, was observed as a day of Thanksgiving and praise. It has been a lovely day—cool, delicious air, golden, gladdening sunlight, deep blue sky, with soft white clouds floating over it. Had we no other causes the glory and beauty of the day alone make it a day for which to give thanks. But we have other causes, great and glorious, which unite to make this peculiarly a day of thanksgiving and praise. It has been a general holiday. According to Gen. Saxton's orders an animal was killed on each plantation that the people might to-day eat fresh meat, which is a great luxury to them, and indeed to all of us here.

This morning a large number—Superintendents, teachers and freed people, assembled in the little Baptist church. It was a sight that I shall not soon forget—that crowd of eager, happy black faces from which the shadow of slavery had forever passed. "Forever free!" "Forever free!" Those magical words were all the time singing themselves in my soul, and never before have I felt so truly grateful to God. The singing was, as usual, very beautiful. I thought I had never heard my favorite "Down in the Lonesome Valley" so well sung.

After an appropriate prayer and sermon by Rev. Mr. Phillips, Gen. Saxton made a short but spirited speech to the people—urging the young men to enlist in the regiment now forming under Col. T. W. Higginson. That was the first intimation I had had of Mr. H[igginson]'s being down here. I am greatly rejoiced thereat. He seems to me of all fighting men the one best fitted to command a regiment of colored soldiers. The mention of his [name] recalled the happy days passed last summer in Massachusetts, when day after day, in the streets of W[orcester] we used to see the indefatigable *Capt.* H[igginson] drilling his white company. I never saw him so full of life and energy—entering with his whole soul into his work—without thinking what a splendid general he w'ld make. And that too may come about. Gen. Saxton said to-day that he hoped to see him commander of an army of black men. The Gen. told the people how nobly Mr. H[igginson] had stood by Anthony Burns, in the old dark days, even suffering imprisonment for his sake; and assured [them] that they might feel sure of meeting no injustice under the leadership of such a man; that he w'ld see to it that they were not wronged in any way.

Then he told them the story of Robert Small[s], and added. "To-day Rob[ert] came to see me. I asked him how he was getting on in the store which he is keeping for the freed people. He said he was doing very well—making fifty dollars a week, sometimes, "But" said he "Gen. I'm going to stop keeping store. I'm going to enlist." "What," said I. "Are you going to enlist when you can make fifty doll[ar]s a week keeping store?" "Yes Sir," he replied "I'm going to enlist as a private in the black regiment. How can I expect to keep my freedom if I'm not willing to fight for it? Suppose the Secesh sh'ld get back here again? what good w'ld my fifty doll[ar]s do me then? Yes, Sir I sh'ld enlist if I were making a thousand dollars a week.

Mrs. [Frances D.] Gage then made a few beautiful and earnest remarks. She told the people about the slaves in Santa Cruz, how they rose and conquered their masters, and declared themselves free, and no one dared to oppose them. And how, soon after, the governor rode into the marketplace and proclaimed emancipation to all people of the Danish W[est] I[ndies]. She then made a beautiful appeal to the mothers, urging them not to keep back their sons from the war fearing they might be killed but to send them forth willingly and gladly as she had done hers, to fight for liberty. It must have been something very novel and strange to them to hear a woman speak in public, but they listened with great attention and seemed much moved by what she said.

Then Gen. Saxton made a few more remarks. I think what he said will have much effect on the young men here. There has been a good deal of distrust about joining the regiment. The soldiers were formerly so unjustly treated by the Government. But they trust Gen. Saxton. He told them what a victory the black troops had lately won on the Georgian coast, and what a great good they had done for their race in winning; they had proved to their enemies that the black man can and will fight for his freedom. After the Gen. had done speaking the people [sang] "Marching Along," with great spirit.

After church there was a wedding. This is a very common occurrence here. Of course the bridal costumes are generally very unique and comical, but the principal actors are fortunately quite unconscious of it, and look so proud and happy while enjoying this—one of the many

privileges that freedom has bestowed upon them —that it is quite pleasant to see them.

Beside the Gen. and Mrs. G[age] there were several other strangers present;—ladies from the North who come down here to teach.

In Miss T[owne]'s box came my parcel—so long looked for—containing letters from my dear Mary S[hepard], [and] Aunt M[argaretta] . . . and a Liberator, the first that I have seen since leaving home. How great a pleasure it is to see it. It is familiar and delightful to look upon as the face of an old friend. It is of an old date—Oct. 31st but it is not the less welcome for that. And what a significant fact it is that one may now sit here in safety—here in the rebellious little Palmetto State and read the Liberator, and display it to one's friends, rejoicing over it in the fulness of one's heart as a very great treasure. It is fitting that we sh'ld give to this—the Pioneer Paper in the cause of human rights—a hearty welcome to the land where, until so recently, those rights have been most barbarously trampled upon. We do not forget that it is in fact directly traceable to the exertions of the editor of this paper and those who have labored so faithfully with him, that the Northern people now occupy in safety the S[outh] C[arolina] Shore; that freedom now blesses it, that it is, for the first time, a place worth living in.

This eve. commenced a long letter to Mr. [William Lloyd] Garrison, composed partly of to-day's journalism, and partly of other things that I thought w'ld interest him. He can publish it in the Liberator, if he thinks it worth printing, which I do not.

Truly this has been a delightful day to me. I recal [*sic*] with pleasure the pleasant Thanksgiving Days passed in N[ew] E[ngland] in Mass[achusetts] which I believe I am in the habit of considering as *all* N[ew] E[ngland]. But this has been the happiest, the most jubilant Thanksgiving Day of my life. We hear of cold weather and heavy snowstorms up in the North land. But here roses and oleanders are blooming in the open air. Figs and oranges are ripening, the sunlight is warm and bright, and over all shines gloriously the blessed light of Freedom—Freedom forevermore!—

Friday, Nov. 28.   Kept store nearly all day, and found constant sources of interest and amusement in it. I had nearly forgotten to tell you, dear A., to tell you about a very old man—Dr. Crofts, they call him—(his name is Scipio rightly) who came into the store yesterday. He was rejoicing over the new state of things here, and said to Mr. Hunn. "Don't hab me feelings hurt now. Used to hab me feelings hurt all de time. But don't hab em hurt now, no more." Poor old soul! We rejoiced with him that he and many like him no longer have their "feelings hurt," as in the old time.

This eve. finished my letter to Mr. G[arrison]. . . . Mr. H[unn] brought me a paper from the office—a Boston Transcript, sent by Sarah P[utnam]. It is pleasant to see a Boston paper.

Saturday, Nov. 29. Have decorated our little sitting room with ivy and autumn leaves and berries till it looks quite bright. Have hung a wreath of ivy around my lovely [picture] Eva[ngeline] which makes her, if possible, lovelier than ever. We have a clock, which is quite a treasure here. It is like the face of an old friend. . . . This eve. devoured "Aurora Leigh" for the *very manyth* time. Every time I read it I discover new beauty in it.

Life Among the Freedmen

November 30, 1862–February 14, 1863

Sunday, Nov. 30. Farewell Autumn! It seems so very long since we came here, and yet, as they pass, the days seem short enough. But to look back upon the time seems very long.

Attended church. Mr. Thorpe, one of the young Superintendents, a N[ew] E[ngland] man, was so kind as to send his wagon for us. L[izzie] did not feel well enough to go, but I went and had a very pleasant drive with old Jack—Mr. T[horpe]'s foreman, as he told me. He is a *very* polite old man, and seemed quite pleased and proud at driving a lady. It was very kind in Mr. T[horpe]. I like him much, and Mr. L. Phillips also. The latter invited me to come and get some slips from his garden. And oh, dear A. he has japonicas in bloom. I shall not go, of course, but live in hourly hope that he will be moved by the spirit to bring me some japonicas.

Mr. P[hillips], the minister, is an excellent man, but certainly not an interesting preacher. To-day he was unusually dull, and I got very tired. I thought I sh'ld certainly go to sleep. Fortunately I did not. We had a bit of a Sunday School. Taught the children a hymn—"Heaven is my Home." After church three couples were married.

This eve. heard Harry read, then the children came in, and sang for us, and had a regular

"shout" in the piazza, of which, of course Prince was the leader. He is the most comical creature I ever saw. Besides the old songs they sang two new ones, so singular that I must try to note down the words—some of them. But of the tune and manner of singing it is impossible to give any idea. The first is—

> Old elder, old elder, wher hab you been
> When de gospel been flourishin
> All over dis world
> I have somethin fur to tell you
> From the secret of my heart
>   Marry King Jesus
> And no more to part.

Then

> Young sister, young sister where hab you been etc.
>   "   bruder   " bruder "   "   "   "
>   "   member " member "   "   "   "

Another commences

> My mudder's gone to glory and I want to git dere too
> Till dis warfare's over hallelujah
>   Chorus—Hallelujah, hallelujah
> Till dis warfare's over, hallelujah, etc.
>   All de members gone to glory, etc.
>   Then chorus.
> Cinda gnaw my sin, hallelujah.
>   Chorus

The singular hymn that I heard them sing in school one day, about the graveyard begins thus.—

> I wonder where my mudder gone,
>   Sing oh graveyard!
> Graveyard ought to know me
>   Sing Jerusalem!
> Oh carry my mudder in de graveyard
>   Sing etc.
> Oh grass grow in de graveyard
>   Sing etc.
> Lay my body in de graveyard
>   Sing etc.

It is a very strange wild thing.

I am quite in love with one of the children here —little Amaretta who is neice [*sic*] to our good old Amaretta. She is a cunning little kittenish thing with such a gentle demure look. She is not quite black, and has pretty close hair, but delicate features. She is bright too. I love the child. Wish I c[ou]ld take her for my own.

Am in a writing mood to-night, and think I will give to you, my dearest A. a more minute description of the people around than I've yet given to anyone. I shall write down their names too, that I may remember them always. Don't know them thoroughly enough yet to say much about their characters.

To begin with the older ones. First there is old Harriet. She is a very kind, pleasant old soul. Comes from Darien, G[eorgi]a. Her parents were Africans. She speaks a *very* foreign tongue. Three of her children have been sold from her. Her master's son killed somebody in a duel, and was obliged to "pay money" H[arriet] says. I suppose she means to give bail. And she and her children were sold to this place, to raise the money. Then there is her daughter Tillah. Poor creature, she has a dear little baby, Annie, who for weeks has been dangerously ill with whooping cough and fever. Our good Miss T[owne] attends it, and does all that can be done, but the baby is still very ill. For Tillah's sake I hope it will get well. She is devoted to it night and day. T[illah]'s husband is a gallant looking young soldier—a member of the black regiment.

His mother, Bella, is rather a querulous body. But who can blame her? She has had enough to try her sorely. One by one her children at a tender age have been dragged from her to work in the cotton fields. She herself has been made to work when most unfit for it. She has had to see her own children cruelly beaten. Is it strange that these things sh'ld have embittered her? But she has much of the milk of human kindness left her yet. She nurses the poor baby faithfully, and often, old as she is, sits up the entire night with it. Harry is another of her sons. I have told you, dear A. how bright, how eager to learn, he is. His wife, Tamar, is a good-natured, easy soul. She has several nice little children, and the baby— Mary Lincoln—as Mr. R[uggles] the Superintendent has named her—is a very cunning little creature, an especial pet of ours.

Celia is one of the best women on the place. She is a cripple. Her feet and limbs were so badly frozen by exposure that her legs were obliged to be amputated just above the knees. But she manages to get about almost as actively as any of the others. Her husband, Thomas, has been a soldier, and is now quite ill with pneumonia. She had several children—Rose, who is our little maid, Olivia the eldest, Dolly, a bright little thing who goes to school with me every morn. and who likes to go. Lastly Aiken, whose proper name is Thomas. He is an odd lit[tle] fellow, very much spoiled. Amaretta, Celia's sister is our laundress and cook. I like her very much.

Then there is Wilhelmina, a mulatto (the others are all black). She comes from Virginia, and speaks therefore quite intelligibly. She is a good sensible woman, and both she and her husband Rob[er]t, —who is one of my night pupils—are most anxious for their three little ones to learn.

Cupid our major-domo, is as obliging as possible. A shrewd fellow, who knows well what he is about. His wife Patience, is Tamar's sister, and lives across the creek at Pollywana. Their children —two of them—come to our school. They are good scholars.

I do enjoy hearing Cupid and Harry tell about the time that the Secesh had to flee. The time of the "gun shoot," as they call the taking of Bay Point, which is opposite Hilton Head. It delights them greatly to recal [*sic*] that time. Their master had the audacity to venture back even while the Union Troops were occupying Beaufort. H[arry] says he tried to persuade him to go back with him, assuring him that the Yankees w'ld shoot them all when they came. "Bery well sur," he replied "if I go wid you I be good as dead, so if I got to dead, I might's well dead here as anywhere. So I'll stay and wait for the Yankees." He told me that he knew all the time that his master was not telling the truth. Cupid says the master told the people to get all the furniture together and take it over to Pollywana, and to stay on that side themselves. "So" says Cupid, "dey c'ld jus' swap us all up in a heap and geder us up an' put us in de boat. And he told me to row Patience and de chilens down to a certain pint, and den I c'ld come back if I choose." "Jus' as if I was gwine to be sich a goat" adds Cupid, with a look and gesture of ineffable contempt. The *finale* of the story is that the people left the premises and hid themselves so that when the master returned not one of all his "faithful servants" was to be found to go into slavery with him, and he was obliged to return, a disappointed, but it is to be hoped, a wiser man.

Monday, Dec. 1. The first day of winter. It is hard to realize it here. Tis almost as warm as June to-day, and almost as lovely.

Tuesday, Dec. 2. After school went with the children to the Episcopal Church, where Miss M[urray] played on the organ "Sound the Loud Timbrel," while the children sang. They enjoyed it very much. Fear some of it is rather too difficult for them, but Miss M[urray] is determined they shall learn it, and I hope they will. It w'ld be so very appropriate.

The road to the church is very beautiful. It is lined with the noble live oaks, and carpeted with brown pine leaves. The woods looked particularly inviting to-day. One tree—a green tree was all a'flame in the sunlight. Every leaf looked as if it were steeped in rosy wine. Have rarely seen so beautiful a sight. Miss M[urray] and I secured as many of the leaves as we c'ld carry. I wanted to bring away the whole tree.

Found a letter awaiting me at home—a kind letter from my dear Mrs. P[utnam]. It was very pleasant to hear from her. But why does not Henry write? I feel very anxious at not hearing from him. Fear he must be ill. Every day I expect a letter from him, and every day, am disappointed. Has he forgotten his stupid little sister, I wonder? Or is he ill. I do wish I c'ld know. This eve. gave Harry his lesson.

Wednesday, Dec. 3. Wrote to Jane this morn —Miss T[owne] was so kind as to let me have her [Anti-Slavery] Standard of Nov. 22. It is full of interesting matter. I *devoured* Mr. Phillips' fine Music Hall speech. Mr. French's account of the victory won by the blacks troops on the Georgian coast is very interesting. They did splendidly. I feel quite proud of them. See that Lucy McKim has set to music some of the songs of the "contrabands" here. She has sent "Poor Rosy, poor gal" as the first of a series, to Dwight's Journal [of Music]. It is much liked.

Thursday, Dec. 4. After school went again to the Episcopal Church with the children. Miss M[urray] and I preferred walking. Gathered some more of those exquisite leaves. After the children had done singing and all had gone, stayed some time and practiced on the organs—some of my old pieces, and one or two from the book of Church music, among them "Sound the Loud Timbrel" which I am anxious to learn so as to relieve Miss M[urray]. Tis hard for me to learn the simplest thing. Have forgotten so many of my notes. Had a good long walk home in the light rain, which I enjoyed much.

Heard to my surprise, that Wilhelmina has a little girl. Shall suggest as a name, Jessie Fremont, dear to all lovers of freedom.

Friday, Dec. 5. Rained all day so that I c[ou]ldn't go to school. Has been a sad day. Heard this afternoon of the death of the young Mr. Phillips of whom I've already spoken to you. It was very sudden; after only a few day's illness. Do not know when anything has made me feel so sad. He was a good young man, much loved by all

the people. Saw him last Sunday at church in perfect health. And now he is dead. My heart aches for his poor mother. He was an only son. It will be a terrible shock to her. It has cast a gloom over every thing here. His people grieve for him much.

Another death—to-night. One of the old men has just come in to tell us of the death of his little grandson—Hercules—or "Harkles," as they call it. The little fellow has been ill a long time with whooping cough and fever; and now he has gone to rest.

Sunday, Dec. 7. Poor Mr. P[hillips] was buried to-day, or rather the funeral services were said at the church. The body is to be sent home. Was not well enough to go, but Mr H[unn] says there were many people there, and that they were much affected. Everybody who knew him loved him. His poor, poor mother I can only think of her with her aching heart.

Little "Harkles" was buried, across the creek, this morn. This afternoon the people had a meeting in front of his grandparents' cabin. There was singing—a kind of funeral chant—very sad and dismal, and then an old preacher made a prayer, and afterwards a few remarks. I did not stay to hear him but went in to see poor Tillah's baby, who is worse to-day. The poor little creature looks very ill. I fear poor Tillah must lose it.

This eve. wrote a long letter to Henry. We did not have our usual singing. The children said it was too cold. And truly it has been wintry to-day. I cant get warm.

Monday, Dec. 8. Almost froze in school to-day. It was intensely cold. Grew milder at night, and the children came in. They have been singing *gloriously* all the eve. Several new hymns were sung. I will try to note them down for you dear A. I cant describe to you the effect that the singing has on me to-night. I believe I was quite *lifted out* of myself. Oh it was glorious! They all sing beautifully; but one of our girls, Grace, has the strongest voice for a child that I ever heard. And Aaron—the leader has really a magnificent voice. I want you dearest, I want everybody to hear his wonderful singing. . . .

Thursday, Dec. 11. After lessons we went again to the Epis[copal] Church and practiced the hymn with the children. The woods around seemed more beautiful than ever. I longed to explore some of those lovely paths.

Came home, and soon afterward, to my great grief, heard that poor Tillah's dear little baby was dead. It was really a shock to me; for only this morn. we thought the little creature seemed better. I hastened at once to the cabin. The baby had just died, and lay on old Nella's lap, looking as if it were sleeping sweetly. The poor mother sat by looking so very sad. My heart aches for her. During eight weeks she has been constantly devoted to this child—her only little girl—and we hoped she w'ld be rewarded by having it spared to her. But it has gone to heaven. It was one of the loveliest, most interesting babies I ever saw. We are going to bury it to-morrow, over at Polawany; I'm so sorry that William, its father, will not get to see it. It looks very lovely. Its death is a great grief to its mother and grandparents, and a sorrow to us all.

Friday, Dec. 12. This morn. Mr. R[uggles] beaming with delight, informed me that there was a large mail in by the "Star of the South." I'm afraid I answered somewhat impatiently that I was disgusted with mails, and that I wasn't going to expect any more. I had been so often disappointed. Nevertheless I *did* expect, despite myself. I did hope for those letters this time. And when we heard that there were letters for us at The Oaks, we at once despatched our trusty Cupid there. With what a beating heart did I await his coming. Calm outwardly, but what a flutter of expectation within. I never sh'ld have thought that I sh'ld become so *insane* about letters.

At last Cupid came, and only *one* letter for me, and that not from home. It was entirely unexpected —from Mr. McK[im]. Certainly it was very kind in him to write to me. He reminds me that he expects to have a line from me. And indeed I ought to have written to him before. But I am *so* disappointed. Why do I not hear from Mary S[hepard]? I thought she w'ld certainly have written to me during her vacation. I am very much troubled at not hearing from her, and from H[enry]. Aunt M[argaretta] has probably written and put her letter in the box, which I suppose will not get here for a month. I am quite sick at heart to-night, and must go to bed. . . .

Sunday, Dec. 14. What a night last night was! A night worth telling you about, dear A. We retired early. I was very sleepy, but what with the headache, the fleas, and Miss H[unn]'s *tremendous* snoring I got very nervous, and it was a long time before I c'ld get to sleep. At last sleep came. It seemed to me that I hadn't slept more than ten minutes when I was awakened by what seemed to me terrible screams coming from the direction of the Quarters. Three or four times they were repeated, and then, with infinite difficulty I succeeded in awaking Miss Hunn. We both heard the shrieks repeated. I thought somebody was insane or dying, or that something terrible had happened. Sometimes I thought it might be that the rebels had forced a landing, and were trying to carry off the people. We were in a state of great alarm; and sleep was impossible. At last the sounds ceased. And then near day, I had a short and troubled sleep which did me no good. Consequently I felt rather wretched this morn. but the day was so beautiful [I] determined to go to church.

L[izzie Hunn] and I started, but met Mr. T[horpe]'s wagon in the lane, coming for us. How very kind he is. But I am hardly willing to be under such an obligation to a stranger. And yet we can't very well refuse. How very sad Mr. T[horpe] looked to-day. I know he must greatly miss Mr. Phillips, with whom he was so intimate. I pity him.

There were several new arrivals at church to-day. Among them Miss T[owne]'s sister—Miss Rosa T[owne]. She does not look at all like Miss Laura. Is very fair, and has light hair; an English looking person, as I told her sister. A Miss Ware was also there. . . . A lovely but good face. . . .

Nearly everybody was looking gay and happy; and yet I came home with the blues. Threw myself on the bed, and for the first time since I have been here, felt very lonely and pitied myself. But I have reasoned myself into a more sensible mood and am better now. Let me not forget again that I came not here for friendly sympathy or for anything else but to work, and to work hard. Let me do that faithfully and well. To-night answered Mr. McK[im]'s letter, and commenced one to my dear A[nnie] about whom I feel very anxious.

There, dear A, I have forgotten to tell you the cause of our fright last night. Two of the colored soldiers had come to visit their friends who live across the creek. And they blew a kind of whistle that they have so that somebody on the opposite side might send a boat over for them. That was the shrieking we heard. And it seems we were the only people who heard it on the place. And yet it was heard across the creek. They must be sound sleepers here. The rebels w'ld have a good chance to land without being discovered.

Monday, Dec. 15. Had a perfectly *immense* school to-day. 147., of whom I had 58, at least two thirds of whom were tiny A. B. C. people.

Hardly knew what to do with them at first. But I like a large school. It is inspiriting. Miss Rosa T[owne] was there. Had a good long talk with her while her sister and Miss M[urray] went doctoring. Like her exceedingly. She is very social and enthusiastic. She is delighted with things down here. Never heard the children sing so well as they did to-day. There were so many of them. It was quite grand. . . .

Wednesday, Dec. 17. This eve. Mr. R[uggles] . . . spent a little time with us. I like Mr. R[uggles]. He seems to me a whole-souled kind hearted man. The negroes like him much. I asked him a little about the people on his plantations. Some are industrious, but many are not inclined to work, he says. But he thinks it is because they are so ir-regularly and poorly paid. He thinks if they were promptly and fully paid they w'ld work willingly. I think he is a true friend of the people; but some of the Sup[erintendent]s seem to be strongly pre-judiced against them, and they have a contemptu-ous way of speaking of them that I do not like. It shows a lack of sympathy with them. Such people sh'ld not come here.

Miss H[unn] told me an interesting story of a man who was in the store this afternoon. He had been carried off by the rebels about a year ago and left a wife and children on this island. It was not until a short time since that he had a chance to get away from Jacksonboro'—the place to which he had been taken. He and two relatives, a man and a woman, got away in the night while the family were in bed. They traveled a long distance on foot, and at last reached a stream, which they had no convenience for crossing. He made a kind of raft out of a board and some part of a ruined house, and they crossed in safety. They concealed themselves in the woods during the day, and traveled at night. They came to another stream, and again he built a raft, this time from the roof of the piazza of an old house near. On this they crossed to little Edisto, where they procured a boat from a boat-house and in this went to the blockading fleet. The captain of one of the gun-boats took them and provided them with a boat on which they came to this island. He said it was "almost like death" to his family to see him. They had feared they sh'ld never see him again. He expressed himself very grateful to the Lord for his escape. He said the Lord had been merciful to him. He was a God of mercy and Justice. He said "Put your faith in the Lord and . . . he will give you talents to do anything." They were several

days making their escape, during which they lived on hominy of which they carried a peck in tin buckets.

Thursday, Dec. 18. A truly *wintry* day. I had not half as many scholars as usual. It was too cold for my "babies" to venture out. But altogether we had nearly a hundred. They were unusually bright to-day, and sang with the greatest spirit. "Sound the Loud Tim," was a grand success.

After school the children went into a little cabin near, where they had kindled a fire, and had a grand "shout." While they were performing, two officers rode up, and asked Miss M[urray] if they might look on. She assented, and they dismounted, and came to the cabin door. The children stopped at first, evidently a little alarmed at the presence of soldiers, then the latter spoke so kindly to them that at last they were reassured, and went on with their "shout" with great spirit. The visitors seemed much interested and amused. . . .

Friday, Dec. 19. Miss M[urray] and I had school to ourselves. Miss T[owne] was not able to come, on account of the illness of her sister and Miss——— [illegible]. Had 127. T'was terribly cold. Mr. Palmer, one of the other teachers on the island, came in towards the close of school. He very kindly assisted us to put away our books. I was pleasantly disappointed in him. He seems much more agreeable than he looks.

Spent most of the afternoon in the store. Had a crowd. Enjoyed it very much. Felt so tired that I went to bed at seven, and consequently missed seeing Mr. and Miss Ruggles who spent the eve. here. Am sorry, for I like them.

Saturday, Dec. 20. Went round to see the people, of whom I haven't seen so much this week, being even unusually busy. Had as usual a very pleasant time talking with them all, big and little.

Came home, and worked busily. Made before school this morn. a red flannel jacket for poor old Harriet who is far from well. The good old woman and her husband seemed very grateful. I wish I c'ld do ten times as much for these people.

This afternoon a soldier, a private from the 8th Maine, came in, and we gave him some dinner. The poor fellow seemed glad to get into a com-fortable house, and talked about his home and his family quite confidentially, and told us how his little brothers ran out when he went to visit his home. He seemed a simple, kindly, good hearted fellow, and I was glad that we gave him a good dinner. These poor privates have rather a hard time of it, I fear. They look weary and forlorn, while the *officers* have a most prosperous, well-to-do look. . . .

Sunday, Dec. 21. Went to church, and victimized myself sitting in a cold church, and listening to the dullest of sermons, but was amply rewarded after church when Mr. Severance came from B[eaufort] and I had four letters—from dear Mary S[hepard], and Hattie [Purvis] . . . and, last and best of all, the kindest letter from the noble Whittier, and with it a beautiful little hymn for our children to sing at the Celebration. Also his photograph—a perfect likeness. How very, very kind it was in him to write it; when he was ill too. It grieves me to hear that his dear sister is ill also. She sends me the kindest messages. I am very, very much obliged to Mr. W[hittier] for everything but his sending my letter to the Transcript, as Mary S[hepard] tells me he did. He ought not to have done that. It was not worth it. How dear Miss M[urray] and I rejoiced over the hymn. With what pleasure we will teach our little ones to sing it.

Monday, Dec. 22. Commenced teaching the children Whittier's hymn. We told them who had written it; what a great friend he is to them, and that he had written it *expressly* for them, whereat they seemed greatly pleased. After school, with some of the larger children we three went into the woods in search of evergreens to decorate the church. Had a delightful ramble and got a quantity of greens. . . .

Tuesday, Dec. 23. We commenced decorating the church, and worked hard till dark. They w'ld insist upon my dressing the pulpit, which I was unwilling to do, for that is the most conspicuous place. Finished it to-day. Made a drapery all around it with the lovely hanging moss, and a heading of casino berries and holly. It looks quite pretty. Came home tired but sat up till after 11 sewing on the little aprons for Christmas presents. I *cannot* realize that Christmas is so near.

Wednesday, Dec. 24. Called the children together, and let them sing for some time and then dismissed them and devoted ourselves to finishing the decorations. Miss M[urray] and Miss T[owne] made the festoons, while I made wreaths for the walls. In the afternoon Miss W[are] came, bringing evergreen letters of the words "His people are Free." . . . It was quite dark when we got through. Miss W[are] was so kind as to drive me home. Sat up till after midnight, finishing my little

Christmas gifts. Saw Christmas morn. But it does not seem like Christmas to me.

Christmas Day 1862. A bright and lovely Christmas day. We were waked early by the people knocking at our window and shouting "Merry Christmas." After breakfast we went out and distributed the presents;—to each of the babies a bright red dress, and to little Jessie a white apron trimmed with crotchet braid, and to each of the other children an apron and an orange. To each of the workers a pie—an apple pie, which pleased them much.

Then we went to school. How pretty the evergreens looked in the bright light, after we had thrown open the windows. T'was a long time before the other teachers got there, and I had to keep all the children from getting restless. I kept them out of doors, and had them sing old songs and new. They sang with great spirit. After the others came, we opened school, and at once commenced distributing the presents. First Miss M[urray]'s class, then mine, then Miss T[owne]'s. Most of the children were much delighted with their gifts, and well they might be, for they were very useful ones,—principally dresses for the girls, and material for shirts and pantaloons for the boys. For the larger ones, also there were little bags, nicely fitted out with sewing utensils which Miss M[urray] and Miss T[owne] arranged. The larger children behaved well, and by great exertions I managed to keep the "babies" quiet.

After the gifts were distributed, they were addressed by Lieut. Col. Billings of the 1st reg[iment] S[outh] C[arolina] Vol[unteers]. He is a N[ew] E[ngland] man of very gentlemanly and pleasing manners.—A good man, and much interested in the people, I sh'ld think. I liked him. Then Mr. Fairfield [?] spoke to them about the birth of Christ. Afterward they sang; Among other things, "John Brown," Whittier's "Hymn," "Sing, oh Graveyard," and "Roll, Jordan Roll." There was no one present beside the teachers, our household, [Lt.] Col. B[illings] [,] Mr. T[horpe], Mr. F[airfield] and Miss Rosa [Towne] and Miss W[are].

I enjoyed the day very much. Was too excited and interested to feel weariness then, but am quite exhausted to-night. The children have been in, singing for us. My pet *petite* Amaretta has a sweet voice and quite strong for such a little one. She was full of music to-night. "All I want to do is sing and shout" she said to me with her pretty, dimply smile. There is something very bewitching about that child. All the children had the shouting spirit to-night. They had several grand shouts in the entry. "Look upon the Lord," which they sang to-night, seems to me the most beautiful of all their shouting tunes. There is something in it that goes to the depths of one's soul.—I am weary and must stop.

Dear friends, up North! my heart is with you to-night. What w'ld I not give for one look at your dear faces, one grasp of your kindly hands! Dear ones! I pray with my whole heart that this may have been to you a very, very happy Christmas.

Friday, Dec. 26. Kept store nearly all day. I like it occasionally. It amuses and interests me. There was one very sensible man in to-day, whose story interested me much. He had been a carpenter, and had been taken up by his master on the mainland, on "the main," as they call it, to help build houses to which the families of the rebels might retreat when the Yankees sh'ld come. His master sent him back again to this island to bring back a boat and some of the people. He was provided with a pass. On reaching the island, he found that the Union troops had come, so he determined (indeed he had determined before) to remain here with his family, as he knew his master w'ld not dare to come back after them. Some of his fellow servants whom he had left on the "main," hearing that the Union troops had come resolved to try to make their escape. They found a boat of the master's, out of which a piece about six feet square had been cut. In the night, secretly, they went to the boat which had been sunk near the edge of the creek, measured the hole, and went to the woods and, after several nights' work, made a piece large enough to fit in. With this they mended the boat, by another night's work, and then sunk it in the same position in which they had found it. The next night five of them embarked, and after passing through many perils in the shape of the enemy's boats, near which they were obliged to pass, and so making very slow progress, for they c'ld travel only at night, and in the day time, ran their boat close up to the shore, out of sight— they at last passed the enemy's lines and reached one of our gunboats in safty [sic]. They were taken on board, and their wants attended to, for their provisions had given out and they were much exhausted. After being there some time they were sent to this island, where their families, who had feared they w'ld never see them again welcomed them rejoicingly. I was much interested in the

story of their escape, and give it for yr especial benefit, Dear A.

Spent the eve. in making wreaths for our windows and my lovely [picture] Eva[ngeline]. . . .

A letter from Sarah P[utnam] delights me much, for it tells me that my dear friend Dr. Rogers, sailed last week for P[ort] R[oyal] so of course he has come in this steamer. I c'ld clap my hands and shout for joy. I am so very, very glad. This is the very place for him, and is he of all men, the man for the place. He is to be surgeon in Col. H[igginson]'s reg[iment] S[outh] C[arolina] Vol-[unteers]. . . . I am most impatient to see him.

Sat. Dec. 27. A rather dreary day. So the less said about it the better. Worked quite hard. The Miss T[owne]s and Miss M[urray] paid us a brief visit. Capt. H[ooper] whom everybody likes, has come, and brought me a letter, which I rec'd wonderingly from Miss M[urray]'s hands. The handwriting was strange to me. It was postmarked "Boston." On opening it I found it to be from a stranger—a lady in W[est] Gloucester, who says she has read with interest my letter in the paper, and expresses her great interest in the work here. A very kind and pretty letter. Enclosed in it was a "Proclamation Song," written by a friend of hers, to be sung to the air "Glory Hallelujah," on 1st Jan. Not exquisite poetry, but a very good and appropriate song. It touched [me] receiving such a letter from a stranger. I think I must write and thank her for it. Had a lovely walk in the woods this morn. Twas almost like June.

Sunday, Dec. 28. At church had the pleasure of seeing Gen. S[axton] and his father, who has come down to visit him. The Gen[eral] presented him to me. He is a pleasant old gentleman, and spoke warmly in praise of Dr. R[ogers] who came on the same steamer with him. His nephew James R[ogers] accompanies him. Saw also the much loved Capt. Hooper, whose looks and manners I like much. He made a very good speech to the people, as also did Gen. S[axton] urging them to enlist, and inviting them all to come to the camp near B[eaufort] on N[ew] Year's Day, and join in the grand Celebration, which is to take place there. I long to go, and hope I shall.

Capt. H[ooper] handed me a letter from my dear Mary S[hepard]. It was unexpected, and so all the more delightful. I sh'ld have been very, very glad to have had letters from home and from H[enry] for Christmas gifts. But so it was not. I must try to be content.

Tuesday, Dec. 30. This eve. Mr. and Miss

R[uggles] spent with us quite pleasantly. It is very rarely we have company, and so I note it down.

Wednesday, Dec. 31. Mr. T[horpe] and Mr. H[ooper] dined with us to-day. I think they are—Mr. T[horpe] especially, the most anti-slavery of the Superintendents. And they are very gentlemenly [*sic*], and I like them. This afternoon Mr. and Mrs. W[ells] called. He is very agreeable, she *not* so agreeable, to me. I count the hours till to-morrow, the glorious, glorious day of freedom.

Thursday, New Year's Day, 1863. The most glorious day this nation has yet seen, *I* think. I rose early—an event here—and early we started, with an old borrowed carriage and a remarkably slow horse. Whither were we going? thou wilt ask, dearest A. To the ferry; thence to Camp Saxton, to the Celebration. From the Ferry to the camp the "Flora" took us.

How pleasant it was on board! A crowd of people, whites and blacks, and a band of music —to the great delight of the negroes. Met on board Dr. and Mrs. Peck and their daughters, who greeted me most kindly. Also Gen. S[axton]'s father whom I like much, and several other acquaintances whom I was glad to see. We stopped at Beaufort, and then proceeded to Camp Saxton, the camp of the 1st Reg[iment] S[outh] C[arolina] Vol[unteer]s. The "Flora" c[ou]ld not get up to the landing, so we were rowed ashore in a row boat.

Just as my foot touched the plank, on landing, a hand grasped mine and well known voice spoke my name. It was my dear and noble friend, Dr. Rogers. I cannot tell you, dear A., how delighted I was to see him; how *good* it was to see the face of a friend from the North, and *such* a friend. I think myself particularly blessed to have him for a friend. Walking on a little distance I found myself being presented to Col. Higginson, whereat I was so much overwhelmed, that I had no reply to make to the very kind and courteous little speech with which he met me. I believe I mumbled something, and grinned like a simpleton, that was all. Provoking, isn't it? that when one is most in need of sensible words, one finds them not.

I *cannot* give a regular chronicle of the day. It is impossible. I was in such a state of excitement. It all seemed, and seems still, like a brilliant dream. Dr. R[ogers] and I talked all the time, I know, while he showed me the camp and all the arrangements. They have a beautiful situation, on the grounds once occupied by a very old fort, "De La Ribanchine," built in 1629 or 30. Some of the walls are still standing. Dr. R[ogers] has made quite a good hospital out of an old gin house. I went over it. There are only a few invalids in it, at present. I saw everything; the kitchens, cooking arrangements, and all. Then we took seats on the platform.

The meeting was held in a beautiful grove, a live-oak grove, adjoining the camp. It is the largest one I have yet seen; but I don't think the moss pendants are quite as beautiful as they are on St. Helena. As I sat on the stand and looked around on the various groups, I thought I had never seen a sight so beautiful. There were the black soldiers, in their blue coats and scarlet pants, the officers of this and other regiments in their handsome uniforms, and crowds of lookers-on, men, women and children, grouped in various attitudes, under the trees. The faces of all wore a happy, eager, expectant look.

The exercises commenced by a prayer from Rev. Mr. Fowler, Chaplain of the reg[iment]. An ode written for the occasion by Prof. Zachos, originally a Greek, now Sup[erintendent] of Paris island—was read by himself, and then sung by the whites. Col. H[igginson] introduced Dr. Brisbane in a few elegant and graceful words. He (Dr. B.) read the President's [Emancipation] Proclamation, which was warmly cheered. Then the beautiful flags presented by Dr. Cheever's Church [in New York] were presented to Col. H[igginson] for the Reg[iment] in an excellent and enthusiastic speech, by Rev. Mr. [Mansfield] French. Immediately at the conclusion, some of the colored people—of their own accord sang "My Country Tis of Thee." It was a touching and beautiful incident, and Col. Higginson, in accepting the flags made it the occasion of some happy remarks. He said *that* tribute was far more effective than any speech he c'ld make. He spoke for some time, and all that he said was grand, glorious. He seemed inspired. Nothing c'ld have been better, more perfect. And Dr. R[ogers] told me afterward that the Col. was much affected. That tears were in his eyes. He is as Whittier says, truly a "sure man." The men all admire and love him. There is a great deal of personal magnetism about him, and his kindness is proverbial. After he had done speaking he delivered the flags to the color-bearers with a few very impressive remarks to them. They each then, Sgt. Prince Rivers and [Cpl.] Robert Sutton, made very good speeches indeed, and were loudly cheered. Gen. Saxton and Mrs. Gage spoke very well. The good Gen. was received with great enthusiasm, and throughout the morning—every little while it seemed to me three cheers were given for him. A Hymn written I believe, by Mr. Judd, was sung, and then all the people united with the Reg[iment] in singing "John Brown." It was grand. During the exercises, it was announced that Fremont was appointed Commander-in-chief of the Army, and this was received with enthusiastic and prolonged cheering. But as it is picket news, I greatly fear that is not true.

We dined with good Dr. R[ogers] at the Col's [T. W. Higginson] table, though, greatly to my regret he, (the Col.) was not there. He partook of some of the oxen, (of which ten had been roasted) with his men. I like his doing that. We had quite a sumptuous dinner. Our party consisted of Dr. R[ogers], Adjutant D[ewhurst], Capt. R[ogers], Mr. and Miss Ware (Mrs. Winsor's brother and sister), Mr. Hall, their cousin, whom I like much, and Mr. and Miss H[unn] and me. We had a merry, delightful dinner. The only part that I did not enjoy was being obliged to read Whittier's Hymn aloud at the table. I wanted Dr. R[ogers] to do it. But he w'ld insist on my doing it. So of course it was murdered. I believe the older I grow the more averse I get to doing anything in public. I have no courage to do such things.

Col. H[igginson] invited us into his tent—a very nice, almost *homelike* one. I noticed a nice secretary, with writing utensils and "Les Miserables" on it. A *wreath* of beautiful oranges hung against the wall, fronting the door. I wanted to have a good look at this tent; but we were hardly seated when the Dr. and Col. were called away for a moment, and Lieut. Col. Billings coming in w'ld insist upon our going into his tent. I did not want to go at all, but he was so *persistent* we had to. I fear he is a somewhat vain person. His tent was very comfortable too, and I noticed quite a large piece of "Secesh" furniture, something between a secretary and a bureau, and quite a collection of photographs and daguerres. But I did not examine them, for my attention was occupied by Col. H[igginson] to whom I showed Whittier's poem, letter and photo. "He looks old," he said to me sadly, as he handed back the picture.

Dr. R[ogers] introduced me to Dr. H[awks] and his wife—pleasant people, and *good* anti-slavery. They mentioned having Liberators with my letters in them. I am sorry they have come down here.

Col. H[igginson] asked me to go out and hear the band play, which I very gladly did. But it stopped just as we stepped outside of the tent. Just then one of the soldiers came up to the Col. and said "Do Cunnel, do ask 'em to play Dixie, just for me, for my lone self." The Col. made the request, but the leader of the band said he feared they w'ld not be able to play the whole tune as they had not the necessary pieces. "Nebber mind," said the man "jus' half a tune will do." It was found impossible to play even that but the leader promised that the next time they came they would be fully prepared to play Dixie for him.

The Dress Parade—the first I had ever seen— delighted me. It was a brilliant sight—the long line of men in their brilliant uniform, with bayonets gleaming in the sunlight. The Col. looked splendid. The Dr. said the men went through with the drill remarkably well. It seemed to me nothing c'ld be more perfect. To me it was a grand triumph —that black regiment doing itself honor in the sight of the white officers, many of whom, doubtless "came to scoff." It was typical of what the race, so long downtrodden and degraded will yet achieve on this Continent.

After the Parade, we went to the Landing, intending to take a boat for Beaufort. But the boat was too crowded, and we decided to wait for another. It was the softest, loveliest moon-light. We sat down among the ruins of the old fort. Just [as soon] as the boat had reached a favorable distance from the shore the band in it commenced playing Home, sweet Home. It was exquisitely beautiful. The lovely moonlight on the water, the perfect stillness around seemed to give new beauty to that ever beautiful old song. And then as my dear friend, Dr. R[ogers] said, "It came *very near* to us all."

Finding the night air damp we went to the tent of Mr. Fowler, the chaplain, whom I like much better in private conversation than as an orator. He is a thoroughly good, earnest man. Thither came Col. H[igginson] and Dr. H[awks]. We sat around the nice fire—the tent has *chimney* and fire place, made by Mr. F[owler]'s own skilful hands. Col. H[igginson] is a perfectly delightful person in private.—So genial, so witty, so kind. But I noticed when he was silent, a careworn almost sad expression on his earnest, noble face. My heart was full when I looked at him. I longed to say "I thank you, I thank you, for that noble glorious speech." And yet I c'ld not. It is always so. I do not know how to talk. Words always fail me when I want them most. The more I feel the more impossible it is for me to speak. It is very provoking. Among other things, Col. H[igginson] said how amusing it was to him—their plan of housekeeping down here. "This morning I was asked 'Well, Colonel, how many oxen shall we roast today.' And I said, just as calmly as I w'ld have ordered a pound or two of beef, at home.— well I think *ten* will do. And then to be consulted as to how many gallons of molasses, and of vinegar, and how many pounds of ginger w'ld be wanted seemed very odd." I wish I c'ld reproduce for you the dry humorous tones in which this was said. We had a pleasant chat, sitting there in the fire-light, and I was most unwilling to go, for besides the happiness of being in the society of the Col. and the Dr. we wanted dreadfully to see the "shout" and grand jubilee which the soldiers were going to have that night. But it was already late, and hearing that the "Flora" was coming we had to hasten to the Landing. I was sorry to say good-bye to Dr. R[ogers]. What an *unspeakable* happiness it was to see him. But I fear for his health. I fear the exposure of a camp life. Am glad to see that he has warm robes and blankets, to keep him comfortable. I wish I c'ld do something for him. He has done so much for me.

Ah, what a grand, glorious day this has been. The dawn of freedom which it heralds may not break upon us at once; but it will surely come, and sooner, I believe, than we have ever dared hope before. My soul is glad with an exceeding great gladness. But before I close, dear A., I must bring our little party safe home to Oaklands. We had a good time on the Flora. L[izzie Hunn] and I promenaded the deck, and sang John Brown, and Whittier's Hymn and "My Country Tis of Thee." And the moon shone bright above us, and the waves beneath, smooth and clear, glistened in the soft moonlight. At Beaufort we took the row boat, and the boatmen sang as they rowed us across. Mr. Hall was with us, and seemed really to appreciate and enjoy everything. I like him. Arrived at St. Helena's we separated, he to go to "Coffin's Point" (a dreadful name, as Dr. R[ogers] says) and we to come hither [Oaklands]. Can't say that I enjoyed the homeward drive very much. T'was so intensely cold, yes *intensely*, for these regions. I fear some of the hot enthusiasm with which my soul was filled got chilled a little but it was only for a short time.

Old friend, my good and dear A. a very, very happy New Year to you! Dear friends in both my Northern homes a happy, happy New Year to you, too! And to us all a year of such freedom as we have never yet known in this boasted but hitherto wicked land. The hymn, or rather one of the hymns that those boat[men] sung [*sic*] is singing itself to me now. The refrain "Religion so . . . sweet" was so sweet and touching in its solemnity.

Sunday, Jan. 4. . . . To-day we had a little celebration at our church, on our own account. Gen. Saxton spoke. Gen. Seymour was present. Mr. [Mansfield] French and others made very good addresses. . . . And our children sang "Sound the Loud Timbrel," and Whittier's Hymn. I thought they did not sing quite so well as usual. But the people seemed pleased. Our children wore badges of red, white and blue, which delighted them much. . . .

This afternoon Mrs. H[unn] arrived with the children. So of course there was great rejoicing in the household. I like her appearance. She seems a gentle, lady-like person. The little girl has a look of refinement.

Monday, Jan. 5. Went to school, but as Miss M[urray] and I were both far from well, and it was damp and chilly, had no school. To-night wrote to Mrs. C[hew] and to Mr. Hunt. I dreaded the last performance.

Wednesday, Jan. 7. Yesterday and to-day quite unwell with a bad cough, and hear that dear Miss M[urray] is quite ill. My good physician, Miss T[owne] came. How kind she is to me. She said she thought it decidedly best that we sh'ld give up school for this week. I demurred at first, but afterward agreed, seeing the prudence of the thing.

This afternoon was lying on the lounge feeling rather ill, and decidedly low-spirited, when the door opened and who sh'ld enter but my dear friend Dr. R[ogers]. Wasn't I glad to see him! It did me never [*sic*] so much good. He came on purpose to see me, but c'ld only stay a very little while. How much I enjoyed that brief visit no words can tell. He is looking well, but from what he said I fear he is *not* well. It grieves me to think it. I was so sorry to have him go.—Dear noble, kind friend! There are few as good as he is. He said he w'ld write to me often if I w'ld write to him. I shall do so gladly, for the sake of having letters from him. I don't deserve it I know. Our people here are very kind; several have been in to see me. I will not, must not be ill here.

Thursday, Jan. 8. Feel better [to]day. Went round to see the people. Then my good Miss

T[owne] came and took me as far as the church, just for the sake of the drive. But she w'ld not let me go in, while she put away the books. Had a very pleasant talk with her by the way. It always does me good just to see her bright, cheerful face. Did some sewing and considerable writing to-day.

Sunday, Jan. 11. Rec'd to-day my hat, and my box of chessmen from Aunt M[argaretta] with a note;—nothing else that I wanted. I am so disappointed, for I needed the things sadly. But it c'ld not be helped. Had also a note from Hat-[tie] and the box of clothing, which I am very glad to get. Drove out to The Oaks for a little while this afternoon.

Monday, Jan. 12. A bright, lovely day. Feel much better. Had school out-of doors—in the bright sunlight. T'was delightful. Imagine our school room, dear A.—the soft brown earth for a carpet; blue sky for a ceiling, and for walls, the grand old oaks with their exquisite moss drapery. I enjoyed it very much. Even the children seemed to appreciate it, and were unusually quiet.

Thursday, Jan. 15. After school drove to the Oaks, and practised for some time. Then went up-stairs and had a pleasant little chat with the ladies in their homelike room. Had a letter mailed to my good friend Whittier. Dear Miss M[urray] is quite unwell which grieves me much. Miss T[owne] sent me the Dec[ember] Atlantic [Monthly]. Enjoyed it this eve. especially Dr. [Oliver Wendell] Holmes excellent article, wherein he speaks of our friend Charles W[?] very pleasantly. It is an excellent No. *That* article is— "My Hunt after the Captain."

Saturday, Jan. 17. Spent the afternoon with Miss R[uggles]. She is a kind soul, though somewhat garrulous. Met there a new arrival, a Mrs. Clarke whom I don't admire particularly, and a Mr. De la croix who seems to me decidedly *lap-dogish [sic]*. Had a delicious tea;—which is worth recording being the first we have taken from home. Miss R[uggles] lent me "Ravenshoe," by Henry Kingsley. Some parts of it are good; others seem to me not worth reading. Don't like him as well as Charles K[ingsley]—his brother.

Sunday, Jan. 18. Had a lovely drive partly through the woods. The pines were singing "the slow song of the sea." It recalled the old Bridge-water [Massachusetts] days, when we used to lie on the brown leaves and listen dreamily to that wondrous song. We lost our way, which made it all the more delightful, of course!—

Monday, Jan. 19. Cold disagreeable day. Was too unwell to go to school. Miss T[owne] came to see me and did me good, as usual with her good medicines and her sunshiny face. Sewed in a most exemplary way. . . .

Friday, Jan. 23. Had a kind little note from my good friend, Dr. R[ogers]. His reg[iment] goes on an expedition to-day. He asks me to pray for their success. And indeed I will, with my whole soul and for his safety, too—dear, kind friend that he is. I wish I c[ou]ld have seen him again before he went. How he rejoices in Gen. Hunter's coming. And how I rejoice with him!

Saturday, Jan. 24. Had to-day the pleasantest visit I've had since I've been here. L[izzie] and I drove to Mr. Thorpe's plantation. . . . The gentlemen took us around to see the people of whom there are 150 on the place. 100 have come from Edisto. There were no houses to accommodate so many, and they had to find shelter in barns, outhouses and any other place they c[ou]ld get. They have constructed rude houses for themselves —many of them—which do not, however afford them much protection in bad weather. I am told that they are all excellent, industrious people.

One old woman interested me deeply. Her name is Daphne, and she is probably at least a hundred years old. She has had fifty grandchildren, sixty-five greatgrandchildren, and three great, great-grandchild[ren]. She is entirely blind, but seems quite cheerful and happy. She told us that she was brought from Africa to this country just after the Revolution. I asked her if she was glad that all her numerous family were now and forever free. Her bright old face grew brighter as she answered. "Oh yes, yes missus." She retains her faculties remarkably well for one so old. It interested me greatly to see her. As Mr. H[?] said "it was worth coming to S[outh] C[arolina] to see that old relic of a past time."

15 of the people on this place escaped from the main land, last spring. Among them was a man named Michael. After they had gone some distance—their masters in pursuit—M[ichael]'s master overtook him in the swamp. A fierce grapple ensued—the master on horseback, the man on foot:—the former drew a pistol and shot the slave through the arm, shattering it dreadfully. Still the brave man fought desperately and at last succeeded in unhorsing the master, and beat him until he was senseless. He then with the rest of the company escaped. With them was a woman named Rina, now a cook at Mr. T[horpe]'s. She was overtaken by her master's cousin, and nearly run

over by his horse. But he, having a liking for her, wheeled his horse around, when he saw who it was, without saying a word, and allowed her to escape.—A story which I record because it is a rare thing to hear anything good of a rebel. I had the pleasure of shaking hands with Rina, and congratulating her on her escape. She is a very neat, sensible looking black woman.

Mr. T[horpe]'s place—which used to be the property of one of the numerous family of Fripps —Thomas by name—is most beautifully situated in the midst of noble pine trees, and on the banks of a large creek which deserves—almost—to be dignified by the name of river. Tis the pleasantest place I've seen yet. And Mr. T[horpe] says it is quite healthy.

Of course we lost our way coming back, and I, in trying to turn the horse, ran up against a tree and there our "*shay*" staid. In vain did L[izzie] and I try to move the horse, and then the wheels. Both were equally immovable, till fortunately we saw a man at a little distance and called him to our aid. With his assistance we soon got righted again. All this I tell you, dear A. as a great secret. W[ou]ldn't have anybody else know of my unskilfulness. Despite this little *contretemps* we had a delightful sunset drive home.

Sunday, Jan. 25. Saw a wonderful sight to-day. 150 people were baptized in the creek near the church. They looked very picturesque—many of them in white aprons, and bright dresses and handkerchiefs. And as they, in procession, marched down to the water, they sang beautifully. The most perfect order and quiet prevailed throughout.

Monday, Jan. 26. Rec'd another kind note from Dr. R[ogers] written prior to the other. In it he gives me some account of what he is doing; and I am so glad to know. It is so good to hear from him, I fear he has not got my note. Not that t'was of much importance, but I w'ld like him to know how constantly I think of him.

Tuesday, Jan. 27. J[?] brought me from B[eaufort] to-day a package from home containing a letter from Aunt M[argaretta], some delicious candy from our good Emma, and a pair of quite nice pants, from Mrs. Chew, sent especially to Cupid. How delighted he was to get them. He c[ou]ldn't say much, but I wish Mrs. C[hew] c'ld have seen the marvelous bows and *scrapings* which he made.

Wednesday, Jan. 28. A memorable day because we had a snowstorm—in miniature. When I got up this morning some of the roofs had a white layer on them, but it did not stay on the ground. The "storm" lasted but a little while. Towards eve. there was another slight attempt at snow, which was unsuccessful. A cold, dreary day. Miss R[uggles] sent me "Say and Seal," and a bunch of lovely white flowers, which it does my soul good to see. She is very kind. . . .

Friday, Jan. 30. Finished "Say and Seal," some of which I like very much. But it is rather religious to suit me. I don't know but it seems to me the author's works have a little *cant* about them. Now Mrs. [Harriet Beecher] Stowe always has something about religion in her books, but it is so differently *administered,* that it is only pleasant and beautiful. . . .

Saturday, Jan. 31. L[izzie] and I went to Beaufort—after bread. We had a lovely row across,—at noon—in the brightest sunlight. But neither going or coming did the boatmen sing, which disappointed me much. The Sergeant said these were not singers—*That* is most surprising. I thought *everybody* sang down here. Certainly every boat crew *ought.* As we drove to the ferry, we noticed how fresh and green everything looked; —so unlike winter. The trees are nearly all evergreen. Bare branches are rarely to be seen. What a lovely morning it was!—like a May morn. up North. Birds singing on every side. Deep green in the pines and "deep delicious blue" in the sky. Why is it that green and blue together are so lovely in Nature, and so *un*lovely elsewhere?

In B[eaufort] we spent nearly all our time at Harriet Tubman's—otherwise "Moses." She is a wonderful woman—a real heroine. Has helped off a large number of slaves, after taking her own freedom. She told us that she used to hide them in the woods during the day and go around to get provisions for them. Once she had with her a man named Joe, for whom a reward of $1500 was offered. Frequently, in different places she found handbills exactly describing him, but at last they reached in safety the Suspension Bridge over the Falls and found themselves in Canada. Until then, she said, Joe had been very silent. In vain had she called his attention to the glory of the Falls. He sat perfectly still—moody, it seemed, and w'ld not even glance at them. But when she said, "Now we are in Can[ada]" he sprang to his feet with a great shout, and sang and clapped his hand [*sic*] in a perfect delirium of joy. So when they got out, and he first touched *free* soil, he shouted and hurrahed "as if he were crazy"— she said.

How exciting it was to hear her tell the story. And to hear her sing the very scraps of jubilant hymns that he sang. She said the ladies crowded around them, and some laughed and some cried. My own eyes were full as I listened to her—the heroic woman! A reward of $10000 was offered for her by the Southerners, and her friends deemed it best that she sh'ld, for a time find refuge in Can[ada]. And she did so, but only for a short time. She came back and was soon at the good brave work again. She is living in B[eaufort] now; keeping an eating house. But she wants to go North, and will probably do so ere long. I am glad I saw her—*very* glad.

At her house we met one of the Superintendents from P[ort] R[oyal] I[sland], a Boston man —Mr. S[?]—who is intelligent and very agreeable. He kindly went with us to Mrs. Hawkes'—the wife of the Sur[geon] 1st Reg[iment] S[outh] C[arolina] V[olunteers] but she was at the camp with her husband who did not go with the Expedition [up the St. Mary's River]. Was sorry not to see her.

Went, afterward, to Mr. Judd's for letters, and found there one from A[nnie]. Am delighted to have it, and to know she is not ill. Mr. J[udd]'s house is beautifully situated. In the same street with Gen. Saxton's. On the Bay—as they call it. Saw the building which was once the Public Library. It is now a shelter for "contrabands" from Fernandino. How disgusted the rebels w'ld be. I suppose they w'ld upturn their aristocratic noses and say "To what base uses etc." It does *me* good to see how the tables are turned. The market place also we saw. Mr. S[?] said doubtless human beings had been sold there. But there is not a certainty of it, as that business was generally transacted in Charleston. The Arsenal is a fine large stone structure—fine—I sh[ou]ld say—for this region. The entrance is guarded by two handsome brass cannon, and a fierce looking sentinel. Nearly all the houses in B[eaufort] have a dismantled, desolate look. Few persons are to be seen in the streets some soldiers and "contrabands." I believe we saw only three ladies. But already Northern improvements have reached this southern town. One of them is a fine new wharf which is a convenience that one wonders how the "Secesh" c'ld have done without. They were an uncivilized people. I noticed more mulattoes there than we have on St. Hel[ena]. Some were very good-looking. Little colored children— of every hue were playing about the streets looking as merry and happy as children ought to look —now that the dark shadow of slavery hangs over them no more.

We did our few errands and were quite ready for the four o'clock boat, which was not, however, ready for us until sometime afterward. I missed the singing, in our row back.

Sunday, Feb. 1. Quite a number of strangers at church to-day,—among them our good Gen. [Saxton]; whom it is always a pleasure to see. Reuben T[omlinson] was there. I was glad to see him. It recalled the old Phila[delphia] days—the pleasantest of them.

This afternoon went into the woods, and gathered some casino berries and beautiful magnolia leaves and exquisite ferns. How beautifully they contrast, on my table, with the daffodils and narcissus which are in full bloom now. Think of these flowers blooming out of doors in Jan[uary] and Feb[ruary]. Isn't it wonderful? I cant tell you how much pleasure they give me. What sunbeams they are to warm and cheer my heart.

Monday, Feb. 2. Have just heard to-night of the return of the 1st Reg[iment]. They came back with laurels and Secesh prisoners. Have heard no particulars, but am *glad*, emphatically glad to know that they come back completely successful. That is grand, glorious! In the joy of my heart sat down and wrote a congratulatory note, to my dear friend, Dr. R[ogers]. I know how rejoiced he must be. Thank God that he and the noble Col. [T. W. Higginson] have come back safe.

Saturday, Feb. 7. One day this week Tina, an excellent woman from Palawana, came in, and told us a very interesting story about two girls, one about ten the other fifteen, who, having been taken by their master up into the country about the time of [the] "Gun Shoot," determined to try to get back to their parents who had been left on this island. They stole away at night, and travelled through woods and swamps, for two days without eating. Sometimes their strength w'ld fail and they w'ld sink down in the swamps, and think they c'ld [go] no further, but they had brave little hearts, and struggled on, till at last they reached Port Royal Ferry. There they were seen by a boatload of people who had also made their escape. The boat was too full to take them but the people, as soon as they reached these islands, told the father of the children, who immediately hastened to the Ferry for them. The poor little creatures ·were almost wild with joy, despite their exhausted state, when they saw their father coming to them.

When they were brought to their mother she fell down "jus' as if she was dead" as Tina expressed it. She was so overpowered with joy. Both children are living on Dalta now. They are said to be very clever. I want to see the heroic little creatures.

Another day, one of the black soldiers came in and gave us *his* account of the Expedition [up the St. Mary's River]. No words of mine, dear A can give you any account of the state of exultation and enthusiasm that he was in. He was eager for another chance at "de Secesh." I asked him what he w[ou]ld do if his master and others sh'ld come back and try to reenslave him. "I'd fight um Miss, I'd fight um till I turned to dust!" He was especially delighted at the ire which the sight of the black troops excited in the minds of certain Secesh women whom they saw. These vented their spleen by calling the men "baboons dressed in soldiers clothes," and telling them that they ought to be at work in their masters' rice swamps, and that they ought to be lashed to death. "And what did you say to them?" I asked. "Oh miss, we only tell um 'Hole your tongue, and dry up.' You see *we* wusn't feared of *dem, dey c[ou]ldn't hurt us now.* Whew! didn't we laugh . . . to see dem so mad!" The spirit of resistance to the Secesh is strong in these men.

Sunday, Feb. 8. . . . Towards night, after the others had gone, Dr. R[ogers] came. Wasn't I glad to see him. He looks none the worse for his late experience. He brought his notes of the Ex-[pedition] taken on the spot, and very kindly read them to us, to-night. They are very, very interesting, more so to me even than Col. H[igginson]'s excellent Report, (which the Dr. also brought) because entering more into particulars. He will not have them printed for which I am sorry. They ought to be [printed]. They, and the report also, show plainly how nobly and bravely the black soldiers can fight. I am delighted. I think the contemptuous white soldiers will cease to sneer soon. Dr. R[ogers] described beautifully the scenes through which they passed, particularly the night journey up St. Mary's River, with the grand old funereal oaks on either side. How strange and solemn it must have been.

At one place, Alberti's Mills, they went up to the plantation and found the mistress, living in solitary splendor. She and her husband (now dead) came from the North, but have lived a long time down South, and had a large plantation and great wealth. Dr. R[ogers] describes Mad[am] A[lberti] as a very superior woman. She spent a long time in trying to convince Dr. R[ogers] that she and her husband had devoted themselves to the good of their slaves, and lamented their ingratitude in all deserting her—as they have all done except one or two petted house servants. Rob[er]t Sutton, now Corporal in the Reg[iment] was formerly her slave, and said the people were cruelly treated, and the jail on the place, where chains and handcuffs were found, bears witness to that.

The soldiers brought off cattle, horses and lumber, all of great value to the Gov[ernment]. They behaved gallantly under fire from the rebels, and entered into their work with zeal. Three of them saved the life of their brave Col. H[igginson]. He, as usual, was at one time in advance, when a rebel pistol was fired at him by an officer, who immediately drew another and was about to take more fatal aim (the Col. not perceiving it) when three of the soldiers seeing his danger, fired at once, killing the rebel officer. Dr. R[ogers] says that several who were badly wounded did not report to him, fearing that they w'ld be obliged to leave their posts. The noble Rob[er]t Sutton whom Col. H[igginson] calls "the Leader of the Expedition" was wounded in three places, and still kept at his post. Dr. R[ogers] speaks of him as does Col. H[igginson]—in the highest terms. He says he thinks he must be the descendant of some Nubian king. He is a grand man. My heart is filled with an exceeding great joy to-night.

I can never thank Dr. R[ogers] sufficiently for bringing me those notes. It was very kind. And it makes me so happy to see him safe back again. The kind, loving words he spoke to me to-night sank deep into my heart. "As a brother," he told me to consider him. And I will gladly do so. He read me Emerson's noble Hymn, written for the grand Jubilee Concert, on Emancipation Day in Boston. Dr. R[ogers] read it to the Reg[iment] he told me, during service, this morning. I am glad. He was in full uniform to-day. Makes a splendid looking officer. I looked at him and his horse with childish admiration.

Monday, Feb. 9. Dr. R[ogers] walked part of the way to school with me, and we had a nice, long talk. He said he wished he lived nearer that he might come in and read to me sometimes. Ah! w[ou]ldn't *I* enjoy that, unspeakably! It is too bad that I can see so seldom the only old friend I have here,—and such a friend! Dear Miss T[owne] was not well enough to be at school to-day. I am very sorry. Miss M[urray] and I did the best we c'ld without her. With what eager interest and delight Miss M[urray] speaks of the success of the Reg[iment]. I believe she is as rejoiced as I am, and that's saying a great deal. It does me good to see it.

Frogmore, Wednesday, Feb. 11. Quite unwell yesterday and to-day. This morn. the Townes—my good physician and her sister—came in and declaring that I needed change of air, forcibly bore me off to Frogmore. Well, I was glad to go, and here I am. The place is delightfully situated, on an arm of the sea, which, at high tide, comes up to within a few feet of the house. There are lovely trees around, and an almost sea air, which is most invigorating after the somewhat oppressive atmosphere farther inland. This is a very large plantation. There are nearly 200 people living on it. Ah! how pleasant this salt smell is. It recalls the dear old Marblehead days.

Thursday, Feb. 12. Have done little else but sleep. It is very quiet here. Have had most delicious rest, both for soul and body. Miss Rosa T[owne] is as kind as possible. Hers is a beautiful kindness, that does one good thoroughly. I love her. . . .

Found the first snowdrop to-day;—a lovely, pure, little darling, growing at the foot of the piazza steps. Welcome, welcome, a thousand times!

Friday, Feb. 13. Miss Laura [Towne] came to-day. To-night some of the little boys came in and danced for us. It was *deliciously* comical. Miss L[aura] rewarded them by giving them belts with bright buckles, which pleased them mightily. To-night there was a bit of a shout in the "Praise House," but there were not enough to make it very enjoyable. They sang beautifully however. One song I have not heard before. Must try to get the words. "Jacob" and "w[ou]ld not let me go," are in it.

Saturday, Feb. 14. Valentine's Day *at home.* Who will send me one? A dark, gloomy, stormy day without, but cheery within. Miss W[?] and Miss M[urray] came to-day, and we have quite a large party—five ladies and two gentlemen. Stormed so much this afternoon they c'ld not go, and will be obliged to spend the night with us. That is *jolly.* I know Mr. F[?] thinks so. *Wasn't* he rejoiced to see Miss M[urray]. Ah! this love. Tis a queer thing, but very amusing—to lookers-on. Helped Miss Rosa fill bags with sewing utensils for the people—a pleasant task. We both enjoyed it.

To-night—a wild stormy night—went out on the piazza and listened to the roaring of the sea. How wild it sounded. Occasionally we c'ld hear a great wave break upon the shore. That sound of the sea is music to my ears. I c'ld not bear to come away from it. It brought N[ew] E[ngland] near to me. But the air is dangerously damp, and I had to tear myself away. Miss L[aura] T[owne] told us some delightfully horrible stories and then Mr. F[?] told us some stories from Vergil, in which he seems well read. We had a very pleasant, social evening.—Good bye, old Journal friend.

Elizabeth Keckley (1825–1905)

During her lifetime of eighty years, Elizabeth Keckley actually lived three lives, each sharply different from the other. First, for thirty years she was a slave, suffering the floggings and other physical and mental harassment that were the lot of the slave. Then, almost as if by magic, the woman who had been a slave became Washington's stylish modiste, serving the highest of official society and eventually becoming the seamstress and intimate friend of Mary Todd Lincoln, the nation's high-strung First Lady. Indeed, some said that Elizabeth Keckley was the only real friend Mrs. Lincoln had in Washington. Her third life began when the Lincoln association ended. It was essentially a long period of twilight memories, from 1870 until her death in 1905. During most of this period, Mrs. Keckley used her skills as a modiste and seamstress in teaching and directing the domestic arts program at Wilberforce University.

The details of her first two lives are recounted in her autobiography, *Behind the Scenes; or Thirty Years a Slave, and Four Years in the White House,* a well-written interior account of slavery that also provides some perceptive insights into the Lincoln family and Washington during the war years. It is written in such a high and elegant style, in the best novelistic diction of the times, that some people have questioned its authenticity. Mrs. Keckley always claimed that she had received very little help on the book, except for some assistance with grammar and certain other constructions from the publisher of the 1868 volume, Mr. G. W. Carleton. When the book was republished in 1931, the charge was again made that the book was ghostwritten, but the Rev. Francis Grimké and others who had been personal friends of Elizabeth Keckley supplied reliable evidence in support of the author's claim that *Behind the Scenes* was indeed her book. And, as historian Benjamin Quarles wryly asserts, the name Elizabeth Keckley is listed as author on the title page.

The principal interest of *Behind the Scenes* is its rather detailed account of life with the Lincolns. This has proven to be of great value to historians and Lincoln specialists. But Mrs. Keckley's description of her life as a slave, although related with a certain amount of reserve and reticence, is of interest also. The reader senses the hopeless monotony of a slave's existence—the floggings, the tensions, the conflicts, the endless concern for the trivial proprieties and insipid amenities of the master–slave relationship. One also senses how quickly a slave's life could suffer radical alteration at a master's whim or some change in family fortunes. It was thus that, as a young woman, Mrs. Keckley (then just "Lizzie") was moved out of a warm family relationship in Virginia to a rather complicated situation in St. Louis, Missouri. Of particular interest was her stay in Hillsboro, North Carolina, for here she not only suffered a brutal and forcible rape, which was the usual lot of a female slave, but something else even more sinister in the catalogue of slavery's evils. For several months, a young Christian minister flogged her every Saturday because he thought it his Christian duty to induce in her a demeanor more fitting for a slave. Such a perversion of Christian principles provides an interesting footnote on the psychology of the depravity of human slavery.

After Mrs. Keckley moved into the White House in 1860, her life style changed. To President Lincoln, she became "Madame Elizabeth." Now the flogging scars on her back were hidden from view by her stylish clothing, and all that Washington saw was a distinguished and graceful woman of great charm and social tact. And, as she recounts so well, one needed great social tact to be the friend of Mary Todd Lincoln. Indeed, much of this part of *Behind the Scenes* amounts to almost an extended psychograph of America's most puzzling First Lady, particularly the long account of Mrs. Lincoln's pathetic attempt to sell her clothes and jewelry following her husband's tragic death.

During her White House years, Mrs. Keckley labored in behalf of the

Union war effort. Of particular concern to her was the pitiable plight of the ex-slaves or contrabands who flocked into the capital city. So she became in early 1862 founder and president of the Contraband Relief Association and traveled to New York and Boston to raise funds for this organization. She made the utmost sacrifice to the war effort when her only son, George Keckley, was killed in action as a Union solider in Missouri.

The sections from *Behind the Scenes* that follow describe Mrs. Keckley's reactions to life in wartime Washington, a brief interlude with the war-weary President, and the death of the President, so soon after his great battlefield victories.

from *Behind the Scenes*

Chapter VII: Washington in 1862–3

In the summer of 1862, freedmen began to flock into Washington from Maryland and Virginia. They came with a great hope in their hearts, and with all their worldly goods on their backs. Fresh from the bonds of slavery, fresh from the benighted regions of the plantation, they came to the Capital looking for liberty, and many of them not knowing it when they found it. Many goods friends reached forth kind hands, but the North is not warm and impulsive. For one kind word spoken, two harsh ones were uttered; there was something repelling in the atmosphere, and the bright joyous dreams of freedom to the slave faded—were sadly altered, in the presence of that stern, practical mother, reality. Instead of flowery paths, days of perpetual sunshine, and bowers hanging with golden fruit, the road was rugged and full of thorns, the sunshine was eclipsed by shadows, and the mute appeals for help too often were answered by cold neglect. Poor dusky children of slavery, men and women of my own race—the transition from slavery to freedom was too sudden for you! The bright dreams were too rudely dispelled; you were not prepared for the new life that opened before you, and the great masses of the North learned to look upon your helplessness with indifference—learned to speak of you as an idle, dependent race. Reason should have prompted kinder thoughts. Charity is ever kind.

One fair summer evening I was walking the streets of Washington, accompanied by a friend, when a band of music was heard in the distance.

We wondered what it could mean, and curiosity prompted us to find out its meaning. We quickened our steps, and discovered that it came from the house of Mrs. Farnham. The yard was brilliantly lighted, ladies and gentlemen were moving about, and the band was playing some of its sweetest airs. We approached the sentinel on duty at the gate, and asked what was going on. He told us that it was a festival given for the benefit of the sick and wounded soldiers in the city. This suggested an idea to me. If the white people can give festivals to raise funds for the relief of suffering soldiers, why should not the well-to-do colored people go to work to do something for the benefit of the suffering blacks? I could not rest. The thought was ever present with me, and the next Sunday I made a suggestion in the colored church, that a society of colored people be formed to labor for the benefit of the unfortunate freedmen. The idea proved popular, and in two weeks "the Contraband Relief Association" was organized, with forty working members.

In September of 1862, Mrs. Lincoln left Washington for New York, and requested me to follow her in a few days, and join her at the Metropolitan Hotel. I was glad of the opportunity to do so, for I thought that in New York I would be able to do something in the interests of our society. Armed with credentials, I took the train for New York, and went to the Metropolitan, where Mrs. Lincoln had secured accommodations for me. The next morning I told Mrs. Lincoln of my project; and she immediately headed my list with a subscription of $200. I circulated among the colored people, and got them thoroughly interested in the subject, when I was called to Boston by Mrs. Lincoln, who wished to visit her son Robert, attending college in that city. I met Mr. Wendell Phillips, and other Boston philanthropists, who gave me all the assistance in their power. We held a mass meeting at the Colored Baptist Church, Rev. Mr. Grimes, in Boston, raised a sum of money, and organized there a branch society. The society was organized by Mrs. Grimes, wife of the pastor, assisted by Mrs. Martin, wife of Rev. Stella Martin. This branch of the main society, during the war, was able to send us over eighty large boxes of goods, contributed exclusively by the colored people of Boston. Returning to New York, we held a successful meeting at the Shiloh Church, Rev. Henry Highland Garnet, pastor. The Metropolitan Hotel, at that time as now, employed colored help. I suggested the object of my mission to Robert Thompson, Steward of the Hotel, who immediately raised quite a sum of money among the dining-room waiters. Mr. Frederick Douglass contributed $200, besides lecturing for us. Other prominent colored men sent in liberal contributions. From England[1] a large quantity of stores was received. Mrs. Lincoln made frequent contributions, as also did the President. In 1863 I was re-elected President of the Association, which office I continue to hold.

For two years after Willie's death the White House was the scene of no fashionable display. The memory of the dead boy was duly respected. In some things Mrs. Lincoln was an altered woman. Sometimes, when in her room, with no one present but myself, the mere mention of Willie's name would excite her emotion, and any trifling memento that recalled him would move her to tears. She could not bear to look upon his picture; and after his death she never crossed the threshold of the Guest's Room in which he died, or the Green Room in which he was embalmed. There was something supernatural in her dread of these things, and something that she could not explain. Tad's nature

was the opposite of Willie's, and he was always regarded as his father's favorite child. His black eyes fairly sparkled with mischief.

.   .   .

Chapter IX: Behind the Scenes

Some of the freedmen and freedwomen had exaggerated ideas of liberty. To them it was a beautiful vision, a land of sunshine, rest, and glorious promise. They flocked to Washington, and since their extravagant hopes were not realized, it was but natural that many of them should bitterly feel their disappointment. The colored people are wedded to associations, and when you destroy these you destroy half of the happiness of their lives. They make a home, and are so fond of it that they prefer it, squalid though it be, to the comparative ease and luxury of a shifting, roaming life. Well, the emancipated slaves, in coming North, left old associations behind them, and the love for the past was so strong that they could not find much beauty in the new life so suddenly opened to them. Thousands of the disappointed, huddled together in camps, fretted and pined like children for the "good old times." In visiting them in the interests of the Relief Society of which I was president, they would crowd around me with pitiful stories of distress. Often I heard them declare that they would rather go back to slavery in the South, and be with their old masters, than to enjoy the freedom of the North. I believe they were sincere in these declarations, because dependence had become a part of their second nature, and independence brought with it the cares and vexations of poverty.

I was very much amused one day at the grave complaints of a good old, simple-minded woman, fresh from a life of servitude. She had never ventured beyond a plantation until coming North. The change was too radical for her, and she could not exactly understand it. She thought, as many others thought, that Mr. and Mrs. Lincoln were the government, and that the President and his wife had nothing to do but to supply the extravagant wants of every one that applied to them. The wants of this old woman, however, were not very extravagant.

"Why, Missus Keckley," said she to me one day, "I is been here eight months, and Missus Lingom an't even give me one shife. Bliss God, childen, if I had ar know dat de Government, and

[1] The Sheffield Anti-Slavery Society of England contributed through Mr. Frederick Douglass, to the Freedmen's Relief Association, $24.00; Aberdeen Ladies' Society, $40.00; Anti-Slavery Society of Edinburgh, Scotland, $48.00; Friends at Bristol, England, $176.00; Birmingham Negro's Friend Society, $50.00. Also received through Mr. Charles R. Douglass, from the Birmingham Society, $33.00.

Mister and Missus Government, was going to do dat ar way, I neber would've comed here in God's wurld. My old missus us't gib me two shifes eber year."

I could not restrain a laugh at the grave manner in which this good old woman entered her protest. Her idea of freedom was two or more old shifts every year. Northern readers may not fully recognize the pith of the joke. On the Southern plantation, the mistress, according to established custom, every year made a present of certain undergarments to her slaves, which articles were always anxiously looked forward to, and thankfully received. The old woman had been in the habit of receiving annually two shifts from her mistress, and she thought the wife of the President of the United States very mean for overlooking this established custom of the plantation.

While some of the emancipated blacks pined for the old associations of slavery, and refused to help themselves, others went to work with commendable energy, and planned with remarkable forethought. They built themselves cabins, and each family cultivated for itself a small patch of ground. The colored people are fond of domestic life, and with them domestication means happy children, a fat pig, a dozen or more chickens, and a garden. Whoever visits the Freedmen's Village now in the vicinity of Washington will discover all of these evidences of prosperity and happiness. The schools are objects of much interest. Good teachers, white and colored, are employed, and whole brigades of bright-eyed dusky children are there taught the common branches of education. These children are studious, and the teachers inform me that their advancement is rapid. I number among my personal friends twelve colored girls employed as teachers in the schools at Washington. The Colored Mission Sabbath School, established through the influence of Gen. Brown at the Fifteenth Street Presbyterian Church, is always an object of great interest to the residents of the Capital, as well as to the hundreds of strangers visiting the city.

.   .   .

Mr. Lincoln was fond of pets. He had two goats that knew the sound of his voice, and when he called them they would come bounding to his side. In the warm bright days, he and Tad would sometimes play in the yard with these goats, for an hour at a time. One Saturday afternoon I went to the White House to dress Mrs. Lincoln. I had nearly completed my task when the President came in. It was a bright day, and walking to the window, he looked down into the yard, smiled, and, turning to me, asked:

"Madam Elizabeth, you are fond of pets, are you not?"

"O yes, sir," I answered.

"Well, come here and look at my two goats. I believe they are the kindest and best goats in the world. See how they sniff the clear air, and skip and play in the sunshine. Whew! what a jump," he exclaimed as one of the goats made a lofty spring. "Madam Elizabeth, did you ever before see such an active goat?" Musing a moment, he continued: "He feeds on my bounty, and jumps with joy. Do you think we could call him a bounty-jumper? But I flatter the bounty-jumper. My goat is far above him. I would rather wear his horns and hairy coat through life, than demean myself to the level of the man who plunders the national treasury in the name of patriotism. The man who enlists into the service for a consideration, and deserts the moment he receives his money but to repeat the play, is bad enough; but the men who manipulate the grand machine and who simply make the bounty-jumper their agent in an outrageous fraud are far worse. They are beneath the worms that crawl in the dark hidden places of earth."

His lips curled with haughty scorn, and a cloud was gathering on his brow. Only a moment the shadow rested on his face. Just then both goats looked up at the window and shook their heads as if they would say "How d'ye do, old friend?"

"See, Madam Elizabeth," exclaimed the President in a tone of enthusiasm, "my pets recognize me. How earnestly they look! There they go again; what jolly fun!" and he laughed outright as the goats bounded swiftly to the other side of the yard. Just then Mrs. Lincoln called out, "Come, Lizabeth; if I get ready to go down this evening I must finish dressing myself, or you must stop staring at those silly goats."

Mrs. Lincoln was not fond of pets, and she could not understand how Mr. Lincoln could take so much delight in his goats. After Willie's death, she could not bear the sight of anything he loved, not even a flower. Costly bouquets were presented to her, but she turned from them with a shudder, and either placed them in a room where she could not see them, or threw them out of the window. She gave all of Willie's toys—

everything connected with him—away, as she said she could not look upon them without thinking of her poor dead boy, and to think of him, in his white shroud and cold grave, was maddening. I never in my life saw a more peculiarly constituted woman. Search the world over, and you will not find her counterpart. After Mr. Lincoln's death, the goats that he loved so well were given away—I believe to Mrs. Lee, *née* Miss Blair, one of the few ladies with whom Mrs. Lincoln was on intimate terms in Washington.

During my residence in the Capital I made my home with Mr. and Mrs. Walker Lewis, people of my own race, and friends in the truest sense of the word.

The days passed without any incident of particular note disturbing the current of life. On Friday morning, April 14th—alas! what American does not remember the day—I saw Mrs. Lincoln but for a moment. She told me that she was to attend the theatre that night with the President, but I was not summoned to assist her in making her toilette. Sherman had swept from the northern border of Georgia through the heart of the Confederacy down to the sea, striking the death-blow to the rebellion. Grant had pursued General Lee beyond Richmond, and the army of Virginia, that had much such stubborn resistance, was crumbling to pieces. Fort Sumter had fallen; —the stronghold first wrenched from the Union, and which had braved the fury of Federal guns for so many years, was restored to the Union; the end of the war was near at hand, and the great pulse of the loyal North thrilled with joy. The dark war-cloud was fading, and a white-robed angel seemed to hover in the sky, whispering "Peace—peace on earth, good-will toward men!" Sons, brothers, fathers, friends, sweethearts were coming home. Soon the white tents would be folded, the volunteer army be disbanded, and tranquillity again reign. Happy, happy day!— happy at least to those who fought under the banner of the Union. There was great rejoicing throughout the North. From the Atlantic to the Pacific, flags were gayly thrown to the breeze, and at night every city blazed with its tens of thousand lights. But scarcely had the fireworks ceased to play, and the lights been taken down from the windows, when the lightning flashed the most appalling news over the magnetic wires. "The President has been murdered!" spoke the swift-winged messenger, and the loud huzza died upon the lips. A nation suddenly paused in the midst of festivity, and stood paralyzed with horror— transfixed with awe.

Oh, memorable day! Oh, memorable night! Never before was joy so violently contrasted with sorrow.

At 11 o'clock at night I was awakened by an old friend and neighbor, Miss M. Brown, with the startling intelligence that the entire Cabinet had been assassinated, and Mr. Lincoln shot, but not mortally wounded. When I heard the words I felt as if the blood had been frozen in my veins, and that my lungs must collapse for the want of air. Mr. Lincoln shot! the Cabinet assassinated! What could it mean? The streets were alive with wondering, awe-stricken people. Rumors flew thick and fast, and the wildest reports came with every new arrival. The words were repeated with blanched cheeks and quivering lips. I waked Mr. and Mrs. Lewis, and told them that the President was shot, and that I must go to the White House. I could not remain in a state of uncertainty. I felt that the house would not hold me. They tried to quiet me, but gentle words could not calm the wild tempest. They quickly dressed themselves, and we sallied out into the street to drift with the excited throng. We walked rapidly towards the White House, and on our way passed the residence of Secretary Seward, which was surrounded by armed soliders, keeping back all intruders with the point of the bayonet. We hurried on, and as we approached the White House, saw that it too was surrounded with soldiers. Every entrance was strongly guarded, and no one was permitted to pass. The guard at the gate told us that Mr. Lincoln had not been brought home, but refused to give any other information. More excited than ever, we wandered down the street. Grief and anxiety were making me weak, and as we joined the outskirts of a large crowd, I began to feel as meek and humble as a penitent child. A gray-haired old man was passing. I caught a glimpse of his face, and it seemed so full of kindness and sorrow that I gently touched his arm, and imploringly asked:

"Will you please, sir, to tell me whether Mr. Lincoln is dead or not?"

"Not dead," he replied, "but dying. God help us!" and with a heavy step he passed on.

"Not dead, but dying! then indeed God help us!"

We learned that the President was mortally wounded—that he had been shot down in his box at the theatre, and that he was not expected to live till morning; when we returned home with heavy hearts. I could not sleep. I wanted to go to Mrs. Lincoln, as I pictured her wild with grief; but then I did not know where to find her, and I must wait till morning. Never did the hours drag so slowly. Every moment seemed an age, and I could do nothing but walk about and hold my arms in mental agony.

Morning came at last, and a sad morning was it. The flags that floated so gayly yesterday now were draped in black, and hung in silent folds at half-mast. The President was dead, and a nation was mourning for him. Every house was draped in black, and every face wore a solemn look. People spoke in subdued tones, and glided whisperingly, wonderingly, silently about the streets.

About eleven o'clock on Saturday morning a carriage drove up to the door, and a messenger asked for "Elizabeth Keckley."

"Who wants her?" I asked.

"I come from Mrs. Lincoln. If you are Mrs. Keckley, come with me immediately to the White House."

I hastily put on my shawl and bonnet, and was driven at a rapid rate to the White House. Everything about the building was sad and solemn. I was quickly shown to Mrs. Lincoln's room, and on entering, saw Mrs. L. tossing uneasily about upon a bed. The room was darkened, and the only person in it besides the widow of the President was Mrs. Secretary Welles, who had spent the night with her. Bowing to Mrs. Welles, I went to the bedside.

"Why did you not come to me last night, Elizabeth—I sent for you?" Mrs. Lincoln asked in a low whisper.

"I did try to come to you, but I could not find you," I answered, as I laid my hand upon her hot brow.

I afterwards learned, that when she had partially recovered from the first shock of the terrible tragedy in the theatre, Mrs. Welles asked:

"Is there no one, Mrs. Lincoln, that you desire to have with you in this terrible affliction?"

"Yes, send for Elizabeth Keckley. I want her just as soon as she can be brought here."

Three messengers, it appears, were successively despatched for me, but all of them mistook the number and failed to find me.

Shortly after entering the room on Saturday morning, Mrs. Welles excused herself, as she said she must go to her own family, and I was left alone with Mrs. Lincoln.

She was nearly exhausted with grief, and when she became a little quiet, I asked and received permission to go into the Guests' Room, where the body of the President lay in state. When I crossed the threshold of the room, I could not help recalling the day on which I had seen little Willie lying in his coffin where the body of his father now lay. I remembered how the President had wept over the pale beautiful face of his gifted boy, and now the President himself was dead. The last time I saw him he spoke kindly to me, but alas! the lips would never move again. The light had faded from his eyes, and when the light went out the soul went with it. What a noble soul was his—noble in all the noble attributes of God! Never did I enter the solemn chamber of death with such palpitating heart and trembling footsteps as I entered it that day. No common mortal had died. The Moses of my people had fallen in the hour of his triumph. Fame had woven her choicest chaplet for his brow. Though the brow was cold and pale in death, the chaplet should not fade, for God had studded it with the glory of the eternal stars.

Folk Literature of Emancipation and Freedom

We'll Soon Be Free

We'll soon be free,
We'll soon be free,
We'll soon be free,
   When de Lord will call us home.
My brudder, how long,
My brudder, how long,
My brudder, how long,
   'Fore we done sufferin' here?
It won't be long [*Thrice.*]

'Fore de Lord will call us home.
We'll walk de miry road [*Thrice.*]
   Where pleasure never dies.
My brudder, how long [*Thrice.*]
   'Fore we done sufferin' here?
We'll soon be free [*Thrice.*]
   When Jesus sets me free.
We'll fight for liberty [*Thrice.*]
   When de Lord will call us home.

Rock About My Saro Jane

I've got a wife an-a five lil chillun
I believ I'll mak a trip on the big Macmillam
O Saro Jane

Chorus:
O there's nothing to do but to set down and sing
And rock about, my Saro Jane
O rock about, my Saro Jane

Biler busted and whistle done blowed
The head cap'n don fell overboard
O Saro Jane

Engine giv a crack and de whistle giv a squall
De engineer gon to de Hole-in-de-Wall
O Saro Jane

Yankees build boats for to shoot dem rebels
My musket's loaded and I'm gonna hold her
   level
O, Saro Jane

Don wid Driber's Dribin'

Don wid driber's dribin',
Don wid driber's dribin',
Don wid driber's dribin',
   Roll, Jordan, roll.

Don wid massa's hollerin',
Don wid massa's hollerin',
Don wid massa's hollerin',
   Roll, Jordan, roll.

Don wid missus' scoldin',
Don wid missus' scoldin',
Don wid missus' scoldin',
   Roll, Jordan, roll.

Sins so heaby dat I cannot get along,
Sins so heaby dat I cannot get along,
Sins so heaby dat I cannot get along,
   Roll, Jordan, roll.

Cast my sins to de bottom ob de sea,
Cast my sins to de bottom ob de sea,
Cast my sins to de bottom ob de sea,
   Roll, Jordan, roll.

Many a Thousand Die

No more driver call for me,
   No more driver call;
No more driver call for me,
   Many a thousand die!

No more peck of corn for me,
   No more peck of corn;
No more peck of corn for me,
   Many a thousand die!

No more hundred lash for me,
   No more hundred lash;
No more hundred lash for me,
   Many a thousand die!

Freedom

Abe Lincoln freed the nigger,
Wid da gun and wid da trigger,
An I ain't ginna git whipped no mo.
Ah got mah ticket
Out of dis heah thicket,
An I'm headin for da golden sho.

O freedom, O freedom,
O freedom after a while,
And before I'd be a slave, I'd be buried in my grave,
And go home to my Lord and be free.

There'll be no more moaning, no more moaning,
No more moaning after a while,
And before I'd be a slave, I'd be buried in my grave,
And go home to my Lord and be free.

No more weeping, no more crying,
No more weeping after a while,
And before I'd be a slave, I'd be buried in my grave,
And go home to my Lord and be free.

There'll be no more kneeling, no more bowing,
No more kneeling after a while,
And before I'd be a slave, I'd be buried in my grave,
And go home to my Lord and be free.

There'll be shouting, there'll be shouting,
There'll be shouting after a while,
And before I'd be a slave, I'd be buried in my grave,
And go home to my Lord and be free.

PART IV

Reconstruction and Reaction: 1865–1915

In his authoritative and well-informed history *The Negro and the Civil War,* Black historian Benjamin Quarles relates an incident in which one of the conquerors of Vicksburg, Admiral David Porter, made a final visit to a plantation a few miles above Vicksburg to have a farewell chat with a very old ex-slave who, befitting the times, called himself "Mr. Contraban' Moses." The time was late 1864, and there was every evidence that a complete Yankee victory was both imminent and inevitable. Atlanta was in ashes; Richmond was beseiged; and a victorious Sherman was about to complete a three-pronged path of devastation through Georgia to the sea. As the Admiral bade "Mr. Contraban'" a fond farewell, the old ex-slave said, "Good-by, Massa Cap'n, I'se mos sorry de war so nigh ober, cos I's feard de niggers won be no more consekence."

These were words of penetrating insight, for the history of the Black man in America from 1865 to 1915 was essentially an embittering and discouraging struggle to be of some "consekence." During the Civil War, the Black man had indeed been of consequence. Approximately 178,985 had fought in the Union Army, and 37,300 had given their lives in order that their enslaved brothers might be free. Four Black sailors and seventeen Black soldiers had been awarded the Medal of Honor for heroism in battle. And there was no doubt during the gray, monotonous,

315

and wearying months of the war that the Black man's present and future status was of considerable consequence both in the halls of Congress and in the White House where a worried President pondered what to do to keep this "new birth of freedom" alive and kicking. Should the slave, once freed, be colonized outside the United States, as emigrationists had advocated? If so, where? Haiti? Liberia? Panama? Or could the country, with its vast resources and potential for expansion, absorb four million former slaves and bring about some effective accommodation between slave and defeated master?

Assuredly, then, both the President and the nation in 1865 were concerned about the lot of the newly freed Black man. But the onsweep of events seemed to confirm the fears of "Mr. Contraban' Moses." First, the apparently well-intentioned Lincoln was assassinated even as, at the war's end, he pondered some effective master plan for postwar rehabilitation of the nation. Then, Southern state legislatures, angered by defeat, pounced with vengeful fury on the four million ex-slaves and with the enactment of the infamous Black Codes stripped them of their civil rights and left them defenseless before marauding night-riders. Fortunately, through the enactment of the Reconstruction Act of March 1867, these codes were struck down; military law was imposed on the South and federal protection was provided for the Black man. Immediately thereafter, Congress presented to the nation the Fourteenth Amendment to the Constitution providing for equal protection for all the nation's citizens, white and Black. Then there followed in 1870 the ratification of the Fifteenth Amendment granting full voting rights to the newly freed Black man. But the Reconstruction years were only a brief bright spot in the Black man's quest for real freedom. By 1880—only fifteen years after Appomattox—the long night of legal segregation had already settled. It seemed that there were no longer people in high places who cared—no Thaddeus Stevens, no Charles Sumner. Gone, too, were the fervid abolitionists. It seemed that by 1880 the Black man had become an embarrassing encumbrance to the industrial North as well as to the agrarian South. This climate of national racial hostility was confirmed when, in 1883, the Supreme Court struck down the Civil Rights Act of 1875, thus leaving the Black man once again powerless before a vengeful South. "Mr. Contraban' Moses" had indeed spoken with prophetic insight. The Black man who had been the concern of American social and political idealists in the mid-1860's had become, by the mid-1880's, the victim of American hostility and cynicism.

Necessarily, the literature that the Black man produced from 1865 to 1915 was of a people systematically excluded from the national mainstream. It reflected the Black man's fears, his frustrations, his anxieties, his blighted hopes. Living in a hostile environment and threatened by emotional and psychological insecurity, Black writers were unable to produce a literature of impressive sweep. Hence, the few genres developed were not essentially belletristic. For instance, the novel, usually considered to be a highly sophisticated literary form, received only moderate development. After 1853, the year William Wells Brown published *Clotel,* the first novel by a Black author, there were several novels; but only a few of those written prior to 1900 now merit critical consideration, although some, like Clarissa Thompson's *Treading the Wine Press* (1886), Mrs. A. E. Johnson's *Clarence and Chlorine, or God's Way* (1890), and Walter H. Stowers' and William H. Anderson's *Appointed, an American Novel* (1894), enjoyed considerable popularity during their day. In the last decade of the century, Frances Watkins Harper, a very popular poet of the period, published her *Iola Leroy, or Shadows Uplifted* (1892), an account of the racial pride of an octoroon during the stressful times of Reconstruction. *Imperium in Imperio* (1899), the first of several novels by Sutton Griggs, has great ideological interest.

Paul Laurence Dunbar and Charles W. Chesnutt appeared as novelists at the end of the century. Dunbar, although far more famous as a poet than as a novelist, produced four novels before his early death in 1906. The first three—*The Uncalled* (1898), *The Love of Landry* (1900), and *The Fanatics* (1901)—all have principal characters who are white. His last novel, *The Sport of the Gods* (1902), attempts to analyze the destructive impact of city life on a young Negro from a rural background. Dunbar's contemporary, Chesnutt, was, in the opinion of many critics, the first master of Black fiction to appear. Starting out as a short story writer for the *Atlantic Monthly* from 1887 until 1900, when W. D. Howells disclosed his racial identity, Chesnutt published his first novel, *The House Behind the Cedars*, in 1900. Thereafter, he published two more novels, *The Marrow of Tradition* (1901) and *The Colonel's Dream* (1905).

All three of Chesnutt's novels are well plotted and well written, but the white literary establishment virtually ignored them. For both Dunbar and Chesnutt made their respective bows as novelists in a period neither encouraging nor receptive to the Black novelist. The mere fact that Walter Hines Page, editor of the *Atlantic Monthly*, chose to repress Chesnutt's racial identity as the author of short stories published in the magazine before 1900 is an index of the racial climate of this period. The pressures of his literary environment notwithstanding, Chesnutt's novels have withstood the test of time and have received considerable critical attention. *The Marrow of Tradition,* for instance, is an extremely well controlled fictional account of a Southern community caught up in flaming racial conflict. Presumably, the Wilmington, North Carolina, race riot of 1898 furnished the author with the core of his plot. The character Josh Green in particular stands out as a Black man of heroic stature; in the race riot that engulfs his community he dies as a man of principle who would "ruther be a dead nigger any day dan a live dog!"

After Chesnutt, the one outstanding novelist who emerged in this period was James Weldon Johnson. When his *Autobiography of an Ex-Coloured Man* appeared in 1912, he was forty-one years old and already an established and honored writer of songs. The novel itself was conceived and written while Johnson was in the consular service in Venezuela and Nicaragua. He elected to publish the novel anonymously. As Johnson later indicated in his autobiography, *Along This Way* (1933), anonymous authorship had good and bad consequences. On the one hand, because the *Autobiography* was well written and had considerable verisimilitude of plot, theme, and character, many thought it to be some-one's real life story. After all, in 1912 there were many instances of Blacks who married whites and were themselves light enough to pass over into the white race. So the novel sold well, exciting comment in both the Black and white communities in America. As Johnson explains in *Along This Way,* speculation about the author was particularly rife among Blacks:

> *I did get a certain pleasure out of anonymity that no acknowledged book could have given me. The authorship of the book excited the curiosity of literate colored people, and there was speculation among them as to who the writer might be.*

Johnson goes on to say in the same passage that on one occasion he was in a group in which a gentleman solemnly "Confessed" that the *Auto-biography* was his real-life story. When the novel was republished in 1925, Johnson listed himself as author, but by that time the "true-story," "human-document" interpretation had taken firm root. Many continued to think that a story that rang so true had to be more than just carefully wrought fiction.

The Black poet between 1865 and 1915, like the Black fiction writer, enjoyed little or no national visibility, with the exception, of course, of Paul Laurence Dunbar. And even his case, as will be noted below, warrants further comment and clarification. Many more Black poets than Black fiction writers appeared before 1900, but they confronted the same Black writer's world. And for the poet, this world of grinding material insecurity and multilevel hostility was particularly frustrating. It was a world that rarely permitted contemplation or esthetic detachment. Accordingly, there were many poets who wrote poems either full of bitter racial protest or dripping with escapist romantic idealism. Poets like James Madison Bell (1826–1902), James Whitfield (1823–1878), and, to some extent, Alberry Whitman (1851–1902) wrote protest poetry reflecting the bitter experiences of the post-Reconstruction period. Theirs was the tradition of George Moses Horton, who, in the late 1820's, although confined in "slavery's night" on "this vile, ac-cursed earth," yearned and hoped for liberty. Other poets such as Anne Plato and Henrietta Ray wrote the poems of romantic escapism. A third identifiable group of poets were the so-called dialect poets. These— James Campbell, Elliot Henderson, and Daniel Davis—wrote poems reflecting the white stereotype of Blacks contented and happy in their carefree world of song and laughter.

As mentioned above, Paul Laurence Dunbar was the one undoubtedly significant Black poet to emerge during this period. Certainly, he was the only one to acquire a truly national reputation. Many Black writers and critics—Braithwaite, Brawley, Redding, Wright—have assessed his poetry and career, and all suggest that there was something tragic about the life of this very gifted man. Dunbar, like Chesnutt, had a white sponsor, William Dean Howells. As a consequence, his *Lyrics of Lowly Life* (1896), for which Howells wrote a very laudatory introduction, became the first volume of poetry by a Black poet to capture nationwide interest. The poems in this volume of poetry are largely in dialect and depict rural Blacks as sentimental and emotional primitives, happy with their outcast lot and ignorant of any protest about their condition. Dunbar was undoubtedly cheered by the success of his 1896 volume, but he was at the same time conscious of the fact, as he wrote to a friend in 1897, "that Mr. Howells has done me irrevocable harm in the dictum he laid down regarding my dialect verse." The poet was eminently right in this conclusion, for his *Lyrics of the Hearthside* (1899), a volume of poetry in nondialect English and standard orthography, was not as popular as the 1896 volume. The fault lay not with Mr. Howells' dictum, however. Dunbar's tragedy ultimately lay with an America that would accept from a Black poet only the shuffling, singing, slow-talking plantation stereotype and not the true poetic utterance of a man who, because of his race, had to "wear the mask" of happiness to cover a world of pain. There is no doubt that Dunbar as an artist felt trapped by his situation. His poem "Sympathy," about a caged bird, suggests this:

> *I know why the caged bird sings, ah me,*
>   *When his wing is bruised and his bosom sore,—*
> *When he beats his bars and he would be free;*
> *It is not a carol of joy or glee,*
>   *But a prayer that he sends from his heart's deep core,*
> *But a plea, that upward to Heaven he flings—*
> *I know why the caged bird sings!*

In the *Collected Poems,* published in 1913, seven years after his death in 1906, less than one third are in dialect. Yet his reputation in literary America rested on his dialect poetry—his "jingles in a broken tongue." In a sense, Dunbar wrote his own tragic epitaph when he wrote these lines:

> *He sang of love when earth was young,*
>   *And Love, itself, was in his lays.*
>   *But ah, the world, it turned to praise*
> *A jingle in a broken tongue.*

If the temper of the period 1865–1915 proved far less than congenial to Dunbar and Chesnutt, it was quite receptive to the genre of Black biography or autobiography. Many persons of proven fame and achievement—John Mercer Langston, Frederick Douglass, Daniel Payne, Booker T. Washington—told their stories of achievement, and these works enjoyed a very durable popularity. There are undoubtedly many reasons for the broad appeal of works in this genre during the last quarter of the nineteenth century; at least two are significant enough to warrant comment. First, post–Civil War America was a land of unbridled expansion and growth by virtue of individual enterprise and initiative. The man who could tell of his successful involvement in this expansion gained the ear of the public. In other words, the America of this period developed a great love for the individual success story, whether recounted by a Black man or by a white man. The opportunities for the Black man to display initiative and enterprise were admittedly restricted and limited, but for what he accomplished within his narrow framework of achievement the nation gave praise. All that was asked was that the Black achiever relate a story of upward progress in the American manner without creating any large waves in the sea of race relations. Accordingly, Booker T. Washington was praised for his rise "up from slavery" to the position of the presidency of Tuskegee Institute, located five miles from the nearest train stop at Chehaw, Alabama. His story received wide circulation. Similarly, Bishop Payne's inspiring story of how he moved from an orphaned childhood as a freeborn Black in Charleston, South Carolina, to a bishopric in the A.M.E. Church and thence to the presidency of Wilberforce University was a heartening story to achievement-loving Americans. Both Washington and Payne had displayed fortitude, endurance, initiative, and enterprise within the prescribed racial context, proving that America could even be a land of opportunity for that Black man who held dear the American values of frugality, industry, overt Christian piety, and the like.

The second observation to be made is that these biographies and autobiographies were very inspirational and encouraging to other Black Americans. Like the slave narratives of an earlier time with their stories of escape and achievement in the face of overwhelming odds, the achieving Black man's story after slavery was, in a sense, a "witness" in print that "hard times didn't have to last always." So the Black biography became a kind of written testimony that the Black man who lived right and worked hard could move into America's promised land. Admittedly, for many Black youths during this period such hopes were a snare and a delusion, but what Daniel did and Booker did gave all young Blacks a sense of racial pride and well-being.

Three additional factors affecting Black literary expression during this period should be noted. First, between 1865 and 1915 increased educational opportunities improved Black literacy levels. No Black poets ablaze with creativity emerged from the somewhat puritanically rigid Black Southern colleges, but a Black reader audience slowly emerged. Later, after 1900, this audience was to provide the critical ballast so necessary for the development of literary expression.

A second factor affecting Black literary expression was the continuing development of a rich folklore tradition. Spirituals, work songs, and gospel hymns grew in number with the rapid development of Black religion. Alienated and excluded from the profits of late nineteenth and early twentieth century American materialism, the Black man turned to his church and his religion for comfort and relief from pain. As a consequence, the Black churches grew stronger and more numerous and the sermons of Black preachers supplied a significant cultural additive to an already fertile folk tradition. As James Weldon Johnson was to demonstrate later during the Harlem Awakening in *God's Trombones,* almost every sermon was a richly wrought piece of folk poetry.

It is also appropriate in this connection to remark on white America's developing interest in Black folklore during this period. This interest started when volunteers working with the Freedmen's Commission during the war heard the songs of ex-slaves on the Sea Islands of Port Royal and St. Helena. These were collected by William Allen, Charles Ware, and Lucy Garrison and published in 1867 under the title *Slave Songs of the United States.* As Richard Dorson notes in his *American Folklore,* "The *Slave Songs* erected a bridge from the obscure subculture of Negro folk music to the broad light of American civilization." Then, in 1880, Joel Chandler Harris published his *Uncle Remus: His Songs and Sayings,* giving to the white world the animal tales of old plantation days. With Harris' second publication, *Nights with Uncle Remus* (1883), interest in the Black folk tradition escalated rapidly. Dorson reports that between 1888, the year the *Journal of American Folklore* was founded, and 1913, over a hundred articles on Black folklore were published in the *Journal.* Obviously, these early folklore publications touched on only a part of the rich repertoire of the Black folk tale. In addition to "Buh Rabbit" and "Tar Baby," there were other folk personalities such as Stagalee, Daddy Jake, John Henry, and Juju Mama—all testifying to the rich variety of Black folklore. Although during the period from 1865 to 1915 certain literary genres developed slowly, this was not true of the Black man's folk literature. With every new and varied experience in his pilgrimage through a weary land, the Black man added something to his rich folk tradition.

A third factor affecting Black literary expression in this period was the emergence and crystallization of the Black literary stereotype. As Ralph Ellison has suggested, this racial stereotyping developed as a kind of defense mechanism for guilt-ridden racists. Given the racial climate of the final twenty-five years of the nineteenth century and the prewar years of the twentieth century, it is easily understood how and why demeaning and degrading Black racial stereotypes saturated the publishing market. In works by white authors, Black characters were stereotyped as laughing, happy, singing niggers or as numbskull, slow-witted, slow-talking niggers or as exotic, immoral, primitive niggers or as loyal, moral, servant niggers or as just plain bad, "no-count" niggers. Inevitably, the publishing houses conspired to perpetuate these stereotypes. As a consequence, Black creative writers such as Paul Laurence Dunbar and Charles Chesnutt found themselves trapped by the publishers' demand for racial stereotyping. As has been seen, both Dunbar and Chesnutt found a protective white sponsor in William Dean Howells, who helped them break the color line in publishing. Significantly, both of these Black writers, donned protective masks—Chesnutt that of racial anonymity and Dunbar that of a plantation happiness buff. Obviously, to counter the publishers' demand for Black racial stereotyping, the creative Black writer of this period had to fashion an effective strategy. Some, like Du Bois, successfully sought out publishers not afflicted with "stereotypism" (Du Bois' publisher of *The Souls of Black Folk* in 1903 was A. C. McClurg and Co.). Others did not fare so well, and Black creative literary output suffered accordingly.

One can gather from much of the foregoing that Black literary expression, although not richly varied, was not of one piece. During the fifty-year span, some matters remained provokingly constant—such as cultural alienation, literary stereotyping, discrimination in the labor and housing markets, and segregation in the use of public accommodations and facilities—but in other respects there were changes as the decades rolled by. For instance, the first fifteen years of the period—from 1865 to 1880—can be designated the period of the Reconstruction. Attitudes of both the participant and the historical analyst toward this particular period of Black history are understandably mixed. In literary activity only William Wells Brown was of some importance, but in the political sphere these were years of heartening achievement and bold venturing. On the other hand, on the sharecropper or grass-roots level, there was testimony of another sort: "Reconstruction times bout like times before 'cepting Yankee stole and tore up a scandalous heap. They tell the Black folks to do something, and then come white folks you live with and say Ku Kluck whup you." By 1880, however, the Yankees, following the Tilden-Hayes compromise, were gone from the Southland, taking their "scandalous" ways with them, and there followed a twenty-year period— from 1880 to 1900—in which the newly freed Black man had to grope his way alone. Facing him was a vengeful and destitute South, an uncharitable and callous North, and a cold and inhospitable West. The Black leader who finally emerged during these parlous times was Booker T. Washington, an educator who counselled racial self-reliance, industrial education, and stoical endurance of racial adversity. In his famous Atlanta Exposition speech in 1895, his response to the then fixed patterns of white hostility was one of conciliation and accommodation. In essence, he endorsed racial separatism. Ironically, one year later, in 1896, the Supreme Court gave a legal nod of concurrence with the now famous Plessy-Ferguson decision. In retrospect, it now appears that Booker T. Washington's leadership actually bore little fruit, despite the far-flung endorsement of his defensive strategy by the white power structure. One historian appropriately describes these twenty years as "the Decades of Disappointment." Another, with equal appropriateness, calls this period "the Nadir of the Black Experience."

The third chronological subdivision of this period—1900 to 1915—was marked by the appearance of William Edward Burghardt Du Bois, a versatile and all-sufficient man of learning. In past years, other scholarly men had been associated with the Black man's cause, notably Reconstruction Congressman Robert Elliott, who was a product of Eton and a skilled linguist—but Du Bois, because of sheer intellectual range and energy, stood alone. His life spanned almost seven decades of the twentieth century, and his unusual accomplishments during the first fifteen years of the century provided an effective prelude to the Harlem Awakening. In the main, during this short time, his achievements were threefold. First, he wrote and published *Souls of Black Folk* (1903), and for the first time a book by a Black man spoke to and for an emerging Black intelligentsia. The essays in *Souls* display a disciplined, critical intellect analyzing and surveying aspects of the Black experience with remarkably keen insight and objective accuracy. Such an explication of ideas was far removed from the biographical or autobiographical testimony of personal achievement that, before 1900, had constituted the Black literary essay. Du Bois' second achievement in the early part of the century was the organization of the Niagara Movement in 1905, thus preparing the way for the founding of the NAACP four years later in 1909. His aggressive and able editorship of *The Crisis* constituted his third achievement. Under his leadership, *The Crisis* ignited smoldering literary fires and prepared the way for the Harlem Awakening. Thus, literarily speaking, the years in which the young Du Bois stood at the helm of leadership were good years. For the first time there seemed to be firm intellectual leadership and an emerging Black intelligentsia. It is significant that out of this period came the first one of a series of excellent twentieth-century Black novels—James Weldon Johnson's *Autobiography of an Ex-coloured Man* (1912). This was certainly a harbinger of things to come—a sign that for the Black writer and man of letters the Awakening was at hand.

The Major Writers

Charles W. Chesnutt (1858–1932)

Unlike his famous contemporary Paul Laurence Dunbar, who knew the South only through the recollections of his parents, Charles Waddell Chesnutt had thorough first-hand experience of life in North Carolina as well as in his native Cleveland. His probing treatment of racial and inter-racial themes North and South earned him the richly deserved title of the outstanding pioneer of Black fiction. Challenging the racist interpretations of Joel Chandler Harris, Thomas Nelson Page, James Lane Allen, Thomas Dixon, and other white writers of the Plantation School, Chesnutt presented a more realistic, less sentimental view of slavery times and the Reconstruction period. The problems and preoccupations of the near-white, such as strained family relations, intraracial prejudice, and passing, received his special attention, for he was himself light enough to pass, but he did not ignore darker characters, ranging from the cunning Uncle Julius of *The Conjure Woman* to the militant and violent Josh Green of *The Marrow of Tradition*. Chesnutt's white characters, too, are widely diverse. He always wrote out of an implacable hostility to the American caste system, which he considered the chief "barrier to the moral progress of the American people," but his literary method at its best relied more on indirection and irony than on overt argument to effect what he called the "moral revolution" necessary to cleanse the national soul. Compared by the influential critic William Dean Howells to such giants as Maupassant, Turgenev, and Henry James, Chesnutt was a careful literary artist, especially in the short story, whose craft as well as themes made him an auspicious early master of Afro-American writing.

Chesnutt was born in Cleveland on June 20, 1858, of parents who had left Fayetteville, North Carolina, two years earlier to escape the increasing repression of free Blacks in the decade before the Civil War. Serving in the Union Army in North Carolina when the war ended, Chesnutt's father soon afterward sent for his wife and two sons to join him in Fayetteville, hoping that Reconstruction would make the South a more favorable place in which to raise a Black family. With the exception of a few months, Chesnutt lived in North Carolina from the age of eight to the age of twenty-five. He augmented his formal education with extensive independent study and tutorial instruction in German, French, and Greek. While only a boy of fourteen and still a pupil at the Howard School in Fayetteville, he began teaching there. Later, he taught in Charlotte and Mt. Zion, North Carolina, and in a country school near Spartanburg, South Carolina, before becoming a principal in Charlotte and then, still not yet twenty, assistant principal and teacher in a new State Normal School in Fayetteville, moving up to principal of this institution in November 1880. All the while he was continuing his own education, both literary and practical. His favorite authors included Shakespeare, Goldsmith, Cowper, Burns, Byron, Dickens, Macaulay, Molière, Dumas, and, among American writers, Harriet Beecher Stowe and Albion W. Tourgée. Cherishing his own literary ambitions, he confided in his journal on May 29, 1880:

I think I must write a book. I am almost afraid to undertake a book so early and with so little experience in composition. But it has been my cherished dream, and I feel an influence that I cannot resist calling me to the task. Besides, I do not know but I am as well prepared as some successful writers. A fair knowledge of the classics, speaking acquaintance with the modern languages, an intimate friendship with literature, etc., seven years' experience in the school room, two years of married life, and a habit of studying character, have I think, left me not entirely unprepared to write even a book.

But in addition to his liberal studies, he had taken the prudent step of mastering stenography. Moving into the larger world of the North in 1883, he found a job as an interviewer and reporter for a Wall Street news agency. Six months later, he moved from New York to Cleveland, where he had accepted employment in the accounting department of a railroad company. Cleveland was to be his home for the next half century. Here he achieved literary fame, business prosperity as a lawyer and legal stenographer, social success, and civic distinction. When he received the Springarn Medal of the NAACP in 1928, he was cited for his "pioneer work as a literary artist depicting the life and struggles of Americans of Negro descent, and for his long and useful career as scholar, worker, and freeman of one of America's greatest cities."

As a writer, Chesnutt excelled in the short story, produced novels of considerable social and historical interest, and contributed thoughtful, lucid nonfiction in the form of essays, speeches, reviews, and a brief biography of Frederick Douglass. He also wrote some dozen poems, half of which were published, as well as an unpublished play. Though it is often asserted that Chesnutt began his literary career with "The Goophered Grapevine," published in *The Atlantic Monthly* of August 1887, he had already published at least sixteen short stories in various newspapers, not to mention several poems and articles and, in his New York days, "a daily column of Wall Street gossip" in the *New York Mail and Express*. "The Goophered Grapevine" did bring him to the attention of a national literary audience, however, and friendships developed with such established liberal white writers as George Washington Cable, Albion W. Tourgée, and Walter Hines Page. His stories continued to appear in major periodicals, especially the *Atlantic,* but he had to wait for more than a decade before they were collected in book form, *The Conjure Woman* and *The Wife of His Youth and Other Stories of the Color Line* both appearing in 1899. In *The Conjure Woman* Chesnutt uses or invents folk material in tales of the ante-bellum South involving magic—"goopher"—performed by old slave conjurers. The picture of slavery that emerges is grimly unlike the sentimentalized and falsified version then widely prevalent, for parents and children are separated, lovers are parted, the lash is applied freely. The repressive power of the master is always present and usually exercised in these stories. On the other hand, the reliance of the slave on "magic," a system of religious belief with African roots, brings him not only solutions to pressing personal problems but also a sense that he is attuned, as the white man is not, to the ultimate mysteries of existence. As interesting as the tales themselves is the framework in which they are placed, with its complex arrangement of points of view. The scene and occasion of each story are established by a white grape grower who has moved to North Carolina from northern Ohio because of his wife's delicate health. This couple, John and Annie, listen to the tale proper narrated in dialect by Uncle Julius, an old ex-slave who is not only a living repository of local legend but also a clever manipulator of his white auditors. The purpose of his manipulation of John, a practical but morally insensitive man, is to protect and provide for his own interests and comforts: income from a vineyard, the use of an old school house, a secret honey-tree, and so on. The manipulation of Annie, a sympathetic and responsive woman, is of a different order, for the design of Uncle Julius is to induce her to recognize the truth about "those horrid days before the War." Like Annie, the reader of *The Conjure Woman* is morally instructed by Uncle Julius. For all of the charm of their telling, these tales point toward the inescapably painful conclusion: "'What a system it was,' she exclaimed, when Julius had finished, 'under which such things were possible.'"

The Wife of His Youth has perhaps less unity than *The Conjure Woman,* but each of the nine stories turns on some problem caused by racial prejudice; as Chesnutt himself put it in a letter to his publisher, "the backbone of this volume is not a character, like Uncle Julius . . . but a subject, as indicated in the title—*The Color Line.*" Two of the stories, "The Wife of His Youth" and "A Matter of Principle," deal with the Blue Vein Society of the Black bourgeoisie in Groveland (Cleveland), a social club based on a system of false values imitative of those of genteel whites. Mr. Ryder of the title story achieves a real victory in meeting his moral crisis by affirming Blackness, but Cicero Clayton of "A Matter of Principle" rejects his Black identity and fails as a human being. Most of the other stories deal with the South, and one, the amusing "Uncle Wellington's Wives," with both South and North. Among the best are "The Sheriff's Children," a study of guilt and suicide and attempted lynching, and "The Passing of Grandison," a superbly ironic reversal of the stereotype of the faithful and contented slave. Irony is indeed the most effective of Chesnutt's literary instruments in his short fiction. His occasional touches of sentimentality and his reliance on coincidence in plotting show him to be a writer of his time, but his ironic probing of the manifold results of racism shows him to be one who can still speak to our own.

Writing in Alain Locke's important collection *The New Negro* (1925), the Black critic William Stanley Braithwaite states that "Mr. Chesnutt is a story-teller of genius transformed by racial earnestness into the novelist of talent." Most critics have agreed that his short stories are more artistically successful than his novels, which are more polemical and less firmly constructed. Perhaps, but his three novels are still very much worth reading for their searching exploration of racial tension in the Reconstruction and post-Reconstruction South. *The House Behind the Cedars* (1900), an expansion of a short story entitled "Rena Walden" written over a decade earlier, is concerned with passing and inter-racial love, but at the end the very light heroine comes home to her people, rejecting the white George Tryon and the mulatto Jeff Wain to die with her hand clasped in that of the Black Frank Fowler. In *The Marrow of Tradition* (1901) Chesnutt treats the disillusionment of Dr. William Miller, a Black physician who idealistically hopes for interracial cooperation as he sets up his practice in the South. His dream is shattered by massive white violence, patterned by the author after the Wilmington, North Carolina, riot of 1898. Chesnutt's last published novel, *The Colonel's Dream* (1905), is similarly gloomy (and realistic) in its assessment of the possibility of Southern racial harmony. Colonel Henry French, a white aristocrat, attempts to overcome such evils as peonage, the convict lease system, and educational, economic, and political discrimination, but is finally driven out of the South. At the close of the work, Chesnutt expresses the hope "that some day our land will be truly free, and the strong will cheerfully help to bear the burdens of the weak, and Justice, the seed, and Peace, the flower, of liberty, will prevail throughout all our borders," but he knew that such a day would be a long time coming. In addition to his published novels, Chesnutt wrote six others, the manuscripts of which are deposited in the library of Fisk University.

Chesnutt's nonfiction is mostly concerned in one way or another with what he once called "the everlasting problem." More than two dozen articles and speeches appeared in a variety of periodicals and books, and many others exist in manuscript form. His adherence to racial justice was unswerving, for as he observed in a letter to an activist in the Niagara Movement, "Agitation for rights is by no means foolish; where rights are denied it is a sacred duty...." But his own forensic proclivities were on the side of restraint and understatement, though he recognized the place of a more militant tone: "I don't blame any one for becoming angry or impatient about the situation in this country. The only way for a colored person to keep calm about it is not to think about it. But there is a certain conservatism in discussion, and a certain philosophical point of view which I think quite as effective as hysterical declamation. But we need both—some to fan the flame and others to furnish the fuel." "The

Disfranchisement of the Negro," contributed in 1903 to a volume of essays by several hands entitled *The Negro Problem,* is a representative example of Chesnutt's work as a social commentator.

All of Chesnutt's books are now in print, five of them in paperback: *The Conjure Woman* (introduction by Robert M. Farnsworth), *The Wife of His Youth* (introduction by Earl Schenck Miers), *The House Behind the Cedars* (introduction by Darwin T. Turner), *The Marrow of Tradition* (introduction by R. M. Farnsworth), and *The Colonel's Dream.* Two of Chesnutt's essays with special literary relevance are "Superstitions and Folk-lore of the South," *Modern Culture,* XIII (May 1901), 231–235, and "Post-bellum, Pre-Harlem," *The Crisis,* XXXVIII (June 1931), 193–194. The most important collection of materials is catalogued by Mildred Freeney and Mary T. Henry in *A List of Manuscripts . . . in the Charles Waddell Chesnutt Collection of . . . Fisk University* (1954).

A very helpful guide to Chesnutt scholarship is Dean H. Keller, "Charles Waddell Chesnutt (1858–1932)," *American Literary Realism,* No. 3 (Summer 1968), pp. 1–4. Helen M. Chesnutt's *Charles Waddell Chesnutt: Pioneer of the Color Line* (1952) is a filial biography, uncritical but charming and especially valuable for the generous quotations from private journals and correspondence. For criticism of Chesnutt's fiction, see the standard literary histories: Vernon Loggins, *The Negro Author* (1931); Sterling Brown, *The Negro in American Fiction* (1937); Benjamin Brawley, *The Negro Genius* (1937); Hugh M. Gloster, *Negro Voices in American Fiction* (1948); and Robert Bone, *The Negro Novel in America* (1958). Sylvia Lyons Render, who wrote her doctoral dissertation on Chesnutt and is preparing a volume on him for Twayne's United States Authors Series, has published an important study of "Tar Heelia in Chesnutt," *CLA Journal,* IX (September 1965), 39–50. Other significant articles are Samuel Sillen, "Charles W. Chesnutt: A Pioneer Negro Novelist," *Masses & Mainstream,* VI (February 1953), 8–14; Russell Ames, "Social Realism in Charles W. Chesnutt," *Phylon,* XIII (Second Quarter 1953), 199–206; Julian D. Mason, Jr., "Charles W. Chesnutt as Southern Author," *The Mississippi Quarterly,* XX (Spring 1967), 77–89; Gerald W. Haslam, "'The Sheriff's Children': Chesnutt's Tragic Racial Parable," *Negro American Literature Forum,* II (Summer 1968), 21–26; June Sochen, "Charles Waddell Chesnutt and the Solution to the Race Problem," *Negro American Literature Forum,* III (Summer 1969), 52–56; R. M. Farnsworth, "Testing the Color Line—Dunbar and Chesnutt," in *The Black American Writer* (1969), Vol. I, edited by C. W. E. Bigsby, and "Charles Chesnutt and the Color Line," in *Minor American Novelists* (1970), edited by Charles Alva Hoyt; and John M. Reilly, "The Dilemma in Chesnutt's The Marrow of Tradition," *Phylon,* XXXII (1971), 31–38. William Dean Howells' early reviews are still worth reading: "Mr. Charles W. Chesnutt's Stories," *The Atlantic Monthly,* LXXXV (May 1900), 699–701, and "A Psychological Counter-Current in Recent Fiction," *North American Review,* CLXXIII (December 1901), 881–883, on *The Marrow of Tradition.*

The Goophered Grapevine

Some years ago my wife was in poor health, and our family doctor, in whose skill and honesty I had implicit confidence, advised a change of climate. I shared, from an unprofessional standpoint, his opinion that the raw winds, the chill rains, and the violent changes of temperature that characterized the winters in the region of the Great Lakes tended to aggravate my wife's difficulty, and would undoubtedly shorten her life if she remained exposed to them. The doctor's advice was that we seek, not a temporary place of sojourn, but a permanent residence, in a warmer and more equable climate. I was engaged at the time in grape-culture in northern Ohio, and, as I liked the business and had given it much study, I decided to look for some other locality suitable for carrying it on. I thought of sunny France, of sleepy Spain, of Southern California, but there were objections to them all. It occurred to me that I might find what I wanted in some one of our own Southern States. It was a sufficient time after the war for conditions in the South to have become somewhat settled; and I was enough of a pioneer to start a new industry, if I could not find a place where grape-culture had been tried. I wrote to a cousin who had gone into the turpentine business in central North Carolina. He assured me, in response to my inquiries, that no better place could be found in the South than the State and neighborhood where he lived; the climate was perfect for health, and, in conjunction with the soil, ideal for grape-culture; labor was cheap, and land could be bought for a mere song. He gave us a cordial invitation to come and visit him while we looked into the matter. We accepted the invitation, and after several days of leisurely travel, the last hundred miles of which were up a river on a sidewheel steamer, we reached our destination, a quaint old town, which I shall call Patesville, because, for one reason, that is not its name. There was a red brick market-house in the public square, with a tall tower, which held a four-faced clock that struck the hours, and from which there pealed out a curfew at nine o'clock. There were two or three hotels, a court-house, a jail, stores, offices, and all the appurtenances of a county seat and a commercial emporium; for while Patesville numbered only four or five thousand inhabitants, of all shades of complexion, it was one of the principal towns in North Carolina, and had a considerable trade in cotton and naval stores. This business activity was not immediately apparent to my unaccustomed eyes. Indeed, when I first saw the town, there brooded over it a calm that seemed almost sabbatic in its restfulness, though I learned later on that underneath its somnolent exterior the deeper currents of life— love and hatred, joy and despair, ambition and avarice, faith and friendship—flowed not less steadily than in livelier latitudes.

We found the weather delightful at that season, the end of summer, and were hospitably entertained. Our host was a man of means and evidently regarded our visit as a pleasure, and we were therefore correspondingly at our ease, and in a position to act with the coolness of judgment desirable in making so radical a change in our lives. My cousin placed a horse and buggy at our disposal, and himself acted as our guide until I became somewhat familiar with the country.

I found that grape-culture, while it had never been carried on to any great extent, was not entirely unknown in the neighborhood. Several planters thereabouts had attempted it on a commercial scale, in former years, with greater or less success; but like most Southern industries, it had felt the blight of war and had fallen into desuetude.

I went several times to look at a place that I thought might suit me. It was a plantation of considerable extent, that had formerly belonged to a wealthy man by the name of McAdoo. The estate had been for years involved in litigation between disputing heirs, during which period shiftless cultivation had well-nigh exhausted the soil. There had been a vineyard of some extent on the place, but it had not been attended to since the war, and had lapsed into utter neglect. The vines—here partly supported by decayed and broken-down trellises, there twining themselves among the branches of the slender saplings which had sprung up among them—grew in wild and unpruned luxuriance, and the few scattered grapes they bore were the undisputed prey of the first comer. The site was admirably adapted to grape-raising; the soil, with a little attention, could not have been better; and with the native grape, the luscious scuppernong, as my main reliance in the beginning, I felt sure that I could introduce and cultivate successfully a number of other varieties.

One day I went over with my wife to show her the place. We drove out of the town over a long wooden bridge that spanned a spreading mill-pond, passed the long whitewashed fence surrounding the county fair-ground, and struck into a road so sandy that the horse's feet sank to the fetlocks. Our route lay partly up hill and partly down, for we were in the sand-hill county; we drove past cultivated farms, and then by abandoned fields grown up in scrub-oak and short-leaved pine, and once or twice through the solemn aisles of the virgin forest, where the tall pines, well-nigh meeting over the narrow road, shut out the sun, and wrapped us in cloistral solitude. Once, at a cross-roads, I was in doubt as to the turn to take, and we sat there waiting ten minutes —we had already caught some of the native infection of restfulness—for some human being to come along, who could direct us on our way. At length a little negro girl appeared, walking straight as an arrow, with a piggin full of water on her head. After a little patient investigation, necessary to overcome the child's shyness, we learned what we wished to know, and at the end of about five miles from the town reached our destination.

We drove between a pair of decayed gateposts —the gate itself had long since disappeared—and up a straight sandy lane, between two lines of rotting rail fence, partly concealed by jimson-weeds and briers, to the open space where a dwelling-house had once stood, evidently a spacious mansion, if we might judge from the ruined chimneys that were still standing, and the brick pillars on which the sills rested. The house itself, we had been informed, had fallen a victim to the fortunes of war.

We alighted from the buggy, walked about the yard for a while, and then wandered off into the adjoining vineyard. Upon Annie's complaining of weariness I led the way back to the yard, where a pine log, lying under a spreading elm, afforded a shady though somewhat hard seat. One end of the log was already occupied by a venerable-looking colored man. He held on his knees a hat full of grapes, over which he was smacking his lips with great gusto, and a pile of grapeskins near him indicated that the performance was no new thing. We approached him

at an angle from the rear, and were close to him before he perceived us. He respectfully rose as we drew near, and was moving away, when I begged him to keep his seat.

"Don't let us disturb you," I said. "There is plenty of room for us all."

He resumed his seat with somewhat of embarrassment. While he had been standing, I had observed that he was a tall man, and, though slightly bowed by the weight of years, apparently quite vigorous. He was not entirely black, and this fact, together with the quality of his hair, which was about six inches long and very bushy, except on the top of his head, where he was quite bald, suggested a slight strain of other than negro blood. There was a shrewdness in his eyes, too, which was not altogether African, and which, as we afterwards learned from experience, was indicative of a corresponding shrewdness in his character. He went on eating the grapes, but did not seem to enjoy himself quite so well as he had apparently done before he became aware of our presence.

"Do you live around here?" I asked, anxious to put him at his ease.

"Yas, suh. I lives des ober yander, behine de nex' san'-hill, on de Lumberton plank-road."

"Do you know anything about the time when this vineyard was cultivated?"

"Lawd bless you, suh, I knows all about it. Dey ain' na'er a man in dis settlement w'at won' tell you ole Julius McAdoo 'uz bawn en raise' on dis yer same plantation. Is you de Norv'n gemman w'at's gwine ter buy de ole vimya'd?"

"I am looking at it." I replied; "but I don't know that I shall care to buy unless I can be reasonably sure of making something out of it."

"Well, suh, you is a stranger ter me, en I is a stranger ter you, en we is bofe strangers ter one anudder, but 'f I 'uz in yo' place, I wouldn' buy dis vimya'd."

"Why not?" I asked.

"Well, I dunno whe'r you b'lieves in cunj'in' er not,—some er de w'ite folks don't, er says dey don't,—but de truf er de matter is dat dis yer ole vimya'd is goophered."

"Is what?" I asked, not grasping the meaning of this unfamiliar word.

"Is goophered,—cunju'd, bewitch'."

He imparted this information with such solemn earnestness, and with such an air of confidential mystery, that I felt somewhat interested, while

Annie was evidently much impressed, and drew closer to me.

"How do you know it is bewitched?" I asked.

"I would n' spec' fer you ter b'lieve me 'less you know all 'bout de fac's. But ef you en young miss dere doan' min' lis'nin' ter a ole nigger run on a minute er two w'ile you er restin', I kin 'splain to you how it all happen'."

We assured him that we would be glad to hear how it all happened, and he began to tell us. At first the current of his memory—or imagination—seemed somewhat sluggish; but as his embarrassment wore off, his language flowed more freely, and the story acquired perspective and coherence. As he became more and more absorbed in the narrative, his eyes assumed a dreamy expression, and he seemed to lose sight of his auditors, and to be living over again in monologue his life on the old plantation.

"Ole Mars Dugal' McAdoo," he began, "bought dis place long many years befo' de wah, en I 'member well w'en he sot out all dis yer part er de plantation in scuppernon's. De vimes growed monst'us fas', en Mars Dugal' made a thousan' gallon er scuppernon' wine eve'y year.

"Now, ef dey's an'thing a nigger lub, nex' ter 'possum, en chick'n, en watermillyums, it's scuppernon's. Dey ain' nuffin dat kin stan' up side'n de scuppernon' fer sweetness; sugar ain't a suckumstance ter scuppernon'. W'en de season is nigh 'bout ober, en de grapes begin ter swivel up des a little wid de wrinkles er ole age,—w'en de skin git sof' en brown,—den de scuppernon' make you smack yo' lip en roll yo' eye en wush fer mo'; so I reckon it ain' very 'stonishin' dat niggers lub scuppernon'.

"Dey wuz a sight er niggers in de naberhood er de vimya'd. Dere wuz ole Mars Henry Brayboy's niggers, en ole Mars Jeems McLean's niggers, en Mars Dugal's own niggers; den dey wuz a settlement er free niggers en po' buckrahs down by de Wim'l'ton Road, en Mars Dugal' had de only vimya'd in de naberhood. I reckon it ain' so much so nowadays, but befo' de wah, in slab'ry times, a nigger did n' mine goin' fi' er ten mile in a night, w'en dey wuz sump'n good ter eat at de yuther een'.

"So atter a w'ile Mars Dugal' begin ter miss his scuppernon's. Co'se he 'cuse' de niggers er it, but dey all 'nied it ter de las'. Mars Dugal' sot spring guns en steel traps, en he en de oberseah sot up nights once't er twice't, tel one night Mars Dugal'—he 'uz a monst'us keerless man—got his leg shot full er cow-peas. But somehow er nudder dey could n' nebber ketch none er de niggers. I dunner how it happen, but it happen des like I tell you, en de grapes kep' on a-goin' des de same.

"But bimeby ole Mars Dugal' fix' up a plan ter stop it. Dey wuz a cunjuh 'oman livin' down 'mongs' de free niggers on de Wim'l'ton Road, en all de darkies fum Rockfish ter Beaver Crick wuz feared er her. She could wuk de mos' powerfulles' kin' er goopher,—could make people hab fits, er rheumatiz, er make 'em des dwinel away en die; en dey say she went out ridin' de niggers at night, fer she wuz a witch 'sides bein' a cunjuh 'oman. Mars Dugal' hearn 'bout Aun' Peggy's doin's, en begun ter 'flect whe'r er no he could n' git her ter he'p him keep de niggers off'n de grapevimes. One day in de spring er de year, ole miss pack' up a basket er chick'n en poun'-cake, en a bottle er scuppernon' wine, en Mars Dugal' tuk it in his buggy en driv ober ter Aun' Peggy's cabin. He tuk de basket in, en had a long talk wid Aun' Peggy.

"De nex' day Aun' Peggy come up ter de vimya'd. De niggers seed her slippin' 'roun', en dey soon foun' out what she 'uz doin' dere. Mars Dugal' had hi'ed her ter goopher de grapevimes. She sa'ntered 'roun' 'mongs' de vimes, en tuk a leaf fum dis one, en a grape-hull fum dat one, en a grape-seed fum anudder one; en den a little twig fum here, en a little pinch er dirt fum dere,—en put it all in a big black bottle, wid a snake's toof en a speckle' hen's gall en some ha'rs fum a black cat's tail, en den fill' de bottle wid scuppernon' wine. W'en she got de goopher all ready en fix', she tuk 'n went out in de woods en buried it under de root uv a red oak tree, en den come back en tole one er de niggers she done goopher de grapevimes, en a'er a nigger w'at eat dem grapes 'ud be sho ter die inside'n twel' mont's.

"Atter dat de niggers let de scuppernon's 'lone, en Mars Dugal' did n' hab no 'casion ter fine no mo' fault; en de season wuz mos' gone, w'en a strange gemman stop at de plantation one night ter see Mars Dugal' on some business; en his coachman, seein' de scuppernon's growin' so nice en sweet, slip 'roun' behine de smoke-house, en et all de scuppernon's he could hole. Nobody did n' notice it at de time, but dat night, on de way home, de gemman's hoss runned away en kill' de coachman. W'en we hearn de noos, Aun' Lucy, de cook, she up 'n say she seed de strange nigger eat'n' er de scuppernon's behine de smoke-house; en den we knowed de goopher had b'en er wukkin'. Den one er de nigger chilluns runned away fum de quarters one day, en got in de scuppernon's, en died de nex' week. W'ite folks say he die' er de fevuh, but de niggers knowed it wuz de goopher. So you k'n be sho de darkies did n' hab much ter do wid dem scuppernon' vimes.

"W'en de scuppernon' season 'uz ober fer dat year, Mars Dugal' foun' he had made fifteen hund'ed gallon er wine; en one er de niggers hearn him laffin' wid de oberseah fit ter kill, en sayin' dem fifteen hund'ed gallon er wine wuz monst'us good intrus' on de ten dollars he laid out on de vimya'd. So I 'low ez he paid Aun' Peggy ten dollars fer to goopher de grapevimes.

"De goopher did n' wuk no mo' tel de nex' summer, w'en 'long to'ds de middle er de season one er de fiel' han's died; en ez dat lef' Mars Dugal' sho't er han's, he went off ter town fer ter buy anudder. He fotch de noo nigger home wid 'im. He wuz er ole nigger, er de color er a gingy-cake, en ball ez a hoss-apple on de top er his head. He wuz a peart ole nigger, do', en could do a big day's wuk.

"Now it happen dat one er de niggers on de nex' plantation, one er ole Mars Henry Brayboy's niggers, had runned away de day befo', en tuk ter de swamp, en ole Mars Dugal' en some er de yuther nabor w'ite folks had gone out wid dere guns en dere dogs fer ter he'p 'em hunt fer de nigger; en de han's on our own plantation wuz all so flusterated dat we fuhgot ter tell de noo han' 'bout de goopher on de scuppernon' vimes. Co'se he smell de grapes en see de vimes, an atter dahk de fus' thing he done wuz ter slip off ter de grapevimes 'dout sayin' nuffin ter nobody. Nex' mawnin' he tole some er de niggers 'bout de fine bait er scuppernon' he et de night befo'.

"W'en dey tole 'im 'bout de goopher on de grapevimes, he 'uz dat tarrified dat he turn pale, en look des like he gwine ter die right in his tracks. De oberseah come up en axed w'at 'uz de matter; en w'en dey tole 'im Henry be'n eatin' er de scuppernon's, en got de goopher on 'im, he gin Henry a big drink er w'iskey, en 'low dat de nex' rainy day he take 'im ober ter Aun' Peggy's, en see ef she would n' take de goopher off'n him, seein' ez he did n' know nuffin erbout it tel he done et de grapes.

"Sho nuff, it rain de nex' day, en de oberseah went ober ter Aun' Peggy's wid Henry. En Aun' Peggy say dat bein' ez Henry did n' know 'bout de goopher, en et de grapes in ign'ance er de conseq'ences, she reckon she mought be able fer ter take de goopher off'n him. So she fotch out er bottle wid some cunjuh medicine in it, en po'd some out in a go'd fer Henry ter drink. He manage ter git it down; he say it tas'e like whiskey wid sump'n bitter in it. She 'lowed dat 'ud keep de goopher off'n him tel de spring; but w'en de sap begin ter rise in de grapevimes he ha' ter come en see her ag'in, en she tell him w'at e's ter do.

"Nex' spring, w'en de sap commence' ter rise in de scuppernon' vime, Henry tuk a ham one night. Whar'd he git de ham? *I* doan know; dey wa'n't no hams on de plantation 'cep'n' w'at 'uz in de smoke-house, but *I* never see Henry 'bout de smoke-house. But ez I wuz a-sayin', he tuk de ham ober ter Aun' Peggy's; en Aun' Peggy tole 'im dat w'en Mars Dugal' begin ter prune de grapevimes, he mus' go en take 'n scrape off de sap whar it ooze out'n de cut een's er de vimes, en 'n'int his ball head wid it; en ef he do dat once't a year de goopher would n' wuk agin 'im long ez he done it. En bein' ez he fotch her de ham, she fix' it so he kin eat all de scuppernon' he want.

"So Henry 'n'int his head wid de sap out'n de big grapevime des ha'f way 'twix' de quarters en de big house, en de goopher nebber wuk agin him dat summer. But de beatenes' thing you eber see happen ter Henry. Up ter dat time he wuz ez ball ez a sweeten' 'tater, but des ez soon ez de young leaves begun ter come out on de grape-vimes, de ha'r begun ter grow out on Henry's head, en by de middle er de summer he had de bigges' head er ha'r on de plantation. Befo' dat, Henry had tol'able good ha'r 'roun' de aidges, but soon ez de young grapes begun ter come, Henry's ha'r begun to quirl all up in little balls, des like dis yer reg'lar grapy ha'r, en by de time de grapes got ripe his head look des like a bunch er grapes. Combin' it did n' do no good; he wuk at it ha'f de night wid er Jim Crow,[1] en think he git it straighten' out, but in de mawnin' de grapes 'ud be dere des de same. So he gin it up, en tried ter keep de grapes down by havin' his ha'r cut sho't.

"But dat wa'n't de quares' thing 'bout de goopher. When Henry come ter de plantation, he wuz gittin' a little ole an stiff in de j'ints. But dat summer he got des ez spry en libely ez any young nigger on de plantation; fac', he got so

[1] A small card, resembling a currycomb in construction, and used by negros in the rural districts instead of a comb.

biggity dat Mars Jackson, de oberseah, ha' ter th'eaten ter whip 'im, ef he did n' stop cuttin' up his didos en behave hisse'f. But de mos' cur'ouses' thing happen' in de fall, when de sap begin ter go down in de grapevimes. Fus', when de grapes 'uz gethered, de knots begun ter straighten out'n Henry's ha'r; en w'en de leaves begin ter fall, Henry's ha'r 'mence' ter drap out; en when de vimes 'uz bar', Henry's head wuz baller'n it wuz in de spring, en he begin ter git ole en stiff in de j'ints ag'in, en paid no mo' 'tention ter de gals dyoin' er de whole winter. En nex' spring, w'en he rub de sap on ag'in, he got young ag'in, en so soopl en libely dat none er de young niggers on de plantation could n' jump, ner dance, ner hoe ez much cotton ez Henry. But in de fall er de year his grapes 'mence' ter straighten out, en his j'ints ter git stiff, en his ha'r drap off, en de rheumatiz begin ter wrastle wid 'im.

"Now, ef you'd 'a' knowed ole Mars Dugal' McAdoo, you'd 'a' knowed dat it ha' ter be a mighty rainy day when he could n' fine sump'n fer his niggers ter do, en it ha' ter be a mighty little hole he could n' crawl thoo, en ha' ter be a monst'us cloudy night when a dollar git by him in de dahkness; en w'en he see how Henry git young in de spring en ole in de fall, he 'lowed ter hisse'f ez how he could make mo' money out'n Henry dan by wukkin' him in de cotton-fiel'. 'Long de nex' spring, atter de sap 'mence' ter rise, en Henry 'n'int 'is head en sta'ted fer ter git young en soopl, Mars Dugal' up 'n tuk Henry ter town, en sole 'im fer fifteen hunder' dollars. Co'se de man w'at bought Henry did n' know nuffin 'bout de goopher, en Mars Dugal' did n' see no 'casion fer ter tell 'im. Long to'ds de fall, w'en de sap went down, Henry begin ter git ole ag'in same ez yuzhal, en his noo marster begin ter git skeered les'n he gwine ter lose his fifteen-hunder'-dollar nigger. He sent fer a mighty fine doctor, but de med'cine did n' 'pear ter do no good; de goopher had a good holt. Henry tole de doctor 'bout de goopher, but de doctor des laff at 'im.

"One day in de winter Mars Dugal' went ter town, en wuz santerin' 'long de Main Street, when who should he meet but Henry's noo marster. Dey said 'Hoddy,' en Mars Dugal' ax 'im ter hab a seegyar; en atter dey run on awhile 'bout de craps en de weather, Mars Dugal' ax 'im, sorter keerless, like ez ef he des thought of it,—

"'How you like de nigger I sole you las' spring?'

"Henry's marster shuck his head en knock de ashes off'n his seegyar.

"'Spec' I made a bad bahgin when I bought dat nigger. Henry done good wuk all de summer, but sence de fall set in he 'pears ter be sorter pinin' away. Dey ain' nuffin pertickler de matter wid 'im—leastways de doctor say so—'cep'n' a tech er de rheumatiz; but his ha'r is all fell out, en ef he don't pick up his strenk mighty soon, I spec' I'm gwine ter lose 'im.'

"Dey smoked on awhile, en bimeby ole mars say, 'Well, a bahgin's a bahgin, but you en me is good fren's, en I doan wan' ter see you lose all de money you paid fer dat nigger; en ef w'at you say is so, en I ain't 'sputin' it, he ain't wuf much now. I 'spec's you wukked him too ha'd dis summer, er e'se de swamps down here don't agree wid de san'-hill nigger. So you des lemme know, en ef he gits any wusser I'll be willin' ter gib yer five hund'ed dollars fer 'im, en take my chances on his livin'.'

"Sho 'nuff, when Henry begun ter draw up wid de rheumatiz en it look like he gwine ter die fer sho, his noo marster sen' fer Mars Dugal', en Mars Dugal' gin him what he promus, en brung Henry home ag'in. He tuk good keer uv 'im dyoin' er de winter,— give 'im w'iskey ter rub his rheumatiz, en terbacker ter smoke, en all he want ter eat,—'caze a nigger w'at he could make a thousan' dollars a year off'n did n' grow on eve'y huckleberry bush.

"Nex' spring, w'en de sap rise en Henry's ha'r commence' ter sprout, Mars Dugal' sole 'im ag'in, down in Robeson County dis time; en he kep' dat sellin' business up fer five year er mo'.' Henry nebber say nuffin 'bout de goopher ter his noo marsters, 'caze he know he gwine ter be tuk good keer uv de nex' winter, w'en Mars Dugal' buy him back. En Mars Dugal' made 'nuff money off'n Henry ter buy anudder plantation ober on Beaver Crick.

"But 'long 'bout de een' er dat five year dey come a stranger ter stop at de plantation. De fus' day he 'uz dere he went out wid Mars Dugal' en spent all de mawnin' lookin' ober de vimya'd, en atter dinner dey spent all de evenin' playin' kya'ds. De niggers soon 'skiver' dat he wuz a Yankee, en dat he come down ter Norf C'lina fer ter l'arn de w'ite folks how to raise grapes en make wine. He promus Mars Dugal' he c'd make de grapevimes b'ar twice't ez many grapes, en dat de noo winepress he wuz a-sellin' would make mo' d'n twice't ez many gallons er wine. En ole Mars Dugal' des drunk it all in, des 'peared ter be bewitch' wid dat Yankee. W'en de darkies see dat

Yankee runnin' 'roun' de vimya'd en diggin' under de grapevimes, dey shuk dere heads, en 'lowed dat dey feared Mars Dugal' losin' his min'. Mars Dugal' had all de dirt dug away fum under de roots er all de scuppernon' vimes, an' let 'em stan' dat away fer a week er mo'. Den dat Yankee made de niggers fix up a mixtry er lime en ashes en manyo, en po' it 'roun' de roots er de grapevimes. Den he 'vise Mars Dugal' fer trim de vimes close't, en Mars Dugal' tuck 'n done eve'ything de Yankee tole him ter do. Dyoin' all er dis time, mind yer, dis yer Yankee wuz libbin' off'n de fat er de lan', at de big house, en playing' kya'ds wid Mars Dugal' eve'y night; en dey say Mars Dugal' los' mo'n a thousan' dollars dyoin' er de week dat Yankee wuz a'-ruinin' de grapevimes.

"W'en de sap ris nex' spring, ole Henry 'n'inted his head ez yuzhal, en his ha'r 'mence' ter grow des de same ez it done eve'y year. De scuppernon' vimes growed monst's fas', en de leaves wuz greener en thicker dan dey eber be'n dyoin' my rememb'ance; en Henry's ha'r growed thicker dan eber, en he 'peared ter git younger 'n younger, en soopler 'n soopler; en seein' ez he wuz sho't er han's dat spring, havin' tuk in consid'able noo groun', Mars Dugal' 'cluded he would n' sell Henry 'tel he git de crap in en de cotton chop'. So he kep' Henry on de plantation.

"But 'long 'bout time fer de grapes ter come on de scuppernon' vimes, dey 'peared ter come a change ober 'em; de leaves withered en swivel' up, en de young grapes turn' yaller, en bimeby eve'ybody on de plantation could see dat de whole vimya'd wuz dyin'. Mars Dugal' tuk 'n water de vimes en done all he could, but 't wa'n' no use: dat Yankee had done bus' de watermillyum. One time de vimes picked up a bit, en Mars Dugal' 'lowed dey wuz gwine ter come out ag'in; but dat Yankee done dug too close under de roots, en prune de branches too close ter de vime, en all dat lime en ashes done burn' de life out'n de vimes, en dey des kep' a-with'in' en a-swivelin'.

"All dis time de goopher wuz a-wukkin'. When de vimes sta'ted ter wither, Henry 'mence' ter complain er his rheumatiz; en when de leaves begin ter dry up, his ha'r 'mence' ter drap out. When de vimes fresh' up a bit, Henry 'd git peart ag'in, en when de vimes wither' ag'in, Henry 'd git ole ag'in, en des kep' gittin' mo' en mo' fitten fer nuffin; he des pined away, en pined away, en fine'ly tuk ter his cabin; en when de big vime whar he got de sap ter 'n'int his head withered en

turned yaller en died, Henry died too,—des went out sorter like a cannel. Dey did n't 'pear ter be nuffin de matter wid 'im, 'cep'n' de rheumatiz, but his strenk des dwinel' away 'tel he did n' hab ernuff lef' ter draw his bref. De goopher had got de under holt, en th'owed Henry dat time fer good en all.

"Mars Dugal' tuk on might'ly 'bout losin' his vimes en his nigger in de same year; en he swo' dat ef he could git holt er dat Yankee he'd wear 'im ter a frazzle, en den chaw up de frazzle; en he'd done it, too, for Mars Dugal' 'uz a monst'us brash man w'en he once git started. He sot de vimya'd out ober ag'in, but it wuz th'ee er fo' year befo' de vimes got ter b'arin' any scuppernon's.

"W'en de wah broke out, Mars Dugal' raise' a comp'ny, en went off ter fight de Yankees. He say he wuz mighty glad dat wah come, en he des want ter kill a Yankee fer eve'y dollar he los' 'long er dat grape-raisin' Yankee. En I 'spec' he would 'a' done it, too, ef de Yankees had n' s'picioned sump'n, en killed him fus'. Atter de s'render ole miss move' ter town, de niggers all scattered 'way fum de plantation, en de vimya'd ain' be'n cultervated sence."

"Is that story true?" asked Annie doubtfully, but seriously, as the old man concluded his narrative.

"It's des ez true ez I'm a-settin' here, miss. Dey's a easy way ter prove it: I kin lead de way right ter Henry's grave ober yander in de plantation buryin'-groun'. En I tell yer w'at, marster, I would n' 'vise you to buy dis yer ole vimya'd, 'caze de goopher's on it yit, en dey ain' no tellin' w'en it's gwine ter crap out."

"But I thought you said all the old vines died."

"Dey did 'pear ter die, but a few un 'em come out ag'in, en is mixed in 'mongs' de yuthers. I ain' skeered ter eat de grapes, 'caze I knows de old vimes fum de noo ones; but wid strangers dey ain' no tellin' w'at mought happen. I would n' 'vise yer ter buy dis vimya'd."

I bought the vineyard, nevertheless, and it has been for a long time in a thriving condition, and is often referred to by the local press as a striking illustration of the opportunities open to Northern capital in the development of Southern industries. The luscious scuppernong holds first rank among our grapes, though we cultivate a great many other varieties, and our income from grapes packed and shipped to the Northern markets is quite considerable. I have not noticed any developments of the goopher in the vineyard, although I have a mild suspicion that our colored assistants do not suffer from want of grapes during the season.

I found, when I bought the vineyard, that Uncle Julius had occupied a cabin on the place for many years, and derived a respectable revenue from the product of the neglected grapevines. This, doubtless, accounted for his advice to me not to buy the vineyard, though whether it inspired the goopher story I am unable to state. I believe, however, that the wages I paid him for his services as coachman, for I gave him employment in that capacity, were more than an equivalent for anything he lost by the sale of the vineyard.

The Wife of His Youth

I

Mr. Ryder was going to give a ball. There were several reasons why this was an opportune time for such an event.

Mr. Ryder might aptly be called the dean of the Blue Veins. The original Blue Veins were a little society of colored persons organized in a certain Northern city shortly after the war. Its purpose was to establish and maintain correct social standards among a people whose social condition presented almost unlimited room for improvement. By accident, combined perhaps with some natural affinity, the society consisted of individuals who were, generally speaking, more white than black. Some envious outsider made the suggestion that no one was eligible for membership who was not white enough to show blue veins. The suggestion was readily adopted by those who were not of the favored few, and since that time the society, though possessing a longer and more pretentious name, had been known far and wide as the "Blue Vein Society," and its members as the "Blue Veins."

The Blue Veins did not allow that any such requirement existed for admission to their circle, but, on the contrary, declared that character and culture were the only things considered; and that if most of their members were light-colored, it was because such persons, as a rule, had had better opportunities to qualify themselves for membership. Opinions differed, too, as to the usefulness of the society. There were those who had been known to assail it violently as a glaring example of the very prejudice from which the colored race had suffered most; and later, when such critics had succeeded in getting on the inside, they had been heard to maintain with zeal and earnestness that the society was a lifeboat, an anchor, a bulwark and a shield,—a pillar of cloud by day and of fire by night, to guide their people through the social wilderness. Another alleged prerequisite for Blue Vein membership was that of free birth; and while there was really no such requirement, it is doubtless true that very few of the members would have been unable to meet it if there had been. If there were one or two of the older members who had come up from the South and from slavery, their history presented enough romantic circumstances to rob their servile origin of its grosser aspects.

While there were no such tests of eligibility, it is true that the Blue Veins had their notions on these subjects, and that not all of them were equally liberal in regard to the things they collectively disclaimed. Mr. Ryder was one of the most conservative. Though he had not been among the founders of the society, but had come in some years later, his genius for social leadership was such that he had speedily become its recognized adviser and head, the custodian of its standards, and the preserver of its traditions. He shaped its social policy, was active in providing for its entertainment, and when the interest fell off, as it sometimes did, he fanned the embers until they burst again into a cheerful flame.

There were still other reasons for his popularity. While he was not as white as some of the Blue Veins, his appearance was such as to confer distinction upon them. His features were of a refined type, his hair was almost straight; he was always neatly dressed; his manners were irreproachable, and his morals above suspicion. He had come to Groveland a young man, and obtaining employment in the office of a railroad company as messenger had in time worked himself up to the position of stationery clerk, having charge of the distribution of the office supplies for the whole company. Although the lack of early training had hindered the orderly development of a naturally fine mind, it had not prevented him from doing a great deal of reading or from forming decidedly literary tastes. Poetry was his passion. He could repeat whole pages of the great English poets; and if his pronunciation was sometimes faulty, his eye, his voice, his gestures, would respond to the changing sentiment with a precision that revealed a poetic soul and disarmed criticism. He was economical, and had saved money; he owned and occupied a very comfortable house on a respectable street. His residence was handsomely furnished, containing among other things a good library, especially rich in poetry, a piano, and some choice engravings. He generally shared his house with some young couple, who looked after his wants and were company for him; for Mr. Ryder was a single man. In the early days of his connection with the Blue Veins he had been regarded as quite a catch, and young ladies and their mothers had manœuvred with much ingenuity to capture him. Not, however, until Mrs. Molly Dixon visited Groveland had any woman ever made him wish to change his condition to that of a married man.

Mrs. Dixon had come to Groveland from Washington in the spring, and before the summer was over she had won Mr. Ryder's heart. She possessed many attractive qualities. She was much younger than he; in fact, he was old enough to have been her father, though no one knew exactly how old he was. She was whiter than he, and better educated. She had moved in the best colored society of the country, at Washington, and had taught in the schools of that city. Such a superior person had been eagerly welcomed to the Blue Vein Society, and had taken a leading part in its activities. Mr. Ryder had at first been attracted by her charms of person, for she was very good looking and not over twenty-five; then by her refined manners and the vivacity of her wit. Her husband had been a government clerk, and at his death had left a considerable life insurance. She was visiting friends in Groveland, and, finding the town and the people to her liking, had prolonged her stay indefinitely. She had not seemed displeased at Mr. Ryder's attentions, but on the contrary had given him every proper encouragement; indeed, a younger and less cautious man would long since have spoken. But he had made up his mind, and had only to determine the time when he would ask her to be his wife. He decided to give a ball in her honor, and at some time during the evening of the ball to offer her his heart and hand. He had no special fears about the outcome, but, with a little touch of romance, he wanted the surroundings to be in harmony with his own feelings when he should have received the answer he expected.

Mr. Ryder resolved that this ball should mark an epoch in the social history of Groveland. He knew, of course,—no one could know better,— the entertainments that had taken place in past years, and what must be done to surpass them. His ball must be worthy of the lady in whose honor it was to be given, and must, by the quality of its guests, set an example for the future. He had observed of late a growing liberality, almost a laxity, in social matters, even among members of his own set, and had several times been forced to meet in a social way persons whose complexions and callings in life were hardly up to the standard which he considered proper for the society to maintain. He had a theory of his own.

"I have no race prejudice," he would say, "but we people of mixed blood are ground between the upper and the nether millstone. Our fate lies between absorption by the white race and extinction in the black. The one does n't want us yet, but may take us in time. The other would welcome us, but it would be for us a backward step. 'With malice towards none, with charity for all,' we must do the best we can for ourselves and those who are to follow us. Self-preservation is the first law of nature."

His ball would serve by its exclusiveness to counteract leveling tendencies, and his marriage with Mrs. Dixon would help to further the upward process of absorption he had been wishing and waiting for.

II

The ball was to take place on Friday night. The house had been put in order, the carpets covered with canvas, the halls and stairs decorated with palms and potted plants; and in the afternoon Mr. Ryder sat on his front porch, which the shade of a vine running up over a wire netting made a cool and pleasant lounging place. He expected to respond to the toast "The Ladies" at the supper, and from a volume of Tennyson—his favorite poet—was fortifying himself with apt quotations. The volume was open at "A Dream of Fair Women." His eyes fell on these lines, and he read them aloud to judge better of their effect:—

> At length I saw a lady within call,
>   Stiller than chisell'd marble, standing there;
> A daughter of the gods, divinely tall,
>   And most divinely fair.

He marked the verse, and turning the page read the stanza beginning,—

> O sweet pale Margaret,
> O rare pale Margaret.

He weighed the passage a moment, and decided that it would not do. Mrs. Dixon was the palest lady he expected at the ball, and she was of a rather ruddy complexion, and of lively disposition and buxom build. So he ran over the leaves until his eye rested on the description of Queen Guinevere:—

> She seem'd a part of joyous Spring:
> A gown of grass-green silk she wore,
> Buckled with golden clasps before;
> A light-green tuft of plumes she bore
> Closed in a golden ring. ·
> . . . .
> She look'd so lovely, as she sway'd
> The rein with dainty finger-tips,
> A man had given all other bliss,
> And all his worldly worth for this,
> To waste his whole heart in one kiss
> Upon her perfect lips.

As Mr. Ryder murmured these words audibly, with an appreciative thrill, he heared the latch of his gate click, and a light footfall sounding on the steps. He turned his head, and saw a woman standing before his door.

She was a little woman, not five feet tall, and proportioned to her height. Although she stood erect, and looked around her with very bright and restless eyes, she seemed quite old; for her face was crossed and recrossed with a hundred wrinkles, and around the edges of her bonnet could be seen protruding here and there a tuft of short gray wool. She wore a blue calico gown of ancient cut, a little red shawl fastened around her shoulders with an old-fashioned brass brooch, and a large bonnet profusely ornamented with faded red and yellow artificial flowers. And she was very black,—so black that her toothless gums, revealed when she opened her mouth to speak, were not red, but blue. She looked like a bit of the old plantation life, summoned up from the past by the wave of a magician's wand, as the poet's fancy had called into being the gracious shapes of which Mr. Ryder had just been reading.

He rose from his chair and came over to where she stood.

"Good-afternoon, madam," he said.

"Good-evenin', suh," she answered, ducking suddenly with a quaint curtsy. Her voice was shrill and piping, but softened somewhat by age. "Is dis yere whar Mistuh Ryduh lib, suh?" she asked, looking around her doubtfully, and glancing into the open windows, through which some of the preparations for the evening were visible.

"Yes," he replied, with an air of kindly patronage, unconsciously flattered by her manner, "I am Mr. Ryder. Did you want to see me?"

"Yas, suh, ef I ain't 'sturbin' of you too much."

"Not at all. Have a seat over here behind the vine, where it is cool. What can I do for you?"

"'Scuse me, suh," she continued, when she had sat down on the edge of a chair, "'scuse me, suh, I 's lookin' for my husban'. I heerd you wuz a big man an' had libbed heah a long time, an' I 'lowed you wouldn't min' ef I 'd come roun' an' ax you ef you'd every heer of a merlatter man by de name er Sam Taylor 'quirin' roun' in de chu'ches ermongs' de people fer his wife 'Liza Jane?"

Mr. Ryder seemed to think for a moment.

"There used to be many such cases right after the war," he said, "but it has been so long that I have forgotten them. There are very few now. But tell me your story, and it may refresh my memory."

She sat back farther in her chair so as to be more comfortable, and folded her withered hands in her lap.

"My name 's 'Liza," she began, "'Liza Jane. W'en I wuz young I us'ter b'long ter Marse Bob Smif, down in ole Missoura. I wuz bawn down dere. W'en I wuz a gal I wuz married ter a man named Jim. But Jim died, an' after dat I married a merlatter man named Sam Taylor. Sam wuz free-bawn, but his mammy and daddy died, an' de w'ite folks 'prenticed him ter my marster fer ter work fer 'im 'tel he wuz growed up. Sam worked in de fiel', an' I wuz de cook. One day Ma'y Ann, ole miss's maid, came rushin' out ter de kitchen, an' says she, "Liza Jane, ole marse gwine sell yo' Sam down de ribber.'

" 'Go way f'm yere," says I; 'my husban' 's free!'

" 'Don' make no diff'ence. I heerd ole marse tell ole miss he wuz gwine take yo' Sam 'way wid 'im ter-morrow, fer he needed money, an' he knowed whar he could git a t'ousan' dollars fer Sam an' no questions axed.'

"W'en Sam come home f'm de fiel' dat night, I tole him 'bout ole marse gwine steal 'im, an' Sam run erway. His time wuz mos' up, an' he swo' dat w'en he wuz twenty-one he would come back an' he'p me run erway, er else save up de money ter buy my freedom. An' I know he'd 'a' done it, fer he thought a heap er me, Sam did. But w'en he come back he did n' fin' me, fer I wuz n' dere. Ole marse had heerd dat I warned Sam, so he had me whip' an' sol' down de ribber.

"Den de wah broke out, an' w'en it wuz ober de cullud folks wuz scattered. I went back ter de ole home; but Sam wuz n' dere, an' I could n' l'arn nuffin' 'bout 'im. But I knowed he'd be'n dere to look fer me an' had n' foun' me, an' had gone erway ter hunt fer me.

"I 's be'n lookin' fer 'im eber sense," she added simply, as though twenty-five years were but a couple of weeks, "an' I knows he 's be'n lookin' fer me. Fer he sot a heap er sto' by me, Sam did, an' I know he 's be'n huntin' fer me all dese years, —'less'n he 's be'n sick er sump'n, so he could n' work, er out'n his head, so he could n' 'member his promise. I went back down de ribber, fer I 'lowed he 'd gone down dere lookin' fer me. I 's be'n ter Noo Orleens, an' Atlanty, an' Charleston, an' Richmon'; an' w'en I 'd be'n all ober de Souf I come ter de Norf. Fer I knows I 'll fin' 'im some er dese days," she added softly, "er he 'll fin' me, an' den we 'll bofe be as happy in freedom as we wuz in de ole days befo' de wah." A smile stole over her withered countenance as she paused a moment, and her bright eyes softened into a far-away look.

This was the substance of the old woman's story. She had wandered a little here and there. Mr. Ryder was looking at her curiously when she finished.

"How have you lived all these years?" he asked.

"Cookin', suh. I 's a good cook. Does you know anybody w'at needs a good cook, suh? I 's stoppin' wid a cullud fam'ly roun' de corner yonder 'tel I kin git a place."

"Do you really expect to find your husband? He may be dead long ago."

She shook her head emphatically, "Oh no, he ain' dead. De signs an' de tokens tells me. I dremp three nights runnin' on'y dis las' week dat I foun' him."

"He may have married another woman. Your slave marriage would not have prevented him, for you never lived with him after the war, and without that your marriage does n't count."

"Would n' make no diff'ence wid Sam. He would n' marry no yuther 'ooman 'tel he foun' out 'bout me. I knows it," she added. "Sump'n 's be'n tellin' me all dese years dat I 's gwine fin' Sam 'fo' I dies."

"Perhaps he 's outgrown you, and climbed up in the world where he would n't care to have you find him."

"No, indeed, suh," she replied, "Sam ain' dat kin' er man. He wuz good ter me, Sam wuz, but he wuz n' much good ter nobody e'se, fer he wuz one er de triflin'es' han's on de plantation. I 'spec's ter haf ter suppo't 'im w'en I fin' 'im, fer he nebber would work 'less'n he had ter. But den he wuz free, an' he did n' git no pay fer his work, an' I don' blame 'im much. Mebbe he 's done better sence he run erway, but I ain' 'spectin' much."

"You may have passed him on the street a hundred times during the twenty-five years, and not have known him; time works great changes."

She smiled incredulously. "I 'd know 'im 'mongs' a hund'ed men. Fer dey wuz n' no yuther merlatter man like my man Sam, an' I could n' be mistook. I 's toted his picture roun' wid me twenty-five years."

"May I see it?" asked Mr. Ryder. "It might help me to remember whether I have seen the original."

As she drew a small parcel from her bosom he saw that it was fastened to a string that went around her neck. Removing several wrappers, she brought to light an old-fashioned daguerreotype in a black case. He looked long and intently at the portrait. It was faded with time, but the features were still distinct, and it was easy to see what manner of man it had represented.

He closed the case, and with a slow movement handed it back to her.

"I don't know of any man in town who goes by that name," he said, "nor have I heard of any one making such inquiries. But if you will leave me your address, I will give the matter some attention, and if I find out anything I will let you know."

She gave him the number of a house in the neighborhood, and went away, after thanking him warmly.

He wrote the address on the fly-leaf of the volume of Tennyson, and, when she had gone, rose to his feet and stood looking after her curiously. As she walked down the street with mincing step, he saw several persons whom she passed turn and look back at her with a smile of kindly amusement. When she had turned the corner, he went upstairs to his bedroom, and stood for a long time before the mirror of his dressing-case, gazing thoughtfully at the reflection of his own face.

III

At eight o'clock the ballroom was a blaze of light and the guests had begun to assemble; for there was a literary programme and some routine business of the society to be gone through with before the dancing. A black servant in evening dress waited at the door and directed the guests to the dressing-rooms.

The occasion was long memorable among the colored people of the city; not alone for the dress and display, but for the high average of intelligence and culture that distinguished the gathering as a whole. There were a number of school-teachers, several young doctors, three or four lawyers, some professional singers, an editor, a lieutenant in the United States army spending his furlough in the city, and others in various polite callings; these were colored, though most of them would not have attracted even a casual glance because of any marked difference from white people. Most of the ladies were in evening costume, and dress coats and dancing pumps were the rule among the men. A band of string music, stationed in an alcove behind a row of palms, played popular airs while the guests were gathering.

The dancing began at half past nine. At eleven o'clock supper was served. Mr. Ryder had left the ballroom some little time before the intermission, but reappeared at the supper-table. The spread was worthy of the occasion, and the guests did full justice to it. When the coffee had been served, the toast-master, Mr. Solomon Sadler, rapped for order. He made a brief introductory speech, complimenting host and guests, and then presented in their order the toasts of the evening.

They were responded to with a very fair display of after-dinner wit.

"The last toast," said the toast-master, when he reached the end of the list, "is one which must appeal to us all. There is no one of us of the sterner sex who is not at some time dependent upon woman,—in infancy for protection, in manhood for companionship, in old age for care and comforting. Our good host has been trying to live alone, but the fair faces I see around me to-night prove that he too is largely dependent upon the gentler sex for most that makes life worth living, —the society and love of friends,—and rumor is at fault if he does not soon yield entire subjection to one of them. Mr. Ryder will now respond to the toast,—The Ladies."

There was a pensive look in Mr. Ryder's eyes as he took the floor and adjusted his eye-glasses. He began by speaking of woman as the gift of Heaven to man, and after some general observations on the relations of the sexes he said: "But perhaps the quality which most distinguishes woman is her fidelity and devotion to those she loves. History is full of examples, but has recorded none more striking than one which only to-day came under my notice."

He then related, simply but effectively, the story told by his visitor of the afternoon. He gave it in the same soft dialect, which came readily to his lips, while the company listened attentively and sympathetically. For the story had awakened a responsive thrill in many hearts. There were some present who had seen, and others who had heard their fathers and grandfathers tell, the wrongs and sufferings of this past generation, and all of them still felt, in their darker moments, the shadow hanging over them. Mr. Ryder went on:—

"Such devotion and confidence are rare even among women. There are many who would have searched a year, some who would have waited five years, a few who might have hoped ten years; but for twenty-five years this woman has retained her affection for and her faith in a man she has not seen or heard of in all that time.

"She came to me to-day in the hope that I might be able to help her find this long-lost husband. And when she was gone I gave my fancy rein, and imagined a case I will put to you.

"Suppose that this husband, soon after his escape, had learned that his wife had been sold away, and that such inquiries as he could make brought no information of her whereabouts.

Suppose that he was young, and she much older than he; that he was light, and she was black; that their marriage was a slave marriage, and legally binding only if they chose to make it so after the war. Suppose, too, that he made his way to the North, as some of us have done, and there, where he had larger opportunities, had improved them, and had in the course of all these years grown to be as different from the ignorant boy who ran away from fear of slavery as the day is from the night. Suppose, even, that he had qualified himself, by industry, by thrift, and by study, to win the friendship and be considered worthy the society of such people as these I see around me to-night, gracing my board and filling my heart with gladness; for I am old enough to remember the day when such a gathering would not have been possible in this land. Suppose, too, that, as the years went by, this man's memory of the past grew more and more indistinct, until at last it was rarely, except in his dreams, that any image of this bygone period rose before his mind. And then suppose that accident should bring to his knowledge the fact that the wife of his youth, the wife he had left behind him,—not one who had walked by his side and kept pace with him in his upward struggle, but one upon whom advancing years and a laborious life had set their mark,—was alive and seeking him, but that he was absolutely safe from recognition or discovery, unless he chose to reveal himself. My friends, what would the man do? I will presume that he was one who loved honor, and tried to deal justly with all men. I will even carry the case further, and suppose that perhaps he had set his heart upon another, whom he had hoped to call his own. What would he do, or rather what ought he to do, in such a crisis of a lifetime?

"It seemed to me that he might hesitate, and I imagined that I was an old friend, a near friend, and that he had come to me for advice; and I argued the case with him. I tried to discuss it impartially. After we had looked upon the matter from every point of view, I said to him, in words that we all know:—

> This above all: to thine own self be true,
> And it must follow, as the night the day,
> Thou canst not then be false to any man.

Then, finally, I put the question to him, 'Shall you acknowledge her?'

"And now, ladies and gentlemen, friends and companions, I ask you, what should he have done?"

There was something in Mr. Ryder's voice that stirred the hearts of those who sat around him. It suggested more than mere sympathy with an imaginary situation; it seemed rather in the nature of a personal appeal. It was observed, too, that his look rested more especially upon Mrs. Dixon, with a mingled expression of renunciation and inquiry.

She had listened, with parted lips and streaming eyes. She was the first to speak: "He should have acknowledged her."

"Yes," they all echoed, "he should have acknowledged her."

"My friends and companions," responded Mr. Ryder, "I thank you, one and all. It is the answer I expected, for I knew your hearts."

He turned and walked toward the closed door of an adjoining room, while every eye followed him in wondering curiosity. He came back in a moment, leading by the hand his visitor of the afternoon, who stood startled and trembling at the sudden plunge into this scene of brilliant gayety. She was neatly dressed in gray, and wore the white cap of an elderly woman.

"Ladies and gentlemen," he said, "this is the woman, and I am the man, whose story I have told you. Permit me to introduce to you the wife of my youth."

The Passing of Grandison

I

When it is said that it was done to please a woman, there ought perhaps to be enough said to explain anything; for what a man will not do to please a woman is yet to be discovered. Nevertheless, it might be well to state a few preliminary facts to make it clear why young Dick Owens tried to run one of his father's negro men off to Canada.

In the early fifties, when the growth of anti-slavery sentiment and the constant drain of fugitive slaves into the North had so alarmed the slaveholders of the border States as to lead to the passage of the Fugitive Slave Law, a young white man from Ohio, moved by compassion for the sufferings of a certain bondman who happened to have a "hard master," essayed to help the slave to freedom. The attempt was discovered and frustrated; the abductor was tried and convicted for slave-stealing, and sentenced to a term of imprisonment in the penitentiary. His death, after the expiration of only a small part of the sentence, from cholera contracted while nursing stricken fellow prisoners, lent to the case a melancholy interest that made it famous in anti-slavery annals.

Dick Owens had attended the trial. He was a youth of about twenty-two, intelligent, handsome, and amiable, but extremely indolent, in a graceful and gentlemanly way; or, as old Judge Fenderson put it more than once, he was lazy as the Devil,— a mere figure of speech, of course, and not one that did justice to the Enemy of Mankind. When asked why he never did anything serious, Dick would good-naturedly reply, with a well-modulated drawl, that he did n't have to. His father was rich; there was but one other child, an unmarried daughter, who because of poor health would probably never marry, and Dick was therefore heir presumptive to a large estate. Wealth or social position he did not need to seek, for he was born to both. Charity Lomax had shamed him into studying law, but notwithstanding an hour or so a day spent at old Judge Fenderson's office, he did not make remarkable headway in his legal studies.

"What Dick needs," said the judge, who was fond of tropes, as became a scholar, and of horses, as was befitting a Kentuckian, "is the whip of necessity, or the spur of ambition. If he had either, he would soon need the snaffle to hold him back."

But all Dick required, in fact, to prompt him to the most remarkable thing he accomplished before he was twenty-five, was a mere suggestion from Charity Lomax. The story was never really known to but two persons until after the war, when it came out because it was a good story and there was no particular reason for its concealment.

Young Owens had attended the trial of this slave-stealer, or martyr,—either or both,—and, when it was over, had gone to call on Charity Lomax, and, while they sat on the veranda after sundown, had told her all about the trial. He was a good talker, as his career in later years disclosed, and described the proceedings very graphically.

"I confess," he admitted, "that while my principles were against the prisoner, my sympathies were on his side. It appeared that he was of good family, and that he had an old father and mother, respectable people, dependent upon him for support and comfort in their declining years. He had been led into the matter by pity for a negro whose master ought to have been run out of the county long ago for abusing his slaves. If it had been merely a question of old Sam Brigg's negro, nobody would have cared anything about it. But father and the rest of them stood on the principle of the thing, and told the judge so, and the fellow was sentenced to three years in the penitentiary."

Miss Lomax had listened with lively interest.

"I've always hated old Sam Briggs," she said emphatically, "ever since the time he broke a negro's leg with a piece of cordwood. When I hear of a cruel deed it makes the Quaker blood that came from my grandmother assert itself. Personally I wish that all Sam Briggs's negroes would run away. As for the young man, I regard him as a hero. He dared something for humanity. I could love a man who would take such chances for the sake of others."

"Could you love me, Charity, if I did something heroic?"

"You never will, Dick. You're too lazy for any use. You'll never do anything harder than playing cards or fox-hunting."

"Oh, come now, sweetheart! I've been courting you for a year, and it's the hardest work imaginable. Are you never going to love me?" he pleaded.

His hand sought hers, but she drew it back beyond his reach.

"I'll never love you, Dick Owens, until you have done something. When that time comes, I'll think about it."

"But it takes so long to do anything worth mentioning, and I don't want to wait. One must read two years to become a lawyer, and work five more to make a reputation. We shall both be gray by then."

"Oh, I don't know," she rejoined. "It does n't require a lifetime for a man to prove that he is a man. This one did something, or at least tried to."

"Well, I'm willing to attempt as much as any other man. What do you want me to do, sweetheart? Give me a test."

"Oh, dear me!" said Charity, "I don't care what you *do,* so you do *something.* Really, come to think of it, why should I care whether you do anything or not?"

"I'm sure I don't know why you should, Charity," rejoined Dick humbly, "for I'm aware that I'm not worthy of it."

"Except that I do hate," she added, relenting slightly, "to see a really clever man so utterly lazy and good for nothing."

"Thank you, my dear; a word of praise from you has sharpened my wits already. I have an idea! Will you love me if *I* run a negro off to Canada?"

"What nonsense!" said Charity scornfully. "You must be losing your wits. Steal another man's slave, indeed, while your father owns a hundred!"

"Oh, there'll be no trouble about that," responded Dick lightly; "I'll run off one of the old man's; we've got too many anyway. It may not be quite as difficult as the other man found it, but it will be just as unlawful, and will demonstrate what I am capable of."

"Seeing's believing," replied Charity. "Of course, what you are talking about now is merely absurd. I'm going away for three weeks, to visit my aunt in Tennessee. If you're able to tell me, when I return, that you've done something to prove your quality, I'll—well, you may come and tell me about it."

II

Young Owens got up about nine o'clock next morning, and while making his toilet put some questions to his personal attendant, a rather bright looking young mulatto of about his own age.

"Tom," said Dick.

"Yas, Mars Dick," responded the servant.

"I'm going on a trip North. Would you like to go with me?"

Now, if there was anything that Tom would have liked to make, it was a trip North. It was something he had long contemplated in the abstract, but had never been able to muster up sufficient courage to attempt in the concrete.

He was prudent enough, however, to dissemble his feelings.

"I would n't min' it, Mars Dick, ez long ez you'd take keer er me an' fetch me home all right."

Tom's eyes belied his words, however, and his young master felt well assured that Tom needed only a good opportunity to make him run away. Having a comfortable home, and a dismal prospect in case of failure, Tom was not likely to take any desperate chances; but young Owens was satisfied that in a free State but little persuasion would be required to lead Tom astray. With a very logical and characteristic desire to gain his end with the least necessary expenditure of effort, he decided to take Tom with him, if his father did not object.

Colonel Owens had left the house when Dick went to breakfast, so Dick did not see his father till luncheon.

"Father," he remarked casually to the colonel, over the fried chicken, "I'm feeling a trifle run down. I imagine my health would be improved somewhat by a little travel and change of scene."

"Why don't you take a trip North?" suggested his father. The colonel added to paternal affection a considerable respect for his son as the heir of a large estate. He himself had been "raised" in comparative poverty, and had laid the foundations of his fortune by hard work; and while he despised the ladder by which he had climbed, he could not entirely forget it, and unconsciously manifested, in his intercourse with his son, some of the poor man's deference toward the wealthy and well-born.

"I think I'll adopt your suggestion, sir," replied the son, "and run up to New York; and after I've been there awhile I may go on to Boston for a week or so. I've never been there, you know."

"There are some matters you can talk over with my factor in New York." rejoined the colonel, "and while you are up there among the Yankees, I hope you'll keep your eyes and ears open to find out what the rascally abolitionists are saying and doing. They're becoming altogether too active for our comfort, and entirely too many ungrateful niggers are running away. I hope the conviction of that fellow yesterday may discourage the rest of the breed. I'd just like to catch any one trying to run off one of my darkeys. He'd get short shrift; I don't think any Court would have a chance to try him."

"They are a pestiferous lot," assented Dick, "and dangerous to our institutions. But say, father, if I go North I shall want to take Tom with me."

Now, the colonel, while a very indulgent father, had pronounced views on the subject of negroes, having studied them, as he often said, for a great many years, and, as he asserted oftener still, understanding them perfectly. It is scarcely worth while to say, either, that he valued more highly than if he had inherited them the slaves he had toiled and schemed for.

"I don't think it safe to take Tom up North," he declared, with promptness and decision. "He's a good enough boy, but too smart to trust among those low-down abolitionists. I strongly suspect him of having learned to read, though I can't imagine how. I saw him with a newspaper the other day, and while he pretended to be looking at a woodcut, I'm almost sure he was reading the paper. I think it by no means safe to take him."

Dick did not insist, because he knew it was useless. The colonel would have obliged his son in any other matter, but his negroes were the outward and visible sign of his wealth and station, and therefore sacred to him.

"Whom do you think it safe to take?" asked Dick. "I suppose I'll have to have a body-servant."

"What's the matter with Grandison?" suggested the colonel. "He's handy enough, and I reckon we can trust him. He's too fond of good eating, to risk losing his regular meals; besides, he's sweet on your mother's maid, Betty, and I've promised to let 'em get married before long. I'll have Grandison up, and we'll talk to him. Here, you boy Jack," called the colonel to a yellow youth in the next room who was catching flies and pulling their wings off to pass the time, "go down to the barn and tell Grandison to come here."

"Grandison," said the colonel, when the negro stood before him, hat in hand.

"Yas, marster."

"Have n't I always treated you right?"

"Yas, marster."

"Have n't you always got all you wanted to eat?"

"Yas, marster."

"And as much whiskey and tobacco as was good for you, Grandison?"

"Y-a-s, marster."

"I should just like to know, Grandison, whether you don't think yourself a great deal better off than those poor free negroes down by the plank road, with no kind master to look after them and no mistress to give them medicine when they're sick and—and"—

"Well, I sh'd jes' reckon I is better off, suh, dan dem low-down free niggers, suh! Ef anybody ax 'em who dey b'long ter, dey has ter say nobody, er e'se lie erbout it. Anybody ax me who I b'longs ter, I ain' got no 'casion ter be shame' ter tell 'em, no suh, 'deed I ain', suh!"

The colonel was beaming. This was true gratitude, and his feudal heart thrilled at such appreciative homage. What cold-blooded, heartless monsters they were who would break up this blissful relationship of kindly protection on the one hand, of wise subordination and loyal dependence on the other! The colonel always became indignant at the mere thought of such wickedness.

"Grandison," the colonel continued, "your young master Dick is going North for a few weeks, and I am thinking of letting him take you along. I shall send you on this trip, Grandison, in order that you may take care of your young master. He will need some one to wait on him, and no one can ever do it so well as one of the boys brought up with him on the old plantation. I am going to trust him in your hands, and I'm sure you'll do your duty faithfully, and bring him back home safe and sound—to old Kentucky."

Grandison grinned. "Oh yas, marster, I'll take keer er young Mars Dick."

"I want to warn you, though, Grandison," continued the colonel impressively, "against these cussed abolitionists, who try to entice servants from their comfortable homes and their indulgent masters, from the blue skies, the green fields, and the warm sunlight of their southern home, and send them away off yonder to Canada, a dreary country, where the woods are full of wildcats and wolves and bears, where the snow lies up to the eaves of the houses for six months of the year, and the cold is so severe that it freezes your breath and curdles your blood; and where, when runaway niggers get sick and can't work, they are turned out to starve and die, unloved and uncared for. I reckon, Grandison, that you have too much sense to permit yourself to be led astray by any such foolish and wicked people."

"'Deed, suh, I would n' low none er dem cussed, low-down abolitioners ter come nigh me, suh. I'd—I'd—would I be 'lowed ter hit 'em, suh?"

"Certainly, Grandison," replied the colonel, chuckling, "hit 'em as hard as you can. I reckon they'd rather like it. Begad, I believe they would! It would serve 'em right to be hit by a nigger!"

"Er ef I did n't hit 'em, suh," continued Grandison reflectively, "I'd tell Mars Dick, en *he'd* fix 'em. He'd smash de face off'n 'em, suh, I jes' knows he would."

"Oh yes, Grandison, your young master will protect you. You need fear no harm while he is near."

"Dey won't try ter steal me, will dey, marster?" asked the negro, with sudden alarm.

"I don't know, Grandison," replied the colonel, lighting a fresh cigar. "They 're a desperate set of lunatics, and there 's no telling what they may resort to. But if you stick close to your young master, and remember always that he is your best friend, and understands your real needs, and has your true interests at heart, and if you will be careful to avoid strangers who try to talk to you, you 'll stand a fair chance of getting back to your home and your friends. And if you please your master Dick, he 'll buy you a present, and a string of beads for Betty to wear when you and she get married in the fall."

"Thanky, marster, thanky, suh," replied Grandison, oozing gratitude at every pore; "you is a good marster, to be sho', suh; yas, 'deed you is. You kin jes' bet me and Mars Dick gwine git 'long jes' lack I wuz own boy ter Mars Dick. En it won't be my fault ef he don' want me fer his boy all de time, w'en we come back home ag'in."

"All right, Grandison, you may go now. You need n't work any more to-day, and here 's a piece of tobacco for you off my own plug."

"Thanky, marster, thanky, marster! You is de bes' marster any nigger ever had in dis worl'." And Grandison bowed and scraped and disappeared round the corner, his jaws closing around a large section of the colonel's best tobacco.

"You may take Grandison," said the colonel to his son. "I allow he 's abolitionist-proof."

III

Richard Owens, Esq., and servant from Kentucky, registered at the fashionable New York hostelry for Southerners in those days, a hotel where an atmosphere congenial to Southern institutions was sedulously maintained. But there were negro waiters in the dining-room, and mulatto bell-boys, and Dick had no doubt that Grandison, with the native gregariousness and garrulousness of his race, would foregather and palaver with them sooner or later, and Dick hoped that they would speedily inoculate him with the virus of freedom. For it was not Dick's intention to say anything to his servant about his plan to free him, for obvious reasons. To mention one of them, if Grandison should go away, and by legal process be recaptured, his young master's part in the matter would doubtless become known, which would be embarrassing to Dick, to say the least. If, on the other hand, he should merely give Grandison sufficient latitude, he had no doubt he would eventually lose him. For while not exactly skeptical about Grandison's perfervid loyalty, Dick had been a somewhat keen observer of human nature, in his own indolent way, and based his expectations upon the force of the example and argument that his servant could scarcely fail to encounter. Grandison should have a fair chance to become free by his own initiative; if it should become necessary to adopt other measures to get rid of him, it would be time enough to act when the necessity arose; and Dick Owens was not the youth to take needless trouble.

The young master renewed some acquaintances and made others, and spent a week or two very pleasantly in the best society of the metropolis, easily accessible to a wealthy, well-bred young Southerner, with proper introductions. Young women smiled on him, and young men of convivial habits pressed their hospitalities; but the memory of Charity's sweet, strong face and clear blue eyes made him proof against the blandishments of the one sex and the persuasions of the other. Meanwhile he kept Grandison supplied with pocket-money, and left him mainly to his own devices. Every night when Dick came in he hoped he might have to wait upon himself, and every morning he looked forward with pleasure to the prospect of making his toilet unaided. His hopes, however, were doomed to disappointment, for every night when he came in Grandison was on hand with a bootjack, and a nightcap mixed for his young master as the colonel had taught him to mix it, and every morning Grandison appeared with his master's boots blacked and his clothes brushed and laid his linen out for the day.

"Grandison," said Dick one morning after finishing his toilet "this is the chance of your life to go around among your own people and see how they live. Have you met any of them?"

"Yas suh, I's seen some of 'em. But I don' keer nuffin fer 'em suh. Dey 're diffe'nt f'm de niggers down ou' way. Dey 'lows dey 're free, but dey ain' got sense 'nuff ter know dey ain' half as well off as dey would be down Souf, whar dey 'd be 'preciated."

When two weeks had passed without any apparent effect of evil example upon Grandison, Dick resolved to go on to Boston where he thought the atmosphere might prove more favorable to his ends. After he had been at the Revere House for a day or two without losing Grandison, he decided upon slightly different tactics.

Having ascertained from a city directory the addresses of several well-known abolitionists, he wrote them each a letter something like this:

DEAR FRIEND AND BROTHER:—

A wicked slaveholder from Kentucky, stopping at the Revere House, has dared to insult the liberty-loving people of Boston by bringing his slave into their midst. Shall this be tolerated? Or shall steps be taken in the name of liberty to rescue a fellow-man from bondage? For obvious reasons I can only sign myself,

A FRIEND OF HUMANITY.

That his letter might have an opportunity to prove effective, Dick made it a point to send Grandison away from the hotel on various errands. On one of these occasions Dick watched him for quite a distance down the street. Grandison had scarcely left the hotel when a long-haired, sharp-featured man came out behind him, followed him, soon overtook him, and kept along beside him until they turned the next corner. Dick's hopes were roused by this spectacle, but sank correspondingly when Grandison returned to the hotel. As Grandison said nothing about the encounter, Dick hoped there might be some self-consciousness behind this unexpected reticence, the results of which might develop later on.

But Grandison was on hand again when his master came back to the hotel at night, and was in attendance again in the morning, with hot water, to assist at his master's toilet. Dick sent him on further errands from day to day, and upon one occasion came squarely up to him—

inadvertently of course—while Grandison was engaged in conversation with a young white man in clerical garb. When Grandison saw Dick approaching, he edged away from the preacher and hastened toward his master, with a very evident expression of relief upon his countenance.

"Mars Dick," he said, "dese yer abolitioners is jes' pesterin' de life out er me tryin' ter git me ter run away. I don' pay no 'tention ter 'em, but dey riles me so sometimes dat I 'm feared I 'll hit some of 'em some er dese days, an' dat mought git me inter trouble. I ain' said nuffin' ter you 'bout it, Mars Dick, fer I did n' wanter 'sturb yo' min'; but I don' like it, suh; no, suh, I don'! Is we gwine back home 'fo' long, Mars Dick?"

"We 'll be going back soon enough," replied Dick somewhat shortly, while he inwardly cursed the stupidity of a slave who could be free and would not, and registered a secret vow that if he were unable to get rid of Grandison without assassinating him, and were therefore compelled to take him back to Kentucky, he would see that Grandison got a taste of an article of slavery that would make him regret his wasted opportunities. Meanwhile he determined to tempt his servant yet more strongly.

"Grandison," he said next morning, "I'm going away for a day or two, but I shall leave you here. I shall lock up a hundred dollars in this drawer and give you the key. If you need any of it, use it and enjoy yourself,—spend it all if you like,—for this is probably the last chance you 'll have for some time to be in a free State, and you 'd better enjoy your liberty while you may."

When he came back a couple of days later and found the faithful Grandison at his post, and the hundred dollars intact, Dick felt seriously annoyed. His vexation was increased by the fact that he could not express his feelings adequately. He did not even scold Grandison; how could he, indeed, find fault with one who so sensibly recognized his true place in the economy of civilization, and kept it with such touching fidelity?

"I can't say a thing to him," groaned Dick. "He deserves a leather medal, made out of his own hide tanned. I reckon I 'll write to father and let him know what a model servant he has given me."

He wrote his father a letter which made the colonel swell with pride and pleasure. "I really think," the colonel observed to one of his friends, "that Dick ought to have the nigger interviewed by the Boston papers, so that they may see how contented and happy our darkeys really are."

Dick also wrote a long letter to Charity Lomax, in which he said, among many other things, that if she knew how hard he was working, and under what difficulties, to accomplish something serious for her sake, she would no longer keep him in suspense, but overwhelm him with love and admiration.

Having thus exhausted without result the more obvious methods of getting rid of Grandison, and diplomacy having also proved a failure, Dick was forced to consider more radical measures. Of course he might run away himself, and abandon Grandison, but this would be merely to leave him in the United States, where he was still a slave, and where, with his notions of loyalty, he would speedily be reclaimed. It was necessary, in order to accomplish the purpose of his trip to the North, to leave Grandison permanently in Canada, where he would be legally free.

"I might extend my trip to Canada," he reflected, "but that would be too palpable. I have it! I 'll visit Niagara Falls on the way home, and lose him on the Canada side. When he once realizes that he is actually free, I 'll warrant that he 'll stay."

So the next day saw them westward bound, and in due course of time, by the somewhat slow conveyances of the period, they found themselves at Niagara. Dick walked and drove about the Falls for several days, taking Grandison along with him on most occasions. One morning they stood on the Canadian side, watching the wild whirl of the waters below them.

"Grandison," said Dick, raising his voice above the roar of the cataract, "do you know where you are now?"

"I 's wid you, Mars Dick; dat 's all I keers."

"You are now in Canada, Grandison, where your people go when they run away from their masters. If you wished, Grandison, you might walk away from me this very minute, and I could not lay my hand upon you to take you back."

Grandison looked around uneasily.

"Let 's go back ober de ribber, Mars Dick. I 's feared I 'll lose you ovuh heah, an' den I won' hab no marster, an' won't nebber be able to git back home no mo'."

Discouraged, but not yet hopeless, Dick said, a few minutes later,—

"Grandison, I 'm going up the road a bit, to the inn over yonder. You stay here until I return. I 'll not be gone a great while."

Grandison's eyes opened wide and he looked somewhat fearful.

"Is dey any er dem dadblasted abolitioners roun' heah, Mars Dick?"

"I don't imagine that there are," replied his master, hoping there might be. "But I 'm not afraid of *your* running away, Grandison. I only wish I were," he added to himself.

Dick walked leisurely down the road to where the whitewashed inn, built of stone, with true British solidity, loomed up through the trees by the roadside. Arrived there he ordered a glass of ale and a sandwich, and took a seat at a table by a window, from which he could see Grandison in the distance. For a while he hoped that the seed he had sown might have fallen on fertile ground, and that Grandison, relieved from the restraining power of a master's eye, and finding himself in a free country, might get up and walk away; but the hope was vain, for Grandison remained faithfully at his post, awaiting his master's return. He had seated himself on a broad flat stone, and, turning his eyes away from the grand and awe-inspiring spectacle that lay close at hand, was looking anxiously toward the inn where his master sat cursing his ill-timed fidelity.

By and by a girl came into the room to serve his order, and Dick very naturally glanced at her; and as she was young and pretty and remained in attendance, it was some minutes before he looked for Grandison. When he did so his faithful servant had disappeared.

To pay his reckoning and go away without the change was a matter quickly accomplished. Retracing his footsteps toward the Falls, he saw, to his great disgust, as he approached the spot where he had left Grandison, the familiar form of his servant stretched out on the ground, his face to the sun, his mouth open, sleeping the time away, oblivious alike to the grandeur of the scenery, the thunderous roar of the cataract, or the insidious voice of sentiment.

"Grandison," soliloquized his master, as he stood gazing down at his ebony encumbrance, "I do not deserve to be an American citizen; I ought not to have the advantages I possess over you; and I certainly am not worthy of Charity Lomax, if I am not smart enough to get rid of you. I have an idea! You shall yet be free, and I will be the instrument of your deliverance. Sleep on, faithful and affectionate servitor, and dream of the blue grass and the bright skies of old

Kentucky, for it is only in your dreams that you will ever see them again!"

Dick retraced his footsteps towards the inn. The young woman chanced to look out of the window and saw the handsome young gentleman she had waited on a few minutes before, standing in the road a short distance away, apparently engaged in earnest conversation with a colored man employed as hostler for the inn. She thought she saw something pass from the white man to the other, but at that moment her duties called her away from the window, and when she looked out again the young gentleman had disappeared, and the hostler, with two other young men of the neighborhood, one white and one colored, were walking rapidly towards the Falls.

IV

Dick made the journey homeward alone, and as rapidly as the conveyances of the day would permit. As he drew near home his conduct in going back without Grandison took on a more serious aspect than it had borne at any previous time, and although he had prepared the colonel by a letter sent several days ahead, there was still the prospect of a bad quarter of an hour with him; not, indeed, that his father would upbraid him, but he was likely to make searching inquiries. And notwithstanding the vein of quiet recklessness that had carried Dick through his preposterous scheme, he was a very poor liar, having rarely had occasion or inclination to tell anything but the truth. Any reluctance to meet his father was more than offset, however, by a stronger force drawing him homeward, for Charity Lomax must long since have returned from her visit to her aunt in Tennessee.

Dick got off easier than he had expected. He told a straight story, and a truthful one, so far as it went.

The colonel raged at first, but rage soon subsided into anger, and anger moderated into annoyance, and annoyance into a sort of garrulous sense of injury. The colonel thought he had been hardly used; he had trusted this negro, and he had broken faith. Yet, after all, he did not blame Grandison so much as he did the abolitionists, who were undoubtedly at the bottom of it.

As for Charity Lomax, Dick told her, privately of course, that he had run his father's man, Grandison, off to Canada, and left him there.

"Oh, Dick," she had said with shuddering alarm, "what have you done? If they knew it they'd send you to the penitentiary, like they did that Yankee."

"But they don't know it," he had replied seriously; adding, with an injured tone, "you don't seem to appreciate my heroism like you did that of the Yankee; perhaps it's because I wasn't caught and sent to the penitentiary. I thought you wanted me to do it."

"Why, Dick Owens!" she exclaimed. "You know I never dreamed of any such outrageous proceeding.

"But I presume I'll have to marry you," she concluded, after some insistence on Dick's part, "if only to take care of you. You are too reckless for anything; and a man who goes chasing all over the North, being entertained by New York and Boston society and having negroes to throw away, needs some one to look after him."

"It's a most remarkable thing," replied Dick fervently, "that your views correspond exactly with my profoundest convictions. It proves beyond question that we were made for one another."

They were married three weeks later. As each of them had just returned from a journey, they spent their honeymoon at home.

A week after the wedding they were seated, one afternoon, on the piazza of the colonel's house, where Dick had taken his bride, when a negro from the yard ran down the lane and threw open the big gate for the colonel's buggy to enter. The colonel was not alone. Beside him, ragged and travel-stained, bowed with weariness, and upon his face a haggard look that told of hardship and privation, sat the lost Grandison.

The colonel alighted at the steps.

"Take the lines, Tom," he said to the man who had opened the gate, "and drive round to the barn. Help Grandison down,—poor devil, he's so stiff he can hardly move!—and get a tub of water and wash him and rub him down, and feed him, and give him a big drink of whiskey, and then let him come round and see his young master and his new mistress."

The colonel's face wore an expression compounded of joy and indignation,—joy at the restoration of a valuable piece of property; indignation for reasons he proceeded to state.

"It's astounding, the depths of depravity the human heart is capable of! I was coming along the road three miles away, when I heard some one call me from the roadside. I pulled up the mare, and who should come out of the woods but Grandison. The poor nigger could hardly crawl along, with the help of a broken limb. I was never more astonished in my life. You could have knocked me down with a feather. He seemed pretty far gone,—he could hardly talk above a whisper,—and I had to give him a mouthful of whiskey to brace him up so he could tell his story. It's just as I thought from the beginning, Dick; Grandison had no notion of running away; he knew when he was well off, and where his friends were. All the persuasions of abolition liars and runaway niggers did not move him. But the desperation of those fanatics knew no bounds; their guilty consciences gave them no rest. They got the notion somehow that Grandison belonged to a nigger-catcher, and had been brought North as a spy to help capture ungrateful runaway servants. They actually kidnaped him—just think of it!—and gagged him and bound him and threw him rudely into a wagon, and carried him into the gloomy depths of a Canadian forest, and locked him in a lonely hut, and fed him on bread and water for three weeks. One of the scoundrels wanted to kill him, and persuaded the others that it ought to be done; but they got to quarreling about how they should do it, and before they had their minds made up Grandison escaped, and, keeping his back steadily to the North Star, made his way, after suffering incredible hardships, back to the old plantation, back to his master, his friends, and his home. Why, it 's as good as one of Scott's novels! Mr. Simms or some other one of our Southern authors ought to write it up."

"Don't you think, sir," suggested Dick, who had calmly smoked his cigar throughout the colonel's animated recital, "that that kidnaping yarn sounds a little improbable? Is n't there some more likely explanation?"

"Nonsense, Dick; it 's the gospel truth! Those infernal abolitionists are capable of anything—everything! Just think of their locking the poor, faithful nigger up, beating him, kicking him, depriving him of his liberty, keeping him on bread and water for three long, lonesome weeks, and he all the time pining for the old plantation!"

There were almost tears in the colonel's eyes at the picture of Grandison's sufferings that he conjured up. Dick still professed to be slightly skeptical, and met Charity's severely questioning eye with bland unconsciousness.

The colonel killed the fatted calf for Grandison, and for two or three weeks the returned wanderer's life was a slave's dream of pleasure. His fame spread throughout the county, and the colonel gave him a permanent place among the house servants, where he could always have him conveniently at hand to relate his adventure to admiring visitors.

About three weeks after Grandison's return the colonel's faith in sable humanity was rudely shaken, and its foundations almost broken up. He came near losing his belief in the fidelity of the negro to his master,—the servile virtue most highly prized and most sedulously cultivated by the colonel and his kind. One Monday morning Grandison was missing. And not only Grandison, but his wife, Betty the maid; his mother, aunt Eunice; his father, uncle Ike; his brothers, Tom and John, and his little sister Elsie, were likewise absent from the plantation; and a hurried search and inquiry in the neighborhood resulted in no information as to their whereabouts. So much valuable property could not be lost without an effort to recover it, and the wholesale nature of the transaction carried consternation to the hearts of those whose ledgers were chiefly bound in black. Extremely energetic measures were taken by the colonel and his friends. The fugitives were traced, and followed from point to point, on their northward run through Ohio. Several times the hunters were close upon their heels, but the magnitude of the escaping party begot unusual vigilance on the part of those who sympathized with the fugitives, and strangely enough, the underground railroad seemed to have had its tracks cleared and signals set for this particular train. Once, twice, the colonel thought he had them, but they slipped through his fingers.

One last glimpse he caught of his vanishing property, as he stood, accompanied by a United States marshal, on a wharf at a port on the south shore of Lake Erie. On the stern of a small steamboat which was receding rapidly from the wharf, with her nose pointing toward Canada, there stood a group of familiar dark faces, and the look they cast backward was not one of longing for the fleshpots of Egypt. The colonel saw Grandison point him out to one of the crew of the vessel, who waved his hand derisively toward the colonel. The latter shook his fist impotently—and the incident was closed.

Paul Laurence Dunbar (1872–1906)

When the Honorable Frederick Douglass opened up the Haiti Pavilion at the Chicago World's Fair in 1893, he employed as his assistant a frail young man from Dayton, Ohio. This young man was to become Black America's first nationally known poet, but in 1893 he was both abysmally poor and relatively unknown. Every free moment he had was devoted to peddling copies of his first volume of verse, *Oak and Ivy,* and he had desperate need of the $5.00 weekly wage he received at the Haiti Pavilion.

The association of the venerable Frederick Douglass and the youthful Paul Laurence Dunbar at the Chicago Fair was, in some respects, a happy historical accident. It was good for the shy young poet to get to know the stentorian-voiced orator and veteran of almost a century of crisis and struggle. In 1893, Douglass was seventy-six years old and at the end of his spectacular career. In fact, within two years from this date, the great voice that had once been the conscience of a guilt-ridden America was silenced by death. So a great man, in the twilight of his years, met another man who, at the age of only twenty-one, was groping his way toward his own brief period of fame. Thirteen years later, Dunbar too was dead.

In 1893, however, there was a lot of untapped poetry in the young Dunbar, and soon it came pouring forth—from as rich a vein of lyricism as America had ever seen. First there came *Majors and Minors* in 1895, followed by *Lyrics of Lowly Life* in 1896 and *Lyrics of the Hearthside* in 1899. Fame of a sort came to him when America's foremost literary critic of the time, William Dean Howells, wrote a favorable review of *Majors and Minors*. With such influential sponsorship, the young Black poet's literary career was assured. Howells not only arranged for Dodd, Mead to publish *Lyrics of Lowly Life* but wrote an introduction full of praise for Dunbar's poetry, particularly for his dialect pieces. In Howells' view, Dunbar was the first Black poet to "feel the Negro life aesthetically and express it lyrically." Within a short time after the publication of *Lyrics of Lowly Life,* Dunbar came to realize that the enthusiastic endorsement of his dialect poetry actually placed some limitation on his acceptance as a full-fledged poet and man of literature. Actually, Howells' judgment was more of a social reaction than a literary evaluation. To white America in the 1890's and early 1900's a Black poet could only be fully acceptable if he presented lyrical pictures of contented ex-slaves written in what appeared to be the gentle folk accents and speech patterns of ex-slaves. Indeed, Dunbar's portraits of a dancing, contented Black people, living a rural life free of hunger, illness, and privation, comforted white America and eased its guilty conscience.

Despite his disappointment over the implications of Howells' endorsement, Dunbar proceeded to produce poetry, short stories, and novels at a rapid rate. After *Lyrics of Lowly Life,* published in 1896, the poet had only ten years of living and writing left, and in this decade, harried as he was by a debilitating illness, his literary output was prodigious. Between 1896 and 1906, the year of his death, he wrote and published four novels, three more volumes of verse, and four volumes of short stories. Admittedly, all that he produced during this decade of productivity was not of high literary quality. Generally speaking, his poetry was better than his short stories were, and his short stories were better than his novels. But by 1899, a year in which he spent some time in Denver, Colorado, he knew that he was incurably ill with tuberculosis, and this fact is of importance in evaluating the amazing breadth of his literary output. During this time, too, there were poetry readings or "recitals" in large Northern cities, collaborative efforts with the Black musician Coleridge Taylor, whom he had met in London, and some attempt to work with Black dramatists such as Rosamund and James Weldon Johnson in producing Black musical revues in New York City.

One can get a good critical overview of Dunbar's poetry by examining *The Complete Poems,* published in 1913, seven years after the poet's death. Over two thirds of the poems are in standard English, and many of these have the bittersweet melancholy of the Romantic who finds life tedious and emotionally unfulfilling. Life is like a prison, and people of talent are "caged" birds who can only overcome the pain of their imprisonment through song. And for Black people, life is the kind of prison in which one has to "wear the mask that grins and lies." In reality, there is "never a laugh but the moans come double." Even for the poet with the gift of song there is only "the boon of Death."

However, the general tone of the poet's dialect poetry is quite different, especially that depicting the life of the typical Black peasant in his traditional rural environment. These poems radiate a warm humanity and seem to suggest that, whatever the continuing calamities that beset the Black man in his urban environment, good living, good eating, and good times were to be had "down home." Dunbar's picture is overdrawn, idealized, and sentimentalized, but he describes enough of the salvageable good memories of life on the farm or plantation to provoke a nostalgic reaction in the reader. No poems deal with the depressing economics of Southern rural living, and no poems deal with brutal night riders who burn, pillage, and kill. But there are a lot of poems that celebrate the warm joys of Thanksgiving and Christmas when "good hunting" and "good cooking" have piled the table high with irresistible goodies. The Black man in Dunbar country eats well; for him there are no dietary deficiencies—no rickets, no pellagra, no protein starvation. Instead, there is a round of good eating:

We had wheat bread white ez cotton an' a egg pone jes like gol',
Hog jole, bilin' hot an' steamin', roasted shoat an' ham sliced cold. . . .

Add to this "hot chittlin's," "gread big sweet pertaters, layin' by de possum's side," and a coon cooked in his own gravy, and one has a sample of good eating that even today would make a Northern urban "soul-food" specialist envious.

The dialect pieces, however, describe more than good eating. There is good fellowship, even between "Christuns" and "sinnahs." The children are described with skill and tender delicacy, and there is every evidence of a high quality of family solidarity long before this became a matter of concern in American social thought. Even the love affairs turn out well, with no aftermath of bitterness, death, or dying.

So the folk heroes of Dunbar's dialect poetry lived in something of a never-never land of economic, social, and emotional fulfillment. Actually, the Black man's headlong flight from the rural South, in progress even during the poet's lifetime, is conclusive proof that this idyllic rural life was a figment of Dunbar's poetic imagination or, at best, a literary half-truth that shows what could have been or should have been in order to ease the pain of what actually did happen.

Although little of Dunbar's prose fiction is read today, some mention of his work in this genre should be made. As indicated above, his short stories—of which there are four volumes and some yet uncollected stories published in *Lippincott's Magazine*—are not as good as his poetry but are substantially better than any of his novels, with the possible exception of his last novel, *The Sport of the Gods*. Primarily, his stories have the same range of subject matter found in his early dialect poetry. The titles given three of the volumes confirm this: *Folks from Dixie* published in 1898, *In Old Plantation Days* in 1903, and *The Heart of Happy Hollow* in 1904. All, including *The Strength of Gideon and Other Stories* (1900), were published by Dodd, Mead, presumably because there was thought to be a market for innocuous tales dealing with the Black man's folk experiences during and just after the Civil War. The stories are almost completely devoid of racial protest, but one notable exception is "The Lynching of Jube Benson," in which a white man is tortured by remorse over his participation in the lynching of a loyal and friendly Black named Jube. But even this story contains no denunciation of this infamous crime; in fact, Dr. Melville's closing pronouncement at the end of the story—"Gentlemen, that was my last lynching"—is almost comic in its anticlimactic absurdity. In general, however, the stories present stereotypes—the chivalrous plantation aristocrat (white) and the happy and loyal servant (Black)—that, in the light of history, can only be considered racially demeaning.

The four novels—*The Uncalled* (1898), *The Love of Landry* (1900), *The Fanatics* (1901), and *The Sport of the Gods* (1902)—have even less literary merit. *The Sport of the Gods* is the only one with major Black characters and a theme concerned with the hard realities of the Black man's lot in the degenerate South and his bitter fate in the urban North. Structurally, it is not a good novel, but it is one that suggests that had Dunbar lived he might have mastered the skills necessary to write about the trauma of the rural Black man's adjustment to the corrupt ways of the big Northern city.

Dunbar's literary reputation has not prospered in the almost seventy years since his death, in spite of his having striven so hard for fame. Few scholars have rushed to become Dunbar specialists. However, his prose fiction has received some critical attention in standard surveys of Black fiction such as Hugh Gloster's *Negro Voices in American Fiction* (1948) and Robert Bone's *The Negro Novel in America* (1965). Similarly, his poetry has provoked critical comment in Sterling Brown's *The Negro in Poetry and Drama* (1937) and in Saunders Redding's *To Make a Poet Black* (1939). But in all of these years no authoritative Dunbar scholar has emerged. Benjamin Brawley, whose *Paul Laurence Dunbar: Poet of His People* was published by the University of North Carolina in 1936, came closest to playing this role. Prior to writing this highly laudatory biography, Brawley had written an appreciative essay, "Dunbar Thirty Years After," for the *Southern Workman* in 1930 that supplemented his comments and critical observations on the poet and his work in *The Negro in Literature and Art* (1929). See also Victor Lawson's *Dunbar Critically Examined* (1941), Virginia Cunningham's *Paul Laurence Dunbar and His Song* (1947), and Jean Gould's *That Dunbar Boy: The Story of America's Famous Negro Poet* (1958). Within recent years, the one outstanding critical study of Dunbar has been produced by a French literary critic. This is Jean Wagner's *Les poètes nègres des États-Unis: Le sentiment racial et religieux dans la poèsie de P. L. Dunbar à L. Hughes* (1963). Probably, Black America's current critical mood toward the poet who charmed white America with his "jingle in a broken tongue" so many years ago is summarized in the title of Darwin Turner's recent essay—"Paul Laurence Dunbar: The Rejected Symbol," *The Journal of Negro History*, LII (1967), 1–13.

We Wear the Mask

We wear the mask that grins and lies,
It hides our cheeks and shades our eyes,—
This debt we pay to human guile;
With torn and bleeding hearts we smile,
And mouth with myriad subtleties.

We smile, but, O great Christ, our cries
To thee from tortured souls arise.
We sing, but oh the clay is vile
Beneath our feet, and long the mile;
But let the world dream otherwise,
    We wear the mask!

Why should the world be overwise,
In counting all our tears and sighs?
Nay, let them only see us, while
    We wear the mask.

The Colored Soldiers

If the muse were mine to tempt it
   And my feeble voice were strong,
If my tongue were trained to measures,
   I would sing a stirring song.
I would sing a song heroic
   Of those noble sons of Ham,
Of the gallant colored soldiers
   Who fought for Uncle Sam!

In the early days you scorned them,
   And with many a flip and flout
Said "These battles are the white man's,
   And the whites will fight them out."
Up the hills you fought and faltered,
   In the vales you strove and bled,
While your ears still heard the thunder
   Of the foes' advancing tread.

Then distress fell on the nation,
   And the flag was drooping low;
Should the dust pollute your banner?
   No! the nation shouted, No!
So when War, in savage triumph,
   Spread abroad his funeral pall—
Then you called the colored soldiers,
   And they answered to your call.

And like hounds unleashed and eager
   For the life blood of the prey,
Sprung they forth and bore them bravely
   In the thickest of the fray.
And where'er the fight was hottest,
   Where the bullets fastest fell,
There they pressed unblanched and fearless
   At the very mouth of hell.

Ah, they rallied to the standard
   To uphold it by their might;
None were stronger in the labors,
   None were braver in the fight.
From the blazing breach of Wagner
   To the plains of Olustee,
They were foremost in the fight
   Of the battles of the free.

And at Pillow! God have mercy
   On the deeds committed there,
And the souls of those poor victims
   Sent to Thee without a prayer.
Let the fulness of Thy pity
   O'er the hot wrought spirits sway
Of the gallant colored soldiers
   Who fell fighting on that day!

Yes, the Blacks enjoy their freedom,
   And they won it dearly, too;
For the life blood of their thousands
   Did the southern fields bedew.
In the darkness of their bondage,
   In the depths of slavery's night,
Their muskets flashed the dawning,
   And they fought their way to light.

They were comrades then and brothers,
   Are they more or less to-day?
They were good to stop a bullet
   And to front the fearful fray.
They were citizens and soldiers,
   When rebellion raised its head;
And the traits that made them worthy,—
   Ah! those virtues are not dead.

They have shared your nightly vigils,
   They have shared your daily toil;
And their blood with yours commingling
   Has enriched the Southern soil.
They have slept and marched and suffered
   'Neath the same dark skies as you,
They have met as fierce a foeman,
   And have been as brave and true.

And their deeds shall find a record
   In the registry of Fame;
For their blood has cleansed completely
   Every blot of Slavery's shame.
So all honor and all glory
   To those noble sons of Ham—
The gallant colored soldiers
   Who fought for Uncle Sam!

Ships That Pass in the Night

Out in the sky the great dark clouds are massing;
  I look far out into the pregnant night,
Where I can hear a solemn booming gun
  And catch the gleaming of a random light,
That tells me that the ship I seek is passing,
    passing.

My tearful eyes my soul's deep hurt are glassing;
  For I would hail and check that ship of ships.
I stretch my hands imploring, cry aloud,
  My voice falls dead a foot from mine own lips,
And but its ghost doth reach that vessel, passing,
    passing.

O Earth, O Sky, O Ocean, both surpassing,
  O heart of mine, O soul that dreads the dark!
Is there no hope for me? Is there no way
  That I may sight and check that speeding bark
Which out of sight and sound is passing, passing?

Ere Sleep Comes Down to Soothe the Weary Eyes

Ere sleep comes down to soothe the weary eyes,
  Which all the day with ceaseless care have
    sought
The magic gold which from the seeker flies;
  Ere dreams put on the gown and cap of thought,
And make the waking world a world of lies,—
  Of lies most palpable, uncouth, forlorn,
That say life's full of aches and tears and sighs,—
  Oh, how with more than dreams the soul is
    torn,
Ere sleep comes down to soothe the weary eyes.

Ere sleep comes down to soothe the weary eyes,
  How all the griefs and heartaches we have
    known
Come up like pois'nous vapors that arise
  From some base witch's caldron when the crone,
To work some potent spell, her magic plies.
  The past which held its share of bitter pain,
Whose ghost we prayed that Time might exorcise,
  Comes up, is lived and suffered o'er again,
Ere sleep comes down to soothe the weary eyes.

Ere sleep comes down to soothe the weary eyes,
  What phantoms fill the dimly lighted room;
What ghostly shades in awe-creating guise
  Are bodied forth within the teeming gloom.
What echoes faint of sad and soul-sick cries,
  And pangs of vague inexplicable pain
That pay the spirit's ceaseless enterprise,
  Come thronging through the chambers of the
    brain,
Ere sleep comes down to soothe the weary eyes.

Ere sleep comes down to soothe the weary eyes,
  Where ranges forth the spirit far and free?
Through what strange realms and unfamiliar
    skies
  Tends her far course to lands of mystery?
To lands unspeakable—beyond surmise,
  Where shapes unknowable to being spring,
Till, faint of wing, the Fancy fails and dies
  Much wearied with the spirit's journeying,
Ere sleep comes down to soothe the weary eyes.

Ere sleep comes down to soothe the weary eyes,
  How questioneth the soul that other soul,—
The inner sense which neither cheats nor lies,
  But self exposes unto self, a scroll
Full writ with all life's acts unwise or wise,
  In characters indelible and known;
So, trembling with the shock of sad surprise,
  The soul doth view its awful self alone,
Ere sleep comes down to soothe the weary eyes.

When sleep comes down to seal the weary eyes,
  The last dear sleep whose soft embrace is
    balm,
And whom sad sorrow teaches us to prize
  For kissing all our passions into calm,
Ah, then, no more we heed the sad world's
    cries,
Or seek to probe th' eternal mystery,
Or fret our souls at long-withheld replies,
  At glooms through which our visions cannot
    see,
When sleep comes down to seal the weary eyes.

Dawn

An angel, robed in spotless white,
Bent down and kissed the sleeping Night.
Night woke to blush; the sprite was gone.
Men saw the blush and called it Dawn.

The Party

Dey had a gread big pahty down to Tom's de othah night;
Was I dah? You bet! I nevah in my life see sich a sight;
All de folks f'om fou' plantations was invited, an' dey come,
Dey come troopin' thick ez chillun when dey hyeahs a fife an' drum.
Evahbody dressed deir fines'—Heish yo' mouf an' git away,
Ain't seen no sich fancy dressin' sense las' quah'tly meetin' day;
Gals all dressed in silks an' satins, not a wrinkle ner a crease,
Eyes a-battin', teeth a-shinin', haih breshed back ez slick ez grease;
Sku'ts all tucked an' puffed an' ruffled, evah blessed seam an' stitch;
Ef you 'd seen 'em wif deir mistus, could n't swahed to which was which.
Men all dressed up in Prince Alberts, swaller-tails 'u'd tek yo' bref!
I cain't tell you nothin' 'bout it, y' ought to seen it fu' yo'se'f.
Who was dah? Now who you askin'? How you 'spect I gwine to know?
You mus' think I stood an' counted evahbody at de do.'
Ole man Babah's house-boy Isaac, brung dat gal, Malindy Jane,
Huh a-hangin' to his elbow, him a-struttin' wif a cane;
My, but Hahvey Jones was jealous! seemed to stick him lak a tho'n;
But he laughed with Viney Cahteh, tryin' ha'd to not let on,
But a pusson would 'a' noticed f'om de d'rection of his look,
Dat he was watchin' ev'ry step dat Ike an' Lindy took.
Ike he foun' a cheer an' asked huh: "Won't you set down?" wif a smile,
An' she answe'd up a-bowin', "Oh, I reckon 't ain't wuth while."
Dat was jes' fu' style, I reckon, 'cause she sot down jes' de same,
An' she stayed dah 'twell he fetched huh fu' to jine some so't o' game;
Den I hyeahd huh sayin' propah, ez she riz to go away,
"Oh, you raly mus' excuse me, fu' I hardly keers to play."
But I seen huh in a minute wif de othahs on de flo',
An' dah was n't any one o' dem a-playin' any mo';
Comin' down de flo' a-bowin' an' a-swayin' an' a-swingin',
Puttin' on huh high-toned mannahs all de time dat she was singin':
"Oh, swing Johnny up an' down, swing him all aroun',
Swing Johnny up an' down, swing him all aroun',
Oh, swing Johnny up an' down, swing him all aroun'
Fa' you well, my dahlin'."
Had to laff at ole man Johnson, he 's a caution now, you bet—
Hittin' clost onto a hunderd, but, he 's spry an' nimble yet;
He 'lowed how a-so't o' gigglin', "I ain't ole, I 'll let you see.
D'ain't no use in gittin' feeble, now, you youngstahs jes' watch me,"
An' he grabbed ole Aunt Marier,—weighs th'ee hunderd mo' er less,
An' he spun huh 'roun' de cabin swingin' Johnny lak de res'.

Evahbody laffed an' hollahed: "Go it! Swing huh, Uncle Jim!"
An' he swung huh too, I reckon, lak a youngstah, who but him.
Dat was bettah 'n young Scott Thomas, tryin' to be so awful smaht.
You know wehn dey gits to singin' an' dey comes to dat ere paht:
  "In some lady's new brick house,
  In some lady's gyahden.
    Ef you don't let me out, I will jump out,
  So fa' you well, my dahlin'."
Den dey 's got a circle 'roun' you, an' you 's got to break de line;
Well, dat dahky was so anxious, lak to bust hisse'f a-tryin';
Kep' on blund'rin' 'roun' an' foolin' 'twell he giv' one gread big jump,
Broke de line, an lit head-fo'most in de fiah-place right plump;
Hit 'ad fiah in it, mind you; well, I thought my soul I 'd bust,
Tried my best to keep f'om laffin', but hit seemed like die I must!
Y' ought to seen dat man a-scramblin' f'om de ashes an' de grime.
Did it bu'n him! Sich a question, why he did n't give it time:
Th'ow'd dem ashes and dem cindahs evah which-a-way I guess,
An' you nevah did, I reckon, clap yo' eyes on sich a mess;
Fu' he sholy made a picter an' a funny one to boot,
Wif his clothes all full o' ashes an' his face all full o' soot.
Well, hit laked to stopped de pahty, an' I reckon lak ez not
Dat it would ef Tom's wife, Mandy, had n't happened on de spot,
To invite us out to suppah—well, we scrambled to de table,
An' I 'd lak to tell you 'bout it— what we had—but I ain't able,
Mention jes' a few things, dough I know I had n't orter,
Fu' I know 't will staht a hank'rin' an' yo' mouf 'll 'mence to worter.
We had wheat bread white ez cotton an' a egg pone jes like gol',
Hog jole, bilin' hot an' steamin' roasted shoat an' ham sliced cold—
Look out! What 's de mattah wif you? Don't be fallin' on de flo';
Ef it 's go'n' to 'fect you dat way, I won't tell you nothin' mo'.
Dah now—well, we had hot chittlin's—now you 's tryin' ag'in to fall,
Cain't you stan' to hyeah about it? S'pose you 'd been an' seed it all;
Seed dem gread big sweet pertaters, layin' by de possum's side,
Seed dat coon in all his gravy, reckon den you 'd up and died!
Mandy 'lowed "you all mus' 'scuse me, d' wa'n't much upon my she'ves,
But I 's done my bes' to suit you, so set down an' he'p yo'se'ves."
Tom, he 'lowed: "I don't b'lieve in 'pologisin' an' perfessin',
Let 'em tek it lak dey ketch it. Eldah Thompson, ask de blessin'."
Wish you'd seed dat colo'ed preachah cleah his th'oat an' bow his head;
One eye shet, an' one eye open,—dis is evah wud he said:
"Lawd, look down in tendah mussy on sich generous hea'ts ez dese;
Make us truly thankful, amen. Pass dat possum, ef you please!"
Well, we eat and drunk ouah po'tion, 'twell dah was n't nothin' lef,
An' we felt jes' like new sausage, we was mos' nigh stuffed to def!
Tom, he knowed how we 'd be feelin', so he had de fiddlah 'roun',
An' he made us cleah de cabin fu' to dance dat suppah down.
Jim, de fiddlah, chuned his fiddle, put some rosum on his bow,
Set a pine box on de table, mounted it an' let huh go!
He 's a fiddlah, now I tell you, an' he made dat fiddle ring,
'Twell de ol'est an' de lamest had to give deir feet a fling.
Jigs, cotillions, reels an' breakdowns, cordrills an' a waltz er two;
Bless yo' soul, dat music winged 'em an' dem people lak to flew.
Cripple Joe, de old rheumatic, danced dat flo' f'om side to middle,

Th'owed away his crutch an' hopped it; what's rheumatics 'ginst a fiddle?
Eldah Thompson got so tickled dat he lak to los' his grace,
Had to tek bofe feet an' hol' dem so 's to keep 'em in deir place
An' de Christuns an' de sinnahs got so mixed up on dat flo',
Dat I don't see how dey 'd pahted ef de trump had chanced to blow.
Well, we danced dat way an' capahed in de mos' redic'lous way,
'Twell de roostahs in de bahnyard cleahed deir th'oats an' crowed fu' day.
Y' ought to been dah, fu' I tell you evahthing was rich an' prime,
An' dey ain't no use in talkin', we jes had one scrumptious time!

A Negro Love Song

Seen my lady home las' night,
    Jump back, honey, jump back.
Hel' huh han' an' sque'z it tight,
    Jump back, honey, jump back.
Hyeahd huh sigh a little sigh,
Seen a light gleam f'om huh eye,
An' a smile go flittin' by—
    Jump back, honey, jump back.

Hyeahd de win' blow thoo de pine,
    Jump back, honey, jump back.
Mockin'-bird was singin' fine,
    Jump back, honey, jump back.
An' my hea't was beatin' so,
When I reached my lady's do',
Dat I could n't ba' to go—
    Jump back, honey, jump back.

Put my ahm aroun' huh wais',
    Jump back, honey, jump back.
Raised huh lips an' took a tase,
    Jump back, honey, jump back.
Love me, honey, love me true?
Love me well ez I love you?
An' she answe'd, "'Cose I do"—
    Jump back, honey, jump back.

When Malindy Sings

G'way an' quit dat noise, Miss Lucy—
    Put dat music book away;
What 's de use to keep on tryin'?
    Ef you practise twell you 're gray,
You cain't sta't no notes a-flyin'
    Lak de ones dat rants and rings
F'om de kitchen to de big woods
    When Malindy sings.

You ain't got de nachel o'gans
    Fu' to make de soun' come right,
You ain't got de tu'ns an' twistin's
    Fu' to make it sweet an' light.
Tell you one thing now, Miss Lucy,
    An' I 'm tellin' you fu' true,
When hit comes to raal right singin',
    'T ain't no easy thing to do.

Easy 'nough fu' folks to hollah,
    Lookin' at de lines an' dots,
When dey ain't no one kin sence it,
    An' de chune comes in, in spots;
But fu' real melojous music,
    Dat jes' strikes yo' hea't and clings,
Jes' you stan' an' listen wif me
    When Malindy sings.

Ain't you nevah hyeahd Malindy?
    Blessed soul, tek up de cross!
Look hyeah, ain't you jokin', honey?
    Well, you don't know whut you los'.
Y' ought to hyeah dat gal a-wa'blin',
    Robins, la'ks, an' all dem things.
Heish dey moufs an' hides dey faces
    When Malindy sings.

Fiddlin' man jes' stop his fiddlin'.
  Lay his fiddle on de she'f;
Mockin'-bird quit tryin' to whistle,
  'Cause he jes' so shamed hisse'f.
Folks a-playin' on de banjo
  Drap dey fingahs on de strings—
Bless yo' soul—fu'gits to move em,
  When Malindy sings.

She jes' spreads huh mouf and hollahs,
  "Come to Jesus," twell you hyeah
Sinnahs' tremblin' steps and voices
  Timid-lak a-drawin' neah;
Den she tu'ns to "Rock of Ages,"
  Simply to de cross she clings;
An' you fin' yo' teahs a-drappin'
  When Malindy sings.

Who dat says dat humble praises
  Wif de Master nevah counts?
Heish yo' mouf, I hyeah dat music,
  Ez hit rises up an' mounts—
Floatin' by de hills an' valleys,
  Way above dis buryin' sod,
Ez hit makes its way in glory
  To de very gates of God!

Oh, hit 's sweetah dan de music
  Of an edicated band;
An hit 's dearah dan de battle's
  Song o' triumph in de lan'.
It seems holier dan evenin'
  When de solemn chu'ch bell rings,
Ez I sit an' ca'mly listen
  While Malindy sings.

Towsah, stop dat ba'kin', hyeah me!
  Mandy, mek dat chile keep still;
Don't you hyeah de echoes callin'
  F'om de valley to de hill?
Let me listen, I can hyeah it,
  Th'oo de bresh of angels' wings,
Sof' an' sweet, "Swing Low, Sweet Chariot,"
  Ez Malindy sings.

Sympathy

I know what the caged bird feels, alas!
  When the sun is bright on the upland slopes;
When the wind stirs soft through the springing
    grass,
And the river flows like a stream of glass;
  When the first bird sings and the first bud opes,
And the faint perfume from its chalice steals—
I know what the caged bird feels!

I know why the caged bird beats his wing
  Till its blood is red on the cruel bars;
For he must fly back to his perch and cling
When he fain would be on the bough a-swing;
  And a pain still throbs in the old, old scars
And they pulse again with a keener sting—
I know why he beats his wing!

I know why the caged bird sings, ah me,
  When his wing is bruised and his bosom sore,—
When he beats his bars and would be free;
It is not a carol of joy or glee,
  But a prayer that he sends from his heart's deep
    core,
But a plea, that upward to Heaven, he flings—
I know why the caged bird sings!

Harriet Beecher Stowe

She told the story, and the whole world wept
    At wrongs and cruelties it had not known
    But for this fearless woman's voice alone.
    She spoke to consciences that long had slept:
Her message, Freedom's clear reveille, swept
    From heedless hovel to complacent throne.
    Command and prophecy were in the tone
    And from its sheath the sword of justice leapt.
Around two peoples swelled a fiery wave,
    But both came forth transfigured from the
        flame.
Blest be the hand that dared be strong to save,
    And blest be she who in our weakness came—
    Prophet and priestess! At one stroke she gave
    A race to freedom and herself to fame.

Soliloquy of a Turkey

Dey 's a so't o' threatenin' feelin' in de blowin' of
    de breeze,
    An' I 's feelin' kin' o' squeamish in de night;
I 's a-walkin' 'roun' a-lookin' at de diffunt style o'
    trees,
    An' a-measurin' dey thickness an' dey height.
Fu' dey 's somep'n mighty 'spicious in de looks
    de da'kies give,
    Ez dey pass me an' my fambly on de groun',
So it 'curs to me dat lakly, ef I caihs to try an' live,
    It concehns me fu' to 'mence to look erroun'.

Dey 's a cu'ious kin' o' shivah runnin' up an'
    down my back,
    An' I feel my feddahs rufflin' all de day,
An' my laigs commence to trimble evah blessid
    step I mek;
    W'en I sees a ax, I tu'ns my head away.
Folks is go'gin' me wid goodies, an' dey 's treatin'
    me wid caih,
    An' I 's fat in spite of all dat I kin do.
I 's mistrus'ful of de kin'ness dat 's erroun' me
    evahwhaih,
    Fu' it 's jes' too good, an' frequent, to be true.

Snow 's a-fallin' on de medders, all erroun' me
    now is white,

But I 's still kep' on a-roostin' on de fence;
Isham comes an' feels my breas'bone, an' he hefted
    me las' night,
    An' he 's gone erroun' a-grinnin' evah sence.
'T ain't de snow dat meks me shivah; 't ain't de
    col' dat meks me shake;
    'T ain't de wintah-time itse'f dat 's 'fectin'
    me;
But I t'ink de time is comin', an' I 'd bettah mek
    a break,
    Fu' to set wid Mistah Possum in his tree.

W'en you hyeah de da'kies singin', an' de quah-
    tahs all is gay,
    'T ain't de time fu' birds lak me to be 'erroun';
W'en de hick'ry chips is flyin', an' de log 's been
    ca'ied erway,
    Den hit 's dang'ous to be roostin' nigh he
    groun'.

Grin on, Isham! Sing on, da'kies! But I flop my
    wings an' go
    Fu' de sheltah of de ve'y highest tree,
Fu' dey 's too much close ertention—an' dey 's
    too much fallin' snow—
    An' it 's too nigh Chris'mus mo'nin' now
    fu' me.

The Poet

He sang of life, serenely sweet,
  With, now and then, a deeper note.
  From some high peak, nigh yet remote,
He voiced the world's absorbing beat.

He sang of love when earth was young,
  And Love, itself, was in his lays.
  But ah, the world, it turned to praise
A jingle in a broken tongue.

In the Morning

'Lias! 'Lias! Bless de Lawd!
Don' you know de day 's erbroad?
Ef you don' git up, you scamp,
Dey 'll be trouble in dis camp.
T'ink I gwine to let you sleep
W'ile I meks yo' boa'd an' keep?
Dat 's a putty howdy-do—
Don' you hyeah me, 'Lias—you?

Bet ef I come crost dis flo'
You won' fin' no time to sno'.
Daylight all a-shinin in
W'ile you sleep—w'y hit's a sin!
Ain't de can'le-light enough
To bu'n widout a snuff,
But you go de mo'nin' thoo
Bu'nin' up de daylight too?

'Lias, don' you hyeah me call?
No use tu'nin' to'ds de wall;
I kin hyeah dat mattuss squeak;
Don' you hyeah me w'en I speak?
Dis hyeah clock done struck off six—
Ca'line, bring me dem ah sticks!
Oh, you down, suh; huh, you down—
Look hyeah, don' you daih to frown.

Ma'ch yo'se'f an' wash yo' face,
Don' you splattah all de place;
I got somep'n else to do,
'Sides jes' cleanin' aftah you.
Tek dat comb an' fix yo' haid—
Looks jes' lak a feddah baid.
Look hyeah, boy, I let you see
You sha' n't roll yo' eyes at me.

Come hyeah; bring me dat ah strap!
Boy, I 'll whup you 'twell you drap;
You done felt yo'se'f too strong,
An' you sholy got me wrong.
Set down at dat table thaih;
Jes' you whimpah ef you daih!
Evah mo'nin' on dis place,
Seem lak I mus' lose my grace.

Fol' yo' han's an' bow yo' haid—
Wait ontwell de blessin' 's said;
"Lawd, have mussy on ouah souls—"
(Don' you daih to tech dem rolls—)
"Bless de food we gwine to eat—"
(You set still—I *see* yo' feet;
You jes' try dat trick agin!)
"Gin us peace an' joy. Amen!"

A Death Song

Lay me down beneaf de willers in de grass,
Whah de branch 'll go a-singin' as it pass.
  An' w'en I 's a-layin' low,
  I kin hyeah it as it go
Singin', "Sleep, my honey, tek yo' res' at las'."

Lay me nigh to whah hit meks a little pool,
An' de watah stan's so quiet lak an' cool,
  Whah de little birds in spring,
  Ust to come an' drink an' sing,
An' de chillen waded on dey way to school.

  Let me settle w'en my shouldahs draps dey load
  Nigh enough to hyeah de noises in de road;
    Fu' I t'ink de las' long res'
    Gwine to soothe my sperrit bes'
  Ef I 's layin' 'mong de t'ings I 's allus knowed.

Compensation

Because I had loved so deeply,
   Because I had loved so long,
God in His great compassion
   Gave me the gift of song.

Because I have loved so vainly,
   And sung with such faltering breath,
The Master in infinite mercy
   Offers the boon of Death.

Jimsella

No one could ever have accused Mandy Mason of being thrifty. For the first twenty years of her life conditions had not taught her the necessity for thrift. But that was before she had come North with Jim. Down there at home one either rented or owned a plot of ground with a shanty set in the middle of it, and lived off the products of one's own garden and coop. But here it was all very different: one room in a crowded tenement house, and the necessity of grinding day after day to keep the wolf—a very terrible and ravenous wolf—from the door. No wonder that Mandy was discouraged and finally gave up to more than her old shiftless ways.

Jim was no less disheartened. He had been so hopeful when he first came, and had really worked hard. But he could not go higher than his one stuffy room, and the food was not so good as it had been at home. In this state of mind, Mandy's shiftlessness irritated him. He grew to look on her as the source of all his disappointments. Then, as he walked Sixth or Seventh Avenue, he saw other coloured women who dressed gayer than Mandy, looked smarter, and did not wear such great shoes. These he contrasted with his wife, to her great disadvantage.

"Mandy," he said to her one day, "why don't you fix yo'se'f up an' look like people? You go 'roun' hyeah lookin' like I dunno what."

"Why n't you git me somep'n' to fix myse'f up in?" came back the disconcerting answer.

"Ef you had any git up erbout you, you 'd git somep'n' fu' yo'se'f an' not wait on me to do evahthing."

"Well, ef I waits on you, you keeps me waitin', fu' I ain' had nothin' fit to eat ner waih since I been up hyeah."

"Nev' min'! You 's mighty free wid yo' talk now, but some o' dese days you won't be so free.

You 's gwine to wake up some mo'nin' an' fin' dat I 's lit out; dat 's what you will."

"Well, I 'low nobody ain't got no string to you."

Mandy took Jim's threat as an idle one, so she could afford to be independent. But the next day had found him gone. The deserted wife wept for a time, for she had been fond of Jim, and then she set to work to struggle on by herself. It was a dismal effort, and the people about her were not kind to her. She was hardly of their class. She was only a simple, honest countrywoman, who did not go out with them to walk the avenue.

When a month or two afterward the sheepish Jim returned, ragged and dirty, she had forgiven him and taken him back. But immunity from punishment spoiled him, and hence of late his lapses had grown more frequent and of longer duration.

He walked in one morning, after one of his absences, with a more than usually forbidding face, for he had heard the news in the neighbourhood before he got in. During his absence a baby had come to share the poverty of his home. He thought with shame at himself, which turned into anger, that the child must be three months old and he had never seen it.

"Back ag'in, Jim?" was all Mandy said as he entered and seated himself sullenly.

"Yes, I 's back, but I ain't back fu' long. I jes' come to git my clothes. I 's a-gwine away fu' good."

"Gwine away ag'in! Why, you been gone fu' nigh on to fou' months a'ready. Ain't you nevah gwine to stay home no mo'?"

"I tol' you I was gwine away fu' good, did n't I? Well, dat 's what I mean."

"Ef you did n't want me, Jim, I wish to Gawd

dat you 'd 'a' lef' me back home among my folks, whaih people knowed me an' would 'a' give me a helpin' han. Dis hyeah No'f ain't no fittin' place fu' a lone colo'ed ooman less 'n she got money."

"It ain't no place fu' nobody dat 's jes' lazy an' no 'count."

"I ain't no' count. I ain't wuffless. I does de bes' I kin. I been wo'kin' like a dog to try an' keep up while you trapsein' 'roun', de Lawd knows whaih. When I was single I could git out an' mek my own livin'. I did n't ax nobody no odds; but you wa'n't satisfied ontwell I ma'ied you, an' now, when I 's tied down wid a baby, dat 's de way you treats me."

The woman sat down and began to cry, and the sight of her tears angered her husband the more.

"Oh, cry!" he exclaimed. "Cry all you want to. I reckon you 'll cry yo' fill befo' you gits me back. What do I keer about de baby! Dat 's jes' de trouble. It wa' n't enough fu' me to have to feed an' clothe you a-layin' 'roun' doin' nothin', a baby had to go an' come too."

"It 's yo'n, an' you got a right to tek keer of it, dat 's what you have. I ain't a-gwine to waih my soul-case out a-tryin' to pinch along an' sta've to def at las'. I 'll kill myse'f an' de chile, too, fus'."

The man looked up quickly. "Kill yo'se'f," he said. Then he laughed. "Who evah hyeahed tell of a niggah killin' hisse'f?"

"Nev' min', nev' min', you jes' go on yo' way rejoicin'. I 'spect you runnin' 'roun' aftah some-body else—dat 's de reason you cain't nevah stay at home no mo'."

"Who tol' you dat?" exclaimed the man, fiercely. "I ain't runnin' aftah nobody else— 't ain't none o' yo' business ef I is."

The denial and implied confession all came out in one breath.

"Ef hit ain't my bus'ness, I 'd like to know whose it gwine to be. I 's yo' lawful wife an' hit 's me dat 's a-sta'vin' to tek keer of yo' chile."

"Doggone de chile; I 's tiahed o' hyeahin' 'bout huh."

"You done got tiahed mighty quick when you ain't nevah even seed huh yit. You done got tiahed quick, sho."

"No, an' I do' want to see huh, neithah."

"You do' know nothin' 'bout de chile, you do' know whethah you wants to see huh er not."

"Look hyeah, ooman, don't you fool wid me. I ain't right, nohow!"

Just then, as if conscious of the hubbub she had raised, and anxious to add to it, the baby awoke and began to wail. With quick mother instinct, the black woman went to the shabby bed, and, taking the child in her arms, began to croon softly to it: "Go s'eepy, baby; don' you be 'f'aid; mammy ain' gwine let nuffin' hu't you, even ef pappy don't wan' look at huh li'l face. Bye, bye, go s'eepy, mammy's li'l gal." Un-consciously she talked to the baby in a dialect that was even softer than usual. For a moment the child subsided, and the woman turned angrily on her husband: "I don' keer whethah you evah sees dis chile er not. She 's a blessed li'l angel, dat 's what she is, an' I 'll wo'k my fingahs off to raise huh, an' when she grows up, ef any nasty niggah comes erroun' mekin' eyes at huh, I 'll tell huh 'bout huh pappy an' she 'll stay wid me an' be my comfo't."

"Keep yo' comfo't. Gawd knows I do' want huh."

"De time 'll come, though, an' I kin wait fu' it. Hush-a-bye, Jimsella."

The man turned his head slightly.

"What you call huh?"

"I calls huh Jimsella, dat 's what I calls huh, 'ca'se she de ve'y spittin' image of you. I gwine to jes' lun to huh dat she had a pappy, so she know she 's a hones' chile an' kin hol' up huh haid."

"Oomph!"

They were both silent for a while, and then Jim said, "Huh name ought to be Jamsella— don't you know Jim 's sho't fu' James?"

"I don't keer what it 's sho't fu'." The woman was holding the baby close to her breast and sobbing now. "It was n't no James dat come a-cou'tin' me down home. It was jes' plain Jim. Dat 's what de mattah, I reckon you done got to be James." Jim did n't answer, and there was another space of silence, only interrupted by two or three contented gurgles from the baby.

"I bet two bits she don't look like me," he said finally, in a dogged tone that was a little tinged with curiosity.

"I know she do. Look at huh yo'se'f."

"I ain' gwine look at huh."

"Yes, you 's 'fraid—dat 's de reason."

"I ain' 'fraid nuttin' de kin'. What I got to be 'fraid fu'? I reckon a man kin look at his own darter. I will look jes' to spite you."

He could n't see much but a bundle of rags,

from which sparkled a pair of beady black eyes. But he put his finger down among the rags. The baby seized it and gurgled. The sweat broke out on Jim's brow.

"Cain't you let me hold de baby a minute?" he said angrily. "You must be 'fraid I 'll run off wid huh." He took the child awkwardly in his arms.

The boiling over of Mandy's clothes took her to the other part of the room, where she was busy for a few minutes. When she turned to look for Jim, he had slipped out, and Jimsella was lying on the bed trying to kick free of the coils which swaddled her.

At supper-time that evening Jim came in with a piece of "shoulder-meat" and a head of cabbage.

"You 'll have to git my dinnah ready fu' me to ca'y to-morrer. I 's wo'kin' on de street, an I cain't come home twell night."

"Wha', what!" exclaimed Mandy, "den you ain' gwine leave, aftah all."

"Don't bothah me, ooman," said Jim. "Is Jimsella 'sleep?"

W. E. B. Du Bois (1868–1963)

When William Edward Burghardt Du Bois died on the evening of August 27, 1963, tens of thousands of Americans were en route in the March on Washington for Jobs and Freedom. To most of them, the event seemed the beginning of a new epoch in race relations, the dusk of dawn of the new day that Du Bois had prophesied and struggled for almost a century to bring about. Traveling on chartered buses, many of the marchers were unaware of the old man's death until A. Philip Randolph, another venerable warrior for racial justice, announced it sadly to the great throng assembled before the Lincoln Memorial. The initial reaction of sorrow was quickly followed by the calm assurance that Du Bois' work was being done, that his vision was at that moment being fulfilled. But Du Bois himself had died in Accra a Ghanaian citizen, having renounced the citizenship of his native land and joined the Communist Party. He had given up on America, a fact that the optimism of the moment made it difficult for the marchers to remember. Nearly a decade after his death—the decade of Watts and Selma and Detroit and Hough and Newark, the decade of the martyrdom of Malcolm X and Martin Luther King and Fred Hampton—one wonders whether the pessimism of Du Bois was not a more nearly accurate assessment of the national soul than the sanguine expectations of the marchers on Washington. At any rate, Du Bois lies buried on the Ghana coast, not in the Berkshire hills of his boyhood.

The road from Great Barrington, Massachusetts, where Du Bois was born on February 23, 1868, to Accra was long and arduous, but it was filled with achievements of a variety, scope, and profundity that make plausible the claim of John Oliver Killens that "he was the greatest American intellectual of the twentieth century." Born "with a flood of Negro blood, a strain of French, a bit of Dutch, but thank God! no 'Anglo-Saxon,'" Du Bois had a poor but relatively happy New England childhood. While still in high school he began his long writing career by serving as a correspondent for newspapers in New York and in Springfield, Massachusetts. After graduation, in spite of insufficient funds, he dreamed of attending Harvard, but he chose instead to accept the help of some local churches and enroll at Fisk University in Nashville. There he discovered his Blackness and made a lifelong commitment to his people: "A new loyalty and allegiance replaced my Americanism: henceforward I was a Negro." Teaching in rural Black schools in Tennessee during summer vacations further expanded his awareness of the beauty of the souls of Black folk, and his editorship of the *Fisk Herald* in his senior year provided his first racial forum.

After graduating from Fisk in 1888, Du Bois entered Harvard as a junior. There he studied under such giants as William James, Josiah Royce, and George Santayana in philosophy, Nathaniel Shaler in geology, Barret Wendell in English, and Albert Bushnell Hart in history, men who recognized his abilities and gave him encouragement and sometimes friendship. In his social life, however, Du Bois stood proudly aloof from his white classmates, preferring the company of Black students and Black Bostonians. When he graduated *cum laude* in 1890, he felt the need for further preparation and study in order to be able to apply "philosophy to an historical interpretation of race relations. . . ." "I was trying," he recalls in his *Autobiography,* "to take my first steps toward sociology as the science of human action." After two years of graduate work at Harvard, he spent another two years at the University of Berlin on a Slater Fund Fellowship. Here, as at Harvard, he studied under some of the most distinguished minds of the late nineteenth century: Gustav Schmoller, Adolf Wagner, Heinrich von Treitschke, and Max Weber. Traveling widely in Europe, he was delighted by the absence of color consciousness among Europeans and impressed by their mellow civilization. But he knew that his life's work was elsewhere, in "the rise of the Negro people, taking for granted that their best development means the best development of the world." Du Bois returned to America in 1894, now at last ready to begin.

In a brief résumé only some of the major landmarks in the vast terrain of Du Bois' writings can be indicated, but they will suffice to suggest the magnitude of his achievement. During the two years of his first academic appointment as professor of Greek and Latin at Wilberforce University, he completed work for the Harvard doctorate. His thesis, *The Suppression of the African Slave-Trade to the United States of America, 1638–1870,* received the singular distinction of being selected as the inaugural volume of the Harvard Historical Studies series in 1896 and remains the standard treatment today. Another major contribution to Afro-American history was *Black Reconstruction in America* (1935), an indispensable corrective to the racist interpretations of Reconstruction history by William Archibald Dunning and his followers. Far from being the corrupt and ignorant barbarians of Southern legend, Du Bois shows that Black Reconstruction politicians tended to be no less honest and educated than their white colleagues, North and South. Furthermore, he shows that they supported progressive social measures, which, if passed and supported, would have made the South an economic, social, and political democracy instead of the racist oligarchy that it became. The real betrayal, *Black Reconstruction in America* argues, was not of the nation and the South by Black men, but vice versa. Both *The Suppression of the African Slave-Trade* and *Black Reconstruction* are specialized works of historical scholarship, but Du Bois could also work on a larger canvas. *The Negro* (1915) is a sketch of Black people throughout history in both Africa and the New World. The same large subject is more fully treated in *Black Folk, Then and Now: An Essay in the History and Sociology of the Negro Race* (1939), and eight years later he placed Africa in the context of global history in *The World and Africa* (1947). As historian Du Bois has told the Black man's story with scholarship and with passion, qualities that he made compatible.

After *The Suppression of the African Slave-Trade,* most of Du Bois' historical works have a strong admixture of sociology. In sociology proper, his most impressive single achievement is *The Philadelphia Negro* (1899), for which he did research during a year's appointment as assistant instructor in sociology at the University of Pennsylvania. Based on painstaking empirical investigation, including some five thousand personal interviews conducted by Du Bois himself, *The Philadelphia Negro* is one of the great pioneer works of urban and ethnic sociology. The sociologist E. Digby Baltzell has recently asserted that "there has not been a scholarly study of the American Negro in the twentieth century which has not referred to and utilized the empirical findings, the research methods, and the theoretical point of view of this seminal book." Of equal importance is the groundbreaking series of eighteen monographs resulting from conferences at Atlanta University conducted by Du Bois mainly during his tenure there as professor of economics and history from 1897 to 1910. Together, these studies touch on almost all aspects of Black life. No more comprehensive sociological inquiry was to be made until Gunnar Myrdal's *An American Dilemma* in 1944.

While still at Atlanta University, Du Bois wrote *John Brown* (1909) for the American Crisis Biographies series. The author called this "one of the best written of my books." It was a labor of love, for Du Bois considered Brown "the man who of all Americans has perhaps come nearest to touching the real souls of black folks." Autobiographer as well as biographer, Du Bois examined his own life in the opening chapter and elsewhere in *Darkwater* (1920). Two decades later, he published *Dusk of Dawn: An Essay Toward an Autobiography of a Race Concept* (1940), a full-scale treatment of "the Problem" (racism) as experienced during the first seventy years of his life. Finally, he wrote his magisterial work *The Autobiography of W. E. B. Du Bois: A Soliloquy on Viewing My Life from the Last Decade of Its First Century* (completed in 1960, published in abridged form in China, the Soviet Union, and East Germany in 1964 and 1965, published in its entirety in 1968). More than personal records, these autobiographical writings interweave the Du Bois narrative with the great public events and issues with which his life was inextricably involved.

Du Bois' career as an imaginative writer began in the first decade of the twentieth century with poems contributed to *The Independent* and *The Horizon*. He turned to poetry again in his extreme old age. A posthumous collection of *Selected Poems* was published by the Ghana University Press in 1965. In drama he wrote "The Christ of the Andes" in 1908, and five years later, on the fiftieth anniversary of the Emancipation Proclamation, his historical pageant entitled "The Star of Ethiopia" was produced first in New York and Washington, later in Philadelphia and Los Angeles. In fiction he was more productive, writing his first novel in 1911 and his fifth and last exactly fifty years later. *The Quest for the Silver Fleece* (1911) is a sociological novel about the Southern cotton economy and its effects on Black life. *Dark Princess*, appearing at the height of the Harlem Renaissance in 1928, relates the struggle of the Black man in America to the revolutionary unrest of the dark peoples of Asia and Africa. Prophetic as always, Du Bois in this novel envisions the solidarity of the Third World against their white oppressors and exploiters. Finally, when he was almost ninety, he began *The Black Flame* trilogy, a vast fictional panorama of Afro-American history from the end of Reconstruction to the mid-1950's. *The Ordeal of Mansart* (1957), *Mansart Builds a School* (1959), and *Worlds of Color* (1961) trace the lives of four generations of the Mansart family in the full context of the racial experience that the author had lived and helped to shape.

Du Bois' imaginative writing was always ancillary to his scholarly and racial interests. But if his poetry, fiction, and drama embody historical and sociological themes, one may also say that his intellectual writings are often infused with a poetic style and spirit. Especially is this true of some of his best books, such as *The Souls of Black Folk* (1903) and *Darkwater* (1920), which range widely over his interests and ideas in a variety of moods and modes. In *The Souls of Black Folk* the reader may sample history, sociology, biography, economic analysis, educational theory, social commentary, and even fiction in the fourteen chapters, but the work holds together because of its "poetic" style, its recurrent metaphors and phrases, its chapter epigraphs of poetry and music, and its pervasive anti-Washingtonianism. Among Du Bois' early books, *The Souls of Black Folk* is the most essential for the general reader, as is the *Autobiography* among the later works.

In addition to his own books and pamphlets, Du Bois contributed hundreds of articles, editorials, and reviews to dozens of books, magazines, and newspapers. His work as editor of *The Crisis,* the organ of the NAACP, from 1910 to 1934 was perhaps the most sustained and uncompromising single effort in the history of racial protest in America. As a scholarly editor, he founded *Phylon* in 1940 at Atlanta University. As early as 1909 he had projected an "Encyclopedia Africana" that would preserve and expand the store of knowledge about Black people. This labor occupied him intermittently for the rest of his life, *Encyclopedia of the Negro: Preparatory ·Volume* appearing in 1945. The twilight years in Ghana were devoted mainly to this task.

The complex development of Du Bois' ideas can only be hinted at here. Initially, he strove to bring a scientific rigor to the study of Black America in the hope that the dissemination of facts would itself ameliorate racial relations. Shortly afterward, he began to oppose the Washingtonian program with its emphasis on vocational training and its acquiescence to white supremacy. As he wrote in *The Souls of Black Folk,* "Work, culture, liberty,—all these we need, not singly but together, not successively but together, each growing and aiding each. . . ." To correct Washington's overemphasis on work, and in rebellion against his dominance in Black affairs, Du Bois placed his own stress on culture and liberty, urging higher education for "the talented tenth" and full political and civil rights for all. To implement his ideas, he organized in 1905 the Niagara Movement, which merged four years later with a group of white liberals to form the NAACP. From its founding through the 1920's, this organization worked vigorously against suffrage restrictions, segregation, and lynching and other forms of mob violence.

Even earlier than the Niagara Movement, Du Bois had become interested in the problems of Africa as well as Afro-Americans. In 1900 he attended the First Pan-African Conference in London, and from then on he was the great architect of Pan-Africanism, a movement reacting against the oppression and exploitation of Africa by white colonial powers and looking toward a Black Africa independent and united. Du Bois was the moving force in subsequent Pan-African Congresses in 1919, 1921, 1923, 1927, and 1945. It was fitting that in 1961 he accepted the invitation of President Kwame Nkrumah to take up residence in Ghana, the first ex-colonial Black African nation. Du Bois had lived to see his Pan-African dream becoming reality.

During his student days in Germany, Du Bois took his first tentative steps toward the political left. Though not yet thoroughly familiar with Marxist economic analysis, he was flirting with Socialists as the Niagara Movement got under way, and he joined the Socialist Party in 1910, resigning, however, in 1912. In the 1920's he began to read Marx carefully, and in 1926 he visited the Soviet Union and was impressed by what he saw. During the 1930's, he considered himself a Marxist Socialist, though he criticized the Communist Party for its ineptitude in dealing with Black problems. As he moved farther left during the 1940's and 1950's, his influence tended to wane except among Communists, especially after his indictment by the Department of Justice early in 1951 for "failure to register as agent of a foreign principal" in connection with his work as chairman of the Peace Information Center. The charge was absurd and Du Bois was acquitted, but not before he had suffered deep humiliation from this example of Cold War political persecution. He spent most of 1958 and 1959 in the Soviet Union and China, and in 1961, at the age of ninety-three, he joined the Communist Party of the United States.

The legacy of W. E. B. Du Bois as writer, thinker, and racial leader may well prove to be more durable than that of any other Afro-American of the twentieth century. Less charismatic as a personality than Marcus Garvey or Martin Luther King or Malcom X, his interests ranged wider and his analysis went deeper. As President Nnamdi Azikiwe of Nigeria has written: "His influence as a writer and reformer will never diminish and the monument to his greatness, vividly apparent in his many published works, will always serve to guide men and women everywhere in the holy crusade for human freedom."

Du Bois' full-length books not mentioned above include *The Gift of Black Folk* (1924), *Color and Democracy: Colonies and Peace* (1945), and *In Battle for Peace: The Story of My 83rd Birthday* (1952). Three useful collections of short pieces are *An ABC of Color* (1963), edited by John Oliver Killens; *W. E. B. Du Bois: A Reader* (1970), edited by Meyer Weinberg, who includes a partial list of Du Bois' vast output of pamphlets and articles; and the two volumes of *W. E. B. Du Bois Speaks: Speeches and Addresses* (1970), edited by Philip S. Foner.

Two important studies are Francis L. Broderick's *W. E. B. Du Bois, Negro Leader in a Time of Crisis* (1959) and Elliott M. Rudwick's *W. E. B. Du Bois: A Study in Minority Group Leadership* (1960 and 1968). Leslie Alexander Lacy's *Cheer the Lonesome Traveler* (1970) is a recent life. Herbert Aptheker, Du Bois' literary executor, is working on an authorized biography. A special Du Bois issue of *Freedomways* (Winter 1965) has been reprinted by Beacon Press as *Black Titan: W. E. B. Du Bois* (1970). Some books containing evaluations of Du Bois are Vernon Loggins, *The Negro Author* (1931); Benjamin Brawley, *The Negro Genius* (1937); Edwin R. Embree, *13 Against the Odds* (1944); Hugh M. Gloster, *Negro Voices in American Fiction* (1948); Robert Bone, *The Negro Novel in America* (1958); Earl E. Thorpe, *Negro Historians in the United States* (1958) and *The Mind of the Negro* (1961); August Meier, *Negro Thought in America 1880–1915* (1963); Harold Cruse, *The Crisis of the Negro Intellectual* (1967); Lerone Bennett, Jr., *Pioneers in Protest* (1968); and George R. Metcalf, *Black Profiles* (1970).

See also the following articles: Robert M. Lovett, "Du Bois," *Phylon*, II (1941), 214–218; M. L. Chaffee, "William E. B. Du Bois' Concept of the Racial Problem in the United States," *Journal of Negro History*, XLI (1956), 241–258; Truman Nelson, "W. E. B. Du Bois: Prophet in Limbo," *The Nation*, CLXXXVI (January 25, 1958), 76–79; Sidney Finkelstein, "W. E. B. Du Bois' Trilogy: A Literary Triumph," *Mainstream*, XIV (October 1961), 6–17; Martin Duberman, "Du Bois as Prophet," *The New Republic*, CLVIII (March 23, 1968), 36–39; Irving Howe, "Remarkable Man, Ambiguous Legacy," *Harper's Magazine*, CCXXXVI (March 1968), 143–149; Martin Luther King, Jr., "Honoring Dr. Du Bois," *Freedomways*, VIII (1968), 104–111; Richard Kostelanetz, "Fiction of a Negro Politics: The Neglected Novels of W. E. B. Du Bois," *Xaxier University Studies*, VII, No. 2 (1968), 5–39; Peter Shaw, "The Uses of Autobiography," *The American Scholar*, XXXVIII (1969), 136, 138, 140, 142, 144; Vincent Harding, "W. E. B. Du Bois and the Black Messianic Vision," *Freedomways*, IX (1969), 44–58; Lenneal J. Henderson, "W. E. B. Du Bois: Black Scholar and Prophet," *The Black Scholar*, I (January–February 1970), 48–57; Earl Ofari, "W. E. B. Du Bois and Black Power," *Black World*, XIX (August 1970), 26–28; and Andrew G. Paschal, "The Spirit of W. E. B. Du Bois," *The Black Scholar*, II (October 1970), 17–28 (February 1971), 38–50.

from *The Souls of Black Folk**

V: Of the Wings of Atalanta

O black boy of Atlanta!
But half was spoken;
The slave's chains and the master's
Alike are broken;
The one curse of the races
Held both in tether;
They are rising—all are rising—
The black and white together.

WHITTIER

South of the North, yet north of the South, lies the City of a Hundred Hills, peering out from the shadows of the past into the promise of the future. I have seen her in the morning, when the first flush of day had half-roused her; she lay gray and still on the crimson soil of Georgia; then the blue smoke began to curl from her chimneys, the tinkle of bell and scream of whistle broke the silence, the rattle and roar of busy life slowly gathered and swelled, until the seething whirl of the city seemed a strange thing in a sleepy land.

Once, they say, even Atlanta slept dull and drowsy at the foot-hills of the Alleghanies, until the iron baptism of war awakened her with its sullen waters, aroused and maddened her, and left her listening to the sea. And the sea cried to the hills and the hills answered the sea, till the city rose like a widow and cast away her weeds, and toiled for her daily bread; toiled steadily, toiled cunningly,—perhaps with some bitterness, with a touch of *réclame*,—and yet with real earnestness, and real sweat.

It is a hard thing to live haunted by the ghost of an untrue dream; to see the wide vision of empire fade into real ashes and dirt; to feel the pang of the conquered, and yet know that with all the Bad that fell on one black day, something was vanquished that deserved to live, something killed that in justice had not dared to die; to know that with the Right that triumphed, triumphed something of Wrong, something sordid and mean, something less than the broadest and best. All this is bitter hard; and many a man and city and people have found in it excuse for sulking, and brooding, and listless waiting.

Such are not men of the sturdier make; they of Atlanta turned resolutely toward the future; and

* Musical notation has been deleted from the songs.

that future held aloft vistas of purple and gold:— Atlanta, Queen of the cotton kingdom; Atlanta, Gateway to the Land of the Sun; Atlanta, the new Lachesis, spinner of web and woof for the world. So the city crowned her hundred hills with factories, and stored her shops with cunning handiwork, and stretched long iron ways to greet the busy Mercury in his coming. And the Nation talked of her striving.

Perhaps Atlanta was not christened for the winged maiden of dull Bœotia; you know the tale, —how swarthy Atalanta, tall and wild, would marry only him who out-raced her; and how the wily Hippomenes laid three apples of gold in the way. She fled like a shadow, paused, startled over the first apple, but even as he stretched his hand, fled again; hovered over the second, then, slipping from his hot grasp, flew over river, vale, and hill; but as she lingered over the third, his arms fell round her, and looking on each other, the blazing passion of their love profaned the sanctuary of Love, and they were cursed. If Atlanta be not named for Atalanta, she ought to have been.

Atalanta is not the first or the last maiden whom greed of gold has led to defile the temple of Love; and not maids alone, but men in the race of life, sink from the high and generous ideals of youth to the gambler's code of the Bourse; and in all our Nation's striving is not the Gospel of Work befouled by the Gospel of Pay? So common is this that one-half think it normal; so unquestioned, that we almost fear to question if the end of racing is not gold, if the aim of man is not rightly to be rich. And if this is the fault of America, how dire a danger lies before a new land and a new city, lest Atlanta, stooping for mere gold, shall find that gold accursed!

It was no maiden's idle whim that started this hard racing; a fearful wilderness lay about the feet of that city after the War,—feudalism, poverty, the rise of the Third Estate, serfdom, the re-birth of Law and Order, and above and between all, the Veil of Race. How heavy a journey for weary feet! what wings must Atalanta have to flit over all this hollow and hill, through sour wood and sullen water, and by the red waste of sun-baked clay! How fleet must Atalanta be if she will not be tempted by gold to profane the Sanctuary!

The Sanctuary of our fathers has, to be sure, few Gods,—some sneer, "all too few." There is the thrifty Mercury of New England, Pluto of the North, and Ceres of the West; and there, too, is the half-forgotten Apollo of the South, under whose ægis the maiden ran,—and as she ran she forgot him, even as there in Bœotia Venus was forgot. She forgot the old ideal of the Southern gentleman,—that new-world heir of the grace and courtliness of patrician, knight, and noble; forgot his honor with his foibles, his kindliness with his carelessness, and stooped to apples of gold,—to men busier and sharper, thriftier and more unscrupulous. Golden apples are beautiful—I remember the lawless days of boyhood, when orchards in crimson and gold tempted me over fence and field—and, too, the merchant who has dethroned the planter is no despicable *parvenu*. Work and wealth are the mighty levers to lift this old new land; thrift and toil and saving are the highways to new hopes and new possibilities; and yet the warning is needed lest the wily Hippomenes tempt Atalanta to thinking that golden apples are the goal of racing, and not mere incidents by the way.

Atlanta must not lead the South to dream of material prosperity as the touchstone of all success; already the fatal might of this idea is beginning to spread; it is replacing the finer type of Southerner with vulgar money-getters; it is burying the sweeter beauties of Southern life beneath pretence and ostentation. For every social ill the panacea of Wealth has been urged,—wealth to overthrow the remains of the slave feudalism; wealth to raise the "cracker" Third Estate; wealth to employ the black serfs, and the prospect of wealth to keep them working; wealth as the end and aim of politics, and as the legal tender for law and order; and, finally, instead of Truth, Beauty, and Goodness, wealth as the ideal of the Public School.

Not only is this true in the world which Atlanta typifies, but it is threatening to be true of a world beneath and beyond that world,—the Black World beyond the Veil. To-day it makes little difference to Atlanta, to the South, what the Negro thinks or dreams or wills. In the soul-life of the land he is to-day, and naturally will long remain, unthought of, half forgotten; and yet when he does come to think and will and do for himself,—and let no man dream that day will

never come,—then the part he plays will not be one of sudden learning, but words and thoughts he has been taught to lisp in his race-childhood. To-day the ferment of his striving toward self-realization is to the strife of the white world like a wheel within a wheel: beyond the Veil are smaller but like problems of ideals, of leaders and the led, of serfdom, of poverty, of order and subordination, and, through all, the Veil of Race. Few know of these problems, few who know notice them; and yet there they are, awaiting student, artist, and seer,—a field for somebody sometime to discover. Hither has the temptation of Hippomenes penetrated; already in this smaller world, which now indirectly and anon directly must influence the larger for good or ill, the habit is forming of interpreting the world in dollars. The old leaders of Negro opinion, in the little groups where there is a Negro social consciousness, are being replaced by new; neither the black preacher nor the black teacher leads as he did two decades ago. Into their places are pushing the farmers and gardeners, the well-paid porters and artisans, the businessmen,—all those with property and money. And with all this change, so curiously parallel to that of the Other-world, goes too the same inevitable change in ideals. The South laments to-day the slow, steady disappearance of a certain type of Negro,—the faithful, courteous slave of other days, with his incorruptible honesty and dignified humility. He is passing away just as surely as the old type of Southern gentleman is passing, and from not dissimilar causes,—the sudden transformation of a fair far-off ideal of Freedom into the hard reality of bread-winning and the consequent deification of Bread.

In the Black World, the Preacher and Teacher embodied once the ideals of this people,—the strife for another and a juster world, the vague dream of righteousness, the mystery of knowing; but to-day the danger is that these ideals, with their simple beauty and weird inspiration, will suddenly sink to a question of cash and a lust for gold. Here stands this black young Atalanta, girding herself for the race that must be run; and if her eyes be still toward the hills and sky as in the days of old, then we may look for noble running; but what if some ruthless or wily or even thoughtless Hippomenes lay golden apples before her? What if the Negro people be wooed from a strife for righteousness, from a love of knowing, to regard dollars as the be-all and end-all of life? What if to the Mammonism of America be added the rising Mammonism of the re-born South, and the Mammonism of this South be reinforced by the budding Mammonism of its half-awakened black millions? Whither, then, is the new-world quest of Goodness and Beauty and Truth gone glimmering? Must this, and that fair flower of Freedom which, despite the jeers of latter-day striplings, sprung from our fathers' blood, must that too degenerate into a dusty quest of gold,—into lawless lust with Hippomenes?

The hundred hills of Atlanta are not all crowned with factories. On one, toward the west, the setting sun throws three buildings in bold relief against the sky. The beauty of the group lies in its simple unity:—a broad lawn of green rising from the red street with mingled roses and peaches; north and south, two plain and stately halls; and in the midst, half hidden in ivy, a larger building, boldly graceful, sparingly decorated, and with one low spire. It is a restful group,—one never looks for more; it is all here, all intelligible. There I live, and there I hear from day to day the low hum of restful life. In winter's twilight, when the red sun glows, I can see the dark figures pass between the halls to the music of the night-bell. In the morning, when the sun is golden, the clang of the day-bell brings the hurry and laughter of three hundred young hearts from hall and street, and from the busy city below,—children all dark and heavy-haired,—to join their clear young voices in the music of the morning sacrifice. In a half-dozen class-rooms they gather then,—here to follow the love-song of Dido, here to listen to the tale of Troy divine; there to wander among the stars, there to wander among men and nations,—and elsewhere other well-worn ways of knowing this queer world. Nothing new, no time-saving devices,—simply old time-glorified methods of delving for Truth, and searching out the hidden beauties of life, and learning the good of living. The riddle of existence is the college curriculum that was laid before the Pharaohs, that was taught in the groves by Plato, that formed the *trivium* and *quadrivium,* and is to-day laid before the freedmen's sons by Atlanta University. And this course of study will not change; its methods will grow more deft and effectual, its content richer by toil of scholar and sight of seer; but the true college will ever have one goal,—not to earn meat, but to know the end and aim of that life which meat nourishes.

The vision of life that rises before these dark eyes has in it nothing mean or selfish. Not at Oxford or at Leipsic, not at Yale or Columbia, is there an air of higher resolve or more unfettered striving; the determination to realize for men, both black and white, the broadest possibilities of life, to seek the better and the best, to spread with their own hands the Gospel of Sacrifice,—all this is the burden of their talk and dream. Here, amid a wide desert of caste and proscription, amid the heart-hurting slights and jars and vagaries of a deep race-dislike, lies this green oasis, where hot anger cools, and the bitterness of disappointment is sweetened by the springs and breezes of Parnassus; and here men may lie and listen, and learn of a future fuller than the past, and hear the voice of Time:

> Entbehren sollst du, sollst entbehren.

They made their mistakes, those who planted Fisk and Howard and Atlanta before the smoke of battle had lifted; they made their mistakes, but those mistakes were not the things at which we lately laughed somewhat uproariously. They were right when they sought to found a new educational system upon the University: where, forsooth, shall we ground knowledge save on the broadest and deepest knowledge? The roots of the tree, rather than the leaves, are the sources of its life; and from the dawn of history, from Academus to Cambridge, the culture of the University has been the broad foundation-stone on which is built the kindergarten's A B C.

But these builders did make a mistake in minimizing the gravity of the problem before them; in thinking it a matter of years and decades; in therefore building quickly and laying their foundation carelessly, and lowering the standard of knowing, until they had scattered haphazard through the South some dozen poorly equipped high schools and miscalled them universities. They forgot, too, just as their successors are forgetting, the rule of inequality:—that of the million black youth, some were fitted to know and some to dig; that some had the talent and capacity of university men, and some the talent and capacity of blacksmiths; and that true training meant neither that all should be college men nor all artisans, but that the one should be made a missionary of culture to an untaught people, and the other a free workman among serfs. And to seek to make the blacksmith a scholar is almost as silly as the more modern scheme of making the scholar a blacksmith; almost, but not quite.

The function of the university is not simply to

teach bread-winning, or to furnish teachers for the public schools, or to be a centre of polite society; it is, above all, to be the organ of that fine adjustment between real life and the growing knowledge of life, an adjustment which forms the secret of civilization. Such an institution the South of to-day sorely needs. She has religion, earnest, bigoted:—religion that on both sides the Veil often omits the sixth, seventh, and eighth commandments, but substitutes a dozen supplementary ones. She has, as Atlanta shows, growing thrift and love of toil; but she lacks that broad knowledge of what the world knows and knew of human living and doing, which she may apply to the thousand problems of real life to-day confronting her. The need of the South is knowledge and culture,—not in dainty limited quantity, as before the war, but in broad busy abundance in the world of work; and until she has this, not all the Apples of Hesperides, be they golden and bejewelled, can save her from the curse of the Bœotian lovers.

The Wings of Atalanta are the coming universities of the South. They alone can bear the maiden past the temptation of golden fruit. They will not guide her flying feet away from the cotton and gold; for—ah, thoughtful Hippomenes!—do not the apples lie in the very Way of Life? But they will guide her over and beyond them, and leave her kneeling in the Sanctuary of Truth and Freedom and broad Humanity, virgin and undefiled. Sadly did the Old South err in human education, despising the education of the masses, and niggardly in the support of colleges. Her ancient university foundations dwindled and withered under the foul breath of slavery; and even since the war they have fought a failing fight for life in the tainted air of social unrest and commercial selfishness, stunted by the death of criticism, and starving for lack of broadly cultured men. And if this is the white South's need and danger, how much heavier the danger and need of the freedmen's sons! how pressing here the need of broad ideals and true culture, the conservation of soul from sordid aims and petty passions! Let us build the Southern university—William and Mary, Trinity, Georgia, Texas, Tulane, Vanderbilt, and the others—fit to live; let us build, too, the Negro universities:—Fisk, whose foundation was ever broad; Howard, at the heart of the Nation; Atlanta at Atlanta, whose ideal of scholarship has been held above the temptation of numbers. Why not here, and perhaps elsewhere, plant deeply and

for all time centres of learning and living, colleges that yearly would send into the life of the South a few white men and a few black men of broad culture, catholic tolerance, and trained ability, joining their hands to other hands, and giving to this squabble of the Races a decent and dignified peace?

Patience, Humility, Manners, and Taste, common schools and kindergartens, industrial and technical schools, literature and tolerance,—all these spring from knowledge and culture, the children of the university. So must men and nations build, not otherwise, not upside down.

Teach workers to work,—a wise saying; wise when applied to German boys and American girls; wiser when said of Negro boys, for they have less knowledge of working and none to teach them. Teach thinkers to think,—a needed knowledge in a day of loose and careless logic; and they whose lot is gravest must have the carefulest training to think aright. If these things are so, how foolish to ask what is the best education for one or seven or sixty million souls! shall we teach them trades, or train them in liberal arts? Neither and both: teach the workers to work and the thinkers to think; make carpenters of carpenters, and philosophers of philosophers, and fops of fools. Nor can we pause here. We are training not isolated men but a living group of men,—nay, a group within a group. And the final product of our training must be neither a psychologist nor a brickmason, but a man. And to make men, we must have ideals, broad, pure, and inspiring ends of living,—not sordid money-getting, not apples of gold. The worker must work for the glory of his handiwork, not simply for pay; the thinker must think for truth, not for fame. And all this is gained only by human strife and longing; by ceaseless training and education; by founding Right on righteousness and Truth on the unhampered search for Truth; by founding the common school on the university, and the industrial school on the common school; and weaving thus a system, not a distortion, and bringing a birth, not an abortion.

When night falls on the City of a Hundred Hills, a wind gathers itself from the seas and comes murmuring westward. And at its bidding, the smoke of the drowsy factories sweeps down upon the mighty city and covers it like a pall, while yonder at the University the stars twinkle above Stone

Hall. And they say that yon gray mist is the tunic of Atalanta pausing over her golden apples. Fly, my maiden, fly, for yonder comes Hippomenes!

. . .

XIV: The Sorrow Songs

I walk through the churchyard
  To lay this body down;
I know moon-rise, I know star-rise;
I walk in the moonlight, I walk in the starlight;
I'll lie in the grave and stretch out my arms,
I'll go to judgment in the evening of the day,
And my soul and thy soul shall meet that day,
  When I lay this body down.

NEGRO SONG

They that walked in darkness sang songs in the olden days—Sorrow Songs—for they were weary at heart. And so before each thought that I have written in this book I have set a phrase, a haunting echo of these weird old songs in which the soul of the black slave spoke to men. Ever since I was a child these songs have stirred me strangely. They came out of the South unknown to me, one by one, and yet at once I knew them as of me and of mine. Then in after years when I came to Nashville I saw the great temple builded of these songs towering over the pale city. To me Jubilee Hall seemed ever made of the songs themselves, and its bricks were red with the blood and dust of toil. Out of them rose for me morning, noon, and night, bursts of wonderful melody, full of the voices of my brothers and sisters, full of the voices of the past.

Little of beauty has America given the world save the rude grandeur God himself stamped on her bosom; the human spirit in this new world has expressed itself in vigor and ingenuity rather than in beauty. And so by fateful chance the Negro folk-song—the rhythmic cry of the slave—stands to-day not simply as the sole American music, but as the most beautiful expression of human experience born this side the seas. It has been neglected, it has been, and is, half despised, and above all it has been persistently mistaken and misunderstood; but notwithstanding, it still remains as the singular spiritual heritage of the nation and the greatest gift of the Negro people.

Away back in the thirties the melody of these slave songs stirred the nation, but the songs were soon half forgotten. Some, like "Near the lake where drooped the willow," passed into current airs and their source was forgotten; others were caricatured on the "minstrel" stage and their memory died away. Then in war-time came the singular Port Royal experiment after the capture of Hilton Head, and perhaps for the first time the North met the Southern slave face to face and heart to heart with no third witness. The Sea Islands of the Carolinas, where they met, were filled with a black folk of primitive type, touched and moulded less by the world about them than any others outside the Black Belt. Their appearance was uncouth, their language funny, but their hearts were human and their singing stirred men with a mighty power. Thomas Wentworth Higginson hastened to tell of these songs, and Miss McKim and others urged upon the world their rare beauty. But the world listened only half credulously until the Fisk Jubilee Singers sang the slave songs so deeply into the world's heart that it can never wholly forget them again.

There was once a blacksmith's son born at Cadiz, New York, who in the changes of time taught school in Ohio and helped defend Cincinnati from Kirby Smith. Then he fought at Chancellorsville and Gettysburg and finally served in the Freedman's Bureau at Nashville. Here he formed a Sunday-school class of black children in 1866, and sang with them and taught them to sing. And then they taught him to sing, and when once the glory of the Jubilee songs passed into the soul of George L. White, he knew his life-work was to let those Negroes sing to the world as they had sung to him. So in 1871 the pilgrimage of the Fisk Jubilee Singers began. North to Cincinnati they rode,—four half-clothed black boys and five girl-women,—led by a man with a cause and a purpose. They stopped at Wilberforce, the oldest of Negro schools, where a black bishop blessed them. Then they went, fighting cold and starvation, shut out of hotels, and cheerfully sneered at, ever northward; and ever the magic of their song kept thrilling hearts, until a burst of applause in the Congregational Council at Oberlin revealed them to the world. They came to New York and Henry Ward Beecher dared to welcome them, even though the metropolitan dailies sneered at his "Nigger Minstrels." So their songs conquered till they sang across the land and across the sea, before Queen and Kaiser, in Scotland and Ireland, Holland and Switzerland. Seven years they sang, and brought back a hundred and fifty thousand dollars to found Fisk University.

Since their day they have been imitated—sometimes well, by the singers of Hampton and Atlanta, sometimes ill, by straggling quartettes. Caricature has sought again to spoil the quaint beauty of the music, and has filled the air with many debased melodies which vulgar ears scarce know from the real. But the true Negro folk-song still lives in the hearts of those who have heard them truly sung and in the hearts of the Negro people.

What are these songs, and what do they mean? I know little of music and can say nothing in technical phrase, but I know something of men, and knowing them, I know that these songs are the articulate message of the slave to the world. They tell us in these eager days that life was joyous to the black slave, careless and happy. I can easily believe this of some, of many. But not all the past South, though it rose from the dead, can gainsay the heart-touching witness of these songs. They are the music of an unhappy people, of the children of disappointment; they tell of death and suffering and unvoiced longing toward a truer world, of misty wanderings and hidden ways.

The songs are indeed the siftings of centuries; the music is far more ancient than the words, and in it we can trace here and there signs of development. My grandfather's grandmother was seized by an evil Dutch trader two centuries ago; and coming to the valleys of the Hudson and Housatonic, black, little, and lithe, she shivered and shrank in the harsh north winds, looked longingly at the hills, and often crooned a heathen melody to the child between her knees, thus:

> Do ba-na co-ba, ge-ne me, ge-ne me!
> Do ba-na co-ba, ge-ne me, ge-ne me!
> Ben d' nu-li, nu-li, nu-li, nu-li, ben d' le.

The child sang it to his children and they to their children's children, and so two hundred years it has travelled down to us and we sing it to our children, knowing as little as our fathers what its words may mean, but knowing well the meaning of its music.

This was primitive African music; it may be seen in larger form in the strange chant which heralds "The Comin of John":

> You may bury me in the East,
> You may bury me in the West,
> But I'll hear the trumpet sound in that morning,

—the voice of exile.

Ten master songs, more or less, one may pluck from this forest of melody—songs of undoubted Negro origin and wide popular currency, and songs peculiarly characteristic of the slave. One

of these I have just mentioned. Another whose strains begin this book is "Nobody knows the trouble I've seen." When, struck with a sudden poverty, the United States refused to fulfil its promises of land to the freedmen, a brigadier-general went down to the Sea Islands to carry the news. An old woman on the outskirts of the throng began singing this song; all the mass joined with her, swaying. And the soldier wept.

The third song is the cradle-song of death which all men know,—"Swing low, sweet chariot,"—whose bars begin the life story of "Alexander Crummell." Then there is the song of many waters, "Roll, Jordan, roll," a mighty chorus with minor cadences. There were many songs of the fugitive like that which opens "The Wings of Atalanta," and the more familiar "Been a-listening." The seventh is the song of the End and the Beginning—"My Lord, what a mourning! when the stars begin to fall"; a strain of this is placed before "The Dawn of Freedom." The song of groping—"My way's cloudy"—begins "The Meaning of Progress"; the ninth is the song of this chapter—"Wrestlin' Jacob, the day is a-breaking,"—a pæan of hopeful strife. The last master song is the song of songs—"Steal away," —sprung from "The Faith of the Fathers."

There are many others of the Negro folk-songs as striking and characteristic as these, as, for instance, the three strains in the third, eighth, and ninth chapters; and others I am sure could easily make a selection on more scientific principles. There are, too, songs that seem to me a step removed from the more primitive types: there is the maze-like medley, "Bright sparkles," one phrase of which heads "The Black Belt"; the Easter carol, "Dust, dust and ashes"; the dirge, "My mother's took her flight and gone home"; and that burst of melody hovering over "The Passing of the First-Born"—"I hope my mother will be there in that beautiful world on high."

These represent a third step in the development of the slave song, of which "You may bury me in the East" is the first, and songs like "March on" (chapter six) and "Steal away" are the second. The first is African music, the second Afro-American, while the third is a blending of Negro music with the music heard in the foster land. The result is still distinctively Negro and the method of blending original, but the elements are both Negro and Caucasian. One might go further and find a fourth step in this development, where the songs of white America have been distinctively influenced by the slave songs or have incorporated whole phrases of Negro melody, as "Swanee River" and "Old Black Joe." Side by side, too, with the growth has gone the debasements and imitations—the Negro "minstrel" songs, many of the "gospel" hymns, and some of the contemporary "coon" songs,—a mass of music in which the novice may easily lose himself and never find the real Negro melodies.

In these songs, I have said, the slave spoke to the world. Such a message is naturally veiled and half articulate. Words and music have lost each other and new and cant phrases of a dimly understood theology have displaced the older sentiment. Once in a while we catch a strange word of an unknown tongue, as the "Mighty Myo," which figures as a river of death; more often slight words or mere doggerel are joined to music of singular sweetness. Purely secular songs are few in number, partly because many of them were turned into hymns by a change of words, partly because the frolics were seldom heard by the stranger, and the music less often caught. Of nearly all the songs, however, the music is distinctly sorrowful. The ten master songs I have mentioned tell in word and music of trouble and exile, of strife and hiding; they grope toward some unseen power and sigh for rest in the End.

The words that are left to us are not without interest, and, cleared of evident dross, they conceal much of real poetry and meaning beneath conventional theology and unmeaning rhapsody. Like all primitive folk, the slave stood near to Nature's heart. Life was a "rough and rolling sea" like the brown Atlantic of the Sea Islands; the "Wilderness" was the home of God, and the "lonesome valley" led to the way of life. "Winter'll soon be over," was the picture of life and death to a tropical imagination. The sudden wild thunder-storms of the South awed and impressed the Negroes,—at times the rumbling seemed to them "mournful," at times imperious:

> My Lord calls me,
> He calls me by the thunder,
> The trumpet sounds it in my soul.

The monotonous toil and exposure is painted in many words. One sees the ploughmen in the hot, moist furrow, singing:

> Dere's no rain to wet you,
> Dere's no sun to burn you,
> Oh, push along, believer,
> I want to go home.

The bowed and bent old man cries, with thrice-repeated wail:

> O Lord, keep me from sinking down,

and he rebukes the devil of doubt who can whisper:

> Jesis is dead and God's gone away.

Yet the soul-hunger is there, the restlessness of the savage, the wail of the wanderer, and the plaint is put in one little phrase:

> My soul wants something that's new, that's new

Over the inner thoughts of the slaves and their relations one with another the shadow of fear ever hung, so that we get but glimpses here and there, and also with them, eloquent omissions and silences. Mother and child are sung, but seldom father; fugitive and weary wanderer call for pity and affection, but there is little of wooing and wedding; the rocks and the mountains are well known, but home is unknown. Strange blending of love and helplessness sings through the refrain:

> Yonder's my ole mudder,
> Been waggin' at de hill so long;
> 'Bout time she cross over,
> Git home bime-by.

Elsewhere comes the cry of the "motherless" and the "Farewell, farewell, my only child."

Love-songs are scarce and fall into two categories—the frivolous and light, and the sad. Of deep successful love there is ominous silence, and in one of the oldest of these songs there is a depth of history and meaning:

> Poor Rosy, poor gal;
> Poor Rosy, poor gal;
> Rosy break my poor heart,
> Heav'n shall-a-be my home.

A black woman said of the song, "It can't be sung without a full heart and a troubled sperrit." The same voice sings here that sings in the German folk-song:

> Jetz Geh i' an's brunele, trink' aber net.

Of death the Negro showed little fear, but talked of it familiarly and even fondly as simply a crossing of the waters, perhaps—who knows?—back to his ancient forests again. Later days transfigured his fatalism, and amid the dust and dirt the toiler sang:

> Dust, dust and ashes, fly over my grave,
> But the Lord shall bear my spirit home.

The things evidently borrowed from the surrounding world undergo characteristic change when they enter the mouth of the slave. Especially is this true of Bible phrases. "Weep, O captive daughter of Zion," is quaintly turned into "Zion, weep-a-low," and the wheels of Ezekiel are turned every way in the mystic dreaming of the slave, till he says:

There's a little wheel a-turnin' in-a-my heart.

As in olden time, the words of these hymns were improvised by some leading minstrel of the religious band. The circumstances of the gathering, however, the rhythm of the songs, and the limitations of allowable thought, confined the poetry for the most part to single or double lines, and they seldom were expanded to quatrains or longer tales, although there are some few examples of sustained efforts, chiefly paraphrases of the Bible. Three short series of verses have always attracted me,—the one that heads this chapter, of one line of which Thomas Wentworth Higginson has fittingly said, "Never, it seems to me, since man first lived and suffered was his infinite longing for peace uttered more plaintively." The second and third are descriptions of the Last Judgment,—the one a late improvisation, with some traces of outside influence:

Oh, the stars in the elements are falling,
And the moon drips away into blood,
And the ransomed of the Lord are returning unto God,
Blessed be the name of the Lord.

And the other earlier and homelier picture from the low coast lands:

Michael, haul the boat ashore,
Then you'll hear the horn they blow,
Then you'll hear the trumpet sound,
Trumpet sound the world around,
Trumpet sound for rich and poor,
Trumpet sound the Jubilee,
Trumpet sound for you and me.

Through all the sorrow of the Sorrow Songs there breathes a hope—a faith in the ultimate justice of things. The minor cadences of despair change often to triumph and calm confidence. Sometimes it is faith in life, sometimes a faith in death, sometimes assurance of boundless justice in some fair world beyond. But whichever it is, the meaning is always clear: that sometime, somewhere, men will judge men by their souls and not by their skins. Is such a hope justified? Do the Sorrow Songs sing true?

The silently growing assumption of this age is that the probation of races is past, and that the backward races of to-day are of proven inefficiency and not worth the saving. Such an assumption is the arrogance of peoples irreverent toward Time and ignorant of the deeds of men. A thousand years ago such an assumption, easily possible, would have made it difficult for the Teuton to prove his right to life. Two thousand years ago such dogmatism, readily welcome, would have scouted the idea of blond races ever leading civilization. So wofully unorganized is sociological knowledge that the meaning of progress, the meaning of "swift" and "slow" in human doing, and the limits of human perfectability, are veiled, unanswered sphinxes on the shores of science. Why should Æschylus have sung two thousand years before Shakespeare was born? Why has civilization flourished in Europe, and flickered, flamed, and died in Africa? So long as the world stands meekly dumb before such questions, shall this nation proclaim its ignorance and unhallowed prejudices by denying freedom of opportunity to those who brought the Sorrow Songs to the Seats of the Mighty?

Your country? How came it yours? Before the Pilgrims landed we were here. Here we have brought our three gifts and mingled them with yours: a gift of story and song—soft, stirring melody in an ill-harmonized and unmelodious land; the gift of sweat and brawn to beat back the wilderness, conquer the soil, and lay the foundations of this vast economic empire two hundred years earlier than your weak hands could have done it; the third, a gift of the Spirit. Around us the history of the land has centred for thrice a hundred years; out of the nation's heart we have called all that was best to throttle and subdue all that was worst; fire and blood, prayer and sacrifice, have billowed over this people, and they have found peace only in the altars of the God of Right. Nor has our gift of the Spirit been merely passive. Actively we have woven ourselves with the very warp and woof of this nation,—we fought their battles, shared their sorrow, mingled our blood with theirs, and generation after generation have pleaded with a headstrong, careless people to despise not Justice, Mercy, and Truth, lest the nation be smitten with a curse. Our song, our toil, our cheer, and warning have been given to this nation in blood-brotherhood. Are not these gifts worth the giving? Is not this work and striving? Would America have been America without her Negro people?

Even so is the hope that sang in the songs of my fathers well sung. If somewhere in this whirl and chaos of things there dwells Eternal Good, pitiful yet masterful, then anon in His good time America shall rend the Veil and the prisoned shall go free. Free, free as the sunshine trickling down the morning into these high windows of mine, free as yonder fresh young voices welling up to me from the caverns of brick and mortar below—swelling with song, instinct with life, tremulous treble and darkening bass. My children, my little children, are singing to the sunshine, and thus they sing:

> Let us cheer the weary traveller,
> Cheer the weary traveller,
> Let us cheer the weary traveller
> Along the heavenly way.

And the traveller girds himself, and sets his face toward the Morning, and goes his way.

The After-Thought

Hear my cry, O God the Reader; vouchsafe that this my book fall not still-born into the world-wilderness. Let there spring, Gentle One, from out its leaves vigor of thought and thoughtful deed to reap the harvest wonderful. Let the ears of a guilty people tingle with truth, and seventy millions sigh for the righteousness which exalteth nations, in this drear day when human brotherhood is mockery and a snare. Thus in Thy good time may infinite reason turn the tangle straight, and these crooked marks on a fragile leaf be not indeed

THE END

Resolutions at Harpers Ferry, 1906

The men of the Niagara Movement, coming from the toil of the year's hard work, and pausing a moment from the earning of their daily bread, turn toward the nation and again ask in the name of ten million the privilege of a hearing. In the past year the work of the Negro hater has flourished in the land. Step by step the defenders of the rights of American citizens have retreated. The work of stealing the black man's ballot has progressed and the fifty and more representatives of stolen votes still sit in the nation's capital. Discrimination in travel and public accommodation has so spread that some of our weaker brethren are actually afraid to thunder against color discrimination as such and are simply whispering for ordinary decencies.

Against this the Niagara Movement eternally protests. We will not be satisfied to take one jot or tittle less than our full manhood rights. We claim for ourselves every single right that belongs to a freeborn American, political, civil and social; and until we get these rights we will never cease to protest and assail the ears of America. The battle we wage is not for ourselves alone, but for all true Americans. It is a fight for ideals, lest this, our common fatherland, false to its founding, become in truth the land of the Thief and the home of the Slave—a by-word and a hissing among the nations for its sounding pretensions and pitiful accomplishment.

Never before in the modern age has a great and civilized folk threatened to adopt so cowardly a creed in the treatment of its fellow-citizens, born and bred on its soil. Stripped of verbiage and subterfuge and in its naked nastiness, the new American creed says: fear to let black men even try to rise lest they become the equals of the white. And this is the land that professes to follow Jesus Christ. The blasphemy of such a course is only matched by its cowardice.

In detail our demands are clear and unequivocal.

First. We would vote; with the right to vote goes everything: freedom, manhood, the honor of your wives, the chastity of your daughters, the right to work, and the chance to rise; let no man listen to those who deny this.

We want full manhood suffrage, and we want it now, henceforth and forever.

Second. We want discrimination in public accommodation to cease. Separation in railway and street cars, based simply on race and color, is un-American, undemocratic, and silly. We protest against all such discrimination.

Third. We claim the right of freemen to walk, talk and be with them that wish to be with us. No man has the right to choose another man's friends, and to attempt to do so is an impudent interference with the most fundamental human privilege.

Fourth. We want the laws enforced against rich as well as poor; against Capitalist as well as Laborer; against white as well as black. We are not more lawless than the white race, we are more often arrested, convicted and mobbed. We want justice even for criminals and outlaws. We want the Constitution of the country enforced. We want Congress to take charge of the Congressional elections. We want the Fourteenth Amendment carried out to the letter and every State disfranchised in Congress which attempts to disfranchise its rightful voters. We want the Fifteenth Amendment enforced and no State allowed to base its franchise simply on color.

The failure of the Republican Party in Congress at the session just closed to redeem its pledge of 1904 with reference to suffrage conditions at the South seems a plain, deliberate, and premeditated breach of promise, and stamps that party as guilty of obtaining votes under false pretense.

Fifth. We want our children educated. The school system in the country districts of the South is a disgrace and in few towns and cities are the Negro schools what they ought to be. We want the national government to step in and wipe out illiteracy in the South. Either the United States will destroy ignorance or ignorance will destroy the United States.

And when we call for education, we mean real education. We believe in work. We ourselves are workers, but work is not necessarily education. Education is the development of power and ideal. We want our children trained as intelligent human beings should be, and we will fight for all time against any proposal to educate black boys and girls simply as servants and underlings, or simply for the use of other people. They have a right to know, to think, to aspire.

These are some of the chief things which we want. How shall we get them? By voting where we may vote; by persistent, unceasing agitation; by hammering at the truth; by sacrifice and work.

We do not believe in violence, neither in the despised violence of the raid nor the lauded violence of the soldier, nor the barbarous violence of the mob; but we do believe in John Brown, in that incarnate spirit of justice, that hatred of a lie, that willingness to sacrifice money, reputation, and life itself on the altar of right. And here on the scene of John Brown's martyrdom, we reconsecrate ourselves, our honor, our property to the final emancipation of the race for whose freedom John Brown died.

A Litany of Atlanta*

O Silent God, Thou whose voice afar in mist and mystery hath left our ears an-hungered in these fearful days—
Hear us, good Lord!

Listen to us, Thy children: our faces dark with doubt, are made a mockery in Thy sanctuary. With uplifted hands we front Thy heaven, O God, crying:
We beseech Thee to hear us, good Lord!

We are not better than our fellows, Lord, we are but weak and human men. When our devils do deviltry, curse Thou the doer and the deed: curse them as we curse them, do to them all and more than ever they have done to innocence and weakness, to womanhood and home.
Have mercy upon us, miserable sinners!

And yet whose is the deeper guilt? Who made these devils? Who nursed them in crime and fed them on injustice? Who ravished and debauched their mothers and their grandmothers? Who bought and sold their crime, and waxed fat and rich on public iniquity?
Thou knowest, good God!

Is this Thy justice, O Father, that guile be easier than innocence, and the innocent crucified for the guilt of the untouched guilty?
Justice, O Judge of men!

* Written in response to the Atlanta riot of 1906.

Wherefore do we pray? Is not the God of the fathers dead? Have not seers seen in Heaven's halls Thine hearsed and lifeless form stark amidst the black and rolling smoke of sin, where all along bow bitter forms of endless dead?

Awake, Thou that sleepest!

Thou art not dead, but flown afar, up hills of endless light, thru blazing corridors of suns, where worlds do swing of good and gentle men, of women strong and free—far from the cozenage, black hypocrisy and chaste prostitution of this shameful speck of dust!

Turn again, O Lord, leave us not to perish in our sin!

From lust of body and lust of blood
Great God deliver us!

From lust of power and lust of gold,
Great God deliver us!

From the leagued lying of despot and of brute,
Great God deliver us!

A city lay in travail, God our Lord, and from her loins sprang twin Murder and Black Hate. Red was the midnight; clang, crack and cry of death and fury filled the air and trembled underneath the stars when church spires pointed silently to Thee. And all this was to sate the greed of greedy men who hide behind the veil of vengeance!

Bend us Thine ear, O Lord!

In the pale, still morning we looked upon the deed. We stopped our ears and held our leaping hands, but they—did they not wag their heads and leer and cry with bloody jaws: *Cease from Crime!* The word was mockery, for thus they train a hundred crimes while we do cure one.

Turn again our captivity, O Lord!

Behold this maimed and broken thing; dear God it was an humble black man who toiled and sweat to save a bit from the pittance paid him. They told him: *Work and Rise.* He worked. Did this man sin? Nay, but some one told how some one said another did—one whom he had never seen nor known. Yet for that man's crime this man lieth maimed and murdered, his wife naked to shame, his children, to poverty and evil.

Hear us, O heavenly Father!

Doth not this justice of hell stink in Thy nostrils, O God? How long shall the mounting flood of innocent blood roar in Thine ears and pound in our hearts for vengeance? Pile the pale frenzy of blood-crazed brutes who do such deeds high on Thine altar, Jehovah Jireh, and burn it in hell forever and forever!

Forgive us, good Lord; we know not what we say!

Bewildered we are, and passion-tost, mad with the madness of a mobbed and mocked and murdered people; straining at the armposts of Thy Throne, we raise our shackled hands and charge Thee, God, by the bones of our stolen fathers, by the tears of our dead mothers, by the very blood of Thy crucified Christ: *What meaneth this?* Tell us the Plan; give us the Sign!

Keep not thou silence, O God!

Sit no longer blind, Lord God, deaf to our prayer and dumb to our dumb suffering. Surely Thou too art not white, O Lord, a pale, bloodless, heartless thing?

Ah! Christ of all the Pities!

Forgive the thought! Forgive these wild, blasphemous words. Thou art still the God of our black fathers, and in Thy soul's soul sit some soft darkenings of the evening, some shadowings of the velvet night.

But whisper—speak—call, great God, for Thy silence is white terror to our hearts! The way, O God, show us the way and point us the path.

Whither? North is greed and South is blood; within, the coward, and without, the liar. Whither? To death?

Amen! Welcome dark sleep!

Whither? To life? But not this life, dear God, not this. Let the cup pass from us, tempt us not beyond our strength, for there is that clamoring and clawing within, to whose voice we would not listen, yet shudder lest we must, and it is red, Ah! God! It is a red and awful shape.

Selah!

In yonder East trembles a star.

Vengeance is mine; I will repay, saith the Lord!

Thy will, O Lord, be done!
Kyrie Eleison!

Lord, we have done these pleading, wavering words.
We beseech Thee to hear us, good Lord!

We bow our heads and hearken soft to the sobbing of women and little children.
We beseech Thee to hear us, good Lord!

Our voices sink in silence and in night.
Hear us, good Lord!

In night, O God of a godless land!
Amen!

In silence, O Silent God.
Selah!

The Immediate Program of the American Negro (1915)

The immediate program of the American Negro means nothing unless it is mediate to his great ideal and the ultimate ends of his development. We need not waste time by seeking to deceive our enemies into thinking that we are going to be content with a half loaf, or by being willing to lull our friends into a false sense of our indifference and present satisfaction.

The American Negro demands equality—political equality, industrial equality and social equality; and he is never going to rest satisfied with anything less. He demands this in no spirit of braggadocio and with no obsequious envy of others, but as an absolute measure of self-defense and the only one that will assure to the darker races their ultimate survival on earth.

Only in a demand and a persistent demand for essential equality in the modern realm of human culture can any people show a real pride of race and a decent self-respect. For any group, nation or race to admit for a moment the present monstrous demand of the white race to be the inheritors of the earth, the arbiters of mankind and the sole owners of a heritage of culture which they did not create, nor even improve to any greater extent than the other great division of men—to admit such pretense for a moment is for the race to write itself down immediately as indisputably inferior in judgment, knowledge and common sense.

The equality in political, industrial and social life which modern men must have in order to live, is not to be confounded with sameness. On the contrary, in our case, it is rather insistence upon the right of diversity;—upon the right of a human being to be a man even if he does not wear the same cut of vest, the same curl of hair or the same color of skin. Human equality does not even entail, as is sometimes said, absolute equality of opportunity; for certainly the natural inequalities of inherent genius and varying gift make this a dubious phase. But there is a more and more clearly recognized minimum of opportunity and maximum of freedom to be, to move and to think, which the modern world denies to no being which it recognizes as a real man.

These involve both negative and positive sides. They call for freedom on the one hand and power on the other. The Negro must have political freedom; taxation without representation is tyranny. American Negroes of to-day are ruled by tyrants who take what they please in taxes and give what they please in law and administration, in justice and in injustice; and the great mass of black people must stand helpless and voiceless before a condition which has time and time again caused other peoples to fight and die.

The Negro must have industrial freedom. Between the peonage of the rural South, the oppression of shrewd capitalists and the jealousy of certain trade unions, the Negro laborer is the most exploited class in the country, giving more hard toil for less money than any other American, and have less voice in the conditions of his labor.

In social intercourse every effort is being made to-day from the President of the United States and the so-called Church of Christ down to saloons and boot-blacks to segregate, strangle and spiritually starve Negroes so as to give them the least possible chance to know and share civilization.

These shackles must go. But that is but the beginning. The Negro must have power; the power of men, the right to do, to know, to feel and to express that knowledge, action and spiritual gift. He must not simply be free from the political tyranny of white folk, he must have the right to vote and to rule over the citizens, white and black, to the extent of his proven foresight and ability. He must have a voice in the new industrial democracy which is building and the power to see to it that his children are not in the next generation trained to be the mudsills of society. He must have the right to social intercourse with his fellows. There was a time in the atomic individualistic group when "social intercourse" meant merely calls and tea-parties; to-day social intercourse means theatres, lectures, organizations, churches, clubs, excursions, travel, hotels,—it means in short Life; to bar a group from such methods of thinking, living and doing is to bar them from the world and bid them create a new world;—a task to which no single group is to-day equal; it is to crucify them and taunt them with not being able to live.

What now are the practical steps which must be taken to accomplish these ends?

First of all before taking steps the wise man knows the object and end of his journey. There are those who would advise the black man to pay little or no attention to where he is going so long as he keeps moving. They assume that God or his vice-gerent the White Man will attend to the steering. This is arrant nonsense. The feet of those that aimlessly wander land as often in hell as in heaven. Conscious self-realization and self-direction is the watchword of modern man, and the first article in the program of any group that will survive must be the great aim, equality and power among men.

The practical steps to this are clear. First we must fight obstructions; by continual and increasing effort we must first make American courts either build up a body of decisions which will protect the plain legal rights of American citizens or else make them tear down the civil and political rights of all citizens in order to oppress a few. Either result will bring justice in the end. It is lots of fun and most ingenious just now for courts to twist law so as to say I shall not live here or vote there, or marry the woman who wishes to marry me. But when to-morrow these decisions throttle all freedom and overthrow the foundation of democracy and decency, there is going to be some judicial house cleaning.

We must *secondly* seek in legislature and congress remedial legislation; national aid to public school education, the removal of all legal discriminations based simply on race and color,

and those marriage laws passed to make the seduction of black girls easy and without legal penalty.

Third, the human contact of human beings must be increased; the policy which brings into sympathetic touch and understanding, men and women, rich and poor, capitalist and laborer, Asiatic and European, must bring into closer contact and mutual knowledge the white and black people of this land. It is the most frightful indictment of a country which dares to call itself civilized that it has allowed itself to drift into a state of ignorance where ten million people are coming to believe that all white people are liars and thieves, and the whites in turn to believe that the chief industry of Negroes is raping white women.

Fourth only the publication of the truth repeatedly and incisively and uncompromisingly can secure that change in public opinion which will correct these awful lies. THE CRISIS, our record of the darker races, must have a circulation not of 35,000 chiefly among colored folk but of at least 250,000 among all men who believe in men. It must not be a namby-pamby box of salve, but a voice that thunders fact and is more anxious to be true than pleasing. There should be a campaign of tract distribution— short well written facts and arguments—rained over this land by millions of copies, particularly in the South, where the white people know less about the Negro than in any other part of the civilized world. The press should be utilized—the 400 Negro weeklies, the great dailies and eventually the magazines, when we get magazine editors who will lead public opinion instead of following afar with resonant brays. Lectures, lantern-slides and moving pictures, co-operating with a bureau of information and eventually becoming a Negro encyclopedia, all these are efforts along the line of making human beings realize that Negroes are human.

Such is the program of work against obstructions. Let us now turn to constructive effort. This may be summed up under (1) economic co-operation (2) a revival of art and literature (3) political action (4) education and (5) organization.

Under economic co-operation we must strive to spread the idea among colored people that the accumulation of wealth is for social rather than individual ends. We must avoid, in the advancement of the Negro race, the mistakes of ruthless exploitation which have marked modern economic history. To this end we must seek not simply home ownership, small landholding and saving accounts, but also all forms of co-operation, both in production and distribution, profit sharing, building and loan associations, systematic charity for definite, practical ends, systematic migration from mob rule and robbery, to freedom and enfranchisement, the emancipation of women and the abolition of child labor.

In art and literature we should try to loose the tremendous emotional wealth of the Negro and the dramatic strength of his problems through writing, the stage, pageantry and other forms of art. We should resurrect forgotten ancient Negro art and history, and we should set the black man before the world as both a creative artist and a strong subject for artistic treatment.

In political action we should organize the votes of Negroes in such congressional districts as have any number of Negro voters. We should systematically interrogate candidates on matters vital to Negro freedom and uplift. We should train colored voters to reject the bribe of office and to accept only decent legal enactments both for their own uplift and for the uplift of laboring classes of all races and both sexes.

In education we must seek to give colored children free public school training. We must watch with grave suspicion the attempt of those who, under the guise of vocational training, would fasten ignorance and menial service on the Negro

for another generation. Our children must not in large numbers, be forced into the servant class; for menial service is still, in the main, little more than an antiquated survival of impossible conditions. It has always been as statistics show, a main cause of bastardy and prostitution and despite its many marvelous exceptions it will never come to the light of decency and honour until the house servant becomes the Servant in the House. It is our duty then, not drastically but persistently, to seek out colored children of ability and genius, to open up to them broader, industrial opportunity and above all, to find that Talented Tenth and encourage it by the best and most exhaustive training in order to supply the Negro race and the world with leaders, thinkers and artists.

For the accomplishment of all these ends we must organize. Organization among us already has gone far but it must go much further and higher. Organization is sacrifice. It is sacrifice of opinions, of time, of work and of money, but it is, after all, the cheapest way of buying the most priceless of gifts—freedom and efficiency. I thank God that most of the money that supports the National Association for the Advancement of Colored People comes from black hands; a still larger proportion must so come, and we must not only support but control this and similar organizations and hold them unwaveringly to our objects, our aims and our ideals.

In Black (1920)

It was in Chicago. John Haynes Holmes was talking.

He said: "I met two children—one as fair as the dawn—the other as beautiful as the night." Then he paused. He had to pause for the audience guffawed in wild merriment. Why?

It was a colored audience. Many of them were black. Some black faces there were as beautiful as the night.

Why did they laugh?

Because the world had taught them to be ashamed of their color.

Because for 500 years men had hated and despised and abused black folk.

And now in strange, inexplicable transposition the rising blacks laugh at themselves in nervous, blatant, furtive merriment.

They laugh because they think they are expected to laugh—because all their poor hunted lives they have heard "black" things laughed at.

Of all the pitiful things of this pitiful race problem, this is the pitifullest. So curious a mental state tends to further subtleties. Colored folk, like all folk, love to see themselves in pictures; but they are afraid to see the types which the white world has caricatured. The whites obviously seldom picture brown and yellow folk, but for five centuries they have exhausted every ingenuity of trick, of ridicule and caricature on black folk: "grinning" Negroes, "happy" Negroes, "gold dust twins", "Aunt Jemimas", "solid" headed tacks—everything and anything to make Negroes ridiculous. As a result if THE CRISIS puts a black face on its cover our 500,000 colored readers do not see the actual picture—they see the caricature that white folks intend when *they* make a black face. In the last few years a thoughtful, clear eyed artist, Frank Walts, has done a number of striking portraits for THE CRISIS. Mainly he has treated black faces; and regularly protests have come to us from various colored sources. His lovely portrait of the bright-eyed boy, Harry Elam, done in thoughtful sympathy, was approved by few Negroes. Our photograph of a woman of Santa Lucia, with its strength and humor and fine swing of head, was laughed at by many.

Why?

"O—er—it was not because they were black," stammer some of my office companions, "but they are *too* black. No people were ever so—"

Nonsense! Do white people complain because their pictures are too white? They ought to, but they do not. Neither do we complain if we are photographed a shade "light".

No. It is not that we are ashamed of our color and blood. We are instinctively and almost unconsciously ashamed of the caricatures done of our darker shades. Black *is* caricature in our half conscious thought and we shun in print and paint that which we love in life. How good a dark face looks to us in a strange white city! How the black soldiers, despite their white French sweethearts, yearned for their far-off "brown-skins". A mighty and swelling human consciousness is leading us joyously to embrace the darker world, but we remain afraid of black pictures because they are the cruel reminders of the crimes of Sunday "comics" and "Nigger" minstrels.

Off with these thought-chains and inchoate soul-shrinkings, and let us train ourselves to see beauty in black.

from *The Autobiography of W. E. B. Du Bois*

Communism

I have studied socialism and communism long and carefully in lands where they are practiced and in conversation with their adherents, and with wide reading. I now state my conclusion frankly and clearly: I believe in communism. I mean by communism, a planned way of life in the production of wealth and work designed for building a state whose object is the highest welfare of its people and not merely the profit of a part. I believe that all men should be employed according to their ability and that wealth and services should be distributed according to need. Once I thought that these ends could be attained under capitalism, means of production privately owned, and used in accord with free individual initiative. After earnest observation I now believe that private ownership of capital and free enterprise are leading the world to disaster. I do not believe that so-called "people's capitalism" has in the United States or anywhere replaced the ills of private capitalism and shown an answer to socialism. The corporation is but the legal mask behind which the individual owner of wealth hides. Democratic government in the United States has almost ceased to function. A fourth of the adults are disfranchised, half the legal voters do not go to the polls. We are ruled by those who control wealth and who by that power buy or coerce public opinion.

I resent the charge that communism is a conspiracy: Communists often conspire as do capitalists. But it is false that all Communists are criminals and that communism speaks and exists mainly by means of force and fraud. I shall therefore hereafter help the triumph of communism in every honest way that I can: without deceit or hurt; and in any way possible, without war; and with goodwill to all men of all colors, classes and creeds. If, because of this belief and such action, I become the victim of attack and calumny, I will react in the way that seems to me best for the world in which I live and which I have tried earnestly to serve. I know well that the triumph of communism will be a slow and difficult task, involving mistakes of every sort. It will call for progressive change in human nature and a better type of manhood than is common today. I believe this possible, or otherwise we will continue to lie, steal and kill as we are doing today.

Who now am I to have come to these conclusions? And of what if any significance are my deductions? What has been my life and work and of what meaning to mankind? The final answer to these questions, time and posterity must make. But perhaps it is my duty to contribute whatever enlightenment I can. This is the excuse for this writing which I call a Soliloquy.

. . .

Postlude

Returning to America in 1959 after my great journey, I was welcomed home; not simply by my friends but by my government. In Sweden it was feared I might not as a member of the World Peace Council be allowed to land in England. But Pritt and Belfrage took hold and I received every courtesy. I had tea on the terrace of the House of Lords with a viscount, an earl, and two ladies; also on the terrace of the House of Commons, I had tea where I had last been entertained by Kier Hardie. I met several members of Parliament, and spent many Sunday afternoons with Donald Ogden Stewart and Ella Winter. There I met James Aldrich and Katherine Hepburn. I saw Paul Robeson and his splendid production of *Othello*. Lawrence Bradshaw, sculptor of the great head of Karl Marx, did my head.

The cabin on the *Liberté* as we returned was large and airy, and the voyage smooth and pleasant. But how would the United States receive us? We had openly spent ten weeks in China, and spoken widely and broadcast. There was some hasty last minute telephoning from the boat, I am sure, but all went well. Our passports were not seized, and the chief inspector of Customs passed our bags quickly and welcomed us home. Our relatives and friends swarmed to greet us. I was unable to understand why Scott Nearing and Waldo Frank should be forbidden to do what as yet I have been unrebuked for doing openly and proudly. However, three months later when the Supreme Court agreed to consider the cases of Waldo Frank and William Worthy, the State Department demanded our passports. We asked delay until the Supreme Court made its verdict. This was granted.

I am a little puzzled now about the ordering of my life. Several times in the past I find that I have prepared for death and death has not come. Always on my desk lies a calendar of my own devising with daily and hourly tasks; with plans for the week and next week, the month and months ahead and the sentinel of my main task for the year. This year-part is now getting uncertain. Even months are no longer absolutely mine, yet I am reasonably content and although my strength warns me not to try to work as many hours as once I did, yet I work and work regularly and with some efficiency, from day to day.

As I recall, I have long faced the inevitability of death and not tried to dodge the thought. In early manhood I wrote:

"I saw a mother, black and seared and iron-haired, who had watched her boy through college, for men to jeer at and discourage and tempt until he sought women and whiskey and died. She crept on a winter's Sunday into a Cathedral of St. John The Divine and crouched there where a comfortable red and yellow angel sat sunning her ample limbs 'To Keep the Memory of Obadiah James Green'—a stock-gambler. And there she rested while the organ warbled the overture to *Der Feischutz*, and the choir asserted 'My Jesus! As Thou wilt.' The priest intoned: 'Come unto Me all ye that labor and are heavy laden and I will give you rest! For my yoke is easy and my burden light.' And the window-angel moved a fat wing and murmured: 'except niggers!'

"In that dark day when all friends gathered round shall sigh: as he goes to that full dreadful home where earth shall move away and these dim eyes shall strain to scenes all glorious, shall they see on that morning round the wide, white throne a glorified Negro Problem? If so, Father of Mercies, send me to Hell."

At 50, after a serious operation I wrote:

"Last year I looked death in the face and found its lineaments not unkind. But it was not my time. Yet in nature some time soon and in the fullness of days I shall die, quietly, I trust, with my face turned South and eastward; and, dreaming or dreamless I shall, I am sure, enjoy death as I have enjoyed life."

At 60 years of age I wrote again:

"For long years we of the world gone wild, have looked into the face of death and smiled. Through all our bitter tears we knew how beautiful it was to die for that which our souls called sufficient. Like all true beauty this thing of dying was so simple, so matter-of-fact. The boy clothed in his splendid youth stood before us and laughed in his own jolly way—went and was gone. Suddenly the world was full of the fragrance of sacrifice. We left our digging and burden-bearing; we turned from our scraping and twisting of things and words; we paused from our hurrying hither and thither and walking up and down, and asked in half whisper: 'Death—is this life? And is its beauty real or false?'

"Here, then, is beauty and ugliness, a wide vision of world-sacrifice, a fierce gleam of world-hate. Which is life and what is death and how shall we face so tantalizing a contradiction? Any explanation must necessarily be subtle and involved. No pert and easy word of encouragement, no merely dark despair, can lay hold of the roots of these things. And first and before all, we cannot forget that this world is beautiful. Grant all its ugliness and sin—the petty, horrible snarl of its putrid threads, which few have seen more near or more often than I—notwithstanding all this, the beauty of the world is not to be denied.

"And then—the Veil, the Veil of color. It drops as drops the night on southern seas—vast, sudden, unanswering. There is Hate behind it, and Cruelty and Tears. As one peers through its intricate, unfathomable pattern of ancient, old, old design, one sees blood and guilt and misunderstanding. And yet it hangs there, this Veil, between then and now, between Pale and Colored and Black and White—between You and Me. Surely it is but a thought-thing, tenuous, intangible; yet just as surely is it true and terrible and not in our little day may you and I lift it. We may feverishly unravel its edges and even climb slow with giant shears to where its ringed and gilded top nestles close to the throne of Eternity. But as we work and climb we shall see through streaming eyes and hear with aching ears, lynching and murder, cheating and despising, degrading and lying, so flashed and flashed through this vast hanging darkness that the Doer never sees the Deed and the Victim knows not the Victor and Each hate All in wild and bitter ignorance. Listen, O Isles, to those voices from within the Veil, for they portray the most human hurt of the Twentieth Cycle of that poor Jesus who was called the Christ!

"At last to us all comes happiness, there in the Court of Peace, where the dead lie so still and calm and good. If we were not dead we would lie and listen to the flowers grow. We would hear the birds sing and see how the rain rises and blushes and burns and pales and dies in beauty. We would see spring, summer, and the red riot of autumn, and then in winter, beneath the soft white snow, sleep and dream of dreams. But we know that being dead, our Happiness is a fine and finished thing and that ten, a hundred, and a thousand years, we shall lie at rest, unhurt in the Court of Peace."

From then until now the wraith of Death has followed me, slept with me and awakened me and accompanied my day. Only now it is more commonplace and reasonable. It is the end and without ends there can be no beginnings. Its finality we must not falsify. It is our great debt to the Soviet Union that it alone of nations dared stop that lying to children which so long disgraced our schools. We filled little minds with fairy tales of religious dogma which we ourselves never believed. We filled their thoughts with pictures of barbarous revenge called God which contradicted all their inner sense of decency. We repeated folk tales of children without fathers, of death which was life, of sacrifice which was shrewd investment and ridiculous pictures of an endless future. The Soviets have stopped this. They allow a child to grow up without religious lies and with mature mind make his own decision about the world without scaring him into Hell or rewarding him with a silly Heaven.

We know that Death is the End of Life. Even when we profess to deny this we know that this hope is mere wishful thinking, pretense broidered with abject and cowardly Fear. Our endless egotism cannot conceive a world without Us and yet we know that this will happen and the world be happier for it.

I have lived a good and full life. I have finished my course. I do not want to live this life again. I have tasted its delights and pleasures; I have known its pain, suffering and despair. I am tired, I am through. For the souls who follow me; for that little boy born Christmas day before last, my great grandson and his compeers, I bequeath all that waits to be done, and Holy Time what a task, forever!

I have seen miracles in my life. As a boy we did not have the possibility of miracles emphasized in our schools. In the weekly Sunday School, we studied the bible with its tales of the impossible but I remember distinctly that I questioned the validity of some of them, like that story of Jonah. In other words I was brought up in the shadow of modern science where all that happens had a cause and there were many things unlikely to happen. For instance, then flying by man was not to be thought of and we talked of flying as impossible and joked at man's attempts. Yet I read of the first successful flights; and myself in 1921 flew from Paris to London. I have flown tens of thousands of miles since, over land and sea. I visited the Paris World's Fair in 1900, and was astonished to see automobiles on the streets; not many but perhaps a dozen in a day. I lived to see the jokes about the possibility of these motors displacing the horse fade away and automobiles fill the streets and cover the nations.

I remember when first, in an American city, seeing the streets lighted by electricity; the lights blinked and sputtered but in a few years electric bulbs supplanted the gas lights of my boyhood. Then came the gas-filled balloons rising in the sky and men crossed the Atlantic in Zeppelins. Soon came the horror of Hiroshima and I began to feel the vast possibilities of man's brain and his coming conquest of the air. But the most startling miracle of my time before the year 1958, was Sputnik. This went beyond the internal combustion engine, the airplane and balloon; beyond the electric light and the bursting atom. This was beyond mere utility into the realm of Knowledge and the triumph of Reason. It taught the United States the superiority of Communist thought and calculation. It stopped our sneers at Soviet education.

Then this year came the climax; the triumph of thought over power and space that was the greatest miracle of which I ever dreamed. Not yet have I been able to comprehend its meaning, or to realize that it is today actually possible to send a human being to the stars. A Frenchman once said, "I know but two beautiful things on earth: the stars above us and the feeling of duty within us." Now that we have pierced the heavens, we are more sure of making Mankind willing and eager to do right.

I have lived to an age of life which is increasingly distasteful to this nation. Unless by 60 a man has gained possession of enough of money to support himself, he faces the distinct possibility of starvation. He is liable to lose his job and to refusal if he seeks another. At 70 he is frowned upon by the church and if he is foolish enough to survive until 90, he is often regarded as a freak. This is because in the face of human experience the United States has discovered that Youth knows more than Age. When a man of 35 becomes president of a great institution of learning or United States Senator or head of a multi-million dollar corporation, a cry of triumph rings in the land. Why? To pretend that 15 years bring of themselves more wisdom and understanding than 50 is a contradiction in terms. Given a born

fool, a hundred years will not make him wise; but given an idiot, he will not be wise at 20. Youth is more courageous than age because it knows less. Age is wiser than youth because it knows more. This all mankind has affirmed from Egypt and China five thousand years ago, to Britain and Germany today. Only the United States knows better. I would have been hailed with approval if I had died at 50. At 75 my death was practically requested. If living does not give value, wisdom and meaning to life, then there is no sense in living at all. If immature and inexperienced men rule the earth, then the earth deserves what it gets: the repetition of age-old mistakes, and wild welcome for what men knew a thousand years ago was disaster.

I do not apologize for living long. High on the ramparts of this blistering hell of life, as it must appear to most men, I sit and see the Truth. I look it full in the face, and I will not lie about it, neither to myself nor to the world. I see my country as what Cedric Belfrage aptly characterizes as a "Frightened Giant" afraid of the Truth, afraid of Peace. I see a land which is degenerating and faces decadence unless it has sense enough to turn about and start back. It is no sin to fail. It is the habit of men. It is disaster to go on when you know you are going wrong. I judge this land not merely by statistics or reading lies agreed upon by historians. I judge by what I have seen, heard, and lived through for near a century.

There was a day when the world rightly called Americans honest even if crude; earning their living by hard work; telling the truth no matter whom it hurt; and going to war only in what they believed a just cause after nothing else seemed possible. Today we are lying, stealing, and killing. We call all this by finer names: Advertising, Free Enterprise, and National Defense. But names in the end deceive no one; today we use science to help us deceive our fellows; we take wealth that we never earned and we are devoting all our energies to kill, maim and drive insane, men, women, and children who dare refuse to do what we want done. No nation threatens us. We threaten the world.

Our President says that Foster Dulles was the wisest man he knew. If Dulles was wise, God help our fools—the fools who rule us and are today running wild in order to shoot a football into the sky where Sputnik rolls in peace around the earth. And they know why we fail, these military masters of men: we haven't taught our children mathematics and physics. No, it is because we have not taught our children to read and write or to behave like human beings and not like hoodlums. Every child on my street is whooping it up with toy guns and big boys with real pistols. When Elvis Presley goes through the motions of copulation on the public stage it takes the city police force to hold back teen-age children from hysteria. The highest ambition of an American boy today is to be a millionaire. The highest ambition of an American girl is to be a movie star. Of the ethical actions which lie back of these ideals, little is said or learned. What are we doing about it? Half the Christian churches of New York are trying to ruin the free public schools in order to install religious dogma in them; and the other half are too interested in Venezuelan oil to prevent the best center in Brooklyn from fighting youthful delinquency, or prevent a bishop from kicking William Howard Melish into the street and closing his church. Which of the hundreds of churches sitting half empty protests about this? They hire Billy Graham to replace the circus in Madison Square Garden.

Howard Melish is one of the few Christian clergymen for whom I have the highest respect. Honest and conscientious, believing sincerely in much of the Christian dogma, which I reject, but working honestly and without hypocrisy, for the guidance of the young, for the uplift of the poor and ignorant, and for the betterment of his city and his country, he has been driven from his work and his career ruined by a vindictive bishop of his church, with no effective protest from most of the Christian ministry and membership or of the people of the United States. The Melish case is perhaps at once the most typical and frightening illustration of present American religion and my reaction. Here is a young man of ideal character, of impeccable morals; a hard worker, especially among the poor and unfortunate, with fine family relations. His father had helped build one of the most popular Episcopal churches in the better part of Brooklyn. He himself had married a well-educated woman, and had three sons in school. The community about it was changing from well-to-do people of English and Dutch descent, to white-collar and laboring folk of Italian, Negro and Puerto Rican extraction. Trinity church, under the Melishes, adapted itself to changing needs and invited neighborhood membership. It was not a large church, but it was doing the best work among the young and foreign-born of any institution in Brooklyn.

The young rector took one step for which the bishop, most of his fellow clergymen and the well-to-do community, with its business interests, pilloried him. He joined and became an official of the National Council of American-Soviet Friendship. He was accused immediately of favoring communism, and to appease criticism he gave up his official position in this organization, but refused to resign his membership. Allegedly for this reason the bishop, most of the clergy and the well-to-do community proceeded to force him out of the church. The real reason behind their fight was anger because a rich, white, "respectable" church was being surrendered to workers and Negroes. It became a renewed battle between Episcopal authority and democratic rule. That his parish wanted to retain Melish as rector was unquestionable. Through the use of technicalities in the canon law and in accord with the decision of Catholic judges who believed in Episcopal power, Howard Melish lost his church, had his life work ruined, the church itself closed, and its local influence ended. There was vigorous protest against this by a few devoted colleagues, many of them Jews and liberals. But the great mass of the Episcopal church membership was silent and did nothing.

All this must not be mentioned even if you know it and see it. America must never be criticized even by honest and sincere men. America must always be praised and extravagently praised, or you lose your job or are ostracized or land in jail. Criticism is treason, and treason or the hint of treason testified to by hired liars may be punished by shameful death. I saw Ethel Rosenberg lying beautiful in her coffin beside her mate. I tried to stammer futile words above her grave. But not over graves should we shout this failure of justice, but from the housetops of the world.

Honest men may and must criticize America. Describe how she has ruined her democracy, sold out her jury system, and led her seats of justice astray. The only question that may arise is whether this criticism is based on truth, not whether it has been openly expressed.

What is truth? What can it be when the President of the United States, guiding the nation, stands up in public and says: "*The world also thinks of us as a land which has never enslaved anyone.*" Everyone who heard this knew it was not true. Yet here stands the successor of George Washington who bought, owned, and sold slaves; the successor of Abraham Lincoln who freed four million slaves after they had helped him win victory over the slaveholding South. And so far as I have seen, not a single periodical, not even a Negro weekly, has dared challenge or even criticize that falsehood.

Perhaps the most extraordinary characteristic of current America is the attempt to reduce life to buying and selling. Life is not love unless love is sex and bought and sold. Life is not knowledge save knowledge of technique, of science for destruction. Life is not beauty except beauty for sale. Life is not art unless its price is high and it is sold for profit. All life is production for profit, and for what is profit but for buying and selling again?

Even today the contradictions of American civilization are tremendous. Freedom of political discussion is difficult; elections are not free and fair. Democracy is for us to a large extent unworkable. In business there is a tremendous amount of cheating and stealing; gambling in card games, on television and on the stock exchange is widely practiced. It is common custom for distinguished persons to sign books, articles, and speeches that they did not write; for men of brains to compose and sell opinions which they do not believe. Ghost writing is a profession. The greatest power in the land is not thought or ethics, but wealth, and the persons who exercise the power of wealth are not necessarily its owners, but those who direct its use, and the truth about this direction is so far as possible kept a secret. We do not know who owns our vast property and resources, so that most of our argument concerning wealth and its use must be based on guess work. Those responsible for the misuse of wealth escape responsibility, and even the owners of capital often do not know for what it is being used and how. The criterion of industry and trade is the profit that it accrues, not the good which it does either its owners or the public. Present profit is valued higher than future need. We waste materials. We refuse to make repairs. We cheat and deceive in manufacturing goods. We have succumbed to an increased use of lying and misrepresentation. In the last ten years at least a thousand books have been published to prove that the fight to preserve Negro slavery in America was a great and noble cause, led by worthy men of eminence.

I know the United States. It is my country and the land of my fathers. It is still a land of magnificent possibilities. It is still the home of noble souls and generous people. But it is selling its birthright. It is betraying its mighty destiny. I was born on its soil and educated in its schools. I have served my country to the best of my ability. I have never knowingly broken its laws or unjustly attacked its reputation. At the same time I have pointed out its injustices and crimes and blamed it, rightly as I believe, for its mistakes. It has given me education and some of its honors, for which I am thankful.

Today the United States is the leading nation in the world, which apparently believes that war is the only way to settle present disputes and difficulties. For this reason it is spending fantastic sums of money, and wasting wealth and energy on the preparation for war, which is nothing less than criminal. Yet the United States dare not stop spending money for war. If she did her whole economy, which is today based on preparation for war, might collapse. Therefore, we prepare for a Third World War; we spread our soldiers and arms over the earth and we bribe every nation we can to become our allies. We are taxing our citizens into poverty, crime and unemployment, and systematically distorting the truth about socialism. We have used the horror of germ warfare. Some of our leaders are ready to use it again.

The use of history for distortion and not for education has led to another of our greatest present evils; and that is to make fear of socialism and communism so great that we have withdrawn our efforts toward the education of children, the war on disease, and the raising of the standards of living. We encourage the increase of debt to finance present enjoyment; and above all we use news gathering and opinion, radio and television, magazines and books, to make most Americans believe that the threat of war, especially on the part of the Soviet Union against the United States, justifies heavy taxation and tremendous expenditure for war preparation.

This propaganda began when our tremendous profits from the First World War encouraged American business to believe that the United States was about to replace Great Britain as ruler of most of mankind. The rise and spread of socialism contradicted this ambition, and made the projected American century quail in fright before the century of communism. We determined therefore to overthrow communism by brute force. Gradually we discovered the impossibility of this, unless we risked suicide. We saw communism increasing education, science and productivity. We now face the possibility of co-existence with the communist world, and competition between the methods of capitalism and the methods of socialism. It is at this crisis that I had the opportunity to live seven months in a world of socialism, which is striving toward communism as an ideal.

This is what I call decadence. It could not have happened 50 years ago. In the day of our fiercest controversy we have not dared thus publicly to silence opinion. I have lived through disagreement, vilification, and war and war again. But in all that time, I have never seen the right of human beings to think so challenged and denied as today.

The day after I was born, Andrew Johnson was impeached. He deserved punishment as a traitor to the poor Southern whites and poorer freedmen. Yet during his life no one denied him the right to defend himself. A quarter of a century ago, I tried to state and carry into realization unpopular ideas against a powerful opposition—in the white South, in the reactionary North, and even among my own people. I found my thought being misconstrued and I planned an organ of propaganda, *The Crisis,* where I would be free to say what I believed. This was no easy sailing. My magazine reached but a fraction of the nation. It was bitterly attacked and once the government suppressed it. But in the end I maintained a platform of radical thinking on the Negro question which influenced many minds. War and depression ended my independence of thought and forced me to return to teaching, but with the certainty that I had at least started a new line of belief and action. Then they stopped my teaching.

As a result of my work and that of others, the Supreme Court began to restore democracy in the South and finally outlawed discrimination in public services based on color. This caused rebellion in the South which the nation is afraid to meet. The Negro stands bewildered an attempt is made by appointments to unimportant offices and trips abroad to bribe him into silence. His art and literature cease to function. Only the children like those at Little Rock stand and fight.

The Yale sophomore who replaced a periodical of brains by a book of pictures concealed in advertisements, proposed that America rule the world. This failed because we could not rule ourselves. But Texas to the rescue, as Johnson proposes that America take over outer space. Somewhere beyond the Moon there must be sentient creatures rolling in inextinguishable laughter at the antics of our Earth.

We tax ourselves into poverty and crime so as to make the rich richer and the poor poorer and more evil. We know the cause of this: it is to permit our rich business interests to stop socialism and to prevent the ideals of communism from ever triumphing on earth. The aim is impossible. Socialism progresses and will progress. All we can do is to silence and jail its promoters and make world war on communism. I believe in socialism. I seek a world where the ideals of communism will triumph—to each according to his need, from each according to his ability. For this I will work as long as I live. And I still live.

I just live. I plan my work, but plan less for shorter periods. I live from year to year and day to day. I expect snatches of pain and discomfort to come and go. And then reaching back to my archives, I whisper to the great Majority: To the Almighty Dead, into whose pale approaching faces, I stand and stare; you whose thoughts, deeds and dreams have made men wise with all wisdom and stupid with utter evil. In every name of God, bend out and down, you who are the infinite majority of all mankind and with your thoughts, deeds, dreams and memories, overwhelm, outvote, and coerce this remnant of human life which lingers on, imagining themselves wisest of all who have lived just because they still survive. Wither with wide revelation will they go with their stinking pride and empty boasting, whose ever recurring lies only you the Dead have known all too well? Teach living man to jeer at this last civilization which seeks to build heaven on Want and Ill of most men and vainly builds on color and hair rather than on decency of hand and heart. Let your memories teach these wilful fools all which you have forgotten and ruined and done to death.

You are not and yet you are: your thoughts, your deeds, above all your dreams still live. So too, your deeds and what you forgot—these lived as your bodies died. With these we also live and die, realize and kill. Our dreams seek Heaven, our deeds plumb Hell. Hell lies about us in our Age: blithely we push into its stench and flame. Suffer us not, Eternal Dead to stew in this Evil—the Evil of South Africa, the Evil of Mississippi; the Evil of Evils which is what we hope to hold in

Asia and Africa, in the southern Americas and islands of the Seven Seas. Reveal, Ancient of Days, the Present in the Past and prophesy the End in the Beginning. For this is a beautiful world; this is a wonderful America, which the founding fathers dreamed until their sons drowned it in the blood of slavery and devoured it in greed. Our children must rebuild it. Let then the Dream of the Dead rebuke the Blind who think that what is will be forever and teach them that what was worth living for must live again and that which merited death must stay dead. Teach us, Forever Dead, there is no Dream but Deed, there is no Deed but Memory.

History

George Washington Williams[*]

from *History of the Negro Race in America from 1619 to 1880*

Chapter XIII: The Colony of New York

So the mild system of domestic slavery introduced by the Dutch now received the sanction of positive British law. Most of the slaves in the Province of New York, from the time they were first introduced, down to 1664, had been the property of the West-India Company. As such they had small plots of land to work for their own benefit, and were not without hope of emancipation some day. But under the English government the condition of the slave was clearly defined by law and one of great hardships. On the 24th of October, 1684, an Act was passed in which slavery was for the first time regarded as a legitimate institution in the Province of New York under the English government.[1]

The slave-trade grew. New York began to feel the necessity of a larger number of slaves. In 1702 her "most gracious majesty," Queen Anne, among many instructions to the royal governor, directed that the people "take especial care, that God Almighty be devoutly and duly served," and that the "Royal African Company of England" "take especial care that the said Province may have a constant and sufficient supply of merchantable Negroes, at moderate rates."[2] It was a marvellous zeal that led the good queen to build up the Church of England alongside of the institution of human slavery. It was an impartial zeal that sought their mutual growth,—the one intended by our divine Lord to give mankind absolute liberty, the other intended by man to rob mankind of the great boon of freedom! But with the sanction of statutory legislation, and the silent acquiescence of the Church, the foundations of the institution of slavery were firmly laid in the approving conscience of a selfish public. Dazzled by prospective riches, and unscrupulous in the methods of accumulations, the people of the Province of New York clamored for more exacting laws by which to govern the slaves.[3] Notwithstanding Lord Cornbury had received the following instructions from the crown, "you shall endeavor to get a law passed for the restraining of any inhuman severity . . . to find out the best means to facilitate and encourage the conversion of Negroes and Indians to the Christian religion," the Colonial Assembly (the same year, 1702) passed severe laws against the slaves. It was "*An Act for regulating slaves,*" but was quite lengthy and specific. It was deemed "*not lawful to trade with negro slaves,*" and the violation of this law was followed by fine and imprisonment. "*Not above three slaves may meet together:*" if they did they were liable to be whipped by a justice of the peace, or sent to jail. "*A common whipper to be appointed,*" showed that the justices had more physical exercise than they cared for. "*A slave not to strike a freeman,*" indicated that the slaves in New York as in

[1] Journals, etc., N.Y., vol. i. p. xiii.
[2] Dunlap's Hist. of N.Y., vol. i. p. 260.

[3] Booth's Hist. of N.Y., vol. i. pp. 270–272.

[*] For headnote see p. 257.

Virginia were accounted as heathen. "*Penalty for concealing slaves,*" and the punishment of Negroes for stealing, etc., were rather severe, but only indicated the temper of the people at that time.[4]

The recommendations to have Negro and Indian slaves baptized gave rise to considerable discussion and no little alarm. As was shown in the chapter on Virginia, the proposition to baptize slaves did not meet with a hearty indorsement from the master-class. The doctrine had obtained in most of the colonies, that a man was a freeman by virtue of his membership in a Christian church, and hence eligible to office. To escape the logic of this position, the dealer in human flesh sought to bar the door of the Church against the slave. But in 1706 "*An Act to encourage the baptizing of Negro, Indian, and mulatto slaves,*" was passed in the hope of quieting the public mind on this question.

Whereas divers of her Majesty's good Subjects, Inhabitants of this Colony, now are, and have been willing that such Negroe, Indian, and Mulatto Slaves, who belong to them, and desire the same, should be baptized, but are deterred and hindered therefrom by reason of a groundless Opinion that hath spread itself in this Colony, that by the baptizing of such Negro, Indian, or Mulatto Slave, they would become Free, and ought to be set at liberty. In order therefore to put an end to all such Doubts and scruples as have, or hereafter at any time may arise about the same—

Be it enacted, &c., that the baptizing of a Negro, Indian, or Mulatto Slave shall not be any cause or reason for the setting them or any of them at liberty.

And be it, &c., that all and every Negro, Indian, Mulatto and Mestee bastard child and children, who is, are, and shall be born of any Negro, Indian, or Mestee, shall follow the state and condition of the mother and be esteemed, reputed, taken and adjudged a slave and slaves to all intents and purposes whatsoever.

Provided always, and be it, &c., That no slave whatsoever in this colony shall at any time be admitted as a witness for or against any freeman in any case, matter or cause, civil or criminal, whatsoever.[5]

So when the door of the Christian Church was opened to the Negro, he was to appear at the sacred altar with his chains on. Though emancipated from the bondage of Satan, he nevertheless remained the abject slave of the Christian colonists. Claiming spiritual kinship with Christ, the Negro could be sold at the pleasure of his master, and his family hearthstone trodden down by the slave-dealer. The humane feature of the system of slavery under the simple Dutch government, of allowing slaves to acquire an interest in the soil, was now at an end. The tendency to manumit faithful slaves called forth no approbation. The colonists grew cold and hard-fisted. They saw not God's image in the slave,—only so many dollars. There were no strong men in the pulpits of the colony who dared brave the avaricious spirit of the times. Not satisfied with colonial legislation, the municipal government of the city of New York passed, in 1710,[6] an ordinance forbidding Negroes, Indians, and Mulatto slaves from appearing "in the streets after nightfall without a lantern with a lighted candle in it."[7] The year before, a slave-market was erected at the foot of Wall Street, where slaves of every description were for sale. Negroes, Indians, and Mulattoes; men, women, and children; the old, the middle-aged, and the young,—all, as sheep in shambles, were daily declared the property of the highest cash-bidder. And what of the few who secured their freedom? Why, the law of 1712 declared that no Negro, Indian, or Mulatto that shall hereafter be set free "shall hold any land or real estate, but the same shall escheat."[8] There was, therefore, but little for

---

[4] On the 22d of March, 1680, the following proclamation was issued: "Whereas, several inhabitants within this city have and doe dayly harbour, entertain and countenance Indian and neger slaves in their houses, and to them sell and deliver wine, rum, and other strong liquors, for which they receive money or goods which by the said Indian and negro slaves is pilfered, purloyned, and stolen from their several masters, by which the publick peace is broken, and the damage of the master is produced, etc., therefore they are prohibited, etc.; and if neger or Indian slave make application for these forbidden articles, immediate information is to be given to his master or to the mayor or oldest alderman."—DUNLAP, vol. ii. Appendix, p. cxxviii.

[5] Bradford Laws, p. 81.

[6] The ordinance referred to was re-enacted on the 22d of April, 1731, and reads as follows: "No Negro, Mulatto, or Indian slave, above the age of fourteen, shall presume to appear in any of the streets, or in any other place of this city on the south side of Fresh Water, in the night time, above an hour after sunset, without a lanthorn and candle in it (unless in company with his owner or some white belonging to the family). Penalty, the watch-house that night; next day, prison, until the owner pays 4*s.*, and before discharge, the slave to be whipped not exceeding forty lashes."—DUNLAP, vol. ii. Appendix, p. clxiii.

[7] Booth, vol. i. p. 271.

[8] Hurd's Bondage and Freedom, vol. i. p. 281.

the Negro in either state,—bondage or freedom. There was little in this world to allure him, to encourage him, to help him. The institution under which he suffered was one huge sepulchre, and he was buried alive.

The poor grovelling worm turns under the foot of the pedestrian. The Negro winched under his galling yoke of British colonial oppression.

A misguided zeal and an inordinate desire of conquest had led the Legislature to appropriate ten thousand pounds sterling toward an expedition to effect the conquest of Canada. Acadia had just fallen into the hands of Gov. Francis Nicholson without firing a gun, and the news had carried the New Yorkers off their feet. "On to Canada!" was the shibboleth of the adventurous colonists; and the expedition started. Eight transports, with eight hundred and sixty men, perished amid the treacherous rocks and angry waters of the St. Lawrence. The troops that had gone overland returned in chagrin. The city was wrapped in gloom: the Legislature refused to do any thing further; and here the dreams of conquest vanished. The city of New York was thrown on the defensive. The forts were repaired, and every thing put in readiness for an emergency. Like a sick man the colonists started at every rumor. On account of bad faith the Iroquois were disposed to mischief.

In the feeble condition of the colonial government, the Negro grew restless. At the first, as previously shown, the slaves were very few, but now, in 1712, were quite numerous. The Negro, the Quaker, and the Papist were a trinity of evils that the colonists most dreaded. The Negro had been badly treated; and an attempt on his part to cast off the yoke was not improbable, in the mind of the master-class. The fears of the colonists were at length realized. A Negro riot broke out. A house was burned, and a number of white persons killed; and, had it not been for the prompt and efficient aid of the troops, the city of New York would have been reduced to ashes.

Now, what was the condition of the slaves in the Christian colony of New York? They had no family relations: for a long time they lived together by common consent. They had no property, no schools, and, neglected in life, were abandoned to burial in a common ditch after death. They dared not lift their hand to strike a Christian or a Jew. Their testimony was excluded by the courts, and the power of their masters over their bodies extended sometimes to life and limb.

This condition of affairs yielded its bitter fruit at length.

Here we see the effects of that blind and wicked policy which induced England to pamper her merchants and increase her revenues, by positive instructions to the governors of her colonies, strictly enjoining them (for the good of the African company, and for the emoluments expected from the assiento contract), to fix upon America a vast negro population, torn from their homes and brought hither by force. New York was at this time filled with negroes; every householder who could afford to keep servants, was surrounded by blacks, some pampered in indolence, all carefully kept in ignorance, and considered, erroneously, as creatures whom the white could not do without, yet lived in dread of. They were feared, from their numbers, and from a consciousness, however stifled, that they were injured and might seek revenge or a better condition.[9]

The Negro plot of 1741 furnishes the most interesting and thrilling chapter in the history of the colony of New York. Unfortunately for the truth of history, there was but one historian[10] of the affair, and he an interested judge; and what he has written should be taken *cum grano salis.* His book was intended to defend the action of the court that destroyed so many innocent lives, but no man can read it without being thoroughly convinced that the decision of the court was both illogical and cruel. There is nothing in this country to equal it, except it be the burning of the witches at Salem. But in stalwart old England the Popish Plot in 1679, started by Titus Oates, is the only occurrence in human history that is so faithfully reproduced by the Negro plot. Certainly history repeats itself. Sixty-two years of history stretch between the events. One tragedy is enacted in the metropolis of the Old World, the other in the metropolis of the New World. One was instigated by a perjurer and a heretic, the other by an indentured servant, in all probability from a convict ship. The one was suggested by the hatred of the Catholics, and the other by hatred of the Negro. And in both cases the evidence that convicted and condemned innocent men and women was wrung from the lying lips of doubtful characters by an overwrought zeal on the part of the legal authorities.

Titus Oates, who claimed to have discovered the *"Popish Plot,"* was a man, of the most execrable character. He was the son of an

[9] Dunlap, vol. i. p. 323.
[10] Judge Daniel Horsemanden.

Anabaptist, took orders in the Church, and had been settled in a small living by the Duke of Norfolk. Indicted for perjury, he effected an escape in a marvellous manner. While a chaplain in the English navy he was convicted of practices not fit to be mentioned, and was dismissed from the service. He next sought communion with the Church of Rome, and made his way into the Jesuit College of St. Omers. After a brief residence among the students, he was deputed to perform a confidential mission to Spain, and, upon his return to St. Omers, was dismissed to the world on account of his habits, which were very distasteful to Catholics. He boasted that he had only joined them to get their secrets. Such a man as this started the cry of the Popish Plot, and threw all England into a state of consternation. A chemist by the name of Tongue, on the 12th of August, 1678, had warned the king against a plot that was directed at his life, etc. But the king did not attach any importance to the statement until Tongue referred to Titus Oates as his authority. The latter proved himself a most arrant liar while on the stand: but the people were in a credulous state of mind, and Oates became the hero of the hour;[11] and under his wicked influence many souls were hurried into eternity. Read Hume's account of the Popish Plot, and then follow the bloody narrative of the Negro plot of New York, and see how the one resembles the other.

Some mysterious design was still suspected in every enterprise and profession: arbitrary power and Popery were apprehended as the scope of all projects: each breath or rumor made the people start with anxiety: their enemies, they thought, were in their very bosom, and had gotten possession of their sovereign's confidence. While in this timorous, jealous disposition, the cry of a *plot* all on a sudden struck their ears: they were wakened from their slumber, and like men affrightened and in the dark, took every figure for a spectre. The terror of each man became the source of terror to another. And a universal panic being diffused, reason and argument, and common-sense and common humanity, lost all influence over them. From this disposition of men's minds we are to account for the progress of the *Popish Plot,* and the credit given to it; an event which would otherwise appear prodigious and altogether inexplicable.[12]

On the 28th of February, 1741, the house of one Robert Hogg, Esq., of New-York City, a mer-

[11] Hume, vol. vi. pp. 171–212.
[12] Ibid., vol. vi. p. 171.

chant, was robbed of some fine linen, medals, silver coin, etc. Mr. Hogg's house was situated on the corner of Broad and Mill Streets, the latter sometimes being called Jew's Alley. The case was given to the officers of the law to look up.

The population of New-York City was about ten thousand, about two thousand of whom were slaves. On the 18th of March the chapel in the fort took fire from some coals carelessly left by an artificer in a gutter he had been soldering. The roof was of shingles; and a brisk wind from the south-east started a fire, that was not observed until it had made great headway. In those times the entire populace usually turned out to assist in extinguishing fires; but, this fire being in the fort, the fear of an explosion of the magazine somewhat checked their usual celerity on such occasions. The result was, that all the government buildings in the fort were destroyed. A militia officer by the name of Van Horne, carried away by the belief that the fire was purposely set by the Negroes, caused the beating of the drums and the posting of the "night watch." And for his vigilance he was nicknamed "Major Drum." The "Major's" apprehensions, however, were contagious. The fact that the governor reported the true cause of the fire to the Legislature had but little influence in dispossessing the people of their fears of a Negro plot. The next week the chimney of Capt. Warren's house near the fort took fire, but was saved with but slight damage. A few days after this the storehouse of a Mr. Van Zandt was found to be on fire, and it was said at the time to have been occasioned by the carelessness of a smoker. In about three days after, two fire-alarms were sounded. One was found to be a fire in some hay in a cow-stable near a Mr. Quick's house. It was soon extinguished. The other alarm was on account of a fire in the kitchen loft of the dwelling of a Mr. Thompson. On the next day coals were discovered under the stables of a Mr. John Murray on Broadway. On the next morning an alarm called the people to the residence of Sergeant Burns, near the fort; and in a few hours the dwelling of a Mr. Hilton, near Fly Market, was found to be on fire. But the flames in both places were readily extinguished. It was thought that the fire was purposely set at Mr. Hilton's as a bundle of tow was found near the premises. A short time before these strange fires broke out, a Spanish vessel, partly manned by Spanish Catholic Negroes, had been brought into the port of New York as a prize. All the crew that were

Negroes were hurried into the Admiralty Court; where they were promptly condemned to slavery, and an order issued for their sale. The Negroes pleaded their freedom in another country, but had no counsel to defend them. A Capt. Sarly purchased one of these Negroès. Now, Capt. Sarly's house adjoined that of Mr. Hilton's; and so, when the latter's house was discovered to be on fire, a cry was raised, "The Spanish Negroes! The Spanish! Take up the Spanish Negroes!" Some persons took it upon themselves to question Capt. Sarly's Negro about the fires, and it is said that he behaved in an insolent manner; whereupon he was sent to jail. A magistrate gave orders to the constables to arrest and incarcerate the rest of the Spanish Negroes. The magistrates held a meeting the same day, in the afternoon; and, while they were deliberating about the matter, another fire broke out in Col. Phillipes's storehouse. Some of the white people cried "Negro! Negro!" and "Cuff Phillipes!" Poor Cuff, startled at the cry, ran to his master's house, from whence he was dragged to jail by an excited mob. Judge Horsemanden says,—

Many people had such terrible apprehensions on this occasion that several Negroes (many of whom had assisted to put out the fire) who were met in the streets, were hurried away to jail; and when they were there they were continued some time in confinement before the magistrates could spare time to examine into their several cases.[13]

Let the reader return now to the robbery committed in Mr. Hogg's house on the 28th of February. The officers thought they had traced the stolen goods to a public house on the North River, kept by a person named John Hughson. This house had been a place of resort for Negroes; and it was searched for the articles, but nothing was found. Hughson had in his service an indentured servant,—a girl of sixteen years,—named Mary Burton. She intimated to a neighbor that the goods were concealed in Hughson's house, but that it would be at the expense of her life to make this fact known. This information was made known to the sheriff, and he at once apprehended the girl and produced her before Alderman Banker. This benevolent officer promised the girl her freedom on the ground that she should tell all she knew about the missing property. For prudential reasons the Alderman ordered Mary Burton to be taken to the City Hall,

[13] Horsemanden's Negro Plot, p. 29.

corner Wall and Nassua Streets. On the 4th of March the justices met at the City Hall. In the mean while John Hughson and his wife had been arrested for receiving stolen goods. They were now examined in the presence of Mary Burton. Hughson admitted that some goods had been brought to his house, produced them, and turned them over to the court. It appears from the testimony of the Burton girl that another party, dwelling in the house of the Hughson's, had taken part in receiving the stolen articles. She was a girl of bad character, called Margaret Sorubiero, *alias* Solinburgh, *alias* Kerry, but commonly called Peggy Carey. This woman had lived in the home of the Hughsons for about ten months, but at one time during this period had remained a short while at the house of John Rommes, near the new Battery, but had returned to Hughson's again. The testimony of Mary Burton went to show that a Negro by the name of Cæsar Varick, but called Quin, on the night in which the burglary was committed, entered Peggy's room through the window. The next morning Mary Burton saw "speckled linen" in Peggy's room, and that the man Varick gave the deponent two pieces of silver. She further testified that Varick drank two mugs of punch, and bought of Hughson a pair of stockings, giving him a lump of silver; and that Hughson and his wife received and hid away the linen.[14] Mr. John Varick (it was spelled Vaarck then), a baker, the owner of Cæsar, occupied a house near the new Battery, the kitchen of which adjoined the yard of John Romme's house. He found some of Robert Hogg's property under his kitchen floor, and delivered it to the mayor. Upon this revelation Romme fled to New Jersey, but was subsequently captured at Brunswick. He had followed shoemaking and tavern-keeping, and was, withal, a very suspicious character.

Up to this time nothing had been said about a Negro plot. It was simply a case of burglary. Hughson had admitted receiving certain articles, and restored them; Mr. Varick had found others, and delivered them to the mayor.

[14] As far back as 1684 the following was passed against the entertainment of slaves: "No person to countenance or entertain any negro or Indian slave, or sell or deliver to them any strong liquor, without liberty from his master, or receive from them any money or goods; but, upon any offer made by a slave, to reveal the same to the owner, or to the mayor, under penalty of £5."—Dunlap, vol. ii. Appendix, p. cxxxiii.

The reader will remember that the burglary took place on the 28th of February; that the justices arraigned the Hughsons, Mary Burton, and Peggy Carey on the 4th of March; that the first fire broke out on the 18th, the second on the 25th, of March, the third on the 1st of April, and the fourth and fifth on the 4th of April; that on the 5th of April coals were found disposed so as to burn a haystack, and that the day following two houses were discovered to be on fire.

On the 11th of April the Common Council met. The following gentlemen were present: John Cruger, Esq., mayor; the recorder, Daniel Horsemanden; aldermen, Gerardus Stuyvesant, William Romaine, Simon Johnson, John Moore, Christopher Banker, John Pintard, John Marshall; assistants, Henry Bogert, Isaac Stoutenburgh, Philip Minthorne, George Brinckerhoff, Robert Benson, and Samuel Lawrence. Recorder Horsemanden suggested to the council that the governor be requested to offer rewards for the apprehension of the incendiaries and all persons implicated, and that the city pay the cost, etc. It was accordingly resolved that the lieutenant-governor be requested to offer a reward of one hundred pounds current money of the Province to any white person, and pardon, if concerned; and twenty pounds, freedom, and, if concerned, pardon to any slave (the master to be paid twenty-five pounds); and to any free Negro, Mulatto, or Indian, forty-five pounds and pardon, if concerned. The mayor and the recorder (Horsemanden), called upon Lieut.-Gov. Clark, and laid the above resolve before him.

The city was now in a state of great excitement. The air was peopled with the wildest rumors.

On Monday the 13th of April each alderman, assistant, and constable searched his ward. The militia was called out, and sentries posted at the cross-streets. While the troops were patrolling the streets, the aldermen were examining Negroes in reference to the origin of the fires. Nothing was found. The Negroes denied all knowledge of the fires or a plot.

On the 21st of April, 1741, the Supreme Court convened.[15] Judges Frederick Phillipse and Daniel Horsemanden called the *grand jury*. The members were as follows: Robert Watts, merchant, foreman; Jeremiah Latouche, Joseph Read, Anthony Rutgers, John M'Evers, John Cruger, jun., John Merrit, Adoniah Schuyler,

[15] Horsemanden's Negro Plot, p. 33.

Isaac DePeyster, Abraham Ketteltas, David Provoost, Rene Hett, Henry Beeckman, jun., David van Horne, George Spencer, Thomas Duncan, and Winant Van Zandt,—all set down as merchants,—a respectable, intelligent, and influential grand jury! Judge Phillipse informed the jury that the people "have been put into many frights and terrors," in regard to the fires; that it was their duty to use "all lawful means" to discover the guilty parties, for there was "much room to suspect" that the fires were not accidental. He told them that there were many persons in jail upon whom suspicion rested; that arson was felony at common law, even though the fire is extinguished, or goes out itself; that arson was a deep crime, and, if the perpetrators were not apprehended and punished, "who can say he is safe, or where will it end?" The learned judge then went on to deliver a moral lecture against the wickedness of selling "penny drams" to Negroes, without the consent of their masters. In conclusion, he charged the grand jury to present "all conspiracies, combinations and other offences."

It should be kept in mind that Mary Burton was only a witness in the burglary case already mentioned. Up to that time there had been no fires. The fires, and wholesale arrests of innocent Negroes, followed the robbery. But the grand jury called Mary Burton to testify in reference to the fires. She refused to be sworn. She was questioned concerning the fires, but gave no answer. Then the proclamation of the mayor, offering protection, pardon, freedom, and one hundred pounds, was read. It had the desired effect. The girl opened her mouth, and spake all the words that the jury desired. At first she agreed to tell all she knew about the stolen goods, but would say nothing about the fires. This declaration led the jury to infer that she could, but would not say any thing about the fires. After a moral lecture upon her duty in the matter in the light of eternal reward, and a reiteration of the proffered reward that then awaited her wise decision, her memory brightened, and she immediately began to tell *all* she knew. She said that a Negro named Prince, belonging to a Mr. Auboyman, and Prince (Varick) brought the goods, stolen from Mr. Hogg's house, to the house of her master, and that Hughson, his wife, and Peggy (Carey) received them; further, that Cæsar, Prince, and Cuffee (Phillipse) had frequently met at Hughson's tavern, and discoursed about burning the fort; that they had said they would go down to the Fly (the east end of the city), and burn the entire place; and that Hughson and his wife had assented to these insurrectionary remarks, and promised to assist them. She added, by way of fulness and emphasis, that when a handful of wretched slaves, seconded by a miserable and ignorant white tavern-keeper, should have lain the city in ashes, and murdered eight or nine thousand persons,—then Cæsar should be governor, Hughson king, and Cuffee supplied with abundant riches! The loquacious Mary remembered that this intrepid trio had said, that when they burned the city it would be in the night, so they could murder the people as they came out of their homes. It should not be forgotten that *all* the fires broke out in the daytime!

It is rather remarkable and should be observed, that this wonderful witness stated that her master, John Hughson, had threatened to poison her if she told anybody that the stolen goods were in his house; that all the Negroes swore they would burn her if she told; and that, when they talked of burning the town during their meetings, there were no white persons present save her master, mistress, and Peggy Carey.

The credulous Horsemanden tells us that "the evidence of a conspiracy," not only to burn the city, but also "to destroy and murder the people," was most "astonishing to the grand jury!" But that any white person should confederate with slaves in such a wicked and cruel purpose was astounding beyond measure! And the grand jury was possessed of the same childlike faith in the ingenious narrative of the wily Mary. In their report to the judges, they set forth in strong terms their faith in the statements of the deponent, and required the presence of Peggy Carey. The extent of the delusion of the judges, jury, and people may be seen in the fact, that, immediately upon the report of the jury, the judges summoned the entire bar of the city of New York to meet them. The following gentlemen responded to the call: Messrs. Murray, Alexander, Smith, Chambers, Nichols, Lodge, and Jameson. All the lawyers were present except the attorney-general. By the act of 1712, "for preventing, suppressing and punishing the conspiracy and insurrection of negroes and other slaves,"[16] a justice of the peace could try the refractory slaves at once. But here

[16] Bradford's Laws, pp. 141–144.

was a deep, dark, and bloody plot to burn the city and murder its inhabitants, in which *white* persons were implicated. This fact led the learned judges to conclude it wise and prudent to refer this whole matter to the Supreme Court. And the generous offer of the *entire* bar of New-York City to assist, in turns, in every trial, should remain evermore an indestructible monument to their unselfish devotion to their city, the existence of which was threatened by less than a score of ignorant, penniless Negro slaves!

By the testimony of Mary Burton, Peggy Carey stood convicted as one of the conspirators. She had already languished in jail for more than a month. The judges thought it advisable to examine her in her cell. They tried to cajole her into criminating others; but she stoutly denied all knowledge of the fires, and said "that if she should accuse anybody of any such thing, she must accuse innocent persons, and wrong her own soul."

On the 24th of April, Cæsar Varick, Prince Auboyman, John Hughson, his wife, and Peggy Carey were arraigned for felony, and pleaded not guilty. Cæsar and Prince were first put on trial. As they did not challenge the jury, the following gentlemen were sworn: Messrs. Roger French, John Groesbeck, John Richard, Abraham Kipp, George Witts, John Thurman, Patrick Jackson, Benjamin Moore, William Hammersley, John Lashiere, Joshua Sleydall, and John Shurmer. "Guilty!" as charged in the indictment. They had committed the robbery, so said the jury.

On the 3d of May one Arthur Price, a common thief, was committed to jail for theft. He occupied a cell next to the notorious Peggy Carey. In order to bring himself into favor with the judges, he claimed to have had a conversation with Peggy through the hole in the door. Price says she told him that "she was afraid of those fellows" (the Negroes); that if they said any thing in any way involving her she would hang every one of them; that she did not care to go on the stand again unless she was called; that when asked if she intended to set the town on fire she said no; but she knew about the plot; that Hughson and his wife "were sworn with the rest;" that she was not afraid of "Prince, Cuff, Cæsar, and Fork's Negro—not Cæsar, but another," because they "were all true-hearted fellows." This remarkable conversation was flavored throughout with the vilest species of profanity. Notwithstanding this interview was between a common Irish prostitute and a wretched sneak-thief, it had great weight with the solemn and upright judges.

In the midst of this trial, seven barns were burnt in the town of Hackinsack. Two Negroes were suspected of the crime, but there was not the slightest evidence that they were guilty. But one of them said that he had discharged a gun at the party who set his master's barn on fire, but did not kill any one. The other one was found loading a gun with two bullets. This was enough to convict. They were burnt alive at a stake. This only added fuel to the flame of public excitement in New York.

On the 6th of May (Wednesday) two more arrests were made,—Hughson's daughter Sarah, suspected of being a confederate, and Mr. Sleydall's Negro Jack,—on suspicion of having put fire to Mr. Murray's haystack. On the same day the judges arraigned the white persons implicated in the case,—John Hughson, his wife, and Peggy Carey. The jury promptly found them guilty of "receiving stolen goods." "Peggy Carey," says Recorder Horsemanden, "seeming to think it high time to do something to recommend herself to mercy, made a voluntary confession." This vile, foul-mouthed prostitute takes the stand, and gives a new turn to the entire affair. She removes the scene of the conspiracy to another tavern near the new Battery, where John Romme had made a habit of entertaining, *contrary to law,* Negro slaves. Peggy had seen many meetings at this place, particularly in December, 1740. At that time she mentioned the following Negroes as being present: Cuff, Brash, Curacoa, Cæsar, Patrick, Jack, Cato; but *her* especial Cæsar Varick was not implicated! Romme administered an oath to all these Negroes, and then made a proposition to them; viz., that they should destroy the fort, burn the town, and bring the spoils to him. He engaged to divide with them, and take them to a new country, where he would give them their freedom. Mrs. Romme was present during this conversation; and, after the Negroes had departed, she and the deponent (Peggy) were sworn by Romme to eternal secrecy. Mrs. Romme denied swearing to the conspiracy, but acknowledged that her husband had received stolen goods, that he sold drams to Negroes who kept game-fowls there; but that never more than three Negroes came at a time. She absconded in great fright. It has been mentioned that Peggy Carey had lived at the tavern of John Romme for a short time, and that articles belonging to Mr. Hogg had

been found under the kitchen floor of the house next to Romme's.

The judges evidently reasoned that all Negroes would steal, or that stealing was incident upon or implied by the condition of the slave. Then Romme kept a "tippling-house," and defied the law by selling "drams" to Negroes. Now, a man who keeps a "tippling-house" was liable to encourage a conspiracy.

A full list of the names of the persons implicated by Peggy was handed to the proper officers, and those wicked persons apprehended. They were brought before the redoubtable Peggy for identification. She accused them of being sworn conspirators. They all denied the charge. Then they were turned over to Mary Burton; and she, evidently displeased at Peggy's attempt to rival her in the favor of the powerful judges, testified that she knew them not. But it was vain. Peggy had the ear of the court, and the terror-stricken company was locked up in the jail. Alarmed at their helpless situation, the ignorant Negroes began "to accuse one another, as it would seem, by way of injuring an enemy and guarding themselves."

Cæsar and Prince, having been tried and convicted of felony, were sentenced to be hanged. The record says,—

Monday, 11th of May. Cæsar and Prince were executed this day at the gallows, according to sentence: they died very stubbornly, without confessing *any thing about the conspiracy:* and denied that *they knew any thing about it to the last.* The body of Cæsar was accordingly hung in chains.[17]

On the 13th of May, 1741, a solemn fast was observed; "because many houses and dwellings had been fired about our ears, without any discovery of the cause or occasion of them, which had put us into the utmost consternation." Excitement ran high. Instead of getting any light on the affair, the plot thickened.

On the 6th of May, Hughson, his wife, and Peggy Carey had been tried and found guilty, as has already been stated. Sarah Hughson, daughter of the Hughsons, was in jail. Mary Burton was the heroine of the hour. Her word was law. Whoever she named was produced in court. The sneak-thief, Arthur Price, was employed by the judges to perform a mission that was at once congenial to his tastes and in harmony with his criminal education. He was sent among the

[17] Horsemanden's Negro Plot, p. 60.

incarcerated Negroes to administer punch, in the desperate hope of getting more "confessions!" Next, he was sent to Sarah Hughson to persuade her to accuse her father and mother of complicity in the conspiracy. He related a conversation he had with Sarah, but she denied it to his teeth with great indignation. This vile and criminal method of securing testimony of a conspiracy never brought the blush to the cheek of a single officer of the law. "None of these things moved" them. They were themselves so completely lost in the general din and excitement, were so thoroughly convinced that a plot existed, and that it was their duty to prove it in some manner or other,—that they believed every thing that went to establish the guilt of any one.

Even a feeble-minded boy was arrested, and taken before the grand jury. He swore that he knew nothing of the plot to burn the town, but the kind magistrates told him that if he would tell the truth he should not be hanged. Ignorant as these helpless slaves were, they now understood "telling the truth" to mean to criminate some one in the plot, and thus gratify the inordinate hunger of the judges and jury for testimony relating to a "conspiracy." This Negro imbecile began his task of telling "what he knew," which was to be rewarded by allowing him to leave without being hung! He deposed that Quack desired him to burn the fort; that Cuffee said he would fire one house, Curacoa Dick another, and so on *ad infinitum*. He was asked by one of the learned gentlemen, "what the Negroes intended by all this mischief?" He answered, "To kill all the gentlemen and take their wives; that one of the fellows already hanged, was to be an officer in the Long Bridge Company, and the other, in the Fly Company."[18]

On the 25th of May a large number of Negroes were arrested. The boy referred to above (whose name was Sawney, or Sandy) was called to the stand again on the 26th, when he grew very talkative. He said that "at a meeting of Negroes he was called in and frightened into undertaking to burn the slip Market;" that he witnessed some of the Negroes in their attempts to burn certain houses; that at the house of one Comfort, he, with others, was sworn to secrecy and fidelity to each other; said he was never at either tavern, Hughson's nor Romme's; and ended his revelations by accusing a woman of setting fire to a

[18] The city of New York was divided into parts at that time, and comprised two militia districts.

house, and of murdering her child. As usual, after such confessions, more arrests followed. Quack and Cuffee were tried and convicted of felony, "for wickedly and maliciously conspiring with others to burn the town and murder the inhabitants." This was an occasion to draw forth the eloquence of the attorney-general; and in fervid utterance he pictured the Negroes as "monsters, devils, etc." A Mr. Rosevelt, the master of Quack, swore that his slave was home when the fire took place in the fort; and Mr. Phillipse, Cuffee's master, testified as much for his servant. But this testimony was not what the magistrates wanted: so they put a soldier on the stand who swore that Quack *did* come to the fort the day of the fire; that his wife lived there, and when he insisted on going in he (the sentry) knocked him down, but the officer of the guard passed him in. Lawyer Smith, "whose eloquence had disfranchised the Jews," was called upon to sum up. He thought too much favor had been shown the Negroes, in that they had been accorded a trial as if they were freemen; that the wicked Negroes might have been proceeded against in a most summary manner; that the Negro witnesses had been treated with too much consideration; that "the law requires no oath to be administered to them; and, indeed, it would be a profanation of it to administer it to a heathen in a legal form;" that "the monstrous ingratitude of this black tribe is what exceedingly aggravates their guilt;" that their condition as slaves was one of happiness and peace; that "they live without care; are commonly better fed and clothed than the poor of most Christian countries; they are indeed slaves," continued the eloquent and logical attorney, "but under the protection of the law: none can hurt them with impunity; but notwithstanding all the kindness and tenderness with which they have been treated among us, yet this is the second attempt of this same kind that this brutish and bloody species of mankind have made within one age!" Of course the jury knew their duty, and merely went through the form of going out and coming in immediately with a verdict of "guilty." The judge sentenced them to be chained to a stake and burnt to death,—"and the Lord have mercy upon your poor wretched souls." His Honor told them that "they should be thankful that their feet were caught in the net; that the mischief had fallen upon their own pates." He advised them to consider the tenderness and humanity with which they had been treated; that they were the most abject wretches, the very outcasts of the nations of the earth; and, therefore, they should look to their souls, for as to their bodies, they would be burnt.

These poor fellows were accordingly chained to the stake the next Sunday; but, before the fuel was lighted, Deputy Sheriff More and Mr. Rosevelt again questioned Quack and Cuffee, and reduced their confessions to paper, for they had stoutly protested their innocence while in court. In hope of being saved they confessed, in substance, that Hughson contrived to burn the town, and kill the people; that a company of Negroes voted Quack the proper person to burn the fort, because his wife lived there; that he did set the chapel on fire with a lighted stick; that Mary Burton had told the truth, and that she could implicate many more if she would, etc. All this general lying was done with the understanding that the confessors were to be reprieved until the governor could be heard from. But a large crowd had gathered to witness the burning of these poor Negroes, and they compelled the sheriff to proceed with the ceremonies. The convicted slaves were burned.

On the 1st of June the boy Sawney was again put upon the witness-stand. His testimony led to the arrest of more Negroes. He charged them with having been sworn to the plot, and with having sharp penknives with which to kill white men. One Fortune testified that he never knew of houses where conspirators met, nor did he know Hughson, but accuses Sawney, and Quack who had been burnt. The next witness was a Negro girl named Sarah. She was frightened out of her senses. She foamed at the mouth, uttered the bitterest imprecations, and denied all knowledge of a conspiracy. But the benevolent gentlemen who conducted the trial told her that others had said certain things in proof of the existence of a conspiracy, that the only way to save her life was to acknowledge that there had been a conspiracy to burn the town and kill the inhabitants. She then assented to all that was told her, and thereby implicated quite a number of Negroes; but, when her testimony was read to her, she again denied all. She was without doubt a fit subject for an insane-asylum rather than for the witness-stand, in a cause that involved so many human lives.

It will be remembered that John Hughson, his wife, and daughter had been in the jail for a long time. He now desired to be called to the witness-stand. He begged to be sworn, that in the most solemn manner he might deny all knowl-

edge of the conspiracy, and exculpate his wife and child. But the modest recorder reminded him of the fact that he stood convicted as a felon already, that he and his family were doomed to be hanged, and that, therefore, it would be well for him to "confess all." He was sent back to jail unheard. Already condemned to be hung, the upright magistrates had Hughson tried again for "conspiracy" on the 4th of June! The indictments were three in number: *First,* that Hughson, his wife, his daughter, and Peggy Carey, with three Negroes, Cæsar, Prince, and Cuffee, conspired in March last to set fire to the house in the fort. *Second,* That Quack (already burnt) did set fire to and burn the house, and that the prisoners, Hughson, his wife, daughter Sarah, and Peggy, encouraged him so to do. *Third,* That Cuffee (already burnt) did set fire to Phillipse's house, and burnt it; and they, the prisoners, procured and encouraged him so to do. Hughson, his family, and Peggy pleaded not guilty to all the above indictments. The attorney-general delivered a spirited address to the jury, which was more forcible than elegant. He denounced the unlucky Hughson as "infamous, inhuman, an arch-rebel against God, his king, and his country,—a devil incarnate," etc. He was ably assisted by eminent counsel for the king,—Joseph Murray, James Alexander, William Smith, and John Chambers. Mary Burton was called again. She swore that Negroes used to go to Hughson's at night, eat and drink, and sometimes buy provisions; that Hughson did swear the Negroes to secrecy in the plot; that she herself had seen seven or eight guns and swords, a bag of shot, and a barrel of gunpowder at Hughson's house; that the prisoner told her he would kill her if she ever revealed any thing she knew or saw; wanted her to swear like the rest, offered her silk gowns, and gold rings,—but none of those tempting things moved the virtuous Mary. Five other witnesses testified that they heard Quack and Cuffee say to Hughson while in jail, "This is what you have brought us to." The Hughsons had no counsel, and but three witnesses. One of them testified that he had lived in Hughson's tavern about three months during the past winter, and had never seen Negroes furnished entertainment there. The two others said that they had never seen any evil in the man nor in his house, etc.

"William Smith, Esq." now took the floor to sum up. He told the jury that it was "black and hellish" to burn the town, and then kill them all;

that John Hughson, by his complicity in this crime, had made himself blacker than the Negroes; that the credit of the witnesses was good, and that there was nothing left for them to do but to find the prisoners guilty, as charged in the indictment. The judge charged the jury, that the evidence against the prisoners "is ample, full, clear, and satisfactory. They were found guilty in twenty minutes, and on the 8th of June were brought into court to receive sentence. The judge told them that they were guilty of a terrible crime; that they had not only made Negroes their equals, but superiors, by waiting upon, keeping company with, entertaining them with meat, drink, and lodging; that the most amazing part of their conduct was their part in a plot to burn the town, and murder the inhabitants,—to have consulted with, aided, and abetted the "black seed of Cain," was an unheard of crime,—that although "with uncommon assurance they deny the fact, and call on God, as a witness of their innocence, He, out of his goodness and mercy, has confounded them, and proved their guilt, to the satisfaction of the court and jury." After a further display of forensic eloquence, the judge sentenced them "to be hanged by the neck 'till dead," on Friday, the 12th of June, 1741.

The Negro girl Sarah, referred to above, who was before the jury on the 1st of June in such a terrified state of body and mind, was re-called on the 5th of June. She implicated twenty Negroes, whom she declared were present at the house of Comfort, whetting their knives, and avowing that "they would kill white people." On the 6th of June, Robin, Cæsar, Cook, Cuffee, and Jack, another Cuffee, and Jamaica were arrested, and put upon trial on the 8th of June. It is a sad fact to record, even at this distance, that these poor blacks, without counsel, friends, or money, were tried and convicted upon the evidence of a poor ignorant, hysterical girl, and the "dying confession" of Quack and Cuffee, who "confessed" with the understanding that they should be free! Tried and found guilty on the 8th, without clergy or time to pray, they were burned at the stake the next day! Only Jack found favor with the court, and that favor was purchased by perjury. He was respited until it "was found how well he would deserve further favor." It was next to impossible to understand him, so two white gentlemen were secured to act as interpreters. Jack testified to having seen Negroes at Hughson's tavern; that "when they

were eating, he said they began to talk about setting the houses on fire:" he was so good as to give the names of about fourteen Negroes whom he heard say that they would set their masters' houses on fire, and then rush upon the whites and kill them; that at one of these meetings there were five or six Spanish Negroes present, whose conversation he could not understand; that they waited a month and a half for the Spaniards and French to come, but when they came not, set fire to the fort. As usual, more victims of these confessors swelled the number already in the jail; which was, at this time, full to suffocation.

On the 19th of June the lieutenant-governor issued a proclamation of freedom to all who would "confess and discover" before the 1st of July. Several Indians were in the prison, charged with conspiracy. The confessions and discoveries were numerous. Every Negro charged with being an accomplice of the unfortunate wretches that had already perished at the stake began to accuse some one else of complicity in the plot. They all knew of many Negroes who were going to cut the white people's throats with penknives; and when the town was in flames they were to "meet at the end of Broadway, next to the fields!" And it must be recorded, to the everlasting disgrace of the judiciary of New York, that scores of ignorant, helpless, and innocent Negroes—and a few white people too—were convicted upon the confessions of the terror-stricken witnesses! There is not a court to-day in all enlightened Christendom that would accept as evidence—not even circumstantial—the incoherent utterances of these Negro "confessors." And yet an intelligent (?) New York court thought the evidence "clear (?), and satisfactory!"

But the end was not yet reached. A new turn was to be given to the notorious Mary Burton. The reader will remember that she said that there never were any white persons present when the burning of the town was the topic of conversation, except her master and mistress and Peggy Carey. But on the 25th of June the budding Mary accused Rev. John Ury, a reputed Catholic priest, and a schoolmaster in the town, and one Campbell, also a school-teacher, of having visited Hughson's tavern with the conspirators.

On the 26th of June, nine more Negroes were brought before the court and arraigned. Seven pleaded guilty in the hope of a reprieve: two were tried and convicted upon the testimony of Mary Burton. Eight more were arraigned, and pleaded guilty; followed by seven more, some of whom pleaded guilty, and some not guilty. Thus, in one day, the court was enabled to dispose of twenty-four persons.

On the 27th of June, one Adam confessed that he knew of the plot, but said he was enticed into it by Hughson, three years before; that Hughson told him that he knew a man who could forgive him all his sins. So between John Hughson's warm rum, and John Ury's ability to forgive sin, the virtuous Adam found all his scruples overcome; and he took the oath. A Dr. Hamilton who lodged at Holt's and the latter also, are brought into court as accused of being connected with the plot. It was charged that Holt directed his Negro Joe to set fire to the play-house at the time he should indicate. At the beginning of the trial only four white persons were mentioned; but now they began to multiply, and barrels of powder to increase at a wonderful rate. The confessions up to this time had been mere repetitions. The arrests were numerous, and the jail crowded beyond its capacity. The poor Negroes implicated were glad of an opportunity to "confess" against some one else, and thereby save their own lives. Recorder Horsemanden says, "Now many negroes began to squeak, in order to lay hold of the benefit of the proclamation." He deserves the thanks of humanity for his frankness! For before the proclamation there were not more than seventy Negroes in jail; but, within eight days after it was issued, thirty more frightened slaves were added to the number. And Judge Horsemanden says, "'Twas difficult to find room for them, nor could we see any likelihood of stopping the impeachments." The Negroes turned to accusing white persons, and seven or eight were arrested. The sanitary condition of the prison now became a subject of grave concern. The judges and lawyers consulted together, and agreed to pardon some of the prisoners to make room in the jail. They also thought it prudent to lump the confessions, and thereby facilitate their work; but the confessions went on, and the jail filled up again.

The Spanish Negroes taken by an English privateer, and adjudged to slavery by the admiralty court, were now taken up, tried, convicted, and sentenced to be hung. Five others received sentence the same day.

The bloody work went on. The poor Negroes in the jail, in a state of morbid desperation, turned upon each other the blistering tongue of accusation. They knew that they were accusing each other innocently,—as many confessed afterwards,—but this was the last straw that these sinking people could see to catch at, and this they did involuntarily. "Victims were required; and those who brought them to the altar of Moloch, purchased their own safety, or, at least, their lives."

On the 2d of July, one Will was produced before Chief-Justice James DeLancy. He plead guilty, and was sentenced to be burnt to death on the 4th of July. On the 6th of July, eleven plead guilty. One Dundee implicates Dr. Hamilton with Hughson in giving Negroes rum and swearing them to the plot. A white man by the name of William Nuill deposed that a Negro—belonging to Edward Kelly, a butcher—named London swore by God that if he should be arrested and cast into the jail, he would hang or burn all the Negroes in New York, guilty or not guilty. On this same day five Negroes were hanged. One of them was "hung in chains" upon the same gibbet with Hughson. And the Christian historian says "the town was amused" on account of a report that Hughson had turned black and the Negro white! The vulgar and sickening description of the condition of the bodies, in which Mr. Horsemanden took evident relish, we withhold from the reader. It was rumored that a Negro doctor had administered poison to the convicts, and hence the change in the bodies after death.

In addition to the burning of the Negro Will, on the 4th of July, was the sensation created by his accusing two white soldiers, Kane and Kelly, with complicity in the conspiracy. Kane was examined the next day: said that he had never been to the house of John Romme; acknowledged that he had received a stolen silver spoon, given to his wife, and sold it to one Van Dype, a silversmith; that he never knew John Ury, etc. Knowing Mary Burton was brought forward,—as she always was when the trials began to lag,—and accused Kane. He earnestly denied the accusation at first, but finally confessed that he was at Hughson's in reference to the plot on two separate occasions, but was induced to go there "by Corker, Coffin, and Fagan." After his tongue got limbered up, and his memory refreshed, he criminated Ury. He implicated Hughson's father and three brothers, Hughson's mother-in-law, an old fortune-teller, as being parties to the plot as sworn "to burn, and kill;" that Ury christened some of the Negroes, and even had the temerity to attempt to proselyte him, Kane; that Ury asked him if he could read Latin, could he read English; to both questions he answered no; that the man Coffin read to him, and descanted upon the benefits of being a Roman Catholic; that they could forgive sins, and save him from hell; and that if he had not gone away from their company they might have seduced him to be a Catholic; that one Conolly, on Governor's Island, admitted that he was "bred up a priest;" that one Holt, a dancing-master, also knew of the plot; and then described the mystic ceremony of swearing the plotters. He said, "There was a black ring made on the floor, about a foot and a half in diameter; and Hughson bid every one put off the left shoe and put their toes within the ring; and Mrs. Hughson held a bowl of punch over their heads, as the Negroes stood around the circle, and Hughson pronounced the oath above mentioned, (something like a freemason's oath and penalties,) and every negro severally repeated the oath after him, and then Hughson's wife fed them with a draught out of the bowl."

This was "new matter," so to speak, and doubtless broke the monotony of the daily recitals to which their honors had been listening all summer. Kane was about to deprive Mary Burton of her honors; and, as he could not write, he made his mark. A peddler named Coffin was arrested and examined. He denied all knowledge of the plot, never saw Hughson, never was at his place, saw him for the first time when he was executed; had never seen Kane but once, and then at Eleanor Waller's, where they drank beer together. But the court committed him. Kane and Mary Burton accused Edward Murphy. Kane charged David Johnson, a hatter, as one of the conspirators; while Mary Burton accuses Andrew Ryase, "little Holt," the dancing-master, John Earl, and seventeen soldiers,—all of whom were cast into prison.

On the 16th of July nine Negroes were arraigned: four plead guilty, two were sentenced to be burnt, and the others to be hanged. On the next day seven Negroes plead guilty. One John Schultz came forward, and made a deposition that perhaps had some little influence on the court and the community at large. He swore that a Negro man slave, named Cambridge, belonging to Christopher Codwise, Esq., did on the 9th of June, 1741, confess to the deponent, in the presence of Codwise and Richard Baker, that the confession he had made before Messrs. Lodge and Nichols was entirely false; viz., that he had con-

fessed himself guilty of participating in the conspiracy; had accused a Negro named Cajoe through fear; that he had heard some Negroes talking together in the jail, and saying that if they did not confess they would be hanged; that what he said about Horsefield Cæsar was a lie; that he had never known in what section of the town Hughson lived, nor did he remember ever hearing his name, until it had become the town talk that Hughson was concerned in a plot to burn the town and murder the inhabitants.

This did not in the least abate the zeal of Mary Burton and William Kane. They went on in their work of accusing white people and Negroes, receiving the approving smiles of the magistrates. Mary Burton says that John Earl, who lived in Broadway, used to come to Hughson's with ten soldiers at a time; that these white men were to command the Negro companies; that John Ury used to be present; and that a man near the Mayor's Market, who kept a shop where she (Mary Burton) got rum from, a doctor, by nationality a Scotchman, who lived by the Slip, and another dancing-master, named Corry, used to meet with the conspirators at Hughson's tavern.

On the 14th of July, John Ury was examined, and denied ever having been at Hughson's or knowing any thing about the conspiracy; said he never saw any of the Hughsons, nor did he know Peggy Carey. But William Kane, the soldier, insisted that Ury did visit the house of Hughson. Ury was again committed. On the next day eight persons were tried and convicted upon the evidence of Kane and Mary Burton. The jail was filling up again, and the benevolent magistrates pardoned fourteen Negroes. Then they turned their judicial minds to the case of William Kane *vs.* John Ury. First, he was charged with having counselled, procured, and incited a Negro slave, Quack, to burn the king's house in the fort: to which he pleaded not guilty. Second, that being a priest, made by the authority of the pretended See of Rome, he had come into the Province and city of New York after the time limited by law against Jesuits and Popish priests, passed in the eleventh year of William III., and had remained for the space of seven months; that he had announced himself to be an ecclesiastical person, made and ordained by the authority of the See of Rome; and that he had appeared so to be by celebrating masses and granting absolution, etc. To these charges Ury pleaded not guilty, and requested a copy of the indictments, but was only allowed a copy of the second; and pen, ink, and paper grudgingly granted him. His private journal was seized, and a portion of its contents used as evidence against him. The following was furnished to the grand jury:—

Arrived at Philadelphia the 17th of February, 1738. At Ludinum, 5th March.—To Philadelphia, 29th April.—Began school at Burlington, 18th June. Omilta Jacobus Atherthwaite, 27th July.—Came to school at Burlington, 23d January, 1740.—Saw ———, 7th May.—At five went to Burlington, to Piercy, the madman.—Went to Philadelphia, 19th May.—Went to Burlington, 18th June.—At six in the evening to Penefack, to Joseph Ashton.—Began school at Dublin under Charles Hastie, at eight pounds a year, 31st July, ———, 15th October, ———, 27th ditto.—Came to John Croker (at the Fighting Cocks), New York, 2d November.— I boarded gratis with him, 7th November,—Natura Johannis Pool, 26th December.—I began to teach with John Campbell, 6th April, 1741.—Baptized Timothy Ryan, born 18th April, 1740, son of John Ryan and Mary Ryan, 18th May.—Pater Confessor Butler, two Anni, no sacramentum non confessio.[19]

On the 21st of July, Sarah Hughson, who had been respited, was put on the witness-stand again. There were some legal errors in the indictments against Ury, and his trial was postponed until the next term; but he was arraigned on a new indictment. The energies of the jury and judges received new life. Here was a man who was a Catholic,— or had been a Catholic,—and the spirit of religious intolerance asserted itself. Sarah Hughson remembered having seen Ury at her father's house on several occasions; had seen him make a ring with chalk on the floor, make all the Negroes stand around it, while he himself would stand in the middle, with a cross, and swear the Negroes. This was also "new matter:" nothing of this kind was mentioned in the first confession. But this was not all. She had seen Ury preach to the Negroes, forgive their sins, and baptize some of them! She said that Ury wanted her to confess to him, and that Peggy confessed to him in French.

On the 24th of July, Elias Desbroses, confectioner, being called, swore that Ury had come to his shop with one Webb, a carpenter, and inquired for sugar-bits, or wafers, and asked him "whether a minister had not his wafers of him? or, whether that paste, which the deponent showed him, was not made of the same ingredients as the Luthern minister's?" or words to

that effect: the deponent told Ury that if he desired such things a joiner would make him a mould; and that when he asked him whether he had a congregation, Ury "waived giving him an answer."

On the 27th of July, Mr. Webb, the carpenter, was called to the witness-stand and testified as follows: That he had met Ury at John Croker's (at the Fighting Cocks), where he became acquainted with him; that he had heard him read Latin and English so admirably that he employed him to teach his child; that finding out that he was a school-teacher, he invited him to board at his house without charge; that he understood from him that he was a non-juring minister, had written a book that had drawn the fire of the Church, was charged with treason, and driven out of England, sustaining the loss of "a living" worth fifty pounds a year; that on religious matters the deponent could not always comprehend him; that the accused said Negroes were only fit for slaves, and to put them above that condition was to invite them to cut your throats. The observing Horsemanden was so much pleased with the above declaration, that he gives Ury credit in a footnote for understanding the dispositions of Negroes![20] Farther on Mr. Webb says, that, after one Campbell removed to Hughson's, Ury went thither, and so did the deponent on three different times, and heard him read prayers after the manner of the Church of England; but in the prayer for the king he only mentioned "our sovereign lord the King," and not "King George." He said that Ury pleaded against drunkenness, debauchery, and Deists; that he admonished every one to keep his own minister; that when the third sermon was delivered one Mr. Hildreth was present, when Ury found fault with certain doctrines, insisted that good works as well as faith were necessary to salvation; that he announced that on a certain evening he would preach from the text, "Upon this rock I will build my church, and the gates of hell shall not prevail against it; and whosoever sins ye remit, they are remitted, and whosoever sins ye retain, they are retained."

The judges, delighted with this flavor added to the usually dry proceedings, thought they had better call Sarah Hughson; that if she were grateful for her freedom she would furnish the testimony their honors desired. Sarah was

---

[19] Dunlap, vol. i. p. 344.

[20] Horsemanden's Negro Plot, p. 284.

accordingly called. She is recommended for mercy. She is, of course, to say what is put in her mouth, to give testimony such as the court desires. So the fate of the poor schoolmaster was placed in the keeping of the fateful Sarah.

On the 28th of July another grand jury was sworn, and, like the old one, was composed of merchants. The following persons composed it: Joseph Robinson, James Livingston, Hermanus Rutgers, jun., Charles LeRoux, Abraham Boelen, Peter Rutgers, Jacobus Roosevelt, John Auboyneau, Stephen Van Courtlandt, jun., Abraham Lynsen, Gerardus Duyckinck, John Provost, Henry Lane, jun., Henry Cuyler, John Roosevelt, Abraham DePeyster, Edward Hicks, Joseph Ryall, Peter Schuyler, and Peter Jay.[21]

Sarah Hughson had been pardoned. John Ury was brought into court, when he challenged some of the jury. William Hammersley, Gerardus Beekman, John Shurmur, Sidney Breese, Daniel Shatford, Thomas Behenna, Peter Fresneau, Thomas Willett, John Breese, John Hastier, James Tucker, and Brandt Schuyler were sworn to try him. Barring formalities, he was arraigned upon the old indictment; viz., felony, in inciting and exciting the Negro slave Quack to set fire to the governor's house. The king's counsel were the attorney-general, Richard Bradley, and Messrs. Murray, Alexander, Smith, and Chambers. Poor Ury had no counsel, no sympathizers. The attorney-general, in an opening speech to the jury, said that certain evidence was to be produced showing that the prisoner at the bar was guilty as charged in the indictment; that he had a letter that he desired to read to them, which had been sent to Lieut.-Gov. Clark, written by Gen. Oglethorpe ("the visionary Lycurgus of Georgia"), bearing date of the 16th of May. The following is a choice passage from the letter referred to:—

Some intelligence I had of a villanous design of a very extraordinary nature, and if true very important, viz., that the Spaniards had employed emissaries to burn all the magazines and considerable towns in the English North America, and thereby to prevent the subsisting of the great expedition and fleet in the West Indies; and for this purpose many priests were employed, who pretended to be physicians, dancing-masters, and other such kinds of occupations, and under that pretence to get admittance and confidence in families.[22]

[21] Horsemanden's Negro Plot, p. 286.
[22] Colonial Hist. of N.Y., vol. vi. p. 199.

The burden of his effort was the wickedness of Popery and the Roman-Catholic Church. The first witness called was the irrepressible Mary Burton. She began by rehearsing the old story of setting fire to the houses: but this time she varied it somewhat; it was not the fort that was to be burnt first, but Croker's, near a coffee-house, by the long bridge. She remembered the ring drawn with chalk, saw things in it that looked like rats (the good Horsemanden throws a flood of light upon this otherwise dark passage by telling his reader that it was the Negroes' black toes!); that she peeped in once and saw a black thing like a child, and Ury with a book in his hand, and at this moment she let a silver spoon drop, and Ury chased her, and would have caught her, had she not fallen into a bucket of water, and thus marvellously escaped! But the rule was to send this curious Mary to bed when any thing of an unusual nature was going on. Ury asked her some questions.

Prisoner.—You say you have seen me several times at Hughson's, what clothes did I usually wear?
Mary Burton.—I cannot tell what clothes you wore particularly.
Prisoner.—That is strange, and know me so well?

She then says several kinds, but particularly, or chiefly, a riding-coat, and often a brown coat, trimmed with black.

Prisoner.—I never wore such a coat. What time of the day did I used to come to Hughson's?
M. Burton.—You used chiefly to come in the night-time, and when I have been going to bed I have seen you undressing in Peggy's room, as if you were to lie there; but I cannot say that you did, for you were always gone before I was up in the morning.
Prisoner.—What room was I in when I called Mary, and you came up, as you said?
M. Burton.—In the great room, up stairs.
Prisoner.—What answer did the Negroes make, when I offered to forgive them their sins, as you said?
M. Burton.—I don't remember.[23]

William Kane, the soldier, took the stand. He was very bold to answer all of Ury's questions. He saw him baptize a child, could forgive sins, and wanted to convert him! Sarah Hughson was next called, but Ury objected to her because she had been convicted. The judge informed him that she had been pardoned, and was, therefore, competent as a witness. Judge Horsemanden was careful to produce newspaper scraps to prove

[23] Horsemanden's Negro Plot, pp. 292, 293.

that the court of France had endeavored to create and excite revolts and insurrections in the English colonies, and ended by telling a pathetic story about an Irish schoolmaster in Ulster County who drank the health of the king of Spain![24] This had great weight with the jury, no doubt. Poor Ury, convicted upon the evidence of three notorious liars, without counsel, was left to defend himself. He addressed the jury in an earnest and intelligent manner. He showed where the evidence clashed; that the charges were not in harmony with his previous character, the silence of Quack and others already executed. He showed that Mr. Campbell took possession of the house that Hughson had occupied, on the 1st of May; that at that time Hughson and his wife were in jail, and Sarah in the house; that Sarah abused Campbell, and that he reproved her for the foul language she used; and that this furnished her with an additional motive to accuse him; that he never knew Hughson or any of the family. Mr. John Croker testified that Ury never kept company with Negroes, nor did he receive them at Croker's house up to the 1st of May, for all the plotting was done before that date; that he was a quiet, pious preacher, and an excellent schoolmaster; that he taught Webb's child, and always declared himself a non-juring clergyman of the Church of England. But the fatal revelation of this friend of Ury's was, that Webb made him a desk; and the jury thought they saw in it an altar for a Catholic priest! That was enough. The attorney-general told the jury that the prisoner was a Romish priest, and then proceeded to prove the exceeding sinfulness of that Church. Acknowledging the paucity of the evidence intended to prove him a priest, the learned gentleman hastened to dilate upon all the dark deeds of Rome, and thereby poisoned the minds of the jury against the unfortunate Ury. He was found guilty, and on the 29th of August, 1741, was hanged, professing his innocence, and submitting cheerfully to a cruel and unjust death as a servant of the Lord.[25]

The trials of the Negroes had continued, but were somewhat overshadowed by that of the reputed Catholic priest. On the 18th of July seven Negroes were hanged, including a Negro doctor named Harry. On the 23d of July a number of white persons were fined for keeping disorderly houses,—entertaining Negroes; while nine Negroes were, the same day, released from jail on account of a lack of evidence! On the 15th of August a Spanish Negro was hanged. On the 31st of August, Corry (the dancing-master), Ryan, Kelly, and Coffin—all white persons—were dismissed because no one prosecuted; while the reader must have observed that the evidence against them was quite as strong as that offered against any of the persons executed, by the lying trio Burton, Kane, and Sarah. But Mr. Smith the historian gives the correct reason why these trials came to such a sudden end.

The whole summer was spent in the prosecutions; every new trial led to further accusations: a coincidence of slight circumstances, was magnified by the general terror into violent presumptions; tales collected without doors, mingling with the proofs given at the bar, poisoned the minds of the jurors; and the sanguinary spirit of the day suffered no check till Mary, the capital informer, bewildered by frequent examinations and suggestions, lost her first impressions, and began to touch characters, which malice itself did not dare to suspect.[26]

The 24th of September was solemnly set apart for public thanksgiving for the escape of the citizens from destruction!

As we have already said, this "Negro plot" has but one parallel in the history of civilization. It had its origin in a diseased public conscience, inflamed by religious bigotry, accelerated by hired liars, and consummated in the blind and bloody action of a court and jury who imagined themselves sitting over a powder-magazine. That a robbery took place, there was abundant evidence in the finding of some of the articles, and the admissions of Hughson and others; but there was not a syllable of competent evidence to show that there was an organized plot. And the time came, after the city had gotten back to its accustomed quietness, that the most sincere believers in the "Negro plot" were converted to the opinion that the zeal of the magistrates had not been "according to knowledge." For they could not have failed to remember that the Negroes were considered heathen, and, therefore, not sworn by the court; that they were not allowed counsel; that the evidence was indirect, contradictory, and malicious, while the trials were hasty and unfair. From the 11th of May to the 29th of August, one hundred and fifty-four

---

[24] Ibid., pp. 298, 299, note.
[25] Horsemanden's Negro Plot, pp. 221, 222.

[26] Smith's Hist. of N.Y., vol. ii. pp. 59, 60.

Negroes were cast into prison; fourteen of whom were burnt, eighteen hanged, seventy-one transported, and the remainder pardoned. During the same space of time twenty-four whites were committed to prison; four of whom were executed, and the remainder discharged. The number arrested was one hundred and seventy-eight, thirty-six executed, and seventy-one transported! What a terrible tragedy committed in the name of law and Christian government! Mary Burton, the Judas Iscariot of the period, received her hundred pounds as the price of the blood she had caused to be shed; and the curtain fell upon one of the most tragic events in all the history of New York or of the civilized world.[27]

The legislature turned its attention to additional legislation upon the slavery question. Severe laws were passed against the Negroes. Their personal rights were curtailed until their condition was but little removed from that of the brute creation. We have gone over the voluminous records of the Province of New York, and have not found a single act calculated to ameliorate the condition of the slave.[28] He was hated, mistrusted, and feared. Nothing was done, of a friendly character, for the slave in the Province of New York, until threatening dangers from without taught the colonists the importance of husbanding all their resources. The war between the British colonies in North America and the mother country gave the Negro an opportunity to level, by desperate valor, a mountain of prejudice, and wipe out with his blood the dark stain of 1741. History says he did it.

[27] "On the 6th of March, 1742, the following order was passed by the Common Council: 'Ordered, that the indentures of Mary Burton be delivered up to her, and that she be discharged from the remainder of her servitude, and three pounds paid her, to provide necessary clothing.' The Common Council had purchased her indentures from her master, and had kept her and them, until this time."—DUNLAP, vol. ii. Appendix, p. clxvii.

[28] On the 17th of November, 1767, a bill was brought into the House of Assembly "to prevent the unnatural and unwarrantable custom of enslaving mankind, and the importation of slaves into this province." It was changed into an act "for laying an impost on Negroes imported." This could not pass the governor and council; and it was afterward known that Benning I. Wentworth, the governor of New Hampshire, had received instructions not to pass any law "imposing duties on negroes imported into that province." Hutchinson of Massachusetts had similar instructions. The governor and his Majesty's council knew this at the time.

Autobiography

Booker T. Washington (1856–1915)

In 1902, W. E. B. Du Bois, then a professor at Atlanta University, wrote of Booker T. Washington:

Today he stands as the one recognized spokesman of his ten million fellows and one of the most notable figures in a nation of seventy millions.

Although the rest of "Of Mr. Booker T. Washington and Others" is less than complimentary to Washington, this statement describing the fame and achievement of the distinguished president and founder of Tuskegee Institute rings true. Actually, the miracle of Booker T. Washington is not that he rose from the powerlessness and ignorance of slavery to a position of unexampled power and prestige but that his rise to fame occurred during the "nadir" of Black achievements and aspirations. As Kelly Miller points out in an initially anonymous article on "Washington's Policy" published in the *Boston Transcript* in 1903, Washington's influence and prestige spiraled upward while the rest of Black America saw every political advance and civil liberty extinguished by an angry and vindictive South. Kelly Miller describes the "Washington Years" as follows:

. . . the last vestige of political power has been swept away. Civil privileges have been restricted; educational opportunities . . . have been curtailed; the industrial situation . . . has become ominous and uncertain, while the feeling between the races is constantly growing more acute and threatening.

In attempting to probe the causes for the enormous success of Washington, who was born of a white slaveholding father and a Black slave mother in Franklin County, Virginia, one courts the danger of sliding into dangerous but oft-repeated half-truths. One half-truth is that Washington was a skilled accommodationist who sold his soul and his race to the white power structure for reasons of personal gain and privilege. Another half-truth is that he scorned the need for Black political rights and civil liberties and emphasized, instead, the need for strategies to promote Black economic adaptation along lines acceptable to the white power structure. A third half-truth is that Washington was unyielding in his opposition to higher education for Black people and fought against the development and improvement of colleges and universities such as Howard, Fisk, Morehouse, and Atlanta.

Enough historical and biographical information has been gathered to show that these statements present only partial pictures of Booker T. Washington. In the first place, one must understand, as an essential background fact, that Washington was preeminently a man of his times—a man not only having a rare sense of historical timing but one who, in the words of Du Bois, enjoyed "a thorough oneness with his age." And Washington's age was, as Kelly Miller asserted, not an age of "moral giants" but an age of "commercial princes." Living in a period of unprecedented economic and industrial expansion, Washington sought by every device, covert and overt, to involve the recently freed Black man in America's economic expansion. In attempting to achieve this objective, he became very much the pragmatic realist, fully aware that accommodations and adaptations would have to be made to counter the overt hostility of the nation's white majority. He also knew, as a pragmatic realist, that the South was the region in which the Black man would have to initiate his involvement in American business and economic growth. Here in the South were the Black man's roots, his power of numbers. But Washington's pragmatic realism also told him that the South—where there had been 2500 Black people lynched between 1885 and 1900 and an enormous number of invidious decrees and ordinances passed that militated against the welfare and well-being of Blacks—was the most unlikely region in which the Black man's economic rehabilitation and development could occur. Certainly, to gain the kind of economic foothold he envisioned called for great daring and consummate skill. As Du Bois indicated, however, Washington knew the "heart of the South from birth and training." He knew that it was a tormented, guilt-ridden land. And he knew, long before Faulkner emerged to write about it, that the South had a penchant for sadistic violence and masochistic bloodletting—that there could be sudden, freakish storms of violence to drench the magnolias with Black men's blood. Washington also knew the South's love of form and ritual; he knew the white prerogatives it honored and the Black sanctions it demanded; and he was aware of the ambivalence of the love–hate relationship between Black and white and the delicately wrought system of racial etiquette designed to keep it in balance. Knowing all this, Washington still maintained as his basic objective the movement of the Black peasant out of his windowless, weather-beaten cabin and onto the road of economic involvement. For this period and region, Washington faced a most formidable task, and it is now clear that his success was minimal.

However, the disparaging half-truths about Booker T. Washington have lingered, not because his success was minimal, but because the white power structure, North and South, rewarded him with power and prestige for his unfailing good will and racial congeniality. It seemed as though he received the white world's acclaim because what he attempted to do did not disturb the status quo; he provided minimal Black achievement within traditional political and economic structures. By 1910 it was evident that Washington had been granted more power than any Black man has ever enjoyed before or since. No presidential or governmental appointments involving Black people during the Roosevelt and Taft administrations were made without his approval. Professor Robert Brisbane in *The Black Vanguard* not only provides evidence in support of Washington's strong political influence but asserts that he exerted considerable control over Black public opinion through the *New York Age* and the *Washington Bee,* two Black newspapers in which the "Tuskegee Machine" held a controlling interest. In fact, Brisbane asserts, the "Tuskegee Machine" monitored every racial movement from William Monroe Trotter's plans for radical activism to the plans for the annual Niagara Conferences sponsored by Du Bois and his associates.

And yet no one can doubt the zeal and sincerity of the man who walked and hitchhiked over five hundred miles—from Malden on the Kanawha River in West Virginia—to enroll as a student at Hampton Institute on the Virginia tidewater, nor can one underestimate the overwhelming odds facing him in a volatile, hostile South. In many respects, his argument for the value of vocational education as a steppingstone to some form of Black economic power was sound, provided, of course, that there were some sound assurances that American Labor would open its union ranks to Black artisans and tradesmen. His endless preaching about Black self-help and self-discipline was also good advice, provided, of course, that the white power structure would help in the psychological rehabilitation of the Black man.

We now know that American Labor never did voluntarily open its ranks to Black artisans and that twentieth-century white America, through all of its communication media, strove to give the Black man an extremely uncomplimentary self-image. When one speculates on why a man of Washington's foresight and power could not have read the racial signs and portents with a little more accuracy, the answer could be that American optimism blinded him to the realities of the situation. Or it could be that he did not read enough of the Black man's past in America—of Remond, Garnet, Wells Brown, or Delany. These men all could have told him about their bitter disappointments in America's poorly kept promises. Or he might have broadened his intellectual range and vision by reading the literature of revolution—the writings of Marx and others who held that political revolution was the *sine qua non* for economic change. There is evidence that Washington even misread the Black Reconstruction, construing it to be an era of tragic error rather than a time of Black achievement. On one occasion he said:

> *No influence could ever make me desire to go back to the conditions of Reconstruction days to secure the ballot for the Negro. That was an order of things that was bad for the Negro and bad for the white man.*

So, throughout all of his days Booker T. Washington scorned the value of Black officeholding and never openly fought for a restoration of the ballot. There is now some evidence to indicate that he did give substantial but surreptitious financial support to the Black man's fight for the franchise in Louisiana, Georgia, and Alabama. His efforts bore no fruit, however, for no leader can lead a people to power without first eradicating the conditions that render them powerless. All of the great engineers of social change have acted on this basic premise. But Washington chose to be politic rather than political.

Nor was he agonized by what Du Bois called the Black man's sense of double consciousness—that sense of being both a Black man and an American. Unlike Crummell, Garnet, Delany, and Trotter, who were tortured by having "two souls, two thoughts . . . two warring ideals in one dark body," Booker T. Washington was singularly free of inner conflicts about his dedication to America with its worship of property and material substance. This may have been one of the causes for the deep rift that developed between him and radical Northern university intellectuals such as Forbes of Amherst and Trotter of Harvard. They never developed the unassailable faith in the American way that he did.

However controversial his methods and objectives, few can doubt that Washington worked hard to achieve them. Certainly, the high point in his career was his famous speech at the Atlanta Cotton States and International Exposition in 1895 in which he accepted social and legal segregation but promised racial friendship and cooperation. This singular event launched him on a heavy speaking schedule that took him to every major city in the nation. In addition to this and his continuing responsibilities as president and founder of Tuskegee Institute, he also found time to write and publish twelve books. Most important of these are his strong autobiography, *Up From Slavery* (1901), and his *The Future of the American Negro* (1899), which, according to some critics, contains the clearest expression of Washington's philosophy. It is in this book that he first mentions the "impatient extremists" among Northern Negroes whose "ill-considered, incendiary utterances . . . tend to add to the burdens of our people in the South rather than relieve them." He also wrote a *Life of Frederick Douglass* (1907), picturing him as a successful and militant accommodationist to the American way of life.

Recently, there has been a revival of critical interest in the life and philosophy of Booker T. Washington. August Meier has written a very interesting monograph designed to provide a new perspective on Washington in "Toward a Reinterpretation of Booker T. Washington," *Journal of Southern History,* XXIII (May 1957), 220–227, and he has also provided a historical review of Washington's period in his *Negro Thought in America—1880–1915: Racial Ideologies in the Age of Booker T. Washington* (1963). Also of interest are Hugh Hawkins' edition of *Booker T. Washington and His Critics* (1962) and Samuel Spencer's *Booker T. Washington and the Negro's Place in American Life* (1955). Finally, Robert Brisbane's *The Black Vanguard* (1970) gives a spirited account of the workings of the "Tuskegee Machine" and the series of vehement confrontations between Trotter and Washington. The University of Illinois Press will publish fifteen volumes of *The Booker T. Washington Papers,* edited by Louis R. Harlan, who is also preparing a biography of Washington.

from *Up from Slavery*

Chapter 7: Early Days at Tuskegee

During the time that I had charge of the Indians and the night-school at Hampton, I pursued some studies myself, under the direction of the instructors there. One of these instructors was the Rev. Dr. H. B. Frissell, the present Principal of the Hampton Institute, General Armstrong's successor.

In May, 1881, near the close of my first year in teaching the night-school, in a way that I had not dared expect, the opportunity opened for me to begin my life-work. One night in the chapel, after the usual chapel exercises were over, General Armstrong referred to the fact that he had received a letter from some gentlemen in Alabama asking him to recommend some one to take charge of what was to be a normal school for the coloured people in the little town of Tuskegee in that state. These gentlemen seemed to take it for granted that no coloured man suitable for the position could be secured, and they were expecting the General to recommend a white man for the place. The next day General Armstrong sent for me to come to his office, and, much to my surprise, asked me if I thought I could fill the position in Alabama. I told him that I would be willing to try. Accordingly, he wrote to the people who had applied to him for the information, that he did not know of any white man to suggest, but if they would be willing to take a coloured man, he had one whom he could recommend. In this letter he gave them my name.

Several days passed before anything more was heard about the matter. Some time afterward, one Sunday evening during the chapel exercises, a messenger came in and handed the General a telegram. At the end of the exercises he read the telegram to the school. In substance, these were its words: "Booker T. Washington will suit us. Send him at once."

There was a great deal of joy expressed among the students and teachers, and I received very hearty congratulations. I began to get ready at once to go to Tuskegee. I went by way of my old home in West Virginia, where I remained for several days, after which I proceeded to Tuskegee. I found Tuskegee to be a town of about two thousand inhabitants, nearly one-half of whom were coloured. It was in what was known as the Black Belt of the South. In the county in which Tuskegee is situated the coloured people outnumbered the whites by about three to one. In some of the adjoining and near-by counties the proportion was not far from six coloured persons to one white.

I have often been asked to define the term "Black Belt." So far as I can learn, the term was first used to designate a part of the country which was distinguished by the colour of the soil. The part of the country possessing this thick, dark, and naturally rich soil was, of course, the part of the South where the slaves were most profitable, and consequently they were taken there in the largest numbers. Later and especially since the war, the term seems to be used wholly in a political sense—that is, to designate the counties where the black people outnumbered the white.

Before going to Tuskegee I had expected to find there a building and all the necessary apparatus ready for me to begin teaching. To my disappointment, I found nothing of the kind. I did find, though, that which no costly building and apparatus can supply—hundreds of hungry, earnest souls who wanted to secure knowledge.

Tuskegee seemed an ideal place for the school. It was in the midst of the great bulk of the Negro population, and was rather secluded, being five miles from the main line of railroad, with which it was connected by a short line. During the days of slavery, and since, the town had been a centre for the education of the white people. This was an added advantage, for the reason that I found the white people possessing a degree of culture and education that is not surpassed by many localities. While the coloured people were ignorant, they had not, as a rule degraded and weakened their bodies by vices such as are common to the lower class of people in the large cities. In general, I found the relations between the two races pleasant. For example, the largest, and I think at that time the only hardware store in the town was owned and operated jointly by a coloured man and a white man. This copartnership continued until the death of the white partner.

I found that about a year previous to my going to Tuskegee some of the coloured people who had heard something of the work of education being done at Hampton had applied to the state Legislature, through their representatives, for a small appropriation to be used in starting a normal school in Tuskegee. This request the Legislature had complied with to the extent of granting an annual appropriation of two thousand dollars. I soon learned, however, that this money could be used only for the payment of the salaries of the instructors, and that there was no provisions for securing land, buildings, or apparatus. The task before me did not seem a very encouraging one. It seemed much like making bricks without straw. The coloured people were overjoyed, and were constantly offering their services in any way in which they could be of assistance in getting the school started.

My first task was to find a place in which to open the school. After looking the town over with some care, the most suitable place that could be secured seemed to be a rather dilapidated shanty near the coloured Methodist church, together with the church itself as a sort of assembly-room. Both the church and the shanty were in about as bad condition as was possible. I recall that during the first months of school that I taught in this building it was in such poor repair that, whenever it rained, one of the older students would very kindly leave his lessons to hold an umbrella over me while I heard the recitations of the others. I remember, also, that on more than one occasion my landlady held an umbrella over me while I ate breakfast.

At the time I went to Alabama the coloured people were taking considerable interest in politics, and they were very anxious that I should become one of them politically, in every respect. They seemed to have a little distrust of strangers in this regard. I recall that one man, who seemed to have been designated by the others to look after my political destiny, came to me on several

occasions and said, with a good deal of earnestness: "We wants you to be sure to vote jes' like we votes. We can't read de newspapers very much, but we knows how to vote, an' we wants you to vote jes' like we votes." He added: "We watches de white man, and we keeps watching de white man till we finds out which way de white man's gwine to vote; an' when we finds out which way de white man's gwine to vote, den we votes 'xactly de other way. Den we know we's right."

I am glad to add, however, that at the present time the disposition to vote against the white man merely because he is white is largely disappearing, and the race is learning to vote from principle, for what the voter considers to be for the best interests of both races.

I reached Tuskegee, as I have said, early in June, 1881. The first month I spent in finding accommodations for the school, and in travelling through Alabama, examining into the actual life of the people, especially in the country districts, and in getting the school advertised among the class of people that I wanted to have attend it. The most of my travelling was done over the country roads, with a mule and a cart or a mule and a buggy wagon for conveyance. I ate and slept with the people, in their little cabins. I saw their farms, their schools, their churches. Since, in the case of the most of these visits, there had been no notice given in advance that a stranger was expected, I had the advantage of seeing the real, everyday life of the people.

In the plantation districts I found that, as a rule the whole family slept in one room, and that in addition to the immediate family there sometimes were relatives, or others not related to the family, who slept in the same room. On more than one occasion I went outside the house to get ready for bed, or to wait until the family had gone to bed. They usually contrived some kind of a place for me to sleep, either on the floor or in a special part of another's bed. Rarely was there any place provided in the cabin where one could bathe even the face and hands, but usually some provision was made for this outside the house, in the yard.

The common diet of the people was fat pork and corn bread. At times I have eaten in cabins where they had only corn bread and "black-eye peas" cooked in plain water. The people seemed to have no other idea than to live on this fat meat and corn bread,—the meat, and the meal of which the bread was made, having been bought at a high price at a store in town, notwithstanding the fact that the land all about the cabin homes could easily have been made to produce nearly every kind of garden vegetable that is raised anywhere in the country. Their one object seemed to be to plant nothing but cotton; and in many cases cotton was planted up to the very door of the cabin.

In these cabin homes I often found sewing-machines which had been bought, or were being bought, on instalments, frequently at a cost of as much as sixty dollars, or showy clocks for which the occupants of the cabins had paid twelve or fourteen dollars. I remember that on one occasion when I went into one of these cabins for dinner, when I sat down to the table for a meal with the four members of the family, I noticed that, while there were five of us at the table, there was but one fork for the five of us to use. Naturally there was an awkward pause on my part. In the opposite corner of that same cabin was an organ for which the people told me they were paying sixty dollars in monthly instalments. One fork, and a sixty-dollar organ!

In most cases the sewing-machine was not used, the clocks were so worthless that they did not keep correct time—and if they had, in nine cases out of ten there would have been no one in the family who could have told the time of day—while the organ, of course, was rarely used for want of a person who could play upon it.

In the case to which I have referred, where the family sat down to the table for the meal at which I was their guest, I could see plainly that this was an awkward and unusual proceeding, and was done in my honour. In most cases, when the family got up in the morning, for example, the wife would put a piece of meat in a frying-pan and put a lump of dough in a "skillet," as they called it. These utensils would be placed on the fire, and in ten or fifteen minutes breakfast would be ready. Frequently the husband would take his bread and meat in his hand and start for the field, eating as he walked. The mother would sit down in a corner and eat her breakfast, perhaps from a plate and perhaps directly from the "skillet" or frying-pan, while the children would eat their portion of the bread and meat while running about the yard. At certain seasons of the year, when meat was scarce, it was rarely that the children who were not old enough or strong enough to work in the fields would have the luxury of meat.

The breakfast over, and with practically no attention given to the house, the whole family would, as a general thing, proceed to the cotton-field. Every child that was large enough to carry a hoe was put to work, and the baby—for usually there was at least one baby—would be laid down at the end of the cotton row, so that its mother could give it a certain amount of attention when she had finished chopping her row. The noon meal and the supper were taken in much the same way as the breakfast.

All the days of the family would be spent after much this same routine, except Saturday and Sunday. On Saturday the whole family would spend at least half a day, and often a whole day, in town. The idea in going to town was, I suppose, to do shopping, but all the shopping that the whole family had money for could have been attended to in ten minutes by one person. Still, the whole family remained in town for most of the day, spending the greater part of the time in standing on the streets, the women, too often, sitting about somewhere smoking or dipping snuff. Sunday was usually spent in going to some big meeting. With few exceptions, I found that the crops were mortgaged in the counties where I went, and that the most of the coloured farmers were in debt. The state had not been able to build schoolhouses in the country districts, and, as a rule, the schools were taught in churches or in log cabins. More than once, while on my journeys, I found that there was no provision made in the house used for school purposes for heating the building during the winter, and consequently a fire had to be built in the yard, and teacher and pupils passed in and out of the house as they got cold or warm. With few exceptions, I found the teachers in these country schools to be miserably poor in preparation for their work, and poor in moral character. The schools were in session from three to five months. There was practically no apparatus in the schoolhouses, except that occasionally there was a rough blackboard. I recall that one day I went into a schoolhouse—or rather into an abandoned log cabin that was being used as a schoolhouse—and found five pupils who were studying a lesson from one book. Two of these, on the front seat, were using the book between them; behind these were two others peeping over the shoulders of the first two, and behind the four was a fifth little fellow who was peeping over the shoulders of all four.

What I have said concerning the character of

the schoolhouses and teachers will also apply quite accurately as a description of the church buildings and the ministers.

I met some very interesting characters during my travels. As illustrating the peculiar mental processes of the country people, I remember that I asked one coloured man, who was about sixty years old, to tell me something of his history. He said he had been born in Virginia, and sold into Alabama in 1845. I asked him how many were sold at the same time. He said, "There were five of us; myself and brother and three mules."

In giving all these descriptions of what I saw during my month of travel in the country around Tuskegee, I wish my readers to keep in mind the fact that there were many encouraging exceptions to the conditions which I have described. I have stated in such plain words what I saw, mainly for the reason that later I want to emphasize the encouraging changes that have taken place in the communities, not wholly by the work of the Tuskegee school but by that of other institutions as well.

Chapter 8: Teaching School in a Stable and a Hen-House

I confess that what I saw during my month of travel and investigation left me with a very heavy heart. The work to be done in order to lift these people up seemed almost beyond accomplishing. I was only one person, and it seemed to me that the little effort which I could put forth could go such a short distance toward bringing about results. I wondered if I could accomplish anything, and if it were worth while for me to try.

Of one thing I felt more strongly convinced than ever, after spending this month in seeing the actual life of the coloured people, and that was that, in order to lift them up, something must be done more than merely to imitate New England education as it then existed. I saw more clearly than ever the wisdom of the system which General Armstrong had inaugurated at Hampton. To take the children of such people as I had been among for a month, and each day give them a few hours of mere book education, I felt would be almost a waste of time.

After consultation with the citizens of Tuskegee, I set July 4, 1881, as the day for the opening of the school in the little shanty and church which had been secured for its accommodation. The white

people, as well as the coloured, were greatly interested in the starting of the new school, and the opening day was looked forward to with much earnest discussion. There were not a few white people in the vicinity of Tuskegee who looked with some disfavour upon the project. They questioned its value to the coloured people, and had a fear that it might result in bringing about trouble between the races. Some had the feeling that in proportion as the Negro received education, in the same proportion would his value decrease as an economic factor in the state. These people feared the result of education would be that the Negroes would leave the farms, and that it would be difficult to secure them for domestic service.

The white people who questioned the wisdom of starting this new school had in their minds pictures of what was called an educated Negro, with a high hat, imitation gold eye-glasses, a showy walking-stick, kid gloves, fancy boots, and what not—in a word, a man who was determined to live by his wits. It was difficult for these people to see how education would produce any other kind of a coloured man.

In the midst of all the difficulties which I encountered in getting the little school started, and since then through a period of nineteen years, there are two men among all the many friends of the school in Tuskegee upon whom I have depended constantly for advice and guidance; and the success of the undertaking is largely due to these men, from whom I have never sought anything in vain. I mention them simply as types. One is a white man and an ex-slaveholder, Mr. George W. Campbell; the other is a black man and an ex-slave, Mr. Lewis Adams. These were the men who wrote to General Armstrong for a teacher.

Mr. Campbell is a merchant and banker, and had had little experience in dealing with matters pertaining to education. Mr. Adams was a mechanic, and had learned the trades of shoe-making, harness-making, and tinsmithing during the days of slavery. He had never been to school a day in his life, but in some way he had learned to read and write while a slave. From the first, these two men saw clearly what my plan of education was, sympathized with me, and supported me in every effort. In the days which were darkest financially for the school, Mr. Campbell was never appealed to when he was not willing to extend all the aid in his power. I do not know two men, one an ex-slaveholder, one an ex-slave, whose advice and judgment I would feel more like following in everything which concerns the life and development of the school at Tuskegee than those of these two men.

I have always felt that Mr. Adams, in a large degree, derived his unusual power of mind from the training given his hands in the process of mastering well three trades during the days of slavery. If one goes to-day into any Southern town, and asks for the leading and most reliable coloured man in the community, I believe that in five cases out of ten he will be directed to a Negro who learned a trade during the days of slavery.

On the morning that the school opened, thirty students reported for admission. I was the only teacher. The students were about equally divided between the sexes. Most of them lived in Macon County, the county in which Tuskegee is situated and of which it is the county-seat. A great many more students wanted to enter the school, but it had been decided to receive only those who were above fifteen years of age, and who had previously received some education. The greater part of the thirty were public-school teachers, and some of them were nearly forty years of age. With the teachers came some of their former pupils, and when they were examined it was amusing to note that in several cases the pupil entered a higher class than did his former teacher. It was also interesting to note how many big books some of them had studied, and how many high-sounding subjects some of them claimed to have mastered. The bigger the book and the longer the name of the subject, the prouder they felt of their accomplishment. Some had studied Latin, and one or two Greek. This they thought entitled them to special distinction.

In fact, one of the saddest things I saw during the month of travel which I have described was a young man, who had attended some high school, sitting down in a one-room cabin, with grease on his clothing, filth all around him, and weeds in the yard and garden, engaged in studying French grammar.

The students who came first seemed to be fond of memorizing long and complicated "rules" in grammar and mathematics, but had little thought or knowledge of applying the rules to the everyday affairs of their life. One subject which they liked to talk about, and tell me that they had mastered, in arithmetic, was "banking and discount," but I soon found out that neither they nor almost any one in the neighborhood in which

they lived had ever had a bank account. In registering the names of the students, I found that almost every one of them had one or more middle initials. When I asked what the "J" stood for, in the name of John J. Jones, it was explained to me that this was a part of his "entitles." Most of the students wanted to get an education because they thought it would enable them to earn more money as school-teachers.

Notwithstanding what I had said about them in these respects, I have never seen a more earnest and willing company of young men and women than these students were. They were all willing to learn the right thing as soon as it was shown them what was right. I was determined to start them off on a solid and thorough foundation, so far as their books were concerned. I soon learned that most of them had the merest smattering of the high-sounding things that they had studied. While they could locate the Desert of Sahara or the capital of China on an artificial globe, I found out that the girls could not locate the proper places for the knives and forks on an actual dinner-table, or the places on which the bread and meat should be set.

I had to summon a good deal of courage to take a student who had been studying cube root and "banking and discount," and explain to him that the wisest thing for him to do first was thoroughly to master the multiplication table.

The number of pupils increased each week, until by the end of the first month there were nearly fifty. Many of them, however, said that, as they could remain only for two or three months, they wanted to enter a high class and get a diploma the first year if possible.

At the end of the first six weeks a new and rare face entered the school as co-teacher. This was Miss Olivia A. Davidson, who later became my wife. Miss Davidson was born in Ohio, and received her preparatory education in the public schools of that state. When little more than a girl, she heard of the need of teachers in the South. She went to the state of Mississippi and began teaching there. Later she taught in the city of Memphis. While teaching in Mississippi, one of her pupils became ill with smallpox. Every one in the community was so frightened that no one would nurse the boy. Miss Davidson closed her school and remained by the bedside of the boy night and day until he recovered. While she was at her Ohio home on her vacation, the worst epidemic of yellow fever broke out in Memphis, Tenn., that perhaps has ever occurred in the South. When she heard of this, she at once telegraphed the Mayor of Memphis, offering her services as a yellow-fever nurse, although she had never had the disease.

Miss Davidson's experience in the South showed her that the people needed something more than mere book-learning. She heard of the Hampton system of education, and decided that this was what she wanted in order to prepare herself for better work in the South. The attention of Mrs. Mary Hemenway, of Boston, was attracted to her rare ability. Through Mrs. Hemenway's kindness and generosity, Miss Davidson, after graduating at Hampton, received an opportunity to complete a two years' course of training at the Massachusetts State Normal School at Framingham.

Before she went to Framingham, some one suggested to Miss Davidson that, since she was so very light in colour, she might find it more comfortable not to be known as a coloured woman in this school in Massachusetts. She at once replied that under no circumstances and for no considerations would she consent to deceive any one in regard to her racial identity.

Soon after her graduation from the Framingham institution, Miss Davidson came to Tuskegee, bringing into the school many valuable and fresh ideas as to the best methods of teaching, as well as a rare moral character and a life of unselfishness that I think has seldom been equalled. No single individual did more toward laying the foundations of the Tuskegee Institute so as to insure the successful work that has been done there than Olivia A. Davidson.

Miss Davidson and I began consulting as to the future of the school from the first. The students were making progress in learning books and in developing their minds; but it became apparent at once that, if we were to make any permanent impression upon those who had come to us for training, we must do something besides teach them mere books. The students had come from homes where they had had no opportunities for lessons which would teach them how to care for their bodies. With few exceptions, the homes in Tuskegee in which the students boarded were but little improvement upon those from which they had come. We wanted to teach the students how to bathe; how to care for their teeth and clothing. We wanted to teach them what to eat,

and how to eat it properly, and how to care for their rooms. Aside from this, we wanted to give them such a practical knowledge of some one industry, together with the spirit of industry, thrift, and economy, that they would be sure of knowing how to make a living after they had left us. We wanted to teach them to study actual things instead of mere books alone.

We found that most of our students came from the country districts, where agriculture in some form or other was the main dependence of the people. We learned that about eighty-five percent of the coloured people in the Gulf states depended upon agriculture for their living. Since this was true, we wanted to be careful not to educate our students out of sympathy with agricultural life, so that they would be attracted from the country to the cities, and yield to the temptation of trying to live by their wits. We wanted to give them such an education as would fit a large proportion of them to be teachers, and at the same time cause them to return to the plantation districts and show the people there how to put new energy and new ideas into farming, as well as into the intellectual and moral and religious life of the people.

All these ideas and needs crowded themselves upon us with a seriousness that seemed well-nigh overwhelming. What were we to do? We had only the little old shanty and the abandoned church which the good coloured people of the town of Tuskegee had kindly loaned us for the accommodation of the classes. The number of students was increasing daily. The more we saw of them and the more we travelled through the country districts, the more we saw that our efforts were reaching, to only a partial degree, the actual needs of the people whom we wanted to lift up through the medium of the students whom we should educate and send out as leaders.

The more we talked with the students, who were then coming to us from several parts of the state, the more we found that the chief ambition among a large proportion of them was to get an education so that they would not have to work any longer with their hands.

This is illustrated by a story told of a coloured man in Alabama, who, one hot day in July, while he was at work in a cotton-field, suddenly stopped, and, looking toward the skies, said "O Lawd, de cotton am so grassy, de work am so hard, and the sun am so hot dat I b'lieve dis darky am called to preach!"

About three months after the opening of the school, and at the time when we were in the greatest anxiety about our work, there came into the market for sale an old and abandoned plantation which was situated about a mile from the town of Tuskegee. The mansion house—or "big house," as it would have been called—which had been occupied by the owners during slavery, had been burned. After making a careful examination of this place, it seemed to be just the location that we wanted in order to make our work effective and permanent.

But how were we to get it? The price asked for it was very little—only five hundred dollars—but we had no money, and we were strangers in the town and had no credit. The owner of the land agreed to let us occupy the place if we could make a payment of two hundred and fifty dollars down, with the understanding that the remaining two hundred and fifty dollars must be paid within a year. Although five hundred dollars was cheap for the land, it was a large sum when one did not have any part of it.

In the midst of the difficulty I summoned a great deal of courage and wrote to my friend General J. F. B. Marshall, the Treasurer of the Hampton Institute, putting the situation before him and beseeching him to lend me the two hundred and fifty dollars on my own personal responsibility. Within a few days a reply came to the effect that he had no authority to lend me money belonging to the Hampton Institute, but that he would gladly lend me the amount needed from his own personal funds.

I confess that the securing of this money in this way was a great surprise to me, as well as a source of gratification. Up to that time I never had had in my possession so much money as one hundred dollars at a time, and the loan which I had asked General Marshall for seemed a tremendously large sum to me. The fact of my being responsible for the repaying of such a large amount of money weighed very heavily upon me.

I lost no time in getting ready to move the school on to the new farm. At the time we occupied the place there were standing upon it a cabin, formerly used as the dining room, an old kitchen, a stable, and an old hen-house. Within a few weeks we had all these structures in use. The stable was repaired and used as a recitation-room and very presently the hen-house was utilized for the same purpose.

I recall that one morning, when I told an old coloured man who lived near, and who sometimes helped me, that our school had grown so large that it would be necessary for us to use the hen-house for school purposes, and that I wanted him to help me give it a thorough cleaning out the next day, he replied, in the most earnest manner: "What you mean, boss? You sholy ain't gwine clean out de hen-house in de *day*-time?"

Nearly all the work of getting the new location ready for school purposes was done by the students after school was over in the afternoon. As soon as we got the cabins in condition to be used, I determined to clear up some land so that we could plant a crop. When I explained my plan to the young men, I noticed that they did not seem to take to it very kindly. It was hard for them to see the connection between clearing land and an education. Besides, many of them had been school-teachers, and they questioned whether or not clearing land would be in keeping with their dignity. In order to relieve them from any embarrassment, each afternoon after school I took my axe and led the way to the woods. When they saw that I was not afraid or ashamed to work, they began to assist with more enthusiasm. We kept at the work each afternoon until we had cleared about twenty acres and had planted a crop.

In the meantime Miss Davidson was devising plans to repay the loan. Her first effort was made by holding festivals, or "suppers." She made a personal canvass among the white and coloured families in the town of Tuskegee, and got them to agree to give something, like a cake, a chicken, bread, or pies, that could be sold at the festival. Of course the coloured people were glad to give anything that they could spare, but I want to add that Miss Davidson did not apply to a single white family, so far as I now remember, that failed to donate something; and in many ways the white families showed their interest in the school.

Several of these festivals were held, and quite a little sum of money was raised. A canvass was also made among the people of both races for direct gifts of money, and most of those applied to gave small sums. It was often pathetic to note the gifts of the older coloured people, most of whom had spent their best days in slavery. Sometimes they would give five cents, sometimes twenty-five cents. Sometimes the contribution was a quilt, or a quantity of sugarcane. I recall one old coloured woman, who was about seventy years of age, who came to see me when we were raising money to pay for the farm. She hobbled into the room where I was, leaning on a cane. She was clad in rags; but they were clean. She said: "Mr. Washin'ton, God knows I spent de bes' days of my life in slavery. God knows I's ignorant an' poor; but," she added, "I knows what you an' Miss Davidson is tryin' to do. I knows you is tryin' to make better men an' better women for de coloured race. I ain't got no money, but I wants you to take dese six eggs, what I's been savin' up, an' I wants you to put dese six eggs into de eddication of dese boys an' gals."

Since the work at Tuskegee started, it has been my privilege to receive many gifts for the benefit of the institution, but never any, I think, that touched me so deeply as this one.

. . .

Chapter 13: Two Thousand Miles for a Five-Minute Speech

Soon after the opening of our boarding department, quite a number of students who evidently were worthy, but who were so poor that they did not have any money to pay even the small charges at the school, began applying for admission. This class was composed of both men and women. It was a great trial to refuse admission to these applicants, and in 1884 we established a night-school to accommodate a few of them.

The night-school was organized on a plan similar to the one which I had helped to establish at Hampton. At first it was composed of about a dozen students. They were admitted to the night-school only when they had no money with which to pay any part of their board in the regular day-school. It was further required that they must work for ten hours during the day at some trade or industry, and study academic branches for two hours during the evening. This was the requirement for the first one or two years of their stay. They were to be paid something above the cost of their board, with the understanding that all of their earnings, except a very small part, were to be reserved in the school's treasury, to be used for paying their board in the regular day-school after they had entered that department. The night-school, started in this manner, has grown until there are at present four hundred and fifty-seven students enrolled in it alone.

There could hardly be a more severe test of a student's worth than this branch of the Institute's work. It is largely because it furnishes such a good opportunity to test the backbone of a student that I place such high value upon our night-school. Any one who is willing to work ten hours a day at the brick-yard, or in the laundry, through one or two years, in order that he or she may have the privilege of studying academic branches for two hours in the evening, has enough bottom to warrant being further educated.

After the student has left the night-school he enters the day-school, where he takes academic branches four days in a week, and works at his trade two days. Besides this he usually works at his trade during the three summer months. As a rule, after a student has succeeded in going through the night-school test, he finds a way to finish the regular course in industrial and academic training. No student, no matter how much money he may be able to command, is permitted to go through school without doing manual labour. In fact, the industrial work is now as popular as the academic branches. Some of the most successful men and women who have graduated from the institution obtained their start in the night-school.

While a great deal of stress is laid upon the industrial side of the work at Tuskegee, we do not neglect or overlook in any degree the religious and spiritual side. The school is strictly undenominational, but it is thoroughly Christian, and the spiritual training of the students is not neglected. Our preaching service, prayer-meetings, Sunday-school, Christian Endeavour Society, Young Men's Christian Association, and various missionary organizations, testify to this.

In 1885, Miss Olivia Davidson, to whom I have already referred as being largely responsible for the success of the school during its early history, and I were married. During our married life she continued to divide her time and strength between our home and the work for the school. She not only continued to work in the school at Tuskegee, but also kept up her habit of going North to secure funds. In 1889 she died, after four years of happy married life and eight years of hard and happy work for the school. She literally wore herself out in her never ceasing efforts in behalf of the work that she so dearly loved. During our married life there were born to us two bright, beautiful boys, Booker Taliaferro and Ernest Davidson. The older of these, Booker, has already mastered the brick-maker's trade at Tuskegee.

I have often been asked how I began the practice of public speaking. In answer I would say that I never planned to give any large part of my life to speaking in public. I have always had more of an ambition to *do* things than merely to talk *about* doing them. It seems that when I went North with General Armstrong to speak at the series of public meetings to which I have referred, the President of the National Educational Association, the Hon. Thomas W. Bicknell, was present at one of those meetings and heard me speak. A few days afterward he sent me an invitation to deliver an address at the next meeting of the Educational Association. This meeting was to be held in Madison, Wis. I accepted the invitation. This was, in a sense, the beginning of my public-speaking career.

On the evening that I spoke before the Association there must have been not far from four thousand persons present. Without my knowing it, there were a large number of people present from Alabama, and some from the town of Tuskegee. These white people afterward frankly told me that they went to this meeting expecting to hear the South roundly abused, but were pleasantly surprised to find that there was no word of abuse in my address. On the contrary, the South was given credit for all the praiseworthy things that it had done. A white lady who was teacher in a college in Tuskegee wrote back to the local paper that she was gratified, as well as surprised, to note the credit which I gave the white people of Tuskegee for their help in getting the school started. This address at Madison was the first that I had delivered that in any large measure dealt with the general problem of the races. Those who heard it seemed to be pleased with what I said and with the general position that I took.

When I first came to Tuskegee, I determined that I would make it my home, that I would take as much pride in the right actions of the people of the town as any white man could do, and that I would, at the same time, deplore the wrongdoing of the people as much as any white man. I determined never to say anything in a public address in the North that I would not be willing to say in the South. I early learned that it is a hard matter to convert an individual by abusing him, and that this is more often accomplished by giving credit for all the praiseworthy actions performed than by calling attention alone to all the evil done.

While pursuing this policy I have not failed, at the proper time and in the proper manner, to call attention, in no uncertain terms, to the wrongs which any part of the South has been guilty of. I have found that there is a large element in the South that is quick to respond to straightforward, honest criticism of any wrong policy. As a rule, the place to criticise the South, when criticism is necessary, is in the South—not in Boston. A Boston man who came to Alabama to criticise Boston would not effect so much good, I think, as one who had his word of criticism to say in Boston.

In this address at Madison I took the ground that the policy to be pursued with reference to the races was, by every honourable means, to bring them together and to encourage the cultivation of friendly relations, instead of doing that which would embitter. I further contended that, in relation to his vote, the Negro should more and more consider the interests of the community in which he lived, rather than seek alone to please some one who lived a thousand miles away from him and from his interests.

In this address I said that the whole future of the Negro rested largely upon the question as to whether or not he should make himself, through his skill, intelligence, and character, of such undeniable value to the community in which he lived that the community could not dispense with his presence. I said that any individual who learned to do something better than anybody else—learned to do a common thing in an uncommon manner—had solved his problem, regardless of the colour of his skin, and that in proportion as the Negro learned to produce what other people wanted and must have, in the same proportion would he be respected.

I spoke of an instance where one of our graduates had produced two hundred and sixty-six bushels of sweet potatoes from an acre of ground, in a community where the average production had been only forty-nine bushels to the acre. He had been able to do this by reason of his knowledge of the chemistry of the soil and by his knowledge of improved methods of agriculture. The white farmers in the neighbourhood respected him, and came to him for ideas regarding the raising of sweet potatoes. These white farmers honoured and respected him because he, by his skill and knowledge, had added something to the wealth and comfort of the community in which he lived. I explained that my theory of education for the Negro would not, for example, confine him for all time to farm life—to the production of the best and the most sweet potatoes—but that, if he succeeded in this line of industry, he could lay the foundations upon which his children and grandchildren could grow to higher and more important things in life.

Such, in brief, were some of the views I advocated in this first address dealing with the broad question of the relations of the two races, and since that time I have not found any reason for changing my views on any important point.

In my early life I used to cherish a feeling of ill will toward any one who spoke in bitter terms against the Negro, or who advocated measures that tended to oppress the black man or take from him opportunities for growth in the most complete manner. Now, whenever I hear any one advocating measures that are meant to curtail the development of another. I pity the individual who would do this. I know that the one who makes this mistake does so because of his lack of opportunity for the highest kind of growth. I pity him because I know that he is trying to stop the progress of the world, and because I know that in time the development and the ceaseless advance of humanity will make him ashamed of his weak and narrow position. One might as well try to stop the progress of a mighty railroad train by throwing his body across the track, as to try to stop the growth of the world in the direction of giving mankind more intelligence, more culture, more skill, more liberty, and in the direction of extending more sympathy and more brotherly kindness.

The address which I delivered at Madison, before the National Educational Association, gave me a rather wide introduction in the North and soon after that opportunities began offering themselves for me to address audiences there.

I was anxious, however, that the way might also be opened for me to speak directly to a representative Southern white audience. A partial opportunity of this kind, one that seemed to me might serve as an entering wedge, presented itself in 1893, when the international meeting of Christian Workers was held at Atlanta, Ga. When this invitation came to me, I had engagements in Boston that seemed to make it impossible for me to speak in Atlanta. Still, after looking over my list of dates and places carefully, I found that I could take a train from Boston that would get me into Atlanta about thirty minutes before my address was to be delivered, and that I could remain in that city about sixty minutes before taking another train for Boston. My invitation to speak in Atlanta stipulated that I was to confine my address to five minutes. The question, then, was whether or not I could put enough into a five-minute address to make it worth while for me to make such a trip.

I knew that the audience would be largely composed of the most influential class of white men and women, and that it would be a rare opportunity for me to let them know what we were trying to do at Tuskegee, as well as to speak to them about the relations of the races. So I decided to make the trip. I spoke for five minutes to an audience of two thousand people, composed mostly of Southern and Northern whites. What I said seemed to be received with favour and enthusiasm. The Atlanta papers of the next day commented in friendly terms on my address, and a good deal was said about it in different parts of the country. I felt that I had in some degree accomplished my object—that of getting a hearing from the dominant class of the South.

The demands made upon me for public addresses continued to increase, coming in about equal numbers from my own people and from Northern whites. I gave as much time to these addresses as I could spare from the immediate work at Tuskegee. Most of the addresses in the North were made for the direct purpose of getting funds with which to support the school. Those delivered before the coloured people had for their main object the impressing upon them of the importance of industrial and technical education in addition to academic and religious training.

I now come to that one of the incidents in my life which seems to have excited the greatest amount of interest, and which perhaps went farther than anything else in giving me a reputation that in a sense might be called National. I refer to the address which I delivered at the opening of the Atlanta Cotton states and International Exposition, at Atlanta, Ga., September 18, 1895.

So much has been said and written about this incident, and so many question have been asked me concerning the address, that perhaps I may be excused for taking up the matter with some detail. The five-minute address in Atlanta, which I came from Boston to deliver, was possibly the prime cause for an opportunity being given me to make the second address there. In the spring of 1895 I received a telegram from prominent citizens in Atlanta asking me to accompany a committee from that city to Washington for the purpose of appearing before a committee of Congress in the interest of securing Government help for the Exposition. The committee was composed of about twenty-five of the most prominent and most influential white men of Georgia. All the members of this committee were white men except Bishop Grant, Bishop Gaines, and myself. The mayor and several other city and state officials spoke before the committee. They were followed by the two coloured bishops. My name was the last on the list of speakers. I had never before appeared before such a committee, nor had I ever delivered any address in the capital of the Nation. I had many misgivings as to what I ought to say, and as to the impression that my address would make. While I cannot recall in detail what I said, I remember that I tried to impress upon the committee with all the earnestness and plainness of any language that I could command, that if Congress wanted to do something which would assist in ridding the South of the race question and making friends between the two races, it should, in every proper way, encourage the material and intellectual growth of both races. I said that the Atlanta Exposition would present an opportunity for both races to show what advance they had made since freedom, and would at the same time afford encouragement to them to make still greater progress.

I tried to emphasize the fact that while the Negro should not be deprived by unfair means of the franchise, political agitation alone would not save him, and that back of the ballot he must have property, industry, skill, economy, intelligence, and character, and that no race without these elements could permanently succeed. I said that in granting the appropriation Congress could do something that would prove to be of real and lasting value to both races, and that it was the first great opportunity of the kind that had been presented since the close of the Civil War.

I spoke for fifteen or twenty minutes, and was surprised at the close of my address to receive the hearty congratulations of the Georgia committee and of the members of Congress who were present. The Committee was unanimous in making a favourable report, and in a few days the bill passed Congress. With the passing of this bill the success of the Atlanta Exposition was assured.

Soon after this trip to Washington the directors of the Exposition decided that it would be a fitting recognition of the coloured race to erect a large and attractive building which should be devoted wholly to showing the progress of the Negro since freedom. It was further decided to have the building designed and erected wholly by Negro mechanics. This plan was carried out. In design, beauty, and general finish the Negro Building was equal to the others on the grounds.

After it was decided to have a separate Negro exhibit, the question arose as to who should take charge of it. The officials of the Expositions were anxious that I should assume this responsibility, but I declined to do so, on the plea that the work at Tuskegee at that time demanded my time and strength. Largely at my suggestion, Mr. I. Garland Penn, of Lynchburg, Va., was selected to be at the head of the Negro department. I gave him all the aid that I could. The Negro exhibit, as a whole, was large and creditable. The two exhibits in this department which attracted the greatest amount of attention were those from the Hampton Institute and the Tuskegee Institute. The people who seemed to be the most surprised, as well as pleased, at what they saw in the Negro Building were the Southern white people.

As the day for the opening of the Exposition drew near, the Board of Directors began preparing the programme for the opening exercises. In the discussion from day to day of the various features of this programme, the question came up as to the advisability of putting a member of the Negro race on for one of the opening addresses, since the Negroes had been asked to take such a prominent part in the Exposition. It was argued, further, that such recognition would mark the good feeling prevailing between the two races. Of course there were those who were opposed to any such recognition of the rights of the Negro, but the Board of Directors, composed of men who represented the best and most progressive element in the South, had their way, and voted to invite a black man to speak on the opening day. The next thing was to decide upon the person who was thus to represent the Negro race. After the question had been canvassed for several days, the directors voted unanimously to ask me to deliver one of the opening-day addresses, and in a few days after that I received the official invitation.

The receiving of this invitation brought to me a sense of responsibility that it would be hard for any one not placed in my position to appreciate. What were my feelings when this invitation came to me? I remembered that I had been a slave; that my early years had been spent in the lowest depths of poverty and ignorance, and that I had had little opportunity to prepare me for such a responsibility as this. It was only a few years before that time that any white man in the audience might have claimed me as his slave; and it was easily possible that some of my former owners might be present to hear me speak.

I knew, too, that this was the first time in the entire history of the Negro that a member of my race had been asked to speak from the same platform with white Southern men and women on any important National occasion. I was asked now to speak to an audience composed of the wealth and culture of the white South, the representatives of my former masters. I knew, too, that while the greater part of my audience would be composed of Southern people, yet there would be present a large number of Northern whites, as well as a great many men and women of my own race.

I was determined to say nothing that I did not feel from the bottom of my heart to be true and right. When the invitation came to me, there was not one word of intimation as to what I should say or as to what I should omit. In this I felt that the Board of Directors had paid a tribute to me. They knew that by one sentence I could have blasted, in a large degree, the success of the Exposition. I was also painfully conscious of the fact that, while I must be true to my own race in my utterances, I had it in my power to make such an ill-timed address as would result in preventing any similar invitation being extended to a black man again for years to come. I was equally determined to be true to the North, as well as to the best element of the white South, in what I had to say.

The papers, North and South, had taken up the discussion of my coming speech, and as the time for it drew near this discussion became more and more widespread. Not a few of the Southern white papers were unfriendly to the idea of my speaking. From my own race I received many suggestions as to what I ought to say. I prepared myself as best I could for the address, but as the eighteenth of September drew nearer, the heavier my heart became, and the more I feared that my effort would prove a failure and a disappointment.

The invitation had come at a time when I was very busy with my school work, as it was the beginning of our school year. After preparing my address, I went through it, as I usually do with all those utterances which I consider particularly important, with Mrs. Washington, and she approved of what I intended to say. On the sixteenth of September, the day before I was to start for Atlanta, so many of the Tuskegee teachers expressed a desire to hear my address that I consented to read it to them in a body. When I had done so, and had heard their criticism and comments, I felt somewhat relieved, since they seemed to think well of what I had to say.

On the morning of September 17, together with Mrs. Washington and my three children, I started for Atlanta. I felt a good deal as I suppose a man feels when he is on his way to the gallows. In passing through the town of Tuskegee I met a white farmer who lived some distance out in the country. In a jesting manner this man said: "Washington, you have spoken before the Northern white people, the Negroes in the South, and to us country white people in the South; but in Atlanta, to-morrow, you will have before you the Northern whites, the Southern whites, and the Negroes all together. I am afraid that you have got yourself into a tight place." This farmer diagnosed the situation correctly, but his frank words did not add anything to my comfort.

In the course of the journey from Tuskegee to Atlanta both coloured and white people came to the train to point me out, and discussed with perfect freedom, in my hearing, what was going to take place the next day. We were met by a committee in Atlanta. Almost the first thing that I heard when I got off the train in that city was an expression something like this from an old coloured man near by: "Dat's de man of my race what's gwine to make a speech at de Exposition to-morrow. I'se sho' gwine to hear him."

Atlanta was literally packed, at the time, with people from all parts of this country, and with representatives of foreign governments, as well as with military and civic organizations. The afternoon papers had forecasts of the next day's proceedings in flaring headlines. All this tended to add to my burden. I did not sleep much that night. The next morning, before day, I went carefully over what I intended to say. I also kneeled down and asked God's blessing upon my effort. Right here, perhaps, I ought to add that I make it a rule never to go before an audience, on any occasion, without asking the blessing of God upon what I want to say.

I always make it a rule to make special preparation for each separate address. No two audiences are exactly alike. It is my aim to reach and talk to the heart of each individual audience, taking it into my confidence very much as I would a person. When I am speaking to an audience, I care little for how what I am saying is going to sound in the newspapers, or to another audience, or to an individual. At the time, the audience before me absorbs all my sympathy, thought, and energy.

Early in the morning a committee called to escort me to my place in the procession which was to march to the Exposition grounds. In this procession were prominent coloured citizens in carriages, as well as several Negro military organizations. I noted that the Exposition officials seemed to go out of their way to see that all of the coloured people in the procession were properly placed and properly treated. The procession was about three hours in reaching the Exposition grounds, and during all of this time the sun was shining down upon us disagreeably hot. When we reached the grounds, the heat, together with my nervous anxiety, made me feel as if I were about ready to collapse, and to feel that my address was not going to be a success. When I entered the audience-room, I found it packed with humanity from bottom to top, and there were thousands outside who could not get in.

The room was very large, and well suited to public speaking. When I entered the room, there were vigorous cheers from the coloured portion of the audience, and faint cheers from some of the white people. I had been told, while I had been in Atlanta, that while many white people were going to be present to hear me speak, simply out of curiosity, and that others who would be present would be in full sympathy with me, there was a still larger element of the audience which would consist of those who were going to be present for the purpose of hearing me make a fool of myself, or, at least, of hearing me say some foolish thing, so that they could say to the officials who had invited me to speak, "I told you so!"

One of the trustees of the Tuskegee Institute, as well as my personal friend, Mr. William H. Baldwin, Jr., was at the time General Manager of the Southern Railroad, and happened to be in Atlanta on that day. He was so nervous about the kind of reception that I would have, and the effect that my speech would produce, that he could not persuade himself to go into the building, but walked back and forth in the grounds outside until the opening exercises were over.

Chapter 14: The Atlanta Exposition Address

The Atlanta Exposition, at which I had been asked to make an address as a representative of the Negro race, as stated in the last chapter, was opened with a short address from Governor Bullock. After other interesting exercises, including an invocation from Bishop Nelson, of Georgia, a dedicatory ode by Albert Howell, Jr., and addresses by the President of the Exposition and Mrs. Joseph Thompson, the President of the Woman's Board, Governor Bullock introduced me with the words, "We have with us to-day a representative of Negro enterprise and Negro civilization."

When I arose to speak, there was considerable cheering, especially from the coloured people. As I remember it now, the thing that was uppermost in my mind was the desire to say something that would cement the friendship of the races and bring about hearty cooperation between them. So far as my outward surroundings were concerned, the only thing that I recall distinctly now is that when I got up, I saw thousands of eyes looking intently into my face. The following is the address which I delivered :—

MR. PRESIDENT AND GENTLEMEN OF THE
BOARD OF DIRECTORS AND CITIZENS.

One-third of the population of the South is of the Negro race. No enterprise seeking the material, civil, or moral welfare of this section can disregard this element of our population and reach the highest success. I but convey to you, Mr. President and Directors, the sentiment of the masses of my race when I say that in no way have the value and manhood of the American Negro been more fittingly and generously recognized than by the managers of this magnificent Exposition at every stage of its progress. It is a recognition that will do more to cement the friendship of the two races than any occurrence since the dawn of our freedom.

Not only this, but the opportunity afforded will awaken among us a new era of industrial progress. Ignorant and inexperienced, it is not strange that in the first years of our new life we began at the top instead of at the bottom; that a seat in Congress or the state legislature was more sought than real estate or industrial skill; that the political convention of stump speaking had more attractions than starting a dairy farm or truck garden.

A ship lost at sea for many days suddenly sighted a friendly vessel. From the mast of the unfortunate vessel was seen a signal, "Water, water: we die of thirst!" The answer from the friendly vessel at once came back, "Cast down your bucket where you are." A second time the signal, "Water, water; send us water!" ran up from the distressed vessel, and was answered, "Cast down your bucket where you are." And a third and fourth signal for water was answered, "Cast down your bucket where you are." The captain of the distressed, at last heeding the injunction, cast down his bucket, and it came up full of fresh, sparkling water from the mouth of the Amazon River. To those of my race who depend on bettering their condition in a foreign land or who underestimate the importance of cultivating friendly relations with the Southern white man, who is their next-door neighbour, I would say: "Cast down your bucket where you are"—cast it down in making friends in every manly way of the people of all races by whom we are surrounded.

Cast it down in agriculture, mechanics, in commerce, in domestic service, and in the professions. And in this connection it is well to bear in mind that whatever other sins the South may be called to bear, when it comes to business, pure and simple, it is in the South that the Negro is given a man's chance in the commercial world, and in nothing is this Exposition more eloquent than in emphasizing this chance. Our greatest danger is that in the great leap from slavery to freedom we may overlook the fact that the masses of us are to live by the productions of our hands, and fail to keep in mind that we shall prosper in proportion as we learn to dignify and glorify common labour and put brains and skill into the common occupations of life; shall prosper in proportion as we learn to draw the line between the superficial and the substantial, the ornamental gewgaws of life and the useful. No race can prosper till it learns that there is as much dignity in tilling a field as in writing a poem. It is at the bottom of life we must begin, and not at the top. Nor should we permit our grievances to overshadow our opportunities.

To those of the white race who look to the incoming of those of foreign birth and strange tongue and habits for the prosperity of the South, were I permitted I would repeat what I say to my own race, "Cast down your bucket where you are." Cast it down among the eight millions of Negroes whose habits you know, whose fidelity and love you have tested in days when to have proved treacherous meant the ruin of your firesides. Cast down your bucket among these people who have, without strikes and labour wars, tilled your fields, cleared your forests, builded your railroads and cities, and brought forth treasures from the bowels of the earth, and helped make possible this magnificent representation of the progress of the South. Casting down your bucket among my people, helping and encouraging them as you are doing on these grounds, and to education of head, hand, and heart, you will find that they will buy your surplus land, make blossom the waste places in your fields, and run your factories. While doing this, you can be sure in the future, as in the past, that you and your families will be surrounded by the most patient, faithful, law-abiding, and unresentful people that the world has seen. As we have proved our loyalty to you in the past, in nursing your children, watching by the sick-bed of your mothers and fathers, and often following them with tear-dimmed eyes to their graves, so in the future, in our humble way, we shall stand by you with a devotion that no foreigner can approach, ready to lay down our lives, if need be, in defence of yours, interlacing our industrial, commercial, civil, and religious life with yours in a way that shall make the interests of both races one. In all things that are purely social we can be as separate as the fingers, yet one as the hand in all things essential to mutual progress.

There is no defence or security for any of us except in the highest intelligence and development of all. If anywhere there are efforts tending to curtail the fullest growth of the Negro, let these efforts be turned into stimulating, encouraging, and making him the most useful and intelligent citizen. Effort or means so invested will pay a thousand per cent interest. These efforts will be twice blessed—"blessing him that gives and him that takes."

There is no escape through law of man or God from the inevitable:—

The laws of changeless justice bind
Oppressor with oppressed;
And close as sin and suffering joined
We march to fate abreast.

Nearly sixteen millions of hands will aid you in pulling the load upward, or they will pull against you the load downward. We shall constitute one-third and more of the ignorance and crime of the South, or one-third its intelligence and progress; we shall contribute one-third to the business and industrial prosperity of the South, or we shall prove a veritable body of death, stagnating, depressing, retarding every effort to advance the body politic.

Gentlemen of the Exposition, as we present to you our humble effort at an exhibition of our progress, you must not expect overmuch. Starting thirty years ago with ownership here and there in a few quilts and pumpkins and chickens (gathered from miscellaneous sources), remember the path that has led from these to the inventions and production of agricultural implements, buggies, steam-engines, newspapers, books, statuary, carving, paintings, the management of drug-stores and banks, has not been trodden without contact with thorns and thistles. While we take pride in what we exhibit as a result of our independent efforts, we do not for a moment forget that our part in this exhibition would fall far short of your expectations but for the constant help that has come to our educational life, not only from the Southern states, but especially from Northern philanthropists, who have made their gifts a constant stream of blessing and encouragement.

The wisest among my race understand that the agitation of questions of social equality is the extremest folly, and that progress in the enjoyment of all the privileges that will come to us must be the result of severe and constant struggle rather than of artificial forcing. No race that has anything to contribute to the markets of the world is long in any degree ostracized. It is important and right that all privileges of the law be ours, but it is vastly more important that we be prepared for the exercises of these privileges. The opportunity to earn a dollar in a factory just now is worth infinitely more than the opportunity to spend a dollar in an opera-house.

In conclusion, may I repeat that nothing in thirty years has given us more hope and encouragement, and drawn us so near to you of the white race, as this opportunity offered by the Exposition; and here bending, as it were, over the altar that represents the results of the struggles of your race and mine, both starting practically empty-handed three decades ago, I pledge that in your effort to work out the great and intricate problem which God has laid at the doors of the South, you shall have at all times the patient, sympathetic help of my race; only let this be constantly in mind, that, while from representations in these buildings of the product of field, of forest, of mine, of factory, letters, and art, much good will come, yet far above and beyond material benefits will be that higher good, that, let us pray God, will come, in a blotting out of sectional differences and racial animosities and suspicions, in a determination to administer absolute justice, in a willing obedience among all classes to the mandates of law. This, then, coupled with our material prosperity, will bring into our beloved South a new heaven and a new earth.

The first thing that I remember, after I had finished speaking, was that Governor Bullock rushed across the platform and took me by the hand, and that others did the same. I received so many and such hearty congratulations that I found it difficult to get out of the building. I did not appreciate to any degree, however, the impression which my address seemed to have made, until the next morning, when I went into the business part of the city. As soon as I was recognized, I was surprised to find myself pointed out and surrounded by a crowd of men who wished to shake hands with me. This was kept up on every street on to which I went, to an extent which embarrassed me so much that I went back to my boarding-place. The next morning I returned to Tuskegee. At the station in Atlanta, and at almost all of the stations at which the train stopped between that city and Tuskegee, I found a crowd of people anxious to shake hands with me.

The papers in all parts of the United States published the address in full, and for months afterward there were complimentary editorial references to it. Mr. Clark Howell, the editor of the Atlanta *Constitution,* telegraphed to a New York paper, among other words, the following, "I do not exaggerate when I say that Professor Booker T. Washington's address yesterday was one of the most notable speeches, both as to character and as to the warmth of its reception, ever delivered to a Southern audience. The address was a revelation. The whole speech is a platform upon which blacks and whites can stand with full justice to each other."

The Boston *Transcript* said editorially: "The speech of Booker T. Washington at the Atlanta Exposition, this week, seems to have dwarfed all the other proceedings and the Exposition itself. The sensation that it has caused in the press has never been equalled."

I very soon began receiving all kinds of propositions from lecture bureaus, and editors of magazines and papers, to take the lecture platform, and to write articles. One lecture bureau offered me fifty thousand dollars, or two hundred dollars a night and expenses, if I would place my services at its disposal for a given period. To all these communications I replied that my life-work was at Tuskegee; and that whenever I spoke it must be in the interests of the Tuskegee school and my race, and that I would enter into no arrangements that seemed to place a mere commercial value upon my services.

Some days after its delivery I sent a copy of my address to the President of the United States, the Hon. Grover Cleveland. I received from him the following autographed reply:—

GRAY GABLES, BUZZARD'S BAY, MASS.,
OCTOBER 6, 1895.

BOOKER T. WASHINGTON, ESQ.:

MY DEAR SIR: I thank you for sending me a copy of your address delivered at the Atlanta Exposition.

I thank you with much enthusiasm for making the address. I have read it with intense interest, and I think the Exposition would be fully justified if it did not do more than furnish the opportunity for its delivery. Your words cannot fail to delight and encourage all who wish well for your race; and if our coloured fellow-citizens do not from your utterances gather new hope and form new determinations to gain every valuable advantage offered them by their citizenship, it will be strange indeed.

Yours very truly,
GROVER CLEVELAND.

Later I met Mr. Cleveland, for the first time, when, as President, he visited the Atlanta Exposition. At the request of myself and others he consented to spend an hour in the Negro Building, for the purpose of inspecting the Negro exhibit and of giving the coloured people in attendance an opportunity to shake hands with him. As soon as I met Mr. Cleveland I became impressed with his simplicity, greatness, and rugged honesty. I have met him many times since then, both at public functions and at his private residence in Princeton, and the more I see of

him the more I admire him. When he visited the Negro Building in Atlanta he seemed to give himself up wholly, for that hour, to the coloured people. He seemed to be as careful to shake hands with some old coloured "auntie" clad partially in rags, and to take as much pleasure in doing so, as if he were greeting some millionaire. Many of the coloured people took advantage of the occasion to get him to write his name in a book or on a slip of paper. He was as careful and patient in doing this as if he were putting his signature to some great state document.

Mr. Cleveland has not only shown his friendship for me in many personal ways, but has always consented to do anything I have asked of him for our school. This he has done, whether it was to make a personal donation or to use his influence in securing the donations of others. Judging from my personal acquaintance with Mr. Cleveland, I do not believe that he is conscious of possessing any colour prejudice. He is too great for that. In my contact with people I find that, as a rule, it is only the little, narrow people who live for themselves, who never read good books, who do not travel, who never open up their souls in a way to permit them to come into contact with other souls—with the great outside world. No man whose vision is bounded by colour can come into contact with what is highest and best in the world. In meeting men, in many places, I have found that the happiest people are those who do the most for others; the most miserable are those who do the least. I have also found that few things, if any, are capable of making one so blind and narrow as race prejudice. I often say to our students, in the course of my talks to them on Sunday evenings in the chapel, that the longer I live and the more experience I have of the world, the more I am convinced that, after all, the one thing that is most worth living for—and dying for, if need be—is the opportunity of making some one else more happy and more useful.

The coloured people and the coloured newspapers at first seemed to be greatly pleased with the character of my Atlanta address, as well as with its reception. But after the first burst of enthusiasm began to die away, and the coloured people began reading the speech in cold type, some of them seemed to feel that they had been hypnotized. They seemed to feel that I had been too liberal in my remarks toward the Southern whites, and that I had not spoken out strongly enough for what they termed the "rights" of the race. For a while there was a reaction, so far as a certain element of my own race was concerned, but later these reactionary ones seemed to have been won over to my way of believing and acting.

While speaking of changes in public sentiment, I recall that about ten years after the school at Tuskegee was established, I had an experience that I shall never forget. Dr. Lyman Abbott, then the pastor of Plymouth Church, and also editor of the *Outlook* (then the *Christian Union*), asked me to write a letter for his paper giving my opinion of the exact condition, mental and moral, of the coloured ministers in the South, as based upon my observations. I wrote the letter, giving the exact facts as I conceived them to be. The picture painted was a rather black one—or, since I am black, shall I say "white"? It could not be otherwise with a race but a few years out of slavery, a race which had not had time or opportunity to produce a competent ministry.

What I said soon reached every Negro minister in the country, I think, and the letters of condemnation which I received from them were not few. I think that for a year after the publication of this article every association and every conference or religious body of any kind, of my race, that met, did not fail before adjourning to pass a resolution condemning me, or calling upon me to retract or modify what I had said. Many of these organizations went so far in their resolutions as to advise parents to cease sending their children to Tuskegee. One association even appointed a "missionary" whose duty it was to warn the people against sending their children to Tuskegee. This missionary had a son in the school, and I noticed that, whatever the "missionary" might have said or done with regard to others, he was careful not to take his son away from the institution. Many of the coloured papers, especially those that were the organs of religious bodies, joined in the general chorus of condemnation or demands for retraction.

During the whole time of the excitement, and through all the criticism, I did not utter a word of explanation or retraction. I knew that I was right, and that time and the sober second thought of the people would vindicate me. It was not long before the bishops and other church leaders began to make a careful investigation of the conditions of the ministry, and they found out that I was right. In fact, the oldest and most influential bishop in one branch of the Methodist Church said that my words were far too mild.

Very soon public sentiment began making itself felt, in demanding a purifying of the ministry. While this is not yet complete by any means, I think I may say, without egotism, and I have been told by many of our most influential ministers, that my words had much to do with starting a demand for the placing of a higher type of men in the pulpit. I have had the satisfaction of having many who once condemned me thank me heartily for my frank words.

The change of the attitude of the Negro ministry, so far as regards myself, is so complete that at the present time I have no warmer friends among any class than I have among the clergymen. The improvement in the character and life of the Negro ministers is one of the most gratifying evidences of the progress of the race. My experience with them, as well as other events in my life, convince me that the thing to do, when one feels sure that he has said or done the right thing, and is condemned, is to stand still and keep quiet. If he is right, time will show it.

In the midst of the discussion which was going on concerning my Atlanta speech, I received the letter which I give below, from Dr. Gilman, the President of Johns Hopkins University, who had been made chairman of the judges of award in connection with the Atlanta Exposition:—

> JOHNS HOPKINS UNIVERSITY, BALTIMORE,
> President's office, September 30, 1895.
> DEAR MR. WASHINGTON: Would it be agreeable to you to be one of the Judges of Award in the Department of Education at Atlanta? If so, I shall be glad to place your name upon the list. A line by telegraph will be welcomed.
>
> > Yours very truly,
> > D. C. GILMAN.

I think I was even more surprised to receive this invitation than I had been to receive the invitation to speak at the opening of the Exposition. It was to be a part of my duty, as one of the jurors, to pass not only upon the exhibits of the coloured schools, but also upon those of the white schools. I accepted the position, and spent a month in Atlanta in performance of the duties which it entailed. The board of jurors was a large one, consisting in all of sixty members. It was about equally divided between Southern white people and Northern white people. Among them were college presidents, leading scientists and men of letters, and specialists in many subjects. When the group of jurors to which I was assigned met for organization, Mr. Thomas Nelson Page, who was one of the number, moved that

I be made secretary of that division, and the motion was unanimously adopted. Nearly half of our division were Southern people. In performing my duties in the inspection of the exhibits of white schools I was in every case treated with respect, and at the close of our labours I parted from my associates with regret.

I am often asked to express myself more freely than I do upon the political condition and the political future of my race. These recollections of my experience in Atlanta give me the opportunity to do so briefly. My own belief is, although I have never before said so in so many words, that the time will come when the Negro in the South will be accorded all the political rights which his ability, character, and material possessions entitle him to. I think, though, that the opportunity to freely exercise such political rights will not come in any large degree through outside or artificial forcing, but will be accorded to the Negro by the Southern white people themselves, and that they will protect him in the exercise of those rights. Just as soon as the South gets over the old feeling that it is being forced by "foreigners," or "aliens," to do something which it does not want to do, I believe that the change in the direction that I have indicated is going to begin. In fact, there are indications that it is already beginning in a slight degree.

Let me illustrate my meaning. Suppose that some months before the opening of the Atlanta Exposition there had been a general demand from the press and public platform outside the South that a Negro be given a place on the opening programme, and that a Negro be placed upon the board of jurors of award. Would any such recognition of the race have taken place? I do not think so. The Atlanta officials went as far as they did because they felt it to be a pleasure, as well as a duty, to reward what they considered merit in the Negro race. Say what we will, there is something in human nature which we cannot blot out, which makes one man, in the end, recognize and reward merit in another, regardless of colour or race.

I believe it is the duty of the Negro—as the greater part of the race is already doing—to deport himself modestly in regard to political claims, depending upon the slow but sure influences that proceed from the possession of property, intelligence, and high character for the full recognition of his political rights. I think that the according of the full exercise of political rights is going to be a matter of natural, slow growth, not an over-night, gourd-vine affair. I do not believe that the Negro should cease voting, for a man cannot learn the exercise of self-government by ceasing to vote any more than a boy can learn to swim by keeping out of the water, but I do believe that in his voting he should more and more be influenced by those of intelligence and character who are his next-door neighbours.

I know coloured men who, through the encouragement, help, and advice of Southern white people, have accumulated thousands of dollars' worth of property, but who, at the same time, would never think of going to those same persons for advice concerning the casting of their ballots. This, it seems to me, is unwise and unreasonable, and should cease. In saying this I do not mean that the Negro should truckle, or not vote from principle, for the instant he ceases to vote from principle he loses the confidence and respect of the Southern white man even.

I do not believe that any state should make a law that permits an ignorant and poverty-stricken white man to vote, and prevents a black man in the same condition from voting. Such a law is not only unjust, but it will react, as all unjust laws do, in time; for the effect of such a law is to encourage the Negro to secure education and property, and at the same time it encourages the white man to remain in ignorance and poverty. I believe that in time, through the operation of intelligence and friendly race relations, all cheating at the ballot box in the South will cease. It will become apparent that the white man who begins by cheating a Negro out of his ballot soon learns to cheat a white man out of his, and that the man who does this ends his career of dishonesty by the theft of property or by some equally serious crime. In my opinion, the time will come when the South will encourage all of its citizens to vote. It will see that it pays better, from every standpoint, to have healthy, vigorous life than to have that political stagnation which always results when one-half of the population has no share and no interest in the Government.

As a rule, I believe in universal, free suffrage, but I believe that in the South we are confronted with peculiar conditions that justify the protection of the ballot in many of the states, for a while at least, either by an educational test, a property test, or by both combined; but whatever tests are required, they should be made to apply with equal and exact justice to both races.

Race and Politics

Robert Brown Elliott (1842–1884)

Born in Boston of West Indian parents of unmixed African descent on August 11, 1842, Robert Brown Elliott became one of the most eloquent and learned of Black Reconstruction politicians. His education was excellent—primary schooling in Boston and Jamaica, followed by six years of study in England at High Holborn Academy, which he entered in 1853, and Eton College, from which he was graduated in 1859. He then read law in London with Sergeant Fitzherbert. His formal education was followed by travel around the British Isles and to South America. Though still a young man in his early twenties when he joined the Union Navy during the Civil War, he had learned much of both books and the world.

After the war Elliott established residence in South Carolina, where he worked as printer and then editor for the *Charleston Leader* (later called the *Missionary Record*), a Black newspaper. His articles brought him public notice, and in 1868 he was elected a delegate to the Constitutional Convention of South Carolina, the first exercise of Black power in American politics. The positions he took during the deliberations of this body were a forecast of his later record as a progressive legislator—support of such measures as a homestead provision and compulsory free public education and opposition to suffrage restrictions, such as the poll tax and literacy tests, that would diminish the number of Black voters. Following the convention, Elliott was elected to the reconstituted House of Representatives of South Carolina, where he served from July 1868 to October 1870. Again he supported enlightened measures far ahead of his time, such as the abolition of capital punishment (except for premeditated murder). Widely recognized as the ablest member of the South Carolina legislature, he quickly assumed the additional responsibilities of the chairmanship of the Republican State Executive Committee, serving until 1876, and the adjutant generalship of the state militia, to which he was appointed on March 25, 1869.

It was only natural, then, that this rising politician would be elected to the Forty-second United States Congress, defeating his Democratic opponent by the decisive vote of 20,564 to 13,997. His election to the Forty-third Congress was much more lopsided—21,627 to 1,094. Elliott's record in Congress was consistent with the progressive posture he had taken in state politics. His main interest was domestic affairs, but he also sympathized with anti-imperialist struggles abroad, introducing a petition late in 1873 "to accord to the struggling patriots of the Cuban Republic belligerent rights." His most important contributions as a congressman, however, were his two great speeches in 1871 and 1874. The first was delivered on April 1 in support of a bill to enforce the Fourteenth Amendment against the terrorist tactics of the Ku Klux Klan and other racist groups. The second speech pitted Elliott against some of the white South's leading spokesmen, including Alexander H. Stephens of Georgia, formerly Vice-President of the Confederacy. This speech, delivered on January 6, 1874, and reprinted here, supported H.R. No. 796, one of the most meaningful civil rights bills ever presented in Washington. With learning, irony, eloquence, and passion, Elliott demolished his opponents' arguments and presented an irrefutably cogent case for the responsibility of the federal government to protect the democratic rights of its citizens.

A strong Civil Rights Act was passed in 1875, but Elliott lived to see it overthrown by the Supreme Court in 1883. One disappointment after another confronted him as he fought to consolidate and extend the advances made by Black Reconstruction. Resigning from Congress in May 1874, he returned to South Carolina politics as sheriff, followed by his election once again to the state legislature, where he became Speaker of the House. Further campaigns for elective office—United States Senator and state attorney-general—failed as resurgent racism under the leadership of Wade Hampton ended Reconstruction in South Carolina and re-established Democratic rule in 1876 and 1877. For the next several years Elliott practiced law and then served as an agent of the United States Treasury Department before moving finally to New Orleans, where he died on August 9, 1884.

Elliott's last years were embittered by the loss of civil rights so painfully won by his people. "Although clothed with the rights of citizenship by the provisions of the Constitution of the United States," he told President-elect Garfield early in 1881, "yet still in all the Southern States we are but citizens in name and not in fact." Black Reconstruction was over.

Elliott's congressional speeches may be found in the appropriate volumes of the *Congressional Globe* and the *Congressional Record*. Carter G. Woodson reprints Elliott's eulogy of Charles Sumner in *Negro Orators and Their Orations* (1925). Biographical sketches of Elliott appear in William J. Simmons, *Men of Mark: Eminent, Progressive and Rising* (1887); John W. Cromwell, *The Negro in American History* (1914); and Benjamin Brawley, *Negro Builders and Heroes* (1937). For detailed accounts of the political background, see Alrutheus A. Taylor, *The Negro in South Carolina During the Reconstruction* (1924), and Joel Williams, *After Slavery: The Negro in South Carolina During Reconstruction, 1861–1877* (1965).

Speech on the Civil Rights Bill Delivered in the United States Congress, January 6, 1874

While I am sincerely grateful for this high mark of courtesy that has been accorded to me by this House, it is a matter of regret to me that it is necessary at this day that I should rise in the presence of an American Congress to advocate a bill which simply asserts equal rights and equal public privileges for all classes of American citizens. I regret, sir, that the dark hue of my skin may lend a color to the imputation that I am controlled by motives personal to myself in my advocacy of this great measure of national justice. Sir, the motive that impels me is restricted by no such narrow boundary, but is as broad as your Constitution. I advocate it, sir, because it is right. The bill, however, not only appeals to your justice, but it demands a response from your gratitude.

In the events that led to the achievement of American Independence the Negro was not an inactive or unconcerned spectator. He bore his part bravely upon many battle fields, although uncheered by that certain hope of political elevation which victory would secure to the white man. The tall granite shaft, which a grateful State has reared above its sons who fell in defending Fort Griswold against the attack of Benedict Arnold, bears the name of Jordan, Freeman, and other brave men of the African race who there cemented with their blood the corner-stone of the Republic. In the State which I have the honor in part to represent the rifle of the black man rang out against the troops of the British crown in the darkest days of the American Revolution. Said General Greene, who has been justly termed the Washington of the North, in a letter written by him to Alexander Hamilton, on the 10th day of January, 1781, from the vicinity of Camden, South Carolina:

There is no such thing as national character or national sentiment. The inhabitants are numerous, but they would be formidable abroad rather than at home. There is a great spirit of enterprise among the black people, and those that come out as volunteers are not a little formidable to the enemy.

At the battle of New Orleans, under the immortal Jackson, a colored regiment held the extreme right of the American line unflinchingly, and drove back the British column that pressed upon them, at the point of the bayonet. So marked was their valor on that occasion that it evoked from their great commander the warmest encomiums, as will be seen from his dispatch announcing the brilliant victory.

As the gentleman from Kentucky, (Mr. Beck), who seems to be the leading exponent on this floor of the party that is arrayed against the principle of this bill, has been pleased, in season and out of season, to cast odium upon the negro and to vaunt the chivalry of his State, I may be pardoned for calling attention to another portion of the same dispatch. Referring to the various regiments under his command, and their conduct on that field which terminated the second war of American Independence, General Jackson says:

At the very moment when the entire discomfiture of the enemy was looked for with a confidence amounting to certainty, the Kentucky reinforcements, in whom so much reliance had been placed, ingloriously fled.

In quoting this indisputable piece of history, I do so only by way of admonition and not to question the well-attested gallantry of the true Kentuckian, and to suggest to the gentleman that it would be well that he should not flaunt his heraldry so proudly while he bears this bar-sinister on the military escutcheon of his State—a State which answered the call of the Republic in 1861, when treason thundered at the very gates of the capital, by coldly declaring her neutrality in the impending struggle. The Negro, true to that patriotism and love of country that have ever characterized and marked his history on this continent, came to the aid of the Government in its efforts to maintain the Constitution. To that Government he now appeals; that Constitution he now invokes for protection against outrage and unjust prejudices founded upon caste.

But, sir, we are told by the distinguished gentleman from Georgia (Mr. Stephens) that Congress has no power under the Constitution to pass such a law, and that the passage of such an act is in direct contravention of the rights of the States. I cannot assent to any such proposition. The constitution of a free government ought always to be construed in favor of human rights. Indeed, the thirteenth, fourteenth, and fifteenth amendments, in positive words, invest Congress with the power to protect the citizen in his civil and political rights. Now, sir, what are civil rights? Rights natural, modified by civil society. Mr. Lieber says:

By civil liberty is meant, not only the absence of individual restraint, but liberty within the social system and political organism—a combination of principles and laws which acknowledge, protect, and favor the dignity of man.... Civil liberty is the result of man's two-fold character as an individual and social being, so soon as both are equally respected.— Leiber on *Civil Liberty,* Page 25.

Alexander Hamilton, the right-hand man of Washington in the perilous days of the then infant Republic, the great interpreter and expounder of the Constitution, says:

Natural liberty is a gift of the beneficent Creator to the whole human race; civil liberty is founded on it; civil liberty is only natural liberty modified and secured by civil society.—Hamilton's *History of the American Republic,* vol. 1, page 70.

In the French constitution of June, 1793, we find this grand and noble declaration:

Government is instituted to insure to man the free use of his natural and inalienable rights. These rights are equality, liberty, security, property. All men are equal by nature and before the law.... Law is the same for all, be it protective or penal. Freedom is the power by which man can do what does not interfere with the rights of another; its basis is nature, its standard is justice, its protection is law, its moral boundary is the maxim: "Do not unto others what you do not wish they should do unto you."

Are we then, sir, with the amendments to our Constitution staring us in the face; with these grand truths of history before our eyes; with innumerable wrongs daily inflicted upon five million citizens demanding redress, to commit this question to the diversity of State legislation? In the words of Hamilton—

Is it the interest of the Government to sacrifice individual rights to the preservation of the rights of an artificial being, called States? There can be no truer principle than this, that every individual of the community at large has an equal right to the protection of Government. Can this be a free Government if partial distinctions are tolerated or maintained?

The rights contended for in this bill are among "the sacred rights of mankind, which are not to be rummaged for among old parchments or musty records; they are written as with a sunbeam, in the whole volume of human nature, by the hand of the Divinity itself, and can never be erased or obscured by mortal power."

But the Slaughter-house cases!—the Slaughterhouse cases!

The honorable gentleman from Kentucky, always swift to sustain the failing and dishonored cause of proscription, rushes forward and flaunts in our faces the decision of the Supreme Court of the United States in the Slaughter-house cases, and in that act he has been willingly aided by the gentleman from Georgia. Hitherto, in the contests which have marked the progress of the cause of equal civil rights, our opponents have appealed sometimes to custom, sometimes to prejudice, more often to pride of race, but they have never sought to shield themselves behind the Supreme Court. But now, for the first time, we are told that we are barred by a decision of that court, from which there is no appeal. If this be true we must stay our hands. The cause of equal civil rights must pause at the command of a power whose edicts must be obeyed till the fundamental law of our country is changed.

Has the honorable gentleman from Kentucky considered well the claim he now advances? If it were not disrespectful I would ask, has he ever read the decision which he now tells us is an insuperable barrier to the adoption of this great measure of justice?

In the consideration of this subject, has not the judgment of the gentleman from Georgia been warped by the ghost of the dead doctrines of State-rights? Has he been altogether free from prejudices engendered by long training in that school of politics that well-nigh destroyed this Government?

Mr. Speaker, I venture to say here in the presence of the gentleman from Kentucky, and the gentleman from Georgia, and in the presence of the whole country, that there is not a line or word, not a thought or dictum even, in the decision of the Supreme Court in the great Slaughter-house cases which casts a shadow of doubt on the right of Congress to pass the pending bill, or to adopt such other legislation as it may judge proper and necessary to secure perfect equality before the law to every citizen of the Republic. Sir,

I protest against the dishonor now cast upon our Supreme Court by both the gentleman from Kentucky and the gentleman from Georgia. In other days, when the whole country was bowing beneath the yoke of slavery, when press, pulpit, platform, Congress, and courts felt the fatal power of the slave oligarchy, I remember a decision of that court which no American now reads without shame and humiliation. But those days are past. The Supreme Court of today is a tribunal as true to freedom as any department of this Government, and I am honored with the opportunity of repelling a deep disgrace which the gentleman from Kentucky, backed and sustained as he is by the gentleman from Georgia, seeks to put upon it.

What were these Slaughter-house cases? The gentleman should be aware that a decision of any court should be examined in the light of the exact question which is brought before it for decision. That is all that gives authority to any decision.

The State of Louisiana, by act of her Legislature, had conferred on certain persons the exclusive right to maintain stock-landings and slaughter-houses within the city of New Orleans, or the parishes of Orleans, Jefferson, and Saint Bernard, in that State. The corporation which was thereby chartered were invested with the sole and exclusive privilege of conducting and carrying on the livestock, landing, and slaughter-house business within the limits designated.

The supreme court of Louisiana sustained the validity of the act conferring these exclusive privileges, and the plaintiffs in error brought the case before the Supreme Court of the United States for review. The plaintiffs in error contended that the act in question was void, because, first, it established a monopoly which was in derogation of common right and in contravention of the common law; and, second, that the grant of such exclusive privileges was in violation of the thirteenth and fourteenth amendments of the Constitution of the United States.

It thus appears from a simple statement of the case that the question which was before the court was not whether a State law which denied to a particular portion of her citizens the rights conferred on her citizens generally, on account of race, color, or previous condition of servitude, was unconstitutional because in conflict with the recent amendments, but whether an act which conferred on certain citizens exclusive privileges for police purposes was in conflict therewith, because imposing an involuntary servitude forbidden by the thirteenth amendment, or abridging the rights and immunities of citizens of the United States, or denying the equal protection of the laws, prohibited by the fourteenth amendment.

On the part of the defendants in error it was maintained that the act was the exercise of the ordinary and unquestionable power of the State to make regulation for the health and comfort of society—the exercise of the police power of the State, defined by Chancellor Kent to be "the right to interdict unwholesome trades, slaughter-houses, operations offensive to the senses, the deposit of powder, the application of steam-power to propel cars, the building with combustible materials, and the burial of the dead in the midst of dense masses of population, on the general and rational principle that every person ought so to use his own property as not to injure his neighbors, and that private interests must be made subservient to the general interests of the community."

The decision of the Supreme Court is to be found in the 16th volume of Wallace's Reports, and was delivered by Associate Justice Miller. The court holds, first, that the act in question is a legitimate and warrantable exercise of the police power of the State in regulating the business of stock-handling and slaughtering in the city of New Orleans and the territory immediately contiguous. Having held this, the court proceeds to discuss the question whether the conferring of exclusive privileges, such as those conferred by the act in question, is the imposing of an involuntary servitude, the abridging of the rights and immunities of citizens of the United States, or the denial to any person within the jurisdiction of the State of the equal protection of the laws.

That the act is not the imposition of an involuntary servitude the court holds to be clear, and they next proceed to examine the remaining questions arising under the fourteenth amendment. Upon this question the court holds that the leading and comprehensive purpose of the thirteenth, fourteenth, and fifteenth amendments was to secure the complete freedom of the race, which, by the events of the war, had been wrested from the unwilling grasp of their owners. I know no finer or more just picture, albeit painted in the neutral tints of true judicial impartiality, of the motives and events which led to these amendments. Has the gentleman from Kentucky read these passages which I now quote? Or has the gentleman from Georgia considered well the force of the language therein used? Says the court on page 70:

The process of restoring to their proper relations with the Federal Government and with the other States those which had sided with the rebellion, undertaken under the proclamation of President Johnson in 1865, and before the assembling of Congress, developed the fact that, notwithstanding the formal recognition by those States of the abolition of slavery, the condition of the slave race would, without further protection of the Federal Government, be almost as bad as it was before. Among the first acts of legislation adopted by several of the States in the legislative bodies which claimed to be in their normal relations with the Federal Government, were laws which imposed upon the colored race onerous disabilities and burdens, and curtailed their rights in the pursuit of life, liberty and property to such an extent that their freedom was of little value, while they had lost the protection which they had received from their former owners from motives both of interest and humanity.

They were in some States forbidden to appear in the towns in any other character than menial servants. They were required to reside on and cultivate the soil, without the right to purchase or own it. They were excluded from any occupations of gain, and were not permitted to give testimony in the courts in any case where a white man was a party. It was said that their lives were at the mercy of bad men, either because the laws for their protection were insufficient or were not enforced.

These circumstances, whatever of falsehood or misconception may have been mingled with their presentation, forced upon the statesmen who had conducted the Federal Government in safety through the crisis of rebellion, and who supposed that by the thirteenth article of amendment they had secured the result of their labors, the conviction that something more was necessary in the way of constitutional protection to the unfortunate race who had suffered so much. They accordingly passed through Congress the proposition for the fourteenth amendment, and they declined to treat as restored to their full participation in the Government of the Union the States which had been in insurrection until they ratified that article by a formal vote of their legislative bodies.

Before we proceed to examine more critically the provisions of this amendment, on which the plaintiffs in error rely, let us complete and dismiss the history of the recent amendments, as that history relates to the general purpose which pervades them all. A few years' experience satisfied the thoughtful men who had been the authors of the other two amendments that, notwithstanding the restraints of those articles

on the States and the laws passed under the additional powers granted to Congress, these were inadequate for the protection of life, liberty, and property, without which freedom to the slave was no boon. They were in all those States denied the right of suffrage. The laws were administered by the white man alone. It was urged that a race of men distinctively marked as was the Negro, living in the midst of another and dominant race, could never be fully secured in their person and their property without the right of suffrage.

Hence the fifteenth amendment, which declares that "the right of a citizen of the United States to vote shall not be denied or abridged by any State on account of race, color, or previous condition of servitude." The Negro having, by the fourteenth amendment, been declared to be a citizen of the United States, is thus made a voter in every State of the Union.

We repeat, then, in the light of this recapitulation of events almost too recent to be called history, but which are familiar to us all, and on the most casual examination of the language of these amendments, no one can fail to be impressed with the one pervading purpose found in them all, lying at the foundation of each, and without which none of them would have been even suggested: we mean the freedom of the slave race, the security and firm establishment of that freedom, and the protection of the newly-made freeman and citizen from the oppressions of those who had formerly exercised unlimited dominion over him. It is true that only the fifteenth amendment in terms mentions the Negro by speaking of his color and his slavery. But it is just as true that each of the other articles was addressed to the grievances of that race, and designed to remedy them, as the fifteenth.

These amendments, one and all, are thus declared to have as their all-pervading design and end the security to the recently enslaved race, not only their nominal freedom, but their complete protection from those who had formerly exercised unlimited dominion over them. It is in this broad light that all these amendments must be read, the purpose to secure the perfect equality before the law of all citizens of the United States. What you give to one class you must give to all; what you deny to one class you shall deny to all, unless in the exercise of the common and universal police power of the State you find it needful to confer exclusive privileges on certain citizens, to be held and exercised still for the common good of all.

Such are the doctrines of the Slaughter-house Cases—doctrines worthy of the Republic, worthy of the age, worthy of the great tribunal which thus loftily and impressively enunciates them. Do they—I put it to any man, be he lawyer or not; I put it to the gentleman from Georgia—do they give color even to the claim that this Congress may not now legislate against a plain discrimination made by State laws or State customs against that very race for whose complete freedom and protection these great amendments were elaborated and adopted? Is it pretended, I ask the honorable gentleman from Kentucky or the honorable gentleman from Georgia—is it pretended anywhere that the evils of which we complain, our exclusion from the public inn, from the saloon and table of the steamboat, from the sleeping-coach on the railway, from the right of sepulture in the public burial-ground, are an exercise of the police power of the State? Is such oppression and injustice nothing but the exercise by the State of the right to make regulations for the health, comfort, and security of all her citizens? Is it merely enacting that one man shall so use his own as not to injure another's? Are the colored people to be assimilated to an unwholesome trade or to combustible materials, to be interdicted, to be shut up within prescribed limits? Let the gentleman from Kentucky or the gentleman from Georgia answer. Let the country know to what extent even the audacious prejudice of the gentleman from Kentucky will drive him, and how far even the gentleman from Georgia will permit himself to be led captive by the unrighteous teachings of a false political faith.

If we are to be likened in legal view to "unwholesome trades," to "large and offensive collections of animals," to "noxious slaughterhouses," to "the offal and stench which attend on certain manufactures," let it be avowed. If that is still the doctrine of the political party to which the gentlemen belong, let it be put upon record. If State laws which deny us the common rights and privileges of other citizens, upon no possible or conceivable ground save one of prejudice, or of "taste," as the gentleman from Texas termed it, and as I suppose the gentlemen will prefer to call it, are to be placed under the protection of a decision which affirms the right of a State to regulate the police of her great cities, then the decision is in conflict with the bill before us. No man will dare maintain such a doctrine. It is as shocking to the legal mind as it is offensive to the heart and conscience of all who love justice or respect manhood. I am astonished that the gentleman from Kentucky or the gentleman from Georgia should have been so grossly misled as

to rise here and assert that the decision of the Supreme Court in these cases was a denial to Congress of the power to legislate against discriminations on account of race, color, or previous condition of servitude, because that court has decided that exclusive privileges conferred for the common protection of the lives and health of the whole community are not in violation of the recent amendments. The only ground upon which the grant of exclusive privileges to a portion of the community is ever defended is that the substantial good of all is promoted; that in truth it is for the welfare of the whole community that certain persons should alone pursue certain occupations. It is not the special benefit conferred on the few that moves the legislature, but the ultimate and real benefit of all, even of those who are denied the right to pursue those specified occupations. Does the gentleman from Kentucky say that my good is promoted when I am excluded from the public inn? Is the health or safety of the community promoted? Doubtless his prejudice is gratified. Doubtless his democratic instincts are pleased; but will he or his able coadjutor say that such exclusion is a lawful exercise of the police power of the State, or that it is not a denial to me of the equal protection of the laws? They will not so say.

But each of these gentlemen quote at some length from the decision of the court to show that the court recognizes a difference between citizenship of the United States and citizenship of the States. That is true, and no man here who supports this bill questions or overlooks the difference. There are privileges and immunities which belong to me as a citizen of the United States, and there are other privileges and immunities which belong to me as a citizen of my State. The former are under the protection of the Constitution and laws of the United States, and the latter are under the protection of the constitution and laws of my State. But what of that? Are the rights which I now claim—the right to enjoy the common public conveniences of travel on public highways, of rest and refreshment at public inns, of education in public schools, of burial in public cemeteries—rights which I hold as a citizen of the United States or of my State? Or, to state the question more exactly, is not the denial of such privileges to me a denial to me of the equal protection of the laws? For it is under this clause of the fourteenth amendment that we place the present bill, no State shall "deny to any person within its jurisdiction the equal protection of the laws." No matter, therefore, whether his rights are held under the United States or under his particular State, he is equally protected by this amendment. He is always and everywhere entitled to the equal protection of the laws. All discrimination is forbidden; and while the rights of citizens of a State as such are not defined or conferred by the Constitution of the United States, yet all discrimination, all denial of equality before the law, all denial of the equal protection of the laws, whether State or national laws, is forbidden.

The distinction between the two kinds of citizenship is clear, and the Supreme Court have clearly pointed out this distinction, but they have nowhere written a word or line which denies to Congress the power to prevent a denial of equality of rights, whether those rights exist by virtue of citizenship of the United States or of a State. Let honorable members mark well this distinction. There are rights which are conferred on us by the United States. There are other rights conferred on us by the States of which we are individually the citizens. The fourteenth amendment does not forbid a State to deny to all its citizens any of those rights which the State itself has conferred, with certain exceptions, which are pointed out in the decision which we are examining. What it does forbid is inequality, is discrimination, or, to use the words of the amendment itself, is the denial "to any person within its jurisdiction the equal protection of the laws." If a State denies to me rights which are common to all her other citizens, she violates this amendment, unless she can show, as was shown in the Slaughter-house Cases, that she does it in the legitimate exercise of her police power. If she abridges the rights of all her citizens equally, unless those rights are specially guarded by the Constitution of the United States, she does not violate this amendment. This is not to put the rights which I hold by virtue of my citizenship of South Carolina under the protection of the national Government; it is not to blot out or overlook in the slightest particular the distinction between rights held under the United States and the rights held under the States; but it seeks to secure equality, to prevent discrimination, to confer as complete and ample protection on the humblest as on the highest.

The gentleman from Kentucky, in the course of the speech to which I am now replying, made a reference to the State of Massachusetts which betrays again the confusion which exists in his mind on this precise point. He tells us that Massachusetts excludes from the ballot-box all who cannot read and write, and points to that fact as the exercise of a right which this bill would abridge or impair. The honorable gentleman from Massachusetts (Mr. Dawes) answered him truly and well, but I submit that he did not make the best reply. Why did he not ask the gentleman from Kentucky if Massachusetts had ever discriminated against any of her citizens on account of color, or race, or previous condition of servitude? When did Massachusetts sully her proud record by placing on her statute-book any law which admitted to the ballot the white man and shut out the black man? She has never done it; she will not do it; she cannot do it so long as we have a Supreme Court which reads the Constitution of our country with the eyes of justice; nor can Massachusetts or Kentucky deny to any man, on account of his race, color, or previous condition of servitude, that perfect equality of protection under the laws so long as Congress shall exercise the power to enforce, by appropriate legislation, the great and unquestionable securities embodied in the fourteenth amendment to the Constitution.

But, sir, a few words more as to the suffrage regulation of Massachusetts. It is true that Massachusetts in 1857, finding that her illiterate population was being constantly augmented by the continual influx of ignorant emigrants, placed in her constitution the least possible limitation consistent with manhood suffrage to stay this tide of foreign ignorance. Its benefit has been fully demonstrated in the intelligent character of the voters of that honored Commonwealth, reflected so conspicuously in the able Representatives she has today upon this floor. But neither is the inference of the gentleman from Kentucky legitimate, nor do the statistics of the census of 1870, drawn from his own State, sustain his astounding assumption. According to the statistics we find the whole white population of that State is 1,098,692; the whole colored population 222,210. Of the whole white population who cannot write we find 201,077; of the whole colored population who cannot write, 126,048; giving us, as will be seen, 96,162 colored persons who can write to 897,615 white persons who can write. Now, the ratio of the colored population to the white is as 1 to 5, and the ratio of the illiterate colored population to the whole colored population is as 1 to 2; the ratio of the illiterate white population is to the whole white population is as 1 to 5. Reducing this, we have only a preponderance of three-tenths in favor of the whites as to literacy, notwithstanding the advantages which they have always enjoyed and do now enjoy of free-school privileges, and this, too, taking solely into account the single item of being unable to write; for with regard to the inability to read, there is no discrimination in the statistics between the white and colored population. There is, moreover, a peculiar felicity in these statistics with regard to the State of Kentucky, quoted so opportunely for me by the honorable gentleman; for I find that the population of the State, both with regard to its white and colored populations, bears the same relative rank in regard to the white and colored population of the United States; and, therefore, while one Negro would be disfranchised were the limitation of Massachusetts put in force, nearly three white men would at the same time be deprived of the right of suffrage—a consummation which I think would be far more acceptable to the colored people of that State than to the whites.

Now, sir, having spoken as to the intention of the prohibition imposed by Massachusetts, I may be pardoned for a slight inquiry as to the effect of this prohibition. First, it did not in any way abridge or curtail the exercise of the suffrage by any person who at that time enjoyed such right. Nor did it discriminate between the illiterate native and the illiterate foreigner. Being enacted for the good of the entire Commonwealth, like all just laws, its obligations fell equally and impartially upon all its citizens. And as a justification for such a measure, it is a fact too well known almost for mention here that Massachusetts had, from the beginning of her history, recognized the inestimable value of an educated ballot, by not only maintaining a system of free schools, but also enforcing an attendance thereupon, as one of the safeguards for the preservation of a real republican form of government. Recurring then, sir, to the possible contingency alluded to by the gentleman from Kentucky, should the State of Kentucky, having first established a system of common schools whose doors shall swing open freely to all, as contemplated by the provisions of this bill, adopt a provision similar to that of Massachusetts, no one would have cause justly to complain. And if in the coming years the result of such legislation should produce a constituency rivaling that of the old Bay State, no one would be more highly gratified than I.

Mr. Speaker, I have neither the time nor the inclination to notice the many illogical and forced conclusions, the numerous transfers of terms, of the vulgar insinuations which further incumber the argument of the gentleman from Kentucky. Reason and argument are worse than wasted upon those who meet every demand for political and civil liberty by such ribaldry as this— extracted from the speech of the gentleman from Kentucky:

I suppose there are gentlemen on this floor who would arrest, imprison, and fine a young woman in any State of the South if she were to refuse to marry a Negro man on account of color, race, or previous condition of servitude, in the event of his making her a proposal of marriage, and her refusing on that ground. That would be depriving him of a right he had under the amendment, and Congress would be asked to take it up and say, "This insolent white woman must be taught to know that it is a misdemeanor to deny a man marriage because of race, color, or previous condition of servitude"; and Congress will be urged to say after a while that that sort of thing must be put a stop to, and your conventions of colored men will come here asking you to enforce that right.

Now, sir, recurring to the venerable and distinguished gentleman from Georgia (Mr. Stephens), who has added his remonstrance against the passage of this bill, permit me to say that I share in the feeling of high personal regard for that gentleman which pervades this House. His years, his ability, and his long experience in public affairs entitle him to the measure of consideration which has been accorded to him on this floor. But in this discussion I cannot and I will not forget that the welfare and rights of my whole race in this country are involved. When, therefore, the honorable gentleman from Georgia lends his voice and influence to defeat this measure, I do not shrink from saying that it is not from him that the American House of Representatives should take lessons in matters touching human rights or the joint relations of the State and national governments. While the honorable gentleman contented himself with harmless speculations in his study, or in the columns of a newspaper, we might well smile at the impotence of his efforts to turn back the advancing tide of opinion and progress; but, when he comes again upon this national arena, and throws himself with all his power and influence across the path which leads to the full enfranchisement of my race, I meet him only as an adversary; nor shall age or any other consideration restrain me from saying that he now offers his Government, which he has done his utmost to destroy, a very poor return for its magnanimous treatment, to come here and seek to continue, by the assertion of doctrines obnoxious to the true principles of our Government, the burdens and oppressions which rest upon five millions of his countrymen who never failed to lift their earnest prayers for the success of this Government when the gentleman was seeking to break up the Union of these States and to blot the American Republic from the galaxy of nations. [Loud applause.]

Sir, it is scarcely twelve years since that gentleman shocked the civilized world by announcing the birth of a government which rested on human slavery as its corner-stone. The progress of events has swept away that pseudo-government, which rested on greed, pride, and tyranny; and the race whom he then ruthlessly spurned and trampled on are here to meet him in debate, and to demand that the rights which are enjoyed by their former oppressors—who vainly sought to overthrow a Government which they could not prostitute to the base uses of slavery—shall be accorded to those who even in the darkness of slavery kept their allegiance true to freedom and the Union. Sir, the gentleman from Georgia has learned much since 1861; but he is still a laggard. Let him put away entirely the false and fatal theories which have so greatly marred an otherwise enviable record. Let him accept, in its fullness and beneficence, the great doctrine that American citizenship carries with it every civil and political right which manhood can confer. Let him lend his influence, with all his masterly ability, to complete the proud structure of legislation which makes this nation worthy of the great declaration which heralded its birth, and he will have done that which will most nearly redeem his reputation in the eyes of the world, and best vindicate the wisdom of that policy which has permitted him to regain his seat upon this floor.

To the diatribe of the gentleman from Virginia (Mr. Harris), who spoke on yesterday, and who so far transcended the limits of decency and propriety as to announce upon this floor that his remarks were addressed to white men alone, I shall have no word of reply. Let him feel that a Negro was not only too magnanimous to smite him in his weakness, but was even charitable enough to grant him the mercy of his silence. [Laughter and applause on the floor and in the galleries.] I shall, sir, leave to others less charitable the unenviable and fatiguing task of sifting out of that mass of chaff the few grains of sense that may, perchance, deserve notice. Assuring the gentleman that the Negro in this country aims at a higher degree of intellect than that exhibited by him in this debate, I cheerfully commend him to the commiseration of all intelligent men the world over—black men as well as white men.

Sir, equality before the law is now the broad, universal, glorious rule and mandate of the Republic. No State can violate that. Kentucky and Georgia may crowd their statute-books with retrograde and barbarous legislation; they may rejoice in the odious eminence of their consistent hostility to all the great steps of human progress which have marked our national history since slavery tore down the stars and stripes on Fort Sumter; but, if Congress shall do its duty, if Congress shall enforce the great guarantees which the Supreme Court has declared to be the one pervading purpose of all the recent amendments, then their unwise and unenlightened conduct will fall with the same weight upon the gentlemen from those States who now lend their influence to defeat this bill, as upon the poorest slave who once had no rights which the honorable gentlemen were bound to respect.

But, sir, not only does the decision in the Slaughter-house Cases contain nothing which suggests a doubt of the power of Congress to pass the pending bill, but it contains an express recognition and affirmance of such power. I quote now from page 81 of the volume:

"Nor shall any State deny to any person within its jurisdiction the equal protection of the laws."

In the light of the history of these amendments, and the pervading purpose of them, which we have already discussed, it is not difficult to give a meaning to this clause. The existence of laws in the States where the newly emancipated Negroes resided, which discriminated with gross injustice and hardship against them as a class, was the evil to be remedied by this clause, and by it such laws are forbidden.

If, however, the States did not conform their laws to its requirements, then, by the fifth section of the article of amendment, Congress was authorized to enforce it by suitable legislation. We doubt very much whether any action of a State not directed by way of discrimination against the Negroes as a class, or on account of their race, will ever be held to come within the purview of this provision. It is so clearly a provision for that race and that emergency, that a strong case would be necessary for its application to any other. But as it is a State that is to be dealt with, and not alone the validity of its laws, we may safely leave that matter until Congress shall have exercised its power, or some case of State oppression, by denial of equal justice in its courts shall have claimed a decision at our hands.

No language could convey a more complete assertion of the power of Congress over the subject embraced in the present bill than is here expressed. If the States do not conform to the requirements of this clause, if they continue to deny to any person within their jurisdiction the equal protection of the laws, or as the Supreme Court had said, "deny equal justice in its courts," then Congress is here said to have power to enforce the constitutional guarantee by appropriate legislation. That is the power which this bill now seeks to put in exercise. It proposes to enforce the constitutional guarantee against inequality and discrimination by appropriate legislation. It does not seek to confer new rights, nor to place rights conferred by State citizenship under the protection of the United States, but simply to prevent and forbid inequality and discrimination on account of race, color, or previous condition of servitude. Never was there a bill more completely within the constitutional power of Congress. Never was there a bill which appealed for support more strongly to that sense of justice and fair-play which has been said, and in the main with justice, to be a characteristic of the Anglo-Saxon race. The Constitution warrants it; the Supreme Court sanctions it; justice demands it.

Sir, I have replied to the extent of my ability to the arguments which have been presented by the opponents of this measure. I have replied also to some of the legal propositions advanced by gentlemen on the other side; and now that I am about to conclude, I am deeply sensible of the imperfect manner in which I have performed the task. Technically, this bill is to decide upon the civil status of the colored American citizen; a point disputed at the very formation of our present Government, when by a short-sighted policy, a policy repugnant to true republican government, one Negro counted as three-fifths of a man. The logical result of this mistake of the

framers of the Constitution strengthened the cancer of slavery, which finally spread its poisonous tentacles over the southern portion of the body-politic. To arrest its growth and save the nation we have passed through the harrowing operation of internecine war, dreaded at all times, resorted to at the last extremity, like the surgeon's knife, but absolutely necessary to extirpate the disease which threatened with the life of the nation the overthrow of civil and political liberty on this continent. In that dire extremity the members of the race which I have the honor in part to represent—the race which pleads for justice at your hands today, forgetful of their inhuman and brutalizing servitude at the South, their degradation and ostracism at the North—flew willingly and gallantly to the support of the national Government. Their sufferings, assistance, privations, and trials in the swamps and in the rice-fields, their valor on the land and on the sea, is a part of the ever-glorious record which makes up the history of a nation preserved, and might, should I urge the claim, incline you to respect and guarantee their rights and privileges as citizens of our common Republic. But I remember that valor, devotion, and loyalty are not always rewarded according to their just deserts, and that after the battle some who have borne the brunt of the fray may, through neglect or contempt, be assigned to a subordinate place, while the enemies in war may be preferred to the sufferers.

The results of the war, as seen in reconstruction, have settled forever the political status of my race. The passage of this bill will determine the civil status, not only of the Negro, but of any other class of citizens who may feel themselves discriminated against. It will form the cap-stone of that temple of liberty, begun on this continent under discouraging circumstances, carried on in spite of the sneers of monarchists and the cavils of pretended friends of freedom, until at last it stands in all its beautiful symmetry and proportions, a building the grandest which the world has ever seen, realizing the most sanguine expectations and the highest hopes of those who, in the name of equal, impartial, and universal liberty, laid the foundation stones.

The Holy Scriptures tell us of an humble handmaiden who long, faithfully and patiently gleaned in the rich fields of her wealthy kinsman; and we are told further that at last, in spite of her humble antecedents, she found complete favor in his sight. For over two centuries our race has "reaped down your fields." The cries and woes which we have uttered have "entered into the ears of the Lord of Sabaoth," and we are at last politically free. The last vestiture only is needed— civil rights. Having gained this, we may, with hearts overflowing with gratitude, and thankful that our prayer has been granted, repeat the prayer of Ruth: "Entreat me not to leave thee, or to return from following after thee; for whither thou goest, I will go; and where thou lodgest, I will lodge; thy people shall be my people, and thy God my God; where thou diest, will I die, and there will I be buried; the Lord do so to me, and more also, if aught but death part thee and me." [Great applause.]

Blanche K. Bruce (1841–1898)

It is one of history's fascinating ironies that Mississippi, with its long and sustained record of racial violence, produced America's three most eminent Black Reconstruction politicians. These were John R. Lynch, Hiram K. Revels, and Blanche K. Bruce. Of the three, John Lynch was undoubtedly the most enterprising and the most gifted. Starting out as Speaker of the Mississippi House at the young age of twenty-four, he eventually served two full terms as a Congressman and became the confidante of Presidents during this turbulent period in American history. Hiram Revels was the best educated of the three, having finished college in Ohio to prepare for the ministry and then, following his short career as a United States Senator, becoming the first president of Alcorn College in Lorman, Mississippi. But, if one's success is measured by the distance one travels, Blanche K. Bruce was the most successful of the three. Born a slave in Prince Edward County, Virginia, he escaped as a young man and until the war spent his time wandering as a fugitive. Four years after the end of the war, in 1869, he wandered down to Mississippi to try his hand at farming, the only career for which he was prepared.

He picked the right state at the right time, for he arrived just when the political reconstruction and reorganization of the state were beginning to take place under the aegis of the newly formed Republican Party. John R. Lynch in his *The Facts of Reconstruction* (1913) records Bruce's small steady stairsteps to ultimate political success. First he was elected to the humble post of sergeant-at-arms of the state senate in the new Republican-dominated legislature of 1870. Then, when the legislature adjourned, Bruce was sent to Bolivar County in 1871 in the rich Mississippi Delta country to become county assessor. After discharging his functions as assessor quite creditably, he was next appointed sheriff and tax collector of that county. From this position he was elected to the United States Senate, becoming the only Black person in his century to gain and hold a seat for a full term.

One or two other facts should be noted about Blanche K. Bruce. First, he had a great sense of political timing. John Lynch records how he turned down his party's request that he accept the nomination for lieutenant-governor of Mississippi in 1873. Lynch's account is as follows:

> *After going over the field very carefully it was decided that there was just one man possessing the necessary qualifications—B. K. Bruce of Bolivar County. He, it was decided, was just the man for the place, and to him the nomination was to be tendered. . . . But Mr. Bruce positively declined. He could not be induced under any circumstances to change his mind. He was fixed in his determination not to allow his name to be used for the office of Lieutenant-Governor, and from that determination he could not be moved.*

Later, it was revealed that Bruce's firm declination was based on a sound strategy to hold himself open and available to be a candidate for the United States Senate to fill the unexpired term of Senator Ames, who was elected governor by the Republicans in 1874. This proved to be a wise decision, for the state elections of 1875 became a blood bath for Black candidates and for Black voters and an overwhelming, if illegal, victory for the resurgent all-white Democratic Party. By this time Bruce was safely ensconced in Washington and remained there until 1881—a post-Reconstruction symbol of what might have been had there been no Hayes-Tilden Compromise over white electoral votes following the presidential election of 1876 and no withdrawal of Federal troops and protection from the South.

A second point to be made about Blanche Bruce is that he used his high office in the Senate to speak out fearlessly against the crimes perpetrated against Black men in his own state and in other states of the South—hence, his speech on the Senate floor charging the all-white Democratic Party with high crimes and bloody misdeameanors in the election of 1875 and his speech in a futile defense of the right of P. B. S. Pinchback to have his seat in the Senate despite the irregularities charged in Pinchback's election.

Third, Blanche K. Bruce had a relentless kind of "survival power" amid what were truly perilous times for a Black Republican from Mississippi. For he went to Washington virtually on the eve of the violent overthrow of Black Republicanism in Mississippi. His very introduction to the Senate, when Senator Alcorn—an ex-Confederate general from Mississippi and an ex-Republican—refused to escort him for presentation to the Senate, demonstrated that his six-year term was to be spent amid hostility and loneliness. Yet he persevered until his term expired in 1881, and he was able to move to an appointment in the Department of the Treasury. The adversities of slavery and slavery's grim aftermath had given him both the courage and the wisdom to endure.

As indicated above, John R. Lynch's *The Facts of Reconstruction* (1913) contains a precise account of Bruce's contributions as a Reconstruction politician. More recent works that discuss his career are Vernon L. Wharton, *The Negro in Mississippi, 1865–1890* (1947); John Hope Franklin, *Reconstruction After the Civil War* (1961); and Kenneth M. Stampp, *The Era of Reconstruction* (1965).

Address Delivered to the United States Senate in Behalf of Admitting P. B. S. Pinchback, March 3, 1876

When I entered upon my duties here as Senator from Mississippi, the question ceased to be novel, and had already been elaborately and exhaustively discussed. So far as opportunity has permitted me to do so, I have dispassionately examined the question in the light of the discussion, and I venture my views now with the diffidence inspired by my limited experience in the consideration of such questions and by a just appreciation of the learning and ability of the gentlemen who have already attempted to elucidate and determine this case.

I believe, Mr. President, whatever seeming informalities may attach to the manner in which the will of the people was ascertained, Mr. Pinchback is the representative of a majority of the legal voters of Louisiana, and is entitled to a seat in the Senate. In the election of 1872, the white population of the state exceeded, by the census of 1872, the colored population by about two thousand, including in the white estimate 6,300 foreigners, only half of whom were naturalized. This estimate, at the same ratio in each race, would give a large majority of colored voters. The census and registration up to 1872 substantially agree, and both sustain this conclusion. The census of 1875, taken in pursuance of an article of the State constitution, gives, after including the foreign population (naturalized and unnaturalized) in the white aggregate, a majority of 45,695 colored population.

This view of the question is submitted not as determining the contest, but as an offset to the allegation that Mr. Pinchback does not fairly represent the popular will of the State, and as a presumption in favor of the legal title of the assembly that elected him.

The State government elected in 1872, and permanently inaugurated in January, 1873, in the face of contest and opposition, obtained for its authority recognition of the inferior and supreme courts of the State. When organized violence threatened its existence and the United States Government was appealed to for troops to sustain it, the national Executive, in pursuance of his constitutional authority and duty, responded to the demand made for help, prefacing said action by an authoritative declaration, made through the Attorney General, addressed to Lieutenant-Governor Pinchback, then Acting Governor, of date of December 17, 1872, that said Pinchback was "recognized as the lawful executive of Louisiana, and the body assembled at Mechanics' Institute as the lawful Legislature of the State"; and similar recognition of his successor was subsequently given. When in September, 1874, an attempt was made to overthrow the government, the President again interposed with the Army and Navy for its protection and the maintenance of its authority.

This government has proceeded to enact and enforce laws for three years, which not only affect life, liberty, and property, but which have received the general obedience of the citizens of the State. The present government also has frequently been brought in official contact with the United States Congress—through its legislatures of 1873 and 1875, by memorials and joint resolutions addressed to the respective Houses; and through its executive, by credentials, borne by Congressmen and by Senators—and in no instance has the sufficiency of the executive's credentials been questioned, in either House, except in the matter of the senatorial claimant.

Now, Sir, shall we admit by our action on this case that for three years the State of Louisiana has not had a lawful Legislature; that its laws have been made by an unauthorized mob; that the President of the United States actively, and Congress, by non-action at least, have sustained and perpetuated this abnormal, illegal, wrongful condition of things, thereby justifying and provoking the indignant and violent protests of one portion of the people of that State, and inviting them to renewed and continued agitation and violence? Such action by us would be unjust to the claimant, a great wrong to the people who sent him here, and cruel even to that class who have awaited an opportunity to bring to their support the overwhelming moral power of the nation in the pursuit of their illusion—which has so nearly ruined the future of that fair State—a government based upon the prejudices of caste.

I respectfully ask attention of Senators to another view of this subject, which is not without weight in determining the obligations of this body to the State of Louisiana and in ascertaining the title of the claimant. If the assumption that the present government inaugurated in 1873 is without legal authority and usurpation is true, the remedy for the state of things was to be found in the exercise of Congress through the joint action of the two Houses of the powers conferred under the guaranteeing clause of the Constitution relative to republican forms of government in the several States.

Failing to exercise her power and perform her duty in this direction, and thus practically perpetuating the present government, I submit that, in my judgment, we cannot now ignore our obligation to give the State her full representation on the score of the alleged irregularity of the government through which she has expressed her will; and there does seem to me, in this connection, something incongruous in the proposition that we may impose upon the people a government without legal sanction and demand their obedience to and support thereof, said government meanwhile determining the character of its successions and thus perpetuating its talent, and yet are powerless to admit a Senator elected thereby.

In my judgment, this question shall at this juncture be considered and decided not on abstract but practical grounds. Whatever wrongs have been done and mistakes made in Louisiana by either party, the present order of things is accepted by the people of the State and by the nation, and will be maintained as final settlement of the political issues that have divided the people there; and no changes in the administration of public affairs can or will be made except by the people, through the ballot, under the existing government and laws of the Commonwealth.

Under these circumstances, holding the question in abeyance is, in my judgment, an unconstitutional deprivation of a State, and a provocation of popular disquietude; and in the interest of goodwill and good government, the most judicious and consistent course is to admit the claimant to his seat.

I desire, Mr. President, to make a personal reference to the claimant. I would not attempt one or deem one proper were it not that his personal character has been assailed.

As a father, I know him to be affectionate; as a husband, the idol of a pleasant home and cheerful fireside; as a citizen, loyal, brave, and true. And in his character and success we behold an admirable illustration of the excellence of our republican institutions.

Speech to the United States Senate on Mississippi Election, Delivered March 31, 1876

The conduct of the late election in Mississippi affected not merely the fortunes of the partisans—as the same were necessarily involved in the defeat or success of the respective parties to the contest—but put in question and jeopardy the sacred rights of the citizens; and the investigation contemplated in the pending resolution has for its object not the determination of the question whether the offices shall be held and the public affairs of the State be administered by democrats or republicans, but the higher and more important end, the protection in all their purity and significance of the political rights of the people and the free institutions of the country.

The evidence in hand and accessible will show beyond peradventure that in many parts of the State corrupt and violent influences were brought to bear upon the registrars of voters, thus materially affecting the character of the voting or poll lists; upon the inspectors of election, prejudicially and unfairly, thereby changing the number of votes cast; and finally threats and violence were practiced directly upon the masses of voters in such measures and strength as to produce grave apprehensions for personal safety and as to deter them from the exercise of their political franchises.

It will not accord with the laws of nature or history to brand colored people a race of cowards. On more than one historic field, beginning in 1776 and coming down to the centennial year of the Republic, they have attested in blood their courage as well as a love of liberty. I ask Senators to believe that no consideration of fear or personal danger has kept us quiet and forbearing under the provocations and wrongs that have so sorely tried our souls. But feeling kindly towards our white fellow-citizens, appreciating the good purposes and offices of the better classes, and, above all, abhorring war of races, we determined to wait until such time as an appeal to the good sense and justice of the American people could be made.

The sober American judgment must obtain in the South as elsewhere in the Republic, that the only distinctions upon which parties can be safely organized and in harmony with our institutions are differences of opinion relative to principles and policies of government, and that differences of religion, nationality, or race can neither with safety nor propriety be permitted for a moment to enter into the party contests of the day. The unanimity with which the colored voters act with a party is not referable to any race prejudice on their part. On the contrary, they invite the political co-operation of their white brethren, and vote as a unit because proscribed as such. They deprecate the establishment of the color line by the opposition, not only because the act is unwise, but because it isolates them from the white men of the South and forces them, in sheer self-protection, and against their inclination, to act seemingly upon the basis of a race prejudice that they neither respect nor entertain. They not only recognize the equality of citizenship and the right of every man to hold without proscription any position of honor and trust to which the confidence of the people may elevate him; but owing nothing to race, birth, or sur-

roundings, they above all other classes, in the community, are interested to see prejudices drop out of both politics and the businesses of the country, and success in life proceed upon the integrity and merit of the man who seeks it. . . . But withal, as they progress in intelligence and appreciation of the dignity of their prerogatives as citizens, they as an evidence of growth begin to realize the significance of the proverb, "When thou doest well for thyself, men shall praise thee"; and are disposed to exact the same protection and concessions of rights that are conferred upon other citizens by the Constitution, and that too without humiliation involved in the enforced abandonment of their political convictions.

I have confidence, not only in my country and her institutions, but in the endurance, capacity and destiny of my people. We will, as opportunity offers and ability serves, seek our places, sometimes in the field of literary arts, science and the professions. More frequently mechanical pursuits will attract and elicit our efforts; more still of my people will find employment and livelihood as the cultivators of the soil. The bulk of this people—by surroundings, habits, adaptation, and choice will continue to find their homes in the South and constitute the masses of its yeomanry. We will there, probably of our own volition and more abundantly than in the past, produce the great staples that will contribute to the basis of foreign exchange, and in giving the nation a balance of trade and minister to the wants and comforts and build up the prosperity of the whole land. Whatever our ultimate position in the composite civilization of the Republic and whatever varying fortunes attend our career, we will not forget our instincts for freedom nor our love for country.

Poetry

Albery A. Whitman (1851–1902)

Albery A. Whitman, like other Black writers of his generation, led a life of formidable activity and variety. Born a slave, he was "emancipated" in 1863, and, although he had little formal education, he became a prominent minister in the A.M.E. Church and the most prolific Black poet of his time. At first, he was a school teacher and then, encouraged by Bishop Daniel Payne, he developed into a forceful and articulate itinerant preacher throughout the Middle West.

Writing poetry, however, was Whitman's main calling. Starting with his first work, *Essay on the Ten Plagues and Other Miscellaneous Poems,* written some time before 1873, he wrote more poetry, in terms of sheer volume, than any of his literary contemporaries. His first published poem, *Leelah Misled* (1873), does not treat a racial theme, but it does introduce what was to become the Whitman formula in long narrative melodramatic poetry. His next poem, *Not a Man and Yet a Man,* aptly bears this out. It appeared in 1877; unlike *Leelah Misled,* it is racial in theme, but, like the earlier poem, it is an example of long poetic narration surfeited with melodramatic incident. This poem also suffers from the dubious distinction of being, up until that time, the longest poem composed by a Black writer. *Not a Man and Yet a Man* is set in slavery times and deals with the varied romantic fortunes of a strong-hearted slave hero named Rodney. Early in the story, he rescues his master's fair-haired daughter from certain death at the hands of marauding Indians. When she is about to bestow upon him a fitting romantic reward, the minions of the "system" quickly sell him South. There, with more appropriateness, he falls in love with Leeona, a beautiful Black slave girl, and, after many hazards and mishaps and thrilling adventures, these two find love, happiness, and freedom in Canada. Needless to say, in the aftermath of the Civil War and in the floodtide of American Romanticism, there were many "Rodneys and Leeonas" appearing in the fiction and poetry of the 1870's and 1880's.

Whitman's best-known work is *Rape of Florida* (1884), an epic poem about the tragedy of the American Indian after the manner of Longfellow's *Hiawatha.* Written in Spenserian stanzas and many cantos, it was reissued in 1885 with slight modifications under the title *Twasinta's Seminoles; or, Rape of Florida.* Although the poem cannot be termed a fully successful literary effort, Whitman's epic does bespeak great literary resourcefulness and considerable poetic craftsmanship, particularly in terms of metrical virtuosity. Indeed, no Black poet used a greater variety of meters in his poetry than did Whitman, ranging all the way from various forms of the couplet in *Not a Man and Yet a Man* to the *ottava rima* in his last work, *Idyl of the South*.

Evidently, the public reception accorded both *Not a Man* and *Rape of Florida* was encouraging, for both poems were reprinted in 1890, together with an earlier collection of miscellaneous poems entitled *Drifted Leaves*. A very reliable index of Whitman's widespread popularity was his appearance, along with other Black luminaries, at the Chicago World's Fair on "Colored American Day," August 25, 1893. Sharing the platform with Douglass, a very youthful Dunbar, and others, Whitman recited a poem entitled "The Freedman's Triumphant Song," written especially for the occasion. From this same platform, the poet's wife, Caddie Whitman, recited "The Veteran," one of the poems from *Drifted Leaves*.

Whitman's last work was *An Idyl of the South, an Epic Poem in Two Parts*. The first part, *The Octoroon*, which appeared in 1901, is very much like Vashon's *A Life-Day* in plot and setting. Here again is the standard master–slave love affair with all of the attendant tensions, sighs, and palpitations. The second part of the epic, *The Southland's Charms and Freedom's Magnitude*, appeared in 1902, the year of Whitman's death. This section contains a somewhat surprising apologia for the antebellum South, indicative either of a discernible decline in the poet's racial zeal or of the toll popular success takes of some poets.

Sterling Brown's *Negro Poetry and Drama* (1937) provides a short but incisive evaluation of Whitman's poetry. Vernon Loggins' *The Negro Author* (1931) also contains a good critical account. A fuller critical statement and assessment can be found in William H. Robinson's edition of *Early Black American Poets* (1969). Fortunately, plans have been made to publish a collected edition of this very prolific Black American's poems and sermons.

from *Rape of Florida*

Canto I

I

The negro slave by Swanee river sang;
Well-pleased he listened to his echoes ringing;
For in his heart a secret comfort sprang,
When Nature seemed to join his mournful singing.
To mem'ry's cherished objects fondly clinging;
His bosom felt the sunset's patient glow,
And spirit whispers into weird life springing,
Allured to worlds he trusted yet to know,
And lightened for a while life's burdens here
  below.

II

The drowsy dawn from many a low-built shed,
Beheld his kindred driven to their task;
Late evening saw them turn with weary tread
And painful faces back; and dost thou ask
How sang these bondmen? how their suff'rings
  mask?
Song is the soul of sympathy divine,
And hath an inner ray where hope may bask;
Song turns the poorest waters into wine,
Illumines exile hearts and makes their faces
  shine.

III

The negro slave by Swanee river sang,
There soon the human hunter rode along;
And eagerly behind him came a gang
Of hounds and men,—the bondman hushed his
    song—
Around him came a silent, list'ning throng;
"Some runaway!" he muttered; said no more,
But sank from view the growing corn among;
And though deep pangs his wounded spirit bore,
He hushed his soul, and went on singing as
    before.

IV

So fared the land where slaves were groaning
    yet—
Where beauty's eyes must feed the lusts of men!
'Tis as when horrid dreams we half forget,
Would then relate, and still relate again—
Ah! cold abhorrence hesitates my pen!
The heavens were sad, and hearts of men were
    faint;
Philanthropy implored and wept, but then
The wrong, unblushing trampled on Restraint,
With feeble Law sat by and uttered no complaint.

V

"Fly and be free!" a whisper comes from heaven,
"Thy cries are heard!" the bondman's up and
    gone!
To grasp the dearest boon to mortals given,
He frantic flies, unaided and alone.
To him the red man's dwellings are unknown;
But he can crave the freedom of his race,
Can find his harvests in the desert sown,
And in the cypress forest's dark embrace
A pathway to his lonely habitations trace.

VI

The sable slave, from Georgia's utmost bounds,
Escapes for life into the Great Wahoo.
Here he has left afar the savage hounds
And human hunters that did late pursue;
There in the hommock darkly hid from view,
His wretched limbs are stretched awhile to rest,
Till some kind Seminole shall guide him thro'
To where by hound nor hunter more distrest,
He in a flow'ry home, shall be the red man's guest.

VII

If tilled profusion does not crown the view,
Nor wide-ranged farms begirt with fences spread;
The cultivated plot is well to do;
And where no slave his groaning life has led,
The songs of plenty fill the lowliest shed.
Who could wish more, when Nature, always
    green,

Brings forth fruit-bearing woods and fields of
    bread?
Wish more, where cheerful valleys bloom between,
And herds browse on the hills, where winter ne'er
    has been?

    .   .   .

X

Fair Florida! whose scenes could so enhance—
Could in the sweetness of the earth excel!
Wast thou the Seminole's inheritance?
Yea, it was thee he loved, and loved so well!
'Twas 'neath thy palms and pines he strove to
    dwell.
Not savage, but resentful to the knife,
For these he sternly struggled—sternly fell!
Thoughtful and brave, in long uneven strife,
He held the verge of manhood mid the heights of
    life.

XI

A wild-born pride endeared him to thy soil!
When roamed his herds without a keeper's care—
Where man knew not the pangs of slavish toil!
And where thou didst not blooming pleasures
    spare,
But well allotted each an ample share,
He loved to dwell: Oh! isn't the goal of life
Where man has plenty and to man is fair?
When free from avarice's pinch and strife,
Is earth not like the Eden-home of man and wife?

    .   .   .

XIX

Oh! sing it in the light of freedom's morn,
Tho' tyrant wars have made the earth a grave;
The good, the great, and true, are, if so, born,
And so with slaves, *chains do not make the slave!*
If high-souled birth be what the mother gave,—
If manly birth, and manly to the core,—
Whate'er the test, the man will he behave!
Crush him to earth and crush him o'er and o'er,
A man he'll rise at last and meet you as before.

XX

So with our young Atlassa,[1] hero-born,—
Free as the air within his palmy shade,
The nobler traits that do the man adorn,
In him were native: Not the music made
In Tampa's forests or the everglade
Was fitter than in this young Seminole

[1] "Atlassa," was Wild Cat, or Cooacoochee—an
eminent Seminole chieftain. He went with his people
to Fort Smith and the Indian Territory and thence to
South Rosa, Mexico, where [he] died at a very
advanced age, not long ago. I had the honor of
meeting two of his nephews, very intelligent gentlemen,
in 1884.—The Author.

Was the proud spirit which did life pervade,
And glow and tremble in his ardent soul—
Which, lit his inmost-self, and spurned all mean
    control.

XXI

Than him none followed chase with nimbler feet,
None readier in the forest council rose;
To speak for war, e'er sober and discreet,
In battle stern, but kind to fallen foes;
He led the *charge,* but halted,—slow to close
The vexed retreat: In front of battle he,
Handsome and wild his proud form would
    expose;
But in the cheering van of victory,
Gentle and brave he was the real chief to see.

XXII

Lo! mid a thousand warriors where he stands,
Pride of all hearts and idol of his race!
Look how the chieftains of his war-tried bands
Kindle their courage in his valiant face!
And as his lips in council open, trace
How deep suspense her earnest furrows makes
On ev'ry brow! How rings the forest-place
With sounding cheers! when native valor wakes
His dark intrepid eyes, and he their standard
    takes!

XXIII

Proud spirit of the hommock-bounded home
Well wast thy valor like a buckler worn!
And when the light of other times shall come,—
When history's muse shall venture to adorn
The brow of all her children hero-born,—
When the bold truth to man alike assigns
The place he merits, of no honor shorn;
The wreath shall be, that thy proud brow
    entwines,
As green as Mickasukie's everlasting pines!

XXIV

Well bled thy warriors at their leader's side!
Well stood they the oppressor's wasting fire;
For years sweep on, and in their noiseless tide,
Bear down the mem'ries of the past! The dire
And gloomful works of tyrants shall expire,
Till naught survives, save truth's great victories;
Then shall the voyager on his way aspire
To ponder what vast wrecks of time he sees
And on Fame's temple columns read their
    memories!

XXV

Not so with Osceola, thy dark mate;
The hidden terror of the hommock, he
Sat gloomily and nursed a bitter hate,—
The white man was his common enemy—

He rubbed the burning wounds of injury,
And plotted in his dreadful silent gloom;
As dangerous as a rock within the sea.
And when in fray he showed his fearless plume,
Revenge made sweet the blows that dealt the
    white man's doom.

XXVI

The pent-up wrath that rankled in his breast,
O'er smould'ring embers shot a lurid glare,
And wrongs that time itself had not redrest,
In ghost-like silence stalked and glimmered there.
And from the wizard caverns of despair,
Came voice and groan, reminding o'er and o'er
The outrage on his wife so young and fair;
And so, by heaven and earth and hell he swore
To treat in council with the white man never more.

XXVII

Such were the chiefs who led their daring braves
In many a battle nobly lost or won,
And consecrated Mickasukie's graves
To that sweet province of the summer sun!
And still shall history forgetful run?
Shall legend too be mute? then Poesy,
Divinest chronicler of deeds well done,
From the blest shrine and annals of the free,
Sing forth thy praise and man shall hear
    attentively.

XXVIII

The poorest negro coming to their shore,
To them was brother—their own flesh and
    blood,—
They sought his wretched manhood to restore,—
They found his hidings in the swampy wood,
And brought him forth—in arms before him
    stood,—
The citizens of God and sovran earth,—
They shot straight forward looks with flame
    imbued,
Till in him manhood sprang, a noble birth,
And warrior-armed he rose to all that manhood's
    worth.

XXIX

On the dark front of battle often seen,
Or holding dang'rous posts through dreadful
    hours,—
In ranks obedient, in command serene,
His comrades learn to note the tested powers
Which prove that valor is not always ours,
Be whomsoever we: A common race
Soon from this union flows—soon rarest flowers
Bloom out and smile in beauty's blending grace,
And rivals they become for love's sublimest
    place.

XXX

The native warrior leads his ebon maid,
The dark young brave his bloom-hued lover
  wins;
And where soft spruce and willows mingle
  shade,
Young life mid sunniest hours its course begins:
All Nature pours its never-ending dins
In groves of rare-hued leaf without'n end,—
'Tis as if Time, forgetting Eden's sins,
Relents, and spirit visitors descend
In love's remembered tokens, earth once more to
  blend.

XXXI

The sleepy mosses wave within the sun,
And on the dark elms climbs the mistletoe;
Great tangled vines through pendant branches
  run,
And hang their purple clusters far below;
The old pines wave their summits to and fro,
And dancing to the earth, impatient light
Touches the languid scene, to quickly go,
Like some gay spirit in its sunny plight,
That, visiting the earth, did glance and take its
  flight.

.   .   .

James Edwin Campbell (1860?–1905?)

James Campbell's most impressive distinction in the history of Black literature is that he was the first Black poet to write in Black plantation dialect and his dialect most nearly approximates the speech of the plantation. At least, that is the opinion of critics such as Saunders Redding and Sterling Brown. Not much is actually known about the literary career of this poet. Born in Pomeroy, Ohio, just as the Civil War was beginning, he ultimately became a journalist in Chicago, after attending Miami University in Oxford, Ohio. Just when he wrote "Ol' Doc' Hyar" is not exactly known, but it is assumed that it and other dialect pieces were written sometime in the 1880's when Campbell was working in Chicago. These poems were later collected and published in a volume entitled *Echoes from the Cabin and Elsewhere* in 1905.

A close examination of Campbell's dialect pieces reveals a realistic, unliterary approach to Black folk speech and, in some instances, a touch of Gullah speech patterns. For instance, the line in "Ol' Doc' Hyar"

> *He grab up he hat an' grab up he cane,*
> *Den—"blam!" go de do'—he gone lak de train*

has a "geechee" or Gullah lilt to it. This poem also contains a clear social message. "Ol' Doc' Hyar" who lives in a mighty fine house on a mighty high hill cares nothing for the welfare of his patients. His medical philosophy is expressed in the lines

> *"Ef pahsons git well ur pahsons git wu's,*
> *Money got ter come een de Ol' Hyar's pu's."*

In other words, Campbell could write good satire as well as good dialect verse.

James Campbell's poetry receives effective comment and analysis in
Saunders Redding's *To Make A Poet Black* (1939) and in Sterling Brown's
Negro Poetry and Drama (1969). Several of his poems can also be found
in William H. Robinson's *Early Black American Poets* (1969).

Ol' Doc' Hyar

Ur ol' Hyar lib in ur house on de hill,
He hunner yurs ol' an' nebber wuz ill;
He yurs dee so long an' he eyes so beeg,
An' he laigs so spry dat he dawnce ur jeeg;
He lib so long that he know ebbry tings
'Bout de beas'ses dat walks an' de bu'ds dat
    sings—
                Dis Ol' Doc' Hyar,
                Whar lib up dar
Een ur mighty fine house on ur mighty high hill.

He doctah fur all de beas'ses an' bu'ds—
He put on he specs an' he use beeg wu'ds,
He feel dee pu's' den he look mighty wise,
He pull out he watch an' he shet boofe eyes;
He grab up he hat an' grab up he cane,
Den—"blam!" go de do'—he gone lak de train,
                Dis O' Doc' Hyar,
                Whar lib up dar
Een ur mighty fine house on ur mighty high hill.

Mistah B'ar fall sick—dee sont fur Doc' Hyar,
"Oh, Doctah, come queeck, an' see Mr. B'ar;
He mighty nigh daid des sho' ez you b'on!"
"Too much ur young peeg, too much ur green
    co'n,"
Ez he put on he hat, said Ol' Doc' Hyar;

"I'll tek 'long meh lawnce, an' lawnce Mistah
    B'ar,"
                Said Ol' Doc' Hyar,
                Whar lib up dar
Een ur mighty fine house on ur mighty high hill.

Mistah B'ar he groaned, Mistah B'ar he
    growled,
W'ile de ol' Miss B'ar an' de chillen howled;
Doctah Hyar tuk out he sha'p li'l lawnce,
An' pyu'ced Mistah B'ar twel he med him
    prawnce
Den grab up he hat an' grab up he cane
"Blam!" go de do' an' he gone lak de train,
                Dis Ol' Doc' Hyar,
                Whar lib up dar
Een ur mighty fine house on ur mighty high hill.

But de vay naix day Mistah B'ar he daid;
Wen dee tell Doc' Hyar, he des scratch he haid:
"Ef pahsons git well ur pahsons git wu's,
Money got ter come een de Ol' Hyar's pu's;
Not wut folkses does, but fur wut dee know
Does de folkses git paid"—an' Hyar larfed low,
                Dis sma't Ol' Hyar,
                Whar lib up dar
Een de mighty fine house on de mighty high hill!

When Ol' Sis' Judy Pray

When ol' Sis' Judy pray,
De teahs come stealin' down my cheek,
De voice ur God widin me speak';
I see myse'f so po' an' weak,
Down on my knees de cross I seek,
When ol' Sis' Judy pray.

When ol' Sis' Judy pray,
De thun'ers ur Mount Sin-a-i
Comes rushin' down f'um up on high—
De Debbil tu'n his back an' fly
While sinnahs loud fur pa'don cry,
When ol' Sis' Judy pray.

When ol' Sis' Judy pray,
Ha'd sinnahs trimble in dey seat
Ter hyuh huh voice in sorro' 'peat:
(While all de chu'ch des sob an' weep)
"O Shapa'd, dese, dy po' los' sheep!"
When ol' Sis' Judy pray.

When ol' Sis' Judy pray,
De whole house hit des rock an' moan
Ter see huh teahs an' hyuh huh groan;
Dar's somepin' in Sis' Judy's tone
Dat melt all ha'ts dough med ur stone
When ol' Sis' Judy pray.

When ol' Sis' Judy pray,
Salvation's light comes pourin' down—
Hit fills de chu'ch an' all de town—
Why, angels' robes go rustlin' 'roun,
An' hebben on de yurf am foun',
When ol' Sis' Judy pray.

When ol' Sis' Judy pray,
My soul go sweepin' up on wings,
An' loud de chu'ch wid "Glory!" rings,
An' wide de gates ur Jahsper swings
Twel you hyuh ha'ps wid golding strings,
When ol' Sis' Judy pray. . . .

William Stanley Braithwaite (1878–1962)

The literary and poetic career of William Stanley Braithwaite spanned at least three fairly distinct literary periods. When he published his first volume of poetry entitled *Lyrics of Life and Love* in 1904, his competitor was Paul Laurence Dunbar, whose *Lyrics of Love and Laughter* had just been published in 1903. In 1908, two years after Dunbar's death, Braithwaite published his second volume of poetry, *The House of Falling Leaves,* and in 1913, the year in which Dunbar's *Collected Poems* were published, he initiated his annual edition of *Anthology of Magazine Verse.* Thus, his initial poetic output occurred during the period largely dominated by Dunbar. However, Braithwaite's poetry was not in any way influenced by Dunbar. He wrote no dialect poetry after the manner of Dunbar. In fact, there is little in Braithwaite's verse that even reflects the influence of then popular American poets such as James Whitcomb Riley. Rather, he wrote Keatsian poetry in the style of the post-Romantic British poets. Apparently, Braithwaite, born of West Indian parentage in Boston, developed no burning sense of identity with the Black experience, or at least this is not reflected in his poetry.

In addition to his temporal association with the period of Dunbar, Braithwaite was also productive during the period of the Harlem Renaissance. During this time, he continued to edit the annual *Anthology of Magazine Verse,* submitted occasional poems to *Opportunity* and other literary periodicals, and worked as a literary critic on the editorial staff of the *Boston Transcript.* However, he was only tangentially involved with the literary ferment in Harlem. Rather, his literary scope at this time was influenced by other new thrusts and developments in American poetry. Relatively unknown poets such as Edgar Lee Masters, Vachel Lindsay, and Carl Sandburg were introduced to the American public in the pages of the annual *Anthology of Magazine Verse.*

With the onset of the Depression in the 1930's and the demise of the *Boston Transcript* as well as the cessation of his annual *Anthology,* Braithwaite joined the English faculty of the nation's first all-Black separate graduate school at Atlanta University. This experience, in a sense, put him more closely in touch with the Black world—at least, with the world of Black literary academia. Although in his brief autobiographical statement in *Caroling Dusk* Braithwaite had asserted that his literary roots lay in the intellectual incentives and ideals of an "ancestry of British gentlemen," his Atlanta experience enriched his critical perspective and broadened his literary scope. No longer could critics charge him with dilettantism and a lack of social and racial relevance. In fact, the Atlanta of the late 1930's and early 1940's—with Du Bois, Mercer Cook, Rayford Logan, and others—was a kind of Black intellectual mecca. Serving on the Atlanta University English faculty during this period was thus a beneficial experience for the poet and critic who for so long had viewed himself as a proper Bostonian of British heritage.

The Atlanta experience, in a sense, rounded off Braithwaite's literary career. His *Selected Poems* were published in 1948, but thereafter he wrote no more poetry. The publication of this volume occurred in his seventieth year, thus ending a long career of sustained literary creativity.

Unfortunately, like Dunbar, Braithwaite has not received much critical attention. Saunders Redding in *To Make a Poet Black* (1939) mentions him as the master of a "pretty and skillful" kind of poetry and as a literary figure of "perverted energy" who somehow existed outside of Black experience. Much more favorable treatment is accorded him in Benjamin Brawley's *The Negro in Literature and Art* (1929), but Brawley's critical assessments are always more appreciative than critical. Braithwaite's work as a critic and anthologist has similarly been neglected, although Fronzell Spellman gives this aspect of his career due notice in her article "The Twentieth Century's Greatest Negro Anthologist," *Negro History Bulletin*, XXVI (1963), 137. Philip Butcher has written "W. S. Braithwaite's Southern Exposure: Resumé and Revelation," *The Southern Literary Journal*, III (Spring 1971), 3–17.

Rhapsody

I am glad daylong for the gift of song,
For time and change and sorrow;
For the sunset wings and the world-end things
Which hang on the edge of tomorrow.
I am glad for my heart whose gates apart
Are the entrance-place of wonders,
Where dreams come from the rush and din
Like sheep from the rains and thunders.

Scintilla

I kissed a kiss in youth
Upon a dead man's brow;
And that was long ago—
And I'm a grown man now.
It's lain there in the dust
Thirty years and more—
My lips that set a light
At a dead man's door.

The Watchers

Two women on the lone wet strand,
  (*The wind's out with a will to roam*)
The waves wage war on rocks and sand,
  (*And a ship is long due home.*)

The sea sprays in the women's eyes—
  (*Hearts can writhe like the sea's wild foam*)
Lower descend the tempestuous skies,
  (*For the wind's out with a will to roam.*)

"O daughter, thine eyes be better than mine,"
  (*The waves ascend high as yonder dome*)
"North or south is there never a sign?"
  (*And a ship is long due home.*)

They watched there all the long night through—
  (*The wind's out with a will to roam*)
Wind and rain and sorrow for two,—
  (*And heaven on the long reach home.*)

Sandy Star

I: SCULPTURED WORSHIP
The zones of warmth around his heart,
  No alien airs had crossed;
But he awoke one morn to feel
  The magic numbness of autumnal frost.

His thoughts were a loose skein of threads,
  And tangled emotions, vague and dim;
And sacrificing what he loved
  He lost the dearest part of him.

In sculptured worship now he lives,
  His one desire a prisoned ache;
If he can never melt again
  His very heart will break.

II: LAUGHING IT OUT
He had a whim and laughed it out
  Upon the exit of a chance;
He floundered in a sea of doubt—
  If life was real—or just romance.

Sometimes upon his brow would come
  A little pucker of defiance;
He totalled in a word the sum
  Of all man made of facts and science.

And then a hearty laugh would break,
  A reassuring shrug of shoulder;
And we would from his fancy take
  A faith in death which made life bolder.

III: EXIT
No, his exit by the gate
  Will not leave the wind ajar;
He will go when it is late
  With a misty star.

One will call, he cannot see;
  One will call, he will not hear;
He will take no company
  Nor a hope or fear.

We shall smile who loved him so—
  They who gave him hate will weep;
But for us the winds will blow
  Pulsing through his sleep.

IV: THE WAY
He could not tell the way he came,
  Because his chart was lost:
Yet all his way was paved with flame
  From the bourne he crossed.

He did not know the way to go,
  Because he had no map:
He followed where the winds blow—
  And the April sap.

He never knew upon his brow
  The secret that he bore,—
And laughs away the mystery now
  The dark's at his door.

V: ONUS PROBANDI
No more from out the sunset,
  No more across the foam,
No more across the windy hills
  Will Sandy Star come home.

He went away to search it
  With a curse upon his tongue.
And in his hand the staff of life,
  Made music as it swung.

I wonder if he found it,
   And knows the mystery now—
Our Sandy Star who went away,
   With the secret on his brow.

Fenton Johnson (1888–1958)

Fenton Johnson was one of the many gifted Black poets who appeared during World War I, and he became a poetic spokesman for the Black man so newly settled in the urban North. Born in Chicago and educated at the University of Chicago and Northwestern University, Johnson had first-hand knowledge of Northern racial conflict but only vicarious knowledge of the bitter misery of the rural Black South. But his ancestral roots ran deep, so his poetry reflects two strains—a "down-home" musical spirituality and an "up-home" bluesy, big-city futility.

His three volumes of poetry were all published within a three-year period—*A Little Dreaming* in 1913, *Visions of Dusk* in 1915, and *Songs of the Soil* in 1916. He also wrote a collection of short stories, *Tales of Darkest America,* published in 1920.

In many ways, Johnson's "up-home" poetry reflects the dual influence of Carl Sandburg's urban realism and Edgar Lee Masters' grim and sardonic pessimism. Civilization is old and tired, says Johnson, the Black man is old and tired, sin and vice soon conquer virtue and godliness, and "gin is better than all the water in Lethe" in the big city. So Fenton Johnson's is the voice of the Northern Black caught up in the toils of urban living. But all is not despair and melancholy in his poetry. At times the glory of Blackness shines through, and he sings of his people as "the stardust folk / Striving folk" who have come to that point in their deep night of despair "where the moon rays dip" and "star-gleams shine."

In addition to his volumes of poetry, Fenton Johnson published separate poems in many of the leading literary journals of his day. He was also a dramatist, and several of his plays were presented at the old Pekin Theater in Chicago.

After 1920, Johnson published little and apparently "sat out" the Harlem Renaissance and the gray years of the Depression. One critic has suggested that in Johnson's day Black urban America was not ready for Black poetic protest on urban themes. Today, a half century later, the Black urban poet has a large emotionally involved Black ghetto audience that Fenton Johnson did not. The city he prophetically saw as a consuming monster was then to the migrant Black a bright haven. Ironically, time has proven Johnson right; the mirage of the city as a refuge from man's inhumanity has faded away, and America today is confronted with the stark ugliness of the ghetto.

Saunders Redding's *To Make a Poet Black* (1939) presents a balanced analysis of Johnson's poetry. Selections of his work may also be found in all major anthologies of Black literature. It should also be noted that an unpublished collection of Johnson's poems is in the manuscript collection of the Fisk University Library.

Tired *

I am tired of work; I am tired of building up somebody else's civilization.
Let us take a rest, M'Lissy Jane.
I will go down to the Last Chance Saloon, drink a gallon or two of gin, shoot a game or two of dice and sleep the rest of the night in one of Mike's barrels.
You will let the old shanty go to rot, the white people's clothes turn to dust, and the Calvary Baptist Church sink to the bottomless pit.
You will spend your days forgetting you married me and your nights hunting the warm gin Mike serves the ladies in the rear of the Last Chance Saloon.
Throw the children into the river; civilization has given us too many. It is better to die than to grow up and find that you are colored.
Pluck the stars out of the heavens. The stars mark our destiny. The stars marked my destiny.
I am tired of civilization.

The Scarlet Woman *

Once I was good like the Virgin Mary and the Minister's wife.
My father worked for Mr. Pullman and white people's tips; but he died two days after his insurance expired.
I had nothing, so I had to go to work.
All the stock I had was a white girl's education and a face that enchanted the men of both races.
Starvation danced with me.
So when Big Lizzie, who kept a house for white men, came to me with tales of fortune that I could reap from the sale of my virtue I bowed my head to Vice.
Now I can drink more gin than any man for miles around.
Gin is better than all the water in Lethe.

* These poems are published with the kind permission of Arna Bontemps, curator of the James Weldon Johnson Memorial Collection of the Yale University Library and literary executor of Fenton Johnson.

Folk Literature

Tale

The Talkin Mule

Ole feller one time had uh mule. His name wuz Bill. Evah mawnin ole man go to ketch him, he say, "Come roun, Bill!"

So, one mawnin when he sleep late, he havin his coffee an he sen his son to ketch Ole Bill. He say, "Go down dere, Boy, an bring dat mule up heah!"

Boy, he sech a fas Aleck, he grab de bridle an wen down to de fiel to ketch Ole Bill. When he get thar, he say, "Come roun, Bill."

De mule he look roun at him. So boy say agin, "Come roun, Bill. Ain no us you rollin yo eyes at me. Paw wants you dis mawning, so come stick yo haid in dis bridle."

Mule he keep a-lookin at him an den he say, "Evah mawnin it's 'Come roun, Bill! Come roun, Bill!' Don hahdly git no res fo it's 'Come roun, Bill!'"

Dat boy he tho down dat bridle an away he scat to de house. "Paw, Paw," he say, "Dat mule he a talkin mule! He talkin!"

Paw say, "Boy, gwan tellin them lies. Gwan an ketch dat mule lak ah don tol ya, else ahm gonna ketch you wid sumpn on yo backside!"

Boy he say, "Nawsuh, dat mule gon to talkin, Paw. I ain goin neah no talkin mule."

Ole man say to ole lady, "See whut a lie dat boy is tellin." So he gits out an goes on down to de fiel to git de mule hissef. When he git thar, he hollar, "Come roun, Bill!"

Ole mule he look roun an say, "Evah mawnin, it's 'Come roun, Bill!'"

Now, ole man he hav uh lil fice dog go wid him evahwhuh he go so when he lit out licty-split to de house, lil fice right behin him. Ole man say to de ole lady, "Dat boy ain lyin. He tellin da troof. Dat mule is talkin. I ain nevah heard a mule talk befo."

Lil fice say, "Me neither."

Ole man now he really skeered. So he jump up an start runnin agin. Thu de woods he go, lictysplit, lak he bout to run hissef to def. Finely, he reach a stump an sit down to ketch he bref an he say, "Lawd, Ize so tied don know whut to do." An lil fice he sit down in fron an he a-pantin an hasslin for his bref an he say, "Me too."

Dat ole man he still runnin!

Prison Songs

No Mo Cane on dis Brazis *

It ain't no mo cane on dis Brazis,
Dey don grine it all in molazzis.

Well, de cap'n standin an lookin an cryin,
Well, it gittin so col, my row's behine.

Cap'n, doncha do me like ya did po Shine,
You drive dat bully till he wen stone-blind.

Cap'n, Cap'n you mus be blind,
Keep on hollin an I almos flyin.

* See the Acknowledgments for credit.

Ninety-nine years so jumpin long,
To be here rollin an cain go home.

Ef I had a sentence like ninety-nine yeah,
All de dogs on de Brazis won't keep me heah.

B'lieve I'll do like ol' Riley,
Ol' Riley walked de big Brazis.

Well, de dog sargint got worried and couldn't
  go,
Ol' Rattler wen to howlin kaze de tracks too ol.

Oughta com on de rivah in 1904,
You could fine a dead man on every turn row.

Oughta com on de rivah in 1910,
Dey wuz drivin de wimmin jest like de men.

Wake up dead men, an help drive my row,
Wake up dead men, an help drive my row.

Some in de buildin, an some on de farm,
Some in de graveyard, an some goin home.

Wake up, lifetime, hol up yo haid,
Well, you may git a pahdon an you may drop
  dead.

Go down, Ol' Hannah,[1] doncha rise no mo,
Ef you rise in de mawnin, bring Judgment Day.

[1] [The sun about 3–4 P.M.—Editors' note]

Go Down, Ol' Hannah

Go down ol' Hannah,
  Won you rise no mo?
Go down ol' Hannah,
  Won you rise no mo?

Lawd, if you rise,
  Bring Judgment on.
Lawd, if you rise,
  Bring Judgment on.

Oh, did you hear
  What the cap'n said?
Oh, did you hear
  What the cap'n said?

That if you work
  He'll treat you well,
And if you don
  He'll give you hell.

Oh, go down ol' Hannah,
  Won you rise no mo?
Won you go down, ol' Hannah,
  Won you rise no mo?

Oh, long-time man,
  Hold up yo haid.
Well, you may get a pardon
  An you may drop daid.

Lawdy, nobody feels sorry
  For de life-time man.
Nobody feels sorry
  For de life-time man.

Po Laz'us *

High Shayiff tol de depitty—Hanh!
"Go out an bring me Laz'us"—Hanh!
High Shayiff tol de depitty—Hanh!
"Go out an bring me Laz'us—Hanh!
Bring him dead or alive, Lawd, Lawd—Hanh!
Bring him dead or alive"—Hanh!

De depitty he gins to wonder—Hanh!
Whuh in de worl he could fin him—Hanh!
De depitty he gins to wonder—Hanh!
Whuh in de worl he could fin him—Hanh!
Well-a, Ah don know, Lawd, Lawd—Hanh!
Ah jes don know—Hanh!

O dey foun po' Laz'us—Hanh!
Way out tween two mountins—Hanh!
O dey foun po Laz'us—Hanh!
Way out tween two mountins—Hanh!
And dey blowed him down, Lawd, Lawd—Hanh!
Dey blowed him down—Hanh!

Ol' Laz'us tol de depitty—Hanh!
He nevah be arrested—Hanh!
Ol' Laz'us tol de depitty—Hanh!
He nevah be arrested—Hanh!
By no one man, Lawd, Lawd—Hanh!
By no one man—Hanh!

* See the Acknowledgments for credit.

So dey shot po Laz'us—Hanh!
Shot him wid a great big number—Hanh!
Dey shot po Laz'us—Hanh!
Shot him wid a great big number—Hanh!
Number Forty-five, Lawd, Lawd—Hanh!
Number Forty-five—Hanh!

An dey taken po Laz'us—Hanh!
An lay him on de commisary county—Hanh!
Dey taken po Laz'us—Hanh!
An lay him on de commisary county—Hanh!
Den dey walks away, Lawd, Lawd—Hanh!
Dey walks away—Hanh!

Laz'us tol de depitty—Hanh!
"Gimme a cool drink a water"—Hanh!
Laz'us tol de depitty—Hanh!
"Gimme a cool drink a water—Hanh!
Jes fo Ah die, Lawd, Lawd—Hanh!
Jes fo Ah die"—Hanh!

Laz'us sister run—Hanh!
An tol huh Mama—Hanh!
Laz'us sister run—Hanh!
An tol huh Mama—Hanh!
"Po Laz'us daid, Lawd, Lawd—Hanh!
Po Laz'us daid"—Hanh!

Laz'us mama—Hanh!
Lay down huh sewin—Hanh!
Laz'us mama—Hanh!
Lay down huh sewin—Hanh!
She gin to cry, Lawd, Lawd—Hanh!
She gin to cry—Hanh!

Laz'us sister—Hanh!
Couldn't go to de fun'l—Hanh!
Laz'us sister—Hanh!
Couldn't go to de fun'l—Hanh!
Didn't have no shoes, Lawd, Lawd—Hanh!
Didn't have no shoes—Hanh!

Cap'n, did you heah—Hanh!
All yo mens gonna leave you—Hanh!
Cap'n, did you heah—Hanh!
All yo mens gonna leave you—Hanh!
Nex payday, Lawd, Lawd—Hanh!
Nex payday—Hanh!

Another Man Don Gon *

Another man don gon,
Another man don gon,
From the county farm,
Another man don gon.

He had a long chain on,
He had a long chain on,
He had a long chain on,
He had a long chain on.

He killed another man,
He killed another man,
He killed another man,
He killed another man.

Bad Man Songs

Railroad Bill

Railroad Bill, he a mighty bad coon,
Shot da shayiff by da light of de moon.

He had a .38 special as long as his arm,
"Gonna kill evahbody evah don me wrong."

* See the Acknowledgments for credit.

Stackerlee and de Debbil

Stackerlee he tol da debbil,
Say, "Come on, les have some fun,
You stick me wid yo pitchfork,
I shoot you wid mah .41."

"Take dat pitchfork, Tom Debbil,
An lay it on da shef;
I'm dat bad man, Stackerlee,
An I'm gonna rule Hell by mysef."

John Hardy *

John Hardy stood at the gamblin table,
Didn't have no intres in the game,
Up stepped a yella gal and threw a dollar down,
Said, "Deal John Hardy in the game, poor boy,
Deal John Hardy in the game."

John Hardy took that yella gal's money
And then he began to play,
Said, "The man that wins mah yella gal's dollah
I'll lay him in his lonesome grave, poor boy,
I'll lay him in his lonesome grave."

John Hardy drew to a four-card straight,
And the Chinaman drew to a pair,
John failed to catch and the Chinaman won,
And he left him sitting dead in his chair, poor boy,
And he left him sitting dead in his chair.

John started to catch that East-Bound train,
So dark he could not see,
Up stepped the police and took him by the arm,
Said, "Johnny come go with me, poor boy,
Johnny come go with me."

John Hardy's Daddy came to him,
Come for to go his bail,
No bail was allowed for a murderin man,
So they shoved John Hardy back in jail, poor boy,
They shoved John Hardy back in jail.

They took John Hardy to the hangin groun,
They hung him there to die,
And the very las word I heard him say,
"Mah forty gun never tol a lie, poor boy,
Mah forty gun never tol a lie."

The Blues

Shorty George †

Well-a, Shorty George, he ain' no fren o mine
Well-a, Shorty George, he ain' no fren o mine
Taken all de wimmins and leave de mens behin.

O when I get back to Dallas, gonna walk an tell
O when I get back to Dallas, gonna walk an tell
Dat de Fort Ben bottom am a burnin' hell.

My mama died, Lord, when Ize a lad
My mama died, Lord, when Ize a lad
Since then I been nuthin but bad.

Got a letter fum my baby, "Come at once she's dyin"
Got a letter fum my baby, "Come at once she's dyin"
She warn't dead but slowly dyin.

How can you blame po man fum cryin
How can you blame po man fum cryin
When he babe ain't dead but slowly dyin?

* See the Acknowledgments for credit.
† Shorty George was the name given the train that on specified Sundays and holidays brought sweethearts and wives to visit the prisoners at Sugarland, Texas. See the Acknowledgments for credit.

Well-a, followed her down to de buryin groun
Well-a, followed her down to de buryin groun
You oughta heerd me holla when they let her down.

I took my babe to de buryin groun
I took my babe to de buryin groun
I never knowed I loved her till the coffin soun.

Goin Down the Road

I'm goin down this road feelin bad,
Lawd, I'm goin down this road feelin bad,
Well, I'm goin down this road feelin bad, Lawd, Lawd,
An I ain't gonna be treated thisaway.

I ain't got but one old lousy dime,
Lawd, I ain't got but one lousy dime,
Well, I ain't got but one old lousy dime, Lawd, Lawd,
But I'll find me a new dollar some old day.

I'm goin where the climate suits mah close,
Lawd, I'm goin where the climate suits mah close,
Well, I'm goin where the climate suits mah close, Lawd, Lawd,
Cause I ain't gonna be treated thisaway.

I'm goin where the water tastes like wine,
Lawd, I'm goin where the water tastes like wine,
Well, I'm goin where the water tastes like wine, Lawd, Lawd,
Cause this water round here tastes like turpentine.

I'm tired of lyin in this jail,
Lawd, I'm tired of lyin in this jail,
Well, I'm tired of lyin in this jail, Lawd, Lawd,
And I ain't gonna be treated thisaway.

Who'll stir yo gravy when I'm gon,
Lawd, who'll stir yo gravy when I'm gon,
Well, who'll stir yo gravy when I'm gon, Lawd, Lawd,
When I'm gon to mah long, lonesome home.

Pity a Poor Boy

Pity a poor boy? Pity a poor boy?
You ain't goin' to pity me down.
Oh, pity a poor boy! Pity a poor boy!
But you ain't goin' to pity me down.

I'm water logged, I'm fire bound,
I'm climbin' up a mountain on-a slippery groun',
My head's under water
But I ain't goin' drown.
And you ain't goin' to pity me,
Ain't goin' to pity me down.

Pity me down! Pity me down! Pity me down!
Oh, why you want to pity me down?
Oh, pity me down! Pity me down!
But you ain't goin' to pity me down.

I'm fallin' down, I'm stumblin' on,
I'm tryin' to make a livin',
But my money's all gone.
Got my toe holt broken, but I'm climbin' on,
And you ain't goin' to pity me down,
Ain't goin' to pity me down.

Pity me? Don't pity me!
You ain't goin' to pity me down.

Dink's Blues

Ef I had wings like Noah's dove
I'd fly up de river to de man I love
Fare thee well, O honey, fare thee well.

Ize gotta man an he's long an tall
Moves just lak a cannonball
Fare thee well, O honey, fare thee well.

One o these days an it won be long
Call my name an I'll be gone
  Fare thee well, O honey, fare thee well.

Member one night, a-drizzlin rain
Roun my heart I felt a pain
  Fare thee well, O honey, fare thee well.

When I wo my ap'on low
Couldn't keep you fum out ma do
  Fare thee well, O honey, fare thee well.

Now I wears my ap'on high
Scacely sees you passin by
  Fare thee well, O honey, fare thee well.

Now my ap'on's up to my chin
You pass my do an won't come in
  Fare thee well, O honey, fare thee well.

Ef I had listened to what my mama said
I'd be at home in my mama's bed
  Fare thee well, O honey, fare thee well.

Frankie Baker

Frankie Baker was a good gal
Everybody knows.
She paid a hundred dollars flat
For the makin' of a suit o' clothes
  For her man.
  He didn't treat her right.

Frankie went down to the corner,
She bought a bottle o' beer.
Frankie says to the bartender,
Have Albert Britton been here?
  He is my man.
  He don't treat me right.

Frankie went up Hogan's Alley,
Thought she heard a bulldog bark.
T'warn't nothin' but her good man
Tryin' to dodge her in the dark.
  He was her man.
  He didn't treat her right.

Frankie says to Albert,
Just run now if you can.
I got a razor in my pocket
And a pistol in my hand.
  You are my man.
  You don't treat me right.

She shot him in the shoulder.
He fell down on the floor.
Rooty-toot-toot and rooty-toot-toot,
She shot that man some more.
  He was her man.
  He didn't treat her right.

Frankie says to the doctor,
Help me if you can.
Here's a thousand dollars cold
For the savin' of my man.
  He is my man,
  But he didn't treat me right.

Doctor says to Frankie,
He cannot get well.
You done filled him full o' holes
And shot him plumb to hell.
  He was your man.
  He didn't treat you right.

Frankie went to Albert's mother's house,
She fell down on her knees.
Mother, I have killed your only son,
Forgive me, if you please.
  He was my man.
  He ain't done me right.

Judge Gridley says to Frankie,
Frankie, tell me if you can,
WHY did you shoot that
Big tall yellow man?
  Judge, he was my man.
  He ain't done me right.

Judge Gridley says to Frankie,
Frankie, please tell me
WHY did you shoot that man
In the third degree?
  He was your man
  If he didn't treat you right.

Frankie said to the Judge,
Judge it came to pass,
I didn't shoot him in no third degree—
I shot him in his yas, yas, yas!
  He was my man.
  He didn't treat me right.

Lillies of the valley,
Roses sure smell nice.
Flowers all over poor Albert,
He thought he was in Paradise.
  He was her man.
  He didn't treat her right.

Frankie's in the jail house.
Hear her weep and moan,
Cryin' for poor Albert,
And her pillow ain't nothin' but stone.
    He was her man.
    He didn't treat her right.

Listen, all you good gals,
Two things you can choose—
Livin' with a low-down man,
Or them low-down jail-house blues.
    Better keep your man—
    Even if he don't treat you right.

Work Songs

Casey Jones

On a Sunday morning it begins to rain,
Round the curve sped a passenger train,
Under de cab lay po Casey Jones.
He's a good engineer, but he's dead an gone,
Dead an gone, dead an gone,
Kaze he's been on the cholly so long.

Casey Jones was a good engineer,
Tol' his fireman not to have no fear,
"All I want's a lil water an coal,
Peep out de cab an see de drivers roll,
See de drivers roll, see de drivers roll."
Kaze he's been on the cholly so long.

When we got within a mile of the place,
Old number 4 stared us right in the face,
Conductor pulled his watch, mumbled and said,
"We may make it, but we'll all be dead,
All be dead, all be dead."
Kaze he's been on the cholly so long.

When Casey's wife heard dat Casey was daid,
She was in de kitchun makin up braid;
She say, "Go to bed, chullun an hol yo breath,
Yall all git a pension at yo daddy's death,
At yo daddy's death, at yo daddy's death,
Kaze he's been on the cholly so long."

John Henry

Some say he's from Georgia,
Some say he's from Alabam,
But it's wrote on the rock at the Big Ten Tunnel,
John Henry's a East Virginia Man,
John Henry's a East Virginia Man.

John Henry he could hammah,
He could whistle, he could sing,
He went to the mountain early in the mornin'
To hear his hammah ring,
To hear his hammah ring.

John Henry went to the section boss,
Says the section boss what kin you do?
Says Ah can line a track, Ah kin histe a jack,
Ah kin pick and shovel, too,
Ah kin pick and shovel, too.

John Henry went to the tunnel
An' they put him in lead to drive,
The rock was so tall and John Henry so small
That he laid down his hammah and he cried,
That he laid down his hammah and he cried.

The steam drill was on the right han' side,
John Henry was on the left,
Says before Ah let this steam drill beat me down,
Ah'll hammah myself to death,
Ah'll hammah myself to death.

Oh the cap'n said to John Henry,
Ah bleeve this mountain's sinkin' in.
John Henry said to the cap'n, Oh my!
Tain't nothin' but my hammah suckin' wind,
Tain't nothin' but my hammah suckin' wind.

John Henry had a pretty liddle wife,
She come all dressed in blue.
An' the last words she said to him,
John Henry Ah been true to you,
John Henry Ah been true to you.

John Henry was on the mountain,
The mountain was so high,
He called his pretty liddle wife,
Said Ah kin almos' touch the sky,
Said Ah kin almos' touch the sky.

Who gonna shoe yoh pretty liddle feet,
Who gonna glove yoh han',
Who gonna kiss yoh rosy cheeks,
An' who gonna be yoh man,
An' who gonna be yoh man?

Papa gonna shoe my pretty liddle feet,
Mama gonna glove my han',
Sistah gonna kiss my rosy cheeks,
An' Ah ain't gonna have no man,
An' Ah ain't gonna have no man.

Then John Henry he did hammah,
He did make his hammah soun',
Says now one more lick fore quittin' time,
An' Ah'll beat this steam drill down,
An' Ah'll beat this steam drill down.

The hammah that John Henry swung,
It weighed over nine poun',
He broke a rib in his left han' side,
An' his intrels fell on the groun',
An' his intrels fell on the groun'.

All the women in the West
That heard of John Henry's death,
Stood in the rain, flagged the east bound train,
Goin' where John Henry dropped dead,
Goin' where John Henry dropped dead.

They took John Henry to the White House,
An' buried him in the san',
An' every locomotive come roarin' by,
Says there lays that steel drivin' man,
Says there lays that steel drivin' man.

Dis Hammer

Take dis hammer—Hanh! Take it to da cap'n—
    Hanh!
Tell him I'm gon, tell him I'm gon.—Hanh!

If he ask you—Hanh! wuz I runnin?—Hanh!
Tell him Ize flyin, tell him Ize flyin.—Hanh!

If he ask you—Hanh! wuz I laffin?—Hanh!
Tell him Ize cryin, tell him Ize cryin.—Hanh!

I don wan no—Hanh! col i'on shackles—Hanh!
Around my leg, around my leg.—Hanh!

I don wan no—Hanh! pease, cawnbraid an
    molasses—Hanh!

Dey hurts mah pride, dey hurts mah pride.—
    Hanh!

Cap'n call me—Hanh! "a nappy head devil,"—
    Hanh!
Dat ain mah name, dat ain mah name.—Hanh!

Cap'n gotta big gun—Hanh! an he try to play
    bad—Hanh!
Gon take it in da mawnin, if he mak me mad.—
    Hanh!

I'm gonna make these—Hanh! few days I started
    —Hanh!
Den I'm goin home, den I'm goin home.—Hanh!

Rainbow Roun Mah Shoulder

Evahwhuh I, whuh I look dis mawnin,
Looks lak rain, looks lak rain.

I gotta rainbow, tied all roun mah shoulder,
Ain gonna rain, ain gonna rain.

I don walk till, walk till mah feets gone to rollin,
Jes lak a wheel, jes lak a wheel.

Evah mailday, I gets a letter,
"My son come home, my son come home."

Dat ol letter read about dyin,
Mah tears run down, mah tears run down.

I'm gonna break right, break right pas dat shooter,
I'm goin home, Lawd, I'm goin home.

Railroad Section Leader's Song

Ef ah could, ah sholy would,
Stan on da rock whuh Moses stood.

Mary, Martha, Luke an John,
All dem sciples dead an gon.

Ah gotta woman in Jennielee Square,
Ef you wanna die easy, lemme ketch you there.

Lil Evaline, settin in da shade,
Figurin on da money I ain't made.

Jack de rabbit, Jack de bear,
Cancha move it jus a hair?

All ah hate bout linin track,
Dese ol bars bout to break mah back.

You keep talkin bout da joint ahead,
Never say nawthin bout mah hog an bread.

Way down yonder in da holla of da fiel,
Angels wukkin on da chayet wheel.

Reason I stay wid my cap'n so long,
He giv me biscuits to rear back on.

Jes lemme tell ya whut da cap'n jes done,
Looked at his watch and he looked at da sun.

Ho, Boys, it ain time.
Ho, Boys, you cain't quit.
Ho, Boys, it ain time.
Sun ain gone down yit.

Long-Line Skinner's Blues

I've got a belly full of whiskey and a headful of
gin,
The doctor says will kill me but he don say when.
I'm a long-line skinner an my home's out wes',
Lookin' for the woman that'll love me bes'.

See pretty mama, pretty mama, look whut you
done done,
You made your daddy love you now your man
done come.
I'm a long-line skinner and my home's out wes'.
Lookin' for the gal, Lord, that'll love me bes'.

I'm way down in the bottom skinnin mules for
John Ryan,

Puttin my initials, honey, on a mule's behine
With my long whip line, babe, with my long whip
line,
Lookin for the woman who can ease my worried
mine.

When the weather it gits chilly, gonna pack up
my line,
Cause I ain't skinnin mules, Lawd, in the winter
time.
Yes, I'm a long-line skinner an my home's out
wes',
An I'm lookin for the woman that'll love me the
bes'.

PART V

Renaissance and Radicalism: 1915–1945

In the early morning hours of November 14, 1915, Booker T. Washington lay dying at Tuskegee, exhausted by his years of strenuous labor for the cause of industrial education for Blacks. For two decades, since the death of Frederick Douglass, Washington had wielded unparalleled if not unchallenged power as a leader of his race. His message was survival and progress through accommodation and compromise with the racist establishment. If political and social equality could not be quickly attained in the New South, at least some measure of economic security could be achieved by hard work and a realistic assessment of race relations.

But for all the glittering and well-publicized philanthropic support of Tuskegee Institute, the overall economic progress of Blacks under the Washingtonian program had been minimal. The sharecropping system still chained most rural Southern Blacks to an economic bondage not far removed from slavery itself. Washington's anachronistic emphasis on the independent artisan did not prepare urban Blacks for increasing industrialization, from which they were largely excluded in any event by the racism of organized labor. The policy of conciliation had failed even to attain the modest economic goals that Washington had proposed. Furthermore, lynching, rioting, and other forms of racist violence continued to take a fearful annual toll of Black lives. Clearly, new directions of racial leadership were needed if the problem of the color line, which W. E. B. Du Bois had designated as early as 1903 as the central problem of the twentieth century, was to be met.

Du Bois himself, of course, had been taking such directions for a decade in the Niagara Movement and the National Association for the Advancement of Colored People. As the brilliant editor of *The Crisis,* Du Bois helped to lead the uncompromising fight of the NAACP against racist violence and discrimination. One important legal victory was won in 1915 when the Supreme Court outlawed the grandfather clause used to disfranchise Black voters. Shortly after the establishment of the NAACP, the National Urban League was formed. Only a month before Washington's death, a Harvard-trained historian, Carter G. Woodson, organized the Association for the Study of Negro Life and History, which was to become an important agency in developing Black pride through a scholarly investigation of the Black past. These developments and others were creating a collective mood of confidence and assertiveness—at least among the "talented tenth"—from which would emerge the New Negro and the Harlem Renaissance.

But the awakening of the intelligentsia was accompanied by and related to a demographic shift of the Black population that is perhaps the most crucial fact of Afro-American history in the twentieth century. The Great Migration of rural Blacks from the South to the urban North grew out of a combination of economic crisis and social pressure. Driven from the fields by the boll weevil, low wages, floods, soil exhaustion, and agricultural mechanization, as well as by racist violence and injustice, Blacks began the trek North in 1915 and 1916, lured on by the favorable market for their labor created by the decrease in European immigration occasioned by World War I. By 1920 hundreds of thousands had arrived in New York, Chicago, Detroit, Philadelphia, Cleveland, and other urban centers. The flow continued throughout the 1920's before tapering off during the Depression, to be renewed during and after World War II. Bewildering, disruptive, and often disillusioning or even traumatic, the move to the North nevertheless had elements of an epic adventure. Without the air of excitement, opportunity, and drama created in Northern cities during the 1920's by the Great Migration, the outburst of literary energy in the decade would hardly have been possible.

Another great historical event with both an unsettling and a stimulating effect on Black life was the war itself. If the purpose of the war was to make the world safe for democracy, as President Woodrow Wilson insisted, perhaps unequivocal support of the war effort by Black people would contribute toward making the American "democracy" safer for them. With this hope Black servicemen and civilians alike performed enthusiastically despite the discouraging obstacles of Jim Crow in the military and racist violence on the home front such as continued lynchings and the East St. Louis riot of 1917. For the two hundred thousand Black soldiers who went to France, including forty-two thousand combat troops, the good will shown by white Frenchmen was a revelation. Together with a fully justified pride in their own performance, this fraternal spirit of the French induced in the overseas Black troops a mood of intensified impatience with American racial prejudice.

Back in the states, however, this mood confronted an equally determined mood of white racist reaction. Riot after riot in the bloody summer of 1919 inflicted massive Black casualties and prompted Claude McKay to write "If We Must Die," which ends:

> *Like men we'll face the murderous, cowardly pack,*
> *Pressed to the wall, dying but fighting back!*

In the urban centers, especially, the sense of disillusionment and desperation was growing rapidly as the 1920's began.

This collective awareness of a common plight heightened a feeling of racial identity and solidarity. One important expression this feeling took, especially among the Black masses, was Garveyism. Marcus Garvey arrived in Harlem from his native Jamaica in 1916 to promulgate his ideas of Black nationalism, "to establish a Universal Confraternity among the race," and "to promote the sp. it of race pride and love," among other goals. Garvey's organization, the Universal Negro Improvement Association, gained few American adherents at first, but after the war it grew rapidly. In August 1920, twenty-five thousand Blacks, including representatives from three continents, packed Madison Square Garden to hear Garvey's demand for a free Africa controlled by the world's four hundred million Black people. Garvey's career suffered serious reversals when he was imprisoned for mail fraud in 1925 and then deported late in 1927, but his impact had been undeniable. The *New York Amsterdam News* explained his appeal in this way: "It is because Marcus Garvey made black people proud of their race. In a world where black is despised, he taught them that black is beautiful. He taught them to admire and praise black things and black people. . . . They rallied to him because he heard and responded to the heart beat of his race." Though none of the important writers of the Harlem Renaissance was a Garveyite— and several of them were openly critical—in certain ways their movement was a literary manifestation of a similar nationalistic impulse. At the very least, it was a literary movement characterized by racial assertiveness and expressiveness. As such, it reflected the historical developments out of which it grew: the aggressive protest of the NAACP and the ferment created by the Great Migration, World War I and its aftermath, and Garveyism.

A number of Black men and women of letters were already well established as the 1920's began. Dunbar was dead and Chesnutt was silent, but William Stanley Braithwaite, a Bostonian of West Indian parentage, had enjoyed wide recognition as poet, critic, and anthologist since the early years of the century. During the war years, the conservative critic and poet Benjamin G. Brawley began his long series of genteel assessments of Black literature. A number of poets had published in the first two decades of the century: James David Corrothers, Leslie Pinckney Hill, Fenton Johnson, Georgia Douglas Johnson, Alice Dunbar Nelson, and Angelina Weld Grimké are among the more important. By far the most influential precursors of the Harlem Renaissance, however, were W. E. B. Du Bois and James Weldon Johnson.

With *The Suppression of the African Slave Trade to America, 1638–1870* (1896) and *The Philadelphia Negro* (1899), W. E. B. Du Bois had achieved distinction as both historian and sociologist before the turn of the century. By 1920, at the age of fifty-two, he was already an elder statesman. In addition to his roles as scholarly investigator, editor, and racial leader, he had ventured into belles lettres. His *The Souls of Black Folk* (1903) included fiction, biography, and autobiography, as well as essays in history and social analysis. An allegorical novel entitled *The Quest of the Silver Fleece* had appeared in 1911, to be followed at the height of the Harlem Renaissance by *Dark Princess* (1928) and at the end of his life by the Black Flame trilogy (1957, 1959, 1961). In 1920 *Darkwater* collected essays and poems, including among the latter "A Litany of Atlanta," written fourteen years earlier after a race riot in that city. By the example of his achievement, then, as well as by precept, Du Bois was encouraging younger writers of fiction, drama, essays, and poetry as the Harlem Renaissance got under way.

A man of interests and achievements almost as diverse as those of Du Bois, James Weldon Johnson arrived in New York in the early years of the century for a brilliant if brief career in the musical theater before serving half a dozen years in the diplomatic corps. His anonymously published novel, *The Autobiography of an Ex-Coloured Man,* appeared in 1912 and was reissued under Johnson's name in 1927. In poetry, his collection *Fifty Years and Other Poems* (1917) celebrated Black history, and his poetic rendition of folk sermons, *God's Trombones,* which appeared ten years later, was a superb realization of a major task of the Harlem Renaissance: to give serious literary treatment to folk material. The several editions of *The Book of American Negro Poetry,* which Johnson first brought out in 1922, helped to popularize Black poets, and the long introduction was a major critical statement of the need to break away from the stultifying dialect tradition of Dunbar and his followers. *Black Manhattan,* appearing at the end of the Renaissance in 1930, contains an evaluation of the literary movement to which Johnson himself contributed so much.

In *Black Manhattan,* Johnson writes: "The most outstanding phase of the development of the Negro in the United States during the past decade has been the recent literary and artistic emergence of the individual creative artist; and New York has been, almost exclusively, the place where that emergence has taken place." Five years earlier, Alain Locke, another major interpreter of the Renaissance, had indicated the reason for Harlem's prominence: "In Harlem, Negro life is seizing upon its first chances for group expression and self-determination. It is—or promises to be—a race capital." In a strict sense, "Harlem *Renaissance*" is not a wholly accurate term for this literary movement, because it was more a birth than a rebirth; as Locke points out, it was the *first* opportunity for a collective literary expression of Black writers, in contrast to the typically solitary efforts that had characterized previous Afro-American literature. Furthermore, "*Harlem* Renaissance" is somewhat misleading in view of the fact that of the most important participants in the movement, only Countee Cullen seems to have been a native New Yorker, and some of the leading writers—Claude McKay and Langston Hughes, for example—lived elsewhere during most of the 1920's. But in a larger sense "Harlem Renaissance" is appropriate enough, for Harlem certainly was the center of activity, and "Renaissance" suggests something of the vigor, versatility, and achievement of the period.

The development of Harlem as a "race capital" was comparatively recent. At the turn of the century most of Manhattan's Black people lived in the Tenderloin and San Juan Hill districts downtown. In 1904 the Lenox Avenue subway line was completed to 145th Street, and Philip A. Payton, Jr., an enterprising Black speculator, organized the Afro-American Realty Company. Under this dual impetus, the Black population of Harlem increased markedly, so that by 1915 the figure was approximately fifty thousand and by 1920 the Great Migration had added another twenty thousand. At the end of the 1920's there were 164,566 Black people living in Harlem, making it the most densely populated Black area in the world. Not only were novelists and poets lured to this "Negro mecca," but also artists such as Aaron Douglas, Palmer Hayden, Hale Woodruff, and Richmond Barthé, musicians such as W. C. Handy, J. Rosamond Johnson (the brother of James Weldon Johnson), and Duke Ellington, dramatists such as Garland Anderson and Wallace Thurman, actors such as Bert Williams, Charles Gilpin, and Paul Robeson, social scientists such as Charles S. Johnson and Ira De A. Reid, political journalists such as A. Philip Randolph, Chandler Owen, and P. M. H. Savory. Clearly the Harlem Renaissance was not merely a literary movement, but an immensely exciting general cultural ferment whose ramifications extended into every area of Black life. And its arena was a neighborhood of vivid color and pulsating vitality different in spirit and mood from white New York. This difference was emphasized repeatedly by Renaissance writers, as in the following passage by Rudolph Fisher:

> *Not just a change of complexion. A completely dissimilar atmosphere. Sidewalks teeming with leisurely strollers, at once strangely dark and bright. Boys in white trousers, berets, and green shirts, with slickened black heads and proud swagger. Bareheaded girls in crisp organdy dresses, purple, canary, gay scarlet. And laughter, abandoned strong Negro laughter, some falling full on the ear, some not heard at all, yet sensed—the warm life-breath of the tireless carnival to which Harlem's heart quickens in summer.*

One of the most salient practical reasons for the concentration of Black literary activity in Harlem was the publishing opportunities that New York afforded. Downtown, major houses such as Alfred A. Knopf, Boni and Liveright, Harper, Viking Press, and Harcourt, Brace were opening up to Black writers. Equally important, several magazines vied with each other in stimulating the work of the younger writers. In March 1925 Alain Locke edited a Harlem issue of *Survey Graphic,* published later the same year in an enlarged version as *The New Negro,* one of the landmarks of the movement. Under the editorship of W. E. B. Du Bois and the sponsorship of the NAACP, *The Crisis* had served as a major racial forum since 1910. Beginning with the issue of November 1919, Jessie Redmond Fauset, herself a poet and novelist, served as literary editor of this magazine and welcomed the work of the younger writers. *Opportunity,* the organ of the Urban League, was a more handsomely produced magazine than *The Crisis* and at least as instrumental in fostering Black talent after its inception in 1923 under the editorship of Charles S. Johnson, a brilliant social scientist who later became president of Fisk University. Not only did *Opportunity* publish works by most of the Renaissance writers, but it provided employment for two of them: Eric Walrond as business manager from August 1925 to February 1927, and Countee Cullen as assistant editor from January 1927 to September 1928. In 1927 Charles S. Johnson edited and *Opportunity* published a collection entitled *Ebony and Topaz,* somewhat along the lines of Alain Locke's *The New Negro.* Both *The Crisis* and *Opportunity* conducted literary contests for cash prizes provided by such white patrons as Amy B. Spingarn, Casper Holstein, and Carl Val Vechten. Organizational support, financial and otherwise, was necessary for such magazines and collections as these, but little magazines, operating on the proverbial shoestring, were also started. *The Messenger,* a militant socialist journal edited by A. Philip Randolph and Chandler Owen, managed to last more than a decade (1917–1928). Not so fortunate were the strictly literary magazines promoted by Wallace Thurman, *Fire!!* and *Harlem,* which lasted only one issue each. Consciously avant-garde, they outraged the conservative Black critics, one of whom fumed in print: "I have just thrown *Fire* into the fire."

The four principal Renaissance writers who achieved their first major recognition in the 1920's—Claude McKay, Jean Toomer, Countee Cullen, and Langston Hughes—were quite diverse in background, personality, and technique, though certain common themes bring them together as members of a literary movement. McKay and Toomer were a decade older than Cullen and Hughes, but all four wrote much of their best work before the age of thirty.

A West Indian, Claude McKay had published two books of verse in Jamaican dialect before coming to the United States in 1912 to study agriculture, briefly at Tuskegee and for a longer period at Kansas State College. Manhattan Island was a more logical destination than Manhattan, Kansas, however, and McKay moved in 1915 to New York, where he was active in radical political and literary circles while supporting himself by a series of menial jobs. A third volume of poetry was published in London in 1920, but McKay's American reputation was not established until two years later when *Harlem Shadows* appeared. Leaving the United States in 1923 to attend the Third International in Moscow, he spent the rest of the decade in Europe and North Africa, not returning to this country until after the Renaissance had subsided. His first two novels, *Home to Harlem* (1928) and *Banjo* (1929), are major fictional landmarks in the movement, however, just as *Harlem Shadows* was in poetry. As poet, McKay wrote both powerful sonnets of racial protest and also poems on such traditional Romantic themes as love and celebration of Nature. In the latter a note of poignant nostalgia for Jamaica is often struck. There are in McKay's imagination—and imagery—qualities of tropical luxuriance, warmth, and color that constitute his own variety of négritude. At the same time, as a self-conscious intellectual he remains somewhat detached from the spontaneous joy he observes in Black life. These two sides of his nature are represented by the intellectual Ray and the emotional Jake of *Home to Harlem.*

Jean Toomer was also deeply attracted to Black folk life, but unable finally to relate to it. A member of the Black bourgeoisie of Washington, D.C., Toomer was educated (for brief periods) at the University of Wisconsin, the University of Chicago, the City College of New York, and New York University, before going South in 1922 as a principal and teacher in a Black school in Sparta, Georgia. Here for several months he sought out his racial identity and heritage, transforming his experiences and observations into the exquisitely beautiful sketches, stories, and poems of the first part of *Cane* (1923). The second part is set in the urban North of Washington and Chicago, where the problem of the double consciousness of the Black American is more severe. If the character Kabnis of the last part of *Cane* may be considered at least in part autobiographical, Toomer himself, a very light-skinned man, was not successful in affirming his Blackness, but *Cane* remains a beautiful, moving, often puzzling artistic record of his effort to do so. For the rest of his life Toomer evaded his racial identity and plunged into mysticism and religion. He continued to write, but publishers repeatedly rejected his manuscripts, rightfully considering them inferior to *Cane.*

Countee Cullen and Langston Hughes were still in their teens in 1922 when McKay published *Harlem Shadows,* but a few years later they had both written their own poetic classics of the Renaissance, Cullen's *Color* (1925) and Hughes' *The Weary Blues* (1926). Similar as prodigies, Cullen and Hughes were strikingly different as men and poets. Cullen was raised in Harlem by his grandmother until her death in 1916, when he was adopted by Frederick Cullen, a genteel A.M.E. minister. After graduating from De Witt Clinton High School, New York University, and Harvard, Cullen capped his education with a tour of Europe before returning to Harlem. By this time he was an established poet, and in the next three years three more volumes of his verse appeared, as well as *Caroling Dusk,* an anthology of Black poetry. By training, temperament, and preference, Cullen was a Romantic poet—specifically, an ardent disciple of John Keats. Much of his poetry is nonracial, concerning itself with the Keatsian themes of love, spring, youth, the longing for death, and the power of the poetic imagination. But Cullen could not escape his Blackness altogether. A few poems frankly celebrate Blackness, but more often a somewhat more ambivalent attitude toward questions of racial identity and heritage emerges, as in "From the Dark Tower," "Yet Do I Marvel," and "Heritage."

The long and prolific literary career of Langston Hughes began in high school in Cleveland, and his first important recognition came when he was only nineteen—the appearance of "The Negro Speaks of Rivers" in the June 1921 issue of *The Crisis*. Unlike Cullen, Hughes was never ambivalent about his racial heritage; in "The Negro Speaks of Rivers" he celebrates the Black historical experience, especially in its spiritual dimension, its development of "soul." Though some of Hughes' poetry is nonracial, most of it falls into three categories: themes and variations on Black music ("The Weary Blues," "Jazzonia," "Dream Boogie"), racial affirmation ("Dream Variation," "Harlem Sweeties," "Me and the Mule"), and racial protest ("I, Too, Sing America," "Song for a Dark Girl," "Merry-Go-Round"). After *The Weary Blues* and *Fine Clothes to the Jew* (1927), his poems were periodically collected in eight subsequent volumes, the last being the posthumous *The Panther and the Lash* (1967). Much of his best work in poetry, however, was done during the Renaissance. Of his voluminous later work in fiction, drama, history, biography, autobiography, translation, juveniles, and anthologies, perhaps the most durable will prove to be the charming Simple stories, which Hughes wrote during the last twenty-five years of his life. Of the whole range of Afro-American literature, these richly humorous but often biting sketches of a not-so-simple "Negro Everyman" have been the most widely read and enjoyed by Black readers. From first to last, Langston Hughes was a literary race man, extolling, in the phrase of Conrad Kent Rivers, "all things black and beautiful." From a young Bohemian poet of the Harlem Renaissance, he became finally a Harlem institution, the grand old man of Black letters.

In addition to McKay, Toomer, Cullen, and Hughes, other Black voices were heard in the 1920's. Jessie Fauset, Walter White, and Nella Larsen wrote novels concerned with the problems of the Black middle class, especially those light enough to pass. The novels of George Schuyler and Wallace Thurman satirize the paradoxes of American color consciousness. Two accomplished local-color short story writers were Eric Walrond, whose *Tropic Death* presents a gloomy view of Black life in the Caribbean, and Rudolph Fisher, who dealt with Harlem scenes. In poetry Arna Bontemps, Waring Cuney, Sterling A. Brown, Frank Horne, Gwendolyn B. Bennett, Helene Johnson, and others contributed to the ebulliently youthful tone of the decade.

The Harlem Renaissance has sometimes been treated as a minor appendage to the larger American literary movement of the 1920's. To do so is to ignore or distort some of its most distinctive features, for its primary importance is as a cultural expression of a racial experience. Nevertheless, some mention of parallel developments in white drama and fiction is needed to place Afro-American writing of the decade in its full context. Black themes and characters had fascinated a number of nineteenth-century writers—James Fenimore Cooper, Harriet Beecher Stowe, Herman Melville, George Washington Cable, Mark Twain, Thomas Nelson Page, Albion W. Tourgée, Joel Chandler Harris, and Stephen Crane, to name only the most important—but in the 1920's the supposedly primitive energy and vitality of Black life exerted a particularly strong attraction on the American literary imagination. In drama, Ridgely Torrence's *Three Plays for a Negro Theatre* (1917) had pioneered in breaking through the minstrel tradition into a more sympathetic and realistic folk drama. Paul Green's *In Abraham's Bosom* (1924), *Porgy* (1927) by DuBose and Dorothy Heyward, and Marc Connelly's *The Green Pastures* (1930) were further steps in the same direction. Eugene O'Neill, the greatest of all American dramatists, also had a special interest in Black themes. Though his understanding of Black people was far from perfect, *The Emperor Jones* (1920) and *All God's Chillun Got Wings* (1923) gave a new dramatic dignity and stature to Black characters, qualities considerably enhanced by the acting genius of Charles Gilpin and Paul Robeson in starring roles. In fiction, too, there was a pronounced interest in Black material. Two friends and literary associates of Jean Toomer, for example, wrote novels ascribing primitive virtues to Black characters. Accompanied by Toomer, Waldo Frank passed for Black on a trip in the Deep South in 1922—more than forty years before the similar experiment of John Howard Griffin—to gather material for *Holiday* (1923), a novel of racial conflict in which John Cloud, a Black Christ-figure, is lynched for a crime of which he is innocent. Sherwood Anderson, whose prose is strikingly similar to Toomer's, contrasts the repressed and sterile lives of whites to the rich sensuality of Blacks in *Dark Laughter* (1925). Southern novelists also began to treat Black life with a new respect. If the work of Julia Peterkin, DuBose Heyward, T. S. Stribling, and William Faulkner is not without paternalistic condescension, at least it represents a substantial improvement over the overt racism of most prior Southern writers. A special word must be said concerning Carl Van Vechten. No one on the New York literary and social scene did more to bring Black writers and singers to the attention of whites than this highly sophisticated novelist and critic. His novel *Nigger Heaven* (1926) attempted to depict Harlem life among both the intellectuals and the underworld. Widely resented by Blacks because of the title, the book was defended by Van Vechten's friends James Weldon Johnson and Langston Hughes. Whatever the merits of *Nigger Heaven* (McKay's *Home to Harlem* is a similar but better book), Van Vechten's effective promotion and patronage of the Harlem Renaissance made him an invaluable white ally—"one of the most vital factors," James Weldon Johnson thought, "in bringing about the artistic emergence of the Negro in America."

Such were some of the circumstances and participants of the Harlem Renaissance. It remains to note briefly some of the issues and themes of the movement. One such issue was the conflict between gentility and Bohemianism, between literary Puritanism and Freudianism. Partly this was a generational dispute, for such senior figures as Du Bois and Braithwaite were reared in a fastidious late Victorian literary culture that made them hostile to the boldness and candor of McKay and Hughes. In his *Crisis* review, Du Bois complained: "*Home to Harlem* for the most part nauseates me, and after the dirtier parts of its filth I feel distinctly like taking a bath." To expose Harlem low life to white readers, the literary conservatives feared, was not only to flout the accepted standards of good taste, but to confirm white stereotypes about Black sexuality and irresponsibility; it almost amounted to racial betrayal. For both literary and social reasons, then, it would be better to write well-mannered fiction about the Black middle class à la Jessie Fauset and Nella Larsen or "correct" poetry in conventional forms, such as that of Countee Cullen (who married the daughter of Du Bois).

Such cautious considerations could not contain the rebellious spirits of McKay, Toomer, Hughes, Thurman, and others. In 1934 Benjamin Brawley was still deploring jazz, free verse, the cult of the primitive, and sensationalism, but the prevailing mood had been expressed by Hughes in 1926:

> We younger Negro artists who create now intend to express our individual dark-skinned selves without fear or shame. If white people are pleased we are glad. If they are not, it doesn't matter. We know we are beautiful. And ugly too. The tom-tom cries and the tom-tom laughs. If colored people are pleased we are glad. If they are not, their displeasure doesn't matter either. We build our temples for tomorrow, strong as we know how, and we stand on top of the mountain, free within ourselves.

The smugness and artificiality of both the Black middle class and American society in general were rejected in favor of the "primitive" virtues of spontaneity, joy, energy, sensuality. Thus the African past was affirmed, not ignored or disparaged. Folklore and folk music were admired and imitated. Above all, a racial self-awareness and pride were engendered that brought a sense of liberation from white standards and values. The best writers of the Harlem Renaissance were saying and singing, in their various ways, that Black was indeed beautiful.

Then came the Great Depression. Always last hired and first fired, Blacks suffered sooner, longer, and more profoundly than whites the disastrous effects of the vast economic dislocation of the 1930's. In the South, the cotton economy was hit so hard that the number of Black tenant farmers and sharecroppers decreased by some two hundred thousand from 1930 to 1940. Industrial workers North and South were laid off or displaced by whites. By 1932 fifty-six per cent of Blacks were unemployed. To meet the crisis the new President, Franklin D. Roosevelt, instituted a number of relief measures beginning in 1933 that proved highly beneficial to large segments of the Black population. New Deal agencies frequently indulged in racial discrimination, however, despite the efforts of Roosevelt's "Black Cabinet," a group of advisors including Robert C. Weaver, Eugene Kinckle Jones, Robert L. Vann, Mary McLeod Bethune, the poet Frank S. Horne, Laurence A. Oxley, and others. Nevertheless, the hope offered by Roosevelt—and by his highly popular wife, Eleanor —induced Black voters to shift away from their traditional allegiance to the Republican Party. In 1934 Arthur Mitchell was elected to the House of Representatives as the first Black Democratic Congressman. In 1936 Roosevelt carried the Black vote.

Another response to economic and social crisis in the 1930's was the formation in 1935 of the Committee for Industrial Organization (later called the Congress of Industrial Organizations) by John L. Lewis of the United Mine Workers and other union leaders dissatisfied with the more conservative craft union leadership that dominated the American Federation of Labor. Unlike the AFL, the CIO recognized the importance of organizing all industrial workers regardless of race. For the first time in American Labor history, Black workers were becoming part of the union movement.

At the same time, the Communist Party was making a serious bid for Black support and participation. James W. Ford, a Black man, was the Communist vice-presidential candidate in 1932, 1936, and 1940. Another important Black Communist was Benjamin J. Davis, Jr., who was elected to the New York City Council in 1943. The Party had some success, too, in arousing Blacks in the ghettos of Chicago and New York to resist evictions during the Depression. On the other hand, the Communist Party never attracted a really sizable Black following, though it did influence a number of Black intellectuals, of whom Richard Wright was the most important.

Another interracial movement of considerable importance was led by Father Divine, who began operations shortly after World War I. During the 1930's and 1940's his followers numbered in the thousands. Whatever one thinks of the legitimacy of his claim to be God, his charisma was undeniable. Furthermore, his "heavens" or Peace Missions performed a valuable social service by providing food and shelter to the poor and homeless at nominal charges.

Other social, political, and religious movements were predominantly or exclusively Black. The National Negro Congress was formed in 1936 as a broad coalition of Black groups. In early 1941 A. Philip Randolph began to develop plans for a massive March on Washington to press demands for employment of Black workers in defense plants. As the target date of July 1 approached, President Roosevelt finally capitulated to the pressure and issued Executive Order 8802 banning racial discrimination in defense industries and government. Other movements during the 1930's protested the trial of the Scottsboro boys charged with rape in Alabama and boycotted stores with discriminatory employment policies ("Don't Buy Where You Can't Work!"). Occasionally social tensions erupted into violence, as in the Harlem riot of 1935. Two Black leaders who were to achieve greater fame at a later time got their start in the 1930's. Adam Clayton Powell, Jr., was a key organizer of the Greater New York Coördinating Committee, which used "nonviolent direct social action" such as picket lines to expand economic opportunity. Beginning in 1930, Elijah Muhammed worked patiently to spread his religious and social teachings and to expand the membership of the Nation of Islam (Black Muslims), though he had to wait until the 1950's and 1960's to see the full fruition of his efforts.

World War II brought some alleviation of the economic problems of Black people, even though compliance with Roosevelt's executive order concerning fair employment was spotty. But the war raised other issues equally troubling. Jim Crow was universal in the armed services, and the Navy at first used Blacks only in menial capacities. Because many training bases were in the South, Black trainees from the North were often subject to the most overt kinds of discrimination. Riots were common at military installations in many parts of the country. Larger riots took place in Detroit, New York, and Los Angeles during the war years. The bitter irony of his participation in the war effort was not lost on the Black man. Fighting against Nazism and its myth of Aryan superiority, he had to contend with America's own variety of virulent racism.

The historical context of Afro-American literature from 1930 to 1945, then, was economic crisis, social tension, and world war. Only a literature of protest, most Black writers thought, was an adequate response to the exigencies of the time. Consequently, several established Black writers turned to the left. W. E. B. Du Bois, who had flirted with socialism for years, embraced Marxism in the early 1930's, though he often criticized the Communist Party. The poetry of Langston Hughes written during the 1930's often looks to Leninism as the wave of the future. Sterling Brown's *Southern Road* (1932) has overtones of class struggle as well as racial conflict. Even Countee Cullen found that "Scottsboro, Too, Is Worth Its Song."

But the central figure in Black literature during the 1930's and early 1940's was Richard Wright. From a Deep Southern childhood and youth characterized by racial injustice, a broken family, inadequate educational opportunity, and poverty, Wright fled to Chicago in 1927. A few years later he found himself writing radical poetry—agitprop verse—under the auspices of the John Reed Club, a literary and artistic organization affiliated with the Communist Party. He then turned to fiction while working on the Writers Project of the Works Progress Administration, first in Chicago and then in New York. His first published book was *Uncle Tom's Children* (1938), a collection of four long stories concerned with racial violence in the South. Not only were the separate stories of a high caliber, but they were so arranged and related as to develop a theme of militant collectivism as the only meaningful response to white power. *Uncle Tom's Children* brought Wright literary recognition, but his powerful novel *Native Son* (1940) brought him fame such as no other Black Writer had enjoyed. And justly so, for the almost unbearably intense story of Bigger Thomas, a Chicago youth whose rebelliousness involves him in murder and leads him to the electric chair, is both a central document of the American racial dilemma and a novel of high artistic merit. Together with *Black Boy* (1945), a moving autobiographical testament of Wright's years in Mississippi, Arkansas, and Tennessee, *Native Son* and *Uncle Tom's Children* constitute the enduring legacy of the first phase of the literary career of America's greatest Black writer.

Wright was only one of a number of Black intellectuals affiliated with the Federal Writers Project of the WPA. Sterling Brown rendered an important administrative service as Editor of Negro Affairs. Arna Bontemps worked on the Project in Chicago, as did Margaret Walker, whose book of poetry *For My People* appeared in 1942 in a prestigious series published by Yale University Press. The young poet Robert E. Hayden worked on the Project in Detroit. Frank Yerby is now best known as a writer of best sellers, but he was a WPA author who began his career with such protest stories as "Health Card" and "Roads Going Down." Other novelists working for the Project included Claude McKay, William Attaway, Ralph Ellison, and Willard Motley. The first novels of Motley and Ellison did not appear until well after the end of the war. Attaway's first novel, *Let Me Breathe Thunder* (1939), is a Steinbeckian tale of Depression drifters. His second novel, *Blood on the Forge* (1941), is an impressive fictional treatment of the Great Migration. In all the authors whom it affected, the Federal Writers Project tended to fortify social concern and intensify protest, as well as provide the means for material survival.

Most of the radical Black writers of the 1930's and 1940's dealt with the urban North, but two novelists wrote essentially apolitical works drawing on their intimate knowledge of Black folk life in the rural South. George Wylie Henderson's *Ollie Miss* (1935), set in Alabama, and Zora Neale Hurston's *Their Eyes Were Watching God* (1937), set in Florida, are evocative, sensitive portrayals of Black womanhood confronting personal problems not directly related to racial conflict. But these were exceptions to the general literary trend. It is perhaps not too misleading an oversimplification to say that the dominant theme of Afro-American literature from 1915 to 1930 was racial affirmation, and the dominant theme from 1930 to 1945 was radical racial protest.

The Major Writers

James Weldon Johnson (1871–1938)

Like his contemporary W. E. B. Du Bois, James Weldon Johnson was a man of diverse talents, interests, and activities. Born in Jacksonville, Florida, on June 17, 1871, Johnson was raised in a cultivated family who had moved from Nassau to the mainland two years earlier. His father was a self-educated headwaiter at a fashionable resort hotel. A talented, artistic woman, his mother taught at the Stanton Public School for Blacks and inculcated in her children a love for reading and music. After completing work at Stanton in 1887, Johnson entered the preparatory division of Atlanta University. The years Johnson spent at Atlanta were pleasant and sometimes adventurous, but filled with a sense of mission. Like Du Bois at Fisk, Johnson at Atlanta had the invaluable experience of teaching one summer in a rural Black school. "It was this period," he recalls in his autobiography, "that marked the beginning of my psychological change from boyhood to manhood. It was this period which marked also the beginning of my knowledge of my own people as a 'race.'"

With this experience and an A.B. from the collegiate division of Atlanta University, Johnson returned to Jacksonville in 1894 to assume the principalship at Stanton, which now had a thousand pupils. Not only was his administration so successful that he was able to add high school grades to the school, but he found time to found and edit a newspaper, *The Daily American,* which lasted for eight months. In the fall of 1896 he began to spend his spare time reading law, and he passed the Florida bar examination some twenty months later.

Meanwhile, his younger brother, John Rosamond Johnson, had returned to Jacksonville from Boston, where he had studied music and had worked in the musical theater. Combining their talents, the two brothers wrote *Toloso,* a satirical comic opera on United States imperialism in the Spanish-American War. Rosamond supplied the music and J. W. wrote the libretto. When school was dismissed for the summer of 1899, they went to New York hoping to get their work produced. They were unsuccessful, but the effort introduced them to some of the most brilliant luminaries of the musical stage, including Oscar Hammerstein and Bob Cole, the latter a versatile theatrical man who later teamed with the brothers to form the famous musical team of Cole and Johnson. After spending the following two summers in New York, J. W. Johnson decided to give up his career in education and make his fortune in Tin-Pan Alley. Together with Bob Cole, the Johnson brothers produced a steady flow of hit songs, including "The Maiden with the Dreamy Eyes," "My Castle on the Nile," "Under the Bamboo Tree," "The Congo Love Song," and many others. Their theatrical engagements took them across the United States and even to Europe.

In his spare time from 1903 to 1906 J. W. Johnson undertook graduate study at Columbia University in English and drama, forming a close friendship with Brander Matthews, a well-known critic and professor. To him Johnson confided his serious literary ambitions. When the Broadway glamor began to fade, he decided to accept an appointment in the foreign service as a reward for Republican campaign activities in 1904. As United States Consul in Puerto Cabello, Venezuela, from 1906 to 1909, he had ample leisure to devote to literary pursuits. His second consular assignment, in revolution-torn Nicaragua (1909–1912), kept him more occupied, but he managed to complete *The Autobiography of an Ex-Coloured Man* (1912), a novel begun while Johnson was a student of Brander Matthews, and to write more poems.

Denied preferment because of the Democratic victory in the elections of 1912, Johnson left the consular service. After a year and a half in Jacksonville, he went back to New York, where he became the editorialist for *The New York Age*. Efforts to revive his career as a Broadway songwriter failed, but he continued to write poetry, publishing *Fifty Years and Other Poems* in 1917. At the end of 1916 he had joined the NAACP as field secretary, becoming general secretary in 1920, crucial positions that he filled with distinction until 1930, leading the fight against lynching, winning a series of civil rights cases, investigating American imperialism in Haiti. "I got immense satisfaction out of the work which was the main purpose of the National Association for the Advancement of Colored People," he has written, "at the same time, I struggled constantly not to permit that part of me which was the artist to become entirely submerged." In addition to his creative work, he rendered valuable service as critic and anthologist during the Harlem Renaissance, especially in *The Book of American Negro Poetry* (1922), *The Book of American Negro Spirituals* (1925), and *The Second Book of Negro Spirituals* (1926).

At the end of 1930 Johnson resigned as general secretary of the NAACP to accept the Adam K. Spence Chair of Creative Literature at Fisk University. The last years of his life were devoted to writing, teaching at Fisk, and lecturing at New York University. On June 26, 1938, he was killed in a grade crossing accident while on vacation in Maine.

As writer Johnson made major contributions to Afro-American literature in fiction, poetry, and nonfiction. He did not acknowledge his authorship of the anonymously published *The Autobiography of an Ex-Coloured Man* until it was reissued in 1927. At that time it made a remarkable impact, though earlier it had been little noticed. Compared to other Black novels before the Harlem Renaissance, it is notable for the complexity of characterization of its protagonist, a light-skinned man with ambivalent feelings toward his racial identity. Wishing to make a commitment to his people, he instead drifts aimlessly from Atlanta to Jacksonville to New York to Europe before finally deciding to pass as white. Achieving at the end of the story the white goal of material success and marrying a white woman, he nevertheless realizes the moral failure attendant on his denial of race.

Johnson's first book of poetry, *Fifty Years and Other Poems,* contains a section of sixteen "Jingles and Croons," dialect poems after the manner of Paul Laurence Dunbar. Though some of these, such as "Sence You Went Away" and "Brer Rabbit, You's de Cutes' of 'Em All," are charming, Johnson came to feel, as he explains in the preface to *The Book of American Negro Poetry,* that the dialect tradition had come to a dead end. The remaining four dozen poems of *Fifty Years and Other Poems* show great variety—protest verse, vignettes of tropical life, translations from Spanish and German poetry, melancholy meditations, among other types. The title poem, written to celebrate the fiftieth anniversary of the Emancipation Proclamation, was called by Brander Matthews "one of the noblest commemorative poems yet written by any American." More unified is *God's Trombones: Seven Negro Sermons in Verse* (1927). Relying on rhythm, idiom, and imagery rather than dialect to convey an authentic folk quality, Johnson, despite his personal agnosticism, expresses movingly in these poems some of the profundity of Black religious feeling. Three years after *God's Trombones* he printed privately a bitterly satirical poem on racial prejudice "written while meditating upon heaven and hell and democracy and war and America and the Negro Gold Star Mothers." This was included as the title poem of *Saint Peter Relates an Incident: Selected Poems* (1935), a final volume that contained the best of *Fifty Years and Other Poems* and a few new poems.

Finally, one must not overlook Johnson's nonfiction. In addition to his voluminous journalism, he wrote *Black Manhattan* (1930), an informal history of Black people in New York, especially valuable on theatrical, musical, and literary life; *Along This Way* (1933), a long, sophisticated, and thoughtful autobiography, as urbane as the man himself; and *Negro Americans, What Now?* (1934), his final assessment of the American racial situation.

Except for Ellen Tarry's *Young Jim* (1967), a sketch of the young Johnson for juveniles, there is no biography. Miles M. Jackson, Jr., has carefully edited "Letters to a Friend: Correspondence From James Weldon Johnson to George A. Towns," *Phylon,* XXIX (1968), 182–198. See also Jackson's "James Weldon Johnson," *Black World,* XIX (June 1970), 32–34. The September 1938 issue of *The Crisis* contains numerous memorial tributes to Johnson.

For criticism see the following: Benjamin Brawley, *The Negro Genius* (1937); Sterling A. Brown, *Negro Poetry and Drama* (1937) and *The Negro in American Fiction* (1937); Saunders Redding, *To Make a Poet Black* (1939); Hugh M. Gloster, *Negro Voices in American Fiction* (1948); Robert A. Bone, *The Negro Novel in America* (1958); Arna Bontemps, the introduction to *The Autobiography of an Ex-Coloured Man* (1960); Eugenia W. Collier, "James Weldon Johnson: Mirror of Change," *Phylon*, XXI (1960), 351–359; E. C. Tate, "Sentiment and Horse Sense: James Weldon Johnson's Style," *Negro History Bulletin*, XXV (April 1962), 152–154; Jean Wagner, *Les poètes nègres des États-Unis* (1963), an excellent study; Stephen H. Bronz, *Roots of Negro Racial Consciousness* (1964); Harold Cruse, *The Crisis of the Negro Intellectual* (1967); Eugene Levy, "Ragtime and Race Pride: The Career of James Weldon Johnson," *Journal of Popular Culture*, I (1968), 357–370; S. P. Fullinwider, *The Mind and Mood of Black America: 20th Century Thought* (1969); Richard Kostelanetz, "The Politics of Passing: The Fiction of James Weldon Johnson," *Negro American Literature Forum*, III (1969), 22–24, 29; and Robert E. Fleming, "Contemporary Themes in Johnson's *Autobiography of an Ex-Coloured Man*," *Negro American Literature Forum*, IV (1970), 120–124, 141, and "Irony as a Key to Johnson's *The Autobiography of an Ex-Coloured Man*," *American Literature*, XLIII (1971), 83–96.

from *The Book of American Negro Poetry*

Preface

A people may become great through many means, but there is only one measure by which its greatness is recognized and acknowledged. The final measure of the greatness of all peoples is the amount and standard of the literature and art they have produced. The world does not know that a people is great until that people produces great literature and art. No people that has produced great literature and art has ever been looked upon by the world as distinctly inferior.

The status of the Negro in the United States is more a question of national mental attitude toward the race than of actual conditions. And nothing will do more to change that mental attitude and raise his status than a demonstration of intellectual parity by the Negro through the production of literature and art.

Is there likelihood that the American Negro will be able to do this? There is, for the good reason that he possesses the innate powers. He has the emotional endowment, the originality and artistic conception, and, what is more important, the power of creating that which has universal appeal and influence.

I make here what may appear to be a more startling statement by saying that the Negro has already proved the possession of these powers by being the creator of the only things artistic that have yet sprung from American soil and been universally acknowledged as distinctive American products.

These creations by the American Negro may be summed up under four heads. The first two are the Uncle Remus stories, which were collected by Joel Chandler Harris, and the "spirituals" or slave songs, to which the Fisk Jubilee Singers made the public and the musicians of both the United States and Europe listen. The Uncle Remus stories constitute the greatest body of folk lore that America has produced, and the "spirituals" the greatest body of folk song. I shall speak of the "spirituals" later because they are more than folk songs, for in them the Negro sounded the depths, if he did not scale the heights, of music.

The other two creations are the cakewalk and ragtime.

· · ·

It may be surprising to many to see how little of the poetry being written by Negro poets today is being written in Negro dialect. The newer Negro poets show a tendency to discard dialect; much of the subject-matter which went into the making of traditional dialect poetry, 'possums, watermelons, etc., they have discarded altogether, at least, as poetic material. This tendency will, no doubt, be regretted by the majority of white readers; and, indeed, it would be a distinct loss if the American Negro poets threw away this quaint and musical folk speech as a medium of expression. And yet, after all, these poets are working through a problem not realized by the reader, and, perhaps, by many of these poets themselves not realized consciously. They are trying to break away from, not Negro dialect itself, but the limitations on Negro dialect imposed by the fixing effects of long convention.

The Negro in the United States has achieved or been placed in a certain artistic niche. When he is thought of artistically, it is as a happy-go-lucky, singing, shuffling, banjo-picking being or as a more or less pathetic figure. The picture of him is in a log cabin amid fields of cotton or along the levees. Negro dialect is naturally and by long association the exact instrument for voicing this phase of Negro life; and by that very exactness it is an instrument with but two full stops, humor and pathos. So even when he confines himself to purely racial themes, the Aframerican poet realizes that there are phases of Negro life in the United States which cannot be treated in the dialect either adequately or artistically. Take, for example, the phases rising out of life in Harlem, that most wonderful Negro city in the world. I do not deny that a Negro in a log cabin is more picturesque than a Negro in a Harlem flat, but the Negro in the Harlem flat is here, and he is but part of a group growing everywhere in the country, a group whose ideals are becoming increasingly more vital than those of the traditionally artistic group, even if its members are less picturesque.

What the colored poet in the United States needs to do is something like what Synge did for the Irish; he needs to find a form that will express the racial spirit by symbols from within rather than by symbols from without, such as the mere mutilation of English spelling and pronunciation. He needs a form that is freer and larger than dialect, but which will still hold the racial flavor; a form expressing the imagery, the idioms, the peculiar turns of thought, and the distinctive humor and pathos, too, of the Negro, but which will also be capable of voicing the deepest and highest emotions and aspirations, and allow of the widest range of subjects and the widest scope of treatment.

Negro dialect is at present a medium that is not capable of giving expression to the varied conditions of Negro life in America, and much less is it capable of giving the fullest interpretation of Negro character and psychology. This is no indictment against the dialect as dialect, but against the mold of convention in which Negro dialect in the United States has been set. In time these conventions may become lost, and the colored poet in the United States may sit down to write in dialect without feeling that his first line will put the general reader in a frame of mind which demands that the poem be humorous or pathetic. In the meantime, there is no reason why these poets should not continue to do the beautiful things that can be done, and done best, in the dialect.

In stating the need for Aframerican poets in the United States to work out a new and distinctive form of expression I do not wish to be understood to hold any theory that they should limit themselves to Negro poetry, to racial themes; the sooner they are able to write *American* poetry spontaneously, the better. Nevertheless, I believe that the richest contribution the Negro poet can make to the American literature of the future will be the fusion into it of his own individual artistic gifts. . . .

Sence You Went Away

Seems lak to me de stars don't shine so bright,
Seems lak to me de sun done loss his light,
Seems lak to me der's nothin' goin' right,
　Sence you went away.

Seems lak to me de sky ain't half so blue,
Seems lak to me dat ev'ything wants you,
Seems lak to me I don't know what to do,
　Sence you went away.

Seems lak to me dat ev'ything is wrong,
Seems lak to me de day's jes twice ez long,
Seems lak to me de bird's forgot his song,
    Sence you went away.

Seems lak to me I jes can't he'p but sigh,
Seems lak to me ma th'oat keeps gittin' dry,
Seems lak to me a tear stays in ma eye,
    Sence you went away.

Fifty Years (1863–1913)

O brothers mine, today we stand
    Where half a century sweeps our ken,
Since God, through Lincoln's ready hand,
    Struck off our bonds and made us men.

Just fifty years—a winter's day,
    As runs the history of a race;
Yet, as we look back o'er the way,
    How distant seems our starting place!

Look farther back! Three centuries!
    To where a naked, shivering score,
Snatched from their haunts across the seas,
    Stood, wide-eyed, on Virginia's shore.

Then let us here erect a stone,
    To mark the place, to mark the time;
As witness to God's purpose shown,
    A pledge to hold this day sublime.

A part of His unknown design,
    We've lived within a mighty age;
And we have helped to write a line
    On history's most wondrous page.

A few black bondmen strewn along
    The borders of our eastern coast,
Now grown a race, ten million strong,
    An upward, onward, marching host.

Far, far the way that we have trod,
    From slave and pagan denizens,
To freedmen, freemen, sons of God,
    Americans and Citizens.

For never let the thought arise
    That we are here on sufferance bare;
Outcasts asylumed 'neath these skies,
    And aliens without part or share.

This land is ours by right of birth,
    This land is ours by right of toil;
We helped to turn its virgin earth,
    Our sweat is in its fruitful soil.

Where once the tangled forest stood,
    Where flourished once rank weed and thorn,
Behold the path-traced, peaceful wood,
    The cotton white, the yellow corn.

To gain these fruits that have been earned,
    To hold these fields that have been won,
Our arms have strained, our backs have burned,
    Bent bare beneath a ruthless sun.

That Banner which is now the type
    Of victory on field and flood—
Remember, its first crimson stripe
    Was dyed by Attucks' willing blood.

And never yet has come the cry—
    When that fair flag has been assailed—
For men to do, for men to die,
    That we have faltered or have failed.

We've helped to bear it, rent and torn,
    Through many a hot-breath'd battle breeze;
Held in our hands, it has been borne
    And planted far across the seas.

And never yet—O haughty Land,
    Let us, at least, for this be praised—
Has one black, treason-guided hand
    Ever against that flag been raised.

Then should we speak but servile words,
    Or shall we hang our heads in shame?
Stand back of new-come foreign hordes,
    And fear our heritage to claim?

No! Stand erect and without fear,
    And for our foes let this suffice—
We've brought a rightful sonship here,
    And we have more than paid the price.

And yet, my brothers, well I know
    The tethered feet, the pinioned wings,
The spirit bowed beneath the blow,
    The heart grown faint from wounds and
        stings;

The staggering force of brutish might,
  That strikes and leaves us stunned and dazed;
The long, vain waiting through the night
  To hear some voice for justice raised.

Full well I know the hour when hope
  Sinks dead, and round us everywhere
Hangs stifling darkness, and we grope
  With hands uplifted in despair.

Courage! Look out, beyond, and see
  The far horizon's beckoning span!
Faith in your God-known destiny!
  We are a part of some great plan.

Because the tongues of Garrison
  And Phillips now are cold in death,
Think you their work can be undone?
  Or quenched the fires lit by their breath?

Think you that John Brown's spirit stops?
  That Lovejoy was but idly slain?
Or do you think those precious drops
  From Lincoln's heart were shed in vain?

That for which millions prayed and sighed,
  That for which tens of thousands fought,
For which so many freely died,
  God cannot let it come to naught.

O Black and Unknown Bards

O black and unknown bards of long ago,
How came your lips to touch the sacred fire?
How, in your darkness, did you come to know
The power and beauty of the minstrel's lyre?
Who first from midst his bonds lifted his eyes?
Who first from out the still watch, lone and long,
Feeling the ancient faith of prophets rise
Within his dark-kept soul, burst into song?

Heart of what slave poured out such melody
As "Steal Away to Jesus"? On its strains
His spirit must have nightly floated free,
Though still about his hands he felt his chains.
Who heard great "Jordan roll"? Whose starward
  eye
Saw chariot "swing low"? And who was he
That breathed that comforting, melodic sigh,
"Nobody Knows de Trouble I See"?

What merely living clod, what captive thing,
Could up toward God through all its darkness
  grope,
And find within its deadened heart to sing
These songs of sorrow, love, and faith, and hope?
How did it catch that subtle undertone,
That note in music heard not with the ears?
How sound the elusive reed so seldom blown,
Which stirs the soul or melts the heart to tears?

Not that great German master in his dream
Of harmonies that thundered amongst the stars
At the creation, ever heard a theme
Nobler than "Go Down, Moses." Mark its bars,
How like a mighty trumpet-call they stir
The blood. Such are the notes that men have sung
Going to valorous deeds; such tones there were
That helped make history when Time was
  young.

There is a wide, wide wonder in it all,
That from degraded rest and servile toil
The fiery spirit of the seer should call
These simple children of the sun and soil.
O black slave singers, gone, forgot, unfamed,
You—you alone, of all the long, long line
Of those who've sung untaught, unknown,
  unnamed,
Have stretched out upward, seeking the divine.

You sang not deeds of heroes or of kings;
No chant of bloody war, no exulting pæan
Of arms-won triumphs; but your humble strings
You touched in chord with music empyrean.
You sang far better than you knew; the songs
That for your listeners' hungry hearts sufficed
Still live—but more than this to you belongs:
You sang a race from wood and stone to Christ.

The White Witch

O brothers mine, take care! Take care!
The great white witch rides out tonight,
Trust not your prowess nor your strength;
Your only safety lies in flight;
For in her glance there is a snare,
And in her smile there is a blight.

The great white witch you have not seen?
Then, younger brothers mine, forsooth,
Like nursery children you have looked
For ancient hag and snaggle-tooth;
But no, not so; the witch appears
In all the glowing charms of youth.

Her lips are like carnations red,
Her face like new-born lilies fair,
Her eyes like ocean waters blue,
She moves with subtle grace and air,
And all about her head there floats
The golden glory of her hair.

But though she always thus appears
In form of youth and mood of mirth,
Unnumbered centuries are hers,
The infant planets saw her birth;
The child of throbbing Life is she,
Twin sister to the greedy earth.

And back behind those smiling lips,
And down within those laughing eyes,
And underneath the soft caress
Of hand and voice and purring sighs,
The shadow of the panther lurks,
The spirit of the vampire lies.

For I have seen the great white witch,
And she has led me to her lair,
And I have kissed her red, red lips
And cruel face so white and fair;
Around me she has twined her arms,
And bound me with her yellow hair.

I felt those red lips burn and sear
My body like a living coal;
Obeyed the power of those eyes
As the needle trembles to the pole;
And did not care although I felt
The strength go ebbing from my soul.

Oh! she has seen your strong young limbs,
And heard your laughter loud and gay,
And in your voices she has caught
The echo of a far-off day,
When man was closer to the earth;
And she has marked you for her prey.

She feels the old Antæan strength
In you, the great dynamic beat
Of primal passions, and she sees
In you the last besieged retreat
Of love relentless, lusty, fierce,
Love pain-ecstatic, cruel-sweet.

O, brothers mine, take care! Take care!
The great white witch rides out tonight.
O, younger brothers mine, beware!
Look not upon her beauty bright;
For in her glance there is a snare,
And in her smile there is a blight.

Fragment

The hand of Fate cannot be stayed,
The course of Fate cannot be steered,
By all the gods that man has made,
Nor all the devils he has feared,
Not by the prayers that might be prayed
In all the temples he has reared.

See! In your very midst there dwell
Ten thousand thousand blacks, a wedge
Forged in the furnaces of hell,
And sharpened to a cruel edge
By wrong and by injustice fell,
And driven by hatred as a sledge.

A wedge so slender at the start—
Just twenty slaves in shackles bound—
And yet which split the land apart
With shrieks of war and battle sound,
Which pierced the nation's very heart,
And still lies cankering in the wound.

Not all the glory of your pride,
Preserved in story and in song,
Can from the judging future hide,
Through all the coming ages long,
That though you bravely fought and died,
You fought and died for what was wrong.

'Tis fixed—for them that violate
The eternal laws, naught shall avail
Till they their error expiate;
Nor shall their unborn children fail
To pay the full required weight
Into God's great, unerring scale.

Think not repentance can redeem,
That sin his wages can withdraw;
No, think as well to change the scheme
Of worlds that move in reverent awe;
Forgiveness is an idle dream,
God is not love, no, God is law.

Go Down Death—A Funeral Sermon

Weep not, weep not,
She is not dead;
She's resting in the bosom of Jesus.
Heart-broken husband—weep no more;
Grief-stricken son—weep no more;
Left-lonesome daughter—weep no more;
She's only just gone home.

Day before yesterday morning,
God was looking down from his great, high heaven,
Looking down on all his children,
And his eye fell on Sister Caroline,
Tossing on her bed of pain.
And God's big heart was touched with pity,
With the everlasting pity.

And God sat back on his throne,
And he commanded that tall, bright angel
   standing at his right hand:
Call me Death!
And that tall, bright angel cried in a voice
That broke like a clap of thunder:
Call Death!—Call Death!
And the echo sounded down the streets of heaven
Till it reached away back to that shadowy place,
Where Death waits with his pale, white horses.

And Death heard the summons,
And he leaped on his fastest horse,
Pale as a sheet in the moonlight.
Up the golden street Death galloped,
And the hoofs of his horse struck fire from the gold,
But they didn't make no sound.
Up Death rode to the Great White Throne,
And waited for God's command.

And God said: Go down, Death, go down,
Go down to Savannah, Georgia,
Down in Yamacraw,
And find Sister Caroline.
She's borne the burden and heat of the day,
She's labored long in my vineyard,
And she's tired—
She's weary—
Go down, Death, and bring her to me.

And Death didn't say a word,
But he loosed the reins on his pale, white horse,
And he clamped the spurs to his bloodless sides,
And out and down he rode,
Through heaven's pearly gates,
Past suns and moons and stars;
On Death rode,
And the foam from his horse was like a comet in
   the sky;
On Death rode,
Leaving the lightning's flash behind;
Straight on down he came.

While we were watching round her bed,
She turned her eyes and looked away,
She saw what we couldn't see;
She saw Old Death. She saw Old Death
Coming like a falling star.
But Death didn't frighten Sister Caroline;
He looked to her like a welcome friend.
And she whispered to us: I'm going home,
And she smiled and closed her eyes.

And Death took her up like a baby,
And she lay in his icy arms,
But she didn't feel no chill.
And Death began to ride again—
Up beyond the evening star,
Out beyond the morning star,
Into the glittering light of glory,
On to the Great White Throne.
And there he laid Sister Caroline
On the loving breast of Jesus.

And Jesus took his own hand and wiped away
   her tears,
And he smoothed the furrows from her face,
And the angels sang a little song,
And Jesus rocked her in his arms,
And kept a-saying: Take your rest,
Take your rest, take your rest.

Weep not—weep not,
She is not dead;
She's resting in the bosom of Jesus.

Claude McKay (1889-1948)

A Jamaican peasant who became a cosmopolitan citizen of the world, a dedicated political radical and religious freethinker who ended his life as a convert to Roman Catholicism, a Black nationalist many of whose friends were white, a primitivist and a modernist, a key figure in the Harlem Renaissance who spent most of the 1920's wandering over Europe and North Africa, Claude McKay was a fascinatingly paradoxical figure whose adventurous life and vivid poetry and fiction constitute one of the most interesting chapters in Afro-American literary history.

McKay was born in the small village of Sunny Ville in the hills of central Jamaica on September 15, 1889. His parents were proud and sturdy rural people. His mother was a compassionate, altruistic woman whose "rich, warm love," her son remembered, encompassed not only her family but everyone else, especially the poor and unfortunate. His father, Thomas Francis McKay, was somewhat sterner. He retained a strong sense of his African past, telling his children the legends and customs of the Ashanti people from whom he descended. The physical environment of McKay's youth was beautiful, and the lives of the people, however poor, had a collective integrity of shared values. Speaking of the folk songs he learned as a boy, McKay called them "community songs for community work. They were not made in the mind of an individual intent on his individualism. They grew from a way of life." Predominantly Black, this way of life had assimilated other elements—Chinese, East Indian, Sephardic Jewish—into "a garden of mixed humanity." However far he wandered from his island home, McKay never lost his nostalgia for its love, beauty, and communal stability, values that he contrasted to the egoism, materialism, and racism of American life.

The two chief intellectual tutors of McKay's youth were his elder brother, an agnostic schoolteacher, and Walter Jekyll (Squire Gensir of McKay's novel *Banana Bottom*), an intellectual English resident of Jamaica who collected island folklore. Through these men McKay had access to books, and he devoured poets and philosophers with equal relish: Dante, Villon, Milton, Pope, Goethe, Byron, Shelley, Keats, Leopardi, Baudelaire, Whitman, Schopenhauer, Herbert Spencer. With such intellectual vistas opening for the youth, it was inevitable that he would not be long satisfied with the trade of wheelwright and cabinetmaker, to which he was apprenticed when he was seventeen, or with service in the Jamaican constabulary in Kingston in 1909. The poetic vocation was more attractive, and in 1912 he published his first two collections of verse, *Songs of Jamaica* and *Constab Ballads,* the former with a preface by Walter Jekyll. Most of the poems in both volumes are in Jamaican dialect. *Songs of Jamaica* treats mainly rural peasant life; *Constab Ballads* depicts the harsher urban existence of Kingston, where the poet had more directly encountered racism and moral degradation. The Jamaica that he tended to remember in later life was that of his lovely and loved Clarendon Hills, but with a scholarship won by his poems he was ready in 1912 to move to a larger arena, the United States.

Although Black Jamaicans held both white and Black American visitors to the island in low esteem, the myth of America as the "golden land of education and opportunity" (McKay's phrase) prevailed. Considerable disillusionment resulted, however, from his few months as a student of agriculture at Tuskegee Institute and then his two years at Kansas State College in Manhattan; in 1914, with a legacy that he hoped would tide him over until he could establish a literary position, he moved to New York.

When bad investments consumed his capital, McKay was forced to live a hand-to-mouth existence as a kitchen helper in New England hotels and as a Pullman waiter on trains out of New York, among other menial jobs. But he was writing all the while, and late in 1917 he achieved his first important literary recognition in America when *The Seven Arts,* a major literary magazine edited by James Oppenheim, Waldo Frank, and Van Wyck Brooks, published two of his sonnets under the pseudonym Eli Edwards. Soon afterward he met Frank Harris, man of letters and editor of *Pearson's Magazine,* whose forceful personality and enthusiastic encouragement provided the young poet with an experience so stimulating that years later he was to make it the subject of the first chapter of his autobiography. After some of his poems appeared in *Pearson's,* other editorial doors began to open, notably that of the radical intellectual Max Eastman, whose magazine *The Liberator* published McKay's "The Dominant White" in the April 1919 issue and nine more poems (including "If We Must Die") as well as an editorial tribute in the July issue of the same year. Later, from March 1921 to June 1922, McKay was a key member of the editorial staff of *The Liberator,* and his name continued on the masthead through the final issue of October 1924. In addition to poems, he contributed essays and reviews to this important radical journal.

In the early 1920's McKay achieved recognition in England as well as in America. His second volume of verse, *Constab Ballads,* had been published in England. When he arrived in London for the first time in 1919, he found himself in surroundings familiar from his childhood reading and education. He met George Bernard Shaw and other radical white writers and journalists, and also frequented a colored soldiers' club in Drury Lane that he described in a series of articles he sent back to the *Negro World,* a Garveyite publication in New York. Further experience in radical journalism was gained with Sylvia Pankhurst on the *Workers' Dreadnought.* In 1920 C. K. Ogden published some two dozen of McKay's poems in the *Cambridge Magazine,* and later in the same year *Spring in New Hampshire and Other Poems* appeared. In the preface to this volume the brilliant critic I. A. Richards, Ogden's colleague at Cambridge, called McKay's poetry among "the best work that the present generation is producing in this country."

McKay's American reputation was not secured until the publication of *Harlem Shadows* in 1922. This collection of passionate and vibrant poems is the first great literary achievement of the Harlem Renaissance.

Like Countee Cullen but unlike Langston Hughes, McKay favored traditional poetic forms, especially the sonnet, for his "most lawless and revolutionary passions and moods."

These moods, together with his chronic wanderlust, took him away from Harlem again in 1922, this time for a period of twelve years. The first year was spent in Russia, where McKay as a Black leftist poet was lionized and eulogized by both the Bolshevik leaders and the Russian masses. By the time *Pravda* published his poem "Petrograd: May Day, 1923," McKay had met Trotsky, Bukharin, Lunarcharsky, Radek, and Zinoviev, and he had seen and felt "The presence and the simple voice of Lenin." This "Magic Pilgrimage" to the Soviet Union, as he called it, had made him a world figure as well as an Anglo-American one.

McKay spent the middle 1920's in France, mostly in Paris, Toulon, Marseilles, Nice, and Antibes. Here he wrote his first novel, *Home to Harlem* (1928), and gathered material for his second, *Banjo* (1929), which he began in Marseilles and completed in Spain and Morocco. While living in North Africa he turned back in his fiction to the first subject of his poetry—Jamaican peasant life. The two resulting books were a collection of short stories, *Gingertown* (1932), which also treats Harlem life, and a novel, *Banana Bottom* (1933).

The last fourteen years of McKay's life (1934–1948) were anticlimactic. Back in the States, he found that his creative impulse was waning and his health was failing. His important autobiography *A Long Way from Home* came out in 1937 and the impressionistic treatise *Harlem: Negro Metropolis* in 1940, but no more important fiction or poetry. In 1938 he formed a friendship with Ellen Tarry, a Black Catholic writer of children's books. Her influence resulted finally in his conversion to Roman Catholicism in October 1944, less than four years before his death.

Near the end of his life McKay wrote a recollection of his childhood that he considered to be "the farewell testimony of a man who was bitter because he loved, who was both right and wrong because he hated the things that destroyed love, who tried to give back to others a little of what he had got from them and the continuous adventure of being a black man in a white society. Happily, as I move on, I see that adventure changing for those who will come after me. For this is the century of the coloured world." Claude McKay was prophet as well as poet.

A Long Way from Home should be supplemented by two revealing autobiographical essays: "Boyhood in Jamaica," *Phylon*, XIV (1953), 134–145, and "Why I Became a Catholic," *Ebony*, I (March 1946), 32. See also McKay's "A Negro to his Critics," *New York Herald Tribune Books*, March 6, 1932, pp. 1, 6. Ellen Tarry recalls her friendship with McKay in *The Third Door* (1955).

There is no book-length study of McKay. General accounts of his literary career may be found in Saunders Redding, *To Make a Poet Black* (1939); Robert A. Smith, "Claude McKay: An Essay in Criticism," *Phylon*, IX (1948), 270–273; Stephen A. Bronz, *Roots of Racial Consciousness* (1964); Wayne Cooper, "Claude McKay and the New Negro of the

1920's," *Phylon,* XXV (1964), 297–306; George E. Kent, "The Soulful Way of Claude McKay," *Black World,* XX (November 1970), 37–51; and Eugenia Collier, "The Four-Way Dilemma of Claude McKay," available from the Center for African and Afro-American Studies at Atlanta University. Sister Mary Conroy, whose doctoral dissertation was on McKay, has traced an important theme in "The Vagabond Motif in the Writings of Claude McKay," *Negro American Literature Forum,* V (1971), 15–23. McKay's poetry is treated in Sterling A. Brown, *Negro Poetry and Drama* (1937); Blyden Jackson, "The Essential McKay," *Phylon,* XIV (1953), 216–217; Jean Wagner, *Les poètes nègres des États-Unis* (1963), the most detailed study; and Wilfred Carty, "Four Shadows of Harlem," *Negro Digest,* XVIII (August 1969), 22–25, 83–92. McKay's fiction is examined in the two standard studies, Hugh M. Gloster's *Negro Voices in American Fiction* (1948) and Robert A. Bone's *The Negro Novel in America* (1958). See also Kenneth Ramchand, "Claude McKay and *Banana Bottom,*" *Southern Review,* IV (1970), 53–66, and Jacqueline Kaye, "Claude McKay's 'Banjo,'" *Présence Africaine,* No. 73 (1970), pp. 165–169.

Spring in New Hampshire

To J. L. J. F. E.

Too green the springing April grass,
  Too blue the silver-speckled sky,
For me to linger here, alas,
  While happy winds go laughing by,
Wasting the golden hours indoors,
Washing windows and scrubbing floors.

Too wonderful the April night,
  Too faintly sweet the first May flowers,
The stars too gloriously bright,
  For me to spend the evening hours,
When fields are fresh and streams are leaping,
Wearied, exhausted, dully sleeping.

My Mother

I

Reg wished me to go with him to the field.
I paused because I did not want to go;
But in her quiet way she made me yield,
Reluctantly, for she was breathing low.
Her hand she slowly lifted from her lap
And, smiling sadly in the old sweet way,
She pointed to the nail where hung my cap.
Her eyes said: I shall last another day.
But scarcely had we reached the distant place,
When over the hills we heard a faint bell ringing.
A boy came running up with frightened face—
We knew the fatal news that he was bringing.
I heard him listlessly, without a moan,
Although the only one I loved was gone.

II

The dawn departs, the morning is begun,
The Trades come whispering from off the seas,
The fields of corn are golden in the sun,
The dark-brown tassels fluttering in the breeze;
The bell is sounding and children pass,
Frog-leaping, skipping, shouting, laughing
    shrill,
Down the red road, over the pasture-grass,
Up to the schoolhouse crumbling on the hill.
The older folk are at their peaceful toil,
Some pulling up the weeds, some plucking corn,
And others breaking up the sun-baked soil.
Float, faintly-scented breeze, at early morn
Over the earth where mortals sow and reap—
Beneath its breast my mother lies asleep.

Flame-Heart

So much I have forgotten in ten years,
So much in ten brief years! I have forgot
What time the purple apples come to juice,
And what month brings the shy forget-me-not.
I have forgot the special, startling season
Of the pimento's flowering and fruiting;
What time of year the ground doves brown the
    fields
And fill the noonday with their curious fluting.
I have forgotten much, but still remember
The poinsettia's red, blood-red, in warm
    December.

I still recall the honey-fever grass,
But cannot recollect the high days when
We rooted them out of the ping-wing path
To stop the mad bees in the rabbit pen.
I often try to think in what sweet month
The languid painted ladies used to dapple
The yellow by-road mazing from the main,
Sweet with the golden threads of the rose-
    apple.
I have forgotten—strange—but quite remember
The poinsettia's red, blood-red, in warm
    December.

What weeks, what months, what time of the
    mild year
We cheated school to have our fling at tops?
What days our wine-thrilled bodies pulsed with
    joy
Feasting upon blackberries in the copse?
Oh some I know! I have embalmed the days,
Even the sacred moments when we played,
All innocent of passion, uncorrupt,
At noon and evening in the flame-heart's shade.
We were so happy, happy, I remember,
Beneath the poinsettia's red in warm December.

The Tropics in New York

Bananas ripe and green, and ginger-root,
    Cocoa in pods and alligator pears,
And tangerines and mangoes and grape fruit,
    Fit for the highest prize at parish fairs,

Set in the window, bringing memories
    Of fruit-trees laden by low-singing rills,
And dewy dawns, and mystical blue skies
    In benediction over nun-like hills.

My eyes grew dim, and I could no more gaze;
    A wave of longing through my body swept,
And, hungry for the old, familiar ways,
    I turned aside and bowed my head and wept.

If We Must Die

If we must die, let it not be like hogs
Hunted and penned in an inglorious spot,
While round us bark the mad and hungry dogs,
Making their mock at our accursed lot.

If we must die, O let us nobly die,
So that our precious blood may not be shed
In vain; then even the monsters we defy
Shall be constrained to honor us though dead!

O kinsmen! we must meet the common foe!
Though far outnumbered let us show us brave,
And for their thousand blows deal one
    deathblow!

What though before us lies the open grave?
Like men we'll face the murderous, cowardly
    pack,
Pressed to the wall, dying, but fighting back!

The Lynching

His Spirit in smoke ascended to high heaven.
His father, by the cruelest way of pain,
Had bidden him to his bosom once again;
The awful sin remained still unforgiven.
All night a bright and solitary star
(Perchance the one that ever guided him,
Yet gave him up at last to Fate's wild whim)
Hung pitifully o'er the swinging char.

Day dawned, and soon the mixed crowds came
    to view
The ghastly body swaying in the sun.
The women thronged to look, but never a one
Showed sorrow in her eyes of steely blue.

And little lads, lynchers that were to be,
Danced round the dreadful thing in fiendish glee.

Like a Strong Tree

Like a strong tree that in the virgin earth
Sends far its roots through rock and loam and
    clay,
And proudly thrives in rain or time of dearth,
When dry waves scare the rain-come sprites
    away;
Like a strong tree that reaches down deep,
    deep,
For sunken water, fluid underground,

Where the great-ringed unsightly blind worms
    creep,
And queer things of the nether world abound:
So would I live in rich imperial growth,
Touching the surface and the depth of things,
Instinctively responsive unto both,
Tasting the sweets of being, fearing no stings,
Sensing the subtle spell of changing forms,
Like a strong tree against a thousand storms.

Tiger

The white man is a tiger at my throat,
Drinking my blood as my life ebbs away,
And muttering that his terrible striped coat
Is Freedom's and portends the Light of Day.
Oh white man, you may suck up all my blood
And throw my carcass into potter's field,
But never will I say with you that mud
Is bread for Negroes! Never will I yield.

Europe and Africa and Asia wait
The touted New Deal of the New World's hand!
New systems will be built on race and hate,
The Eagle and the Dollar will command.
Oh Lord! My body, and my heart too, break—
The tiger in his strength his thirst must slake!

The Desolate City

My spirit is a pestilential city,
With misery triumphant everywhere,
Glutted with baffled hopes and human pity.
Strange agonies make quiet lodgement there:
Its sewers, bursting, ooze up from below
And spread their loathsome substance through
    its lanes,
Flooding all areas with their evil flow
And blocking all the motions of its veins:
Its life is sealed to love or hope or pity,
My spirit is a pestilential city.

Above its walls the air is heavy-wet,
Brooding in fever mood and hanging thick
Round empty tower and broken minaret,
Settling upon the tree tops stricken sick
And withered under its contagious breath.
Their leaves are shrivelled silver, parched
    decay,
Like wilting creepers trailing underneath
The chalky yellow of a tropic way.
Round crumbling tower and leaning minaret,
The air hangs fever-filled and heavy-wet.

And all its many fountains no more spurt;
Within the dammed-up tubes they tide and
    foam,
Around the drifted sludge and silted dirt,
And weep against the soft and liquid loam.
And so the city's ways are washed no more,
All is neglected and decayed within,
Clean waters beat against its high-walled
    shore
In furious force, but cannot enter in:
The suffocated fountains cannot spurt,
They foam and rage against the silted dirt.

Beneath the ebon gloom of mounting rocks
The little pools lie poisonously still,
And birds come to the edge in forlorn flocks,
And utter sudden, plaintive notes and shrill,
Pecking at strangely gray-green substances;
But never do they dip their bills and drink.
They twitter, sad beneath the mournful trees,
And fretfully flit to and from the brink,
In little gray-brown, green-and-purple flocks,
Beneath the jet-gloom of the mounting rocks.

And green-eyed moths of curious design,
With gold-black wings and rarely silver-dotted,
On nests of flowers among those rocks recline,
Bold, burning blossoms, strangely leopard-
    spotted,
But breathing deadly poison from their lips.
And every lovely moth that wanders by,
And from the blossoms fatal nectar sips,
Is doomed to dropping stupor, there to die;
All green-eyed moths of curious design
That on the fiercely-burning blooms recline.

Oh cold as death is all the loveliness,
That breathes out of the strangeness of the scene,
And sickening like a skeleton's caress,
Of clammy clinging fingers, long and lean.
Above it float a host of yellow flies,
Circling in changeless motion in their place,
That came down snow-thick from the freighted
    skies,
Swarming across the gluey floor of space:
Oh cold as death is all the loveliness,
And sickening like a skeleton's caress.

There was a time when, happy with the birds,
The little children clapped their hands and
    laughed;
And midst the clouds the glad winds heard their
    words
And blew down all the merry ways to waft
The music through the scented fields of flowers.
Oh sweet were children's voices in those days,
Before the fall of pestilential showers,
That drove them forth far from the city's ways:
Now never, nevermore their silver words
Will mingle with the golden of the birds.

Gone, gone forever the familiar forms
To which the city once so dearly clung,
Blown worlds beyond by the destroying storms
And lost away like lovely songs unsung.
Yet life still lingers, questioningly strange,
Timid and quivering, naked and alone,
Against the cycle of disruptive change,
Though all the fond familiar forms are gone,
Forever gone, the fond familiar forms;
Blown worlds beyond by the destroying storms.

America

Although she feeds me bread of bitterness,
And sinks into my throat her tiger's tooth,
Stealing my breath of life, I will confess
I love this cultured hell that tests my youth!
Her vigor flows like tides into my blood,
Giving me strength erect against her hate.
Her bigness sweeps my being like a flood.

Yet as a rebel fronts a king in state,
I stand within her walls with not a shred
Of terror, malice, not a word of jeer.
Darkly I gaze into the days ahead,
And see her might and granite wonders there,
Beneath the touch of Time's unerring hand,
Like priceless treasures sinking in the sand.

Harlem Shadows

I hear the halting footsteps of a lass
In Negro Harlem when the night lets fall
Its veil. I see the shapes of girls who pass
To bend and barter at desire's call.
Ah, little dark girls who in slippered feet
Go prowling through the night from street to
street!

Through the long night until the silver break
Of day the little gray feet know no rest;
Through the lone night until the last snow-flake
Has dropped from heaven upon the earth's
white breast,
The dusky, half-clad girls of tired feet
Are trudging, thinly shod, from street to street.

Ah, stern harsh world, that in the wretched way
Of poverty, dishonor and disgrace,
Has pushed the timid little feet of clay,
The sacred brown feet of my fallen race!
Ah, heart of me, the weary, weary feet
In Harlem wandering from street to street.

The Harlem Dancer

Applauding youths laughed with young
prostitutes
And watched her perfect, half-clothed body
sway;
Her voice was like the sound of blended flutes
Blown by black players upon a picnic day.
She sang and danced on gracefully and calm,
The light gauze hanging loose about her form;
To me she seemed a proudly-swaying palm

Grown lovelier for passing through a storm.
Upon her swarthy neck black shiny curls
Luxuriant fell; and tossing coins in praise,
The wine-flushed, bold-eyed boys, and even the
girls,
Devoured her shape with eager, passionate
gaze;
But looking at her falsely-smiling face,
I knew her self was not in that strange place.

The White House*

Your door is shut against my tightened face,
And I am sharp as steel with discontent;
But I possess the courage and the grace
To bear my anger proudly and unbent.
The pavement slabs burn loose beneath my
    feet,
A chafing savage, down the decent street;
And passion rends my vitals as I pass,
Where boldly shines your shuttered door of
    glass.
Oh, I must search for wisdom every hour,
Deep in my wrathful bosom sore and raw,
And find in it the superhuman power
To hold me to the letter of your law!
Oh, I must keep my heart inviolate
Against the potent poison of your hate.

St. Isaac's Church, Petrograd

Bow down my soul in worship very low
And in the holy silences be lost.
Bow down before the marble Man of Woe,
Bow down before the singing angel host.
What jewelled glory fills my spirit's eye,
What golden grandeur moves the depths of me!
The soaring arches lift me up on high,
Taking my breath with their rare symmetry.

Bow down my soul and let the wondrous light
Of beauty bathe thee from her lofty throne,
Bow down before the wonder of man's might.
Bow down in worship, humble and alone,
Bow lowly down before the sacred sight
Of man's Divinity alive in stone.

Flower of Love

The perfume of your body dulls my sense.
    I want nor wine nor weed; your breath alone
Suffices. In this moment rare and tense
    I worship at your breast. The flower is
    blown,
The saffron petals tempt my amorous mouth,
    The yellow heart is radiant now with dew
Soft-scented, redolent of my loved South;
    O flower of love! I give myself to you.

Uncovered on your couch of figured green,
    Here let us linger indivisible.
The portals of your sanctuary unseen
    Receive my offering, yielding unto me.
Oh, with our love the night is warm and deep!
    The air is sweet, my flower, and sweet the
    flute
Whose music lulls our burning brain to sleep,
    While we lie loving, passionate and mute.

A Memory of June

When June comes dancing on the death of
    May,
    With scarlet roses tinting her green breast,
And mating thrushes ushering in her day,
    And Earth on tiptoe for her golden
    guest,

I always see the evening when we met—
    The first of June baptized in tender rain—
And walked home through the wide streets,
    gleaming wet,
    Arms locked, our warm flesh pulsing with
    love's pain.

* "My title was symbolic . . . it had no reference to the official residence of the President of the United States. . . . The title 'White Houses' changed the whole symbolic intent and meaning of the poem, making it appear as if the burning ambition of the black malcontent was to enter white houses in general." Claude McKay: *A Long Way from Home* (1937), pp. 313–314.

I always see the cheerful little room,
    And in the corner, fresh and white, the
        bed,
Sweet scented with a delicate perfume,
    Wherein for one night only we were wed;

Where in the starlit stillness we lay mute,
    And heard the whispering showers all night
        long,
And your brown burning body was a lute
    Whereon my passion played his fevered song.

    When June comes dancing on the death of May,
        With scarlet roses staining her fair feet,
    My soul takes leave of me to sing all day
        A love so fugitive and so complete.

Memorial

Your body was a sacred cell always,
    A jewel that grew dull in garish light,
An opal which beneath my wondering gaze
    Gleamed rarely, softly throbbing in the night.

I touched your flesh with reverential hands,
    For you were sweet and timid like a flower
That blossoms out of barren tropic sands,
    Shedding its perfume in one golden hour.

You yielded to my touch with gentle grace,
    And though my passion was a mighty wave
That buried you beneath its strong embrace,
    You were yet happy in the moment's grave.

Still more than passion consummate to me,
    More than the nuptials immemorial sung,
Was the warm thrill that melted me to see
    Your clean brown body, beautiful and young;

The joy in your maturity at length,
    The peace that filled my soul like cooling wine,
When you responded to my tender strength,
    And pressed your heart exulting into mine.

How shall I with such memories of you
    In coarser forms of love fruition find?
No, I would rather like a ghost pursue
    The fairy phantoms of my lonely mind.

from *Home to Harlem*

II: Arrival

Jake was paid off. He changed a pound note he had brought with him. He had fifty-nine dollars. From South Ferry he took an express subway train for Harlem.

Jake drank three Martini cocktails with cherries in them. The price, he noticed, had gone up from ten to twenty-five cents. He went to Bank's and had a Maryland fried-chicken feed—a big one with candied sweet potatoes.

He left his suitcase behind the counter of a saloon on Lenox Avenue. He went for a promenade on Seventh Avenue between One Hundred and Thirty-fifth and One Hundred and Fortieth Streets. He thrilled to Harlem. His blood was hot. His eyes were alert as he sniffed the street like a hound. Seventh Avenue was nice, a little too nice that night.

Jake turned off on Lenox Avenue. He stopped before an ice-cream parlor to admire girls sipping ice-cream soda through straws. He went into a cabaret....

A little brown girl aimed the arrow of her eye at him as he entered. Jake was wearing a steel-gray English suit. It fitted him loosely and well, perfectly suited his presence. She knew at once that Jake must have just landed. She rested her chin on the back of her hands and smiled at him. There was something in his attitude, in his hungry wolf's eyes, that went warmly to her. She was brown, but she had tinted her leaf-like face to a ravishing chestnut. She had on an orange scarf over a green frock, which was way above her knees, giving an adequate view of legs lovely in fine champagne-colored stockings....

Her shaft hit home.... Jake crossed over to her table. He ordered Scotch and soda.

"Scotch is better with soda or even water," he said. "English folks don't take whisky straight, as we do."

But she preferred ginger ale in place of soda. The cabaret singer, seeing that they were making up to each other, came expressly over to their table and sang. Jake gave the singer fifty cents. . . .

Her left hand was on the table. Jake covered it with his right.

"Is it clear sailing between us, sweetie?" he asked.

"Sure thing. . . . You just landed from over there?"

"Just today!"

"But there wasn't no boat in with soldiers today, daddy."

"I made it in a special one."

"Why, you lucky baby! . . . I'd like to go to another place, though. What about you?"

"Anything you say, I'm game," responded Jake.

They walked along Lenox Avenue. He held her arm. His flesh tingled. He felt as if his whole body was a flaming wave. She was intoxicated, blinded under the overwhelming force.

But nevertheless she did not forget her business. "How much is it going to be, daddy?" she demanded.

"How much? *How* much? Five?"

"Aw no, daddy. . . ."

"Ten?"

She shook her head.

"Twenty, sweetie!" he said, gallantly.

"Daddy," she answered, "I wants fifty."

"Good," he agreed. He was satisfied. She was responsive. She was beautiful. He loved the curious color on her cheek.

They went to a buffet flat on One Hundred and Thirty-seventh Street. The proprietress opened the door without removing the chain and peeked out. She was a matronly mulatto woman. She recognized the girl, who had put herself in front of Jake, and she slid back the chain and said, "Come right in."

The windows were heavily and carefully shaded. There was beer and wine, and there was plenty of hard liquor. Black and brown men sat at two tables in one room, playing poker. In the other room a phonograph was grinding out a "blues," and some couples were dancing, thick as maggots in a vat of sweet liquor, and as wriggling.

Jake danced with the girl. They shuffled warmly, gloriously about the room. He encircled her waist with both hands, and she put both of hers up to his shoulders and laid her head against his breast. And they shuffled around.

"Harlem! Harlem!" thought Jake. "Where else could I have all this life but Harlem? Good old Harlem! Chocolate Harlem! Sweet Harlem! Harlem, I've got you' number down. Lenox Avenue, you're a bear, I know it. And, baby honey, sure enough youse a pippin for your pappy. Oh, boy!" . . .

After Jake had paid for his drinks, that fifty-dollar note was all he had left in the world. He gave it to the girl. . . .

"Is we going now, honey?" he asked her.

"Sure, daddy. Let's beat it." . . .

Oh, to be in Harlem again after two years away. The deep-dyed color, the thickness, the closeness of it. The noises of Harlem. The sugared laughter. The honey-talk on its streets. And all night long, ragtime and "blues" playing somewhere, . . . singing somewhere, dancing somewhere! Oh, the contagious fever of Harlem. Burning everywhere in dark-eyed Harlem. . . . Burning now in Jake's sweet blood. . . .

He woke up in the morning in a state of perfect peace. She brought him hot coffee and cream and doughnuts. He yawned. He sighed. He was satisfied. He breakfasted. He washed. He dressed. The sun was shining. He sniffed the fine dry air. Happy, familiar Harlem.

"I ain't got a cent to my name," mused Jake, "but ahm as happy as a prince, all the same. Yes, I is."

He loitered down Lenox Avenue. He shoved his hand in his pocket—pulled out the fifty-dollar note. A piece of paper was pinned to it on which was scrawled in pencil:

"Just a little gift from a baby girl to a honey boy!"

Jean Toomer (1894–1967)

Jean Toomer's life was motivated by a quest for meaning, for certainty, for a sense of psychological stability in a world of chaos and flux. At times he thought that he had discovered his answer—in the vanishing integrity of Black rural life in the South, in the Freudian mysticism of George Ivanovitch Gurdjieff, in the Society of Friends—but he periodically found it necessary to renew the search. "Perhaps . . .," he wrote in his late fifties, "our lot on this earth is to seek and to search. Now and again we find just enough to enable us to carry on. I now doubt that any of us will completely find and be found in this life."

Much of Toomer's sense of insecurity stemmed from his unhappy childhood. His mother was Nina Pinchback Toomer, the daughter of P. B. S. Pinchback, who had been an important Reconstruction politician in Louisiana but was living in reduced financial and social circumstances in Washington, D.C., in the 1890's. Toomer never knew his father, who abandoned his wife after a year of marriage. Living with his embittered grandfather, the boy turned away from his unhappy family life and grew more introspective. When his very light-skinned grandfather moved the family from the white neighborhood where they lived to Florida Avenue in the upper-class Black area, the adolescent Toomer found "more emotion, more rhythm, more color, more gaiety" in life, but at the same time he was troubled by his nascent sexuality. After graduation from Dunbar High School, he moved restlessly from one college to another: the University of Wisconsin, the Massachusetts College of Agriculture, the American College of Physical Training in Chicago (see the story "Bona and Paul" in *Cane*), the University of Chicago, New York University, and the City College of New York. Never did he stay at one institution long enough to become a serious degree candidate. Similarly, he afterward moved from one job to another: selling automobiles in Chicago, teaching physical education in Wisconsin, working in a shipyard in New Jersey. In his middle twenties at the end of World War I, Toomer returned to his grandfather in Washington a confused and disoriented young man.

Then he began to write, placing poems and stories in such avant-garde little magazines as *The Double Dealer, Broom, The Liberator, The Crisis, The Little Review, S 4 N, Secession, The Modern Review, Nomad, Prairie,* and *Opportunity*. He formed close friendships in a group of New York intellectuals that included Waldo Frank, Paul Rosenfeld, Hart Crane, Kenneth Burke, Gorham P. Munson, and Alfred Stieglitz. In 1921 Toomer accepted a temporary position in rural Sparta, Georgia, as superintendent of a small Black school. In the four months he spent there he soaked up the essence of the region and its people that he was to distill in the first and third parts of *Cane* (1923).

Cane contains short stories, sketches, poems, and a novella-play, but it is a unified work of art, not merely a collection. Its unity is achieved through structure, style, and theme. The book is divided into three parts. In the first, the setting is rural Georgia and the subject the life of Black folk in both its physical and psychic dimensions. Frustration and tragedy touch these lives, but they nevertheless retain a measure of spiritual integrity and a luxuriantly poetic beauty that is much rarer in Washington and Chicago, the settings of the second part of *Cane.* Here Black life is corrupted and rendered sterile by the materialism of an urban society dominated by white values. In the final section, "Kabnis," a neurotic Black intellectual has come South to teach and to attempt to seek out the roots of his racial identity, his ancestral soul. He fails, as Toomer himself in a similar sense failed in his later life. But the book itself is a superb success in its evocation of Black soul-beauty. Its word-music, its haunting recurrent images of dusk and cane, its experimental prose, its surrealistic touches, its brooding sensuality—all of these qualities are orchestrated into one of the greatest artistic triumphs of Afro-American literature.

After *Cane,* Toomer once again fell into a state of psychological disarray. In quest of the elusive principle of unity, he turned, together with several other intellectuals of his group, to the philosophies of F. Matthias Alexander, P. D. Ouspensky, and, especially, George I. Gurdjieff, a Russian who combined elements of Yoga, religious mysticism, and Freud into a system he called Unitism. As an ardent disciple, Toomer spent the summer of 1924 and several summers thereafter at the Gurdjieff Institute in France, and he taught the Gurdjieffian message in New York and Chicago. Among his pupils were Wallace Thurman, Aaron Douglas, Nella Larsen, and Margery Latimer, the last named a white writer whom he married in 1931 but who died in childbirth the following year. He remarried, again to a white woman, in 1934. At times he seemed to wish to deny his racial identity, as when he said soon after his second marriage: "I do not know whether colored blood flows through my veins." The more likely explanation is that he was attempting to transcend racial categories altogether. "I am of no particular race," he asserted, "I am of the human race, a man at large in the human world, preparing a new race." His vision of the new race in the new America is expressed in his long poem "Blue Meridian" (1936).

Toomer continued to write after the appearance of *Cane,* but he had difficulty getting published. Darwin T. Turner, who has examined the Toomer manuscript collection at Fisk University, reports "two novels, two books of poems, a collection of stories, books of non-fiction, two books of aphorisms," as well as some half-dozen plays, three of which were written in the early 1920's. His work after *Cane,* published and unpublished, became more and more abstract, more and more disconnected from physical reality. In the 1940's he turned to the Quaker faith for spiritual sustenance. He died on March 30, 1967.

In addition to the material published in *Cane,* Toomer published the following: "Balo," in *Plays of Negro Life* (1927), edited by Alain Locke and Montgomery Gregory; "Winter on Earth," in *The Second American*

Caravan (1928), edited by Alfred Kreymborg and others; "York Beach," a novella, in *The New American Caravan* (1929), edited by Alfred Kreymbourg and others; "Race Problems and Modern Society," in *Problems of Civilization* (1929), edited by Baker Brownell; *Essentials: Definitions and Aphorisms* (1931), privately printed; "As the Eagle Soars," *The Crisis*, XLI (1932), 116; "The Hill," an essay, in *America & Alfred Stieglitz* (1934), edited by Waldo Frank and others; *Work-Ideas I* and *Living Is Developing*, pamphlets privately printed in 1937; and two Quaker pamphlets, *An Interpretation of Friends Worship* (1947) and *The Flavor of Man* (1949). Excerpts from his unpublished autobiography, "Earth-Being," appeared in *The Black Scholar*, II (January 1971), 3–13.

Darwin Turner outlines criticism of Toomer through 1967 in *A Bibliographical Guide to the Study of Southern Literature* (1969), edited by Louis D. Rubin, Jr. Early appreciations include Waldo Frank's foreword to *Cane* (1923); Paul Rosenfeld's chapter in *Men Seen* (1925); Gorham B. Munson's "The Significance of Jean Toomer," *Opportunity*, III (1925), 262–263, and *Destinations* (1928); and Eugene Holmes' "Jean Toomer— Apostle of Beauty," *Opportunity*, X (1932), 252–254, 260. *Cane* is treated by Hugh M. Gloster in *Negro Voices in American Fiction* (1948) and by Robert A. Bone in *The Negro Novel in America* (1958). More recent studies include Jean Wagner, *Les poètes nègres des États-Unis* (1963); Arna Bontemps, "The Negro Renaissance: Jean Toomer and the Harlem Writers of the 1920's," in *Anger, and Beyond* (1966), edited by Herbert Hill, and the introduction to the paperback reprint of *Cane* (1969); S. P. Fullinwider, "Jean Toomer: Lost Generation, or Negro Renaissance?" *Phylon*, XXVII (1966), 396–403, and *The Mind and Mood of Black America: 20th Century Thought* (1969); Darwin Turner, "The Failure of a Playwright," *CLA Journal*, X (1967), 308–318, "And Another Passing," *Negro American Literature Forum*, I (1967), 3–4, "Jean Toomer's *Cane*," *Negro Digest*, XVIII (January 1969), 54–61, and two headnotes in *Black American Literature* (1970), which prints three of Toomer's hitherto unpublished poems; William J. Goede, "Jean Toomer's Ralph Kabnis: Portrait of the Negro Artist as a Young Man," *Phylon*, XXX (1969), 73–85; Todd Lieber, "Design and Movement in *Cane*," *CLA Journal*, XIII (1969), 35–50; Benjamin F. McKeever, "*Cane* as Blues," *Negro American Literature Forum*, IV (1970), 61–63; Clifford Mason, "Jean Toomer's Black Authenticity," *Black World*, XX (November 1970), 70–76; John M. Reilly, "The Search for Black Redemption: Jean Toomer's *Cane*," *Studies in the Novel*, II (1970), 312–324; Rafael A. Cancel, "Male and Female Interrelationship in Toomer's *Cane*," *Negro American Literature Forum*, V (1971), 25–31; and Sister Mary Kathryn Grant, "Images of Celebration in *Cane*," *Negro American Literature Forum*, V (1971), 32–34, 36. Mabel Dillard, whose 1967 Ohio University doctoral dissertation was on Toomer, is collaborating with Darwin Turner on a biographical-critical study.

from *Cane*

Karintha

Her skin is like dusk on the eastern horizon,
O cant you see it, O cant you see it,
Her skin is like dusk on the eastern horizon
. . . When the sun goes down.

Men had always wanted her, this Karintha, even as a child, Karintha carrying beauty, perfect as dusk when the sun goes down. Old men rode her hobby-horse upon their knees. Young men danced with her at frolics when they should have been dancing with their grown-up girls. God grant us youth, secretly prayed the old men. The young fellows counted the time to pass before she would be old enough to mate with them. This interest of the male, who wishes to ripen a growing thing too soon, could mean no good to her.

Karintha, at twelve, was a wild flash that told the other folks just what it was to live. At sunset, when there was no wind, and the pine-smoke from over by the sawmill hugged the earth, and you couldnt see more than a few feet in front, her sudden darting past you was a bit of vivid color, like a black bird that flashes in light. With the other children one could hear, some distance off, their feet flopping in the two-inch dust. Karintha's running was a whir. It had the sound of the red dust that sometimes makes a spiral in the road. At dusk, during the hush just after the sawmill had closed down, and before any of the women had started their supper-getting-ready songs, her voice, high-pitched, shrill, would put one's ears to itching. But no one ever thought to make her stop because of it. She stoned the cows and beat her dog, and fought the other children. . . Even the preacher, who caught her at mischief, told himself that she was as innocently lovely as a November cotton flower. Already, rumors were out about her. Homes in Georgia are most often built on the two-room plan. In one, you cook and eat, in the other you sleep, and there love goes on. Karintha had seen or heard, perhaps she had felt her parents loving. One could but imitate one's parent's, for to follow them was the way of God. She played "home" with a small boy who was not afraid to do her bidding. That started the whole thing. Old men could no longer ride her hobby-horse upon their knees. But young men counted faster.

Her skin is like dusk,
O cant you see it,
Her skin is like dusk,
When the sun goes down.

Karintha is a woman. She who carries beauty, perfect as dusk when the sun goes down. She has been married many times. Old men remind her that a few years back they rode her hobby-horse upon their knees. Karintha smiles, and indulges them when she is in the mood for it. She has contempt for them. Karintha is a woman. Young men run stills to make her money. Young men go to the big cities and run on the road. Young men go away to college. They all want to bring her money. These are the young men who thought that all they had to do was to count time. But Karintha is a woman, and she has had a child. A child fell out of her womb onto a bed of pine-needles in the forest. Pine-needles are smooth and sweet. They are elastic to the feet of rabbits. . . A sawmill was nearby. Its pyramidal sawdust pile smouldered. It is a year before one completely burns. Meanwhile, the smoke curls up and hangs in odd wraiths about the trees, curls up, and spreads itself out over the valley. . . Weeks after Karintha returned home the smoke was so heavy you tasted it in water. Some one made a song:

Smoke is on the hills. Rise up.
Smoke is on the hills, O rise
And take my soul to Jesus.

Karintha is a woman. Men do not know that the soul of her was a growing thing ripened too soon. They bring their money; they will die not having found it out. . . Karintha at twenty, carrying beauty, perfect as dusk when the sun goes down. Karintha. . .

Her skin is like dusk on the eastern horizon,
O cant you see it, O cant you see it,
Her skin is like dusk on the eastern horizon
. . . When the sun goes down.

Goes down. . .
. . . .

Song of the Son

Pour O pour that parting soul in song,
O pour it in the sawdust glow of night,
Into the velvet pine-smoke air to-night,
And let the valley carry it along.
And let the valley carry it along.

O land and soil, red soil and sweet-gum tree,
So scant of grass, so profligate of pines,
Now just before an epoch's sun declines
Thy son, in time, I have returned to thee,
Thy son, I have in time returned to thee.

In time, for though the sun is setting on
A song-lit race of slaves, it has not set;
Though late, O soil, it is not too late yet
To catch thy plaintive soul, leaving, soon gone,
Leaving, to catch thy plaintive soul soon gone.

O Negro slaves, dark purple ripened plums,
Squeezed, and bursting in the pine-wood air,
Passing, before they stripped the old tree bare
One plum was saved for me, one seed becomes

An everlasting song, a singing tree,
Caroling softly souls of slavery,
What they were, and what they are to me,
Caroling softly souls of slavery.

. . .

Fern

Face flowed into her eyes. Flowed in soft cream foam and plaintive ripples, in such a way that wherever your glance may momentarily have rested, it immediately thereafter wavered in the direction of her eyes. The soft suggestion of down slightly darkened, like the shadow of a bird's wing might, the creamy brown color of her upper lip. Why, after noticing it, you sought her eyes, I cannot tell you. Her nose was aquiline, Semitic. If you have heard a Jewish cantor sing, if he has touched you and made your own sorrow seem trivial when compared with his, you will know my feeling when I follow the curves of her profile, like mobile rivers, to their common delta. They were strange eyes. In this, that they sought nothing—that is, nothing that was obvious and tangible and that one could see, and they gave the impression that nothing was to be denied. When a woman seeks, you will have observed, her eyes deny. Fern's eyes desired nothing that you could give her; there was no reason why they should withhold. Men saw her eyes and fooled themselves. Fern's eyes said to them that she was easy. When she was young, a few men took her, but got no joy from it. And then, once done, they felt bound to her (quite unlike their hit and run with other girls), felt as though it would take them a lifetime to fulfill an obligation which they could find no name for. They became attached to her, and hungered after finding the barest trace of what she might desire. As she grew up, new men who came to town felt as almost everyone did who ever saw her: that they would not be denied. Men were everlastingly bringing her their bodies. Something inside of her got tired of them, I guess, for I am certain that for the life of her she could not tell why or how she began to turn them off. A man in fever is no trifling thing to send away. They began to leave her, baffled and ashamed, yet vowing to themselves that some day they would do some fine thing for her: send her candy every week and not let her know whom it came from, watch out for her wedding-day and give her a magnificent something with no name on it, buy a house and deed it to her, rescue her from some unworthy fellow who had tricked her into marrying him. As you know, men are apt to idolize or fear that which they cannot understand, especially if it be a woman. She did not deny them, yet the fact was that they were denied. A sort of superstition crept into their consciousness of her being somehow above them. Being above them meant that she was not to be approached by anyone. She became a virgin. Now a virgin in a small southern town is by no means the usual thing, if you will believe me. That the sexes were made to mate is the practice of the South. Particularly, black folks were made to mate. And it is black folks whom I have been talking about thus far. What white men thought of Fern I can arrive at only by analogy. They let her alone.

Anyone, of course, could see her, could see her eyes. If you walked up the Dixie Pike most any time of day, you'd be most like to see her resting listless-like on the railing of her porch, back propped against a post, head tilted a little forward because there was a nail in the porch post just where her head came which for some reason or other she never took the trouble to pull out. Her eyes, if it were sunset, rested idly where the sun, molten and glorious, was pouring down between the fringe of pines. Or maybe they gazed at the gray cabin on the knoll from which an evening folk-song was coming. Perhaps they followed a cow that had been turned loose to roam and feed on cotton-stalks and corn leaves. Like as not they'd settle on some vague spot above the horizon, though hardly a trace of wistfulness would come to them. If it were dusk, then they'd wait for the search-light of the evening train which you could see miles up the track before it flared across the Dixie Pike, close to her home. Wherever they looked, you'd follow them and then waver back. Like her face, the whole countryside seemed to flow into her eyes. Flowed into them with the soft listless cadence of Georgia's South. A young Negro, once, was looking at her, spellbound, from the road. A white man passing in a buggy had to flick him with his whip if he was to get by without running him over. I first saw her on her porch. I was passing with a fellow whose crusty numbness (I was from the North and suspected of being prejudiced and stuck-up) was melting as he found me warm. I asked him who she was. "That's Fern," was all I that could get from him. Some folks already thought that I was given to nosing around; I let it go at that, so far as questions were concerned. But at first sight of her I felt as if I heard a Jewish cantor sing. As if his singing rose above the unheard chorus of a folk-song. And I felt bound to her. I too had my dreams: something I would do for her. I have knocked about from town to town too much not to know the futility of mere change of place. Besides, picture if you can, this cream-colored solitary girl sitting at a tenement window looking down on the indifferent throngs of Harlem. Better that she listen to folk-songs at dusk in Georgia, you would say, and so would I. Or, suppose she came up North and married. Even a doctor or a lawyer, say, one who would be sure to get along—that is, make money. You and I know, who have had experience in such things, that love is not a thing like prejudice which can be bettered by changes of town. Could men in Washington, Chicago, or New York, more than the men of Georgia, bring her something left vacant by the bestowal of their bodies? You and I know men in these cities will have to say, they could not. See her out and out a prostitute along State Street in Chicago. See her move into a southern town where white men are more aggressive. See her become a white man's concubine... Something I must do for her. There was myself. What could I do for her? Talk, of course. Push back the fringe of pines

upon new horizons. To what purpose? and what for? Her? Myself? Men in her case seem to lose their selfishness. I lost mine before I touched her. I ask you, friend (it makes no difference if you sit in the Pullman or the Jim Crow as the train crosses her road), what thoughts would come to you—that is, after you'd finished with the thoughts that leap into men's minds at the sight of a pretty woman who will not deny them; what thoughts would come to you, had you seen her in a quick flash, keen and intuitively, as she sat there on her porch when your train thundered by? Would you have got off at the next station and come back for her to take her where? Would you have completely forgotten her as soon as you reached Macon, Atlanta, Augusta, Pasadena, Madison, Chicago, Boston, or New Orleans? Would you tell your wife or sweetheart about a girl you saw? Your thoughts can help me, and I would like to know. Something I would do for her. . .

One evening I walked up the Pike on purpose, and stopped to say hello. Some of her family were about, but they moved away to make room for me. Damn if I knew how to begin. Would you? Mr. and Miss So-and-So, people, the weather, the crops, the new preacher, the frolic, the church benefit, rabbit and possum hunting, the new soft drink they had at old Pap's store, the schedule of the trains, what kind of town Macon was, Negro's migration north, boll-weevils, syrup, the Bible—to all these things she gave a yassur or nassur, without further comment. I began to wonder if perhaps my own emotional sensibility had played one of its tricks on me. "Lets take a walk," I at last ventured. The suggestion, coming after so long an isolation, was novel enough, I guess, to surprise. But it wasnt that. Something told me that men before me had said just that as a prelude to the offering of their bodies. I tried to tell her with my eyes. I think she understood. The thing from her that made my throat catch, vanished. Its passing left her visible in a way I'd thought, but never seen. We walked down the Pike with people on all the porches gaping at us. "Doesnt it make you mad?" She meant the row of petty gossiping people. She meant the world. Through a cane-brake that was ripe for cutting, the branch was reached. Under a sweet-gum tree, and where reddish leaves had dammed the creek a little, we sat down. Dusk, suggesting the almost imperceptible procession of giant trees, settled with a purple haze about the cane. I felt strange, as I always do in Georgia, particularly at dusk. I felt that things unseen to men were tangibly immediate. It would not have surprised me had I had a vision. People have them in Georgia more often than you would suppose. A black woman once saw the mother of Christ and drew her in charcoal on the court-house wall. . . When one is on the soil of one's ancestors, most anything can come to one. . . From force of habit, I suppose, I held Fern in my arms—that is, without at first noticing it. Then my mind came back to her. Her eyes, unusually weird and open, held me. Held God. He flowed in as I've seen the countryside flow in. Seen men. I must have done something—what, I dont know, in the confusion of my emotion. She sprang up. Rushed some distance from me. Fell to her knees, and began swaying, swaying. Her body was tortured with something it could not let out. Like boiling sap it flooded arms and fingers till she shook them as if they burned her. It found her throat, and spattered inarticulately in plaintive, convulsive sounds, mingled with calls to Christ Jesus. And then she sang, brokenly. A Jewish cantor singing with a broken voice. A child's voice, uncertain, or an old man's. Dusk hid her; I could hear only her song. It seemed to me as though she were pounding her head in anguish upon the ground. I rushed to her. She fainted in my arms.

There was talk about her fainting with me in the canefield. And I got one or two ugly looks from town men who'd set themselves up to protect her. In fact, there was talk of making me leave town. But they never did. They kept a watch-out for me, though. Shortly after, I came back North. From the train window I saw her as I crossed her road. Saw her on her porch, head tilted a little forward where the nail was, eyes vaguely focused on the sunset. Saw her face flow into them, the countryside and something that I call God, flowing into them. . . Nothing ever really happened. Nothing ever came to Fern, not even I. Something I would do for her. Some fine unnamed thing. . . And, friend, you? She is still living, I have reason to know. Her name,

against the chance that you might happen down that way, is Fernie May Rosen.

.   .   .

Portrait in Georgia

Hair—braided chestnut, coiled like a lyncher's rope,
Eyes—fagots,
Lips—old scars, or the first red blisters,
Breath—the last sweet scent of cane,
And her slim body, white as the ash of black flesh after flame.

.   .   .

Seventh Street

Money burns the pocket, pocket hurts,
Bootleggers in silken shirts,
Ballooned, zooming Cadillacs,
Whizzing, whizzing down the street-car tracks.

Seventh Street is a bastard of Prohibition and the War. A crude-boned, soft-skinned wedge of nigger life breathing its loafer air, jazz songs and love, thrusting unconscious rhythms, black reddish blood into the white and whitewashed wood of Washington. Stale soggy wood of Washington. Wedges rust in soggy wood. . . Split it! In two! Again! Shred it! . . the sun. Wedges are brilliant in the sun; ribbons of wet wood dry and blow away. Black reddish blood. Pouring for crude-boned soft-skinned life, who set you flowing? Blood suckers of the War would spin in a frenzy of dizziness if they drank your blood. Prohibition would put a stop to it. Who set you flowing? White and whitewash disappear in blood. Who set you flowing? Flowing down the smooth asphalt of Seventh Street, in shanties, brick office buildings, theaters, drug stores, restaurants, and cabarets? Eddying on the corners? Swirling like a blood-red smoke up where the buzzards fly in heaven? God would not dare to suck black red blood. A Nigger God! He would duck his head in shame and call for the Judgment Day. Who set you flowing?

Money burns the pocket, pocket hurts,
Bootleggers in silken shirts,
Ballooned, zooming Cadillacs,
Whizzing, whizzing down the street-car tracks.

.   .   .

Blue Meridian

It is a new America,
To be spiritualized by each new American.

> *Black Meridian, black light,*
> *Dynamic atom-aggregate,*
> *Lay sleeping on an inland lake.*

Lift, lift, thou waking forces!
Let us feel the energy of animals,
The energy of rumps and bull-bent heads
Crashing the barrier to man.
It must spiral on!
A million million men, or twelve men,
Must crash the barrier to the next higher form.

> Beyond plants are animals,
> Beyond animals is man,
> Beyond man is the universe.

> The Big Light,
> Let the Big Light in!

O thou, Radiant Incorporal,
The I of earth and of mankind, hurl
Down these seaboards, across this continent,
The thousand-rayed discus of thy mind,
And above our walking limbs unfurl
Spirit-torsos of exquisite strength!

The Mississippi, sister of the Ganges,
Main artery of earth in the western world,
Is waiting to become
In the spirit of America, a sacred river.
Whoever lifts the Mississippi
Lifts himself and all America;
Whoever lifts himself
Makes that great brown river smile.
The blood of earth and the blood of man
Course swifter and rejoice when we spiritualize.

We—priest, clown, scientist, technician,
Artist, rascal, worker, lazybones,
This is the whole—
Individuals and people,
This is the whole that stood with Adam
And has come down to us,
Never to be less,
Whatever side is up, however viewed,
Whatever the vicissitudes,
The needs of evolution that bring
Emphasis upon a part—
Man himself, his total body and soul,
This is the moving whole.

Men of the East, men of the West,
Men in life, men in death,
Americans and all countrymen—
Growth is by admixture from less to more,
Preserving the great granary intact,
Through cycles of death and life,
Each stage a pod,
Perpetuating and perfecting
An essence identical in all,
Obeying the same laws, unto the same goal,
That far-distant objective,
By ways both down and up,
Down years ago, now struggling up.

So lift, lift, thou waking forces!

The old gods, led by an inverted Christ,
A shaved Moses, a blanched Lemur,
And a moulting Thunderbird,
Withdrew into the distance and died,
Their dust and seed falling down
To fertilize the seven regions of America.

We are waiting for a new God.

The old peoples—
The great European races sent wave after wave
That washed the forests, the earth's rich loam,
Grew towns with the seeds of giant cities,
Made roads, laid silver rails,
Sang of their swift achievement
And died, displaced by machines.
They say that near the end
It was a world of crying men and hard women,
A city of goddam and Jehovah
Baptized in finance
Without benefit of saints,
Of dear defectives
Winnowing their likenesses from synthetic rock
Sold by national organizations of undertakers.

Someone said:
  Blood cannot mix with the stuff upon our
        boards
    As water with flour to make bread,
    Nor have we yeast, nor have we fire.
    Not iron, not chemicals or money
    Are animate to suffer and rejoice,
    Not what we have become, this angel-dough,
    But slowly die, never having birth
    Above the body, above its pain and nerves,
    To beat pavements, stand in lines,
    Fill space and drive motor-cars.

Another cried:
  It is because of thee, O Life,
  That the first prayer ends in the last curse.

Another sang:
  Late minstrels of the restless earth,
  No muteness can be granted thee,
  Lift thy laughing energies
  To that white point which is a star.

The great African races sent a single wave
And singing riplets to sorrow in red fields,
Sing a swan song, to break rocks
And immortalize a hiding water boy.

    I'm leaving the shining ground, brothers,
    I sing because I ache,
    I go because I must,
    Brothers, I am leaving the shining ground;
    Don't ask me where,
    I'll meet you there,
    I'm leaving the shining ground.

    But we must keep keep keep
        the watermelon—
    He moaned, O Lord, Lord,
    This bale will break me—
    But we must keep keep
        the watermelon.

The great red race was here.
In a land of flaming earth and torrent-rains,
Of red sea-plains and majestic mesas,
At sunset from a purple hill
The gods came down;
They serpentined into pueblo,
And a white-robed priest
Danced with them five days and nights;
But pueblo, priest, and Shalakos
Sank into the sacred earth
To fertilize the seven regions of America.

    Hé-ya, hé-yo, hé-yo,
    Hé-ya, hé-yo, hé-yo,
    The ghosts of buffaloes,
    A lone eagle feather,
    An untamed Navajo,
    Hé-ya, hé-yo, hé-yo,
    Hé-ya, hé-yo, hé-yo.

We are waiting for a new people.

When the Spirit of mankind conceived
A New World in America, and dreamed
The human structure rising from this base,
The land was as a vacant house to new
        inhabitants,

A vacuum compelled by Nature to be filled.
Spirit could not wait to time-select,
Weighing in wisdom each piece,
Fitting each right thing into each right place,
But had to act, trusting the vision of the possible,
Had to bring vast life to this vast plot,
Drawing, in waves of inhabitation,
All the peoples of the earth,
Later to weed out, organize, assimilate.
And thus we are—
Gathered by the snatch of accident,
Selected with the speed of fate,
The alien and the belonging,
All belonging now,
Not yet made one and aged.

O thou, Radiant Incorporal,
The I of earth and of mankind, hurl
Down these seaboards, across this continent,
The thousand-rayed discus of thy mind,
And blend our bodies to one flesh,
And blend this body to mankind.

The east coast is masculine,
The west coast is feminine,
The middle region is the child—
Reconciling force
And generator of symbols.

    Thou, great fields, waving thy growths
        across the world,
    Couldst thou find the seed which started
        thee?
    Can you remember the first great hand to
        sow?
    Have you memory of His intention?
    Great plains, and thou, mountains,
    And thou, stately trees, and thou,
    America, sleeping and producing with the
        seasons,
    No clever dealer can divide,
    No machine or scheme can undermine thee.

The prairie's sweep is flat infinity,
The city's rise is perpendicular to farthest star,
I stand where the two directions intersect,
At Michigan Avenue and Walton Place,
Parallel to my countrymen,
Right-angled to the universe.

It is a new America,
To be spiritualized by each new American,
To be taken as a golden grain
And lifted, as the wheat of our bodies,
To matter uniquely man.

I would give my life to see inscribed
Upon the arch of our consciousness
These words: Understanding, Conscience,
      Ability.
Let new eyes see this statue in the bay,
Let this be quarantine to unbend dreams,
Let old eyes see it in Wall Street and the Loop,
And through this clearing house
Let all pass checks who may.

But out of our past comes hell,
Rushing us, sweeping us,
Winding us, blinding us,
Mistakes and hates,
Out of our past they come,
And they are hell.

The eagle, you should know, American,
Is a sublime and bloody bird,
A living dynamo
Capable of spiritualizing and sensualizing,
One or the other predominantly;
Its spread from tip to tip denotes extremes
Of affirming and denying,
Producing, destroying—
And the majestic flight may disappear;
Now the eagle is a flying-machine,
One wing is broken,
The plunge to earth is panic before death;
Newspapers have forgotten the first Lindbergh—
Flight-symbol of the alone to the Alone—
They headline Al Capone,
For all I know he may be reincarnated
      Robinhood;
I do know there is force gone wrong.

   I met a girl upon the streets—
   "So you are, eh, ready for anything,
   A fly little bum? It's OK with me.
   Let's go to a night club
   Where we men who disembowel the day
   Drink and coax reluctant lust.
   We're all niggers now—get me?
   Black niggers, white niggers—take your
      choice,
   In any case come jazz with me,
   Make the place as swank as you like,
   I've got millions, they all know me,
   And, kid, who knows, it may be
   Our luck to see the dancing Wow,
   The Bold Bitch of Babylon."
   She said—
   "Yes, I too have let friends suffer for a day,
   I see yesterday and tomorrow—

You then must convince me that you know
The yesterday before birth, the after-death
      tomorrow,
The now of man and woman—
So will I believe you worthy to let me."

(That nature which man should have,
That faith which woman should have in man,
That depth and beauty of relationship,
That after chaos they may manifest again
And build their worlds.)

An airplane, with broken wing,
In a tail-spin,
Descends with terrifying speed—
"Don't put me on the spot!"—
From beings to no-things,
From human beings to grotesques,
From men and women to manikins,
From forms to chaoses—

Crash!

Of what avail that with neon lights
We make gas-tanks look like Christmas trees?
Of what avail the battle
Of the school-books and the guns?

   Blood cannot mix with the stuff upon our
      boards
   As water with flour to make bread,
   Nor have we yeast, nor have we fire;
   Not steel, not chemicals or money
   Are spirited to suffer and rejoice,
   Not what we have become, this angel-dough,
   But slowly die, never having birth
   Above the body, above its ego and hungers,
   To sit at desks, stand in lines,
   Fill space and pass time
   Within a prison system all of wardens.

Nor does it help to know that thus
The pioneers and puritans have legacied us,
They, indentured to all men before them.

   Nor can we eat, though food is here,
   Nor can we breathe, though the universe is
      air,
   Nor can we move, though the planet speeds,
   Nor can we circulate, though Nature flows,
   Nor can we love and bear love's fruit
   Though we are living and life is everywhere.
   It is because of thee, O Man,
   That the first prayer ends in the last curse.

In truth, in no ordinary way
Can anyone quit any racket.

Men and women—
It begins with us,
So we must end it.

On what vermilion peak will squad-cars cluster
When the universe sounds judgment-day,
Vigilant for what gong-alarm
To get what anti-cosmic outlaws?
Down what rosy-golden streets will the black
            cars cruise,
Watchful for what syndicate
Of racketeers and hijackers,
And where the bull-pen, what the bars,
And who the men who will thus help God?

        Men,
        Men and women—
        Liberate!

Yet, in this crashing land
Terrorized by bullet-athletes,
I unbolt windows and ten-cents greet
A happy simple thing—
An organ grinder with jaunty hat,
With wayward roaming feet,
And his monkey,
Sauntering along a spring street,
Diddle-lidle-le, diddle-lidle-le.

        Late minstrels of the restless earth,
        No muteness can be granted thee,
        Lift thy laughing energies
        To that white point which is a star.

There is land—I have worked it with my hands,
There are materials for every known and
            unknown need of man,
There are houses built and more to build,
Calling to the builder and the genius in each
            person,
There are men, there are women,
There are all the coming generations,
There is Life—
On land are shadows not of trees or clouds,
On materials marks not made by Nature,
On men and women ravages no animal could
            make,
On children brands,
On life a blight not put by God—
Gargoyle shadows,
Finger marks,
Ghosts like us,
A blight in an image recognized,
I having seen myself—
O Man, that thy mask

Streaks the space between the sun and earth,
Streaks the air between thyself and thyself.

Driven by what the cosmos has put in me,
Let me then affirm to those, the mazed,
Who like myself have seen self-streaks,
Who too have felt the sear
And would rather suffer it than pass it on,
That there is a great detour,
Purgatories by many names,
And a highway just beyond where all roads end,
Along which, despite the prowlers of this planet,
Man and woman can love each other,
Find their plot, build their world,
Live this life with unstreaked dignity
And lift a rainbow to the heavens.

        White Meridian, white light,
        Dynamic atom-aggregate,
        Lay waking on an inland lake.

To depression
The stock of débris descends,
Down go its greed-events,
Control by fear, prejudice, and murder.
Let go!
What value this, paper of the past,
Engraved, ingrained, but meaningless?
What life, that for words and figures,
For power to spend and rear vain monuments,
Two hold guns and the rest are destitute?
Let go—and we'll carry all America in our
            hearts.
This is no ship we want to sink with,
But wreckage;
This is no ark through deluge into the future,
But wreckage manned by homesick ghosts.
Let go!
Let it go that we may live.
A pin, a watch-fob, a card of identification,
A name, pain, and emptiness,
A will to perpetuate what has been, blind
To distinctions between the useful and the
            useless,
And, of course, an ego.
Let go!
That which you have held has got hold of you
And would sink you as it goes down.
A chair of pessimism, a desk of disillusion,
Doors and windows of despair,
Denials run wild,
Rampant negatives—
A fine suite, it is said—
A modern office

Machined and ventilated
For everything but man.
Walk from it,
Wake from it,
From the terrible mistake
That we who have power are less than we
                                should be.
Join that staff whose left hand is
Demolishing defectives,
Whose right is setting up a mill
And a wheel therein, its rim of power,
Its spokes of knowledge, its hub of conscience—
And in that same heart we will hold all life.
It is the world we live in,
Then let us live in it.

Islanders, newly come upon the continents,
If to live against annihilation,
Must outgrow themselves and their old places,
Disintegrate tribal integrators,
And fix, as their center of gravity,
The symbol of universal man—
Lest the continents shrink to islands,
Lest man, bristling upon himself, explode.

So I, once an islander, proclaim,
Not as if I were the first,
But remembering one who went before me,

Our crocks are adequate and breathed upon,
Shaped first by hand, now machined,
But not whole. Cracks are in them,
Lids close out the radiant air,
Close in unholy rust,
And we, incontinent
Or small by shrinkage,
As if souls were denim,
Are tight after the wash of experience.
Yet we are not, nor are we made
Of cheap materials;
Throughout we are perpetuating stuff,
Existing in every world conceived by man,
Enduring in the real world itself,
Made to flow and expand
Through fasts and feasts,
Through sufferings and ecstasies
To balance, and the sacred reconciliation.

Mend and clean, and then—

Uncase the races,
Open this pod,
Free man from this shrinkage,
Not from the reality itself,
But from the unbecoming and enslaving behavior

Associated with our prejudices and preferences.
Eliminate these;
I am, we are, simply of the human race.

Uncase the nations,
Open this pod,
Keep the real but destroy the false;
We are of the human nation.

Uncase the regions—
Occidental, Oriental, North, South—
We are of Earth.

Free the sexes,
I am neither male nor female nor in-between;
I am of sex, with male differentiations.

Open the classes;
I am, we are, simply of the human class.

Expand the fields—
Those definitions which fix fractions
    and lose wholes—
I am of the field of being,
We are beings.

Uncase the religions;
I am religious.

Uncase, unpod whatever impedes, until,
Having realized pure consciousness of being,
Sensing, feeling and understanding
That we are beings,
Co-existing with others in an inhabited universe,
We will be free to use rightly with reason
Our own and other human functions.

In another Wall Street of the world
The stock of value ascends.
What then am I bid,
By what free arm and yielding hand,
Offering what currency,
For this—

Matrons of shrinkage,
Feed not on these children,
But rather break your arms
Than impede their growth;
Lift those shadows,
Cut the binds of apron-strings,
That young gods may dance.

The skins have dried, so let them pass,
So let those who once lived and gathered,
Release all seeds to us,
That we in turn may plant and gather
And pass on to those to come
Sound grain, right soil, air, rain and sun.

The cold white eye is in cold storage,
Down is the ad that reads,
"A dime to heaven in an elevator,"
And in this sacred factory
Of minerals, plants, animals and man,
Right direction is in his hands—
Man, master of himself and husbandman
Of earth and growths and every breathing
        creature,
Thus to live, thus to work, thus to love.

It is a new America . . .
In brand new cities,
Slanting up incredible buildings,
Bright pilasters are pathways to the sun.

I held a fair position as men rate things,
Even enviable—
I could taste flavors in a grain of sand,
My eyes saw loveliness,
And I had learned to peal the wind,
In short, I was a lucky fellow,
People shook my hand, said nice things,
And sometimes slapped me on the back;
Curious, then, that I, of all people,
In the month of the nasty mouth,
Should have found myself caught
In a backbay leased by public and private
        scavengers;
Such was the case—but I found
A river flowing backward to its source.

I met a woman—
Much that I am I owe to her,
For she was going where I was going,
Except that on the way we parted.
She, individualized and beautiful,
Remarkable beyond most,
Followed, at one turn, her picture of herself—
The will of modern woman, biased by pain and
        pride away from man—
And thereafter went off,
Having thus re-tasted dominance.
She divided us, she divided me,
So that had I stayed or tried to follow
I would have stopped, lost my way, lost
        myself,
Lost the thing that woman wants essentially.
Now she has entered a world, all hers only;
It is for her to say if it is hers or not.
Now and again I see her, hardly know
She is that woman who was going as I was,
But feel, deep beneath the layers,
Gratitude—and the task of man.

Upon my phonograph are many records
Played on sides in sacred and profane extremes;
Sometimes I hear Gregorian chants
Or the exquisite pure air for a G string;
Sometimes I hear Duke Ellington
Or Eddy Duchin sing popular contemporary;
And some rare times
I hear myself, the unrecorded,
Sing the flow of I,
The notes and language not of this experience,
Sing I am,
As the flow of I pauses,
Then passes through my water-wheel—
And those radiant realities, the living others,
The people identical in being.

Water-wheel, as the relentless stream flows
To turn thee to thy function,
Send thy power to the stones
That they may grind, that we may live,
And do it excellently,
But may thy motions sometimes pause,
May you be still within the flow
That always was and always will be.

Sun upon clean water is the radiance of
        creation—
And once, far out in the vast spread,
Our eyes beheld a sacrament;
Her face was marvelously bright,
My brain was fiery with internal stars,
I felt certain I had brought
The gods to earth and men to heaven;
I blessed her, drawing with the fingers
Of my spirit the figure of the cross;
I said to her—
"All my senses will remember you as sweet,
Your essence is my wonder."

      Sweetheart of the lake!
      Marvel of the prairies with starry eyes!
      Angel child! Princess of earth!
      Girl of the mesas and the great red plains!
      Star of the sky! Joy of the sun!
      Pride of the eagle! Beloved of the
        thunder-bird!

It is a new America

Fifty times walk up the Palmolive Building
Or the Empire State, following the pilasters,
And, if it is the Empire State, you will find
On top at last a curious mooring-mast,
If the Palmolive, a curious revolving light;
Above you will arch a strange universe,

Below you will spread a strange earth,
Beside you will stand a strange man.

To be spiritualized by each new American

Curious engine, compact of gleaming steel,
Trees, bone, blood, and compressed steam,
Your cabin is the captain's house,
Your whistle is the eagle's scream,
Accelerate your driving-rods—
Irresistible the whirling drive of great wheels.
Thundering black fire-being, down
          straight-a-ways
You roar with demonic speed, leaving
In your wake evident world-rails;
The double accents of your rods proclaim,
"My captain has new fuel and direction,
He will thunder me past semaphores,
Through blocks of all dimensions,
Past waiting stations and waiting beings,
Past all determined symmetries,
Beyond my head-light's searching reach . . ."
Irresistible the whirling drive of great wheels.

Each new American—
To be taken as a golden grain
And lifted, as the wheat of our bodies,
To matter superbly human.

The old gods, led by an inverted Christ,
A shaved Moses, a blanched Lemur,
And a moulting dollar,
Withdrew into the distance and died,
Their dust and seed sifting down
To fertilize the seven regions of America.
This new God we have—
Man at last triumphant over not-man.

The old peoples—
The great European races sent wave after wave
That washed the forests, the earth's rich loam,
Grew towns with the seeds of giant cities,
Made roads, laid silver rails,
Factoried superb machines,
Died, and came alive again
To demonstrate the integrity of individuals,
A commonwealth of reason, conscience, and
          great acts.

   Blood does mix with the stuff upon our
      boards
   As water with flour to make bread,
   And we have yeast, and we have fire;
   To implement ourselves by things,—
   We suffer and create—what we are,
   What we have become, Americans,

   To live in body and all births;
   And we can eat, and we can breathe,
   And we can move, and we can circulate,
   And we can love and bear love's fruit
   For we are men and women living.

The great African races sent a single wave
And singing riplets to sorrow in red fields,
Sing a swan song, to break rocks
And immortalize a hiding water boy.

   Earth is earth, ground is ground,
   All shining if loved.
   Love does not brand as slave or peon
   Any man, but feels his hands,
   His touch upon his work,
   And welcomes death that liberates
   The poet, American among Americans,
   Man at large among men.

The great red race was here.
In a land of flaming earth and torrent-rains,
Of red sea-plains and majestic mesas,
At sunset from a purple hill
The Gods came down;
They serpentined into pueblo,
And a white-robed priest
Danced with them five days and nights;
And pueblo, priest, and Shalakos
Sank into the sacred earth
To resurrect—
To project into this conscious world
An example of the organic;
To enact a mystery among facts—
The mime-priest in the market-place,
Daubed with mud to grace the fecund,
Clown, satirist, and invocator,
Free dancer—
In the Corn Dance, the Kosharé.

A strong yes, a strong no,
With these we move and make drama,
Yet say nothing of the goal.
Black is black, white is white,
East is east, west is west,
Is truth for the brain of contrasts;
Yet here the high way of the third,
The blue man, the purple man
Foretold by ancient minds who knew,
Not the place, not the name,
But the resultant of yes and no
Struggling for birth through ages.

We who exist today are the new people,
Born of elevated rock and lifted branches,

A race called the Americans—
Not to call this name but to live the reality,
Not to stop at it, but to respond to man;
And we are the old people; we are witnesses
That behind us there extends
An unbroken chain of ancestors, linking us
To all who ever lived and will live;
Of millions of fathers through a million years
We are the breathing receptacles.

Mankind is a cross,
Joined as a cross irrevocably—
The solid stream sourcing in the remote past,
Ending in far off distant years,
Is the perpendicular;
The planetary wash of those now living
Forms the transverse bar . . .

O thou, Relentless Stream . . .

The Mississippi, sister of the Ganges,
Main artery of earth in the western world,
Is a sacred river
In the spirit of our people;
Whoever lifts the Mississippi
Lifts himself and all mankind,
Whoever lifts himself
Makes that great brown river smile;
The blood of earth and the blood of man
Course swifter and rejoice when we spiritualize.

The west is masculine,
The east is feminine,
The middle region is the child—
Reconciling force
And generator of symbols,
Source of a new force—

My life is given to have
Fixed in our consciousness,
Materialized in life without celebrity,
This actual: wisdom empowered.

> No split spirit can divide,
> No dead soul can undermine thee,

Thou, great coasts and harbors,
Mountains, lakes, and plains,
Thou art the majestic base
Of cathedral people,
America,
The seed which started thee has grown.

The prairie's sweep is flat infinity,
The city's rise is perpendicular to farthest star,
I stand where the two directions intersect,
At Michigan Avenue and Walton Place,
Parallel to my countrymen,
Right-angled to the universe.

> *Blue Meridian, banded-light,*
> *Dynamic atom-aggregate,*
> *Awakes upon the earth;*
> *In his left hand he holds elevated rock,*
> *In his right hand he holds lifted branches,*
> *He dances the dance of the Blue Meridian*
> *And dervishes with the seven regions of*
> > *America.*

Lift, lift, thou waking forces!
Let us have the energy of man,
The force of brain and heart and limbs
Moving on and on
Through the terms of life on earth
And then beyond
To aid the operations of the cosmos.

> Beyond plants are animals,
> Beyond animals is man,
> Beyond man is God.

> The Big Light,
> Let the Big Light in!

O thou, Radiant Incorporal,
The I of our universe, hurl
Down these seaboards, across these continents,
The thousand-rayed discus of thy mind,
And above our waking limbs unfurl
Spirit-torsos of exquisite strength!

Langston Hughes (1902–1967)

When Langston Hughes died in 1967, his years of literary productivity had spanned almost half a century. In a sense, he was a literary phenomenon, for he was one of the first Black men of literature who strove to make a productive and profitable career out of his writing. This he accomplished in spite of the overwhelming obstacles faced by a Black writer from the 1920's to the 1950's. He was also a literary phenomenon in the sheer variety of his literary output. With the possible exception of formal literary criticism, he wrote in every genre. Throughout his four decades of literary creativity, he wrote poetry, drama, and fiction, assembled anthologies, and collaborated in the translation of many of his works. He also found time to travel extensively, participate in somewhat complicated annual lecture tours, and remain well informed about everything that was taking place or about to take place on the Black literary rialto.

Accordingly, he wrote against a background of incessant activity and movement, and his two autobiographies—*The Big Sea* (1940) and *I Wonder as I Wander* (1956)—are the written record of this movement. But throughout all of his activity one thing remained constant. Wherever he went, Langston Hughes remained the literary explicator and interpreter of the social, cultural, spiritual, and emotional experiences of Black America. From his first published poem, "The Negro Speaks of Rivers," in 1921 to his last volume of poetry, *The Panther and the Lash,* in 1967, he sought to explore the nooks and crannies of the Black Experience, particularly in its urban dimensions. Life in urban Black America, as typified by Harlem, became for this well-attuned and well-adjusted man of literature a life of swirling emotion, from the fury of violent racial confrontation, death, and murder in the streets, to the subtle nuances of blues singers in the nightclubs, to the glory shouting of gospel singers in the storefront churches on Sunday mornings.

For Langston Hughes, Harlem was more than a place or a setting. His interest as a writer was in its people—in their manners, their talk, their gestures of bravado, their dances, their clothes, their thoughts, and their dreams, both deferred and interred. So, though he traveled extensively, Harlem remained his spiritual, esthetic, and emotional home. And even though it changed from a place of bright artistic effervescence in the 1920's to a place of gray squalor and urban blight during the 1950's and 1960's, Hughes remained to "dig" the sounds, colors, and rhythms of his people.

Actually, his life began far from Harlem. Born in Joplin, Missouri, he spent his youth crisscrossing the Middle West—first to Lawrence, Kansas, to live with a grandmother whose husband, Sheridan Leary, had died with John Brown at Harpers Ferry. Then, after it became clear that his father and mother were permanently separated, he followed his mother to Detroit and finally to Cleveland, where he finished high school and first began to write poetry. After graduation, he spent almost two years living in Mexico with his father, who had become a business man of considerable means there. In *The Big Sea,* Hughes recounts the tortured relationship between the sternly business-like father and the dreamy, poetical son. This relationship ended after a disastrous first year at Columbia University in 1921, and for the next four years—until a "patron" assisted him in enrolling at Lincoln University in 1925— Langston Hughes traveled.

However, in the same year that he left Columbia, he published "The Negro Speaks of Rivers" in the *Crisis,* so a firm beginning had been made on a poetic career. By the time he returned to America to work in Washington, D.C., it was clear that his literary career was to be a successful undertaking. Not only did the well-known poet Vachel Lindsay praise his poetry, but in 1925 he won the first prize for poetry from *Opportunity* magazine. At Lincoln University he won the Witter Bynner Prize for undergraduate poetry, and on holidays and during summer vacations he became a habitué of Black literary Harlem. His chapter on "The Harlem Literati" in *The Big Sea* describes this time of ferment and excitement when being Negro "was in vogue" both up-town and downtown. Moreover, Hughes earned a special standing with other Renaissance writers such as Wallace Thurman, Arna Bontemps, Zora Neale Hurston, and Gwendolyn Bennett with his first book of poetry, *The Weary Blues,* published in 1926. This was quickly followed by a second volume in 1927 entitled *Fine Clothes to the Jew.* When in 1930 he turned to prose fiction and published *Not Without Laughter,* it became quite evident that few of his contemporaries would be able to match his productive pace or his literary versatility.

The great Depression of the 1930's found Langston Hughes rather comfortably ensconced as the bard of Harlem. Like other writers of this period, he traveled to Russia and visited war-torn Spain, but the poems, plays, and short stories that he wrote were all about the Black Experience in America and life in Harlem. He enjoyed a rather unusual success in 1936 when his play *Mulatto* ran for a year on Broadway, and somehow, by never slackening his pace, he made a living with his pen—a remarkable accomplishment for a Black writer during the Depression.

Langston Hughes' literary career took a new and significant direction when, during the war years of the 1940's, he created the character of Jesse B. Semple. Simple, as he came to be called, had just the right blend of qualities to be Black America's new spokesman—just enough urban humor, cynicism, and sardonic levity and just enough down-home simplicity, mother-wit, innocence, and naïveté. As this character rounded and took shape during the 1950's, he developed into a sort of Black Everyman whose feet hurt and whose subjects and verbs rarely agreed but whose racial perceptions reflected great wisdom and depth of insight. As the anecdotes and stories about Simple swelled into four volumes, Hughes was consistently able to maintain a neatly balanced characterization. At times, Simple is full of pain; at times, he is full of wise tolerance; at times, he is vocally indignant at the Black man's lot; but he is never consumed by anger or overwhelmed by fear or para-lyzed by racial paranoia. In other words, Simple is in and of the urban ghetto during the bad times of the postwar years, but he is singularly free of the psychological inhibitions of a ghetto dweller. Simple is not on welfare or on dope, and nowhere about him is there the "mark of oppression."

Some critics believe that in the stories and anecdotes of the life of Jesse B. Semple we have the true mark of Langston Hughes' literary genius. His character has no tragic grandeur, but he never sinks into caricature. Rather, he symbolizes a coolly comic view of Black and white America, and this is Hughes' perspective of the Black man's experience. In his long and extensive career as a man of literature, Hughes wrote of the bitter tragedy of being a "mulatto" or of having a life full of frustration and dreams "deferred" or of being a "minstrel man" who laughs to hide his pain, but in the characterization of Jesse B. Semple is Hughes' comic view. It is a socially salutary comic view proclaiming that out of the complexities of modern urban living and the mountainous mass of human error, "simple" men will emerge to pronounce "simple" truths and provide "simple" solutions. Much that he had written before Simple—*The Ways of White Folks, Laughing to Keep from Crying*—Langston Hughes wrote for the white world. With Jesse B. Semple he came "home" to "dig and be dug by" his own people.

Works of criticism on the poetry, prose, and drama of Hughes are almost as voluminous as his own output. Fortunately, Darwin Turner's *Afro-American Writers* (1970) provides a fairly complete listing of critical essays about Langston Hughes. Of the works listed, Arthur Davis' essays on the poetry are excellent, and James Emanuel's work on the fiction is similarly perceptive. There is also an excellent classified and annotated bibliography of the writings of Langston Hughes by Therman O'Daniel entitled "Langston Hughes: A Selected Classified Bibliography," *CLA Journal,* XI (1967), 349–366.

Books on Hughes include James Emanuel, *Langston Hughes* (1967); Donald C. Dickinson, *A Bio-Bibliography of Langston Hughes, 1902–1967* (1967); Milton Meltzer, *Langston Hughes: A Biography* (1968); and Charlemae Rollins, *Black Troubador: Langston Hughes* (1970). Three journals have collected essays on Hughes: *Negro Digest* (September 1967), *Freedomways* (Spring 1968), and *CLA Journal* (June 1968).

The Negro Speaks of Rivers

I've known rivers:
I've known rivers ancient as the world and
  older than the flow of human blood in human
  veins.

My soul has grown deep like the rivers.

I bathed in the Euphrates when dawns were
  young.
I built my hut near the Congo and it lulled me
  to sleep.

I looked upon the Nile and raised the pyramids
  above it.
I heard the singing of the Mississippi when Abe
  Lincoln went down to New Orleans, and I've
  seen its muddy bosom turn all golden in the
  sunset.

I've known rivers:
Ancient, dusky rivers.

My soul has grown deep like the rivers.

Mother to Son

Well, son, I'll tell you:
Life for me ain't been no crystal stair.
It's had tacks in it,
And splinters,
And boards torn up,
And places with no carpet on the floor—
Bare.
But all the time
I'se been a-climbin' on,
And reachin' landin's,
And turnin' corners,
And sometimes goin' in the dark
Where there ain't been no light.
So boy, don't you turn back.
Don't you set down on the steps
'Cause you finds it's kinder hard.
Don't you fall now—
For I'se still goin', honey,
I'se still climbin',
And life for me ain't been no crystal stair.

Jazzonia

Oh, silver tree!
Oh, shining rivers of the soul.

In a Harlem cabaret
Six long-headed jazzers play.
A dancing girl whose eyes are bold
Lifts high a dress of silken gold.

Oh, singing tree!
Oh, shining rivers of the soul!

Were Eve's eyes
In the first garden
Just a bit too bold?
Was Cleopatra gorgeous
In a gown of gold?

Oh, shining tree!
Oh, silver rivers of the soul!

In a whirling cabaret
Six long-headed jazzers play.

Dream Variation

To fling my arms wide
In some place of the sun,
To whirl and to dance
Till the white day is done.
Then rest at cool evening
Beneath a tall tree
While night comes on gently,
    Dark like me—
That is my dream!

To fling my arms wide
In the face of the sun,
Dance! Whirl! Whirl!
Till the quick day is done.
Rest at pale evening . . .
A tall, slim tree . . .
Night coming tenderly
    Black like me.

I, Too

I, too, sing America.

I am the darker brother.
They send me to eat in the kitchen
When company comes,
But I laugh,
And eat well,
And grow strong.

Tomorrow,
I'll be at the table

When company comes.
Nobody'll dare
Say to me,
"Eat in the kitchen,"
Then.

Besides,
They'll see how beautiful I am
And be ashamed—

I, too, am America.

The Weary Blues

Droning a drowsy syncopated tune,
Rocking back and forth to a mellow croon,
   I heard a Negro play.
Down on Lenox Avenue the other night
By the pale dull pallor of an old gas light
   He did a lazy sway . . . .
   He did a lazy sway . . . .
To the tune o' those Weary Blues.
With his ebony hands on each ivory key
He made that poor piano moan with melody.
   O Blues!
Swaying to and fro on his rickety stool
He played that sad raggy tune like a musical
   fool.
   Sweet Blues!
Coming from a black man's soul.
   O Blues!
In a deep song voice with a melancholy tone
I heard that Negro sing, that old piano moan—

"Ain't got nobody in all this world,
   Ain't got nobody but ma self.
   I's gwine to quit ma frownin'
   And put ma troubles on the shelf."
Thump, thump, thump, went his foot on the
   floor.
He played a few chords then he sang some
   more—
   "I got the Weary Blues
   And I can't be satisfied.
   Got the Weary Blues
   And can't be satisfied—
   I ain't happy no mo'
   And I wish that I had died."
And far into the night he crooned that tune.
The stars went out and so did the moon.
The singer stopped playing and went to bed
While the Weary Blues echoed through his head
He slept like a rock or a man that's dead.

Cross

My old man's a white old man
And my old mother's black.
If ever I cursed my white old man
I take my curses back.

If ever I cursed my black old mother
And wished she were in hell,
I'm sorry for that evil wish
And now I wish her well.

My old man died in a fine big house.
My ma died in a shack.
I wonder where I'm gonna die,
Being neither white nor black?

Bound No'th Blues

Goin' down the road, Lawd,
Goin' down the road.
Down the road, Lawd,
Way, way down the road.
Got to find somebody
To help me carry this load.

Road's in front o' me,
Nothin' to do but walk.
Road's in front o' me,
Walk . . . an' walk . . . an' walk.
I'd like to meet a good friend
To come along an' talk.

Hates to be lonely,
Lawd, I hates to be sad.
Says I hates to be lonely,
Hates to be lonely an' sad,
But ever' friend you finds seems
Like they try to do you bad.

Road, road, road, O!
Road, road . . . road . . . road, road!
Road, road, road, O!
On the no'thern road.
These Mississippi towns ain't
Fit fer a hoppin' toad.

Brass Spittoons

Clean the spittoons, boy.
  Detroit,
  Chicago,
  Atlantic City,
  Palm Beach.
Clean the spittoons.
The steam in hotel kitchens,
And the smoke in hotel lobbies.
And the slime in hotel spittoons:
Part of my life.
  Hey, boy!
  A nickel,
  A dime,
  A dollar,
Two dollars a day.
  Hey, boy!
  A nickel,
  A dime,
  A dollar,
  Two dollars

Buy shoes for the baby.
House rent to pay.
Gin on Saturday,
Church on Sunday.
  My God!
Babies and gin and church
And women and Sunday
All mixed with dimes and
Dollars and clean spittoons
And house rent to pay.
  Hey, boy!
A bright bowl of brass is beautiful to the Lord.
Bright polished brass like the cymbals
Of King David's dancers,
Like the wine cups of Solomon.
  Hey, boy!
A clean spittoon on the altar of the Lord.
A clean bright spittoon all newly polished—
At least I can offer that.
  Com'mere, boy!

Song for a Dark Girl

Way Down South in Dixie
  (Break the heart of me)
They hung my black young lover
  To a cross roads tree.

Way Down South in Dixie
  (Bruised body high in air)
I asked the white Lord Jesus
  What was the use of prayer.

Way Down South in Dixie
(Break the heart of me)
Love is a naked shadow
On a gnarled and naked tree.

Sylvester's Dying Bed

I woke up this mornin'
'Bout half-past three.
All de womens in town
Was gathered round me.

Sweet gals was a-moanin',
"Sylvester's gonna die!"
And a hundred pretty mamas
Bowed their heads to cry.

I woke up little later
'Bout half-past fo',
De doctor 'n' undertaker's
Both at ma do'.

Black gals was a-beggin',
"You can't leave us here!"

Brown-skins cryin' "Daddy!
Honey! Baby! Don't go, dear!"

But I felt ma times' a-comin',
And I know'd I's dyin' fast.
I seed de River Jerden
A-creepin' muddy past—
But I's still Sweet Papa 'Vester,
Yes, sir! Long as life do last!

So I hollers, "Com'ere, babies,
Fo' to love yo' daddy right!"
And I reaches up to hug 'em—
When de Lawd put out de light.

Then everything was darkness
In a great . . . big . . . night.

Ballad of the Landlord

Landlord, landlord,
My roof has sprung a leak.
Don't you 'member I told you about it
Way last week?

Landlord, landlord,
These steps is broken down.
When you come up yourself
It's a wonder you don't fall down.

Ten Bucks you say I owe you?
Ten Bucks you say is due?
Well, that's Ten Bucks more'n I'll pay you
Till you fix this house up new.

What? You gonna get eviction orders?
You gonna cut off my heat?
You gonna take my furniture and
Throw it in the street?

Um-huh! You talking high and mighty.
Talk on—till you get through.

You ain't gonna be able to say a word
If I land my fist on you.

Police! Police!
Come and get this man!
He's trying to ruin the government
And overturn the land!

Copper's whistle!
Patrol bell!
Arrest.

Precinct Station.
Iron cell.
Headlines in press:

MAN THREATENS LANDLORD

∴

TENANT HELD NO BAIL

∴

JUDGE GIVES NEGRO 90 DAYS IN COUNTY JAIL

Dream Boogie

Good morning, daddy!
Ain't you heard
The boogie-woogie rumble
Of a dream deferred?

Listen closely:
You'll hear their feet
Beating out and beating out a—

You think
It's a happy beat?

Listen to it closely:
Ain't you heard

something underneath
like a—

What did I say?

Sure,
I'm happy!
Take it away!

Hey, pop!
Re-bop!
Mop!

Y-e-a-h!

from *The Big Sea*

I've Known Rivers

That November the First World War ended. In Cleveland, everybody poured into the streets to celebrate the Armistice. Negroes, too, although Negroes were increasingly beginning to wonder where, for them, was that democracy they had fought to preserve. In Cleveland, a liberal city, the color line began to be drawn tighter and tighter. Theaters and restaurants in the downtown area began to refuse to accommodate colored people. Landlords doubled and tripled the rents at the approach of a dark tenant. And when the white soldiers came back from the war, Negroes were often discharged from their jobs and white men hired in their places.

The end of the war! But many of the students at Central kept talking, not about the end of the war, but about Russia, where Lenin had taken power in the name of the workers, who made everything, and who would now own everything they made. "No more pogroms," the Jews said, "no more race hatred, no more landlords." John Reed's *Ten Days That Shook the World* shook Central High School, too.

The daily papers pictured the Bolsheviki as the greatest devils on earth, but I didn't see how they could be that bad if they had done away with race hatred and landlords—two evils that I knew well at first hand.

My father raised my allowance that year, so I was able to help my mother with the expenses of our household. It was a pleasant year for me, for I was a senior. I was elected Class Poet and Editor of our Year Book. As an officer in the drill corps, I wore a khaki uniform and leather puttees, and gave orders. I went calling on a little brownskin girl, who was as old as I was— seventeen—but only in junior high school, because she had just come up from the poor schools of the South. I met her at a dance at the Longwood Gym. She had big eyes and skin like rich chocolate. Sometimes she wore a red dress that was very becoming to her, so I wrote a poem about her that declared:

When Susanna Jones wears red
Her face is like an ancient cameo
Turned brown by the ages.

Come with a blast of trumpets,
Jesus!

When Susanna Jones wears red
A queen from some time-dead Egyptian night
Walks once again.

Blow trumpets, Jesus!

And the beauty of Susanna Jones in red
Burns in my heart a love-fire sharp like pain.

Sweet silver trumpets,
Jesus!

I had a whole notebook full of poems by now, and another one full of verses and jingles. I always tried to keep verses and poems apart, although I saw no harm in writing verses if you felt like it, and poetry if you could.

June came. And graduation. Like most graduations, it made you feel both sorry and glad: sorry to be leaving and glad to be going. Some students were planning to enter college, but not many, because there was no money for college in most of Central's families.

My father had written me to come to Mexico again to discuss with him my future plans. He hinted that he would send me to college if I intended to go, and he thought I had better go.

I didn't want to return to Mexico, but I had a feeling I'd never get any further education if I didn't, since my mother wanted me to go to work and be, as she put it, "of some use to her." She demanded to know how I would look going off to college and she there working like a dog!

I said I thought I could be of more help to her once I got an education than I could if I went to work fresh out of high school, because nobody could do much on the salary of a porter or a bus boy. And such jobs offered no advancement for a Negro.

But about my going to join my father, my mother acted much as she had done the year before. I guess it is the old story of divorced parents who don't like each other, and take their grievances out on the offspring. I got the feeling then that I'd like to get away from home altogether, both homes, and that maybe if I went to Mexico one more time, I could go to college somewhere in some new place, and be on my own.

So I went back to Toluca.

My mother let me go to the station alone, and I felt pretty bad when I got on the train. I felt bad for the next three or four years, to tell the truth, and those were the years when I wrote most of my poetry. (For my best poems were all written when I felt the worst. When I was happy, I didn't write anything.)

The one of my poems that has perhaps been most often reprinted in anthologies, was written on the train during this trip to Mexico when I was feeling very bad. It's called "The Negro Speaks of Rivers" and was written just outside St. Louis, as the train rolled toward Texas.

It came about in this way. All day on the train I had been thinking about my father and his strange dislike of his own people. I didn't understand it, because I was a Negro, and I liked Negroes very much. One of the happiest jobs I had ever had was during my freshman year in high school, when I worked behind the soda fountain for a Mrs. Kitzmiller, who ran a refreshment parlor on Central Avenue in the heart of the colored neighborhood. People just up from the South used to come in for ice cream and sodas and watermelon. And I never tired of hearing them talk, listening to the thunderclaps of their laughter, to their troubles, to their discussions of the war and the men who had gone to Europe from the Jim Crow South, their complaints over the high rent and the long overtime hours that brought what seemed like big checks, until the weekly bills were paid. They seemed to me like the gayest and the bravest people possible —these Negroes from the Southern ghettos— facing tremendous odds, working and laughing and trying to get somewhere in the world.

I had been in to dinner early that afternoon on the train. Now it was just sunset, and we crossed the Mississippi, slowly, over a long bridge. I looked out the window of the Pullman at the great muddy river flowing down toward the heart of the South, and I began to think what that river, the old Mississippi, had meant to Negroes in the past—how to be sold down the river was the worst fate that could overtake a slave in times of bondage. Then I remembered reading how Abraham Lincoln had made a trip down the Mississippi on a raft to New Orleans, and how he had seen slavery at its worst, and had decided within himself that it should be removed from American life. Then I began to think about other rivers in our past—the Congo, and the Niger, and the Nile in Africa—and the thought came to me: "I've known rivers," and I put it down on the back of an envelope I had in my pocket, and within the space of ten or fifteen minutes, as the train gathered speed in the dusk, I had written this poem, which I called "The Negro Speaks of Rivers":

I've known rivers:
I've known rivers ancient as the world and older than the flow of human blood in human veins.

My soul has grown deep like the rivers.

I bathed in the Euphrates when dawns were young.
I built my hut near the Congo and it lulled me to sleep.
I looked upon the Nile and raised the pyramids above it.
I heard the singing of the Mississippi when Abe Lincoln went down to New Orleans, and I've seen its muddy bosom turn all golden in the sunset.

I've known rivers:
Ancient, dusky rivers.

My soul has grown deep like the rivers.

No doubt I changed a few words the next day, or maybe crossed out a line or two. But there are seldom many changes in my poems, once they're down. Generally, the first two or three lines come to me from something I'm thinking about, or looking at, or doing, and the rest of the poem (if there is to be a poem) flows from those first few lines, usually right away. If there is a chance to put the poem down then, I write it down. If not, I try to remember it until I get to a pencil and paper; for poems are like rainbows: they escape you quickly.

.   .   .

Harlem Literati

The summer of 1926, I lived in a rooming house on 37th Street, where Wallace Thurman and Harcourt Tynes also lived. Thurman was then managing editor of the *Messenger,* a Negro magazine that had a curious career. It began by being very radical, racial, and socialistic, just after the war. I believe it received a grant from the Garland Fund in its early days. Then it later became a kind of Negro society magazine and a plugger for Negro business, with photographs of prominent colored ladies and their nice homes in it. A. Phillip Randolph, now President of the Brotherhood of Sleeping Car Porters, Chandler Owen, and George S. Schuyler were connected with it. Schuyler's editorials, à la Mencken, were the most interesting things in the magazine, verbal brickbats that said sometimes one thing, sometimes another, but always vigorously. I asked Thurman what kind of magazine the *Messenger* was, and he said it reflected the policy of whoever paid off best at the time.

Anyway, the *Messenger* bought my first short stories. They paid me ten dollars a story. Wallace Thurman wrote me that they were very bad stories, but better than any others they could find, so he published them.

Thurman had recently come from California to New York. He was a strangely brilliant black boy, who had read everything, and whose critical mind could find something wrong with everything he read. I have no critical mind, so I usually either like a book or don't. But I am not capable of liking a book and then finding a million things wrong with it, too—as Thurman was capable of doing.

Thurman had read so many books because he could read eleven lines at a time. He would get from the library a great pile of volumes that would have taken me a year to read. But he would go through them in less than a week, and be able to discuss each one at great length with anybody. That was why, I suppose, he was later given a job as a reader at Macaulay's—the only Negro reader, so far as I know, to be employed by any of the larger publishing firms.

Later Thurman became a ghost writer for *True Story* and other publications, writing under all sorts of fantastic names, like Ethel Belle Mandrake or Patrick Casey. He did Irish and Jewish and Catholic "true confessions." He collaborated with William Jordan Rapp on plays and novels. Later he ghosted books. In fact, this quite dark young Negro is said to have written *Men, Women, and Checks.*

Wallace Thurman wanted to be a great writer, but none of his own work ever made him happy. *The Blacker the Berry,* his first book, was an important novel on a subject little dwelt upon in Negro fiction—the plight of the very dark Negro woman, who encounters in some communities a double wall of color prejudice within and without the race. His play, *Harlem,* considerably distorted for box office purposes, was, nevertheless, a compelling study—and the only one in the theater—of the impact of Harlem on a Negro family fresh from the South. And his *Infants of the Spring,* a superb and bitter study of the bohemian fringe of Harlem's literary and artistic life, is a compelling book.

But none of these things pleased Wallace Thurman. He wanted to be a *very* great writer, like Gorki or Thomas Mann, and he felt that he was merely a journalistic writer. His critical mind, comparing his pages to the thousands of other pages he had read, by Proust, Melville, Tolstoy, Galsworthy, Dostoyevski, Henry James, Sainte-Beauve, Taine, Anatole France, found his own pages vastly wanting. So he contented himself by writing a great deal for money, laughing bitterly at his fabulously concocted "true stories," creating two bad motion pictures of the "Adults Only" type for Hollywood, drinking more and more gin, and then threatening to jump out of windows at people's parties and kill himself.

During the summer of 1926, Wallace Thurman,

Zora Neale Hurston, Aaron Douglas, John P. Davis, Bruce Nugent, Gwendolyn Bennett, and I decided to publish "a Negro quarterly of the arts" to be called *Fire*—the idea being that it would burn up a lot of the old, dead conventional Negro-white ideas of the past, *épater le bourgeois* into a realization of the existence of the younger Negro writers and artists, and provide us with an outlet for publication not available in the limited pages of the small Negro magazines then existing, the *Crisis, Opportunity,* and the *Messenger*—the first two being house organs of inter-racial organizations, and the latter being God knows what.

Sweltering summer evenings we met to plan *Fire*. Each of the seven of us agreed to give fifty dollars to finance the first issue. Thurman was to edit it, John P. Davis to handle the business end, and Bruce Nugent to take charge of distribution. The rest of us were to serve as an editorial board to collect material, contribute our own work, and act in any useful way that we could. For artists and writers, we got along fine and there were no quarrels. But October came before we were ready to go to press. I had to return to Lincoln, John Davis to Law School at Harvard, Zora Hurston to her studies at Barnard, from whence she went about Harlem with an anthropologist's ruler, measuring heads for Franz Boas.

Only three of the seven had contributed their fifty dollars, but the others faithfully promised to send theirs out of tuition checks, wages, or begging. Thurman went on with the work of preparing the magazine. He got a printer. He planned the layout. It had to be on good paper, he said, worthy of the drawings of Aaron Douglas. It had to have beautiful type, worthy of the first Negro art quarterly. It had to be what we seven young Negroes dreamed our magazine would be—so in the end it cost almost a thousand dollars, and nobody could pay the bills.

I don't know how Thurman persuaded the printer to let us have all the copies to distribute but he did. I think Alain Locke, among others, signed notes guaranteeing payments. But since Thurman was the only one of the seven of us with a regular job, for the next three or four years his checks were constantly being attached and his income seized to pay for *Fire*. And whenever I sold a poem, mine went there, too—to *Fire*.

None of the older Negro intellectuals would have anything to do with *Fire*. Dr. DuBois in the *Crisis* roasted it. The Negro press called it all sorts of bad names, largely because of a green and purple story by Bruce Nugent, in the Oscar Wilde tradition, which we had included. Rean Graves, the critic for the *Baltimore Afro-American,* began his review by saying: "I have just tossed the first issue of *Fire* into the fire." Commenting upon various of our contributors, he said: "Aaron Douglas who, in spite of himself and the meaningless grotesqueness of his creations, has gained a reputation as an artist, is permitted to spoil three perfectly good pages and a cover with his pen and ink hudge pudge. Countee Cullen has written a beautiful poem in his 'From a Dark Tower,' but tries his best to obscure the thought in superfluous sentences. Langston Hughes displays his usual ability to say nothing in many words."

So *Fire* had plenty of cold water thrown on it by the colored critics. The white critics (except for an excellent editorial in the *Bookman* for November, 1926) scarcely noticed it at all. We had no way of getting it distributed to bookstands or news stands. Bruce Nugent took it around New York on foot and some of the Greenwich Village bookshops put it on display, and sold it for us. But then Bruce, who had no job, would collect the money and, on account of salary, eat it up before he got back to Harlem.

Finally, irony of ironies, several hundred copies of *Fire* were stored in the basement of an apartment where an actual fire occurred and the bulk of the whole issue was burned up. Even after that Thurman had to go on paying the printer.

Now *Fire* is a collector's item, and very difficult to get, being mostly ashes.

That taught me a lesson about little magazines. But since white folks had them, we Negroes thought we could have one, too. But we didn't have the money.

Wallace Thurman laughed a long bitter laugh. He was a strange kind of fellow, who liked to drink gin, but *didn't* like to drink gin; who liked being a Negro, but felt it a great handicap; who adored bohemianism, but thought it wrong to be a bohemian. He liked to waste a lot of time, but he always felt guilty wasting time. He loathed crowds, yet he hated to be alone. He almost always felt bad, yet he didn't write poetry.

Once I told him if I could feel as bad as he did *all* the time, I would surely produce wonderful books. But he said you had to know how to *write,* as well as how to feel bad. I said I didn't have to know how to feel bad, because, every so often, the blues just naturally overtook me, like a blind beggar with an old guitar:

You don't know,
You don't know my mind—
When you see me laughin',
I'm laughin' to keep from cryin'.

About the future of Negro literature Thurman was very pessimistic. He thought the Negro vogue had made us all too conscious of ourselves, had flattered and spoiled us, and had provided too many easy opportunities for some of us to drink gin and more gin, on which he thought we would always be drunk. With his bitter sense of humor, he called the Harlem literati, the "niggerati."

Of this "niggerati," Zora Neale Hurston was certainly the most amusing. Only to reach a wider audience, need she ever write books— because she is a perfect book of entertainment in herself. In her youth she was always getting scholarships and things from wealthy white people, some of whom simply paid her just to sit around and represent the Negro race for them, she did it in such a racy fashion. She was full of side-splitting anecdotes, humorous tales, and tragi-comic stories, remembered out of her life in the South as a daughter of a travelling minister of God. She could make you laugh one minute and cry the next. To many of her white friends, no doubt, she was a perfect "darkie," in the nice meaning they give the term—that is a naïve, childlike, sweet, humorous, and highly colored Negro.

But Miss Hurston was clever, too—a student who didn't let college give her a broad *a* and who had great scorn for all pretensions, academic or otherwise. That is why she was such a fine folk-lore collector, able to go among the people and never act as if she had been to school at all. Almost nobody else could stop the average Harlemite on Lenox Avenue and measure his head with a strange-looking, anthropological device and not get bawled out for the attempt, except Zora, who used to stop anyone whose head looked interesting, and measure it.

When Miss Hurston graduated from Barnard she took an apartment in West 66th Street near the park, in that row of Negro houses there. She moved in with no furniture at all and no money, but in a few days friends had given her every-thing, from decorative silver birds, perched atop the linen cabinet, down to a footstool. And on Saturday night, to christen the place, she had a *hand*-chicken dinner, since she had forgotten to say she needed forks.

She seemed to know almost everybody in New York. She had been a secretary to Fannie Hurst, and had met dozens of celebrities whose friend-ship she retained. Yet she was always having terrific ups-and-downs about money. She tells this story on herself, about needing a nickel to go downtown one day and wondering where on earth she would get it. As she approached the subway, she was stopped by a blind beggar hold-ing out his cup.

"Please help the blind! Help the blind! A nickel for the blind!"

"I need money worse than you today," said Miss Hurston, taking five cents out of his cup. "Lend me this! Next time, I'll give it back." And she went on downtown.

Harlem was like a great magnet for the Negro intellectual, pulling him from everywhere. Or perhaps the magnet was New York—but once in New York, he had to live in Harlem, for rooms were hardly to be found elsewhere unless one could pass for white or Mexican or Eurasian and perhaps live in the Village—which always seemed to me a very arty locale, in spite of the many real artists and writers who lived there. Only a few of the New Negroes lived in the Village, Harlem being their real stamping ground.

The wittiest of these New Negroes of Harlem, whose tongue was flavored with the sharpest and saltiest humor, was Rudolph Fisher, whose stories appeared in the *Atlantic Monthly*. His novel, *Walls of Jericho,* captures but slightly the raciness of his own conversation. He was a young medical doctor and X-ray specialist, who always fright-ened me a little, because he could think of the most incisively clever things to say—and I could never think of anything to answer. He and Alain Locke together were great for intellectual wise-cracking. The two would fling big and witty words about with such swift and punning in-nuendo that an ordinary mortal just sat and looked wary for fear of being caught in a net of witticisms beyond his cultural ken. I used to wish I could talk like Rudolph Fisher. Besides being a good writer, he was an excellent singer, and had sung with Paul Robeson during their college days. But I guess Fisher was too brilliant and too talented to stay long on this earth. During the same week, in December, 1934, he and Wallace Thurman both died.

Thurman died of tuberculosis in the charity ward at Bellevue Hospital, having just flown back to New York from Hollywood.

Dear Dr. Butts

"Do you know what has happened to me?" said Simple.

"No."

"I'm out of a job."

"That's tough. How did that come about?"

"Laid off—they're converting again. And right now, just when I am planning to get married this spring, they have to go changing from civilian production to war contracts, installing new machinery. Manager says it might take two months, might take three or four. They'll send us mens notices. If it takes four months, that's up to June, which is no good for my plans. To get married a man needs money. To stay married he needs more money. And where am I? As usual, behind the eight-ball."

"You can find another job meanwhile, no doubt."

"That ain't easy. And if I do, they liable not to pay much. Jobs that pay good money nowadays are scarce as hen's teeth. But Joyce says she do not care. She is going to marry me, come June anyhow—even if she has to pay for it herself. Joyce says since I paid for the divorce, she can pay for the wedding. But I do not want her to do that."

"Naturally not, but maybe you can curtail your plans somewhat and not have so big a wedding. Wedlock does not require an elaborate ceremony."

"I do not care if we don't have none, just so we get locked. But you know how womens is. Joyce has waited an extra year for her great day. Now here I am broke as a busted bank."

"How're you keeping up with your expenses?"

"I ain't. And I don't drop by Joyce's every night like I did when I was working. I'm embarrassed. Then she didn't have to ask me to eat. Now she does. In fact, she insists. She says, 'You got to eat somewheres. I enjoy your company. Eat with me.' I do, if I'm there when she extends the invitation. But I don't go looking for it. I just sets home and broods, man, and looks at my four walls, which gives me plenty of time to think. And do you know what I been thinking about lately?"

"Finding work, I presume."

"Besides that?"

"No. I don't know what you've been thinking about."

"Negro leaders, and how they're talking about how great democracy is—and me out of a job. Also how there is so many leaders I don't know that the white folks know about, because they are always in the white papers. Yet *I'm* the one they are supposed to be leading. Now, you take that little short leader named Dr. Butts, I do not know him, except in name only. If he ever made a speech in Harlem it were not well advertised. From what I reads, he teaches at a white college in Massachusetts, stays at the Commodore when he's in New York, and ain't lived in Harlem for ten years. Yet he's leading me. He's an article writer, but he does not write in colored papers. But lately the colored papers taken to reprinting parts of what he writes—otherwise I would have never seen it. Anyhow, with all this time on my hands these days, I writ him a letter last night. Here, read it."

Harlem, U.S.A.
One Cold February Day

Dear Dr. Butts,

I seen last week in the colored papers where you have writ an article for The New York Times *in which you say America is the greatest country in the world for the Negro race and Democracy the greatest kind of government for all,* but *it would be better if there was equal education for colored folks in the South, and if everybody could vote, and if there were not Jim Crow in the army, also if the churches was not divided up into white churches and colored churches, and if Negroes did not have to ride on the back seats of busses South of Washington.*

Now, all this later part of your article is hanging onto your but. *You start off talking about how great American democracy is, then you* but *it all over the place. In fact, the* but *end of your see-saw is so far down on the ground I do not believe the other end can ever pull it up. So me myself, I would not write no article for no* New York Times *if I had to put in so many* buts. *I reckon maybe you come by it naturally, though, that being your name, dear Dr. Butts.*

I hear tell that you are a race leader, but I do not know who you lead because I have not heard tell of you before and I have not laid eyes on you. But if you are leading me, make me know it, because I do not read the New York Times *very often*, *less I happen to pick up a copy blowing around in the subway, so I did not know you were my leader. But since you are my leader, lead on, and see if I will follow behind your* but—*because there is more behind that* but *than there is in front of it.*

Dr. Butts, I am glad to read that you writ an article in The New York Times, *but also* sometime *I wish you would write one in the colored papers and let me know how to get out from behind all these* buts *that are staring me in the face. I know America is a great country* but—*and it is that* but *that has been keeping me where I is all these years. I can't get over it, I can't get under it, and I can't get around it, so what am I supposed to do? If you are leading me, lemme see. Because we have too many colored leaders now that nobody knows until they get from the white papers to the colored papers and from the colored papers to me who has never seen hair nor hide of you. Dear Dr. Butts, are you hiding from me—and leading me, too?*

From the way you write, a man would think my race problem was made out of nothing but buts. But *this,* but *that, and, yes, there is Jim Crow in Georgia* but—. *America admits they bomb folks in Florida—*but Hitler gassed the Jews. Mississippi is bad—*but Russia is worse. Detroit slums are awful—*but compared to the slums in India, Detroit's Paradise Valley is Paradise.

Dear Dr. Butts, Hitler is dead. I don't live in Russia. India is across the Pacific Ocean. And I do not hope to see Paradise no time soon. I am nowhere near some of them foreign countries you are talking about being so bad. I am here! And you know as well as I do, Mississippi is hell. There ain't no but *in the world can make it out different. They tell me when Nazis gas you, you die slow. But when they put a bomb under you like in Florida, you don't have time to say your prayers. As for Detroit, there is as much difference between Paradise Valley and Paradise as there is between* heaven and Harlem. *I don't know nothing about India, but I been in Washington, D.C. If you think there ain't slums there, just take your* but *up Seventh Street late some night, and see if you still got it by the time you get to Howard University.*

I should not have to be telling you these things. You are colored just like me. To put a but *after all this Jim Crow fly-papering around our feet is just like telling a hungry man, "But Mr. Rockefeller has got plenty to eat." It's just like telling a joker with no overcoat in the winter time, "But you will be hot next summer." The fellow is liable to haul off and say, "I am hot now!" And bop you over your head.*

Are you in your right mind, dear Dr. Butts? Or are you just writing? Do you really think a new day is dawning? Do you really think Christians are having a change of heart? I can see you now taking your pen in hand to write, "But just last year the Southern Denominations of Hell-Fired Salvation resolved to work toward Brotherhood." In fact, that is what you already writ. Do you think Brotherhood means colored to them Southerners?

Do you reckon they will recognize you for a brother, Dr. Butts, since you done had your picture taken in the Grand Ballroom of the Waldorf-Astoria shaking hands at some kind of meeting with five hundred white big-shots and five *Negroes, all* five *of them Negro leaders, so it said underneath the picture? I did not know any of them Negro leaders by sight, neither by name, but since it says in the white papers that they are leaders, I reckon they are. Anyhow, I take my pen in hand to write you this letter to ask you to make yourself clear to me. When you answer me, do not write no "so-and-so-and-so but—." I will not take* but *for an answer. Negroes have been looking at Democracy's* but *too long. What we want to know is how to get rid of that* but.

Do you dig me, dear Dr. Butts?

> *Sincerely very truly,*
> Jesse B. Semple

Countee Cullen (1903–1946)

The literary career of Countee Cullen provides an excellent illustration of what W. E. B. Du Bois meant by the "double consciousness" that so often burdens the Black man in America—the consciousness of being both an American and a Black man. Countee Cullen's academic training in the public schools of New York City, at New York University, and at Harvard University conformed to the best traditions in American education. He earned a Phi Beta Kappa key at New York University, and during his graduate study at Harvard he enrolled in a poetry-writing course under Robert Hillyer, where he gained practice in writing every form of English verse, from Spenserian stanzas to rime royal and *terza rima.* Consequently, when his first book of poems, *Color,* was published in 1925, the author quite understandably emerged as something of a Black Keats, concerned with lyrical definitions of truth and beauty and goodness and their seeming transiency in the world of time and circumstance.

But there was another side to Countee Cullen—another level of consciousness. He was ever aware of his racial heritage and background. Even the titles given his volumes of poetry—*Color, Copper Sun, Ballad of a Brown Girl*—indicate an emotional and social involvement with race and color. Moreover, the poem "Heritage," in which the poet tries to define his relationship to his African past and answer the question "What is Africa to me?" reveals his involvement with racial roots to be somewhat confused. His conclusion is that in order to avoid being consumed by the fiery memories of his African racial past, one must "quench" his pride and "cool" his blood and try not to remember the beat of "Great drums throbbing through the air." To those who would charge that here is not an authentic racial consciousness but rather a sort of Romantic primitivism, there is in the poem "From the Dark Tower" the outspoken promise that Black people "were not made eternally to weep" and that there will come a time of harvest and consummation when they too will "reap / The golden increment of bursting fruit." But although there is nowhere in the finely wrought lyrics of Countee Cullen anything approaching the rhetoric of Blackness, and, as Saunders Redding states, the tom-tom beat in his verse is never above a faint whisper, there was a Black side to his experience that was in apparent, if occasional, conflict with the white side of his experience.

The works of Countee Cullen come more clearly into focus in comparison with those of Langston Hughes, one of his Harlem Renaissance contemporaries. Both published first volumes of poetry in the middle 1920's, Cullen's *Color* coming out in 1925 and Hughes' *The Weary Blues* in 1926. Before that golden decade ended, Cullen had produced three additional volumes of verse and, as assistant editor of *Opportunity* magazine, had edited an anthology of works by young poets entitled *Caroling Dusk.* Hughes published one more volume of verse, *Fine*

Clothes to the Jew, before the decade ended and then turned to fiction in *Not Without Laughter,* written during his Lincoln University years and published in 1930. By this time, Cullen's interests, too, were being directed toward fiction, and in 1932 he published his novel, *One Way to Heaven.* Both writers also wrote poetry for children, Langston Hughes collaborating with Arna Bontemps to produce *Popo and Fifina: Children of Haiti* in 1932 and Cullen publishing *The Last Zoo* in 1940. Indeed, one could push the seeming career parallels even further in that each author became involved in musical comedy writing, Cullen collaborating with Arna Bontemps in the early 1940's to convert Bontemps' novel *God Sends Sunday* into the musical *St. Louis Woman* and Hughes producing in the late 1950's his *Simply Heavenly.* However, the similarities in their careers should not be overemphasized. The sharp differences between Hughes as poet and author and Cullen as poet and author are quite obvious when one compares, say, two dramatic works written in the middle 1930's—*Mulatto* by Hughes and *The Medea* by Cullen. As the title of Hughes' play suggests, it is concerned with the social and moral effects of miscegenation on Southern social structures. It speaks to immediate problems that were then matters of overwhelming concern to the South and to the North; as a consequence, the play had a year's successful run on Broadway in the middle of the Depression years. Cullen's *The Medea,* on the other hand, reflects a different interest. In the first place, it is a poetic drama and hence not meant to be acted but rather to be evaluated for its literary qualities as a work of translation. That is, where *Mulatto* was a dramatic success, Cullen's *The Medea* was a literary achievement. *Mulatto* speaks to twentieth-century America mired in racial sin and immorality. *The Medea* speaks of the rise and fall of a great woman whose story had nothing to do with race or social doctrines but instead was concerned with the consuming passions of woman as she emerged in the Graeco-Roman world. Thus, *The Medea* represents the "other" side of Cullen's consciousness, and *Mulatto* reveals Hughes' continuing preoccupation with the Black man's status in America. Cullen worked assiduously to become a man of literature, and is accepted by scholars and writers because of his craftsmanship and skill and not because of his race. Hughes, on the other hand, involved himself ever more deeply with Harlem and the creation of Jesse B. Semple, Black folk philosopher *par excellence.*

Cullen's poetry receives critical comment in Saunders Redding's *To Make a Poet Black* (1939), Benjamin Brawley's *The Negro Genius* (1937), Jean Wagner's *Les poètes nègres des États-Unis* (1963), Stephen H. Bronz's *Roots of Negro Racial Consciousness* (1964), and Blanche E. Ferguson's *Countee Cullen and the Harlem Renaissance* (1966). Several good critical essays are also to be found in *Phylon,* including Bertram Woodruff's "The Poetic Philosophy of Countee Cullen," I (1940), 213–223; and Arthur Davis' "The Alien-and-Exile Theme in Countee Cullen's Racial Poems," XIV (1953), 390–400. Margaret Perry's *A Bio-Bibliography of Countee P. Cullen, 1903–1946* (1971) is indispensable. Many of Cullen's papers are deposited in the Atlanta University Library.

Yet Do I Marvel

I doubt not God is good, well-meaning, kind,
And did He stoop to quibble could tell why
The little buried mole continues blind,
Why flesh that mirrors Him must someday die,
Make plain the reason tortured Tantalus
Is baited by the fickle fruit, declare
If merely brute caprice dooms Sisyphus
To struggle up a never-ending stair.
Inscrutable His ways are, and immune
To catechism by a mind too strewn
With petty cares to slightly understand
What awful brain compels His awful hand.
Yet do I marvel at this curious thing:
To make a poet black, and bid him sing!

A Brown Girl Dead

With two white roses on her breasts,
   White candles at head and feet,
Dark Madonna of the grave she rests;
   Lord Death has found her sweet.

Her mother pawned her wedding ring
   To lay her out in white;
She'd be so proud she'd dance and sing
   To see herself tonight.

Incident

Once riding in Old Baltimore,
   Heart-filled, head-filled with glee,
I saw a Baltimorean
   Keep looking straight at me.

Now I was eight and very small,
   And he was no whit bigger,
And so I smiled, but he poked out
   His tongue and called me, "Nigger."

I saw the whole of Baltimore
   From May until December;
Of all the things that happened there
   That's all that I remember.

Heritage

For Harold Jackman

What is Africa to me:
Copper sun or scarlet sea,
Jungle star or jungle track,
Strong bronzed men, or regal black
Women from whose loins I sprang
When the birds of Eden sang?
One three centuries removed
From the scenes his fathers loved,
Spicy grove, cinnamon tree,
What is Africa to me?

So I lie, who all day long
Want no sound except the song
Sung by wild barbaric birds
Goading massive jungle herds,
Juggernauts of flesh that pass
Trampling tall defiant grass
Where young forest lovers lie,
Plighting troth beneath the sky.
So I lie, who always hear,
Though I cram against my ear

Both my thumbs, and keep them there,
Great drums throbbing through the air.
So I lie, whose fount of pride,
Dear distress, and joy allied,
Is my somber flesh and skin,
With the dark blood dammed within
Like great pulsing tides of wine
That, I fear, must burst the fine
Channels of the chafing net
Where they surge and foam and fret.

Africa? A book one thumbs
Listlessly, till slumber comes.
Unremembered are her bats
Circling through the night, her cats
Crouching in the river reeds,
Stalking gentle flesh that feeds
By the river brink; no more
Does the bugle-throated roar
Cry that monarch claws have leapt
From the scabbards where they slept.
Silver snakes that once a year
Doff the lovely coats you wear,
Seek no covert in your fear
Lest a mortal eye should see;
What's your nakedness to me?
Here no leprous flowers rear
Fierce corollas in the air;
Here no bodies sleek and wet,
Dripping mingled rain and sweat,
Tread the savage measures of
Jungle boys and girls in love.
What is last year's snow to me,
Last year's anything? The tree
Budding yearly must forget
How its past arose or set—
Bough and blossom, flower, fruit,
Even what shy bird with mute
Wonder at her travail there,
Meekly labored in its hair.
One three centuries removed
From the scenes his fathers loved,
Spicy grove, cinnamon tree,
What is Africa to me?

So I lie, who find no peace
Night or day, no slight release
From the unremittant beat
Made by cruel padded feet
Walking through my body's street.
Up and down they go, and back.
Treading out a jungle track.

So I lie, who never quite
Safely sleep from rain at night—
I can never rest at all
When the rain begins to fall;
Like a soul gone mad with pain
I must match its weird refrain;
Ever must I twist and squirm,
Writhing like a baited worm,
While its primal measures drip
Through my body, crying, "Strip!
Doff this new exuberance.
Come and dance the Lover's Dance!"
In an old remembered way
Rain works on me night and day.

Quaint, outlandish heathen gods
Black men fashion out of rods,
Clay, and brittle bits of stone,
In a likeness like their own,
My conversion came high-priced;
I belong to Jesus Christ,
Preacher of humility,
Heathen gods are naught to me.

Father, Son, and Holy Ghost,
So I make an idle boast;
Jesus of the twice-turned cheek,
Lamb of God, although I speak
With my mouth thus, in my heart
Do I play a double part.
Ever at Thy glowing altar
Must my heart grow sick and falter,
Wishing He I served were black,
Thinking then it would not lack
Precedent of pain to guide it,
Let who would or might deride it;
Surely then this flesh would know
Yours had borne a kindred woe.
Lord, I fashion dark gods, too,
Daring even to give You
Dark despairing features where,
Crowned with dark rebellious hair,
Patience wavers just so much as
Mortal grief compels, while touches
Quick and hot, of anger, rise
To smitten cheek and weary eyes.
Lord, forgive me if my need
Sometimes shapes a human creed.
All day long and all night through,
One thing only must I do:
Quench my pride and cool my blood,
Lest I perish in the flood,

Lest a hidden ember set
Timber that I thought was wet
Burning like the dryest flax,
Melting like the merest wax,

Lest the grave restore its dead.
Not yet has my heart or head
In the least way realized
They and I are civilized.

For John Keats, Apostle of Beauty

Not writ in water nor in mist,
Sweet lyric throat, thy name.
Thy singing lips that cold death kissed
Have seared his own with flame.

For Paul Laurence Dunbar

Born of the sorrowful of heart
Mirth was a crown upon his head;
Pride kept his twisted lips apart
In jest, to hide a heart that bled.

She of the Dancing Feet Sings

To Ottie Graham

And what would I do in heaven, pray,
  Me with my dancing feet,
And limbs like apple boughs that sway
  When the gusty rain winds beat?

And how would I thrive in a perfect place
  Where dancing would be sin,
With not a man to love my face,
  Nor an arm to hold me in?

The seraphs and the cherubim
  Would be too proud to bend
To sing the faery tunes that brim
  My heart from end to end.

The wistful angels down in hell
  Will smile to see my face,
And understand, because they fell
  From that all-perfect place.

To John Keats, Poet. At Springtime

I cannot hold my peace, John Keats;
There never was a spring like this;
It is an echo, that repeats
My last year's song and next year's bliss.
I know, in spite of all men say

Of Beauty, you have felt her most.
Yea, even in your grave her way
Is laid. Poor, troubled, lyric ghost,
Spring never was so fair and dear
As Beauty makes her seem this year.

I cannot hold my peace, John Keats,
I am as helpless in the toil
Of Spring as any lamb that bleats
To feel the solid earth recoil
Beneath his puny legs. Spring beats
Her tocsin call to those who love her,
And lo! the dogwood petals cover
Her breasts with drifts of snow, and sleek
White gulls fly screaming to her, and hover
About her shoulders, and kiss her cheek,
While white and purple lilacs muster
A strength that bears them to a cluster
Of color and odor; for her sake
All things that slept are now awake.

And you and I, shall we lie still,
John Keats, while Beauty summons us?
Somehow I feel your sensitive will
Is pulsing up some tremulous

Sap road of a maple tree, whose leaves
Grow music as they grow, since your
Wild voice is in them, a harp that grieves
For life that opens death's dark door.
Though dust, your fingers still can push
The Vision Splendid to a birth,
Though now they work as grass in the hush
Of the night on the broad sweet page of the earth.

"John Keats is dead," they say, but I
Who hear your full insistent cry
In bud and blossom, leaf and tree,
Know John Keats still writes poetry.
And while my head is earthward bowed
To read new life sprung from your shroud,
Folks seeing me must think it strange
That merely spring should so derange
My mind. They do not know that you,
John Keats, keep revel with me, too.

From the Dark Tower

We shall not always plant while others reap
The golden increment of bursting fruit,
Not always countenance, abject and mute,
That lesser men should hold their brothers cheap;
Not everlastingly while others sleep
Shall we beguile their limbs with mellow flute
Not always bend to some more subtle brute;
We were not made eternally to weep.

The night whose sable breast relieves the stark
White stars is no less lovely being dark,
And there are buds that cannot bloom at all
In light, but crumple, piteous, and fall;
So in the dark we hide the heart that bleeds,
And wait, and tend our agonizing seeds.

Threnody for a Brown Girl

Weep not, you who love her;
What rebellious flow
Grief undams shall recover
Whom the gods bid go?
Sorrow rising like a wall,
Bitter, blasphemous,
What avails it to recall
Beauty back to us?

Think not this grave shall keep her,
This marriage-bed confine;
Death may dig it deep and deeper;
She shall climb it like a vine.
Body that was quick and sentient,
Dear as thought or speech,
Death could not with one trenchant
Blow snatch out of reach.

She is nearer than the word
Wasted on her now,
Nearer than the swaying bird
On its rhythmic bough.
Only were our faith as much
As a mustard seed,
Aching, hungry hands might touch
Her as they touch a reed.

Life who was not loth to trade her
Unto death, has done
Better than he planned, has made her
Wise as Solomon.
Now she knows the Why and Wherefore,
Troublous Whence and Whither,
Why men strive and sweat, and care for
Bays that droop and wither.

All the stars she knows by name,
End and origin thereof,
Knows if love be kin to shame,
If shame be less than love.
What was crooked now is straight,
What was rough is plain;
Grief and sorrow have no weight
Now to cause her pain.

Plain to her why fevered blisters
Made her dark hands run,
While her favored, fairer sisters
Neither wrought nor spun;
Clear to her the hidden reason
Men daily fret and toil,
Staving death off for a season
Till soil return to soil.

One to her are flame and frost;
Silence is her singing lark;
We alone are children, lost,
Crying in the dark.
Varied feature now, and form,
Change has bred upon her;
Crush no bug nor nauseous worm
Lest you tread upon her.

Pluck no flower lest she scream;
Bruise no slender reed,
Lest it prove more than it seem,
Lest she groan and bleed.
More than ever trust your brother,
Read him golden, pure;
It may be she finds no other
House so safe and sure.

Set no poet carving
Rhymes to make her laugh;
Only live hearts starving
Need an epitaph.
Lay upon her no white stone
From a foreign quarry;
Earth and sky be these alone
Her obituary.

Swift as startled fawn or swallow,
Silence all her sound,
She has fled; we cannot follow
Further than this mound.
We who take the beaten track
Trying to appease
Hearts near breaking with their lack,
We need elegies.

Variations on a Theme

The Loss of Love

1

This house where Love a little while abode,
Impoverished completely of him now,
Of every vestige bare, drained like a bough
Wherefrom the all-sustaining sap has flowed
Away, yet bears upon its front bestowed
A cabalistic legend telling how
Love for a meagre space deigned to allow
It summer scent before the winter snowed.
Here rots to ruin a splendor proudly calm,
A skeleton whereof the clean bones wear
Their indigence relieved of any qualm
For purple robes that once were folded there.
The mouldy Coliseum draws upon
Our wonder yet . . . no less Love's Parthenon.

2

All through an empty place I go,
And find her not in any room;
The candles and the lamps I light
Go down before a wind of gloom.

Thick-spraddled lies the dust about,
A fit, sad place to write her name
Or draw her face the way she looked
That legendary night she came.

A Song of Sour Grapes

I wish your body were in the grave,
Deep down as a grave may be,
Or rotting under the deepest wave
That ever ploughed the sea.

I wish I never had seen your face,
Or the sinuous curve of your mouth,
Dear as a straw to a man who drowns
Or rain to a land in drouth.

I would that your mother had never borne
Your father's seed to fruit,
That meadow rats had gnawed his corn
Before it gathered root.

That Bright Chimeric Beast

That bright chimeric beast
Conceived yet never born,
Save in the poet's breast,
The white-flanked unicorn,
Never may be shaken
From his solitude;
Never may be taken
In any earthly wood.

That bird forever feathered,
Of its new self the sire,
After aeons weathered,
Reincarnate by fire,
Falcon may not nor eagle
Swerve from his eyrie,
Nor any crumb inveigle
Down to an earthly tree.

That fish of the dread regime
Invented to become
The fable and the dream
Of the Lord's aquarium,
Leviathan, the jointed
Harpoon was never wrought
By which the Lord's anointed
Will suffer to be caught.

Bird of the deathless breast,
Fish of the frantic fin,
That bright chimeric beast
Flashing the argent skin,—
If beasts like these you'd harry,
Plumb then the poet's dream;
Make it your aviary,
Make it your wood and stream.

There only shall the swish
Be heard of the regal fish;
There like a golden knife
Dart the feet of the unicorn,
And there, death brought to life,
The dead bird be reborn.

Little Sonnet to Little Friends

Let not the proud of heart condemn
Me that I mould my ways to hers,
Groping for healing in a hem
No wind of passion ever stirs;
Nor let them sweetly pity me
When I am out of sound and sight;
They waste their time and energy;
No mares encumber me at night.

Always a trifle fond and strange,
And some have said a bit bizarre,
Say, "Here's the sun," I would not change
It for my dead and burnt-out star.
Shine as it will, I have no doubt
Some day the sun, too, may go out.

Therefore, Adieu

Now you are gone, and with your unreturning
  goes
All I had thought in spite of you would stay;
Now draws forever to its unawakening close
The beauty of the bright bandanna'd day.

Now sift in ombrous flakes and revolutions
  slow
My dreams descending from my heady sky.
The balm I kept to cool my grief in (leaves of
  snow)
Now melts, with your departure flowing by.

I knew, indeed, the straight unswerving track
  the sun
Took to your face (as other ecstasies)
Yet I had thought some faith to me in them;
  they run
From me to you as fly to honey, bees.

Avid, to leave me neither fevered joy nor ache,
Only of soul and body vast unrest.
Sun, moon, and stars should be enough; why
  must you take
The feeling of the heart out of the breast?

Now I who dreamed before I died to shoot one
  shaft
Of courage from a warped and crooked bow,
Stand utterly forsaken, stripped of that small
  craft
I had, watching with you all prowess go.

Nothing Endures

Nothing endures,
Not even love,
Though the warm heart purrs
Of the length thereof.

Though beauty wax,
Yet shall it wane;
Time lays a tax
On the subtlest brain.

Let the blood riot,
Give it its will;
It shall grow quiet,
It shall grow still.

Nirvana gapes
For all things given;
Nothing escapes,
Love not even.

Black Majesty

After reading John W. Vandercook's chronicle of sable glory

These men were kings, albeit they were black,
Christophe and Dessalines and L'Ouverture;
Their majesty has made me turn my back
Upon a plaint I once shaped to endure.
These men were black, I say, but they were
  crowned
And purple-clad, however brief their time.
Stifle your agony; let grief be drowned;
We know joy had a day once and a clime.

Dark gutter-snipe, black sprawler-in-the-mud,
A thing men did a man may do again.
What answer filters through your sluggish
  blood
To these dark ghosts who knew so bright a
  reign?
"Lo, I am dark, but comely," Sheba sings.
"And we were black," three shades reply, "but
  kings."

Magnets

The straight, the swift, the debonair,
Are targets on the thoroughfare
For every kind appraising eye;
Sweet words are said as they pass by.
But such a strange contrary thing
My heart is, it will never cling
To any bright unblemished thing.
Such have their own security,
And little need to lean on me.

The limb that falters in its course,
And cries, "Not yet!" to waning force;
The orb that may not brave the sun;
The bitter mouth, its kissing done;
The loving heart that must deny
The very love it travels by;
What most has need to bend and pray,
These magnets draw my heart their way.

A Negro Mother's Lullaby

After visiting John Brown's grave

Hushaby, hushaby, dark one at my knee;
  Slumber you softly, nor pucker, nor frown;
  Though some may be bonded, you shall be
      free,
  Thanks to a man . . . Osawatamie Brown.
    His sons are high fellows,
    An Archangel is he,
    And they doff their bright haloes
    To none but the Three.

Hushaby, hushaby, sweet darkness at rest,
  Two there have been who their lives laid
      down
  That you might be beautiful here at my breast:
  Our Jesus and . . . Osawatamie Brown.
    His sons are high fellows,

    An Archangel is he,
    And they doff their bright haloes
    To none but the Three.

Hushaby, hushaby, when a man, not a slave,
  With freedom for wings you go through the
      town,
  Let your love be dew on his evergreen grave;
  Sleep, in the name of Osawatamie Brown.
    Rich counsel he's giving
    Close by the throne,
    Tall he was living
    But now taller grown.

    His sons are high fellows,
    An Archangel is he,
    And they doff their bright haloes
    To none but the Three.

Richard Wright (1908–1960)

Born near Natchez, Mississippi—one of the most racist areas of the most racist state—Richard Wright grew up to be one of the greatest of all Black writers. He had achieved at the time of his death in Paris world-wide fame as novelist, autobiographer, and social critic. His pilgrimage from Mississippi to Memphis to Arkansas to Mississippi again to Memphis again and, in 1927, to the South Side of Chicago epitomizes an important chapter in Black social history, just as his intellectual journey from

Marxism to existentialism to Third Worldism typifies a pattern often repeated by other writers on the left.

Most of the themes and attitudes of Wright's fiction resulted from the oppressive conditions of his childhood and youth. No other American writer has surmounted such difficult barriers in achieving literary distinction: racial prejudice, poverty, family disorganization, and a poor education. As a Black child in the South, Wright suffered from white oppression both through personal experience and observation and through the pervasive fear and tension engendered by the Jim Crow system. In the ghettoes of Chicago and New York, where he lived during his twenties, racial prejudice was less overt than in the Deep South, but still quite formidable. During his first thirty years, Wright also suffered from a state of destitution that frequently, in his childhood, entailed actual physical hunger and malnutrition, as well as inadequate clothing and shelter. During the Depression, Wright and his family in Chicago were on relief. Since he was barely five years of age his family had consisted of himself, his younger brother, and his mother, for his father had abandoned them in Memphis to live with another woman. For a brief period, the young Wright was committed to an orphanage. After his mother's health began to fail in 1919, Wright's brother went North to live with relatives, and Wright himself lived with relatives in Mississippi, principally his maternal grandparents in Jackson. The Jackson household was dominated by his grandmother, a fanatic Seventh-Day Adventist whose lasting hostility Wright incurred quickly. Before going to Memphis alone in 1925, Wright had moved some twenty times. Thus his early years totally lacked the stabilizing influence of an ordered family life. Nor did his education provide any compensation for his other handicaps. His formal schooling consisted of a few years in segregated Southern schools, ending with his graduation from a Jackson junior high school. Often even this inferior education was disrupted by his frequent moves and by his raggedness and hunger, which made attendance sporadic and concentration difficult. His environment outside of school was indifferent when not hostile to learning, especially that not directly related to economic advancement. His grandmother, furthermore, objected to secular books, especially novels, on religious grounds and refused to have them in her house. Wright's reading was confined mostly to such cheap fiction as escaped the surveillance of his relatives.

These handicaps—racial, economic, familial, and educational—reinforced each other in a cruel way. Only when Wright fled to Memphis did he begin to find some measure of alleviation, for there he roomed with a family whose emotional warmth was freely extended to him. In Memphis he also became interested in serious literature, reading Mencken, Dreiser, Sinclair Lewis, Sherwood Anderson, and others. But the racial and economic problems remained. After two years in Memphis, Wright moved North again—to Chicago.

The decade that Wright spent in Chicago continued his education in American race relations, plunged him into the Communist movement, and initiated his serious literary career. With the advent of the

Depression, Wright's sense of personal despair merged into the collective unrest of the urban proletariat. By the fall of 1933 he was attending meetings of the Chicago John Reed Club, and soon after he joined the Communist Party. His first writing for such leftist literary magazines as *Left Front, New Masses,* and *International Literature* consisted of proletarian poetry, most of it rather crude, expressing his new political enlightenment. After the John Reed Club disbanded in 1935, a group of Black Chicago writers gathered around Wright, whose interests were now turning to fiction. Before moving to New York in May 1937, he had written most of *Lawd Today* and at least two of the four stories in *Uncle Tom's Children*.

Though *Lawd Today,* published posthumously in 1963, is clearly an apprentice work, it is not without merit. Depicting graphically a typically sordid day in the blighted life of a Black postal clerk in Chicago, the novel reveals also the social forces responsible for his—and his race's—plight. The setting of *Uncle Tom's Children* (1938), Wright's first published book, is the rural South. In each of the stories of this work, racial conflict results in physical violence. In their response to white oppression, however, the protagonists move from individual flight in "Big Boy Leaves Home" through protection of the family in "Down by the Riverside" and "Long Black Song" to the directed, collective resistance of "Fire and Cloud." The stories have considerable individual distinction, but their interrelationships give the entire work an impressive measure of unity and developing meaning.

The success of *Uncle Tom's Children* enabled Wright to turn from his writing for the New York Writer's Project and his reporting for the *Daily Worker* to work on a novel. This appeared early in 1940 as *Native Son,* Wright's most substantial achievement in fiction. Drawing on his experiences in the South, his equally intimate knowledge of Black urban life in the North, and his Communist ideology, Wright created in Bigger Thomas a powerful, painful, and undeniably real portrait of a rebellious young Black man formed—or deformed—by the American racial system. *Native Son* may be viewed in its bitter protest as a representative document of its time, indeed as the climax of a decade of socially conscious fiction, but it should also be regarded as a successful novel skillfully constructed and intensely rendered, with a strong characterization of Bigger and a suggestive symbolic pattern. Though the novel had its detractors, most reviewers and critics—white, Black, Communist, and foreign—have given *Native Son* their enthusiastic endorsement.

The last two decades of Wright's life began with a flurry of activity on behalf of the Communist Party, then a gradual disengagement, and finally a complete break in 1944. During the early 1940's, his major literary endeavors were autobiographical, culminating in 1945 in *Black Boy,* in many respects his best book. Restless after its completion, Wright visited France in 1946 and then returned the following year to establish permanent residence. He was received eagerly by Jean-Paul Sartre and the other members of *Les Temps Modernes* group. Wright's next novel, *The Outsider* (1953), shows clearly the influence of his immersion in existentialism.

Wright produced six books in his remaining seven years. Two of these, *Savage Holiday* (1954) and *The Long Dream* (1958), were novels. The other four consisted of one collection of lectures, *White Man, Listen!* (1957), and three books of travel and sociopolitical comment concerning Africa—*Black Power* (1954), Asia—*The Color Curtain* (1956), and Spain—*Pagan Spain* (1957). At the time of his death, in November 1960, he was busily at work on several literary projects, one of which was *Eight Men* (1961), a collection of short stories, radio plays, a novella, and an autobiographical essay. Spanning almost the entire range of his literary career, *Eight Men* prompted James Baldwin to make the profound observation that "Wright's unrelentingly bleak landscape was not merely that of the Deep South, or of Chicago, but that of the world, of the human heart."

Other important works by Wright include the dramatic version of *Native Son* (1941), written in collaboration with Paul Green; *12 Million Black Voices* (1941), a "folk history of the Negro in the United States"; and contributions to *The God That Failed* (1950), edited by Richard Crossman, and *Soon, One Morning* (1963), edited by Herbert Hill.

Constance Webb's *Richard Wright: A Biography* (1968) is inadequate in many ways, but it has a good checklist of almost all of Wright's published work compiled by Michel Fabre and Edward Margolies. Fabre is preparing what may well be a definitive biography of Wright, and Margolies is editing Wright's letters. Thomas Knipp has already edited *Richard Wright: Letters to Joe C. Brown* (1968). A recent brief biography is John A. Williams, *The Most Native of Sons* (1970).

For a guide to Wright scholarship, see Russell C. Brignano's "Richard Wright: A Bibliography of Secondary Sources," *Studies in Black Literature,* II (Summer 1971), 19–25. The four major critical studies are Edward Margolies, *The Art of Richard Wright* (1969); Dan McCall, *The Example of Richard Wright* (1969); Russell C. Brignano, *Richard Wright: An Introduction to the Man and His Works* (1970); and Keneth Kinnamon, *The Emergence of Richard Wright: A Study in Literature and Society* (1972). Robert Bone's *Richard Wright* (1969) and Milton and Patricia Rickels' *Richard Wright* (1970) are introductory pamphlets. *Negro Digest* (December 1968), *CLA Journal* (June 1969), *Studies in Black Literature* (Autumn 1970), and *New Letters* (Winter 1971) have devoted special issues to Wright. Richard Abcarian has collected reviews, critical essays, and other materials in *Richard Wright's Native Son: A Critical Handbook* (1970), and Donald B. Gibson has included six major evaluations in *Five Black Writers* (1970). Among the many other important essays, the following may be mentioned: Ralph Ellison, "Richard Wright's Blues," reprinted in this anthology; James Baldwin, "Everybody's Protest Novel," reprinted in this anthology, and "Many Thousands Gone" in *Notes of a Native Son* (1955) and three pieces in *Nobody Knows My Name* (1961) under the collective title of "Alas, Poor Richard";

Arthur P. Davis, "'The Outsider' as a Novel of Race," *The Midwest Journal*, VII (Winter 1955–56), 320–326; Nathan A. Scott, Jr., "Search for Beliefs: Fiction of Richard Wright," *The University of Kansas City Review*, XXIII (1956), 19–24, 131–138, and "No Point of Purchase," *The Kenyon Review*, XXIII (1961), 337–343; Saunders Redding, "Richard Wright: An Evaluation," *AMSAC Newsletter*, III (December 30, 1960), 3–6; Hoyt W. Fuller, "On the Death of Richard Wright," *Southwest Review*, XLVI (1961), vi–vii, 334–337; Henry F. Winslow, "Richard Nathaniel Wright: Destroyer and Preserver (1908–1960)," *The Crisis*, LXIX (1962), 149–163, 187; Irving Howe, "Black Boys and Native Sons," *Dissent*, X (1963), 353–368; Harold Cruse, *The Crisis of the Negro Intellectual* (1967), pp. 181–189; Keneth Kinnamon, "The Pastoral Impulse in Richard Wright," *Midcontinent American Studies Journal*, X (1969), 41–47, and "Richard Wright: Proletarian Poet," *Concerning Poetry*, II (1969), 39–50; Richard Kostelanetz, "The Politics of Unresolved Quests in the Novels of Richard Wright," *Xavier University Studies*, VIII (1969), 31–64; Donald B. Gibson, "Wright's Invisible Native Son," *American Quarterly*, XXI (1969), 728–738; James Nagel, "Images of 'Vision' in *Native Son*," *University Review*, XXXVI (December 1969), 109–115; Warren French, "The Lost Potential of Richard Wright," in *The Black American Writer* (1969), edited by C. W. E. Bigsby, I, 125–142; Stanley Edgar Hyman, "Richard Wright Reappraised," *The Atlantic*, CCXXV (March 1970), 127–128, 130–132; Lloyd W. Brown, "Stereotypes in Black and White: The Nature of Perception in Wright's *Native Son*," *Black Academy Review*, I (Fall 1970), 35–44; and Blyden Jackson, "Richard Wright in a Moment of Truth," *The Southern Literary Journal*, III (Spring 1971), 3–17.

The Ethics of Living Jim Crow

An Autobiographical Sketch

I

My first lesson in how to live as a Negro came when I was quite small. We were living in Arkansas. Our house stood behind the railroad tracks. Its skimpy yard was paved with black cinders. Nothing green ever grew in that yard. The only touch of green we could see was far away, beyond the tracks, over where the white folks lived. But cinders were good enough for me and I never missed the green growing things. And anyhow cinders were fine weapons. You could always have a nice hot war with huge black cinders. All you had to do was crouch behind the brick pillars of a house with your hands full of gritty ammunition. And the first woolly black head you saw pop out from behind another row of pillars was your target. You tried your very best to knock it off. It was great fun.

I never fully realized the appalling disadvantages of a cinder environment till one day the gang to which I belonged found itself engaged in a war with the white boys who lived beyond the tracks. As usual we laid down our cinder barrage, thinking that this would wipe the white boys out. But they replied with a steady bombardment of broken bottles. We doubled our cinder barrage, but they hid behind trees, hedges, and the sloping embankments of their lawns. Having no such fortifications, we retreated to the brick pillars of our homes. During the retreat a broken milk bottle caught me behind the ear, opening a deep gash which bled profusely. The sight of blood pouring over my face completely demoralized our ranks. My fellow-combatants left me standing paralyzed in the center of the yard, and scurried for their homes. A kind neighbor saw me and rushed me to a doctor, who took three stitches in my neck.

I sat brooding on my front steps, nursing my wound and waiting for my mother to come from work. I felt that a grave injustice had been done me. It was all right to throw cinders. The greatest harm a cinder could do was leave a bruise. But broken bottles were dangerous; they left you cut, bleeding, and helpless.

When night fell, my mother came from the white folks' kitchen. I raced down the street to meet her. I could just feel in my bones that she would understand. I knew she would tell me exactly what to do next time. I grabbed her hand and babbled out the whole story. She examined my wound, then slapped me.

"How come yuh didn't hide?" she asked me. "How come yuh awways fightin'?"

I was outraged, and bawled. Between sobs I told her that I didn't have any trees or hedges to hide behind. There wasn't a thing I could have used as a trench. And you couldn't throw very far when you were hiding behind the brick pillars of a house. She grabbed a barrel stave, dragged me home, stripped me naked, and beat me till I had a fever of one hundred and two. She would smack my rump with the stave, and, while the skin was still smarting, impart to me gems of Jim Crow wisdom. I was never to throw cinders any more. I was never to fight any more wars. I was never, never, under any conditions, to fight *white* folks again. And they were absolutely right in clouting me with the broken milk bottle. Didn't I know she was working hard every day in the hot kitchens of the white folks to make money to take care of me? When was I ever going to learn to be a good boy? She couldn't be bothered with my fights. She finished by telling me that I ought to be thankful to God as long as I lived that they didn't kill me.

All that night I was delirious and could not sleep. Each time I closed my eyes I saw monstrous white faces suspended from the ceiling, leering at me.

From that time on, the charm of my cinder yard was gone. The green trees, the trimmed hedges, the cropped lawns grew very meaningful, became a symbol. Even today when I think of white folks, the hard, sharp outlines of white houses surrounded by trees, lawns, and hedges are present somewhere in the background of my mind. Through the years they grew into an overreaching symbol of fear.

It was a long time before I came in close contact with white folks again. We moved from Arkansas to Mississippi. Here we had the good fortune not to live behind the railroad tracks, or close to white neighborhoods. We lived in the very heart of the local Black Belt. There were black churches and black preachers; there were black schools and black teachers; black groceries and black clerks. In fact, everything was so solidly black that for a long time I did not even think of white folks, save in remote and vague terms. But this could not last forever. As one grows older one eats more. One's clothing costs more. When I finished grammar school I had to go to work. My mother could no longer feed and clothe me on her cooking job.

There is but one place where a black boy who knows no trade can get a job, and that's where the houses and faces are white, where the trees, lawns, and hedges are green. My first job was with an optical company in Jackson, Mississippi. The morning I applied I stood straight and neat before the boss, answering all his questions with sharp yessirs and nosirs. I was very careful to pronounce my *sirs* distinctly, in order that he might know that I was polite, that I knew where I was, and that I knew he was a *white* man. I wanted that job badly.

He looked me over as though he were examining a prize poodle. He questioned me closely about my schooling, being particularly insistent about how much mathematics I had had. He seemed very pleased when I told him I had had two years of algebra.

"Boy, how would you like to try to learn something around here?" he asked me.

"I'd like it fine, sir," I said, happy. I had visions of "working my way up." Even Negroes have those visions.

"All right," he said. "Come on."

I followed him to the small factory.

"Pease," he said to a white man of about thirty-five, "this is Richard. He's going to work for us."

Pease looked at me and nodded.

I was then taken to a white boy of about seventeen.

"Morrie, this is Richard, who's going to work for us."

"Whut yuh sayin' there, boy!" Morrie boomed at me.

"Fine!" I answered.

The boss instructed these two to help me, teach me, give me jobs to do, and let me learn what I could in my spare time.

My wages were five dollars a week.

I worked hard, trying to please. For the first month I got along O.K. Both Pease and Morrie seemed to like me. But one thing was missing. And I kept thinking about it. I was not learning anything and nobody was volunteering to help me. Thinking they had forgotten that I was to learn something about the mechanics of grinding lenses, I asked Morrie one day to tell me about the work. He grew red.

"Whut yuh tryin' t' do, nigger, git smart?" he asked.

"Naw; I ain' tryin' t' git smart," I said.

"Well, don't, if yuh know whut's good for yuh!"

I was puzzled. Maybe he just doesn't want to help me, I thought. I went to Pease.

"Say, are yuh crazy, you black bastard?" Pease asked me, his gray eyes growing hard.

I spoke out, reminding him that the boss had said I was to be given a chance to learn something.

"Nigger, you think you're *white*, don't you?"

"Naw, sir!"

"Well, you're acting mighty like it!"

"But, Mr. Pease, the boss said . . ."

Pease shook his fist in my face.

"This is a *white* man's work around here, and you better watch yourself!"

From then on they changed toward me. They said good-morning no more. When I was just a bit slow in performing some duty, I was called a lazy black son-of-a-bitch.

Once I thought of reporting all this to the boss. But the mere idea of what would happen to me if Pease and Morrie should learn that I had "snitched" stopped me. And after all, the boss was a white man too. What was the use?

The climax came at noon one summer day. Pease called me to his work-bench. To get to him I had to go between two narrow benches and stand with my back to a wall.

"Yes, sir," I said.

"Richard, I want to ask you something," Pease began pleasantly, not looking up from his work.

"Yes, sir," I said again.

Morrie came over, blocking the narrow passage between the benches. He folded his arms, staring at me solemnly.

I looked from one to the other, sensing that something was coming.

"Yes, sir," I said for the third time.

Pease looked up and spoke very slowly.

"Richard, *Mr.* Morrie here tells me you call me *Pease.*"

I stiffened. A void seemed to open up in me. I knew this was the show-down.

He meant that I had failed to call him *Mr.* Pease. I looked at Morrie. He was gripping a steel bar in his hands. I opened my mouth to speak, to protest, to assure Pease that I had never called him simply *Pease,* and that I had never had any intentions of doing so, when Morrie grabbed me by the collar, ramming my head against the wall.

"Now, be careful, nigger!" snarled Morrie, baring his teeth. "I heard yuh call 'im *Pease!* 'N' if yuh say yuh didn't, yuh're callin' me a *lie,* see?" He waved the steel bar threateningly.

If I had said: No, sir, Mr. Pease, I never called you *Pease,* I would have been automatically calling Morrie a liar. And if I had said: Yes, sir Mr. Pease, I called you *Pease,* I would have been pleading guilty to having uttered the worst insult that a Negro can utter to a southern white man. I stood hesitating, trying to frame a neutral reply.

"Richard, I asked you a question!" said Pease. Anger was creeping into his voice.

"I don't remember calling you *Pease,* Mr. Pease," I said cautiously. "And if I did, I sure didn't mean . . ."

"You black son-of-a-bitch! You called me *Pease,* then!" he spat, slapping me till I bent sideways over a bench. Morrie was on top of me, demanding:

"Didn't yuh call 'im *Pease?* If yuh say yuh didn't, I'll rip yo' gut string loose with this bar, yuh black granny dodger! Yuh can't call a white man a lie 'n' git erway with it, you black son-of-a-bitch!"

I wilted. I begged them not to bother me. I knew what they wanted. They wanted me to leave.

"I'll leave," I promised. "I'll leave right *now.*"

They gave me a minute to get out of the

factory. I was warned not to show up again, or tell the boss.

I went.

When I told the folks at home what had happened, they called me a fool. They told me that I must never again attempt to exceed my boundaries. When you are working for white folks, they said, you got to "stay in your place" if you want to keep working.

II

My Jim Crow education continued on my next job, which was portering in a clothing store. One morning, while polishing brass out front, the boss and his twenty-year-old son got out of their car and half dragged and half kicked a Negro woman into the store. A policeman standing at the corner looked on, twirling his nightstick. I watched out of the corner of my eye, never slackening the strokes of my chamois upon the brass. After a few minutes, I heard shrill screams coming from the rear of the store. Later the woman stumbled out, bleeding, crying, and holding her stomach. When she reached the end of the block, the policeman grabbed her and accused her of being drunk. Silently, I watched him throw her into a patrol wagon.

When I went to the rear of the store, the boss and his son were washing their hands at the sink. They were chuckling. The floor was bloody and strewn with wisps of hair and clothing. No doubt I must have appeared pretty shocked, for the boss slapped me reassuringly on the back.

"Boy, that's what we do to niggers when they don't want to pay their bills," he said, laughing.

His son looked at me and grinned.

"Here, hava cigarette," he said.

Not knowing what to do, I took it. He lit his and held the match for me. This was a gesture of kindness, indicating that even if they had beaten the poor old woman, they would not beat me if I knew enough to keep my mouth shut.

"Yes, sir," I said, and asked no questions.

After they had gone, I sat on the edge of a packing box and stared at the bloody floor till the cigarette went out.

That day at noon, while eating in a hamburger joint, I told my fellow Negro porters what had happened. No one seemed surprised. One fellow, after swallowing a huge bite, turned to me and asked:

"Huh! Is tha' all they did t' her?"

"Yeah. Wasn't tha' enough?" I asked.

"Shucks! Man, she's a lucky bitch!" he said, burying his lips deep into a juicy hamburger. "Hell, it's a wonder they didn't lay her when they got through."

III

I was learning fast, but not quite fast enough. One day, while I was delivering packages in the suburbs, my bicycle tire was punctured. I walked along the hot, dusty road, sweating and leading my bicycle by the handle-bars.

A car slowed at my side.

"What's the matter boy?" a white man called.

I told him my bicycle was broken and I was walking back to town.

"That's too bad," he said. "Hop on the running board."

He stopped the car. I clutched hard at my bicycle with one hand and clung to the side of the car with the other.

"All set?"

"Yes, sir," I answered. The car started.

It was full of young white men. They were drinking. I watched the flask pass from mouth to mouth.

"Wanna drink, boy?" one asked.

I laughed as the wind whipped my face. Instinctively obeying the freshly planted precepts of my mother, I said:

"Oh, no!"

The words were hardly out of my mouth before I felt something hard and cold smash me between the eyes. It was an empty whisky bottle. I saw stars, and fell backwards from the speeding car into the dust of the road, my feet becoming entangled in the steel spokes of my bicycle. The white men piled out and stood over me.

"Nigger, ain't yuh learned no better sense'n tha' yet?" asked the man who hit me. "Ain' yuh learned t' say *sir* t' a white man yet?"

Dazed, I pulled to my feet. My elbows and legs were bleeding. Fists doubled, the white man advanced, kicking my bicycle out of the way.

"Aw, leave the bastard alone. He's got enough," said one.

They stood looking at me. I rubbed my shins, trying to stop the flow of blood. No doubt they felt a sort of contemptuous pity, for one asked:

"Yuh wanna ride t' town now, nigger? Yuh reckon yuh know enough t' ride now?"

"I wanna walk," I said, simply.

Maybe it sounded funny. They laughed.

"Well, walk, yuh black son-of-a-bitch!"

When they left they comforted me with:

"Nigger, yuh sho better be damn glad it wuz us yuh talked t' tha' way. Yuh're a lucky bastard, 'cause if yuh'd said tha' t' somebody else, yuh might've been a dead nigger now."

IV

Negroes who have lived South know the dread of being caught alone upon the streets in white neighborhoods after the sun has set. In such a simple situation as this the plight of the Negro in America is graphically symbolized. While white strangers may be in these neighborhoods trying to get home, they can pass unmolested. But the color of a Negro's skin makes him easily recognizable, makes him suspect, converts him into a defenseless target.

Late one Saturday night I made some deliveries in a white neighborhood. I was pedaling my bicycle back to the store as fast as I could, when a police car, swerving toward me, jammed me into the curbing.

"Get down and put up your hands!" the policeman ordered.

I did. They climbed out of the car, guns drawn, faces set, and advanced slowly.

"Keep still!" they ordered.

I reached my hands higher. They searched my pockets and packages. They seemed dissatisfied when they could find nothing incriminating. Finally, one of them said:

"Boy, tell your boss not to send you out in white neighborhoods after sundown."

As usual, I said:

"Yes, sir."

V

My next job was as hall-boy in a hotel. Here my Jim Crow education broadened and deepened. When the bell-boys were busy, I was often called to assist them. As many of the rooms in the hotel were occupied by prostitutes, I was constantly called to carry them liquor and cigarettes. These women were nude most of the time. They did not bother about clothing, even for bell-boys. When you went into their rooms, you were supposed to take this nakedness for granted, as though it startled you no more than a blue vase or a red rug. Your presence awoke in them no sense of shame, for you were not regarded as human. If they were alone, you could steal sidelong glimpses at them. But if they were receiving men, not a flicker of your eyelids could show. I remember one incident vividly. A new woman, a huge, snowy-skinned blonde, took a room on my floor. I was sent to wait upon her. She was in bed with a thick-set man; both were nude and uncovered. She said she wanted some liquor and slid out of bed and waddled across the floor to get her money from a dresser drawer. I watched her.

"Nigger, what in hell you looking at?" the white man asked me, raising himself upon his elbows.

"Nothing," I answered, looking miles deep into the blank wall of the room.

"Keep your eyes where they belong, if you want to be healthy!" he said.

"Yes, sir."

VI

One of the bell-boys I knew in this hotel was keeping steady company with one of the Negro maids. Out of a clear sky the police descended upon his home and arrested him, accusing him of bastardy. The poor boy swore he had had no intimate relations with the girl. Nevertheless, they forced him to marry her. When the child arrived, it was found to be much lighter in complexion than either of the two supposedly legal parents. The white men around the hotel made a great joke of it. They spread the rumor that some white cow must have scared the poor girl while she was carrying the baby. If you were in their presence when this explanation was offered, you were supposed to laugh.

VII

One of the bell-boys was caught in bed with a white prostitute. He was castrated and run out of town. Immediately after this all the bell-boys and hall-boys were called together and warned. We were given to understand that the boy who had been castrated was a "mighty, mighty lucky bastard." We were impressed with the fact that next time the management of the hotel would not be responsible for the lives of "trouble-makin' niggers." We were silent.

VIII

One night, just as I was about to go home, I met one of the Negro maids. She lived in my direction, and we fell in to walk part of the way home together. As we passed the white night-watchman, he slapped the maid on her buttock. I turned around, amazed. The watchman looked at me with a long, hard, fixed-under stare. Suddenly he pulled his gun and asked:

"Nigger, don't yuh like it?"

I hesitated.

"I asked yuh don't yuh like it?" he asked again, stepping forward.

"Yes, sir," I mumbled.

"Talk like it, then!"

"Oh, yes, sir!" I said with as much heartiness as I could muster.

Outside, I walked ahead of the girl, ashamed to face her. She caught up with me and said:

"Don't be a fool! Yuh couldn't help it!"

This watchman boasted of having killed two Negroes in self-defense.

Yet, in spite of all this, the life of the hotel ran with an amazing smoothness. It would have been impossible for a stranger to detect anything. The maids, the hall-boys, and the bell-boys were all smiles. They had to be.

IX

I had learned my Jim Crow lessons so thoroughly that I kept the hotel job till I left Jackson for Memphis. It so happened that while in Memphis I applied for a job at a branch of the optical company. I was hired. And for some reason, as long as I worked there, they never brought my past against me.

Here my Jim Crow education assumed quite a different form. It was no longer brutally cruel, but subtly cruel. Here I learned to lie, to steal, to dissemble. I learned to play that dual role which every Negro must play if he wants to eat and live.

For example, it was almost impossible to get a book to read. It was assumed that after a Negro had imbibed what scanty schooling the state furnished he had no further need for books. I was always borrowing books from men on the job. One day I mustered enough courage to ask one of the men to let me get books from the library in his name. Surprisingly, he consented. I cannot help but think that he consented because he was a Roman Catholic and felt a vague sympathy for Negroes, being himself an object of hatred. Armed with a library card, I obtained books in the following manner: I would write a note to the librarian, saying: "Please let this nigger boy have the following books." I would then sign it with the white man's name.

When I went to the library, I would stand at the desk, hat in hand, looking as unbookish as possible. When I received the books desired I would take them home. If the books listed in the note happened to be out, I would sneak into the lobby and forge a new one. I never took any chances guessing with the white librarian about what the fictitious white man would want to read. No doubt if any of the white patrons had suspected that some of the volumes they enjoyed had been in the home of a Negro, they would not have tolerated it for an instant.

The factory force of the optical company in Memphis was much larger than that in Jackson, and more urbanized. At least they liked to talk, and would engage the Negro help in conversation whenever possible. By this means I found that many subjects were taboo from the white man's point of view. Among the topics they did not like to discuss with Negroes were the following: American white women; the Ku Klux Klan; France, and how Negro soldiers fared while there; French women; Jack Johnson; the entire northern part of the United States; the Civil War; Abraham Lincoln; U. S. Grant; General Sherman; Catholics; the Pope; Jews; the Republican Party; slavery; social equality; Communism; Socialism; the 13th and 14th Amendments to the Constitution; or any topic calling for positive knowledge or manly self-assertion on the part of the Negro. The most accepted topics were sex and religion.

There were many times when I had to exercise a great deal of ingenuity to keep out of trouble. It is a southern custom that all men must take off their hats when they enter an elevator. And especially did this apply to us blacks with rigid force. One day I stepped into an elevator with my arms full of packages. I was forced to ride with my hat on. Two white men stared at me coldly. Then one of them very kindly lifted my hat and placed it upon my armful of packages. Now the most accepted response for a Negro to make under such circumstances is to look at the white man out of the corner of his eyes and grin. To have said: "Thank you!" would have made the white man *think* that you *thought* you were receiving from him a personal service. For such an act I have seen Negroes take a blow in the mouth. Finding the first alternative distasteful, and the second dangerous, I hit upon an acceptable course of action which fell safely between these two poles. I immediately—no sooner than my hat was lifted—pretended that my packages were about to spill, and appeared deeply distressed with keeping them in my arms. In this fashion I evaded having to acknowledge his service, and, in spite of adverse circumstances, salvaged a slender shred of personal pride.

How do Negroes feel about the way they have to live? How do they discuss it when alone among themselves? I think this question can be answered in a single sentence. A friend of mine who ran an elevator once told me:

"Lawd, man! Ef it wuzn't fer them polices 'n' them ol' lynch-mobs, there wouldn't be nothin' but uproar down here!"

Big Boy Leaves Home

I

Yo mama don wear no drawers . . .
Clearly, the voice rose out of the woods, and died away. Like an echo another voice caught it up:
Ah seena when she pulled em off . . .
Another, shrill, cracking, adolescent:
N she wash'd 'em in alcohol . . .
Then a quartet of voices, blending in harmony, floated high above the tree tops:
N she hung 'em out in the hall . . .
Laughing easily, four black boys came out of the woods into cleared pasture. They walked lollingly in bare feet, beating tangled vines and bushes with long sticks.
"Ah wished Ah knowed some mo lines t tha song."
"Me too."
"Yeah, when yuh gits t where she hangs em out in the hall yuh has t stop."
"Shucks, whut goes wid *hall?*"
"*Call.*"
"*Fall.*"
"*Wall.*"
"*Quall.*"
They threw themselves on the grass, laughing.
"Big Boy?"
"Huh?"
"Yuh know one thing?"
"Whut?"
"Yuh sho is crazy!"
"Crazy?"
"Yeah, yuh crazys a bed-bug!"

"Crazy bout whut?"
"Man, whoever hearda *quall.*"
"Yuh said yuh wanted something t go wid *hall,* didnt yuh?"
"Yeah, but whuts a *quall?*"
"Nigger, a *qualls a quall.*"
They laughed easily, catching and pulling long green blades of grass with their toes.
"Waal, ef a *qualls a quall,* whut IS a *quall?*"
"Oh, Ah know."
"Whut?"
"Tha ol song goes something like this:

Yo mama don wear no drawers,
Ah seena when she pulled em off,
N she washed em in alcohol,
N she hung em out in the hall,
N then she put em back on her QUALL!"

They laughed again. Their shoulders were flat to the earth, their knees propped up, and their faces square to the sun.
"Big Boy, yuhs CRAZY!"
"Don ax me nothin else."
"Nigger, yuhs CRAZY!"
They fell silent, smiling, drooping the lids of their eyes softly against the sunlight.
"Man, don the groun feel warm?"
"Jus lika bed."
"Jeeesus, Ah could stay here ferever."
"Me too."
"Ah kin feel tha ol sun goin all thu me."
"Feels like mah bones is warm."
In the distance a train whistled mournfully.
"There goes number fo!"

"Hittin on all six!"

"Highballin it down the line!"

"Bound for up Noth, Lawd, bound for up Noth!"

They began to chant, pounding bare heels in the grass.

> *Dis train boun fo Glory*
> *Dis train, Oh Hallelujah*
> *Dis train bound fo Glory*
> *Dis train, Oh Hallelujah*
> *Dis train bound fo Glory*
> *Ef yuh ride no need fer fret er worry*
> *Dis train, Oh Hallelujah*
> *Dis train . . .*
>
> *Dis train don carry no gambler*
> *Dis train, Oh Hallelujah*
> *Dis train don carry no gambler*
> *Dis train, Oh Hallelujah*
> *Dis train don carry no gambler*
> *No fo day creeper er midnight rambler*
> *Dis train, Oh Hallelujah*
> *Dis train . . .*

When the song ended they burst out laughing, thinking of a train bound for Glory.

"Gee, thas a good ol song!"

"Huuuuummmmmmmmmman . . ."

"Whut?"

"Geeee whiiiiiiz . . ."

"Whut?"

"Somebody don let win! Das whut!"

Buck, Bobo and Lester jumped up. Big Boy stayed on the ground, feigning sleep.

"Jeeesus, tha sho stinks!"

"Big Boy!"

Big Boy feigned to snore.

"Big Boy!"

Big Boy stirred as though in sleep.

"Big Boy!"

"Hunh?"

"Yuh rotten inside!"

"Rotten?"

"Lawd, cant yuh smell it?"

"Smell whut?"

"Nigger, yuh mus gotta bad col!"

"*Smell what?*"

"NIGGER, YUH BROKE WIN!"

Big Boy laughed and fell back on the grass, closing his eyes.

"The hen whut cackles is the hen whut laid the egg."

"We ain no hens."

"Yuh cackled, didnt yuh?"

The three moved off with noses turned up.

"C mon!"

"Where yuh-all goin?"

"T the creek fer a swim."

"Yeah, les swim."

"Naw buddy naw!" said Big Boy, slapping the air with a scornful palm.

"Aa, c mon! Don be a heel!"

"N git *lynched*? Hell naw!"

"He ain gonna see us."

"How yuh know?"

"Cause he ain."

"Yuh-all go on. Ahma stay right here," said Big Boy.

"Hell, let im stay! C mon, les go," said Buck.

The three walked off, swishing at grass and bushes with sticks. Big Boy looked lazily at their backs.

"Hey!"

Walking on, they glanced over their shoulders.

"Hey, niggers!"

"C mon!"

Big Boy grunted, picked up his stick, pulled to his feet, and stumbled off.

"Wait!"

"C mon!"

He ran, caught up with them, leaped upon their backs, bearing them to the ground.

"Quit, Big Boy!"

"Gawddam, nigger!"

"Git t hell offa me!"

Big Boy sprawled in the grass beside them, laughing and pounding his heels in the ground.

"Nigger, whut yuh think we is, hosses?"

"How come yuh awways hoppin on us?"

"Lissen, wes gonna doubt-team on yuh one of these days n beat yo ol ass good."

Big Boy smiled.

"Sho nough?"

"Yeah, don yuh like it?"

"We gonna beat yuh sos yuh cant walk!"

"N dare yuh t do nothin erbout it!"

Big Boy bared his teeth.

"C mon! Try it now!"

The three circled around him.

"Say, Buck, yuh grab his feets!"

"N yuh git his head, Lester!"

"N Bobo, yuh git berhin n grab his arms!"

Keeping more than arm's length, they circled round and round Big Boy.

"C mon!" said Big Boy, feinting at one and then the other.

Round and round they circled, but could not

seem to get any closer. Big Boy stopped and braced his hands on his hips.

"Is all three of yuh-all scareda me?"

"Les git im some other time," said Bobo, grinning.

"Yeah, we kin ketch yuh when yuh ain thinkin," said Lester.

"We kin trick yuh," said Buck.

They laughed and walked together.

Big Boy belched.

"Ahm hongry," he said.

"Me too."

"Ah wished Ah hada big hot pota bellybusters!"

"Cooked wid some good ol salty ribs . . ."

"N some good ol egg cornbread . . ."

"N some buttermilk . . ."

"N some hot peach cobbler swimming in juice . . ."

"Nigger, hush!"

They began to chant, emphasizing the rhythm by cutting at grass with sticks.

> *Bye n bye*
> *Ah wanna piece of pie*
> *Pies too sweet*
> *Ah wanna piece of meat*
> *Meats too red*
> *Ah wanna piece of bread*
> *Breads too brown*
> *Ah wanna go t town*
> *Towns too far*
> *Ah wanna ketch a car*
> *Cars too fas*
> *Ah fall n break mah ass*
> *Ahll understan it better bye n bye . . .*

They climbed over a barbed-wire fence and entered a stretch of thick woods. Big Boy was whistling softly, his eyes half-closed.

"LES GIT IM!"

Buck, Lester, and Bobo whirled, grabbed Big Boy about the neck, arms, and legs, bearing him to the ground. He grunted and kicked wildly as he went back into weeds.

"Hol im tight!"

"Git his arms! Git his arms!"

"Set on his legs so he cant kick!"

Big Boy puffed heavily, trying to get loose.

"WE GOT YUH NOW, GAWDDAMMIT, WE GOT YUH NOW!"

"Thas a Gawddam lie!" said Big Boy. He kicked, twisted, and clutched for a hold on one and then the other.

"Say, yuh-all hep me hol his arms!" said Bobo.

"Aw, we got this bastard now!" said Lester.

"Thas a Gawddam lie!" said Big Boy again.

"Say, yuh-all hep me hol his arms!" called Bobo.

Big Boy managed to encircle the neck of Bobo with his left arm. He tightened his elbow scissorslike and hissed through his teeth:

"Yuh got me, ain yuh?"

"Hol im!"

"Les beat this bastard's ass!"

"Say, hep me hol his *arms!* Hes got aholda mah *neck!*" cried Bobo.

Big Boy squeezed Bobo's neck and twisted his head to the ground.

"Yuh got me, ain yuh?"

"Quit, Big Boy, yuh chokin me; yuh hurtin mah neck!" cried Bobo.

"Turn me loose!" said Big Boy.

"Ah ain got yuh! Its the others whut got yuh!" pleaded Bobo.

"Tell them others t git t hell offa me or Ahma break yo neck," said Big Boy.

"Ssssay, yyyuh-all gggit ooooffa Bbig Boy. Hhhes got me," gurgled Bobo.

"Cant yuh hol im?"

"Nnaw, hhes ggot mmah nneck . . ."

Big Boy squeezed tighter.

"N Ahma break it too les yuh tell em t git t hell offa me!"

"Ttturn mmmeee llloose," panted Bobo, tears gushing.

"Cant yuh hol im, Bobo?" asked Buck.

"Nnaw, yuh-all tturn im lloose; hhhes got mah nnneck . . ."

"Grab his neck, Bobo . . ."

"Ah cant; yugurgur . . ."

To save Bobo, Lester and Buck got up and ran to a safe distance. Big Boy released Bobo, who staggered to his feet, slobbering and trying to stretch a crick out of his neck.

"Shucks, nigger, yuh almos broke mah neck," whimpered Bobo.

"Ahm gonna break yo ass nex time," said Big Boy.

"Ef Bobo coulda hel yuh we woulda had yuh," yelled Lester.

"Ah wuznt gonna let im do that," said Big Boy.

They walked together again, swishing sticks.

"Yuh see," began Big Boy, "when a ganga guys jump on yuh, all yuh gotta do is just put the heat on one of them n make im tell the others t let up, see?"

"Gee, thas a good idee!"

"Yeah, thas a good idee!"

"But yuh almos broke mah neck, man," said Bobo.

"Ahma smart nigger," said Big Boy, thrusting out his chest.

II

They came to the swimming hole.

"Ah ain goin in," said Bobo.

"Done got scared?" asked Big Boy.

"Naw, Ah ain scared . . ."

"How come yuh ain goin in?"

"Yuh know ol man Harvey don erllow no niggers t swim in this hole."

"N jus las year he took a shot at Bob fer swimmin in here," said Lester.

"Shucks, ol man Harvey ain studyin bout us niggers," said Big Boy.

"Hes at home thinking about his jelly-roll," said Buck.

They laughed.

"Buck, yo mins lowern a snakes belly," said Lester.

"Ol man Harveys too doggone ol t think erbout jelly-roll," said Big Boy.

"Hes dried up; all the saps don lef him," said Bobo.

"C mon, les go!" said Big Boy.

Bobo pointed.

"See tha sign over yonder?"

"Yeah."

"Whut it say?"

"NO TRESPASSIN," read Lester.

"Know whut tha mean?"

"Mean ain no dogs n niggers erllowed," said Buck.

"Waal, wes here now," said Big Boy. "Ef he ketched us even like this thered be trouble, so we just as waal go on in . . ."

"Ahm wid the nex one!"

"Ahll go ef anybody else goes!"

Big Boy looked carefully in all directions. Seeing nobody, he began jerking off his overalls.

"LAS ONE INS A OL DEAD DOG!"

"THAS YOU MA!"

"THAS YO PA!"

"THAS BOTH YO MA N YO PA!"

They jerked off their clothes and threw them in a pile under a tree. Thirty seconds later they stood, black and naked, on the edge of the hole under a sloping embankment. Gingerly Big Boy touched the water with his foot.

"Man, this waters col," he said.

"Ahm gonna put mah cloes back on," said Bobo, withdrawing his foot.

Big Boy grabbed him about the waist.

"Like hell yuh is!"

"Git outta the way, nigger!" Bobo yelled.

"Throw im in!" said Lester.

"Duck im!"

Bobo crouched, spread his legs, and braced himself against Big Boy's body. Locked in each other's arms, they tussled on the edge of the hole, neither able to throw the other.

"C mon, les me n yuh push em in."

"O.K."

Laughing, Lester and Buck gave the two locked bodies a running push. Big Boy and Bobo splashed, sending up silver spray in the sunlight. When Big Boy's head came up he yelled:

"Yuh bastard!"

"Tha wuz yo ma yuh pushed!" said Bobo, shaking his head to clear the water from his eyes.

They did a surface dive, came up and struck out across the creek. The muddy water foamed. They swam back, waded into shallow water, breathing heavily and blinking eyes.

"C mon in!"

"Man, the waters fine!"

Lester and Buck hesitated.

"Les wet em," Big Boy whispered to Bobo.

Before Lester and Buck could back away, they were dripping wet from handsful of scooped water.

"Hey, quit!"

"Gawddam, nigger; Tha waters col!"

"C mon in!" called Big Boy.

"We jus as waal go on in now," said Buck.

"Look n see ef anybodys comin."

Kneeling, they squinted among the trees.

"Ain nobody."

"C mon, les go."

They waded in slowly, pausing each few steps to catch their breath. A desperate water battle began. Closing eyes and backing away, they shunted water into one another's faces with the flat palms of hands.

"Hey, cut it out!"

"Yeah, Ahm bout drownin!"

They came together in water up to their navels, blowing and blinking. Big Boy ducked, upsetting Bobo.

"Look out, nigger!"

"Don holler so loud!"

"Yeah, they kin hear yo ol big mouth a mile erway."

"This waters too col fer me."

"Thas cause it rained yistiddy."

They swam across and back again.

"Ah wish we hada bigger place t swim in."

"The white folks got plenty swimmin pools n we ain got none."

"Ah useta swim in the ol Missippi when we lived in Vicksburg."

Big Boy put his head under the water and blew his breath. A sound came like that of a hippopotamus.

"C mon, les be hippos."

Each went to a corner of the creek and put his mouth just below the surface and blew like a hippopotamus. Tiring, they came and sat under the embankment.

"Look like Ah gotta chill."

"Me too."

"Les stay here n dry off."

"Jeeesus, Ahm col!"

They kept still in the sun, suppressing shivers. After some of the water had dried off their bodies they began to talk through clattering teeth.

"Whut would yuh do ef ol man Harveyd come erlong right now?"

"Run like hell!"

"Man, Ahd run so fas hed thinka black streaka lightnin shot pass im."

"But spose he hada gun?"

"Aw, nigger, shut up!"

They were silent. They ran their hands over wet, trembling legs, brushing water away. Then their eyes watched the sun sparkling on the restless creek.

Far away a train whistled.

"There goes number seven!"

"Headin fer up Noth!"

"Blazin it down the line!"

"Lawd, Ahm goin Noth some day."

"Me too, man."

"They say colored folks up Noth is got ekual rights."

They grew pensive. A black winged butterfly hovered at the water's edge. A bee droned. From somewhere came the sweet scent of honeysuckles. Dimly they could hear sparrows twittering in the woods. They rolled from side to side, letting sunshine dry their skins and warm their blood. They plucked blades of grass and chewed them.

"Oh!"

They looked up, their lips parting.

"Oh!"

A white woman, poised on the edge of the opposite embankment, stood directly in front of them, her hat in her hand and her hair lit by the sun.

"Its a woman!" whispered Big Boy in an underbreath. "A *white* woman!"

They stared, their hands instinctively covering their groins. Then they scrambled to their feet. The white woman backed slowly out of sight. They stood for a moment, looking at one another.

"Les git outta here!" Big Boy whispered.

"Wait till she goes erway."

"Les run, theyll ketch us here naked like this!"

"Mabbe theres a man wid her."

"C mon, les git our cloes," said Big Boy.

They waited a moment longer, listening.

"Whut t hell! Ahma git mah cloes," said Big Boy.

Grabbing at short tufts of grass, he climbed the embankment.

"Don run out there now!"

"C mon back, fool!"

Bobo hesitated. He looked at Big Boy, and then at Buck and Lester.

"Ahm goin wid Big Boy n git mah cloes," he said.

"Don run out there naked like tha, fool!" said Buck. "Yuh don know whos out there!"

Big Boy was climbing over the edge of the embankment.

"C mon," he whispered.

Bobo climbed after. Twenty-five feet away the woman stood. She had one hand over her mouth. Hanging by fingers, Buck and Lester peeped over the edge.

"C mon back; that womans scared," said Lester.

Big Boy stopped, puzzled. He looked at the woman. He looked at the bundle of clothes. Then he looked at Buck and Lester.

"C mon, les git our cloes!"

He made a step.

"Jim!" the woman screamed.

Big Boy stopped and looked around. His hands hung loosely at his sides. The woman, her eyes wide, her hand over her mouth, backed away to the tree where their clothes lay in a heap.

"Big Boy, come back here n wait till shes gone!"

Bobo ran to Big Boy's side.

"Les go home! Theyll ketch us here," he urged.

Big Boy's throat felt tight.

"Lady, we wanna git our cloes," he said.

Buck and Lester climbed the embankment and stood indecisively. Big Boy ran toward the tree.

"Jim!" the woman screamed. "Jim! Jim!"

Black and naked, Big Boy stopped three feet from her.

"We wanna git our cloes," he said again, his words coming mechanically.

He made a motion.

"You go away! You go away! I tell you, you go away!"

Big Boy stopped again, afraid. Bobo ran and snatched the clothes. Buck and Lester tried to grab theirs out of his hands.

"You go away! You go away! You go away!" the woman screamed.

"Les go!" said Bobo, running toward the woods.

CRACK!

Lester grunted, stiffened, and pitched forward. His forehead struck a toe of the woman's shoes.

Bobo stopped, clutching the clothes. Buck whirled. Big Boy stared at Lester, his lips moving.

"Hes gotta gun; hes gotta gun!" yelled Buck, running wildly.

CRACK!

Buck stopped at the edge of the embankment, his head jerked backward, his body arched stiffly to one side; he toppled headlong, sending up a shower of bright spray to the sunlight. The creek bubbled.

Big Boy and Bobo backed away, their eyes fastened fearfully on a white man who was running toward them. He had a rifle and wore an army officer's uniform. He ran to the woman's side and grabbed her hand.

"You hurt, Bertha, you hurt?"

She stared at him and did not answer.

The man turned quickly. His face was red. He raised the rifle and pointed it at Bobo. Bobo ran back, holding the clothes in front of his chest.

"Don shoot me, Mistah, don shoot me . . ."

Big Boy lunged for the rifle, grabbing the barrel.

"You black sonofabitch!"

Big Boy clung desperately.

"Let go, you black bastard!"

The barrel pointed skyward.

CRACK!

The white man, taller and heavier, flung Big Boy to the ground. Bobo dropped the clothes, ran up, and jumped onto the white man's back.

"You black sonsofbitches!"

The white man released the rifle, jerked Bobo to the ground, and began to batter the naked boy with his fists. Then Big Boy swung, striking the man in the mouth with the barrel. His teeth caved in, and he fell, dazed. Bobo was on his feet.

"C mon, Big Boy, les go!"

Breathing hard, the white man got up and faced Big Boy. His lips were trembling, his neck and chin wet with blood. He spoke quietly.

"Give me that gun, boy!"

Big Boy leveled the rifle and backed away.

The white man advanced.

"Boy, I say give me that gun!"

Bobo had the clothes in his arms.

"Run, Big Boy, run!"

The man came at Big Boy.

"Ahll kill yuh; Ahll kill yuh!" said Big Boy.

His fingers fumbled for the trigger.

The man stopped, blinked, spat blood. His eyes were bewildered. His face whitened. Suddenly, he lunged for the rifle, his hands outstretched.

CRACK!

He fell forward on his face.

"Jim!"

Big Boy and Bobo turned in surprise to look at the woman.

"Jim!" she screamed again, and fell weakly at the foot of the tree.

Big Boy dropped the rifle, his eyes wide. He looked around. Bobo was crying and clutching the clothes.

"Big Boy, Big Boy . . ."

Big Boy looked at the rifle, started to pick it up, but didn't. He seemed at a loss. He looked at Lester, then at the white man; his eyes followed a thin stream of blood that seeped to the ground.

"Yuh done killed im," mumbled Bobo.

"Les go home!"

Naked, they turned and ran toward the wood. When they reached the barbed-wire fence they stopped.

"Les git our cloes on," said Big Boy.

They slipped quickly into overalls. Bobo held Lester's and Buck's clothes.

"Whut we gonna do wid these?"

Big Boy stared. His hands twitched.

"Leave em."

They climbed the fence and ran through the woods. Vines and leaves switched their faces. Once Bobo tripped and fell.

"C mon!" said Big Boy.

Bobo started crying, blood streaming from his scratches.

"Ahm scared!"

"C mon! Don cry! We wanna git home fo they ketches us!"

"Ahm scared!" said Bobo again, his eyes full of tears.

Big Boy grabbed his hand and dragged him along.

"C mon!"

III

They stopped when they got to the end of the woods. They could see the open road leading home, home to ma and pa. But they hung back, afraid. The thick shadows cast from the trees were friendly and sheltering. But the wide glare of sun stretching out over the fields was pitiless. They crouched behind an old log.

"We gotta git home," said Big Boy.

"Theys gonna lynch us," said Bobo, half-questioningly.

Big Boy did not answer.

"Theys gonna lynch us," said Bobo again.

Big Boy shuddered.

"Hush!" he said. He did not want to think of it. He could not think of it; there was but one thought, and he clung to that one blindly. He had to get home, home to ma and pa.

Their heads jerked up. Their ears had caught the rhythmic jingle of a wagon. They fell to the ground and clung flat to the side of a log. Over the crest of the hill came the top of a hat. A white face. Then shoulders in a blue shirt. A wagon drawn by two horses pulled into full view.

Big Boy and Bobo held their breath, waiting. Their eyes followed the wagon till it was lost in dust around a bend of the road.

"We gotta git home," said Big Boy.

"Ahm scared," said Bobo.

"C mon! Les keep t the fields."

They ran till they came to the cornfields. Then they went slower, for last year's corn stubbles bruised their feet.

They came in sight of a brickyard.

"Wait a minute," gasped Big Boy.

They stopped.

"Ahm goin on t mah home n yuh better go on t yos."

Bobo's eyes grew round.

"Ahm scared!"

"Yuh better go on!"

"Lemme go wid yuh; theyll ketch me . . ."

"Ef yuh kin git home mabbe yo folks kin hep yuh t git erway."

Big Boy started off. Bobo grabbed him.

"Lemme go wid yuh!"

Big Boy shook free.

"Ef yuh stay here theys gonna lynch yuh!" he yelled, running.

After he had gone about twenty-five yards he turned and looked; Bobo was flying through the woods like the wind.

Big Boy slowed when he came to the railroad. He wondered if he ought to go through the streets or down the track. He decided on the tracks. He could dodge a train better than a mob.

He trotted along the ties, looking ahead and back. His cheek itched, and he felt it. His hand came away smeared with blood. He wiped it nervously on his overalls.

When he came to his back fence he heaved himself over. He landed among a flock of startled chickens. A bantam rooster tried to spur him. He slipped and fell in front of the kitchen steps, grunting heavily. The ground was slick with greasy dishwater.

Panting, he stumbled through the doorway.

"Lawd, Big Boy, whuts wrong wid yuh?"

His mother stood gaping in the middle of the floor. Big Boy flopped wordlessly onto a stool, almost toppling over. Pots simmered on the stove. The kitchen smelled of food cooking.

"Whuts the matter, Big Boy?"

Mutely, he looked at her. Then he burst into tears. She came and felt the scratches on his face.

"Whut happened t yuh, Big Boy? Somebody been botherin yuh?"

"They after me, Ma! They after me . . ."

"Who!"

"Ah . . . Ah . . . We . . ."

"Big Boy, whuts wrong wid yuh?"

"He killed Lester n Buck," he muttered simply.

"Killed!"

"Yessum."

"Lester n Buck!"

"Yessum, Ma!"

"How killed?"

"He shot em, Ma!"

"Lawd Gawd in Heaven, have mercy on us all! This is mo trouble, mo trouble," she moaned, wringing her hands.

"N Ah killed im, Ma . . ."

She stared, trying to understand.

"Whut happened, Big Boy?"

"We tried t git our cloes from the tree . . ."

"Whut tree?"

"We wuz swimmin, Ma. N the white woman. . ."

"*White* woman? . . ."

"Yessum. She wuz at the swimmin hole . . ."

"Lawd have mercy! Ah knowed yuh boys wuz gonna keep on till yuh got into somethin like this!"

She ran into the hall.

"Lucy!"

"Mam?"

"C mere!"

"Mam?"

"C mere, Ah say!"

"Whutcha wan, Ma? Ahm sewin."

"Chile, will yuh c mere like Ah ast yuh?"

Lucy came to the door holding an unfinished apron in her hands. When she saw Big Boy's face she looked wildly at her mother.

"Whuts the matter?"

"Wheres Pa?"

"He's out front, Ah reckon."

"Git im, quick!"

"Whuts the matter, Ma?"

"Go git yo Pa, Ah say!"

Lucy ran out. The mother sank into a chair, holding a dish rag. Suddenly, she sat up.

"Big Boy, Ah thought yuh wuz at school?"

Big Boy looked at the floor.

"How come yuh didnt go t school?"

"We went t the woods."

She sighed.

"Ah done done all Ah kin fer yuh, Big Boy. Only Gawd kin help yuh now."

"Ma, don let em git me; dont let em git me . . ."

His father came into the doorway. He stared at Big Boy, then at his wife.

"Whuts Big Boy inter now?" he asked sternly.

"Saul, Big Boys done gone n got inter trouble wid the white folks."

The old man's mouth dropped, and he looked from one to the other.

"Saul, we gotta git im erway from here."

"Open yo mouth n talk! Whut yuh been doin?" The old man gripped Big Boy's shoulders and peered at the scratches on his face.

"Me n Lester n Buck n Bobo wuz out on ol man Harveys place swimmin . . ."

"Saul, its a *white* woman!"

Big Boy winced. The old man compressed his lips and stared at his wife. Lucy gaped at her brother as though she had never seen him before.

"Whut happened? Can't yuh-all talk?" the old man thundered, with a certain helplessness in his voice.

"We wuz swimmin," Big Boy began, "n then a white woman comes up t the hole. We got up right erway t git our cloes sos we could git erway, n she started screamin. Our cloes wuz right by the tree where she wuz standin, n when we started t git em she jus screamed. We told her we wanted our cloes . . . Yuh see, Pa, she wuz standin right *by* our cloes; n when we went t git em she jus screamed . . . Bobo got the cloes, n then he shot Lester . . ."

"*Who* shot Lester?"

"The white man."

"Whut white man?"

"Ah dunno, Pa. He wuz a soljer, n he had a rifle."

"A soljer?"

"Yessuh."

"A *soljer?*"

"Yessuh, Pa. A soljer."

The old man frowned.

"N then whut yuh-all do?"

"Waal, Buck said, 'Hes gotta gun!' N we started runnin. N then he shot Buck, n he fell in the swimmin hole. We didn't see im no mo . . . He wuz close on us then. He looked at the white woman n then he started t shoot Bobo. Ah grabbed the gun, n we started fightin. Bobo jumped on his back. He started beatin Bobo. Then Ah hit im wid the gun. Then he started at me n Ah shot im. Then we run . . ."

"Who seen?"

"Nobody."

"Wheres Bobo?"

"He went home."

"Anybody run after yuh-all?"

"Nawsuh."

"Yuh see anybody?"

"Nawsuh. Nobody but a white man. But he didnt see us."

"How long fo yuh-all lef the swimmin hole?"

"Little while ergo."

The old man nervously brushed his hand across his eyes and walked to the door. His lips moved, but no words came.

"Saul, whut we gonna do?"

"Lucy," began the old man, "go t Brother Sanders n tell im Ah said c mere; n go t Brother Jenkins n tell im Ah said c mere; n go t Elder Peters n tell im Ah said c mere. N don say nothin t nobody but whut Ah tol yuh. N when yuh git thu come straight back. Now go!"

Lucy dropped her apron across the back of a chair and ran down the steps. The mother bent over, crying and praying. The old man walked slowly over to Big Boy.

"Big Boy?"

Big Boy swallowed.

"Ahm talkin t yuh!"

"Yessuh."

"How come yuh didnt go t school this mawnin?"

"We went t the woods."

"Didnt yo ma send yuh t school?"

"Yessuh."

"How come yuh didn't go?"

"We went t the woods."

"Don yuh know thas wrong?"

"Yessuh."

"How come yuh go?"

Big Boy looked at his fingers, knotted them, and squirmed in his seat.

"AHM TALKIN T YUH!"

His wife straghtened up and said reprovingly:

"Saul!"

The old man desisted, yanking nervously at the shoulder straps of his overalls.

"How long wuz the woman there?"

"Not long."

"Wuz she young?"

"Yessuh. Lika gal."

"Did yuh-all say anythin t her?"

"Nawsuh. We jus said we wanted our cloes."

"N what she say?"

"Nothin, Pa. She jus backed erway t the tree n screamed."

The old man stared, his lips trying to form a question.

"Big Boy, did yuh-all bother her?"

"Nawsuh, Pa. We didn't *touch* her."

"How long fo the white man come up?"

"Right erway."

"Whut he say?"

"Nothin. He jus cussed us."

Abruptly the old man left the kitchen.

"Ma, cant Ah go fo they ketches me?"

"Sauls doin whut he kin."

"Ma, Ma, Ah don wan em t ketch me . . ."

"Sauls doin whut he kin. Nobody but the good Lawd kin hep us now."

The old man came back with a shotgun and leaned it in a corner. Fascinatedly, Big Boy looked at it.

There was a knock at the front door.

"Liza, see whos there."

She went. They were silent, listening. They could hear her talking.

"Whos there?"

"Me."

"Who?"

"Me, Brother Sanders."

"C mon in. Sauls waitin fer yuh."

Sanders paused in the doorway, smiling.

"Yuh sent fer me, Brother Morrison?"

"Brother Sanders, wes in deep trouble here."

Sanders came all the way into the kitchen.

"Yeah?"

"Big Boy done gone n killed a white man."

Sanders stopped short, then came forward, his face thrust out, his mouth open. His lips moved several times before he could speak.

"A *white* man?"

"They gonna kill me; they gonna kill me!" Big Boy cried, running to the old man.

"Saul, cant we git im erway somewhere?"

"Here now, take it easy; take it easy," said Sanders, holding Big Boy's wrists.

"They gonna kill me; they gonna lynch me!"

Big Boy slipped to the floor. They lifted him to a stool. His mother held him closely, pressing his head to her bosom.

"Whut we gonna do?" asked Sanders.

"Ah done sent fer Brother Jenkins n Elder Peters."

Sanders leaned his shoulders against the wall. Then, as the full meaning of it all came to him, he exclaimed:

"Theys gonna git a mob! . . ." His voice broke off and his eyes fell on the shotgun.

Feet came pounding on the steps. They turned toward the door. Lucy ran in crying. Jenkins followed. The old man met him in the middle of the room, taking his hand.

"Wes in bad trouble here, Brother Jenkins. Big Boy's done gone n killed a white man. Yuh-alls gotta hep me . . ."

Jenkins looked hard at Big Boy.

"Elder Peters says hes comin," said Lucy.

"When all this happen?" asked Jenkins.

"Near bout a hour ergo, now," said the old man.

"Whut we gonna do?" asked Jenkins.

"Ah wanna wait till Elder Peters come," said the old man helplessly.

"But we gotta work fas ef we gonna do anythin," said Sanders. "Well git in trouble jus standin here like this."

Big Boy pulled away from his mother.

"Pa, lemme go now! Lemme go now!"

"Be still, Big Boy!"

"Where kin yuh go?"

"Ah could ketch a freight!"

"Thas *sho* death!" said Jenkins. "Theyll be watchin em all!"

"Kin yuh-all hep me wid some money?" the old man asked.

They shook their heads.

"Saul, whut kin we do? Big Boy cant stay here."

There was another knock at the door.

The old man backed stealthily to the shotgun.

"Lucy, go!"

Lucy looked at him, hesitating.

"Ah better go," said Jenkins.

It was Elder Peters. He came in hurriedly.

"Good evenin, everbody!"

"How yuh, Elder?"

"Good evenin."

"How yuh today?"

Peters looked around the crowded kitchen.

"Whuts the matter?"

"Elder, wes in deep trouble," began the old man. "Big Boy n some mo boys . . ."

". . . Lester n Buck n Bobo . . ."

". . . wuz over on ol man Harveys place swimmin . . ."

"N he don like us niggers *none,*" said Peters emphatically. He widened his legs and put his thumbs in the armholes of his vest.

". . . n some white woman . . ."

"Yeah?" said Peters, coming closer.

". . . comes erlong n the boys tries t git their cloes where they done lef em under a tree. Waal, she started screamin n all, see? Reckon she thought the boys wuz after her. Then a white man in a soljers suit shoots two of em . . ."

". . . Lester n Buck . . ."

"Huummm," said Peters. "Tha wuz ol man Harveys son."

"Harveys son?"

"Yuh mean the one tha wuz in the Army?"

"Yuh mean Jim?"

"Yeah," said Peters. "The papers said he wuz here fer a vacation from his regiment. N tha woman the boys saw wuz jes erbout his wife . . ."

They stared at Peters. Now that they knew what white person had been killed, their fears became definite.

"N whut else happened?"

"Big Boy shot the man . . ."

"Harveys *son?*"

"He had t, Elder. He wuz gonna shoot im ef he didnt . . ."

"Lawd!" said Peters. He looked around and put his hat back on.

"How long ergo wuz this?"

"Mighty near an hour, now, Ah reckon."

"Do the white folks know yit?"

"Don know, Elder."

"Yuh-all better git this boy outta here right now," said Peters. "Cause ef yuh don theres gonna be a lynchin . . ."

"Where kin Ah go, Elder?" Big Boy ran up to him.

They crowded around Peters. He stood with his legs wide apart, looking up at the ceiling.

"Mabbe we kin hide im in the church till he kin git erway," said Jenkins.

Peters' lips flexed.

"Naw, Brother, thall never do! Theyll git im there sho. N anyhow, ef they ketch im there itll ruin us all. We gotta git the boy outta town . . ."

Sanders went up to the old man.

"Lissen," he said in a whisper. "Mah son, Will, the one whut drives fer the Magnolia Express Comny, is taking a truck o goods t Chicawgo in the mawnin. If we kin hide Big Boy somewhere till then, we kin put im on the truck . . ."

"Pa, please, lemma go wid Will when he goes in the mawnin," Big Boy begged.

The old man stared at Sanders.

"Yuh reckon thas safe?"

"Its the only thing yuh *kin* do," said Peters.

"But where we gonna hide im till then?"

"Whut time yo boy leavin out in the mawnin?"

"At six."

They were quiet, thinking. The water kettle on the stove sang.

"Pa, Ah knows where Will passes erlong wid the truck out on Bullards Road. Ah kin hide in one of them ol kilns . . ."

"Where?"

"In one of them kilns we built . . ."

"But theyll git yuh there," wailed the mother.

"But there ain no place else fer im t go."

"Theres some holes big ernough fer me t git in n stay till Will comes erlong," said Big Boy. "Please, Pa, lemme go fo they ketches me . . ."

"Let im go!"

"Please, Pa . . ."

The old man breathed heavily.

"Lucy, git his things!"

"Saul, theyll git im out there!" wailed the mother, grabbing Big Boy.

Peters pulled her away.

"Sister Morrison, ef yuh don let im go n git erway from here hes gonna be caught shos theres a Gawd in Heaven!"

Lucy came running with Big Boy's shoes and pulled them on his feet. The old man thrust a battered hat on his head. The mother went to the stove and dumped the skillet of corn pone into her apron. She wrapped it, and unbuttoning Big Boy's overalls, pushed it into his bosom.

"Heres somethin fer yuh t eat; n pray, Big Boy, cause thas all anybody kin do now . . ."

Big Boy pulled to the door, his mother clinging to him.

"Let im go, Sister Morrison!"

"Run fas, Big Boy!"

Big Boy raced across the yard, scattering the chickens. He paused at the fence and hollered back:

"Tell Bobo where Ahm hidin n tell im t c mon!"

IV

He made for the railroad, running straight toward the sunset. He held his left hand tightly over his heart, holding the hot pone of corn bread there. At times he stumbled over the ties, for his shoes were tight and hurt his feet. His throat burned from thirst; he had had no water since noon.

He veered off the track and trotted over the crest of a hill, following Bullard's Road. His feet slipped and slid in the dust. He kept his eyes straight ahead, fearing every clump of shrubbery, every tree. He wished it were night. If he could only get to the kilns without meeting anyone. Suddenly a thought came to him like a blow. He recalled hearing the old folks tell tales of blood-hounds, and fear made him run slower. None of them had thought of that. Spose blood-houns wuz put on his trail? Lawd! Spose a whole pack of em, foamin n howlin, tore im t pieces? He went limp and his feet dragged. Yeah, thas whut they wuz gonna send after im, blood-houns! N then thered be no way fer im t dodge! Why hadnt Pa let im take tha shotgun? He stopped. He oughta go back n git tha shotgun. And then when the mob came he would take some with him.

In the distance he heard the approach of a train. It jarred him back to a sharp sense of danger. He ran again, his big shoes sopping up and down in the dust. He was tired and his lungs were bursting from running. He wet his lips, wanting water. As he turned from the road across a plowed field he heard the train roaring at his heels. He ran faster, gripped in terror.

He was nearly there now. He could see the black clay on the sloping hillside. Once inside a kiln he would be safe. For a little while, at least. He thought of the shotgun again. If he only had something! Someone to talk to . . . Thas right! Bobo! Bobod be wid im. Hed almost fergot Bobo. Bobod bringa gun; he knowed he would. N tergether they could kill the whole mob. Then in the mawning theyd git inter Will's truck n go far erway, t Chicawgo . . .

He slowed to a walk, looking back and ahead. A light wind skipped over the grass. A beetle lit on his cheek and he brushed it off. Behind the dark pines hung a red sun. Two bats flapped against that sun. He shivered, for he was growing cold; the sweat on his body was drying.

He stopped at the foot of the hill, trying to choose between two patches of black kilns high above him. He went to the left, for there lay the ones he, Bobo, Lester, and Buck had dug only last week. He looked around again; the landscape was bare. He climbed the embankment and stood before a row of black pits sinking four and five feet deep into the earth. He went to the largest and peered in. He stiffened when his ears caught the sound of a whir. He ran back a few steps and poised on his toes. Six foot of snake slid out of the pit and went into coil. Big Boy looked around wildly for a stick. He ran down the slope, peering into the grass. He stumbled over a tree limb. He picked it up and tested it by striking it against the ground.

Warily, he crept back up the slope, his stick poised. When about seven feet from the snake he stopped and waved the stick. The coil grew tighter, the whir sounded louder, and a flat head reared to strike. He went to the right, and the flat head followed him, the blue-black tongue darting forth; he went to the left, and the flat head followed him there too.

He stopped, teeth clenched. He had to kill this snake. Jus had t kill im! This wuz the safest pit on on the hillside. He waved the stick again, looking at the snake before, thinking of a mob behind. The flat head reared higher. With stick over shoulder, he jumped in, swinging. The stick sang through the air, catching the snake on the side of the head, sweeping him out of coil. There was a brown writhing mass. Then Big Boy was upon him, pounding blows home, one on top of the other. He fought viciously, his eyes red, his teeth bared in a snarl. He beat till the snake lay still; then he stomped it with his heel, grinding its head into the dirt.

He stopped, limp, wet. The corners of his lips were white with spittle. He spat and shuddered.

Cautiously, he went to the hole and peered. He longed for a match. He imagined whole nests of them in there waiting. He put the stick into the hole and waved it around. Stooping, he peered again. It mus be awright. He looked over the hillside, his eyes coming back to the dead snake. Then he got to his knees and backed slowly into the hole.

When inside he felt there must be snakes all about him, ready to strike. It seemed he could see and feel them there, waiting tensely in coil. In the dark he imagined long white fangs ready to sink into his neck, his side, his legs. He wanted to come out, but kept still. Shucks, he told himself, ef there wuz any snakes in here they sho woulda done bit me by now. Some of his fear left, and he relaxed.

With elbows on ground and chin on palms, he settled. The clay was cold to his knees and thighs, but his bosom was kept warm by the hot pone of corn bread. His thirst returned and he longed for a drink. He was hungry, too. But he did not want to eat the corn pone. Naw, not now. Mabbe after erwhile, after Bobo came. Then theyd both eat the corn pone.

The view from his hole was fringed by the long tufts of grass. He could see all the way to Bullard's Road, and even beyond. The wind was blowing, and in the east the first touch of dusk was rising. Every now and then a bird floated past, a spot of wheeling black printed against the sky. Big Boy sighed, shifted his weight, and chewed at a blade of grass. A wasp droned. He heard number nine, far away and mournful.

The train made him remember how they had dug these kilns on long hot summer days, how they had made boilers out of big tin cans, filled them with water, fixed stoppers for steam, cemented them in holes with wet clay, and built fires under them. He recalled how they had danced and yelled when a stopper blew out of a boiler, letting out a big spout of steam and a shrill whistle. There were times when they had the whole hillside blazing and smoking. Yeah, yuh see, Big Boy wuz Casey Jones n wuz speedin it down the gleamin rails of the Southern Pacific. Bobo had number

two on the Santa Fe. Buck wuz on the Illinoy Central. Lester the Nickel Plate. Lawd, how they shelved the wood in! The boiling water would almost jar the cans loose from the clay. More and more pineknots and dry leaves would be piled under the cans. Flames would grow so tall they would have to shield their eyes. Sweat would pour off their faces. Then, suddenly, a peg would shoot high into the air, and

Pssseeeezzzzzzzzzzzzzzzzzzzzzzzz . . .

Big Boy sighed and stretched out his arm, quenching the flames and scattering the smoke. Why didn't Bobo c mon? He looked over the fields; there was nothing but dying sunlight. His mind drifted back to the kilns. He remembered the day when Buck, jealous of his winning, had tried to smash his kiln. Yeah, that ol sonofabitch! Naw, Lawd! He didn't go t say tha! Whut wu he thinkin erbout? Cussin the dead! Yeah, po ol Buck wuz dead now. N Lester too. Yeah, it wuz awright fer Buck t smash his kiln. Sho. N he wished he hadnt socked ol Buck so hard tha day. He wuz sorry fer Buck now. N he sho wished he hadnt cussed po ol Bucks ma, neither. Tha wuz sinful! Mabbe Gawd would git im fer tha? But he didnt go t do it! Po Buck! Po Lester! Hed never treat anybody like tha ergin, never . . .

Dusk was slowly deepening. Somewhere, he could not tell exactly where, a cricket took up a fitful song. The air was growing soft and heavy. He looked over the fields, longing for Bobo . . .

He shifted his body to ease the cold damp of the ground, and thought back over the day. Yeah, hed been dam right erbout not wantin t go swimmin. N ef hed followed his right min hed neverve gone n got inter all this trouble. At first hed said naw. But shucks, somehow hed just went on wid the res. Yeah, he shoulda went on t school tha mawnin, like Ma told im t do. But, hell, who wouldn't git tireda school? T hell wid school! Tha wuz the big trouble, awways drivin a guy t school. He wouldnt be in all this trouble now ef it wuznt fer that Gawddam school! Impatiently, he took the grass out of his mouth and threw it away, demolishing the little red school house . . .

Yeah, ef they had all kept still n quiet when tha ol white woman showed-up, mabbe shedve went on off. But yuh never kin tell erbout these white folks. Mabbe she wouldntve went. Mabbe tha white man woulda killed all of em! All *fo* of em! Yeah, yuh never kin tell erbout white folks. Then, ergin, mabbe tha white woman woulda went on off n laffed. Yeah, mabbe tha white man woulda

said: *Yuh nigger bastards git t hell outta here!*
Yuh know Gawddam well yuh don berlong here!
N then they woulda grabbed their cloes n run
like all hell . . . He blinked the white man away.
Where wuz Bobo? Why didnt he hurry up n c
mon?

He jerked another blade and chewed. Yeah, ef
pa had only let im have tha shotgun! He could
stan off a whole mob wid a shotgun. He looked
at the ground as he turned a shotgun over in his
hands. Then he leveled it at an advancing white
man. *Boooom!* The man curled up. Another came.
He reloaded quickly, and let him have what the
other had got. He too curled up. Then another
came. He got the same medicine. Then the whole
mob swirled around him, and he blazed away,
getting as many as he could. They closed in; but,
by Gawd, he had done his part, hadnt he? N the
newspapersd say: NIGGER KILLS DOZEN OF
MOB BEFO LYNCHED! Er mabbe theyd say:
TRAPPED NIGGER SLAYS TWENTY BEFO
KILLED! He smiled a little. Tha wouldn't be so
bad, would it? Blinking the newspaper away, he
looked over the fields. Where wuz Bobo? Why
didnt he hurry up n c mon?

He shifted, trying to get a crick out of his legs.
Shucks, he wuz gittin tireda this. N it wuz almos
dark now. Yeah, there wuz a little bittie star way
over yonder in the eas. Mabbe tha white man
wuznt dead? Mabbe they wuznt even lookin fer
im? Mabbe he could go back home now? Naw,
better wait erwhile. Thad be bes. But, Lawd, ef he
only had some water! He could hardly swallow,
his throat was so dry. Gawddam them white folks!
Thas all they wuz good fer, t run a nigger down
lika rabbit! Yeah, they git yuh in a corner n then
they let yuh have it. A thousan of em! He shivered,
for the cold of the clay was chilling his bones.
Lawd, spose they found im here in this hole? N
wid nobody t hep im? . . . But ain no use in thinkin erbout tha; wait till trouble come fo yuh start
fightin it. But ef tha mob came one by one hed
wipe em all out. Clean up the whole bunch. He
caught one by the neck and choked him long and
hard, choked him till his tongue and eyes popped
out. Then he jumped upon his chest and stomped
him like he had stomped that snake. When he had
finished with one, another came. He choked him
too. Choked till he sank slowly to the ground,
gasping . . .

"Hoalo!"

Big Boy snatched his fingers from the white
man's neck and looked over the fields. He saw
nobody. Had someone spied him? He was sure
that somebody had hollered. His heart pounded.
But, shucks, nobody couldnt see im here in this
hole . . . But mabbe theyd seen im when he wuz
comin n had laid low n wuz now closin in on im!
Praps they wuz signalin fer the others? Yeah,
they wuz creepin up on im! Mabbe he oughta git
up n run . . . Oh! Mabbe tha wuz Bobo! Yeah,
Bobo! He oughta clim out n see ef Bobo wuz
lookin fer im . . . He stiffened.

"Hoalo!"

"Hoalo!"

"Wheres yuh?"

"Over here on Bullards Road!"

"C mon over!"

"Awright!"

He heard footsteps. Then voices came again,
low and far away this time.

"Seen anybody?"

"Naw. Yuh?"

"Naw."

"Yuh reckon they got erway?"

"Ah dunno. Its hard t tell."

"Gawddam them sonofabitchin niggers!"

"We oughta kill ever black bastard in this
country!"

"Waal, Jim got two of em, anyhow."

"But Bertha said there wuz *fo!*"

"Where in hell they hidin?"

"She said one of em wuz named Big Boy, or
somethin like tha."

"We went t his shack lookin fer im."

"Yeah?"

"But we didnt fin im."

"These niggers stick tergether; they don never
tell on each other."

"We looked all thu the shack n couldnt fin hide
ner hair of im. Then we drove the ol woman n
man out n set the shack on fire . . ."

"Jeesus! Ah wished Ah coulda been there!"

"Yuh shoulda heard the ol nigger woman
howl . . ."

"Hoalo!"

"C mon over!"

Big Boy eased to the edge and peeped. He saw
a white man with a gun slung over his shoulder
running down the slope. Wuz they gonna search
the hill? Lawd, there wuz no way fer im t git
erway now; he wuz caught! He shoulda knowed
theyd git im here. N he didnt hava thing, notta
thing t fight wid. Yeah, soon as the bloodhouns
came theyd fin im. Lawd, have mercy! Theyd
lynch im right here on the hill . . . Theyd git im

n tie im t a stake n burn im erlive! Lawd! Nobody but the good Lawd could hep im now, nobody . . .

He heard more feet running. He nestled deeper. His chest ached. Nobody but the good Lawd could hep now. They wuz crowdin all round im n when they hada big crowd theyd close in on im. Then itd be over . . . The good Lawd would have t hep im, cause nobody could hep im now, nobody . . .

And then he went numb when he remembered Bobo. Spose Bobod come now? Hed be caught sho! Both of em would be caught! Theyd make Bobo tell where he wuz! Bobo oughta not try to come now. Somebody oughta tell im . . . But there wuz nobody; there wuz no way . . .

He eased slowly back to the opening. There was a large group of men. More were coming. Many had guns. Some had coils of rope slung over shoulders.

"Ah tell yuh they still here, somewhere . . ."

"But we looked all over!"

"What t hell! Wouldnt do t let em git erway!"

"Naw. Ef they git erway notta woman in this town would be safe."

"Say, whuts tha yuh got?"

"Er pillar."

"Fer whut?"

"Feathers, fool!"

"Chris! Thisll be hot ef we kin ketch them niggers!"

"Ol Anderson said he wuz gonna bringa barrela tar!"

"Ah got some gasoline in mah car ef yuh need it."

Big Boy had no feelings now. He was waiting. He did not wonder if they were coming after him. He just waited. He did not wonder about Bobo. He rested his cheek against the cold clay, waiting.

A dog barked. He stiffened. It barked again. He balled himself into a knot at the bottom of the hole, waiting. Then he heard the patter of dog feet.

"Look!"

"Whuts he got?"

"Its a snake!"

"Yeah, the dogs foun a snake!"

"Gee, its a big one!"

"Shucks, Ah wish he could fin one of them sonofabitchin niggers!"

The voices sank to low murmurs. Then he heard number twelve, its bell tolling and whistle crying

as it slid along the rails. He flattened himself against the clay. Someone was singing:

" *We'll hang ever nigger t a sour apple tree . . .* "

When the song ended there was hard laughter. From the other side of the hill he heard the dog barking furiously. He listened. There was more than one dog now. There were many and they were barking their throats out.

"Hush, Ah hear them dogs!"

"When theys barkin like tha theys foun somethin!"

"Here they come over the hill!"

"WE GOT IM! WE GOT IM!"

There came a roar. Tha mus be Bobo; tha mus be Bobo . . . In spite of his fear, Big Boy looked. The road, and half of the hillside across the road, were covered with men. A few were at the top of the hill, stenciled against the sky. He could see dark forms moving up the slopes. They were yelling.

"By Gawd, we got im!"

"C mon!"

"Where is he?"

"Theyre bringin im over the hill!"

"Ah got a rope fer im!"

"Say, somebody go n git the others!"

"Where is he? Cant we see im, Mister?"

"They say Berthas comin, too."

"Jack! Jack! Don leave me! Ah wanna see im!"

"Theyre bringin im over the hill, sweetheart!"

"AH WANNA BE THE FIRS T PUT A ROPE ON THA BLACK BASTARDS NECK!"

"Les start the fire!"

"Heat the tar!"

"Ah got some chains t chain im."

"Bring im over this way!"

"Chris, Ah wished Ah hada drink . . ."

Big Boy saw men moving over the hill. Among them was a long dark spot. Tha mus be Bobo; tha mus be Bobo theys carryin . . . Theyll git im here. He oughta git up n run. He clamped his teeth and ran his hand across his forehead, bringing it away wet. He tried to swallow, but could not; his throat was dry.

They had started the song again:

" *We'll hang ever nigger t a sour apple tree . . .* "

There were women singing now. Their voices made the song round and full. Song waves rolled over the top of pine trees. The sky sagged low, heavy with clouds. Wind was rising. Sometimes cricket cries cut surprisingly across the mob song. A dog had gone to the utmost top of the hill. At each lull of the song his howl floated full into the night.

Big Boy shrank when he saw the first tall flame light the hillside. Would they see im here? Then he remembered you could not see into the dark if you were standing in the light. As flames leaped higher he saw two men rolling a barrel up the slope.

"Say, gimme a han here, will yuh?"

"Awright, heave!"

"C mon! Straight up! Git t the other end!"

"Ah got the feathers here in this pillar!"

"BRING SOME MO WOOD!"

Big Boy could see the barrel surrounded by flames. The mob fell back, forming a dark circle. Theyd fin im here! He had a wild impulse to climb out and fly across the hills. But his legs would not move. He stared hard, trying to find Bobo. His eyes played over a long dark spot near the fire. Fanned by wind, flames leaped higher. He jumped. That dark spot had moved. Lawd, thas Bobo; thas Bobo . . .

He smelt the scent of tar, faint at first, then stronger. The wind brought it full into his face, then blew it away. His eyes burned and he rubbed them with his knuckles. He sneezed.

"LES GIT SOURVINEERS!"

He saw the mob close in around the fire. Their faces were hard and sharp in the light of the flames. More men and women were coming over the hill. The long dark spot was smudged out.

"Everbody git back!"

"Look! Hes gotta finger!"

"C MON! GIT THE GALS BACK FROM THE FIRE!"

"Hes got one of his ears, see?"

"Whuts the matter!"

"A woman fell out! Fainted, Ah reckon . . ."

The stench of tar permeated the hillside. The sky was black and the wind was blowing hard.

"HURRY UP N BURN THE NIGGER FO IT RAINS!"

Big Boy saw the mob fall back, leaving a small knot of men about the fire. Then, for the first time, he had a full glimpse of Bobo. A black body flashed in the light. Bobo was struggling, twisting; they were binding his arms and legs.

When he saw them tilt the barrel he stiffened. A scream quivered. He knew the tar was on Bobo. The mob fell back. He saw a tar-drenched body glistening and turning.

"THE BASTARDS GOT IT!"

There was a sudden quiet. Then he shrank violently as the wind carried, like a flurry of snow, a widening spiral of white feathers into the night. The flames leaped tall as the trees. The scream came again. Big Boy trembled and looked. The mob was running down the slopes, leaving the fire clear. Then he saw a writhing white mass cradled in yellow flame, and heard screams, one on top of the other, each shriller and shorter than the last. The mob was quiet now, standing still, looking up the slopes at the writhing white mass gradually growing black, growing black in a cradle of yellow flame.

"PO ON MO GAS!"

"Gimme a lif, will yuh!"

Two men were struggling, carrying between them a heavy can. They set it down, tilted it, leaving it so that the gas would trickle down to the hollowed earth around the fire.

Big Boy slid back into the hole, his face buried in clay. He had no feelings now, no fears. He was numb, empty, as though all blood had been drawn from him. Then his muscles flexed taut when he heard a faint patter. A tiny stream of cold water seeped to his knees, making him push back to a drier spot. He looked up; rain was beating in the grass.

"Its rainin!"

"C mon, les git t town!"

". . . don worry, when the fire git thu wid im hell be gone . . ."

"Wait, Charles! Don leave me; its slippery here . . ."

"Ahll take some of yuh ladies back in mah car . . ."

Big Boy heard the dogs barking again, this time closer. Running feet pounded past. Cold water chilled his ankles. He could hear raindrops steadily hissing.

Now a dog was barking at the mouth of the hole, barking furiously, sensing a presence there. He balled himself into a knot and clung to the bottom, his knees and shins buried in water. The bark came louder. He heard paws scraping and felt the hot scent of dog breath on his face. Green eyes glowed and drew nearer as the barking, muffled by the closeness of the hole, beat upon his eardrums. Backing till his shoulders pressed against the clay, he held his breath. He pushed out his hands, his fingers stiff. The dog yawped louder, advancing, his bark rising sharp and thin. Big Boy rose to his knees, his hands before him.

Then he flattened out still more against the bottom, breathing lungsful of hot dog scent, breathing it slowly, hard, but evenly. The dog came closer, bringing hotter dog scent. Big Boy could go back no more. His knees were slipping and slopping in the water. He braced himself, ready. Then, he never exactly knew how—he never knew whether he had lunged or the dog had lunged—they were together, rolling in the water. The green eyes were beneath him, between his legs. Dognails bit into his arms. His knees slipped backward and he landed full on the dog; the dog's breath left in a heavy gasp. Instinctively, he fumbled for the throat as he felt the dog twisting between his knees. The dog snarled, long and low, as though gathering strength. Big Boy's hands traveled swiftly over the dog's back, groping for the throat. He felt dognails again and saw green eyes, but his fingers had found the throat. He choked, feeling his fingers sink; he choked, throwing back his head and stiffening his arms. He felt the dog's body heave, felt dognails digging into his loins. With strength flowing from fear, he closed his fingers, pushing his full weight on the dog's throat. The dog heaved again, and lay still . . . Big Boy heard the sound of his own breathing filling the hole, and heard shouts and footsteps above him going past.

For a long, long time he held the dog, held it long after the last footstep had died out, long after the rain had stopped.

V

Morning found him still on his knees in a puddle of rainwater, staring at the stiff body of a dog. As the air brightened he came to himself slowly. He held still for a long time, as though waking from a dream, as though trying to remember.

The chug of a truck came over the hill. He tried to crawl to the opening. His knees were stiff and a thousand needle-like pains shot from the bottom of his feet to the calves of his legs. Giddiness made his eyes blur. He pulled up and looked. Through brackish light he saw Will's truck standing some twenty-five yards away, the engine running. Will stood on the runningboard, looking over the slopes of the hill.

Big Boy scuffled out, falling weakly in the wet grass. He tried to call to Will, but his dry throat would make no sound. He tried again.

"Will!"

Will heard, answering:

"Big Boy, c mon!"

He tried to run, and fell. Will came, meeting him in the tall grass.

"C mon," Will said, catching his arm.

They struggled to the truck.

"Hurry up!" said Will, pushing him onto the runningboard.

Will pushed back a square trapdoor which swung above the back of the driver's seat. Big Boy pulled through, landing with a thud on the bottom. On hands and knees he looked around in the semi-darkness.

"Wheres Bobo?"

Big Boy stared.

"Wheres Bobo?"

"They got im."

"When?"

"Las night."

"The mob?"

Big Boy pointed in the direction of a charred sapling on the slope of the opposite hill. Will looked. The trapdoor fell. The engine purred, the gears whined, and the truck lurched forward over the muddy road, sending Big Boy on his side.

For a while he lay as he had fallen, on his side, too weak to move. As he felt the truck swing around a curve he straightened up and rested his back against a stack of wooden boxes. Slowly, he began to make out objects in the darkness. Through two long cracks fell thin blades of daylight. The floor was of smooth steel, and cold to his thighs. Splinters and bits of sawdust danced with the rumble of the truck. Each time they swung around a curve he was pulled over the floor; he grabbed at corners of boxes to steady himself. Once he heard the crow of a rooster. It made him think of home, of ma and pa. He thought he remembered hearing somewhere that the house had burned, but could not remember where . . . It all seemed unreal now.

He was tired. He dozed, swaying with the lurch. Then he jumped awake. The truck was running smoothly, on gravel. Far away he heard two short blasts from the Buckeye Lumber Mill. Unconsciously, the thought sang through his mind: Its six erclock . . .

The trapdoor swung in. Will spoke through a corner of his mouth.

"How yuh comin?"

"Awright."

"How they git Bobo?"

"He wuz comin over the hill."

"Whut they do?"

"They burnt im . . . Will, Ah wan some water; mah throats like fire . . ."

"Well git some when we pas a fillin station."

Big Boy leaned back and dozed. He jerked awake when the truck stopped. He heard Will get out. He wanted to peep through the trapdoor, but was afraid. For a moment, the wild fear he had known in the hole came back. Spose theyd search n fin im? He quieted when he heard Will's footstep on the runningboard. The trapdoor pushed in. Will's hat came through, dripping.

"Take it, quick!"

Big Boy grabbed, spilling water into his face.

The truck lurched. He drank. Hard cold lumps of brick rolled into his hot stomach. A dull pain made him bend over. His intestines seemed to be drawing into a tight knot. After a bit it eased, and he sat up, breathing softly.

The truck swerved. He blinked his eyes. The blades of daylight had turned brightly golden. The sun had risen.

The truck sped over the asphalt miles, sped northward, jolting him, shaking out of his bosom the crumbs of corn bread, making them dance with the splinters and sawdust in the golden blades of sunshine.

He turned on his side and slept.

Oratory and Essays

Marcus Garvey (1887–1940)

Probably no Black leader has moved so profoundly so many Black people during his own lifetime as did Marcus Garvey. Though most of his specific proposals and projects did not come to material fruition, he stimulated a revolution in Black consciousness more far-reaching in its implications than the mere financial success of the Black Star Line or the Negro Factories Corporation could possibly have been. "I shall teach the black man to see beauty in himself," Garvey declared, and millions learned the lesson.

Marcus Garvey was born on August 17, 1887, in the coastal town of St. Ann's Bay, Jamaica, the son of a sternly authoritarian father and a gentle mother. Lacking an extensive formal education, the elder Garvey was nevertheless a bookish man, and his son grew up with a deep respect for learning, attending local schools during childhood and later studying law briefly in London. At the age of fourteen, however, he was forced by lack of funds to interrupt his education and begin work as an apprentice printer. His background in this trade, first in St. Ann's Bay and then in Kingston, was to serve him well in his many journalistic ventures.

In 1907 the twenty-year-old Garvey participated as a leader in a printers' strike in Kingston that was broken and that resulted in his being blacklisted. This experience disillusioned him about the utility of established labor unions in the cause of the Black worker, but it confirmed his belief in the necessity of some kind of collective action. While working afterward in the government printing office in Kingston he edited a periodical called *Garvey's Watchman* and then turned his always abundant energies to the formation of a political group, the National Club, whose organ was pointedly named *Our Own*. Next the young Black nationalist journeyed to Costa Rica, where he worked as a timekeeper on a banana plantation and observed at first hand the ruthless exploitation of Black labor by the United Fruit Company. Further travels in Panama, Ecuador, Nicaragua, Honduras, Colombia, and Venezuela confirmed the bitter truth: everywhere Black workers were oppressed and exploited. His organizational and journalistic efforts in Central America had not been successful, but back in Jamaica Garvey continued to ponder the question of what could be done to alleviate the suffering of his brothers.

Parts of the answer were soon to be supplied by two of the most important influences on the development of Garvey's thought, Duse Mohammed Ali and Booker T. Washington. Traveling to London in 1912, Garvey met the former, a Black Egyptian from whom he learned much about the injustices inherent in the British colonial system. Even more importantly, Duse Mohammed Ali stimulated the young Jamaican's interest in all things African. While in London, Garvey also read Washington's *Up from Slavery,* which intensified his desire to become a racial leader: "I asked: 'Where is the black man's Government? Where is his King and his kingdom? Where is his President, his country, and his ambassador, his army, his navy, his men of big affairs?' I could not find them, and then I declared, 'I will help to make them.'" When he returned to Jamaica in the summer of 1914, he set about organizing the movement that was to consume his energies for the rest of his life and to grow into the largest expression of the Black nationalistic impulse of the era, the Universal Negro Improvement Association, which had the ultimate goal of "uniting all the Negro peoples of the world into one great body to establish a country and Government absolutely their own."

Garvey's initial efforts on behalf of the UNIA in Jamaica were so impeded by the mulatto caste, traditionally hostile to darker-skinned Blacks, that he decided to shift his scene of operations to the United States. Arriving in Harlem on March 23, 1916, Garvey stepped into a situation of restless ferment brought about by the war and the great migration of Southern Blacks to Northern cities. This situation was to prove ideal for his purposes. Traveling through the country observing racial conditions, talking to the "so-called Negro leaders" (as he sneeringly called them), discovering their dangerous alliance with white philanthropists, Garvey recognized clearly both the need and the opportunity for the magnetic leadership that he could provide. From the handful of West Indians who attended his first meetings in Harlem in 1917, his following grew by scores and then by hundreds and thousands, especially after the establishment early in 1918 of the New York UNIA newpaper, the *Negro World,* which was published weekly for the next sixteen years. By the summer of 1919, Garvey claimed for the UNIA thirty branches and two million members. Perhaps these figures are somewhat inflated, but the immense success of the first international convention of the organization in August 1920 made it clear to the most skeptical that Garvey's massive support was unprecedented in Black history.

For the next several years, however, Garvey and the UNIA suffered a series of debilitating reverses. The Black Star Line, Garvey's ambitious scheme to develop a fleet of merchant ships owned and operated by Blacks, was a victim of inexperience, mismanagement, undercapitalization, and heavy repair expenses. Thousands of Garveyites lost their small investments in this enterprise. Even more serious in the eyes of many Blacks was Garvey's flirtation with the Ku Klux Klan. Believing the Klan to represent overtly the racist attitudes held covertly by most white

Americans, he hoped to elicit Klan support for migration of Blacks to Africa. But Blacks who hoped to achieve their civil rights in the United States were horrified. Finally, the legal entanglements that plagued Garvey during most of his adult life culminated in his highly questionable conviction in a mail fraud case and his imprisonment for a five-year term beginning on February 8, 1925. This sentence was commuted after he had served almost three years, but he was immediately deported, ending in December 1927 the American phase of his career.

In his last thirteen years Garvey witnessed the decline and disintegration of the UNIA, despite his indefatigable attempts to recapture his earlier triumphs. After travels in the Caribbean and Central America, he visited England, France, Switzerland, and Canada. He made little real impact in the white countries, but his ringing oratory was as prophetic as ever: "Now we have started to speak, and I am only the forerunner of an awakened Africa that shall never go back to sleep." Back in Jamaica in 1929, he dedicated himself to political activity, protest against the poverty of the Black masses, and new journalistic endeavors (*Black Man* and *The New Jamaica*), but the hostility of the Jamaican establishment, both white and colored, was too great to be overcome. In 1935 Garvey moved to London and a life of lonely penury until his death in 1940.

During the thrust toward racial integration in the United States from the 1940's to the 1960's, the name of Marcus Garvey was seldom invoked. When he was mentioned, it was often in derision of his alleged megalomania, his ostentatious displays, his unrealized schemes of a return to Africa. But as the 1970's begin in a nationalistic mood, Black people can reassess Garvey for his permanent importance. Black pride, the unity of African peoples in and out of Africa, the beauty of Blackness, cooperative Black economic activity, the rejection of white religion, the understanding of white racism as a historical constant, distrust of white radicalism—all of these concepts and attitudes so prevalent today were pioneered by Marcus Garvey. As early as 1920 he formulated this definition of racial leadership: "The Uncle Tom nigger has got to go, and his place must be taken by the new leader of the Negro race. That man will not be a white man with a black heart, nor a black man with a white heart, but a black man with a black heart." More than any other racial leader before Malcolm X, Marcus Garvey fulfilled the terms of this definition.

An essential collection of Garvey's writings and speeches is *Philosophy and Opinions of Marcus Garvey* (1923 and 1926). The two original volumes, edited by his second wife Amy Jacques Garvey, were reprinted as a single volume in 1967 with an introduction by E. U. Essien-Udom and again in 1969 with a preface by H. R. Lynch. Much of Garvey's journalism and oratory is not easily available, but one important essay may be found in most college libraries: "The Negro's Greatest Enemy," *Current History*, XVIII (1923), 951–957.

A reliable scholarly biography is Edmund David Cronon's *Black Moses: The Story of Marcus Garvey and the Universal Negro*

Improvement Association (1955). Amy Jacques Garvey wrote *Garvey and Garveyism* (1963), reprinted recently with an introduction by John Henrik Clarke. Briefer accounts of the man and his movement may be found in Mary White Ovington, *Portraits in Color* (1927); James Weldon Johnson, *Black Manhattan* (1930); Claude McKay, *Harlem: Negro Metropolis* (1940); Roi Ottley, '*New World A-Coming*' (1943); Gunnar Myrdal, *An American Dilemma* (1944); Joel A. Rogers, *World's Great Men of Color,* Vol. II (1946); Arna Bontemps and Jack Conroy, *Anyplace But Here* (1966); Adolph Edwards, *Marcus Garvey, 1887–1940* (1967); Lerone Bennett, Jr., *Pioneers in Protest* (1968); and Robert H. Brisbane, *The Black Vanguard* (1970).

Speech Delivered at Liberty Hall N.Y.C. During Second International Convention of Negroes, August 1921

Four years ago, realizing the oppression and the hardships from which we suffered, we organized ourselves into an organization for the purpose of bettering our condition, and founding a government of our own. The four years of organization have brought good results, in that from an obscure, despised race we have grown into a mighty power, a mighty force whose influence is being felt throughout the length and breadth of the world. The Universal Negro Improvement Association existed but in name four years ago, today it is known as the greatest moving force among Negroes. We have accomplished this through unity of effort and unity of purpose, it is a fair demonstration of what we will be able to accomplish in the very near future, when the millions who are outside the pale of the Universal Negro Improvement Association will have linked themselves up with us.

By our success of the last four years we will be able to estimate the grander success of a free and redeemed Africa. In climbing the heights to where we are today, we have had to surmount difficulties, we have had to climb over obstacles, but the obstacles were stepping stones to the future greatness of this Cause we represent. Day by day we are writing a new history, recording new deeds of valor performed by this race of ours. It is true that the world has not yet valued us at our true worth but we are climbing up so fast and with such force that every day the world is chang-

ing its attitude towards us. Wheresoever you turn your eyes today you will find the moving influence of the Universal Negro Improvement Association among Negroes from all corners of the globe. We hear among Negroes the cry of "Africa for the Africans." This cry has become a positive, determined one. It is a cry that is raised simultaneously the world over because of the universal oppression that effects the Negro. You who are congregated here tonight as Delegates representing the hundreds of branches of the Universal Negro Improvement Association in different parts of the world will realize that we in New York are positive in this great desire of a free and redeemed Africa. We have established this Liberty Hall as the centre from which we send out the sparks of liberty to the four corners of the globe, and if you have caught the spark in your section, we want you to keep it a-burning for the great Cause we represent.

There is a mad rush among races everywhere towards national independence. Everywhere we hear the cry of liberty, of freedom, and a demand for democracy. In our corner of the world we are raising the cry for liberty, freedom and democracy. Men who have raised the cry for freedom and liberty in ages past have always made up their minds to die for the realization of the dream. We who are assembled in this Convention as Delegates representing the Negroes of the world give out the same spirit that the fathers of liberty in this country gave out over one hundred years ago. We give out a spirit that knows no compromise, a spirit that refuses to turn back, a spirit that says "Liberty or Death," and in prosecution of this great ideal—the ideal of a free and redeemed Africa, men may scorn, men may spurn us, and may say that we are on the wrong side of life, but let me tell you that way in which you are travelling is just the way all peoples who are free have travelled in the past. If you want liberty you yourselves must strike the blow. If you must be free you must become so through your own effort, through your own initiative. Those who have discouraged you in the past are those who have enslaved you for centuries and it is not expected that they will admit that you have a right to strike out at this late hour for freedom, liberty and democracy.

At no time in the history of the world, for the last five hundred years, was there ever a serious attempt made to free Negroes. We have been camouflaged into believing that we were made free by Abraham Lincoln. That we were made free by Victoria of England, but up to now we are still slaves, we are industrial slaves, we are social slaves, we are political slaves, and the new Negro desires a freedom that has no boundary, no limit. We desire a freedom that will lift us to the common standard of all men, whether they be white men of Europe or yellow men of Asia, therefore, in our desire to lift ourselves to that standard we shall stop at nothing until there is a free and redeemed Africa.

I understand that just at this time while we are endeavoring to create public opinion and public sentiment in favor of a free Africa, that others of our race are being subsidized to turn the attention of the world toward a different desire on the part of Negroes, but let me tell you that we who make up this Organization know no turning back, we have pledged ourselves even unto the last drop of our sacred blood that Africa must be free. The enemy may argue with you to show you the impossibility of a free and redeemed Africa, but I want you to take as your argument the thirteen colonies of America, that once owed their sovereignity to Great Britain, that sovereignity has been destroyed to make a United States of America. George Washington was not God Almighty. He was a man like any Negro in this building, and if he and his associates were able to make a free America, we too can make a free Africa. Hampden, Gladstone, Pitt and Disraeli were not the representatives of God in the person of Jesus Christ. They were but men, but in their time they worked for the expansion of the British Empire, and today they boast of a British Empire upon which "the sun never sets." As Pitt and Gladstone were able to work for the expansion of the British Empire, so you and I can work for the expansion of a great African Empire. Voltaire and Mirabeau were not Jesus Christs, they were but men like ourselves. They worked and overturned the French Monarchy. They worked for the Democracy which France now enjoys, and if they were able to do that, we are able to work for a democracy in Africa. Lenine and Trotzky were not Jesus Christs, but they were able to overthrow the despotism of Russia, and today they have given to the world a Social Republic, the first of its kind. If Lenine and Trotzky were able to do that for Russia, you and I can do that for Africa. Therefore, let no man, let no power on earth, turn you from this sacred cause of liberty. I prefer to die at this moment rather than not to work for the freedom of Africa. If liberty is good for certain sets of humanity it is good for all. Black men, Colored men, Negroes have as much right to be free as any other race that God Almighty ever created, and we desire freedom that is unfettered, freedom that is unlimited, freedom that will give us a chance and opportunity to rise to the fullest of our ambition and that we cannot get in countries where other men rule and dominate.

We have reached the time when every minute, every second must count for something done, something achieved in the cause of Africa. We need the freedom of Africa now, therefore, we desire the kind of leadership that will give it to us as quickly as possible. You will realize that not only individuals, but governments are using their influence against us. But what do we care about the unrighteous influence of any government? Our cause is based upon righteousness. And anything that is not righteous we have no respect for, because God Almighty is our leader and Jesus Christ our standard bearer. We rely on them for that kind of leadership that will make us free, for it is the same God who inspired the Psalmists to write "Princes shall come out of Egypt and Ethiopia shall stretch out her hands unto God." At this moment methinks I see Ethiopia stretching forth her hands unto God and methinks I see the Angel of God taking up the standard of the Red, the Black and the Green, and saying "Men of the Negro Race, Men of Ethiopia, follow me."

Tonight we are following. We are following 400,000,000 strong. We are following with a determination that we must be free before the wreck of matter, before the crash of worlds.

It falls to our lot to tear off the shackles that bind Mother Africa. Can you do it? You did it in the Revolutionary War. You did it in the Civil War; You did it at the Battles of the Marne and Verdun; You did it in Mesopotamia. You can do it marching up the battle heights of Africa. Let the world know that 400,000,000 Negroes are prepared to die or live as free men. Despise us as much as you care. Ignore us as much as you care. We are coming 400,000,000 strong. We are coming with our woes behind us, with the memory of suffering behind us—woes and suffering of three hundred years—they shall be our inspiration. My bulwark of strength in the conflict for freedom in Africa, will be the three hundred years of persecution and hardship left behind in this Western Hemisphere. The more I remember the suffering of my fore-fathers, the more I remember the lynchings and burnings in the Southern States of America, the more I will fight on even though the battle seems doubtful. Tell me that I must turn back, and I laugh you to scorn. Go on! Go on! Climb ye the heights of liberty and cease not in well doing until you have planted the banner of the Red, the Black and the Green on the hilltops of Africa.

Speech Delivered at Madison Square Garden, March 1924

In Honor of the Return to America of the Delegation Sent to Europe and Africa by the Universal Negro Improvement Association to Negotiate for the Repatriation of Negroes to a Homeland of Their Own in Africa

Fellow Citizens:

The coming together, all over this country, of fully six million people of Negro blood, to work for the creation of a nation of their own in their motherland, Africa, is no joke.

There is now a world revival of thought and action, which is causing peoples everywhere to bestir themselves towards their own security, through which we hear the cry of Ireland for the Irish, Palestine for the Jew, Egypt for the Egyptian, Asia for the Asiatic, and thus we Negroes raise the cry of Africa for the Africans, those at home and those abroad.

Some people are not disposed to give us credit for having feelings, passions, ambitions and desires like other races; they are satisfied to relegate us to the back-heap of human aspirations; but this is a mistake. The Almighty Creator made us men, not unlike others, but in his own image; hence, as a race, we feel that we, too, are entitled to the rights that are common to humanity.

The cry and desire for liberty is justifiable, and is made holy everywhere. It is sacred and holy to the Anglo-Saxon, Teuton and Latin; to the Anglo-American it precedes that of all religions, and now come the Irish, the Jew, the Egyptian, the Hindoo, and, last but not least, the Negro, clamoring for their share as well as their right to be free.

All men should be free—free to work out their own salvation. Free to create their own destinies. Free to nationally build up themselves for the upbringing and rearing of a culture and civilization of their own. Jewish culture is different from Irish culture. Anglo-Saxon culture is unlike Teutonic culture. Asiatic culture differs greatly from European culture; and, in the same way, the world should be liberal enough to allow the Negro latitude to develop a culture of his own. Why should the Negro be lost among the other races and nations of the world and to himself? Did nature not make of him a son of the soil? Did the Creator not fashion him out of the dust of the earth?—out of that rich soil to which he bears such a wonderful resemblance?—a resemblance that changes not, even though the ages have flown? No, the Ethiopian cannot change his skin; and so we appeal to the conscience of the white world to yield us a place of national freedom among the creatures of present-day temporal materialism.

We Negroes are not asking the white man to turn Europe and America over to us. We are not asking the Asiatic to turn Asia over for the accommodation of the blacks. But we are asking a just and righteous world to restore Africa to her scattered and abused children.

We believe in justice and human love. If our rights are to be respected, then, we, too, must respect the rights of all mankind; hence, we are ever ready and willing to yield to the white man the things that are his, and we feel that he, too, when his conscience is touched, will yield to us the things that are ours.

We should like to see a peaceful, prosperous and progressive white race in America and Europe; a peaceful, prosperous and progressive yellow race in Asia, and, in like manner, we want, and we demand, a peaceful, prosperous and progressive black race in Africa. Is that asking too much? Surely not. Humanity, without any immediate human hope of racial oneness, has drifted apart, and is now divided into separate and distinct groups, each with its own ideals and aspirations. Thus, we cannot expect any one race to hold a monopoly of creation and be able to keep the rest satisfied.

Distinct Racial Group Idealism

From our distinct racial group idealism we feel that no black man is good enough to govern the white man, and no white man good enough to rule the black man; and so of all races and peoples. No one feels that the other, alien in race, is good enough to govern or rule to the exclusion of native racial rights. We may as well, therefore, face the question of superior and inferior races. In twentieth century civilization there are no inferior and superior races. There are backward peoples, but that does not make them inferior. As far as humanity goes, all men are equal, and especially where peoples are intelligent enough to know what they want. At this time all peoples know what they want—it is liberty. When a people have sense enough to know that they ought to be free, then they naturally become the equal of all, in the higher calling of man to know and direct himself. It is true that economically and scientifically certain races are more progressive than others; but that does not imply superiority. For the Anglo-Saxon to say that he is superior because he introduced submarines to destroy life, or the Teuton because he compounded liquid gas to outdo in the art of killing,

and that the Negro is inferior because he is backward in that direction is to leave one's self open to the retort "Thou shalt not kill," as being the divine law that sets the moral standard of the real man. There is no superiority in the one race economically monopolizing and holding all that would tend to the sustenance of life, and thus cause unhappiness and distress to others; for our highest purpose should be to love and care for each other, and share with each other the things that our Heavenly Father has placed at our common disposal; and even in this, the African is unsurpassed, in that he feeds his brother and shares with him the product of the land. The idea of race superiority is questionable; nevertheless, we must admit that, from the white man's standard, he is far superior to the rest of us, but that kind of superiority is too inhuman and dangerous to be permanently helpful. Such a superiority was shared and indulged in by other races before, and even by our own, when we boasted of a wonderful civilization on the banks of the Nile, when others were still groping in darkness; but because of our unrighteousness it failed, as all such will. Civilization can only last when we have reached the point where we will be our brother's keeper. That is to say, when we feel it righteous to live and let live.

No Exclusive Right to the World

Let no black man feel that he has the exclusive right to the world, and other men none, and let no white man feel that way, either. The world is the property of all mankind, and each and every group is entitled to a portion. The black man now wants his, and in terms uncompromising he is asking for it.

The Universal Negro Improvement Association represents the hopes and aspirations of the awakened Negro. Our desire is for a place in the world; not to disturb the tranquillity of other men, but to lay down our burden and rest our weary backs and feet by the banks of the Niger, and sing our songs and chant our hymns to the God of Ethiopia. Yes, we want rest from the toil of centuries, rest of political freedom, rest of economic and industrial liberty, rest to be socially free and unmolested, rest from lynching and burning, rest from discrimination of all kinds.

Out of slavery we have come with our tears and

sorrows, and we now lay them at the feet of American white civilization. We cry to the considerate white people for help, because in their midst we can scarce help ourselves. We are strangers in a strange land. We cannot sing, we cannot play on our harps, for our hearts are sad. We are sad because of the tears of our mothers and the cry of our fathers. Have you not heard the plaintive wail? It is your father and my father burning at stake; but, thank God, there is a larger humanity growing among the good and considerate white people of this country, and they are going to help. They will help us to recover our souls.

As children of captivity we look forward to a new day and a new, yet ever old, land of our fathers, the land of refuge, the land of the Prophets, the land of the Saints, and the land of God's crowning glory. We shall gather together our children, our treasures and our loved ones, and, as the children of Israel, by the command of God, faced the promised land, so in time we shall also stretch forth our hands and bless our country.

Good and dear America that has succored us for three hundred years knows our story. We have watered her vegetation with our tears for two hundred and fifty years. We have built her cities and laid the foundations of her imperialism with the mortar of our blood and bones for three centuries, and now we cry to her for help. Help us, America, as we helped you. We helped you in the Revolutionary War. We helped you in the Civil War, and, although Lincoln helped us, the price is not half paid. We helped you in the Spanish-American War. We died nobly and courageously in Mexico, and did we not leave behind us on the stained battlefields of France and Flanders our rich blood to mark the poppies' bloom, and to bring back to you the glory of the flag that never touched the dust? We have no regrets in service to America for three hundred years, but we pray that America will help us for another fifty years until we have solved the troublesome problem that now confronts us. We know and realize that two ambitious and competitive races cannot live permanently side by side, without friction and trouble, and that is why the white race wants a white America and the black race wants and demands a black Africa.

Let white America help us for fifty years honestly, as we have helped her for three hundred

years, and before the expiration of many decades there shall be no more race problem. Help us to gradually go home, America. Help us as you have helped the Jews. Help us as you have helped the Irish. Help us as you have helped the Poles, Russians, Germans and Armenians.

The Universal Negro Improvement Association proposes a friendly co-operation with all honest movements seeking intelligently to solve the race problem. We are not seeking social equality; we do not seek intermarriage, nor do we hanker after the impossible. We want the right to have a country of our own, and there foster and re-establish a culture and civilization exclusively ours. Don't say it can't be done. The Pilgrims and colonists did it for America, and the new Negro, with sympathetic help, can do it for Africa.

Back to Africa

The thoughtful and industrious of our race want to go back to Africa, because we realize it will be our only hope of permanent existence. We cannot all go in a day or year, ten or twenty years. It will take time under the rule of modern economics, to entirely or largely depopulate a country of a people, who have been its residents for centuries, but we feel that, with proper help for fifty years, the problem can be solved. We do not want all the Negroes in Africa. Some are no good here, and naturally will be no good there. The no-good Negro will naturally die in fifty years. The Negro who is wrangling about and fighting for social equality will naturally pass away in fifty years, and yield his place to the progressive Negro who wants a society and country of his own.

Negroes are divided into two groups, the industrious and adventurous, and the lazy and dependent. The industrious and adventurous believe that whatsoever others have done it can do. The Universal Negro Improvement Association belongs to this group, and so you find us working, six million strong, to the goal of an independent nationality. Who will not help? Only the mean and despicable "who never to himself hath said, this is my own, my native land." Africa is the legitimate, moral and righteous home of all Negroes, and now, that the time is coming for all to assemble under their own vine and fig tree, we feel it our duty to arouse every Negro to a consciousness of himself.

White and black will learn to respect each other when they cease to be active competitors in the same countries for the same things in politics and society. Let them have countries of their own, wherein to aspire and climb without rancor. The races can be friendly and helpful to each other, but the laws of nature separate us to the extent of each and every one developing by itself.

We want an atmosphere all our own. We would like to govern and rule ourselves and not be encumbered and restrained. We feel now just as the white race would feel if they were governed and ruled by the Chinese. If we live in our own districts, let us rule and govern those districts. If we have a majority in our communities, let us run those communities. We form a majority in Africa and we should naturally govern ourselves there. No man can govern another's house as well as himself. Let us have fair play. Let us have justice. This is the appeal we make to white America.

Alain Locke (1886–1954)

As both catalyst and interpreter of Afro-American culture, Alain Leroy Locke has had few peers. With an intellectual versatility rivaling that of W. E. B. Du Bois or James Weldon Johnson, he was a literary and drama critic, philosopher, art and music historian, anthropologist, educator, and educational theorist. A cosmopolitan humanist, he supported the philosophical principles of cultural pluralism and value relativism, but no one labored more effectively in the role he described as "philosophical midwife to a generation of younger Negro poets, writers, artists. . . ."

Locke was born an only son in Philadelphia, a city to which he later imputed a "provincialism flavored by urbanity and [a] petty bourgeois psyche with the Tory slant. . . ." After preparatory work at Central High School and the Philadelphia School of Pedagogy, he entered Harvard University in 1904, graduating three years later with a highly distinguished record. From 1907 to 1910 he studied at Oxford as the first Black Rhodes Scholar. With an Oxonian B. Litt. he went on to the University of Berlin for another year of advanced work in philosophy, and he also attended lectures by Henri Bergson in Paris. His long association with Howard University began in 1912 with his appointment as "Assistant Professor of the Teaching of English and Instructor in Philosophy and Education." Back at Harvard in 1916–1917, he wrote a doctoral thesis on "The Problem of Classification in Theory of Value." From 1918 to his retirement in 1953 he was professor of philosophy at Howard, though he took leave from time to time for research and for lecturing in Haiti and at Fisk University, the University of Wisconsin, the New School for Social Research, City College of New York, and the Salzburg Seminar in American Studies.

On March 1, 1925, *The Survey* magazine issued a special number entitled "Harlem, Mecca of the New Negro," edited by Locke. Assembling his material under three headings—"The Greatest Negro Community in the World," "The Negro Expresses Himself," and "Black and White—

Studies in Race Contacts"—he included among his contributors such established figures as Du Bois, J. W. Johnson, and Kelly Miller; the young racial leaders Walter White, Charles S. Johnson, and Elise Johnson McDougald; a group of young writers consisting of McKay, Toomer, Cullen, Hughes, Rudolph Fisher, Angelina Grimké, and Anne Spencer; and such white writers as Melville J. Herskovits, Konrad Bercovici, and Albert C. Barnes. Enhanced by the striking drawings of Winold Reiss, the issue had a phenomenal success. Late in the same year Locke's *The New Negro* appeared. In this volume eleven of the essays (some with considerable revision), many of the poems, and one of the short stories were taken from *The Survey*, but Locke added much new material: seven short stories, several poems, a play, two folk tales, eleven more essays, and extensive bibliographies. Six essays that had appeared in *The Survey* were omitted. *The New Negro*, with its illustrations and designs by Reiss, Aaron Douglass, Walter Von Ruckteschell, and Miguel Covarrubias, was as visually striking as it was intellectually exciting. All in all a remarkable job of creative editing, the work provided a forum for some of the younger talent, brought a measure of cohesion to the Harlem Renaissance by bringing older and younger writers together, and announced to all the world that the New Negro had arrived. During the remainder of his life, Locke continued to stimulate through his writings and personal contacts the cultural ferment in Black America of which *The New Negro* is a major landmark.

Locke's own writings on Afro-American culture include *Plays of Negro Life* (1927, edited with Montgomery Gregory), *The Negro and His Music* (1936), *Negro Art: Past and Present* (1936), *The Negro in Art: A Pictorial Record of the Negro Artist and of the Negro Theme in Art* (1940), and *Le rôle du nègre dans la culture des Amériques* (1943). He did not live to complete the projected great synthesis of his studies of Black culture in America, but using his plan and his materials Margaret Just Butcher published *The Negro in American Culture* in 1956. One of Locke's most useful contributions, especially to the student of literature, was the brilliant series of annual comprehensive reviews of books on Black topics appearing in *Opportunity* and *Phylon* from the 1930's to the early 1950's.

Locke's important philosophical essay "Values and Imperatives," prefaced by a fascinating autobiographical sketch, appears in *American Philosophy Today and Tomorrow* (1935), edited by Horace M. Kallen and Sidney Hook. For Locke's philosophical position see also "Pluralism and Ideological Peace" in *Freedom and Experience* (1947), edited by Sidney Hook and Milton R. Konvitz.

Robert E. Martin's useful but incomplete "Bibliography of the Writings of Alain Leroy Locke" appears in *The New Negro Thirty Years Afterward* (1955), an important Howard University publication that also includes memoirs of Locke and studies of the Harlem Renaissance by some of his colleagues and friends. For additional commentary on Locke see the following: William Stanley Braithwaite, "Alain Locke's Relationship to the Negro in American Literature," *Phylon*, XVIII (1957), 166–173;

Eugene C. Holmes, "Alain Locke—Philosopher, Critic, Spokesman," *The Journal of Philosophy*, LIV (1957), 113–118, "Alain Leroy Locke: A Sketch," *Phylon*, XX (1959), 82–89, and "Alain Locke and the New Negro Movement," *Negro American Literature Forum*, II (1968), 60–68; Horace M. Kallen, "Alain Locke and Cultural Pluralism," *The Journal of Philosophy*, LIV (1957), 119–127; Gene Ulansky, "The Integrated Careers of Alain Locke, Philosopher of the New Negro," *The Negro History Bulletin*, XXVI (1963), 240–243; Robert Hayden, preface to the Atheneum edition of *The New Negro* (1968); and S. P. Fullinwider, *The Mind and Mood of Black America: 20th Century Thought* (1969).

The New Negro

In the last decade something beyond the watch and guard of statistics has happened in the life of the American Negro and the three norns who have traditionally presided over the Negro problem have a changeling in their laps. The Sociologist, the Philanthropist, the Race-leader are not unaware of the New Negro, but they are at a loss to account for him. He simply cannot be swathed in their formulæ. For the younger generation is vibrant with a new psychology; the new spirit is awake in the masses, and under the very eyes of the professional observers is transforming what has been a perennial problem into the progressive phases of contemporary Negro life.

Could such a metamorphosis have taken place as suddenly as it has appeared to? The answer is no; not only because the New Negro is not here, but because the Old Negro had long become more of a myth than a man. The Old Negro, we must remember, was a creature of moral debate and historical controversy. His has been a stock figure perpetuated as an historical fiction partly in innocent sentimentalism, partly in deliberate reactionism. The Negro himself has contributed his share to this through a sort of protective social mimicry forced upon him by the adverse circumstances of dependence. So for generations in the mind of America, the Negro has been more of a formula than a human being—a something to be argued about, condemned or defended, to be "kept down," or "in his place," or "helped up," to be worried with or worried over, harassed or patronized, a social bogey or a social burden. The thinking Negro even has been induced to share this same general attitude, to focus his attention on controversial issues, to see himself in the distorted perspective of a social problem. His shadow, so to speak, has been more real to him than his personality. Through having had to appeal from the unjust stereotypes of his oppressors and traducers to those of his liberators, friends and benefactors he has had to subscribe to the traditional positions from which his case has been viewed. Little true social or self-understanding has or could come from such a situation.

But while the minds of most of us, black and white, have thus burrowed in the trenches of the Civil War and Reconstruction, the actual march of development has simply flanked these positions, necessitating a sudden reorientation of view. We have not been watching in the right direction; set North and South on a sectional axis, we have not noticed the East till the sun has us blinking.

Recall how suddenly the Negro spirituals revealed themselves; suppressed for generations under the stereotypes of Wesleyan hymn harmony, secretive, half-ashamed, until the courage of being natural brought them out—and behold, there was folk-music. Similarly the mind of the Negro seems suddenly to have slipped from under the tyranny of social intimidation and to be shaking off the psychology of imitation and implied inferiority. By shedding the old chrysalis of the Negro problem we are achieving something like a spiritual emancipation. Until recently, lacking self-understanding, we have been almost as much of a problem to ourselves as we still are to others. But the decade that found us with a problem has left us with only a task. The multitude perhaps feels as yet only a strange relief and a new vague urge, but the thinking few know that in the reaction the vital inner grip of prejudice has been broken.

With this renewed self-respect and self-dependence, the life of the Negro community is bound to enter a new dynamic phase, the buoyancy from within compensating for whatever pressure there may be of conditions from without. The migrant masses, shifting from countryside to city, hurdle several generations of experience at a leap, but more important, the same thing happens spiritually in the life-attitudes and self-expression of the Young Negro, in his poetry, his art, his education and his new outlook, with the additional advantage, of course, of the poise and greater certainty of knowing what it is all about. From this comes the promise and warrant of a new leadership. As one of them has discerningly put it:

> We have tomorrow
> Bright before us
> Like a flame.
>
> Yesterday, a night-gone thing
> A sun-down name.
>
> And dawn today
> Broad arch above the road we came.
> We march!

This is what, even more than any "most creditable record of fifty years of freedom," requires that the Negro of to-day be seen through other than the dusty spectacles of past controversy. The day of "aunties," "uncles" and "mammies" is equally gone. Uncle Tom and Sambo have passed on, and even the "Colonel" and "George" play barnstorm rôles from which they escape with relief when the public spotlight is off. The popular melodrama has about played itself out, and it is time to scrap the fictions, garret the bogeys and settle down to a realistic facing of facts.

First we must observe some of the changes which since the traditional lines of opinion were drawn have rendered these quite obsolete. A main change has been, of course, that shifting of the Negro population which has made the Negro problem no longer exclusively or even predominantly Southern. Why should our minds remain sectionalized, when the problem itself no longer is? Then the trend of migration has not only been toward the North and the Central Midwest, but city-ward and to the great centers of industry—the problems of adjustment are new, practical, local and not peculiarly racial. Rather they are an integral part of the large industrial and social problems of our present-day democracy. And finally, with the Negro rapidly in process of class differentiation, if it ever was warrantable to regard and treat the Negro *en masse* it is becoming with every day less possible, more unjust and more ridiculous.

In the very process of being transplanted, the Negro is being transformed.

The tide of Negro migration, northward and city-ward, is not to be fully explained as a blind flood started by the demands of war industry coupled with the shutting off of foreign migration, or by the pressure of poor crops coupled with increased social terrorism in certain sections of the South and Southwest. Neither labor demand, the boll-weevil nor the Ku Klux Klan is a basic factor, however contributory any or all of them may have been. The wash and rush of this human tide on the beach line of the northern city centers is to be explained primarily in terms of a new vision of opportunity, of social and economic freedom, of a spirit to seize, even in the face of an extortionate and heavy toll, a chance for the improvement of conditions. With each successive wave of it, the movement of the Negro becomes more and more a mass movement toward the larger and the more democratic chance—in the Negro's case a deliberate flight not only from countryside to city, but from medieval America to modern.

Take Harlem as an instance of this. Here in Manhattan is not merely the largest Negro community in the world, but the first concentration in history of so many diverse elements of Negro life. It has attracted the African, the West Indian, the Negro American; has brought together the Negro of the North and the Negro of the South; the man from the city and the man from the town and village; the peasant, the student, the business man, the professional man, artist, poet, musician, adventurer and worker, preacher and criminal, exploiter and social outcast. Each group has come with its own separate motives and for it own special ends, but their greatest experience has been the finding of one another. Proscription and prejudice have thrown these dissimilar elements into a common area of contact and interaction. Within this area, race sympathy and unity have determined a further fusing of sentiment and experience. So what began in terms of segregation becomes more and more, as its elements mix and react, the laboratory of a great race-welding. Hitherto, it must be admitted that American Negroes have been a race more in name than in fact, or to be exact, more in sentiment than in experience. The chief bond between them has been that of a common condition rather than a common consciousness; a problem in common rather than a life in common. In Harlem, Negro life is seizing upon its first chances for group expression and self-determination. It is—or promises at least to be—a race capital. That is why our comparison is taken with those nascent centers of folk-expression and self-determination which are playing a creative part in the world to-day. Without pretense to their political significance, Harlem has the same rôle to play for the New Negro as Dublin has had for the New Ireland or Prague for the New Czechoslovakia.

Harlem, I grant you, isn't typical—but it is significant, it is prophetic. No sane observer, however sympathetic to the new trend, would contend that the great masses are articulate as yet, but they stir, they move, they are more than physically restless. The challenge of the new intellectuals among them is clear enough—the "race radicals" and realists who have broken with the old epoch of philanthropic guidance, sentimental appeal and protest. But are we after all only reading into the stirrings of a sleeping giant the dreams of an agitator? The answer is in the migrating peasant. It is the "man farthest down" who is most active in getting up. One of the most characteristic symptoms of this is the professional man, himself migrating to recapture his constituency after a vain effort to maintain in some Southern corner what for years back seemed an established living and clientele. The clergyman following his errant flock, the physician or lawyer trailing his clients, supply the true clues. In a real sense it is the rank and file who are leading, and the leaders who are following. A transformed and transforming psychology permeates the masses.

When the radical leaders of twenty years ago spoke of developing race-pride and stimulating race-consciousness, and of the desirability of race solidarity, they could not in any accurate degree have anticipated the abrupt feeling that has surged up and now pervades the awakened centers. Some of the recognized Negro leaders and a powerful section of white opinion identified with "race work" of the older order have indeed attempted to discount this feeling as a "passing phase," an attack of "race nerves" so to speak, an "aftermath of the war," and the like. It has not abated, however, if we are to gauge by the present tone and temper of the Negro press, or by the shift in popular support from the officially recognized and orthodox spokesmen to those of the independent, popular, and often radical type who are unmistakable symptoms of a new order. It is a social disservice to blunt the fact that the Negro of the Northern centers has reached a stage where tutelage, even of the most interested and well-intentioned sort, must give place to new relationships, where positive self-direction must be reckoned with in ever increasing measure. The American mind must reckon with a fundamentally changed Negro.

The Negro too, for his part, has idols of the tribe to smash. If on the one hand the white man has erred in making the Negro appear to be that which would excuse or extenuate his treatment of him, the Negro, in turn, has too often unnecessarily excused himself because of the way he has been treated. The intelligent Negro of to-day is resolved not to make discrimination an extenuation for his shortcomings in performance, individual or collective; he is trying to hold himself at par, neither inflated by sentimental allowances nor depreciated by current social discounts. For this he must know himself and be known for precisely what he is, and for that reason he welcomes the new scientific rather than the old sentimental interest. Sentimental interest in the Negro has ebbed. We used to lament this as the falling off of our friends; now we rejoice and pray to be delivered both from self-pity and condescension. The mind of each racial group has had a bitter weaning, apathy or hatred on one side matching disillusionment or resentment on the other; but they face each other to-day with the possibility at least of entirely new mutual attitudes.

It does not follow that if the Negro were better known, he would be better liked or better treated. But mutual understanding is basic for any subsequent coöperation and adjustment. The effort toward this will at least have the effect of remedying in large part what has been the most unsatisfactory feature of our present stage of race relationships in America, namely the fact that the more intelligent and representative elements of the two race groups have at so many points got quite out of vital touch with one another.

The fiction is that the life of the races is separate,

and increasingly so. The fact is that they have touched too closely at the unfavorable and too lightly at the favorable levels.

While inter-racial councils have sprung up in the South, drawing on forward elements of both races, in the Northern cities manual laborers may brush elbows in their everyday work, but the community and business leaders have experienced no such interplay or far too little of it. These segments must achieve contact or the race situation in America becomes desperate. Fortunately this is happening. There is a growing realization that in social effort the co-operative basis must supplant long-distance philanthropy, and that the only safeguard for mass relations in the future must be provided in the carefully maintained contacts of the enlightened minorities of both race groups. In the intellectual realm a renewed and keen curiosity is replacing the recent apathy; the Negro is being carefully studied, not just talked about and discussed. In art and letters, instead of being wholly caricatured, he is being being seriously portrayed and painted.

To all of this the New Negro is keenly responsive as an augury of a new democracy in American culture. He is contributing his share to the new social understanding. But the desire to be understood would never in itself have been sufficient to have opened so completely the protectively closed portals of the thinking Negro's mind. There is still too much possibility of being snubbed or patronized for that. It was rather the necessity for fuller, truer self-expression, the realization of the unwisdom of allowing social discrimination to segregate him mentally, and a counter-attitude to cramp and fetter his own living—and so the "spite-wall" that the intellectuals built over the "color-line" has happily been taken down. Much of this reopening of intellectual contacts has centered in New York and has been richly fruitful not merely in the enlarging of personal experience, but in the definite enrichment of American art and letters and in the clarifying of our common vision of the social tasks ahead.

The particular significance in the re-establishment of contact between the more advanced and representative classes is that it promises to offset some of the unfavorable reactions of the past, or at least to re-surface race contacts somewhat for the future. Subtly the conditions that are molding a New Negro are molding a new American attitude.

However, this new phase of things is delicate; it will call for less charity but more justice; less help, but infinitely closer understanding. This is indeed a critical stage of race relationships because of the likelihood, if the new temper is not understood, of engendering sharp group antagonism and a second crop of more calculated prejudice. In some quarters, it has already done so. Having weaned the Negro, public opinion cannot continue to paternalize. The Negro to-day is inevitably moving forward under the control largely of his own objectives. What are these objectives? Those of his outer life are happily already well and finally formulated, for they are none other than the ideals of American institutions and democracy. Those of his inner life are yet in process of formation, for the new psychology at present is more of a consensus of feeling than of opinion, of attitude rather than of program. Still some points seem to have crystallized.

Up to the present one may adequately describe the Negro's "inner objectives" as an attempt to repair a damaged group psychology and reshape a warped social perspective. Their realization has required a new mentality for the American Negro. And as it matures we begin to see its effects; at first, negative, iconoclastic, and then positive and constructive. In this new group psychology we note the lapse of sentimental appeal, then the development of a more positive self-respect and self-reliance; the repudiation of social dependence, and then the gradual recovery from hyper-sensitiveness and "touchy" nerves, the repudiation of the double standard of judgment with its special philanthropic allowances and then the sturdier desire for objective and scientific appraisal; and finally the rise from social disillusionment to race pride, from the sense of social debt to the responsibilities of social contribution, and of setting the necessary working and commonsense acceptance of restricted conditions, the belief in ultimate esteem and recognition. Therefore the Negro to-day wishes to be known for what he is, even in his faults and shortcomings, and scorns a craven and precarious survival at the price of seeming to be what he is not. He resents being spoken of as a social ward or minor, even by his own, and to being regarded a chronic patient for the sociological clinic, the sick man of American Democracy. For the same reasons, he himself is through with those social nostrums and panaceas, the so-called "solutions" of his "problem," with which he and the country have been so liberally dosed in the past. Religion, freedom, education, money—in turn, he has ardently hoped for and peculiarly trusted these things; he still believes in them, but not in blind trust that they alone will solve his life-problem.

Each generation, however, will have its creed, and that of the present is the belief in the efficacy of collective effort, in race co-operation. This deep feeling of race is at present the mainspring of Negro life. It seems to be the outcome of the reaction to proscription and prejudice; an attempt, fairly successful on the whole, to convert a defensive into an offensive position, a handicap into an incentive. It is radical in tone, but not in purpose and only the most stupid forms of opposition, misunderstanding or persecution could make it otherwise. Of course, the thinking Negro has shifted a little toward the left with the world-trend, and there is an increasing group who affiliate with radical and liberal movements. But fundamentally for the present the Negro is radical on race matters, conservative on others, in other words, a "forced radical," a social protestant rather than a genuine radical. Yet under further pressure and injustice iconoclastic thought and motives will inevitably increase. Harlem's quixotic radicalisms call for their ounce of democracy to-day lest to-morrow they be beyond cure.

The Negro mind reaches out as yet to nothing but American wants, American ideas. But this forced attempt to build his Americanism on race values is a unique social experiment, and its ultimate success is impossible except through the fullest sharing of American culture and institutions. There should be no delusion about this. American nerves in sections unstrung with race hysteria are often fed the opiate that the trend of Negro advance is wholly separatist, and that the effect of its operation will be to encyst the Negro as a benign foreign body in the body politic. This cannot be—even if it were desirable. The racialism of the Negro is no limitation or reservation with respect to American life; it is only a constructive effort to build the obstructions in the stream of his progress into an efficient dam of social energy and power. Democracy itself is obstructed and stagnated to the extent that any of its channels are closed. Indeed they cannot be selectively closed. So the choice is not between one way for the Negro and another way for the rest, but between American institutions frustrated on the one hand and American ideals progressively fulfilled and realized on the other.

There is, of course, a warrantably comfortable feeling in being on the right side of the country's professed ideals. We realize that we cannot be undone without America's undoing. It is within the gamut of this attitude that the thinking Negro faces America, but with variations of mood that are if anything more significant than the attitude itself. Sometimes we have it taken with the defiant ironic challenge of McKay:

> Mine is the future grinding down to-day
> Like a great landslip moving to the sea,
> Bearing its freight of débris far away
> Where the green hungry waters restlessly
> Heave mammoth pyramids, and break and roar
> Their eerie challenge to the crumbling shore.

Sometimes, perhaps more frequently as yet, it is taken in the fervent and almost filial appeal and counsel of Weldon Johnson's:

> O Southland, dear Southland!
> Then why do you still cling
> To an ideal age and a musty page,
> To a dead and useless thing?

But between defiance and appeal, midway almost between cynicism and hope, the prevailing mind stands in the mood of the same author's *To America*, an attitude of sober query and stoical challenge:

> How would you have us, as we are?
> Or sinking 'neath the load we bear,
> Our eyes fixed forward on a star,
> Or gazing empty at despair?
>
> Rising or falling? Men or things?
> With dragging pace or footsteps fleet?
> Strong, willing sinews in your wings,
> Or tightening chains about your feet?

More and more, however, an intelligent realization of the great discrepancy between the American social creed and the American social practice forces upon the Negro the taking of the moral advantage that is his. Only the steadying and sobering effect of a truly characteristic gentleness of spirit prevents the rapid rise of a definite cynicism and counter-hate and a defiant superiority feeling. Human as this reaction would be, the majority still deprecate its advent, and would gladly see it forestalled by the speedy amelioration of its causes. We wish our race pride to be a healthier, more positive achievement than a feeling based upon a realization of the shortcomings of others. But all paths toward the attainment of a sound social attitude have been difficult; only a relatively few enlightened minds have been able as the phrase puts it "to rise above" prejudice. The ordinary man has had until recently only a hard choice between the alternatives of supine and humiliating submission and stimulating but hurtful counter-prejudice. Fortunately from some inner, desperate resourcefulness has recently sprung up the simple expedient of fighting prejudice by mental passive resistance, in other words by trying to ignore it. For the few, this manna may perhaps be effective, but the masses cannot thrive upon it.

Fortunately there are constructive channels opening out into which the balked social feelings of the American Negro can flow freely.

Without them there would be much more pressure and danger than there is. These compensating interests are racial but in a new and enlarged way. One is the consciousness of acting as the advance-guard of the African peoples in their contact with Twentieth Century civilization; the other, the sense of a mission of rehabilitating the race in world esteem from that loss of prestige for which the fate and conditions of slavery have so largely been responsible. Harlem, as we shall see, is the center of both these movements; she is the home of the Negro's "Zionism." The pulse of the Negro world has begun to beat in Harlem. A Negro newspaper carrying news material in English, French and Spanish, gathered from all quarters of America, the West Indies and Africa has maintained itself in Harlem for over five years. Two important magazines, both edited from New York, maintain their news and circulation consistently on a cosmopolitan scale. Under American auspices and backing, three pan-African congresses have been held abroad for the discussion of common interests, colonial questions and the future cooperative development of Africa. In terms of the race question as a world problem, the Negro mind has leapt, so to speak, upon the parapets of prejudice and extended its cramped horizons. In so doing it has linked up with the growing group consciousness of the dark-peoples and is gradually learning their common interests. As one of our writers has recently put it: "It is imperative that we understand the white world in its relations to the non-white world." As with the Jew, persecution is making the Negro international.

As a world phenomenon this wider race consciousness is a different thing from the much asserted rising tide of color. Its inevitable causes are not of our making. The consequences are not necessarily damaging to the best interests of civilization. Whether it actually brings into being new Armadas of conflict or argosies of cultural exchange and enlightenment can only be decided by the attitude of the dominant races in an era of critical change. With the American Negro, his new internationalism is primarily an effort to recapture contact with the scattered peoples of African derivation. Garveyism may be a transient, if spectacular, phenomenon, but the possible rôle of the American Negro in the future development of Africa is one of the most constructive and universally helpful missions that any modern people can lay claim to.

Constructive participation in such causes cannot help giving the Negro valuable group incentives, as well as increased prestige at home and abroad. Our greatest rehabilitation may possibly come through such channels, but for the present, more immediate hope rests in the revaluation by white and black alike of the Negro in terms of his artistic endowments and cultural contributions, past and prospective. It must be increasingly recognized that the Negro has already made very substantial contributions, not only in his folk-art, music especially, which has always found appreciation, but in larger, though humbler and less acknowledged ways. For generations the Negro has been the peasant matrix of that section of America which has most undervalued him, and here he has contributed not only materially in labor and in social patience, but spiritually as well. The South has unconsciously absorbed the gift of his folk-temperament. In less than half a generation it will be easier to recognize this, but the fact remains that a leaven of humor, sentiment, imagination and tropic nonchalance has gone into the making of the South from a humble, unacknowledged source. A second crop of the Negro's gifts promises still more largely. He now becomes a conscious contributor and lays aside the status of a beneficiary and ward for that of a collaborator and participant in American civilization. The great social gain in this is the releasing of our talented group from the arid fields of controversy and debate to the productive fields of creative expression. The especially cultural recognition they win should in turn prove the key to that revaluation of the Negro which must precede or accompany any considerable further betterment of race relationships. But whatever the general effect, the present generation will have added the motives of self-expression and spiritual development to the old and still unfinished task of making material headway and progress. No one who understandingly faces the situation with its substantial accomplishment or views the new scene with its still more abundant promise can be entirely without hope. And certainly, if in our lifetime the Negro should not be able to celebrate his full initiation into American democracy, he can at least, on the warrant of these things, celebrate the attainment of a significant and satisfying new phase of group development, and with it a spiritual Coming of Age.

Walter White (1893–1955)

Like his predecessors and colleagues W. E. B. Du Bois and James Weldon Johnson, Walter White brought to his leadership role in the NAACP a broad culture as well as an unremitting and fearless dedication to racial justice. At the age of twelve he was already thoroughly familiar with the books on the family shelf—Shakespeare, Dickens, Thackeray, Trollope, and some of the Harvard Classics—supplemented by volumes borrowed from the library of the First Congregational Church of Atlanta, Georgia, of which his postman father was a devout member. Both moral rectitude and a respect for learning were inculcated in young Walter from early childhood through his undergraduate days at Atlanta University, from which he was graduated in 1916. His lifelong commitment to the struggle against racism was forged on the anvil of the terrifying Atlanta race riots of 1906, when he affirmed the Blackness of his identity despite his white skin, blue eyes, and blond hair. Though he would use his white appearance as a convenient disguise in service to the anti-racist cause (as recorded in the following essay), he never seemed confused in his own mind about who he was.

The young White's leadership in a fight to improve educational opportunities for Blacks in Atlanta brought him in 1917 to the attention of James Weldon Johnson, field secretary of the NAACP, who offered him the position of assistant secretary of the organization. In this capacity White served from 1918 to 1931, when he succeeded Johnson as chief executive officer, holding this position for most of the next quarter century. Thus for the better part of four decades he devoted himself to the work of the NAACP, at the risk of being lynched in the early days and in spite of recurrent cardiac seizures in the later years. He investigated forty-one lynchings and eight race riots, supported Pan-Africanism, lobbied tirelessly for antilynching legislation and other reforms, fought against racism in the defense industry and in the armed services during World War II, advised the American delegation at the founding of the United Nations, and lived to see the culmination of his efforts to desegregate public education in the Supreme Court decision of 1954. As racial leader, Walter White's period of influence was long, his energy inexhaustible, and his achievement impressive.

But he somehow found time to write. His first two books were novels, *Fire in the Flint* (1924) and *Flight* (1926). The former tells the story of a Black Georgian who returns home to practice after a medical education in the North. His doomed effort to improve health and economic conditions among his people brings him into conflict with the white establishment and ends in his death by lynching. *Flight* treats the theme of passing. The light-skinned New Orleans protagonist realizes finally that the sacrifices she must make in living as a white are greater than any rewards her false status can bring.

White's finest book, however, is *Rope and Faggot* (1929), the best nonfictional treatment of lynching ever written. No one else has personally reported as many lynchings as White, but the book is more than sensationalistic reportage. As the author later recalled, it is "a study of the complex influences—economic, political, religious, sexual— behind the gruesome, and too little understood, phenomenon. . . ." Other results of racism were explored in *A Rising Wind* (1945), concerning the treatment of Black soldiers in World War II as witnessed by White in the European and North African theaters; *A Man Called White* (1948), a masterly autobiography worthy of comparison with those of Douglass, Washington, Johnson, McKay, Hughes, Wright, Malcolm X, and Du Bois; and a final assessment of the American racial situation in *How Far the Promised Land?* (1955). Like so many other Black leaders and intellectuals, Walter White managed to reconcile the claims of action and thought by making them complementary.

In addition to his full-length works, White contributed two "Little Blue Books" to the Haldeman-Julius series: *The American Negro and His Problems* (1927) and *The Negro's Contribution to American Culture* (1928). Among his many valuable essays and articles, two may be singled out: "Negro Literature," in *American Writers on American Literature* (1931), edited by John A. Macy; and "Why I Remain a Negro," *The Saturday Review of Literature*, XXX (October 11, 1947), 13–14, 49–52.

For an informal account of most of White's years after his autobiography was written, see *A Gentle Knight: My Husband, Walter White* (1956) by Poppy Cannon, his second wife. Three interesting sketches are Mary White Ovington's in *Portraits in Color* (1927); Roy Wilkins' in *Rising Above Color* (1943), edited by Philip Henry Lotz; and Edwin R. Embree's in *13 Against the Odds* (1944). White's two novels are treated briefly in Benjamin Brawley, *The Negro Genius* (1937); Hugh M. Gloster, *Negro Voices in American Fiction* (1948); and Robert Bone, *The Negro Novel in America* (1958).

I Investigate Lynchings

Nothing contributes so much to the continued life of an investigator of lynchings and his tranquil possession of all his limbs as the obtuseness of the lynchers themselves. Like most boastful people who practice direct action when it involves no personal risk, they just can't help talk about their deeds to any person who manifests even the slightest interest in them.

Most lynchings take place in small towns and rural regions where the natives know practically nothing of what is going on outside their own immediate neighborhoods. Newspapers, books, magazines, theatres, visitors and other vehicles for the transmission of information and ideas are usually as strange among them as dry-point etchings. But those who live in so sterile an atmosphere usually esteem their own perspicacity in about the same degree as they are isolated from the world of ideas. They gabble on *ad infinitum,* apparently unable to keep from talking.

In any American village, North or South, East or West, there is no problem which cannot be solved in half an hour by the morons who lounge about the village store. World peace, or the lack of it, the tariff, sex, religion, the settlement of the war debts, short skirts, Prohibition, the carryings-on of the younger generation, the superior moral rectitude of country people over city dwellers (with a wistful eye on urban sins)—all these controversial subjects are disposed of quickly and finally by the bucolic wise men. When to their isolation is added an emotional fixation such as the rural South has on the Negro, one can sense the atmosphere from which spring the Heflins, the Ku Kluxers, the two-gun Bible-beaters, the lynchers and the anti-evolutionists. And one can see why no great amount of cleverness or courage is needed to acquire information in such a forlorn place about the latest lynching.

Professor Earle Fiske Young of the University of Southern California recently analyzed the lynching returns from fourteen Southern States for thirty years. He found that in counties of less than 10,000 people there was a lynching rate of 3.2 per 100,000 of population; that in those of from 10,000 to 20,000 the rate dropped to 2.4; that in those of from 20,000 to 30,000, it was 2.1 per cent; that in those of from 30,000 to 40,000, it was 1.7, and that thereafter it kept on going down until in counties with from 300,000 to 800,000 population it was only 0.05.

Of the forty-one lynchings and eight race riots I have investigated for the National Association for the Advancement of Colored People during the past ten years all of the lynchings and seven of the riots occurred in rural or semi-rural communities. The towns ranged in population from around one hundred to ten thousand or so. The lynchings were not difficult to inquire into because of the fact already noted that those who perpetrated them were in nearly every instance simple-minded and easily fooled individuals. On but three occasions were suspicions aroused by my too definite questions or by informers who had seen me in other places. These three times I found it rather desirable to disappear slightly in advance of reception committees imbued with the desire to make an addition to the lynching record. One other time the possession of a light skin and blue eyes (though I consider myself a colored man) almost cost me my life when (it was during the Chicago race riots in 1919) a Negro shot at me thinking me to be a white man.

II

In 1918 a Negro woman, about to give birth to a child, was lynched with almost unmentionable brutality along with ten men in Georgia. I reached the scene shortly after the butchery and while excitement yet ran high. It was a prosperous community. Forests of pine trees gave rich returns in turpentine, tar and pitch. The small towns where the farmers and turpentine hands traded were fat and rich. The main streets of the largest of these towns were well paved and lighted. The stores were well stocked. The white inhabitants belonged to the class of Georgia crackers—lanky, slow of movement and of speech, long-necked, with small eyes set close together, and skin tanned by the hot sun to a reddish-yellow hue.

As I was born in Georgia and spent twenty years of my life there, my accent is sufficiently Southern to enable me to talk with Southerners and not arouse their suspicion that I am an outsider. (In the rural South hatred of Yankees is not much less than hatred of Negroes.) On the morning of my arrival in the town I casually dropped into the store of one of the general merchants who, I had been informed, had been one of the leaders of the mob. After making a small purchase I engaged the merchant in conversation. There was, at the time, no other customer in the store. We spoke of the weather, the possibility of good crops in the Fall, the political situation, the latest news from the war in Europe. As his manner became more and more friendly I ventured to mention guardedly the recent lynchings.

Instantly he became cautious—until I hinted that I had great admiration for the manly spirit the men of the town had exhibited. I mentioned the newspaper accounts I had read and confessed that I had never been so fortunate as to see a lynching. My words or tone seemed to disarm his suspicions. He offered me a box on which to sit, drew up another one for himself, and gave me a bottle of Coca-Cola.

"You'll pardon me, Mister," he began, "for seeming suspicious but we have to be careful. In ordinary times we wouldn't have anything to worry about, but with the war there's been some talk of the Federal Government looking into lynchings. It seems there's some sort of law during wartime making it treason to lower the man power of the country."

"In that case I don't blame you for being careful," I assured him. "But couldn't the Federal government do something if it wanted to when a lynching takes place, even if no war is going on at the moment?"

"Naw," he said, confidently, obviously proud of the opportunity of displaying his store of information to one whom he assumed knew nothing whatsoever about the subject. "There's no such law, in spite of all the agitation by a lot of fools who don't know the niggers as we do. States' rights won't permit Congress to meddle in lynching in peace time."

"But what about your State government—your Governor, your sheriff, your police officers?"

"Humph! Them? We elected them to office didn't we? And the niggers, we've got them disfranchised, ain't we? Sheriffs and police and Governors and prosecuting attorneys have got too much sense to mix in lynching-bees. If they do they know they might as well give up all idea of running for office any more—if something worse don't happen to them—" This last with a tightening of the lips and a hard look in the eyes.

I sought to lead the conversation into less dangerous channels. "Who was the white man who was killed—whose killing caused the lynchings?" I asked.

"Oh, he was a hard one, all right. Never paid his debts to white men or niggers and wasn't liked much around here. He was a mean 'un all right, all right."

"Why, then, did you lynch the niggers for killing such a man?"

"It's a matter of safety—we gotta show niggers that they mustn't touch a white man, no matter how low-down and ornery he is."

Little by little he revealed the whole story. When he told of the manner in which the pregnant woman had been killed he chuckled and slapped his thigh and declared it to be "the best show, Mister, I ever did see. You ought to have heard the wench howl when we strung her up."

Covering the nausea the story caused me as best I could, I slowly gained the whole story, with the names of the other participants. Among them were prosperous farmers, business men, bankers, newspaper reporters and editors, and several law enforcement officers.

My several days of discreet inquiry began to arouse suspicions in the town. On the third day of my stay I went once more into the store of the man with whom I had first talked. He asked me to wait until he had finished serving the sole customer. When she had gone he came from behind the counter and with secretive manner and lowered voice he asked, "You're a government man, ain't you?" (An Agent of the Federal Department of Justice was what he meant.)

"Who said so?" I countered.

"Never mind who told me; I know one when I see him," he replied, with a shrewd harshness in his face and voice.

Ignorant of what might have taken place since last I talked with him, I thought it wise to learn all I could and say nothing which might commit me. "Don't you tell anyone I am a government man; if I *am* one, you're the only one in town who knows it," I told him cryptically. I knew that within an hour everybody in town would share his "information."

An hour or so later I went at nightfall to the little but not uncomfortable hotel where I was staying. As I was about to enter a Negro approached me and, with an air of great mystery, told me that he had just heard a group of white men discussing me and declaring that if I remained in the town overnight "something would happen" to me.

The thought raced through my mind before I replied that it was hardly likely that, following so terrible a series of lynchings, a Negro would voluntarily approach a supposedly white man whom he did not know and deliver such a message. He had been sent, and no doubt the persons who sent him were white and for some reason did not dare tackle me themselves. Had they dared there would have been no warning in advance—simply an attack. Though I had no weapon with me, it occurred to me that there was no reason why two should not play at the game of bluffing. I looked straight into my informant's eyes and said, in as convincing a tone as I could muster: "You go back to the ones who sent you and tell them this: that I have a damned good automatic and I know how to use it. If anybody attempts to molest me tonight or at any other time, somebody is going to get hurt."

That night I did not take off my clothes nor did I sleep. Ordinarily in such small Southern towns everyone is snoring by nine o'clock. That night, however, there was much passing and re-passing of the hotel. I learned afterward that the merchant had, as I expected, told generally that I was an agent of the Department of Justice, and my empty threat had served to reinforce his assertion. The Negro had been sent to me in the hope that I might be frightened enough to leave before I had secured evidence against the members of the mob. I remained in the town two more days. My every movement was watched, but I was not molested. But when, later, it became known that not only was I not an agent of the Department of Justice but a Negro, the fury of the inhabitants of the region was unlimited—particularly when it was found that evidence I gathered had been placed in the hands of the Governor of Georgia. It happened that he was a man genuinely eager to stop lynching—but restrictive laws against which he had appealed in vain effectively prevented him from acting upon the evidence. And the Federal government declared itself unable to proceed against the lynchers.

III

In 1926 I went to a Southern State for a New York newspaper to inquire into the lynching of two colored boys and a colored woman. Shortly after reaching the town I learned that a certain lawyer knew something about the lynchers. He proved to be the only specimen I have ever encountered in much travelling in the South of the Southern gentleman so beloved by fiction writers of the older school. He had heard of the lynching before it occurred and, fruitlessly, had warned the judge and the prosecutor. He talked frankly about the affair and gave me the names of certain men who knew more about it than he did. Several of them lived in a small town nearby where the only industry was a large cotton mill. When I asked him if he would go with me to call on these people he peered out of the window at the descending sun and said, somewhat anxiously, I thought, "I will go with you if you will promise to get back to town before sundown."

I asked why there was need of such haste. "No one would harm a respectable and well-known person like yourself, would they?" I asked him.

"Those mill hands out there would harm anybody," he answered.

I promised him we would be back before sundown—a promise that was not hard to make, for if they would harm this man I could imagine what they would do to a stranger!

When we reached the little mill town we passed through it and, ascending a steep hill, our car stopped in front of a house perched perilously on the side of the hill. In the yard stood a man with iron grey hair and eyes which seemed strong enough to bore through concrete. The old lawyer introduced me and we were invited into the house. As it was a cold afternoon in late Autumn the gray-haired man called a boy to build a fire.

I told him frankly I was seeking information about the lynching. He said nothing but left the room. Perhaps two minutes later, hearing a sound at the door through which he had gone, I looked up and there stood a figure clad in the full regalia of the Ku Klux Klan. I looked at the figure and the figure looked at me. The hood was then removed and, as I suspected, it was the owner of the house.

"I show you this," he told me, "so you will know that what I tell you is true."

This man, I learned, had been the organizer and kleagle of the local Klan. He had been quite honest in his activities as a Kluxer, for corrupt officials and widespread criminal activities had caused him and other local men to believe that the only cure rested in a secret extra-legal organization. But he had not long been engaged in promoting the plan before he had the experience of other believers in Klan methods. The very people whose misdeeds the organization was designed to correct gained control of it. This man then resigned and ever since had been living in fear of his life. He took me into an adjoining room after removing his Klan robe and there showed me a considerable collection of revolvers, shot guns, rifles and ammunition.

We then sat down and I listened to as hair-raising a tale of Nordic moral endeavor as it has ever been my lot to hear. Among the choice bits were stories such as this: The sheriff of an adjoining county the year before had been a candidate for reëlection. A certain man of considerable wealth had contributed largely to his campaign fund, providing the margin by which he was reëlected. Shortly afterwards a married woman with whom the sheriff's supporter had been intimate quarreled one night with her husband. When the cuckold charged his wife with infidelity, the gentle creature waited until he was asleep, got a large butcher knife, and then artistically carved him up. Bleeding more profusely than a pig in the stock yards, the man dragged himself to the home of a neighbor several hundred yards distant and there died on the door-step. The facts were notorious, but the sheriff effectively blocked even interrogation of the widow!

I spent some days in the region and found that the three Negroes who had been lynched were about as guilty of the murder of which they were charged as I was. Convicted in a court thronged with armed Klansmen and sentenced to death, their case had been appealed to the State Supreme Court, which promptly reversed the conviction, remanded the appellants for new trials, and severely criticized the judge before whom they had been tried. At the new trial the evidence against one of the defendants so clearly showed his innocence that the judge granted a motion to dismiss, and the other two defendants were obviously as little guilty as he. But as soon as the motion to dismiss was granted the defendant was rearrested on a trivial charge and once again lodged in jail. That night the mob took the prisoners to the outskirts of the town, told them to run, and as they set out pumped bullets into their backs. The two boys died instantly. The woman was shot in several places, but was not immediately killed. One of the lynchers afterwards laughingly told me that

"we had to waste fifty bullets on the wench before one of them stopped her howling."

Evidence in affidavit form indicated rather clearly that various law enforcement officials, including the sheriff, his deputies, various jailers and policemen, three relatives of the then Governor of the State, a member of the State Legislature and sundry individuals prominent in business, political and social life of the vicinity, were members of the mob.

The revelation of these findings after I had returned to New York did not add to my popularity in the lynching region. Public sentiment in the State itself, stirred up by several courageous newspapers, began to make it uncomfortable for the lynchers. When the sheriff found things getting a bit too unpleasant he announced that he was going to ask the grand jury to indict me for "bribery and passing for white." It developed that the person I was supposed to have paid money to for execution of an affidavit was a man I had never seen in the flesh, the affidavit having been secured by the reporter of a New York newspaper.

An amusing tale is connected with the charge of passing. Many years ago a bill was introduced in the Legislature of that State defining legally as a Negro any person who had one drop or more of Negro blood. Acrimonious debate in the lower house did not prevent passage of the measure, and the same result seemed likely in the State Senate. One of the Senators, a man destined eventually to go to the United States Senate on a campaign of vilification of the Negro, rose at a strategic point to speak on the bill. As the story goes, his climax was: "If you go on with this bill you will bathe every county in blood before nightfall. And, what's more, there won't be enough white people left in the State to pass it."

When the sheriff threatened me with an indictment for passing as white, a white man in the State with whom I had talked wrote me a long letter asking me if it were true that I had Negro blood. "You did not tell me nor anyone else in my presence," he wrote, "that you were white except as to your name. I had on amber-colored glasses and did not take the trouble to scrutinize your color, but I really did take you for a white man, and, according to the laws of——, you may be." My information urged me to sit down and figure out mathematically the exact percentage of Negro blood that I possessed and, if it proved to be less than one-eighth, to sue for libel those who had charged me with passing.

This man wrote of the frantic efforts of the whites of his State to keep themselves thought of as white. He quoted an old law to the effect that "it was not slander to call one a Negro because everybody could see that he was not: but it was slanderous to call him a mulatto."

IV

On another occasion a serious race riot occurred in Tulsa, Okla., a bustling town of 100,000 inhabitants. In the early days Tulsa had been a lifeless and unimportant village of not more than five thousand people, and its Negro residents had been forced to live in what was considered the least desirable section of the village, down near the railroad. Then oil was discovered nearby and almost overnight the village grew into a prosperous town. The Negroes prospered along with the whites, and began to erect comfortable homes, business establishments, a hotel, two cinemas and other enterprises, all of these springing up in the section to which they had been relegated. This was, as I have said, down near the railroad tracks. The swift growth of the town made this hitherto disregarded land of great value for business purposes. Efforts to purchase the land from the Negro owners at prices far below its value were unavailing. Having built up the neighborhood and knowing its value, the owners refused to be victimized.

One afternoon in 1921 a Negro messenger boy went to deliver a package in an office building on the main street of Tulsa. His errand done, he rang the bell for the elevator in order that he might descend. The operator, a young white girl, on finding that she had been summoned by a Negro, opened the door of the car ungraciously. Two versions there are of what happened then. The boy declared that she started the car on its downward plunge when he was only halfway in, and that to save himself from being killed he had to throw himself into the car, stepping on the girl's foot in doing so. The girl, on the other hand, asserted that the boy attempted to rape her in the elevator. The latter story, at best, seemed highly dubious—that an attempted criminal assault would be made by any person in an open elevator of a crowded office building on the main street of a town of 100,000 inhabitants—and in open day-light!

Whatever the truth, the local press, with scant investigation, published lurid accounts of the alleged assault. That night a mob started to the jail to lynch the Negro boy. A group of Negroes offered their services to the jailer and sheriff in protecting the prisoner. The offer was declined, and when the Negroes started to leave the sheriff's office a clash occurred between them and the mob. Instantly the mob swung into action.

The Negroes, outnumbered, were forced back to their own neighborhood. Rapidly the news spread of the clash and the numbers of mobbers grew hourly. By daybreak of the following day the mob numbered around five thousand, and was armed with machine-guns, dynamite, rifles, revolvers and shotguns, cans of gasoline and kerosene, and—such are the blessings of invention!—airplanes. Surrounding the Negro section, it attacked, led by men who had been officers in the American army in France. Outnumbered and out-equipped, the plight of the Negroes was a hopeless one from the beginning. Driven further and further back, many of them were killed or wounded, among them an aged man and his wife, who were slain as they knelt at prayer for deliverance. Forty-four blocks of property were burned after homes and stores had been pillaged.

I arrived in Tulsa while the excitement was at its peak. Within a few hours I met a commercial photographer who had worked for five years on a New York newspaper and he welcomed me with open arms when he found that I represented a New York paper. From him I learned that special deputy sheriffs were being sworn in to guard the town from a rumoured counter-attack by the Negroes. It occurred to me that I could get myself sworn in as one of these deputies.

It was even easier to do this than I had expected. That evening in the City Hall I had to answer only three questions—name, age, and address. I might have been a thug, a murderer, an escaped convict, a member of the mob itself which had laid waste a large area of the city—none of these mattered; my skin was apparently white, and that was enough. After we—some fifty or sixty of us—had been sworn in, solemnly declaring we would do our utmost to uphold the laws and constitutions of the United States and the State of Oklahoma, a villainous-looking man next me turned and remarked casually, even with a note of happiness in his voice: "Now you can go out and shoot any nigger you see and the law'll be behind you."

As we stood in the wide marble corridor of the not unimposing City Hall waiting to be assigned to automobiles which were to patrol the city during the night, I noticed a man, clad in the uniform of a captain of the United States Army, watching me closely. I imagined I saw in his very swarthy face (he was much darker than I, but was classed as a white man while I am deemed a Negro) mingled inquiry and hostility. I kept my eye on him without appearing to do so. Tulsa would not have been a very healthy place for me that night had my race or my previous investigations of other race riots been known there. At last the man seemed certain he knew me and started toward me.

He drew me aside into a deserted corner on the excuse that he had something he wished to ask me, and I noticed that four other men with whom he had been talking detached themselves from the crowd and followed us.

Without further introduction or apology my dark-skinned newly-made acquaintance, putting his face close to mine and looking into my eyes with a steely, unfriendly glance, demanded challengingly:

"You say that your name is White?"

I answered affirmatively.

"You say you're a newspaper man?"

"Yes, I represent the New York———. Would you care to see my credentials?"

"No, but I want to tell you something. There's an organization in the South that doesn't love niggers. It has branches everywhere. You needn't ask me the name—I can't tell you. But it has come back into existence to fight this damned nigger Advancement Association. We watch every movement of the officers of this nigger society and we're out to get them for putting notions of equality into the heads of our niggers down South here."

There could be no question that he referred to the Ku Klux Klan on the one hand and the National Association for the Advancement of Colored People on the other. As coolly as I could, the circumstances being what they were, I took a cigarette from my case and lighted it, trying to keep my hands from betraying my nervousness. When he finished speaking I asked him:

"All this is very interesting, but what, if anything, has it to do with the story of the race riot here which I've come to get?"

For a full minute we looked straight into each other's eyes, his four companions meanwhile crowding close about us. At length his eyes fell. With a shrug of his shoulders and a half-apologetic smile, he replied as he turned away, "Oh, nothing except I wanted you to know what's back of the trouble here."

It is hardly necessary to add that all that night, assigned to the same car with this man and his four companions, I maintained a considerable vigilance. When the news stories I wrote about the riot (the boy accused of attempted assault was acquitted in the magistrate's court after nearly one million dollars of property and a number of lives had been destroyed) revealed my identity— that I was a Negro and an officer of the Advancement Society—more than a hundred anonymous letters threatening my life came to me. I was also threatened with a suit for criminal libel by a local paper, but nothing came of it after my willingness to defend it was indicated.

V

A narrower escape came during an investigation of an alleged plot by Negroes in Arkansas to "massacre" all the white people of the State. It later developed that the Negroes had simply organized a co-operative society to combat their economic exploitations by landlords, merchants, and bankers, many of whom openly practiced peonage. I went as a representative of a Chicago newspaper to get the facts. Going first to the capital of the State, Little Rock, I interviewed the Governor and other officials and then proceeded to the scene of the trouble, Phillips county, in the heart of the cotton-raising area close to the Mississippi.

As I stepped from the train at Elaine, the county seat, I was closely watched by a crowd of men. Within half an hour of my arrival I had beeen asked by two shopkeepers, a restaurant waiter, and a ticket agent why I had come to Elaine, what my business was, and what I thought of the recent riot. The tension relaxed somewhat, when I implied I was in sympathy with the mob. Little by little suspicion was lessened and then, the people being eager to have a metropolitan newspaper give their side of the story, I was shown "evidence" that the story of the massacre plot was well-founded, and not very clever attempts were made to guide me away from the truth.

Suspicion was given new birth when I pressed

my inquiries too insistently concerning the share-cropping and tenant-farming system, which works somewhat as follows: Negro farmers enter into agreements to till specified plots of land, they to receive usually half of the crop for their labor. Should they be too poor to buy food, seed, clothing and other supplies, they are supplied these commodities by their landlords at designated stores. When the crop is gathered the landowner takes it and sells it. By declaring that he has sold it at a figure far below the market price and by refusing to give itemized accounts of the supplies purchased during the year by the tenant, a landlord can (and in that region almost always does) so arrange it that the bill for supplies always exceeds the tenant's share of the crop. Individual Negroes who had protested against such thievery had been lynched. The new organization was simply a union to secure relief through the courts, which relief those who profited from the system meant to prevent. Thus the story of a "massacre" plot.

Suspicion of me took definite form when word was sent to Phillips county from Little Rock that it had been discovered that I was a Negro, though I knew nothing about the message at the time. I walked down West Cherry street, the main thoroughfare of Elaine, one day on my way to the jail, where I had an appointment with the sheriff, who was going to permit me to interview some of the Negro prisoners who were charged with being implicated in the alleged plot. A tall, heavy-set Negro passed me and, *sotto voce,* told me as he passed that he had something important to tell me, and that I should turn to the right at the next corner and follow him. Some inner sense bade me obey. When we had got out of sight of other persons the Negro told me not to go to the jail, that there was great hostility in the town against me and that they planned harming me. In the man's manner there was something which made me certain he was telling the truth. Making my way to the railroad station, since my interview with the prisoners, (the sheriff and jailer being present), was unlikely to add anything to my story, I was able to board one of the two trains a day out of Elaine. When I explained to the conductor—he looked at me so inquiringly—that I had no ticket because delays in Elaine had given me no time to purchase one, he exclaimed, "Why, Mister, you're leaving just when the fun is going to start! There's a damned yaller nigger down here passing for white and the boys are going to have some fun with him."

I asked him the nature of the fun.

"Wal, when they get through with him," he explained grimly, "he won't pass for white no more."

Fiction

Rudolph Fisher (1897–1934)

One of the wittiest writers and talkers of the Harlem Renaissance, Rudolph Fisher during his brief life combined brilliantly literary and medical careers. The son of the Reverend John Wesley Fisher, he was born in Washington, D.C., but grew up in Providence, Rhode Island, where he attended Brown University. His undergraduate study, concentrating in English and biology, brought him membership in Phi Beta Kappa and other honors. After taking the A.B. in 1919 and the M.A. in 1920, he left Brown to return to his native Washington to enter the Howard University Medical School. After taking the M.D. degree with highest honors in 1924, he interned for a year at Freedmen's Hospital in Washington, then moved to New York for advanced biological research at Columbia University and specialization in roentgenology, working for a time in the X-ray division of the New York Department of Health.

Even as Fisher was pursuing his medical studies and contributing articles to scientific journals, he was also turning his hand to fiction. In the February 1925 issue of *The Atlantic Monthly* appeared "The City of Refuge," the first of several stories on the theme of the urban adjustment required of Southern Black migrants to Harlem. Other stories followed in *The Atlantic Monthly, McClure's, The Survey, Redbook, Junior Red Cross News, Metropolitan,* and *Story,* as well as *The Crisis, Opportunity,* and Black newspapers. He also wrote two novels, the satirical *The Walls of Jericho* (1928) and *The Conjure-Man Dies: A Mystery Tale of Dark Harlem* (1932), a detective story. The latter was dramatized and produced at the Lafayette Theatre in Harlem as *Conjur Man Dies* in 1936, more than a year after Fisher's death.

Unlike many of his colleagues of the Harlem Renaissance, Fisher was as much concerned with the ordinary man in the street as he was with the educated class or the inhabitants of the jazz world. All types of Blacks appear in *The Walls of Jericho,* from the poolroom habitué to the society ball snob, but most of Fisher's short stores concentrate on the folk. Often bewildered, exploited, and deceived, they nevertheless manage to survive and sometimes to triumph in their struggle with the city.

Fisher's fiction is discussed briefly in Benjamin Brawley, *The Negro Genius* (1937); Sterling Brown, *The Negro in American Fiction* (1937);

and Hugh M. Gloster, *Negro Voices in American Fiction* (1948). Doris E. Abramson examines *Conjur Man Dies* in *Negro Playwrights in the American Theatre 1925–1959* (1969). See also Waters E. Turpin's analysis of the short story "Miss Cynthie" in "Four Short Fiction Writers of the Harlem Renaissance—Their Legacy of Achievement," *CLA Journal*, XI (1967), 59–72, and William H. Robinson, Jr.'s helpful preface to the paperback edition of *The Walls of Jericho* (1969).

The City of Refuge

I

Confronted suddenly by daylight, King Solomon Gillis stood dazed and blinking. The railroad station, the long, white-walled corridor, the impassible slot machine, the terrifying subway train—he felt as if he had been caught up in the jaws of a steam-shovel, jammed together with other helpless lumps of dirt, swept blindly along for a time, and at last abruptly dumped.

There had been strange and terrible sounds: 'New York! Penn Terminal—all change!' 'Pohter, hyer, pohter, suh?' Shuffle of a thousand soles, clatter of a thousand heels, innumerable echoes. Cracking rifle-shots—no, snapping turnstiles. 'Put a nickel in!' 'Harlem? Sure. This side —next train.' Distant thunder, nearing. The screeching onslaught of the fiery hosts of hell, headlong, breath-taking. Car doors rattling, sliding, banging open. 'Say, wha' d'ye think this is, a baggage car?' Heat, oppression, suffocation—eternity—'Hundred 'n turdy-fif' next!' More turnstiles. Jonah emerging from the whale.

Clean air, blue sky, bright sunlight.

Gillis set down his tan-cardboard extension-case and wiped his black, shining brow. Then slowly, spreadingly, he grinned at what he saw: Negroes at every turn; up and down Lenox Avenue, up and down One Hundred and Thirty-Fifth Street; big, lanky Negroes, short, squat Negroes; black ones, brown ones, yellow ones; men standing idle on the curb, women, bundle-laden, trudging reluctantly homeward, children rattle-trapping about the sidewalks; here and there a white face drifted along, but Negroes predominantly, overwhelmingly everywhere. There was assuredly no doubt of his whereabouts. This was Negro Harlem.

Back in North Carolina Gillis had shot a white man and, with the aid of prayer and an automo-bile, probably escaped a lynching. Carefully avoiding the railroads, he had reached Washington in safety. For his car a Southwest bootlegger had given him a hundred dollars and directions to Harlem; and so he had come to Harlem.

Ever since a traveling preacher had first told him of the place, King Solomon Gillis had longed to come to Harlem. The Uggams were always talking about it; one of their boys had gone to France in the draft and, returning, had never got any nearer home than Harlem. And there were occasional 'colored' newspapers from New York: newspapers that mentioned Negroes without comment, but always spoke of a white person as 'So-and-so, white.' That was the point. In Harlem, black was white. You had rights that could not be denied you; you had privileges, protected by law. And you had money. Everybody in Harlem had money. It was a land of plenty. Why, had not Mouse Uggam sent back as much as fifty dollars at a time to his people in Waxhaw?

The shooting, therefore, simply catalyzed whatever sluggish mental reaction had been already directing King Solomon's fortunes toward Harlem. The land of plenty was more than that now: it was also the city of refuge.

Casting about for direction, the tall newcomer's glance caught inevitably on the most conspicuous thing in sight, a magnificent figure in blue that stood in the middle of the crossing and blew a whistle and waved great white-gloved hands. The Southern Negro's eyes opened wide; his mouth opened wider. If the inside of New York had mystified him, the outside was amazing him. For there stood a handsome, brass-buttoned giant directing the heaviest traffic Gillis had ever seen; halting unnumbered tons of automobiles and trucks and wagons and pushcarts and streetcars; holding them at bay with one hand while he swept similar tons peremptorily on with the other; ruling the wide crossing with supreme self-assurance; and he, too, was a Negro!

Yet most of the vehicles that leaped or crouched at his bidding carried white passengers. One of these overdrove bounds a few feet and Gillis heard the officer's shrill whistle and gruff reproof, saw the driver's face turn red and his car draw back like a threatened pup. It was beyond belief—impossible. Black might be white, but it couldn't be that white!

'Done died an' woke up in Heaven,' thought King Solomon, watching, fascinated; and after a while, as if the wonder of it were too great to believe simply by seeing, 'Cullud policemans!' he said, half aloud; then repeated over and over, with greater and greater conviction, 'Even got cullud policemans—even got cullud—'

'Where y' want to go, big boy?'

Gillis turned. A little, sharp-faced yellow man was addressing him.

'Saw you was a stranger. Thought maybe I could help y' out.'

King Solomon located and gratefully extended a slip of paper. 'Wha' dis hyeh at, please, suh?'

The other studied it a moment, pushing back his hat and scratching his head. The hat was a tall-crowned, unindented brown felt; the head was brown patent-leather, its glistening brush-back flawless save for a suspicious crimpiness near the clean-grazed edges.

'See that second corner? Turn to the left when you get there. Number forty-five's about halfway the block.'

'Thank y', suh.'

'You from—Massachusetts?'

'No, suh, Nawth Ca'lina.'

'Is 'at so? You look like a Northerner. Be with us long?'

'Til I die,' grinned the flattered King Solomon.

'Stoppin' there?'

'Reckon I is. Man in Washin'ton 'lowed I'd find lodgin' at dis ad-dress.'

'Good enough. If y' don't, maybe I can fix y' up. Harlem's pretty crowded. This is me.' He proffered a card.

'Thank y', suh,' said Gillis, and put the card in his pocket.

The little yellow man watched him plod flat-footedly on down the street, long awkward legs never quite straightened, shouldered extension-case bending him sidewise, wonder upon wonder halting or turning him about. Presently, as he proceeded, a pair of bright-green stockings caught and held his attention. Tony, the shop-keeper, was crossing the sidewalk with a bushel basket of apples. There was a collision; the apples rolled; Tony exploded; King Solomon apologized. The little yellow man laughed shortly, took out a notebook, and put down the address he had seen on King Solomon's slip of paper.

'Guess you're the shine I been waitin' for,' he surmised.

As Gillis, approaching his destination, stopped to rest, a haunting notion grew into an insistent idea. 'Dat li'l yaller nigger was a sho' 'nuff gen'man to show me de road. Seem lak I knowed him befo'—' He pondered. That receding brow, that sharp-ridged, spreading nose, that tight upper lip over the two big front teeth, that chinless jaw— He fumbled hurriedly for the card he had not looked at and eagerly made out the name.

'Mouse Uggam, sho' 'nuff! Well, dog-gone!'

II

Uggam sought out Tom Edwards, once a Pullman porter, now prosperous proprietor of a cabaret, and told him:—

'Chief, I got him: a baby jess in from the land o' cotton and so dumb he thinks ante bellum's an old woman.'

'Where'd you find him?'

'Where you find all the jay birds when they first hit Harlem—at the subway entrance. This one come up the stairs, batted his eyes once or twice, an' froze to the spot—with his mouth open. Sure sign he's from 'way down behind the sun an' ripe f' the pluckin'.'

Edwards grinned a gold-studded, fat-jowled grin. 'Gave him the usual line, I suppose?'

'Did n't miss. An' he fell like a ton o' bricks. 'Course I've got him spotted, but damn 'f I know jess how to switch em' on to him.'

'Get him a job around a store somewhere. Make out you're befriendin' him. Get his confidence.'

'Sounds good. Ought to be easy. He's from my state. Maybe I know him or some of his people.'

'Make out you do, anyhow. Then tell him some fairy tale that 'll switch your trade to him. The cops 'll follow the trade. We could even let Froggy flop into some dumb white cops hands and "confess" where he got it. See?'

'Chief, you got a head, no lie.'

'Don't lose no time. And remember, hereafter, it's better to sacrifice a little than to get squealed on. Never refuse a customer. Give him a little credit. Humor him along till you can get rid of him safe. You don't know what that guy that died may have said; you don't knows who 's on to you now. And if they get you—I don't know you.'

'They won't get *me*,' said Uggam.

King Solomon Gillis sat meditating in a room half the size of his hencoop back home, with a single window opening into an airshaft.

An airshaft: cabbage and chitterlings cooking; liver and onions sizzling, sputtering; three player-pianos out-plunking each other: a man and woman calling each other vile things; a sick, neglected baby wailing; a phonograph broadcasting blues; dishes clacking; a girl crying heartbrokenly; waste noises, waste odors of a score of families, seeking issue through a common channel; pollution from bottom to top—a sewer of sounds and smells.

Contemplating this, King Solomon grinned and breathed, 'Dog-gone!' A little later, still gazing into the sewer, he grinned again. 'Green stockin's,' he said; 'loud green!' The sewer gradually grew darker. A window lighted up opposite revealing a woman in camisole and petticoat, arranging her hair. King Solomon, staring vacantly, shook his head and grinned yet again. 'Even got cullud policemans!' he mumbled softly.

III

Uggam leaned out of the room's one window and spat maliciously into the dinginess of the airshaft. 'Damn glad you got him,' he commented, as Gillis finished his story. 'They 's a thousand shines in Harlem would change places with you in a minute jess f' the honor of killin' a cracker.'

'But I did n't go to do it. 'T was a accident.'

'That 's the only part to keep secret.'

'Know whut dey done? Dey killed five o' Mose Joplin's hawses 'fo he lef'. Put groun' glass in de feed-trough. Sam Cheevers come up on three of 'em one night pizenin' his well. Bleesom beat Crinshaw out o' sixty acres o' lan' an' a year's crops. Dass jess how 't is. Soon 's a nigger make a li'l sump'n he better git to leavin'. An' 'fo long ev'ybody's goin' be lef'!'

'Hope to hell they don't all come here.'

The doorbell of the apartment rang. A crescendo of footfalls in the hallway culminated in a sharp rap on Gillis's door. Gillis jumped. Nobody but a policeman would rap like that. Maybe the landlady had been listening and had called in the law. It came again, loud, quick, angry. King Solomon prayed that the policeman would be a Negro.

Uggam stepped over and opened the door. King Solomon's apprehensive eyes saw framed therein, instead of a gigantic officer, calling for him, a little blot of a creature, quite black against even the darkness of the hallway, except for a dirty wide-striped silk shirt, collarless, with the sleeves rolled up.

'Ah hahve bill fo' Mr. Gillis.' A high, strongly accented Jamaican voice, with its characteristic singsong intonation, interrupted King Solomon's sigh of relief.

'Bill? Bill fo' me? What kin' o' bill?'

'Wan bushel appels. T'ree seventy-fife.'

'Apples? I ain' bought no apples.' He took the paper and read aloud, laboriously, 'Antonio Gabrielli to K. S. Gillis, Doctor—'

'Mr. Gabrielli say, you not pays him, he send policemon.'

'What I had to do wid 'is apples?'

'You bumps into him yesterday, no? Scatter appels everywhere—on de sidewalk, in de gutter. Kids pick up an' run away. Others all spoil. So you pays.'

Gillis appealed to Uggam. 'How 'bout it, Mouse?'

'He 's a damn liar. Tony picked up most of 'em; I seen him. Lemme look at that bill—Tony never wrote this thing. This baby 's jess playin' you for a sucker.'

'Ain' had no apples, ain' payin' fo' none,' announced King Solomon, thus prompted. 'Did n't have to come to Harlem to git cheated. Plenty o' dat right wha' I come fum.'

But the West Indian warmly insisted. 'You cahn't do daht, mon. Whaht you t'ink, 'ey? Dis mon loose 'is appels an' 'is money too?'

'What diff'ence it make to you, nigger?'

'Who you call nigger, mon? Ah hahve you understahn'—'

'Oh, well, white folks, den. What all you got t' do wid dis hyeh, anyhow?'

'Mr. Gabrielli send me to collect bill!'

'How I know dat?'

'Do Ah not bring bill? You t'ink Ah steal t'ree dollar, 'ey?'

'Three dollars an' sebenty-fi' cent,' corrected Gillis. ''Nuther thing: wha' you ever see me befo'? How do you know dis is me?'

'Ah see you, sure. Ah help Mr. Gabrielli in de store. When you knocks down de baskette appels, Ah see. Ah follow you. Ah know you comes in dis house.'

'Oh, you does? An' how come you know my name an' flat an' room so good? How come dat?'

'Ah fin' out. Sometime Ah brings up here vegetables from de store.'

'Humph! Mus' be workin' on shares.'

'You pays, 'ey? You pays me or de policemon?'

'Wait a minute,' broke in Uggam, who had been thoughtfully contemplating the bill. 'Now listen, big shorty. You haul hips on back to Tony. We got your menu all right'—he waved the bill—'but we don't eat your kind o' cookin', see?'

The West Indian flared. 'Whaht it is to you, 'ey? You can not mind your own business? Ah hahve not spik to you!'

'No, brother. But this is my friend, an' I'll be john-browned if there's a monkey-chaser in Harlem can gyp him if I know it, see? Bes' thing f' you to do is catch air, toot sweet.'

Sensing frustration, the little islander demanded the bill back. Uggam figured he could use the bill himself, maybe. The West Indian hotly persisted; he even menaced. Uggam pocketed the paper and invited him to take it. Wisely enough, the caller preferred to catch air.

When he had gone, King Solomon sought words of thanks.

'Bottle it,' said Uggam. 'The point is this: I figger you got a job.'

'Job? No I ain't! Wha' at?'

'When you show Tony this bill, he'll hit the roof and fire that monk.'

'What ef he do?'

'Then you up 'n ask f' the job. He'll be too grateful to refuse. I know Tony some, an' I'll be there to put in a good word. See?'

King Solomon considered this. 'Sho' needs a job, but ain' after stealin' none.'

'Stealin'? 'T would n't be stealin'. Stealin''s what that damn monkey-chaser tried to do from you. This would be doin' Tony a favor an' gettin' y'self out o' the barrel. What's the hold-back?'

'What make you keep callin' him monkey-chaser?'

'West Indian. That's another thing. Any time

y' can knife a monk, do it. They's too damn many of 'em here. They're an achin' pain.'

'Jess de way white folks feels 'bout niggers.'

'Damn that. How' bout it? Y' want the job?'

'Hm—well—I'd ruther be a policeman.'

'Policeman?' Uggam gasped.

'M–hm. Dass all I wants to be, a policeman, so I can police all de white folks right plumb in jail!'

Uggam said seriously, 'Well, y' might work up to that. But it takes time. An' y've got to eat while y're waitin'.' He paused to let this penetrate. 'Now, how 'bout this job at Tony's in the meantime? I should think y'd jump at it.'

King Solomon was persuaded.

'Hm—well—reckon I does,' he said slowly.

'Now y're tootin'!' Uggam's two big front teeth popped out in a grin of genuine pleasure. 'Come on. Let's go.'

IV

Spitting blood and crying with rage, the West Indian scrambled to his feet. For a moment he stood in front of the store gesticulating furiously and jabbering shrill threats and unintelligible curses. Then abruptly he stopped and took himself off.

King Solomon Gillis, mildly puzzled, watched him from Tony's doorway. 'I jess give him a li'l shove,' he said to himself, 'an' he roll' clean 'cross de sidewalk.' And a little later, disgustedly, 'Monkey-chaser!' he grunted, and went back to his sweeping.

'Well, big boy, how y' comin' on?'

Gillis dropped his broom. 'Hay-o, Mouse. Wha' you been las' two-three days?'

'Oh, around. Gettin' on all right here? Had any trouble?'

'Deed I ain't—'ceptin' jess now I had to throw 'at li'l jigger out.'

'Who? The monk?'

'M–hm. He sho' Lawd doan like me in his job. Look like he think I stole it from him, stiddy him tryin' to steal from me. Had to push him down sho' 'nuff 'fo I could get rid of 'im. Den he run off talkin' Wes' Indi'man an' shakin' his fis' at me.'

'Ferget it.' Uggam glanced about. 'Where's Tony?'

'Boss man? He be back direckly.'

'Listen—like to make two or three bucks a day extra?'

'Huh?'

'Two or three dollars a day more 'n what you 're gettin' already?'

'Ain' I near 'nuff in jail now?'

'Listen.' King Solomon listened. Uggam had n't been in France for nothing. Fact was, in France he 'd learned about some valuable French medicine. He 'd brought some back with him,—little white pills,—and while in Harlem had found a certain druggist who knew what they were and could supply all he could use. Now there were any number of people who would buy and pay well for as much of this French medicine as Uggam could get. It was good for what ailed them, and they did n't know how to get it except through him. But he had no store in which to set up an agency and hence no single place where his customers could go to get what they wanted. If he had, he could sell three or four times as much as he did.

King Solomon was in a position to help him now, same as he had helped King Solomon. He would leave a dozen packages of the medicine—just small envelopes that could all be carried in a coat pocket—with King Solomon every day. Then he could simply send his customers to King Solomon at Tony's store. They 'd make some trifling purchase, slip him a certain coupon which Uggam had given them, and King Solomon would wrap the little envelope of medicine with their purchase. Must n't let Tony catch on, because he might object, and then the whole scheme would go gaflooey. Of course it would n't really be hurting Tony any. Would n't it increase the number of his customers?

Finally, at the end of each day, Uggam would meet King Solomon some place and give him a quarter for each coupon he held. There 'd be at least ten or twelve a day—two and a half or three dollars plumb extra! Eighteen or twenty dollars a week!

'Dog-gone!' breathed Gillis.

'Does Tony ever leave you heer alone?'

'M–hm. Jess started dis mawnin'. Doan nobody much come round 'tween ten 'an twelve, so he done took to doin' his buyin' right 'long 'bout dat time. Nobody hyeh but me fo' 'n hour or so.'

'Good. I'll try to get my folks to come 'round here mostly while Tony's out, see?'

'I doan miss.'

'Sure y' get the idea, now?' Uggam carefully explained it all again. By the time he had finished, King Solomon was wallowing in gratitude.

'Mouse, you sho' is been a friend to me. Why, 'f 't had n' been fo' you—'

'Bottle it,' said Uggam. 'I'll be round to your room to-night with enough stuff for to-morrer, see? Be sure 'n be there.'

'Won't be nowha' else.'

'An' remember, this is all jess between you n' me.'

'Nobody else but,' vowed King Solomon.

Uggam grinned to himself as he went on his way. 'Dumb Oscar! Wonder how much can we make before the cops nab him? French medicine —Hmph!'

V

Tony Gabrielli, an oblate Neapolitan of enormous equator, wabbled heavily out of his store and settled himself over a soap box.

Usually Tony enjoyed sitting out front thus in the evening, when his helper had gone home and his trade was slackest. He liked to watch the little Gabriellis playing over the sidewalk with the little Levys and Johnsons; the trios and quartettes of brightly dressed, dark-skinned girls merrily out for a stroll; the slovenly gaited, darker men, who eyed them up and down and commented to each other with an unsuppressed 'Hot damn!' or 'Oh no, now!'

But tonight Tony was troubled. Something was wrong in the store; something was different since the arrival of King Solomon Gillis. The new man had seemed to prove himself honest and trustworthy, it was true. Tony had tested him, as he always tested a new man, by apparently leaving him alone in charge for two or three mornings. As a matter of fact, the new man was never under more vigilant observation than during these two or three mornings. Tony's store was a modification of the front rooms of his flat and was in direct communication with it by way of a glass-windowed door in the rear. Tony always managed to get back into his flat via the side-street entrance and watch the new man through this unobtrusive glass-windowed door. If anything excited his suspicion, like unwarranted interest in the cash register, he walked unexpectedly out of this door to surprise the offender in the act. Thereafter he would have no more such trouble. But he had not succeeded in seeing King Solomon steal even an apple.

What he had observed, however, was that the

number of customers that came into the store during the morning's slack hour had pronouncedly increased in the last few days. Before, there had been three or four. Now there were twelve or fifteen. The mysterious thing about it was that their purchases totaled little more than those of the original three or four.

Yesterday and to-day Tony had elected to be in the store at the time when, on the other days, he had been out. But Gillis had not been overcharging or short-changing; for when Tony waited on the customers himself—strange faces all—he found that they bought something like a yeast cake or a five-cent loaf of bread. It was puzzling. Why should strangers leave their own neighborhoods and repeatedly come to him for a yeast cake or loaf of bread? They were not new neighbors. New neighbors would have bought more variously and extensively and at different times of day. Living near by, they would have come in, the men often in shirtsleeves and slippers, the women in kimonos, with boudoir caps covering their lumpy heads. They would have sent in strange children for things like yeast cakes and loaves of bread. And why did not some of them come in at night when the new helper was off duty?

As for accosting Gillis on suspicion, Tony was too wise for that. Patronage had a queer way of shifting itself in Harlem. You lost your temper and let slip a single ' *nègre*.' A week later you sold your business.

Spread over his soap box, with his pudgy hands clasped on his preposterous paunch, Tony sat and wondered. Two men came up, conspicuous for no other reason than that they were white. They displayed extreme nervousness, looking about as if afraid of being seen; and when one of them spoke to Tony it was in a husky, toneless, blowing voice, like the sound of a dirty phonograph record.

'Are you Antonio Gabrielli?'

'Yes, sure.' Strange behavior for such lusty-looking fellows. He who had spoken unsmilingly winked first one eye then the other, and indicated by a gesture of his head that they should enter the store. His companion looked cautiously up and down the Avenue, while Tony, wondering what ailed them, rolled to his feet and puffingly led the way.

Inside, the spokesman snuffled, gave his shoulders a queer little hunch, and asked, 'Can you fix us up, buddy?' The other glanced rest-

lessly about the place as if he were constantly hearing unaccountable noises.

Tony thought he understood clearly now. 'Booze, 'ey?' he smiled. 'Sorry—I no got.'

'Booze? Hell, no!' The voice dwindled to a throaty whisper. 'Dope. Coke, milk, dice—anything. Name your price. Got to have it.'

'Dope?' Tony was entirely at a loss. 'What 's a dis, dope?'

'Aw, lay off, brother. We 're in on this. Here.' He handed Tony a piece of paper. 'Froggy gave us a coupon. Come on. You can't go wrong.'

'I no got,' insisted the perplexed Tony; nor could he be budged on that point.

Quite suddenly the manner of both men changed. 'All right,' said the first angrily, in a voice as robust as his body. 'All right, you 're clever, You no got. Well, you will get. You 'll get twenty years!'

'Twenty year? Whadda you talk?'

'Wait a minute, Mac,' said the second caller. 'Maybe the wop 's on the level. Look here, Tony, we 're officers, see? Policemen.' He produced a badge. 'A couple of weeks ago a guy was brought in dying for the want of a shot, see? Dope—he needed some dope—like this—in his arm. See? Well, we tried to make him tell us where he 'd been getting it, but he was too weak. He croaked next day. Evidently he had n't had money enough to buy any more.

'Well, this morning a little nigger that goes by the name of Froggy was brought into the precinct pretty well doped up. When he finally came to, he swore he got the stuff here at your store. Of course, we 've just been trying to trick you into giving yourself away, but you don't bite. Now what's your game? Know anything about this?'

Tony understood. 'I dunno,' he said slowly; and then his own problem, whose contemplation his callers had interrupted, occurred to him. 'Sure!' he exclaimed. 'Wait. Maybeso I know somet'ing.'

'All right. Spill it.'

'I got a new man, work-a for me.' And he told them what he had noted since King Solomon Gillis came.

'Sounds interesting. Where is this guy?'

'Here in da store—all day.'

'Be here to-morrow?'

'Sure. All day.'

'All right. We 'll drop in to-morrow and give him the eye. Maybe he 's our man.'

'Sure. Come ten o'clock. I show you,' promised Tony.

VI

Even the oldest and rattiest cabarets in Harlem have sense of shame enough to hide themselves under the ground—for instance, Edwards's. To get into Edwards's you casually enter a dimly lighted corner saloon, apparently—only apparently—a subdued memory of brighter days. What was once the family entrance is now a side entrance for ladies. Supporting yourself against close walls, you crouchingly descend a narrow, twisted staircase until, with a final turn, you find yourself in a glaring, long, low basement. In a moment your eyes become accustomed to the haze of tobacco smoke. You see men and women seated at wire-legged, white-topped tables, which are covered with half-empty bottles and glasses; you trace the slow-jazz accompaniment you heard as you came down the stairs to a pianist, a cornetist, and a drummer on a little platform at the far end of the room. There is a cleared space from the foot of the stairs, where you are standing, to the platform where this orchestra is mounted, and in it a tall brown girl is swaying from side to side and rhythmically proclaiming that she has the world in a jug and the stopper in her hand. Behind a counter at your left sits a fat, bald, tea-colored Negro, and you wonder if this is Edwards—Edwards, who stands in with the police, with the political bosses, with the importers of wines and worse. A white-vested waiter hustles you to a seat and takes your order. The song's tempo changes to a quicker; the drum and the cornet rip out a fanfare, almost drowning the piano; the girl catches up her dress and begins to dance. . . .

Gillis's wondering eyes had been roaming about. They stopped.

'Look, Mouse!' he whispered. 'Look a-yonder!'

'Look at what?'

'Dog-gone if it ain' de self-same gal!'

'Wha' d' ye mean, self-same girl?'

'Over yonder, wi' de green stockin's. Dass de gal made me knock over dem apples fust day I come to town. 'Member? Been wishin' I could see her ev'y sence.'

'What for?' Uggam wondered.

King Solomon grew confidential. 'Ain' but two things in this world, Mouse, I really wants. One is to be a policeman. Been wantin' dat ev'y sence I seen dat cullud traffic-cop dat day. Other is to git myse'f a gal lak dat one over yonder!'

'You'll do it,' laughed Uggam, 'if you live long enough.'

'Who dat wid her?'

'How 'n hell do I know?'

'He cullud?'

'Don't look like it. Why? What of it?'

'Hm—nuthin'—'

'How many coupons y' got to-night?'

'Ten.' King Solomon handed them over.

'Y' ought to 've slipt 'em to me under the table, but it's all right now, long as we got this table to ourselves. Here's y' medicine for to-morrer.'

'Wha'?'

'Reach under the table.'

Gillis secured and pocketed the medicine.

'An' here's two-fifty for a good day's work.' Uggam passed the money over. Perhaps he grew careless; certainly the passing this time was above the table, in plain sight.

'Thanks, Mouse.'

Two white men had been watching Gillis and Uggam from a table near by. In the tumult of merriment that rewarded the entertainer's most recent and daring effort, one of these men, with a word to the other, came over and took the vacant chair beside Gillis.

'Is your name Gillis?'

''T ain' nuthin' else.'

Uggam's eyes narrowed.

The white man showed King Solomon a police officer's badge.

'You're wanted for dope-peddling. Will you come along without trouble?'

'Fo' what?'

'Violation of the narcotic law—dope-selling.'

'Who—me?'

'Come on, now, lay off that stuff. I saw what happened just now myself.' He addressed Uggam. 'Do you know this fellow?'

'Nope. Never saw him before to-night.'

'Did n't I just see him sell you something?'

'Guess you did. We happened to be sittin' here at the same table and got to talkin'. After a while I says I can't seem to sleep nights, so he offers me sump'n he says 'll make me sleep, all right. I don't know what it is, but he says he uses it himself an' I offers to pay him what it cost him.

That's how I come to take it. Guess he's got more in his pocket there now.'

The detective reached deftly into the coat pocket of the dumfounded King Solomon and withdrew a packet of envelopes. He tore off a corner of one, emptied a half-dozen tiny white tablets into his palm, and sneered triumphantly. 'You'll make a good witness,' he told Uggam.

The entertainer was issuing an ultimatum to all sweet mammas who dared to monkey round her loving man. Her audience was absorbed and delighted, with the exception of one couple—the girl with the green stockings and her escort. They sat directly in the line of vision of King Solomon's wide eyes, which, in the calamity that had descended upon him, for the moment saw nothing.

'Are you coming without trouble?'

Mouse Uggam, his friend. Harlem. Land of plenty. City of refuge—city of refuge. If you live long enough—

Consciousness of what was happening between the pair across the room suddenly broke through Gillis's daze like flame through smoke. The man was trying to kiss the girl and she was resisting. Gillis jumped up. The detective, taking the act for an attempt at escape, jumped with him and was quick enough to intercept him. The second officer came at once to his fellow's aid, blowing his whistle several times as he came.

People overturned chairs getting out of the way, but nobody ran for the door. It was an old crowd. A fight was a treat; and the tall Negro could fight.

'Judas Priest!'

'Did you see that?'

'Damn!'

White—both white. Five of Mose Joplin's horses. Poisoning a well. A year's crops. Green stockings—white—white—

'That's the time, papa!'

'Do it, big boy!'

'Good night!'

Uggam watched tensely, with one eye on the door. The second cop had blown for help—

Downing one of the detectives a third time and turning to grapple again with the other, Gillis found himself face to face with a uniformed black policeman.

He stopped as if stunned. For a moment he simply stared. Into his mind swept his own words like a forgotten song, suddenly recalled:—

'Cullud policemans!'

The officer stood ready, awaiting his rush.

'Even—got—cullud—policemans—'

Very slowly King Solomon's arms relaxed; very slowly he stood erect; and the grin that came over his features had something exultant about it.

Eric Walrond (1898-1966)

The scenes of Caribbean life so vividly and intensely etched in *Tropic Death* were derived from the experiences of the first two decades of Eric Walrond's life. Born in Georgetown, British Guiana, in 1898, Walrond moved to Barbados at the age of eight and later to the Panama Canal Zone, where thousands of West Indian laborers were employed in digging the Canal. His early education at St. Stephen's Boys' School in Black Rock, Barbados, and Canal Zone public schools was supplemented from 1913 to 1916 by tutorial instruction in Colon, after which he was employed in the Health Department at Cristobal, on the Atlantic entrance to the Canal. He also worked as a reporter on *The Panama Star and Herald* before leaving for New York in 1918.

After three years at the City College of New York, Walrond was ready to continue his career as a journalist, first as an editor of the *Brooklyn and Long Island Informer*. Next he joined the staff of the *Negro World*, the main organ of Garveyism, though afterward he severely criticized the Jamaican leader. From late 1925 to early 1927 he was business manager of *Opportunity*. Beginning in 1922, his articles and stories appeared frequently in such leading periodicals as *The New Republic, Current History, The Messenger, The Smart Set, Opportunity, The New Age, The Independent, Vanity Fair, The Saturday Review of Literature, Success Magazine,* and *Argosy All-Story Magazine.* Cultivating his special talent for impressionistic short fiction with the aid of extension writing courses at Columbia University, he published *Tropic Death* in 1926.

The ten grim stories of this volume depict Black life—and often death— in Barbados, the Canal Zone, and British Guiana. Direct white oppression is only one of the threats faced by Walrond's characters. Disaster may also come to them in the form of starvation ("Drought") or leprosy ("Tropic Death") or *obeah* ("The Black Pin"). Degradation, the ruler of these lives, is resisted bravely if vainly. Natural and human forces of overpowering magnitude finally work their will. But the author's familiarity with his material, his easy mastery of West Indian dialects, and his vibrant, nervous, impressionistic prose style that catches the color, the glaring heat, and the opulent life of the Black tropics—all these combine to achieve what Langston Hughes has called "a certain hard poetic beauty."

Except for Jean Toomer, no Harlem Renaissance writer of prose fiction made a more auspicious debut than Eric Walrond. Like Toomer, unfortunately, he turned out to be a one-book author. Leaving New York, he traveled in Europe and lived for a considerable time in France. His last years were spent in London, where he died in 1966 while writing a book concerned with the Panama Canal.

Tropic Death has been reissued with an introduction by Arna Bontemps. Two of Walrond's stories about Black life in New York are "Miss Kenny's Marriage," *The Smart Set,* LXXII (September 1923), 73–80, and "City Love," in *The American Caravan* (1927), edited by Van Wyck Brooks, Alfred Kreymborg, Lewis Mumford, and Paul Rosenfeld, pp. 485–493. The reader who wishes to sample Walrond's journalism may begin with "On Being Black," *The New Republic,* XXXII (November 1, 1922), 244–246; "The New Negro Faces America," *Current History,* XVII (February 1923), 786–788, on Black leadership; "The Black City," *The Messenger,* VI (January 1924), 13–14, on Harlem; "The Negro Exodus from the South," *Current History,* XVIII (September 1923), 942–944, one of several articles Walrond wrote on the Great Migration; and "Imperator Africanus, Marcus Garvey: Menace or Promise?" *The Independent,* CXIV (January 3, 1925), 8–11.

Very little has been written on Walrond. Brief treatments appear in Sterling Brown, *The Negro in American Fiction* (1937), and Hugh M. Gloster, *Negro Voices in American Fiction* (1948). Two especially interesting reviews are Robert Herrick, "Tropic Death," *The New Republic,* XLVIII (November 10, 1926), 332, and Langston Hughes, "Marl-Dust and West Indian Sun," *New York Herald Tribune Books,* December 5, 1926, p. 9.

Subjection

Of a sudden the sun gave Ballet an excuse to unbend and straighten himself up, his young, perspiring back cricking in the upward swing. He hurled the pick furiously across the dusty steel rail, tugged a frowsy, sweat-moist rag out of his overall pocket and pushed back his cap, revealing a low, black brow embroidered by scraps of crisp, straggly hair. He fastened, somewhat obliquely, white sullen eyes on the Marine. Irrefutably, by its ugly lift, Ballet's mouth was in on the rising rebellion which thrust a flame of smoke into the young Negro's eyes.

"Look at he, dough," he said, "takin' exvantage o' de po 'lil' boy. A big able hog like dat."

Toro Point resounded to the noisy rhythm of picks swung by gnarled black hands. Sun-baked rock stones flew to dust, to powder. In flashing unison rippling muscle glittered to the task of planing a mound of rocky earth dredged up on the barren seashore.

Songs seasoned the rhythm. And the men sang on and swung picks, black taciturn French colonials, and ignored Ballet, loafing, beefing. . . .

The blows rained. The men sang—blacks, Island blacks—Turks Island, St. Vincent, the Bahamas—

Diamond gal cook fowl botty giv' de man

"I'll show you goddam niggers how to talk back to a white man—"

About twelve, thirteen, fourteen men, but only the wind rustled. A hastening breath of wind, struck dead on the way by the grueling presence of the sun.

A ram-shackle body, dark in the ungentle spots exposing it, jogged, reeled and fell at the tip of a white bludgeon. Forced a dent in the crisp caked earth. An isolated ear lay limp and juicy, like some exhausted leaf or flower, half joined to the tree whence it sprang. Only the sticky milk flooding it was crimson, crimsoning the dust and earth.

"Unna is a pack o' men, ni'," cried Ballet, outraged, "unna see de po' boy get knock' down an' not a blind one o' wunna would a len' he a han'. Unna is de mos'—"

But one man, a Bajan creole, did whip up the courage of voice. "Good God, giv' he a chance, ni'. Don' kick he in de head now he is 'pon de

groun'—" and he quickly, at a nudge and a hushed, "Hey, wha' do you? Why yo' don't tek yo' hand out o' yo' matey' saucepan?" from the only other creole, lapsed into ruthless impassivity.

"Hey, you!" shouted Ballet at last loud enough for the Marine to hear, "why—wha' you doin'? Yo' don' know yo' killin' dat boy, ni'?"

"Le' all we giv' he a han' boys—"

"Ah know I ain't gwine tetch he."

"Nor me."

"Nor me needah."

"Who gwine giv' me a han', ni'?"

"Ain't gwine get meself in no trouble. Go mixin' meself in de backra dem business—"

"Hey, Ballet, if yo' know wha' is good fo' yo'self, yo' bess min' yo' own business, yo' hear wha' me tell yo', yah."

"Wha' yo' got fi' do wit' it? De boy ain't got no business talkin' back to de marinah man—"

"Now he mek up he bed, let 'im lie down in it."

Shocked at sight of the mud the marine's boots left on the boy's dusty, crinkly head, Ballet mustered the courage of action. Some of the older heads passed on, awed, incredulous.

"Yo' gwine kill dat boy," said Ballet, staggering up to the marine.

"You mind yer own goddam business, Smarty, and go back to work," said the marine. He guided an unshaking yellow-spotted finger under the black's warm, dilating nostrils. "Or else—"

He grew suddenly deathly pale. It was a pallor which comes to men on the verge of murder. Mouth, the boy at issue, one of those docile, half-white San Andres coons, was a facile affair. Singly, red-bloodedly one handled it. But here, with this ugly, thick-lipped, board-chested upstart, there was need for handling of an error-less sort.

"I'll git you yet," the marine said, gazing at Ballet quietly, "I'll fill you full of lead yet, you black bastard!"

"Why yo' don't do it now," stuttered Ballet, taking a hesitating step forward, "yo' coward, yo'—a big able man lik' yo' beatin' a lil' boy lik' dat. Why yo' don' hit me? Betcha yo' don' put down yo' gun an' fight me lik' yo' got any guts."

The marine continued to stare at him. "I'll git you yet," he said, "I'll git you yet, Smarty, don't kid yourself." And he slowly moved on.

The boy got up. The sun kept up its irrepressible sizzling. The men minded their business.

Ballet, sulking, aware of the marine on the stony hedge, aware of the red, menacing eyes glued on him, on every single move he made, furtively broke rocks.

.   .   .

"Boy, yo' ain't gwine t' wuk teeday, ni'? Git up!"

Exhausted by the orgy of work and evensong, Ballet snored, rolled, half asleep.

"Get up, ni' yo' ain't hear de *korchee* blowin' fi' go to wuk, ni?"

"Ugh—ooo—ooo—"

"Yo' ent hear me, ni? Um is six o'clock, boy, get up befo' yo' is late. Yo' too lazy, get up, a big, lazy boy lik' yo'—"

Sitting at the head of the cot, a Bible in one hand, Ballet's mother kept shaking him into wakefulness. In the soft flush of dawn bursting in on the veranda, Mirrie's restless gum-moist eyes fell on her son's shining black shoulders. He was sprawled on the canvas, a symbol of primordial force, groaning, half-awake.

"Hey, wha' is to become o' dis boy, ni?" she kept on talking to the emerging flow of light, "Why yo' don't go to bed at night, ni? Stayin' out evah night in de week. Spanishtown, Spanishtown, Spanishtown, evah night—tek heed, ni, tek heed, yo' heah—when yo' run into trouble don' come an' say Ah didn't tell yo'."

To Ballet this was the song of eternity. From the day Mirrie discovered through some vilely unfaithful source the moments there were for youths such as he, in the crimson shades of *el barrio*, the psalms of rage and despair were chanted to him.

His thin, meal-yellow singlet stiffened, ready to crack. He continued snoring. Frowsy body *fuses,* night sod, throttled the air on the dingy narrow porch on which they both contrived to sleep.

She shook him again. "Get up—yo' hear de *korchee* blowin' fo' half pas' six. Time to go to wuk, boy."

Ballet slowly rose—the lower portions of him arching upwards.

The dome of the equator swirled high above Colon—warmth, sticky sweat, heat, malaria, flies—here one slept coverless. Mechanically uttering words of prayer drilled into him by Mirrie, he raised himself up on the stain-blotched cot, salaamed, while Mirrie piously turned her face to the sun.

When he had finished, Ballet, still half asleep, angled his way into his shirt, dragged on his blue pants, took down the skillet from the ledge and went to the cess-pool to bathe his face.

"Yo' know, mahmie," he said to Mirrie as he returned, wiping his eyes with the edge of his shirt sleeve, "I don't feel lik' goin' to work dis mornin'—"

"Why, bo?"

"Oh, Ah dunno." He sat down to tea.

"Yo' too lazy," she blurted out. "Yo' want to follow all o' dem nasty vagabonds an' go roun' de streets an' interfere wit' people. Yo' go to work, sah, an' besides, who is to feed me if yo' don' wuk? Who—answer me dat! Boy, yo' bes' mek up yo' min' an' get under de heel o' de backra."

Peeling the *conkee* off the banana leaf encasing it, Ballet's glistening half-dried eyes roved painfully at the austere lines on his mother's aged face.

"Ah don' wan' fo' go—"

"Dah is wha' Ah get fo' bringin' unna up. Ungrateful vagybond! Dah is wha' Ah get fo' tyin' up my guts wit' plantation trash, feedin' unna—jes' lik' unna wuthliss pappy. But yo' go long an' bring me de coppers when pay day come. Dah is all Ah is Axin' yo' fo' do. Ah too old fo' wash de backra dem dutty ole clothes else unna wouldn't hav' to tu'n up unna backside when Ah ax unna fo' provide anyt'ing fo' mah."

"Oh, yo' mek such a fuss ovah nutton," he sulked.

A stab of pain corrugated Ballet's smooth black brow. His mother's constant dwelling on the dearth of the family fortunes produced in him a sundry set of emotions—escape in rebellion and refusal to do as against a frenzied impulse to die retrieving things.

The impulse to do conquered, and Ballet rose, seized the skillet containing the *conkee* for his midday meal and started.

A fugitive tear, like a pendant pearl, paused on Mirrie's wrinkled, musk-brown face.

"Son, go' long—an tek care o' yo'self."

Light-heartedly Ballet galloped down the stairs. Half-way to the garbage-strewn piazza, he paused to lean over the banister and peep into the foggy depths of the kitchen serving the occupants of the bawdy rooms on the street-level of the tenement.

"Up orready?" shouted Ballet, throwing a sprig of cane peeling at a plump black figure engaged in the languid task of turning with a long flat piece of board a *tache* of bubbling starch.

In a disorderly flight to the piazza one foot landed on the seed of a part-skinned alligator pear. He deftly escaped a fall. Quickly righting himself, he made for the misty, stewy inclosure—dashing under clothes lines, overturning a bucket of wash blue, nearly bursting a hole in some one's sunning, gleaming sheet.

Dark kitchen; slippery and smoky; unseen vermin and strange upgrowth of green snaky roots swarmed along the sides of washtubs, turpentine cans, *taches,* stable ironware.

Presiding over one of the *taches* was a girl. She was slim, young, fifteen years old. Her feet were bare, scales, dirt black, dirt white, sped high up her legs. The fragment of a frock, some peasant thing, once colored, once flowered, stood stiff, rigid off the tips of her curving buttocks.

Grazing the ribs of the *tache* with the rod, Blanche, blithely humming

> Wha' de use yo' gwine shawl up
> Now dat yo' character gone—
> Dicky jump, Dicky jump
> Ah wan' fi' lie down!

was unaware of Ballet slowly crouching behind her.

Becoming clairvoyantly tongue-tied, Blanche suddenly turned, and Ballet came up to her.

Exerting a strange ripe magic over him, the girl cried, "Yo' frighten me, Ballet, how yo' dey?

"Too bad 'bout las' night," she said, in the low lulling tones of a West Indian servant girl, lifting not an eyebrow, and continuing to stir the thickening starch.

"An' me had me min' 'pon it so bad," the boy said, an intense gleam entering his eyes.

"So it dey," responded Blanche, "sometime it hav' obtusions, de neddah time de road are clear."

"Dat a fac'," the boy concurred sorrowfully, "it fatify de *coza* so dat a man can ha'dly sit down an' say 'well, me gwine do dis dis minute an' me gwine do dis dat,' fo' de devil is jes' as smaht as de uddah man uptop."

"Up cose," said Blanche in her most refined manner, "Ah, fi' me notion is to tek de milk fom de cow when him are willin' fi' giv' it, wheddah it are in de mawnin' time or in de even' time—

"Wha' yo' are doin', Ballet, wait—let me put down de stick—wait, Ah say—yo' in a hurry?"

"Wha' Sweetbred, dey? Him gone t' wuk orready?"

"Yes—me don' know but it are seem to me lik' some time muss eclapse befo' dere is any life ah stir in dis kitchen—"

"Oh, Blanche!"

"Yo' bes' be careful, Ballet, fo' de las' time Ah had fi' scrouch aroun' fi' hooks an' eyes an' dat dyam John Chinaman 'im not gwine giv' me anyt'ing beout me giv' 'im somet'ing."

"All right—dere—Blanche—wait—"

"Yo' know what 'im say to me de uddah dey? Me wuz—wait, tek yo' time, Ballet, de cock is jus' a crow, it are soon yet—oh, don't sweet—

"'Im say to me dat Ah mus' giv' 'im somet'ing. An' me say to 'im, 'but John, yo' no me husban' —'an' yo' know wha' de dyam yallah rascal say 'im say 'but me no fo' yo' husban' too'?"

Her hair was hard, but the marble floor of the kitchen undoubtedly helped to stiffen its matty, tangled plaits. And in spite of the water daily splashing over the tanks and *taches* on to the ground, her strong young body took nothing diminishing from it. Only, unquestioningly the force of such a wiry, gluey, gummy impact as theirs left her heels a little broader, and a readier prey for chiggers, by virtue of the constantly widening crevices in them, her hair a little more difficult to comb, and her dress in a suspiciously untidy mood.

Emerging from the slippery darkness of the kitchen, Ballet dashed up Eighth Street. A Colon sunrise streamed in on its lazy inert life. Opposite, some of the disciples of the High Priest of the Ever-Live, Never-Die Sect sat moping, not fully recovered from the flowing mephitic languor of the evening's lyrical excesses.

All the way up the street, Ballet met men of one sort or another trekking to work—on tipsy depot wagons, shovels, picks, forks sticking out like spikes; on foot, alone, smoking pipes, hazily concerned.

Grog shops, chink stores and brothels were closed. The tall, bare, paneled doors were fastened. The sun threw warmth and sting under verandas;

shriveled banana peels to crusts; darkened the half-eaten chunks of soft pomegranates left by some extravagant epicurean, gave manna to big husky wasps foregathering wherever there was light, sun, warmth. . . .

Up on the verandas there dark, bright-skirted, flame-lipped girls, the evening before, danced in squares, holding up the tips of their flimsy dresses, to the *coombia* of creole island places. Creole girls led, thwarted, wooed and burned by *obeah*-working, weed-smoking St. Lucian men. Jamaica girls, fired by an inextinguishable warmth, danced, whirling, wheeling, rolling, rubbing, spinning their posteriors and their hips, in circles, their breasts like rosettes of flame, quivering to the rhythm of the *mento*—conceding none but the scandalously sexless. Spanish girls, white ones, yellow ones, brown ones, furiously gay, furiously concerned over the actualities of beauty.

Over a bar of dredged in earth, Ballet sped. In the growing sunlight figures slowly made for the converging seacoast.

Work-folk yelled to Ballet tidings of the dawn. . . .

"Why yo' don' tek de chiggahs out o' yo' heel an' walk lik' yo' got life in yo' body—"

"Yo' gwine be late, too."

"Yo' go 'long, bo, Oi ent hurrin' fo' de Lawd Gawd Heself dis mawnin'—"

Ahead a vision of buxom green cocoa palms spread like a crescent—from the old rickety wooden houses walled behind the preserves of the quarantine station all the way past the cabins of the fishing folk and dinky bathhouses for the blacks to the unseemly array of garbage at the dump. Out to the seacoast and the writhing palms swarmed men from Coolie Town, Bottle Alley, Bolivar Street, Boca Grande, Silver City.

As he approached the edge of the sea, Ballet waded through grass which rose higher and thicker, whose dew lay in glimmering crystal moistures. Beyond the palm trees opened a vista of the river, the color of brackish water. Empty cocoanut husks cluttered the ground. Sitting on upturned canoes men smoked pipes and sharpened tools, murmuring softly. All across the bay labor boats formed a lane, a lane to Toro Point, shining on the blue horizon.

Drawing nearer the crux of things, Mouth ran up to Ballet and put an unsteady, excited grip on his shoulder.

"Ballet, bettah don' go t' wuk teeday—"

Scorn and disdain crossed Ballet's somber black face.

"Wha' is dah?" he said, refusing to hear his ears.

"Ah, say, don' go t' wuk teeday—stan' home—"

"Why, boy?"

"Dah marine is lookin' fo' yo'."

"Lookin' fo' me?" Ballet stuck a skeptical finger in the pit of his stomach. "Wha' he lookin' fo' me fo'?" A quizzical frown creased his brow.

"He say yo' had no business to jook yo' mout' in de ruction yestiddy. Dat yo' too gypsy an' if yo' know bes' fo' yo'self—"

"Oh, le' he come," cried Ballet, "de blind coward, le' he come—"

A ruffian Q. M. paced up and down the water front, brandishing a staff, firing skyrockets of tobacco spit to right and left, strode up. "Don't stand there, boys, getta move on! Jump in this boat—another one's coming—no time to waste—jump in there!"

A marine lieutenant, pistol in hand, superintended the embarkment. A squad of khakied men paraded the strip of seashore.

Ballet joined the cowed obedient retinue limping to the boats. Curiously, in the scramble to embark the water boy got lost.

"Oh, Oi ain't do nutton. Can't do me nutton."

The passage was swift and safe through swelling seas growing darker and deadlier as the tide mounted. Glumly the men sat, uttering few words, standing up as the boat neared the other side of the river and jumping prematurely ashore, getting their feet wet.

Men gathered on pump cars and on the Toro Point river edge sawing wood to help clear the jungle or sharpening their machetes.

Gangs were forming. Driven by marines, platoons of black men went to obscure parts of the Toro Point bush to cut paths along the swirling lagoon back to the Painted City. Fierce against the sun moaning men jogged with drills on their backs, pounding to dust tons of mortared stone paving lanes through the heathen unexplored jungle.

In the crowd of men, Ballet saw a face leering at him. It was a white face—the face of a scowling marine. . . .

Rockingly, dizzily, it glowed up at him. He was freckled, the pistol in his belt carelessly at hand and he slovenly sported a bayonet rifle.

"Hey—you—I'm talking to you—"

Afraid, unable to fathom the gleam penetrating the depths of the man's eyes, Ballet started running.

"Stand up and take yer medicine, yer goddam skunk," cried the marine; "hey, stop that man—"

Nothing for a black boy, probably a laborer, or a water boy, to do a hide and seek with a tipsy marine. . . .

"Stop that man—"

Ballet flew. He scaled hurdles. He bumped into men. Ugly French colonial words, epithets deserving of a dog, were hurled at him. Impatient, contemptuous Jamaican, colored by a highly British accent, caught at him like shreds.

About to penetrate the dense interior of the jungle, the men sang, soothed the blades of their cutlasses, sang pioneer sea songs, pioneer gold songs. . . .

> Comin' Ah tell yo'!
> One mo' mawin', buoy,

There was a toolshed set a little ways in. Into it Ballet burst. But a hut, it yet had an "upstairs," and up these the boy scrambled wildly.

Behind a wagon wheel sent up there to the wheelwright to be mended, Ballet, breathing hard, heard the marine enter.

Downstairs. A pause. A search. The top of a barrel blammed shut. Imagine—a boy in a barrel of tar. Ludicrous—laughter snuffed out. Heavy steps started upward, upward. . . .

"Where the hell are yer, yer lousy bastard—yer—come sticking in yer mouth where yer hadn't any goddam business? Minding somebody else's business. I'll teach you niggers down here how to talk back to a white man. Come out o' there, you black bastard."

Behind the wheel, bars dividing the two, Ballet saw the dread khaki—the dirt-caked leggings.

His vision abruptly darkened.

Vap, vap, vap—

Three sure, dead shots.

In the Canal Record, the Q. M. at Toro Point took occasion to extol the virtues of the Department which kept the number of casualties in the recent native labor uprising down to one.

Wallace Thurman (1902–1934)

The luminaries of the Harlem Renaissance came to New York from a number of unlikely origins, one of which was Salt Lake City, Utah, the birthplace of Wallace Thurman. White life was dull in this Mormon city, and of Black life Thurman was to write that "there has been and is certainly nothing about him [the Utah Black] to inspire anyone to do anything save perhaps drink gin with gusto, and develop new technique for the contravention of virginity." After graduation from high school Thurman studied medicine at the University of Utah for a couple of years, but a nervous breakdown, harbinger of later neurotic tendencies, forced him to withdraw. He then completed his education in the more cosmopolitan atmosphere of the University of Southern California, graduating in 1925 and leaving for Harlem in the same year.

To the already supercharged atmosphere of the Harlem Renaissance, Thurman added his own nervous, restless brilliance. As he wrote,

> *Three years in Harlem have seen me become a New Negro (for no reason at all and without my consent), a poet (having had 2 poems published by generous editors), an editor (with a penchant for financially unsound publications), an erotic (see articles on Negro*

life and literature in The Bookman, New Republic, Independent, World Tomorrow, etc.), an actor (I was a denizen of Cat Fish Row in Porgy), a husband (having been married all of six months), a novelist (viz: The Blacker the Berry. Macauley's, Feb. 1, 1929: $2.50), a playwright (being co-author of Black Belt). Now—what more could one do?

His editorial activity included work on *The Messenger* in 1926, and, in the same year, publication of *Fire,* an avant-garde "Negro quarterly of the arts" which lasted only one issue. On this lively and iconoclastic but poorly financed venture, Thurman was joined by other young writers and artists—Zora Neale Hurston, Langston Hughes, Aaron Douglas, John P. Davis, Bruce Nugent, and Gwendolyn Bennett. Exactly two years later, in November 1928, Thurman issued another magazine, *Harlem,* but despite such contributors as Alain Locke, George Schuyler, Walter White, and Langston Hughes, it too folded after the first number.

Thurman wrote two three-act plays with some help, mainly structural, from a white playwright named William Jourdan Rapp. One, *Jeremiah, the Magnificent,* was never produced, but the other, *Harlem,* ran for ninety-three performances after its opening on February 20, 1929. Growing out of a short story published in *Fire* ("Cordelia the Crude, a Harlem Sketch"), the play was first entitled *Black Mecca* and then *Black Belt.* In its final form *Harlem: A Melodrama of Negro Life in Harlem* tells the story of the struggle of the Williams family from South Carolina to survive in their new Northern home. The play contains sensationalistic elements including a wildly erotic dance and a shoot-out between two gamblers, but in the main it is a vivid and powerful treatment of the grinding problems of ghetto life.

As a novelist Thurman wrote three books, two alone and one in collaboration with Abraham L. Furman, a white writer. *The Blacker the Berry* (1929) treats the theme of intraracial color prejudice. The heroine, Emma Lou Morgan, is a very dark girl "born in a semi-white world, totally surrounded by an all-white one, and those few dark elements that had forced their way in had either been shooed away or else greeted with derisive laughter." From this community, Boise, Idaho, Emma Lou goes to Los Angeles and then to Harlem, but she can escape neither the handicaps imposed by the notion that light is right nor her own resulting self-hatred. In 1932 Thurman published his second and third novels, *Infants of the Spring* and *The Interne* (with A. L. Furman). *The Interne,* a problem novel on medical abuses in an urban hospital, has no special racial import. *Infants of the Spring,* on the other hand, is a mordant satire on the Harlem Renaissance, which the author thought had fallen far short of its potential. Hugh M. Gloster has written, with some justice, that the novel "reveals an author morbid in outlook, diffuse in thinking, and destructive in purpose." Nevertheless, every serious student of the Harlem Renaissance must come to grips with this fictional critique by one of its most talented participants.

Talented Thurman certainly was, but a genius he was not. "He wanted to be a *very* great writer, like Gorki or Thomas Mann," his friend Langston Hughes recalled, "and he felt that he was merely a journalistic writer." The resulting bitterness and despair led him to hack writing for confessions magazines and for Hollywood, to excessive drinking, to suicide threats, to France, and finally to an early death from tuberculosis in the charity ward of Bellevue Hospital on December 22, 1934.

Each issue of *The Messenger* from April to September 1926 contains contributions by Thurman: essays, reviews, and the short story "Grist in the Mill," reprinted here. Four important essays that appeared elsewhere are "Negro Artists and the Negro," *The New Republic*, LII (August 31, 1927), 37–39; "Nephews of Uncle Remus," *The Independent*, CXIX (September 24, 1927), 296–298; "Harlem Facets," *The World Tomorrow*, X (November 1927), 465–467; and "Negro Poets and Their Poetry," *The Bookman*, LXVII (July 1928), 555–561.

William H. Robinson, Jr., and Therman B. O'Daniel sketch Thurman's literary career in their introductions to recent reprints of *The Blacker the Berry*, as does Gerald Haslam in "Wallace Thurman: A Western Renaissance Man," *Western American Literature*, VI (Spring 1971), 53–59. Doris E. Abramson's *Negro Playwrights in the American Theatre 1925–1959* (1969) adds biographical details to a critique of *Harlem*. Sterling Brown's *The Negro in American Fiction* (1937) and Hugh M. Gloster's *Negro Voices in American Fiction* (1948) both treat *The Blacker the Berry* and *Infants of the Spring*, but not *The Interne*. Finally, no one interested in Thurman should overlook Langston Hughes' reminiscences in *The Big Sea* (1940; see the excerpt reprinted in this anthology) and Dorothy West's in "Elephant's Dance," *Black World*, XX (November 1970), 77–85.

Grist in the Mill

This is indeed an accidental cosmos, so much so, that even the most divine mechanism takes an occasional opportunity to slip a cog and intensify the reigning chaos. And to make matters more intriguing, more terrifying, there seems to be a universal accompaniment of mocking laughter, coming from the ethereal regions as well as from the more mundane spheres, to each mishap whether that mishap be experienced by a dislodged meteor, a moon-bound planet, a sun-shrunken comet, or a determined man. All of which serves to make this universe of ours a sometimes comic spectacle, serves to push all unexpected cosmic experience just over the deviating border line that divides the comic from the tragic, for there is always something delightfully humorous in an accident even if that accident be as earthly, as insignificant (cosmically speaking) and as fatal as was the accident of Colonel Charles Summers, the second, of Louisiana.

Colonel Charles Summers, the second, was a relic; an anachronistic relic from pre-civil war days, being one of those rare sons of a dyed-in-the-wool southern father who had retained all the traditionary characteristics of his patrician papa. Even his aristocratic blood had escaped being diluted by poor white corpuscles making him indeed a phenomenal person among the decadent first families of the decadent south. Colonel Charles Summers, the second, was your true reborn Confederate, your true transplanted devotee of the doctrines of Jeff Davis, your true contemporary Colonel Charles Summers, the first, even to the petty affectation of an unearned military title, and a chronic case of pernicious anæmia.

It was on one of those placid days when a wary human is always expecting the gods to play a scurvy trick upon him, one of those days when smiling nature might be expected to smirk at any moment, one of those days when all seems to be too well with the world that the first act of Colonel Summers' accident occurred. He should have sensed that all was not to be well with him on that day, for long, lonely, isolated years of living with and nursing a dead ideal, had made him peculiarly atune to the ever variant vibrations of his environment. He had little companionship, for there were few kindred souls in the near vicinity. His wife, to him, was practically non-existent, being considered a once useful commodity now useless. He had no children, had not wanted any, for fear that they would become too seared with the customs and mannerisms of the moment to complacently follow in his footsteps. He could not abide the poor white or mongrel aristocrats who were his neighbors. He shrank from contact with the modern world, and preserved his feudal kingdom religiously, passionately, safeguarding it from the unsympathetic outside. Hence he communed with himself and with nature, and became intensely aware of his own mental and psychical reactions and premonitions, so aware, in fact, that he privately boasted that no accident could befall him without his first receiving a sensory warning, but, of course, he forgot to be aware at the proper time, even tho the day was rampant with danger signals.

Mrs. Summers was an unemotional ninny, being one of those backwoods belles whom the fates failed to attend properly at birth. Her only basis of recognition in this world at all was that she was a direct descendant of an old southern family. She was one of those irritating persons who never think about a thing nor yet feel about it. Rather she met all phenomena dispassionately, practically, and seemed to be more mechanical than most other humans. When an interne from the hospital brought her the news that only a blood transfusion would save her husband's life, she accepted that without the slightest suggestion of having received a shock; and she had accepted the news of his sunstroke, induced by walking beneath a torrid, noonday Louisiana sun, and which had resulted in an acute aggravation of his chronic illness in the same "well, that's no news" manner.

"Blood transfusion," she stated rather than queried, "well, why not?"

"We thought, madame," the interne was polite, "that you might be able to suggest"—

She gave a little shrug, the nearest approach to the expression of an emotion that she ever allowed herself. "I am no physician," and the door was closed deliberately, yet normally.

The hospital staff was thus placed in an embarrassing dilemma, for there was no professional blood donor available, and no volunteers forthcoming either from the village center or the outlying plantations. One must suffer from not having friends as well as suffer from having them—so the Colonel's life line continued to fray, his wife made perfunctory visits, and continued to appear disinterested, while the hospital staff pondered and felt criminal, not too criminal, you know, for they remembered that the Colonel had most insultingly refrained from ever donating to their building or upkeep fund, yet they could not let him die while there was a possible chance of saving him, so being both human and humanitarian they played a joke on the doughty old Colonel and at the same time saved his life.

.   .   .

Zacharia Davis had a suppressed desire, and the suppression of that desire was necessarily more potent than the desire itself, for Zacharia wished to make a happy hegira to the northland, and being in the south decided that it was best to keep this desire under cover until such time came that he would have what he called the "necessary mazuma."

Zacharia had been born and schooled in Illinois, and had been perfectly willing to remain there until a certain war-time conscription measure had made Mexico seem more desirable. Once in Mexico he had remained until the ink of the Armistice signatures had been dry five years, and then he had recrossed the border into the cattle lands of western Texas. There he had parked, and attempted to amass sufficient coin to enable him to return to and dazzle Chicago's south side black belt, but an untimely discovery of a pair of loaded dice on his person during an exciting crap game had made it necessary for him to journey by night, and by freight to the cane-brake country of Southern Louisiana.

Here he had occupied himself by doing odd jobs about the various plantations and village shops, and by gambling down by the river bottom at night with the rice field and cane-brake laborers. He avoided trouble either with his fellow black men who were somewhat suspicious of this smooth talking "furriner," and with that white portion of his environment that demanded his quiescent respect. Consciously he adopted a protective cloak of meekness, and at first glance could not be distinguished from the native southern blacks; in fact, only a keen analyst could have discerned that Zacharia was continually laughing at all those about him, both white and black, and that he, unlike the southern native Negro suffered little, even unconsciously, and laughed much. Then, too, Zacharia washed the hospital windows every Saturday morning, and was thus drawn into the little comedy in which Colonel Summers was to play the star role.

Meanwhile there were other factors working to deter Zacharia from ever realizing the fruition of his desire. The sheriff of the parish had finally decided to clamp down on the river bottom gambling activities where there had lately been a siege of serious cuttings and fatal shootings. Of course, normally it did not matter if all the "coons" insisted upon killing one another, but it did matter when northern migration was at its highest peak, and labor was both scarce and valuable to the plantation owners and it was at the instigation of these persons that the sheriff was moved to act. He planned his raid secretly and carefully, seeking the aid of the local K. K. K., and the more adventurous villagers. They had no intention of using firearms or of jailing any of the game participants. Neither did they have any intention of stopping the games completely. They merely hoped to lessen the attendance, and to inspire caution in those who would attend about the advisability of carrying firearms and knives.

Of course, it was in line with Zacharia's general luck that he should be in the midst of a winning streak on the night when the eager vigilantes swooped down upon the river bottom rendezvous like revengeful phantoms in the moonlight, and proceeded to do their chosen duty. And, of course, it was in line with Zacharia's general procedure to forego immediate flight in order to gather up forsaken cash piles.

There was much confusion there in the damp darkness. The fiery, white demons reveled in the raucous riot they had created, while the scuttling blacks cursed and cried out against the lash

sting and the club beat. The rendezvous was surrounded, there was only one means of escape, the river, and the cornered ones shrank back from its cold, slimy, swift currents. Hysteria descended upon the more terrified. Knives were drawn, and temporarily reflected the gleaming moonlight as they were hurled recklessly into the mad white-black crowd. Periodic pistol shots punctuated the hoarse shouts of the conquerors and the pained moans of the vanquished. Torchlight flares carried by the invaders gave the scene the color and passion of a Walpurgis night. Marsh grass was trampled, its dew turned red by dripping blood. And the river—the muddy river—became riotous with struggling men, and chuckled to itself as an occasional body was unable to withstand the current, or unable to reach the other shore.

There was much more confusion there in the damp darkness. Bleeding heads emitted mournful groans, emitted fresh blood streams, more groans, more blood, and then grew still, grew horribly inanimate. Wounded bodies squirmed and moaned. The flares were all extinguished. The river was once more quietly rippling undisturbed by super-imposed freight. The roundup had commenced, the injured whites were being carefully carried into the village hospital, while the wounded blacks were being dragged to jail. Thus the night wore on, and seemed a little weary of having witnessed such a carnal spectacle, such elemental chaos.

Among those hapless blacks who regained consciousness in the crowded jail was Zacharia, who was nonchalantly nursing a cracked head, and a sock full of coin. Being in jail was no novelty, nor was having a cracked head an entirely new experience, but the sock of money, the sock that contained his pecuniary emancipation, the sock that contained the "necessary mazuma," ah, that was new, saliently new, and comforting.

The town was in an uproar. A deputy sheriff had died from a knife wound inflicted by some infuriated black during the conflict. No one had expected any of the invaders to come back wounded. No one had considered that the cornered colored man might stand at bay like a wild, jungle animal, and fight back. Everyone had considered the whole episode as an unusual chance to sock a few niggers upon the head, and to flay a few black hides with a long unused lash, but instead most of the blacks had fought their way to freedom, only a mere handful of the more seriously wounded were in custody, and they were being claimed by their plantation employers. Moreover, the hospital was overcrowded with wounded whites, and now, this death, this death of a white man at the hands of a nigger. Of course, some one had to pay. The plantation owners were not willing to part with any of their hired help, considering the cultivation of the rice and sugar cane crop of more importance now than the punishment of some unknown assailant. Oh, yes, catch some one and punish him, but don't take this nigger of mine, who is one of my best workmen, seemed to be the general attitude.

No one came to claim Zacharia, and he remained in his cell, awaiting to be released, and amusing himself meanwhile by trying to compute in his mind just how much money his beloved sock, so carefully hidden away, contained. No one came to claim him and finally he was accused of having murdered the deputy sheriff.

The trial was conducted rather leisurely. There was no hurry to cash in on the mob's vengeance. Their call for blood had been satiated by that river bottom battle. It was enough that they had a victim in custody whom they could torture at will, and whom they could put to death legally. Thus Zacharia found himself a participant in a mock trial, found himself being legally railroaded to the gallows, found himself being kept away from freedom—from Chicago—when he had the cash, the long desired cash. He was too amazed at first to realize just how completely he had been enveloped by a decidedly hostile environment. Realization came slowly, and noticeably. His bronze colored face grew wan and sickly. His beady eyes became more and more screwed up until it seemed as if they would completely retreat into the protective folds of their wrinkled sockets. Even the firm lower lip, his one sign of forceful character, drooped, and mutely asked for pity.

He was found guilty, and made ready to take his journey to the state penitentiary where he would be held until the date set for his hanging. The date of his departure drew near, and Zacharia became pitifully panic stricken. The four walls of his lousy cell seemed to be gyrating mirrors sordidly reflecting his certain doom. The bars running diagonally across the cell door and standing upright in the cell window all seemed to assume the personality of ballet dancers

attired in hemp, and forming twirling circular figures, lunging at him with menacing loops. Everything choked him, his food—the air—even thought. Incipient nausea tortured him. And then one thought flashed across his mind, lingered there, shimmering with the glorified heat of potential hope. A spasm of grotesque smiles distorted the uneven, thick features, and the quivering lips called to the guards, and begged them to send for Colonel Summers.

Had Zacharia asked for anyone else besides Colonel Summers his request would have been either roughly refused, or rudely ignored, but to have a condemned "nigger" ask for old stuck up Colonel Summers, well, well, well, what a chance for some fun at the Colonel's expense. The question was would the Colonel come. In all probability he wouldn't. Since he had recovered from that last illness of his he had drawn more and more into himself. His wife had imported a sister for company, but the Colonel continued to tramp about his plantation, continued to commune with himself.

It was sheer accident that Colonel Summers happened to be in town on the same day that Zacharia had asked to see him. His wife's sister had had an attack of indigestion. In fact it seemed to Colonel Summers that she was always having an attack of something. And she was always having prescriptions filled, always dispatching a servant to the drug store. Damned frump, the Colonel called her. Worrisum bitch, was what the black servants called her. However, on this day she had sent for medicine twice, and each time the little black boys had come back with the wrong brand, so impatient at both his sister-in-law, the stupid black boys, and the crafty druggist, the Colonel went into town himself.

Of course, once there the Colonel did the usual thing, id est. wandered aimlessly about the streets and enjoyed himself by cursing the activities of these ambitious, pettily so, of course, poor trash. And in his wanderings he walked past the jail, was hailed, stopped to see what the insolent fellow wanted, gaped slightly when he heard, and without a word, or without an idea why he did so except that his pride would not let him appear to be placed at a disadvantage, strode into the jail, and asked to see Zacharia.

Fifteen minutes later the amused eavesdropping guards and jail loiterers rushed into the cell passageway to see the Colonel striking through the bars with his cane, perspiring dreadfully, his face inordinately infused with blood, and to find Zacharia cowed against the further wall, his face a study in perplexity and pleading, his lips whimpering, "I didn't lie, I didn't lie, it was me, it was me," on and on in ceaseless reiteration.

The surprised and amused men plied the old Colonel with questions in a vain effort to find out what was wrong, but the old southern gentleman was incoherent with rage, and sick, both in body and in mind. He seemed on the verge of collapse and the more solicitous men in the group attempted to lead him into the warden's quarters where he could lie down. Someone even suggested a doctor, but all were overruled by Colonel Summers, who had meanwhile regained some of his strength and cried out, "The hospital, the hospital," and to the hospital the men carried him, not knowing that he did not wish to go there for treatment, or that he was seeking for verification—verification of what the doomed Zacharia had told him.

Twenty-four hours later he was taken home, babbling, unconscious, and pitiful. The hospital authorities had verified Zacharia's statement, and Colonel Summers now knew that it was the black man's blood that had saved his life.

    .   .   .

It commenced to rain about twilight time. Colonel Summers suddenly sat up in his bed, the most ambitious move that he had made in a week. He was alone in the room, alone with himself, and his fear, alone in the defeated twilight.

The rain drops increased in volume and velocity. Colonel Summers threw the covers back, struggled out of the bed, and staggered laboriously to the panel mirror set in his clothes closet door. Eagerly, insanely he peered into it, and what he saw there evidently pleased him, for the drawn features relaxed a trifle, and only the eyes, the weak, pitiful eyes, remained intensely animate as they peered and peered into the mirror. Then his strength gave out, and he sank with a groan to the floor.

The rain drops began to come down in torrents, urged on by a rising wind. Colonel Summers once more drew himself up with the aid of the door knob, and once more peered and peered into the mirror. By this time he had ripped his night shirt from him, and stood there naked, his wasted body perspiring from the effort. Soon his strength gave out again, and as he sank to the floor there was a peaceful half smile

striving for expression on his pained and fear-racked face.

"Still white, still white," he muttered, and then more loudly, "still white, still white, still white," the voice became hoarse again, "still white, thank God, A'hm still white."

Night came, greeted by the whistle of the frolicsome wind and the ceaseless chorus of the scampering rain drops. The bedroom became dark, and once more gaining consciousness the naked Colonel crawled across the carpeted floor to the nearest window. The darkness frightened him, he was seeking for light, and since the interior offered none, he sought for it or a reflection of it through the window panes. But on the outside was also the black night plus the cachinnating rain drops, and the playful wind. He shrank back in abject terror only to be confronted with the same terrifying darkness behind him.

He looked out of the window once more. A flash of lightning provided the wanted light, but it brought no release, brought only additional terror, for the tree tops, glistening wet and swaying with the wind, assumed the shapes of savage men, rhythmically moving to the tune of a tom-tom, rhythmically tossing to the intermittent thud of the reverberating thunder.

"Darkies," he murmured, and tried to draw away from the window, "My God—darkies." Then the scene changed. His insane eyes set in a bearded skull conjured up strange figures when the lightning flashed. Each tree assumed a definite personality. That broken limb dangling from the tree just beyond the fence was Zacharia, and as it gyrated wildly in the mad night, it seemed to whisper to the wind, "He is my brother, my brother, my brother," while the wind broadcasted the whisper through the night. And then that tallest tree so close to the house was himself, a black reproduction of himself with savage sap surging through its veins. It too reveled in the wildness of the night; it too exulted in being pelted by the wind-driven rain drops and in responding to the rough rhythm of the thunder-gods tom-tom.

Someone lit a light in the hall, and laid their hand on the door knob preparatory to opening the door to the Colonel's room. Then someone else across the hall called, and the first person released their grip on the knob and treaded softly away.

The Colonel fell prostrate to the floor, and attempted to burrow his head deep into the thick protective nap of the carpet. He felt an inky blackness enveloping him, his whole form seemed to be seared with some indigo stain that burned and burned like an avid acid. Then his body began to revolt against this dusky intruder, began to writhe and wriggle upon the floor, began to twitch and turn, trying to rub itself clean, trying to shed this super-imposed cloak, but the blackness could not be shed—it was sprouting from the inside, and being fertilized by the night.

Time passed. Voices were heard whispering in the hall. A door closed. More whispering. Out-doors all was jubilantly mad. In the bedroom the Colonel still lay upon the floor, panting, perspiring, exhausted from his insane efforts. His reason was now completely gone. His last ounce of life was being slowly nibbled away. The blackness became more intense, and then a black crow, stranded, befuddled by the storm, sought refuge upon the window ledge, and finding none there cawed out in distress, and to the dying maniac on the floor, it seemed to caw, "nigaw, nigaw, nigaw"———

Someone opened the door, turned on the light, and screamed.

Zora Neale Hurston (1903–1960)

Growing up in the all-Black town of Eatonville, Florida, where she was born on January 7, 1903, Zora Neale Hurston was spared the early abrasive contacts with racist whites that so deeply influenced almost all other Afro-American writers. By the time she encountered racism she was self-possessed and self-confident enough to cope with it, and it plays a relatively minor role in her fiction.

Not that her youth was not difficult in other ways. Her philandering father tried to crush her spirit, but she was defended by her mother, who urged all eight of the children to be ambitious, to "jump at de sun." After his wife's death when Zora was nine, John Hurston quickly remarried, and Zora despised her stepmother. For several years she wandered from the house of one relative or friend to that of another, homeless and unloved. During this time her schooling was interrupted, a particularly severe hardship for a bright and curious girl. Life in her married brother's home was not much better. At the age of sixteen, however, she began work as a maid for a white singer in a theatrical company. After eighteen months she found herself in Baltimore, eager to renew her education.

After a period of waiting on tables, she returned to school, first at night and then in the high school department of Morgan College for two years. Going to Howard University in nearby Washington for college work, she was influenced by Lorenzo D. Turner of the Department of English and Alain Locke, who encouraged her writing efforts as a fellow member of The Stylus, a campus literary group. One of her stories, "Drenched in Light," was published by Charles S. Johnson in *Opportunity,* December 1924. Following her story to New York early in 1925, she won second prize in the *Opportunity* competition for both short story ("Spunk") and play (*Color Struck*). With this recognition she became secretary to the white novelist Fannie Hurst, won a scholarship to Barnard College, and became a full-fledged member of the Harlem Renaissance. At Barnard she was a favorite pupil of the great Franz Boas, who diverted her chief interest from English to anthropology. After graduating in 1928, she spent the next four years in anthropological research in Harlem and the South, specializing in folklore.

Almost all of Miss Hurston's writings reflect her immersion in Black folk life, which she had both lived and studied. The *Opportunity* stories, "Sweat" (published in Wallace Thurman's *Fire*), and "The Gilded Six-Bits" (published in *Story,* 1933, and reprinted here) all take place in the Southern Black community (sometimes actually identified as Eatonville) that she knew so well. The same is true of her first two novels, *Jonah's Gourd Vine* (1934) and *Their Eyes Were Watching God* (1937). The former may best be described as a biographical novel, the protagonist, John Buddy Pearson, bearing a striking resemblance to the author's father. *Their Eyes Were Watching God,* composed in a few weeks in Haiti in the aftermath of an intense love affair, is a sensitive, poetic story of a Black woman's search for fulfillment through love. After two unhappy marriages to materialistic men, Janie marries a rounder named Tea Cake. For all his hedonism, he brings to Janie a love that opens her to a total experience of life. A later novel, *Seraph on the Suwanee* (1948), treats the lives of poor whites.

As a folklorist Miss Hurston made a major contribution in *Mules and Men* (1935). The vivid material in this collection was drawn mainly from Polk County, Florida, with its phosphate mines, turpentine camps, and juke joints, and from the hoodoo rites of New Orleans. A trip to Haiti and Jamaica produced *Tell My Horse* (1938), a further exploration into folk magic. Finally, *Moses, Man of the Mountain* (1939) combines fiction, folklore, and religion in an unusual amalgam.

Going to California in the early 1940's, Miss Hurston wrote for Warner Brothers Studio and worked on her autobiography, *Dust Tracks on a Road* (1942). She then taught drama for a time at North Carolina College in Durham, but in the 1950's she lost contact with many of her friends. She was living in poverty in Fort Pierce, Florida, when she died at the age of fifty-seven.

In addition to *Opportunity* and *Fire,* Miss Hurston's work appeared in *The Messenger* and *Ebony and Topaz* during the Harlem Renaissance and in Nancy Cunard's *Negro Anthology* (1934), *The Survey, Journal of American Folklore, American Mercury,* and *Negro Digest* during the 1930's and 1940's.

Biographical sketches and reminiscences include B. Alsterlund, "Zora Neale Hurston," *Wilson Bulletin for Librarians,* XIII (1939), 586; Langston Hughes, *The Big Sea* (1940), pp. 238–240 (reprinted in this anthology); *Current Biography,* III (May 1942), 46–48; Harry Warfel, *American Novelists of Today* (1951), p. 223; and Fannie Hurst, "Zora Hurston: A Personality Sketch," *The Yale University Library Gazette,* XXXV (1960), 17–22. For criticism of Miss Hurston's fiction see Benjamin Brawley, *The Negro Genius* (1937); Sterling Brown, *The Negro in American Fiction* (1937); Hugh M. Gloster, *Negro Voices in American*

Fiction (1948); Robert A. Bone, *The Negro Novel in America* (1958); S. P. Fullinwider, *The Mind and Mood of Black America: 20th Century Thought* (1969); and Evelyn Thomas Helmick, "Zora Neale Hurston," *The Carrell, Journal of the University of Miami Library,* II (June and December 1970), 1–19. Miss Hurston's use of folklore is explored in Blyden Jackson, "Some Negroes in the Land of Goshen," *Tennessee Folklore Society Bulletin,* XIX (1953), 103–107, and James W. Byrd, "Zora Neale Hurston: A Novel Folklorist," *Tennessee Folklore Society Bulletin,* XXI (1955), 37–41. L. Neal's introduction to *Dust Tracks on a Road* (1971) is valuable.

The Gilded Six-Bits

It was a Negro yard around a Negro house in a Negro settlement that looked to the payroll of the G and G Fertilizer works for its support.

But there was something happy about the place. The front yard was parted in the middle by a sidewalk from gate to door-step, a sidewalk edged on either side by quart bottles driven neck down into the ground on a slant. A mess of homey flowers planted without a plan but blooming cheerily from their helter-skelter places. The fence and house were whitewashed. The porch and steps scrubbed white.

The front door stood open to the sunshine so that the floor of the front room could finish drying after its weekly scouring. It was Saturday. Everything clean from the front gate to the privy house. Yard raked so that the strokes of the rake would make a pattern. Fresh newspaper cut in fancy edge on the kitchen shelves.

Missie May was bathing herself in the galvanized washtub in the bedroom. Her dark-brown skin glistened under the soapsuds that skittered down from her wash rag. Her stiff young breasts thrust forward aggressively like broad-based cones with the tips lacquered in black.

She heard men's voices in the distance and glanced at the dollar clock on the dresser.

"Humph! Ah'm way behind time t'day! Joe gointer be heah 'fore Ah git mah clothes on if Ah don't make haste."

She grabbed the clean meal sack at hand and dried herself hurriedly and began to dress. But before she could tie her slippers, there came the ring of singing metal on wood. Nine times.

Missie May grinned with delight. She had not seen the big tall man come stealing in the gate and creep up the walk grinning happily at the joyful mischief he was about to commit. But she knew that it was her husband throwing silver dollars in the door for her to pick up and pile beside her plate at dinner. It was this way every Saturday afternoon. The nine dollars hurled into the open door, he scurried to a hiding place behind the cape jasmine bush and waited.

Missie May promptly appeared at the door in mock alarm.

"Who dat chunkin' money in mah do'way?" she demanded. No answer from the yard. She leaped off the porch and began to search the shrubbery. She peeped under the porch and hung over the gate to look up and down the road. While she did this, the man behind the jasmine darted to the china berry tree. She spied him and gave chase.

"Nobody ain't gointer be chunkin' money at me and Ah not do 'em nothin'," she shouted in mock anger. He ran around the house with Missie May at his heels. She overtook him at the kitchen door. He ran inside but could not close it after him before she crowded in and locked with him in a rough and tumble. For several minutes the two were a furious mass of male and female energy. Shouting, laughing, twisting, turning, tussling, tickling each other in the ribs; Missie May clutching onto Joe and Joe trying, but not too hard, to get away.

"Missie May, take yo' hand out mah pocket!" Joe shouted out between laughs.

"Ah ain't, Joe, not lessen you gwine gimme whateve' it is good you got in yo' pocket. Turn it go, Joe, do Ah'll tear yo' clothes."

"Go on tear 'em. You de one dat pushes de needles round heah. Move yo' hand Missie May."

"Lemme git dat paper sack out yo' pocket. Ah bet its candy kisses."

"Tain't. Move yo' hand. Woman ain't got no business in a man's clothes nohow. Go away."

Missie May gouged way down and gave an upward jerk and triumphed.

"Unhhunh! Ah got it. It 'tis so candy kisses. Ah knowed you had somethin' for me in yo' clothes. Now Ah got to see whut's in every pocket you got."

Joe smiled indulgently and let his wife go through all of his pockets and take out the things that he had hidden there for her to find. She bore off the chewing gum, the cake of sweet soap, the pocket handkerchief as if she had wrested them from him, as if they had not been bought for the sake of this friendly battle.

"Whew! dat play-fight done got me all warmed up." Joe exclaimed. "Got me some water in de kittle?"

"Yo' water is on de fire and yo' clean things is cross de bed. Hurry up and wash yo'self and git changed so we kin eat. Ah'm hongry." As Missie said this, she bore the steaming kettle into the bedroom.

"You ain't hongry, sugar," Joe contradicted her. "Youse jes' a little empty. Ah'm de one whut's hongry. Ah could eat up camp meetin', back off 'ssociation, and drink Jurdan dry. Have it on de table when Ah git out de tub."

"Don't you mess wid mah business, man. You git in yo' clothes. Ah'm a real wife, not no dress and breath. Ah might not look lak one, but if you burn me, you won't git a thing but wife ashes."

Joe splashed in the bedroom and Missie May fanned around in the kitchen. A fresh red and white checked cloth on the table. Big pitcher of buttermilk beaded with pale drops of butter from the churn. Hot fried mullet, crackling bread, ham hock atop a mound of string beans and new potatoes, and perched on the window-sill a pone of spicy potato pudding.

Very little talk during the meal but that little consisted of banter that pretended to deny affection but in reality flaunted it. Like when Missie May reached for a second helping of the tater pone. Joe snatched it out of her reach.

After Missie May had made two or three unsuccessful grabs at the pan, she begged, "Aw, Joe gimme some mo' dat tater pone."

"Nope, sweetenin' is for us men-folks. Y'all pritty lil frail eels don't need nothin' lak dis. You too sweet already."

"Please, Joe."

"Naw, naw. Ah don't want you to git no sweeter than whut you is already. We goin' down de road a lil piece t'night so you go put on yo' Sunday-go-to-meetin' things."

Missie May looked at her husband to see if he was playing some prank. "Sho nuff, Joe?"

"Yeah. We goin' to de ice cream parlor."

"Where de ice cream parlor at, Joe?"

"A new man done come heah from Chicago and he done got a place and took and opened it up for a ice cream parlor, and bein' as it's real swell, Ah wants you to be one de first ladies to walk in dere and have some set down."

"Do Jesus, Ah ain't knowed nothin' 'bout it. Who de man done it?"

"Mister Otis D. Slemmons, of spots and places —Memphis, Chicago, Jacksonville, Philadelphia and so on."

"Dat heavy-set man wid his mouth full of gold teethes?"

"Yeah. Where did you see 'im at?"

"Ah went down to de sto' tuh git a box of lye and Ah seen 'im standin' on de corner talkin' to some of de mens, and Ah come on back and went to scrubbin' de floor, and he passed and tipped his hat whilst Ah was scourin' de steps. Ah thought Ah never seen *him* befo'."

Joe smiled pleasantly. "Yeah, he's up to date. He got de finest clothes Ah ever seen on a colored man's back."

"Aw, he don't look no better in his clothes than you do in yourn. He got a puzzlegut on 'im and he so chuckle-headed, he got a pone behind his neck."

Joe looked down at his own abdomen and said wistfully, "Wisht Ah had a build on me lak he got. He ain't puzzle-gutted, honey. He jes' got a corperation. Dat make 'm look lak a rich white man. All rich mens is got some belly on 'em."

"Ah seen de pitchers of Henry Ford and he's a spare-built man and Rockefeller look lak he ain't got but one gut. But Ford and Rockefeller and dis Slemmons and all de rest kin be as many-gutted as dey please, Ah'm satisfied wid you jes' lak you is, baby. God took pattern after a pine tree and built you noble. Youse a pritty man, and if Ah knowed any way to make you mo' pritty still Ah'd take and do it."

Joe reached over gently and toyed with Missie May's ear. "You jes' say dat cause you love me, but Ah know Ah can't hold no light to Otis D. Slemmons. Ah ain't never been nowhere and Ah ain't got nothin' but you."

Missie May got on his lap and kissed him and

he kissed back in kind. Then he went on. "All de womens is crazy 'bout 'im everywhere he go."

"How you know dat, Joe?"

"He tole us so hisself."

"Dat don't make it so. His mouf is cut cross-ways, ain't it? Well, he kin lie jes' lak anybody else."

"Good Lawd, Missie! You womens sho is hard to sense into things. He's got a five-dollar gold piece for a stick-pin and he got a ten-dollar gold piece on his watch chain and his mouf is jes' crammed full of gold teethes. Sho wisht it wuz mine. And whut make it so cool, he got money 'cumulated. And womens give it all to 'im."

"Ah don't see whut de womens see on 'im. Ah wouldn't give 'im a wink if de sheriff wuz after 'im."

"Well, he tole us how de white womens in Chicago give 'im all dat gold money. So he don't 'low nobody to touch it at all. Not even put dey finger on it. Dey tole 'im not to. You kin make 'miration at it, but don't tetch it."

"Whyn't he stay up dere where dey so crazy 'bout 'im?"

"Ah reckon dey done made 'im vast-rich and he wants to travel some. He say dey wouldn't leave 'im hit a lick of work. He got mo' lady people crazy 'bout him than he kin shake a stick at."

"Joe, Ah hates to see you so dumb. Dat stray nigger jes' tell y'all anything and y'all b'lieve it."

"Go 'head on now, honey and put on yo' clothes. He talkin' 'bout his pritty womens—Ah want 'im to see *mine*."

Missie May went off to dress and Joe spent the time trying to make his stomach punch out like Slemmons' middle. He tried the rolling swagger of the stranger, but found that his tall bone-and-muscle stride fitted ill with it. He just had time to drop back into his seat before Missie May came in dressed to go.

On the way home that night Joe was exultant. "Didn't Ah say ole Otis was swell? Can't he talk Chicago talk? Wuzn't dat funny whut he said when great big fat ole Ida Armstrong come in? He asted me, 'Who is dat broad wid de forte shake?' Dat's a new word. Us always thought forty was a set of figgers but he showed us where it means a whole heap of things. Sometimes he don't say forty, he jes' say thirty-eight and two and dat mean de same thing. Know whut he tole me when Ah wuz payin' for our ice cream? He say, 'Ah have to hand it to you, Joe. Dat wife of

yours is jes' thirty-eight and two. Yessuh, she's forte!' Ain't he killin'?"

"He'll do in case of a rush. But he sho is got uh heap uh gold on 'im. Dat's de first time Ah ever seed gold money. It lookted good on him sho nuff, but it'd look a whole heap better on you."

"Who, me? Missie May youse crazy! Where would a po' man lak me git gold money from?"

Missie May was silent for a minute, then she said, "Us might find some goin' long de road some time. Us could."

"Who would be losin' gold money round heah? We ain't even seen none dese white folks wearin' no gold money on dey watch chain. You must be figgerin' Mister Packard or Mister Cadillac goin' pass through heah."

"You don't know whut been lost 'round heah. Maybe somebody way back in memorial times lost they gold money and went on off and it ain't never been found. And then if we wuz to find it, you could wear some 'thout havin' no gang of womens lak dat Slemmons say he got."

Joe laughed and hugged her. "Don't be so wishful 'bout me. Ah'm satisfied de way Ah is. So long as Ah be yo' husband, Ah don't keer 'bout nothin' else. Ah'd ruther all de other womens in de world to be dead than for you to have de toothache. Less we go to bed and git our night rest."

It was Saturday night once more before Joe could parade his wife in Slemmons' ice cream parlor again. He worked the night shift and Saturday was his only night off. Every other evening around six o'clock he left home, and dying dawn saw him hustling home around the lake where the challenging sun flung a flaming sword from east to west across the trembling water.

That was the best part of life—going home to Missie May. Their white-washed house, the mock battle on Saturday, the dinner and ice cream parlor afterwards, church on Sunday nights when Missie out-dressed any woman in town—all, everything was right.

One night around eleven the acid ran out at the G. and G. The foreman knocked off the crew and let the steam die down. As Joe rounded the lake on his way home, a lean moon rode the lake in a silver boat. If anybody had asked Joe about the moon on the lake, he would have said he hadn't paid it any attention. But he saw it with his feelings. It made him yearn painfully for Missie. Creation obsessed him. He thought about children. They had been married more than a year now. They had money put away. They ought to be making little feet for shoes. A little boy child would be about right.

He saw a dim light in the bedroom and decided to come in through the kitchen door. He could wash the fertilizer dust off himself before presenting himself to Missie May. It would be nice for her not to know that he was there until he slipped into his place in bed and hugged her back. She always liked that.

He eased the kitchen door open slowly and silently, but when he went to set his dinner bucket on the table he bumped it into a pile of dishes, and something crashed to the floor. He heard his wife gasp in fright and hurried to reassure her.

"Iss me, honey. Don't git skeered."

There was a quick, large movement in the bedroom. A rustle, a thud, and a stealthy silence. The light went out.

What? Robbers? Murderers? Some varmint attacking his helpless wife, perhaps. He struck a match, threw himself on guard and stepped over the door-sill into the bedroom.

The great belt on the wheel of Time slipped and eternity stood still. By the match light he could see the man's legs fighting with his breeches in his frantic desire to get them on. He had both chance and time to kill the intruder in his helpless condition—half in and half out of his pants—but he was too weak to take action. The shapeless enemies of humanity that live in the hours of Time had waylaid Joe. He was assaulted in his weakness. Like Samson awakening after his haircut. So he just opened his mouth and laughed.

The match went out and he struck another and lit the lamp. A howling wind raced across his heart, but underneath its fury he heard his wife sobbing and Slemmons pleading for his life. Offering to buy it with all that he had. "Please, suh, don't kill me. Sixty-two dollars at de sto'. Gold money."

Joe just stood. Slemmons looked at the window, but it was screened. Joe stood out like a rough-backed mountain between him and the door. Barring him from escape, from sunrise, from life.

He considered a surprise attack upon the big clown that stood there laughing like a chessy cat. But before his fist could travel an inch, Joe's own rushed out to crush him like a battering ram. Then Joe stood over him.

"Git into yo' damn rags, Slemmons, and dat quick."

Slemmons scrambled to his feet and into his vest and coat. As he grabbed his hat, Joe's fury overrode his intentions and he grabbed at Slemmons with his left hand and struck at him with his right. The right landed. The left grazed the front of his vest. Slemmons was knocked a somersault into the kitchen and fled through the open door. Joe found himself alone with Missie May, with the golden watch charm clutched in his left fist. A short bit of broken chain dangled between his fingers.

Missie May was sobbing. Wails of weeping without words. Joe stood, and after awhile he found out that he had something in his hand. And then he stood and felt without thinking and without seeing with his natural eyes. Missie May kept on crying and Joe kept on feeling so much and not knowing what to do with all his feelings, he put Slemmons' watch charm in his pants pocket and took a good laugh and went to bed.

"Missie May, whut you cryin' for?"

"Cause Ah love you so hard and Ah know you don't love *me* no mo'."

Joe sank his face into the pillow for a spell then he said huskily, "You don't know de feelings of dat yet, Missie May."

"Oh Joe, honey, he said he wuz gointer give me dat gold money and he jes' kept on after me—"

Joe was very still and silent for a long time. Then he said, "Well, don't cry no mo', Missie May. Ah got yo' gold piece for you."

The hours went past on their rusty ankles. Joe still and quiet on one bed-rail and Missie May wrung dry of sobs on the other. Finally the sun's tide crept upon the shore of night and drowned all its hours. Missie May with her face stiff and streaked towards the window saw the dawn come into her yard. It was day. Nothing more. Joe wouldn't be coming home as usual. No need to fling open the front door and sweep off the porch, making it nice for Joe. Never no more breakfast to cook; no more washing and starching of Joe's jumper-jackets and pants. No more nothing. So why get up?

With this strange man in her bed, she felt embarrassed to get up and dress. She decided to wait till he had dressed and gone. Then she would get up, dress quickly and be gone forever beyond reach of Joe's looks and laughs. But he never moved. Red light turned to yellow, then white.

From beyond the no-man's land between them came a voice. A strange voice that yesterday had been Joe's.

"Missie May, ain't you gonna fix me no breakfus'?"

She sprang out of bed. "Yeah, Joe. Ah didn't reckon you wuz hongry."

No need to die today. Joe needed her for a few more minutes anyhow.

Soon there was a roaring fire in the cook stove. Water bucket full and two chickens killed. Joe loved fried chicken and rice. She didn't deserve a thing and good Joe was letting her cook him some breakfast. She rushed hot biscuits to the table as Joe took his seat.

He ate with his eyes in his plate. No laughter, no banter.

"Missie May, you ain't eatin' yo' breakfus'."

"Ah don't choose none, Ah thank yuh."

His coffee cup was empty. She sprang to refill it. When she turned from the stove and bent to set the cup beside Joe's plate, she saw the yellow coin on the table tween them.

She slumped into her seat and wept into her arms.

Presently Joe said calmly, "Missie May, you cry too much. Don't look back lak Lot's wife and turn to salt."

The sun, the hero of every day, the impersonal old man that beams as brightly on death as on birth, came up every morning and raced across the blue dome and dipped into the sea of fire every evening. Water ran down hill and birds nested.

Missie knew why she didn't leave Joe. She couldn't. She loved him too much, but she could not understand why Joe didn't leave her. He was polite, even kind at times, but aloof.

There were no more Saturday romps. No ringing silver dollars to stack beside her plate. No pockets to rifle. In fact the yellow coin in his trousers was like a monster hiding in the cave of his pockets to destroy her.

She often wondered if he still had it, but nothing could have induced her to ask nor yet to explore his pockets to see for herself. Its shadow was in the house whether or no.

One night Joe came home around midnight and complained of pains in the back. He asked Missie to rub him down with liniment. It had been three months since Missie had touched his body and it all seemed strange. But she rubbed him. Grateful for the chance. Before morning, youth

triumphed and Missie exulted. But the next day, as she joyfully made up their bed, beneath her pillow she found the piece of money with the bit of chain attached.

Alone to herself, she looked at the thing with loathing, but look she must. She took it into her hands with trembling and saw first thing that it was no gold piece. It was a gilded half dollar. Then she knew why Slemmons had forbidden anyone to touch his gold. He trusted village eyes at a distance not to recognize his stick-pin as a gilded quarter, and his watch charm as a four-bit piece.

She was glad at first that Joe had left it there. Perhaps he was through with her punishment. They were man and wife again. Then another thought came clawing at her. He had come home to buy from her as if she were any woman in the long house. Fifty cents for her love. As if to say that he could pay as well as Slemmons. She slid the coin into his Sunday pants pocket and dressed herself and left his house.

Half way between her house and the quarters she met her husband's mother, and after a short talk she turned and went back home. Never would she admit defeat to that woman who prayed for it nightly. If she had not the substance of marriage she had the outside show. Joe must leave *her*. She let him see she didn't want his old gold four-bits too.

She saw no more of the coin for some time though she knew that Joe could not help finding it in his pocket. But his health kept poor, and he came home at least every ten days to be rubbed.

The sun swept around the horizon, trailing its robes of weeks and days. One morning as Joe came in from work, he found Missie May chopping wood. Without a word he took the ax and chopped a huge pile before he stopped.

"You ain't got no business choppin' wood, and you know it."

"How come? Ah been choppin' it for de last longest."

"Ah ain't blind. You makin' feet for shoes."

"Won't you be glad to have a lil baby chile, Joe?"

"You know dat 'thout astin' me."

"Iss gointer be a boy chile and de very spit of you."

"You reckon, Missie May?"

"Who else could it look lak?"

Joe said nothing, but he thrust his hand deep into his pocket and fingered something there.

It was almost six months later Missie May took to bed and Joe went and got his mother to come wait on the house.

Missie May was delivered of a fine boy. Her travail was over when Joe came in from work one morning. His mother and the old women were drinking great bowls of coffee around the fire in the kitchen.

The minute Joe came into the room his mother called him aside.

"How did Missie May make out?" he asked quickly.

"Who, dat gal? She strong as a ox. She gointer have plenty mo'. We done fixed her wid de sugar and lard to sweeten her for de nex' one."

Joe stood silent awhile.

"You ain't ast 'bout de baby, Joe. You oughter be mighty proud cause he sho is de spittin' image of yuh, son. Dat's yourn all right, if you never git another one, dat un is yourn. And you know Ah'm mighty proud too, son, cause Ah never thought well of you marryin' Missie May cause her ma used tuh fan her foot around right smart and Ah been mighty skeered dat Missie May wuz gointer git misput on her road."

Joe said nothing. He fooled around the house till late in the day then just before he went to work, he went and stood at the foot of the bed and asked his wife how she felt. He did this every day during the week.

On Saturday he went to Orlando to make his market. It had been a long time since he had done that.

Meat and lard, meal and flour, soap and starch. Cans of corn and tomatoes. All the staples. He fooled around town for awhile and bought bananas and apples. Way after while he went around to the candy store.

"Hello, Joe," the clerk greeted him. "Ain't seen you in a long time."

"Nope, Ah ain't been heah. Been round in spots and places."

"Want some of them molasses kisses you always buy?"

"Yessuh." He threw the gilded half dollar on the counter. "Will dat spend?"

"Whut is it, Joe? Well, I'll be doggone! A gold-plated four-bit piece. Where'd you git it, Joe?"

"Offen a stray nigger dat come through Eatonville. He had it on his watch chain for a charm—goin' round making out iss gold money. Ha ha! He had a quarter on his tie pin and it wuz all golded up too. Tryin' to fool people. Makin' out he so rich and everything. Ha! Ha! Tryin' to tole off folkses wives from home."

"How did you git it, Joe? Did he fool you, too?"

"Who, me? Naw suh! He ain't fooled me none. Know whut Ah done? He come round me wid his smart talk. Ah hauled off and knocked 'im down and took his old four-bits way from 'im. Gointer buy my wife some good ole lasses kisses wid it. Gimme fifty cents worth of dem candy kisses."

"Fifty cents buys a mighty lot of candy kisses, Joe. Why don't you split it up and take some chocolate bars, too. They eat good, too."

"Yessuh, dey do, but Ah wants all dat in kisses. Ah got a lil boy chile home now. Tain't a week old yet, but he kin suck a sugar tit and maybe eat one them kisses hisself."

Joe got his candy and left the store. The clerk turned to the next customer. "Wisht I could be like these darkies. Laughin' all the time. Nothin' worries 'em."

Back in Eatonville, Joe reached his own front door. There was the ring of singing metal on wood. Fifteen times. Missie May couldn't run to the door, but she crept there as quickly as she could.

"Joe Banks, Ah hear you chunkin' money in mah do'way. You wait till Ah got mah strength back and Ah'm gointer fix you for dat."

Chester Himes (1909–   )

Along with Frank Yerby, Chester Bomar Himes has been one of the most productive Black novelists, with sixteen novels published as well as numerous short stories. This large body of fiction ranges widely over many aspects of Black life in diverse social classes, from the criminals of his early prison stories and his later series of detective thrillers to the World War II shipyard worker of *If He Hollers Let Him Go* (1945), the union organizer of *Lonely Crusade* (1947), the decorous middle-class family of *The Third Generation* (1954), the Bohemian novelist of *The Primitive* (1955), and the promiscuous Harlem sophisticates of *Pinktoes* (1965). Always these protagonists are presented against the background of a fully realized social milieu.

Born in Jefferson City, Missouri, Himes grew up in the South and Middle West. His middle-class family suffered stresses and strains, some of them caused by his light-skinned mother and some of them caused by his own rebelliousness. While still in high school he worked as a busboy in a fashionable hotel, where he acquired the experience necessary for his short story "Salute to the Passing" (reprinted here). After graduating from high school in Cleveland, he matriculated at Ohio State University, but in his second semester he was required to withdraw for disciplinary reasons. Soon he was working for a Cleveland gambler, and by the end of 1928 he had been sentenced to twenty years in the Ohio State Penitentiary for armed robbery. There he received his real "education," as Malcolm X, Eldridge Cleaver, and Etheridge Knight were later to do. He witnessed, for example, the catastrophic prison fire of 1930 that killed 320 convicts and became the subject of his first nationally circulated short story, "To What Red Hell?" (1934). His novel *Cast the First Stone* (1952) is also based on prison life. By the time he went out on parole in 1936 he had already published stories in *Esquire, Abbott's Monthly Magazine, Coronet,* and *The Bronzeman*.

Released from prison, Himes returned to Cleveland, where he was befriended by Langston Hughes, then engaged as a playwright for Karamu House, and by the white novelist Louis Bromfield. He worked for the Ohio Writers Project for a while before going to the West Coast. In Los Angeles he became familiar with both the Hollywood scene and the Communist movement, and in San Francisco he worked in the shipyards. His first two novels, *If He Hollers Let Him Go* and *Lonely Crusade,* draw on these experiences.

Since 1955 Himes has lived as an expatriate in Europe, for many years in France and more recently in Spain. Since 1957 he has published a series of detective novels, first in French, that have been highly popular with European readers. The protagonists, two Black detectives named Coffin Ed Smith and Gravedigger Jones, frolic through a series of adventures filled with violence, sex, and macabre comedy. Of these qualities, violence is the most prevalent, for Himes believes it to be the central characteristic of American life. If the Black man is ever to achieve his freedom in America, Himes thinks, it must be through massive violence: "After all, Americans live by violence, and violence achieves —regardless of what anyone says, regardless of the distaste of the white community—its own ends."

A partial bibliography appears as a supplement to John A. Williams' lengthy interview of Himes in *Amistad 1* (1970), edited by John A. Williams and Charles F. Harris. Another recent interview appeared in

The Times (London), June 28, 1969, p. 22. A biographical sketch is included in Harry Warfel's *American Novelists of Today* (1951). For criticism see James Baldwin, "History as Nightmare," *The New Leader,* XXX (October 25, 1947), 11, 15; Robert A. Bone, *The Negro Novel in America* (1958); David Littlejohn, *Black on White* (1966); and, especially, Edward Margolies, *Native Sons* (1968) and "The Thrillers of Chester Himes," *Studies in Black Literature,* I (Summer 1970), 1–11.

Salute to the Passing

When Dick Small pushed through the service hall into the main dining room, he sensed an exasperation in the general mood of the diners with that surety of feeling which twenty years as headwaiter at the Park Manor Hotel had bestowed on him. The creased, careful smile adorning his brown face knotted with self reproach. He should have been there sooner.

His roving gaze searched quickly for flaws in the service. There was fat Mr. McLaughlin knuckling the table impatiently as he awaited— Dick was quite sure that it was broiled lobster that Mr. McLaughlin was so impatiently awaiting. And Mrs. Shipley was frowning with displeasure at the dirty dishes which claimed her elbow room as she endeavored to lean closer to her boon companion, Mrs. Hamilton, and impart in a theatrical whisper a choice morsel of spicy gossip—Dick had no doubt that it was both choice and spicy. When Mr. Lyons lifted his glass to take another sip of iced water, he found to his extreme annoyance that there was no more iced water to be sipped, and even from where he stood, Dick could see Mr. Lyon's forbearance abruptly desert him.

The white-jacketed colored waiters showed a passable alacrity, Dick observed without censor. But direction was lacking. The captain, heavy-footed and slow, plodded about in a stew of indecision.

Dick clapped his hands. "Fill those glasses for that deuce there," he directed the busboy who had sprung to his side. "Take an ashstand to the party at that center table. Clear up those ladies." He left the busboy spinning in his tracks; turned to the captain who came rushing over. "I'll take it over now, son. You slip into a white jacket and bring in Mr. McLaughlin's lobster."

His presence was established and the wrinkles of exasperation ironed smoothly out.

The captain nodded and flashed white teeth, relieved. He turned away, turned back. "Chief, Mr. Erskine has a party of six for six-thirty. I gave it to Pat. Here's the bill of fare." He gave Dick a scrawled note.

Dick pocketed the note and for an instant he stood quite still in the center of the room, head cocked to one side as if deferentially listening. A hum of cultured voices engaged in leisurely conversation; the gentle clatter of silver on fine china, the slight scrape of a chair, the tinkle of ice in glasses, the aroma of hot coffee and savory, well-cooked food, the sight of unhurried dining and hurried service, all blended into an atmosphere ineffably dear to his heart. For directing the service of this dining room in a commendable manner was the ultimate aim of his life. It was as much a part of him as the thin spot in his meticulously brushed hair or the habitual immaculateness of the tuxedoes which draped his slight, spright frame. He was one of the last of his kind, the black headwaiter, a passing American institution.

But the press of duty left no time for idle reflection. He went to Mr. Erskine's table and scanned the setup. After a moment's study, he leaned across the table and aligned a fork, smoothed an infinitesimal wrinkle from the linen, shifted the near candlestick just a wee bit to the left. Then he rocked back on his heels and allowed his eyes to smile. He was pleased.

He nodded commendation to Pat, tan and lanky, who was spooning ice cubes into the upturned glasses, and Pat acknowledged it with his roguish grin.

"Here's the bill of fare, Pat." His voice was quick and crisp. "Put your cocktails on ice and have everything prepared by a quarter after six."

Glancing at the wall clock he noticed that it

was already nearly six. He stepped away, wondering detachedly at the cause for the early rush, circled an unoccupied table and came back, frowning slightly. "This is usually Mrs. Van Denter's table, Pat. Why did the captain decide to put that party of six here?"

"Cap called the desk, chief," Pat explained. "They said Mrs. Van Denter had gone into the country to spend a week with her sister."

"You know how contrary she is. Been that way for twenty years to my knowing, ever since her husband died and . . ." he caught himself and stopped abruptly, ashamed of himself. . . . "Put your reserved card on, Pat." A snap had come into his voice. "Always put your reserved card on first, then . . ."

The sight of Mrs. Van Denter coming through the entrance archway choked him. She made straight for her table, ploughing everyone aside who got in her way. This evening she looked slightly forbidding, her grayish, stoutish, sixtyish appearance looking rockier than ever and the tight seam of her mouth carrying an overload of obstinacy. At first glance he thought that she had had a Martini too many, but as she lumbered closer with her elephantine directness, he decided that it came from her disposition instead of her digestion.

Perhaps she and her sister had had a rift, he reflected, bowing to her with more than his customary deference. "How are you this evening, Mrs. Van Denter?" he smiled. After a brief pause he began an apology, "I am very sorry to have to change you, Mrs. Van Denter, but the captain was under the impression that you were in the country. . . ."

She brushed him aside and aimed her solid body for the table on which Pat had just placed the reserved sign. He turned quickly to follow her, his mouth momentarily slack. There was the hint of a race. But she won.

And for all of the iced glasses and party silver and crimped napkins and bowl of roses and engraved name cards at each plate, for all of the big black-lettered sign which read, *Reserved,* staring up into her face, she reached for the nearest chair, pulled it out and planted her plump body into it with sickening finality. Then she reached for an iced glass.

Dick placed a menu card before her and signaled Pat to take her order, his consternation under control now so that his actions registered no more than a natural desire to serve. He picked up the bowl of flowers and the reserved card and placed them on another table, then moved casually away in both thought and body.

At the third table he stopped for a moment to address the stately, white-haired lady seated there. "How do you do, Mrs. Hughes. And this is your sister, Mrs. Walpole, of Boston, I am sure.

"We're delighted to have you with us again, Mrs. Walpole. I remember quite well when you visited us before."

Mrs. Hughes smiled cordially and Mrs. Walpole said, "I've been here several times before."

"But I was referring to your last visit; it was in August three years ago."

"What a remarkable memory," Mrs. Walpole murmured.

Dick allowed himself a moment's complacence. Why have a memory if he couldn't share it? But when he moved away it carried him deeper into the past, when the black man was America's principal servant and the black headwaiter the pampered protege of millionaires and royalty among his own people. Not that he had ever let it go to his head, he quickly amended. Not in his thirty years of service had he once gotten out of his place. The reflection brought a glow of pride. But it was quickly followed by the disturbing thought that now was an era of change. The black headwaiter was giving way to white hostesses, foreigners, to all sorts of people who claimed to be servants. He was saddened by the thought. Would there ever again be a black man as big as a black headwaiter? he asked himself. A black man who could serve a Senator's steak and have a fellow lodge member appointed to a position in Washington, who could stop a busy industrialist and save a Negro school. . . .

When he spoke again his voice was brusk. "Clear that table!" he ordered a busboy as if he alone was to blame for the change of things.

A party of seven at a center table demanded his personal attention and he was cheered again. "Good evening, Mr. and Mrs. Seedle," he greeted the elderly hosts, knowing that they would not consider the service sufficient until he made his appearance. "And how is this young gentleman?" he inquired of the seven-year-old smart aleck seated beside them.

"I'm all right, Dick," the boy replied, "but I'm not no gentleman 'cause gramma just said so. . . ."

"Arnold!" Mrs. Seedle rebuked.

"Fill these glasses," Dick directed a busy waiter to hide his smile, then filled them himself before the startled waiter had a chance to protest.

He looked about for a busboy. Seeing none at hand, he hurried across the room, irritation lumping in his face.

"What's the matter with you, are you deaf?" he demanded, shaking the boy's shoulder.

"No sir, I—I—er—"

"Go get the salad tray and present it to that party of seven," he snapped, then hurried away in his loping gait to greet Mrs. Collar, eighty and cross, who hesitated undecidedly under the entrance archway.

"It's a rather nasty night, Mrs. Collar," he remarked by way of greeting, seating her in a corner nook. "It doesn't seem to be able to make up its mind whether to rain or sleet, but I feel that it will clear up by tomorrow."

Mrs. Collar looked up at him over the rim of her ancient spectacles. "That isn't any encouragement to me," she replied in her harsh, unconciliatory voice. "I'm going out *tonight*."

Confusion took the smoothness out of Dick's speech. "I—er, I wouldn't be surprised if it cleared up very shortly. It seems . . ."

"Well, make up your mind!" she snapped, scanning the menu.

He smiled deprecatingly, signaling to a waiter. "I'm afraid I'd make a poor weather-man."

"You should concentrate your efforts on the service," she advised sharply.

He turned away from her, reproached, and started kitchenward to recruit more waiters from the room service department. He just must have more waiters, the management should realize that. . . . Something about one of the waiters on duty halted him. He glanced down, glanced up again. "What kind of polish do you use, son?" he inquired disarmingly.

"Paste," the waiter replied, unthinkingly.

He let his gaze drop meaningly to the waiter's unshined shoes. "Try liquid next time, son," he suggested, passing on through the service hall into the kitchen.

Beyond the range, over by the elevator, where the room service was stationed, a waiter lounged indolently by a table and yelled at the closed elevator doors, "Knock-knock!"

Dick drew up quietly behind him, heard the slightly muffled reply from within the elevator, "Who's there?"

"Mr. Small!" Dick said crisply.

The waiter jumped. His hand flew up and knocked over a glass of water on the clean linen. The elevator doors popped open, emitting two other waiters in an impressive hurry.

"If you fellows don't care to work—" he began.

But they did care to work. He rushed them into the dining room. Following, he quickly scanned the sidestand, exploring for negligence. But the pitchers were filled and the butter was iced. The silver was neatly arranged in the drawers. A slight expression of commendation came into his smile. Busboys such as that would make good waiters some day.

Then his thoughts turned back to the guests. Without any question, he realized that these people were his life. They took up his time, his thoughts, his energy. He was interested in them, interested in their private lives and their individual prosperity. His most vital emotions derived coloring from theirs; when they were pleased, he was pleased, when they were hurt, he was hurt, when they failed or prospered in their respective endeavors it had a personal bearing on the course of his life. Each day, as he stood looking over them, he received some quality of character from them which instilled in him a certain dignity.

Now his gaze drifted slowly from face to face, reading the feelings and emotions of each with an uncanny perception. For a moment his cup was filled to overflowing. He felt a bond between himself and these people, the age-old bond between servant and master.

There were Tommy and Jackie Rightmire, the polo playing twins, he noticed with a glow of pride for their achievements. And several tables distant, he saw their sister dining with a Spanish count whom he had never been quite able to admire.

Then suddenly Mrs. Andrews came through the entrance archway and beat a hard-heeled, determined path straight toward the rear of the room where Mr. Andrews, her spouse, and a Mrs. Winnings, a comely divorcee, were dining together behind the slight screen of a rear column. Mrs. Andrews was older than her husband, and showed it, and reputedly was very jealous of his affections.

Knowing this, Dick's compelling thought was to avoid catastrophe, for catastrophe it would be, he sincerely felt, should she chance upon her husband's animated tete-a-tete. He headed her off just in time.

"Right this way, Mrs. Andrews," he began, pulling a chair from a conspicuously placed center table.

"No, no, not that," she refused with a gesture, "I want something remote, quiet. I'm expecting a friend." Her eyes dared him to think more than that which she had explicitly stated, which, he was fully cognizant, it was not his prerogative to do.

"Then this will be just the thing for you," he purred smoothly, seating her across the dining room from her husband with her back toward him and the column between them.

"Thank you, this will be just fine." She smiled, pleased, and he had the feeling of a golfer who has just scored a hole in one.

Strolling casually away, he noticed Mrs. Van Denter preparing to leave and went over to her table. "Was your dinner enjoyable, Madame?" he inquired, bowing again with slightly exaggerated deference.

Dinner, enjoyable or not, had not softened the stone of Mrs. Van Denter's face. "Dick," she snapped, "I find your obsequiousness a bit repugnant." Then she plodded smilelessly away.

He upbraided himself. That was twice in one day that he had drawn criticism. But there was no time to explore into the causes, for the table of two women needed clearing. He went in search of a busboy.

The boy whom he found was a greenhorn. Although it was his second day on the job he was still shy about approaching people and taking their plates. So he slipped up behind the nearer lady, a thin, overly made-up widow with a lashing voice, and reached from behind her for her plate. She had just leaned forward to whisper when she saw his stealthily reaching hand.

"Oh!" she gasped, her sharp mouth going slack like a fish's.

The boy went panicky, fearing that he had offended her. He snatched at the plate in a hurry to get away. But the thin lady jerked it away from him, spilling a bone to the table. By this time the boy was frightened. He grabbed again for the plate.

The lady twisted angrily around in her chair. "Let go!" she shrieked.

The boy released it and jumped backward, his nostrils flaring, his eyes white-rimmed in his black face.

"Always taking my plate before I'm finished!" the lady shrilled caustically.

The boy kept backing away from her and at a safe distance turned and hurried toward the kitchen doorway. Dick started after him, intending to school him in the manner of clearing tables, but by the time he reached the kitchen the boy was downstairs changing into his street clothes. He sent the captain down to bring him back, but he was too frightened to try again.

"Well, he wouldn't have made a waiter, anyway," Dick remarked, and added philosophically, "Good servants are born servants. Take my father; he was his master's butler. A field hand won't make a good servant. . . ." But noticing that a raised window was annoying a stag party of four in the rear corner, he broke off and hurried over to close it.

Afterwards he paused in a half-bow, inquiring solicitously, "Are you being taken care of, gentlemen?"

On closer observation he saw that they were all drunk and not gentlemen after all.

"That's a good looking tux, boy," one remarked. "Where'd you get it? Steal it?"

"No sir, I purchased it. . . ."

"What makes you black?" another cut in. A laugh spurted.

Dick's smile was constant. "God did, gentlemen," he said and moved away.

At a center table a high pressure voice was saying, "Just talked to the Governor. He said. . . ." Dick turned his glance obliquely and noticed a late-comer pull out a chair opposite a comely young matron. Why, of course, that was her husband, but she was the one who signed the checks, and who was the other woman he had seen him with the other day?

The sight of old Mr. Woodford standing in the entrance archway snapped his line of thought before he could recall and he hurried forward to meet him.

"And how are you this evening, Mr. Woodford, sir?" he greeted, then added without awaiting a reply, knowing there would be none, "Right this way, sir. I reserved your table for you."

He received Mr. Woodford's grudging nod and led the way rearward, head cocked and arms swinging, recalling reluctantly the time when Mr. Woodford had been genial and talkative and worth many millions. Since the stock crash he had been broke and now he was glum, with blood-shot eyes from drinking too much.

When he moved away his actions were slowed, groggy, as if he had taken a severe beating. The old order was passing, he told himself, suddenly realizing that in a very short time he would be beyond the sixty mark. Sixty was old for a waiter in a busy hotel. . . . He shook himself as if awakening from a bad dream, stepped forward with a brave show of energy.

Perhaps he wasn't looking, perhaps he could not see, but he bumped into a busboy with a loaded tray. China crashed on the tiled floor, silver rang. The sudden shatter shook the room. He patted the stooping boy on the shoulder, the unusual show of feeling leaving the boy slightly flustered, turned quickly away, head held high, refusing to notice the shattered crockery. By his refusal to notice it, he averted attention.

But by now the dinner rush was gradually subsiding. Dick was first made aware of it by the actions of his waiters. They had begun to move about with a languor which bespoke of liberal tips. He glanced at the clock. It was eight-thirty.

He released the first shift with the ironic suggestion, "Don't disappoint your money, boys."

Watching their happy departure, he was aware that before the hour passed they would be hanging over their favorite bar. A frown of disapproval crossed his face. Well, it was their business, but the first one that stepped into this dining room with the smell of liquor on his breath would be immediately discharged, he promised himself.

Then his attention was drawn to a drunken party at a center table. Overflow from the bar, no doubt. His frown deepened. The coarseness of their speech and actions spread a personal humiliation within him. He always pictured the guests as infallible criterions of gentility, and it hurt him to be disappointed.

Some one of the party made a risqué remark and everyone laughed. The nearby waiter smothered his laugh in a napkin.

Dick rushed over and chastened him with a severe voice. "Take that napkin from your face! Get some side towels and use them. And don't ever let me catch you using a napkin in that manner." His harshness was an outlet.

He moved toward the side windows, trying to stifle the buildup of emotion in his mind. The guests were always right, and a waiter was always impersonal in action and in thought, no matter what occurred—that was the one rigid rule in the waiters' code. But now it helped him but a very little. He decided that he must be tired.

George, tall and dark-skinned, passed him. He noticed that George needed new tuxedo trousers. He didn't say anything, for he knew also that George had a high-yellow woman who took most of his money. It wouldn't be long now before George would need another job.

But he thought no more about it for he had just noticed Mr. Spivat, half-owner of the hotel, dining alone at a wall table. He went over and spoke to him. "Nasty weather we're having, Mr. Spivat."

"Yes, it is, Dick," Mr. Spivat replied absently, scanning the late edition.

The window behind Mr. Spivat drew Dick's gaze. He looked out into the dark night. Park foliage across the street was a thick blackness, wet in the sleet and rain. On a distant summit, the Museum was a chiseled stone block in white light, hanging from the starless night by invisible strings. Street lights in the foreground showed a stone wall bordering the park, a strip of sidewalk, slushy pavement. A car turned the corner, its headlights stabbing into the darkness. The purr of a motor sounded faintly as it passed; the red tail light bobbed lingeringly into the bog of distant darkness. Dick stared into the void after it, feeling very tired. He thought of a chicken farm in the country where he could get off of his feet. But he knew that he would never be satisfied away from a dining room. With a vague, undefined regret, he thought of his son who was now a young doctor and not making anything at it. Nowadays colored boys didn't want to be servants, he reflected with his nearest approach to bitterness. Perhaps it was for the best, who knew? A father couldn't live his son's life. But to head a lineage of headwaiters— He sighed.

When he turned back, traces of an inner weariness showed in the edges of his smile, making it ragged. But his eyes were as sharp as ever. They lingered a moment on the slightly hobbling white-coated figure of Bishop. A little stooped was Bishop, a little paunched, a little gray, with a moon face and soiled eyes and rough skin of midnight blue. A good name, Bishop, a descriptive name, Dick thought with a half smile.

He noticed Bishop lurch once and followed him into the kitchen, overtaking him at the pantry. He spun him about and sniffed his breath, catching the scent of mints and a very faint odor of alcohol.

"You haven't been drinking again, have you, Bishop?" he asked sharply.

Bishop forced a laugh as if to dispel such an

idea. "Nosuh, Chief. Been rubbin' my leg with rubbin' alcohol. That's what you smell. My neuritis is troublin' me a lot."

Dick nodded sympathetically. "You need to watch your diet, Bishop," he advised. "Go home when you serve that dessert."

Bishop bobbed his head, rubbing his hands together. "Thank you, Chief."

Following him back into the dining room, Dick noticed that it was Mr. Spivat whom he was serving. He frowned, trying to recall whether he or the captain had assigned him to Mr. Spivat. He certainly wouldn't have if he had known how badly he was limping for Mr. Spivat was convinced, anyway, that the majority of Negro waiters drank too much. And Bishop did appear drunk.

It all happened so quickly that Dick couldn't move.

Bishop's right leg buckled as he placed the cream pitcher. He jacknifed forward on his knee. Cream flew in a thin sheet over the front of Mr. Spivat's dark blue suit.

Mr. Spivat blanched, then ripened like a russet apple. He got slowly to his feet, controlling himself.

Dick was there in three swift strides, applying a cold damp towel to Mr. Spivat's suit. "Clean up, George," he directed the other waiter, trying to avert the drama which he felt engulfing them. "Sorry, Mr. Spivat, sir. Sorry, sir. The boy's got a bad case of neuritis; it's very bad during this nasty weather. I'll lay him off until it gets better."

But cold damp towels could not help Mr. Spivat's suit, nor expressions of sorrow allay his quiet rage. "Dick, see that this man gets his money, and if I ever see him in this hotel again I'll fire the whole bunch of you. I have no tolerance for a drunken waiter."

Dick motioned Bishop from the dining room and followed behind. He had the checker make out a requisition for Bishop's pay and had another waiter take it out to the *maitre de hotel's* office. It was for an even thirteen dollars.

Bishop stood at a respectful distance, his shoulders drooping, his whole body sagging, wordless and very sad. Dick could not meet the dog-like plea of his eyes. He knew that Bishop had liked serving Mr. Spivat. He recalled how Bishop and Mr. Spivat used to talk baseball during the season.

After a time Bishop said irrelevently, a slight protest in his voice, "I got seven kids."

Dick looked down at Bishop's feet. Big feet they were, with broken arches from shouldering heavy trays on adamant concrete. Big and flat and knotty. He felt in his pockets, discovered a twenty-dollar bill. He pressed it into Bishop's hand.

"I wasn't drunk, Chief. Nosuh, I swear I wasn't," Bishop said.

Dick wanted to believe that, but he couldn't. Bishop as a rule didn't eat mints; he didn't like sweets of any kind. But mints would help kill the odor of whiskey on his breath. He sighed. He knew that Bishop would drink. There was very little of the likes and dislikes and habits of all his waiters, of their family affairs and personal lives, that he did not know.

"Accidents will happen, son," he said. "Yours just cost you your job. Try not to let it happen again. If there's anything I can do for you, let me know. Anything reasonable. And even if it isn't reasonable, come and let me say so." He stood quite still for a moment, his face weary.

Then he shook it all from his mind. He blinked his eyes clear of the picture of a dejected black face, donned his creased, careful smile and pushed through the service hall into the dining room, his head cocked to one side as if deferentially listening.

It required a special effort.

Poetry

Two Women Poets of the Harlem Renaissance: Angelina Grimké (1880–1958) and Anne Spencer (1882–   )

Both Angelina Grimké and Anne Spencer began writing poetry before the Harlem Renaissance actually began, but their poetry first appeared in anthologies during that period, notably in Countee Cullen's *Caroling Dusk*. One quickly notes that their poetry is somewhat conventional and, like much of the poetry of Braithwaite and Cullen, nonracial in theme. But, considering the period in which they wrote, these are not limitations. In the poetry of both there is great sensitivity and emotional acuity. Each strives for the arresting image to express some unique aspect of personal experience. In her poem "Lines to a Nasturtium," Miss Spencer, for instance, plays with the paradox of a beauty that attracts and fulfills but in the very act of fulfilling also destroys. Similarly, Miss Grimké, using a death-wish image, writes of wishing to drown in the beauty of a Mona Lisa's eyes. Both, obviously, studied their neo-Romantic models well.

The great appeal of this kind of poetry, however, is that it communicates a uniquely private experience. Neither Miss Spencer nor Miss Grimké is writing for a group or a class or a race, nor do they use the language of complex cerebration and emotional compression. Rather there is the direct attempt to present and define an emotional experience.

Historically, this is poetry of a period lying somewhere between the time of Dunbar and the time of Langston Hughes. The dialect vogue is passé, and the pungent, racy language of Black urban realism has not yet come into popular use. So each poet writes from her personal and private mountaintop of experience, free to explore subtle emotional nuances as her poetic gifts permit.

Angelina Grimké*

A Mona Lisa

1

I should like to creep
Through the long brown grasses
  That are your lashes;
I should like to poise
  On the very brink
Of the leaf-brown pools
  That are your shadowed eyes;
I should like to cleave
  Without sound,
Their glimmering waters,
  Their unrippled waters,

I should like to sink down
  And down
    And down . . . .
      And deeply drown.

2

Would I be more than a bubble breaking?
  Or an ever-widening circle
  Ceasing at the marge?
Would my white bones
  Be the only white bones
Wavering back and forth, back and forth
  In their depths?

Grass Fingers

Touch me, touch me,
Little cool grass fingers,
Elusive, delicate grass fingers.
With your shy brushings,
Touch my face—
My naked arms—
My thighs—

My feet.
Is there nothing that is kind?
You need not fear me.
Soon I shall be too far beneath you,
For you to reach me, even,
With your tiny, timorous toes.

Anne Spencer*

Lines to a Nasturtium

A Lover Muses

Flame-flower, Day-torch, Mauna Loa,
I saw a daring bee, today, pause, and soar,
  Into your flaming heart;
Then did I hear crisp crinkled laughter
As the furies after tore him apart?
  A bird, next, small and humming,

Looked into your startled depths and
  fled . . .
Surely, some dread sight, and dafter
  Than human eyes as mine can see,
Set the stricken air waves drumming
  In his flight.

* For headnote see p. 626.

Day-torch, Flame-flower, cool-hot Beauty,
I cannot see, I cannot hear your fluty
Voice lure your loving swain,
But I know one other to whom you are in
    beauty
Born in vain;
Hair like the setting sun,
Her eyes a rising star,

Motions gracious as reeds by Babylon, bar
All your competing;
Hands like, how like, brown lilies sweet,
Cloth of gold were fair enough to touch her
    feet . . .
Ah, how the senses flood at my repeating,
As once in her fire-lit heart I felt the furies
Beating, beating.

Letter to My Sister

It is dangerous for a woman to defy the gods;
To taunt them with the tongue's thin tip,
Or strut in the weakness of mere humanity,
Or draw a line daring them to cross;
The gods who own the searing lightning,
The drowning waters, the tormenting fears,
The anger of red sins . . .
Oh, but worse still if you mince along timidly—
Dodge this way or that, or kneel, or pray,
Or be kind, or sweat agony drops,
Or lay your quick body over your feeble young,

If you have beauty or plainness, if celibate,
Or vowed—the gods are Juggernaut,
Passing over each of us . . .
    Or this you may do:
Lock your heart, then quietly,
And, lest they peer within,
Light no lamp when dark comes down.
Raise no shade for sun,
Breathless must your breath come thru,
If you'd die and dare deny
The gods their godlike fun!

Arna Bontemps (1902–   )

In the portion of *The Big Sea* dealing with the Harlem Renaissance, Langston Hughes attributes to Arna Bontemps a second dimension not accorded any of his other literary confreres. Not only was Bontemps a poet and writer of great skill and ability, but he was also a stable family man—a symbol of social stability in a circle of some unstable literary associates. Wallace Thurman was impatient, mercurial, hypersensitive, and brilliant; Zora Neale Hurston was unpredictable, brash, demanding, and brilliant; but Arna Bontemps, looking like "a young edition of Dr. DuBois," was comfortably married *and* brilliant.

His literary career, since those early days of froth and ferment, has developed in a sound and predictably consistent pattern. In the beginning of his career he was a poet, publishing in the literary magazines of the time from 1924 to 1931. His poems "Golgotha Is a Mountain" and "The Return" won the Alexander Pushkin prize offered by *Opportunity* in 1926 and 1927, and his "A Black Man Talks of Reaping" won a *Crisis* first prize in 1927. Then, in the next decade, Bontemps turned to prose fiction, publishing *God Sends Sunday* in 1931, *Black Thunder* in 1936, and *Drums at Dusk* in 1939. Of these, *Black Thunder* stands out as a fictional version of the Gabriel Prosser slave rebellion in Virginia in 1800. Unlike

Styron's *Nat Turner* of a later generation, Bontemps' historical novel won no prizes, but in 1936 it was a significant "first" in this particular genre of Black literature.

In the late 1930's, Arna Bontemps took an unusual step for a creative writer: he went back to school. He had already earned an undergraduate degree from Pacific Union College in 1923; to this he now added a degree in library science, thus expanding his possibilities as an editor and historian of the Black Experience. In the meantime, he developed an interest in juvenile fiction. Starting with *You Can't Pet a Possum* in 1934 and continuing to *Lonesome Boy* in 1955, Bontemps produced six novels in this category, showing very early a concern for the important part youth must play in solving America's pressing social and moral problems.

In his later years, Arna Bontemps has turned his attention to editing. As early as 1941 he had edited *Golden Slippers, An Anthology of Poetry for Young Readers.* In 1949 he joined with Langston Hughes to produce another anthology, *Poetry of the Negro, 1746–1949.* His later anthologies—*Book of Negro Folklore* (prepared in collaboration with Langston Hughes in 1958), *American Negro Poetry* (1963), and *Great Slave Narratives* (1969)—all share two important qualities. First, by the nature of their content they fully support and encourage the revolution of rising expectations among Black people in America, providing the stimulus of the written record to fire racial pride and reveal the depth and breadth of the Black man's heritage. Second, in all of them are literary and historical introductions written by Bontemps that reflect great erudition and critical authority. In the *Book of Negro Folklore,* for instance, he provides a short but incisive introductory essay, showing the relationships among the various kinds of folk material and relating the bestiaries, spirituals, folk sermons, and blues to various aspects of the Black man's long racial experience in Africa, in the Caribbean, and in America. Similarly, his introduction to *American Negro Poetry* presents a historical overview of Black poetry from its eighteenth-century beginnings in America to the unfolding richness of the present generation of poets. Throughout this short essay his method is explicative rather than argumentative; he finds no need to be defensive about Black poetry. His conclusion is that Black poetry and Black music and Black art do not need to seek out a white American mainstream; they have their own mainstream. Finally, the introduction to *Great Slave Narratives* is a scholarly essay on the history and significance of the very important genre of the slave narrative. All Black autobiographical writing, asserts Bontemps, has its roots in this genre. From Olaudah Equiano in 1789 through Booker T. Washington to James Baldwin, autobiography has been the Black man's major form of literature, blending dramatic action with social and moral protest. All of these narratives score white injustice and outline personal strategies for Black survival, but this emphasis is combined with action-paced episodes that provide suspenseful and exciting reading. It is Bontemps' very logical conclusion that racial prejudice is the only reason America has tended to neglect this important genre of the Black man's literature.

Thus, within recent years, the man who began as a poet of the Harlem Renaissance and spent the 1930's, 1940's, and 1950's writing prose fiction has become an editor and critic of considerable stature. Like other creative writers turned critic, Arna Bontemps knows where he is going because he knows where he has been. Having written creatively, he now knows what to say about creative writing, and there is no doubt that his critical insights will continue to be invaluable in improving and broadening the understanding and appreciation of the Black literary heritage. In the meantime, as the poems that follow prove, his poetry has retained its excellence over the years.

Critical comments on Bontemps' prose fiction can be found in Hugh M. Gloster's *Negro Voices in American Fiction* (1948) and in Robert A. Bone's *The Negro Novel in America* (1965). Sterling Brown also provides incisive comment on *Black Thunder* in his *The Negro in American Fiction* (1969). Significantly, the best general comment on the status, promise, and commitment of the Black novelist is contained in Bontemps' own essay, "Jean Toomer and the Harlem Writers of the 1920's," originally printed in Herbert Hill's edition of critical essays entitled *Anger, and Beyond* (1966) and reprinted in Robert Hemenway's *The Black Novelist* (1970). For a checklist of Bontemps' books, see *Black World*, XX (September 1971), 78–79.

A Black Man Talks of Reaping

I have sown beside all waters in my day.
I planted deep, within my heart the fear
That wind or fowl would take the grain away.
I planted safe against this stark, lean year.

I scattered seed enough to plant the land
In rows from Canada to Mexico,
But for my reaping only what the hand
Can hold at once is all that I can show.

Yet what I sowed and what the orchard yields
My brother's sons are gathering stalk and root,
Small wonder then my children glean in fields
They have not sown, and feed on bitter fruit.

Reconnaissance

After the cloud embankments,
The lamentation of wind,
And the starry descent into time,
We came to the flashing waters and shaded
  our eyes
From the glare.

Alone with the shore and the harbor,
The stems of the cocoanut trees,
The fronds of silence and hushed music,
We cried for the new revelation
And waited for miracles to rise.

Where elements touch and merge,
Where shadows swoon like outcasts on the sand
And the tired moment waits, its courage gone—
There were we

In latitudes where storms are born.

Nocturne at Bethesda

I thought I saw an angel flying low,
I thought I saw the flicker of a wing
Above the mulberry trees; but not again.
Bethesda sleeps. This ancient pool that healed
A host of bearded Jews does not awake.

This pool that once the angels troubled does not
    move.
No angel stirs it now, no Saviour comes
With healing in His hands to rise the sick
And bid the lame man leap upon the ground.

The golden days are gone. Why do we wait
So long upon the marble steps, blood
Falling from our open wounds? and why
Do our black faces search the empty sky?
Is there something we have forgotten? some
    precious thing
We have lost, wandering in strange lands?

There was a day, I remember now,
I beat my breast and cried, "Wash me, God,
Wash me with a wave of wind upon
The barley; O quiet One, draw near, draw near!
Walk upon the hills with lovely feet
And in the waterfall stand and speak.

"Dip white hands in the lily pool and mourn
Upon the harps still hanging in the trees
Near Babylon along the river's edge,
But oh, remember me, I pray, before
The summer goes and rose leaves lose their
    red."

The old terror takes my heart, the fear
Of quiet waters and of faint twilights.
There will be better days when I am gone
And healing pools where I cannot be healed.
Fragrant stars will gleam forever and ever
Above the place where I lie desolate.

Yet I hope, still I long to live.
And if there can be returning after death
I shall come back. But it will not be here;
If you want me you must search for me
Beneath the palms of Africa. Or if
I am not there then you may call to me
Across the shining dunes, perhaps I shall
Be following a desert caravan.

I may pass through centuries of death
With quiet eyes, but I'll remember still
A jungle tree with burning scarlet birds.
There is something I have forgotten, some
    precious thing.
I shall be seeking ornaments of ivory,
I shall be dying for a jungle fruit.

          You do not hear, Bethesda.
O still green water in a stagnant pool!
Love abandoned you and me alike.
There was a day you held a rich full moon
Upon your heart and listened to the words
Of men now dead and saw the angels fly.
There is a simple story on your face;
Years have wrinkled you. I know, Bethesda!
You are sad. It is the same with me.

Southern Mansion

Poplars are standing there still as death
And ghosts of dead men
Meet their ladies walking
Two by two beneath the shade
And standing on the marble steps.

There is a sound of music echoing
Through the open door
And in the field there is
Another sound tinkling in the cotton:
Chains of bondmen dragging on the ground.

> The years go back with an iron clank,
> A hand is on the gate,
> A dry leaf trembles on the wall.
> Ghosts are walking.
> They have broken roses down
> And poplars stand there still as death.

Sterling A. Brown (1901–   )

As an editor, critic, poet, and teacher of literature, Sterling A. Brown has exerted considerable influence on the direction and development of Black literature over the past forty years. Like Langston Hughes, Countee Cullen, and Arna Bontemps, he first appeared on the literary scene during the Harlem Renaissance. With a Phi Beta Kappa key from Williams College and a master's degree from Harvard, he seemed to be especially trained for a career as a literary academician. But Brown's creative instincts and strong belief in the artistic and emotional superiority of his people soon turned him away from "literary" literature to folk literature—to the blues and the spirituals. His emphasis on Black folk literature added another significant dimension to the Harlem Renaissance, for Sterling Brown brought a well-honed critical intelligence to his fruitful encounter with this aspect of the Black Experience. The result was that Black academia began to rub shoulders with the unlettered blues shouter and riverbottom folk singer. Ma Rainey, Bessie Smith, and Blind Lemon Jefferson gained a critical and appreciative audience, and the Black folk singer retrieved a long-overdue artistic standing among Black people. This has been Sterling Brown's major contribution.

Inevitably, Sterling Brown's keen interest in folk literature affected his own poetry in style, theme, and content. His poems have the same terseness, dramatic ellipsis, and abbreviated narration. There is also a concern with the realistic and the earthly. The most distinctive quality of the poems in *Southern Road* (1932), however, is their hard-hitting emphasis on social protest. The title poem has rather distinct ballad qualities—rhythmic repetition, narrative compression, and monosyllabic emphasis—but protest against racial injustice irradiates the poem. The singer is a "po' los' boy" sentenced to life and a day on the chain gang. Similarly, old Lem presents his rationalization of his own powerlessness before the white power structure:

> *They don't come by ones*
> *They don't come by twos*
> *But they come by tens.*

Sterling Brown's work as a critic is best seen in his two rather long critical essays—*Negro Poetry and Drama* and *The Negro in American Fiction*—published originally in 1937 and then reissued in the Atheneum series in 1969. After a thirty-year lapse, his critical perceptions remain remarkably accurate and precise. Predictably, in *Negro Poetry* he devotes an entire chapter to "the rich field of folk-poetry," defying chronology somewhat to show the sharp contrasts between the "literary" writers of dialect and those who were truly masters of the art of folk speech. As the title indicates, *The Negro in American Fiction* goes beyond fiction written only by Blacks and examines the vast amount of fiction by white authors that presents various unflattering stereotypes of the Negro. However, both essays have tersely presented literary explications, and there is little or no effort to define the literary, social, or cultural milieu that may have shaped the point of view of a given work.

Sterling Brown's most significant task was editing *The Negro Caravan* in collaboration with Arthur Davis and Ulysses Lee. After its publication in 1941 it quickly became a standard reference text in Black literature. Its particular appeal is the section on Black folk literature, which has a very effective and informative critical introduction to the various subdivisions of folk literature, from spirituals and slave seculars to the blues and folk sermons. In his introductory essay, Brown discusses the various interpretations by white critics such as Guy Johnson and Newman Ivy White concerning the origin and nature of the Black man's folk songs and stories. These interpretations, Brown indicates, usually supported the majority view that the Black man accepted and enjoyed both slavery and his place in American society. Brown, on the other hand, argues that the spirituals were carefully worded protest songs against slavery and its inhumanity.

Saunders Redding has a short but pithy critical appraisal of Sterling Brown as poet and critic in his *To Make a Poet Black* (1939). Similarly, Robert Bone assesses his overall contribution to Black literature in the introduction to the Atheneum edition of *Negro Poetry and Drama* and *The Negro in American Fiction*. See also Jean Wagner's *Les poètes nègres des États-Unis* (1963) and Stephen A. Henderson's "A Strong Man Called Sterling Brown," *Black World,* XIX (September 1970), 5–12.

Old Lem

I talked to old Lem
And old Lem said:
  "They weigh the cotton
They store the corn
    We only good enough
    To work the rows;
They run the commissary
They keep the books
    We gotta be grateful
    For being cheated;
Whippersnapper clerks

Call us out of our name
    We got to say mister
    To spindling boys
They make our figgers
Turn somersets
We buck in the middle
    Say, "Thankyuh, sah.'
      They don't come by ones
      They don't come by twos
      But they come by tens.

"They got the judges
They got the lawyers
They got the jury-rolls
They got the law
  They don't come by ones
They got the sheriffs
They got the deputies
  They don't come by twos
They got the shotguns
They got the rope
  We git the justice
  In the end
  And they come by tens.

"Their fists stay closed
Their eyes look straight
  Our hands stay open
  Our eyes must fall
  They don't come by ones
They got the manhood
They got the courage
  They don't come by twos
  We got to slink around,
  Hangtailed hounds.
They burn us when we dogs

They burn us when we men
  They come by tens. . . .

"I had a buddy
Six foot of man
Muscled up perfect
Game to the heart
  They don't come by ones
Outworked and outfought
Any man or two men
  They don't come by twos
He spoke out of turn
At the commissary
They gave him a day
To git out the county.
He didn't take it.
He said "Come and get me."
They came and got him.
  And they came by tens.
He stayed in the county—
He lays there dead.

  They don't come by ones
  They don't come by twos
  But they come by tens."

Strong Men

The strong men keep coming on.
  —Sandburg

They dragged you from homeland,
They chained you in coffles,
They huddled you spoon-fashion in filthy hatches,
They sold you to give a few gentlemen ease.

They broke you in like oxen,
They scourged you,
They branded you,
They made your women breeders,
They swelled your numbers with bastards. . . .
They taught you the religion they disgraced.

You sang:
  Keep a-inchin' along
  Lak a po' inch worm. . . .

You sang:
  Bye and bye
  I'm gonna lay down dis heaby load. . . .

You sang:
  Walk togedder, chillen,
  Dontcha git weary. . . .

    The strong men keep a-comin' on
    The strong men git stronger.

They point with pride to the roads you built
  for them,
They ride in comfort over the rails you laid
  for them.
They put hammers in your hands
And said—Drive so much before sundown.

You sang:
  Ain't no hammah
  In dis lan',
  Strikes lak mine, bebby,
  Strikes lak mine.

They cooped you in their kitchens,
They penned you in their factories,

They gave you the jobs that they were too good
   for,
They tried to guarantee happiness to themselves
By shunting dirt and misery to you.

You sang:
  Me an' muh baby gonna shine, shine
  Me an' muh baby gonna shine.
    The strong men keep a-comin' on
    The strong men git stronger. . . .

They bought off some of your leaders
You stumbled, as blind men will . . .
They coaxed you, unwontedly soft-voiced. . . .
You followed a way.
Then laughed as usual.
They heard the laugh and wondered;
Uncomfortable;
Unadmitting a deeper terror. . . .
    The strong men keep a-comin' on
    Gittin' stronger. . . .

What, from the slums
Where they have hemmed you,
What, from the tiny huts
They could not keep from you—
What reaches them
Making them ill at ease, fearful?
Today they shout prohibition at you
"Thou shalt not this"
"Thou shalt not that"
"Reserved for whites only"
You laugh.

One thing they cannot prohibit—
    The strong men . . . coming on
    The strong men gittin' stronger.
    Strong men. . . .
    Stronger. . . .

Margaret Walker (1915–   )

Margaret Walker's "For My People" is the title poem of her first volume of poetry, which was published by Yale University Press in 1942. The poem itself had originally appeared in *Poetry* magazine in 1937 and hence reflects the mood and temper of the Depression years rather than the war years. But even in 1937 the poem struck a new note; none of the Black poets in the Harlem Renaissance had written like Margaret Walker. Not only does the poem vibrate with racial consciousness and social protest, but it also has a kind of verbal brilliance heretofore not seen in Black poetry. The verbal arpeggios and the alliteration remind one of both the Black folk sermon and the free verse techniques of Carl Sandburg. However, underneath the flow of words is order and coherence; it is all a celebration of "my people."

Margaret Walker's training for the career of poet and writer started early. Her father was a minister in the Methodist Episcopal Church in Alabama and Louisiana, and she learned that a good sermon could be a kind of poetry and a good poem a kind of sermon. Moreover, as she explains in the introductory notes to *Jubilee,* her prize-winning novel of 1966, hers was a "talking" family, who discussed anecdotes and incidents of the past, issues and events of the present, and prospects and possibilities for the future. Thus, she grew up in an atmosphere of racial awareness; Black history was all around her—good times and bad times, slave times and free times.

Margaret Walker completed her undergraduate work at Northwestern University in Evanston, Illinois, in 1937. It was an exciting time for a young writer to be in the Chicago area. WPA writing projects had brought a cluster of impecunious young writers to the area. Some were Black; some were white; some, like Richard Wright, became famous; some drifted off into anonymity or into military service and were never heard of again. But social protest was everywhere, and leftist social thought was the order of the day. To the leftist social thinker well read in Communist literature, the American Black man was prima facie evidence of capitalist exploitation. So as a people they had to be lifted out of both their oppression and depression so that there would be no more Scottsboro cases, no more hunger, no more confusion. In support of such a hope, Margaret Walker wrote her poem for her people, praying for a "new earth" and "another world." The poem has the quality of sustained verbal zest as it tries to define in words the genius of Negro life in America. The Black man is presented throughout as victim— "distressed and disturbed and deceived and devoured" by the forces of oppression. In many ways it is a sermon on social injustice.

Margaret Walker's other literary achievement, *Jubilee,* is a historical novel. It and her later poetry are discussed in the introduction to Part VI, because this segment of her work belongs to the present-day period of Black literature.

For My People

For my people everywhere singing their slave songs repeatedly: their dirges and their ditties and their blues and jubilees, praying their prayers nightly to an unknown god, bending their knees humbly to an unseen power;

For my people lending their strength to the years: to the gone years and the now years and the maybe years, washing ironing cooking scrubbing sewing mending hoeing plowing digging planting pruning patching dragging along never gaining never reaping never knowing and never understanding;

For my playmates in the clay and dust and sand of Alabama backyards playing baptizing and preaching, and doctor and jail and soldier and school and mama and cooking and playhouse and concert and store and Miss Choomby and hair and company;

For the cramped bewildered years we went to school to learn to know the reasons why and the answers to and the people who and the places where and the days when, in memory of the bitter hours when we discovered we were black and poor and small and different and nobody wondered and nobody understood;

For the boys and girls who grew in spite of these things to be Man and Woman, to laugh and dance and sing and play and drink their wine and religion and success, to marry their playmates and bear children and then die of consumption and anemia and lynching;

For my people thronging 47th Street in Chicago and Lenox Avenue in New York and Rampart Street in New Orleans, lost disinherited dispossessed and HAPPY people filling the cabarets and taverns and other people's pockets needing bread and shoes and milk and land and money and Something—Something all our own;

For my people walking blindly, spreading joy, losing time being lazy, sleeping when hungry, shouting when burdened, drinking when hopeless, tied and shackled and tangled among ourselves by the unseen creatures who tower over us omnisciently and laugh;

For my people blundering and groping and floundering in the dark of churches and schools and clubs and societies, associations and councils and committees and conventions, distressed and disturbed and deceived and devoured by money-hungry glory-craving leeches, preyed on by facile force of state and fad and novelty by false prophet and holy believer;

For my people standing staring trying to fashion a better way from confusion from hypocrisy and misunderstanding, trying to fashion a world that will hold all the people all the faces all the adams and eves and their countless generations;

Let a new earth rise. Let another world be born. Let a bloody peace be written in the sky. Let a second generation full of courage issue forth, let a people loving freedom come to growth, let a beauty full of healing and a strength of final clenching be the pulsing in our spirits and our blood. Let the martial songs be written, let the dirges disappear. Let a race of men now rise and take control!

Drama

Willis Richardson (1897–   )

Willis Richardson made his debut as a dramatist during the Harlem Renaissance. Presently a retired postal clerk living in Washington, D.C., he has enjoyed a long and productive career as a playwright and drama anthologist. His first anthology was *Plays and Pageants from the Life of the Negro,* published by Associated Publishers in 1930. This was followed by *Negro History in Thirteen Plays,* which Richardson, with May Miller as coeditor, produced for Associated Publishers in 1935. Twenty years later, in 1955, he published a collection of plays for children entitled *The King's Dilemma.* But the high point of his illustrious career as a dramatist occurred at its beginning, when he received the *Crisis* prize for his play ''The Broken Banjo'' in 1925.

When Richardson started writing plays about Black life, the prospects for an active and well-supported Black theater were not encouraging. The professional Broadway theater had long been hostile to any form of large-scale Black participation. It is true that *Shuffle Along* and other Black musicals were immensely popular during the 1920's, but this development was something of an isolated phenomenon. Indeed, serious drama by and about Blacks during this period was limited to the tributary theater movement, involving private theater groups such as the Gilpin Players of Cleveland and the Lafayette Players of Harlem. However, the development of these private theater groups was prematurely cut off by the advent of the Depression in the 1930's. There was also a developing interest in theater and drama in several of the Black colleges, but during the 1920's this was of minor significance.

The reasons for the less than favorable climate of the professional theater when Willis Richardson wrote his prize-winning play were many and complex. One primary reason was that, following the mid-nineteenth century emphasis on blackface minstrelsy, the theater in America became surfeited with demeaning racial stereotypes that alienated Black actors and Black playwrights. However, there was some change for the better when Ridgely Torrence wrote and produced in 1917 three one-act plays expressly ''written for the Negro theater.'' Torrence's plays were followed by Eugene O'Neill's tradition-breaking *The Emperor Jones,* which in the early 1920's gave the Black man a new status as a participating actor in professional theater. Both Torrence and

O'Neill broke the tradition of stereotyped roles for Black actors, and their break-throughs suggested that in the lives of Black people there was enough drama to fill a thousand stages.

By 1925 the problem was one of direction and emphasis. As Alain Locke defined it, the question was should the Black man develop a drama of "discussion and social analysis" or a drama of "expression and artistic interpretation." Or, to put the matter more specifically, should an emerging Black playwright like Willis Richardson write "problem" plays addressed to finding solutions for racial dilemmas or plays celebrating the Black man's folk life. In a sense, Angelina Grimké's *Rachel,* presented in Washington, D.C., in 1916, had already hinted a direction and an emphasis, for the plot concerns the struggle of a Black girl whose father had been lynched by a white mob. By the mid-1930's, Paul Green began to write about the stark tragedy of the Black man's life in the rural South, and Langston Hughes produced his *Mulatto.* By this time it had become clear that the emphasis was to be on a drama of "discussion and social analysis." Richardson's *Broken Banjo* is an early example of this sort of drama.

There are several articles that have been written to describe the state of drama during the Harlem Renaissance. Two dependable and authoritative sources are Frederick Bond's *The Negro and the Drama* (1940) and Loften Mitchell's *Black Drama* (1967). Doris Abramson's *Negro Playwrights in the American Theater* (1969) is also good but does not treat any events prior to 1925.

The Broken Banjo

A Folk Tragedy

Characters

MATT TURNER
EMMA, his wife
SAM, her brother
ADAM, her cousin
A POLICEMAN

Scene: A tenement room in the Negro district.
Time: Contemporary.

First performance by the Krigwa Players, New York, August 1, 1925.

THE DINING ROOM *of* MATT *and* EMMA TURNER *is dull and dark looking, with a door at the right leading to the outside and a door at the left leading through the kitchen. There is a square table in the center of the room with two chairs, the only ones in the room, near it. A cupboard is at the rear, and at the right of this is a window. At the left side below the door is a small closet concealed by curtains. When the play begins* MATT, *a short, strongly-built man of thirty, is sitting at the left of the table picking his banjo. He is not by any means a good player, but his desire to play well is his religion. He plays on for a few moments until his wife,* EMMA, *a woman of twenty-seven, appears at the kitchen door.*

EMMA. (*In disagreeable tones*) Matt, for God's sake stop that noise!

MATT. (*Looking up and stopping for a moment*) What the devil's the matter with you?

EMMA. Ah got a headache and Ah'm tired o'

hearin' that bum music. It's a wonder you wouldn't find somethin' else to do. You can come out in the back yard and split me some wood if you want to.

MATT. Didn't Ah work all night? You think Ah'm goin' to work all night, then come home and split wood in the daytime? If you don't like this music put your head in a bag, then you won't hear it.

EMMA. You ain't got no feelin's for nobody but yourself. You just got that old job, and before you got it Ah had to work my hands almost off to keep things goin'; this is the thanks Ah get for what Ah done.

MATT. You needn't throw that in ma face; you didn't have to work if you didn't want to.

EMMA. If Ah hadn't worked, we'd 'a' gone to the poorhouse.

MATT. Maybe we would 'a' been better off.

EMMA. If you wasn't so selfish you'd get along better; but you don't care a thing about nobody or nothin' but that old banjo.

MATT. Have Ah got any cause to care about anything else?

EMMA. How about me?

MATT. Well, that's different. If Ah didn't care nothin' about you Ah'd 'a' been gone long ago. But what about me? Don't everybody in town hate me? Don't your whole family despise the very ground Ah walk on?

EMMA. It ain't their fault.

MATT. It is their fault. Didn't they all try to stop me from comin' to see you? Didn't Ah have to beat the devil out o' that black brother and cousin o' yours before they'd let me alone? And don't they hate me?

EMMA. (*Defending her family*) Now don't start to callin' nobody black, 'cause you ain't got no room to call nobody black. Sam and Adam is just as light as you.

MATT. Maybe they is, but they ain't as honest; and they ain't nothin' but loafin' jailbirds.

EMMA. Ah don't see where you get nothin' by throwin' that at me.

MATT. You know it's the truth; and you know Ah ain't never been to jail.

EMMA. It ain't too late, don't be braggin'.

MATT. You talk like you'd like to see me go to jail.

EMMA. You ought to have better sense than that.

MATT. Well, here's somethin' Ah want to tell you about Sam and Adam before Ah forget it.

EMMA. What?

MATT. Ah want you to keep 'em out o' here. They don't do nothin' but loaf around all the time and come here to eat everything they c'n get.

EMMA. Sam and Adam ain't doin' nobody no harm.

MATT. Yes, they is; they're doin' me harm.

EMMA. How's they doin' you harm?

MATT. They come here and eat up ma grub, then go around and talk about me. Ah wouldn't mind you givin' 'em a bite now and then if they was friends o' mine.

EMMA. Is you got any friends at all?

MATT. No, Ah ain't got no friends. Ain't nobody likes me but you, and you ain't crazy about me.

EMMA. Well, you oughtn't to be so disagreeable, then you'd have some friends.

MATT. Ah don't know, Ah reckons Ah get along just as well without 'em.

EMMA. No, you don't. Ain't nobody that gets along just as well without friends.

MATT. When you ain't got so many friends you ain't got so many people to come around and eat you up.

EMMA. Ain't nothin' in bein' so stingy.

MATT. Ah ain't givin' nobody nothin'; that's why Ah'm tellin' you to tell them two fools to keep out o' here.

EMMA. Ah ain't goin' to insult nobody.

MATT. If you don't tell 'em, Ah will; cause Ah don't want 'em in here. That settles it.

EMMA. Ah ain't after makin' no more enemies. We got enemies enough.

MATT. You don't look out for ma interest much.

EMMA. Yes, Ah do; Ah'm thinkin' for you every minute o' ma life, but you don't know it. You never will know it till you get in a big pinch.

MATT. There ain't no use o' us quarrellin'. We quarrel too much anyhow, Ah reckon.

EMMA. Ah reckon we do. (*He begins to pick the banjo again, and after looking at him for a moment half fondly, she goes back to the kitchen. There are a few moments of silence save the picking of the banjo. Presently* EMMA *reappears at the door and addresses* MATT *in kinder tones*) MATT?

MATT. Huh?

EMMA. Is you got any money?

MATT. No.

EMMA. That's mighty funny.

MATT. Funny how?

EMMA. You workin' every night makin' good wages, and you don't give me nothin' but the money to run the house. What does you do with the rest of it? (MATT *is silent*) You mean you ain't got a cent, Matt?

MATT. Ah ain't got no spare money.

EMMA. No spare money?

MATT. No.

EMMA. Well, what is you got?

MATT. Ah got five dollars Ah been savin' to buy some music with.

EMMA. You wouldn't buy music when Ah need the money for somethin' else, would you, Matt?

MATT. What you need money for?

EMMA. Ah needs shoes, for one thing.

MATT. Ah need shoes too.

EMMA. (*Coming forward and showing her worn shoes*) Look at mine.

MATT. (*Looking at them*) They is pretty bad.

EMMA. There ain't nothin' to 'em but uppers.

MATT. How much your shoes goin' to cost?

EMMA. Ah don't know. You can get 'em second-handed if you want to. You ought to get a good secondhanded pair for two or three dollars.

MATT. Ah tell you what Ah'll do.

EMMA. What?

MATT. Ah'll get you them shoes if you'll tell Sam and Adam to keep out o' here.

EMMA. Why don't you tell 'em, Matt?

MATT. Ah'll tell you the truth, Emma; Ah don't want to tell 'em 'cause Ah don't want to have no trouble. Time Ah tell 'em to stay out Ah know they'll start a' argument, then Ah'll have to beat 'em up like Ah done once before. And Ah get tired o' fightin' some time, 'deed Ah do.

EMMA. Ah'll tell 'em, then.

MATT. (*Rising*) All right, Ah'll get the shoes.

EMMA. Go out the alley through the back way to that Jew store. Ah seen some secondhanded ones in the window.

MATT. What size you want?

EMMA. Sevens.

MATT. What kind?

EMMA. Black. That's the only kind Ah ever wear.

MATT. A pair o' black sevens. All right, if Ah can't get 'em there, Ah'll get 'em somewhere else. (*He goes out through the kitchen leaving his banjo on the table.* EMMA *picks up the banjo, looks at it and shakes her head. As she puts it down and starts back to the kitchen* SAM *and* ADAM *enter from the other door.* SAM *is thirty-three, taller than* MATT, *but not so sturdily built.* ADAM *is thirty, about* MATT's *height, but not so stout as* MATT. *Both are careless loafers; the former is gruff, with a mean temper; the latter is lively and playful.*)

ADAM. (*As they enter*) Hi, Emma.

EMMA. (*Stopping in the doorway and speaking in unwelcome tones*) Hi.

SAM. (*Roughly*) What's the matter with you?

EMMA. Nothin'.

SAM. Got anything to eat?

EMMA. No.

ADAM. That's mighty funny. You used to always have somethin' to eat around here.

EMMA. Don't you-all never think about nothin' but eatin'? (SAM *and* ADAM *look at each other puzzled.*)

SAM. (*Sitting at the left of the table*) Is you and Matt been fussin' this mornin'?

EMMA. No.

ADAM. (*Sitting on the table*) Somethin' must be wrong; you never did act like this before.

EMMA. Ain't nothin' wrong with me.

SAM. (*Looking towards the kitchen*) Seems like Ah smell cabbage. Ain't you cookin' cabbage?

EMMA. Yes.

SAM. Thought you didn't have nothin' to eat?

EMMA. Them cabbage is for Matt's dinner.

SAM. Can't we have some?

EMMA. No, Ah ain't goin' to let you all eat up his dinner.

ADAM. Ah know what's the matter now, Sam.

SAM. (*Turning to him*) What?

ADAM. Matt's been spoonin' with huh and turned huh against us.

EMMA. (*Angrily*) You go to the devil! (*She goes quickly to the kitchen.*)

SAM. Ah'll bet that damn bully's been talkin' about us.

ADAM. Ah'll bet so too. Lend me your knife.

SAM. (*Handing* ADAM *the knife*) Ah'd like to run this between his ribs.

ADAM. (*Taking the knife and a match from his pocket*) Don't let him see you first.

SAM. He ain't as bad as you think he is.

ADAM. (*Making a toothpick with the match*) Ah'll always remember how he beat us up once.

SAM. He won't never beat us up again. Ah got him in the palm o' ma hand.

ADAM. (*Putting the knife into his pocket*) How you goin' to stop him from beatin' us up?

SAM. (*Holding out his hand*) Wait a minute. Gimme that knife.

ADAM. Lemme keep it a day or two.

SAM. No, give it right back here now.

ADAM. Ah'll give it back to you tomorrow.

SAM. (*Catching him by the pocket*) No, give it right here now.

ADAM. What's the use o' bein' so mean?

SAM. (*Looking him in the eye and speaking more firmly*) Gimme that knife here!

ADAM. (*Putting the knife on the table*) Don't be such a sorehead.

SAM. You better stop kidding with me. Ah don't feel like kiddin' today. Ah feel like runnin' this knife in a certain feller's ribs.

ADAM. Don't cut at him and miss him, 'cause if you do you know what'll happen.

SAM. Ain't nothin' goin' to happen. Didn't Ah say Ah had him in the palm o' ma hand?

ADAM. (*Laughing*) You tryin' to kid me?

SAM. No, Ah ain't kiddin'. Ah don't kid when Ah talk about him. Ah could tell you a thing or two if Ah wanted to. You know they ain't caught the one that killed old man Shelton yet.

ADAM. (*Interested*) You talk like you know somethin'.

SAM. You bet your life Ah know somethin'.

ADAM. What is it?

SAM. That's all right, Ah'll talk at the right time. Watch me call huh in here and bawl huh out. (*Calling*) Emma! Emma!

EMMA. (*From the kitchen*) What?

SAM. Come here. (*Emma comes to the kitchen door.*)

EMMA. What you want?

SAM. Is Matt been talkin' about me?

EMMA. What would Matt be talkin' about you for?

SAM. Ain't no use o' lyin', Ah know somethin's been goin' on. Now what is it?

EMMA. If you want to get told Ah'll tell you, all right. Matt don't want you and Adam hangin' around here eatin' up his grub.

SAM. Oh, he don't, don't he?

EMMA. No.

SAM. Ah reckon you don't, neither.

EMMA. That ain't for me to say; Matt rents the house and buys the grub, and it's up to him to say who he wants 'round and who he don't.

ADAM. Ah told you Matt had been lovin' with huh.

SAM. Well, Matt better be careful: Ah know a thing or two about him.

EMMA. Now there ain't no use o' you goin' makin' up nothin' on Matt.

SAM. Ah ain't makin' up nothin'; this is the truth. Ah seen it with ma own eyes.

EMMA. (*Interested*) You seen what?

SAM. Ah know it's goin' to knock you bald-headed when Ah tell you.

EMMA. You better be careful how you talk about Matt; that's all Ah got to say.

SAM. Careful or not careful, Matt killed old man Shelton and Ah seen him do it.

EMMA. It's a lie! You know it's a lie!

SAM. No, it ain't no lie. Ah seen him do it, and if he ain't careful how he acts with me Ah'll get him strung up by his neck.

EMMA. Don't everybody know the one that killed old man Shelton got away and ain't never been caught?

SAM. Matt's the one that got away and ain't never been caught.

EMMA. You can't make nobody believe that. If you had 'a' knowed that about Matt you'd 'a' told it long ago much as you hate him.

SAM. Ah didn't tell it cause he's your husband and Ah didn't want to put you in a hole; but now you turned against me and Ah don't care.

EMMA. Ah ain't turned against you.

SAM. Yes, you is. You don't even believe what Ah'm sayin' now.

EMMA. Ain't no way for you to make me believe that.

SAM. It ain't, ain't it? Well, Ah'll tell you just how it happened.

EMMA. You gettin' ready to make up somethin' now.

SAM. Ah was standin' right in the bushes when Ah seen Matt comin' along pickin' his banjo and not watchin' where he was walkin'. He walked right in old man Shelton's potato patch. Then old man Shelton ran out and started to beatin' Matt over the head with his stick. He hit Matt once or twice, but the next time Matt put up his banjo to knock off the lick, and the lick broke the banjo. That made Matt so mad that before he knowed it he had picked up a rock and hit old man Shelton right in the head, and the old feller fell like a log. Matt grabbed his banjo and beat it and they ain't caught him yet.

EMMA. Ah know you don't think Ah'm believin' that.

SAM. That's all right, Ah'll prove it when he comes in here.

EMMA. You sure got to prove it to me. Ah don't believe a word you say. You all let me alone anyhow, and let me cook ma husband's dinner. (*She goes into the kitchen.*)

ADAM. It's mighty funny you ain't said nothin' to me about that before now.

SAM. Didn't Ah tell you Ah was holdin' ma tongue cause Ah didn't want to get Emma in bad? You wouldn't want me to hurt ma own sister, would you?

ADAM. Seems like you might 'a' told me anyhow, long as we been runnin' together. You didn't think Ah'd pimp, did you?

SAM. (*Closing the whole matter*) Ain't no use to argue about it now. (*He takes the banjo up and looks at it.*) This old thing's give that guy a lot o' trouble. (*He tries to pick the banjo, but is not successful.*)

ADAM. (*Taking hold of the banjo*) Lemme show you how to pick it.

SAM. (*Still holding on to it*) No, you can't pick it.

EMMA. (*Appearing at the kitchen door*) You-all better put that banjo down before you break it.

SAM. Let go the thing, Adam; and quit your playin'! (*He pulls the banjo suddenly from ADAM's hand and it accidentally strikes the table and is broken.*)

EMMA. (*Coming forward*) Now look what you done! You broke that banjo and Matt's goin' to raise the devil!

SAM. (*To ADAM*) Ah told you to quit your kiddin'!

ADAM. If you had 'a' let me have the thing—

EMMA. (*Snatching the banjo from SAM*) Ain't no use o' makin' excuses now! The thing's broke! What you goin' to do about it?

SAM. Ah ain't goin' to do nothin' about it.

EMMA. Both of you better get out o' here before Matt comes back.

SAM. We ain't scared o' Matt long as we know what we know.

EMMA. Ah'm goin' to hide this thing 'cause Ah don't want to see nobody hurt. (*She puts the banjo into the closet.*)

SAM. Don't worry, ain't nobody goin' to get hurt.

EMMA. (*Listening*) Ah believe Ah hear him comin' now.

SAM. Let him come. (*They are silent until MATT enters from the kitchen with a package under his arm.*)

ADAM. Hi, Matt.

MATT. (*Shortly*) Hi. (*To EMMA in a different tone*) Here's the shoes, Emma. (*He takes the shoes to the table and as he puts them down notices that the banjo is not there.*)

MATT. Where's ma banjo?

EMMA. You don't want no banjo now. Lemme see the shoes.

MATT. No, Ah want ma banjo. Who moved it?

EMMA. Ah moved it. Wait till you get your dinner, then get it.

MATT. (*Striking the table with his open hand*) Ah want it right now, right now!

EMMA. Matt, for God's sake, don't be thinkin' about that old banjo all the time.

MATT. (*Beginning to look around*) Ah'll find it myself. (*He goes to the cupboard, and in his eagerness pulls the drawer and all its contents out on the floor.*)

EMMA. (*Beginning to untie the package*) Ah'm goin' to look at these shoes.

MATT. (*Turning to her*) Don't touch them shoes till Ah find ma banjo! Now, where is it?

EMMA. (*After a pause pointing to the curtains*) In there. (MATT *reaches behind the curtains and brings out the banjo.*)

MATT. (*In consternation*) Broke! Who the devil broke this banjo? (*All are silent*) Emma, who broke ma banjo?

EMMA. (*Pleading with him*) Don't make no trouble, Matt; please don't make no trouble.

MATT. (*Taking the shoes from the table*) If you don't tell me who broke ma banjo Ah'm goin' to take these shoes right back! (EMMA *is silent*) All right, back they go!

EMMA. (*As he starts out*) Don't take 'em back, Matt! Don't take 'em back!

MATT. Who broke it, then?

EMMA. Sam broke it! Sam and Adam!

MATT. (*Throwing the shoes on the table and starting for SAM*) Ah'll fix you, you black dog! (SAM *leaves the chair quickly and jumps behind the table.* MATT *takes the chair up to throw it at him.*)

SAM. Don't you hit me with that chair! Ah know who killed old man Shelton! (MATT *holds the chair in the air as if he is fastened in that position and stares at SAM in wonder*) Ain't no use o' looking at me like that. Ah seen you when you hit him with that rock. (MATT *lets the chair come slowly to the floor.* SAM *coming around the table and snapping his fingers in MATT's face*) You ain't so smart now, is you? You ain't so anxious to smash that chair over ma head, is you? Ah got you where Ah want you now! Ah got you in the palm o' ma hand! (MATT *does not speak, but goes quietly over to the hall door and locks it, putting the key into his pocket. He comes back to the table.*) Who the devil you think you're scarin' by lockin' that door? (MATT *goes over and locks the kitchen door before he speaks.*)

MATT. (*Coming to the table again*) You might have me in the palm o' your hand, but you won't have me there long.

EMMA. For God's sake, Matt! What you goin' to do?

MATT. You keep out o' this!

SAM. You can't scare me now.

ADAM. (*At last finding his voice*) No, you can't scare us now with what we know on you.

MATT. What you-all know on me ain't goin' to do you no good, 'cause ain't neither one of you goin' out o' this house till you swear by the God that made you you won't never say no more about me and old man Shelton.

SAM. How you goin' to make us swear?

MATT. (*More determined and angry*) Ah'm goin' to beat you till you do, or keep you right here and starve you to death! (*To* EMMA) Bring that Bible out here, Emma! (EMMA *gets the Bible from behind the curtains and puts it on the table.*)

MATT. Ah know both of you believe in God and the devil and heaven and hell, 'cause you ain't got the guts not to; and you goin' to raise your right hands and swear on this book!

SAM. (*Taking the knife from his pocket*) If you lay your hands on me Ah'll stick this knife in you!

MATT. (*Reaching behind the curtains and bringing out an ax handle*) Ain't no use for you to start that 'cause Ah can settle you with one lick on the head!

ADAM. Aw, we'll swear; what's the use o' fightin' about it?

MATT. Come on, then; and be quick about it!

SAM. Don't you do it, Adam!

ADAM. Ah ain't goin' to stay in here all day. (ADAM *comes around and puts his left hand on the Bible.*)

MATT. Lift up your right hand! (ADAM *raises his right hand.*)

MATT. Do you swear by the God that made you you won't never say nothin' about me and old man Shelton?

ADAM. Yes.

MATT. Don't say that! Say "Ah do"!

ADAM. Ah do.

MATT. (*To* SAM *who turns away*) Now it's your turn!

SAM. You'll have a nice time makin' me swear!

MATT. If you don't swear Ah'm goin' to keep you right here and beat the devil out o' you till you change your mind!

ADAM. (*Winking at* SAM *while* MATT *is glaring at him*) Come on and do it, Sam; Ah want to get out o' here.

MATT. If he don't come on he'll be sorry for it!

SAM. (*After looking steadily at* ADAM *for a moment*) All right, Ah'll swear not to tell.

MATT. No, you don't! You can't play that with me! Come on around here to this Bible! (SAM *goes to the table, puts his left hand on the Bible and raises his right hand.*)

MATT. Do you swear by the God that made you you won't never say nothin' about me and old man Shelton?

SAM. Ah do.

MATT. Now both of you can go; and don't never put your foot in here no more. (*He throws the key over on the floor.*)

ADAM. (*As he picks up the key*) We'll go, all right.

SAM. (*After the door is unlocked*) We'll go, but Ah'll get even with you one way or the other!

MATT. (*Starting towards them angrily*) Get out o' here! (*They hasten out closing the door behind them.*)

MATT. (*Coming back to the table after unlocking the kitchen door*) Ah didn't think that would ever get out about old man Shelton; but you can never can tell.

EMMA. Ah didn't know you had done that, Matt.

MATT. Ah didn't think nobody did. Ah didn't mean to kill him. When he broke ma banjo, Ah hit him harder than Ah thought.

EMMA. What you goin' to do now?

MATT. Nothin' but keep quiet about it.

EMMA. Yes, you is goin' to do somethin', too. You goin' to make your get-away.

MATT. Get-away for what? Didn't they swear not to tell?

EMMA. And when they was swearin' Ah seen Adam winkin' at Sam. Swearin' don't amount to a row o' pins with them.

MATT. They'd be scared to tell after swearin' on the Bible.

EMMA. Don't you believe it. Soon as Sam gets full o' moonshine whiskey he'll tell everything he knows and that he don't know, too. He'll forget he ever seen a Bible.

MATT. Ah don't feel like runnin' from nobody.

EMMA. Sam's mad now; and Sam mad is just like Sam drunk, he'll do anything. (*There is a pause while* EMMA *awaits* MATT's *decision*) Well, if you won't get ready, Ah'll get you ready. (*She hurries out through the hall door.* MATT *sits resting his head on his hands. Presently* EMMA *returns with a bundle of clothes which she puts on the table as she hurries to the kitchen. In a few moments she returns, wrapping some bread in a paper. She puts the bread in with the clothes.*)

MATT. Ah reckon you're right about goin', Emma.

EMMA. Ah know Ah'm right. They're gettin' ready to play some trick on you. Ah seen it in their eyes.

MATT. Where must Ah go? Ah ain't got a cent.

EMMA. That's all right, you go out the back way across the fields to Uncle Silas and get him to row you across the river. When you get over, beat it to Aunt Linda's and tell huh to hide you till Ah come.

MATT. You reckon Uncle Silas'll take me over? He don't like me. Nobody never did like me.

EMMA. Tell him Ah said so. He'll do it for me.

MATT. When you comin'?

EMMA. Ah'll start out in the mornin'.

MATT. But how about the money? We'll need money if we're goin' anywhere.

EMMA. That's all right about the money. Ah got a hund'ed and forty dollars sewed up in ma mattress. Ah been denyin' maself things that Ah wanted and needed and savin' a little at a time, cause Ah knowed with that temper o' yours you'd get in trouble one time or the other.

MATT. (*Taking the bundle in one hand and the banjo in the other and going to the kitchen door*) Ah reckon Ah been a mighty poor husband to you, but you been a mighty good wife to me, Emma; and if we ever get out o' this trouble, Ah'm goin' to turn over a new leaf. Ah'm goin' now and don't you be long comin'.

EMMA. Ah'll be there first thing in the mornin'.

MATT. All right, so long.

EMMA. (*Starting towards him as if to kiss him*) So long, Matt. (*While* MATT *is hesitating at the kitchen door* SAM *and* ADAM *enter hurriedly through the other door followed by an officer.*)

SAM. (*Pointing to* MATT) There he is!

OFFICER. Wait a minute, Matt; Ah want you.

MATT. (*Still standing in the doorway*) What you want with me?

OFFICER. Sam told me all about old man Shelton.

SAM. Ah told you Ah'd fix you, you bully!

MATT. (*Dropping his banjo and bundle and quickly getting his club*) All right, if you want me, take me!

OFFICER. (*Pointing a warning finger at* MATT) There ain't no use for you to try that, you can't get away with it.

EMMA. (*Catching* MATT's *arm and holding him*) Don't do that, Matt! Don't do it! You'll just get in more trouble!

MATT. Ah'm in all the trouble Ah can get in! It can't be no worse!

EMMA. Yes, it can be worse! They won't give you but ten or fifteen years for old man Shelton 'cause you didn't mean to do that, but if you kill this man they'll hang you!

MATT. (*Surrendering*) Ah reckon you're right, Emma; you always been right and Ah always been wrong. If Ah ever get out o' this Ah'll have sense enough to mind what you say. (*Allowing her to take the club from him, he goes to the officer*) Ah'm ready.

SAM. Better put the irons on him.

OFFICER. That's all right, he'll go.

MATT. (*Turning to* EMMA *as they are about to go*) Goodbye, Emma.

EMMA. (*Standing at the left of the table, her whole body trembling*) Goodbye, Matt. (*As they close the door* EMMA *raises her hands to her eyes as if to hold back the tears.*)

CURTAIN

Folk Literature

Political Songs

Garvey

Garvey, Garvey, is a big man
To take his folks to monkey-land.
If he does, I'm sure I can
Stay right here with Uncle Sam.

When I get on the other side
I'll buy myself a mango.
Grab myself a monkey gal
And do the monkey tango.

When a monkey-chaser dies
Don't need no undertaker.
Just throw him in the Harlem River
He'll float back to Jamaica.

Joe Turner

They tell me that Joe Turner's come and gone,
Oh Lord!
They tell me that Joe Turner's come and gone,
Got my man and gone.
He come with forty links of chain,
Oh, Lord!
He come with forty links of chain,
Got my man and gone.

A Breakdown

Ol' Ant Kate, She Died So Late

Ol' Ant Kate, she died so late
She couldn't get in at the Heaven gate.
The angels met her with a great big club,
Knocked her right back in the washing tub.

Hear dat trumpet sound?
Stand up and don't fall down,
Slip and slide around,
Till yo shoes don't have no tacks.

Join dat 'lection band,
Better join it while you can,
If you don't join dat 'lection band,
Gonna drive you outta this land.

The Blues

The Blues Come fum Texas

The blues come fum Texas
   Lopin lak a mule,
The blues come a-walkin
   Lak a nuchul fool.

Blues run a rabbit,
   Run him a solid mile.
When the blues ketch him,
   He holler like a baby chile.

Woke up this mawnin,
   Blues all round my bed.
Went to eat breakfuss,
   Blues all in my bread.

Good mawning, blues,
   How do you do?
Good mawnin, blues,
   How do you do?
He say, "I'm feelin fine,
   How is you?"

St. James Infirmary Blues

I went down to St. James Infirmary,
   My baby there she lay,
Out on a cold, cold table.
   Well, I looked an I turned away.
What's my baby's chances,
   I asked old Dr. Tharp.
     "By six o'clock this evenin
     She'll be playin a golden harp."

Let her go, let her go,
   God bless her,
Wherever she may be.
She can hunt this wide world over,
   But she'll never find another man
     like me.

Just Blues

I got a sweet black gal
Lives down by the railroad track,
A sweet black gal
Down by the railroad track,
And everytime she cries
The tears run down her back.

Cryin', baby, have mercy,
Baby, have mercy on me!
Baby, baby, baby,
Have mercy, mercy on me!
If this is your mercy,
What can your pity be?

I rolled and I tumbled
And I tossed the whole night through,
Rolled and tumbled and
Tossed the whole night through.
I could not rest in peace, babe,
For worryin' about you.

I feel just like a log
Floating on the deep blue sea,
Log, log, log, log,
On the deep blue sea,
A-worryin' and a-driftin'
'Cause nobody cares for me.

Can't read, can't write,
Gonna buy me a telephone.
Can't read, can't write,
Gonna buy a telephone.
Gonna talk to my baby
Till she comes back home.

White folks, white folks,
Please don't give my gal a job.
White folks, don't give my
Ugly old gal no job.
She's a married woman and I
Don't want her to work too hard.

I got something on my mind
That sure do worry me.
Something on my mind that
Sure do worry me—
Tain't my present, tain't my future,
It's just my old time used-to-be.

Southern Blues

House catch on fire
And ain't no water around,
If your house catch on fire,
Ain't no water around,
Throw yourself out the window,
Let it burn on down.

I went to the gypsy
To have my fortune told,
I went to the gypsy
To have my fortune told,
She said, "Dog-gone you, girlie,
Dog-gone your hard-luck soul!"

I turned around and
Went to that gypsy next door.
I turned around and
Went to that gypsy next door.
She said, "You can get a man
Anywhere you go."

Let me be your ragdoll
Until your china comes.
Let me be your ragdoll
Until your china comes.
If he keeps me ragged,
He's got to rag it some.

Easy Rider

Easy rider, see what you done done, Lawd, Lawd,
Made me love you, now yo sweet man done come,
Gonna love you, baby, right on to Kingdom come.

When you see me comin,
    Hist yo windas high, Lawd, Lawd,
When you see me comin,
    Hist yo windas high.
You know darn well
    I ain't gonna pass you by.

When you see me leavin,
    Hang yo haid an cry, Lawd, Lawd,
When you see me leavin,
    Hang yo haid an cry.
Gonna love you
    Til the day I die.

If I was a cap'n on some western train, Lawd, Lawd,
If I was a cap'n on some western train,
I'd keep on a-goin
    An never come back again.

I'm goin buy me a shotgun long as I am tall,
    Lawd, Lawd,
Gonna buy me a shotgun long as I am tall.
If you don't treat me right,
    You ain't goin ta hav no haid atall.

If I was a catfish swimmin in the deep blue sea,
    Lawd, Lawd,
If I was a catfish swimmin in the deep blue sea,
I'd keep these putty wimmins from fussin
    over me.

Put It Right Here or Keep It Out There

I've had a man for fifteen years, give him his room and board;
Once he was like a Cadillac, now he's like an old worn-out Ford;
He never brought me a lousy dime and put it in my hand;
So there'll be some changes from now on, according to my plan:

He's got to get it, bring it, and put it right here,
Or else he's goin' to keep it out there;
If he must steal it, beg it, or borrow it somewhere,
Long as he gets it, I don't care.

I'm tired of buyin' porkchops to grease his fat lips,
And he has to find another place for to park his old hips;
He must get it, and bring it, and put it right here,
Or else he's goin' to keep it out there.

The bee gets the honey and brings it to the comb,
Else he's kicked out of his home sweet home.
To show you that they brings it, watch the dog and the cat;
Everything even brings it, from a mule to a gnat.

The rooster gets the worm and brings it to the hen;
That oughta be a tip to all you no-good men.
The groundhog even brings it and puts it in his hole,
So my man is got to bring it—doggone his soul.

He's got to get it, bring it, and put it right here,
Or else he's goin' to keep it out there.
If he must steal it, beg it, borrow it somewhere,
Long as he gets it, chile, I don't care.

I'm goin' to tell him like the Chinaman when you don't bring-um check
You don' get-um laundry, if you break-um neck;
You got to get it, bring it, and put it right here,
Or else you goin' to keep it out there.

Fables

The Signifying Monkey

The Monkey and the Lion
Got to talking one day.
Monkey looked down and said, Lion,
I hear you's king in every way.
But I know somebody
Who do not think that is true—
He told me he could whip
The living daylights out of you.
Lion said, Who?
Monkey said, Lion,
He talked about your mama
And talked about your grandma, too,
And I'm too polite to tell you
What he said about you.
Lion said, Who said what? Who?
Monkey in the tree,
Lion on the ground.
Monkey kept on signifying
But he didn't come down.
Monkey said, His name is Elephant—
He stone sure is not your friend.
Lion said, He don't need to be
Because today will be his end.
Lion took off through the jungle
Lickity-split,
Meaning to grab Elephant
And tear him bit to bit. Period!
He come across Elephant copping a righteous
      nod
Under a fine cool shady tree.
Lion said, You big old no-good so-and-so,
It's either you or me.
Lion let out a solid roar
And bopped Elephant with his paw.
Elephant just took his trunk
And busted old Lion's jaw.
Lion let out another roar,
Reared up six feet tall.
Elephant just kicked him in the belly
And laughed to see him drop and fall.
Lion rolled over,
Copped Elephant by the throat.
Elephant just shook him loose
And butted him like a goat,
Then he tromped him and he stomped him

Till the Lion yelled, Oh, no!
And it was near-nigh sunset
When Elephant let Lion go.
The signifying Monkey
Was still setting in his tree
When he looked down and saw the Lion.
Said, Why, Lion, who can that there be?
Lion said, It's me.
Monkey rapped, Why, Lion,
You look more dead than alive!
Lion said, Monkey, I don't want
To hear your jive-end jive.
Monkey just kept on signifying,
Lion, you for sure caught hell—
Mister Elephant's done whipped you
To a fare-thee-well!
Why, Lion, you look like to me
You been in the precinct station
And had the third-degree,
Else you look like
You been high on gage
And done got caught
In a monkey cage!
You ain't no king to me.
Facts, I don't think that you
Can even as much as roar—
And if you try I'm liable
To come down out of this tree and
Whip your tail some more.
The Monkey started laughing
And jumping up and down.
But he jumped so hard the limb broke
And he landed—*bam!*—on the ground.
When he went to run, his foot slipped
And he fell flat down.
Grr-rrr-rr-r! The Lion was on him
With his front feet and his hind.
Monkey hollered, Ow!
Lion said, You little flea-bag you!
Why, I'll eat you up alive.
I wouldn't a-been in this fix a-tall
Wasn't for your signifying jive.
Please, said Monkey, Mister Lion,
If you'll just let me go,
I got something to tell you, *please,*

I think you ought to know.
Lion let the Monkey loose
To see what his tale could be—
And Monkey jumped right back on up
Into his tree.
What I was gonna tell you, said Monkey,
Is you square old so-and-so,
If you fool with me I'll get

Elephant to whip your head some more.
Monkey, said the Lion,
Beat to his unbooted knees,
You and all your signifying children
Better stay up in them trees.
Which is why today
Monkey does his signifying
A-way-up out of the way.

Shine and the Titanic

It was 1912 when the awful news got around
That the great Titanic was sinking down.
Shine came running up on deck, told the Captain, "Please,
The water in the boiler room is up to my knees."

Captain said, "Take your black self on back down there!
I got a hundred-fifty pumps to keep the boiler room clear."
Shine went back in the hole, started shovelling coal,
Singing, "Lord, have mercy, Lord, on my soul!"

Just then half the ocean jumped across the boiler room deck.
Shine yelled to the Captain, "The water's 'round my neck!"
Captain said, "Go back! Neither fear nor doubt!
I got a hundred more pumps to keep the water out."

"Your words sound happy and your words sound true,
But this is one time, Cap, your words won't do.
I don't like chicken and I don't like ham—
And I don't believe your pumps is worth a damn!"

The old Titanic was beginning to sink.
Shine pulled off his clothes and jumped in the brink.
He said, "Little fish, big fish, and shark fishes, too,
Get out of my way because I'm coming through."

Captain on bridge hollered, "Shine, Shine, save poor me,
And I'll make you as rich as any man can be."
Shine said, "There's more gold on land than there is on sea."
And he swimmed on.

Jay Gould's millionary daughter came running up on deck
With her suitcase in her hand and her dress 'round her neck.
She cried, "Shine, Shine, save poor me!
I'll give you everything your eyes can see."
Shine said, "There's more on land than there is on sea."
And he swimmed on.

Big fat banker begging, "Shine, Shine, save poor me!
I'll give you a thousand shares of T and T."
Shine said, "More stocks on land than there is on sea."
And he swimmed on.

When all them white folks went to heaven,
Shine was in Sugar Ray's Bar drinking Seagrams Seven.

PART VI

The Present Generation: Since 1945

Ralph Ellison's essays in *Shadow and Act* contain many provocative comments on the Black man's art, literature, and culture in twentieth-century America. One of his more perceptive generalizations is that at crucial times in its history America always develops a "new moral awareness" and rediscovers its Black minority. It is as if, Ellison explains, the nation as it is propelled by historical necessity "down the pitch-black road" of national commitment rounds a sudden curve, and there, like an unbridged raging river, is Black America. The end of World War II in 1945 plunged America into just such an unexpected situation. All of a sudden, eight hundred thousand Black veterans, full of high hopes and aspirations for full citizenship, were flooding back home, and, all of a sudden, a Great Migration of four hundred thousand Blacks from the South had inundated Northern and Eastern and Western urban centers. These changes forcibly brought white America to a new awareness of the Black presence and forced the nation to begin anew its search for answers to questions that had gone unanswered since 1865.

Richard Wright's great novel *Native Son* (1940) furnished a key to the developing Black mood of the 1940's. As the decade unfolded, the hero of the novel, Bigger Thomas, seemed to remove himself from the pages of fiction to become an Everyman prototype for Black youth in urban ghettos across the land. If there had ever been any question about a Black writer's need to write out of the context of the Black Experience, by 1945 *Native Son* and Bigger Thomas had fully proved the need. Moreover, Richard Wright's experience as a Black creative artist in America revealed that Black literary expression was inextricably linked to Black political, social, and economic experience.

But by 1947 Wright had left for more hospitable shores, leading the number of Black expatriates who were to flee to European capitals and major cities. The reason for his flight can best be told by a review of the Black man's frustrating fight in the 1940's for full integration into the mainstream of American life. Sensitive artists like Wright did not have the patience or stamina to endure the law's delay even though the NAACP's brilliant team of civil rights lawyers—Houston, Hastie, and Marshall—mounted in the 1940's the most sustained legal assault on segregation and racial bigotry ever recorded in American constitutional history. If Wright had stayed in America, he might conceivably have become another Chesnutt, drifting into self-imposed literary silence, or another Dunbar, dying early in spirit and body. For, in the 1940's, despite the legal gains made on all fronts to win hitherto withheld political and social rights, America was still, literarily speaking, almost entirely lily-white. For instance, Frank Yerby chose in his novels to sever his connections with the Black world in plot, character, theme, and authorial posture. His self-removal deprived him of his Blackness, but brought him instant success as a popular "American" novelist. Positive proof of America's literary whiteness in the 1940's can be found in the sparse representation of Black authors in the literary histories of the times. For instance, Eisinger's *Fiction of the Forties,* published as late as 1963, devotes a maximum of two pages to Wright, Ann Petry, and Willard Motley and none to any other Black novelist.

Nevertheless, the years between Wright's departure in the late 1940's and Ellison's emergence in the early 1950's were noteworthy for many developments in Black literature. First, out of the Black colleges of the South there emerged a critical coterie whose members began to provide articulate and perceptive comment on the fiction, poetry, and drama of Black writers. In a sense, Saunders Redding, Arthur Davis, Hugh Gloster, Sterling Brown, Melvin Tolson, Nick Aaron Ford, Margaret Just Butcher, Nancy Bullock McGhee, Nathan Scott, and others were literary academicians and hence in the tradition of Alain Locke, who had served so well in giving focus and direction to the Harlem Renaissance. But their writing lacked the hortatory elegance of Locke; rather, they formulated their critical opinions with objective precision, giving no quarter and little brotherly sympathy to the Black writer who failed to perform well. Trained in Northern graduate schools, they rigorously applied the critical standards of the white literary establishment. And their incisive criticism bore good fruit, for the Black creative writer came to recognize he now had a critical audience. He might satirize, ridicule, and even castigate the Black academic community, as did both Chester Himes and Ralph Ellison, but many other writers, such as Langston Hughes, developed good rapport with the Black academic literary critics. Hughes' own zealous search for the best in Black creative thinking and writing became a sound stimulus for improving literary expression.

Secondly, most of these academic critics were, befitting the times, literary "mainstreamers," believing that the Black writer's goal should be full integration into the mainstream of American literary life. On occasion, they interrupted their critical assessment to prognosticate. For instance, Hugh Gloster, in an essay on "Race and the Negro Writer" (1950), applauded what he termed "the gradual emancipation of the Negro writer from the fetters of racial chauvinism." The Black man of letters, he proudly asserted, was going to become "an American writer as free as any of his national confrères to tap the rich literary resources of our land and its people." Similarly, Saunders Redding, in an essay on "American Negro Literature" (1949), proclaimed his belief that the Black writer had at last found a white audience. He cited as proof Willard Motley and Frank Yerby, who, using so-called white material, attracted a large white readership, and also two Black women poets, Margaret Walker and Gwendolyn Brooks. Margaret Walker had won the Yale Poetry Prize for her volume of poetry *For My People* at the beginning of the decade, and Gwendolyn Brooks had won the Pulitzer Prize for poetry for her *Annie Allen* at the end of the decade. To Professor Redding these literary events seemed to be a solid index of some integration into America's literary mainstream.

Thus, despite Wright's flight and Yerby's turnabout, the general critical consensus during the 1940's was that the Black writer could and would be merged into American literary life and lose his distinctive Black literary identity. Critical hindsight now indicates that the academic critics erred in both their hope and their predictions, although their point of view assuredly reflected the *Zeitgeist.* The phenomenal success of the NAACP's fight against legal segregation contributed to this spirit. Moreover, in 1946 President Truman, by executive order, created a Commission on Civil Rights. The Commission's report, *To Secure These Rights,* issued in 1947, contained thirty-four recommendations for integrating the Black minority into the mainstream of American life. But the concern for integration went far beyond the NAACP and the White House. Even as the Charter of the United Nations was being formed, in 1946 Secretary of State Dean Acheson publicly decried "the adverse effect" of American racial discrimination on the execution and implementation of American foreign policy. Then, after the official formation of the United Nations, Black Americans themselves made two efforts to seek redress of their grievances before this newly established court of world opinion. The first, in 1946, was entitled "A Petition to the United Nations on Behalf of Thirteen Million Oppressed Negro Citizens of America." The second, in 1947, was a much longer petition, prepared by Dr. W. E. B. Du Bois and other scholars on behalf of the NAACP. Ironically, the first petition received no reply whatsoever; the second, consisting of six chapters and 155 pages, was flatly rejected by American delegates but supported and endorsed, probably as a Cold War ploy, by the Soviet membership of the United Nations Commission on Human Rights. Admittedly, these high-level decisions taken in high places were frustrating setbacks, but they did not stay the thrust toward integration in the late 1940's—and the literary mainstreamers appeared to be in good company. The armed forces were integrated; legal barriers fell in the graduate and professional schools of Southern public and private universities; the all-white primary became a legal and political anachronism.

However, the literary mainstreamers faced a large problem, unique in literature and the creative arts. This problem assumed focus and pointed emphasis when, in 1949, James Baldwin published an article in *Partisan Review* entitled "Everybody's Protest Novel." At the time he wrote the article Baldwin was serving a sort of literary novitiate, preparing himself for his first novel, *Go Tell It on the Mountain* (1953). Part of the young novelist's preparation had been spent in long discussions with Richard Wright about the proper role of Black fiction, and the article reports the differences that developed between them regarding the place of protest in Black literature and art. Essentially, Wright, the older writer who had developed under the shadow of the Scottsboro case and had been schooled by the Depression and American Communism, contended that all good literature had to be protest literature; Baldwin, younger and more idealistic, argued that the best literature should deal with universals and rise above the mundane levels of social protest. The protest novel, he wrote, fails as an art form because it rejects life and ignores the human being, "his beauty, dread, and power." The protest writer's paramount concern, Baldwin argued, is not humanity and its burdens but specific problems and their solutions. And usually the protest writer's world of vision is narrowed to fit his protest.

Although at the time Baldwin's statements per se caused no large ripples of concern (they created more concern when they were republished in *Notes of a Native Son* in 1955), the issue he had raised was full of implications for those literary mainstreamers who believed that the Black writer should and could be integrated into American literary life. For Baldwin's argument led to certain questions that had to be answered: To what extent could a Black writer focus on his racial experiences and use his art to protest his social situation and still be "in"? To what extent could he stay in Bronzeville in theme and subject matter and keep a white audience? To what extent should he strive to keep a white audience? Does protest of any kind impair the artistic merit of a novel, a poem, or a short story? As early as 1926, Langston Hughes had argued that the Black writer, ensconced on his "mountaintop of creativity," should write freely of his Black experience, regardless of the needs and demands of his audience, Black or white. And Richard Wright had demonstrated that an artistically well-made work of fiction could be a powerful protest against a system that locked Bigger Thomas and the rest of Uncle Tom's children and grandchildren in urban and rural ghettos. But in the cold time of World War II's aftermath, the question still remained whether there was now a larger world of concern for the Black writer—a world threatened by atomic annihilation, devoid of spiritual and emotional security, and still shaken by horrifying memories of Nazism. To this question, one of the mainstreaming literary academicians, Professor Nick Aaron Ford, provided a thoughtful answer. In his "Blueprint for Negro Authors" (1950), he argued that the Black writer must continue a purposeful preoccupation with racial themes, for only he could understand and communicate "the tragedy, the pathos, and the humor of being a Negro in America." But, he insisted, this must be done with skill and expert craftsmanship, so that the result would be more than social propaganda and protest. The result, he concluded, could be a work of art quite acceptable in the mainstream of literary expression. In a sense, Professor Ford's blueprint would have satisfied both Wright and Baldwin. Fortunately, in 1952 an event occurred that provided an answer to both the proponents and opponents of the literature of social protest. Ralph Ellison's *Invisible Man* settled the matter, for his Black hero was both blood brother to Bigger Thomas and first cousin to Camus' Meurseult and Dostoevsky's underground man. Viewed from one perspective, Ellison's hero was a symbol of American social and moral protest; viewed from another, he was the midcentury existential man, trapped in godless uncertainties and meaningless absurdities.

Ellison's great novel thus not only settled the question of the admissibility of social protest, but it linked the dispossessed American Black man with the dispossessed throughout the world. World War II had left half of Western Europe's people maimed and broken, and out of this human rubble there had gradually emerged the negative philosophy of existentialism. Man, the existentialist argued, could entertain no extravagant hopes for his moral, religious, or social salvation. The only certainties were birth and death—the first a calamitous accident, the second a fortuitous release from the absurdity of human existence. Ellison's hero's odyssey from the South to the North fully confirmed that this was so. Given the existential postulates, the whether-or-not of social protest became an extraneous issue. America was no longer a land vibrant with opportunity but part of a world in which there were only dazzling negatives. In such a world even integration began to lose its luster. As Julian Mayfield was to suggest in 1960 in his essay "Into the Mainstream and Oblivion," the mainstream was a "nowhere." Given this kind of world, not even the versatile, articulate Langston Hughes could find a preacher's mound, much less a mountaintop. And, given this kind of world, a Black man like Ellison's hero could not even eat his yams in peace.

Thus, by the mid-1950's the Black literary climate began to undergo subtle changes. There was greater recognition by white critics, but, ironically, this did not mean as much as the prognosticators of the 1940's had thought. For his *Invisible Man* Ellison received the National Book Award and has, since that time, published *Shadow and Act* and been busy on his second novel, but the case of Gwendolyn Brooks is more to the point. Her meticulous craftsmanship and disciplined lyrical expression in *Annie Allen* fully merited the Pulitzer Prize, but this award did not bring Miss Brooks instant integration into the white literary establishment

Instead, it led to other poems that, in grim and sparse language, point out the desperate existential dilemma of America's Black man. She wrote, for instance, of Rudolph Reed, who was "oaken" and manly and yet was murdered by his white neighbors on a "street of bitter white." And in another poem, she wrote out her conclusion that America's Black man, inured to suffering, pain, and sorrow, has become, like the blinded Oedipus, a tragic figure of great moral strength and perception. In "Riders to the Blood-Red Wrath" this new Black man speaks with a tone of confident self-assertion:

> *Democracy and Christianity*
> *Recommence with me.*
>
> *And I ride ride I ride on to the end—*
> *Where glowers my continuing Calvary.*

Thus, after Ellison's *Invisible Man* new and significant directions became discernible in Black literature. Assimilation into the mainstream was no longer a need or a demand. The Black man's dilemma in America had become a worldwide issue, somehow identifiable with the world's postwar concern with problems of personal identity and invisibility. For the rapid escalation of automated means for destroying the human race dwarfed individuals of every race into insignificance. In this shift of emphasis, the Black man's lack of identity became a *cause célèbre* for Western liberals everywhere. James Baldwin has already been mentioned in another context; by 1953 he had emerged as a novelist to aid and abet this shift in emphasis. His *Go Tell It on the Mountain* (1953) is a penetrating study of the identity crisis of a Black adolescent, trapped both in an unstable, sin-ridden ghetto family and in a hell-and-brimstone storefront religion. In a way, Baldwin's troubled Black youth is like Salinger's troubled white youth of *The Catcher in the Rye;* both are trying to adjust to an immoral and hypocritical adult world. But there the similarity ends. Baldwin's John Grimes is confined to a ghetto and controlled by the cultural and economic deprivation of the ghetto. Salinger's Holden Caulfield, on the other hand, suffers his identity crisis in the lap of affluence.

Following this first novel, Baldwin turned to the essay, and in an elegantly lucid and precise style continued to probe the psychological, political, and metaphysical parameters of the Black Experience. Some of these essays—notably, *Notes of a Native Son* (1955) and *Nobody Knows My Name* (1961)—were written during and between expatriate sojourns in France and other parts of Europe and hence reflect a composite of many points of view. In the mid-1950's he also produced a second novel, *Giovanni's Room* (1956), which, although it does not deal directly with the Black Experience in America, strongly suggests the essential Baldwinian view that the identity problem is not the Black man's alone—a male homosexual, caught up in the pressures of an aggressively heterosexual society, can have similar identity problems.

Viewed in retrospect, there is no doubt that Baldwin's novels and essays popularized the Black man's cause and linked his identity problems with those of Black, Brown, and Yellow people everywhere the white man had ruled as colonial overlord. Indeed, by the mid-1950's when colonialism was on its deathbed, the search for both an ethnic and historical identity by the colored peoples of the world became a matter of pressing significance. In such a context, men again began to speak of *négritude*, a complex of values affirming a worldwide and culturally unifying creed of Blackness. In the years immediately preceding World War II, three Black scholars in Paris—Senghor of Senegal, Césaire of Martinique, and Damas of French Guiana—had formulated a creed that stressed "the sum total of cultural values of the Negro World." Now, in the mid-1950's, *négritude* became a revitalized concept as the shackles of colonialism began to fall from newly emerging African nations. Ghana, Senegal, Guinea, The Ivory Coast, Nigeria—all achieved independence in fairly rapid succession. Against this background of events, Blackness acquired an international dignity and positive cultural meaning it had never before known in the Western world.

Even as this cultural concept of Blackness was crystallizing, two events occurred in America—one in the late 1940's and one in the middle 1950's —that were to determine Black literary activity and race relations in America for many decades to come. The first event occurred in 1948 in a maximum security prison in Concord, Massachusetts, when Malcolm Little, formerly a Harlem racketeer known as "Big Red," was first exposed to Black Muslimism. By the time Malcolm X was installed as minister of Black Muslim Temple No. 7 in Harlem in 1954, he had become a vocal, articulate, abrasive, and charismatic spokesman for America's greatest Black separatist cult. This new kind of racial militancy acquired a large following, particularly among Black youth, and stimulated considerable literary activity devoted to the cause of a militant Black separatism.

The second event occurred at the end of 1955 in Montgomery, Alabama, when Mrs. Rosa Parks refused to give up her seat on a transit bus to a white person as prescribed by Montgomery's segregationist city ordinance. Her arrest and the ensuing Black protest and boycott brought into prominence a hitherto unknown Baptist minister, Dr. Martin Luther King, Jr. His leadership in the civil rights confrontations of the late 1950's and early 1960's in both the North and South produced an aura of achievement that glowed around the world and, like the Black separatism of Malcolm X, stimulated a stronger Black awareness and increased Black literary activity. Both Malcolm X and Martin Luther King, Jr., were assassinated in the 1960's, but their charismatic leadership caught the imagination of young people everywhere. The wave of Black militancy that resulted brought about an outburst of literary creativity that crested in the "Searing Sixties." Indeed, by the mid-1960's more Black writers were writing than ever before. Unlike the increased literary activity of the Harlem Renaissance of an earlier period, however, the new literary awakening was nationwide and not limited to Harlem; in fact, it linked the aspirations of American Black people to those of the Third World. Moreover, the new literary movement differed from the Harlem Renaissance in two other important respects. First, as will be demonstrated in greater detail below, much of the literature is separatist, political, and revolutionary in tone and subject matter. Secondly, its authors are proudly and aggressively disdainful of traditional or mainstream esthetics and literary standards.

As early as 1949, Gwendolyn Brooks had, with the insight of the truly vatic poet, predicted a time when a Black leader, dedicated to nonviolence like Martin Luther King, would emerge to orchestrate nonviolent civil rights protest and "muzzle the note / With hurting love.... Devote / the bow to silks and honey. Be remote / A while from malice and from murdering." But, as the decade of the 1960's unfolded, it became evident that there were few Black writers who, like the Gwendolyn Brooks of 1949, wished to celebrate the glory and grandeur of nonviolent civil rights protest. Rather, to the young writers of the 1960's, *négritude* and a militant Black separatism had far more emotional and esthetic appeal. Worsening conditions in the great sprawling urban ghettos hardened the mood of protest, and young Black writers began to write plays, poems, and novels reflecting their cynicism, bitterness, and disillusionment with all institutions of the Establishment. As will be seen, they write with an explicit verbal directness and revolutionary zeal shocking to middle-class tastes and values.

Predictably, the richest outpouring was in poetry. Older poets—Sterling Brown, Melvin Tolson, Langston Hughes, Owen Dodson, Arna Bontemps, Gwendolyn Brooks, Margaret Danner, Robert Hayden, and others—continued to write and are represented both in Rosey Pool's 1962 anthology and in Arna Bontemps' 1963 anthology. In a sense, their poetry links the mood and tensions of the "Searing Sixties" with the mood and tensions of the "Fallacy-Ridden Forties," bridging a gap between a time of militant Black separatism with a time of militant integrationism. Also represented in these anthologies are younger figures such as LeRoi Jones, Mari Evans, Calvin Hernton, Naomi Madgett, and Lance Jeffers. Because the times had changed—because Martin Luther King, Jr., had marched and Malcolm X had preached—even in the poems of the older poets as well as in those of the younger group who emerged in the 1950's there is now a new note reflecting both a prideful awareness of Black culture and history and a bitter, agonizing awareness of ghetto hopelessness. For instance, Gwendolyn Brooks delves into the Black ghetto to write of "Way-Out Morgan," who, on a certain night, was busy "collecting guns / in a tiny fourth-floor room" to prepare for his "Day of Debt-pay" to redress ancient racial wrongs. Similarly, few poems stress ghetto hopelessness as poignantly as hers about young Black pool players:

We real cool. We
Left school. We

Lurk late. We
Strike straight. We

Sing sin. We
Thin Gin. We

> *Jazz June. We*
> *Die soon.*

Following the big-city ghetto riots of the middle 1960's, however, a completely new poetry was born—new in style, content, and emphasis. The poets who are writing this new poetry are gifted, young, caustic, cynical, committed revolutionaries. Their spiritual and esthetic leader is LeRoi Jones—not the LeRoi Jones who received his M.A. degree from Columbia University, but a new and transformed LeRoi Jones, a man who was jailed during the flaming Newark riot and emerged as Imamu Amiri Baraka. To Jones and his followers—Don Lee, Nikki Giovanni, Sonia Sanchez, Etheridge Knight, A. B. Spellman and others—a Black poem is not just another esthetic happening but a searing political statement designed to further the cause of social and poltical revolution. For these poets, poems are weapons to maim and guns to kill—"Assassin poems . . . that wrestle cops into alleys / and take their weapons leaving them dead / with their tongues pulled out and sent to Ireland." Accordingly, only rarely does the poetry of this new breed of poet bring the reader into the realm of the poet's emotional privacy. Admittedly, there are exceptions to this generalization. Etheridge Knight, in one of his poems written at Indiana State Prison, recalls a poignant, private memory of life in Arkansas:

> *I shinnied with Bea up a mulberry tree*
> *When we were young and Arkansas was the world;*
> *At sundown, among the leaves and worms,*
> *We kissed, as bullbats swooped for gnats.*
>
> *Beatrice now clicks down Sixty Third Street*
> *In high and fire-red heels*
> *And in Arkansas, in the evenings*
> *The bullbats still catch gnats.*

Similarly, Sonia Sanchez in her "Poem at Thirty" writes of personal reminiscences:

> *I want to tell*
> *you about me*
> *about nights on a*
> *brown couch when*
> *i wrapped my*
> *bones in lint*
> *and refused to move.*

But such poems are exceptions. Usually, this new poet speaks not for himself or herself, but for a cause and for a collectivity—a Black collectivity. As Nikki Giovanni says, the discipline of the revolution does not permit one to write "a beautiful green tree poem" or a "big blue sky poem." And LeRoi Jones or Amiri Baraka is even more explicit:

> *Let there be no love poems written*
> *until love can exist freely and*
> *cleanly.*

There is no time or need for personal revelation and private reflection; there is time only for public declarations and revolutionary assertions to discipline the Black man to live in a burned-out ghetto of charred beams, splintered glass, and roasted rats. In such a place, all Black women, writes Nikki Giovanni, live lives "tied up to unhappiness . . . in a filthy house / with yesterday's watermelon / and monday's tears." And in such a place and at such a time young Black men have no more instinctive, intuitive smiles; if they smile at all, Don Lee says, their smiles are fixed and come slowly "like the gradual / movement of tomatoes in a near empty ketchup bottle."

Not only do these poets avoid personal revelations, but many of their poems exhort the faithful to remain true to the cause of revolution and maintain the discipline befitting a committed revolutionary. Do not, says Don Lee, be a "part-time revolutionist" who talks Black in the daytime and sleeps white in the night-time. Do not, he says, confuse a "cool" outward pseudorevolutionary appearance with true revolutionary commitment. A "double-natural" and "tailor-made dashikis" and "Hand-carved ivory tikis from the Mother-land" provide a revolutionary appearance merely and do not necessarily represent the truly dedicated mover and shaker. Do not, says Sonia Sanchez, use pseudorevolutionary ardor as an excuse for sexual promiscuity; one can read and understand Fanon without sex. Do not, says Amiri Baraka, believe that drug addiction can help the revolutionary cause; rather, he demands that Black poets write "knock-off poems for dope-peddling . . . slick, half-white politicians."

Apart from these obviously unique poetic characteristics—the refusal to write out their own emotional immediacy and privacy and their commitment to a demanding revolutionary discipline—the Black revolutionary poets of the "Searing Sixties" share much with other poets of their time. They are, like the Beat poets of the 1950's, fond of verbal directness; their verse is sprinkled profusely with explicit four-letter words. Like Charles Olson and the projective verse poets, the Black revolutionary poets also scorn form and rhyme and seem to produce the kind of breath-conditioned poetry that can be better declaimed than read. Indeed, Black revolutionary poetry almost demands a "preacher-man" delivery, with incantations, dramatic pauses, inflections, and some body movements. Thus, the message of the poem becomes one with the delivery of the poem. Or, to put it another way, Black revolutionary poetry must be "creatively" read or spoken. One also finds in revolutionary poetry of this type the same studied disdain of bourgeois capitalism, Western European history, and institutionalized religion found in avant-garde poetry of the 1960's.

The Black literary renaissance in poetic expression exceeds what has occurred in fiction or in drama, although there have been significant new directions in the these genres, also. In fiction, no new Ellisons or Richard Wrights have emerged, but several new, young short story writers have appeared—Paule Marshall, Loyle Harrison, Martin Hamer, Ernest Gaines, and William Melvin Kelley. Kelley also produced three novels during the 1960's. His first, *A Different Drummer* (1962), was an award-winning novel, and his two succeeding novels—*A Drop of Patience* (1965) and *dem* (1967)—fully lived up to the promise of the first. Probably the most significant Black writer of fiction to develop is John A. Williams. His third novel, *The Man Who Cried I Am* (1967), has all of the necessary ingredients for good fiction—a good plot, excellent characterization, and a series of expatriate settings bubbling with international intrigue. There is racial protest, but the Black guys are not all good or the white guys all bad. In fact, Max Reddick, the Black hero who holds in his keeping the infamous King Alfred Plan for radical removal and detention of all American Blacks, receives his death at the hands of two Black CIA agents. The principal interest of the novel, however, is not its fast-moving plot but the characterization of Harry Ames, a Black expatriate novelist whose death precipitates the major action of the novel. Harry Ames is Richard Wright, and Williams' portrait recaptures the man vividly and completely. Also portrayed from real life is James Baldwin in the character of Marion Dawes. All in all, the novel furnishes excellent brief cameos and vignettes of life among the Black literary expatriates. Its great merit is that it leaves the reader pretty well convinced that, given the history of racial confrontation in America, the existence of a King Alfred Plan is not only possible but probable. In his novel *Night Song* (1961), Williams first experimented with real-life characterization. The character this time is the great musician Charlie "Yardbird" Parker. However, *Night Song* is not successful in sustaining and explaining the characterization.

At least four writers of the early or late 1940's and early 1950's also continued to write fiction in the 1960's. How they adjusted to the new literary climate deserves some comment. The first is James Baldwin, whose popularity soared in the 1950's not only because of his two very notable novels but also because of the polished style of his essays, in which he analyzed the Black man's identity crisis. In the 1960's he published two more novels—*Another Country* and *Tell Me How Long the Train's Been Gone*. In the first, Baldwin presents a cluster of characters of several races and from several regions, all of whom are suffering from identity problems. As they grope their way through the traumas of urban life, they futilely but repeatedly try to use sex to save themselves. Then, Eric Jones appears, full of solutions and panaceas. A white Alabaman homosexual, with bisexual skills, he has enjoyed a sybaritic expatriation in France. When he returns to New York, the troubled and fragmented characters of the novel begin to find a point of focus for effective self-acceptance. At first glance, Eric looms forth as an anti-heroic homosexual, but he is merely another inhabitant of Giovanni's room. Leo Proudhammer of *Tell Me How Long the Train's Been Gone* is similarly confusing in his characterization. As in the earlier novel, bisexual activity assumes primary importance in determining events and outcomes, and Proudhammer, a Black actor, performs heroically and without peer in this particular area of human activity. What he does and what he says, however, add little or nothing to the reader's understanding of the human condition. Because neither of the novels Baldwin published in the

1960's can be described as well constructed and because his essays are so very well made, it seems that the essay may be the genre best suited to his literary talents.

Another writer who merits comment is Margaret Walker. In 1966, twenty-four years after winning the Yale Poetry Prize for her volume of poems *For My People,* she published a prize-winning novel that in many respects is a unique achievement. In the first place, it demonstrates her enduring versatility as a writer; many of her literary associates of the late 1930's and early 1940's have long been silent. In the second place, *Jubilee* as a prize-winning historical novel stands alone in Black fiction. There have been attempts by other Black writers to probe the anguish and the achievements of the past—Pauli Murray's *Proud Shoes,* for example—but these were usually anecdotal or biographical. They never had the structure or totality of a work of art. *Jubilee* is just such a work of art. It is a well-made historical novel that presents slavery times and the bitter times afterward with ruthless honesty and objectivity. No autobiographical reflections or episodes obtrude to mar the story line. Moreover, the characterization of Vyry, the heroine, is extremely well conceived and gives dramatic continuity to the several plots of the novel. Finally, Miss Walker researched her material well—*Jubilee* contains a lot of Black history at a time when Black history has begun to have an increased importance, and an author who can convert the raw facts of a painful past into a work of art must possess great skill and self-discipline.

Richard Wright, who was one of Margaret Walker's literary associates and friends during the late 1930's and early 1940's, died in 1960. His *Lawd Today* was published posthumously in the early 1960's. Unfortunately, it is a rather poor valedictory for a man who during his lifetime had scaled the heights of literary achievement. One might wonder whether Wright would have retained his power as a writer had he remained in the United States, although such a speculation is more applicable in the case of *The Long Dream,* written in the 1950's, than to *Lawd Today,* which was actually written in the mid-1930's. Jake Jackson, the hero of *Lawd Today,* bears a remarkable resemblance to Cross Damon, hero of *The Outsider* (1953). Both are postal clerks who are progressively victimized by the clutch of urban circumstance and by their own appetites. In fact, Damon's story begins with the kind of multiple entrapment with which Jake Jackson's story ends. The principal difference is that, by 1950, Wright was able to supply some existential solutions that give Damon a little more time. In the end, he, too, becomes another Black male stripped of everything except his anger. Thus, *Lawd Today,* written early in Wright's career, suggests that his views changed little in thirty years. Essentially, the Black man in Wright's fiction is a victim of horrendous social and environmental forces. His violence and anger provide a pattern of reaction, but there are no viable solutions for extricating him from his dilemma. And Jake treats his women with the same callousness and offensive brutality with which Damon treats his women. Indeed, the Black woman does not fare at all well in Wright's fiction. One critic, George Kent, suggests that his portrayal of Black women, and other women as well, may reflect his "highly tensioned" relationship with his mother and the other women in his life. In any event, Wright's view of Black urban America never really changed to keep pace with the sweep of events.

Fortunately, such has not been true of another longtime literary expatriate, Chester Himes. Although he left to escape America's noxious literary climate, this novelist has remained in touch with the changing temper of Black urban life. Accordingly, the anger and frustration of *Lonely Crusade* are gone, replaced by the ebullience of Black detective fiction. His Harlem settings are authentic, and the mixture of swift melodrama, sex, and Black ghettoese has made his detective fiction very popular, both in America and abroad. Admittedly, detective novels are not the highest form of literature, but Himes' are well plotted, suspenseful, and entertaining. If Himes sustains his present rate of output, he may become the "Black Yerby" of the 1970's.

Shakespeare's Hamlet said that in drama one finds "the abstract and brief chronicles of the time," and this is abundantly true of the plays being written by the young Black playwrights—Lonne Elder, Ed Bullins, Douglas Ward, Adrienne Kennedy, and Amiri Baraka. Like the poems of the young Black revolutionary poets, these plays are written for Black audiences, and the social and political messages are always direct and revolutionary. Whereas James Weldon Johnson, some forty years ago, pondered the dilemma of the Black artist schizophrenically trying to please both a Black and a white audience, today's Black playwright writes in open defiance and callous disregard of the white audience and directs his words solely to the Black world. Each playwright attempts to follow Hamlet's prescription about abstracting and chronicling the time; their plays delve into the grimy depths of Black life, either in an urban ghetto, a rural ghetto, or a small-town ghetto in the South. Every aspect of ghetto life is examined—prostitution, homosexuality, drug addiction, thievery, and racial and class strife. These plays, then, are far removed from, say, *Anna Lucasta,* an immensely popular postwar play that probed the emotional and sexual problems of a stereotypical beautiful but benighted octoroon. They are also far removed from Lorraine Hansberry's *Raisin in the Sun.* This play has its setting in a Black community and delves deeply into the conflicts of the Black family, but the new breed of revolutionary dramatists would say that *Raisin in the Sun* is "hung up" in its concern with white middle-class values such as industry, frugality, dependability, and economic responsibility, and would add that Blackness appears to be more burdensome than beautiful in Miss Hansberry's play.

The leading playwright in this group is the provocative and dynamic Amiri Baraka, whose plays—*The Toilet, The Slave, Dutchman, Black Mass, Slave Ship*—reflect what he calls the "iconology" of the revolutionary theater movement. His announced objective is to force change and, by working "black nigger magic," cleanse the world of hate and ugliness and restore virtue. Slightly less revolutionary in technique and theme is Ed Bullins, whose *Clara's Ole Man* and *Goin' a Buffalo* take the audience into the heartland of the ghetto where the characters live lives of existential desperation. Not only are the determinants of happiness and success radically different in Bullins' ghetto world, but violence is always present and strikes suddenly and unexpectedly. It is a world where it is unwise to trust or love or be kind or gracious. So in *Goin' a Buffalo* Art betrays his best friend Curt for reasons of loot and lust, and in *Clara's Ole Man* Jack, the college prepster, is beaten up because Big Girl cannot tolerate anyone who might threaten her lesbian relationship with Clara. One of the best plays of this group is Lonne Elder's *Ceremonies in Dark Old Men*. The mood of this play is dark and threatening; although there is never the swift physical violence of a Bullins play, there is simply no humor, no levity. The build-up of tension in the play is relentless as "Old Man" Parker attempts to become an economic somebody amid economic nobodies. In the effort his fragmented family fragments further, and, when he tries to assert a semblance of patriarchal authority, he becomes a Black Don Quixote jousting with windmills. The best choice for a Black old man is to play checkers. Elder's play demonstrates great skill and dramatic craftsmanship. All the messages about ghetto life and its impact on Black society are there, but none stand out so forcefully that *Ceremonies in Dark Old Men* becomes a message play. Through fine timing and characterization, Elder reveals a universe where, although many things are possible to insure the dignity of man, few are probable.

In some of these plays there is the same caustic, flippant humor found in Don Lee's poetry. For instance, Douglas Turner Ward's *Day of Absence* describes the devastating effects when all the Blacks make a prearranged departure from a small Southern town on a given day. The results, on the surface, are hilarious; the white town is immobilized for want of Black services. However, Ward's play leaves one with the overwhelming paradox: how can people so needed be at the same time so degraded? Another kind of needling truth is behind the action of *Happy Ending*. Here the playwright presents a satire on "Black thievery," a stereotype long resented by Blacks. But the sting of the satire is removed, because the victims are wealthy white employers of two sisters, who, as maids, have been engaged in systematic, in-depth thievery for years. As Ward unfolds his plot, the white family is about to break up and hence the opportunity to steal all those consumer goods is about to be cut off. Fortunately, the white victims decide to remain together, and there is a "happy ending"—Black thievery from wealthy whites can continue. Ward's point is that for residents of the Black ghetto theft of needed goods is excusable in an affluent society.

Thus, Black literature since World War II has been marked by ever-increasing literary activity of unprecedented scope and magnitude. During the twenty-five-year period, the tempo of literary protest against the Black man's condition in America has gradually increased from the integrationist clamor of the late 1940's and early 1950's to the revolutionary Black militant separatism of the late 1960's. There is no doubt that the fervor accompanying this mood of new militant Blackness has produced a ferment of literary activity. More young Black poets, novelists, dramatists, and critics are writing today than ever before. Undoubtedly, Black literary activity will increase during the 1970's, and, as America approaches its two-hundredth anniversary in 1976, it is interesting to compare the Black literary climate of 1776 with what the developing racial and literary climate can be expected to be in 1976. In the 1770's, as in the 1970's, the repressed social status of the Black minority and the immorality of such repression were the motivating concerns for writers such as Olaudah Equiano and Tom Paine. Moreover, the decade of the 1770's was filled with discussion of the rights of man and his inalienable right to pursue happiness and justice and liberty. In such a climate, Tom Paine published his first abolitionist essay, "African Slavery in America" (1776). In that same year, the first abolitionist society was formed in Philadelphia, inspired, no doubt, by Chief Justice Mansfield's decision in the famous Somerset case in England in 1772, which, in effect, set free some fourteen thousand slaves in the mother country. In other words, as the American colonies were preparing to sever their ties with England and become a nation, a growing climate of opinion seemed to favor freeing the sizable number of slaves in the new nation. Unfortunately, none of this was reflected in the writing of the two Black poets of this period. Both Phillis Wheatley and Jupiter Hammon were slaves, but they apparently were too establishment-oriented to protest their servile condition in their poetry. In the 1770's all of the heady talk of freedom, liberty, and equality came to naught; there were no Black protest writers to support and endorse a freedom movement, and there was no literate free Black audience to seize the opportunity to exploit the mood of the times. Although influential persons such as Franklin, Lafayette, Condorcet, and the Polish patriot Kosciusko joined the abolitionist cause, freedom for the American slave was not to be realized during that time two hundred years ago when Americans first began to mouth their slogans of liberty, freedom, and equality. Then, after 1794 and the invention of the cotton gin, slavery became the Western world's most profitable enterprise, and the opportunity was lost. The nineteenth century saw America drift into an attitude of compromise and equivocation over its greatest moral and social problem.

Today, two hundred years later, this attitude of compromise and equivocation still exists. Although the children and grandchildren of former Black slaves are free of slavery's bonds, racial oppression, discrimination, and segregation still remain. The difference, however, is that now there are thousands of Black writers to protest the Black man's condition in prose, poetry, and drama. In the hundred-year-old history of the Black man's freedom from slavery in America, the Black writer has become increasingly significant, proving again the close link between economic and social gains and literary expression and protest. Many Black literary voices will be heard as America celebrates her two-hundredth anniversary. Not only will these Black writers speak for the 22 million Black Americans, but they will speak to the some 180 million other Americans about the new birth of freedom that must come if 1976 is to fulfill the long-delayed promise of 1776.

The Major Writers

Melvin B. Tolson (1898–1966)

When Melvin B. "Cap" Tolson died in 1966, the Black literary world lost one of its most colorful personalities and one of its truly gifted poets. As Karl Shapiro implies in his introduction to *Harlem Gallery* (1965), Tolson was never a mainstreamer in his poetry, his politics, or his pedagogy. Indeed, he was not even an "Afro-American" mainstreamer, for as an individual artist he wanted no fetters on his creativity. For this reason, his poetry is incomparable, in the literal sense of the word.

The key to Tolson as poet, teacher, and man is his irrepressible and zestful iconoclasm. In all of his writings—in his plays, his poems, his occasional pieces—there is enormous indignation against the status quo and the conformists who support and endorse the status quo. Tolson frequently expressed his bitterness at not being recognized and rewarded by the white literary power structure, but, when members of that group came forward, following *Libretto for the Republic of Liberia* (1953), to give him long-overdue honors, he was singularly unmoved. These few words of praise brought no significant changes in his life and career; he still remained an eloquent and articulate outsider. After all, what other poet, Black or white, had ever been elected mayor of Langston, Oklahoma, four times? What other poet, Black or white, had ever served as poet laureate of an African nation that had had its start as a home and refuge for ex-slaves and free Blacks? Tolson enjoyed being different and "otherwise." In "Psi," one of the sections of *Harlem Gallery,* the poet describes the "Negro artist" as a "flower of the gods, whose growth / is dwarfed at an early stage." But this is a generalized complaint on behalf of the Negro artist and not a personal protest. One is inclined to believe that Tolson enjoyed being both a Black man and a "Negro artist." His status conferred upon him freedom to carp and criticize with typically Tolsonian irony and cutting innuendo. Only as a Negro artist could he escape what he termed the "Sodom of Gylt / and the Big White Boss" and spew forth his splendid poetic rage against any and all establishments.

During his poetic career, Tolson produced three volumes of poetry. The first, *Rendezvous with America* (1944), includes the famed "Dark Symphony," which won the National Poetry Prize in a contest sponsored by the American Negro Exposition in Chicago in 1940. Then, in 1953, after

668

being commissioned to write a poem in celebration of the Liberian Centennial and International Exposition, he wrote *Libretto for the Republic of Liberia*. His final volume, *Harlem Gallery,* was originally designed to be the prologue of an extensive poetic odyssey of the Black man's experience in America. Unfortunately, death intervened and the great epic was never completed.

Tolson's poetry is distinctive in many ways. First, there is the ever-present iconoclasm that vibrates in almost every line, particularly in *Harlem Gallery*. In addition, there is a word flow in his poetry reminiscent of Dylan Thomas. At times, ideas are temporarily submerged in plunging streams of foreign phrases and multiple literary and mythological references from the Graeco-Roman world, the Judeo-Christian world, and the world of Black America. For example, in the last stanza of "Psi," he writes of the good ship *Défineznegro* and how, in trying to reach the "archipelago / Nigeridentité. / In the Strait of Octoroon / off black Scylla," it sank "in the abyss / (*Vanitas vanitatum!*) / of white Charybdis." Despite the mingling of many ideas from many backgrounds and cultures, there is an ordered disorder here; classical imagery is blended with the symbolism of Black–white racial confrontation in a stanza whose tone is generally Coleridgean and Romantic (all is seen in "*a Vision in a Dream*"). A better example of this Tolsonian mixture is the following self-describing stanza, also from "Psi":

> *A Pelagian with the* raison d'être *of a Negro,*
> *I cannot say I have outwitted dread,*
> *for I am conscious of the noiseless tread*
> *of the Yazoo tiger's ball-like pads behind me*
> *in the dark*
> *as I trudge ahead*
> *up and up . . . that Lonesome Road . . . up and up.*

In this passage, many apparently unrelated matters are given intelligible poetic coherence—early Christian church history, the Black man's problems in America, his continual fear in the jungle of American racial experience where the powerful white tigers attack by night, and the great challenge of travel up the blues-cluttered "Lonesome Road." Pulling all of these diverse matters together, one may interpret this stanza to say that the Black man in America has not been deterred by fears and anxieties but has pushed on, with existential courage, up the road of progress. Obviously, the Tolsonian method of poetic statement precludes brevity and succinctness and emphasizes, rather, a kind of verbal "overkill" through and by which a cluster of dissimilar concepts and ideas somehow cohere into poetic truth.

As Karl Shapiro suggests in his introduction to *Harlem Gallery,* Tolson's poetry has been relatively neglected, and, although he is represented in all the major anthologies, his work has provoked little critical response to date. It may be safely predicted, however, that a work like *Harlem Gallery* will not long be ignored. It has a complexity of theme and method that will eventually attract critical attention and establish Melvin Tolson as one of the major poets of the mid-twentieth century.

Although there has been no full-length critical study of Tolson's poetry, there have been several short articles. Among these are Allen Tate, "Preface to *Libretto for the Republic of Liberia*," *Poetry*, LXXVI (1950), 216–218; Karl Shapiro, "Melvin B. Tolson, Poet," *Negro Digest*, XIV (May 1965), 75–77; Dan McCall, "The Quicksilver Sparrow of Melvin B. Tolson," *American Quarterly*, XVIII (1966), 538–542; and Sarah Webster Fabio, "Who Speaks Negro?" *Negro Digest*, XVI (December 1966), 54–58. Finally, Melvin Tolson as poet speaks for himself in an interview conducted by Professor M. W. King and printed in Herbert Hill's edition of *Anger, and Beyond* (1966), pp. 181–195; the interview is significantly and appropriately entitled "A Poet's Odyssey."

Dark Symphony

I: ALLEGRO MODERATO

Black Crispus Attucks taught
  Us how to die
Before white Patrick Henry's bugle breath
Uttered the vertical
  Transmitting cry:
"Yea, give me liberty, or give me death."

And from that day to this
  Men black and strong
For Justice and Democracy have stood,
Steeled in the faith that Right
  Will conquer Wrong
And Time will usher in one brotherhood.

No Banquo's ghost can rise
  Against us now
And say we crushed men with a tyrant's boot
Or pressed the crown of thorns
  On Labor's brow,
Or ravaged lands and carted off the loot.

II: LENTO GRAVE

The centuries-old pathos in our voices
Saddens the great white world,
And the wizardry of our dusky rhythms
Conjures up shadow-shapes of ante-bellum years:

Black slaves singing *One More River to Cross*
In the torture tombs of slave ships,
Black slaves singing *Steal Away to Jesus*
In jungle swamps,
Black slaves singing *The Crucifixion*
In slave pens at midnight,
Black slaves singing *Swing Low, Sweet Chariot*
In cabins of death,
Black slaves singing *Go Down, Moses*
In the canebrakes of the Southern Pharaohs.

III: ANDANTE SOSTENUTO

They tell us to forget
The Golgotha we tread . . .
We who are scourged with hate,
A price upon our head.
They who have shackled us
Require of us a song,
They who have wasted us
Bid us o'erlook the wrong.

They tell us to forget
Democracy is spurned.
They tell us to forget
The Bill of Rights is burned.
Three hundred years we slaved,
We slave and suffer yet:
Though flesh and bone rebel,
They tell us to forget!

Oh, how can we forget
Our human rights denied?
Oh, how can we forget
Our manhood crucified?
When Justice is profaned
And plea with curse is met,
When Freedom's gates are barred,
Oh, how can we forget?

IV: TEMPO PRIMO

The New Negro strides upon the continent
In seven league boots . . .
The New Negro
Who sprang from the vigor-stout loins
Of Nat Turner, gallows-martyr for Freedom,
Of Joseph Cinquez, Black Moses of the Amistad
 Mutiny,

Of Frederick Douglass, oracle of the Catholic
Man,
Of Sojourner Truth, eye and ear of Lincoln's
legions,
Of Harriet Tubman, St. Bernard of the
Underground Railroad.

V: LARGHETTO

None in the Land can say
To us black men Today:
You send the tractors on their bloody path,
And create Oakies for *The Grapes of Wrath.*
You breed the slum that breeds a *Native Son*
To damn the good earth Pilgrim Fathers won.

None in the Land can say
To us black men Today:
You dupe the poor with rags-to-riches tales,
And leave the workers empty dinner pails.
You stuff the ballot box, and honest men
Are muzzled by our demogogic din.

None in the Land can say
To us black men Today:
You smash stock markets with your coined
blitzkriegs
And make a hundred million guinea pigs.
You counterfeit our Christianity,
And bring contempt upon Democracy.

None in the Land can say
To us black men Today:
You prowl when citizens are fast asleep,
And hatch Fifth Column plots to blast the deep
Foundations of the State and leave the Land
A vast Sahara with a Fascist brand.

None in the Land can say
To us black men Today:
You send flame-gutting tanks, like swarms of
flies,
And plump a hell from dynamiting skies.
You fill machine-gunned towns with rotting
dead—
A No Man's Land where children cry for bread.

VI: TEMPO DI MARCIA

Out of abysses of Illiteracy,
Through labyrinths of Lies,
Across wastelands of Disease . . .
We advance!

Out of dead-ends of Poverty,
Through wildernesses of Superstition,
Across barricades of Jim Crowism . . .
We advance!

With the Peoples of the World . . .
We advance!

from *Harlem Gallery*

PSI

Black Boy,
let me get up from the white man's Table
of Fifty Sounds
in the kitchen; let me gather the crumbs
and cracklings
of this autobio-fragment,
before the curtain with the skull and bones
descends.

Many a *t* in the ms.
I've left without a cross,
many an *i* without a dot.
A dusky Lot
with a third degree and a second wind and a
seventh turn
of pitch-and-toss,
my psyche escaped the Sodom of Gylt
and the Big White Boss.

Black Boy,
you stand before your heritage,
naked and agape;
cheated like a mockingbird
pecking at a Zuexian grape,
pressed like an awl to do
duty as a screw-
driver, you
ask the American Dilemma in you:
"If the trying plane
of Demos fail,
what will the trowel
of Uncle Tom avail?"

Black Boy,
in this race, at this time, in this place,
to be a Negro artist is to be
a flower of the gods, whose growth
is dwarfed at an early stage—
a Brazilian owl moth,

a giant among his own in an acreage
dark with the darkman's designs,
where the milieu moves back downward like
the sloth.

Black Boy,
true—you
have not
dined and wined
(*ignoti nulla cupido*)
in the El Dorado of aeried Art,
for unreasoned reasons;
and your artists, not so lucky as the Buteo,
find themselves without a
skyscrape sanctuary
in the
season of seasons:
in contempt of the contemptible,
refuse the herb of grace, the rue
of Job's comforter;
take no
lie-tea in lieu
of Broken Orange Pekoe.
Doctor Nkomo said: "*What* is he who smacks
his lips when dewrot eats away the golden
grain
of self-respect exposed like flax
to the regions of sun and rain?"

Black Boy,
every culture,
every caste,
every people,
every class,
facing the barbarians
with lips hubris-curled,
believes its death rattle omens
the *Dies Irae* of the world.

Black Boy,
summon Boas and Dephino,
Blumenbach and Koelreuter,
from their posts
around the gravestone of Bilbo,
who, with cancer in his mouth,
orated until he quaked the magnolias of the
South,
while the pocketbooks of his weeping black
serfs
shriveled in the drouth;
summon the ghosts
of scholars with rams' horns from Jericho
and facies in letters from Jerusalem,
so

we may ask them:
"What is a Negro?"

Black Boy,
what's in a peoples' name that wries the brain
like the neck of a barley bird?
Can sounding brass create
an ecotype with a word?

Black Boy,
beware of the thin-bladed mercy
stroke, for one drop of Negro blood
(V. *The Black Act of the F. F. V.*)
opens the flood-
gates of the rising tide of color
and jettisons
the D. A. R. in the Heraclitean flux
with Uncle Tom and
Crispus Attucks.
The Black Belt White,
painstaking as a bedbug in
a tenant farmer's truckle bed,
rabbit-punched old Darrow
because
he quoted Darwin's sacred laws
(instead of the Lord God Almighty's)
and grabbed that the Catarrhine ape
(the C from a Canada goose nobody knows)
appears,
after X's of years,
in the vestigial shape
of the Nordic's thin lips, his aquiline nose,
his straight hair,
orangutanish on legs and chest and head.
Doctor Nkomo, a votary of touch-and-go,
who can stand the gaff
of Negrophobes and, like Aramis,
parry a thrust with a laugh,
said:

"In spite of the pig in the python's coils,
in spite of Blake's lamb in the jaws of the
tiger,
Nature is kind, even in the raw: she toils
. . . aeons and aeons and aeons . . .
gives the African a fleecy canopy
to protect the seven faculties of the brain
from burning convex lens of the sun;
she foils
whiteness
(without disdain)
to bless the African
(as Herodotus marvels)
with the birthright of a burnt skin for work
or fun;

she roils
the Aryan
(as his eye and ear repose)
to give the African an accommodation nose
that cools the drying-up air;
she entangles the epidermis in broils
that keep the African's body free from lice-
infested hair.
As man to man,
the Logos is
Nature is on the square
with the African.
If a black man circles the rim
of the Great White World, he will find
(even if Adamness has made him half blind)
the bitter waters of Marah *and*
the fresh fountains of Elim."

Although his transition
was a far cry
from Shakespeare to Sardou,
the old Africanist's byplay gave
no soothing feverfew
to the Dogs in the Zulu Club;
said he:
"A Hardyesque artistry
of circumstance
divides the Whites and Blacks in life,
like the bodies of the dead
eaten by vultures
in the tower of Silence.
Let, then, the man with the maggot in his
head
lean . . . lean . . . lean
on race or caste or class,
for the wingless worms of blowflies shall grub,
dry and clean,
the stinking skeletons of these,
when the face of the macabre weather-
cock turns to the torrid wind of misanthropy;
and later their bones shall be swept together
(like the Parsees')
in the Sepulchre of Anonymity."
A Zulu Wit cleared away his unsunned
mood with dark laughter;
but I sensed the thoughts of Doctor Nkomo
pacing nervously to and fro
like Asscher's after
he'd cleaved the giant Cullinan Diamond.

Black Boy,
the vineyard is the fittest place
in which to booze (with Omar) and study

soil and time and integrity—
the telltale triad of grape and race.

Palates that can read the italics
of *salt* and *sugar* know
a grapevine
transplanted from Bordeaux
to Pleasant Valley
cannot give grapes that make a Bordeaux
wine.

Like the sons of the lone mother of dead
empires,
who boasted their ancestors,
page after page—
wines are peacocky
in their vintage and their age,
disdaining the dark ways of those engaging
in the profits
of chemical aging.
.   When the bluebirds sing
their perennial anthem
a capriccio, in the Spring,
the sap begins to move up the stem
of the vine, and the wine in the bed of the deep
cask stirs in its winter sleep.
Its bouquet
comes with the years, dry or wet;
so the connoisseurs say:
"The history of the wine
is repeated by the vine."

Black Boy,
beware of wine labels,
for the Republic does not guarantee
what the phrase "Château Bottled" means—
the estate, the proprietor, the quality.
This ignominy will baffle you, Black Boy,
because the white man's law
has raked your butt many a time
with fang and claw.
Beware of the waiter who wraps
a napkin around your Clos Saint Thierry,
if Chance takes you into high-hat places
open to all creeds and races
born to be or not to be.
Beware of the pop
of a champagne cork:
like the flatted fifth and octave jump in **Bebop**,
it is theatrical
in Vicksburg or New York.
Beware of the champagne cork
that does not swell up like your ma when she
had you—*that*

comes out flat,
because the bottle of wine
is dead . . . dead
like Uncle Tom and the Jim Crow Sign.
Beware . . . yet
your dreams in the Great White World
shall be unthrottled
by pigmented and unpigmented lionhearts,
for we know *without no*
every people, by and by, produce its
"Château Bottled."

White Boy,
as regards the ethnic origin
of Black Boy and me,
the *What* in Socrates' "*Tò ti?*"
is for the musk-ox habitat of anthropologists;
but there is another question,
dangerous as a moutaba tick,
secreted in the house
of every Anglo-Saxon sophist and hick:

Who is a Negro?
(I am a White in deah ole Norfolk.)
Who is a White?
(I am a Negro in little old New York.)
Since my mongrelization is invisible
and my Negroness a state of mind conjured up
by Stereotypus, I am a chameleon
on *that* side of the Mason-Dixon
that a white man's conscience
is not on.
My skin is as white
as a Roman's toga when he sought an office
on the sly;
my hair is as blond
as xanthein;
my eyes are as blue
as the hawk's-eye.
At the Olympian powwow of curators,
when I revealed my Negroness,
my peers became shocked like virgins in a
house
where satyrs tattooed on female thighs
heralds of success.

White Boy,
counterfeit scholars have used
the newest brush-on Satinlac,
to make our ethnic identity
crystal clear for the lowest IQ
in every mansion and in every shack.
Therefore,
according to the myth that Negrophobes
bequeath

to the Lost Gray Cause, since Black Boy is
the color
of betel-stained teeth,
he and I
(from ocular proof
that cannot goof)
belong to races
whose dust-of-the-earth progenitors
the Lord God Almighty created
of different bloods,
in antipodal places.
However,
even the F. F. V. pate
is aware that laws defining a Negro
blackjack each other with*in* and with*out* a
state.
The Great White World, White Boy, leaves
you in a sweat
like a pitcher with three runners on the bases;
and, like Kant, you seldom get
your grammar straight—yet,
you are the wick that absorbs the oil in my
lamp,
in all kinds of weather;
and we are teeth in the pitch wheel
that work together.

White Boy,
when I hear the word *Negro* defined,
why does it bring to mind
the chef, the gourmand, the belly-god,
the disease of Kings, the culinary art
in alien lands, Black Mammy in a Dixie big
house,
and the dietitian's chart?
Now, look at Black Boy scratch his head!
It's a stereotypic gesture of Uncle Tom,
a learned Gentleman of Color said
in his monumental tome,
The *Etiquette of the New Negro,*
which,
the publishers say,
by the way,
should be in every black man's home.

The Negro is a dish in the white man's
kitchen—
a potpourri,
an ola-podrida,
a mixie-maxie,
a hotchpotch of lineal ingredients;
with UN guests at his table,
the host finds himself a Hamlet on the spot,
for, in spite of his catholic pose,

the Negro dish is a dish nobody knows:
to some . . . tasty,
like an exotic condiment—
to others . . . unsavory
and inelegant.

White Boy,
the Negro dish is a mix
like . . . and *un*like
pimiento brisque, chop suey,
eggs à la Goldenrod, and eggaroni;
tongue-and-corn casserole, mulligan stew,
baked fillets of halibut, and cheese fondue;
macaroni milanaise, egg-milk shake,
mullagatawny soup, and sour-milk cake.

Just as the Chinese lack
an ideogram for "to be,"
our lexicon has no definition
for an ethnic amalgam like Black Boy and me.

Behold a Gordian knot without
the *beau geste* of an Alexander's sword!
Water, O Modern Mariner, water, everywhere,
unfit for *vitro de trina* glass
or the old-oaken-bucket's gourd!

For dark hymens on the auction block,
the lord of the mansion knew the macabre
score:
not a dog moved his tongue,
not a lamb lost a drop of blood to protect a
door.
O
Xenos of Xanthos,
what midnight-to-dawn lecheries,
in cabin and big house,

produced these brown hybrids and yellow
motleys?

White Boy,
Buchenwald is a melismatic song
whose single syllable is sung to blues notes
to dark wayfarers who listen for the gong
at the crack of doom along
. . . that Lonesome Road . . .
before they travel on.

A Pelagian with the *raison d'être* of a Negro,
I cannot say I have outwitted dread,
for I am conscious of the noiseless tread
of the Yazoo tiger's ball-like pads behind me
in the dark
as I trudge ahead,
up and up . . . that Lonesome Road . . . up
and up.

In a Vision in a Dream,
from the frigid seaport of the proud
Xanthochroid,
the good ship *Défineznegro*
sailed fine, under an unabridged moon,
to reach the archipelago
Nigeridentité.
In the Strait of Octoroon,
off black Scylla,
after the typhoon Phobos, out of the
Stereotypus Sea,
had rived her hull and sail to a T,
the *Défineznegro* sank the rock
and disappeared in the abyss
(*Vanitas vanitatum!*)
of white Charybdis.

Robert Hayden (1913–   )

Few Black poets now living can rival Robert Hayden in the longevity
of his poetic career. His first book of poems, *Heart-Shape in the Dust,*
was published in 1940, and he has been represented in every major
anthology of Black literature since *The Negro Caravan* appeared in 1941.
His output does not compare with the multi-genre productivity of
Langston Hughes, but Hayden's latest volume of poetry, *Words in the
Mourning Time* (1970), confirms that he has been able to sustain a high
quality of writing over the years.

Like many of his poetic contemporaries—Wilbur, Lowell, Ciardi, and others—Robert Hayden came to poetic maturity in the protective climate of academia. For all of them, this has been a mixed blessing. A positive consequence is that the poet of the academy is always in the forefront of controversy. This has been true of Ciardi both at Harvard and at Rutgers, and this was abundantly true of Hayden at Fisk when, in the early 1960's, he had a series of meaningful encounters with the proponents of a Black literary esthetic. Such a poet cannot remain a recluse, untouched by the flow of ideas; within such an emotional and intellectual context he can be poetically rejuvenated, as Hayden evidently was in the 1960's. But the academy as poetic environment can have adverse consequences, also. Sometimes it can produce poetry that has more intellectual brilliance than poetic content; philosophic profundity sometimes replaces passionate simplicity. Certainly, this is true of Hayden's "Ballad of Remembrance," in which "Contrived ghosts / rapped to metronome clack of lavalieres" and in which there is a "sallow vendeuse / of prepared tarnishes and jokes of nacre and ormolu." Moreover, the academic environment sometimes can provide a life that is more burdensome than poetically stimulating and hence inhibit productivity. On balance, however, as a poet of the academy Robert Hayden has fared well, and his recent return to the University of Michigan and the subsequent publication of *Words in the Mourning Time* augur continued success.

Although he has been widely published over the years in magazines and anthologies, Hayden's production of single volumes of poetry has been scant. In addition to his 1971 volume, he published *A Ballad of Remembrance* privately in London in 1962 and *Selected Poems* in 1966, and edited an anthology of poetry by American Black poets entitled *Kaleidoscope* in 1967. Of these, the poems in *Selected Poems* are the most exciting. Here one finds evidence of the poet's searing encounter with the Black Experience, although he insists that these poems were written by a poet, not by a Black poet. His position, restated forcefully in *Kaleidoscope,* is that no poet, Black or white, should be restricted to racial themes and that any effort to evaluate him as a Black poet is both racially chauvinistic and politically doctrinaire. In a sense, the so-called Black Experience poems in the 1966 volume—"Runagate Runagate," "Middle Passage," "Frederick Douglass," and others—prove his point that a skilled and experienced poet free of political or racial mandates can make significant and esthetically valid statements about any aspect of man's experience that he chooses. Hayden's insistence that the poet must have this freedom enriches and deepens his poetry. By striving for a broader awareness of the human condition, he can arrive at a deeper understanding of the significance of the Black Experience. A portion of the title poem in *Words in the Mourning Time* contains a further clarification of his position:

> *We must not be frightened nor cajoled*
> *into accepting evil as deliverance from evil.*
> *We must go on struggling to be human,*
> *though monsters of abstractions*
> *police and threaten us.*

> *Reclaim now, now renew the vision of*
> *a human world where godliness*
> *is possible and man*
> *is neither gook nigger honkey*
> *wop nor kike*
> *but man*
> *permitted to be man.*

These lines have a refreshing humanism—a humanism that cannot be surrendered to a political creed or buried under new esthetic theories. As long as he believes "godliness is possible," Robert Hayden will be able to write poems like "Runagate Runagate" and probe the moral and spiritual depths of the Black Experience as only a skilled and practised poet can do.

The poetry of Robert Hayden has received little published critical attention. Two articles of note are Rosey Pool, "Robert Hayden, Poet Laureate," *Negro Digest* (now *Black World*), XV (June 1966), 39–43, and D. Galler, "Three Recent Volumes," *Poetry,* CX (1967), 268. Julius Lester also provides a provocative critical comment on *Words in the Mourning Time* in *The New York Times Book Review,* January 24, 1971, p. 4.

Frederick Douglass

When it is finally ours, this freedom, this
  liberty, this beautiful
and terrible thing, needful to man as air,
usable as earth; when it belongs at last to all,
when it is truly instinct, brain matter, diastole,
  systole,
reflex action; when it is finally won; when it is
  more
than the gaudy mumbo jumbo of politicians:
this man, this Douglass, this former slave, this
  Negro
beaten to his knees, exiled, visioning a world
where none is lonely, none hunted, alien,
this man, superb in love and logic, this man
shall be remenbered. Oh, not with statues'
  rhetoric,
not with legends and poems and wreaths of
  bronze alone,
but with the lives grown out of his life, the
  lives
fleshing his dream of the beautiful, needful
  thing.

Runagate Runagate

Runs falls rises stumbles on from darkness into
  darkness
and the darkness thicketed with shapes of
  terror
and the hunters pursuing and the hounds
  pursuing
and the night cold and the night long and the
  river
to cross and the jack-muh-lanterns beckoning
  beckoning
and blackness ahead and when shall I reach
  that somewhere

morning and keep on going and never turn
  back and keep on going

             Runagate
                  Runagate
                       Runagate

Many thousands rise and go
many thousands crossing over

                O mythic North
            O star-shaped yonder Bible city

Some go weeping and some rejoicing
some in coffins and some in carriages
some in silks and some in shackles

          Rise and go or fare you well

No more auction block for me
no more driver's lash for me

    If you see my Pompey, 30 yrs of age,
    new breeches, plain stockings, negro shoes;
    if you see my Anna, likely young mulatto
    branded E on the right cheek, R on the
      left,
    catch them if you can and notify
      subscriber.
    Catch them if you can, but it won't be easy.
    They'll dart underground when you try to
      catch them,
    plunge into quicksand, whirlpools, mazes,
    turn into scorpions when you try to catch
      them.
And before I'll be a slave
I'll be buried in my grave

    North star and bonanza gold
    I'm bound for the freedom, freedom-bound
    and oh Susyanna don't you cry for me

            Runagate

                Runagate

           II
Rises from their anguish and their power,

          Harriet Tubman,

        woman of earth, whipscarred,
        a summoning, a shining

        Mean to be free

And this was the way of it, brethren
    brethren,
way we journeyed from Can't to Can.
Moon so bright and no place to hide,
the cry up and the patterollers riding.
hound dogs belling in bladed air.
And fear starts a-murbling, Never make it,
we'll never make it. *Hush that now,*
and she's turned upon us, levelled pistol
glinting in the moonlight:
Dead folks can't jaybird-talk, she says;
you keep on going now or die, she says.

Wanted   Harriet Tubman   alias The General
alias Moses   Stealer of Slaves

In league with Garrison Alcott Emerson
Garrett Douglass Thoreau John Brown

Armed and known to be Dangerous

Wanted   Reward   Dead or Alive

    Tell me, Ezekiel, oh tell me do you see
    mailed Jehovah coming to deliver me?

Hoot-owl calling in the ghosted air,
five times calling to the hants in the air.
Shadow of a face in the scary leaves,
shadow of a voice in the talking leaves:

    Come ride-a my train

    Oh that train, ghost-story train
    through swamp and savanna movering
      movering,
    over trestles of dew, through caves of the
      wish,
    Midnight special on a sabre track movering
      movering,
    first stop Mercy and the last Hallelujah.

    Come ride-a my train

        Mean mean mean to be free.

Homage to the Empress of the Blues

Because there was a man somewhere in a candystripe silk shirt,
gracile and dangerous as a jaguar and because a woman moaned
for him in sixty-watt gloom and mourned him Faithless Love
Twotiming Love Oh Love Oh Careless Aggravating Love,

She came out on the stage in yards of pearls, emerging like a
favorite scenic view, flashed her golden smile and sang.

Because grey laths began somewhere to show from underneath
torn hurdygurdy lithographs of dollfaced heaven;
and because there was those who feared alarming fists of snow
on the door and those who feared the riot-squad of statistics,

She came out on the stage in ostrich feathers, beaded satin, and
shone that smile on us and sang.

A Ballad of Remembrance

Quadroon mermaids, Afro angels, black saints
balanced upon the switchblades of that air
and sang. Tight streets unfolding to the eye
like fans of corrosion and elegiac lace
crackled with their singing: Shadow of time.
  Shadow of blood.

Shadow, echoed the Zulu king, dangling
from a cluster of balloons. Blood,
whined the gun-metal priestess, floating
over the courtyard where dead men diced.

What will you have? she inquired, the sallow
  vendeuse
of prepared tarnishes and jokes of nacre and
  ormolu,
what but those gleamings, oldrose graces,
manners like scented gloves? Contrived ghosts
rapped to metronome clack of lavalieres.

Contrived illuminations riding a threat
of river, masked Negroes wearing chameleon
satins gaudy now as a fortuneteller's
dream of disaster, lighted the crazy flopping
dance of love and hate among joys, rejections.

Accommodate, muttered the Zulu king,
toad on a throne of glaucous poison jewels.
Love, chimed the saints and the angels and the
  mermaids.
Hate, shrieked the gun-metal priestess
from her spiked bellcollar curved like a
  fleur-de-lis:

As well have a talon as a finger, a muzzle as a
  mouth,
as well have a hollow as a heart. And she
  pinwheeled
away on coruscations of laughter, scattering
those others before her like foil stars.

But the dance continued—now among
  metaphorical
doors, coffee cups floating poised
hysterias, decors of illusion; now among
mazurka dolls offering death's-heads
of cocaine roses and real violets.

Then you arrived, meditative, ironic,
richly human; and your presence was shore
  where I rested
released from the hoodoo of that dance, where I
  spoke
with my true voice again.

And therefore this is not only a ballad of
  remembrance
for the down-South arcane city with death
in its jaws like gold teeth and archaic
  cusswords;
not only a token for the troubled generous friends
held in the fists of that schizoid city like
  flowers,
but also, Mark Van Doren,
a poem of remembrance, a gift, a souvenir for
  you.

Tour 5

The road winds down through autumn
   hills
in blazonry of farewell scarlet
and recessional gold,
past cedar groves, through static villages
whose names are all that's left
of Choctaw, Chickasaw.

We stop a moment in a town
watched over by Confederate sentinels,
buy gas and ask directions of a rawboned
   man
whose eyes revile us as the enemy.

Shrill gorgon silence breaths behind
his taut civility
and in the ever-tautening air,
dark for us despite its Indian summer glow.
We drive on, following the route
of highwaymen and phantoms,

Of slaves and armies.
Children, wordless and remote,
wave at us from kindling porches.
And now the land is flat for miles,
the landscape lush, metallic, flayed,
its brightness harsh as bloodstained swords.

Mourning Poem for the Queen of Sunday

Lord's lost Him His mockingbird,
His fancy warbler;
Satan sweet-talked her,
four bullets hushed her.
Who would have thought
she'd end that way?

Four bullets hushed her. And the world a-clang
   with evil.
Who's going to make old hardened sinner men
   tremble now
and the righteous rock?
Oh who and oh who will sing Jesus down
to help with struggling and doing without and
   being colored
all through blue Monday?
Till way next Sunday?

All those angels
in their cretonne clouds and finery
the true believer saw

when she rared back her head and sang,
all those angels are surely weeping.
Who would have thought
she'd end that way?

Four holes in her heart. The gold works
   wrecked.
But she looks so natural in her big bronze
   coffin
among the Broken Hearts and Gates-Ajar,
it's as if any moment she'd lift her head
from its pillow of chill gardenias
and turn this quiet into shouting Sunday
and make folks forget what she did on Monday.

Oh, Satan sweet-talked her,
and four bullets hushed her.
Lord's lost Him His diva,
His fancy warbler's gone.
Who would have thought,
who would have thought she'd end that way?

Middle Passage

Jesús, Estrella, Esperanza, Mercy:

  Sails flashing to the wind like weapons,
  sharks following the moans the fever and
    the dying;

horror the corposant and compass rose.

Middle Passage:
      voyage through death
           to life upon these shores.

"10 April 1800—
Blacks rebellious. Crew uneasy. Our
  linguist says
their moaning is a prayer for death,
ours and their own. Some try to starve
  themselves.
Lost three this morning leaped with crazy
  laughter
to the waiting sharks, sang as they went
  under."

Desire, Adventure, Tartar, Ann:

Standing to America, bringing home
black gold, black ivory, black seed.

> *Deep in the festering hold thy father lies,*
> *of his bones New England pews are made,*
> *those are altar lights that were his eyes.*

Jesus Savior Pilot Me
Over Life's Tempestuous Sea

We pray that thou wilt grant, O Lord,
safe passage to our vessels bringing
heathen souls unto Thy chastening.

Jesus Saviour

"8 bells. I cannot sleep, for I am sick
with fear, but writing eases fear a little
since still my eyes can see these words take
  shape
upon the page & so I write, as one
would turn to exorcism. 4 days scudding,
but now the sea is calm again.
  Misfortune
follows in our wake like sharks (our
  grinning
tutelary gods). Which one of us
has killed an albatross? A plague among
our blacks—Ophthalmia: blindness—& we
have jettisoned the blind to no avail.
It spreads, the terrifying sickness spreads.
Its claws have scratched sight from the
  Capt.'s eyes
& there is blindness in the fo'c'sle
& we must sail 3 weeks before we come
to port."

> *What port awaits us, Davy Jones'*
> *or home? I've heard of slavers drifting,*
> *drifting,*
> *playthings of wind and storm and chance,*
> *their crews*
> *gone blind, the jungle hatred*
> *crawling up on deck.*

Thou Who Walked On Galilee

"Deponent further sayeth *The Bella J*
left the Guinea Coast
with cargo of five hundred blacks and odd
for the barracoons of Florida:

"That there was hardly room 'tween-decks
  for half
the sweltering cattle stowed spoon-fashion
  there;
that some went mad of thirst and tore
  their flesh
and sucked the blood:

"That Crew and Captain lusted with the
  comeliest
of the savage girls kept naked in the
  cabins;
that there was one they called The Guinea
  Rose
and they cast lots and fought to lie with
  her:

"That when the Bo's'n piped all hands, the
  flames
spreading from starboard already were
  beyond
control, the negroes howling and their
  chains
entangled with the flames:

"That the burning blacks could not be
  reached,
that the Crew abandoned ship,
leaving their shrieking negresses behind,
that the Captain perished drunken with the
  wenches:

"Further Deponent sayeth not."

Pilot Oh Pilot Me

II

Aye, lad, and I have seen those factories,
Gambia, Rio Pongo, Calabar;
have watched the artful mongos baiting traps
of war wherein the victor and the vanquished

Were caught as prizes for our barracoons.
Have seen the nigger kings whose vanity
and greed turned wild black hides of Fellatah,
Mandingo, Ibo, Kru to gold for us.

And there was one—King Anthracite we named
  him—
fetish face beneath French parasols
of brass and orange velvet, impudent mouth
whose cups were carven skulls of enemies:

He'd honor us with drum and feast and conjo
and palm-oil-glistening wenches deft in love,
and for tin crowns that shone with paste,
red calico and German-silver trinkets

Would have the drums talk war and send
his warriors to burn the sleeping villages
and kill the sick and old and lead the young
in coffles to our factories.

Twenty years a trader, twenty years,
for there was wealth aplenty to be harvested
from those black fields, and I'd be trading still
but for the fevers melting down my bones.

III
Shuttles in the rocking loom of history,
the dark ships move, the dark ships move,
their bright ironical names
like jests of kindness on a murderer's mouth;
plough through thrashing glister toward
fata morgana's lucent melting shore,
weave toward New World littorals that are
mirage and myth and actual shore.

Voyage through death,
                          voyage whose chartings
                                     are unlove.

A charnel stench, effluvium of living death
spreads outward from the hold,
where the living and the dead, the horribly
    dying,
lie interlocked, lie foul with blood and
    excrement.

> *Deep in the festering hold thy father lies,*
> *the corpse of mercy rots with him,*
> *rats eat love's rotten gelid eyes.*

> *But, oh, the living look at you*
> *with human eyes whose suffering accuses*
> *   you,*
> *whose hatred reaches through the swill of*
> *   dark*
> *to strike you like a leper's claw.*

> *You cannot stare that hatred down*
> *or chain the fear that stalks the watches*
> *and breathes on you its fetid scorching*
> *   breath;*
> *cannot kill the deep immortal human wish,*
> *the timeless will.*

> "But for the storm that flung up
>   barriers

of wind and wave, *The Amistad,*
    señores,
would have reached the port of
    Príncipe in two,
three days at most; but for the storm
    we should
have been prepared for what befell.
Swift as the puma's leap it came. There
    was
that interval of moonless calm filled
    only
with the water's and the rigging's
    usual sounds,
then sudden movement, blows and
    snarling cries
and they had fallen on us with
    machete
and marlinspike. It was as though the
    very
air, the night itself were striking us.
Exhausted by the rigors of the storm,
we were no match for them. Our men
    went down
before the murderous Africans. Our
    loyal
Celestino ran from below with gun
and lantern and I saw, before the cane-
knife's wounding flash, Cinquez,
that surly brute who calls himself a
    prince,
directing, urging on the ghastly work.
He hacked the poor mulatto down,
    and then
he turned on me. The decks were
    slippery
when daylight finally came. It sickens
    me
to think of what I saw, of how these
    apes
threw overboard the butchered bodies
    of
our men, true Christians all, like so
    much jetsam.
Enough, enough. The rest is quickly
    told:
Cinquez was forced to spare the two
    of us
you see to steer the ship to Africa,
and we like phantoms doomed to rove
    the sea
voyaged east by day and west by
    night,
deceiving them, hoping for rescue,

prisoners on our own vessel, till
at length we drifted to the shores of this
your land, America, where we were freed
from our unspeakable misery. Now we
demand, good sirs, the extradition of
Cinquez and his accomplices to La
Havana. And it distresses us to know
there are so many here who seem inclined
to justify the mutiny of these blacks.
We find it paradoxical indeed
that you whose wealth, whose tree of liberty
are rooted in the labor of your slaves
should suffer the august John Quincy Adams
to speak with so much passion of the right

of chattel slaves to kill their lawful masters
and with his Roman rhetoric weave a hero's
garland for Cinquez. I tell you that
we are determined to return to Cuba
with our slaves and there see justice done. Cinquez—
or let us say 'the Prince'—Cinquez shall die."

The deep immortal human wish,
the timeless will:

Cinquez its deathless primaveral image,
life that transfigures many lives.

Voyage through death
to life upon these shores.

Ralph Ellison (1914–   )

In his recollections of childhood, Richard Wright emphasized the negative. Ralph Ellison, on the other hand, usually accentuates the positive when interviewers ask him about his early years in Oklahoma City, where he was born in 1914 and where he lived until his departure for Tuskegee Institute in 1933. His father, Lewis Alfred Ellison, had spent an adventurous youth that took him to China in the Spanish-American War, and he was an intellectual adventurer as well—an avid reader who named his son Ralph Waldo Ellison and exposed the boy to books while he was still a toddler. The elder Ellison died when Ralph was three, but his influence was to endure in the developing imagination of his son. If one may say that Ellison "inherited" his interest in books from his father, one may also locate the genesis of his concern with social and political matters in his mother. A strong and militant Black woman raised on a Georgia farm, she organized for the Socialist Party in the year of his birth and later defied the segregationist policies of Governor "Alfalfa Bill" Murray.

A third abiding interest of Ellison's life was also formed in his Oklahoma childhood—music. Both the classical music taught in school and the vital jazz being created by such personal friends as Jimmy Rushing and Charlie Christian appealed so deeply to Ellison that he became an accomplished jazz trumpeter at the same time that he was preparing to enter Tuskegee Institute to study composing.

For all its segregation and racism, then, the Oklahoma of Ellison's youth was not without a certain frontier fluidity, freedom, and openness that instilled in him a sense of possibility and creativity. A governing concept of his boyhood, as he has recalled on more than one occasion, was that of the Renaissance Man. He and his friends "discussed mastering ourselves and everything in sight as though no such thing as racial discrimination existed."

At Tuskegee in Alabama, however, Ellison found himself in a much more repressive atmosphere. Disappointed in Tuskegee as a locus of racial values, he turned from the frivolous pursuit of popularity and prestige through athletics and campus politics to immure himself in the library. There he discovered *The Waste Land* of T. S. Eliot. His musical career continued, but even before leaving the campus to find summer work in New York in 1936 his reading was becoming more and more a central activity of his life.

In New York (Ellison did not return to Tuskegee) the shift from music to literature as the chief mode of his creative impulse was accelerated by the influence of Richard Wright. Having admired one of Wright's poems (probably "We of the Streets") for its affinity with the poetry of Eliot, Ellison was eager to meet him after Wright moved to New York from Chicago in 1937. Introduced by Langston Hughes, Wright and Ellison struck up a close personal, literary, and political friendship. Wright directed the younger man to "those works in which writing was discussed as a craft . . . to Henry James' prefaces, to Conrad, to Joseph Warren Beach and to the letters of Dostoievsky." He invited Ellison to contribute to *New Challenge,* a Harlem literary magazine that he edited, and his story "The Man Who Lived Underground" was to provide the *donnée* of *Invisible Man.* Ellison has denied that his work was deeply influenced by Wright, but the evidence of his early fiction and essays, appearing in such magazines as *The New Masses, Direction, Common Ground, Negro Story, The Negro Quarterly* (which Ellison edited 1942–1943), and *Tomorrow,* indicates otherwise. Langston Hughes was probably correct in claiming that for Ellison "Wright became a sort of literary god for a time."

While serving in the Merchant Marine near the end of World War II, Ellison was encouraged by a publisher to begin work on a novel. This turned out to be *Invisible Man* (1952), which is both the most artistically satisfying work of fiction by a Black writer and one of the most profound explorations of the meaning of the Black Experience in America. The search of the unnamed protagonist for both individual identity and racial meaning in his passage from innocence to experience in a chaotic American society struck deeply responsive chords in readers of all races. Whatever Ellison's future achievement may be, *Invisible Man* stands, in the opinion of many critics, as the finest American novel of the postwar period.

Since the publication of *Invisible Man* Ellison has taught and lectured widely in both America and Europe. In the mid-1950's he lectured in Germany and Austria before going to Rome on a National American Academy of Arts and Letters fellowship. Back in the United States in 1958, he taught at Bard College, the University of Chicago, and Rutgers

University until 1964. Recently he has become Albert Schweitzer Professor in the Humanities at New York University. He has also been a visiting fellow at Yale and a lecturer at many other leading institutions, Columbia, Fisk, Antioch, Princeton, UCLA, Oberlin, and Illinois among them.

Shadow and Act, Ellison's second book, appeared in 1964. This collection of essays, reviews, and interviews from more than two decades is arranged under three categories: "The Seer and the Seen"—literary and folklore topics; "Sound and the Mainstream"—Black music; and "The Shadow and the Act"—Afro-American culture and society in relation to the total national pattern. Thus the very organization of *Shadow and Act* reflects the primary concerns—books, music, and race—he has retained from his childhood and youth. A man always conscious of his roots, Ralph Ellison takes special pride in two of the many honors he has received: in 1963 Tuskegee Institute, which he had left without graduating, awarded him an honorary Ph.D. in Humane Letters, and in 1967 he was recognized, along with the Indian ballerina Maria Tallchief, by the Oklahoma State Legislature for his outstanding contribution to the creative arts.

Since 1955 Ellison has been at work on a long novel concerning the Black religious experience and politics. Its characters include Daddy Hickman, a revivalist preacher, and Reverend Bliss, a younger white protégé who becomes a racist United States Senator. The several excerpts from this work in progress that have been published suggest that the long wait for its appearance will at last be amply rewarded.

Some of Ellison's uncollected early short stories are "Slick Gonna Learn," *Direction,* September 1938, pp. 10–11, 14, 16; "Mister Toussan," *The New Masses,* XLI (November 4, 1941), 19–20; "That I Had the Wings," *Common Ground,* III (Summer 1943), 30–37; "In a Strange Country," *Tomorrow,* III (July 1944), 41–44; "Flying Home," in *Cross Section* (1944), edited by Edwin Seaver; "King of the Bingo Game," *Tomorrow,* IV (November 1944), 29–33; and "Afternoon," *Negro Story,* I (March–April 1945), 3–8. Three later stories are "Did You Ever Dream Lucky?" *New World Writing #5* (1954), pp. 134–145; "A Coupla Scalped Indians," *New World Writing #9* (1956), pp. 225–236; and "Out of the Hospital and Under the Bar" (first conceived as part of *Invisible Man*), in *Soon, One Morning* (1963), edited by Herbert Hill, pp. 243–290. Uncollected essays and reviews appeared in *The New Masses* and *The Negro Quarterly* in the early 1940's. Excerpts from Ellison's work in progress have appeared in several periodicals. For a full listing of these and all other works by Ellison, see "A Bibliography of Ralph Ellison's Published Writings," *Studies in Black Literature,* II (Autumn 1971), 25–28, by Bernard Benoit and Michel Fabre.

No biography or full-length critical study has been written, but much of interest can be found in interviews with Ellison, two of which are reprinted in *Shadow and Act,* and one in *The Black American Writer* (1969), edited by C. W. E. Bigsby. Two important interviews conducted by young Black writers appeared in *Harper's Magazine,* CCXXXIV (March 1967), 76–80, 83–86, 88, 90, 93–95, and *The Atlantic,* CCXXVI (December 1970), 45–60. John M. Reilly has edited *Twentieth Century Interpretations of Invisible Man: A Collection of Critical Essays* (1970), and Donald B. Gibson includes four important critical essays on Ellison in *Five Black Writers* (1970). The March 1970 *CLA Journal* and the December 1970 *Black World* are special Ellison issues. See also John Corry, "An American Novelist Who Sometimes Teaches," *The New York Times Magazine,* November 20, 1956, pp. 54–55, 179–180, 182–185, 187, 196; Robert A. Bone, *The Negro Novel in America* (1958); Ihab Hassan, *Radical Innocence: The Contemporary American Novel* (1961); Irving Howe, "Black Boys and Native Sons," *Dissent,* X (1963), 353–368; Robert Penn Warren, "The Unity of Experience," *Commentary,* XXXIX (1965), 91–96; Richard Kostelanetz, "The Politics of Ellison's Booker: *Invisible Man* as Symbolic History," *Chicago Review,* XIX, ii (1967), 5–26, and "Ralph Ellison: Novelist as Brown Skinned Aristocrat," *Shenandoah,* XX (Summer 1969), 56–77; Gene Bluestein, "The Blues as Literary Theme," *Massachusetts Review,* VIII (1967), 593–617; Nancy M. Tischler, "Negro Literature and Classic Form," *Contemporary Literature,* X (1969), 352–365; and Thomas A. Vogler, "*Invisible Man:* Somebody's Protest Novel," *The Iowa Review,* I (Spring 1970), 64–82.

Richard Wright's Blues

If anybody ask you
who sing this song,
Say it was ole [Black Boy]
done been here and gone.[1]

As a writer, Richard Wright has outlined for himself a dual role: to discover and depict the meaning of Negro experience; and to reveal to both Negroes and whites those problems of a psychological and emotional nature which arise between them when they strive for mutual understanding.

Now, in *Black Boy,* he has used his own life to probe what qualities of will, imagination and intellect are required of a Southern Negro in order to possess the meaning of his life in the United States. Wright is an important writer, perhaps the most articulate Negro American, and what he has to say is highly perceptive. Imagine Bigger Thomas projecting his own life in lucid prose, guided, say, by the insights of Marx and Freud, and you have an idea of this autobiography.

Published at a time when any sharply critical

approach to Negro life has been dropped as a wartime expendable, it should do much to redefine the problem of the Negro and American Democracy. Its power can be observed in the shrill manner with which some professional "friends of the Negro people" have attempted to strangle the work in a noose of newsprint.

What in the tradition of literary autobiography is it like, this work described as a "great American autobiography"? As a non-white intellectual's statement of his relationship to Western culture, *Black Boy* recalls the conflicting pattern of identification and rejection found in Nehru's *Toward Freedom.* In its use of fictional techniques, its concern with criminality (sin) and the artistic sensibility, and in its author's judgment and rejection of the narrow world of his origin, it recalls Joyce's rejection of Dublin in *A Portrait of the Artist.* And as a psychological document of life under oppressive conditions, it recalls *The House of the Dead,* Dostoievsky's profound study of the humanity of Russian criminals.

Such works were perhaps Wright's literary guides, aiding him to endow his life's incidents with communicable significance; providing him

[1] Signature formula used by blues singers at conclusion of song.

with ways of seeing, feeling and describing his environment. These influences, however, were encountered only after these first years of Wright's life were past and were not part of the immediate folk culture into which he was born. In that culture the specific folk-art form which helped shape the writer's attitude toward his life and which embodied the impulse that contributes much to the quality and tone of his autobiography was the Negro blues. This would bear a word of explanation:

The blues is an impulse to keep the painful details and episodes of a brutal experience alive in one's aching consciousness, to finger its jagged grain, and to transcend it, not by the consolation of philosophy but by squeezing from it a near-tragic, near-comic lyricism. As a form, the blues is an autobiographical chronicle of personal catastrophe expressed lyrically. And certainly Wright's early childhood was crammed with catastrophic incidents. In a few short years his father deserted his mother, he knew intense hunger, he became a drunkard begging drinks from black stevedores in Memphis saloons; he had to flee Arkansas, where an uncle was lynched; he was forced to live with a fanatically religious grandmother in an atmosphere of constant bickering; he was lodged in an orphan asylum; he observed the suffering of his mother, who became a permanent invalid, while fighting off the blows of the poverty-stricken relatives with whom he had to live; he was cheated, beaten and kicked off jobs by white employees who disliked his eagerness to learn a trade; and to these objective circumstances must be added the subjective fact that Wright, with his sensitivity, extreme shyness and intelligence, was a problem child who rejected his family and was by them rejected.

Thus along with the themes, equivalent descriptions of milieu and the perspectives to be found in Joyce, Nehru, Dostoievsky, George Moore and Rousseau, *Black Boy* is filled with blues-tempered echoes of railroad trains, the names of Southern towns and cities, estrangements, fights and flights, deaths and disappointments, charged with physical and spiritual hungers and pain. And like a blues sung by such an artist as Bessie Smith, its lyrical prose evokes the paradoxical, almost surreal image of a black boy singing lustily as he probes his own grievous wound.

In *Black Boy,* two worlds have fused, two cultures merged, two impulses of Western man become coalesced. By discussing some of its cul-

tural sources I hope to answer those critics who would make of the book a miracle and of its author a mystery. And while making no attempt to probe the mystery of the artist (who Hemingway says is "forged in injustice as a sword is forged"), I do hold that basically the prerequisites to the writing of *Black Boy* were, on the one hand, the microscopic degree of cultural freedom which Wright found in the South's stony injustice, and, on the other, the existence of a personality agitated to a state of almost manic restlessness. There were, of course, other factors, chiefly ideological; but these came later.

Wright speaks of his journey north as

. . . taking a part of the South to transplant in alien soil, to see if it could grow differently, if it could drink of new and cool rains, bend in strange winds, respond to the warmth of other suns, and perhaps, to bloom. . . .

And just as Wright, the man, represents the blooming of the delinquent child of the autobiography, just so does *Black Boy* represent the flowering—cross-fertilized by pollen blown by the winds of strange cultures—of the humble blues lyric. There is, as in all acts of creation, a world of mystery in this, but there is also enough that is comprehensible for Americans to create the social atmosphere in which other black boys might freely bloom.

For certainly, in the historical sense, Wright is no exception. Born on a Mississippi plantation, he was subjected to all those blasting pressures which in a scant eighty years have sent the Negro people hurtling, without clearly defined trajectory, from slavery to emancipation, from log cabin to city tenement, from the white folks' fields and kitchens to factory assembly lines; and which, between two wars, have shattered the wholeness of its folk consciousness into a thousand writhing pieces.

Black Boy describes this process in the personal terms of *one* Negro childhood. Nevertheless, several critics have complained that it does not "explain" Richard Wright. Which, aside from the notion of art involved, serves to remind us that the prevailing mood of American criticism has so thoroughly excluded the Negro that it fails to recognize some of the most basic tenets of Western democratic thought when encountering them in a black skin. They forget that human life possesses an innate dignity and mankind an innate sense of nobility; that all men possess the tendency to dream and the compulsion to make their dreams reality; that the need to be ever dissatisfied and the urge ever to seek satisfaction is implicit in the human organism; and that all men are the victims and the beneficiaries of the goading, tormenting, commanding and informing activity of that imperious process known as the Mind—the Mind, as Valéry describes it, "armed with its inexhaustible questions."

Perhaps all this (in which lies the very essence of the human, and which Wright takes for granted) has been forgotten because the critics recognize neither Negro humanity nor the full extent to which the Southern community renders the fulfillment of human destiny impossible. And while it is true that *Black Boy* presents an almost unrelieved picture of a personality corrupted by brutal environment, it also presents those fresh, human responses brought to its world by the sensitive child:

There was the *wonder* I felt when I first saw a brace of mountainlike, spotted, black-and-white horses clopping down a dusty road . . . the *delight* I caught in seeing long straight rows of red and green vegetables stretching away in the sun . . . the faint, cool kiss of *sensuality* when dew came on to my cheeks . . . the vague *sense of the infinite* as I looked down upon the yellow, dreaming waters of the Mississippi . . . the echoes of *nostalgia* I heard in the crying strings of wild geese . . . the *love* I had for the mute regality of tall, moss-clad oaks . . . the hint of *cosmic cruelty* that I *felt* when I saw the curved timbers of a wooden shack that had been warped in the summer sun . . . and there was the *quiet terror* that suffused my senses when vast hazes of gold washed earthward from star-heavy skies on silent nights. . . .[2]

And a bit later, his reactions to religion:

Many of the religious symbols appealed to my sensibilities and I responded to the dramatic vision of life held by the church, feeling that to live day by day with death as one's sole thought was to be so compassionately sensitive toward all life as to view all men as slowly dying, and the trembling sense of fate that welled up, sweet and melancholy, from the hymns blended with the sense of fate that I had already caught from life.

There was also the influence of his mother—so closely linked to his hysteria and sense of suffering—who (though he only implies it here) taught him, in the words of the dedication prefacing *Native Son,* "to revere the fanciful and the imaginative." There were also those white men—

[2] Italics mine.

the one who allowed Wright to use his library privileges and the other who advised him to leave the South, and still others whose offers of friendship he was too frightened to accept.

Wright assumed that the nucleus of plastic sensibility is a human heritage: the right and the opportunity to dilate, deepen and enrich sensibility—democracy. Thus the drama of *Black Boy* lies in its depiction of what occurs when Negro sensibility attempts to fulfill itself in the undemocratic South. Here it is not the individual that is the immediate focus, as in Joyce's *Stephen Hero,* but that upon which his sensibility was nourished.

Those critics who complain that Wright has omitted the development of his own sensibility hold that the work thus fails as art. Others, because it presents too little of what they consider attractive in Negro life, charge that it distorts reality. Both groups miss a very obvious point: That whatever else the environment contained, it had as little chance of prevailing against the overwhelming weight of the child's unpleasant experiences as Beethoven's Quartets would have of destroying the stench of a Nazi prison.

We come, then, to the question of art. The function, the psychology, of artistic selectivity is to eliminate from art form all those elements of experience which contain no compelling significance. Life is as the sea, art a ship in which man conquers life's crushing formlessness, reducing it to a course, a series of swells, tides and wind currents inscribed on a chart. Though drawn from the world, "the organized significance of art," writes Malraux, "is stronger than all the multiplicity of the world; . . . that significance alone enables man to conquer chaos and to master destiny."

Wright saw his destiny—that combination of forces before which man feels powerless—in terms of a quick and casual violence inflicted upon him by both family and community. His response was likewise violent, and it has been his need to give that violence significance which has shaped his writings.

What were the ways by which other Negroes confronted their destiny?

In the South of Wright's childhood there were three general ways: They could accept the role created for them by the whites and perpetually resolve the resulting conflicts through the hope and emotional cartharsis of Negro religion; they could repress their dislike of Jim Crow social relations while striving for a middle way of respectability, becoming—consciously or unconsciously—the accomplices of the whites in oppressing their brothers; or they could reject the situation, adopt a criminal attitude, and carry on an unceasing psychological scrimmage with the whites, which often flared forth into physical violence.

Wright's attitude was nearest the last. Yet in it there was an all-important qualitative difference: it represented a groping for *individual* values, in a black community whose values were what the young Negro critic, Edward Bland, has defined as "pre-individual." And herein lay the setting for the extreme conflict set off, both within his family and in the community, by Wright's assertion of individuality. The clash was sharpest on the psychological level, for, to quote Bland:

In the pre-individualistic thinking of the Negro the stress is on the group. Instead of seeing in terms of the individual, the Negro sees in terms of "races," masses of peoples separated from other masses according to color. Hence, an act rarely bears intent against him as a Negro individual. He is singled out not as a person but as a specimen of an ostracized group. He knows that he never exists in his own right but only to the extent that others hope to make the race suffer vicariously through him.

This pre-individual state is induced artificially —like the regression to primitive states noted among cultured inmates of Nazi prisons. The primary technique in its enforcement is to impress the Negro child with the omniscience and omnipotence of the whites to the point that whites appear as ahuman as Jehovah, and as relentless as a Mississippi flood. Socially it is effected through an elaborate scheme of taboos supported by a ruthless physical violence, which strikes not only the offender but the entire black community. To wander from the paths of behavior laid down for the group is to become the agent of communal disaster.

In such a society the development of individuality depends upon a series of accidents, which often arise, as in Wright's case, from conditions within the Negro family. In Wright's life there was the accident that as a small child he could not distinguish between his fair-skinned grandmother and the white women of the town, thus developing skepticism as to their special status. To this was linked the accident of his having no close contacts with whites until after the child's normal formative period.

But these objective accidents not only link forward to these qualities of rebellion, criminality and intellectual questioning expressed in Wright's work today. They also link backward into the shadow of infancy where environment and consciousness are so darkly intertwined as to require the skill of a psychoanalyst to define their point of juncture. Nevertheless, at the age of four, Wright set the house afire and was beaten near to death by his frightened mother. This beating, followed soon by his father's desertion of the family, seems to be the initial psychological motivation of his quest for a new identification. While delirious from this beating Wright was haunted "by huge wobbly white bags like the full udders of a cow, suspended from the ceiling above me [and] I was gripped by the fear that they were going to fall and drench me with some horrible liquid . . ."

It was as though the mother's milk had turned acid, and with it the whole pattern of life that had produced the ignorance, cruelty and fear that had fused with mother-love and exploded in the beating. It is significant that the bags were of the hostile color white, and the female symbol that of the cow, the most stupid (and, to the small child, the most frightening) of domestic animals. Here in dream symbolism is expressed an attitude worthy of an Orestes. And the significance of the crisis is increased by virtue of the historical fact that the lower-class Negro family is matriarchal; the child turns not to the father to compensate if he feels mother-rejection, but to the grandmother, or to an aunt—and Wright rejected both of these. Such rejection leaves the child open to psychological insecurity, distrust and all of those hostile environmental forces from which the family functions to protect it.

One of the Southern Negro family's methods of protecting the child is the severe beating—a homeopathic dose of the violence generated by black and white relationships. Such beatings as Wright's were administered for the child's own good; a good which the child resisted, thus giving family relationships an undercurrent of fear and hostility, which differs qualitatively from that found in patriarchal middle-class families, because here the severe beating is administered by the mother, leaving the child no parental sanctuary. He must ever embrace violence along with maternal tenderness, or else reject, in his helpless way, the mother.

The division between the Negro parents of

Wright's mother's generation, whose sensibilities were often bound by their proximity to the slave experience, and their children, who historically and through the rapidity of American change stand emotionally and psychologically much farther away, is quite deep. Indeed, sometimes as deep as the cultural distance between Yeats' *Autobiographies* and a Bessie Smith blues. This is the historical background to those incidents of family strife in *Black Boy* which have caused reviewers to question Wright's judgment of Negro emotional relationships.

We have here a problem in the sociology of sensibility that is obscured by certain psychological attitudes brought to Negro life by whites.

The first is the attitude which compels whites to impute to Negroes sentiments, attitudes and insights which, as a group living under certain definite social conditions, Negroes could not humanly possess. It is the identical mechanism which William Empson identifies in literature as "pastoral." It implies that since Negroes possess the richly human virtues credited to them, then their social position is advantageous and should not be bettered; and, continuing syllogistically, the white individual need feel no guilt over his participation in Negro oppression.

The second attitude is that which leads whites to misjudge Negro passion, looking upon it as they do, out of the turgidity of their own frustrated yearning for emotional warmth, their capacity for sensation having been constricted by the impersonal mechanized relationships typical of bourgeois society. The Negro is idealized into a symbol of sensation, of unhampered social and sexual relationships. And when *Black Boy* questions their illusion they are thwarted much in the manner of the occidental who, after observing the erotic character of a primitive dance, "shacks up" with a native woman—only to discover that far from possessing the hair-trigger sexual responses of a Stork Club "babe," she is relatively phlegmatic.

The point is not that American Negroes are primitives, but that as a group their social situation does not provide for the type of emotional relationships attributed them. For how could the South, recognized as a major part of the backward third of the nation, nurture in the black, most brutalized section of its population, those forms of human relationships achievable only in the most highly developed areas of civilization?

Champions of this "Aren't-Negroes-Wonderful?" school of thinking often bring Paul Robeson and Marian Anderson forward as examples of highly developed sensibility, but actually they are only its *promise*. Both received their development from an extensive personal contact with European culture, free from the influences which shape Southern Negro personality. In the United States, Wright, who is the only Negro literary artist of equal caliber, had to wait years and escape to another environment before discovering the moral and ideological equivalents of his childhood attitudes.

Man cannot express that which does not exist—either in the form of dreams, ideas or realities—in his environment. Neither his thoughts nor his feelings, his sensibility nor his intellect are fixed, innate qualities. They are processes which arise out of the interpenetration of human instinct with environment, through the process called experience; each changing and being changed by the other. Negroes cannot possess many of the sentiments attributed to them because the same changes in environment which, through experience, enlarge man's intellect (and thus his capacity for still greater change) also modify his feelings; which in turn increase his sensibility, i.e., his sensitivity, to refinements of impression and subtleties of emotion. The extent of these changes depends upon the quality of political and cultural freedom in the environment.

Intelligence tests have measured the quick rise in intellect which takes place in Southern Negroes after moving north, but little attention has been paid to the mutations effected in their sensibilities. However, the two go hand in hand. Intellectual complexity is accompanied by emotional complexity; refinement of thought, by refinement of feeling. The movement north affects more than the Negro's wage scale, it affects his entire psychosomatic structure.

The rapidity of Negro intellectual growth in the North is due partially to objective factors present in the environment, to influences of the industrial city and to a greater political freedom. But there are also changes within the "inner world." In the North energies are released and given *intellectual* channelization—energies which in most Negroes in the South have been forced to take either a *physical* form or, as with potentially intellectual types like Wright, to be expressed as nervous tension, anxiety and hysteria. Which is nothing mysterious. The human organism responds to environmental stimuli by converting them into either physical and/or intellectual energy. And what is called hysteria is suppressed intellectual energy expressed physically.

The "physical" character of their expression makes for much of the difficulty in understanding American Negroes. Negro music and dances are frenziedly erotic; Negro religious ceremonies violently ecstatic; Negro speech strongly rhythmical and weighted with image and gesture. But there is more in this sensuousness than the unrestraint and insensitivity found in primitive cultures; nor is it simply the relatively spontaneous and undifferentiated responses of a people living in close contact with the soil. For despite Jim Crow, Negro life does not exist in a vacuum, but in the seething vortex of those tensions generated by the most highly industrialized of Western nations. The welfare of the most humble black Mississippi sharecropper is affected less by the flow of the seasons and the rhythm of natural events than by the fluctuations of the stock market; even though, as Wright states of his father, the sharecropper's memories, actions and emotions are shaped by his immediate contact with nature and the crude social relations of the South.

All of this makes the American Negro far different from the "simple" specimen for which he is taken. And the "physical" quality offered as evidence of his primitive simplicity is actually the form of his complexity. The American Negro is a Western type whose social condition creates a state which is almost the reverse of the cataleptic trance: Instead of his consciousness being lucid to the reality around it while the body is rigid, here it is the body which is alert, reacting to pressures which the constricting forces of Jim Crow block off from the transforming, concept-creating activity of the brain. The "eroticism" of Negro expression springs from much the same conflict as that displayed in the violent gesturing of a man who attempts to express a complicated concept with a limited vocabulary; thwarted ideational energy is converted into unsatisfactory pantomime, and his words are burdened with meanings they cannot convey. Here lies the source of the basic ambiguity of *Native Son,* wherein in order to translate Bigger's complicated feelings into universal ideas, Wright had to force into Bigger's consciousness concepts and ideas which his intellect could not formulate. Between Wright's skill and knowledge and the potentials of Bigger's mute feelings lay a thousand years of conscious culture.

In the South the sensibilities of both blacks and whites are inhibited by the rigidly defined environment. For the Negro there is relative safety as long as the impulse toward individuality is suppressed. (Lynchings have occurred because Negroes painted their homes.) And it is the task of the Negro family to adjust the child to the Southern milieu: through it the currents, tensions and impulses generated within the human organism by the flux and flow of events are given their distribution. This also gives the group its distinctive character. Which, because of Negroes' suppressed minority position, is very much in the nature of an elaborate but limited defense mechanism. Its function is dual: to protect the Negro from whirling away from the undifferentiated mass of his people into the unknown, symbolized in its most abstract form by insanity, and most concretely by lynching; and to protect him from those unknown forces *within himself* which might urge him to reach out for that social and human equality which the white South says he cannot have. Rather than throw himself against the charged wires of his prison he annihilates the impulses within him.

The pre-individualistic black community discourages individuality out of self-defense. Having learned through experience that the whole group is punished for the actions of the single member, it has worked out efficient techniques of behavior control. For in many Southern communities everyone knows everyone else and is vulnerable to his opinions. In some communities everyone is "related" regardless of blood-ties. The regard shown by the group for its members, its general communal character and its cohesion are often mentioned. For by comparison with the coldly impersonal relationships of the urban industrial community, its relationships are personal and warm.

Black Boy, however, illustrates that this personal quality, shaped by outer violence and inner fear, is ambivalent. Personal warmth is accompanied by an equally personal coldness, kindliness by cruelty, regard by malice. And these opposites are as quickly set off against the member who gestures toward individuality as a lynch mob forms at the cry of rape. Negro leaders have often been exasperated by this phenomenon, and Booker T. Washington (who demanded far less of Negro humanity than Richard Wright) described the

Negro community as a basket of crabs, wherein should one attempt to climb out, the others immediately pull him back.

The member who breaks away is apt to be more impressed by its negative than by its positive character. He becomes a stranger even to his relatives and he interprets gestures of protection as blows of oppression—from which there is no hiding place, because every area of Negro life is affected. Even parental love is given a qualitative balance akin to "sadism." And the extent of beatings and psychological maimings meted out by Southern Negro parents rivals those described by the nineteenth-century Russian writers as characteristic of peasant life under the Czars. The horrible thing is that the cruelty is also an expression of concern, of love.

In discussing the inadequacies for democratic living typical of the education provided Negroes by the South, a Negro educator has coined the term *mis-education*. Within the ambit of the black family this takes the form of training the child away from curiosity and adventure, against reaching out for those activities lying beyond the borders of the black community. And when the child resists, the parent discourages him; first with the formula, "That there's for white folks. Colored can't have it," and finally with a beating.

It is not, then, the family and communal violence described by *Black Boy* that is unusual, but that Wright *recognized* and made no peace with its essential cruelty—even when, like a babe freshly emerged from the womb, he could not discern where his own personality ended and it began. Ordinarily both parent and child are protected against this cruelty—seeing it as love and finding subjective sanction for it in the spiritual authority of the Fifth Commandment, and on the secular level in the legal and extralegal structure of the Jim Crow system. The child who did not rebel, or who was unsuccessful in his rebellion, learned a masochistic submissiveness and a denial of the impulse toward Western culture when it stirred within him.

Why then have Southern whites, who claim to "know" the Negro, missed all this? Simply because they, too, are armored against the horror and the cruelty. Either they deny the Negro's humanity and feel no cause to measure his actions against civilized norms; or they protect themselves from their guilt in the Negro's condition and from their fear that their cooks might poison them, or that their nursemaids might strangle their infant charges, or that their field hands might do them violence, by attributing to them a superhuman capacity for love, kindliness and forgiveness. Nor does this in any way contradict their stereotyped conviction that all Negroes (meaning those with whom they have no contact) are given to the most animal behavior.

It is only when the individual, whether white or black, *rejects* the pattern that he awakens to the nightmare of his life. Perhaps much of the South's regressive character springs from the fact that many, jarred by some casual crisis into wakefulness, flee hysterically into the sleep of violence or the coma of apathy again. For the penalty of wakefulness is to encounter ever more violence and horror than the sensibilities can sustain unless translated into some form of social action. Perhaps the impassioned character so noticeable among those white Southern liberals so active in the Negro's cause is due to their sense of accumulated horror; their passion—like the violence in Faulkner's novels—is evidence of a profound spiritual vomiting.

This compulsion is even more active in Wright and the increasing number of Negroes who have said an irrevocable "no" to the Southern pattern. Wright learned that it is not enough merely to reject the white South, but that he had also to reject that part of the South which lay within. As a rebel he formulated that rejection negatively, because it was the negative face of the Negro community upon which he looked most often as a child. It is this he is contemplating when he writes:

Whenever I thought of the essential bleakness of black life in America, I knew that Negroes had never been allowed to catch the full spirit of Western civilization, that they lived somehow in it but not of it. And when I brooded upon the cultural barrenness of black life, I wondered if clean, positive tenderness, love, honor, loyalty and the capacity to remember were native to man. I asked myself if these human qualities were not fostered, won, struggled and suffered for, preserved in ritual from one generation to another.

But far from implying that Negroes have no capacity for culture, as one critic interprets it, this is the strongest affirmation that they have. Wright is pointing out what should be obvious (especially to his Marxist critics) that Negro sensibility is socially and historically conditioned; that Western culture must be won, confronted like the animal in a Spanish bullfight, dominated by the red shawl of codified experience and brought heaving to its knees.

Wright knows perfectly well that Negro life is a by-product of Western civilization, and that in it, if only one possesses the humanity and humility to see, are to be discovered all those impulses, tendencies, life and cultural forms to be found elsewhere in Western society.

The problem arises because the special condition of Negroes in the United States, including the defensive character of Negro life itself (the "will toward organization" noted in the Western capitalist appears in the Negro as a will to camouflage, to dissimulate), so distorts these forms as to render their recognition as difficult as finding a wounded quail against the brown and yellow leaves of a Mississippi thicket—even the spilled blood blends with the background. Having himself been in the position of the quail—to expand the metaphor—Wright's wounds have told him both the question and the answer which every successful hunter must discover for himself: "Where would I hide if *I* were a wounded quail?" But perhaps that requires more sympathy with one's quarry than most hunters possess. Certainly it requires such a sensitivity to the shifting guises

of humanity under pressure as to allow them to identify themselves with the human content, whatever its outer form; and even with those Southern Negroes to whom Paul Robeson's name is only a rolling sound in the fear-charged air.

Let us close with one final word about the blues: Their attraction lies in this, that they at once express both the agony of life and the possibility of conquering it through sheer toughness of spirit. They fall short of tragedy only in that they provide no solution, offer no scapegoat but the self. Nowhere in America today is there social or political action based upon the solid realities of Negro life depicted in *Black Boy;* perhaps that is why, with its refusal to offer solutions, it is like the blues. Yet in it thousands of Negroes will for the first time see their destiny in public print. Freed here of fear and the threat of violence, their lives have at last been organized, scaled down to possessable proportions. And in this lies Wright's most important achievement: He has converted the American Negro impulse toward self-annihilation and "going-under-ground" into a will to confront the world, to evaluate his experience honestly and throw his findings unashamedly into the guilty conscience of America.

And Hickman Arrives

Three days before the shooting a chartered planeload of Southern Negroes swooped down upon the District of Columbia and attempted to see the Senator. They were all quite elderly; old ladies dressed in little white caps and white uniforms made of surplus nylon parachute material, and men dressed in neat but old-fashioned black suits, wearing wide-brimmed, deep crowned panama hats which, in the Senator's walnut paneled reception room now, they held with a grave ceremonial air. Solemn, uncommunicative, and quietly insistent, they were led by a huge, distinguished-looking old fellow who on the day of the chaotic event was to prove himself, his age notwithstanding, an extraordinarily powerful man. Tall and broad and of an easy dignity, this was the Reverend A. Z. Hickman—better known, as one of the old ladies proudly informed the Senator's secretary, as "God's Trombone."

This, however, was about all they were willing to explain. Forty-four in number, the women with their fans and satchels and picnic baskets, and the men carrying new blue airline take-on bags, they listened intently while Reverend Hickman did their talking.

"Ma'am," Hickman said, his voice deep and resonant as he nodded toward the door of the Senator's private office, "you just tell the Senator that Hickman has arrived. When he hears who's out here he'll know that it's important and want to see us."

"But I've told you that the Senator isn't available," the secretary said. "Just what is your business? Who are you, anyway? Are you his constituents?"

"Constituents?" Suddenly the old man smiled. "No, miss," he said, "the Senator doesn't even have anybody like us in *his* state. We're from down where we're among the counted but not among the heard."

"Then why are you coming here?" she said. "What is your business?"

"He'll tell you, ma'am," Hickman said. "He'll know who we are; all you have to do is tell him that we have arrived. . . ."

The secretary, a young Mississippian, sighed. Obviously these were Southern Negroes of a type she had known all her life—and old ones; yet, instead of being already in herdlike movement toward the door, they were calmly waiting, as though she hadn't said a word. And now she had a suspicion that, for all their staring eyes, she actually didn't exist for them. They just stood there, now looking oddly like a delegation of Asians who had lost their interpreter along the way, and who were trying to tell her something which she had no interest in hearing, through this old man who himself did not know the language. Suddenly they no longer seemed familiar and a feeling of dreamlike incongruity came over her. They were so many that she could no longer see the large abstract paintings which hung along the paneled wall. Nor the framed facsimiles of State Documents which hung above a bust of Vice-President Calhoun. Some of the old women were calmly plying their palm-leaf fans, as though in serene defiance of the droning air-conditioner. Yet she could see no trace of impertinence in their eyes, nor any of the anger which the Senator usually aroused in members of their group. Instead, they seemed resigned; like people embarked upon a difficult journey who were already far beyond the point of no return. Her uneasiness grew, then she blotted out the others by focusing her eyes narrowly upon their leader. And when she spoke again her voice took on a nervous edge.

"I've told you that the Senator isn't here," she said, "and you must realize that he is a busy man who can only see people by appointment. . . ."

"We know, ma'am," Hickman said, "but . . ."

"You don't just walk in here and expect to see him on a minute's notice."

"We understand that, ma'am," Hickman said, looking mildly into her eyes, his close-cut white head tilted to one side, "but this is something that developed of a sudden. Couldn't you reach him by long distance? We'd pay the charges. And I don't even have to talk, miss; you can do the talking. All you have to say is that we have arrived."

"I'm afraid this is impossible," she said.

The very evenness of the old man's voice made her feel uncomfortably young, and now, deciding that she had exhausted all the tried-and-true techniques her region had worked out (short of violence) for getting quickly rid of Negroes, the secretary lost her patience and telephoned for a guard.

They left as quietly as they had appeared, the old minister waiting behind until the last had stepped into the hall, then he turned, and she saw his full height, framed by the doorway, as the others arranged themselves beyond him in the hall. "You're really making a mistake, miss," he said. "The Senator knows us and . . ."

"*Knows* you," she said indignantly. "I've heard Senator Sunraider state that the only colored he knows is the boy who shines shoes at his golf club."

"Oh?" Hickman shook his head as the others exchanged knowing glances.

"Very well, ma'am," Hickman said. "We're sorry to have caused you this trouble. It's just that it's very important that the Senator know that we're on the scene. So I hope you won't forget to tell him that we have arrived, because soon it might be too late."

There was no threat in it; indeed, his voice echoed the odd sadness which she thought she detected in the faces of the others just before the door blotted them from view.

In the hall they exchanged no words, moving silently behind the guard, who accompanied them down to the lobby. They were about to move into the street, when the security-minded chief guard observed their number, stepped up, and ordered them searched.

They submitted patiently, amused that anyone should consider them capable of harm, and for the first time an emotion broke the immobility of their faces. They chuckled and winked and smiled, fully aware of the comic aspect of the situation. Here they were, quiet, old, and obviously religious black folk who because they had attempted to see the man who was considered the most vehement enemy of their people in either house of Congress, were being energetically searched by uniformed security police, and they knew what the absurd outcome would be. They were found to be armed with nothing more dangerous than pieces of fried chicken and ham sandwiches, chocolate cake and sweet-potato fried pies. Some obeyed the guards' commands with exaggerated sprightliness, the old ladies giving their skirts a whirl as they turned in their flat-heeled shoes. When ordered to remove his wide-brimmed hat, one old man held it for the guard to look inside; then, flipping out the sweatband, he gave the crown a tap, causing something to fall to the floor, then waited with a calloused palm extended as the guard bent to retrieve it. Straightening and unfolding the object, the guard saw a worn but neatly creased fifty-dollar bill which he dropped upon the outstretched palm as though it were hot. They watched silently as he looked at the old man and gave a dry, harsh laugh; then as he continued laughing the humor slowly receded behind their eyes. Not until they were allowed to file into the street did they give further voice to their amusement.

"These here folks don't understand nothing," one of the old ladies said. "If we had been the kind to depend on the sword instead of on the Lord, we'd been in our graves long ago—ain't that right Sis' Arter?"

"You said it," Sister Arter said. "In the grave and done long finished mold'ing!"

"Let them worry, our conscience is clear on that. . . ."

"Amen!"

On the sidewalk now, they stood around Reverend Hickman holding a hushed conference, then in a few minutes they had disappeared in a string of taxis and the incident was thought closed.

Shortly afterwards, however, they appeared mysteriously at a hotel where the Senator leased a private suite, and tried to see him. How they knew of this secret suite they would not explain.

Next they appeared at the editorial offices of the newspaper which was most critical of the Senator's methods, but here too they were turned away. They were taken for a protest group, just one more lot of disgruntled Negroes crying for justice as though theirs were the only grievances in the world. Indeed, they received less of a hearing here than elsewhere. They weren't even questioned as to why they wished to see the Senator—which was poor newspaper work, to say the least; a failure of technical alertness, and, as events were soon to prove, a gross violation of press responsibility.

So once more they moved away.

Although the Senator returned to Washington the following day, his secretary failed to report his strange visitors. There were important interviews scheduled and she had understandably classified the old people as just another annoyance. Once the reception room was cleared of their disquieting presence they seemed no more significant than the heavy mail received from white liberals and Negroes, liberal and reactionary alike, whenever the Senator made one of his taunting remarks. She forgot them. Then at about eleven a.m. Reverend Hickman reappeared without the others and started into the building. This time, however, he was not to reach the secretary. One of the guards, the same who had picked up the fifty-dollar bill, recognized him and pushed him bodily from the building.

Indeed, the old man was handled quite roughly, his sheer weight and bulk and the slow rhythm of his normal movements infuriating the guard to that quick, heated fury which springs up in one when dealing with the unexpected recalcitrance of some inanimate object. Say, the huge stone that resists the bulldozer's power or the chest of drawers that refuses to budge from its spot on the floor. Nor did the old man's composure help matters. Nor did his passive resistance hide his distaste at having strange hands placed upon his person. As he was being pushed about, old Hickman looked at the guard with a kind of tolerance, an understanding which seemed to remove his personal emotions to some far, cool place where the guard's strength could never reach them. He even managed to pick up his hat from the sidewalk, where it had been thrown after him, with no great show of breath or hurry, and arose to regard the guard with a serene dignity.

"Son," he said, flicking a spot of dirt from the soft old panama with a white handkerchief, "I'm sorry that this had to happen to you. Here you've worked up a sweat on this hot morning and not a thing has been changed—except that you've interfered with something that doesn't concern you. After all, you're only a guard, you're not a mind-reader. Because if you were, you'd be trying to get me *in* there as fast as you could instead of trying to keep me out. You're probably not even a good guard and I wonder what on earth you'd do if I came here prepared to make some trouble."

Fortunately, there were too many spectators present for the guard to risk giving the old fellow a demonstration and he was compelled to stand silent, his thumbs hooked over his cartridge belt, while old Hickman strolled—or more accurately, *floated* up the walk and disappeared around the corner.

Except for two attempts by telephone, once to the Senator's office and later to his home, the group made no further effort until that afternoon, when Hickman sent a telegram asking Senator Sunraider to phone him at a T Street hotel. A message, which, thanks again to the secretary, the Senator did not see. Following this attempt there was silence.

During the late afternoon the group of closed-mouthed old folk were seen praying quietly within the Lincoln Memorial. An amateur photographer, a high-school boy from the Bronx, was there at the time and it was his chance photograph of the group, standing with bowed heads beneath old Hickman's outspread arms, while facing the great sculpture, that was flashed over the wires following the shooting. Asked why he had photographed that particular group, the boy replied that he had seen them as a "good composition. . . . I thought their faces would make a good scale of grays between the whiteness of the marble and the blackness of the shadows." And for the rest of the day the group appears to have faded into those same peaceful shadows, to remain there until the next morning—when they materialized shortly before chaos erupted.

Forty-four in all, they were sitting in the Senate's visitors' gallery when Senator Sunraider arose to address the body. They sat in compact rows, their faces marked by that impassive expression which American Negroes often share with Orientals, watching the Senator with a remote concentration of their eyes. Although the debate was not one in which they would normally have been interested (being a question not of civil rights, but of foreign aid) they barely moved while the Senator developed his argument, sitting like a row of dark statuary—until, during an aside, the Senator gave way to his obsession and made a quite gratuitous and mocking reference to their people.

It was then that a tall, elderly woman wearing steel-rimmed glasses arose from her chair and stood shaking with emotion, her eyes flashing. Twice she opened her mouth as though to hurl down some retort upon the head of the man holding forth below; but now the old preacher glimpsed her out of the corner of his eye, and, without turning from the scene below, gravely shook his head. For a second she ignored him, then feeling her still standing, he turned, giving her the full force of his gaze, and she reluctantly took her seat, the muscles ridged out about her dark prognathous jaws as she bent forward, resting her elbows upon her knees, her hands tightly clasped, listening. But although a few

whites departed, some angrily shaking their heads over the Senator's remarks, others extending them embarrassed smiles, the rest made no sign. They seemed bound by some secret discipline, their faces remaining composed, their eyes remote as though through some mistake they were listening to a funeral oration for a stranger.

Nevertheless, Reverend Hickman was following the speech with close attention, his gaze playing over the orderly scene below as he tried to identify the men with their importance to the government. So this is where he came to rest, he thought. After all his rambling, this was the goal. Who would have imagined? At first, although he was familiar with his features from the newspapers, he had not recognized the Senator. The remarks, however, were unmistakable. These days, much to the embarrassment of his party and the citizens of his New England state, only Senator Sunraider (certain Southern senators were taken for granted) made such remarks, and Hickman watched him with deep fascination. He's driven to it, Hickman thought, it's so much with him that he probably couldn't stop if he wanted to. He rejected his dedication and his set-asideness, but it's still on him, it's with him night and day.

"Reveren' . . ." Sister Neal had touched his arm and he leaned toward her, still watching the scene.

"Reveren'," she said, "is that him?"

"Yes, that's him all right," he said.

"Well, he sho don't look much like his pictures."

"It's the distance. Up close though you'd recognize him."

"I guess you right," she said. "All those white folks down there don't make him any more familiar either. It's been so long I don't recognize nothing about him now."

"You will," Hickman whispered. "You just watch—see there . . ."

"What?"

"The way he's using his right hand. See how he gets his wrist into it?"

"Yeah, yeah!" she said. "And he would have his little white Bible in his other hand. Sure, I remember."

"That's right. See, I told you. Now watch this. . . ."

"Watch what?"

"There, there it goes. I could just see it coming—see the way he's got his head back and tilted to the side?"

"Yeah—why, Reveren', that's *you!* He's still doing you! Oh, my Lord," he heard her moan, "still doing you after all these years and yet he can say all those mean things he says. . . ."

Hearing a catch in her voice, Hickman turned; she was softly crying.

"Don't, Sister Neal," he said. "This is just life; it's not to be cried over, just understood. . . ."

"Yes, I know. But *seeing* him, Reveren'. I forgave him many times for everything, but seeing him *doing you* in front of all these people and humiliating us at the same time—I don't know, it's just too much."

"He probably doesn't know he's doing it," Hickman said. "Anyway, it's just a gesture, something he picked up almost without knowing it. Like the way you can see somebody wearing his hat in a certain way and start to wearing yours the same way."

"Well, he sure knows when he says something about us," she said.

"Yes, I guess he does. But he's not happy in it, he's driven."

"I'd like to drive him the other way a bit," she said. "I could teach him a few things."

Hickman became silent, listening to the Senator develop his argument, thinking, she's partly right, they take what they need and then git. Then they start doing all right for themselves and pride tells them to deny that they ever knew us. That's the way it's been for a long time. Sure, but not Bliss. There's something else, I don't know what it was but it was something different. . . .

"Reveren'." It was Sister Neal again. "What's he talking about? I mean what's back of it all?"

"This is how the laws are made, Sister."

"Why does he want to give away all that money he's talking about?"

"It's politics. He wants to keep those Asian people and the Africans on our side. . . ."

"Then why is he signifying at those other men and going on?"

"That's because he plans to use those Asian folks to divide the men down there who don't like some of the things he's trying to do over here. He's playing divide and rule, Sister Neal. This way he can even put those Asian leaders in his hip pocket. They need the money he's trying to get for foreign aid so bad that naturally they will have to shut up and stop criticizing the way things go over here. Like the way we're treated, for instance. . . ."

"But will they get the money?"

"Oh, yes, they'll get it."

"Does that mean he's really doing some good?"

"It means that he's doing *some* good in order to do *some* bad."

"Oh?"

"Yes," he said, "and some bad in order to do some good. What I mean is, he's complicated. Part of the time he probably doesn't know what he means to do himself. He just does something."

"So what do you think?"

"Well, I think that although it's mixed, all that which he does about scientific research and things like that is on the good side. But that reactionary stuff he's mixed up in, that's bad."

"You mean his playing around with those awful men from down home?"

"That's right, that's part of it."

"Reveren'," she said, "why would he do things like that?"

"I guess he's in the go-long, Sister Neal. He has to play the game so that he can stay and play the game. . . ."

I guess that's the way it is, he thought. Power is as power does—for power. If I knew anything for sure, would I be sitting here?

Silently he listened to the flight of the Senator's voice and searched for echoes of the past. He had never seen the Senate in session before and was mildly surprised that he could follow most of the course of the debate. It's mainly knowing how to manipulate and use words, he thought. And reading the papers. Yes, and knowing the basic issues, because they seldom change. He sure knows how to use the words; he never forgot that. Imagine, going up there to New England and using all that kind of old Southern stuff, our own stuff, which we never get a chance to use on a broad platform—and making it pay off. It's probably the only thing he took with him that he's still proud of, or simply couldn't do without. Sister Neal's right, some of that he's doing is me all right. I could see it and hear it the moment she spotted it. So I guess I have helped to spread some corruption I didn't know about. Just listen to him down there; he's making somebody mighty uncomfortable because he's got them caught between what they profess to believe and what they feel they can't do without. Yes, and he's having himself a fine time doing it. He's almost laughing a devilish laugh in every word. Master, is that from me too? Did he ever hear me doing that?

He leaned toward Sister Neal again.

"Sister, do you follow what's happening?"

"Some, but not quite," she said.

"Well, I'll tell you," he said. "He is going to get this bill passed and pretty soon the money will start to flowing over there and those Indians, those Hindus, and such won't be able to say a thing about their high morals and his low ones. They have a heap of hungry folks to feed and he's making it possible. Let them talk that way then and they'll sound like a man making a speech on the correct way to dress while he's standing on the corner in a suit of dirty drawers. . . ."

"He's got no principles but he's as smart as ever, ain't he?" she said.

Hickman nodded, thinking, yes, he's smart all right. Born with mother wit. He climbed up that high from nowhere, and now look, he's one of the most powerful men on the floor. Lord, what a country this is. Even his name's not his own name. Made himself from the ground up, you might say. But why this mixed-up way and all this sneering at us who never did more than wish him well? Why this craziness which makes it look sometimes like he does everything else, good and bad, clean-cut and crooked, just so he can have more opportunity to scandalize our name? Ah, but the glory of that baby boy. I could never forget it and that's why we had to hurry here. He has to be seen and I'm the one to see him. I don't know how we're going to do it, but soon's this is over we have to find a way to get to him. I hope Janey was wrong, but any time she goes to the trouble of writing a letter herself, she just about knows what she's talking about. So far though we're ahead, but Lord only knows for how long. If only that young woman had told him we were trying to reach him. . . .

He leaned forward, one elbow resting upon a knee, watching the Senator who was now in the full-throated roar of his rhetoric, head thrown back, his arms outspread—when someone crossed his path of vision.

Two rows below a neatly dressed young man had stood up to leave, and, moving slowly toward the aisle as though still engrossed in the speech, had stopped directly in front of him; apparently to remove a handkerchief from his inside jacket pocket. Why doesn't he move on out of the way, Hickman thought, he can blow his nose when he gets outside—when, leaning around so as to see the Senator, he saw that it was not a handkerchief in the young man's hand, but a pistol. His body seemed to melt. Lord, can this

be it? Can this be the one?, he thought, even as he saw the young man coolly bracing himself, his body slightly bent, and heard the dry, muffled popping begin. Unable to move he sat, still bent forward and to one side, seeing glass like stars from a Fourth of July rocket bursting from a huge chandelier which hung directly in the trajectory of the bullets. Lord, no, he thought, no Master, not this, staring at the dreamlike world of rushing confusion below him. Men were throwing themselves to the floor, hiding behind their high-backed chairs, dashing wildly for the exits; while he could see Bliss still standing as when the shooting began, his arms lower now, but still outspread, with a stain blooming on the front of his jacket. Then, as the full meaning of the scene came home to him, he heard Bliss give surprising voice to the old idiomatic cry,

Lord, LAWD, WHY HAST THOU . . . ?

and staggering backwards and going down, and now he was on his own feet, moving toward the young man.

For all his size Hickman seemed suddenly everywhere at once. First stepping over the back of a bench, his great bulk rising above the paralyzed visitors like a missile, yelling, "No. NO!" to the young man, then lumbering down and reaching for the gun—only to miss it as the young man swerved aside. Then catching sight of the guards rushing, pistols in hand, through the now standing crowd, he whirled, pushing the leader off balance, back into his companion, shouting, "No, don't kill him! Don't kill that Boy! Bliss won't want him killed!" as now some of his old people began to stir. But already now the young man was moving toward the rail, waving a spectator away with his pistol, looking coolly about him as he continued forward; while Hickman, grasping his intention from where he struggled with one of the guards, now trying in beet-faced fury to club him with his pistol, began yelling, "Wait, Wait! Oh, my God, son—WAIT!" holding the guard for all his years like a grandfather quieting a boy throwing a tantrum, "WAIT!" Then calling the strange name, "Severen, wait," and saw the young man throwing him a puzzled, questioning look, then climb over the rail to plunge deliberately head first to the floor below. Pushing the guard from him now, Hickman called a last despairing "Wait" as he stumbled to the rail to stand there crying down as the group of old people quickly surrounded him, the old women pushing and striking at the angry guards with their handbags as they sought to protect him.

For a moment he continued to cry, grasping the rail with his hands and staring down to where the Senator lay twisting upon the dais beside an upturned chair. Then suddenly, in the midst of all the screaming, the shrilling of whistles, and the dry ineffectual banging of the chairman's gavel, he began to sing.

Even his followers were startled. The voice was big and resonant with a grief so striking that the crowd was halted in mid-panic, turning their wide-eyed faces up to where it soared forth to fill the great room with the sound of his astounding anguish. There he stood in the gallery above them, past the swinging chandelier, his white head towering his clustered flock, tears gleaming bright against the darkness of his face, creating with his voice an atmosphere of bafflement and mystery no less outrageous than the shooting which had released it.

"Oh, Lord," he sang, "why hast thou taken our Bliss, Lord? Why now our awful secret son, Lord? . . . Snatched down our poor bewildered foundling, Lord? LORD, LORD, Why hast thou . . . ?"

Whereupon, seeing the Senator trying to lift himself up and falling heavily back, he called out: "Bliss! You were our last hope, Bliss; now Lord have mercy on this dying land!"

As the great voice died away it was as though all had been stunned by a hammer and there was only the creaking sound made by the serenely swinging chandelier. Then the guards moved, and as the old ladies turned to confront them, Hickman called: "No, it's all right. We'll go. Why would we want to stay here? We'll go wherever they say."

They were rushed to the Department of Justice for questioning, but before this could begin, the Senator, who was found to be still alive upon his arrival at the hospital, began calling for Hickman in his delirium. He was calling for him when he entered the operating room and was still calling for him the moment he emerged from the anesthetic, insisting for all his weakness, that the old man be brought to his room. Against the will of the doctors this was done, the old man arriving mute and with the eyes of one in a trance. Following the Senator's insistence that he be allowed to stay with him through the crisis, he was given a chair beside the bed and sank his great bulk

into it without a word, staring listlessly at the Senator, who lay on the bed in one of his frequent spells of unconsciousness. Once he asked a young nurse for a glass of water, but beyond thanking her politely, he made no further comment, offered no explanation for his odd presence in the hospital room.

When the Senator awoke he did not know if it was the shape of a man which he saw beyond him or simply a shadow. Nor did he know if he was awake or dreaming. He seemed to move in a region of grays which revolved slowly before his eyes, ceaselessly transforming shadow and substance, dream and reality. And yet there was still the constant, unyielding darkness which seemed to speak to him silently words which he dreaded to hear. Yet he wished to touch it, but even the idea of movement brought pain and set his mind to wandering. It hurts here, he thought, and here; the light comes and goes behind my eyes. It hurts here and here and there and there. If only the throbbing would cease. Who . . . why . . . what . . . LORD, LORD, LORD WHY HAST THOU . . . Then some seemed to call to him from a long way off, *Senator, do you hear me?* Did the Senator hear? Who? Was the Senator here? And yes, he did, very clearly, yes. And he was. Yes, he was. Then another voice seemed to call, *Bliss?* And he thought is Bliss here? Perhaps. But when he tried to answer he seemed to dream, to remember, to recall to himself an uneasy dream.

It was a bright day and he said, Come on out here, Bliss; I got something to show you. And I went with him through the garden past the apple trees on under the grape arbor to the barn. And there it was, sitting up on two short sawhorses.

Look at that, he said.

It was some kind of long, narrow box. I didn't like it.

I said, What is it?

It's for the service. For the revivals. Remember me and Deacon Wilhite talking about it?

No, sir.

Sho, you remember. It's for you to come up out of. You're going to be resurrected so the sinners can find life ever-lasting. Bliss, a preacher is a man who carries God's load. And that's the whole earth, Bliss boy. The whole earth and all the people. And he smiled.

Oh! I said. I remembered. But before it hadn't meant too much. Since then, Juney had gone away and I had seen one. Juney's was pine painted black, without curves. This was fancy, all carved and covered with white cloth. It seemed to roll and grow beneath my eyes, while he held his belly in his hands, thumbs in trousers top, his great shoes creaking as he walked around it, proudly.

How you like it?

He was examining the lid, swinging it smoothly up and down with his hand. I couldn't see how it was put together. It seemed to be all white cloth bleeding into pink and pink into white again, over the scrolls. Then he let the lid down again and I could see two angels curved in its center. They were blowing long-belled valveless trumpets as they went flying. Behind them, in the egg-shaped space in which they trumpeted and flew, were carved clouds. Their eyes looked down. I said,

Is it for me?

Sho, didn't I tell you? We get it all worked out the way we want it and then, sinners, watch out!

Suddenly I could feel my fingers turn cold at the tips.

But why is it so big, I said. I'm not that tall. In fact, I'm pretty little for my age.

Yeah, but this one has got to last, Bliss. Can't be always buying you one of these like I do when you scuff out your shoes or bust out the seat of your britches.

But my feet won't even touch the end, I said. I hadn't looked inside.

Yeah, but in a few years they will. By time your voice starts to change your feet will be pushing out one end and your head out the other. I don't want even to have to think about another one before then.

But couldn't you get a littler one?

You mean "smaller"—but that's *just* what we don't want, Bliss. If it's too small, they won't notice it or think of it as applying to them. If it's too big, they'll laugh when you come rising up. No, Bliss, it's got to be this size. They have to see it and feel it for what it is, not take it for a toy like one of those little tin wagons or autos. Down there in Mexico one time I saw them selling sugar candy made in this shape, but ain't no use in trying to sugar-coat it. No, sir, Bliss. They have got to see it and know what they're seeing is where they've all got to end up. Bliss, that there sitting right there on those sawhorses is everybody's last clean shirt, as the old saying goes. And they've got to realize that when that sickle starts to cut its swarth, it don't play no favorites.

Everybody goes when that wagon comes, Bliss; babies and grandmaws too, 'cause there simply ain't no exceptions made. Death is like Justice is *supposed* to be. So you see, Bliss, it's got to be of a certain size. Hop in there and let's see how it fits. . . .

No, please. Please, Daddy Hickman. PLEASE!

It's just for a little while, Bliss. You won't be in the dark long, and you'll be wearing your white dress suit with the satin lapels and the long pants with the satin stripes. You'll like that, won't you, Bliss? Sure you will. In that pretty suit? Course! And you breathe through this here tube we fixed here in the lid. See? It comes through right here—you hear what I'm saying, Bliss? All right then, pay attention. Look here at this tube. All you have to do is lay there and breathe through it. Just breathe in and out like you always do; *only through the tube*. And when you hear me say, Suffer the little children . . . you push it up inside the lid, so's they can't see it when Deacon Wilhite goes to open up the lid . . .

But then I won't have any air. . . .

Now don't worry about that, there'll be air enough inside the box. Besides, Deacon Wilhite will open it right away. . . .

But suppose something happens and . . .

Nothing's *going* to happen, Bliss.

Yes, but suppose he forgets?

He won't forget. How's he going to forget when you're the center of the services?

But I'm scaird. In all that darkness and with that silk cloth around my mouth and eyes.

Silk, he said. He looked down at me steadily. What else you want it lined with, Bliss? Cotton? Would you feel any better about it if it was lined with something most folks have to work all their lives and wear every day—weekdays and Sunday? Something that most of our folks never get away from? You don't want that, do you?

He touched my shoulder with his finger. I said, Do you?

I shook my head, shamed.

He watched me, his head to one side. I'd do it myself, Bliss, but it wouldn't mean as much for the people. It wouldn't touch them in the same way. Besides, I'm so big most towns wouldn't have men strong enough to carry me. We don't want to have to break anybody's back just to save their souls, do you, Bliss?

I don't guess so, but . . .

Of course not, he said quickly. And it won't be but a few minutes, Bliss. You can even take Teddy with you—no, I guess you better take your Easter bunny. With your Easter bunny you won't be afraid, will you? Course not. And like I tell you, it will last no longer than it takes for the boys to march you down the aisle. I'll have you some good strong, big fellows, so you don't have to worry about them dropping you. Now, Bliss: you'll hear the music and they'll set it down in front of the pulpit. Then more music and preaching. Then Deacon Wilhite will open the lid. Then I'll say, Suffer the little children, and you sit up, see? I say do you see, Bliss?

Yessuh.

Say *Sir!*

Sir.

Good. Don't talk like I talk; talk like I *say* talk. Words are your business, boy. Not just *the* Word. Words are everything. The key to the Rock, the answer to the Question.

Yes, sir.

Now, when you rise up, you come up slow—don't go bolting up like no jack-in-the-box, understand? You don't want to scair the living daylights out of anybody. You want to come up slow and easy. And be sure you don't mess up your hair. I want the part to be still in it, neat. So don't forget when we close you in—and don't be chewing on no gum or sucking on no sour balls, you hear? Hear me now . . .

Yes, sir, I said. I couldn't turn away my eyes. His voice rolled on as I wondered which of the two with the trumpets was Gabriel. . . .

. . . It depends on the size of the church, Bliss. You listening to me?

Yes, sir.

Well, now when you hear me say, *Suffer the little children,* you sit up slow and, like I tell you, things are going to get quiet as the grave. That's the way it'll be.

He stood silently for a moment, one hand on his chin, the other against his hip, one great leg pushed forward, bending at the knee. He wore striped pants.

Bliss, I almost forgot something important: I better have the ladies get us some flowers. Roses would be good. Red ones. Ain't nobody in this town got any lilies—least not anybody we know. I'm glad I thought of it in time.

Now, Bliss. We'll have it sitting near the pulpit so when you rise up you'll be facing to the side and every living soul will see you. But I don't want you to open your eyes right off. Yes, and you better have your Bible in your hands—and

leave that rabbit down in there. You won't forget that, will you?

No, sir.

Good. And what are you suppose to say when you rise up?

I ask the Lord how come he has forsaken me.

That's right. That's correct, Bliss. But say it with the true feeling, hear? And in good English. That's right, Bliss; in Good Book English. I guess it's 'bout time I started reading you some Shakespeare and Emerson. Yes, it's about time. Who's Emerson? He was a preacher too, Bliss. Just like you. He wrote a heap of stuff and he was what is called a *philosopher.* Main thing though is that he knew that every tub has to sit on its own bottom. Have you remembered the rest of the sermon I taught you?

Yes, sir; but in the dark I . . .

Never mind the dark—when you come to *Why hast Thou forsaken me,* on the *me,* I want you to open your eyes and let your head go back. And you want to spread out your arms wide—like this, see? Lemme see you try it.

Like this?

That's right. That's pretty good. Only you better look sad, too. You got to look like you feel it, Bliss. You want to feel like everybody has put you down. Then you start with, *I am the resurrection and the life*—say it after me:

I am the resurrection . . .

I am the resurrection . . .

. . . And the life . . .

And the life . . .

That's good, but not too fast now. I am the lily of the valley . . .

I'm the lily of the valley . . .

Uh huh, that's pretty good—I am the bright and morning star. . . .

. . . The bright and morning star.

Thy rod . . .

Thy rod and thy staff.

Good, Bliss. I couldn't trap you. That's enough. You must remember that all of those *I*'s have got to be in it. Don't leave out any of those *I*'s, Bliss; because it takes a heap of *I*'s before they can see the true vision or even hear the true word.

Yes, sir. But can I take Teddy too?

Teddy? Just why you got to have that confounded bear with you all the time, Bliss? Ain't the Easter bunny enough? And your little white leather Bible, your kid-bound Word of God? Ain't that enough for you, Bliss?

But it's dark in there and I feel braver with

Teddy. Because you see, Teddy's a bear and bears aren't afraid of the dark.

Never mind all that, Bliss. And don't you start preaching me no sermon; specially none of those you make up yourself. You preach what I been teaching you and there'll be folks enough out there tonight who'll be willing to listen to you. I tell you, Bliss, you're going to make a fine preacher and you're starting at just the right age. You're just a little over six and Jesus Christ himself didn't start until he was twelve. *But you have to go leave that bear alone.* The other day I even heard you preaching to that bear. Bliss, bears don't give a continental about the Word. Did you ever hear tell of a bear of God? Of course not. There's the Lamb of God, and the Holy Dove, and one of the saints, Jerome, had him a lion. And another had him a bull of some kind—probably an old-fashioned airplane, since he had wings—he said under his breath, and Peter had the keys to the Rock. But no bear, Bliss. So you think about that, you hear?

He looked at me with that gentle, joking look, smiling in his eyes and I felt better.

You think you could eat some ice cream?

Oh, yes, sir.

You do? Well, here; take this four-bits and go get us each a pint. You look today like you could eat just about a pint. What I mean is, you look kind of hot.

He leaned back and squinted down.

I can even see the steam rising out of your collar, Bliss. In fact, I suspect you're on fire, so you better hurry. Make mine strawberry. Without a doubt, ice cream is good for a man's belly, and when he has to sing and preach a lot like I do, it's good for his throat too. Wait a second—where'd I put that money? Here it is. I thought I'd lost it. Ice cream is good if you don't overdo it—but I don't guess I have to recommend it to you though, do I, Bliss? 'Cause you're already sunk chin deep in the ice cream habit. Fact, Bliss, if eating ice cream was a sin you'd sail to hell in a freezer. Ha, ha! I'm sorry, now don't look at me like that. I was only kidding, little boy. Here, take this dime and bring us some of those chocolate marshmallow cookies you love so well. Hurry on now, and watch out for those wagons and autos. . . .

Yes, that was how it began, and that was Hickman.

When he laughed his belly shook like a Santa

Claus. A great kettledrum of deep laughter. Huge, tall, slow-moving. Like a carriage of state in ceremonial parade until on the platform, then a man of words evoking action. Black Garrick, Alonzo Zuber, Daddy Hickman.

God's Golden-voiced Hickman
Better known as
GOD'S TROMBONE,

they billed him. Brother A. Z. to Deacon Wilhite, when they were alone. They drank elderberry wine beneath the trees together, discussing the Word; me with a mug of milk and a buttered slice of homemade bread. . . . That was the beginning and we made every church in the circuit. I learned to rise up slow, the white Bible between my palms, my head thrusting sharp into the frenzied shouting and up, up, into the certainty of his mellow voice soaring isolated and calm like a note of spring water burbling in a glade haunted by the counterrhythms of tumbling, nectar-drunk bumblebees.

I used to lie within, trembling. Breathing through the tube, the hot air and hearing the hypnotic music, the steady moaning beneath the rhythmic clapping of hands, trembling as the boys marched me down a thousand aisles on a thousand nights and days. In the dark, trembling in the dark. Lying in the dark while his words seemed to fall like drops of rain upon the resonant lid. Until each time just as the shapes seemed to close in upon me, Deacon Wilhite would raise the lid and I'd rise up slowly, as he taught me, with the white Bible between my palms, careful not to disturb my hair on the tufted pink lining. Trembling now, with the true hysteria in my cry:

LORD, LORD, WHY HAST THOU . . . ?

Then came the night that changed it all. Yes, Bliss is here, for I can see myself, Bliss, again, dropping down from the back of the platform with the seven black-suited preachers in their high-backed chairs onto the soft earth covered with sawdust, hearing the surge of fevered song rising above me as Daddy Hickman's voice sustained a note without apparent need for breath, rising high above the tent as I moved carefully out into the dark to avoid the ropes and tent stakes, walking softly over the sawdust and heading then across the clearing for the trees where Deacon Wilhite and the big boys were waiting. I moved reluctantly as always, yet hurrying; thinking, he still hasn't breathed. He's still up there, hearing Daddy Hickman soaring above the rest like a great dark bird of light, a sweet yet anguished mellowing cry. Still hearing it hovering there as I began to run to where I can see the shadowy figures standing around where it lies white and threatening upon a table set beneath the pines. Leaning huge against a tree off to the side is the specially built theatrical trunk they carried it in. Then I am approaching the table with dragging feet, hearing one of the boys giggling and saying, What you saying there, Deadman? And I look at it with horror—pink, frog-mouthed, with opened lid. Then looking back without answering, I see with longing the bright warmth of the light beneath the tent and catch the surging movements of the worshippers as they rock in time to the song which now seems to rise up to the still, sustained line of Daddy Hickman's transcendent cry. Then Deacon Wilhite said, Come on little preacher, in you go! Lifting me, his hands firm around my ribs, then my feet beginning to kick as I hear the boys giggling, then going inside and the rest of me slipping past Teddy and Easter bunny, prone now and taking my Bible in my hands and the shivery beginning as the tufted top brings the blackness down.

At Deacon Wilhite's signal they raise me and it is as though the earth has fallen away, leaving me suspended in air. I seem to float in the blackness, the jolting of their measured footsteps guided by Deacon Wilhite's precise instructions, across the contoured ground, all coming to me muted through the pink insulation of the padding which lined the bottom, top, and sides, reaching me at blunt points along my shoulders, buttocks, thighs, heels. A beast with twelve disjointed legs coursing along, and I its inner ear, anxiety; its anxious heart; straining to hear if the voice that sustained its line and me still soared. Because I believed that if he breathed while I was trapped inside, I'd never emerge. And hearing the creaking of a handle near my ear, the thump of Cylee's knuckle against the side to let me know he was out there, giggling squint-eyed at my fear. Through the thick satin-choke of the lining the remote singing seeming miles away and the rhythmical clapping of hands coming to me like sharp, bright flashes of lightning, promising rain. Moving along on the tips of their measured strides like a boat in a slow current as I breathe through the tube in the lid of the hot ejaculatory air, hushed now by the entry and passage among them of that ritual coat of silk and satin, my stiff dark costume made necessary to their absurd and eternal play of death and resurrection. . . .

No, not me but another. Bliss. Resting on his lids, black inside, yet he knew that it was pink, a soft, silky pink blackness around his face, covering even his nostrils. Always the blackness. Inside everything became blackness, even the white Bible and Teddy, even his white suit. It was black even around his ears, deadening the sound except for Reverend Hickman's soaring song; which now, noodling up there high above, had taken on the softness of the piece of black velvet cloth from which Grandma Wilhite had made a nice full-dress overcoat—only better, because it had a wide cape for a collar. *Ayee,* but blackness.

He listened intently, one hand gripping the white Bible, the other frozen to Teddy's paw. Teddy was down there where the top didn't open at all, unafraid, a bold bad bear. He listened to the voice sustaining itself of its lyrics, the words rising out of the Word like Ezekiel's wheels; without breath, straining desperately to keep its throbbing waves coming to him, thinking, If he stops to breathe I'll die. My breath will stop too. Just like Adam's if God had coughed or sneezed.

And yet he knew that he was breathing noisily through the tube set in the lid. Hurry, Daddy Hickman, he thought. Hurry and say the word. Please, let me rise up. Let me come up and out into the light and air. . . .

Bliss?

So they were walking me slowly over the smooth ground and I could feel the slight rocking movement as the box shifted on their shoulders. And I thought, That means we're out in the clearing. Trees back there, voices that-a-way, life and light up there. Hurry! They're moving slow, like an old boat drifting down the big river in the night and me inside looking up into the black sky, no moon or stars and all the folks gone far beyond the levees. And I could feel the shivering creeping up my legs now and squeezed Teddy's paw to force it down. Then the rising rhythm of the clapping hands were coming to me like storming waves heard from a distance; like waves that struck the boat and flew off into the black sky like silver sparks from the shaking of the shimmering tambourines, showering at the zenith like the tails of skyrockets. If I could only open my eyes. It hangs heavy-heavy over my lids. Please hurry! Restore my sight. The night is black and I am far . . . far . . . I thought of Easter bunny, he came from the dark inside of a red-and-white striped egg. . . .

And at last they were letting me down, down, down; and I could feel the jar as someone went too fast, as now a woman's shout came to me, seeming to strike the side near my right ear like a flash of lightning streaking jaggedly across a dark night sky.

Jeeeeeeeeeeeeeeeeeeeee-sus! Have mercy, Jeeeee-ee-sus! and the cold quivering flashed up my legs.

Everybody's got to die, sisters and brothers, Daddy Hickman was saying, his voice remote through the dark. That is why each and every one must be redeemed. YOU HAVE GOT TO BE REDEEMED! Yes, even He who was the Son of God and the voice of God to man—even *He* had to die. And what I mean is die as a *man*. So what do you, the lowest of the low, what do you expect you're going to have to do? He had to die in all of man's loneliness and pain because that's the price He had to pay for coming down here and putting on the pitiful, unstable form of man. Have mercy! Even with his godly splendor which could transform the built-in wickedness of man's animal form into an organism that could stretch and strain toward sublime righteousness— Amen! That could show man the highway to progress and toward a more noble way of living— even with all that, even He had to die! Listen to me tell it to you: Even *He* who said, Suffer the little ones to come unto *Me* had to die as a man. And like a man crying from His cross in all of man's pitiful puzzlement at the will of Almighty God! . . .

It was not yet time. I could hear the waves of Daddy Hickman's voice rolling against the sides, then down and back, now to boom suddenly in my ears as I felt the weight of darkness leave my eyes, my face bursting with sweat as I felt the rush of bright air bringing the odor of flowers. I lay there, blinking up at the lights, the satin corrugations of the slanting lid and the vague outlines of Deacon Wilhite, who now was moving aside, so that it seemed as though he had himself been the darkness. I lay there breathing through my nose, deeply inhaling the flowers as I released Teddy's paw and grasped my white Bible with both hands, feeling the chattering and the real terror beginning and an ache in my bladder. For always it was as though it waited for the moment when I was prepared to answer Daddy Hickman's signal to rise up that it seemed to slide like heavy

mud from my face to my thighs and there to hold me like quicksand. Always at the sound of Daddy Hickman's voice I came floating up like a corpse shaken loose from the bottom of a river and the terror rising with me.

We are the children of Him who said, "Suffer . . ." I heard, and in my mind I could see Deacon Wilhite, moving up to stand beside Daddy Hickman at one of the two lecterns, holding on to the big Bible and looking intently at the page as he repeated, "Suffer . . ."

And the two men standing side by side, the one large and dark, the other slim and light brown; the other reverends rowed behind them, their faces staring grim with engrossed attention to the reading of the Word; like judges in their carved, high-backed chairs. And the two voices beginning their call and countercall as Daddy Hickman began spelling out the text which Deacon Wilhite read, playing variations on the verses just as he did with his trombone when he really felt like signifying on a tune the choir was singing:

Suffer, meaning in this workaday instance to *surrender,* Daddy Hickman said.

Amen, Deacon Wilhite said, repeating Surrender.

Yes, meaning to surrender with tears and to feel the anguished sense of human loss. Ho, our hearts bowed down!

Suffer the little ones, Deacon Wilhite said.

The little ones—ah yes! *Our* little ones. He was talking to us too, Daddy Hickman said. Our little loved ones. Flesh of our flesh, soul of *our* soul. Our hope for heaven and our charges in this world. Yes! The little lambs. The promise of our fulfillment, the guarantee of our mortal continuance. The little wases-to-bes-Ha!—Amen! The little used-to-bes that we all were to our mammys and pappys, and with whom we are but one with God. . . .

Oh my Lord, just look how the bright word leaps! Daddy Hickman said. First the babe, then the preacher. The babe father to the man, the man father to us all. A kind father calling for the babes in the morning of their earthly day—yes. Then in the twinkling of an eye, Time slams down and He calls us to come on home!

He said to Come, Brother Alonzo.

Ah yes, to Come, meaning to *approach*. To come up and be counted; to go along with Him, Lord Jesus. To move through the narrow gate bristling with spears, up the hill of Calvary, to climb onto the unyielding cross on which even lil' babies are turned into men. Yes, to come upon the proving ground of the human condition. Vanity dropped like soiled underwear. Pride stripped off like a pair of duckings that've been working all week in the mud. Feet dragging with the gravity of the trial ahead. Legs limp as a pair of worn-out galluses. With eyes dim as a flickering lamp-wick! Read to me, Deacon; line me out some more!

He said volumes in just those words. Brother Alonzo, he said, COME UNTO ME, Deacon Wilhite cried.

Yes! Meaning to take up His burden. At first the little baby-sized load that with the first steps we take weighs less than a butter ball; no more than the sugar tit made up for a year-and-a-half-old child. Then, Lord help us, it grows heavier with each step we take along life's way. Until in that moment it weighs upon us like the headstone of the world. Meaning to come bringing it! Come hauling it! Come dragging it! Come even if you have to crawl! Come limping, come lame; come crying in your Jesus' name—but *Come!* Come with your abuses but come with no excuses. Amen! Let me have it again, Rev. Wilhite. . . ."

Come unto me, the Master said.

Meaning to help the weak and the down-hearted. To stand up to the oppressors. To suffer and hang from the cross for standing up for what you believe. Meaning to undergo His initiation into the life-everlasting. Oh yes, and to Cry, Cry, Cry . . . Eyeeeee.

I could hear the word rise and spread to become the great soaring trombone note of Daddy Hickman's singing voice now and it seemed somehow to arise there in the box with me, shaking me fiercely as it rose to float with throbbing pain up to him again, who now seemed to stand high above the tent. And trembling I tensed myself and rose slowly from the waist in the controlled manner Daddy Hickman had taught me, feeling the terror gripping my chest like quicksand, feeling the opening of my mouth and the spastic flexing of my diaphragm as the words rushed to my throat to join his resounding cry:

Lord . . . Lord . . .

. . . Why . . .

. . . Hast Thou . . .

Forsaken me . . . I cried, but now Daddy Hickman was opening up and bearing down:

. . . More Man than men and yet in that world-destroying-world-creating moment just a little

child calling to His Father. . . . HEAR THE LAMB A-CRYING ON THE TREE!

LORD, LORD, I cried, WHY HAST THOU FORSAKEN ME?

Amen, Daddy Hickman said, Amen!

Then his voice came faster, explosive with gut-toned preacher authority:

The father of no man who yet was Father to all men—the human-son-side of God—Great God A-mighty! Calling out from the agony of the cross! Ho, open up your downcast eyes and see the beauty of the living Word. . . . All babe, and yet in the mysterious moment, ALL MAN. Him who had taken up the burden of all the little children crying, LORD. . . .

Lord, I cried.

Crying plaintive as a baby sheep . . .

. . . Baaaaaaaaa! . . .

Yes, the little Lamb crying with the tongue of man . . .

. . . LORD . . .

. . . Crying to the Father . . .

. . . Lord, LORD . . .

. . . Calling to his pappy . . .

. . . Lord, Lord, why hast . . .

Amen! LORD, WHY . . .

. . . Hast Thou . . .

Forsaken . . . me . . .

Aaaaaaaaaaah!

WHY HAST THOU FORSAKEN ME, LORD?

I screamed the words in answer and now I wanted to cry, to be finished, but the sound of Daddy Hickman's voice told me that this was not the time, that the words were taking him where they wanted him to go. I could hear him beginning to walk up and down the platform behind me, pacing in his great black shoes, his voice rising above his heavy tread, his great chest heaving.

Crying—Amen! Crying, Lord, Lord—Amen! On a cross on a hill, His arms spread out like my mammy told me it was the custom to stretch a runaway slave when they gave him the water cure. When they forced water into his mouth until water filled up his bowels and he lay swollen and drowning on the dry land. Drinking water, breathing water, water overflowing his earth-bound lungs like a fish drowning of air on the parched dry land.

And nailed NAILED to the cross-arm like a coonskin fixed to the side of a barn, yes, but with the live coon still inside the furry garment! Still in possession, with all nine points of the Roman law a fiery pain to consume the house. Yes, every point of law a spearhead of painful injustice. Ah, yes!

Look! His head is lollying! Green gall is drooling from His lips. Drooling as it had in those long sweet, baby days long gone. AH, BUT NOT TIT SO TOUGH NOR PAP SO BITTER AS TOUCHED THE LIPS OF THE DYING LAMB!

There He is, hanging on; hanging on in spite of knowing the way it would have to be. Yes! Because the body of man does not wish to die! It matters not who's inside the ribs, the heart, the lungs. Because the body of man does not sanction death. That's why suicide is but sulking in the face of hope! Ah, man is *tough.* Man is human! Yes, and by definition man is proud. Even when heaven and hell come slamming together like a twelve-pound sledge on a piece of heavy-gauged railroad steel, man is tough and mannish, and *ish* means like . . .

So there He was, stretching from hell-pain to benediction; head in heaven and body in hell—tell me, who said He was weak? Who said He was frail? Because if He was, then we need a new word for *strength,* we need a new word for *courage.* We need a whole new dictionary to capture the truth of that moment.

Ah, but there He is, with the others laughing up at Him, their mouths busted open like melons with rotten seeds—laughing! You know how it was, you've been up there. You've heard that contemptuous sound: IF YOU BE THE KING OF THE JEWS AND THE SON OF GOD, JUMP DOWN! JUMP DOWN, BLACK BASTARD, DIRTY JEW, JUMP DOWN! Scorn burning the wind. Enough halitosis alone to burn up old Moloch and melt him down.

He's bleeding from his side. Hounds baying the weary stag. And yet . . . And yet, His the power and the glory locked in the weakness of His human manifestation, bound by His acceptance of His human limitation, His sacrificial humanhood! Ah, yes, for He *willed* to save man by dying as *man* dies, and He was a heap of man in that moment, let me tell you. He was man raised to his most magnificent image, shining like a prism glass with all the shapes and colors of man, and dazzling all who had the vision to see. Man moved beyond mere pain to godly joy. . . . There He is, with the spikes in His tender flesh. Nailed to the cross. First with it lying flat on the ground, and then being raised in a slow, flesh-

rending, bond-scraping arc, one-hundred-and-eighty degrees—Up, up, UP! Aaaaaaaaaaaah! Until He's upright like the ridge-pole of the House of God. Lord, Lord, Why? See Him, Watch Him! Feel Him! His eyes rolling as white as our eyes, looking to His, our Father, the tendons of His neck roped out, straining like the steel cables of a heavenly curving bridge in a storm. His jaw muscles bursting out like kernels of corn on a hot lid. Yea! His mouth trying to refuse the miserable human questioning of His fated words . . .

Lord, Lord. . . .

Oh, yes, Rev. Bliss. Crying above the laughing ones for whom He left His Father to come down here to save, crying—

Lord, Lord, Why . . . ?

Amen! Crying as no man since—thank you, Jesus—has ever had to cry.

Ah, man, ah, human flesh! This side we all know well. On this weaker, human side we were all up there on the cross, just swarming over Him like microbes. But look at him with me now, look at Him fresh, with the eyes of your most understanding human heart. There He is, hanging on in man-flesh, His face twitching and changing like a field of grain struck by a high wind—hanging puzzled. Bemused and confused. Mystified and teary-eyed, wracked by the realization dawning in the grey matter of His cramped human brain; knowing in the sinews, in the marrow of His human bone, in the living tissue of His most human veins—realizing totally that *man was born to suffer and to die* for other men! There He is, look at Him. Suspended between heaven and hell, hanging on already nineteen centuries of time in one split second of his torment and realizing, I say, realizing in that second of His anguished cry that life in this world is but a zoom between the warm womb and the lonely tomb. Proving for all time, casting the pattern of history forth for all to see in the undeniable concreteness of blood, bone, and human courage before that which has to be borne by every man. Proving, proving that in this lonely, lightning-bug flash of time we call our life on earth we all begin with a slap of a hand across our tender baby bottoms to start us crying the puzzled question with our first drawn breath:

Why was I born? . . . Aaaaaaaah!

And hardly before we can get it out of our mouths, hardly before we can exhale the first lungful of life's anguished air—even before we can think to ask, Lord, What's my true name? Who, Lord, am I?—here comes the bone-crunching slap of a cold iron spade across our cheeks and it's time to cry, WHY, LORD, WHY WAS I BORN TO DIE?

Why, Rev. Bliss? Because we're men, that's why! The initiation into the lodge is hard! The dues are outrageous and what's more, nobody can refuse to join. Oh, we can wear the uniforms and the red-and-purple caps and capes a while, and we can enjoy the feasting and the marching and strutting and the laughing fellowship—then Dong, Dong! and we're caught between two suspensions of our God-given breath. One to begin and the other to end it, a whoop of joy and a sigh of sadness, the pinch of pain and the tickle of gladness, learning charity if we're lucky, faith if we endure, and hope in sheer downright desperation!

That's why, Reveren' Bliss. But now, thank God, because He passed his test like any mannish man—not like a God, but like any pale, frail, weak man who dared to be his father's son . . . Amen! Oh, we must dare to be, brothers and sisters. . . . We must dare, my little children. . . . We must dare in our own troubled times to be our father's own. Yes, and now we have the comfort and the example to help us through from darkness to lightness, a beacon along the way. Ah, but in that flash of light in which we flower and wither and die, we must find Him so that He can find *us,* ourselves. For it is only a quivering moment—then the complicated tongs of life's old good-bad comes clamping down, grabbing us in our tender places, feeling like a bear's teeth beneath our short-hair. Lord, He taught us how to live, yes! And in the sun-drowning awfulness of that moment, He taught us how to die. There He was on the cross, leading His sheep, showing us how to achieve the heritage of our godliness which He in that most pitiful human moment—with spikes in His hands and through His feet, with the thorny crown of scorn studding His tender brow, with the cruel points of Roman steel piercing His side . . . Crying . . .

Lord . . .

. . . Lord . . .

LORD! Amen. Crying from the castrated Roman tree unto his father like an unjustly punished child. And yet, Rev. Bliss, Glory to God, and yet He was guaranteeing with the final expiration of his human breath our everlasting life. . . .

Bliss's throat ached with the building excitement of it all. He could feel the Word working in the crowd now, boiling in the heat of the Word and the weather. Women were shouting and up suddenly to collapse back into their chairs, and far back in the dark he could see someone dressed in white leaping into the air with outflung arms, going up then down—over backwards and up and down again, in a swooning motion which made her seem to float in the air stirred by the agitated movement of women's palm leaf fans. It was long past the time for him to preach St. Mark, but each time he cried Lord, Lord, they shouted and screamed all the louder. Across the platform now he could see Deacon Wilhite lean against the lectern shaking his head, his lips pursed against his great emotion. While behind him, the great preachers in their high-backed chairs thundered out deep staccato Amens, he tried to see to the back of the tent, back where the seams in the ribbed white cloth curved down and were tied in a roll; past where the congregation strained forward or sat rigid in holy transfixation, seeing here and there the hard, bright disks of eyeglasses glittering in the hot, yellow light of lanterns and flares. The faces were rapt and owl-like, gleaming with heat and Daddy Hickman's hot interpretation of the Word. . . .

Then suddenly, right down there in front of the coffin he could see an old white-headed man beginning to leap in holy exaltation, bounding high into the air, and sailing down; then up again, higher than his own head, moving like a jumping jack, with bits of sawdust dropping from his white tennis shoes. A brown old man, whose face was a blank mask, set and mysterious like a picture framed on a wall, his lips tight, his eyes starry, like those of a blue-eyed china doll—soaring without effort through the hot shadows of the tent. Sailing as you sailed in dreams just before you fell out of bed. A holy jumper, Brother Pegue. . . .

Bliss turned to look at Daddy Hickman, seeing the curved flash of his upper teeth and the swell of his great chest as with arms outspread he began to sing . . . when suddenly from the left of the tent he heard a scream.

It was of a different timbre, and when he turned, he could see the swirling movement of a woman's form; strangely, no one was reaching out to keep her from hurting herself, from jumping out of her underclothes and showing her woman-ness as some of the ladies sometimes did. Then he could see her coming on, a tall redheaded woman in a purple-red dress; coming screaming through the soprano section of the big choir where the members, wearing their square, flat-topped caps were standing and knocking over chairs to let her through as she dashed among them striking about with her arms.

She's a sinner coming to testify, he thought. . . . A white? Is she white? hearing the woman scream,

He's mine, MINE! That's Cudworth, my child. My baby. You gipsy niggers stole him, my baby. You robbed him of his birthright!

And he thought, Yes, she's white all right, seeing the wild eyes and the red hair, streaming like a field on fire, coming toward him now at a pace so swift it seemed suddenly dreamlike slow. What's she doing here with us, a white sinner? Moving toward him like the devil in a nightmare, as now a man's voice boomed from far away, Madam, LADY, PLEASE—this here's the House of God!

But even then not realizing that she was clawing and pushing her way toward him. Cudworth, he thought, who's Cudworth? Then suddenly there she was, her hot breath blasting his ear, her pale face shooting down toward him like an image leaping from a toppling mirror, her green eyes wide, her nostrils flaring. Then he felt the bite of her arms locking around him and his head was crushed against her breast, hard into the sharp, sweet woman-smell of her. Me. She means me, he thought, as something strange and painful stirred within him. Then he could no longer breathe. She was crushing his face closer to her, squeezing and shaking him as he felt his Bible slipping from his fingers and tried desperately to hold on. But she screamed again with a sudden movement, her voice bursting hot into the sudden hush. And now he felt his Bible fall irretrievably away in the well-like echo punctuated by the heaving rasp of her breathing as he realized that she was trying to tear him from the coffin.

I'm taking him home to his heritage, he heard. He's mine, you understand, I'm his mother!

It sounded strangely dreamy, like a scene you saw when the big boys told you to open your eyes under the water. Who is she, he thought, where's she taking me? She's strong, but my mother went away, Paradise up high. . . . Then he was looking around at the old familiar grown folks, seeing their bodies frozen in odd postures, like kids playing a game of statue. And he thought They're scaird; she's scairing them all, as his head was snapped around to where he could see Daddy Hickman leaning over the platform just above, bracing his hands against his thighs, his arms rigid and a wild look of disbelief on his great laughing-happy face, as now he shook his head. Then she moved again and as his head came around the scene broke and splashed like quiet water stirred by a stick.

Now he could see the people standing and leaning forward to see, some standing in chairs holding on to the shoulders of those in front, their eyes and mouths opened wide. Then the scene suddenly crumpled like a funny paper in a fireplace. He saw their mouths uttering the same insistent burst of words so loud and strong that he heard only a blur of loud silence. Yet her breathing came hard and clear. His head came around to her now, and he could see a fringe of freckles shooting across the ridge of the straight thin nose like a covey of quail flushing across a field of snow, the wide-glowing green of her eyes. Stiff copper hair was bursting from the pale white temple, reminding him of the wire bristles of Daddy Hickman's "Electric Hairbrush". . . . Then the scene changed again with a serene new sound beginning:

JUST DIG MY GRAVE, he heard. JUST DIG MY GRAVE AND READY MY SHROUD, CAUSE THIS HERE AIN'T HAPPENING! OH, NO, IT AIN'T GOING TO HAPPEN. SO JUST DIG-A MY GRAVE!

It was a short, stooped black woman, hardly larger than a little girl, whose shoulders slanted straight down from her neck inside the white collar of her oversized black dress, and from which her deep and vibrant alto voice seemed to issue as from a source other than her mouth. He could see her coming through the crowd, shaking her head and pointing toward the earth, crying, I SAID DIG IT! I SAID GO GET THE DIGGERS!, the words so intense with negation that they sounded serene, the voice rolling with eerie confidence as now she seemed to float in among the white-uniformed deaconesses who stood at the front to his right. And he could see the women turning to stare questioningly at one another, then back to the little woman, who moved between them, grimly shaking her head. And now he could feel the arms tighten around his body, gripping him like a bear and he was being lifted up, out of the coffin; hearing her scream hotly past his ear, DON'T YOU BLUEGUMS TOUCH ME! DON'T YOU DARE!

And again it was as though they had all receded beneath the water to a dimly lit place where nothing would respond as it should. For at the woman's scream he saw the little woman and the deaconesses pause, just as they should have paused in the House of God as well as in the world outside the House of God—then she was lifting him higher and he felt his body come up until only one foot was still caught on the pink lining, and as he looked down he saw the coffin move. It was going over, slowly, like a turtle falling off a log; then it seemed to rise up of its own will, lazily, as one of the sawhorses tilted, causing it to explode. He felt that he was going to be sick in the woman's arms, for glancing down, he could see the coffin still in motion, seeming to rise up of its own will, lazily, indulgently, like Daddy Hickman turning slowly in pleasant sleep—only it seemed to laugh at him with its pink frog-mouth. Then as she moved him again, one of the sawhorses shifted violently, and he could see the coffin tilt at an angle and heave, vomiting Teddy and Easter bunny and his glass pistol with its colored candy bee-bee bullets, like prizes from a paper horn-of-plenty. Even his white leather Bible was spurted out, its pages fluttering open for everyone to see.

He thought, He'll be mad about my Bible and my bear, feeling a scream start up from where the woman was squeezing his stomach, as now she swung him swiftly around, causing the church tent, the flares, and the people to spin before his eyes like a great tin humming top. Then he felt his head snap forward and back, rattling his teeth—and in the sudden break of movement he saw the deaconesses springing forward even as the spilled images from the toppling coffin quivered vividly before his eyes then fading like a splash of water in bright sunlight—just as a tall woman with short, gleaming hair and steel-rimmed glasses shot from among the deaconesses and as her lenses glittered harshly he saw her mouth come open, causing the other women to freeze and a great silence to explore beneath the upward curve of his own shrill scream. Then he saw her head go back with an angry toss and he felt the sound slap hard against him.

What? Y'all mean to tell *me?* Here in the House-a-God? She's coming in *here*—who? WHOOOO! JUST TELL ME WHO BORN OF MAN'S HOT CONJUNCTION WITH A WOMAN'S SINFUL BOWELS?

And like an eerie echo now, the larger voice of the smaller woman floated up from the sawdust-covered earth, JUST DIG MY GRAVE! I SAY JUST READY MY SHROUD! JUST . . . and the voices booming and echoing beneath the tent like a duet of angry ghosts. Then it was as though something heavy had plunged from a great height into the water, throwing the images into furious motion and he could see the frozen women leap forward.

They came like shadows flying before a torch tossed into the dark, their weight seeming to strike the white woman who held him out of one single, slow, long-floating, space-defying leap, sending her staggering backward and causing her arms to squash the air from his lungs—Aaaaaaaah! Their faces, wet with wrath, loomed before him, seeming to enter where his breath had been, their dark, widespread hands beginning to tear at his body like the claws of great cats with human heads; lifting him screaming clear of earth and coffin and suspending him there between the red-headed woman who now held his head and the others who had seized possession of his legs, arms, and body. And again he felt, but could not hear, his own throat's *Aaaaaaaaaaaaayee!*

The Senator was first aware of the voice, then the dry taste of fever filled his mouth and he had the odd sensation that he had been listening to a foreign language that he knew but had neglected, so that now it was necessary to concentrate upon each word in order to translate its meaning. The very effort seemed to reopen his wounds and now his fingers felt for the button to summon the nurse but the voice was still moving around him, mellow and evocative. He recognized it now, allowing the button to fall as he opened his eyes. Yes, it was Hickman's, still there. And now it was as though he had been listening all along, for Hickman did not pause, his voice flowed on with an urgency which compelled him to listen, to make the connections.

"Well, sir, Bliss," Hickman said, "here comes this white woman pushing over everybody and loping up to the box and it's like hell had erupted at a side show. She rushed up to the box and . . ."

"*Box?*" the Senator said. "You mean coffin, don't you?"

He saw Hickman look up, frowning judiciously

"No, Bliss, I mean 'box'; it ain't actually a coffin till it holds a dead man. . . . So, as I was saying, she rushed up and grabs you in the box and the deaconesses leaped out of their chairs and folks started screaming, and I looked out there for some white folks to come and get her, but couldn't see a single one. So there I was. I could have cried like a baby, because I knew that one miserable woman could bring the whole state down on us. Still there she is, floating up out of nowhere like a puff of poison gas to land right smack in the middle of our meeting. Bliss, it was like God had started playing practical jokes.

"Next thing I know she's got you by the head and Sister Susie Trumball's got one leg and another sister's got the other, and others are snatching you by the arms—talking about King Solomon, he didn't have but *two* women to deal with, I had seven. And one convinced that she's a different breed of cat from the rest. Yes, and the others chock-full of disagreement and out to prove it. I tell you, Bliss, when it comes to chillen, women just ain't gentlemen.

"For a minute there it looked like they were going to snatch you limb from limb and dart off in seven different directions. *And* the folks were getting outraged a mile a minute. Because although you might have forgot it, nothing makes our people madder and will bring them to make a killing-floor stand quicker than to have white folks come bringing their craziness into the church. We just can't stand to have our one place of peace broken up, and nothing'll upset us worse—*unless* it's messing with one of our babies. You could just see it coming on, Bliss. I turned and yelled at them to regard the House of God— when here comes another woman, one of the deaconesses, Sister Bearmasher. She's a six-foot city woman from Birmingham, wearing eye-glasses and who ordinarily was the kindest woman you'd want to see. Soft-spoken and easy going the way some big women get to be because most of the attention goes to the little cute ones. Well, Bliss, she broke it up.

"I saw her coming down the aisle from the rear of the tent and reaching over the heads of the others, and before I could move she's in that woman's head of long red hair like a wild cat in a weaving mill. I couldn't figure what she was up to in all that pushing and tugging, but when they kind of rumbled around and squatted down low like they were trying to grab better holts I could see somebody's shoe and a big comb come sailing out, then they squatted again a couple of times— real fast, and when they come up, she's got all four feet or so of that woman's red hair wrapped around her arm like an ell of copper-colored cloth. And Bliss, she's talking calm and slapping the others away with her free hand like they were babies. Saying, 'Y'all just leave her to *me* now, sisters. Everything's going to be all right. She ain't no trouble, darlings; not now. Get on away now, Sis' Trumball. Let her go now. You got rumatism in you shoulder anyway. Y'all let her loose, now. Coming here into the House of God talking about this is *her* child. Since when? I want to know, since *when?* HOLD STILL DARLING!' she tells the white woman. 'NO-BODY WANTS TO HURT YOU, BUT YOU MUST UNDERSTAND THAT YOU HAVE GONE TOO FAR!'

"And that white woman is holding on to you for dear life, Bliss; with her head snubbed back, way back, like a net full of red snappers and flounders being wound up on a ship's winch. And this big amazon of a woman, who could've easily set horses with a Missouri mule, starts then to preaching her own sermon. Saying, 'If this Revern-Bliss-the-Preacher is her child then all the yellow bastards in the nation has got to be hers. So when, I say, so when's she going to testify to all that? You sisters let her go now; just let me have her. Y'all just take that child. Take that child, I say. I love that child cause he's God's child and y'all love that child. So I say take that child out of this foolish woman's sacri-legious hands. TAKE HIM, I SAY! And if this be the time then this is the time. If it's the time to die, then I'm dead. If it's the time to bleed, then I'm bleeding—but take that child. 'Cause what-ever time it is, this is one kind of foolishness that's got to be stopped before it gets any further under way!'

"Well, sir, there you were, Bliss, with the white woman still got holt of you but with her head snubbed back now and her head bucking like a frightened mare's, screaming, 'He's mine, he's mine.' *Claiming* you, boy, claiming you right out of our hands. At least out of those women's hands. Because us men were petrified, thrown out of action by that white woman's nerve. And that big, strong Bearmasher woman threatening to snatch her scalp clean from her head.

"And all the time Sister Bearmasher is preach-ing her sermon. Saying, 'If he was just learning his abc's like the average child instead of being a true, full-fledged preacher of the Gospel you wouldn't want him and you'd yell down destruction on anybody who even signified he was yours—WHERE'S HIS DADDY? YOU AIN'T THE VIRGIN MARY, SO YOU SHO MUST'VE PICKED OUT HIS DADDY. WHO'S THE BLACK MAN YOU PICKED TO DIE?'

"And then, Bliss, women all over the place started to taking it up: 'YES! That's right, who's the man? Amen! Just tell us!' and all like that.... Bliss, I'm a man with great puzzlement about life and I enjoy the wonderment of how things can happen and how folks can act, so I guess I must have been just standing there with my mouth open and taking it all in. But when those women started to making a chorus and working themselves up to do something outrageous, I broke loose. I reached down and grabbed my old trombone and started to blow. But instead of playing something calming, I was so excited that I broke into the 'St. Louis Blues,' like we used to when I was a young hellion and a fight would break out at a dance. Just automatically, you know; and I caught myself on about the seventh note and smeared into 'Listen to the Lambs,' but my lip was set wrong and there I was half laughing at how my sinful days had tripped me up—so that it came out 'Let Us Break Bread Together,' and by that time Deacon Wilhite had come to life and started singing and some of the men joined in—in fact, it was a men's chorus, because those women were still all up in arms. I blew me a few bars then put down that horn and climbed down to the floor to see if I could untangle that mess.

"I didn't want to touch that woman, so I yelled for somebody who knew her to come forward and get her out of there. Because even after I had calmed them a bit, she kept her death grip on you and was screaming, and Sister Bearmasher still had all that red hair wound round her arm and wouldn't let go. Finally a woman named Lula Strothers came through and started to talk to her like you'd talk to a baby and she gave you up. I'm expecting the police or some of her folks by now, but luckily none of them had come out to laugh at us that night. So Bliss, I got you into some of the women's hands and me and Sister Bearmasher got into the woman's rubber-tired buggy and rode off into town. She had two snow-white horses hitched to it, and luckily I had handled horses as a boy, because they were almost wild. And she was screaming and they reared and pitched until I could switch them around; then they hit that midnight road for a fare-thee-well.

"The woman is yelling, trying to make them smash us up, and cursing like a trooper and calling for you—though by the name of Cudworth—while Sister Bearmasher is still got her bound up by the hair. It was dark of the moon, Bliss, and a country road, and we took every curve on two wheels. Yes, and when we crossed a little wooden bridge it sounded like a burst of rifle fire. It seemed like those horses were rushing me to trouble so fast that I'd already be there before I could think of what I was going to say. How on earth was I going to explain what had happened, with that woman there to tell the sheriff something different—with her just *being* with us more important than the truth? I thought about Sister Bearmasher's question about who the man was that had been picked to die, and I tell you, Bliss, I thought that man was me. There I was, hunched over and holding on to those reins for dear life, and those mad animals frothing and foaming in the dark so that the spray from their bits was about to give us a bath and just charging us into trouble. I could have taken a turn away from town, but that would've only made it worse, putting the whole church in danger. So I was bound to go ahead since I was the minister responsible for their bodies as well as their souls. Sister Bearmasher was the only calm one in that carriage. She's talking to that woman as polite as if she was waiting on table or massaging her feet or something. And all the time she's still wound up in the woman's hair.

"But the woman wouldn't stop screaming, Bliss; and she's cussing some of the worst oaths that ever fell from the lips of man. And at a time when we're flying through the dark and I can see the eyes of wild things shining out at us, at first up ahead, then disappearing. And the sound of the galloping those horses made! They were hitting a lick on that road like they were in a battle charge.

"'Revern'?' Sister Bearmasher yelled over to me.

"'Yes, Sister?' I called back over to her.

"'I say, are you praying?'

"'Praying,' I yelled. 'Sister, my whole body and soul is crying out to God, but it's about as much as I can do to hold on to these devilish reins. You just keep that woman's hands from scratching at my face.'

"Well, Bliss, about that time we hit a straightaway, rolling past some fields, and way off to one side I looked and saw somebody's barn on fire. It was like a dream, Bliss. There we was making better time than the Hamiltonian, with foam flying, the woman screeching, leather straining, hooves pounding and Sister Bearmasher no longer talking to the woman but moaning a prayer like she's bending over a washtub somewhere on a peaceful sunny morning. And managing to sound so through all that rushing air. And then, there it was, way off yonder across the dark fields, that big barn filling the night with silent flames. It was too far to see if anyone was there to know about it, and it was too big for anybody except us not to see it; and as we raced on there seemed no possible way to miss it burning across the night. We seemed to wheel around it, the earth was so flat and the road so long and winding. Lonesome, Bliss; that sight was lonesome. Way yonder, isolated and lighting up the sky like a solitary torch. And then as we swung around a curve where the road swept into a lane of trees, I looked through the flickering of the trees and saw it give way and collapse. Then all at once the flames sent a big cloud of sparks to sweep the sky. Poor man, I thought, poor man, as that buggy hit a rough stretch of road. Then I was praying. Boy, I was really praying. I said, 'Lord, bless these bits, these bridles and these reins. Lord, please keep these thin wheels and rubber tires hugging firm to your solid ground, and Lord, bless these hames, these cruppers, and this carriage tongue. Bless the breast-straps, Lord and these straining leather belly-bands.' And Bliss, I listened to those pounding hoofbeats and

felt those horses trying to snatch my arms clear out of their sockets and I said, 'Yea, Lord, and bless this wiffle tree.' Then I thought about that fire and looked over at the white woman and finally I prayed, 'Lord, please bless this wild redheaded woman and that man back there with that burning barn. And Lord, since you know all about Sister Bearmasher and me, all we ask is that you please just keep us steady in your sight.'

"Those horses moved, Bliss. Zip, and we're through the land and passing through a damp place like a swamp, then up a hill through a burst of heat. And all the time, Bliss . . ."

The voice had ceased. Then the Senator heard, "Bliss, are you there, boy?"

"Still here," the Senator said from far away. "Don't stop. I hear."

Then through his blurring eyes he saw the dark shape come closer, and now the voice sounded small as though Hickman stood on a hill somewhere inside his head.

"I say, Bliss, that all the time I should have been praying for you, back there all torn up inside by those women's hands. Because, after all, a lot of prayer and sweat and dedication had gone into that buggy along with the money-greed and show-off pride. Because it held together through all that rough ride even though its wheels were humming like guitar strings, and it took me and Sister Bearmasher to jail and a pretty hot time before they let us go. So there between a baby, a buggy, and a burning barn I prayed the wrong prayer. I left you out Bliss, and I guess right then and there you started to wander. . . ."

Hickman leaned closer now, gazing into the quiet face.

The Senator slept.

Gwendolyn Brooks (1917–   )

In her short but pithy introduction to Etheridge Knight's *Poems from Prison* (1968), Gwendolyn Brooks hails the advent of this new young Black poet with the words: "Vital. Vital. This poetry is a major announcement." She adds that Knight's poetry is filled with a "controlled softness" and a Blackness that is at once "inclusive, possessed . . . terrible and beautiful." Two conclusions may be drawn from Miss Brooks' comments on Etheridge Knight's poetry. First, through her words of introduction Miss Brooks, a poet of an earlier generation, shows that she has the esthetic sensitivity to understand and fully empathize with a poet of a younger generation, a rather rare ability. Secondly, the words Miss Brooks uses in describing the poetry of Knight in 1968 could very aptly have been used to describe her own poetry when she made her first appearance with *A Street in Bronzeville* in 1945. Her poems had a vitality and a freshness and a beautiful Blackness long before any esthetic creed of Blackness had been explicitly formulated.

It should also be observed that Etheridge Knight made his poetic debut at a time when conditions were a little more comfortable for the emerging Black artist than they were during the 1940's. During the "Searing Sixties," the Black artist and poet attained a sense of emotional and psychological security that had never before been a part of the Black Experience. On the other hand, during the war years and the postwar years of the 1940's and 1950's, the influence of the poetic giants of the 1930's—Sandburg, Spender, Pound, Frost, Stevens, and others—was still pervasive. Younger poets such as Ciardi, Wilbur, Lowell, and Shapiro were emerging, but their poetry in form and content reflected the influence of their older counterparts. Indeed, it seemed that, after the devastation of the war and mankind's brush with the horror of atomic power, few people—poets included—had the heart for revolutionary change. So the "new" young poets followed Eliot in their use of symbolism and thematic irony and Pound in their experimentation with a rich variety of new forms. Naturally, the result was intellectualized, academic poetry, and four of the well-known poets—Frost, Ciardi, Lowell, and Wilbur—were in fact associated with academic institutions. By the same token, few, if any, of these poets expressed poetic concern about problems associated with urbanized America—problems rooted in the unprecedented expansion of the urban population. Everywhere in America the farms were emptying into the cities, and Black people in particular were leaving the racial violence of the South to flood the Black ghettos of the North and West. But no poets sang of the pungent odors of the city or of the poverty that continued to persist amid postwar affluence. Then, in 1945, Gwendolyn Brooks appeared to provide the poetic chronicle of her people in Bronzeville as they attempted to make their agonizing adaptations to the rigors of urban living. In theme and form, Miss Brooks provided a new kind of poetic statement and started a trend that moved poetry from the realm of the academic gown to the realm of the big town.

Since the appearance of her *A Street in Bronzeville* in 1945, Gwendolyn Brooks has published six more volumes of poetry—*Annie Allen* in 1949 *The Bean Eaters* in 1961, *Selected Poems* in 1963, *In the Mecca* in 1968, *Riot* in 1969, and *Family Pictures* in 1970. In all of these the hallmark of her poetry is her delicately accurate descriptions of the Black people of the urban North. Usually, she pictures the poor, the haunted, the frustrated, and the deluded, some of whom have been in the city for many troubled decades and others who have just come from the South and are new to city ways. Occasionally, there is a pseudo-success story such as "The Sundays of Satin-Legs Smith," in which, with skillful ironic touches, Miss Brooks portrays a flamboyant weekend pleasure-seeker who has perfected an elaborate escape mechanism to obscure the poverty of his troubled yesterdays. Once, in an interview, Miss Brooks said that her purpose was to "vivify the universal fact" in contemporary settings, but she does not use a large canvas or try, after the manner of Frost or Eliot, to deal with massive enigmas. Her areas of concern are the small, almost imperceptible psychological and economic webs that trap common Black people in their urban enclaves. These people are not heroic, and she does not plead their cause with high rhetoric. One merely listens to a mother agonizing over the children lost through abortion or observes the decline and fall of a young girl, all "sweet and chocolate," who ends up "thoroughly / Derelict and dim and done." There are no "amens" or "hallelujahs" and no fierce regrets or lamentations. Indeed, the troubles of her city dwellers are depicted with almost clinical brevity, and always there is a disciplined emotional reticence—almost like the "apoplectic ice" of the speaker in "Riders to the Blood-Red Wrath."

Of course, most of the young Black poets who emerged in the late 1960's and are now writing do not practice brevity and low-keyed racial rhetoric. And yet, despite the great differences in technique, the younger poets "dig" the poetry of Miss Brooks. They sympathize with her enduring concern for the Black urban poor, and they appreciate her vatic foresightedness about the need to "First fight, Then fiddle." They like the militant bravado of her "Way-Out Morgan," who collects sniper weapons in a "tiny fourth-floor room" and listens "to Blackness stern and blunt and beautiful." And they understand her terse, cryptic summation of the Black man's experience in slavery and afterward when her Black Everyman recalls:

> *I recollect the latter lease and lash*
> *And labor that defiled the bone, that thinned*
> *My blood and blood-line. All my climate my*
> *Foster designers designed and disciplined.*

Don Lee's poem "Gwendolyn Brooks" shows very clearly that to the younger generation of Black poets this "lady 'negro poet'" is "total-real":

> *and everywhere the*
> *lady "negro poet"*
> *appeared the poets were there.*
> *they listened & questioned.*
> *& went home feeling uncomfortable | unsound & so-untogether*
> *they read | re-read | wrote & re-wrote*
> *& came back the next time to tell the lady "negro poet"*
> *how beautiful she was | is & how she had helped them*
> *& she came back with:*
> *how necessary they were and how they've helped her.*

*the poets walked & as space filled the vacuum, between them & the
lady "negro poet"
u could hear one of the blackpoets say:
"bro, they been callin that sister by the wrong name."*

When Miss Brooks first appeared as a poet in 1945 and even when she received the Pulitzer Prize for poetry in 1950, many of the "blackpoets" of Don Lee's generation were not yet born. For them, therefore, she links a troubled past with an uncertain future and is, in a sense, a historian of the Black consciousness. Indeed, her alignment with the new generation of poets shows that the "circle is unbroken"—that, from isolated beginnings to the organized and activist present, Black poets have talked to other Black poets, and this is one way to record an enduring racial history.

Gwendolyn Brooks' long and distinguished career as a poet has provoked considerable written critical reaction. One of the earlier articles is Stanley Kunitz' "Bronze by Gold," *Poetry,* LXXVI (1950), 52–56. Another is J. Crockett's "An Essay on Gwendolyn Brooks," *Negro History Bulletin,* XIX (1955), 37–39. Arthur Davis has also contributed two very good essays on Miss Brooks' poetry. These are "The Black-and-Tan Motif in the Poetry of Gwendolyn Brooks," *CLA Journal,* VI (1962), 90–97; and "Gwendolyn Brooks: A Poet of the Unheroic," *CLA Journal,* VII (1963), 114–125. Also of significance is John L. Brown's "Chicago's Great Lady of Poetry," *Negro Digest* (now *Black World*), XI (December 1961), 53–57. Miss Brooks' poetry has received critical mention in the following general surveys of recent Black poetry: Margaret Walker, "New Poets," *Phylon,* XI (1950), 345–354; Martha Ellison, "Velvet Voices Feed on Bitter Fruit," *Poet and Critic,* IV (Winter 1967–1968), 39–49; and Abraham Chapman, "Black Poetry Today," *Arts in Society,* V (1968), 401–408. Finally, *Dark Symphony* (1968), an anthology edited by James Emanuel and Theodore Gross, contains a good critical introduction to a generous sampling of Miss Brooks' poetry; George Kent's recent "The Poetry of Gwendolyn Brooks," *Black World,* XX (September 1971), 30–43, (October 1971), 36–48, 68–71, is valuable; and James Emanuel demonstrates the possibilities of explication in "A Note on the Future of Negro Poetry," *Negro American Literature Forum,* I (1967), 2–3.

The Mother

Abortions will not let you forget.
You remember the children you got that you did
  not get,
The damp small pulps with a little or with no
  hair,
The singers and workers that never handled the
  air.
You will never neglect or beat
Them, or silence or buy with a sweet.
You will never wind up the sucking-thumb

Or scuttle off ghosts that come.
You will never leave them, controlling your
luscious sigh,
Return for a snack of them, with gobbling
mother-eye.

I have heard in the voices of the wind the voices
of my dim killed children.
I have contracted. I have eased
My dim dears at the breasts they could never
suck.
I have said, Sweets, if I sinned, if I seized
Your luck
And your lives from your unfinished reach,
If I stole your births and your names,
Your straight baby tears and your games,
Your stilted or lovely loves, your tumults, your
marriages, aches, and your deaths,
If I poisoned the beginnings of your breaths,

Believe that even in my deliberateness I was not
deliberate.
Though why should I whine,
Whine that the crime was other than mine?—
Since anyhow you are dead.
Or rather, or instead,
You were never made.

But that too, I am afraid,
Is faulty: oh, what shall I say, how is the truth to
be said?
You were born, you had body, you died.
It is just that you never giggled or planned or
cried.

Believe me, I loved you all.
Believe me, I knew you, though faintly, and I
loved, I loved you
All.

Of De Witt Williams on His Way to
Lincoln Cemetery

He was born in Alabama.
He was bred in Illinois.
He was nothing but a
Plain black boy.

Swing low swing low sweet sweet chariot.
Nothing but a plain black boy.

Drive him past the Pool Hall.
Drive him past the Show.
Blind within his casket,
But maybe he will know.

Down through Forty-seventh Street:
Underneath the L,

And Northwest Corner, Prairie,
That he loved so well.

Don't forget the Dance Halls—
Warwick and Savoy,
Where he picked his women, where
He drank his liquid joy.

Born in Alabama.
Bred in Illinois.
He was nothing but a
Plain black boy.

Swing low swing low sweet sweet chariot.
Nothing but a plain black boy.

Piano After War

On a snug evening I shall watch her fingers,
Cleverly ringed, declining to clever pink,
Beg glory from the willing keys. Old hungers
Will break their coffins, rise to eat and thank.
And music, warily, like the golden rose
That sometimes after sunset warms the west,
Will warm that room, persuasively suffuse

That room and me, rejuvenate a past.
But suddenly, across my climbing fever
Of proud delight—a multiplying cry.
A cry of bitter dead men who will never
Attend a gentle maker of musical joy.
Then my thawed eye will go again to ice.
And stone will shove the softness from my face.

Mentors

For I am rightful fellow of their band.
My best allegiances are to the dead.
I swear to keep the dead upon my mind,
Disdain for all time to be overglad.
Among spring flowers, under summer trees,
By chilling autumn waters, in the frosts
Of supercilious winter—all my days

I'll have as mentors those reproving ghosts.
And at that cry, at that remotest whisper,
I'll stop my casual business. Leave the banquet.
Or leave the ball—reluctant to unclasp her
Who may be fragrant as the flower she wears,
Make gallant bows and dim excuses, then quit
Light for the midnight that is mine and theirs.

"Do Not Be Afraid of No"

"Do not be afraid of no,
Who has so far so very far to go":

New caution to occur
To one whose inner scream set her to cede, for
    softer lapping and smooth fur!

Whose esoteric need
Was merely to avoid the nettle, to not-bleed.

Stupid, like a street
That beats into a dead end and dies there, with
    nothing left to reprimand or meet.

And like a candle fixed
Against dismay and countershine of mixed

Wild moon and sun. And like

A flying furniture, or bird with lattice wing; or
    gaunt thing, a-stammer down a nightmare neon
    peopled with condor, hawk and shrike.

To say yes is to die
A lot or a little. The dead wear capably their
    wry

Enameled emblems. They smell.
But that and that they do not altogether yell is all
    that we know well.

It is brave to be involved,
To be not fearful to be unresolved.

Her new wish was to smile
When answers took no airships, walked a while.

The Children of the Poor

1

People who have no children can be hard:
Attain a mail of ice and insolence:
Need not pause in the fire, and in no sense
Hesitate in the hurricane to guard.
And when wide world is bitten and bewarred
They perish purely, waving their spirits hence
Without a trace of grace or of offense
To laugh or fail, diffident, wonder-starred.
While through a throttling dark we others hear
The little lifting helplessness, the queer
Whimper-whine; whose unridiculous

Lost softness softly makes a trap for us.
And makes a curse. And makes a sugar of
The malocclusions, the inconditions of love.

2

What shall I give my children? who are poor,
Who are adjudged the leastwise of the land,
Who are my sweetest lepers, who demand
No velvet and no velvety velour;
But who have begged me for a brisk contour,
Crying that they are quasi, contraband
Because unfinished, graven by a hand
Less than angelic, admirable or sure.

My hand is stuffed with mode, design, device.
But I lack access to my proper stone.
And plenitude of plan shall not suffice
Nor grief nor love shall be enough alone
To ratify my little halves who bear
Across an autumn freezing everywhere.

3

And shall I prime my children, pray, to pray?
Mites, come invade most frugal vestibules
Spectered with crusts of penitents' renewals
And all hysterics arrogant for a day.
Instruct yourselves here is no devil to pay.
Children, confine your lights in jellied rules;
Resemble graves; be metaphysical mules;
Learn Lord will not distort nor leave the fray.
Behind the scurryings of your neat motif
I shall wait, if you wish: revise the psalm
If that should frighten you: sew up belief
If that should tear: turn, singularly calm
At forehead and at fingers rather wise,
Holding the bandage ready for your eyes.

4

First fight. Then fiddle. Ply the slipping string
With feathery sorcery; muzzle the note
With hurting love; the music that they wrote
Bewitch, bewilder. Qualify to sing

Threadwise. Devise no salt, no hempen thing
For the dear instrument to bear. Devote
The bow to silks and honey. Be remote
A while from malice and from murdering.
But first to arms, to armor. Carry hate
In front of you and harmony behind.
Be deaf to music and to beauty blind.
Win war. Rise bloody, maybe not too late
For having first to civilize a space
Wherein to play your violin with grace.

5

When my dears die, the festival-colored
    brightness
That is their motion and mild repartee
Enchanted, a macabre mockery
Charming the rainbow radiance into tightness
And into a remarkable politeness
That is not kind and does not want to be,
May not they in the crisp encounter see
Something to recognize and read as rightness?
I say they may, so granitely discreet,
The little crooked questionings inbound,
Concede themselves on most familiar ground,
Cold an old predicament of the breath:
Adroit, the shapely prefaces complete,
Accept the university of death.

We Real Cool

The Pool Players.
Seven at the Golden Shovel.

We real cool. We
Left school. We

Lurk late. We
Strike straight. We

Sing sin. We
Thin gin. We

Jazz June. We
Die soon.

The Chicago *Defender* Sends a Man to Little Rock

Fall, 1957

In Little Rock the people bear
Babes, and comb and part their hair
And watch the want ads, put repair
To roof and latch. While wheat toast burns
A woman waters multiferns.

Time upholds or overturns
The many, tight, and small concerns.

In Little Rock the people sing
Sunday hymns like anything,
Through Sunday pomp and polishing.

And after testament and tunes,
Some soften Sunday afternoons
With lemon tea and Lorna Doones.

I forecast
And I believe
Come Christmas Little Rock will cleave
To Christmas tree and trifle, weave,
From laugh and tinsel, texture fast.

In Little Rock is baseball; Barcarolle.
That hotness in July . . . the uniformed figures
    raw and implacable
And not intellectual,
Batting the hotness or clawing the suffering dust.
The Open Air Concert, on the special twilight
    green. . . .
When Beethoven is brutal or whispers to lady-like
    air.
Blanket-sitters are solemn, as Johann troubles to
    lean
To tell them what to mean. . . .

There is love, too, in Little Rock. Soft women
    softly
Opening themselves in kindness,
Or, pitying one's blindness,
Awaiting one's pleasure
In azure
Glory with anguished rose at the root. . . .
To wash away old semi-discomfitures.
They re-teach purple and unsullen blue.

The wispy soils go. And uncertain
Half-havings have they clarified to sures.

In Little Rock they know
Not answering the telephone is a way of rejecting
    life,
That is our business to be bothered, is our
    business
To cherish bores or boredom, be polite
To lies and love and many-faceted fuzziness.

I scratch my head, massage the hate-I-had.
I blink across my prim and pencilled pad.
The saga I was sent for is not down.
Because there is a puzzle in this town.
The biggest News I do not dare
Telegraph to the Editor's chair:
"They are like people everywhere."

The angry Editor would reply
In hundred harryings of Why.

And true, they are hurling spittle, rock,
Garbage and fruit in Little Rock.
And I saw coiling storm a-writhe
On bright madonnas. And a scythe
Of men harassing brownish girls.
(The bows and barrettes in the curls
And braids declined away from joy.)

I saw a bleeding brownish boy. . . .

The lariat lynch-wish I deplored.

The loveliest lynchee was our Lord.

Riders to the Blood-Red Wrath

My proper prudence toward his proper probe
Astonished their ancestral seemliness.
It was a not-nice risk, a wrought risk, was
An indelicate risk, they thought. And an excess.
Howas I handled my discordances
And prides and apoplectic ice, howas
I reined my charger, channeled the fit fume
Of his most splendid honorable jazz
Escaped the closing and averted sight
Waiving all witness except of rotted flowers
Framed in maimed velvet. That mad demi-art
Of ancient and irrevocable hours.
Waiving all witness except of dimnesses
From which extrude beloved and pennant arms
Of a renegade death impatient at his shrine
And keen to share the gases of his charms.

They veer to vintage. Careening from
    tomorrows.
Blaring away from my just genesis.
They loot Last Night. They hug old graves, root
    up
Decomposition, warm it with a kiss

The National Anthem vampires at the blood.
I am a uniform. Not brusque, I bray
Through blur and blunder in a little voice!
This is a tender grandeur, a tied fray!
Under macabres, stratagem and fair
Fine smiles upon the face of holocaust,
My scream! unedited, unfrivolous.
My laboring unlatched braid of heat and frost.
I hurt. I keep that scream in at what pain:

At what repeal of salvage and eclipse.
Army unhonored, meriting the gold, I
Have sewn my guns inside my burning lips.

Did they detect my parleys and replies?
My Revolution pushed his twin the mare,
The she-thing with the soft eyes that conspire
To lull off men, before him everywhere.
Perhaps they could not see what wheedling bent
Her various heart in mottles of submission
And sent her into a firm skirmish which
Has tickled out the enemy's sedition.

They do not see how deftly I endure.
Deep down the whirlwind of good rage I store
Commemorations in an utter thrall.
Although I need not eat them any more.

I remember kings.
A blossoming palace. Silver. Ivory.
The conventional wealth of stalking Africa.
All bright, all Bestial. Snarling marvelously.
I remember my right to roughly run and roar.
My right to raid the sun, consult the moon,
Nod to my princesses or split them open,
To flay my lions, eat blood with a spoon.
You never saw such running and such roaring!—
Nor heard a burgeoning heart so craze and
    pound!—
Nor sprang to such a happy rape of heaven!
Nor sanctioned such a kinship with the ground!

And I remember blazing dementias
Abroad such trade as maddens any man.
. . . The mate and captain fragrantly reviewed
The fragrant hold and presently began

Their retching rampage among their luminous
Black pudding, among the guttural chained
    slime:
Half fainting from their love affair with fetors
That pledged a haughty allegiance for all time.

I recollect the latter lease and lash
And labor that defiled the bone, that thinned
My blood and blood-line. All my climate my
Foster designers designed and disciplined.

But my detention and my massive stain,
And my distortion and my Calvary
I grind into a little light lorgnette
Most sly: to read man's inhumanity.
And I remark my Matter is not all.
Man's chopped in China, in India indented.
From Israel what's Arab is resented.
Europe candies custody and war.

Behind my exposé
I formalize my pity: "*I* shall cite,
Star, and esteem all that which is of woman,
Human and hardly human."

Democracy and Christianity
Recommence with me.

And I ride ride I ride on to the end—
Where glowers my continuing Calvary.
I,
My fellows, and those canny consorts of
Our spread hands in this contretemps-for-love
Ride into wrath, wraith and menagerie

To fail, to flourish, to wither or to win.
We lurch, distribute, we extend, begin.

Way-Out Morgan

Way-out Morgan is collecting guns
in a tiny fourth-floor room.
He is not hungry, ever, though sinfully lean.
He flourishes, ever, on porridge or pat of bean
pudding or wiener soup—fills fearsomely
on visions of Death-to-the-Hordes-of-the-White-
    Men!
Death!
(This is the Maxim painted in big black
above a bed bought at a Champlain rummage
    sale.)
Remembering three local-and-legal beatings, he

rubs his hands in glee,
does Way-out Morgan. Remembering his
    Sister
mob-raped in Mississippi, Way-out Morgan
smacks sweet his lips and adds another gun
and listens to Blackness stern and blunt and
    beautiful,
organ-rich Blackness telling a terrible story.
Way-out Morgan
predicts the Day of Debt-pay shall begin,
the Day of Demon-diamond,
of blood in mouths and body-mouths,

of flesh-rip in the Forum of Justice at last!
Remembering mates in the Mississippi River,
mates with black bodies once majestic, Way-out

postpones a yellow woman in his bed, postpones
wetness and little cries and stomachings—
to consider Ruin.

The Wall

For Edward Christmas

A drumdrumdrum.
Humbly we come.

South of success and east of gloss and glass are
sandals:
flowercloth:
grave hoops of wood or gold, pendant
from black ears, brown ears, reddish-brown
and ivory ears:

black boy-men.
Black
boy-men on roofs fist out "Black Power!" Val,
a little black stampede
in African
images of brass and flowerswirl,
fists out "Black Power!"—tightens pretty eyes,
leans back on mothercountry and is tract,
is treatise through her perfect and tight teeth.

Women in wool hair chant their poetry.

Phil Cohran gives us messages and music
made of developed bone and polished and honed
cult.
It is the Hour of tribe and of vibration,
the day-long Hour. It is the hour
of ringing, rouse, of ferment-festival.

On Forty third and Langley
black furnaces resent ancient

legislatures
of ploy and scruple and practical gelatin.
They keep the fever in,
fondle the fever.

All
worship the Wall.

I mount the rattling wood. Walter
says "She is good." Says "She
our Sister is." In front of me
hundreds of faces, red-brown, brown, black,
    ivory,
yield me hot trust, their yea and their
    Announcement
that they are ready to rile the high-flung ground.
Behind me, Paint.
Heroes.

No child has defiled
the Heroes of this Wall this serious
    Appointment
this still Wing
this Scald this Flute this heavy Light this Hinge.

An emphasis is paroled.
The old decapitations are revised,
the dispossessions beakless.

And we sing.

Loam Norton

Loam
Norton considers Belsen and Dachau,
regrets all old unkindnesses and harms.
... The Lord was their shepherd.
Yet did they want.
Joyfully would they have lain in jungles or
    pastures,
walked beside waters. Their gaunt

souls were not restored, their souls were
    banished.
In the shadow valley
they feared the evil, whether with or without
    God.
They were comforted by no Rod,
no Staff, but flayed by, O besieged by, shot
a-plenty.

The prepared table was the rot or curd of the day.
Anointings were of lice. Blood was the spillage of cups.
Goodness and mercy should follow them all the days of their death.

They should dwell in the house of the Lord forever
and, dwelling, save a place for me.
I am not remote,
not unconcerned. . . .

James Baldwin (1924–   )

A modern master of the essay form, a novelist of great emotional intensity, and a fiery playwright, James Baldwin has been a major literary spokesman of Black America for almost two decades. In the late 1950's and early 1960's, especially, his public voice was that of the national conscience, expressing with eloquence and passion the urgency of Black demands for life, dignity, and justice. At the same time, the private voice of James Baldwin spoke out of a desperately unhappy childhood in asserting his anguished need for love and a meaningful identity. At his best—in *Go Tell It on the Mountain* (1953), *Notes of a Native Son* (1955), *Nobody Knows My Name* (1961), and *The Fire Next Time* (1963)—the public and private voices merge into a literary instrument of great moral and stylistic authority.

Baldwin suffered during childhood because of his family's poverty and the squalor of his Harlem neighborhood, but he suffered even more at the hands of his tyrannical stepfather. An embittered, authoritarian, puritanical migrant to New York from New Orleans, David Baldwin worked at a bottling plant during the week and preached in a storefront church on weekends. Despising James for his illegitimacy and his physical ugliness, this man inflicted psychic wounds on the boy from which he never fully recovered. They were transmuted into art, however, in *Go Tell It on the Mountain,* Baldwin's brilliant and highly autobiographical first novel. Baldwin's personal problems were further complicated by the feminine chores of housecleaning and child tending imposed on him by his mother, who bore eight more children after her marriage in 1927.

Baldwin's intellectual precocity constituted both a defensive weapon and an escape mechanism. Reading avidly from early childhood (*Uncle Tom's Cabin* was his first favorite), young James could compensate for the torment inflicted by a hateful stepfather and teasing schoolmates. And hardly had he begun to read than he began to write. At Frederick Douglass Junior High School in Harlem, where Countee Cullen was one of his teachers, and at DeWitt Clinton High School in the Bronx, he edited student literary magazines and impressed his teachers with his talent. During his high school years, his literary interests divided time with a religious vocation. After his conversion at Mount Calvary of the Pentecostal Faith Church (Mother Horn's Church), he preached for three years and attained a wider following than his own stepfather enjoyed. Baldwin has never, of course, entirely abandoned a homiletic tone.

As his stepfather's paranoiac condition worsened, Baldwin found life at home more and more intolerable. Fleeing Harlem in 1942 for lucrative employment in the booming war economy of New Jersey, he there encountered racial affronts and humiliations in cafés, bars, and elsewhere of a more overt kind than he had previously experienced. Two events in the summer of 1943 intensified his sense of desperation: his stepfather died in a mental hospital, and, only a few hours later, Harlem erupted in a major riot. Both Harlem and New Jersey now seemed impossible for the young Baldwin, not quite twenty; he thought that perhaps Greenwich Village would provide an opportunity for him to begin his serious literary apprenticeship.

In the Village, where he lived until his departure for France in 1948, Baldwin worked in war-related industries during the day and wrote at night. He did not find the peace or emotional stability that he sought, but perhaps the nervous restlessness and rage of these anxious years of the mid-1940's were necessary for the kind of writer that he was in the process of becoming. One very helpful development was his meeting with Richard Wright in the winter of 1944–1945: "He had been my idol since high school," Baldwin has written, "and I, as the fledgling Negro writer, was very shortly in the position of his protégé." Recognizing the talent of the younger man, Wright secured for him his first major literary recognition, a Eugene F. Saxton Memorial Trust Award. This was followed in 1948 by a Rosenwald Fellowship. By this time Baldwin was publishing reviews, articles, and stories in *The Nation, The New Leader, Commentary,* and *Partisan Review,* but he was having troubles with his first novel, not to speak of psychological troubles with basic questions of his racial and sexual identity. To survive, in a literal as well as figurative sense, Baldwin thought it necessary to flee once more. He bought a one-way ticket to France and left the United States, vowing never to return, on November 11, 1948.

In Paris his ordeal did not end, for his poverty was extreme, but he found compensations. One was the completion and publication of *Go Tell It on the Mountain.* Another was his love for Lucien Happersberger, a young Swiss whose close relationship was to provide Baldwin a measure of emotional security for years afterward, as well as material for the novel *Giovanni's Room* (1956). Nevertheless, Baldwin's nervous restlessness had become a permanent character trait. From Paris he wandered to Chartres, to Switzerland, to the South of France, back to the United States for nine months in 1954–1955, when he saw his play *The Amen Corner* produced at Howard University. Afterward his itinerary became even more complicated: back to Paris, nine months in Corsica during 1956–1957, back to the United States in July 1957, followed by his first trip to the American South in the fall of that year. For the last fifteen years he has been an international literary commuter, with New York, Paris, and Istanbul as the major bases, and

Roxbury (where he lived in 1961 with the William Styron family) and Norwalk in Connecticut, Africa, Jackson, Mississippi (where he visited James Meredith and Medgar Evers early in 1963), Puerto Rico, and Hollywood among the many temporary locations.

Since 1957 Baldwin has spent more time in this country than during the preceding nine years. His involvement with the civil rights movement during the late 1950's and early 1960's was intense. His volumes of essays *Notes of a Native Son* (1955) and *Nobody Knows My Name: More Notes of a Native Son* (1961) contain many pieces on racial themes, and *The Fire Next Time* (1963) is one of the major prose statements of Black protest. *Another Country* (1962), a powerful if somewhat sprawling novel of life in Greenwich Village, combines racial and sexual themes, as does in an even more direct way the play *Blues for Mister Charlie* (1964), based on the Emmett Till case and other Mississippi lynchings. In addition to his writing, Baldwin lectured widely, particularly to college audiences, argued the Black cause in 1963 with then Attorney-General Robert Kennedy, participated in the March on Washington in August of the same year, and contributed his time, energy, and resources in numerous other ways.

In the late 1960's Baldwin receded somewhat from public attention as the focus shifted to spokesmen such as Amiri Baraka (LeRoi Jones) and Eldridge Cleaver. His literary career continues, however, as attested by *Nothing Personal* (1964), in which he wrote the text to accompany photographs by his old high-school friend Richard Avedon; *Going to Meet the Man* (1965), a collection of short stories; *Tell Me How Long the Train's Been Gone* (1968), a long novel about a Black actor named Leo Proudhammer; and *A Rap on Race* (1971), tape-recorded conversations with Margaret Mead. Whatever his future career may bring, it is clear that James Baldwin has long since achieved the goal he stated in 1955: "I want to be an honest man and a good writer."

Two useful checklists of both primary and secondary sources compiled by Kathleen A. Kindt and Russell G. Fischer appeared in *Bulletin of Bibliography,* XXIV (1965), 121–130. To supplement these see Fred L. Standley, "James Baldwin: A Checklist 1963–67," *Bulletin of Bibliography,* XXV (1968), 135–136, 160. Fern Marja Eckman's *The Furious Passage of James Baldwin* (1966) is a journalistic biography based on extensive interviews with Baldwin and others. See also Charles E. Adelsen, "A Love Affair: James Baldwin and Istanbul," *Ebony,* XXV (March 1970), 40–42, 44, 46; and John Hall's interview with Baldwin, *Transatlantic Review,* Nos. 37 and 38 (Autumn–Winter 1970–71), pp. 5–14. There is as yet no full-length critical study, but Donald Gibson has a section on Baldwin in his collection of criticism, *Five Black Writers* (1970), and Keneth Kinnamon is collecting criticism for a volume on Baldwin in the Prentice-Hall Twentieth Century Views series. Baldwin is treated in the revised edition of Robert Bone's *The Negro Novel in America* (1965), as well as in Ihab Hassan's *Radical Innocence* (1961), Alfred Kazin's *Contemporaries* (1962), Marcus Klein's *After Alienation* (1964), Calvin Hernton's *White*

Papers for White Americans (1967), and Eldridge Cleaver's *Soul On Ice* (1968).

Only a few of the many critical essays can be mentioned: Richard K. Barksdale, "'Temple of the Fire Baptized,'" *Phylon,* XIV (1953), 326–327; Dan Jacobson, "James Baldwin as Spokesman," *Commentary,* XXXII (1961), 497–502; Julian Mayfield, "And Then Came Baldwin," *Freedomways,* III (1963), 143–155; Maurice Charney, "James Baldwin's Quarrel with Richard Wright," *American Quarterly,* XV (1963), 65–75; Therman B. O'Daniel, "James Baldwin: An Interpretive Study," *CLA Journal,* VII (1963), 37–47; Stephen Spender, "James Baldwin: Voice of a Revolution," *Partisan Review,* XXX (1963), 256–260; John S. Lash, "Baldwin Beside Himself: A Study in Modern Phallicism," *CLA Journal,* VIII (1964), 132–140; David Levin, "Baldwin's Autobiographical Essays: The Problem of Negro Identity," *Massachusetts Review,* V (1964), 239–247; Robert F. Sayre, "James Baldwin's Other Country," in *Contemporary American Novelists* (1964), edited by Harry T. Moore, pp. 158–169; Edward A. Watson, "The Novels of James Baldwin: Case-Book of a 'Lover's War' with the United States," *Massachusetts Review,* VI (1965), 385–402; Theodore Gross, "The World of James Baldwin," *Critique,* VII (1965), 139–149; Charles Newman, "The Lesson of the Master: Henry James and James Baldwin," *Yale Review,* LVI (1966), 45–59; Addison Gayle, "A Defense of James Baldwin," *CLA Journal,* X (1966), 201–208; C. W. E. Bigsby, "The Committed Writer: James Baldwin as Dramatist," *Twentieth Century Literature,* XIII (1967), 39–48; Charlotte Alexander, "The 'Stink of Reality': Mothers and Whores in James Baldwin's Fiction," *Literature and Psychology,* XVIII (1968), 9–26; Irving Howe, "James Baldwin: At Ease in Apocalypse," *Harper's Magazine,* CCXXXVII (September 1968), 92–100; Mike Thelwell, "*Another Country:* Baldwin's New York Novel," in *The Black American Writer* (1969), edited by C. W. E. Bigsby, Vol. I, 181–198; Walter Meserve, "James Baldwin's 'Agony Way,'" in *The Black American Writer* (1969), edited by C. W. E. Bigsby, Vol. II, 171–186; Michel Fabre, "Pères et fils dans *Go Tell It on the Mountain,* de James Baldwin," *Études Anglaises,* XXIII (1970), 47–61; John M. Reilly, "Sonny's Blues': James Baldwin's Image of Black Community," *Negro American Literature Forum,* IV (1970), 56–60; and Albert Gérard, "The Sons of Ham," *Studies in the Novel,* III (1971), 148–164.

Everybody's Protest Novel

In *Uncle Tom's Cabin,* that cornerstone of American social protest fiction, St. Clare, the kindly master, remarks to his coldly disapproving Yankee cousin, Miss Ophelia, that, so far as he is able to tell, the blacks have been turned over to the devil for the benefit of the whites in this world—however, he adds thoughtfully, it may turn out in the next. Miss Ophelia's reaction is, at least, vehemently right-minded: "This is perfectly horrible!" she exclaims. "You ought to be ashamed of yourselves!"

Miss Ophelia, as we may suppose, was speaking

for the author; her exclamation is the moral, neatly framed, and incontestable like those improving mottoes sometimes found hanging on the walls of furnished rooms. And, like these mottoes, before which one invariably flinches, recognizing an insupportable, almost an indecent glibness, she and St. Clare are terribly in earnest. Neither of them questions the medieval morality from which their dialogue springs: black, white, the devil, the next world—posing its alternatives between heaven and the flames—were realities for them as, of course, they were for their creator. They spurned and were terrified of the darkness, striving mightily for the light; and considered from this aspect, Miss Ophelia's exclamation, like Mrs. Stowe's novel, achieves a bright, almost a lurid significance, like the light from a fire which consumes a witch. This is the more striking as one considers the novels of Negro oppression written in our own, more enlightened day, all of which say only: "This is perfectly horrible! You ought to be ashamed of yourselves!" (Let us ignore, for the moment, those novels of oppression written by Negroes, which add only a raging, near-paranoiac postscript to this statement and actually reinforce, as I hope to make clear later, the principles which activate the oppression they decry.)

Uncle Tom's Cabin is a very bad novel, having, in its self-righteous, virtuous sentimentality, much in common with *Little Women*. Sentimentality, the ostentatious parading of excessive and spurious emotion, is the mark of dishonesty, the inability to feel; the wet eyes of the sentimentalist betray his aversion to experience, his fear of life, his arid heart; and it is always, therefore, the signal of secret and violent inhumanity, the mask of cruelty. *Uncle Tom's Cabin*—like its multitudinous, hard-boiled descendants—is a catalogue of violence. This is explained by the nature of Mrs. Stowe's subject matter, her laudable determination to flinch from nothing in presenting the complete picture; an explanation which falters only if we pause to ask whether or not her picture is indeed complete; and what constriction or failure of perception forced her to so depend on the description of brutality— unmotivated, senseless—and to leave unanswered and unnoticed the only important question: what it was, after all, that moved her people to such deeds.

But this, let us say, was beyond Mrs. Stowe's powers; she was not so much a novelist as an im-

passioned pamphleteer; her book was not intended to do anything more than prove that slavery was wrong; was, in fact, perfectly horrible. This makes material for a pamphlet but it is hardly enough for a novel; and the only question left to ask is why we are bound still within the same constriction. How is it that we are so loath to make a further journey than that made by Mrs. Stowe, to discover and reveal something a little closer to the truth?

But that battered word, truth, having made its appearance here, confronts one immediately with a series of riddles and has, moreover, since so many gospels are preached, the unfortunate tendency to make one belligerent. Let us say, then, that truth, as used here, is meant to imply a devotion to the human being, his freedom and fulfillment; freedom which cannot be legislated, fulfillment which cannot be charted. This is the prime concern, the frame of reference; it is not to be confused with a devotion to Humanity which is too easily equated with a devotion to a Cause; and Causes, as we know, are notoriously bloodthirsty. We have, as it seems to me, in this most mechanical and interlocking of civilizations, attempted to lop this creature down to the status of a time-saving invention. He is not, after all, merely a member of a Society or a Group or a deplorable conundrum to be explained by Science. He is—and how old-fashioned the words sound!—something more than that, something resolutely indefinable, unpredictable. In overlooking, denying, evading his complexity— which is nothing more than the disquieting complexity of ourselves—we are diminished and we perish; only within the web of ambiguity, paradox, this hunger, danger, darkness, can we find at once ourselves and the power that will free us from ourselves. It is this power of revelation which is the business of the novelist, this journey toward a more vast reality which must take precedence over all other claims. What is today parroted as his Responsibility—which seems to mean that he must make formal declaration that he is involved in, and affected by, the lives of other people and to say something improving about this somewhat self-evident fact— is, when he believes it, his corruption and our loss; moreover, it is rooted in, interlocked with and intensifies this same mechanization. Both *Gentleman's Agreement* and *The Postman Always Rings Twice* exemplify this terror of the human being, the determination to cut him down to size. And in *Uncle Tom's Cabin* we may find foreshadowing of both: the formula created by the necessity to find a lie more palatable than the truth has been handed down and memorized and persists yet with a terrible power.

It is interesting to consider one more aspect of Mrs. Stowe's novel, the method she used to solve the problem of writing about a black man at all. Apart from her lively procession of field hands, house niggers, Chloe, Topsy, etc.—who are the stock, lovable figures presenting no problem—she has only three other Negroes in the book. These are the important ones and two of them may be dismissed immediately, since we have only the author's word that they are Negro and they are, in all other respects, as white as she can make them. The two are George and Eliza, a married couple with a wholly adorable child—whose quaintness, incidentally, and whose charm, rather put one in mind of a darky bootblack doing a buck and wing to the clatter of condescending coins. Eliza is a beautiful, pious hybrid, light enough to pass—the heroine of *Quality* might, indeed, be her reincarnation—differing from the genteel mistress who has overseered her education only in the respect that she is a servant. George is darker, but makes up for it by being a mechanical genius, and is, moreover, sufficiently un-Negroid to pass through town, a fugitive from his master, disguised as a Spanish gentleman, attracting no attention whatever beyond admiration. They are a race apart from Topsy. It transpires by the end of the novel, through one of those energetic, last-minute convolutions of the plot, that Eliza has some connection with French gentility. The figure from whom the novel takes its name, Uncle Tom, who is a figure of controversy yet, is jet-black, woolyhaired, illiterate; and he is phenomenally forbearing. He has to be; he is black; only through this forbearance can he survive or triumph. (*Cf.* Faulkner's preface to *The Sound and the Fury:* These others were not Compsons. They were black:—They endured.) His triumph is metaphysical, unearthly; since he is black, born without the light, it is only through humility, the incessant mortification of the flesh, that he can enter into communion with God or man. The virtuous rage of Mrs. Stowe is motivated by nothing so temporal as a concern for the relationship of men to one another—or, even, as she would have claimed, by a concern for their relationship to God—but merely by a panic of

being hurled into the flames, of being caught in traffic with the devil. She embraced this merciless doctrine with all her heart, bargaining shamelessly before the throne of grace: God and salvation becoming her personal property, purchased with the coin of her virtue. Here, black equates with evil and white with grace; if, being mindful of the necessity of good works, she could not cast out the blacks—a wretched, huddled mass, apparently, claiming, like an obsession, her inner eye—she could not embrace them either without purifying them of sin. She must cover their intimidating nakedness, robe them in white, the garments of salvation; only thus could she herself be delivered from everpresent sin, only thus could she bury, as St. Paul demanded, "the carnal man, the man of the flesh." Tom, therefore, her only black man, has been robbed of his humanity and divested of his sex. It is the price for that darkness with which he has been branded.

Uncle Tom's Cabin, then, is activated by what might be called a theological terror, the terror of damnation; and the spirit that breathes in this book, hot, self-righteous, fearful, is not different from that spirit of medieval times which sought to exorcize evil by burning witches; and is not different from that terror which activates a lynch mob. One need not, indeed, search for examples so historic or so gaudy; this is a warfare waged daily in the heart, a warfare so vast, so relentless and so powerful that the interracial handshake or the interracial marriage can be as crucifying as the public hanging or the secret rape. This panic motivates our cruelty, this fear of the dark makes it impossible that our lives shall be other than superficial; this, interlocked with and feeding our glittering, mechanical, inescapable civilization which has put to death our freedom.

This, notwithstanding that the avowed aim of the American protest novel is to bring greater freedom to the oppressed. They are forgiven, on the strength of these good intentions, whatever violence they do to language, whatever excessive demands they make of credibility. It is, indeed, considered the sign of a frivolity so intense as to approach decadence to suggest that these books are both badly written and wildly improbable. One is told to put first things first, the good of society coming before niceties of style or characterization. Even if this were incontestable—for what exactly is the "good" of society? —it argues an insuperable confusion, since literature and sociology are not one and the same; it is impossible to discuss them as if they were. Our passion for categorization, life neatly fitted into pegs, has led to an unforeseen, paradoxical distress; confusion, a breakdown of meaning. Those categories which were meant to define and control the world for us have boomeranged us into chaos; in which limbo we whirl, clutching the straws of our definitions. The "protest" novel, so far from being disturbing, is an accepted and comforting aspect of the American scene, ramifying that framework we believe to be so necessary. Whatever unsettling questions are raised are evanescent, titillating; remote, for this has nothing to do with us, it is safely ensconced in the social arena, where, indeed, it has nothing to do with anyone, so that finally we receive a very definite thrill of virtue from the fact that we are reading such a book at all. This report from the pit reassures us of its reality and its darkness and of our own salvation; and "As long as such books are being published," an American liberal once said to me, "everything will be all right."

But unless one's ideal of society is a race of neatly analyzed, hard-working ciphers, one can hardly claim for the protest novels the lofty purpose they claim for themselves or share the present optimism concerning them. They emerge for what they are: a mirror of our confusion, dishonesty, panic, trapped and immobilized in the sunlit prison of the American dream. They are fantasies, connecting nowhere with reality, sentimental in exactly the same sense that such movies as *The Best Years of Our Lives* or the works of Mr. James M. Cain are fantasies. Beneath the dazzling pyrotechnics of these current operas one may still discern, as the controlling force, the intense theological preoccupations of Mrs. Stowe, the sick vacuities of *The Rover Boys*. Finally, the aim of the protest novel becomes something very closely resembling the zeal of those alabaster missionaries to Africa to cover the nakedness of the natives, to hurry them into the pallid arms of Jesus and thence into slavery. The aim has now become to reduce all Americans to the compulsive, bloodless dimensions of a guy named Joe.

It is the peculiar triumph of society—and its loss—that it is able to convince those people to whom it has given inferior status of the reality of this decree; it has the force and the weapons to translate its dictum into fact, so that the allegedly inferior are actually made so, insofar as the societal realities are concerned. This is a more hidden phenomenon now than it was in the days of serfdom, but it is no less implacable. Now, as then, we find ourselves bound, first without, then within, by the nature of our categorization. And escape is not effected through a bitter railing against this trap; it is as though this very striving were the only motion needed to spring the trap upon us. We take our shape, it is true, within and against that cage of reality bequeathed us at our birth; and yet it is precisely through our dependence on this reality that we are most endlessly betrayed. Society is held together by our need; we bind it together with legend, myth, coercion, fearing that without it we will be hurled into that void, within which, like the earth before the Word was spoken, the foundations of society are hidden. From this void—ourselves—it is the function of society to protect us; but it is only this void, our unknown selves, demanding, forever, a new act of creation, which can save us—"from the evil that is in the world." With the same motion, at the same time, it is this toward which we endlessly struggle and from which, endlessly, we struggle to escape.

It must be remembered that the oppressed and the oppressor are bound together within the same society; they accept the same criteria, they share the same beliefs, they both alike depend on the same reality. Within this cage it is romantic, more, meaningless, to speak of a "new" society as the desire of the oppressed, for that shivering dependence on the props of reality which he shares with the *Herrenvolk* makes a truly "new" society impossible to conceive. What is meant by a new society is one in which inequalities will disappear, in which vengeance will be exacted; either there will be no oppressed at all, or the oppressed and the oppressor will change places. But, finally, as it seems to me, what the rejected desire is, is an elevation of status, acceptance within the present community. Thus, the African, exile, pagan, hurried off the auction block and into the fields, fell on his knees before that God in Whom he must now believe; who had made him, but not in His image. This tableau, this impossibility, is the heritage of the Negro in America: *Wash me,* cried the slave to his master, *and I shall be whiter, whiter than snow!* For black is the color of evil; only the robes of the saved are white. It is this cry, implacable on the air and in the skull, that he must live with. Beneath the widely published catalogue of brutality—bringing to mind, somehow, an image, a memory of church-bells burdening the air—is this reality which, in the same nightmare notion, he both flees and rushes to embrace. In America, now, this country devoted to the death of the paradox —which may, therefore, be put to death by one— his lot is as ambiguous as a tableau by Kafka. To flee or not, to move or not, it is all the same; his doom is written on his forehead, it is carried in his heart. In *Native Son,* Bigger Thomas stands on a Chicago street corner watching airplanes flown by white men racing against the sun and "God-damn" he says, the bitterness bubbling up like blood, remembering a million indignities, the terrible, rat-infested house, the humiliation of home-relief, the intense, aimless, ugly bickering, hating it; hatred smoulders through these pages like sulphur fire. All of Bigger's life is controlled, defined by his hatred and his fear. And later, his fear drives him to murder and his hatred to rape; he dies, having come, through this violence, we are told, for the first time, to a kind of life, having for the first time redeemed his manhood. Below the surface of this novel there lies, as it seems to me, a continuation, a complement of that monstrous legend it was written to destroy. Bigger is Uncle Tom's descendant, flesh of his flesh, so exactly opposite a portrait that, when the books are placed together, it seems that the contemporary Negro novelist and the dead New England woman are locked together in a deadly, timeless battle; the one uttering merciless exhortations, the other shouting curses. And, indeed, within this web of lust and fury, black and white can only thrust and counter-thrust, long for each other's slow, exquisite death; death by torture, acid, knives and burning; the thrust, the counter-thrust, the longing making the heavier that cloud which blinds and suffocates them both, so that they go down into the pit together. Thus has the cage betrayed us all, this moment, our life, turned to nothing through our terrible attempts to insure it. For Bigger's tragedy is not that he is cold or black or hungry, not even that he is American, black; but that he has accepted a theology that denies him life, that he admits the possibility of his being sub-human and feels constrained, therefore, to battle for his humanity according to those brutal criteria bequeathed him at his birth. But our humanity is our burden, our life; we need not battle for it; we need only to do what is infinitely more difficult—that is, accept it. The failure of the protest novel lies in its rejection of life, the human being, the denial of his beauty, dread, power, in its insistence that it is his categorization alone which is real and which cannot be transcended.

Sonny's Blues

I read about it in the paper, in the subway, on my way to work. I read it, and I couldn't believe it, and I read it again. Then perhaps I just stared at it, at the newsprint spelling out his name, spelling out the story. I stared at it in the swinging lights of the subway car, and in the faces and bodies of the people, and in my own face, trapped in the darkness which roared outside.

It was not to be believed and I kept telling myself that, as I walked from the subway station to the high school. And at the same time I couldn't doubt it. I was scared, scared for Sonny. He became real to me again. A great block of ice got settled in my belly and kept melting there slowly all day long, while I taught my classes algebra. It was a special kind of ice. It kept melting, sending trickles of ice water all up and down my veins, but it never got less. Sometimes it hardened and seemed to expand until I felt my guts were going to come spilling out or that I was going to choke or scream. This would always be at a moment when I was remembering some specific thing Sonny had once said or done.

When he was about as old as the boys in my classes his face had been bright and open, there was a lot of copper in it; and he'd had wonderfully direct brown eyes, and great gentleness and privacy. I wondered what he looked like now. He had been picked up, the evening before, in a raid on an apartment downtown, for peddling and using heroin.

I couldn't believe it: but what I mean by that is that I couldn't find any room for it anywhere inside me. I had kept it outside me for a long time. I hadn't wanted to know. I had had suspicions, but I didn't name them, I kept putting them away. I told myself that Sonny was wild, but he wasn't crazy. And he'd always been a good boy, he hadn't ever turned hard or evil or disrespectful, the way kids can, so quick, so quick, especially in Harlem. I didn't want to believe that I'd ever see my brother going down, coming to nothing, all that light in his face gone out, in the condition I'd already seen so many others. Yet it had happened and here I was, talking about algebra to a lot of boys who might, every one of them for all I knew, be popping off needles every time they went to the head. Maybe it did more for them than algebra could.

I was sure that the first time Sonny had ever had horse, he couldn't have been much older than these boys were now. These boys, now, were living as we'd been living then, they were growing up with a rush and their heads bumped abruptly against the low ceiling of their actual possibilities. They were filled with rage. All they really knew were two darknesses, the darkness of their lives, which was now closing in on them, and the darkness of the movies, which had blinded them to that other darkness, and in which they now, vindictively, dreamed, at once more together than they were at any other time, and more alone.

When the last bell rang, the last class ended, I let out my breath. It seemed I'd been holding it for all that time. My clothes were wet—I may have looked as though I'd been sitting in a steam bath, all dressed up, all afternoon. I sat alone in the classroom a long time. I listened to the boys outside, downstairs, shouting and cursing and laughing. Their laughter struck me for perhaps the first time. It was not the joyous laughter which—God knows why—one associates with children. It was mocking and insular, its intent was to denigrate. It was disenchanted, and in this, also, lay the authority of their curses. Perhaps I was listening to them because I was thinking about my brother and in them I heard my brother. And myself.

One boy was whistling a tune, at once very complicated and very simple, it seemed to be pouring out of him as though he were a bird, and it sounded very cool and moving through all that harsh, bright air, only just holding its own through all those other sounds.

I stood up and walked over to the window and looked down into the courtyard. It was the beginning of the spring and the sap was rising in the boys. A teacher passed through them every now and again, quickly, as though he or she couldn't wait to get out of that courtyard, to get those boys out of their sight and off their minds. I started collecting my stuff. I thought I'd better get home and talk to Isabel.

The courtyard was almost deserted by the time I got downstairs. I saw this boy standing in the shadow of a doorway, looking just like Sonny. I almost called his name. Then I saw that it wasn't Sonny, but somebody we used to know, a boy from around our block. He'd been Sonny's friend. He'd never been mine, having been too young for me, and, anyway, I'd never liked him. And now, even though he was a grown-up man, he still hung around that block, still spent hours on the street corners, was always high and raggy. I used to run into him from time to time and he'd often work around to asking me for a quarter or fifty cents. He always had some real good excuse, too, and I always gave it to him, I don't know why.

But now, abruptly, I hated him. I couldn't stand the way he looked at me, partly like a dog, partly like a cunning child. I wanted to ask him what the hell he was doing in the school courtyard.

He sort of shuffled over to me, and he said, "I see you got the papers. So you already know about it."

"You mean about Sonny? Yes, I already know about it. How come they didn't get you?"

He grinned. It made him repulsive and it also brought to mind what he'd looked like as a kid. "I wasn't there. I stay away from them people."

"Good for you." I offered him a cigarette and I watched him through the smoke. "You come all the way down here just to tell me about Sonny?"

"That's right." He was sort of shaking his head and his eyes looked strange, as though they were about to cross. The bright sun deadened his damp dark brown skin and it made his eyes look yellow and showed up the dirt in his kinked hair. He smelled funky. I moved a little away from him and I said, "Well, thanks. But I already know about it and I got to get home."

"I'll walk you a little ways," he said. We started walking. There were a couple of kids still loitering in the courtyard and one of them said goodnight to me and looked strangely at the boy beside me.

"What're you going to do?" he asked me. "I mean, about Sonny?"

"Look. I haven't seen Sonny for over a year, I'm not sure I'm going to do anything. Anyway, what the hell *can* I do?"

"That's right," he said quickly, "ain't nothing you can do. Can't much help old Sonny no more, I guess."

It was what I was thinking and so it seemed to me he had no right to say it.

"I'm surprised at Sonny, though," he went on—he had a funny way of talking, he looked straight ahead as though he were talking to himself—"I thought Sonny was a smart boy, I thought he was too smart to get hung."

"I guess he thought so too," I said sharply, "and that's how he got hung. And now about you? You're pretty goddamn smart, I bet."

Then he looked directly at me, just for a minute. "I ain't smart," he said. "If I was smart, I'd have reached for a pistol a long time ago."

"Look. Don't tell *me* your sad story, if it was up to me, I'd give you one." Then I felt guilty—guilty, probably, for never having supposed that the poor bastard *had* a story of his own, much less a sad one, and I asked, quickly, "What's going to happen to him now?"

He didn't answer this. He was off by himself some place. "Funny thing," he said, and from his tone we might have been discussing the quickest way to get to Brooklyn, "when I saw the papers this morning, the first thing I asked myself was if I had anything to do with it. I felt sort of responsible."

I began to listen more carefully. The subway station was on the corner, just before us, and I stopped. He stopped, too. We were in front of a bar and he ducked slightly, peering in, but whoever he was looking for didn't seem to be there. The juke box was blasting away with something black and bouncy and I half watched the barmaid as she danced her way from the juke box to her place behind the bar. And I watched her face as she laughingly responded to something someone said to her, still keeping time to the music. When she smiled one saw the little girl, one sensed the doomed, still-struggling woman beneath the battered face of the semi-whore.

"I never *give* Sonny nothing," the boy said finally, "but a long time ago I come to school high and Sonny asked me how it felt." He paused, I couldn't bear to watch him, I watched the barmaid, and I listened to the music which seemed to be causing the pavement to shake. "I told him it felt great." The music stopped, the barmaid paused and watched the juke box until the music began again. "It did."

All this was carrying me some place I didn't want to go. I certainly didn't want to know how it felt. It filled everything, the people, the houses, the music, the dark, quicksilver barmaid, with menace; and this menace was their reality.

"What's going to happen to him now?" I asked again.

"They'll send him away some place and they'll try to cure him." He shook his head. "Maybe he'll even think he's kicked the habit. Then they'll let him loose"—he gestured, throwing his cigarette into the gutter. "That's all."

"What do you mean, that's *all*?"

But I knew what he meant.

"I *mean,* that's *all.*" He turned his head and looked at me, pulling down the corners of his mouth. "Don't you know what I mean?" he asked, softly.

"How the hell *would* I know what you mean?" I almost whispered it, I don't know why.

"That's right," he said to the air, "how would *he* know what I mean?" He turned toward me again, patient and calm, and yet I somehow felt him shaking, shaking as though he were going to fall apart. I felt that ice in my guts again, the dread I'd felt all afternoon; and again I watched the barmaid, moving about the bar, washing glasses, and singing. "Listen. They'll let him out and then it'll just start all over again. That's what I mean."

"You mean—they'll let him out. And then he'll just start working his way back in again. You mean he'll never kick the habit. Is that what you mean?"

"That's right," he said, cheerfully. "*You* see what I mean."

"Tell me," I said it last, "why does he want to die? He must want to die, he's killing himself, why does he want to die?"

He looked at me in surprise. He licked his lips. "He don't want to die. He wants to live. Don't nobody want to die, ever."

Then I wanted to ask him—too many things. He could not have answered, or if he had, I could not have borne the answers. I started walking. "Well, I guess it's none of my business."

"It's going to be rough on old Sonny," he said. We reached the subway station. "This is your station?" he asked. I nodded. I took one step down. "Damn!" he said, suddenly. I looked up at him. He grinned again. "Damn it if I didn't leave all my money home. You ain't got a dollar on you, have you? Just for a couple of days, is all."

All at once something inside gave and threatened to come pouring out of me. I didn't hate him any more. I felt that in another moment I'd start crying like a child.

"Sure," I said. "Don't sweat." I looked in my wallet and didn't have a dollar, I only had a five. "Here," I said. "That hold you?"

He didn't look at it—he didn't want to look at it. A terrible, closed look came over his face, as though he were keeping the number on the bill a secret from him and me. "Thanks," he said, and now he was dying to see me go. "Don't worry about Sonny. Maybe I'll write him or something."

"Sure," I said. "You do that. So long."

"Be seeing you," he said. I went on down the steps.

And I didn't write Sonny or send him anything for a long time. When I finally did, it was just after my little girl died, he wrote me back a letter which made me feel like a bastard.

Here's what he said:

Dear brother,

You don't know how much I needed to hear from you. I wanted to write you many a time but I dug how much I must have hurt you and so I didn't write. But now I feel like a man who's been trying to climb up out of some deep, real deep and funky hole and just saw the sun up there, outside. I got to get outside.

I can't tell you much about how I got here. I mean I don't know how to tell you. I guess I was afraid of something or I was trying to escape from something and you know I have never been very strong in the head (smile). I'm glad Mama and Daddy are dead and can't see what's happened to their son and I swear if I'd known what I was doing I would never have hurt you so, you and a lot of other fine people who were nice to me and who believed in me.

I don't want you to think it had anything to do with me being a musician. It's more than that. Or maybe less than that. I can't get anything straight in my head down here and I try not to think about what's going to happen to me when I get outside again. Sometime I think I'm going to flip and *never* get outside and sometime I think I'll come straight back. I tell you one thing, though, I'd rather blow my brains out than go through this again. But that's what they all say, so they tell me. If I tell you when I'm coming to New York and if you could meet me, I sure would appreciate it. Give my love to Isabel and the kids and I was sure sorry to hear about little Gracie. I wish I could be like Mama and say the Lord's will be done, but I don't know it seems to me that trouble is the one thing that never does get stopped and I don't know what good it does to blame it on the Lord. But may be it does some good if you believe it.

Your brother,
Sonny

Then I kept in constant touch with him and I sent him whatever I could and I went to meet him when he came back to New York. When I saw him many things I thought I had forgotten came flooding back to me. This was because I had begun, finally, to wonder about Sonny, about the life that Sonny lived inside. This life, whatever it was, had made him older and thinner and it had deepened the distant stillness in which he had always moved. He looked very unlike my baby brother. Yet, when he smiled, when we shook hands, the baby brother I'd never known looked out from the depths of his private life, like an animal waiting to be coaxed into the light.

"How you been keeping?" he asked me.

"All right. And you?"

"Just fine." He was smiling all over his face. "It's good to see you again."

"It's good to see you."

The seven year's difference in our ages lay between us like a chasm: I wondered if these years would ever operate between us as a bridge. I was remembering, and it made it hard to catch my breath, that I had been there when he was born; and I had heard the first words he had ever spoken. When he started to walk, he walked from our mother straight to me. I caught him just before he fell when he took the first steps he ever took in this world.

"How's Isabel?"

"Just fine. She's dying to see you."

"And the boys?"

"They're fine, too. They're anxious to see their uncle."

"Oh, come on. You know they don't remember me."

"Are you kidding? Of course they remember you."

He grinned again. We got into a taxi. We had a lot to say to each other, far too much to know how to begin.

As the taxi began to move, I asked, "You still want to go to India?"

He laughed. "You still remember that. Hell, no. This place is Indian enough for me."

"It used to belong to them," I said.

And he laughed again. "They damn sure knew what they were doing when they got rid of it."

Years ago, when he was around fourteen, he'd

been all hipped on the idea of going to India. He read books about people sitting on rocks, naked, in all kinds of weather, but mostly bad, naturally, and walking barefoot through hot coals and arriving at wisdom. I used to say that it sounded to me as though they were getting away from wisdom as fast as they could. I think he sort of looked down on me for that.

"Do you mind," he asked, "if we have the driver drive alongside the park? On the west side—I haven't seen the city in so long."

"Of course not," I said. I was afraid that I might sound as though I were humoring him, but I hoped he wouldn't take it that way.

So we drove along, between the green of the park and the stony, lifeless elegance of hotels and apartment buildings, toward the vivid, killing streets of our childhood. These streets hadn't changed, though housing projects jutted up out of them now like rocks in the middle of a boiling sea. Most of the houses in which we had grown up had vanished, as had the stores from which we had stolen, the basements in which we had first tried sex, the rooftops from which we had hurled tin cans and bricks. But houses exactly like the houses of our past yet dominated the landscape, boys exactly like the boys we once had been found themselves smothering in these houses, came down into the streets for light and air and found themselves encircled by disaster. Some escaped the trap, most didn't. Those who got out always left something of themselves behind, as some animals amputate a leg and leave it in the trap. It might be said, perhaps, that I had escaped, after all, I was a school teacher; or that Sonny had, he hadn't lived in Harlem for years. Yet, as the cab moved uptown through streets which seemed, with a rush, to darken with dark people, and as I covertly studied Sonny's face, it came to me that what we both were seeking through our separate cab windows was that part of ourselves which had been left behind. It's always at the hour of trouble and confrontation that the missing member aches.

We hit 110th Street and started rolling up Lenox Avenue. And I'd known this avenue all my life, but it seemed to me again, as it had seemed on the day I'd first heard about Sonny's trouble, filled with a hidden menace which was its very breath of life.

"We almost there," said Sonny.

"Almost." We were both too nervous to say anything more.

We lived in a housing project. It hasn't been up long. A few days after it was up it seemed uninhabitably new, now, of course, it's already rundown. It looks like a parody of the good, clean, faceless life—God knows the people who live in it do their best to make it a parody. The beat-looking grass lying around isn't enough to make their lives green, the hedges will never hold out the streets, and they know it. The big windows fool no one, they aren't big enough to make space out of no space. They don't bother with the windows, they watch the TV screen instead. The playground is most popular with the children who don't play at jacks, or skip rope, or roller skate, or swing, and they can be found in it after dark. We moved in partly because it's not too far from where I teach, and partly for the kids; but it's really just like the houses in which Sonny and I grew up. The same things happen, they'll have the same things to remember. The moment Sonny and I started into the house I had the feeling that I was simply bringing him back into the danger he had almost died trying to escape.

Sonny has never been talkative. So I don't know why I was sure he'd be dying to talk to me when supper was over the first night. Everything went fine, the oldest boy remembered him, and the youngest boy liked him, and Sonny had remembered to bring something for each of them; and Isabel, who is really much nicer than I am, more open and giving, had gone to a lot of trouble about dinner and was genuinely glad to see him. And she's always been able to tease Sonny in a way that I haven't. It was nice to see her face so vivid again and to hear her laugh and watch her make Sonny laugh. She wasn't or, anyway, she didn't seem to be, at all uneasy or embarrassed. She chatted as though there were no subject which had to be avoided and she got Sonny past his first, faint stiffness. And thank God she was there, for I was filled with that icy dread again. Everything I did seemed awkward to me, and everything I said sounded freighted with hidden meaning. I was trying to remember everything I'd heard about dope addiction and I couldn't help watching Sonny for signs. I wasn't doing it out of malice. I was trying to find out something about my brother. I was dying to hear him tell me he was safe.

"Safe!" my father grunted, whenever Mama suggested trying to move to a neighborhood which might be safer for children. "Safe, hell! Ain't no place safe for kids, nor nobody."

He always went on like this, but he wasn't, ever, really as bad as he sounded, not even on weekends, when he got drunk. As a matter of fact, he was always on the lookout for "something a little better," but he died before he found it. He died suddenly, during a drunken weekend in the middle of the war, when Sonny was fifteen. He and Sonny hadn't ever got on too well. And this was partly because Sonny was the apple of his father's eye. It was because he loved Sonny so much and was frightened for him, that he was always fighting with him. It doesn't do any good to fight with Sonny. Sonny just moves back, inside himself, where he can't be reached. But the principal reason that they never hit it off is that they were so much alike. Daddy was big and rough and loud-talking, just the opposite of Sonny, but they both had—that same privacy.

Mama tried to tell me something about this, just after Daddy died. I was home on leave from the army.

This was the last time I ever saw my mother alive. Just the same, this picture gets all mixed up in my mind with pictures I had of her when she was younger. The way I always see her is the way she used to be on a Sunday afternoon, say, when the old folks were talking after the big Sunday dinner. I always see her wearing pale blue. She'd be sitting on the sofa. And my father would be sitting in the easy chair, not far from her. And the living room would be full of church folks and relatives. There they sit, in chairs all around the living room, and the night is creeping up outside, but nobody knows it yet. You can see the darkness growing against the windowpanes and you hear the street noises every now and again, or maybe the jangling beat of a tambourine from one of the churches close by, but it's real quiet in the room. For a moment nobody's talking, but every face looks darkening, like the sky outside. And my mother rocks a little from the waist, and my father's eyes are closed. Everyone is looking at something a child can't see. For a minute they've forgotten the children. Maybe a kid is lying on the rug, half asleep. Maybe somebody's got a kid in his lap and is absent-mindedly stroking the kid's head. Maybe there's a kid, quiet and big-eyed, curled up in a big chair in the corner. The silence, the darkness coming, and the darkness in the faces frightens the child obscurely. He hopes that the hand which strokes his forehead will never stop—will never die. He hopes that there will never come a time when the old folks won't be sitting around the living room, talking about where they've come from, and what they've seen, and what's happened to them and their kinfolk.

But something deep and watchful in the child knows that this is bound to end, is already ending. In a moment someone will get up and turn on the light. Then the old folks will remember the children and they won't talk any more that day. And when light fills the room, the child is filled with darkness. He knows that every time this happens he's moved just a little closer to that darkness outside. The darkness outside is what the old folks have been talking about. It's what they've come from. It's what they endure. The child knows that they won't talk any more because if he knows too much about what's happened to *them,* he'll know too much too soon, about what's going to happen to *him.*

The last time I talked to my mother, I remember I was restless. I wanted to get out and see Isabel. We weren't married then and we had a lot to straighten out between us.

There Mama sat, in black, by the window. She was humming an old church song, *Lord, you brought me from a long ways off.* Sonny was out somewhere. Mama kept watching the streets.

"I don't know," she said, "if I'll ever see you again, after you go off from here. But I hope you'll remember the things I tried to teach you."

"Don't talk like that," I said, and smiled. "You'll be here a long time yet."

She smiled, too, but she said nothing. She was quiet for a long time. And I said, "Mama, don't you worry about nothing. I'll be writing all the time, and you be getting the checks. . . ."

"I want to talk to you about your brother," she said, suddenly. "If anything happens to me he ain't going to have nobody to look out for him."

"Mama," I said, "ain't nothing going to happen to you *or* Sonny. Sonny's all right. He's a good boy and he's got good sense."

"It ain't a question of his being a good boy," Mama said, "nor of his having good sense. It ain't only the bad ones, nor yet the dumb ones that gets sucked under." She stopped, looking at me. "Your Daddy once had a brother," she said, and she smiled in a way that made me feel she was in pain. "You didn't never know that, did you?"

"No," I said, "I never knew that," and I watched her face.

"Oh, yes," she said, "your Daddy had a brother." She looked out of the window again. "I know you never saw your Daddy cry. But *I* did—many a time, through all these years."

I asked her, "What happened to his brother? How come nobody's ever talked about him?"

This was the first time I ever saw my mother look old.

"His brother got killed," she said, "when he was just a little younger than you are now. I knew him. He was a fine boy. He was maybe a little full of the devil, but he didn't mean nobody no harm."

Then she stopped and the room was silent, exactly as it had sometimes been on those Sunday afternoons. Mama kept looking out into the streets.

"He used to have a job in the mill," she said, "and, like all young folks, he just liked to perform on Saturday nights. Saturday nights, him and your father would drift around to different place, go to dances and things like that, or just sit around with people they knew, and your father's brother would sing, he had a fine voice, and play along with himself on his guitar. Well, this particular Saturday night, him and your father was coming home from some place, and they were both a little drunk and there was a moon that night, it was bright like day. Your father's brother was feeling kind of good, and he was whistling to himself, and he had his guitar slung over his shoulder. They was coming down a hill and beneath them was a road that turned off from the highway. Well, your father's brother, being always kind of frisky, decided to run down this hill, and he did, with that guitar banging and clanging behind him, and he ran across the road, and he was making water behind a tree. And your father was sort of amused at him and he was still coming down the hill, kind of slow. Then he heard a car motor and that same minute his brother stepped from behind the tree, into the road, in the moonlight. And he started to cross the road. And your father started to run down the hill, he says he don't know why. This car was full of white men. They was all drunk, and when they seen your father's brother they let out a great whoop and holler and they aimed the car straight at him. They was having fun, they just wanted to scare him, the way they do sometimes, you know. But they was drunk. And I guess the

boy, being drunk, too, and scared, kind of lost his head. By the time he jumped it was too late. Your father says he heard his brother scream when the car rolled over him, and he heard the wood of that guitar when it give, and he heard them strings go flying, and he heard them white men shouting, and the car kept on a-going and it ain't stopped till this day. And, time your father got down the hill, his brother weren't nothing but blood and pulp."

Tears were gleaming on my mother's face. There wasn't anything I could say.

"He never mentioned it," she said, "because I never let him mention it before you children. Your Daddy was like a crazy man that night and for many a night thereafter. He says he never in his life seen anything as dark as that road after the lights of that car had gone away. Weren't nothing, weren't nobody on that road, just your Daddy and his brother and that busted guitar. Oh, yes. Your Daddy never did really get right again. Till the day he died he weren't sure but that every white man he saw was the man that killed his brother."

She stopped and took out her handkerchief and dried her eyes and looked at me.

"I ain't telling you all this," she said, "to make you scared or bitter or to make you hate nobody. I'm telling you this because you got a brother. And the world ain't changed."

I guess I didn't want to believe this. I guess she saw this in my face. She turned away from me, toward the window again, searching those streets.

"But I praise my Redeemer," she said at last, "that He called your Daddy home before me. I ain't saying it to throw no flowers at myself, but, I declare, it keeps me from feeling too cast down to know I helped your father get safely through this world. Your father always acted like he was the roughest, strongest man on earth. And everybody took him to be like that. But if he hadn't had *me* there—to see his tears!"

She was crying again. Still, I couldn't move. I said, "Lord, Lord, Mama, I didn't know it was like that."

"Oh, honey," she said, "there's a lot that you don't know. But you are going to find it out." She stood up from the window and came over to me. "You got to hold on to your brother," she said, "and don't let him fall, no matter what it looks like is happening to him and no matter how evil you gets with him. You going to be evil with him many a time. But don't you forget what I told you, you hear?"

"I won't forget," I said. "Don't you worry, I won't forget. I won't let nothing happen to Sonny."

My mother smiled as though she were amused at something she saw in my face. Then, "You may not be able to stop nothing from happening. But you got to let him know you's *there*."

Two days later I was married, and then I was gone. And I had a lot of things on my mind and I pretty well forgot my promise to Mama until I got shipped home on a special furlough for her funeral.

And, after the funeral, with just Sonny and me alone in the empty kitchen, I tried to find out something about him.

"What do you want to do?" I asked him.

"I'm going to be a musician," he said.

For he had graduated, in the time I had been away, from dancing to the juke box to finding out who was playing what, and what they were doing with it, and he had bought himself a set of drums.

"You mean, you want to be a drummer?" I somehow had the feeling that being a drummer might be all right for other people but not for my brother Sonny.

"I don't think," he said, looking at me very gravely, "that I'll ever be a good drummer. But I think I can play a piano."

I frowned. I'd never played the role of the older brother quite so seriously before, had scarcely ever, in fact, *asked* Sonny a damn thing. I sensed myself in the presence of something I didn't really know how to handle, didn't understand. So I made my frown a little deeper as I asked: "What kind of musician do you want to be?"

He grinned. "How many kinds do you think there are?"

"Be *serious*," I said.

He laughed, throwing his head back, and then looked at me. "I *am* serious."

"Well, then, for Christ's sake, stop kidding around and answer a serious question. I mean, do you want to be a concert pianist, you want to play classical music and all that, or—or what?" Long before I finished he was laughing again. "For Christ's *sake*, Sonny!"

He sobered, but with difficulty. "I'm sorry. But you sound so—*scared!*" and he was off again.

"Well, you may think it's funny now, baby, but it's not going to be so funny when you have to make your living at it, let me tell you *that*." I was furious because I knew he was laughing at me and I didn't know why.

"No," he said, very sober now, and afraid, perhaps, that he'd hurt me, "I don't want to be a classical pianist. That isn't what interests me. I mean"—he paused, looking hard at me, as though his eyes would help me to understand, and then gestured helplessly, as though perhaps his hand would help—"I mean, I'll have a lot of studying to do, and I'll have to study *everything*, but, I mean, I want to play *with*—jazz musicians." He stopped. "I want to play jazz," he said.

Well, the word had never before sounded as heavy, as real, as it sounded that afternoon in Sonny's mouth. I just looked at him and I was probably frowning a real frown by this time. I simply couldn't see why on earth he'd want to spend his time hanging around nightclubs, clowning around on bandstands, while people pushed each other around a dance floor. It seemed—beneath him, somehow. I had never thought about it before, had never been forced to, but I suppose I had always put jazz musicians in a class with what Daddy called "good-time people."

"Are you *serious?*"

"Hell, *yes*, I'm serious."

He looked more helpless than ever, and annoyed, and deeply hurt.

I suggested, helpfully: "You mean—like Louis Armstrong?"

His face closed as though I'd struck him. "No. I'm not talking about none of that old-time, down home crap."

"Well, look, Sonny, I'm sorry, don't get mad. I just don't altogether get it, that's all. Name somebody—you know, a jazz musician you admire."

"Bird."

"Who?"

"Bird! Charlie Parker! Don't they teach you nothing in the goddamn army?"

I lit a cigarette. I was surprised and then a little amused to discover that I was trembling. "I've been out of touch," I said. "You'll have to be patient with me. Now. Who's this Parker character?"

"He's just one of the greatest jazz musicians alive," said Sonny, sullenly, his hands in his pockets, his back to me. "Maybe *the* greatest," he added, bitterly, "that's probably why *you* never heard of him."

"All right," I said, "I'm ignorant. I'm sorry. I'll go out and buy all the cat's records right away, all right?"

"It don't," said Sonny, with dignity, "make any difference to me. I don't care what you listen to. Don't do me no favors."

I was beginning to realize that I'd never seen him so upset before. With another part of my mind I was thinking that this would probably turn out to be one of those things kids go through and that I shouldn't make it seem important by pushing it too hard. Still, I didn't think it would do any harm to ask: "Doesn't all this take a lot of time? Can you make a living at it?"

He turned back to me and half leaned, half sat, on the kitchen table. "Everything takes time," he said, "and—well, yes, sure, I can make a living at it. But what I don't seem to be able to make you understand is that it's the only thing I want to do."

"Well, Sonny," I said, gently, "you know people can't always do exactly what they *want* to do—"

"*No,* I don't know that," said Sonny, surprising me. "I think people *ought* to do what they want to do, what else are they alive for?"

"You getting to be a big boy," I said desperately, "it's time you started thinking about your future."

"I'm thinking about my future," said Sonny, grimly. "I think about it all the time."

I gave up. I decided, if he didn't change his mind, that we could always talk about it later. "In the meantime," I said, "you got to finish school." We already decided that he'd have to move in with Isabel and her folks. I knew this wasn't the ideal arrangement because Isabel's folks are inclined to be dicty and they hadn't especially wanted Isabel to marry me. But I didn't know what else to do. "And we have to get you fixed up at Isabel's."

There was a long silence. He moved from the kitchen table to the window. "That's a terrible idea. You know it yourself."

"Do you have a *better* idea?"

He just walked up and down the kitchen for a minute. He was as tall as I was. He had started to shave. I suddenly had the feeling that I didn't know him at all.

He stopped at the kitchen table and picked up my cigarettes. Looking at me with a kind of mocking, amused defiance, he put one between his lips. "You mind?"

"You smoking already?"

He lit the cigarette and nodded, watching me through the smoke. "I just wanted to see if I'd have the courage to smoke in front of you." He grinned and blew a great cloud of smoke to the ceiling. "It was easy." He looked at my face. "Come on, now. I bet you was smoking at my age, tell the truth."

I didn't say anything but the truth was on my face, and he laughed. But now there was something very strained in his laugh. "Sure. And I bet that ain't all you was doing."

He was frightening me a little. "Cut the crap," I said. "We already decided that you was going to go and live at Isabel's. Now what's got into you all of a sudden?"

"*You* decided it," he pointed out. "I didn't decide nothing." He stopped in front of me, leaning against the stove, arms loosely folded. "Look, brother. I don't want to stay in Harlem no more, I really don't." He was very earnest. He looked at me, then over toward the kitchen window. There was something in his eyes I'd never seen before, some thoughtfulness, some worry all his own. He rubbed the muscle of one arm. "It's time I was getting out of here."

"Where do you want to *go,* Sonny?"

"I want to join the army. Or the navy, I don't care. If I say I'm old enough, they'll believe me."

Then I got mad. It was because I was so scared. "You must be crazy. You goddamn fool, what the hell do you want to go and join the *army* for?"

"I just told you. To get out of Harlem."

"Sonny, you haven't even finished *school.* And if you really want to be a musician, how do you expect to study if you're in the *army?*"

He looked at me, trapped, and in anguish. "There's ways. I might be able to work out some kind of deal. Anyway, I'll have the G.I. Bill when I come out."

"*If* you come out." We stared at each other. "Sonny, please. Be reasonable. I know the setup is far from perfect. But we got to do the best we can."

"I ain't learning nothing in school," he said. "Even when I go." He turned away from me and opened the window and threw his cigarette out into the narrow alley. I watched his back. "At least, I ain't learning nothing you'd want me to learn." He slammed the window so hard I thought the glass would fly out, and turned back to me. "And I'm sick of the stink of these garbage cans!"

"Sonny," I said, "I know how you feel. But if you don't finish school now, you're going to be sorry later that you didn't." I grabbed him by the shoulders. "And you only got another year. It ain't so bad. And I'll come back and I swear I'll help you do *whatever* you want to do. Just try to put up with it till I come back. Will you please do that? For me?"

He didn't answer and he wouldn't look at me. "Sonny. You hear me?"

He pulled away. "I hear you. But you never hear anything *I* say."

I didn't know what to say to that. He looked out of the window and then back at me. "OK," he said, and sighed. "I'll try."

Then I said, trying to cheer him up a little, "They got a piano at Isabel's. You can practice on it."

And as a matter of fact, it did cheer him up for a minute. "That's right," he said to himself. "I forgot that." His face relaxed a little. But the worry, the thoughtfulness, played on it still, the way shadows play on a face which is staring into the fire.

But I thought I'd never hear the end of that piano. At first, Isabel would write me, saying how nice it was that Sonny was so serious about his music and how, as soon as he came in from school, or wherever he had been when he was supposed to be at school, he went straight to that piano and stayed there until suppertime. And, after supper, he went back to that piano and stayed there until everybody went to bed. He was at the piano all day Saturday and all day Sunday. Then he bought a record player and started playing records. He'd play one record over and over again, all day long sometimes, and he'd improvise along with it on the piano. Or he'd play one section of the record, one chord, one change, one progression, then he'd do it on the piano. Then back to the record. Then back to the piano.

Well, I really don't know how they stood it. Isabel finally confessed that it wasn't like living with a person at all, it was like living with sound. And the sound didn't make any sense to her, didn't make any sense to any of them—naturally. They began, in a way, to be afflicted by this presence that was living in their home. It was as though Sonny were some sort of god, or monster. He moved in an atmosphere which wasn't like theirs at all. They fed him and he ate, he washed himself, he walked in and out of their door; he

certainly wasn't nasty or unpleasant or rude, Sonny isn't any of those things; but it was as though he were all wrapped up in some cloud, some fire, some vision all his own; and there wasn't any way to reach him.

At the same time, he wasn't really a man yet, he was still a child, and they had to watch out for him in all kinds of ways. They certainly couldn't throw him out. Neither did they dare to make a great scene about that piano because even they dimly sensed, as I sensed, from so many thousands of miles away, that Sonny was at that piano playing for his life.

But he hadn't been going to school. One day a letter came from the school board and Isabel's mother got it—there had, apparently, been other letters but Sonny had torn them up. This day, when Sonny came in, Isabel's mother showed him the letter and asked where he'd been spending his time. And she finally got it out of him that he'd been down in Greenwich Village, with musicians and other characters, in a white girl's apartment. And this scared her and she started to scream at him and what came up, once she began—though she denies it to this day—was what sacrifices they were making to give Sonny a decent home and how little he appreciated it.

Sonny didn't play the piano that day. By evening, Isabel's mother had calmed down but then there was the old man to deal with, and Isabel herself. Isabel says she did her best to be calm but she broke down and started crying. She says she just watched Sonny's face. She could tell, by watching him, what was happening with him. And what was happening was that they penetrated his cloud, they had reached him. Even if their fingers had been a thousand times more gentle than human fingers ever are, he could hardly help feeling they had stripped him naked and were spitting on that nakedness. For he also had to see that his presence, that music, which was life or death to him, had been torture for them and that they had endured it, not at all for his sake, but only for mine. And Sonny couldn't take that. He can take it a little better today than he could then but he's still not very good at it and, frankly, I don't know anybody who is.

The silence of the next few days must have been louder than the sound of all the music ever played since time began. One morning, before she went to work, Isabel was in his room for something and she suddenly realized that all of his records were gone. And she knew for certain that he was gone. And he was. He went as far as the navy would carry him. He finally sent me a postcard from some place in Greece and that was the first I knew that Sonny was still alive. I didn't see him any more until we were both back in New York and the war had long been over.

He was a man by then, of course, but I wasn't willing to see it. He came by the house from time to time, but we fought almost every time we met. I didn't like the way he carried himself, loose and dreamlike all the time, and I didn't like his friends, and his music seemed to be merely an excuse for the life he led. It sounded just that weird and disordered.

Then we had a fight, a pretty awful fight, and I didn't see him for months. By and by I looked him up, where he was living, in a furnished room in the Village, and I tried to make it up. But there were lots of other people in the room and Sonny just lay on his bed, and he wouldn't come downstairs with me, and he treated these other people as though they were his family and I weren't. So I got mad and then he got mad, and then I told him that he might just as well be dead as live the way he was living. Then he stood up and he told me not to worry about him any more in life, that he *was* dead as far as I was concerned. Then he pushed me to the door and the other people looked on as though nothing were happening, and he slammed the door behind me. I stood in the hallway, staring at the door. I heard somebody laugh in the room and then the tears came to my eyes. I started down the steps, whistling to keep from crying, I kept whistling to myself, *You going to need me, baby, one of these cold, rainy days.*

I read about Sonny's trouble in the spring. Little Grace died in the fall. She was a beautiful little girl. But she only lived a little over two years. She died of polio and she suffered. She had a slight fever for a couple of days, but it didn't seem like anything and we just kept her in bed. And we would certainly have called the doctor, but the fever dropped, she seemed to be all right. So we thought it had just been a cold. Then, one day, she was up, playing, Isabel was in the kitchen fixing lunch for the two boys when they'd come in from school, and she heard Grace fall down in the living room. When you have a lot of children you don't always start running when one of them falls, unless they start screaming or something. And, this time, Grace was quiet. Yet, Isabel says

that when she heard that *thump* and then that silence, something happened in her to make her afraid. And she ran to the living room and there was little Grace on the floor, all twisted up, and the reason she hadn't screamed was that she couldn't get her breath. And when she did scream, it was the worst sound, Isabel says, that she'd ever heard in all her life, and she still hears it sometimes in her dreams. Isabel will sometimes wake me up with a low, moaning, strangled sound and I have to be quick to awaken her and hold her to me and where Isabel is weeping against me seems a mortal wound.

I think I may have written Sonny the very day that little Grace was buried. I was sitting in the living room in the dark, by myself, and I suddenly thought of Sonny. My trouble made his real.

One Saturday afternoon, when Sonny had been living with us, or, anyway, been in our house, for nearly two weeks, I found myself wandering aimlessly about the living room, drinking from a can of beer, and trying to work up the courage to search Sonny's room. He was out, he was usually out whenever I was home, and Isabel had taken the children to see their grandparents. Suddenly I was standing still in front of the living room window, watching Seventh Avenue. The idea of searching Sonny's room made me still. I scarcely dared to admit to myself what I'd be searching for. I didn't know what I'd do if I found it. Or if I didn't.

On the sidewalk across from me, near the entrance to a barbecue joint, some people were holding an old-fashioned revival meeting. The barbecue cook, wearing a dirty white apron, his conked hair reddish and metallic in the pale sun, and a cigarette between his lips, stood in the doorway, watching them. Kids and older people paused in their errands and stood there, along with some older men and a couple of very tough-looking women who watched everything that happened on the avenue, as though they owned it, or were maybe owned by it. Well, they were watching this, too. The revival was being carried on by three sisters in black, and a brother. All they had were their voices and their Bibles and a tambourine. The brother was testifying and while he testified two of the sisters stood together, seeming to say, amen, and the third sister walked around with the tambourine outstretched and a couple of people dropped coins into it. Then the brother's testimony ended and the sister who had been taking up the collection dumped the coins into her palm and transferred them to the pocket of her long black robe. Then she raised both hands, striking the tambourine against the air, and then against one hand, and she started to sing. And the two other sisters and the brother joined in.

It was strange, suddenly, to watch, though I had been seeing these street meetings all my life. So, of course, had everybody else down there. Yet, they paused and watched and listened and I stood still at the window. *"Tis the old ship of Zion,"* they sang, and the sister with the tambourine kept a steady, jangling beat, *"it has rescued many a thousand!"* Not a soul under the sound of their voices was hearing this song for the first time, not one of them had been rescued. Nor had they seen much in the way of rescue work being done around them. Neither did they especially believe in the holiness of the three sisters and the brother, they knew too much about them, knew where they lived, and how. The woman with the tambourine, whose voice dominated the air, whose face was bright with joy, was divided by very little from the woman who stood watching her, a cigarette between her heavy, chapped lips, her hair a cuckoo's nest, her face scarred and swollen from many beatings, and her black eyes glittering like coal. Perhaps they both knew this, which was why, when, as rarely, they addressed each other, they addressed each other as Sister. As the singing filled the air the watching, listening faces underwent a change, the eyes focusing on something within; the music seemed to soothe a poison out of them; and time seemed, nearly, to fall away from the sullen, belligerent, battered faces, as though they were fleeing back to their first condition, while dreaming of their last. The barbecue cook half shook his head and smiled, and dropped his cigarette and disappeared into his joint. A man fumbled in his pockets for change and stood holding it in his hand impatiently, as though he had just remembered a pressing appointment further up the avenue. He looked furious. Then I saw Sonny, standing on the edge of the crowd. He was carrying a wide, flat notebook with a green cover, and it made him look, from where I was standing, almost like a schoolboy. The coppery sun brought out the copper in his skin, he was very faintly smiling, standing very still. Then the singing stopped, the tambourine turned into a collection plate again. The furious man dropped in his coins

and vanished, so did a couple of the women, and Sonny dropped some change in the plate, looking directly at the woman with a little smile. He started across the avenue, toward the house. He has a slow, loping walk, something like the way Harlem hipsters walk, only he's imposed on this his own half-beat. I had never really noticed it before.

I stayed at the window, both relieved and apprehensive. As Sonny disappeared from my sight, they began singing again. And they were still singing when his key turned in the lock.

"Hey," he said.

"Hey, yourself. You want some beer?"

"No. Well, maybe." But he came up to the window and stood beside me, looking out. "What a warm voice," he said.

They were singing *If I could only hear my mother pray again!*

"Yes," I said, "and she can sure beat that tambourine."

"But what a terrible song," he said, and laughed. He dropped his notebook on the sofa and disappeared into the kitchen. "Where's Isabel and the kids?"

"I think they went to see their grandparents. You hungry?"

"No." He came back into the living room with his can of beer. "You want to come some place with me tonight?"

I sensed, I don't know how, that I couldn't possibly say no. "Sure. Where?"

He sat down on the sofa and picked up his notebook and started leafing through it. "I'm going to sit in with some fellows in a joint in the Village."

"You mean, you're going to play, tonight?"

"That's right." He took a swallow of his beer and moved back to the window. He gave me a sidelong look. "If you can stand it."

"I'll try," I said.

He smiled to himself and we both watched as the meeting across the way broke up. The three sisters and the brother, heads bowed, were singing *God be with you till we meet again.* The faces around them were very quiet. Then the song ended. The small crowd dispersed. We watched the three women and the lone man walk slowly up the avenue.

"When she was singing before," said Sonny, abruptly, "her voice reminded me for a minute of what heroin feels like sometimes—when it's in your veins. It makes you feel sort of warm and cool at the same time. And distant. And—and sure." He sipped his beer, very deliberately not looking at me. I watched his face. "It makes you feel—in control. Sometimes you've got to have that feeling."

"Do you?" I sat down slowly in the easy chair.

"Sometimes." He went to the sofa and picked up his notebook again. "Some people do."

"In order," I asked, "to play?" And my voice was very ugly, full of contempt and anger.

"Well"—he looked at me with great, troubled eyes, as though, in fact, he hoped his eyes would tell me things he could never otherwise say— "they *think* so. And *if* they think so—!"

"And what do *you* think?" I asked.

He sat on the sofa and put his can of beer on the floor. "I don't know," he said, and I couldn't be sure if he were answering my question or pursuing his thoughts. His face didn't tell me. "It's not so much to *play*. It's to *stand* it, to be able to make it at all. On any level." He frowned and smiled: "In order to keep from shaking to pieces."

"But these friends of yours," I said, "they seem to shake themselves to pieces pretty goddamn fast."

"Maybe." He played with the notebook. And something told me that I should curb my tongue, that Sonny was doing his best to talk, that I should listen. "But of course you only know the ones that've gone to pieces. Some don't—or at least they haven't *yet* and that's just about all *any* of us can say." He paused. "And then there are some who just live, really, in hell, and they know it and they see what's happening and they go right on. I don't know." He sighed, dropped the notebook, folded his arms. "Some guys, you can tell from the way they play, they on something *all* the time. And you can see that, well, it makes something real for them. But of course," he picked up his beer from the floor and sipped it and put the can down again, "they *want* to, too, you've got to see that. Even some of them that say they don't—*some*, not all."

"And what about you?" I asked—I couldn't help it. "What about you? Do *you* want to?"

He stood up and walked to the window and remained silent for a long time. Then he sighed. "Me," he said. Then: "While I was downstairs before, on my way here, listening to that woman sing, it struck me all of a sudden how much suffering she must have had to go through—to

sing like that. It's *repulsive* to think you have to suffer that much."

I said: "But there's no way not to suffer—is there, Sonny?"

"I believe not," he said and smiled, "but that's never stopped anyone from trying." He looked at me. "Has it?" I realized, with this mocking look, that there stood between us, forever, beyond the power of time or forgiveness, the fact that I had held silence—so long!—when he had needed human speech to help him. He turned back to the window. "No, there's no way not to suffer. But you try all kinds of ways to keep from drowning in it, to keep on top of it, and to make it seem— well, like *you*. Like you did something, all right, and now you're suffering for it. You know?" I said nothing. "Well you know," he said, impatiently, "why *do* people suffer? Maybe it's better to do something to give it a reason, *any* reason."

"But we just agreed," I said, "that there's no way not to suffer. Isn't it better, then, just to—take it?"

"But nobody just takes it," Sonny cried, "that's what I'm telling you! *Everybody* tries not to. You're just hung up on the *way* some people try—it's not *your* way!"

The hair on my face began to itch, my face felt wet. "That's not true," I said, "that's not true. I don't give a damn what other people do, I don't even care how they suffer. I just care how *you* suffer." And he looked at me. "Please believe me," I said, "I don't want to see you— die—trying not to suffer."

"I won't," he said, flatly, "die trying not to suffer. At least, not any faster than anybody else."

"But there's no need," I said, trying to laugh, "is there? in killing yourself."

I wanted to say more, but I couldn't. I wanted to talk about will power and how life could be—well, beautiful. I wanted to say that it was all within; but was it? or, rather, wasn't that exactly the trouble? And I wanted to promise that I would never fail him again. But it would all have sounded—empty words and lies.

So I made the promise to myself and prayed that I would keep it.

"It's terrible sometimes, inside," he said, "that's what's the trouble. You walk these streets, black and funky and cold, and there's not really a living ass to talk to, and there's nothing shaking, and there's no way of getting it out—that storm inside. You can't talk it and you can't make love with it, and when you finally try to get with it and play it, you realize *nobody's* listening. So *you've* got to listen. You got to find a way to listen."

And then he walked away from the window and sat on the sofa again, as though all the wind had suddenly been knocked out of him. "Sometimes you'll do *anything* to play, even cut your mother's throat." He laughed and looked at me. "Or your brother's." Then he sobered. "Or your own." Then: "Don't worry. I'm all right now and I think I'll *be* all right. But I can't forget—where I've been. I don't mean just the physical place I've been, I mean where I've *been*. And *what* I've been."

"What have you been, Sonny?" I asked.

He smiled—but sat sideways on the sofa, his elbow resting on the back, his fingers playing with his mouth and chin, not looking at me. "I've been something I didn't recognize, didn't know I could be. Didn't know anybody could be." He stopped, looking inward, looking helplessly young, looking old. "I'm not talking about it now because I feel *guilty* or anything like that—maybe it would be better if I did, I don't know. Anyway, I can't really talk about it. Not to you, not to anybody," and now he turned and faced me. "Sometimes, you know, and it was actually when I was most *out* of the world, I felt that I was in it, that I was *with* it, really, and I could play or I didn't really have to *play*, it just came out of me, it was there. And I don't know how I played, thinking about it now, but I know I did awful things, those times, sometimes, to people. Or it wasn't that I *did* anything to them—it was that they weren't real." He picked up the beer can; it was empty; he rolled it between his palms: "And other times—well, I needed a fix, I needed to find a place to lean, I needed to clear a space to *listen*—and I couldn't find it, and I—went crazy, I did terrible things to *me,* I was terrible *for* me." He began pressing the beer can between his hands, I watched the metal begin to give. It glittered, as he played with it, like a knife, and I was afraid he would cut himself, but I said nothing. "Oh well. I can never tell you. I was all by myself at the bottom of something, stinking and sweating and crying and shaking, and I smelled it, you know? *my* stink, and I thought I'd die if I couldn't get away from it and yet, all the same, I knew that everything I was doing was just locking me in with it. And I didn't know," he paused, still flattening the beer can, "I didn't know, I still *don't* know, something kept telling me that maybe

it was good to smell your own stink, but I didn't think that *that* was what I'd been trying to do—and—who can stand it?" and he abruptly dropped the ruined beer can, looking at me with a small, still smile, and then rose, walking to the window as though it were the lodestone rock. I watched his face, he watched the avenue. "I couldn't tell you when Mama died—but the reason I wanted to leave Harlem so bad was to get away from drugs. And then, when I ran away, that's what I was running from—really. When I came back, nothing had changed, *I* hadn't changed, I was just—older." And he stopped, drumming with his fingers on the windowpane. The sun had vanished, soon darkness would fall. I watched his face. "It can come again," he said, almost as though speaking to himself. Then he turned to me. "It can come again," he repeated. "I just want you to know that."

"All right," I said, at last. "So it can come again, All right."

He smiled, but the smile was sorrowful. "I had to try to tell you," he said.

"Yes," I said. "I understand that."

"You're my brother," he said, looking straight at me, and not smiling at all.

"Yes," I repeated, "yes. I understand that."

He turned back to the window, looking out. "All that hatred down there," he said, "all that hatred and misery and love. It's a wonder it doesn't blow the avenue apart."

We went to the only nightclub on a short, dark street, downtown. We squeezed through the narrow, chattering, jampacked bar to the entrance of the big room, where the bandstand was. And we stood there for a moment, for the lights were very dim in this room and we couldn't see. Then, "Hello, boy," said a voice and an enormous black man, much older than Sonny or myself, erupted out of all that atmospheric lighting and put an arm around Sonny's shoulder. "I been sitting right here," he said, "waiting for you."

He had a big voice, too, and heads in the darkness turned toward us.

Sonny grinned and pulled a little away, and said, "Creole, this is my brother. I told you about him."

Creole shook my hand. "I'm glad to meet you, son," he said, and it was clear that he was glad to meet me *there,* for Sonny's sake. And he smiled, "You got a real musician in *your* family," and he took his arm from Sonny's shoulder and slapped him, lightly, affectionately, with the back of his hand.

"Well. Now I've heard it all," said a voice behind us. This was another musician, and a friend of Sonny's, a coal-black, cheerful-looking man, built close to the ground. He immediately began confiding to me, at the top of his lungs, the most terrible things about Sonny, his teeth gleaming like a lighthouse and his laugh coming up out of him like the beginning of an earthquake. And it turned out that everyone at the bar knew Sonny, or almost everyone; some were musicians, working there, or nearby, or not working, some were simply hangers-on, and some were there to hear Sonny play. I was introduced to all of them and they were all very polite to me. Yet, it was clear that, for them, I was only Sonny's brother. Here, I was in Sonny's world. Or, rather: his kingdom. Here, it was not even a question that his veins bore royal blood.

They were going to play soon and Creole installed me, by myself, at a table in a dark corner. Then I watched them, Creole, and the little black man, and Sonny, and the others, while they horsed around, standing just below the bandstand. The light from the bandstand spilled just a little short of them and, watching them laughing and gesturing and moving about, I had the feeling that they, nevertheless, were being most careful not to step into that circle of light too suddenly: that if they moved into the light too suddenly, without thinking, they would perish in flame. Then, while I watched, one of them, the small, black man, moved into the light and crossed the bandstand and started fooling around with his drums. Then—being funny and being, also, extremely ceremonious—Creole took Sonny by the arm and led him to the piano. A woman's voice called Sonny's name and a few hands started clapping. And Sonny, also being funny and being ceremonious, and so touched, I think, that he could have cried, but neither hiding it nor showing it, riding it like a man, grinned, and put both hands to his heart and bowed from the waist.

Creole then went to the bass fiddle and a lean, very bright-skinned brown man jumped up on the bandstand and picked up his horn. So there they were, and the atmosphere on the bandstand and in the room began to change and tighten. Someone stepped up to the microphone and announced them. Then there were all kinds of murmurs. Some people at the bar shushed others.

The waitress ran around, frantically getting in the last orders, guys and chicks got closer to each other, and the lights on the bandstand, on the quartet, turned to a kind of indigo. Then they all looked different there. Creole looked about him for the last time, as though he were making certain that all his chickens were in the coop, and then he—jumped and struck the fiddle. And there they were.

All I know about music is that not many people ever really hear it. And even then, on the rare occasions when something opens within, and the music enters, what we mainly hear, or hear corroborated, are personal, private, vanishing evocations. But the man who creates the music is hearing something else, is dealing with the roar rising from the void and imposing order on it as it hits the air. What is evoked in him, then, is of another order, more terrible because it has no words, and triumphant, too, for that same reason. And his triumph, when he triumphs, is ours. I just watched Sonny's face. His face was troubled, he was working hard, but he wasn't with it. And I had the feeling that, in a way, everyone on the bandstand was waiting for him, both waiting for him and pushing him along. But as I began to watch Creole, I realized that it was Creole who held them all back. He had them on a short rein. Up there, keeping the beat with his whole body, wailing on the fiddle, with his eyes half closed, he was listening to everything, but he was listening to Sonny. He was having a dialogue with Sonny. He wanted Sonny to leave the shoreline and strike out for the deep water. He was Sonny's witness that deep water and drowning were not the same thing—he had been there, and he knew. And he wanted Sonny to know. He was waiting for Sonny to do the things on the keys which would let Creole know that Sonny was in the water.

And, while Creole listened, Sonny moved, deep within, exactly like someone in torment. I had never before thought of how awful the relationship must be between the musician and his instrument. He has to fill it, this instrument, with the breath of life, his own. He has to make it do what he wants it to do. And a piano is just a piano. It's made out of so much wood and wires and little hammers and big ones, and ivory. While there's only so much you can do with it, the only way to find this out is to try; to try and make it do everything.

And Sonny hadn't been near a piano for over a

year. And he wasn't on much better terms with his life, not the life that stretched before him now. He and the piano stammered, started one way, got scared, stopped; started another way, panicked, marked time, started again; then seemed to have found a direction, panicked again, got stuck. And the face I saw on Sonny I'd never seen before. Everything had been burned out of it, and, at the same time, things usually hidden were being burned in, by the fire and fury of the battle which was occurring in him up there.

Yet, watching Creole's face as they neared the end of the first set, I had the feeling that something had happened, something I hadn't heard. Then they finished, there was scattered applause, and then, without an instant's warning, Creole started into something else, it was almost sardonic, it was *Am I Blue*. And, as though he commanded, Sonny began to play. Something began to happen. And Creole let out the reins. The dry, low, black man said something awful on the drums, Creole answered, and the drums talked back. Then the horn insisted, sweet and high, slightly detached perhaps, and Creole listened, commenting now and then, dry, and driving, beautiful and calm and old. Then they all came together again, and Sonny was part of the family again. I could tell this from his face. He seemed to have found, right there beneath his fingers, a damn brand-new piano. It seemed that he couldn't get over it. Then, for awhile, just being happy with Sonny, they seemed to be agreeing with him that brand-new pianos certainly were a gas.

Then Creole stepped forward to remind them that what they were playing was the blues. He hit something in all of them, he hit something in me, myself, and the music tightened and deepened, apprehension began to beat the air. Creole began to tell us what the blues were all about. They were not about anything very new. He and his boys up there were keeping it new, at the risk of ruin, destruction, madness, and death, in order to find new ways to make us listen. For, while the tale of how we suffer, and how we are delighted, and how we may triumph is never new, it always must be heard. There isn't any other tale to tell, it's the only light we've got in all this darkness.

And this tale, according to that face, that body, those strong hands on those strings, has another aspect in every country, and a new depth in every generation. Listen, Creole seemed to be saying, listen. Now these are Sonny's blues. He made the little black man on the drums know it,

and the bright, brown man on the horn. Creole wasn't trying any longer to get Sonny in the water. He was wishing him Godspeed. Then he stepped back, very slowly, filling the air with the immense suggestion that Sonny speak for himself.

Then they all gathered around Sonny and Sonny played. Every now and again one of them seemed to say, amen. Sonny's fingers filled the air with life, his life. But that life contained so many others. And Sonny went all the way back, he really began with the spare, flat statement of the opening phrase of the song. Then he began to make it his. It was very beautiful because it wasn't hurried and it was no longer a lament. I seemed to hear with what burning he had made it his, with what burning we had yet to make it ours, how we could cease lamenting. Freedom lurked around us and I understood, at last, that he could help us to be free if we would listen, that he would never be free until we did. Yet, there was no battle in his face now. I heard what he had gone through, and would continue to go through until he came to rest in earth. He had made it his: that long line, of which we knew only Mama and Daddy. And he was giving it back, as everything must be given back, so that, passing through death, it can live forever. I saw my mother's face again, and felt, for the first time, how the stones of the road she had walked on must have bruised her feet. I saw the moonlit road where my father's brother died. And it brought something else back to me, and carried me past it, I saw my little girl again and felt Isabel's tears again, and I felt my own tears begin to rise. And I was yet aware that this was only a moment, that the world waited outside as hungry as a tiger, and that trouble stretched above us, longer than the sky.

Then it was over. Creole and Sonny let out their breath, both soaking wet, and grinning. There was a lot of applause and some of it was real. In the dark, the girl came by and I asked her to take drinks to the bandstand. There was a long pause, while they talked up there in the indigo light and after awhile I saw the girl put a Scotch and milk on top of the piano for Sonny. He didn't seem to notice it, but just before they started playing again, he sipped from it and looked toward me, and nodded. Then he put it back on top of the piano. For me, then, as they began to play again, it glowed and shook above my brother's head like the very cup of trembling.

Imamu Amiri Baraka (LeRoi Jones) (1934–   )

Both through his writings and his moral example, Imamu Amiri Baraka has exerted an incalculable influence on a whole generation of young Black writers. From beat poet to racial polemicist to cultural spokesman of Black nationalism, his career has followed a logic of development related both to internal psychological imperatives and to external changes in American society. His painful but finally triumphant pilgrimage "toward the thing I had coming into the world, with no sweat: my blackness" has made much easier similar movements by dozens of other writers. It is not too much to say that Baraka has established the tone and pointed the direction for most Black writing of the 1970's.

Born Everett LeRoi Jones in Newark, New Jersey, on October 7, 1934, he grew up in a middle-class home, his father a postal official and his mother a social worker. A precocious boy, he wrote a comic strip in grade school and science fiction in Barringer High School, from which he was graduated at the age of fifteen. After a lonely year on a science scholarship at the Newark branch of Rutgers University, he transferred to Howard University, where he took a B.A. in English. During three years in the Air Force, he was stationed in such diverse places as Rantoul, Illinois, Puerto Rico, Europe, Africa, and the Middle East. Upon his discharge in 1957 he moved to New York to begin his literary career.

In the late 1950's and early 1960's Jones lived in Greenwich Village and on the Lower East Side, married a white girl, and studied at Columbia University and the New School for Social Research. After taking an M.A. at Columbia he taught first at the New School and then at the University of Buffalo and at Columbia. During these years, Jones was gaining a considerable reputation as poet and editor of the beat generation and as jazz critic for such magazines as *Downbeat, Metronome,* and *Jazz Review.* As poet he contributed to little magazines such as *The Naked Ear, The Floating Bear, Big Table, Combustion, Penny Poems, White Dove Review, Evergreen Review, Outburst, Provincetown Review, Burning Deck, Trobar, Beat Coast East, Quixote, Fuck You | A Magazine of the Arts, Locus Solus, Nomad, Signal, Niagara Frontier Review, The Seasons,* and *Set,* as well as to anthologies and to such established periodicals as *Poetry, The Nation, Beloit Poetry Journal, Massachusetts Review, Yale Literary Magazine,* and *The Village Voice.* His first two volumes of poetry were *Preface to a Twenty Volume Suicide Note* (1961) and *The Dead Lecturer* (1964). Not only was Jones a poet himself, but he was also something of a cultural entrepreneur, establishing in 1958 the Totem Press, which published such beat writers as Allen Ginsberg, Jack Kerouac, Gary Snyder, Philip Whalen, and others. He also edited the magazine *Yugen* and collaborated on *Kulchur* and *The Floating Bear.*

But Jones's acculturation to the white avant-garde was never complete.

This fact is attested not only by the early poem "Hymn to Lanie Poo," but by such an early organizational effort as the On Guard for Freedom Committee, a Harlem interracial group that he organized in 1961. In the mid-1960's his most important writing was dramatic; *The Baptism, The Toilet, Dutchman,* and *The Slave* were all produced in 1964. The anguish and ambivalence of a Black writer's relationship to white bohemia are emphatic in the last two of these, especially, and all four seethe with Jones' disgust for white values, which he expressed on the lecture platform as well as on the stage and in print. Turning his back on Greenwich Village and his white wife, he moved to Harlem to establish the Black Arts Repertory Theatre School. The brief but momentous activity of this group, cut short by political pressure, signified the change in Jones's literary emphasis from protesting to whites to speaking directly to Blacks.

The most recent phase of his career was initiated by his move in 1966 from Harlem home to Newark, where he started the Spirit House and the Spirit House Movers, a theatrical group. While teaching at San Fransicso State College in the spring of 1967, he consulted closely with the cultural nationalist Ron Karenga. Returning to Newark in time for the riot (or insurrection) of July of that year, he was attacked by police and later sentenced to a two-and-a-half to three-year term for illegal possession of a firearm by a judge who made much of his incendiary poetry. Legal appeals have kept him out of prison, but the manifest injustice of his trial only further convinced him of the futility of dealing with white systems. In the same month that he was in the courtroom— January 1968—the BCD (Black Community Development) of Newark was in the process of formation. As one of the three leaders of this movement, Jones assumed the name of Imamu Amiri Baraka and became a minister of the Kawaida faith (Muslim). Wearing African dress and often speaking Swahili, the members of BCD work for the cultural, social, and political autonomy and growth of Black Newark (New Ark). With inexhaustible energy Baraka oversees much of the activity of BCD while continuing to write and to explore the spiritual dimensions of Blackness.

Baraka's writing encompasses all the genres. His early work in poetry, often introspective and quiet, achieves moments of poignance and intense beauty as well as moments of suicidal despair. His poetry after *The Dead Lecturer* has been collected as *Black Magic* (1969), comprising *Sabotage* (poems written from 1961 to 1963), *Target Study* (poems written from 1963 to 1965), and *Black Art* (poems written in 1965 and 1966). The movement during this period is away from European and American forms, whether surrealistic, dadaist, or beat, and toward direct polemical expression, experiments in typography and Black idiom, and a search for spiritual truth. Of his poetry after 1966, which he is reluctant to publish under white auspices, he has said that it "is self-consciously spiritual, and stronger."

Like his poetry, Baraka's plays have changed in both method and theme. He has turned from the preoccupation with homosexuality of *The Baptism* and *The Toilet,* the ambivalent racial antagonism of *Dutchman,* and the nihilistic revolutionism of *The Slave* to the more hopeful revolutionary prospect of *Experimental Death Unit #1* and *Arm Yrself or Harm Yrself,* the Muslim allegory of *A Black Mass,* morality plays such as *Great Goodness of Life* and *Madheart,* the satirical burlesque *J-E-L-L-O,* and the ritual history of *Slave Ship.* Other plays include *The 8th Ditch* and *Home on the Range.* Most critics agree that *Dutchman* is Baraka's most fully realized dramatic achievement, but the usual critical criteria are inapplicable to much of his later work in the theater. His plays are always harrowing or exalting or both, depending upon the spectator's racial, ideological, and emotional perspectives.

Baraka's two works of fiction, *The System of Dante's Hell* (1965) and *Tales* (1967), are fragmentary, impressionistic, often autobiographical narratives usually devoid of plot in any conventional sense but full of vivid images, symbolic episodes, and nightmarish truths. His nonfiction, on the other hand, tends to rely on incisive argument and rhetoric that is carefully controlled, even if hyperbole is a favorite device. *Blues People* (1963) and *Black Music* (1967) explore the social dimension of a prime mode of Black creativity. *Home: Social Essays* (1966) and *Raise Race Rays Raze: Essays Since 1965* (1971) graph the author's move toward Blackness. *Black Value System* (1970) and, with Fundi (Billy Abernathy), *In Our Terribleness* (1970) reveal his present constructive emphasis within a Black framework. Always, whether philosophical or polemical, Baraka's prose reveals a mind of depth as well as agility.

On his own terms, Baraka must now be understood as a Black magician, a poet-priest-prophet of the re-emerging Black nation, an Imamu. On a more personal level, he has helped many readers to discover or recover their Black selves. To white readers he has revealed the painful reality of their own racism.

Baraka has not yet been the subject of a book. Some biographical sources are Saul Gottlieb's interview, "They Think You're an Airplane and You're Really a Bird!" *Evergreen Review,* XI (December 1967), 50–58, 96–97; R. H. Smith, "Jersey Justice and LeRoi Jones," *Publishers' Weekly,* CXCIII (January 15, 1968), 66; Gerald Weales, "The Day LeRoi Jones Spoke on Penn Campus—What Were the Blacks Doing in the Balcony?" *The New York Times Magazine,* May 4, 1969, pp. 38–40, 44, 48, 52, 54, 56, 58; and David Llorens, "Ameer (LeRoi Jones) Baraka," *Ebony,* XXIV (August 1969), 75–78, 80–83, an invaluable account of Baraka's activity in Newark; and Murray Kempton, "Newark: Keeping Up with LeRoi Jones," *The New York Review of Books,* XV (July 2, 1970), 21–23. Four important statements of Baraka's views on Black writing are "Philistinism and the Negro Writer," in *Anger, and Beyond* (1966), edited by Herbert Hill, pp. 51–61; the foreword to *Black Fire* (1968), edited by LeRoi Jones and Larry Neal; "The Black Aesthetic," *Negro Digest,* XVIII (September 1969), 5–6; and "Black (Art) Drama Is the Same as Black Life," *Ebony,* XXVI (February 1971), 74–76, 78, 80, 82.

Books treating Baraka include David Littlejohn, *Black on White* (1966); Harold Cruse, *The Crisis of the Negro Intellectual* (1967); Loften Mitchell, *Black Drama* (1967); Edward Margolies, *Native Sons* (1968); and Doris E. Abramson, *Negro Playwrights in the American Theatre*

1925–1959 (1969). Donald B. Gibson has three essays on Baraka in *Five Black Writers* (1970).

The following critical articles may also be consulted: Denise Levertov, "Poets of the Given Ground," *The Nation,* CXCII (October 14, 1961), 251–252; Phillip Roth, "Channel X: Two Plays on the Race Conflict," *The New York Review of Books,* II (May 28, 1964), 10–13; George Dennison, "The Demagogy of LeRoi Jones," *Commentary,* XXXIX (1965), 67–70; Clarence Major, "The Poetry of LeRoi Jones," *Negro Digest,* XIV (March 1965), 54–56; Hugh Nelson, "LeRoi Jones' *Dutchman:* A Brief Ride on a Doomed Ship," *Educational Theatre Journal,* XX (February 1968), 53–59; Paul Velde, "LeRoi Jones: Pursued by the Furies," *Commonweal,* LXXXVIII (1968), 440–441; Kathryn Jackson, "LeRoi Jones and the New Black Writers of the Sixties," *Freedomways,* IX (1969), 232–247; Maria K. Mootry, "Themes and Symbols in Two Plays by LeRoi Jones," *Negro Digest,* XVIII (April 1969), 42–47; Louis Phillips, "LeRoi Jones and Contemporary Black Drama," in *The Black American Writer* (1969), edited by C. W. E. Bigsby, Vol. II, 203–217; Charlotte Otten, "LeRoi Jones: Napalm Poet," *Concerning Poetry,* III (Spring 1970), 5–11; Daphne S. Reed, "LeRoi Jones: High Priest of the Black Arts Movement," *Educational Theatre Journal,* XXII (1970), 53–59; Tom S. Reck, "Archetypes in LeRoi Jones' *Dutchman,*" *Studies in Black Literature,* I (Spring 1970), 66–68; Cecil M. Brown, "Black Literature and LeRoi Jones," *Black World,* XIX (June 1970), 24–31; Norman Moser, "A Revolutionary Art: Leroi Jones, Ed Bullins, and the Black Revolution," *December,* XII (1970), 180–190; Charles D. Peavy, "Myth, Magic, and Manhood in LeRoi Jones' *Madheart,*" *Studies in Black Literature,* I (Summer 1970), 12–20; Julian Rice, "LeRoi Jones' *Dutchman:* A Reading," *Contemporary Literature,* XII (1971), 42–59; and John Ferguson, "*Dutchman* and *The Slave,*" *Modern Drama,* XIII (1971), 398–405.

Preface to a Twenty Volume Suicide Note

For Kellie Jones, born 16 May 1959

Lately, I've become accustomed to the way
The ground opens up and envelopes me
Each time I go out to walk the dog.
Or the broad edged silly music the wind
Makes when I run for a bus . . .

Things have come to that.

And now, each night I count the stars,
And each night I get the same number.
And when they will not come to be
    counted,
I count the holes they leave.

Nobody sings anymore.

And then last night, I tiptoed up
To my daughter's room and heard her
Talking to someone, and when I opened
The door, there was no one there . . .
Only she on her knees, peeking into

Her own clasped hands.

An Agony. As Now.

I am inside someone
who hates me. I look
out from his eyes. Smell
what fouled tunes come in
to his breath. Love his
wretched women.

Slits in the metal, for sun. Where
my eyes sit turning, at the cool air
the glance of light, or hard flesh
rubbed against me, a woman, a man,
without shadow, or voice, or meaning.

This is the enclosure (flesh,
where innocence is a weapon. An
abstraction. Touch. (Not mine.
Or yours, if you are the soul I had
and abandoned when I was blind and had
my enemies carry me as a dead man
(if he is beautiful, or pitied.

It can be pain. (As now, as all his
flesh hurts me.) It can be that. Or
pain. As when she ran from me into
that forest.
        Or pain, the mind
silver spiraled whirled against the
sun, higher than even old men thought

God would be. Or pain. And the other. The
yes. (Inside his books, his fingers. They
are withered yellow flowers and were never
beautiful.) The yes. You will, lost soul, say
'beauty.' Beauty, practiced, as the tree. The
slow river. A white sun in its wet sentences.

Or, the cold men in their gale. Ecstasy. Flesh
or soul. The yes. (Their robes blown. Their bowls
empty. They chant at my heels, not at yours.)
    Flesh
or soul, as corrupt. Where the answer moves
    too quickly.
Where the God is a self, after all.)

Cold air blown through narrow blind eyes.
    Flesh,
white hot metal. Glows as the day with its sun.
It is a human love, I live inside. A bony skeleton
you recognize as words or simple feeling.

But it has no feeling. As the metal, is hot, it is
    not,
given to love.

It burns the thing
inside it. And that thing
screams.

A Poem for Black Hearts

For Malcolm's eyes, when they broke
the face of some dumb white man, For
Malcolm's hands raised to bless us
all black and strong in his image
of ourselves, For Malcolm's words
fire darts, the victor's tireless
thrusts, words hung above the world
change as it may, he said it, and
for this he was killed, for saying,
and feeling, and being/ change, all
collected hot in his heart, For Malcolm's
heart, raising us above our filthy cities,
for his stride, and his beat, and his address
to the grey monsters of the world, For Malcolm's
pleas for your dignity, black men, for your life,
black men, for the filling of your minds
with righteousness, For all of him dead and

gone and vanished from us, and all of him which
clings to our speech black god of our time.
For all of him, and all of yourself, look up,
black man, quit stuttering and shuffling, look up,
black man, quit whining and stooping, for all of him,
For Great Malcolm a prince of the earth, let nothing in us rest
until we avenge ourselves for his death, stupid animals
that killed him, let us never breathe a pure breath if
we fail, and white men call us faggots till the end of
the earth.

leroy

I wanted to know my mother when she sat
looking sad across the campus in the late 20's
into the future of the soul, there were black angels
straining above her head, carrying life from our ancestors,
and knowledge, and the strong nigger feeling. She sat
(in that photo in the yearbook I showed Vashti) getting into
new blues, from the old ones, the trips and passions
showered on her by her own. Hypnotizing me, from so far
ago, from that vantage of knowledge passed on to her passed on
to me and all the other black people of our time.
When I die, the consciousness I carry I will to
black people. May they pick me apart and take the
useful parts, the sweet meat of my feelings. And leave
the bitter bullshit rotten white parts
alone.

Black People!

What about that bad short you saw last week
on Frelinghuysen, or those stoves and refrigerators, record players
in Sears, Bambergers, Klein's, Hahnes', Chase, and the smaller joosh
enterprises? What about that bad jewelry, on Washington Street, and
those couple of shops on Springfield? You know how to get it, you can
get it, no money down, no money never, money dont grow on trees no
way, only whitey's got it, makes it with a machine, to control you
you cant steal nothin from a white man, he's already stole it he owes
you anything you want, even his life. All the stores will open if you
will say the magic words. The magic words are: Up against the wall mother
fucker this is a stick up! Or: Smash the window at night (these are magic
actions) smash the windows daytime, anytime, together, let's smash the
window drag the shit from in there. No money down. No time to pay. Just
take what you want. The magic dance in the street. Run up and down Broad
Street niggers, take the shit you want. Take their lives if need be, but
get what you want what you need. Dance up and down the streets, turn all
the music up, run through the streets with music, beautiful radios on

Market Street, they are brought here especially for you. Our brothers
are moving all over, smashing at jellywhite faces. We must make our own
World, man, our own world, and we can not do this unless the white man
is dead. Let's get together and killhim my man, let's get to gather the fruit
of the sun, let's make a world we want black children to grow and learn in
do not let your children when they grow look in your face and curse you by
pitying your tomish ways.

The Last Days of the American Empire
(Including Some Instructions for
Black People)

NEWS PICTURES

information

Death throes of the empire. UGLY CRACK-
ERS! Negro policemen with sad twisted eyes.
Strong faces (big Mammas with their arms
folded, lonely children whose future lives you
wonder about), black faces set into America.
There is no America without those whites of
eyes against black skin. . . .

ALL KINDS OF VICTIMS. People being
burned.

What does America mean to you? Does it
mean what these pictures say? Well it do. It sure
do. It surely definitely absolutely does. This is
worldAmerica. You are in the trance of the
White People. You will be escorted to your cell.
In fact you will be pre-born into your cell. "And
there you can be quaint in our lighter moments.
Now, for christ sakes, you have to admit that
Mantan Moreland was funny." (This man I was
talking to meant "amusing.")

Is there anyone in the realworldAmerica who
thinks Slavery Has Been Abolished? Or for that
matter, another irrelevance, would there be someone in the statesies so stoned, as would qualify
America as being less sick than the invention of
Lee Oswald? (Many oil men are inventors, and
they have weird hobbies, like their freakish fake-
man brothers, bombing churchchildren through
the tobacco spit of their brains.)

These pictures should make anybody think.
This is what America looks like now. Where is
the hope? Why should this terrible place not
fall? Who can *dare* defend it? Look at your
LEADERS. What do they look like? Do they look
like you, any of you??? If they do, then you
have something to lose. And chances are you'll
lose it.

It is the blackness of the sufferers, their absolute existence as a *different race,* that cheapens
any further social description as to what, actually,
is going on? Explanation is a selfish act. But The
Man says, What's going on? What do you mean
people are suffering? I didn't realize. . . . What?
That it was real and really happening and real
and really happening, but only to the niggers,
and those white people too stupid to be rich in
this last fat bastion of the white man, doomed
now to go down hard, and eaten, smashed at,
from its insides by its acquisitions, and the
"holiness" of them. Black People will prove to
be the most costly of those acquisitions.

The white eyes of those who say (and with
them the brutal cuteness of the Negro middle
class, who perhaps will never understand what's
really going on till they reexamine the value of
their social connections, *i.e.,* it is a scientific
guess that the white man will not be El Hombre
too much longer, *i.e.,* you cannot fail to recognize
the difference between Boone, Daniel and Boone,
Pat) How can these people live this way? Why
don't they do something? No one ought to deny
the validity of that question. Finally our enemies
are right. Why don't they do something?

Maybe what a few of the white eyes saw, showing up in Bedford Stuyvesant, or St. Francesville,
Louisiana—to catch a part of time-now, to be
exposed to a reality, a basic truth of the world—
filthy makeshift playgrounds, the children's eyes
deep in their black skin, woodplank streets in parts
of black Brooklyn, and summer, everybody outside, children playing on their knees, men sitting or
walking slowly, or staring, or laid out in the
street dying in sneakers—these are truths the
television will not even use as news, except when
the people out on those streets start moving, like

they did "last summer," and being thrashed for at least assuming the dignity of an organism that will react when it is struck. This is the rest of the world. This is what the good white man cannot connect himself with; cannot or will not, it makes no real difference, the results are the same. Most white men I meet say they are not responsible. Perhaps it is best to be left there. To take them at their word, that I'm hip, you are not responsible to the world. But you will be held responsible, anyway, since you own it, you think.

But then, who demands these whippings and bombings? Is J. Edgar Hoover an intelligent man? Will Lyndon B. Johnson submit to an aptitude test? Why isn't automation a help to man? Who is H. L. Hunt? Is there any reason why all the world should be working and dying and growing hopeless with rage, just to feed fat white faces. What is this bullshit?

Black people, if you can steal this expensive book, at your liberal employer's, for instance, though he may even be "a friend of your people" —just remember the only reason you are there in the first place is *for the money, to stay alive, to survive*—steal this book, it will make you very very hot, but even so you will learn that your brothers and sisters are strong, strong, under all the horrors of The White Hell. And in seeing the horrors, and by becoming angry, but even beyond that anger realizing what strength you have— YOU BLACK PEOPLE ARE STRONG, remember that—then you will realize that it is now not even the time to be angry, I mean so angry that you will not remember that you are strong, much stronger than the white eyes. Then you will not need to be angry any longer, you will have gotten to that point, where you will be absolutely rational. Our singing is beautiful, but we can sing while we move. MOVE!

To be rational now in this insane asylum, where we are held prisoner by the inmates. They want us to be their keepers. Do you Negroes like being keepers for these sadists? But to be rational. Rational men would do something to stop the mad, before they destroy not only the asylum, but the rest of the world. There is no reason why we should allow the white man to destroy the world, just because he will not share it, will not share it with the *majority*. The nerve, the stupid arrogance, the ignorance, AND FEAR, in those cracker eyes, those firemen, state patrolmen, the dog holders, all that fear is in the bones of this society. Those mad white policemen are the soul

of this society. And their technology has made them strong. We have accepted that technology, as fact, as useful to our dreams, etc., but its owners are mad because they do not value reality, and therefore they are not real. Hollow Men, Paper Tigers, Closet Queens of the Universe.

Look at those weak fag faces on those patrolmen arresting that beautiful chick, and finally there is something in her face which is stronger than anything in white eyes' life. Because she has had to live in a world of extremes, which is the widening of the consciousness. And this is the "hip" syndrome, simple awareness—America will make you aware if you are black. So that, for instance, in any argument with a liberal white man, finally the black man must grow speechless with rage, because there is always a point beyond which no black-white argument can be pushed with reason. We know what has happened to us, to our mothers and fathers. What more can be said? The black man was brought to the West in chains, he is still in chains. He is still a captive, Negroes, a captive people. What can you say? Look at any pictures of America. They must show the final impasse between white America and Black America. Pictures like these should be used when the black man runs out of words. When the exasperation of explaining his life to justify his desires makes him silent with rage, in the face of *any* white man.

There is an absolute gulf that separates white from black. Slave/SlaveMaster are two different worlds. Segregation reinforces itself, spawns, continues, *separate* cultures. So the Beatles can make millions of dollars putting on a sophisticated coon show, which drives weak white girls into gism fits—all that energy and force, but even so transmuted and disguised. But it is still the Chuck Berrys, the Muddy Waters' etc., who first harnessed that energy. The Ornette Colemans. No matter the use such changed and weakened force might be put to in Winosha, Wisconsin, or by Lynda-Bird's fake Watusi, the real power remains where it naturally falls.

The force of the Negro's life in America has always been very evident in America, no matter the lengths to which white Americans have tried to hide and obfuscate it. But I mean you cannot, for instance, blame any white man for liking Andre Previn more than Cecil Taylor; it is his life that is reflected by his choices (is, in fact, those choices). Most white men in America are closer to Andre Previn than CT or Duke Ellington either, for that matter. White America reflects its energies by its choices. You think that the hero-image in American flicks is homosexual merely by *chance?*

Reality is only useful to people who have some use for it. Otherwise they get something else. But everybody's got to pay some kind of dues, one way or another. It won't even matter, finally, if the person happens to be "innocent"; there is no such thing. If you are alive, now, you are involved with now, even if only by default. You know what "Germans" still means. First of all, now, it means liar. No matter what the man can tell you, *e.g.,* "I was head of the anti-Nazi forces, etc., etc.," the word "German" is sufficient to give any story the shakes. What? you will say. What . . . are you talking about . . . aren't you a German? And that's the end of that. In a few years, "American" will have that connotation, for the rest of the world. (In most of the world it has that connotation already.) And, even more horrible, it will not even matter to the rest of the world that the Negro was "the victim," etc. People will simply ask, Why? And, given the plausibility of supposing that most men would rather not be victims, the fact will remain that any "answer" to that Why? will have to be shaky. The only answer could be, I was in the trance of the whitepeople. But that is a cop out, I'm afraid. Your questioner will not even bother to point out certain obvious alternatives. You will be listed simply as "Coward."

But there are many Negroes now, young and otherwise, who have no use for the role (of victim) the white man has cast him in. Again, look at the black faces. The young boys marching across the street with their signs, or the young fox wet and screaming her defiance, her hatred, but most of all her *will* to live, and to fight back. Look at the young Northern middle-class black lady sitting demurely on the pavement surrounded by cops. Look at her face and posture. You cannot lie to this woman. She knows you're lying. She reads *The Times.* She knows the *New York Times* lies. The poor black man will not even have had to read it to know it lies. "It's whitey's paper, ain't it? What you expect?" Right again. (I looked at a photograph of a black cop arresting a black woman.) Dig for a few seconds, the big spook cop's mouth. He's got his lips pinched together, staring at the lady. BLACK NEW YORK COP SGT. NUMBER 67, YOU KNOW YOU'RE WRONG!! YOU ARE FIGHTING YOUR OWN PEOPLE!

Another sense gotten from any true picture of this society is the isolation of the black man in America. He is a different race from the white man. The poor white has been brain-washed into wanting to kill the black man, so that black man won't get his job or his little girl's drawers. All the immigrants to this country, the Italians, the Irish, the Jews, etc., where are they in this struggle? All the white people in America who have grounds for dissent, and will not dissent. They have had to pay a price for their shaky seat in this enterprise. The dues I spoke of, which even they have to pay, is to be mistreated, used, duped, and still put out on the street to handle America's light work. Where are the Italian Anarchists? The Sacco-Vanzetti frame put them on the skids, and the Mafia takes up the wild strong ones whose lifeneeds still put them outside straightup WASP-AMERICA. The Jewish Radicals, Socialists, Communists, etc., of the 30's, what happened to them? Have they all disappeared into those sullen suburbs hoping Norman Podhoretz or Leslie Fiedler will say something real? The price the immigrants paid to get into America was that they had to become Americans. The black man *cannot* become an American (unless we get a different set of *rules*) because he is black. And even the hopeless CORE representative I met who claimed black men were as evil as white men can never become a white man. Though he might desire it more than anything in the universe. He cannot change the one thing about him that is most important in this place. He must remain, even deluded, a certain kind of black man. The black man's dissent cannot be gotten rid of. It just builds. And builds.

But the white man splits the black man into cadres, "classes," when there is none except blackness—which the white man is the first to realize. Against the filth of America (and with it, the white West—the British, the French, the Germans, the Belgians, the Portuguese, the Dutch, etc., and their ugly little roles in Asia, Africa, Latin America) the black man has to be absolutely *together* in order to survive. But too often, certainly most times in the past, the white man has been able to win out, maintain his stranglehold on us, merely because most of us were so busy looking out for ourselves, which is the "ME ONLY" syndrome, that we were willing to let the worst things in the world happen to our brothers. With black people all over the world dying the most horrible kinds of death imaginable some fools would still be walking around with their behinds in the air saying, "But I'm Cool." Well the word is No You're Not, not as long as one of your brothers and sisters is being messed over by "the man."

Get it together! We must lock arms, take each other's hand, and never stop working until the stone is rolled over this deep stinking hole even some of our "civil rights leaders" speak of as if it were paradise.

Since this book is so expensive, it will fall into the hands of more MC Negroes than people out on the block. (MC meaning middle class or master of ceremonies, and in America the ceremony is blood violence and hatred.)

MC Negroes, I know you can still be made angry too. Perhaps something in the faces of white terrorists will frighten you out from under your shaky cover stories; cover stories like "middle class" or "college trained" or "qualified Negro" or any other fake entrances into this crumbling Rome, which somehow cut off your testicles, usually with the hard cold edge of a dollar bill. ANYBODY CAN PRINT MONEY! BUT NOT EVERYBODY CAN LIVE IN THE WORLD WITH THE PEACEFUL STRENGTH OF THE TRULY VIRTUOUS MAN. (White Americans cannot.)

If you have made some "progress," or somehow got your hands on a good taste of white eyes' loot, keep it moving among your people; also your knowledge. We are in this *together,* let us help each other and begin rolling that huge black stone. *Most* of the world is with us.

I cannot repeat it too many times, nor can any of you black people repeat it too many times to one another. DO NOT ALLOW YOURSELF TO BE SEPARATED from your brothers and sisters, or your culture. This is what makes us think we are weak. But we are not weak. Remember the stories of your parents and grandparents. We have survived over three hundred years of the worst treatment possible, and still come up strong. All Charles has to show for those years is his loot, but the world changes each second, and Charles's hands grow more and more spastic, his lies more and more obvious. For instance, where would the US Olympic Team be without the black man??? This analogy can be extended into any meaningful level of American life. The black man should dig, for

instance, that he is one of the chief reasons this society, these Mad American White People (. . . MAWPS ∴ .) can continue to exercise their will over the rest of the world. We black people, by our labor, are supporting these murderers. It is a paradox, but one no black man should fail to recognize. Even the isolated Negro who has gained "acceptance" into this Gomorrah or the hard-working black man in a "defense" plant or steel mill, must realize the vicious uses his entrance into the mainstream will be put to. All you Negroes making "good livings" now, do you know what the fruits of your labor are being used for? Usually your labors contribute heavily to the murders of nonwhite peoples all over the globe.

Where have all these "police actions" in which the U.S. has taken the major part since the Second World War been happening? And police action is a good phrase because that's what white eye is now—anywhere—a policeman working feverishly to keep the nonwhite peoples down, in colonial or semi-slave positions whether they are American Negroes, Africans, Asians, or Latin Americans. It's all the same. The same mad white people you see in any *Life Magazine* home are our real "ambassadors" all over the world; spiritual cops and cretins. (Do you think that the television series "Burke's Law," where the hero is a white millionaire who is also chief of police, is *accidental?* This is the way these folks think, and what they legitimately aspire to. Ditto, in the case of James Bond, the suave, unbeatable fascist. All these things merely prepare the American's psyche for his role in world domination.)

What I am saying is that there is *no chance* that the American white man will change. Why should he? Isn't this the richest nation in the world? The gross national product rose to $624 billion this year, the growth figure over last year's $584 billion is about $45 billion. This money is not being made because the white eye is ready to "understand" the needs of the world, but because he has been even more successful recently in suppressing those needs. Can there be even one American so out of it as not to realize that this money, this luxury, exists only at the expense of the rest of the world's peoples? Can there be a Negro so out of it as not to understand that the worst racists in South Africa are brothers to the men he sees in our newspapers daily being celebrated for their "humanity"? It is sickening, for instance, to see in our free newspapers accounts every day of how the white man is trying to save the world. This is true. He is trying to save the world—as his personal victory garden and commode. As for instance, in the Congo, where thousands of black people are slaughtered to make the world safe for the white man. The only difference between the Congo and, say, Philadelphia, Mississippi, is the method the white man employs to suppress and murder; essentially, it is the same scene, the same people dying for the same reasons. And of course, they are the same murderers who kill our people all over the globe.

But it sickens me to know that there are supposedly intelligent black people walking around who would actually believe that the Belgians and Americans flew those paratroopers into the Congo for humanitarian reasons. My God! You mean Charles would send planeloads of paratroopers (plus those divisions of white mercenaries) into the Congo to save . . . how many? twenty-one white hostages? and yet still be unable to send even one Vietnamese helicopter to Mississippi to find out who assassinated Medgar Evers, or maybe one Special Forces (anti-liberation "guerillas") to Birmingham, so maybe just one shred of information might be turned up concerning the identities of the dynamite murderers of those four little church children.

Does it make sense to any of you that Uncle Sap will spend millions to "put West Germany back on its feet," and yet have a place such as Harlem in the world's showplace, which they will not spend one honest nickel to alter or intelligently repair. And there are Harlems in every American city where there are great numbers of Negroes. But even more diabolical is this fact, that even the most liberal white man in America does not want to see the existing system really *changed*. What this liberal white man wants is for the black man somehow to be "elevated" Martin Luther King style so that he might be able to enter this society with some kind of general prosperity and join the white man in a truly democratic defense of this cancer, which would make the black man equally culpable for the evil done to the rest of the world. The liberal white man wants the black man to learn to love this America as much as he does, so that the black man will want to murder the world's peoples, his own brothers and sisters Moise

Tshombe style. And let no black man forget all the black traitors all over the world, most of whom, like Tshombe or JaJa Wachuku of Nigeria, have been so brainwashed that they might even think what they are doing (*i.e.,* helping in the murder of thousands of black people) is right. One man, an American Negro, George Schuyler, has even come out on the side of a straightup oppressor, Portugal, defending its actions in Angola where it murdered thousands of black Africans. Black people, do not forget Negroes like this, remember them and every detail of their treason. It will help us to be more scientific.

But these are the Last Days Of The American Empire. Understand that Lyndon Johnson is a war criminal of the not so distant future. Understand that the power structure that controls this country and the world has grown desperate . . . in the face of so much prosperity, but prosperity that is coupled with more unrest than ever before. There are wars of national liberation going on all over the world. The Second World War made emphatic America's newly won security as absolute world ruler, but it also shook up most of the other colonial empires of the world. The need to have that war seen as "A War Against Fascism" contributed dramatically to the organization of many of the world's colonial peoples into armed nationalistic liberation fronts who saw as their task, even after the war against fascism, the eradication of any form of colonialism or imperialism. British, French, and Dutch colonialism suffered almost irreparable losses, but these sorry people are still trying, by one ruse or another, to regain control of their subject peoples. But where before there were only cries of outrage, now these European white eyes are met with bullets and bombs.

There is a war of liberation going on now in America, although the black American has still not gotten hip enough to organize a National Liberation Front that would include all groups and aspirations, and sweep, by the increase of its power, right over this failing power structure, and push these sadists and perverts into the sea. That is the unity that is needed. When will we be strong enough and wise enough to commit ourselves to this kind of unity?

In one sense, when I speak of unity, I mean that seeing one young man being followed menacingly down a road by half the Crackers in Georgia, makes me wonder what it was, specifically, that moved him to do this. I want to know what was he thinking, sprawled in the dust, holding his head, knees pulled up against his chest? I want to know did this young black man really feel that by letting some subhuman super-fools abuse and beat him, he was somehow accomplishing something. That is, I cannot yet understand what kind of mind shift I would have to undergo, for instance, so that I would be convinced, as these rednecks were working me over, that I was doing something to break Charlie's back. The unity I desire would be most apparent when most Black People realized that the murderous philosophies of the Western white man take many curious forms. And that one of the most bizarre methods the man has yet to utilize against black people is to instruct large masses of black people that they are to control their tempers, turn the other cheek, etc., in the presence of, but even more so under the feet and will of, the most brutal killers the world has yet produced.

The kind of unity I would want to see among black Americans would at least produce a huge WHY? when some gentle oppressor talked convincingly about pacifism and nonviolence. In the white West nonviolence means simply doing nothing to change this pitiful society, just do as you have been doing, *e.g.,* suffer, and by some beautiful future-type miracle the minds of the masses of white men will be changed, and they will finally come around to understanding that the majority of peoples in the world deserve to live in that world, no longer plagued by the white man's disgusting habits. But why, WHY, must anyone wait until these cretins . . . change . . . ha ha . . . their famous minds, before people are permitted to live with the simple dignity any man ought to know? Why indeed? The answer is that these askers for nonviolence, *i.e.,* virtuous stagnation, are usually people who would suffer, or at least think they would, if this society were changed with the suddenness of the next second. Even the black man who preaches nonviolence is essentially functioning under the trance of the white people. There are black men who love the white man so dearly, who love, I must suppose, the nice warm feeling of shoe sole on their woolly heads, that they would do nothing to see that the white man relinquishes his stranglehold on the world. But then, there are other black people in America and the rest of the world who will not rest until that stranglehold is broken. So poised

against the image of the young man hugging his knees in the dust, there are also images of young men and old men silhouetted on their porches with their rifles, watchful all through long black Southern nights, men who have no desire to be masters or slaves, but who cannot live in the world as it is without at least attempting to defend what little of the world they know is theirs. I look at an old man sitting next to his gun, or a young man holding his like in a photo to be sent back to a girlfriend, and I wonder about the young man holding his head in the dust. I wonder also about Robert Williams, the ex-NAACP leader from Monroe, North Carolina, who was framed on a kidnapping charge by local officials with the help of the Federal Government simply because he had "advocated" that black men realize that they were living among savages and barbarians and that they must protect themselves and their families, because the Government was made up of these same savages and barbarians. Mr. Williams is in exile in Cuba now for that reason; that he made a few rational statements about the nature of the white American, and what possibly ought to be done when faced with one, and such reasoning is dangerous to the white man, and the white man will have none of it.

The kind of unity I would like to see among black Americans is a unity that would permit most of them to understand that the murder of Patrice Lumumba in the Congo and the murder of Medgar Evers were conducted by the same people. I want them also to realize that a man like Robert Williams faced the same fate, for the same reasons. I want them to realize that any attempt the black man makes to be seen or heard, clearly, honestly, from where he has been made to live during the three-hundred-odd year residency in the West, is always met with repression and violence. Or else such attempts will be subverted by the wills of the holiest of white men, the liberals, who do not want to be our bosses, but our guides. But listen, black men, these liberals are usually agents. That is, even though what these men say might seem to come freely out of an untroubled heart, chances are these words, *e.g.,* "moderation," pacifism, nonviolence, gradualism, etc., etc., seek merely to dim your passion and turn your most rational needs and desires into evil fantasies white (and black) schoolchildren condemn when they are learning to count. Ask the next white liberal you meet, would he be willing to let you, you black man, be his, this white man's, "spiritual guide." And also when the next white man comes up to you and describes the sparkling democratic utopias of the future, remember that he is asking you to pull your knees up against your chest, head hidden, and dream in the dust of never-never land. And when the next missionary comes on to you about nonviolence use his own bible as your lever, pointing out that the God of the Jews was not particularly interested in turning cheeks, *viz.,* all those drowned Egyptians.

But opposed to that image of dreaming in the dust, there is the image of one brother with the sign reading NOW. Look at his face—there's nothing any kind of missionary type could tell this man. He looks like he's beyond all the loads of buckrogers happiness bullshit, and is demanding simple truth. And the sign says NOW, which is clear enough. In news photos all over America there are many other signs of the times: LOVE THY NEIGHBOR (a sign maybe which ought to sit in huge letters in the White House and Pentagon and CIA); WHO NEEDS NIGGERS (from the self-confessed purest of whities); WHERE IS DEMOCRACY (a woman with a very good question): FREEDOM (the most ambiguous term known to man, if Barry Goldwater, the "half-Jewish" Uebermensch, can use it, to rally his 25,000,000, and Martin Luther King can use it, presumably with a different sense intended. But to BG freedom means, like they say, free enterprise, which means OPEN YOUR POCKETS 80 per cent of the world, big white meatface wants to get his rocks off!! That is the freedom to murder, rob, and lie to any people who stand in the way of your own holy luxury.) There is also a sign, on an old beatup Southern store that reads NEGRO KEEP OUT. There are signs like this all over America. And where there are no written signs, brains have been marked, so that the same sentiment leaps out of people's eyes. And finally, the paradox is that these people are right: NEGRO STAY OUT! Because now, when Charles is up tight all over the world, and will of course ask the black lackeys to help him out, it is high time the black man began to make use of the Tonto-syndrome, *i.e.,* leave The Lone Ranger to his own devices, and his own kind of death.

There are pictures of very old black men and women in the news too. Some of the faces look as if they were too old to be lied to. And there is an essential unity existing among these old faces that can no longer be put on by trinkets and fake wampum, and the face of the young man with the NOW sign, just above his eyes. Add to these images, the images of the black men standing on their porches with their rifles looking into a night made unfriendly by the hideousness of the white man's ego, and you will probably get a sense of the powerful emotions and will for release that is crackling in the psyches of the majority of black men today. But there are crucial American social paradoxes that the black man must also understand if he is really to understand the nature of his enemy. For instance, Negroes have been killed and beaten in Mississippi, Alabama, etc., for even attempting to register to vote. In the North, Negroes have long mustered a heavy voting bloc, and because of this have some degree of token political power. But the ugly paradox is to be seen everywhere in the North, the promised land. This token political power can do nothing to change the basic structure of the society. This society, for as long as it has functioned, was never meant to be equitable as far as black men were concerned. It was made for the white man, and the black man was brought here only to be *used,* to promote the luxury of the white man. That was the only reason. It still is the only reason the black man is alive in the West today, that continued exploitative use. But one day, and very soon, the white man might just look up, hip again, and see that the black man has outlived his usefulness. Then the murders will break out in earnest.

So it is a very grim spectacle to see all these Negroes beaten and brutalized for trying to vote, and some ofays must fall on the floor laughing every time they think of it. Because finally in those Southern states, or in the rest of America for that matter, who could you vote for, Negro? I mean, do you really think that by your getting a chance to vote on these criminals who run for political office in America, that somehow you'll be getting closer to peace and social justice? You cannot really think that! I cannot believe that you can still believe that, after so many years of lies and abuse. The choice on almost any level you care to name is roughly like that contest between Lyndon Johnson and Barry Goldwater, in the South most times even worse—and if there's any black man anywhere in the world who thinks that either one of those chumps is working for him, he is laboring under a hideous delusion, or else maybe he is in the Tshombe-bag, which will soon be converted into a shroud.

The main difference right now between the Northern and Southern Negro is that in the South the fight is still for equal rights, civil rights, etc., whereas in the North, the black man already has seen the bad faith of these terms, and has realized now for a long time that these rights we are asked to move toward, are less than abstract rhetoric. Last summer the Northern urban industrial towns popped like mean firecrackers hooked up from ghetto to ghetto. Perhaps next summer these firecrackers will grow even larger —and it was largely in the North, where presumably all these civil rights etc., have been attained, where these most recent demonstrations against white law have taken place. In the South the madness of the oppressors and their stupid henchmen, the poor white, is completely out in the open, the lines already clearly drawn. In the North, because of the lies and chicanery of the Northern industrialist's social form the lines may seem less clearly drawn, the oppressor's hand more heavily veiled, but because of this veil, an even heavier sense of frustration incites the black man to anger. In the South, you know the landscape is for real, in the North they try to tell you it's not. It is the added weight of being lied to, on top of every other indignity, that makes it all so hard to take. And then some white man hearing about oppressed Negroes on television will ask you for a little rational conversation on the subject. This will be a man (this hypothetical questioner) who probably does not know that policemen are menacing subhumans, whose sociocultural conditioning—because they are usually grandsons of immigrants, *i.e.,* poor whites—has usually prepared them to hate niggers even before they get the official instructions (like James Bond) that they are "licensed to kill." The American policeman is the foulest social category in the world today, whether domestic, *e.g.,* "New York's Finest," or international (Humanitarians dropping out of the clouds, etc.).

You may see a barefoot South Carolina Negro,

just grinning quietly—you wonder what's in behind those tired eyes—or you see another man just walking along, outwardly desolate, hands jammed deep in his pockets, and again you wonder, knowing and not knowing. Or you see a scene in Harlem or Bedford Stuyvesant, and know, that even in the North, the ghettoes (compounds) duplicate the South, and only add new frustrations not unlike the old. Sitting on garbage cans, thinking, or sleeping on benches, dreaming, or even pushing those "Jewish airplanes" in the garment center, grown men doing what they call a boy's job, but then still get sharp on weekends and go out hunting foxes. Blind anger sometimes in Georgia or the Bronx; staring at its image will set you off again, thinking of all these strong sweet people, their joy, even of those old hip black moles of men whose only conspicuous association with this century is a button that says, "I am registered, are you?"

What we would see in any realistic photo essay of America would be the image, pinpoints of light which show us the running sore called America. There is hope though, hope in some faces. Even the very young (the boys marching with their signs, the screaming little girls) know what it's all about. A sign says "Everybody wants Freedom." But what is the hope? What can it be? (America will not change because a few blacks and whites can kiss each other, or because Michael Schwerner or Andrew Goodman get themselves murdered. Most of the white kids who go into the South are only trying to save America or save themselves in America; there is more than enough guilt to go round. But there are people all over the world who don't want to see it saved.) Like I was asking, what is the hope? I say if your hope is for the survival of this society, this filthy order, no good. You lose. The hope is that young blacks will remember all of their lives what they are seeing, what they are witness to just by being alive and black in America, and that eventually they will use this knowledge scientifically, and erupt like Mt. Vesuvius to crush in hot lava these willful maniacs who call themselves white Americans.

Nationalism Vs. PimpArt

New talk of Black Art reemerged in America around 1964. It was the Nationalist consciousness reawakened in Black people. The sense of identity, and with that opening, a real sense of purpose and direction. The sense of who and what we were and what we had to do.

We began to understand with the most precise consciousness that we were beings of a particular race and culture, whatever our experience. And that finally, if we were to be saved, we must be saved totally, as a race, because the deathbattle raging around and through us was an actual death struggle between two cultures.

Warfare between that which generates and signifies life and that which is death. As a confusing adjunct to this real war minces "ThE rEVolUTioN" within white society, to make Allen Ginsberg and/or Fulton Sheen comfortable with John Bull's grandson. And that is, will happen. (If you don't have on red, white and blue bellbottoms you must be neckit!)

And all of the above can get in on the vague, integrated, plastic, homosexual "rEVolUTioN" . . . a conglomeration of words, degeneracy, and fake pseudo "act." But for Black people it was (is) critical that we begin to focus on National Liberation, which is what we always meant when we were conscious: National Liberation, the freeing of one nation (culture) from the domination of another.

This was the truth we felt and found, and this is the path we still pursue. Malcolm said (to us) "if you love revolution, you love Black Nationalism." And this consciousness is coming into strong fruition, this legacy of, and movement through, nationalism. Fanon added, "the concepts of nation and culture are inseparable. If you talk about nation you talk about culture." The ways and means of a people, how they live, and what they remember of that life. Their value system. Not merely singing and dancing, or wearing dashikis, tho all life function is to some extent part of a creative motif. Whether war or cornbread. It is a creation of some sensibility. It issues out of some value system. The largest sensibility we deal with now is the national sensibility. *To free the nation is at the same time to free the culture, i.e., the way of life of . . .*

The largest creation, the most exacting manifestation of Euro-American (white) creative motif is, right now, Vietnam. An Absurd White-Comedy. The Ethos (characteristic life-style) of Euro-America is death, about death, and/or dead, or the worship of. Beckett is the prize winner cause he tell about it so cool.

But Nationalism was the move away from this death and degeneracy. To draw away from the dead body, and its spirit. (As Touré says, "decolonialization is not only to get rid of the colonizer, but his spirit as well.") Black Art was first the restoration of LIFE and the restoration of HOPE, that all of the humans would survive the reign of the beasts. But we learned that we could only survive by evolving a different value system from the beast value system. Whether social or esthetic, they are exactly the same. The films of Warhol, when they are about anything, are about ——— people off. (They are exact replicas of American Sensibility.) This can be high art, to people who are interested in ——— people off. But that will not liberate Black people. Campbell's soup cans will not. Some more materialism, if you can dig it, the worship of *things*—sacred to a nation, indicative of that nation's spirit. An artificial commodity.

The Art is The National Spirit. That manifestation of it. Black Art must be the Nationalist's vision given more form and feeling, as a raiser to cut away what is not central to National Liberation. To show that which is. As a humanistic expression Black Art is a raiser, as a spiritual expression it is itself raised. And these are the poles, out of which we create, to raise, or as raised.

The great deluge of nakedness and homosexuality is a "revolution" within the Euro-Am meaning world. The great dope "revolution." All these will change the mores of Euro-Am, they already have. That "revolution" will succeed. But it is not the revolution we spoke of. Though the energy unleashed by our own Black swiftness serves to power the jr. cracker's cry of "rEVolU-TioN." (Witness SDS blackfist minstrel show. Or Rock.) But the Nationalist does not confuse this marxbros type changeover, from old to young white boy, not a regeneration but simply a change of generation in degeneration. The

Nationalist does not confuse this with National Liberation. So the hand grows shakier. We "support" the white revolution of dope and nakedness because it weakens the hand that holds the chain that binds Black people. But we must not confuse the cry of young white boys to be in charge of the pseudo-destruction of America (with a leisure made possible by the same colonialism) with our own necessity. Just because the slavemaster has long hair and smokes bush does nothing to change the fact that he is and will be the slave master until we, yes, *free ourselves*.

And just as the young white boy could pick up "rEVolUTioN" and apply it to his desires, so could some Negroes uncommitted to Nationalism, so emotionally committed to their masters were they, be harnassed as showcase "Black Artists" whose real function was the perpetuation of white cultural imperialism in quaint black face, even funnier, like rag time, in white face over black face over Negro Skin over White Mind. That's heavy ain't it? And where we said Black Art, Negroes with grants were set-up in Soul Food Thea-tuhs to hustle ears, and nostrils, and plenty of I's, in place of the righteous food of the Spirit. Skin was (is) hustled as content. The content was, like Eddie Albee, pizen. The content, was (is) like National Football League Quarterbacks, white.

Black Art is the change of content to the survival of a race and culture, as itself. It is John Coltrane not Mantan Moreland disguised as Lawrence Welk disguised as Mantan Moreland, The Elder Ward of the White State who long ago convinced himself he was Flash Gordone.

In Black Ritual Art, it is Bullins, and Milner, and Garrett, and Marvin X, Yusef Iman, Rob Penny, Furaha, Katibu, Yusef Rahman, Damu, Mchochezi, and Hilary, Barbara Teer, National Black Theater, early Boissiere, Norman Jordan and innumerable young brothers and sisters in Black communications satellites all over the planet.

If the artist is the raised consciousness, and this is what the Black Artist strives to be, the raised consciousness of a people. Precise. Specific. From the particular to the general to the universal to the cosmic, and on back to the single instance of love in the west market street barber shop. (But the Black Man is an artist when he realizes the profundity of his specific placement in the world and seeks to render it into intelligi-

bility to make it meaningful by describing it with his life. There is no such thing as Art and Politics, there is only life, and its many registrations.) If the artist is the raised consciousness, then all that he touches, all that impinges on his consciousness, must be raised. We must be the will of the race toward evolution. We must demand the spiritual by being the spiritual. THE LARGEST WORK OF ART IS THE WORLD ITSELF.

The potential is unlimited. The consciousness of men themselves must be raised. The creation of Cities. Of Institutions. Governments. Treaties. Ceremonies. Public Rituals of The Actual World. The Nation. These are the only things worthy of the true Black Artist's consciousness. The Re-creation of The Actual World. Garvey the artist. Malcolm the artist. Touré the artist. Nyerere the artist. Karenga the artist. &c. In order for the creations of the idea world to be valid they must speak, as Karenga says, Collectively, Functionally, and Committedly. That is, Black Art must be Collective, i.e., the spirit of the whole Nation. It must be Functional, it must have a function in the world to Black people. It must also Commit Black people to the struggle for National Liberation.

But just as robot kneegrows, lustful winduptoys, created by massa in response to the power of Black Nationalism, mack around the pseudo "liberated zones" of America being black, as Weldon Smith says, "for a quick - - - -," in for instance literature, theater, graphics, &c. so there are these same pimps, like the dream fulfillment numbers of panting whiteladies who feared their vaginas would dry up under the sudden late SNCC, late Malcolm decamp of young Black people from out the various villages, Haight-Ashburys, &c, existing in the main area of "the movement" itself.

Frankly the Panthers, no matter the great amounts of sincere but purposefully misled brothers, getting shotup because some nigger was emotionally committed to white people, are extreme examples of Pimp Art gone mad. It is a spooky world when the Negro Ensemble Theater and The Black Panther Party (post Huey) can both suddenly exist as large manipulative symbols of white power and white ideology.

Around the time of Malcolm's death, a Nationalistic spirit moved Black people. There was a sense of Umoja (Unity) that seemed to band us all together against the devil. But with the incarceration of Huey, and the move by

Cleaver into the chief strategist's seat, the Panthers turned left on Nationalism, and turned left on Black people. And the love of Beverly Axelrod has left terrible Marx on the dirty Lenin Black people have been given by some dudes with some dead 1930's white ideology as a freedom suit. Instead of ol' Bayard Rustin, now we gets violent integrationists. Wow!

So the blunt negativism and plain out whiteness of Pimp Art, which would kill us for wanting freedom. Which will show itself on the stage. Or show itself weekend weekout in the streets, by misguided dudes who think by saying "Pick Up The Gun," that the devil will wither up and die, or just by picking up that literal gun, without training, using the same sick value system of the degenerate slavemaster, the same dope, the same liquor, the same dying hippy mentality, that they will liberate all the slave peoples of the world. NO.

It will be a Black Ideology of Change, as perhaps an aggregate of world information, that will free us. Lenin, Marx and Trotsky, or ONeill, Beckett, and the Marat-Sade dude, are just the names of some more "great white men"; there are other dudes who will give you other lists like Washington, Jefferson, Adams, or Paul McCartney, Cream, Grateful Dead, or Mozart, Pinky Lee and the fag with the health tv show. They are just lists of white people.

I can learn from anybody and anything. I could learn something from a pile of Nixon under a stoop. But I will not confuse my identity with its. This is the Nationalist's position. We must survive (and this is the way we *will* survive) as a nation, as a culture. We are against the "depersonalization of African Culture" (to quote Touré again). But we must understand that Black, as Karenga says, is Color (race), Culture, and Consciousness. And Black Art, and any movement for National Liberation, must be all three, if they are to be legitimate.

We know we are Black race, we can look at ourselves, tho I guess there are still dudes who really want to be something other than Black. I think I read about some dude who thought he was an Indian, which would really be weird, like a white mind in a blood's head with an Indian mask on. Can you dig it? That Black is easy, the racial one. The second Black is the culture. Surely you know the difference between John Coltrane and Lawrence Welk. Or DaVinci and Benin. Or myself in my green vine coming around the corner and Robert Lowell. Or between James Brown and Big Brother or Mozart's Mother. Its some difrunce man. I know you know. The attitude that is the culture. Simply, the way people live. The way they bees, feeling. The conglomerate concretization of their feelings, as religion, politics, history, social organization, economic organization, creative motif, and ethos—how they doos it.

Black as consciousness, is the knowledge that we are Black by race and Black by culture, and that we must benefit Black by living, if our life is to have positive meaning. Brother JB is a good example. When he sang "America," he was still Black as color, the song was an example of Afro-American culture, an R&B song for sure, but it did not have the consciousness of Black, so it could not be called Black. To sing lies about America is not beneficial to the Black Nation, therefore it is not conscious of Blackness. It is white manipulation, like a Coca-Cola commercial on a soul station. Colored Form, and like Pimp Art, white content.

So the neo leftist bloods confusing the struggle, they are colored by form but with white content. Dignifying a deathmotion that had been laid to rest, many of us thought, only to see it rise Bela Lugosi style to suck some negroes' blood.

But the rationale is always just a plastic transparent nutout suit to cover the old commitment to whiteness. To white ideas and to white meat. Most of these negroes who will call nationalists racists just feel a draft because they are sleeping white. Racism is a theory, as life motif, of why something is inferior, check out Herodotus and The Teutonic Origins theory of White first, with the rest of life sloping off xenophobically down the scale to bad us. We are not racists; when we accuse white people, it is based on still observable phenomena. No theories. We did not make up colonialism, slavery, slumdeath and murder to justify Nationalism. We are not Nationalists because of the devil. We would be Nationalists if there were no devil.

Fiction

Ann Petry (1911–)

Ann Petry is the only novelist who has written equally well of Black life in the inner city and white life in the New England town. The pattern of her own life brought her into intimate contact with both, giving her a unique fictional perspective that she has sharpened by her conscientious dedication to her craft.

Born in Old Saybrook, Connecticut, of a family of pharmacists and chemists, she took a degree in pharmacy at the University of Connecticut in 1934 and then practiced this profession for four years in her family's drugstores in Old Saybrook and the nearby town of Lyme. However, from an early age her chief interests had been literary, and her marriage in 1938 and subsequent move to New York provided an opportunity, as Marjorie Greene has said, "to get away from bottles and medicinal mixtures on to paper, words, images, and plots."

Her work as a journalist for the Harlem newspapers *Amsterdam News* and *People's Voice* immersed her in the relentless problems of the Black poor. The psychological and social dimensions of these provided the themes of most of her early fiction. As her first published short stories began to appear in *Phylon* and *The Crisis,* an editor at Houghton Mifflin invited her to compete for a fellowship. In 1945 she won this competition with the first five chapters of *The Street,* which was completed and published early in 1946. This powerfully graphic novel of a woman's struggle to survive in Harlem caused a number of critics to place Mrs. Petry in the "School of Wright," but her subsequent career has taken a very different turn.

In 1947 *Country Place* appeared, a distinguished novel of a traditional kind in American literature: the fictional critique of the stagnant, repressive life of the small town. Dealing mainly with white characters, *Country Place* bears comparison with similar works by Sinclair Lewis and Sherwood Anderson. If *The Street* is a novel of Black life and *Country Place* a novel of white life, *The Narrows* (1953) combines the two themes in an intense story of interracial love in a small New England city.

In addition to her three novels, Ann Petry has published a children's book, *The Drugstore Cat* (1949), and two biographies designed for juvenile readers, *Harriet Tubman, Conductor on the Underground Railroad* (1955) and *Tituba of Salem Village* (1964). When her novella "Miss

Muriel" appeared in 1963, it was said to contain "material that will appear in a larger work now in progress." She continues to live and write in her native Connecticut village of Old Saybrook, to which she returned from New York after her initial literary success.

Some of Ann Petry's stories, not yet collected, are "On Saturday the Siren Sounds at Noon," *The Crisis*, L (December 1943), 368–369; "Doby's Gone," *Phylon*, V (1944), 361–366; "Olaf and His Girl Friend," *The Crisis*, LII (May 1945), 135–137, 147; "Like a Winding Sheet," *The Crisis*, LII (November 1945), 317–318, 331–332; "The Necessary Knocking at the Door," *'47—the Magazine of the Year*, I (August 1947), 39–44; "Solo on the Drums," *'47—the Magazine of the Year*, I (October 1947), 105—110; "Bones of Louella Brown," *Opportunity*, XXV (October 1947), 189–192, 226–230; "In Darkness and Confusion," in *Cross Section 1947* (1947), edited by Edwin Seaver, pp. 98–128; "Has Anybody Seen Miss Dora Dean?" *The New Yorker*, XXIV (October 25, 1958), 41–48; "Miss Muriel," in *Soon, One Morning* (1963), edited by Herbert Hill, pp. 166–209; "The New Mirror," *The New Yorker*, XLI (May 29, 1965), 28–36, 38, 40, 43–44, 46, 49–50, 52, 55; and "The Migraine Workers," *Redbook*, CXXXIX (May 1967), 66–67, 125–127. Three important essays by Mrs. Petry are "Harlem," *Holiday*, V (April 1949), 110–116, 163–166, 168; "The Novel as Social Criticism," in *The Writer's Book* (1950), edited by Helen Hull, pp. 32–39; and "The Common Ground," *The Horn Book*, XLI (April 1965), 147–151.

In addition to reviews of her three novels, the reader may consult James W. Ivy, "Ann Petry Talks About First Novel," *The Crisis*, LIII (January 1946), 48–49; Marjorie Greene, "Ann Petry Planned to Write," *Opportunity*, XXIV (April–June 1946), 78–79; Robert Bone, *The Negro Novel in America* (1958); and David Littlejohn, *Black on White* (1966).

Like a Winding Sheet

He had planned to get up before Mae did and surprise her by fixing breakfast. Instead he went back to sleep and she got out of bed so quietly he didn't know she wasn't there beside him until he woke up and heard the queer soft gurgle of water running out of the sink in the bathroom.

He knew he ought to get up but instead he put his arms across his forehead to shut the afternoon sunlight out of his eyes, pulled his legs up close to his body, testing them to see if the ache was still in them.

Mae had finished in the bathroom. He could tell because she never closed the door when she was in there and now the sweet smell of talcum powder was drifting down the hall and into the bedroom. Then he heard her coming down the hall.

"Hi, babe," she said affectionately.

"Hum," he grunted, and moved his arms away from his head, opened one eye.

"It's a nice morning."

"Yeah," he rolled over and the sheet twisted around him, outlining his thighs, his chest. "You mean afternoon, don't ya?"

Mae looked at the twisted sheet and giggled. "Looks like a winding sheet," she said. "A shroud—." Laughter tangled with her words and she had to pause for a moment before she could continue. "You look like a huckleberry—in a winding sheet—"

"That's no way to talk. Early in the day like this," he protested.

He looked at his arms silhouetted against the white of the sheets. They were inky black by contrast and he had to smile in spite of himself and he lay there smiling and savouring the sweet sound of Mae's giggling.

"Early?" She pointed a finger at the alarm clock on the table near the bed, and giggled again. "It's almost four o'clock. And if you don't spring up out of there you're going to be late again."

"What do you mean 'again'?"

"Twice last week. Three times the week before. And once the week before and—"

"I can't get used to sleeping in the day time," he said fretfully. He pushed his legs out from under the covers experimentally. Some of the ache had gone out of them but they weren't really rested yet. "It's too light for good sleeping. And all that standing beats the hell out of my legs."

"After two years you oughtta be used to it," Mae said.

He watched her as she fixed her hair, powdered her face, slipping into a pair of blue denim overalls. She moved quickly and yet she didn't seem to hurry.

"You look like you'd had plenty of sleep," he said lazily. He had to get up but he kept putting the moment off, not wanting to move, yet he didn't dare let his legs go completely limp because if he did he'd go back to sleep. It was getting later and later but the thought of putting his weight on his legs kept him lying there.

When he finally got up he had to hurry and he gulped his breakfast so fast that he wondered if his stomach could possibly use food thrown at it at such a rate of speed. He was still wondering about it as he and Mae were putting their coats on in the hall.

Mae paused to look at the calendar. "It's the thirteenth," she said. Then a faint excitement in her voice. "Why it's Friday the thirteenth." She had one arm in her coat sleeve and she held it there while she stared at the calendar. "I oughtta stay home," she said. "I shouldn't go otta the house."

"Aw don't be a fool," he said. "To-day's payday. And payday is a good luck day everywhere, any way you look at it." And as she stood hesitating he said, "Aw, come on."

And he was late for work again because they spent fifteen minutes arguing before he could con-vince her she ought to go to work just the same. He had to talk persuasively, urging her gently and it took time. But he couldn't bring himself to talk to her roughly or threaten to strike her like a lot of men might have done. He wasn't made that way.

So when he reached the plant he was late and he had to wait to punch the time clock because the day shift workers were streaming out in long lines, in groups and bunches that impeded his progress.

Even now just starting his work-day his legs ached. He had to force himself to struggle past the out-going workers, punch the time clock, and get the little cart he pushed around all night because he kept toying with the idea of going home and getting back in bed.

He pushed the cart out on the concrete floor, thinking that if this was his plant he'd make a lot of changes in it. There were too many standing up jobs for one thing. He'd figure out some way most of 'em could be done sitting down and he'd put a lot more benches around. And this job he had—this job that forced him to walk ten hours a night, pushing this little cart, well, he'd turn it into a sittin-down job. One of those little trucks they used around railroad stations would be good for a job like this. Guys sat on a seat and the thing moved easily, taking up little room and turning in hardly any space at all, like on a dime.

He pushed the cart near the foreman. He never could remember to refer to her as the forelady even in his mind. It was funny to have a woman for a boss in a plant like this one.

She was sore about something. He could tell by the way her face was red and her eyes were half shut until they were slits. Probably been out late and didn't get enough sleep. He avoided looking at her and hurried a little, head down, as he passed her though he couldn't resist stealing a glance at her out of the corner of his eyes. He saw the edge of the light colored slacks she wore and the tip end of a big tan shoe.

"Hey, Johnson!" the woman said.

The machines had started full blast. The whirr and the grinding made the building shake, made it impossible to hear conversations. The men and women at the machines talked to each other but looking at them from just a little distance away they appeared to be simply moving their lips because you couldn't hear what they were saying. Yet the woman's voice cut across the machine sounds—harsh, angry.

He turned his head slowly. "Good Evenin', Mrs. Scott," he said and waited.

"You're late again."

"That's right. My legs were bothering me."

The woman's face grew redder, angrier looking. "Half this shift comes in late," she said. "And you're the worst one of all. You're always late. Whatsa matter with ya?"

"It's my legs," he said. "Somehow they don't ever get rested. I don't seem to get used to sleeping days. And I just can't get started."

"Excuses. You guys always got excuses," her anger grew and spread. "Every guy comes in here late always has an excuse. His wife's sick or his grandmother died or somebody in the family had to go to the hospital," she paused, drew a deep breath. "And the niggers are the worse. I don't care what's wrong with your legs. You get in here on time. I'm sick of you niggers—"

"You got the right to get mad," he interrupted softly. "You got the right to cuss me four ways to Sunday but I ain't letting nobody call me a nigger."

He stepped closer to her. His fists were doubled. His lips were drawn back in a thin narrow line. A vein in his forehead stood out swollen, thick.

And the woman backed away from him, not hurriedly but slowly—two, three steps back.

"Aw, forget it," she said. "I didn't mean nothing by it. It slipped out. It was a accident." The red of her face deepened until the small blood vessels in her cheeks were purple. "Go on and get to work," she urged. And she took three more slow backward steps.

He stood motionless for a moment and then turned away from the red lipstick on her mouth that made him remember that the foreman was a woman. And he couldn't bring himself to hit a woman. He felt a curious tingling in his fingers and he looked down at his hands. They were clenched tight, hard, ready to smash some of those small purple veins in her face.

He pushed the cart ahead of him, walking slowly. When he turned his head, she was staring in his direction, mopping her forehead with a dark blue handkerchief. Their eyes met and then they both looked away.

He didn't glance in her direction again but moved past the long work benches, carefully collecting the finished parts, going slowly and steadily up and down, back and forth the length of the building and as he walked he forced himself to swallow his anger, get rid of it.

And he succeeded so that he was able to think about what had happened without getting upset about it. An hour went by but the tension stayed in his hands. They were clenched and knotted on the handles of the cart as though ready to aim a blow.

And he thought he should have hit her anyway, smacked her hard in the face, felt the soft flesh of her face give under the hardness of his hands. He tried to make his hands relax by offering them a description of what it would have been like to strike her because he had the queer feeling that his hands were not exactly a part of him any more—they had developed a separate life of their own over which he had no control. So he dwelt on the pleasure his hands would have felt—both of them cracking at her, first one and then the other. If he had done that his hands would have felt good now—relaxed, rested.

And he decided that even if he'd lost his job for it he should have let her have it and it would have been a long time, maybe the rest of her life before she called anybody else a nigger.

The only trouble was he couldn't hit a woman. A woman couldn't hit back the same way a man did. But it would have been a deeply satisfying thing to have cracked her narrow lips wide open with just one blow, beautifully timed and with all his weight in back of it. That way he would have gotten rid of all the energy and tension his anger had created in him. He kept remembering how his heart had started pumping blood so fast he had felt it tingle even in the tips of his fingers.

With the approach of night fatigue nibbled at him. The corners of his mouth dropped, the frown between his eyes deepened, his shoulders sagged; but his hands stayed tight and tense. As the hours dragged by he noticed that the women workers had started to snap and snarl at each other. He couldn't hear what they said because of the sound of machines but he could see the quick lip movements that sent words tumbling from the sides of their mouths. They gestured irritably with their hands and scowled as their mouths moved.

Their violent jerky motions told him that it was getting close on to quitting time but somehow he felt that the night still stretched ahead of him, composed of endless hours of steady walking on his aching legs. When the whistle finally blew he went on pushing the cart, unable to believe that it had sounded. The whirring of the machines died away to a murmur and he knew then that he'd really heard the whistle. He stood still for a moment filled with a relief that made him sigh.

Then he moved briskly, putting the cart in the store room, hurrying to take his place in the line forming before the paymaster. That was another thing he'd change, he thought. He'd have the pay envelopes handed to the people right at their benches so there wouldn't be ten or fifteen minutes lost waiting for the pay. He always got home about fifteen minutes late on payday. They did it better in the plant where Mae worked, brought the money right to them at their benches.

He stuck his pay envelope in his pants' pocket and followed the line of workers heading for the subway in a slow moving stream. He glanced up at the sky. It was a nice night, the sky looked packed full to running over with stars. And he thought if he and Mae would go right to bed when they got home from work they'd catch a few hours of darkness for sleeping. But they never did. They fooled around—cooking and eating and listening to the radio and he always stayed in a big chair in the living room and went almost but not quite to sleep and when they finally got to bed it was five or six in the morning and daylight was already seeping around the edges of the sky.

He walked slowly, putting off the moment when he would have to plunge into the crowd hurrying toward the subway. It was a long ride to Harlem and to-night the thought of it appalled him. He paused outside an all-night restaurant to kill time, so that some of the first rush of workers would be gone when he reached the subway.

The lights in the restaurant were brilliant, enticing. There was life and motion inside. And as he looked through the window he thought that everything within range of his eyes gleamed—the long imitation marble counter, the tall stools, the white porcelain topped tables and especially the big metal coffee urn right near the window. Steam issued from its top and a gas flame flickered under it—a lively, dancing, blue flame.

A lot of the workers from his shift—men and women—were lining up near the coffee urn. He watched them walk to the porcelain topped tables carrying steaming cups of coffee and he saw that just the smell of the coffee lessened the fatigue lines in their faces. After the first sip their faces softened, they smiled, they began to talk and laugh.

On a sudden impulse he shoved the door open and joined the line in front of the coffee urn. The line moved slowly. And as he stood there the smell of the coffee, the sound of the laughter and of the voices, helped dull the sharp ache in his legs.

He didn't pay any attention to the girl who was serving the coffee at the urn. He kept looking at the cups in the hands of the men who had been ahead of him. Each time a man stepped out of the line with one of the thick white cups the fragrant steam got in his nostrils. He saw that they walked carefully so as not to spill a single drop. There was a froth of bubbles at the top of each cup and he thought about how he would let the bubbles break against his lips before he actually took a big deep swallow.

Then it was his turn. "A cup of coffee," he said, just as he had heard the others say.

The girl looked past him, put her hands up to her head and gently lifted her hair away from the back of her neck, tossing her head back a little. "No more coffee for awhile," she said.

He wasn't certain he'd heard her correctly and he said, "What?" blankly.

"No more coffee for awhile," she repeated.

There was silence behind him and then uneasy movement. He thought someone would say something, ask why or protest, but there was only silence and then a faint shuffling sound as though the men standing behind him had simultaneously shifted their weight from one foot to the other.

He looked at her without saying anything. He felt his hands begin to tingle and the tingling went all the way down to his finger tips so that he glanced down at them. They were clenched tight, hard, into fists. Then he looked at the girl again. What he wanted to do was hit her so hard that the scarlet lipstick on her mouth would smear and spread over her nose, her chin, out toward her cheeks; so hard that she would never toss her head again and refuse a man a cup of coffee because he was black.

He estimated the distance across the counter and reached forward, balancing his weight on the balls of his feet, ready to let the blow go. And then his hands fell back down to his sides because he forced himself to lower them, to unclench them and make them dangle loose. The effort took his breath away because his hands fought against him. But he couldn't hit her. He couldn't even now bring himself to hit a woman, not even this one, who had refused him a cup of coffee with a toss of her head. He kept seeing the gesture with which she had lifted the length of her blond hair from the back of her neck as expressive of her contempt for him.

When he went out the door he didn't look back. If he had he would have seen the flickering blue flame under the shiny coffee urn being extinguished. The line of men who had stood behind him lingered a moment to watch the people drinking coffee at the tables and then they left just as he had without having had the coffee they wanted so badly. The girl behind the counter poured water in the urn and swabbed it out and as she waited for the water to run out she lifted her hair gently from the back of her neck and tossed her head before she began making a fresh lot of coffee.

But he walked away without a backward look, his head down, his hands in his pockets, raging at himself and whatever it was inside of him that had forced him to stand quiet and still when he wanted to strike out.

The subway was crowded and he had to stand. He tried grasping an overhead strap and his hands were too tense to grip it. So he moved near the train door and stood there swaying back and forth with the rocking of the train. The roar of the train beat inside his head, making it ache and throb, and the pain in his legs clawed up into his groin so that he seemed to be bursting with pain and he told himself that it was due to all that anger-born energy that had piled up in him and not been used and so it had spread through him like a poison—from his feet and legs all the way up to his head.

Mae was in the house before he was. He knew she was home before he put the key in the door of the apartment. The radio was going. She had it tuned up loud and she was singing along with it.

"Hello, Babe," she called out as soon as he opened the door.

He tried to say "hello" and it came out half a grunt and half sigh.

"You sure sound cheerful," she said.

She was in the bedroom and he went and leaned against the door jamb. The denim overalls she wore to work were carefully draped over the back of a chair by the bed. She was standing in front of the dresser, tying the sash of a yellow housecoat around her waist and chewing gum vigorously as she admired her reflection in the mirror over the dresser.

"Whatsa matter?" she said. "You get bawled out by the boss or somep'n?"

"Just tired," he said slowly. "For God's sake do you have to crack that gum like that?"

"You don't have to lissen to me," she said complacently. She patted a curl in place near the side of her head and then lifted her hair away from the back of her neck, ducking her head forward and then back.

He winced away from the gesture. "What you got to be always fooling with your hair for?" he protested.

"Say, what's the matter with you, anyway?" she turned away from the mirror to face him, put her hands on her hips. "You ain't been in the house two minutes and you're picking on me."

He didn't answer her because her eyes were angry and he didn't want to quarrel with her. They'd been married too long and got along too well and so he walked all the way into the room and sat down in the chair by the bed and stretched his legs out in front of him, putting his weight on the heels of his shoes, leaning way back in the chair, not saying anything.

"Lissen," she said sharply. "I've got to wear those overalls again tomorrow. You're going to get them all wrinkled up leaning against them like that."

He didn't move. He was too tired and his legs were throbbing now that he had sat down. Besides the overalls were already wrinkled and dirty, he thought. They couldn't help but be for she'd worn them all week. He leaned further back in the chair.

"Come on, get up," she ordered.

"Oh, what the hell," he said wearily and got up from the chair. "I'd just as soon live in a subway. There'd be just as much place to sit down."

He saw that her sense of humor was struggling with her anger. But her sense of humor won because she giggled.

"Aw, come on and eat," she said. There was a coaxing note in her voice. "You're nothing but a old hungry nigger trying to act tough and—" she paused to giggle and then continued, "You—"

He had always found her giggling pleasant and deliberately said things that might amuse her and then waited, listening for the delicate sound to emerge from her throat. This time he didn't even hear the giggle. He didn't let her finish what she was saying. She was standing close to him and that funny tingling started in his finger tips, went fast up his arms and sent his fist shooting straight for her face.

There was the smacking sound of soft flesh being struck by a hard object and it wasn't until she screamed that he realized he had hit her in the mouth—so hard that the dark red lipstick had blurred and spread over her full lips, reaching up toward the tip of her nose, down toward her chin, out toward her cheeks.

The knowledge that he had struck her seeped through him slowly and he was appalled but he couldn't drag his hands away from her face. He kept striking her and he thought with horror that something inside him was holding him, binding him to this act, wrapping and twisting about him so that he had to continue it. He had lost all control over his hands. And he groped for a phrase, a word, something to describe what this thing was like that was happening to him and he thought it was like being enmeshed in a winding sheet—that was it—like a winding sheet. And even as the thought formed in his mind his hands reached for her face again and yet again.

William Demby (1922–   )

Born in Pittsburgh, William Demby grew up there and in Clarksburg, West Virginia, where his father had a white-collar job with an oil company. His distaste for the drabness and decay, the spiritual and physical exhaustion of the Appalachian coal region is apparent in his first novel, *Beetlecreek* (1950). After matriculating at West Virginia State College, a Black institution, he spent two years in the army, serving most of his time in Italy. While in the service he wrote for the newspaper *Stars and Stripes*. Afterward, at Fisk University, he continued to write, encouraged by poet-professor Robert Hayden, who arrived on the campus in Demby's senior year. Under Hayden's direction and with Demby's contributions, the *Fisk Herald* was an outstanding student newspaper—lively, militant, antifascist. One of Demby's *Herald* stories, "Saint Joey," served as the genesis of *Beetlecreek*.

After graduation from Fisk in 1947, Demby returned to Rome to begin his long expatriation. Interested in art and music as well as literature, he studied at the University of Rome and supported himself by playing the alto saxophone in jazz groups. In the 1950's and early 1960's he worked as a screen writer and translator for European film and television producers, including Roberto Rossellini. Cinematic technique is utilized freely and imaginatively in his second novel, *The Catacombs* (1965). In the mid-1960's Demby returned to the United States and employment in a New York advertising agency and in public relations. He is presently teaching at Staten Island Community College and working on a novel entitled *The Long Bearded Journey*.

The West Virginia setting of *Beetlecreek* is a town economically depressed, socially stagnant, and morally bankrupt. Efforts at human communion on a level beyond the sterile routine of daily life are thwarted by social cruelty and by an ugly death urge that pervades the very atmosphere. Neither Bill Trapp, an old white recluse, nor Johnny Johnson, a Black adolescent, nor his Uncle David, a repressed artist, can achieve fulfillment. Instead, Bill Trapp has his house burned down; Johnny surrenders his moral sensitivity to conform to the senseless violence of a youthful gang; and David escapes the town only to enmesh himself in an equally stultifying relationship with a cheap and domineering woman.

Some of the same elements of paralysis and death are projected on the larger screen of Rome and, indeed, the entire history of Western civilization in *The Catacombs*. But the second novel is more affirmative than the first. If the European tradition and the machine age are moribund, hope emerges from a rejuvenated Christianity, the vitality of Blackness, and the electronics revolution, seemingly disparate forces that Demby's evolutionary vision manages to bring together. Highly innovative in style, use of "cubistic time," and handling of the relation between public and private history, this story of a love affair between an Italian count and a Black American actress-dancer is a work of art that, in the words of one critic, "has probed to the outer limits of contemporary consciousness."

Both of Demby's novels are available in paperback editions, *Beetlecreek* with an afterword by Herbert Hill and *The Catacombs* with an excellent critical introduction, reprinted from *Tri-Quarterly*, by Robert Bone. Bone treats *Beetlecreek* in *The Negro Novel in America* (1958), but see also John F. Bayliss' rebuttal in "*Beetlecreek*: Existential or Human Document?" *Negro Digest*, XIX (November 1969), 70–74. Edward Margolies has a chapter on Demby in *Native Sons* (1968), and Nancy Y. Hoffman deals with "Technique in Demby's *The Catacombs*," *Studies in Black Literature*, II (Summer 1971), 10–13.

The Table of Wishes Come True

He was a heavy set grey haired man with thick, nervous hands. Apprehensively he sat on a chair looking down at thick cables that stretched from under the doorway across the floor to disappear through a crack in the wall. Like snakes they are, he was thinking; and, indeed, with their thick rubber insulation, they did seem alive and ready to trap his feet. This thought gnawed at him so that to assure himself he had to repeat over and over again under his breath: When I go out there, I mustn't step on them . . . By turning his head just a little, he could look out through a tiny window to the control room where a man with a ridiculous mustache (his expression that of a rat contemplating an open floor) sat guarding a panel of instruments. The box-like room was too hot and, irrationally, for there was no real cause for such reasoning, he associated a mysterious clicking sound coming from behind the wall with the stuffiness and lack of ventilation.

There was a day when he was conscious of his

life's real beginning. He was a boy walking home from school kicking his feet through the crisp Fall leaves, conscious of the peace and solemnity of the rich folk's stone mansions on either side of the street. Feeling expansive, at the same time melancholy to see the coral sunset merging with the smoke from the railroad yards in the valley where he lived, he realized suddenly that life was ahead of him to be taken and conquered, that with the strength that thrilled through him under his cordoroy jacket he could pull his destiny up from the sooty houses along the tracks to the cathedral like mansions on this fine street. And out of the sheer ecstasy of this discovery, he gave a whoop and threw his hat higher than the telephone wires. Then, as if at that moment he had signed a pact with his destiny, his life seemed to move ahead with kalaidioscope rapidity, so that in a minute he was sitting with his sister in a drugstore booth eating a chocolate sundae in celebration of his graduation from high school and in two minutes he was in Buffalo undressing in a strange dark hotel that smelled of disinfectant waiting for Milly, his bride, to come from the writing room on their wedding night.

And inevitably, just as there was a day when he was conscious of his life's beginning there came a day when he sensed his life's end. This was a hot parched day in mid-August, the day of the Company's annual employee's picnic. There was no fishing as there had been in other years, for the pond at O'Higgin's Lake was practically dried up in the drought of that year. The beer wasn't cold for the ice melted almost as fast as it was placed in the tubs. Milly was sitting with the other wives under the canvas that had been placed over the roofs of the automobiles. He could hear their voices coming from afar hardly as loud as the sound of flies buzzing around the watermelon rinds at his feet. He was forty-five years old, chief shipping clerk in his department, respected for his caution and reliability. He sat there on a wooden box inside a tottering shanty that at one time had served as a ticket booth. With his fingernail file he carefully scraped away at a potato salad stain on the brand new sport shirt he had bought the day before to wear at the picnic. Ten minutes before a neighbor of his had told him that the new man from Albany was to be made assistant manager, a position he had hoped for ever since the night of the testimonial banquets seven years before when, on the occasion of his being awarded the twenty-year service button, Mr. Owens said in his speech that "who can tell what rewards shall be forthcoming for such an enviable record as this..." Inside that shanty smelling of animal waste, midst the buzzing of insects, he felt the coming of his life's end; and when he heard the shrill whistle announcing the annual softball game between married employees and single employees, he jumped up and ran desperately toward the dusty ball field.

Time ran ahead so quickly then! and there was no stone mansion, nor even children ... so that in more minutes he was being retired and there was only the gold and blue button and a paid up mortgage.

It was almost time for them to come. As always when he was worried, his fingers sought the lapel of his suit to feel the button fastened there that now indicated thirty-five years service with the Company.

Then, for the first time in that sound-proof room, he noticed the loud ticking of his pocket watch. Almost gleefully, as if discovering a toy for the first time, he reached into his vest pocket to get it. In the control room, over the head of the mustached man, was a clock that said thirteen minutes past eight. Joy, in a sudden trickling filled him for his watch showed the same time. This joy brought with it momentary peace and relaxation, a feeling of safety and faith that reassured him that things in the world were as they should be, that nightmare was of the night.

Again came the mysterious clicking noise from behind the wall. What would Milly be doing out there now? He thought of her sitting beside the other ladies all dolled up in her new traveling suit bought especially for the trip. When they stepped from the cab and walked into the hotel lobby, he'd been proud of her in that suit, proud and secretly flattered that she fitted in with it all, that you couldn't tell her from someone who'd lived in the city all their life. At first, everything worked out fine. Even in the restaurant, the one he'd been half afraid to enter because of the foreign name over the door, it seemed that the city had been waiting to greet them, that despite what was always said about the big city there wasn't really any difference between it and the good old home town. Coming out of the restaurant, sucking a toothpick, the souvenir menu tucked safely in his breast pocket, he'd said this to Milly: and then he'd really meant it. For some moments it seemed to him that this was the debt that life had owed him, that this was the reward, the vision he had foreseen that Fall day when as a school boy he had felt his strength and destiny. Only when they left the immense movie theatre (so big he couldn't sit back in the seat because of the nightmare feeling of swinging alone through dark space) to find the crowded streets dark and hostile would he admit that something was wrong.

That evening Milly got into a conversation with a lady she had met in the hotel lobby and though he seldom drank, he'd gone into the bar and had two beers before taking the elevator to their suite on the twenty-third floor. Sitting in the bathroom with his head in his hands he decided he couldn't go through with it. Then he'd heard Milly's uneven step on the heavy carpets. He started to flush the bowl but thought better of it. He spent a long time washing his hands and looking at himself in the mirror before going out to face her.

Why, that woman's been livin' in this very hotel for goin' on eight years, she'd said; husband's dead; believe she said he's some kind of army man; but just think of it her livin' in this expensive hotel and callin' it a home. . . Her eyes were glistening and her hat was pushed way back off her forehead.

Then he told her.

Nonsense, she had said, you're just gettin' cold feet, and after the Wish people payin' all the expenses and all; besides, Harry and Elma'll be listenin' in.

The beer had aggravated his stomach and that night his sleep was woven of strange dreams, one of which he'd had many times before. In this dream he was a bird or an animal, he could not know which, perched on a tree; time after time he would try to spring onto the shoulder of his human self walking along under the tree but every time the human self swept him away with a cruel wipe of the arm.

That evening, only an hour ago (it seemed much longer to him), entering the building so high he dare not look up toward its spiralled top, he'd suddenly become hysterical for no reason at all and miscalculated the swing of the revolving doors, causing himself to be swept around past the entrance. Terrible panic filled him then when he found himself on the street again for he imagined that everyone passing was laughing at him. Milly tried to say something to him that he couldn't hear through the glass. His only thought had been to hide the limp from her for he had hurt his ankle badly.

Once again he glanced at the clock. Eight-fifteen. How much longer before they would come? Beads of sweat had formed on his forehead; the handkerchief bundled up in his hand was soaked through. He remembered the pain in his ankle and reached down to lift his trouser so that he could look at the black and blue gash. Now he got down on one knee. The clicking sound came again. Suddenly he was aware that someone was coming though no sound could penetrate through the doors or wall. When he looked up, sure enough, two men dressed in blue usher uniforms were about to enter the room. One of them carried a long box such as are used to deliver dresses in. Blood rushed to his head. Frantically he lowered his trousers leg, forgetting that the window in his room could not be looked into from the outside.

Mr. Schwartz? one of the men asked.

Involuntarily he had taken a step backwards so that his legs were against the iron seat of the chair. His first attempt at an answer was unsuccessful but somehow he managed to clear his throat and force what he thought was a smile on his face.

The other usher unwrapped the box and pulled out a long garment that looked like a nightgown.

Roll up your trousers, the man commanded.

He was quick to obey for it was a relief now to surrender himself. This uniformed efficiency was something he knew, this closed lip way of giving orders placed him on familiar terrain and lifted him high out of reach of the terrible anxiety of waiting and self dependency he'd felt all these weeks of being retired, weeks of being alone for the first time in his adult life with the unpredictable voice of himself, a voice that haunted his sleep and tarnished his waking hours with the taste of death.

So that now he obeyed the usher's commands until, dressed completely like a baby, complete with pink bonnet, a huge rattle, and an oversized lolly pop, he was pronounced ready to go on.

Boy, you'll kill 'em, one of the ushers said.

Yeah, you're a scream all right, the other added.

The man in the control room was gesturing wildly. Ah, hold your pants, on, the usher snarled, checking his watch with the one in the control room. O.k., let's go, it's eight-fifteen.

Despite his care, he tripped on one of the cables.

Easy now, mister, don't get nervous, ain't nobody goin' to hurt you. . .

He caught the eye of the mustached man in the control room who had been looking at him strangely. An abrupt clash of cymbals and a brass fanfare followed immediately by a deafening roar of laughter saved him from having to think of this look. Only after the laughing died away did he realize that it was his appearance which had caused the commotion. He felt a tug on either elbow. They were leading him to the front of the stage now though the footlights glared so much that at first he could fix his eyes on nothing except the pinkish reflection on the bundled up curtain toward the side of the platform. Then he made out two rows of chairs upon which the women were sitting. With his eyes he sought out Milly but her chair was empty. Milly! he exclaimed to himself, alarmed by her absence. Without her—she who had filled out the penny postcards, she who had listened faithfully to the program for over two years, she who had nearly fainted with joy that evening of the telephone call—without Milly he could never go through with it.

On the other side of the stage was a table filled with glistening objects. This would be the Table of Wishes Come True!

Then he heard someone chuckle and say: This way, sir, or should I say "dumpsy-wumpsy?" The audience roared with appreciation. He was standing in the very center of the stage before a microphone and there was Milly standing beside a nice looking young man who wore a tie of purple curley-cues trimmed in orange. Is this your er-uh . . . husband? the nice looking young man was asking her, his voice quivering with calculated cuteness. The audience's laughter drowned out her reply.

He looked at his wife hoping to get from her some sign, a look perhaps that would tell him that it was all right; but her eyes were narrowed, and her hands, clutched tightly around the opposite ends of a handkerchief, were drained of blood. The idea came to him suddenly that she no longer belonged to him but was an imposter in league with the announcer and the audience; she refused to look at him but stood smiling and nodding her head toward the people as if to say, he imagined, I don't know him, he's none of mine . . . Then he became very cold with a fear he had felt many times in dreams. Always then, as now, it was the terrible awareness of being alone without any possibility of succor that was the real cause of terror. As in the dreams, he wanted to run away, but Milly, the nice looking young man, and the whole audience were there to prevent him. Was there no one he could count on? He shifted his weight. They had tied the ribbon of his bonnet so tight that he was finding it difficult to breathe, yet he dared not lift his hand to unloosen it for fear that even this simple gesture might provoke a fresh outburst of hilarity.

Milly was talking to the announcer and for the moment his gaze was free to wander over to the Table of Wishes Come True. His eyes focused then and he could see that the glistening silver and enamel objects before him were electric roasters, toasters, waffle irons, automatic dish washers, silver sets, a Maid-O-Mat. . . He knew the trade names of all of them for never an evening passed that he didn't leaf dreamily from the back to the front of the many magazines he subscribed to, too tired to read the stories or articles, but content to look at the colored pictures on the advertisements, content to absorb the poetry beneath the picture that extolled the virtue of the object itself as well as the virtue of the life dedicated to its attainment. And seeing them so orderly arranged on the display brought back for a moment the feeling of well being he had felt on entering the hotel when the eager bellboys had snatched his brand new air-lite bag, saying: Oh, you're the Wish people . . . welcome to the city, welcome. . .

But right away the terrible feeling of isolation came back to him; it came with the gust of guffawing laughter that seemed strong enough to blow him off the stage. This time they were laughing at something the nice looking young man had said. He must try to pay attention, he scolded himself. Beyond the footlights he could see that all eyes were looking at him expectantly.

You do-o-o agree that the wife is always right, don't you dumps . . . er-uh, *Mr.* Schwartz, don't you?

He looked toward Milly to take from her expression some clue as to what his reply must be. But again she wouldn't look at him. He nodded his head and again the audience roared with laughter. Looking down toward the front row, he could see the gold fillings in someone's mouth as they laughed. The announcer, too, was laughing softly; from his mouth came a cloud of perfumed breath.

That's a good sport, the nice looking young man was saying; now turn around and close your eyes.

The laughter sweeping over the audience was long and continuous now. How grateful he had been those long evenings for this same uncontrolled laughter when it would enter into the padded softness of his front room to jerk him back into the good-fellow reality of the everyday world, puncturing the bad dreams that had begun coming ever since the day at the picnic when he had sensed his life's end. But now his fear of that great collective guffaw directed at him had become unbearable and he longed for anything that would take him away. If only he dared open his eyes and look at the man in the control room to communicate to this last human being his desperation and need of salvation. He began to feel dizzy.

Abruptly the guffawing stopped and in its place came a great vacuum of silence. Then he felt air rush past his ears and something soft break over his head. He wanted to cry out but so great had become his fear that a strange stoney calm came over him. Someone was turning him around. Again came the terrible laughter.

Thank you, thank you, Mr. A. E. Schwartz from New Castle, Pennsylvania. On behalf of the sponsors of Wishes Come True we thank you for coming out and being such a good sport. The wife is always right... eh, Mr. Schwartz? Yessirree! The wife is always right and to prove it we had Mrs. Schwartz break a dee-liscious old fashioned custard pie right smack over her husband's head—which just goes to prove that the proof of the pie *isn't* in the eating, eh, Mr. Schwartz... Now both of you, if you'll just step over to the Table of Wishes you can choose...

His hands trembled. His breath came in irregular gasps that grinded in his chest. Inside he wept, crying out silently: Give me back the day I first felt my life... show me once again the street! But like Faust standing before the pit, he cried out and gnashed his teeth in vain, for there was no help at that moment; he stood there entirely alone. Custard trickled under his collar. He heard a voice seemingly from far away, a tiny female voice, familiar yet not familiar. For a moment he felt a flicker of hope.

Come on, Albert! Milly hissed, pulling him over to the Wish Table. He focused his eyes. The brightness of the objects dazzled him. He read the numbers backwards on the gage of the automatic roaster that cooked with light rays. His hand reached out to touch a table sized televison set. Milly had linked her arm in his and was squeezing.

He looked at her; her face was flushed and strangely youthful. She was pointing toward the Maid-O-Mat pressure cooker. Isn't it wonderful! Isn't just to-o-o wonderful, she exclaimed.

Paule Marshall (1929–   )

Born in Brooklyn as the Depression began, Paule Marshall grew up as a second-generation Black American. Her parents had immigrated to New York from Barbados a decade earlier, and the "Bajun" cultural style persisted in their home. Thus very early she confronted problems of acculturation as well as racism. She was to turn her childhood experience to literary use not only in a fairly direct way in her first novel, *Brown Girl, Brownstones* (1959), but also in her collection of stories, *Soul Clap Hands and Sing* (1961), and her second novel, *The Chosen Place, the Timeless People* (1969), which deal with cultural as well as racial conflict.

After graduating Phi Beta Kappa from Brooklyn College in 1953, Miss Marshall worked as a librarian in New York and as a journalist for the magazine *Our World,* which sent her on assignment to the West Indies and to Brazil. After the literary success of her first two books, she received fellowship and prize support during the 1960's from the Guggenheim and Ford Foundations, the National Institute of Arts and Letters, the National Endowment for the Arts, and the Yaddo Corporation. As a member of the Association of Artists for Freedom in the mid-1960's, she attacked paternalistic white liberalism and called for a new, more militant, all-Black organization. Having lived for considerable periods in the Caribbean, she now resides with her son in New York.

Brown Girl, Brownstones is a *bildungsroman* about Selina Boyce, a Brooklyn girl whose Barbadian parents cannot come to terms with each other or with the alien city. The novel is equally impressive for its insight into the psychology of maturation, its richly and densely evoked locale, and its poetic but functional prose. From the problems of youth

Miss Marshall turned in her next book to the problems of age. The protagonists of the four stories of *Soul Clap Hands and Sing*—"Barbados," "Brooklyn," "British Guiana," and "Brazil"—must face, like the speaker of Yeats' "Sailing to Byzantium" from which the title of the collection is taken, the physical and mental problems of their decaying bodies, problems posed sharply through conflict with younger, more vital characters. *The Chosen Place, the Timeless People* is a long novel about the heritage of slavery and revolt in a West Indian village. The cultural conflict between the villagers and the staff of a visiting American aid project symbolizes the larger confrontation of the world's darker and lighter peoples, with the oppressed turning on their oppressors even when the latter pose as benefactors. In Miss Marshall's prophetic vision, the time of the timeless people is at last at hand.

Barbados

Dawn, like the night which had preceded it, came from the sea. In a white mist tumbling like spume over the fishing boats leaving the island and the hunched, ghost shapes of the fishermen. In a white, wet wind breathing over the villages scattered amid the tall canes. The cabbage palms roused, their high headdresses solemnly saluting the wind, and along the white beach which ringed the island the casuarina trees began their moaning—a sound of women lamenting their dead within a cave.

The wind, smarting of the sea, threaded a wet skein through Mr. Watford's five hundred dwarf coconut trees and around his house at the edge of the grove. The house, Colonial American in design, seemed created by the mist—as if out of the dawn's formlessness had come, magically, the solid stone walls, the blind, broad windows and the portico of fat columns which embraced the main story. When the mist cleared, the house remained—pure, proud, a pristine white—disdaining the crude wooden houses in the village outside its high gate.

It was not the dawn settling around his house which awakened Mr. Watford, but the call of his Barbary doves from their hutch in the yard. And it was more the feel of that sound than the sound itself. His hands had retained, from the many times a day he held the doves, the feel of their throats swelling with that murmurous, mournful note. He lay abed now, his hands—as cracked and callused as a cane cutter's—filled with the sound, and against the white sheet which flowed out to the white walls he appeared profoundly alone, yet secure in loneliness, contained. His face was fleshless and severe, his black skin sucked deep into the hollow of his jaw, while under a high brow, which was like a bastion raised against the world, his eyes were indrawn and pure. It was as if during all his seventy years, Mr. Watford had permitted nothing to sight which could have affected him.

He stood up, and his body, muscular but stripped of flesh, appeared to be absolved from time, still young. Yet each clenched gesture of his arms, of his lean shank as he dressed in a faded shirt and work pants, each vigilant, snapping motion of his head betrayed tension. Ruthlessly he spurred his body to perform like a younger man's. Savagely he denied the accumulated fatigue of the years. Only sometimes when he paused in his grove of coconut trees during the day, his eyes tearing and the breath torn from his lungs, did it seem that if he could find a place hidden from the world and himself he would give way to exhaustion and weep from weariness.

Dressed, he strode through the house, his step tense, his rough hand touching the furniture from Grand Rapids which crowded each room. For some reason, Mr. Watford had never completed the house. Everywhere the walls were raw and unpainted, the furniture unarranged. In the drawing room with its coffered ceiling, he stood before his favorite piece, an old mantel clock which eked out the time. Reluctantly it whirred five and Mr. Watford nodded. His day had begun.

It was no different from all the days which made up the five years since his return to Barbados. Downstairs in the unfinished kitchen, he prepared his morning tea—tea with canned milk and fried bakes—and ate standing at the stove while lizards skittered over the unplastered walls. Then, belching and snuffling the way a child would, he put on a pith helmet, secured his pants legs with bicycle clasps and stepped into the yard. There he fed the doves, holding them so that their sound poured into his hands and laughing gently—but the laugh gave way to an irritable grunt as he saw the mongoose tracks under the hutch. He set the trap again.

The first heat had swept the island like a huge tidal wave when Mr. Watford, with that tense, headlong stride, entered the grove. He had planted the dwarf coconut trees because of their quick yield and because, with their stunted trunks, they always appeared young. Now as he worked, rearranging the complex of pipes which irrigated the land, stripping off the dead leaves, the trees were like cool, moving presences; the stiletto fronds wove a protective dome above him and slowly, as the day soared toward noon, his mind filled with the slivers of sunlight through the trees and the feel of earth in his hands, as it might have been filled with thoughts.

Except for a meal at noon, he remained in the grove until dusk surged up from the sea; then returning to the house, he bathed and dressed in a medical doctor's white uniform, turned on the lights in the parlor and opened the tall doors to the portico. Then the old women of the village on their way to church, the last hawkers caroling, "Fish, flying fish, a penny, my lady," the roistering saga-boys lugging their heavy steel drums to the crossroad where they would rehearse under the street lamp—all passing could glimpse Mr. Watford, stiff in his white uniform and with his head bent heavily over a Boston newspaper. The papers reached him weeks late but he read them anyway, giving a little savage chuckle at the thought that beyond his world that other world went its senseless way. As he read, the night sounds of the village welled into a joyous chorale against the sea's muffled cadence and the hollow, haunting music of the steel band. Soon the moths, lured in by the light, fought to die on the lamp, the beetles crashed drunkenly against the walls and the night—like a woman offering herself to him—became fragrant with the night-blooming cactus.

Even in America Mr. Watford had spent his evenings this way. Coming home from the hospital, where he worked in the boiler room, he would dress in his white uniform and read in the basement of the large rooming house he owned. He had lived closeted like this, detached, because America—despite the money and property he had slowly accumulated—had meant nothing to him. Each morning, walking to the hospital along the rutted Boston streets, through the smoky dawn light, he had known—although it had never been a thought—that his allegiance, his place, lay elsewhere. Neither had the few acquaintances he had made mattered. Nor the women he had occasionally kept as a younger man. After the first month their bodies would grow coarse to his hand and he would begin edging away.... So that he had felt no regret when, the year before his retirement, he resigned his job, liquidated his properties and, his fifty-year exile over, returned home.

The clock doled out eight and Mr. Watford folded the newspaper and brushed the burnt moths from the lamp base. His lips still shaped the last words he had read as he moved through the rooms, fastening the windows against the night air, which he had dreaded even as a boy. Something palpable but unseen was always, he believed, crouched in the night's dim recess, waiting to snare him.... Once in bed in his sealed room, Mr. Watford fell asleep quickly.

The next day was no different except that Mr. Goodman, the local shopkeeper, sent the boy for coconuts to sell at the racetrack and then came that evening to pay for them and to herald—although Mr. Watford did not know this—the coming of the girl.

That morning, taking his tea, Mr. Watford heard the careful tap of the mule's hoofs and looking out saw the wagon jolting through the dawn and the boy, still lax with sleep, swaying on the seat. He was perhaps eighteen and the muscles packed tightly beneath his lustrous black skin gave him a brooding strength. He came and stood outside the back door, his hands and lowered head performing the small, subtle rites of deference.

Mr. Watford's pleasure was full, for the gestures were those given only to a white man in his time. Yet the boy always nettled him. He sensed a natural arrogance like a pinpoint of light within his dark stare. The boy's stance exhumed a memory buried under the years. He remembered, staring at him, the time when he had worked as a yard boy for a white family, and had had to assume the same respectful pose while their flat, raw, Barbadian voices assailed him with orders. He remembered the muscles in his neck straining as he nodded deeply and a taste like alum on his tongue as he repeated the "Yes, please," as in a litany. But because of their whiteness and wealth, he had never dared hate them. Instead his rancor, like a boomerang, had rebounded, glancing past him to strike all the dark ones like himself, even his mother with her spindled arms and her stomach sagging with a child who was, invariably, dead at birth. He had been the only one of ten to live, the only one to escape. But he had never lost the sense of being pursued by the same dread presence which had claimed them. He had never lost the fear that if he lived too fully he would tire and death would quickly close the gap. His only defense had been a cautious life and work. He had been almost broken by work at the age of twenty when his parents died, leaving him enough money for the passage to America. Gladly had he fled the island. But nothing had mattered after his flight.

The boy's foot stirred the dust. He murmured, "Please, sir, Mr. Watford, Mr. Goodman at the shop send me to pick the coconut."

Mr. Watford's head snapped up. A caustic word flared, but died as he noticed a political button pinned to the boy's patched shirt with "Vote for the Barbados People's Party" printed boldly on it, and below that the motto of the party: "The Old Shall Pass." At this ludicrous touch (for what could this boy, with his splayed and shigoed feet and blunted mind, understand about politics?) he became suddenly nervous, angry. The button and its motto seemed, somehow, directed at him. He said roughly, "Well, come then. You can't pick any coconuts standing there looking foolish!"—and he led the way to the grove.

The coconuts, he knew, would sell well at the booths in the center of the track, where the poor were penned in like cattle. As the heat thickened and the betting grew desperate, they would clamor: "Man, how you selling the water coconuts?" and hacking off the tops they would pour rum into the water within the hollow centers, then tilt the coconuts to their heads so that the rum-sweetened water skimmed their tongues and trickled bright down their dark chins. Mr. Watford had stood among them at the track as a young man, as poor as they were, but proud. And he had always found something unutterably graceful and free in their gestures, something which had roused contradictory feelings in him: admiration, but just as strong, impatience at their easy ways, and shame. . . .

That night, as he sat in his white uniform reading, he heard Mr. Goodman's heavy step and went out and stood at the head of the stairs in a formal, proprietary pose. Mr. Goodman's face floated up into the light—the loose folds of flesh, the skin slick with sweat as if oiled, the eyes scribbled with veins and mottled, bold—as if each blemish there was a sin he proudly displayed or a scar which proved he had met life head-on. His body, unlike Mr. Watford's, was corpulent and, with the trousers caught up around his full crotch, openly concupiscent. He owned the one shop in the village which gave credit and a booth which sold coconuts at the race track, kept a wife and two outside women, drank a rum with each customer at his bar, regularly caned his fourteen children, who still followed him everywhere (even now they were waiting for him in the darkness beyond Mr. Watford's gate) and bet heavily at the races, and when he lost gave a loud hacking laugh which squeezed his body like a pain and left him gasping.

The laugh clutched him now as he flung his pendulous flesh into a chair and wheezed, "Watford, how? Man, I near lose house, shop, shirt and all at race today. I tell you, they got some horses from Trinidad in this meet that's making ours look like they running backwards. Be Jese, I wouldn't bet on a Bajan horse tomorrow if Christ heself was to give me the top. Those bitches might look good but they's nothing 'pon a track."

Mr. Watford, his back straight as the pillar he leaned against, his eyes unstained, his gaunt face planed by contempt, gave Mr. Goodman his cold, measured smile, thinking that the man would be dead soon, bloated with rice and rum—and somehow this made his own life more certain.

Sputtering with his amiable laughter, Mr. Goodman paid for the coconuts, but instead of leaving then as he usually did, he lingered, his eyes probing for a glimpse inside the house. Mr. Watford waited, his head snapping warily; then, impatient, he started toward the door and Mr. Goodman said, "I tell you, your coconut trees bearing fast enough even for dwarfs. You's lucky, man."

Ordinarily Mr. Watford would have waved both the man and his remark aside, but repelled more than usual tonight by Mr. Goodman's gross form and immodest laugh, he said—glad of the cold edge his slight American accent gave the words—"What luck got to do with it? I does care the trees properly and they bear, that's all. Luck! People, especially this bunch around here, is always looking to luck when the only answer is a little brains and plenty of hard work...." Suddenly remembering the boy that morning and the political button, he added in loud disgust, "Look that half-foolish boy you does send here to pick the coconuts. Instead of him learning a trade and going to England where he might find work he's walking about with a political button. He and all in politics now! But that's the way with these down here. They'll do some of every-thing but work. They don't want work!" He gestured violently, almost dancing in anger. "They too busy spreeing."

The chair creaked as Mr. Goodman sketched a pained and gentle denial. "No, man," he said, "you wrong. Things is different to before. I mean to say, the young people nowadays is different to how we was. They not just sitting back and taking things no more. They not so frighten for the white people as we was. No, man. Now take that said same boy, for an example. I don't say he don't like a spree, but he's serious, you see him there. He's a member of this new Barbados People's Party. He wants to see his own color running the government. He wants to be able to make a living right here in Barbados instead of going to any cold England. And he's right!" Mr. Goodman paused at a vehement pitch, then shrugged heavily. "What the young people must do, nuh? They got to look to something ..."

"Look to work!" And Mr. Watford thrust out a hand so that the horned knuckles caught the light.

"Yes, that's true—and it's up to we that got little something to give them work," Mr. Goodman said, and a sadness filtered among the dissipations in his eyes. "I mean to say we that got little something got to help out. In a manner of speaking, we's responsible ..."

"Responsible!" The work circled Mr. Watford's head like a gnat and he wanted to reach up and haul it down, to squash it underfoot.

Mr. Goodman spread his hands; his breathing rumbled with a sigh. "Yes, in a manner of speaking. That's why, Watford man, you got to provide little work for some poor person down in here. Hire a servant at least! 'Cause I gon tell you something ..." And he hitched forward his chair, his voice dropped to a wheeze. "People talking. Here you come back rich from big America and build a swell house and plant 'nough coconut trees and you still cleaning and cooking and thing like some woman. Man, it don't look good!" His face screwed in emphasis and he sat back. "Now, there's this girl, the daughter of a friend that just dead, and she need work bad enough. But I wouldn't like to see she working for these white people 'cause you know how those men will take advantage of she. And she'd make a good servant, man. Quiet and quick so, and nothing a-tall to feed and she can sleep anywhere about the place. And she don't have no boys always around her either...." Still talking, Mr. Goodman eased from his chair and reached the stairs with surprising agility. "You need a servant," he whispered, leaning close to Mr. Watford as he passed. "It don't look good, man, people talking. I gon send she."

Mr. Watford was overcome by nausea. Not only from Mr. Goodman's smell—a stench of salt fish, rum and sweat—but from an outrage which was like a sediment in his stomach. For a long time he stood there almost kecking from disgust, until his clock struck eight, reminding him of the sanctuary within—and suddenly his cold laugh dismissed Mr. Goodman and his proposal. Hurrying in, he locked the doors and windows against the night air and, still laughing, he slept.

The next day, coming from the grove to prepare his noon meal, he saw her. She was standing in his driveway, her bare feet like strong dark roots amid the jagged stones, her face tilted toward the sun—and she might have been standing there always waiting for him. She seemed of the sun, of the earth. The folktale of creation might have been true with her: that along a riverbank a god had scooped up the earth—rich and black and warmed by the sun—and molded her poised head with its tufted braids and then with a whimsical touch crowned it with a sober brown felt hat which should have been worn by some stout English matron in a London suburb, had sculp-tured the passionless face and drawn a screen of gossamer across her eyes to hide the void behind. Beneath her bodice her small breasts were smooth at the crest. Below her waist, her hips branched wide, the place prepared for its load of life. But it was the bold and sensual strength of her legs which completely unstrung Mr. Watford. He wanted to grab a hoe and drive her off.

"What it 'tis you want?" he called sharply.

"Mr. Goodman send me."

"Send you for what?" His voice was shrill in the glare.

She moved. Holding a caved-in valise and a pair of white sandals, her head weaving slightly as though she bore a pail of water there or a tray of mangoes, she glided over the stones as if they were smooth ground. Her bland expression did not change, but her eyes, meeting his, held a vague trust. Pausing a few feet away, she curtsied deeply. "I's the new servant."

Only Mr. Watford's cold laugh saved him from anger. As always it raised him to a height where everything below appeared senseless and insignificant—especially his people, whom the girl embodied. From this height, he could even be charitable. And thinking suddenly of how she had waited in the brutal sun since morning without taking shelter under the nearby tamarind tree, he said, not unkindly, "Well, girl, go back and tell Mr. Goodman for me that I don't need no servant."

"I can't go back."

"How you mean can't?" His head gave its angry snap.

"I'll get lashes," she said simply. "My mother say I must work the day and then if you don't wish me, I can come back. But I's not to leave till night falling, if not I get lashes."

He was shaken by her dispassion. So much so that his head dropped from its disdaining angle and his hands twitched with helplessness. Despite anything he might say or do, her fear of the whipping would keep her there until nightfall, the valise and shoes in hand. He felt his day with its order and quiet rhythms threatened by her intrusion—and suddenly waving her off as if she were an evil visitation, he hurried into the kitchen to prepare his meal.

But he paused, confused, in front of the stove, knowing that he could not cook and leave her hungry at the door, nor could he cook and serve her as though he were the servant.

"Yes, please."

They said nothing more. She entered the room with a firm step and an air almost of familiarity, placed her valise and shoes in a corner and went directly to the larder. For a time Mr. Watford stood by, his muscles flexing with anger and his eyes bounding ahead of her every move, until

feeling foolish and frighteningly useless, he went out to feed his doves.

The meal was quickly done and as he ate he heard the dry slap of her feet behind him—a pleasant sound—and then silence. When he glanced back she was squatting in the doorway, the sunlight aslant the absurd hat and her face bent to a bowl she held in one palm. She ate slowly, thoughtfully, as if fixing the taste of each spoonful in her mind.

It was then that he decided to let her work the day and at nightfall to pay her a dollar and dismiss her. His decision held when he returned later from the grove and found tea awaiting him, and then through the supper she prepared. Afterward, dressed in his white uniform, he patiently waited out the day's end on the portico, his face setting into a grim mold. Then just as dusk etched the first dark line between the sea and sky, he took out a dollar and went downstairs.

She was not in the kitchen, but the table was set for his morning tea. Muttering at her persistence, he charged down the corridor, which ran the length of the basement, flinging open the doors to the damp, empty rooms on either side, and sending the lizards and the shadows long entrenched there scuttling to safety.

He found her in the small slanted room under the stoop, asleep on an old cot he kept there, her suitcase turned down beside the bed, and the shoes, dress and the ridiculous hat piled on top. A loose nightshift muted the outline of her body and hid her legs, so that she appeared suddenly defenseless, innocent, with a child's trust in her curled hand and in her deep breathing. Standing in the doorway, with his own breathing snarled and his eyes averted, Mr. Watford felt like an intruder. She had claimed the room. Quivering with frustration, he slowly turned away, vowing that in the morning he would shove the dollar at her and lead her like a cow out of his house. . . .

Dawn brought rain and a hot wind which set the leaves rattling and swiping at the air like distraught arms. Dressing in the dawn darkness, Mr. Watford again armed himself with the dollar and, with his shoulders at an uncompromising set, plunged downstairs. He descended into the warm smell of bakes and this smell, along with the thought that she had been up before him, made his hand knot with exasperation on the banister. The knot tightened as he saw her, dust swirling at her feet as she swept the corridor, her face bent solemn to the task. Shutting her out with a lifted hand, he shouted, "Don't bother sweeping. Here's a dollar. G'long back."

The broom paused and although she did not raise her head, he sensed her groping through the shadowy maze of her mind toward his voice. Behind the dollar which he waved in her face, her eyes slowly cleared. And, surprisingly, they held no fear. Only anticipation and a tenuous trust. It was as if she expected him to say something kind.

"G'long back!" His angry cry was a plea.

Like a small, starved flame, her trust and expectancy died and she said, almost with reproof, "The rain falling."

To confirm this, the wind set the rain stinging across the windows and he could say nothing, even though the words sputtered at his lips. It was useless. There was nothing inside her to comprehend that she was not wanted. His shoulders sagged under the weight of her ignorance, and with a futile gesture he swung away, the dollar hanging from his hand like a small sword gone limp.

She became as fixed and familiar a part of the house as the stones—and as silent. He paid her five dollars a week, gave her Mondays off and in the evenings, after a time, even allowed her to sit in the alcove off the parlor, while he read with his back to her, taking no more notice of her than he did the moths on the lamp.

But once, after many silent evenings together, he detected a sound apart from the night murmurs of the sea and village and the metallic tuning of the steel band, a low, almost inhuman cry of loneliness which chilled him. Frightened, he turned to find her leaning hesitantly toward him, her eyes dark with urgency, and her face tight with bewilderment and a growing anger. He started, not understanding, and her arm lifted to stay him. Eagerly she bent closer. But as she uttered the low cry again, as her fingers described her wish to talk, he jerked around, afraid that she would be foolish enough to speak and that once she did they would be brought close. He would be forced then to acknowledge something about her which he refused to grant; above all, he would be called upon to share a little of himself. Quickly he returned to his newspaper, rustling it to settle the air, and after a time he felt her slowly, bitterly, return to her silence. . . .

Like sand poured in a careful measure from the hand, the weeks flowed down to August and on the first Monday, August Bank holiday, Mr.

Watford awoke to the sound of the excursion buses leaving the village for the annual outing, their backfire pelleting the dawn calm and the ancient motors protesting the overcrowding. Lying there, listening, he saw with disturbing clarity his mother dressed for an excursion—the white headtie wound above her dark face and her head poised like a dancer's under the heavy outing basket of food. That set of her head had haunted his years, reappearing in the girl as she walked toward him the first day. Aching with the memory, yet annoyed with himself for remembering, he went downstairs.

The girl had already left for the excursion, and although it was her day off, he felt vaguely betrayed by her eagerness to leave him. Somehow it suggested ingratitude. It was as if his doves were suddenly to refuse him their song or his trees their fruit, despite the care he gave them. Some vital past which shaped the simple mosaic of his life seemed suddenly missing. An alien silence curled like coal gas throughout the house. To escape it he remained in the grove all day and, upon his return to the house, dressed with more care than usual, putting on a fresh, starched uniform, and solemnly brushing his hair until it lay in a smooth bush above his brow. Leaning close to the mirror, but avoiding his eyes, he cleaned the white rheum at their corners, and afterward pried loose the dirt under his nails.

Unable to read his papers, he went out on the portico to escape the unnatural silence in the house, and stood with his hands clenched on the balustrade and his taut body straining forward. After a long wait he heard the buses return and voices in gay shreds upon the wind. Slowly his hands relaxed, as did his shoulders under the white uniform; for the first time that day his breathing was regular. She would soon come.

But she did not come and dusk bloomed into night, with a fragrant heat and a full moon which made the leaves glint as though touched with frost. The steel band at the crossroads began the lilting songs of sadness and seduction, and suddenly—like shades roused by the night and the music—images of the girl flitted before Mr. Watford's eyes. He saw her lost amid the carousings in the village, despoiled; he imagined someone like Mr. Goodman clasping her lewdly or tumbling her in the canebrake. His hand rose, trembling, to rid the air of her; he tried to summon his cold laugh. But, somehow, he could not dismiss her as he had always done with everyone else. Instead, he wanted to punish and protect her, to find and lead her back to the house.

As he leaned there, trying not to give way to the desire to go and find her, his fist striking the balustrade to deny his longing, he saw them. The girl first, with the moonlight like a silver patina on her skin, then the boy whom Mr. Goodman sent for the coconuts, whose easy strength and the political button—"The Old Order Shall Pass"—had always mocked and challenged Mr. Watford. They were joined in a tender battle: the boy in a sport shirt riotous with color was reaching for the girl as he leaped and spun, weightless, to the music, while she fended him off with a gesture which was lovely in its promise of surrender. Her protests were little scattered bursts: "But, man, why don't you stop, nuh . . . ? But, you know, you getting on like a real-real idiot. . . ."

Each time she chided him he leaped higher and landed closer, until finally he eluded her arm and caught her by the waist. Boldly he pressed a leg between her tightly closed legs until they opened under his pressure. Their bodies cleaved into one whirling form and while he sang she laughed like a wanton, with her hat cocked over her ear. Dancing, the stones moiling underfoot, they claimed the night. More than the night. The steel band played for them alone. The trees were their frivolous companions, swaying as they swayed. The moon rode the sky because of them.

Mr. Watford, hidden by a dense shadow, felt the tendons which strung him together suddenly go limp; above all, an obscure belief which, like rare china, he had stored on a high shelf in his mind began to tilt. He sensed the familiar specter which hovered in the night reaching out to embrace him, just as the two in the yard were embracing. Utterly unstrung, incapable of either speech or action, he stumbled into the house, only to meet there an accusing silence from the clock, which had missed its eight o'clock winding, and his newspapers lying like ruined leaves over the floor.

He lay in bed in the white uniform, waiting for sleep to rescue him, his hands seeking the comforting sound of his doves. But sleep eluded him and instead of the doves, their throats tremulous with sound, his scarred hands filled with the shape of a woman he had once kept: her skin, which had been almost bruising in its softness; the buttocks and breasts spread under his hands to inspire both cruelty and tenderness. His hands closed to softly crush those forms, and the searing thrust of passion, which he had not felt for years, stabbed his dry groin. He imagined the two outside, their passion at a pitch by now, lying together behind the tamarind tree, or perhaps—and he sat up sharply—they had been bold enough to bring their lust into the house. Did he not smell their taint on the air? Restored suddenly, he rushed downstairs. As he reached the corridor, a thread of light beckoned him from her room and he dashed furiously toward it, rehearsing the angry words which would jar their bodies apart. He neared the door, glimpsed her through the small opening, and his step faltered; the words collapsed.

She was seated alone on the cot, tenderly holding the absurd felt hat in her lap, one leg tucked under her while the other trailed down. A white sandal, its strap broken, dangled from the foot and gently knocked the floor as she absently swung her leg. Her dress was twisted around her body—and pinned to the bodice, so that it gathered the cloth between her small breasts, was the political button the boy always wore. She was dreamily fingering it, her mouth shaped by a gentle, ironic smile and her eyes strangely acute and critical. What had transpired on the cot had not only, it seemed, twisted the dress around her, tumbled her hat and broken her sandal, but had also defined her and brought the blurred forms of life into focus for her. There was a woman's force in her aspect now, a tragic knowing and acceptance in her bent head, a hint about her of Cassandra watching the future wheel before her eyes.

Before those eyes which looked to another world, Mr. Watford's anger and strength failed him and he held to the wall for support. Unreasonably, he felt that he should assume some hushed and reverent pose, to bow as she had the day she had come. If he had known their names, he would have pleaded forgiveness for the sins he had committed against her and the others all his life, against himself. If he could have borne the thought, he would have confessed that it had been love, terrible in its demand, which he had always fled. And that love had been the reason for his return. If he had been honest, he would have whispered—his head bent and a hand shading his eyes—that unlike Mr. Goodman (whom he suddenly envied for his full life) and the boy with his political button (to whom he had lost the girl), he had not been willing to bear the weight of his own responsibility. . . . But all Mr. Watford could admit, clinging there to the wall, was, simply, that he wanted to live—and that the girl held life within her as surely as she held the hat in her hands. If he could prove himself better than the boy, he could win it. Only then, he dimly knew, would he shake off the pursuer which had given him no rest since birth. Hopefully, he staggered forward, his step cautious and contrite, his hands, quivering along the wall.

She did not see or hear him as he pushed the door wider. And for some time he stood there, his shoulders hunched in humility, his skin stripped away to reveal each flaw, his whole self offered in one outstetched hand. Still unaware of him, she swung her leg, and the dangling shoe struck a derisive note. Then, just as he had turned away that evening in the parlor when she had uttered her low call, she turned away now, refusing him.

Mr. Watford's body went slack and then stiffened ominously. He knew that he would have to wrest from her the strength needed to sustain him. Slamming the door, he cried, his voice cracked and strangled, "What you and him was doing in here? Tell me! I'll not have you bringing nastiness round here. Tell me!"

She did not start. Perhaps she had been aware of him all along and had expected his outburst. Or perhaps his demented eye and the desperation rising from him like a musk filled her with pity instead of fear. Whatever, her benign smile held and her eyes remained abstracted until his hand reached out to fling her back on the cot. Then, frowning, she stood up, wobbling a little on the broken shoe and holding the political button as if it was a new power which would steady and protect her. With a cruel flick of her arm she struck aside his hand and, in a voice as cruel, halted him. "But you best move and don't come holding on to me, you nasty, pissy old man. That's all you is, despite yuh big house and fancy furnitures and yuh newspapers from America. You ain't people, Mr. Watford, you ain't people!" And with a look and a lift of her head which made her condemnation final, she placed the hat atop her braids, and turning aside picked up the valise which had always lain, packed, beside the cot—as if even on the first day she had known that this night would come and had been prepared against it. . . .

Mr. Watford did not see her leave, for a pain squeezed his heart dry and the driven blood was a bright, blinding cataract over his eyes. But his inner eye was suddenly clear. For the first time it gazed mutely upon the waste and pretense which had spanned his years. Flung there against the door by the girl's small blow, his body slowly crumpled under the weariness he had long denied. He sensed that dark but unsubstantial figure which roamed the nights searching for him wind him in its chill embrace. He struggled against it, his hands clutching the air with the spastic eloquence of a drowning man. He moaned—and the anguished sound reached beyond the room to fill the house. It escaped to the yard and his doves swelled their throats, moaning with him.

Ernest J. Gaines (1933–   )

Ernest J. Gaines was born on January 15, 1933, in Oscar, Louisiana. His father was employed on a plantation, and young Ernest worked in the fields from an early age. In 1948 the family moved to Vallejo, California, seeking greater opportunity. After high school and two years in the army, Gaines studied at San Francisco State College, receiving the B.A. degree in 1957. Graduate study at Stanford University followed in 1958–1959, with emphasis on the writing of fiction. He received the Joseph Henry Jackson Literary Award in 1959. Since then he has lived quietly in San Francisco, completely dedicated to his craft.

His three novels are *Catherine Carmier* (1964), *Of Love and Dust* (1967), and *The Autobiography of Miss Jane Pittman* (1971). *Bloodline*

(1968) is a collection of five long stories. Gaines' fictional subject is Black life in rural Louisiana—its bleakness, trials, and occasional triumphs. Often he is concerned with the special difficulties of being a man—or a child—in the hostile environment of a racist society. The restrained but intense effects he achieves are the result of complete immersion in his subjects, total and sympathetic understanding of his characters, and impressive literary artistry.

The Sky Is Gray

1

Go'n be coming in a few minutes. Coming round that bend down there full speed. And I'm go'n get out my handkerchief and wave it down, and we go'n get on it and go.

I keep on looking for it, but Mama don't look that way no more. She's looking down the road where we just come from. It's a long old road, and far 's you can see you don't see nothing but gravel. You got dry weeds on both sides, and you got trees on both sides, and fences on both sides, too. And you got cows in the pastures and they standing close together. And when we was coming out here to catch the bus I seen the smoke coming out of the cows's noses.

I look at my mamma and I know what she's thinking. I been with Mama so much, just me and her, I know what she's thinking all the time. Right now it's home—Auntie and them. She's thinking if they got enough wood—if she left enough there to keep them warm till we get back. She's thinking if it go'n rain and if any of them go'n have to go out in the rain. She's thinking 'bout the hog—if he go'n get out, and if Ty and Val be able to get him back in. She always worry like that when she leaves the house. She don't worry too much if she leave me there with the smaller ones, 'cause she know I'm go'n look after them and look after Auntie and everything else. I'm the oldest and she say I'm the man.

I look at my mama and I love my mama. She's wearing that black coat and that black hat and she's looking sad. I love my mama and I want put my arm round her and tell her. But I'm not supposed to do that. She say that's weakness and that's crybaby stuff, and she don't want no crybaby round her. She don't want you to be scared, either. 'Cause Ty's scared of ghosts and she's always whipping him. I'm scared of the dark, too, but I make 'tend I ain't. I make 'tend I ain't 'cause I'm the oldest, and I got to set a good sample for the rest. I can't ever be scared and I can't ever cry. And that's why I never said nothing 'bout my teeth. It's been hurting me and hurting me close to a month now, but I never said it. I didn't say it 'cause I didn't want act like a crybaby, and 'cause I know we didn't have enough money to go have it pulled. But, Lord, it been hurting me. And look like it wouldn't start till at night when you was trying to get yourself little sleep. Then soon 's you shut your eyes—ummm-ummm, Lord, look like it go right down to your heart-string.

"Hurting, hanh?" Ty'd say.

I'd shake my head, but I wouldn't open my mouth for nothing. You open your mouth and let that wind in, and it almost kill you.

I'd just lay there and listen to them snore. Ty there, right 'side me, and Auntie and Val over by the fireplace. Val younger than me and Ty, and he sleeps with Auntie. Mama sleeps round the other side with Louis and Walker.

I'd just lay there and listen to them, and listen to that wind out there, and listen to that fire in the fireplace. Sometimes it'd stop long enough to let me get little rest. Sometimes it just hurt, hurt, hurt. Lord, have mercy.

2

Auntie knowed it was hurting me. I didn't tell nobody but Ty, 'cause we buddies and he ain't go'n tell nobody. But some kind of way Auntie found out. When she asked me, I told her no, nothing was wrong. But she knowed it all the time. She told me to mash up a piece of aspirin and wrap it in some cotton and jugg it down in that hole. I did it, but it didn't do no good. It stopped for a little while, and started right back again. Auntie wanted to tell Mama, but I told her, "Uh-uh." 'Cause I knowed we didn't have any money, and it just was go'n make her mad again. So Auntie told Monsieur Bayonne, and Monsieur Bayonne came over to the house and told me to kneel down 'side him on the fire-place. He put his finger in his mouth and made the Sign of the Cross on my jaw. The tip of Monsieur Bayonne's finger is some hard, 'cause he's always playing on that guitar. If we sit outside at night we can always hear Monsieur Bayonne playing on his guitar. Sometimes we leave him out there playing on the guitar.

Monsieur Bayonne made the Sign of the Cross over and over on my jaw, but that didn't do no good. Even when he prayed and told me to pray some, too, that tooth still hurt me.

"How you feeling?" he say.

"Same," I say.

He kept on praying and making the Sign of the Cross and I kept on praying, too.

"Still hurting?" he say.

"Yes, sir."

Monsieur Bayonne mashed harder and harder on my jaw. He mashed so hard he almost pushed me over on Ty. But then he stopped.

"What kind of prayers you praying, boy?" he say.

"Baptist," I say.

"Well, I'll be—no wonder that tooth still killing him. I'm going one way and he pulling the other. Boy, don't you know any Catholic prayers?"

"I know 'Hail Mary,'" I say.

"Then you better start saying it."

"Yes, sir."

He started mashing on my jaw again, and I could hear him praying at the same time. And, sure enough, after while it stopped hurting me.

Me and Ty went outside where Monsieur Bayonne's two hounds was and we started playing with them. "Let's go hunting," Ty say. "All right," I say; and we went on back in the pasture. Soon the hounds got on a trail, and me and Ty followed them all 'cross the pasture and then back in the woods, too. And then they cornered this little old rabbit and killed him, and me and Ty made them get back, and we picked up the rabbit and started on back home. But my tooth had started hurting me again. It was hurting me plenty now, but I wouldn't tell Monsieur Bayonne.

That night I didn't sleep a bit, and first thing in the morning Auntie told me to go back and let Monsieur Bayonne pray over me some more. Monsieur Bayonne was in his kitchen making coffee when I got there. Soon 's he seen me he knowed what was wrong.

"All right, kneel down there 'side that stove," he say. "And this time make sure you pray Catholic. I don't know nothing 'bout that Baptist, and I don't want know nothing 'bout him."

3

Last night Mama say, "Tomorrow we going to town."

"It ain't hurting me no more," I say. "I can eat anything on it."

"Tomorrow we going to town," she say.

And after she finished eating, she got up and went to bed. She always go to bed early now. 'Fore Daddy went in the Army, she used to stay up late. All of us sitting out on the gallery or round the fire. But now, look like soon 's she finish eating she go to bed.

This morning when I woke up, her and Auntie was standing 'fore the fireplace. She say: "Enough to get there and get back. Dollar and a half to have it pulled. Twenty-five for me to go, twenty-five for him. Twenty-five for me to come back, twenty-five for him. Fifty cents left. Guess I get little piece of salt meat with that."

"Sure can use it," Auntie say. "White beans and no salt meat ain't white beans."

"I do the best I can," Mama say.

They was quiet after that, and I made 'tend I was still asleep.

"James, hit the floor," Auntie say.

I still made 'tend I was asleep. I didn't want them to know I was listening.

"All right," Auntie say, shaking me by the shoulder. "Come on. Today's the day."

I pushed the cover down to get out, and Ty grabbed it and pulled it back.

"You, too, Ty," Auntie say.

"I ain't getting no teef pulled," Ty say.

"Don't mean it ain't time to get up," Auntie say. "Hit it, Ty."

Ty got up grumbling.

"James, you hurry up and get in your clothes and eat your food," Auntie say. "What time y'all coming back?" she say to Mama.

"That 'leven o'clock bus," Mama say. "Got to get back in that field this evening."

"Get a move on you, James," Auntie say.

I went in the kitchen and washed my face, then I ate my breakfast. I was having bread and syrup. The bread was warm and hard and tasted good. And I tried to make it last a long time.

Ty came back there grumbling and mad at me.

"Got to get up," he say. "I ain't having no teefes pulled. What I got to be getting up for?"

Ty poured some syrup in his pan and got a piece of bread. He didn't wash his hands, neither his face, and I could see that white stuff in his eyes.

"You the one getting your teef pulled," he say. "What I got to get up for. I bet if I was getting a teef pulled, you wouldn't be getting up. Shucks; syrup again. I'm getting tired of this old syrup. Syrup, syrup, syrup. I'm go'n take with the sugar diabetes. I want me some bacon sometime."

"Go out in the field and work and you can have your bacon," Auntie say. She stood in the middle door looking at Ty. "You better be glad you got syrup. Some people ain't got that—hard's time is."

"Shucks," Ty say. "How can I be strong."

"I don't know too much 'bout your strength," Auntie say; "but I know where you go'n be hot at, you keep that grumbling up. James, get a move on you; your mama waiting."

I ate my last piece of bread and went in the front room. Mama was standing 'fore the fireplace warming her hands. I put on my coat and my cap, and we left the house.

4

I look down there again, but it still ain't coming. I almost say, "It ain't coming yet," but I keep my mouth shut. 'Cause that's something else she don't like. She don't like for you to say something just for nothing. She can see it ain't coming. I can see it ain't coming, so why say it ain't coming. I don't say it, I turn and look at the river that's back of us. It's so cold the smoke's just raising up from the water. I see a bunch of pool-doos not too far out—just on the other side the lilies. I'm wondering if you can eat pool-doos. I ain't too sure, 'cause I ain't never ate none. But I done ate owls and blackbirds, and I done ate redbirds, too. I didn't want kill the redbirds, but she made me kill them. They had two of them back there. One in my trap, one in Ty's trap. Me

and Ty was go'n play with them and let them go, but she made me kill them 'cause we needed the food.

"I can't," I say. "I can't."

"Here," she say. "Take it."

"I can't," I say. "I can't. I can't kill him, Mama, please."

"Here," she say. "Take this fork, James."

"Please, Mama, I can't kill him," I say.

I could tell she was go'n hit me. I jerked back, but I didn't jerk back soon enough.

"Take it," she say.

I took it and reached in for him, but he kept on hopping to the back.

"I can't, Mama," I say. The water just kept on running down my face. "I can't," I say.

"Get him out of there," she say.

I reached in for him and he kept on hopping to the back. Then I reached in farther, and he pecked me on the hand.

"I can't, Mama," I say.

She slapped me again.

I reached in again, but he kept on hopping out my way. Then he hopped to one side and I reached there. The fork got him on the leg and I heard his leg pop. I pulled my hand out 'cause I had hurt him.

"Give it here," she say, and jerked the fork out my hand.

She reached in and got the little bird right in the neck. I heard the fork go in his neck, and I heard it go in the ground. She brought him out and helt him right in front of me.

"That's one," she say. She shook him off and gived me the fork. "Get the other one."

"I can't, Mama," I say. "I'll do anything, but don't make me do that."

She went to the corner of the fence and broke the biggest switch over there she could find. I knelt 'side the trap, crying.

"Get him out of there," she say.

"I can't, Mama."

She started hitting me 'cross the back. I went down on the ground, crying.

"Get him," she say.

"Octavia?" Auntie say.

'Cause she had come out of the house and she was standing by the tree looking at us.

"Get him out of there," Mama say.

"Octavia," Auntie say, "explain to him. Explain to him. Just don't beat him. Explain to him."

But she hit me and hit me and hit me.

I'm still young—I ain't no more than eight; but

I know now; I know why I had to do it. (They was so little, though. They was so little. I 'member how I picked the feathers off them and cleaned them and helt them over the fire. Then we all ate them. Ain't had but a little bitty piece each, but we all had a little bitty piece, and everybody just looked at me 'cause they was so proud.) Suppose she had to go away? That's why I had to do it. Suppose she had to go away like Daddy went away? Then who was go'n look after us? They had to be somebody left to carry on. I didn't know it then, but I know it now. Auntie and Monsieur Bayonne talked to me and made me see.

5

Time I see it I get out my handkerchief and start waving. It's still 'way down there, but I keep waving anyhow. Then it come up and stop and me and Mama get on. Mama tell me go sit in the back while she pay. I do like she say, and the people look at me. When I pass the little sign that say "White" and "Colored," I start looking for a seat. I just see one of them back there, but I don't take it, 'cause I want my mama to sit down herself. She comes in the back and sit down, and I lean on the seat. They got seats in the front, but I know I can't sit there, 'cause I have to sit back of the sign. Anyhow, I don't want sit there if my mama go'n sit back here.

They got a lady sitting 'side my mama and she looks at me and smiles little bit. I smile back, but I don't open my mouth, 'cause the wind'll get in and make that tooth ache. The lady take out a pack of gum and reach me a slice, but I shake my head. The lady just can't understand why a little boy'll turn down gum, and she reach me a slice again. This time I point to my jaw. The lady understands and smiles little bit, and I smile little bit, but I don't open my mouth, though.

They got a girl sitting 'cross from me. She got on a red overcoat and her hair's plaited in one big plait. First, I make 'tend I don't see her over there, but then I start looking at her little bit. She make 'tend she don't see me, either, but I catch her looking that way. She got a cold, and every now and then she h'ist that little handkerchief to her nose. She ought to blow it, but she don't. Must think she's too much a lady or something.

Every time she h'ist that little handkerchief, the lady 'side her say something in her ear. She shakes her head and lays her hands in her lap again. Then I catch her kind of looking where I'm at. I smile at her little bit. But think she'll smile back? Uh-uh. She just turn up her little old nose and turn her head. Well, I show her both of us can turn us head. I turn mine too and look out at the river.

The river is gray. The sky is gray. They have pool-doos on the water. The water is wavy, and the pool-doos go up and down. The bus go round a turn, and you got plenty trees hiding the river. Then the bus go round another turn, and I can see the river again.

I look toward the front where all the white people sitting. Then I look at that little old gal again. I don't look right at her, 'cause I don't want all them people to know I love her. I just look at her little bit, like I'm looking out that window over there. But she knows I'm looking that way, and she kind of look at me, too. The lady sitting 'side her catch her this time, and she leans over and says something in her ear.

"I don't love him nothing," that little old gal says out loud.

Everybody back there hear her mouth, and all of them look at us and laugh.

"I don't love you, either," I say. "So you don't have to turn up your nose, Miss."

"You the one looking," she say.

"I wasn't looking at you," I say. "I was looking out that window, there."

"Out that window, my foot," she say. "I seen you. Everytime I turned round you was looking at me."

"You must of been looking yourself if you seen me all them times," I say.

"Shucks," she say, "I got me all kind of boy-friends."

"I got girlfriends, too," I say.

"Well, I just don't want you getting your hopes up," she say.

I don't say no more to that little old gal 'cause I don't want have to bust her in the mouth. I lean on the seat where Mama sitting, and I don't even look that way no more. When we get to Bayonne, she jugg her little old tongue out at me. I make 'tend I'm go'n hit her, and she duck down 'side her mama. And all the people laugh at us again.

6

Me and Mama get off and start walking in town. Bayonne is a little bitty town. Baton Rouge is a hundred times bigger than Bayonne. I went to Baton Rouge once—me, Ty, Mama, and Daddy. But that was 'way back yonder, 'fore Daddy went in the Army. I wonder when we go'n see him again. I wonder when. Look like he ain't ever coming back home. . . . Even the pavement all cracked in Bayonne. Got grass shooting right out the sidewalk. Got weeds in the ditch, too; just like they got at home.

It's some cold in Bayonne. Look like it's colder than it is home. The wind blows in my face, and I feel that stuff running down my nose. I sniff. Mama says use that handkerchief. I blow my nose and put it back.

We pass a school and I see them white children playing in the yard. Big old red school, and them children just running and playing. Then we pass a café, and I see a bunch of people in there eating. I wish I was in there 'cause I'm cold. Mama tells me keep my eyes in front where they belong.

We pass stores that's got dummies, and we pass another café, and then we pass a shoe shop, and that bald-head man in there fixing on a shoe. I look at him and I butt into that white lady, and Mama jerks me in front and tells me stay there.

We come up to the courthouse, and I see the flag waving there. This flag ain't like the one we got at school. This one here ain't got but a handful of stars. One at school got a big pile of stars—one for every state. We pass it and we turn and there it is—the dentist office. Me and Mama go in, and they got people sitting everywhere you look. They even got a little boy in there younger than me.

Me and Mama sit on that bench, and a white lady come in there and ask me what my name is. Mama tells her and the white lady goes on back. Then I hear somebody hollering in there. Soon 's that little boy hear him hollering, he starts hollering, too. His mama pats him and pats him, trying to make him hush up, but he ain't thinking 'bout his mama.

The man that was hollering in there comes out holding his jaw. He is a big old man and he's wearing overalls and a jumper.

"Got it, hanh?" another man asks him.

The man shakes his head—don't want open his mouth.

"Man, I thought they was killing you in there," the other man says. "Hollering like a pig under a gate."

The man don't say nothing. He just heads for the door, and the other man follows him.

"John Lee," the white lady says. "John Lee Williams."

The little boy juggs his head down in his mama's lap and holler more now. His mama tells him go with the nurse, but he ain't thinking 'bout his mama. His mama tells him again, but he don't even hear her. His mama picks him up and takes him in there, and even when the white lady shuts the door I can still hear little old John Lee.

"I often wonder why the Lord let a child like that suffer," a lady says to my mama. The lady's sitting right in front of us on another bench. She's got on a white dress and a black sweater. She must be a nurse or something herself, I reckon.

"Not us to question," a man says.

"Sometimes I don't know if we shouldn't," the lady says.

"I know definitely we shouldn't," the man says. The man looks like a preacher. He's big and fat and he's got on a black suit. He's got a gold chain, too.

"Why?" the lady says.

"Why anything?" the preacher says.

"Yes," the lady says. "Why anything?"

"Not us to question," the preacher says.

The lady looks at the preacher a little while and looks at Mama again.

"And look like it's the poor who suffers the most," she says, "I don't understand it."

"Best not to even try," the preacher says. "He works in mysterious ways—wonders to perform."

Right then little John Lee bust out hollering, and everybody turn they head to listen.

"He's not a good dentist," the lady says. "Dr. Robillard is much better. But more expensive. That's why most of the colored people come here. The white people go to Dr. Robillard. Y'all from Bayonne?"

"Down the river," my mama says. And that's all she go'n say, 'cause she don't talk much. But the lady keeps on looking at her, and so she says, "Near Morgan."

"I see," the lady says.

7

"That's the trouble with the black people in this country today," somebody else says. This one here's sitting on the same side me and Mama's sitting, and he is kind of sitting in front of that preacher. He looks like a teacher or somebody that goes to college. He's got on a suit, and he's got a book that he's been reading. "We don't question is exactly our problem," he says. "We should question and question and question— question everything."

The preacher just looks at him a long time. He done put a toothpick or something in his mouth, and he just keeps on turning it and turning it. You can see he don't like that boy with that book.

"Maybe you can explain what you mean," he says.

"I said what I meant," the boy says. "Question everything. Every stripe, every star, every word spoken. Everything."

"It 'pears to me that this young lady and I was talking 'bout God, young man," the preacher says.

"Question Him, too," the boy says.

"Wait," the preacher says. "Wait now."

"You heard me right," the boy says. "His existence as well as everything else. Everything."

The preacher just looks across the room at the boy. You can see he's getting madder and madder. But mad or no mad, the boy ain't thinking 'bout him. He looks at that preacher just 's hard 's the preacher looks at him.

"Is this what they coming to?" the preacher says. "Is this what we educating them for?"

"You're not educating me," the boy says. "I wash dishes at night so that I can go to school in the day. So even the words you spoke need questioning."

The preacher just looks at him and shakes his head.

"When I come in this room and seen you there with your book, I said to myself, 'There's an intelligent man.' How wrong a person can be."

"Show me one reason to believe in the existence of a God," the boys says.

"My heart tells me," the preacher says.

"'My heart tells me,'" the boys says. "'My heart tells me.' Sure, 'My heart tells me.' And as long as you listen to what your heart tells you, you will have only what the white man gives you and nothing more. Me, I don't listen to my heart. The purpose of the heart is to pump blood throughout the body, and nothing else."

"Who's your paw, boy?" the preacher says.

"Why?"

"Who is he?"

"He's dead."

"And your mon?"

"She's in Charity Hospital with pneumonia. Half killed herself, working for nothing."

"And 'cause he's dead and she's sick, you mad at the world?"

"I'm not mad at the world. I'm questioning the world. I'm questioning it with cold logic, sir. What do words like Freedom, Liberty, God, White, Colored mean? I want to know. That's why *you* are sending us to school, to read and to ask questions. And because we ask these questions, you call us mad. No sir, it is not us who are mad."

"You keep saying 'us'?"

"'Us.' Yes—us. I'm not alone."

The preacher just shakes his head. Then he looks at everybody in the room—everybody. Some of the people look down at the floor, keep from looking at him. I kind of look 'way myself, but soon 's I know he done turn his head, I look that way again.

"I'm sorry for you," he says to the boy.

"Why?" the boy says. "Why not be sorry for yourself? Why are you so much better off than I am? Why aren't you sorry for these other people in here? Why not be sorry for the lady who had to drag her child into the dentist office? Why not be sorry for the lady sitting on that bench over there? Be sorry for them. Not for me. Some way or the other I'm going to make it."

"No, I'm sorry for you," the preacher says.

"Of course, of course," the boy says, nodding his head. "You're sorry for me because I rock that pillar you're leaning on."

"You can't ever rock the pillar I'm leaning on, young man. It's stronger than anything man can ever do."

"You believe in God because a man told you to believe in God," the boy says. "A white man told you to believe in God. And why? To keep you ignorant so he can keep his feet on your neck."

"So now we the ignorant?" the preacher says.

"Yes," the boy says. "Yes." And he opens his book again.

The preacher just looks at him sitting there. The boy done forgot all about him. Everybody else make 'tend they done forgot the squabble, too.

Then I see that preacher getting up real slow. Preacher's a great big old man and he got to brace himself to get up. He comes over where the boy is sitting. He just stands there a little while looking down at him, but the boy don't raise his head.

"Get up, boy," preacher says.

The boy looks up at him, then he shuts his book real slow and stands up. Preacher just hauls back and hit him in the face. The boy falls back 'gainst the wall, but he straightens himself up and looks right back at that preacher.

"You forgot the other cheek," he says.

The preacher hauls back and hit him again on the other side. But this time the boy braces himself and don't fall.

"That hasn't changed a thing," he says.

The preacher just looks at the boy. The preacher's breathing real hard like he just run up a big hill. The boy sits down and opens his book again.

"I feel sorry for you," the preacher says. "I never felt so sorry for a man before."

The boy makes 'tend he don't even hear that preacher. He keeps on reading his book. The preacher goes back and gets his hat off the chair.

"Excuse me," he says to us. "I'll come back some other time. Y'all, please excuse me."

And he looks at the boy and goes out the room. The boy h'ist his hand up to his mouth one time to wipe 'way some blood. All the rest of the time he keeps on reading. And nobody else in there say a word.

8

Little John Lee and his mama come out the dentist office, and the nurse calls somebody else in. Then little bit later they come out, and the nurse calls another name. But fast 's she calls somebody in there, somebody's else comes in the place where we sitting, and the room stays full.

The people coming in now, all of them wearing big coats. One of them says something 'bout sleeting, another one says he hope not. Another one says he think it ain't nothing but rain. 'Cause, he says, rain can get awful cold this time of year.

All round the room they talking. Some of them talking to people right by them, some of them talking to people clear 'cross the room, some of them talking to anybody'll listen. It's a little bitty room, no bigger than us kitchen, and I can see everybody in there. The little old room's full of smoke, 'cause you got two old men smoking pipes over by that side door. I think I feel my tooth thumping me some, and I hold my breath and wait. I wait and wait, but it don't thump me no more. Thank God for that.

I feel like going to sleep, and I lean back 'gainst the wall. But I'm scared to go to sleep. Scared 'cause the nurse might call my name and I won't hear her. And Mama might go to sleep, too, and she'll be mad if neither of us heard the nurse.

I look up at Mama. I love my mama. I love my mama. And when cotton come I'm go'n get her a new coat. And I ain't go'n get a black one, either. I think I'm go'n get her a red one.

"They got some books over there," I say. "Want read one of them?"

Mama looks at the books, but she don't answer me.

"You got yourself a little man there," the lady says.

Mama don't say nothing to the lady, but she must've smiled, 'cause I seen the lady smiling back. The lady looks at me a little while, like she's feeling sorry for me.

"You sure got that preacher out here in a hurry," she says to that boy.

The boy looks up at her and looks in his book again. When I grow up I want be just like him. I want clothes like that and I want keep a book with me, too.

"You really don't believe in God?" the lady says.

"No," he says.

"But why?" the lady says.

"Because the wind is pink," he says.

"What?" the lady says.

The boy don't answer her no more. He just reads in his book.

"Talking 'bout the wind is pink," that old lady says. She's sitting on the same bench with the boy and she's trying to look in his face. The boy makes 'tend the old lady ain't even there. He just keeps on reading. "Wind is pink," she says again. "Eh, Lord, what children go'n be saying next?"

The lady 'cross from us bust out laughing.

"That's a good one," she says. "The wind is pink. Yes sir, that's a good one."

"Don't you believe the wind is pink?" the boy says. He keeps his head down in the book.

"Course I believe it, honey," the lady says. "Course I do." She looks at us and winks her eye. "And what color is grass, honey?"

"Grass? Grass is black."

She bust out laughing again. The boy looks at her.

"Don't you believe grass is black?" he says.

The lady quits her laughing and looks at him.

Everybody else looking at him, too. The place quiet, quiet.

"Grass is green, honey," the lady says. "It was green yesterday, it's green today, and it's go'n be green tomorrow."

"How do you know it's green?"

"I know because I know."

"You don't know it's green," the boy says. "You believe it's green because someone told you it was green. If someone had told you it was black you'd believe it was black."

"It's green," the lady says. "I know green when I see green."

"Prove it's green," the boy says.

"Sure, now," the lady says. "Don't tell me it's coming to that."

"It's coming to just that," the boy says. "Words mean nothing. One means no more than the other."

"That's what it all coming to?" that old lady says. That old lady got on a turban and she got on two sweaters. She got a green sweater under a black sweater. I can see the green sweater 'cause some of the buttons on the other sweater's missing.

"Yes ma'am," the boy says. "Words mean nothing. Action is the only thing. Doing. That's the only thing."

"Other words, you want the Lord to come down here and show Hisself to you?" she says.

"Exactly, ma'am," he says.

"You don't mean that, I'm sure?" she says.

"I do, ma'am," he says.

"Done, Jesus," the old lady says, shaking her head.

"I didn't go 'long with that preacher at first," the other lady says; "but now—I don't know. When a person say the grass is black, he's either a lunatic or something's wrong."

"Prove to me that it's green," the boy says.

"It's green because the people say it's green."

"Those same people say we're citizens of these United States," the boy says.

"I think I'm a citizen," the lady says.

"Citizens have certain rights," the boy says. "Name me one right that you have. One right, granted by the Constitution, that you can exercise in Bayonne."

The lady don't answer him. She just looks at him like she don't know what he's talking 'bout. I know I don't.

"Things changing," she says.

"Things are changing because some black men have begun to think with their brains and not their hearts," the boy says.

"You trying to say these people don't believe in God?"

"I'm sure some of them do. Maybe most of them do. But they don't believe that God is going to touch these white people's hearts and change things tomorrow. Things change through action. By no other way."

Everybody sit quiet and look at the boy. Nobody says a thing. Then the lady 'cross the room from me and Mama just shakes her head.

"Let's hope that not all your generation feel the same way you do," she says.

"Think what you please, it doesn't matter," the boy says. "But it will be men who listen to their heads and not their hearts who will see that your children have a better chance than you had."

"Let's hope they ain't all like you, though," the old lady says. "Done forgot the heart absolutely."

"Yes ma'am, I hope they aren't all like me," the boy says. "Unfortunately, I was born too late to believe in your God. Let's hope that the ones who come after will have your faith—if not in your God, then in something else, something definitely that they can lean on. I haven't anything. For me, the wind is pink, the grass is black."

9

The nurse comes in the room where we all sitting and waiting and says the doctor won't take no more patients till one o'clock this evening. My mama jumps up off the bench and goes up to the white lady.

"Nurse, I have to go back in the field this evening," she says.

"The doctor is treating his last patient now," the nurse says. "One o'clock this evening."

"Can I at least speak to the doctor?" my mama asks.

"I'm his nurse," the lady says.

"My little boy's sick," my mama says. "Right now his tooth almost killing him."

The nurse looks at me. She's trying to make up her mind if to let me come in. I look at her real pitiful. The tooth ain't hurting me at all, but Mama say it is, so I make 'tend for her sake.

"This evening," the nurse says, and goes on back in the office.

"Don't feel 'jected, honey," the lady says to Mama. "I been round them a long time—they take you when they want to. If you was white, that's something else; but we the wrong color."

Mama don't say nothing to the lady, and me and her go outside and stand 'gainst the wall. It's cold out there. I can feel that wind going through my coat. Some of the other people come out of the room and go up the street. Me and Mama stand there a little while and we start walking. I don't know where we going. When we come to the other street we just stand there.

"You don't have to make water, do you?" Mama says.

"No, ma'am," I say.

We go on up the street. Walking real slow. I can tell Mama don't know where she's going. When we come to a store we stand there and look at the dummies. I look at a little boy wearing a brown overcoat. He's got on brown shoes, too. I look at my old shoes and look at his'n again. You wait till summer, I say.

Me and Mama walk away. We come up to another store and we stop and look at them dummies, too. Then we go on again. We pass a café where the white people in there eating. Mama tells me keep my eyes in front where they belong, but I can't help from seeing them people eat. My stomach starts to growling 'cause I'm hungry. When I see people eating, I get hungry; when I see a coat, I get cold.

A man whistles at my mama when we go by a filling station. She makes 'tend she don't even see him. I look back and I feel like hitting him in the mouth. If I was bigger, I say; if I was bigger, you'd see.

We keep on going. I'm getting colder and colder, but I don't say nothing. I feel that stuff running down my nose and I sniff.

"That rag," Mama says.

I get it out and wipe my nose. I'm getting cold all over now—my face, my hands, my feet, everything. We pass another little café, but this'n for white people, too, and we can't go in there, either. So we just walk. I'm so cold now I'm 'bout ready to say it. If I knowed where we was going I wouldn't be so cold, but I don't know where we going. We go, we go, we go. We walk clean out of Bayonne. Then we cross the street and we come back. Same thing I seen when I got off the bus this morning. Same old trees, same old walk, same old weeds, same old cracked pave—same old everything.

I sniff again.

"That rag," Mama says.

I wipe my nose real fast and jugg that handkerchief back in my pocket 'fore my hand gets too cold. I raise my head and I can see David's hardware store. When we come up to it, we go in. I don't know why, but I'm glad.

It's warm in there. It's so warm in there you don't ever want to leave. I look for the heater, and I see it over by them barrels. Three white men standing round the heater talking in Creole. One of them comes over to see what my mama want.

"Got any axe handles?" she says.

Me, Mama and the white man start to the back, but Mama stops me when we come up to the heater. She and the white man go on. I hold my hands over the heater and look at them. They go all the way to the back, and I see the white man pointing to the axe handles 'gainst the wall. Mama takes one of them and shakes it like she's trying to figure how much it weighs. Then she rubs her hand over it from one end to the other end. She turns it over and looks at the other side, then she shakes it again, and shakes her head and puts it back. She gets another one and she does it just like she did the first one, then she shakes her head. Then she gets a brown one and do it that, too. But she don't like this one, either. Then she gets another one, but 'fore she shakes it or anything, she looks at me. Look like she's trying to say something to me, but I don't know what it is. All I know is I done got warm now and I'm feeling right smart better. Mama shakes this axe handle just like she did the others, and shakes her head and says something to the white man. The white man just looks at his pile of axe handles, and when Mama pass him to come to the front, the white man just scratch his head and follows her. She tells me come on and we go on out and start walking again.

We walk and walk, and no time at all I'm cold again. Look like I'm colder now 'cause I can still remember how good it was back there. My stomach growls and I suck it in to keep Mama from hearing it. She's walking right 'side me, and it growls so loud you can hear it a mile. But Mama don't say a word.

10

When we come up to the courthouse, I look at the clock. It's got quarter to twelve. Mean we got another hour and a quarter to be out here in the cold. We go and stand 'side a building. Something hits my cap and I look up at the sky. Sleet's falling.

I look at Mama standing there. I want stand close 'side her, but she don't like that. She say that's crybaby stuff. She say you got to stand for yourself, by yourself.

"Let's go back to that office," she says.

We cross the street. When we get to the dentist office I try to open the door, but I can't. I twist and twist, but I can't. Mama pushes me to the side and she twist the knob, but she can't open the door, either. She turns 'way from the door. I look at her, but I don't move and I don't say nothing. I done seen her like this before and I'm scared of her.

"You hungry?" she says. She says it like she's mad at me, like I'm the cause of everything.

"No, ma'am," I say.

"You want eat and walk back, or you rather don't eat and ride?"

"I ain't hungry," I say.

I ain't just hungry, but I'm cold, too. I'm so hungry and cold I want to cry. And look like I'm getting colder and colder. My feet done got numb. I try to work my toes, but I don't even feel them. Look like I'm go'n die. Look like I'm go'n stand right here and freeze to death. I think 'bout home. I think 'bout Val and Auntie and Ty and Louis and Walker. It's 'bout twelve o'clock and I know they eating dinner now. I can hear Ty making jokes. He done forgot 'bout getting up early this morning and right now he's probably making jokes. Always trying to make somebody laugh. I wish I was right there listening to him. Give anything in the world if I was home round the fire.

"Come on," Mama says.

We start walking again. My feet so numb I can't hardly feel them. We turn the corner and go on back up the street. The clock on the courthouse starts hitting for twelve.

The sleet's coming down plenty now. They hit the pave and bounce like rice. Oh, Lord; oh, Lord, I pray. Don't let me die, don't let me die, don't let me die, Lord.

11

Now I know where we going. We going back of town where the colored people eat. I don't care

if I don't eat. I been hungry before. I can stand it. But I can't stand the cold.

I can see we go'n have a long walk. It's 'bout a mile down there. But I don't mind. I know when I get there I'm go'n warm myself. I think I can hold out. My hands numb in my pockets and my feet numb, too, but if I keep moving I can hold out. Just don't stop no more, that's all.

The sky's gray. The sleet keeps on falling. Falling like rain now—plenty, plenty. You can hear it hitting the pave. You can see it bouncing. Sometimes it bounces two times 'fore it settles.

We keep on going. We don't say nothing. We just keep on going, keep on going.

I wonder what Mama's thinking. I hope she ain't mad at me. When summer come I'm go'n pick plenty cotton and get her a coat. I'm go'n get her a red one.

I hope they'd make it summer all the time. I'd be glad if it was summer all the time—but it ain't. We got to have winter, too. Lord, I hate the winter. I guess everybody hate the winter.

I don't sniff this time. I get out my handkerchief and wipe my nose. My hand's so cold I can hardly hold the handkerchief.

I think we getting close, but we ain't there yet. I wonder where everybody is. Can't see a soul but us. Look like we the only two people moving round today. Must be too cold for the rest of the people to move round in.

I can hear my teeth. I hope they don't knock together too hard and make that bad one hurt. Lord, that's all I need, for that bad one to start off.

I hear a church bell somewhere. But today ain't Sunday. They must be ringing for a funeral or something.

I wonder what they doing at home. They must be eating. Monsieur Bayonne might be there with his guitar. One day Ty played with Monsieur Bayonne's guitar and broke one of the strings. Monsieur Bayonne was some mad with Ty. He say Ty wasn't go'n ever 'mount to nothing. Ty can go just like Monsieur Bayonne when he ain't there. Ty can make everybody laugh when he starts to mocking Monsieur Bayonne.

I used to like to be with Mama and Daddy. We used to be happy. But they took him in the Army. Now, nobody happy no more. . . . I be glad when Daddy comes home.

Monsieur Bayonne say it wasn't fair for them to take Daddy and give Mama nothing and give us nothing. Auntie say, "Shhh, Etienne. Don't let them hear you talk like that." Monsieur Bayonne say, "It's God truth. What they giving his children ? They have to walk three and a half miles to school hot or cold. That's anything to give for a paw ? She's got to work in the field rain or shine just to make ends meet. That's anything to give for a husband ?" Auntie say, "Shhh, Etienne, shhh." "Yes, you right," Monsieur Bayonne say. "Best don't say it in front of them now. But one day they go'n find out. One day." "Yes, I suppose so," Auntie say. "Then what, Rose Mary ?" Monsieur Bayonne say. "I don't know, Etienne," Auntie say. "All we can do is us job, and leave everything else in His hand . . ."

We getting closer, now. We getting closer. I can even see the railroad tracks.

We cross the tracks, and now I see the café. Just to get in there, I say. Just to get in there. Already I'm starting to feel little better.

12

We go in. Ahh, it's good. I look for the heater; there 'gainst the wall. One of them little brown ones. I just stand there and hold my hands over it. I can't open my hands too wide cause' they almost froze.

Mama's standing right 'side me. She done unbuttoned her coat. Smoke rises out of the coat, and the coat smells like a wet dog.

I move to the side so Mama can have more room. She opens out her hands and rubs them together. I rub mine together, too, 'cause this keep them from hurting. If you let them warm too fast, they hurt you sure. But if you let them warm just little bit at a time, and you keep rubbing them, they be all right every time.

They got just two more people in the café. A lady back of the counter, and a man on this side the counter. They been watching us ever since we come in.

Mama gets out the handkerchief and count up the money. Both of us know how much money she's got there. Three dollars. No, she ain't got three dollars, 'cause she had to pay us way up here. She ain't got but two dollars and a half left. Dollar and a half to get my tooth pulled, and fifty cents for us to go back on, and fifty cents worth of salt meat.

She stirs the money round with her finger. Most of the money is change 'cause I can hear it rubbing together. She stirs it and stirs it. Then she looks at the door. It's still sleeting. I can hear it hitting 'gainst the wall like rice.

"I ain't hungry, Mama," I say.

"Got to pay them something for they heat," she says.

She takes a quarter out the handkerchief and ties the handkerchief up again. She looks over her shoulder at the people, but she still don't move. I hope she don't spend the money. I don't want her spending it on me. I'm hungry, I'm almost starving I'm so hungry, but I don't want her spending the money on me.

She flips the quarter over like she's thinking. She's must be thinking 'bout us walking back home. Lord, I sure don't want walk home. If I thought it'd do any good to say something, I'd say it. But Mama makes up her own mind 'bout things.

She turns 'way from the heater right fast, like she better hurry up and spend the quarter 'fore she change her mind. I watch her go toward the counter. The man and the lady look at her, too. She tells the lady something and the lady walks away. The man keeps on looking at her. Her back's turned to the man, and she don't even know he's standing there.

The lady puts some cakes and a glass of milk on the counter. Then she pours up a cup of coffee and sets it 'side the other stuff. Mama pays her for the things and comes on back where I'm standing. She tells me sit down at the table 'gainst the wall.

The milk and the cakes's for me; the coffee's for Mama. I eat slow and I look at her. She's looking outside at the sleet. She's looking real sad. I say to myself, I'm go'n make all this up one day. You see, one day, I'm go'n make all this up. I want say it now; I want tell her how I feel right now; but Mama don't like for us to talk like that.

"I can't eat all this," I say.

They ain't got but just three little old cakes there. I'm so hungry right now, the Lord knows I can eat a hundred times three, but I want my mama to have one.

Mama don't even look my way. She knows I'm hungry, she knows I want it. I let it stay there a little while, then I get it and eat it. I eat just on my front teeth, though, 'cause if cake touch that back tooth I know what'll happen. Thank God it ain't hurt me at all today.

After I finish eating I see the man go to the juke box. He drops a nickel in it, then he just stand there a little while looking at the record.

Mama tells me keep my eyes in front where they belong. I turn my head like she say, but then I hear the man coming toward us.

"Dance, pretty?" he says.

Mama gets up to dance with him. But 'fore you know it, she done grabbed the little man in the collar and done heaved him 'side the wall. He hit the wall so hard he stop the juke box from playing.

"Some pimp," the lady back of the counter says. "Some pimp."

The little man jumps up off the floor and starts toward my mama. 'Fore you know it, Mama done sprung open her knife and she's waiting for him.

"Come on," she says. "Come on. I'll gut you from your neighbo to your throat. Come on."

I go up to the little man to hit him, but Mama makes me come and stand 'side her. The little man looks at me and Mama and goes on back to the counter.

"Some pimp," the lady back of the counter says. "Some pimp." She starts laughing and pointing at the little man. "Yes sir, you a pimp, all right. Yes sir-ree."

13

"Fasten that coat, let's go," Mama says.

"You don't have to leave," the lady says.

Mama don't answer the lady, and we right out in the cold again. I'm warm right now—my hands, my ears, my feet—but I know this ain't go'n last too long. It done sleet so much now you got ice everywhere you look.

We cross the railroad tracks, and soon's we do, I get cold. That wind goes through this little old coat like it ain't even there. I got on a shirt and a sweater under the coat, but that wind don't pay them no mind. I look up and I can see we got a long way to go. I wonder if we go'n make it 'fore I get too cold.

We cross over to walk on the sidewalk. They got just one sidewalk back here, and it's over there.

After we go just a little piece, I smell bread cooking. I look, then I see a baker shop. When we get closer, I can smell it more better. I shut my eyes and make 'tend I'm eating. But I keep them shut too long and I butt up 'gainst a telephone post. Mama grabs me and see if I'm hurt. I ain't bleeding or nothing and she turns me loose.

I can feel I'm getting colder and colder, and I look up to see how far we still got to go. Uptown is 'way up yonder. A half mile more, I reckon. I try to think of something. They say think and you won't get cold. I think of that poem, "Annabel Lee." I ain't been to school in so long— this bad weather—I reckon they done passed "Annabel Lee" by now. But passed it or not, I'm sure Miss Walker go'n make me recite it when I get there. That woman don't never forget nothing. I ain't never seen nobody like that in my life.

I'm still getting cold. "Annabel Lee" or no "Annabel Lee," I'm still getting cold. But I can see we getting closer. We getting there gradually.

Soon 's we turn the corner, I see a little old white lady up in front of us. She's the only lady on the street. She's all in black and she's got a long black rag over her head.

"Stop," she says.

Me and Mama stop and look at her. She must be crazy to be out in all this bad weather. Ain't got but a few other people out there, and all of them's men.

"Y'all done ate?" she says.

"Just finish," Mama says.

"Y'all must be cold then?" she says.

"We headed for the dentist," Mama says. "We'll warm up when we get there."

"What dentist?" the old lady says. "Mr. Bassett?"

"Yes, ma'am," Mama says.

"Come on in," the old lady says. "I'll telephone him and tell him y'all coming."

Me and Mama follow the old lady in the store. It's a little bitty store, and it don't have much in there. The old lady takes off her head rag and folds it up.

"Helena?" somebody calls from the back.

"Yes, Alnest?" the old lady says.

"Did you see them?"

"They're here. Standing beside me."

"Good. Now you can stay inside."

The old lady looks at Mama. Mama's waiting to hear what she brought us in here for. I'm waiting for that, too.

"I saw y'all each time you went by," she says. "I came out to catch you, but you were gone."

"We went back of town," Mama says.

"Did you eat?"

"Yes, ma'am."

The old lady looks at Mama a long time, like she's thinking Mama might be just saying that. Mama looks right back at her. The old lady looks at me to see what I have to say. I don't say nothing. I sure ain't going 'gainst my mama.

"There's food in the kitchen," she says to Mama. "I've been keeping it warm."

Mama turns right round and starts for the door.

"Just a minute," the old lady says. Mama stops. "The boy'll have to work for it. It isn't free."

"We don't take no handout," Mama says.

"I'm not handing out anything," the old lady says. "I need my garbage moved to the front. Ernest has a bad cold and can't go out there."

"James'll move it for you," Mama says.

"Not unless you eat," the old lady says. "I'm old, but I have my pride, too, you know."

Mama can see she ain't go'n beat this old lady down, so she just shakes her head.

"All right," the old lady says. "Come into the kitchen."

She leads the way with that rag in her hand. The kitchen is a little bitty little old thing, too. The table and the stove just 'bout fill it up. They got a little room to the side. Somebody in there laying 'cross the bed—'cause I can see one of his feet. Must be the person she was talking to: Ernest or Alnest—something like that.

"Sit down," the old lady says to Mama. "Not you," she says to me. "You have to move the cans."

"Helena?" the man says in the other room.

"Yes, Alnest?" the old lady says.

"Are you going out there again?"

"I must show the boy where the garbage is, Alnest," the old lady says.

"Keep that shawl over your head," the old man says.

"You don't have to remind me. Alnest. Come, boy," the old lady says.

We go out in the yard. Little old back yard ain't no bigger than the store or the kitchen. But it can sleet here just like it can sleet in any big back yard. And 'fore you know it, I'm trembling.

"There," the old lady says, pointing to the cans. I pick up one of the cans and set it right back down. The can's so light, I'm go'n see what's inside of it.

"Here," the old lady says. "Leave that can alone."

I look back at her standing there in the door. She's got that black rag wrapped round her shoulders, and she's pointing one of her little old fingers at me.

"Pick it up and carry it to the front," she says.

I go by her with the can, and she's looking at me all the time. I'm sure the can's empty. I'm sure she could've carried it herself—maybe both of them at the same time. "Set it on the sidewalk by the door and come back for the other one," she says.

I go and come back, and Mama looks at me when I pass her. I get the other can and take it to the front. It don't feel a bit heavier than that first one. I tell myself I ain't go'n be nobody's fool, and I'm go'n look inside this can to see just what I been hauling. First, I look up the street, then down the street. Nobody coming. Then I look over my shoulder toward the door. That little old lady done slipped up there quiet 's mouse, watching me again. Look like she knowed what I was go'n do.

"Ehh, Lord," she says. "Children, children. Come in here, boy, and go wash your hands."

I follow her in the kitchen. She points toward the bathroom, and I go in there and wash up. Little bitty old bathroom, but it's clean, clean. I don't use any of her towels; I wipe my hands on my pants legs.

When I come back in the kitchen, the old lady done dished up the food. Rice, gravy, meat—and she even got some lettuce and tomato in a saucer. She even got a glass of milk and a piece of cake there, too. It looks so good, I almost start eating 'fore I say my blessing.

"Helena?" the old man says.

"Yes, Alnest?"

"Are they eating?"

"Yes," she says.

"Good," he says. "Now you'll stay inside."

The old lady goes in there where he is and I can hear them talking. I look at Mama. She's eating slow like she's thinking. I wonder what's the matter now. I reckon she's thinking 'bout home.

The old lady comes back in the kitchen.

"I talked to Dr. Bassett's nurse," she says. "Dr. Bassett will take you as soon as you get there."

"Thank you, ma'am," Mama says.

"Perfectly all right," the old lady says. "Which one is it?"

Mama nods toward me. The old lady looks at me real sad. I look sad, too.

"You're not afraid, are you?" she says.

"No, ma'am," I say.

"That's a good boy," the old lady says. "Nothing to be afraid of. Dr. Bassett will not hurt you."

When me and Mama get through eating, we thank the old lady again.

"Helena, are they leaving?" the old man says.

"Yes, Alnest."

"Tell them I say good-bye."

"They can hear you, Alnest."

"Good-bye both mother and son," the old man says. "And may God be with you."

Me and Mama tell the old man good-bye, and we follow the old lady in the front room. Mama opens the door to go out, but she stops and comes back in the store.

"You sell salt meat?" she says.

"Yes."

"Give me two bits worth."

"That isn't very much salt meat," the old lady says.

"That's all I have," Mama says.

The old lady goes back of the counter and cuts a big piece off the chunk. Then she wraps it up and puts it in a paper bag.

"Two bits," she says.

"That looks like awful lot of meat for a quarter," Mama says.

"Two bits," the old lady says. "I've been selling salt meat behind this counter twenty-five years. I think I know what I'm doing."

"You got a scale there," Mama says.

"What?" the old lady says.

"Weigh it," Mama says.

"What?" the old lady says. "Are you telling me how to run my business?"

"Thanks very much for the food," Mama says.

"Just a minute," the old lady says.

"James," Mama says to me. I move toward the door.

"Just one minute, I said," the old lady says.

Me and Mama stop again and look at her. The old lady takes the meat out of the bag and unwraps it and cuts 'bout half of it off. Then she wraps it up again and juggs it back in the bag and gives the bag to Mama. Mama lays the quarter on the counter.

"Your kindness will never be forgotten," she says. "James," she says to me.

We go out, and the old lady comes to the door to look at us. After we go a little piece I look back, and she's still there watching us.

The sleet's coming down heavy, heavy now, and I turn up my coat collar to keep my neck warm. My mama tells me turn it right back down.

"You not a bum," she says. "You a man."

William Melvin Kelley (1937–   )

Thoroughly "integrated" in his upbringing and education, William Melvin Kelley in his late twenties began to discover "things inside me that couldn't be explained within the context of Western civilization." At the beginning of his literary career he stressed his concern for the plight of Blacks as individuals, disavowing a sociopolitical role. But by 1965 he announced that the mission of the Black writer was "to help the Negro to find those things that were robbed from him on the shores of Africa, to help repair the damage done to the soul of the Negro in the past three centuries." To do so he must address himself to other Blacks, not to whites. Kelley's third novel, which appeared in 1967, is dedicated to "the Black people in (not of) America." Thus in his later works he has turned to the Afro-American oral tradition, and he has begun to explore his African roots.

Born in New York in 1937, Kelley was brought up in an Italian-American neighborhood in the north Bronx. From the private Fieldston School in New York he went to Harvard, where he studied under the poet Archibald

MacLeish and the novelist John Hawkes. His undergraduate writing
won him the Dana Reed Prize in 1960. With support from the New York
Writers Conference, the Bread Loaf Writers Conference, and the John
Hay Whitney Foundation, he worked on his first novel, published in
1962 as *A Different Drummer*. Since then, Kelley has taught at the New
School for Social Research and the State University of New York at
Geneseo, and has lived in Rome, Paris, and Jamaica. As the author of
four novels and a collection of short stories, he is, in his middle thirties,
one of the important figures of contemporary Black literature.

Kelley's fiction is characterized by an inventive stylistic versatility and
a thematic probing into the meaning of racial relations and the Black
Experience. *A Different Drummer* concerns a mass exodus of Blacks
from a mythical Southern state. Through brilliant manipulation of point
of view, the author explores the effects of this departure on both the
participants and the whites left behind. *Dancers on the Shore* (1964) is a
collection of sixteen short stories of Black life, six of them dealing with a
middle-class family, the Dunfords, and four with a lower-class family, the
Bedlows. The last story, "Cry for Me," concerns Black music, a subject
Kelley returns to in his second novel, *A Drop of Patience* (1965). The
protagonist, Ludlow Washington, is a blind jazz musician who is having an
affair with a white girl named Ragan. He proposes marriage when she
becomes pregnant, but she refuses and deserts him, driving him mad.
Kelley's increasing bitterness toward whites is also apparent in *dem*
(1967), a surrealistic satire on white family life in relation to Black people.
Finally, *Dunfords Travels Everywheres* (1970), the most recent novel, is
a Black equivalent to James Joyce's *Finnegans Wake*, full of linguistic
experimentation and dream sequences. In it Chig Dunford and Carlyle
Bedlow, who both figure importantly in *Dancers on the Shore*, reappear.
The complex relationships between lower-class and middle-class Blacks
have always fascinated Kelley, as in the 1968 short story reprinted here.

Some of Kelley's essays are "If You're Woke You Dig It," *The New
York Times Magazine*, May 20, 1962, pp. 45, 50; "The Ivy League
Negro," *Esquire*, LX (August 1963), 54–56, 108–109; "An American in
Rome," *Mademoiselle*, LX (March 1965), 202, 244–246; "On Racism,
Exploitation, and the White Liberal," *Negro Digest*, XVI (January 1967),
5–12; and "On Africa in the United States," *Negro Digest*, XVII (May
1968), 10–15. See also his contributions to two *Negro Digest* symposia:
"The Task of the Negro Writer as Artist," XIV (April 1965), 64, 78; and
"What Lies Ahead for Black Americans?" XIX (November 1969), 17–19.
A recent short story is "Bumper's Dream," *Black World*, XIX (October
1970), 54–57.

For commentary on Kelley see, in addition to the reviews of his books,
the headnote in *Dark Symphony* (1968), edited by James A. Emanuel
and Theodore L. Gross; Josef Jařab, "The Drop of Patience of the
American Negro," *Philologica Pragensia*, XII (1969), 159–170; and
Robert L. Nadeau, "Black Jesus: A Study of Kelley's *A Different Drummer*," *Studies in Black Literature*, II (Summer 1971), 13–15.

The Dentist's Wife

In Harlem, there once lived a dentist who didn't love his wife. In fact, he was sure she was insane. Even though he'd given her a fantastic wardrobe, a brownstone on the Hill and a cottage on Long Island, she still wasn't satisfied. She wanted one more thing—to cruise around the world. And so he asked her for a divorce.

She refused to give it to him.

He kept asking; she kept refusing; he began to feel trapped. He imagined himself cutting her face up or pouring lye under each eyelid while she slept. He imagined ridding himself of her in many ways, but realized finally only one way was open: He would have to catch her committing adultery.

Not that he was certain she was cheating on him. But he was certain she might be; long before he asked for his divorce, he'd stopped making love to her. Common sense told him that if he was not between her legs, then some other black man could be.

But he could not catch her at it and so decided to hire someone to get under his wife's clothes and to have pictures taken of the event. Someone was Carlyle Bedlow.

Carlyle was sitting in the dentist's chair—two small leather pillows messing his straightened hair—when the dentist made his proposal. Carlyle's mind said yes immediately, but he wanted to see if the dentist was serious and just how much he was offering. He pretended reluctance and also that such a job was beneath him. "Man, you must be crazy. I don't do no shit like that." He pretended to be someone else so well that, for a moment, he forgot the dentist had just pulled his tooth.

"You didn't let me finish." The dentist stood over him, Carlyle's molar clamped between the prongs of his silver pliers. He inspected the tooth, held it so Carlyle could look into its black hole. "You got to take better care of your mouth, Carlyle." He shook his head. "This is a disgrace." He put the pliers and the tooth into a metal dish. "Look, I'm in a spot and it's my only ex-cape. Besides, I ain't mentioned money yet."

"You're hurting me, man, but don't mention it. I don't go in for that kind of stuff. I stick to numbers and warm fur coats." He leaned forward, as if to get up, but the dentist pushed him deeper into his great chair, fingered Carlyle's wound and inserted fresh cotton between cheek and gum.

"The bleeding's stopping." He paused. "Did you ever realize I ain't asking you to do nothing illegal?" He smiled now; the dentist himself had a good dentist. "It's got to be done by somebody and I was just throwing the money your way. All you do is get her clothes off and someone to break in and take pictures."

"Why don't you just ask her for a divorce?" Of course, Carlyle knew, the dentist had already done that.

"You think I hasn't? She won't hear nothing like that. Look, man, I'm in prison with a crazy warden, trying to get me to do all kinds of crazy things." Then he told about his wife's obsession with sailing all around the world.

Carlyle agreed. That did sound crazy. But he still pretended hesitation. "Suppose she really ain't got nobody else? Some women wait. I heard about them. Besides, it ain't my thing."

"She ain't waiting. She's getting some from somewhere. You don't understand how bad it is." He went to the glass door and opened it. "Jean, come in here, will you, baby?"

Entering the office, hand against jaw, Carlyle had noticed Jean's legs even through his pain. He had tried his smile on her, but her lips had not softened, had remained stretched across her teeth. Now she came in almost suspiciously, but smiled at the dentist after she'd closed the door.

"This is my girl."

"Pleased to meet you." Her eyes were black. She was younger, darker and much better built up than the dentist's wife, whom Carlyle had seen once or twice, with the dentist, in Jack O'Gee's Silver Goose Bar and Restaurant.

"I want to marry Jean." The dentist sat down. "And I thought you might help me, out of friendship."

Carlyle nodded, leaned into the small basin beside him and spat. He did not consider the dentist his friend. He did not even have his home phone number. And if he'd had it, Carlyle would never have listed it among his first five choices as a number to call when he was being arrested. He and the dentist met two or three times a month, by accident only, in the Silver Goose.

The dentist waited for Carlyle to straighten up

before he continued. "Now I found me a sane woman and can't live with a crazy one no more. I need those grounds!"

Carlyle glanced at Jean to see if the scheme was new to her. She leaned against the wall near the door, her face empty except for make-up, which was lighter than her skin. "How much you paying?"

"We ain't got no kids." The dentist hesitated and Carlyle knew this, too, was part of the trouble. Carlyle wasn't married, but already he had two children and visited their mothers when he had some money. "That means no support," the dentist hadn't stopped, "and if I get her on adultery, I can cut the alimony down low. So it's worth a thousand if I get my pictures."

It was a better offer than he had expected, but he didn't tell that to the dentist. "Will you throw in my teeth?"

The dentist agreed.

Carlyle climbed out of the dentist's leather chair. "Then, I guess I'll turn legal for a while."

They agreed to meet that night in the Silver Goose. The dentist would bring his wife. Carlyle would sit at their table. After that, they could only hope that the dentist's wife was ready for another new man.

.   .   .

Carlyle was standing at the bar, over his second drink, when they came in. He had seen her only a few times before and his memory had been kind: She looked even less appetizing than he remembered her—in a dull pink dress that hung loosely from narrow shoulders, drowned high, hard breasts and sharp-edged hips. Her face was the color of milk mixed with orange juice, the features squeezed into its center.

Passing by him on the way to the booths at the rear of the Goose, the dentist had not spoken or nodded. But after helping her into a seat and ordering her drink, he returned to the bar and Carlyle. "Bitch didn't want to come, but I told her I sure didn't want to stare at her all night."

Carlyle looked beyond the dentist at his wife. The glass in front of her, a brandy alexander, was already half empty. "What happens to her when she gets drunk?"

"She cries."

Carlyle told the dentist the truth: It couldn't hurt him. "I like your money, but we'll never make it."

"Well, go ahead and try. One thousand dollars is a lot of money."

"You're right." He pushed away from the bar, leaving his drink, which had been stinging the dentist's work, and started toward the booth, the dentist close behind him.

She looked up at them, light-brown eyes in her light-orange face, but she did not speak.

"I ain't seen this nigger in years, Robena." The dentist suddenly pretended great excitement. "We was in the Army together." He introduced them.

Carlyle smiled. "Pleased to meet you." Her hand was cold, filled with tiny bones.

"Have a seat." The dentist motioned him into the booth, next to his wife. As Carlyle was getting settled, she finished her drink, pushed the foamed glass a few inches across the table.

"You want another?" After she nodded the dentist went on selling Carlyle. "We was in Asia. Right, Carlyle?"

"That's right." But so far, Carlyle had been lucky enough to avoid wearing any uniforms.

She looked at him now, seemed not to believe him.

"So how you been, Carlyle?" The dentist did not let him answer. "You do want another drink, don't you?"

She nodded, continuing to study Carlyle.

"What you been doing, man?"

"A little of a lot of things." He reached for his cigarettes, wishing he had smoked for this meeting, trying to decide what to say if she wanted a more precise definition of his livelihood. But then she turned away.

The dentist did not give up. "Carlyle was a male nurse in the dental corps, even pulled some teeth when we had lots of work. He was pretty good at it. I remember the first time I asked him to swing the hammer while I held the chisel. Cat's tooth'd broken off at the root." He started to laugh. "I had to keep telling Carlyle to hit harder. Finally got that sucker out, though. Right, Carlyle?"

"That's right."

The waiter came with her drink. She drained half right away.

"She drinks that like lemonade, huh, Carlyle?"

He did not know what to answer. The dentist had been stupid to ask it. But he forced himself to speak, watching her eyes. "Some people take it better than others."

"And some get falling-down nasty drunk."

She snorted, a short laugh, leaving Carlyle with a silence to fill. "Your wife don't look like that kind." He tried a broad smile.

"Yeah." The dentist finished his drink, put ten dollars on the table and stood up. "I'll be right back." He went toward the rest rooms; but when, 15 minutes later, he had not returned, Carlyle realized he was on his own.

Weather did not interest her, nor Asia, nor even hemlines. She would not speak, gave him no handle. When the ten-dollar bill had dwindled to seven pennies and a dime, he helped her out of the booth, up the stairs to the street and into a taxi.

On the Hill, she handed him a key and he opened her door. He stepped aside, knowing in this situation she would have to ask him inside. "Can you make it all right?"

She nodded and started into the dark house, with his $1000. Then her heels stopped and turned back, but he could not see her pinched face. "You seem too nice to be his friend, Mr. Bedlow." She closed the door in his face.

．　　．　　．

The next day, he paid the dentist a visit. "Man, that was the wrongest thing you could've did, leaving like that. I got to sell myself under your nose."

Bent over his worktable, the dentist was inspecting his tools. "What happened?"

"Nothing. She just sat there and filled up on that ten you left." He was in the dentist's chair, and his jaw, remembering, began to throb. "We worse off than when we started."

"How you figure that?"

"Because now she connects me with an unhappy time. I got to have a chance to sympathize with her. But she didn't tell me nothing. I didn't have the chance to call you a bastard."

The dentist turned around, a small knife in his hand. "I couldn't sit there with that crazy bitch no more. I went to Jean's."

"You have to hold that back if you want this to work. You educated and all, but that was dumb."

"I couldn't help it." He looked unhappy. "So you didn't make progress?"

"Nothing, man. As a matter of fact, I think she knows we ain't Army buddies, because at the end, she sticks her head out the door and tells me I'm too nice to be your friend—Mr. Bedlow."

"She did?" The dentist brightened. "Goddamn! You made it, Carlyle." He jumped, the knife shining in his fist. "Why didn't you tell me that before?"

Carlyle cleared his throat. "Remember you said you wanted to get out before you got crazy, too?" He shook his head. "You too late."

"Listen." The dentist came toward him, waving the knife. "You're too nice to be my friend. That's a compliment."

Just then, Carlyle very much wished he was on his way to a steady customer with a fur coat fresh from some white woman's unlocked car, perfume still strong in its silk lining. "That ain't no compliment. Not the way she said it. She was just getting you."

"You're wrong. I know my wife, man. I'm a bad guy. But you're too nice to be my friend. She's going for it. Time for stage number two." The weekend was coming, he went on. Friday night, Carlyle, Jean, the dentist and his wife would go down to the cottage at the end of Long Island. Jean would pretend to be Carlyle's date. But once they had arrived, Jean and the dentist would have lots of paperwork. Carlyle would be free to seduce the dentist's wife. He was so sure it would work that he told Carlyle to arrange to have someone there to take pictures on Saturday night. He would put the photographer up at a small motel nearby.

There was no arguing with him. Carlyle agreed to come to the office at six that Friday with a suitcase full of attractive sports clothes, the better to trap the dentist's wife.

．　　．　　．

The dentist owned a very big automobile. Carlyle and Jean—her big, beautiful thighs crossed—sat in the back. The dentist's wife stared out of the open right front window at cemeteries, airports, rows of pink and gray houses and, finally, sandy hills covered with stubby Christmas trees and hard, dull-green bushes. Two hours from Harlem, they turned onto a dirt road. Then, even over the engine, Carlyle heard the music, as if they had made a giant circle and returned to the summer jukeboxes of the Avenue.

The community was crowded in the dusk light around a small, bright bay. It did not look like Harlem, but if he had come on it by accident, Carlyle would've known that black people lived there. The music was loud and there was the smell of good food, barbecuing ribs, frying chickens. Carlyle had always believed that black people like the dentist and his wife tried very hard to act white. If so, their music and food gave them away.

The dentist's house was glass and lacquered wood, 30 yards from the beach. They sat around an empty yellow-brick fireplace, flicking their ashes into ceramic trays, while the dentist's wife fixed dinner. Behind her back, the dentist winked, smiled, waved at Jean. Carlyle read a magazine, trying to give them privacy—and wondered if the dentist's wife actually did not know about Jean and the dentist. They ate, drank two or three Scotches apiece, tried to talk and, at 11, gave up and went to bed.

Carlyle had not been in bed at 11 in years, and he awoke in the middle of the night. Listening to the waves, he missed Harlem: cars racing lights on the Avenue, drunks indicting the white man, someone still up and playing music. Unable to get sleep back, he climbed out of bed, removed his black pressing rag and went out into the front yard. Something made him look up and he discovered the stars. In Harlem, he could see only the brightest, strongest ones. But now he saw more stars than sequins on a barmaid's dress, and liked them. He sat, then lay down, careful to keep his hands between the wet grass and his hair.

At first he did not hear her thumping toward him. Then her pinched orange-gray face was peering down at him, her hair wrapped around tiny spiked metal rollers. "You didn't like your bed?" She wore only a nightgown, drab in the starlight.

He sat up quickly. "I couldn't sleep, not enough noise." That sounded funny to him and he laughed quietly.

"I know what you mean." She hesitated for a moment, then sat down next to him. It was going to work, after all. The man did know his wife. Maybe she had some men but was very careful about it.

Lowering herself down beside him, she'd gathered up the nightgown to show him knees as square and hard as fist-sized ivory dice. "It's a nice night, though."

"Yeah." He had not finished judging her legs.

"They're not much, are they? Maybe that's why—" She stopped. "No, that's not why." Then she looked at him. "Mr. Bedlow—"

He did not let her finish, had pushed her onto her back while his name was still soft in the air. It was business, like opening a car door, going through a glove compartment, tossing the road maps aside, hoping to find a portable radio or a wallet. She wrapped her thin arms and legs around him, gasping as if in pain.

On hands and knees, he pulled away from her and discovered she had begun to cry. "Oh, this is bad. This is bad. But . . . I was so hot!" She rolled onto her stomach, muffling sobs in the grass. "This is really bad. I can't do *this*."

He patted her shoulder blades, pulled her nightgown over her buttocks, realizing, as he tried to comfort her, that the dentist had lied to him. If she had been cheating, Carlyle could hope to be President of the United States. Of course, it did not matter, only that he did not want it known that he believed everything people told him.

Finally, he got her to stop crying and sit up. She would not look at him but huddled on the grass, her back to him. "I'm sorry, Mr. Bedlow. I guess you could tell we was having troubles. But I didn't mean to bring you into it."

"Come on, Robena, the sky won't fall down. And call me Carlyle. Mr. Bedlow don't make it now." He moved closer to her, spoke over her shoulder. "What kind of trouble you people got? You own everything, two houses, a big car and all that. So it can't be money." He believed what he said but had asked because now he wanted to know the dentist's weaknesses.

She lowered her chin to her chest. "No, it's not money. Yes, it's money." She raised her head and turned toward him. "How old are you?"

He gave himself a few years.

"I'm thirty-six." She waited, let the number die. "Me and my husband, when we went to school, in Washington, it was different, even from your time. We always thought, at least I did—I mean, now I don't know what he really thought—I mean, we thought it was enough for him to be a dentist. You know what I mean?"

All this had little to do with marriage, the kind he knew. He had expected the usual story, the dentist in the street, running after the many Jeans he'd had before this one. Or perhaps she would think the dentist cheap. He waited.

"But that's not enough anymore. I mean, he's a good dentist, he really is, but they don't care if he's good or not. I always thought they'd care."

They? Carlyle thought. Then he realized she was talking about white people.

"But they don't. It took me a long time to see that; and after, I didn't want to believe it." She paused. "We was raised to believe we had to be best. My momma was always telling me, you got to be best in your class."

Carlyle, too, remembered those words.

"But I was a girl and was only supposed to be the best wife I could be. So when we got married,

I worked so he could go to school full time. He's a good dentist, but it didn't do any good. When he should've been on the staff of a good clinic, he ended up in Harlem. And when he should've—" She stopped, shook her head. "This isn't very interesting, is it?"

One quality Carlyle had developed in his work was patience; he told her to go on, still hoping she would give him something important.

"The point is, when I saw they was lying about caring, I looked into everything they said, and you know what? They lied about everything." She spoke as if still bewildered by her discovery.

"Hell, I known that since I was seven."

She shook her head several times. "No, listen, everything. Even about food. You ever read the small print on a box of ice cream? It's not even ice cream."

"You sound like my little brother." He started to laugh. "He's a Black Jesuit. And you know they crazy."

She ignored him. "What I want is for him to stop working for a year and go around the world. I want to see if what I think is true really is. And I want him to see it. And if it is, maybe we can do just something small. It's not enough for us to sit out here on a little pile of money. I mean, we was supposed to do something good for our race, too." She stopped talking then, sat with her chin on her knees, her nightgown bunched around her thighs, leaving Carlyle disappointed.

Then she stood up. "Well, that's my sad tale. Maybe you'll tell me yours one time." She smiled, for the first time.

In the kitchen, she gave him a cup of instant coffee. He read the label and wondered what kind of chemicals the Xs and Ys were, and what they did to his stomach. When he had finished the coffee, he returned to his room, retied his head and climbed into bed.

.   .   .

The dentist knocked at his door at nine the next morning but did not wait for Carlyle to ask him in. "You made it, didn't you? I knew you could crack it open. Been done before. I hope your man is a good picture taker. My prints got to come out clear!"

Carlyle propped himself against the bed's headboard. "She may not do it again." He had decided he would let the dentist think himself still in charge.

"Go on, man. Everybody knows the first nut is the hardest."

"Maybe so. How you know, anyway?"

"I woke up at three and she wasn't in bed. And neither was you. I figured you was together someplace. What'd you think of it?"

"Ain't the best I ever had."

"Me, too." The dentist came to the bed's foot. "But with the money, you can buy something better." The dentist smiled, good, even white teeth, one gold covered—then closed his lips. "You better drive over to that motel and tell your friend to load his camera."

Carlyle nodded. "What's your plan for today?"

"We're invited to a party. In the late afternoon. We get her drunk, you bring her home, naked, and in bed. I'll make sure you got the house to yourselves." He smiled again. "Me and my Jean'll make sure, someplace." He laughed, turning to the door. "Get your hook in deep."

"I might toss this one back."

He opened the door. "Not in my creek, you won't."

But Carlyle was not so sure.

As he dressed—in short-sleeved pink silk shirt, white bell-bottoms—he tried to decide exactly what to do. Obviously, he wanted to come out the other end with the dentist's $1000. But then the dentist would have to get his pictures. What Carlyle most wanted was to get his money but leave the dentist married to his crazy wife. That would sound good when told in the bars. "That dentist thought he had Carlyle, but then Carlyle Bedlow got down to business, do you hear, business!" That meant he had to get the money before the dentist saw the pictures, bad ones. Pictures in which the woman's face was not quite clear. When he paid the money, the dentist would have to believe the pictures were good. Carlyle heard himself talking: "She passed out, man. I just sat there beside her in my shorts: we pulled back the covers and Hondo snapped away. They so good we might even sell some." But the pictures wouldn't show a thing. He rehearsed his speech while he finished dressing.

He avoided breakfast, wanting the dentist to suffer through a morning with both of his women, imagining that as he drove between the trees on his way to see his friend, the photographer, Hondo Johnson.

"Wait a minute. You saying you don't want the pictures to come out?"

"Right."

"Well, why don't you just give him a blank roll?" Hondo was still in his pajamas, a pullover top, shorts. They were lemon yellow and his legs were brown and shiny. He was sitting on the edge of his motel bed.

"Because, if he ever finds me, I can tell him it was a surprise to me, too. I'll offer to do it again." He was looking into Hondo's mirror, checking his hair. "But he won't go for it, because no man could do it two times to the same woman. And I'm sorry, Doc, but I already spent that money. He ain't got no boys to send after me."

"Come on, man. Why can't we just do it simple? Take the pictures and get the money." Once Hondo thought it was going one way, he did not like to change his plans. He couldn't improvise. But if he knew exactly what to do, it was done. "We'll mess up, man. And I could've used the money."

"We won't lose the money. We'll take insurance pictures. Good ones, with her legs open and all. I know a man downtown'll buy them." And it would be good to have the pictures, just in case the dentist did have some boys. "You satisfied now?"

Hondo nodded but did not look happy. His lips were poked out under his mustache. "Tell me the signal."

"When I turn out the lights." Carlyle hadn't really thought about it.

Hondo started to laugh. "And how'm I supposed to shoot pictures in the dark?" He was pleased to have caught Carlyle.

"You're all right, man." He adjusted his shirt, turned from the mirror. "What about the blinds?"

"That's good. Pull down the blinds, and if they already down, pull them up. Just do something with them blinds." He stood up. "You got that?"

"OK." He liked Hondo. "But I'll try to get her falling-down, so we'll have plenty of time and she won't know nothing. Then we leave. I don't like no drunken broads, anyway."

          .   .   .

It was working. She might even pass out before he got her off the dirt road, into the house and out of her clothes. The party had started at five and now, at ten, was still going. They had eaten— potato salad, fried chicken and greens, on paper plates—drinking steadily. The doctors, lawyers, dentists, big-time hustlers got very loud about baseball, the white man, Harlem after the War, when they were all starting careers. Their children, teenagers, had finally gained control of the phonograph and were dancing hard on the lawn. Carlyle had filled her empty glasses. Finally, he asked her if she wanted to go home. Winking at the dentist, he led her out of the house.

In the moonlight, the dirt of the road, half sand, shone gray. He was supporting her with a hand on her bony rib cage. "How you doing?" He did not really want her to answer and disturb herself.

"I'm doing fine. What did you say?"

"Nothing." They were on the dentist's grass now, circling a clump of lawn chairs and an umbrella table, a few steps from the porch. He saw the bushes move and waved at Hondo.

Taking her straight to her bedroom, he turned on the dim table lamp and began to undress her. She did not resist but was so still that he was not sure she was awake. He put her clothes onto a chair, returned to the bed and pulled the bedcovers from under her. "Thanks, baby." It sounded strange the way she said it. It was meant not for him but for the dentist.

He undressed to his shorts, went to the window and pulled down the blinds.

"What's that?" She raised her head, but it weighed too much.

He tried to imitate the dentist. "Nothing, baby. We need some air, is all."

Hondo was coming. He had banged open the front door, was making his way through the living room, bumping into things. He slid the coffee table out of his way. Carlyle went to the bedroom door. "Hey, man, quiet down. Follow my voice."

"Why didn't you turn on some lights, nigger?" He had almost reached the hallway. Carlyle was at the other end.

"Follow my voice, man."

Now Hondo ran toward him, appeared, in Bermuda shorts and sneakers. Carlyle backed into the room.

Hondo popped into the doorway, stopped. "You expect me to take pictures in this light?" He was disgusted.

"Quiet down, man." Carlyle whispered. "She ain't out yet."

"I got to have more light. I ain't got no infrared attachment." He began to focus his camera on the dentist's naked wife.

"Baby?" She rolled to her side, then back. "Who's that?"

"Ain't nobody. Close your eyes. I'm turning on the top light."

She did not answer. He waited, then switched it on. It was very bright. For a few seconds, he could not see Hondo. "OK now?"

"I think so." He put the camera to his face again. "But I can't be sure until I read the meter."

"Come on, man. We ain't got time for that." She was going to wake up. Somehow he knew it.

"Always got time. What if we ain't got our insurance pictures?" He took a light meter from his pocket, advanced on her, held it over her navel.

Carlyle sat down on the bed. "How you doing, baby?" He patted her shoulder.

Her eyes were closed. "Who was that just now?"

"Just a guy." He leaned over, kissed her cheek.

"I got it now, man." Hondo had moved to the foot of the bed. "One point four. But I got to do it in seconds, so you can't move."

"Who's that voice?" She raised herself to her elbows, looked up into Hondo's lens. "Who's he?"

"OK, now hold it."

But she was already moving, realizing she was with Carlyle, scrambling to the edge of the bed. "He got you to do this."

Carlyle reached out for her, but she broke away and jumped for the closet, "He'll never get one now." She pulled the door behind her.

Carlyle did not follow her. He could easily open the closet door, but that would be useless. She had to be in bed with a man, looking either surprised or happy, but not struggling. "You better come out of there, Robena." He put a threat into his voice but did not mean it. She had to imprison herself while he thought. He knew what he had to do now: convince her to pose for the pictures.

He looked at Hondo, still busy with final adjustments, then stood up. "Listen, baby, you can't stay in there all night. And nobody's coming to rescue you." His mouth was close to the door.

"And nobody's getting a divorce, either." She started to scold him. "I thought you was nice."

"I am. We ain't even into how nice I really am. Come on out."

Hondo sat down on the bed, camera waiting.

"You're not nice." She paused, cleared her nose. "You make love to women for money." She sniffled again.

"That ain't the way it is. I came out here with Jean. Your husband's nurse?"

"I know her. She got a crush on him."

"No, she don't." He waited; she did not speak. "She's with me, but then last night you and me got into something special. But your husband found out. And he said he'd make a lot of trouble for me if I didn't get his pictures. He got me in a terrible spot."

She paused for a moment. "First of all, you didn't even talk to Jean all the way out in the car. And second, where did you get a cameraman so fast?"

The dentist's wife was very smart. "You being real stupid. What you want with a man who don't want you?"

"He does so want me." She did not believe herself.

"No, he don't. He wants Jean. He wants to marry Jean." His voice was cold, the way he talked to white policemen as long as their guns were buried under blue winter coats. "And he's paying me lots of money to get him a divorce."

She waited again, crying behind the closet door. "Well, he's not getting one."

"Listen to me, Robena." He bent closer, softened his tone. "Face it, baby. He don't want you. He don't want anything about you. He don't want to go around the world with you. He thinks you're crazy to want to do that. Give the man his pictures."

And she did.

. . .

They were the clearest pictures any judge would ever see. The woman sat on the bed, bare to the waist. She looked sad, her infidelity uncovered. The young black hoodlum, his hair shiny and slightly waved, was certainly not her husband.

Hondo took no others. Carlyle had decided against trying for the extra money. One thousand was enough. The dentist paid him, in cash, the following Monday evening.

Carlyle had long since turned the money into clothes, a good camel's-hair overcoat, shoes, a few suits, when next he heard from the dentist's wife. She had mailed a postcard to him, care of the Silver Goose. It came from Europe:

Hello. We're here on our honeymoon. My husband is a dentist from [the ink had been smudged] in Africa. Best wishes, Robena (the dentist's wife, remember?).

At first Carlyle did not remember. When he did, he thought about it for a while. . . .

Poetry

Owen Dodson, Dudley Randall, Samuel Allen, Margaret Danner, Mari E. Evans, Etheridge Knight, Conrad Kent Rivers, Don L. Lee, Sonia Sanchez, and Nikki Giovanni

After Gwendolyn Brooks' selection as America's first Black Pulitzer Prize winner in poetry, a curious silence fell upon Black poets in the 1950's. Miss Brooks herself produced no more volumes of poetry until *The Bean Eaters* in 1961. Langston Hughes continued to write prodigiously, but more and more of his creative energies were devoted to developing the Simple stories. Hughes did collaborate with Arna Bontemps to produce two very much needed anthologies—one on Negro poetry and one on Negro folklore—but his real interest seemed to be writing prose. Bontemps, co-editor of these anthologies, had long before turned to prose. Moreover, Margaret Walker, also a poet of some repute, had turned to prose and was busy researching the material for her novel *Jubilee*. This is not to say that Black poets were not writing during the 1950's; many were writing and desperately struggling to publish what they wrote, but all recognized that the 1950's were dominated by fiction writers, specifically the articulate expatriate Richard Wright, Ralph Ellison, and James Baldwin. Wright had established a tradition, and many were attempting to follow in his footsteps—including John Oliver Killens, William Attaway, and Chester Himes. Through their influence there developed a national, almost global concern for the identity problems of American Blacks. By the middle of the decade, Baldwin began to publish his essays to give sharpened focus to the Black man's identity crisis and provide clear evidence of the American Black man's link with the colored people of the colonialized Third World.

One of the Black poets who continued to write despite the apparent indifference to the uses of poetry in the 1950's was Owen Dodson (1914–   ), who had published a volume of poems, *Powerful Long Ladder,* in 1946. However, his primary professional commitment was to the drama program at Howard University. Of his occasional poems, the best is undoubtedly "Yardbird's Skull," a tribute to the legendary great jazz artist, Charlie "Yardbird" Parker. Throughout this short but skillfully wrought elegy, the subject is Yardbird's music and how it will

804

endure long after the singer has gone. Dodson embellishes the standard *ars longa, vita brevis* dichotomy with the image of the skull of the dead musician as a wide-ranging bird flying across the time, space, and wideness of the artistic world of Yardbird Parker:

> *... this skull*
> *Has been with violets ...*
> *This skull has been in air,*
> *Sensed his brother, the swallow,*
> *(Its talent for snow and crumbs).*
> *Flown to lost Atlantis islands,*
> *Places of dreaming, swimming lemmings.*

There is a brief symbolic comparison with Hamlet's Yorick, but the comparison is muted, for Yorick was only a court clown whereas Yardbird made music that reached the horizons.

Other Black poets with developing reputations wrote and published during the 1950's. Like Dodson, Samuel Allen (1917–   ) pursued poetry as an avocation and published his first volume of poems in Germany in 1956 under the pseudonym Paul Vesey. He had the support and encouragement of Richard Wright, whom he had met while studying at the Sorbonne. One of his racial poems is "A Moment Please," in which the poet places in ironic juxtaposition humanity's generally tragic dilemma and the American Black man's particularly tragic dilemma. The poem presents the two positions with commendable succinctness and verbal economy. First, there is the metaphysical dilemma of the "human clan," which continues to exist only through sufferance in an enigmatic and fatalistic universe; in such a philosophical context, man is but the "dupe of space" and the "toy of time." But there is another dimension—the racial dimension—and here there is no room for philosophical detachment; an American Black man remains a "nigger," even though a member of the imperilled human clan. Allen's bitter conclusion appears to be that the American Black man is trapped in overlapping negations—one universal and the other racial, with no suggestion of hope that he will ever escape from such double jeopardy. Somewhat obscured by the widely anthologized "A Moment Please" is another element in Allen's work—a militant and revolutionary impulse that rejects passive acceptance of racism. His "Nat Turner" suggests that another Nat may arise to blaze the "warm red trail" of revolt and elicit from the oppressed "a bloodflecked roar of exultation."

If the 1950's were a sparse period for Black poetry, the 1960's more than compensated for it; during the 1960's, Black poets sprouted up all over America. By the end of the decade not only had poetic giants such as Melvin Tolson, LeRoi Jones, Gwendolyn Brooks, Robert Hayden, and Langston Hughes reappeared with new volumes of poetry but also at least five anthologies of Black poetry were published—Rosey Pool's anthology in 1962, Arna Bontemps' in 1963, Robert Hayden's in 1967, and Clarence Major's and Dudley Randall's in 1969. Among the new Black poets were Donald Henderson, Calvin Hernton, and Joe Johnson, all of whom first published in Harlem's new avant-garde literary publication, *Umbra*. Others—Lance Jeffers, James Emanuel, Ted Joans, Margaret Danner, Mari E. Evans, Conrad Kent Rivers, Russell Atkins, and Julian Bond—made their poetic debuts either in Rosey Pool's anthology or in Arna Bontemps' anthology. And then, as the decade drew to a close, the "Broadside Press" poets appeared through Dudley Randall's series of Broadside Press editions in Detroit and in Hoyt Fuller's *Negro Digest* (now *Black World*). They brought with them new poetic concepts, a new esthetic, and a strong sense of Black ghetto awareness.

Like the spirituals and secular songs of slavery, the new Black poetry of the 1960's burst forth out of a time of racial turmoil. The catalyst for creativity was a series of events beginning with the Montgomery bus boycott and encompassing the nonviolent sit-in demonstrations of the early 1960's and the big-city riots of the mid-1960's. So behind the poets and their songs of bitter protest against racist America were the bombings, the assassinations, the burning ghettos, the screaming sirens, the violent confrontations between white police and Black people, and the cruel awareness of spreading Black poverty amid bounteous white affluence.

The most forthrightly militant spokesmen for the new Black mood in poetry were the Broadside Press poets—so called because their poems are social, political, and moral "broadsides" protesting against the body politic and the Establishment. But before the Broadside Press poets emerged as a definable literary group, other poets were writing protest poetry in the early 1960's that was caustic, bitter, and, at times, mordantly cynical. For instance, in Calvin Hernton's short poem "Street Scene," when the poet hails his "dream," the dream's answer is, "Go to hell, sonofabitch!"

But the poetry became more than bitter militant protest. Under the leadership of LeRoi Jones and others, there developed a Black esthetic that, in some measure, prescribed the guidelines for Black poetic militancy. Under the racial pressures of the late 1950's and early 1960's Jones himself had undergone a metamorphosis, moving from an avant-garde estheticism to a Black nationalism-activism. In the process, he abandoned his "slave" name and became Imamu Amiri Baraka. He also moved out of the mood of deep melancholy and pessimism that permeates many of the poems of his first volume of poetry, *Preface to a Twenty Volume Suicide Note* (1961). But later in the decade he wrote "Black Art," indicating that the pessimism of the earlier years had been replaced by a vigilant and militant activism. Indeed, "Black Art" announces the credo of the new Black esthetic—that the direct objective of all Black artistic expression is to achieve social change and moral and political revolution. Poems, Jones asserts, should be fists and daggers and pistols to clean up the sordid Black ghetto—to "clean out the world for virtue and love."

Inevitably, not all of the militant poetry of the 1960's meets Jones' exacting creed. Margaret Danner, for instance, writes of Africa and of subtle racial confrontations somewhat after the manner of Gwendolyn Brooks. Emotions do not surface and explode in her poetry, but they simmer hotly. Naomi Madgett's "Her Story," on the other hand, states that the only answer to a girl being "big and Black and burly" is to commit suicide.

Mari E. Evans comes closer to the new militancy of social revolution. In her "Status Symbol" she speaks with scathing irony of a society in which the possession of a key to the "white . . . John" bestows a certain kind of social status on a Black person. And her "Black Jam for Dr. Negro" voices the vehement hatred of the Black ghetto-dweller for the antiseptic and somewhat whitened world of the Negro middle class, using the language and idiom of the ghetto to communicate intraracial disdain and distrust:

> *Pullin me in off the corner to wash my face an*
> *cut my afro turn*
> *my collar*
> *down*
> *when that ain't my*
> *thang . . .*
>
> *what you sweatin*
> *baby*
>   *your guts*
> *puked an rotten*
> *waitin*
> *to be defended*

Mari E. Evans' use of Black street speech and Black ghetto idiom is a far cry from the polished poetry of the early Gwendolyn Brooks or the early Robert Hayden. It reflects a trend toward the use of Black folk speech that is eloquently exemplified in the poetry of Sonia Sanchez, Don L. Lee, and other Broadside Press poets. These young poets go far beyond what Wordsworth had in mind when he demanded poetry written in the language of real men. Indeed, one is reminded of the salty street language in Thomas Nashe's prose pieces of the Elizabethan 1590's. The singular difference is that the young Black poets' use of Black ghetto speech is an index of racial self-assertiveness—a way to use the "fist" of language.

However, not all Black poetry of the late 1960's uses a ghetto speech pattern. Conrad Kent Rivers (1933–1968), for instance, wrote in the more traditional poetic idiom, but unfortunately his developing career in literature was interrupted by an untimely death. One of his better poems is a tribute to W. E. B. Du Bois, who died "By African Moonlight and Forgotten Shores." The great scholar's alienation from and rejection by America stand forth clearly in the final lines of the poem and reveal the existential loneliness of his last years:

> *Sage, can there be no more hope for everyman?*
> *Do we walk so close to devils, lose sight of Sun,*
> *struggle against autumnal air, quench thirst of life?*
> *I stand dumb and chilled to understand*
> *your search, your loneliness,*
> *and my own debt for the etchings from those lonely hills*
> *which now and forever hold communion over you.*

Similarly, Rivers' salute to Richard Wright sustains a mood of negation and racial defeatism. The poet asserts that

> *To be born unnoticed*
> *Is to be born black,*
> *And left out of the grand adventure.*

Everywhere there is purposelessness and disorder; even the religion of the Black man brings disorder and confusion and "our father's / Religion warps his life." It is obvious that the many deaths of the 1960's— of Wright, Du Bois, Hughes, King, and others—depressed and discouraged Conrad Kent Rivers, who himself died before the period of self-assertive Blackness of the early 1970's.

The man who serves as a bridge connecting an older generation of poets with a younger generation is Dudley Randall (1914–   ), versatile editor-owner of the Broadside Press. His work as author and poet began in the 1950's, and, after working with Margaret Danner and others in the Boone House cultural center in Detroit in the early 1960's, he founded the Broadside Press in 1965. The initial purpose of the press reflects Randall's background and training as a librarian, for he wanted to open a channel of publication for individual poems by young Black poets for classroom circulation and personal collections. As a poet, Randall has a high proficiency in modern languages that has enabled him to translate Russian and French poems into English. Thus far, he has produced two volumes of poetry—*Poem Counterpoem* (1966) with Margaret Danner and *Cities Burning* (1970). He has also edited *Black Poetry* (1969) and co-edited (with Margaret Burroughs) *Poems on the Life and Death of Malcolm X* (1969). Randall's poetry ranges from erudite translations of Pushkin to cameo portraits of a "Blackberry Sweet" Black girl to poems of social irony such as one about "The Idiot," who respects rough-housing white police. He has also written a much-published dialogue between "Booker T. and W. E. B." that presents the historical controversy between the two race leaders in exceedingly simplistic terms but communicates the poet's strong preference for Du Bois. Undoubtedly, Randall's most notable contribution is not his poetry but the arrangements he has made to facilitate the publication of the poetry of young men and women who, without his aid and counsel, would have remained "Black and Unknown Bards" just as their early forefathers did.

Four relatively young Black poets who have been introduced, with remarkably provocative results, by Dudley Randall's Broadside Press are Don L. Lee, Sonia Sanchez, Nikki Giovanni, and Etheridge Knight. Rarely has a group of Black poets had such a constructively emotional impact on the collective racial ego of Black America, particularly the youth of Black America. Don L. Lee (1942–   ) was the first to make his debut in print with *Think Black* in 1967. Since then, he has published three more volumes of poetry—*Black Pride* (1968), *Don't Cry, Scream* (1969), and *We Walk the Way of the New World* (1970). This is indeed an enviable publishing record for a young poet who is not yet thirty years old. His first volume set the style for other Broadside Press poets. Sonia Sanchez (1935–   ), for instance, published her first volume, *Home Coming,* in 1969 and her second volume, *We a BaddDDD People,* in 1970, using to advantage the precedents introduced by Don L. Lee. Similarly, Nikki Giovanni (1943–   ) published *Black Judgement* in 1969, written in a poetic voice essentially undifferentiated from that of Lee and Sanchez. Only Etheridge Knight (1933–   ) is somewhat different in his approaches and moods. This may be attributable to his being the oldest of the four and to the fact that his first volume of poems published by Broadside—*Poems from Prison* (1968)—was actually written while he was serving a twenty-year term in the Indiana State Prison (fortunately, he was paroled in late November 1968). In his prison poems the strident racial rhetoric of the other Broadside Press poets with whom he has been grouped is somewhat muted. Instead, in Knight's poetry one finds more private reflection and more emotion, recollected not in tranquility but recollected with that tortured perturbation of heart and soul which is the stuff of good poetry.

However, all four poets are committed in their poetry to the cause of political, social, and moral revolution, and all believe that poetry and other forms of artistic expression should serve the ends of revolution. All express a deep pride in Blackness, and all believe that poetry should be written from a racial perspective and should probe the full range of racial confrontation. This they do using ghetto folk speech, without literary embellishments. Theirs is a language of confrontation in which are to be found irony, understatement, and satiric portraiture. Don L. Lee defines this attitude toward a "poetic" language:

> *I ain't seen no poems stop a .38,*
> *I ain't seen no stanzas brake a honkie's head,*
> *I ain't seen no metaphors stop a tank,*
> *I ain't seen no words kill*
> *& if the word was mightier than the sword*
> *Pushkin wouldn't be fertilizing russian soil /*
> *& until my similes can protect me from a night stick*
> *i guess i'll keep my razor*
> *& buy me some more bullets.*

Accordingly, theirs is a poetry of plain and direct statement, such as
Sonia Sanchez' "The Final Solution":

> there is
> no real problem here.
>   we the
> lead/ers of free
>   a/mer/ica
> say. give us your
>   hungry/
>   illiterates/
>   criminals/
>   dropouts/
>   (in others words)
>   your blacks
>   and we will
> let them fight
>   in vietnam
>   defending america's honor.
> we will make responsible
>   citi-
>   zens out of them or
>   kill them trying.

Don L. Lee, in particular, is a master of the satiric portraiture and
ironic understatement that characterize this group of poets. In "Black
Sketches" he writes:

> nat turner
> returned
> &
> killed
> william styron
> &
> his momma too.

And there is his ferocious portrait of a "little nigger" who somehow
became lost in a miasma of "white" hippie liberalism:

> him
> another pipe-smoking faggot
> who lost his balls in
> a double-breasted suit
> walking thru a nadinola commercial
> with a degree in european history.
> little nigger
> choked himself with a hippy's tie
> his momma didn't even know him/
>   .   .   .
> he
> cursed at her in perfect english
> called her:
> Mother-Dear.

Another feature of their poetry is the humanistic concern quite often apparent along with the cynicism and irony. Sonia Sanchez, for instance, expresses deep concern for what drug addiction is doing to young "Black lovers":

> *blk*
> *lovers cannot live*
> *in wite powder that removes*
> *them from they blk selves*
> > *cannot ride*
> *majestic wite horses*
> > *in a machine age.*
> *blk lovers*
> > *must live*
> > *push against the*
> *devils of this world*
> > *against the creeping*
> *witeness of they own minds.*

In other words, these young poets, like other young poets of other places and times, are concerned about the moral imperatives needed to "clean out the world for virtue and love." As Don L. Lee states, the young Black poet wants to "bring new meanings to / the north star" and, with love and understanding, join hands with the beautiful people of the world to "walk a righteous direction / under the moon."

One final comment should be made about the Broadside Press poets. As they continue to write and publish, the hard line of political and revolutionary commitment seems to be softening somewhat to be blended with private wishes, fancies, and insights. Many of Don L. Lee's poems in his latest volume, *We Walk the Way of the New World,* particularly those in the "Blackwoman" section, are filled with gentle personal reminiscences. He writes of a woman whose beauty is like that of "a blackbird resting / on a telephone wire that moves / quietly with the wind." In another poem, he describes women who "are drops of algerian sand / with joyeyes overworked to welcome." Not only does the poet invite the reader into the privacy of his inner fancies and wishes in these poems, but there is more use of poetic language. However, of these poets only Etheridge Knight has thus far explored the desperate tensions and inner loneliness of man. He was imprisoned by steel and concrete within the larger prison of our society, and, as he once wrote,

> *It is hard*
> *To make a poem in prison.*
> *The air lends itself not*
> *to the singer.*
> *The seasons creep by unseen*
> *And spark no fresh fires.*

So, when bitter memories come flooding back of his sister who in the beginning was "the Virgin Mary" but somehow lost her name "in the nameless void" between Nazareth and Bethlehem, what can the imprisoned poet do to dissolve the remembered bitterness and "build a bridge" over the "troubled waters" of memory?

> *And what do I do. I boil my tears in a twisted spoon*
> *And dance like an angel on the point of a needle.*
> *I sit counting syllables like Midas gold.*
> *I am not bold. I cannot yet take hold of the demon*
> *And lift his weight from your black belly,*
> *So I grab the air and sing my song.*

Today, Etheridge Knight enjoys a quasi-freedom in a society desperately in search for a new humanism to save itself from drugs, alcohol, and pollution. As the decade of the 1970's begins, he and the other Broadside Press poets will continue to sing their songs in a desperate attempt to "clean out the world for virtue and love." They will continue to sing of revolution and of the need for rebirth and renewal. Undoubtedly, America will continue to be wracked by racism and other social and economic problems, but one can assume that the fierce idealism of the growing choir of Black poets will have a noticeable effect on the America of the 1970's.

Owen Dodson[*]

Sorrow Is the Only Faithful One

Sorrow is the only faithful one:
The lone companion clinging like a season
To its original skin no matter what the
    variations.

If all the mountains paraded
Eating the valleys as they went
And the sun were a cliffure on the highest peak,

Sorrow would be there between
The sparkling and the giant laughter
Of the enemy when the clouds come down to
    swim.

But I am less, unmagic, black,
Sorrow clings to me more than to doomsday
    mountains
Or erosion scars on a palisade.

Sorrow has a song like a leech
Crying because the sand's blood is dry
And the stars reflected in the lake

Are water for all their twinkling
And bloodless for all their charm.
I have blood, and a song.
SORROW IS THE ONLY FAITHFUL ONE.

[*] For headnote see p. 804.

Yardbird's Skull

For Charlie Parker

The bird is lost,
Dead, with all the music:
Whole sunsets heard the brain's music
Faded to last horizon notes.
I do not know why I hold
This skull, smaller than a walnut's,
Against my ear,
Expecting to hear
The smashed fear
Of childhood from . . . bone;
Expecting to see
Wind nosing red and purple,
Strange gold and magic
On bubbled windowpanes
Of childhood. Shall I hear?
I should hear: this skull

Has been with violets,
Not Yorick, or the gravedigger,
Yapping his yelling story.
This skull has been in air,
Sensed his brother, the swallow,
(Its talent for snow and crumbs).
Flown to lost Atlantis islands,
Places of dreaming, swimming lemmings.
O I shall hear skull skull,
Hear your lame music,
Believe music rejects undertaking,
Limps back.
Remember tiny lasting, we get lonely:
Come sing, come sing, come sing sing
And sing.

Dudley Randall*

Booker T. and W. E. B.

Booker T. Washington and W. E. B. Du Bois

"It seems to me," said Booker T.,
"It shows a mighty lot of cheek
To study chemistry and Greek
When Mister Charlie needs a hand
To hoe the cotton on his land,
And when Miss Ann looks for a cook,
Why stick your nose inside a book?"

"I don't agree," said W. E. B.
"If I should have the drive to seek
Knowledge of chemistry or Greek,
I'll do it. Charles and Miss can look
Another place for hand or cook.
Some men rejoice in skill of hand,
And some in cultivating land,
But there are others who maintain
The right to cultivate the brain."

"It seems to me," said Booker T.,
"That all you folks have missed the boat
Who shout about the right to vote,
And spend vain days and sleepless nights
In uproar over civil rights.
Just keep your mouths shut, do not grouse,
But work, and save, and buy a house."

"I don't agree," said W. E. B.
"For what can property avail
If dignity and justice fail?
Unless you help to make the laws,
They'll steal your house with trumped-up clause.
A rope's as tight, a fire as hot,
No matter how much cash you've got.
Speak soft, and try your little plan,
But as for me, I'll be a man."

"It seems to me," said Booker T.—

"I don't agree,"
Said W. E. B.

* For headnote see p. 808.

Legacy: My South

What desperate nightmare rapts me to this land
Lit by a bloody moon, red on the hills,
Red in the valleys? Why am I compelled
To tread again where buried feet have trod,
To shed my tears where blood and tears have
  flowed?
Compulsion of the blood and of the moon
Transports me. I was molded from this clay.
My blood must ransom all the blood shed here,
My tears redeem the tears. Cripples and
  monsters
Are here. My flesh must make them whole and
  hale.
I am the sacrifice.

See where the halt
Attempt again and again to cross a line
Their minds have drawn, but fear snatches them
  back
Though health and joy wait on the other side.
And there another locks himself in a room
And throws away the key. A ragged scarecrow
Cackles an antique lay, and cries himself
Lord of the world. A naked plowman falls
Famished upon the plow, and overhead
A lean bird circles.

Perspectives

Futile to chide the stinging shower
Or prosecute the thorn
Or set a curse upon the hour
In which my love was born.

All's done, all's vanished, like a sail
That's dwindled down the bay.
Even the mountains vast and tall
The sea dissolves away.

Samuel Allen*

A Moment Please

When I gaze at the sun
  I walked to the subway booth
  for change for a dime.
and know that this great earth
  Two adolescent girls stood there
  alive with eagerness to know
is but a fragment from it thrown
  all in their new found world
  there was for them to know
in heat and flame a billion years ago,
  they looked at me and brightly asked
  "Are you Arabian?"

that then this world was lifeless
  I smiled and cautiously
  —for one grows cautious—
  shook my head.
as, a billion hence,
  "Egyptian?"
it shall again be,
  Again I smiled and shook my head
  and walked away.
what moment is it that I am betrayed,
  I've gone but seven paces now
oppressed, cast down,
    and from behind comes swift the sneer

* For headnote see p. 805.

or warm with love or triumph?
　"Or Nigger?"

　A moment, please
What is it that to fury I am roused?
　for still it takes a moment
What meaning for me
　and now

in this homeless clan
　I'll turn
the dupe of space
　and smile
the toy of time?
　and nod my head.

To Satch

Sometimes I feel like I will never stop
Just go forever
Till one fine morning
I'll reach up and grab me a handful of stars
And swing out my long lean leg

And whip three hot strikes burning down the
　heavens
And look over at God and say
How about that!

Nat Turner

I know a gentle soul whose even fare
Is quiet contemplation with an air
Of melancholy, yet of sweet repose
In all he does or nobly undergoes.
His midnight grief and more, his noonday's tall
Bright hour hover at the brink, break and fall
For him beneath that trackless cosmic tread
Which yields him peace, his ample daily bread.

But his is not my place
Nor role
Nor his my inclination;
For I am long put to it
And I rebel against this fate
And I will raise a voice against it
Till the indifferent doomed, till every demon

Squat in his wet hole,
Shall pause
And break from a unsmiling cackle
Into a bloodflecked roar of exultation;

Though all that yet for me shall come to pass
Is that the restless mist of dawn
Shall yield some cautious sparrow
Picking his lone way
Dumbly to scent
The warm red trail
Whereon the night before
Hammered down against the ground
I rose—
I drove a path.

Margaret Danner[*]

Far from Africa: Four Poems

"are you beautiful still?"

1: GARNISHING THE AVIARY

Our moulting days are in their twilight stage.
These lengthy dreaded suns of draggling plumes.
These days of moods that swiftly alternate
    between

The former preen (ludicrous now) and a down-
    cast rage
Or crestfallen lag, are fading out. The initial
    bloom;
Exotic, dazzling in its indigo, tangerine

Splendor; this rare, conflicting coat had to be
    shed.
Our drooping feathers turn all shades. We spew
This unamicable aviary, gag upon the worm, and
    fling

Our loosening quills. We make a riotous spread
Upon the dust and mire that beds us. We do
    not shoo
So quickly; but the shades of the pinfeathers
    resulting

From this chaotic push, though still exotic,
Blend in more easily with those on the wings
Of the birds surrounding them; garnishing
The aviary, burnishing this zoo.

2: DANCE OF THE ABAKWETA

Imagine what Mrs. Haessler would say
If she could see the Watusi youth dance
Their well-versed initiation. At first glance
As they bend to an invisible barre
You would know that she had designed their
    costumes.

For though they were made of pale beige
    bamboo straw
Their lines were the classic tutu. Nothing varied.
Each was cut short at the thigh and carried
High to a degree of right angles. Nor was there
    a flaw
In their leotards. Made of leopard skin or the
    hide

Of a goat, or the Gauguin-colored Okapi's
    striped coat
They were cut in her reverenced "tradition."
She would have approved their costumes and
    positions.
And since neither Iceland nor Africa is too
    remote
For her vision she would have wanted to form

A "traditional" ballet. Swan Lake, Scheherazade
    or
(After seeing their incredible leaps)
Les Orientales. Imagine the exotic sweep
Of such a ballet, and from the way the music
    pours
Over these dancers (this tinkling of bells, talking
Of drums, and twanging of tan, sandalwood
    harps)
From this incomparable music, Mrs. Haessler of
    Vassar can
Glimpse strains of Tchaikovsky, Chopin
To accompany her undeviatingly sharp
"Traditional" ballet. I am certain that if she
    could
Tutor these potential protégés, as
Quick as Aladdin rubbing his lamp, she would.

3: THE VISIT OF THE PROFESSOR OF AESTHETICS

To see you standing in the sagging bookstore
    door
So filled me with chagrin that suddenly you
    seemed as
Pink and white to me as a newborn, hairless
    mouse. For

I had hoped to delight you at home. Be a furl
Of faint perfume and Vienna's cordlike lace.
To shine my piano till a shimmer of mother-of-
    pearl

Embraced it. To pleasantly surprise you with
    the grace
That transcends my imitation and much worn
"Louis XV" couch. To display my Cathedrals
    and ballets.

[*] For headnote see p. 807.

To plunge you into Africa through my nude
Zulu Prince, my carvings from Benin, forlorn
Treasures garnered by much sacrifice of food.

I had hoped to delight you, for more
Rare than the seven-year bloom of my
Chinese spiderweb fern is a mind like yours

That concedes my fetish for this substance
Of your trade. And I had planned to prove
Your views of me correct at even every chance

Encounter. But you surprised me. And the store
which
Had shown promise until you came, arose
Like a child gone wild when company comes or
a witch

At Hallowe'en. The floor, just swept and
mopped,
Was persuaded by the northlight to deny it.
The muddy rag floor rugs hunched and flopped

Away from the tears in the linoleum that I
wanted
Them to hide. The drapes that I had pleated
In clear orchid and peach feverishly flaunted

Their greasiest folds like a banner.
The books who had been my friends, retreated—
Became as shy as the proverbial poet in manner

And hid their better selves. All glow had been
deleted
By the dirt. And I felt that you whose god is
grace
Could find no semblance of it here. And unaware

That you were scrubbing, you scrubbed your
hands.
Wrung and scrubbed your long white fingers.
Scrubbed

Them as you smiled and I lowered my eyes from
despair.

4: Etta Moten's Attic
(*Filled with mementos of African journeys*)

It was as if Gauguin
had upset a huge paint pot
of his incomparable tangerine,

splashing wherever my startled eyes ran
here and there, and at my very hand on
masques and paintings and carvings not seen

here before, spilling straight as a stripe
spun geometrically in a Nbeble rug
flung over an ebony chair,

or dripping round as a band on a type
of bun the Watusi warriors
make of their pompadoured hair,

splashing high as a sunbird or fly moving
over a frieze of mahogany trees,
or splotching out from low underneath as a
root,

shimmering bright as a ladybug grooving
a green bed of moss, sparkling as a beetle,
a bee, shockingly dotting the snoot

of an ape or the nape of its neck or as clue
to its navel, stamping a Zulu's
intriguing masque, tipping

the lips of a chief of Ashantis who
was carved to his stool so he'd sit
there forever and never fear a slipping

of rule or command, dyeing the skirt
(all askew) that wouldn't stay put on the
Pygmy in spite of his real leather belt,

quickening and charming till we felt the bloom
of veldt and jungle flow through the room.

Mari E. Evans[*]

When in Rome

Marrie dear
the box is full . . .
take
whatever you like
to eat . . .

    (an egg
    or soup
    . . . there ain't no meat.)

there's endive there
and
cottage cheese . . .

    (whew! if I had some
    black-eyed peas . . .)

there's sardines
on the shelves
and such . . .
but

don't
get my anchovies . . .
they cost
too much!

    (me get the
    anchovies indeed!
    what she think, she got—
    a bird to feed?)

there's plenty in there
to fill you up . . .

    (yes'm. just the
    sight's
    enough!

    Hope I lives till I get
    home
    I'm tired of eatin'
    what they eats in Rome . . .)

Black Jam for Dr. Negro

Pullin me in off the corner to wash my face an
cut my afro turn
my collar
down
when that aint my
thang I
walk heels first
nose round an tilted
up
my ancient
eyes
see your thang
baby
an it aint
shit
your thang
puts my eyes out baby
turns my seeking fingers

    into splintering fists
messes up my head
an I scream you out
your thang
is whats wrong
  an you keep
  pilin it on rubbin it
  in
  smoothly
  doin it
  to death

what you sweatin
baby
        your guts
puked an rotten
waitin
to be defended

[*] For headnote see p. 807.

Etheridge Knight*

The Idea of Ancestry

1

Taped to the wall of my cell are 47 pictures: 47 black
faces: my father, mother, grandmothers (1 dead), grand
fathers (both dead), brothers, sisters, uncles, aunts,
cousins (1st & 2nd), nieces, and nephews. They stare
across the space at me sprawling on my bunk. I know
their dark eyes, they know mine. I know their style,
they know mine. I am all of them, they are all of me;
they are farmers, I am a thief, I am me, they are thee.

I have at one time or another been in love with my mother,
1 grandmother, 2 sisters, 2 aunts (1 went to the asylum),
and 5 cousins. I am now in love with a 7 yr old niece
(she sends me letters written in large block print, and
her picture is the only one that smiles at me).

I have the same name as 1 grandfather, 3 cousins, 3 nephews,
and 1 uncle. The uncle disappeared when he was 15, just took
off and caught a freight (they say). He's discussed each year
when the family has a reunion, he causes uneasiness in
the clan, he is an empty space. My father's mother, who is 93
and who keeps the Family Bible, with everybody's birth dates
(and death dates) in it, always mentions him.
There is no
place in her Bible for "whereabouts unknown."

2

Each Fall the graves of my grandfathers call me, the brown
hills and red gullies of mississippi send out their electric
messages, galvanizing my genes. Last yr/like a salmon quitting
the cold ocean—leaping and bucking up his birthstream/I
hitchhiked my way from L.A. with 16 caps in my pocket and a
monkey on my back. and I almost kicked it with the kinfolks.
I walked barefooted in my grandmother's backyard/I smelled the old
land and the woods/I sipped cornwhiskey from fruit jars with the men/
I flirted with the women/I had a ball till the caps ran out
and my habit came down. That night I looked at my grandmother
and split/my guts were screaming for junk/but I was almost
contented/I had almost caught up with me.
(The next day in Memphis I cracked a croaker's crib for a fix.)

This yr there is a gray stone wall damming my stream, and when
the falling leaves stir my genes, I pace my cell or flop on my bunk
and stare at 47 black faces across the space. I am all of them,
they are all of me, I am me, they are thee, and I have no sons
to float in the space between.

* For headnote see p. 809.

2 Poems for Black Relocation Centers

I

Flukum couldn't stand the strain. Flukum
wanted inner and outer order, so
he joined the army where U.S. Manuals made
everything plain—even how to button his shirt,
and how to kill the yellow men. (If Flukum
ever felt hurt or doubt about who his enemy
was, the Troop Information Officer or the Stars
and Stripes straightened him out.)
Plus, we must not forget
that Flukum was paid well to let the Red
Blood. And sin? If Flukum ever thought about
  sin
or Hell for squashing the yellow men, the good
  Chaplain
(Holy by God and by Congress) pointed out
  with
Devilish skill that to kill the colored men was
  not
altogether a sin.

Flukum marched back from the war, straight
  and tall,
and with presents for all: a water pipe for daddy,
teeny tea cups for mama, sheer silk for tittee,
  and

a jade inlaid dagger for me. But, with a smile
on his face in a place just across the bay,
Flukum, the patriot, got shot that same day,
got shot in his great wide chest, bedecked with
  good
conduct ribbons. He died surprised, he had
  thought
the enemy far away on the other side of the sea.

(When we received his belongings they took
  away my dagger.)

II

Dead. He died in Detroit, his beard
was filled with lice; his halo glowed
and his white robe flowed magnificently
over the charred beams and splintered glass;
his stern blue eyes were rimmed with red,
and full of reproach; and the stench: roasted
  rats
and fat baby rumps swept up his nose that
had lost its arch of triumph. He died outraged,
and indecently, shouting impieties and betrayals.
And he arose out of his own ashes. Stripped.
A faggot in steel boots.

Conrad Kent Rivers*

To Richard Wright

You said that your people
Never knew the full spirit of
Western Civilization.
To be born unnoticed
Is to be born black,
And left out of the grand adventure.

Miseducation, denial,
Are lost in the cruelty of oppression.

And the faint cool kiss of sensuality
Lingers on our cheeks.

The quiet terror brings on silent night.
They are driving us crazy. And our father's
Religion warps his life.

To live day by day
  Is not to live at all.

* For headnote see p. 807.

On the Death of William Edward Burghardt Du Bois by African Moonlight and Forgotten Shores

Truth to your mighty winds on dusky shores
    the kingdom bowed down at last,
there you were, the chosen scholar home.

True you were among the earth's unborn
    a sheik of justice and almighty intellect,
killer of liberals, brother to a distant
    universe, not easily explained to bands
of hungry black men experiencing a real truth
    spelled-out, propagated, in slums born
more vigorous each day and year of triumph,
    unemployment, wine and sweet vermouth
        squeezed against death's cool
            cocoa brown hands.

True to your souls of black folk, all hell sweeps
    our land; this moment fulfills your truths
which the State Department burned, Crisis
    censored,
    Marx allowed, and I see you now an old man
opening a door marked entrance, making your
    mark
    for the bravest party you discovered, knowing
full well that none dare give what the NAACP
    demands;

but, somehow hoping your shadow fell over
    all
those trusting black brothers, who depend and
    follow
    the whites of this or any diseased land
instead of their hearts and brains and fountain
    pens;
    men who are ashamed to curse one another,
        to wail
against tyranny, power-structures, famous
    names,
    men against the greatness of themselves.
Sage, can there be no more hope for everyman?
    Do we walk so close to devils, lose sight of
        Sun,
struggle against autumnal air, quench thirst of
    life?
    I stand dumb and chilled to understand
        your search, your loneliness,
and my own debt for the etchings from those
lonely hills
    which now and forever hold communion over
    you.

Don L. Lee*

Assassination

it was wild.

the

bullet hit high.

    (the throat-neck)

& from everywhere:

    the motel, from under bushes and cars,
    from around corners and across streets,
    out of the garbage cans and from rat holes
    in the earth

they came running.

with

guns

drawn

they came running

toward the King—

    all of them

    fast and sure—

as if

the King

was going to fire back.

they came running,

fast and sure,

in the

wrong

direction.

* For headnote see p. 809.

A Poem Looking for a Reader

to be read with a love consciousness

black is not
all inclusive,
there are other colors.
color her warm and womanly,
color her feeling and life,
color her a gibran poem & 4 women of simone.
children will give her color
paint her the color of her
man.

most of all color her
love
a remembrance of life
a truereflection
that we
will
move   u will move with
i want
u
a fifty minute call to blackwomanworld:
      hi baby,
       how u doin?
need u.
listening to
young-holt's, *please sunrise, please.*

to give   i'll give
most personal.
what about the other
scenes: children playing in vacant lots,
      or like the first time u knowingly kissed
       a girl,
      was it joy or just beautifully beautiful.

i
remember at 13
reading chester himes'
cast the first stone and
the eyes of momma when she caught me: read
  on, son.

how will u come:
      like a soulful strut in a two-piece beige
       o-rig'i-nal,
      or afro-down with a beat in yr/walk?
how will love come:
      painless and deep like a razor cut
      or like some cheap 75c movie;
      i think not.

will she be the woman
other men will want
or
will her beauty be
accented with my name on it?

she will come as she would
want her man to come.
she'll come,
she'll come.
i
never wrote a love letter
but
that doesn't mean
i
don't love.

Sonia Sanchez*

Small Comment

the name of the beast is
man or to be more specific

the nature of man is his
bestial nature or to

bring it to its elemental terms
the nature of nature is
the bestial survival of the
fittest the strongest the richest
or to really examine
the scene we cd say that
the nature of any beast is
bestial unnatural and natural
in its struggle for superiority

and survival but to really
be with it we will say that man
is a natural beast bestial in
his lusts natural in his
bestiality and expanding
and growing on the national
scene to be the most
bestial and natural of
any beast. you dig?

Nikki Giovanni*

For Saundra

i wanted to write
a poem
that rhymes
but revolution doesn't lend
itself to be-bopping

then my neighbor
who thinks i hate
asked—do you ever write
tree poems—i like trees
so i thought
i'll write a beautiful green tree poem
peeked from my window
to check the image
noticed the school yard was covered
with asphalt
no green—no trees grow
in manhattan

then, well, i thought the sky
i'll do a big blue sky poem
but all the clouds have winged
low since no-Dick was elected

so i thought again
and it occurred to me
maybe i shouldn't write
at all
but clean my gun
and check my kerosene supply

perhaps these are not poetic
times
at all

* For headnote see p. 809.

Drama

Carlton W. Molette II (1939–   ) and Barbara J. Molette (1940–   )

When New York City's Negro Ensemble Company presented "Rosalee Pritchett" by the young husband-and-wife playwrighting team of Carlton and Barbara Molette, the company presented a play that not only received excellent notices but fully exemplified the company's seasonal emphasis on "themes of Black struggle." The play provides searing insights into the insipidities of a Black middle class so encumbered by the meaning-less values of the white middle class that its bridge-playing members have lost all sense of identification with their race.

Although the Molettes' "Rosalee Pritchett" is one of the first plays in the Black theater to concentrate on the growing dilemmas of the Black middle class, it is, in another sense, a continuation of the analysis of the impact of white values on Black society first seen with telling dramatic effect in Lorraine Hansberry's *A Raisin in the Sun,* which won the New York Drama Critics Circle Award in the 1958–1959 season. But within a ten-year span the evaluation of white middle-class values has changed greatly. In Miss Hansberry's play the values are presented as good, and the Younger family strives to emulate the white middle class with heart-breaking zeal. In the Molettes' one-act play the imitation of society's most meaningless bourgeois practices is condemned. In other words, the development of the Black arts movement in the theater, the increased emphasis on Black pride, and the formulation of a Black esthetic stressing racial revolution have created a climate of tolerance for Black nonparticipation in the white world.

Thus "Rosalee Pritchett" is a timely and moving comment on the ever-changing social values of Black America. In essence, the play proves the absurdity of attempting to gratify pseudo-bourgeois tastes while society is suffering from a prolonged racial nervous breakdown. The Molettes' play is a grim one: none of the characters at the end has learned any-thing regarding renewal and change; indeed, the message seems to be that a massive social paralysis has taken place, fixing situations into racially rigid patterns.

The Molettes are well prepared to contribute to the Black theater. He is associate professor of drama at Spelman College, and she is costume designer and art instructor there.

824

Rosalee Pritchett

Characters

ROSALEE (ROSE) PRITCHETT
DOLLY MAE (DOLL) ANDERSON
MAYBELLE (BELLE) JOHNSON
DORETHA ELLEN (DORRY) SANDERS
ROBERT BARRON
AUGUSTIN (GUS) LOWE
DONALD KING
WILBUR WITTMER
THELMA FRANKLIN

Time: During a riot
Place: A Southern city

Setting

A bridge table and four chairs are set up on one side of the stage. ROSE is on the other side of the stage. The acting area is isolated in a pool of light as the scene opens. ROSE is not physically present in the scenes. She participates in the dialogue just as though she were, and the other characters react to her as if she were.

Playwrights' Notes

We are opposed to the idea of having the Guards played by whites. They should be played by Black men in whiteface makeup. It's not that we have anything against white folks—there are some excellent white actors in the Goodoleusofa, but they just ain't capable of the kind of objectivity that is necessary in the portrayal of those roles.

About the slides—you can takem or leavem. You can use zero slides, fifteen slides, or try to outdo the original production that used about 300 slides on four different rear projection screens. Do your own thang!

About the curtain call—curtain calls say to the audience "the whole thing was make-believe, and it's over now." The audience then leaves the theater unperturbed, satisfied. The audience ought to leave this play perturbed, dissatisfied—so, no curtain call.

"Rosalee Pritchett" was first presented by the Morehouse-Spelman Players at Spelman College, Atlanta, Georgia, on March 23, 1970.

Scene 1

SLIDE CUE 1. Begins with Rose's speech. Various shots of Rose in very middle-class social situations—cocktail party, looking at paintings, in proximity to her "white friends," etc.

ROSE. I am Rosalee Pritchett, wife of Dr. Richard Pritchett. My husband is a prominent physician here in town. He is respected by both whites and Negroes alike. He is even on the governor's blue-ribbon committee to study the racial tension in our community. I guess the riots are still going on. I've been in here for about a week . . . I think. Maybe it has been longer than that. The riots may be over by now. Anyhow, I'm in here . . . in the hospital, because I had a nervous breakdown. I guess you might say I had a nervous breakdown because of the riots.

SLIDE CUE 2. Various shots of the four women playing bridge.

There is soft white music playing in the background throughout the entire scene of the women playing bridge.

DORRY. (*Laughs shrilly from the darkness on the other side of the stage. The lights come up on the bridge players and the music begins. SLIDE CUE 2 begins.*) Didn't you see that movie last night?

BELLE. No, I didn't. What was the name of it?

DORRY. *Teacher's Pet,* starring Clark Gable (*sighs*) and that cute little blonde actress. Ah . . . what's her name . . . Oh, you know.

BELLE. No, Dorry, I don't know.

DORRY. Doris Day. That's who it is. She sure is a good actress. I think I'll get my hair done like she had hers done in the movie.

DOLL. Goddammit, Rose, you trumped my ace again.

ROSE. Sorry. The way the cards were, I thought that dummy had played the ace.

DOLL. You're getting as bad as Dorry and her

playing. (DORRY *sits dreaming with no intention of playing right away.*) Dorry. Dorry!

DORRY. What?

DOLL. Are you playing bridge tonight?

DORRY. Oh! Is it my play? I was just thinking of my menu for tomorrow.

BELLE. What has that got to do with playing from your hand?

DORRY. Oh everything! I was reading an article that said food will help you keep a man.

ROSE. You're worried about keeping Henry?

DORRY. You girls ought to be worried, too. You aren't exactly Playboy Bunnies.

DOLL. Okay, Dorry, now play. You're down this book anyway.

DORRY. You think I'm kidding. Things like peppered steak will really put a man on edge.

BELLE. Hot peppers won't create any kind of heat that a cool glass of water won't cool down.

DORRY. I'm trying to give you advice on how to get a little more fun out of life.

DOLL. We don't have all night. We do have to drive home.

ROSE. Richard was worried about me coming over here to play bridge. But I told him that in our neighborhood, we don't have a thing to worry about. Out here, a woman is safer at night than she would be downtown in broad daylight.

BELLE. Dear partner, shall I come over there and help you play?

DORRY. (*Takes a card from her hand.*) Maybelle Johnson, you don't allow for intelligent thought to take place.

DOLL. Throw down, we have the next two books, anyway. (*Everybody throws down.*)

BELLE. (*Tallying the score.*) Let's see, that puts us two tricks under. I think it's your deal, Doll.

DORRY. (*Picks up cards and gives them to* BELLE.) Anybody getting hungry?

BELLE. Starving. I'm on this diet and I haven't eaten a thing all day. I hope you've made some of those delicious shrimp sandwiches.

DOLL. You aren't serving *us* pepper steaks are you? (*Picks up the other deck, starts to deal.*)

DORRY. Just don't come crawling to me when your husband has taken flight, Doll.

DOLL. Hunh! That will be the day!! (BELLE *starts to shuffle cards.*)

ROSE. Why don't we eat while we play. It's getting late.

DORRY. (*Sarcastically.*) Worried about Richard?

ROSE. I don't have to worry about Richard like you have to worry about Henry! (DORRY *gets up, long pause,* BELLE *stops in mid-shuffle.*)

DOLL. Need some help, Dorry?

DORRY. No, Doll, won't take a minute. Everybody does want coffee? (*All nod in agreement.* DORRY *exits. SLIDES OFF.*)

ROSE. I guess Dorry does need all the help she can get to keep Henry. Being her *friend,* I do worry about her sometimes.

DOLL. Oh, there's nothing wrong with her that a good man couldn't cure her of.

BELLE. How do you know . . .?

DOLL. That doesn't mean I know what kind of man Henry is.

BELLE. Oh!? You don't say?!!!

ROSE. Don't explain that statement, Doll.

DOLL. I won't.

ROSE. (*Doubtfully.*) Do we have time for three more hands?

DOLL. (*Looking at her watch.*) Of course! We still have time for another rubber.

ROSE. What time do you have, Doll?

DOLL. Nine-thirty. Worried about curfew? Rose?

ROSE. Of course not. That curfew doesn't apply to us, here. It's only for them.

BELLE. The thought of those soldiers does make me jittery. Although, Jack was telling me the mayor had asked the governor to end the curfew by next week.

DOLL. Is that committee Jack is on still meeting?

BELLE. Yeah, they've asked Jack, as a lawyer, to see if the governor really has any way legally to keep the soldiers past the crisis.

DOLL. I hope it's over soon. It could interfere with our bridge club.

ROSE. How could they possibly interfere with our bridge club?

DOLL. (*Interrupts* ROSE.) If the National Guard wanted to get nasty, they could start patrolling *our* section.

ROSE. (*Authoritatively.*) For what? We're law-abiding citizens. The riots are not in our area. I don't think we have anything to worry about.

BELLE. True, Jack says that the only thing they're worried about is those niggers that live in the downtown ghetto area. Jack says that they know better than to come stomping around out here. Jack says that if they start any trouble out here he'll have them up to their ears in injunctions.

DOLL. Shall I go ahead and bid?

BELLE. You might as well. No sense waiting for Dorry to come to the table. She's going to take her sweet time anyway. Rose, is Richard treating any of those Negroes that were hurt in the riots? I hear they had asked the doctors in town to take emergency cases to help ease the load at the county hospital.

DOLL. Wait a minute, count your cards. I gave somebody one too many, Belle, count Dorry's cards.

ROSE. No, he's referring them to the clinic. He says that he doesn't want to offend his regular patients. You know, having them in the same waiting room, and all.

BELLE. I see his point. No sense ruining a good practice that has taken years to build.

ROSE. Besides, it's no telling how Richard's white business associates would interpret such a thing. They might think he's mixed up in all this vandalism if he started taking them as patients.

BELLE. . . . Twelve, thirteen, fourteen. Here, I have the extra one. Just pull from my hand, Doll. I haven't looked at them yet.

DOLL. I knew someone should have helped Dorry with the food. Sweet as she is, she's the slowest four women I know. I can't understand how a college professor's wife can be so slow.

BELLE. She must be quicker between the sheets than she is on her feet.

DOLL. (*Laughing.*) I hope so, for Henry's sake.

BELLE. Rose, did you ever contact that woman I was telling you about to help with the deb supper?

ROSE. I called her. But she said that since the curfew was on, she couldn't work at night.

BELLE. What do you mean—couldn't work at night?

ROSE. She said she was afraid to be going home after dark. I thought she'd be anxious to make some money. Poor niggers sure are getting choosy about the kind of work they do.

DOLL. Lord, don't tell me this riot is going to screw up the deb supper.

ROSE. Well, maybe we can come up with somebody else who knows how to fix lobster *à l'américaine.*

DOLL. Lobster *à l'américaine!* I thought we were having lobster thermidor.

ROSE. Don't you remember you were voted down on that idea?

DOLL. But lobster thermidor is much easier to serve. Besides, we'll look like a bunch of pigs sitting up there trying to pull your lobster *à l'américaine* out of a shell.

BELLE. Lobster *à l'américaine sounds* more elegant, Doll. Besides, lobster thermidor ain't nothing but stew.

DOLL. I'm not going to sit at a formal dinner with my $300.00 dress on trying to tackle a lobster in a shell.

BELLE. Who ever we get to cook can take it out of the shell, and then put it back in.

DOLL. Where do you propose to find a nigger that knows how to shell a lobster so that it looks elegant? Now, if we were having the thermidor, the lobster pieces wouldn't have to look pretty.

ROSE. I think you're making a big fuss over something that's already been decided, Doll.

DOLL. Well, since I'm president of the deb society this year, it is going to reflect on me how the dinner turns out.

ROSE. Don't worry, everyone will be thoroughly impressed when the menu is published in the *Daily World.*

DOLL. You better come up with someone who can fix this lobster *à l'américaine* dish, because I'm not about to go to the dinner smelling like some fishmonger from shelling lobster all day.

BELLE. Well, maybe I can get my maid to help out. She's usually pretty good about helping me in emergencies.

DOLL. This is an emergency, honey. I've spent $300.00 on a Cardin and I don't intend for a little riot to spoil it.

ROSE. All this talk about riots almost made me forget something really important. We got a letter from Richard Junior yesterday, and guess what? He has been asked to join a white fraternity at school.

BELLE. Girl! You are moving up in the world.

DOLL. That should give him some good contacts later on in his medical practice.

BELLE. Male or female?

ROSE. I said fraternity, not sorority, Belle.

BELLE. A rich white wife will bring him rich white patients.

DOLL. That is the truth, Rose. Just make sure she isn't trashy, though.

ROSE. Rickie didn't mention anything about white girls in his letter.

DOLL. Take my word for it, he will be if he is in a white fraternity. These days a white girl isn't considered a true liberal if she hasn't been to bed with a Negro.

ROSE. Well . . . I don't know about that, Doll.

DOLL. (*Interrupts* ROSE.) You know you would

be tickled to death. Just make sure her family has money.

BELLE. Right, Rose, a Negro girl with good looks and a little education would be a much better catch than poor white trash. Imagine, Rose and Richard will be yachting with (*tries to think up a rich white name*) the . . . ah . . .

ROSE. (*Evidently liking the thought of such activity joins in the game.*) I won't have time to play bridge with you girls, what with joining the Junior League and the DAR.

BELLE. Mrs. Rosalee Pritchett, wife of Dr. Richard Pritchett, the first Negro woman to join the Daughters of the American Revolution!

DOLL. Maybe you could get us in.

ROSE. Oh, but I couldn't do that! I wouldn't be the only Negro member, then.

DOLL. You're a fair-weather friend. We'll go you one better and divorce our husbands and marry white ones. (*All laugh.* DORRY *comes scurrying in with a tray laden with coffee and sandwiches.*)

DORRY. What have I missed? You all always save the good ones until after I leave.

DOLL. It had nothing to do with sex, Dorry. My, your idea of a minute is a long time.

BELLE. What were you trying to do, starve us? Rose, you don't want anything in your coffee, do you?

ROSE. No. Oh, on second thought, put a little sugar in it.

DORRY. Need to stay sweet for Richard? Speaking of sex. Did I tell you what my gynecologist said? He said . . .

BELLE. Pass me the sandwiches, Dorry.

ROSE. What's that, Dorry?

DOLL. I have time for just about one more rubber. Those sandwiches look good, Dorry.

DORRY. As I was saying, the doctor said that ninety per cent of all female complaints are caused . . .

Lights fade and tape-recorded speeded-up version of the same conversation takes over the conversation of the women.

SLIDE CUE 3. Shots of the women playing bridge just as in SLIDE CUE 2 except that the women are in whiteface makeup and their gestures and facial expressions are slightly exaggerated. The sound speeds up and gets louder; then the sound and slides end abruptly as . . .

Scene 2

Lights go up on ROSE *sitting on a stool in a padded cell. She is just as she was in scene 1, but the women playing bridge are no longer on stage.* ROSE *is isolated in a small pool of light as the scene opens. No slides.*

ROSE. Martial law has been declared by the governor of our great state because the hoodlum element is burning and looting our lovely city. Those same lazy, shiftless niggers you always see hanging out on the street who won't work to support their families are out there stealing, and destroying other people's property. They had to call out the National Guard. Why, the next thing you know, they'll be burning down our Negro businesses. Our Negro businesses have always been a source of tremendous pride to the entire city. Even the white people are proud of our Negro businesses. They had to call out the National Guard. Since all this burning and looting has been going on, nobody's safe. Why, a friend of mine just drove downtown to take her maid home and someone shot her! Can you imagine them shooting another Negro? Of course, they said the police did it. But why would the police shoot a fine law-abiding citizen? You could tell by the way she was dressed and the kind of car she was driving that she wasn't going to cause any trouble. The police don't shoot people like that! Well, I'm glad they called out the National Guard. I feel a lot safer with them patrolling the streets at night. It's no telling what those niggers might try next. Somebody had to take control of the situation, and I'm glad our governor had the courage to stand up for law and order.

Scene 3

The four GUARDSMEN *march on stage to the sound of "The Stars and Stripes Forever." All of them have joined the Reserve to avoid the draft. Their main interest in life is making money. God and country come next. The last thing in the world they want is "combat duty," but they do get a thrill ordering people around at gun point—the pride of absolute power and authority.*

BARRON. Detail, HALT! (*Faces the audience; the three others halt, come to parade rest facing the audience.* BARRON *is an antiseptic-looking man. He is a combination of Listerine, Ban, Dial, and Right Guard.* BARRON *steps forward.*)

SLIDE CUE 4. BARRON *as a "citizen soldier" and as a civilian. A similar slide sequence follows for each of the other* GUARDSMEN *as they introduce themselves.*

Staff Sergeant Robert Barron. I am an insurance executive, age forty-two, I have two teenage daughters. My wife, Dorothy, and I were last year's winners of the Betsy Ross and James Madison awards. I am a member of the Toastmasters Club and the Junior Chamber of Commerce. (*Goes over to stage-left proscenium, leans against it.* LOWE *steps forward. This man has worked hard, barely finished high school. He has made a success of his gas station by winking at the women customers and grabbing their arms. When the men come in, he will shoot the breeze discussing manly things—hunting, fishing, etc. He doesn't feel that he is a man unless he is holding a gun. He is the only one of the group that has carried his M-14 rifle on stage. The others left theirs in the jeep.*)

LOWE. Specialist Four, Augustin (Gus) Lowe. I'm a service station proprietor here in town. I'm thirty-nine years old and the father of four healthy boys. I belong to the National Rifle Association and help out with the Boy Scout troop—you know, hunting and fishing. (*Goes over to stage left, sits on the floor.* DONALD KING *is next. He is nondescript, balding, and wears glasses. Usually very quiet, but a couple of Manhattans, and he is the life of the party.*)

KING. Specialist Five, Donald King, age thirty-seven. I am an accountant for the public utilities firm here in the city. I serve as a deacon in the church and Grand Potentate of my lodge. Grace, my wife, is president of the P.T.A. Children: none. (KING *goes over to* BARRON. *Now, for* WITTMER, *the dippy shoe salesman. Cookey and arrogant. He will lick the boots of any superior to move up a notch. He will also wear a flower that squirts water for laughs.*)

WITTMER. Private First Class, Wilbur Wittmer. I am a shoe salesman. On weekends I sing with the barbershop quartet. I am twenty-six years old. No wife (*implies that he does have some*

children *that he ain't owning up to*), no children. (*Sits.*)

BARRON. (*Steps out from the proscenium.*) Our mission: to protect the city and its citizenry from the forces of anarchy.

LOWE. Hot damn, this ground is cold on my ass!

BARRON. You ought to be used to it by now.

LOWE. I ain't got calluses back there.

WITTMER. Jeez, I hope it stays quiet like this. A couple of more nights like this and maybe they'll let us quit this shitty assignment.

KING. You're getting paid for it, aren't you? Just collect your check and keep your fat mouth shut.

WITTMER. But I'm losing commissions, and also contacts. (*Up.*) Did I tell you about the little redhead that came in today? Missed my big chance having to stomp around here. When she walked in the store, I said, "OH YES!!" (*Accompanied by a few bumps and grinds.*)

LOWE. To her?

WITTMER. (*Quietly.*) To myself. When she sat down, I said, "May I show you something?" (*Holding his penis and winking at* LOWE.) Then I proceeded to show her shoes. After about the fifth pair, I was up to her knees, and had gotten her name. (*Sits.*) Now, here is the sorry ass part of it. She was telling me where she was going to have dinner and then I remembered my "patriotic duty." Now all I can do is sit here, with a hard on, sweat, and think about it.

KING. You're a horny old sonofabitch, you know that?

WITTMER. It's just my manly nature. (*Reaches for his cigarettes.*) When this is over, I'll be able to keep all my women happy again.

BARRON. Wittmer, go keep an eye out. (*Wittmer exits.*) That little punk . . . probably never had a lay in his life. Damn, this ground *is* cold.

KING. I don't mind a bit. I would rather sit here in this alley than chase after those niggers all night.

LOWE. (*Sits fingering his gun.*) It's a goddam shame I haven't had a chance to use this. I wouldn't mind being over there where the action is. First nigger that showed his black ass, I'd shoot the shit outta him. I'm a helluva good shot. Once I shot a crow dead between the eyes. Now, you take my sons, by the time the oldest one is twelve, he'll be able to shoot the warts off a frog. Believe me, that's the way to raise boys.

BARRON. Why don't you go put that weapon in the jeep with the others.

LOWE. Why don't you kiss my ass, Sergeant.

KING. My wife's against guns. But when all this trouble started, she made me get her a gun and show her how to *use* it. She said she'd form an army of mothers to stop the black horde from tearing down the suburbs.

LOWE. I bet she could, too. Everybody is getting damn tired of these niggers trying to take over the whole damned country. We gotta stand up for our rights as American citizens!

BARRON. You got any cigarettes, either of you?

KING. Yeah, should have some. Aw hell! Smoked my last one on our way here.

LOWE. Wittmer should have some. (*Goes over toward* WITTMER—*off stage.*) Wittmer, toss me your cigarettes. (WITTMER *tosses* LOWE *the pack.* LOWE *tosses his rifle to* WITTMER.)

KING. You know, my wife kinda scares me. She keeps this gun for emergency purposes, but she won't keep the gun loaded.

LOWE. Hell, I keep my guns loaded and available.

BARRON. What about your children?

LOWE. What about 'em?

BARRON. Aren't you afraid they'll get hurt?

LOWE. Aw shit, I told you they was good shots. My youngest is already good with a BB gun. Shoots birds and cats and stuff. This coming September, I'm gonna get him a 22 and take him coon hunting.

BARRON. You're taking a chance with the statistics. Every year hundreds of kids get killed playing around with guns.

LOWE. Good god, man, they don't play with the guns. They handle them! They know what they're doing. If I was in combat, I'd rather have them beside me than you clowns. Give us the right equipment, and we could wipe out half the niggers in this town—just the five of us.

KING. If my wife heard you say that, she'd talk your ear off . . . you'd probably end up throwing all your guns away.

LOWE. Well, my wife's the same way. But I just put my foot down and said that I wasn't going to have my sons to grow up to be punks. (BARRON *shrugs, takes a draw on the cigarette, and blows a smoke ring.*)

KING. Wonder if Cassanova's spotted anything.

LOWE. He would shit in his drawers if he did.

BARRON. There's not going to be any trouble way out here.

KING. Hope by this time next week, my feet will

be propped up, I'll have a Manhattan in my hand.

LOWE. We'll be here till them niggers learn where their places is.

BARRON. We're not bothered where we live. We have always had a curfew for the niggers. They have to be out of the area by sundown. I say let them have the goddam city . . . as long as they don't burn it up. They got the whole place smelling like a whorehouse anyway. I don't work downtown anymore since the company moved out to the suburbs. So the only ones I see are the ones that clean up our office. Well, we have one agent in our office, but he's different. Half the time, I think he's white.

LOWE. Is he white enough to screw your daughter?

KING. (*Goes to* LOWE.) Aw hell, Gus, there's one that works in our office too. He's not such a bad guy. I asked him about this rioting the other day and he's just as much against it as you are. He has just as much to lose as you do, maybe even more. He's a helluva lot better educated and he probably makes more money.

LOWE. (*Ignores this affront to his dignity—mainly because he figures* KING *could beat his brains out if the occasion arose.*) Man, has he got you snowed. Don't you know that they all act nice, like that? They'll con you into thinking they're harmless—just waiting for a chance to fuck a white woman.

KING. You know what, Gus? You're out of your damn mind. This man is an accountant with our firm. He's a college graduate.

LOWE. All you college boys think you're so damned smart. I have to work hard for my money—and some damned jigaboo sitting up in an air-conditioned office pushing a friggin' pencil. You probably have him over to your house for dinner! Don't turn you back on him while your wife's around! (*Getting even.*) He'll be humping her right there on your dining room table!

KING. He's never been over to my house! But he and his wife did come to the company Christmas party last year.

LOWE. Oh . . . he's got a wife! What does she look like?

KING. Oh, I don't know. I guess she's pretty good looking for a colored girl.

LOWE. Did you get it?

KING. Get what?

LOWE. That dark meat, boy! They sho-o-ore got some good pussy!

BARRON. Damn, Gus! We're going to have to send you out there with Wittmer to jack off.

LOWE. What's the matter with you guys? Ain't nothing wrong with getting you a little piece a dark meat every now and then—long as you don't catch the clap, or nothing.

BARRON. Gus, Shut up.

LOWE. Maybe I will go keep Wittmer company for a while. (*Gets up—mumbles* Shit, I ain't— *waits to be asked not to leave.*)

BARRON. I wonder what those jigs are gonna try tonight. It's about time for the shooting to start. Probably kill some more of their own people—not to mention ours. Aren't you guys glad I've got political pull?

KING. Yeah, this is a nice secluded spot.

BARRON. Not much of a chance that we'll get shot out here in the nigger suburbs. Nice out here isn't it? Almost like a white neighborhood.

KING. You know, last Sunday in church, one of the members of the congregation stood up and asked for a special collection. Her maid had been burned out completely during the trouble last week. The church gave her a generous offering—over fifty dollars.

BARRON. Fifty dollars? That won't buy much these days.

KING. It doesn't take as much money for them to live on as it does us.

LOWE. I wish somebody would give me some money for starting a riot.

BARRON. That's how they are started, all right.

LOWE. Hunh?

BARRON. These so-called spontaneous rebellions are no damned such a thing. Every single one of them have been planned.

KING. By who?

BARRON. The communists, who else?!?

KING. Wait a minute. That gal didn't get any money for starting a riot. Hell, she was a victim of her own people.

BARRON. She may not have, but there were plenty others who did. The communists are . . .

LOWE. You know, some guy the other day dropped by the station to tell me about some guy who was going to talk about these riots. I ain't never had too much time for politics in any big way. But he sure convinced me. These commies are out to take over any way they can, and these riots are part of their plot. It must be the commies! Niggers ain't smart enough to plan something like this all by themselves.

KING. (*Reluctant to accept what is being said at face value; however, he is reticent about showing his doubt.*) You sure about this?

LOWE. (*To* KING.) You ain't?

KING. (*Decides it best not to further the discussion; gets up and moves away from* BARRON *and* LOWE.) Well . . . yeah, I guess so.

BARRON. This is not a guessing situation. We have documented proof of incidents. We know the names of agents and their contacts. This insurrection they had last week was a trial run. The governor knew what he was doing when he called us in.

LOWE. We're going to stop the pinkos before they burn us all up. Need to line them up against the wall and shoot the shit out of 'em before they have a chance to start another riot. (KING *takes out a little packet of cards from his fatigue jacket. Shuffles through them during the ensuing speech by* BARRON, *and smiles.*)

BARRON. That would be a little hard to do. The "public" would start screaming fascism without even knowing what they were talking about.

LOWE. It's them radicals. They give me a pain in . . . (*Pauses, then turns his back to take a quick piss. While* BARRON *is saying the ensuing speech, the following dialogue is taking place between* LOWE *and* KING. LOWE *sees* KING *smiling.* LOWE *zips up his pants and walks over to* KING.) What the hell you grinning at?

KING. (*Looks up.*) What?

LOWE. Boy, this is no time for smiles.

KING. (*Hands him a card.*) Here.

LOWE. Goddamn . . . get a load of those boobs. (*Lets out a whistle and reaches for another card.*) King, you're all right, after all. Let me see the rest of those. Yeah . . . yeah . . . Go-o-o-o-d-damn!

BARRON. (*Does not really notice that* LOWE *and* KING *are not listening. As* BARRON *starts his speech, fade up* "*God Bless America.*") What we're doing now is trying to convince all of the decent, god-fearing folks like you and King, here, of the international conspiracy that we're up against. We've got socialists, fools, fatheads, and half-brights running our government. It's no wonder that the free-enterprise system is about to go down the drain. This trend towards one-world socialism will destroy us. It's . . . it's treasonous. But we have these people teaching in our schools and making high-level government policy decisions. Our main problem is our involvement with the UN.

I've been fighting to get us out of the UN for years. That's what the James Madison award that I won last year was for. We've even had foreign troops on our soil. But did you hear about it? Of course not! They hushed it up. If we could get an amendment to the constitution forbidding America to join a world government, like the UN, that would go a long way in stopping this creeping socialism. It's up to you and me to stop communism. We've got to get the leaders, destroy them before they destroy our freedom.

LOWE. (*Realizes that* BARRON *is still talking to him.*) Oh yeah . . . show me a commie and I'll blow his guts out.

BARRON. The time will come for that. The biggest problem now is red infiltration.

LOWE. Yeah, everything would be peaceful if pinkos like Markin Luther Coon were stopped before they got started. Had the gall to call himself a man of GOD. Shit, he wasn't no man of my God. Everybody knows that sonofabitch . . . (*Lights start to fade. Red flashing light comes on.* WITTMER *enters, goes near center stage. Other* GUARDSMEN *turn away from audience.*)

WITTMER. HALT! Who goes? (*The* GUARDSMEN *start to turn back around as* WITTMER *goes over to them.*)

SLIDE CUE 5. ROSE *showing look of surprise sitting in her car. Slides continue showing the actual scene indicated by the dialogue.*

ROSE. (*Continues to sit on the stool in the cell and talks to the* GUARDSMEN.) Who's that? What's wrong?

BARRON. STOP!! This is the National Guard. Wittmer, what the hell are you trying to do, anyway, turning on that damn light? How in the hell did I get stuck with a zero like you . . . ?

ROSE. I'm on my way home.

WITTMER. Pull over off the road!

KING. You're under arrest for curfew violation.

BARRON. What?

ROSE. Under arrest?

KING. Yes. You're violating the curfew.

ROSE. I'm on my way home. I live in this neighborhood. I didn't know the curfew applied out here.

BARRON. Out kind of late, aren't you? Curfew is eight o'clock.

LOWE. What did you have to do to get a fine expensive car like this?

ROSE. I beg your pardon!

BARRON. Do you have a permit?

ROSE. Permit?!?

WITTMER. That's what the Sergeant said.

ROSE. I've never heard tell of any permit. My husband is Dr. Pritchett—see the medical tag on the back of the car?

LOWE. What are you doing out this time of night?

ROSE. I'm on my way home from my bridge party.

LOWE. Oh! A bridge party! Niggers play bridge these days.

KING. Do you have any identification? Something to say that you are really Dr. Pritchett's wife?

ROSE. No. Just my driver's license.

BARRON. Where do you work?

ROSE. I'm a housewife.

WITTMER. The Sergeant asked you where did you work?

ROSE. I said I'm a housewife. I don't.

BARRON. Ok, let's see the license.

ROSE. What?

WITTMER. The Sergeant wants the driver's license.

ROSE. Here.

BARRON. You Rosalee Pritchett?

ROSE. Yes.

LOWE. Yessir!

WITTMER. Where do you buy your shoes? Why don't you come see me? I'll give you something that'll make you feel good!

LOWE. Yeah, let me sell you some gasoline sometime. I'll be glad to fill you up. (*Hunches* WITTMER; *they both laugh.*)

KING. You know, Rosie, you're pretty brave to be out so late all by yourself, and all.

WITTMER. Maybe we better escort her home. I'll be glad to volunteer for that detail, Sarge.

ROSE. Thank you, but I can make it home quite well by myself. I live right around the corner.

WITTMER. We wouldn't want you to get lost, now.

ROSE. May I have my driver's license now?

LOWE. Don't be in such a hurry, Rosie.

ROSE. It's Mrs. Pri . . . Pritchett.

WITTMER. Guess she told you.

LOWE. Shut your damned mouth, Private!

ROSE. I've never been stopped before. We've never had any trouble in our neighborhood. This is a nice neighborhood!

BARRON. This is just routine.

LOWE. We're here to protect you, right? (WITTMER *and* KING *nod in agreement.*)

KING. We're here to maintain law and order. We wouldn't want you to get hit by a brick.

LOWE. You wouldn't want a brick to be tossed through that great big windshield on that great big car, now would you?

ROSE. I haven't done anything. May I go now? I'm tired.

WITTMER. Oh you are? Well, maybe you'd like to rest a while with us.

KING. Yeah! We're all tired! Let's everybody just relax and take it easy. (*Makes a grand gesture of welcoming.*)

LOWE. We're glad to see you, Rosie.

WITTMER. Now we have a skirt to grace our company.

ROSE. Please . . . may I leave now?

LOWE. Maybe we could entertain you.

WITTMER. Yeah, we're here to protect you, and entertain you. (*Singing to the tune of "Let Me Entertain You."*) Let me entertain you, Rosie, let me . . .

ROSE. Please, please . . . my husband is expecting me home.

WITTMER. Aw, come on, Rosie. You have to entertain the troops first.

ROSE. Keep your hands off me!

WITTMER. Why, Rosie, we're just being friendly. I mean Mrs. Pritchett. (*Sings "Getting to Know You" down on one knee.*)

BARRON. Little Sinatra, you're not being one damned bit entertaining.

LOWE. Maybe she'd like to entertain us. Come on, Rosie, I'm ready to be . . . ah . . . entertained.

KING. Maybe if we sat down like an audience, she'd give us a show.

LOWE. I'm not sitting on that ground and freeze my ass anymore.

WITTMER. Hey, let's all sit in the car and have a nice intimate show.

ROSE. Oh, God, I just want to go home. Let me go home! Take your hands off me!

BARRON. OK, fellas, that's enough. Knock it off! Wittmer, cut it out! You're going to get all of us in a helluva lot of trouble.

LOWE. What are you? Some kind of nigger lover, or something?

WITTMER. Yeah, whose side are you on, anyhow? We're just having a little fun.

LOWE. Hey, this is a mighty fine car you got here, Rosie. Mind if I sit down and make myself comfortable? (*Drum roll leading into "The Star Spangled Banner."*)

BARRON. Rosie, come on out of that car; let us get a good look at you. (*Pauses.*) Wittmer, turn off that goddamn light!

WITTMER. Right, Sarge! (*Goes over to center stage and returns. Red light goes out.*)

ROSE. Help me!!! Somebody . . . HELP! (*They all start to pull and beat on the imaginary* ROSE, *instigated by* LOWE. *They throw her to the ground and surround her as the lights fade on the* GUARDSMEN. *Lights come on in* ROSE'S *cell while she screams and writhes. She eventually slumps forward.*)

SLIDE CUE 6. Shots of the American flag interspersed with "Americana," e.g. garbage, billboards, Coke signs, etc. Slides continue until the music ends.

KING. We're helping you. Hey, you don't look too bad, Rosie.

LOWE. Relax, Rosie! We're just trying to integrate.

ROSE. No!! Oh DEAR GOD . . . NO-O-O-O!!!! (*Screams, light goes down on* ROSE.)

LOWE. Who ever said a nigger woman was warm? I'm still about to freeze my ass off.

KING. Let me see.

BARRON. She's passed out!

WITTMER. Let's get out of here! (*Exits.*)

BARRON. Put her in the car. Grab her arms, I've got her legs.

LOWE. Always grabbing the best part.

BARRON. Rank has its privileges, Corporal.

KING. Here's her jacket.

BARRON. Hurry up, you bastards! (*All exit. The rest of the lines are yelled from offstage.*)

KING. We aren't leaving her here, are we?

BARRON. Hell, yes! Make sure you don't leave anything in the car. Wittmer, you get a rag out of the jeep and wipe everything off. We can't leave any evidence. (*When music ends, slides fade.*)

Scene 3

ROSE *is still on the other side of the stage. She is very dimly lighted throughout the final scene. The setting is the same as the first scene.* ROSE'S *place has been taken at the bridge table by* THELMA. THELMA *is a newcomer to the group. She is a social climber, younger than the rest of the women present. She is* DOLL'S *partner.*

DORRY *is in the kitchen fixing snacks. Her hand is dummy.*

SLIDE CUE 7. Just like SLIDE CUE 2, but with THELMA *instead of* ROSE. *White music plays throughout the entire scene.*

THELMA. Doll, the deb gala was simply magnificent. I don't know when I have seen such an affair carried out so beautifully. Everything was so ... so elegant. And you looked simply divine in that gorgeous outfit. You know, the little town we were living in before we moved here never had anything that could match this. They had some social affairs, but they were usually so, how shall I put it ... gauche. (*Slides fade.*)

DOLL. (DOLL *and* BELLE *exchange glances.*) Thanks, Thelma. You know, Belle ...

THELMA. My compliments to you, Doll, for that wonderful dish. What was it called? I simply must have the recipe so I can try it out! I am so glad ...

DOLL. Lobster *à l'américaine.* You know, Belle ...

THELMA. Yes! Lobster american. Do you have the recipe?

BELLE. I have it. I'll write it out and give it to you. What were you saying, Doll?

DOLL. Hmmmm ... oh yes, you know, I heard that Rose was still in the hospital.

BELLE. Really? She's been in there for almost a month. Do you know when they're going to release her?

DOLL. They *said* they were going to release her last week.

THELMA. Do they know yet who raped her?

DOLL. Well, not really. She said the National Guard stopped her on her way home that night from our bridge game. I also heard that she's still awfully incoherent and isn't making too much sense.

BELLE. That doesn't make much sense to me. The soldiers weren't patrolling this area. I didn't see any National Guard. Did you, Doll?

DOLL. Well, you know, Rose always did fantasize a bit. Ralph said that Richard had demanded a full-scale investigation of the National Guard, but that General somebody or other had insisted that there were no soldiers stationed anywhere near here that night.

BELLE. Thelma, I believe it's your play. I hope Dorry rushes a little bit with the snacks. I didn't eat anything before I came tonight.

THELMA. I didn't either. I keep saying I am going on a diet.

DOLL. You don't need to diet.

THELMA. Yes I do too. If I don't watch it, everything I eat turns to fat. How do you keep such a trim figure? You always look so cute. No one would ever guess your age. (*Realizes what she has said and tries to rectify it and fails.*) What I mean is ... ah, you look younger than you are.

DOLL. Thanks, Thelma. Have you played yet?

THELMA. Oh no! Sorry. Let's see. Who played what?

DOLL. That's my ace! (THELMA *plays from her hand.*)

BELLE. At least Thelma doesn't trump your aces like Rose always did. Has anybody been thinking about our spring dance? We have absolutely got to think of something different.

THELMA. I have an idea that would just be splendid. We could go Hawaiian. You know, a luau. The decorations could be along the lines of palm trees, with flowers all over the place. We could wear grass skirts. You would look so cute in a grass skirt, Doll.

DOLL. That doesn't sound too bad. At least we won't go through the lobster bit again.

BELLE. That dinner turned out just fine, and you know it. I do like the idea of a luau. We could go way out and serve a roast suckling pig. You know, on a huge tray with parsley all around it and a big apple stuck in his mouth. All this talk about food is making me hungrier. Somebody needs to build a fire under Dorry in there.

THELMA. I'll be glad to do whatever I can to help. I fix a delicious punch that we could serve in coconut shells. Just let me know what needs to be done. I'll be glad to do anything I can.

BELLE. Good, we can always use help. (DORRY *comes scurrying in laden with a tray. There should be four wine glasses on the tray in addition to the plate of sandwiches, coffee cups, and relishes.*)

DORRY. How's your new partner doing, Doll?

THELMA. Oh, I don't know whether I'm doing Doll any good or not. She is such a terrific bridge player. I can really learn so much from her. You see, I am really a novice at playing bridge. In this little town where we were living before we moved here, very few of the girls really played good bridge. Mostly they just talked. It is a real pleasure playing with someone who really knows what they are doing.

DOLL. My, Dorry, we are festive tonight. What's the wine for?

DORRY. It's champagne, Doll. I thought we might celebrate the grand way the deb dinner went off.

THELMA. I was just telling Belle how wonderful the dinner turned out. You all really have a knack for entertaining. It is so delightful having friends such as you. You all must let me host a bridge party.

DOLL. Fine with me. Dorry's been doing it for so long, now.

BELLE. Oh, Dorry, Thelma came up with a great idea for the spring dance—a luau.

DORRY. Oh I like that idea just fine! Let's toast to the luau and hope that it is as big a success as the deb dinner was.

DOLL. You know, girls, we might have to find someplace else to give the spring dance.

BELLE. We'll give it in the armory, like we always ... damn! The National Guard is still using it as headquarters.

DOLL. I know. And offhand I can't think of any place that is as large as the armory is.

DORRY. I thought once the crisis was over that the soldiers were going to stop patrolling at night.

BELLE. This committee that Jack is on has been trying to get the governor to withdraw the troops. Jack says that the governor is afraid that if the soldiers are withdrawn too soon that the rioting will start all over again.

DOLL. What does the governor mean, *too soon?* A month is enough time! The soldiers better be out of the armory within the next two months, or we *will* be in trouble.

DORRY. How are we going to fit that crowd we had last year into anyplace smaller? You know, Thelma, we had over two thousand people. Had you ever seen so many white people at a Negro dance before?

DOLL. It was a good turnout. There must have been over five hundred white folks there.

THELMA. My goodness!

DORRY. We made quite a bit of money ... we didn't keep the money, of course. It went into the deb scholarship fund ... after expenses. We always give two of the outstanding debutantes $200 scholarships for college.

THELMA. Oh, that's nice!

BELLE. Rose did a good job as publicity chairman last year.

DOLL. I hope she is well soon enough to work on publicity this year.

THELMA. Oh, I'll be glad to work on publicity.

BELLE. (*Ignores* THELMA.) It is such a shame that Rose couldn't be there for the deb dinner.

DOLL. Maybe she'll recover from her hysteria in time for the luau.

DORRY. Has she really been hysterical? I guess she would be after being raped like that. Oh well ... Say! Guess where *we're* going for our summer vacation.

DOLL. I haven't the foggiest idea.

DORRY. To one of the islands in the CARA-*BEE*-AN.

THELMA. O-o-o-o-h that sounds fabulous! Have you decided which one yet? I've heard they have the most luxurious hotels. And the service is stupendous. Oh, I envy you just lolling around in the sun and having folks wait on you hand and foot.

DOLL. Dorry, I wouldn't do too much lolling in the sun, if I were you.

DORRY. Oh I might do a little. I'm going to have to show off my new bathing suit. It's almost a bikini. I can't wait to see Henry's reaction when he sees it. It is cut real low in the front and ... (*Tape recorder comes in at a speeded-up rate to drown out the voices of the women.*)

SLIDE CUE 8. *Same as* SLIDE CUE 3, *with* THELMA *instead of* ROSE.

BLACKOUT.

THERE SHOULD BE NO CURTAIN CALL.

Essay

Nathan Hare (1934–   )

A major leader of the Black Studies movement, Nathan Hare was brought up on land his father farmed on shares near Slick, Oklahoma. Attending Langston University, a Black institution in his native state, he was influenced by its most famous faculty member, the poet Melvin B. Tolson. Graduating in 1954, he went to Chicago for graduate study in sociology at Northwestern University and the University of Chicago, receiving from the latter the M.A. in 1957 and the Ph.D. in 1962.

Meanwhile he had started his stormy teaching career. After a year at Virginia State College (1957–1958), he joined the Howard University faculty in 1961 as instructor in sociology and was promoted to assistant professor in 1963. An unorthodox academician, he aroused controversy over his professional boxing, his opposition to the war in Vietnam and the draft, his advocacy of Black power, and his criticism of the Howard administration. After being fired in 1967, he went to San Francisco State College, where he headed a pioneer Black Studies curriculum in the embattled academic year 1968–1969. Once again fired, this time by S. I. Hayakawa, Hare remained in San Francisco. Late in 1969 he began publication of *The Black Scholar,* an important "Journal of Black Studies and Research."

Hare's book *The Black Anglo-Saxons* (1965) carries forward E. Franklin Frazier's critique of the Black middle class, a group, according to Hare, that has largely divested itself of Black values and modes of being in quest of assimilationist goals. Hare himself, now operating free of institutional restraints, is striving to develop concepts of Black Studies truly relevant to the experience, needs, and aspirations of Black people.

Hare's essays and observations have appeared in numerous magazines, among them *The Negro History Bulletin, Phylon, Social Forces, Liberator, Ebony, U.S. News and World Report, Crime and Delinquency, Civil Liberties Bulletin, The Saturday Evening Post, The Saturday Review,* and *The Massachusetts Review.* "Dr. Nathan Hare: Black Power Professor with a Punch," *Sepia,* XVII (April 1968), 50–54, is an illustrated article.

The Challenge of a Black Scholar

The first black scholar I ever knew was a professor at a small Negro college in Oklahoma, at the same time mayor of the town (all-Negro) and poet laureate of Liberia (Africa). Though he had only a bachelor's degree, he easily was the superior of his Ph.D. colleagues in debate and discussion (whenever he could corner them) and used to wind up on occasion telling them that they needed to go back to school.

A scholar is a man who contributes original ideas, new insights and information to the existing fund of knowledge—whether or not he has a string of academic degrees or executes his scholarly activities in a manner appropriate to the traditions and conventions of the existing world of scholarship.

But a scholar is even more than that and a black scholar is still another species apart. It will be an irony of recorded history, we have hypothesized, though almost an axiomatic one, that black scholars will provide the catalysts not only for black liberation but perhaps for the ultimate resolution of America's pathology now infecting, in some form or fashion, the entire world.

On the shoulders of the black scholar falls an enormous task. He must de-colonize his mind so that he may effectively guide other intellectuals and students in their search for liberation.

The white ruler not only distorted and destroyed the educational development of blacks and colonial peoples but also miseducated himself. Thus the society he dominates is increasingly corrupt and bloody with no clear future. The air is filled with pollution and the land and forests are being destroyed as human alienation and conflict remain on the rise.

The connection between white colonialism and its scholarship has always been apparent to blacks and other victims of it. However, an examination of this relationship is in order.

Thorsten Veblen's observations on white scholarship in such books as *The Theory of the Leisure Class* and *The Higher Learning in America,* though decades old, remain quite˙ applicable today. Veblen described the leisure class mentality of the wealthy class who sought to conspicuously display their apartness from the manual worker through the attachment of prestige to non-productive endeavor. Thus education, which was largely private at the time and afforded only by the well-to-do emphasized the abstract as over against the practical. Much time was spent on such matters as syntax, footnotes (implying the leisure to spend on the reading of many books), and the mastery of lofty jargon which, being incomprehensible, could be taken as profound. Even today a student can pass all of his courses with A's but fail to graduate because he flunks the French test though he may never see Paris and would not know enough to communicate well even if he did. Black scholars today, obeying the dictates of scholarly ritualistic tradition, are compelled to footnote, when writing, say, about the slavery era during which their ancestors were forbidden by law and custom to learn to read and write. They must footnote the white slavemasters or historians acceptable to a society which condoned black slavery.

The forces of production which eventually led to over-urbanization and industrialization have produced a concomitant specialization of learning, and a rise of gadgeteering, but the leisure-class legacy has nevertheless remained.

Neither leisure class education nor specialized education is sufficient to transform black consciousness—or white consciousness for that matter—into a revolutionary, creative instrument for dynamic change. Leisure class education creates dilletantes; specialized education creates pragmatists and moral zombies devoid of imagination or compassion in the exercise of their skills.

Black scholars too, members of the "black bourgeoisie" described by the late E. Franklin Frazier have failed in their roles up to now. Aside from a disproportionate number of "house niggers" descendants among them, most received their early training at Negro colleges where the perfunctory trivia of white academia are mimicked and exaggerated. When I taught at Howard University, for example, there were an average of ten mandatory academic (or cap & gown) processionals yearly.

Now there has developed, out of the black studies call for black professors, a mass migration of many such individuals to the staid milieu of the white college faculty, but mainly what they bring there is their Ph.D. degrees and their social fraternity pins, with the same old style of teaching and attitudes toward matters intellectual. They remain isolated and alienated fundamentally from their non-professional fellows, as well as their students, perhaps to an even greater degree than is characteristic of the white professor. Thus whatever scholarly endeavors they execute are prone to be separated and in discord with the needs of their people's struggle. They pant after professorial elevation, conforming to the criteria set forth by white racist administrators, while their people pursue liberation without benefit of a viable ideology or theory.

In the late spring of 1962, E. Franklin Frazier, who had been largely responsible for attracting me to Howard University just before his death, delivered an address at Atlanta University on "The Failure of the Negro Intellectual." This had followed by three decades Carter G. Woodson's *The Miseducation of the American Negro* (based on his experiences in acquiring the master's degree at the University of Chicago and the Ph.D. at Harvard). An expanded and refined version of these two indictments, *The Crisis of the Negro Intellectual,* was published by Harold Cruse. The paradox is that only Cruse, who was not college-trained, has been able, in this era, to write such a book.

Such criticisms have been both well taken and well made, but now is the time to take up the work of DuBois, who actually sought decades earlier to launch a program of black research and scholarship. In an essay entitled, "Science and Empire," DuBois told how, when he went to Atlanta University around the turn of the century, he encountered grave problems which not only obstructed his efforts but eventually led to his firing.

Social thinkers were engaged in vague statements and were seeking to lay down the methods by which, in some distant future, social law analogous to physical law would be discovered. . . . But turning my gaze from fruitless word-twisting and facing the facts of my own social situation and racial world, I determined to put science into sociology through a study of the conditions and problems of my own group. . . . I entered this primarily with the utilitarian object of reform and uplift; in contrast to Herbert Spencer who had issued ten volumes using biological analyses and the trappings of science but without true scientific results, but nevertheless, I wanted to do the work with scientific accuracy. . . . I did not have any clear con-

ception or grasp of the meaning of that industrial imperialism which was beginning to grip the world. . . .

I tried to isolate myself in the ivory tower of race. I wanted to explain the difficulties of race and the ways in which these difficulties caused political and economic troubles. It was this concentration of thought and action and effort that really, in the end, saved my scientific accuracy and search for truth. . . . continually I was forced to consider the economic aspects of world movements as they were developing at the time. Chiefly this was because the group in which I was interested were workers, earners of wages, owners of small bits of land, servants. The labor strikes interested and puzzled me. They were for the most part strikes of workers led by organizations to which Negroes were not admitted.[1]

Eventually, after much persecution from blacks and whites, DuBois came to the conclusion that knowledge is not enough, that people know pretty much what needs to be done, if they would only act. And so, he switched, in his own words, from science to propaganda. Thus we lost the inestimable value of his scientific inquiry with regard to the way in which we should act and how to move other men to action.

The importance of the intellectual in the struggle for national liberation has always been apparent. In a book titled *Black Intellectuals Come to Power,* for instance, the author told how, in Trinidad,

When the People's Educational Movement in 1956 became the People's National Movement, more was changed than just one word in the name of the organization, but much in the way of policy and key personnel had already emerged. The period of pre-party activity not only established the dominant themes on which the party platform would be based, but had also been a time in which the norms of leadership and influence within the organization took shape.[2]

The black scholar must recognize and study this and other movements, their successes and failures, as well as the nature of the oppressor and his ways. To date, there has been a tendency to be preoccupied with the study of his own group alone, influenced in part no doubt by the Establishment-sponsored white research to study the victim, as

---

[1] W. E. B. DuBois, *Dusk of Dawn,* New York: Harcourt, Brace and World, 1940 (Schocken Books Edition, 1968), pp. 50–54.

[2] Ivar Oxaal, *Black Intellectuals Come to Power,* Cambridge: Schenkman Publishing Company, 1967, p. 137.

if to say that his own shortcomings, not the policy of oppression, bring on his problems. Thus there are shelves and shelves of books on blacks. Recently, I received a book called *Black On Blue,* and there are studies of "Negroes and Cotton-Picking in South Georgia," "The Correlation Between Negro Unemployment and the Price of Coons in Creek County, Oklahoma" without an increase in insight and understanding of what is necessary for black liberation. A wealthy foundation not long ago gave $10 million to a group of white scholars to study "the Negro." We black scholars at last have recognized that they have been studying the wrong man. We want $10 million, at the least, to study the white man.

The black scholar suffers from the problem of economic dependency and the Establishment's increasing monopoloy on the world of grants as well as the publication and dissemination of materials. The black scholar must break free from this dependency as well as his fundamental enslavement to Western concepts of scholarship.

Let's examine a few of those concepts. One case in point is the taboo against taking a stand on matters of right and wrong.[3] Objectivity, or its facade, has been made synonymous with neutrality, allowing the scholar to remain ostensibly impartial while catering actually to the wishes of the status quo. Objectivity and impartiality are neither synonymous nor mutually inclusive. As a matter of fact, if a scholar is biased against bias he is possessed by a bias. The belief in neutrality is itself a value-judgment.

On the question of objectivity, the late Louis Wirth, in his prefatory remarks to Karl Mannheim's *Ideology and Utopia,* has written:

It would be naive to suppose that our ideas are entirely shaped by the objects of our contemplation which lie outside of us or that our wishes and our fears have nothing whatever to do with what we perceive or with what will happen. . . . The most important thing, therefore, that we can know about a man is what he takes for granted, and the most elemental and important facts about a society are those that are seldom debated and generally regarded as settled.[4]

The black scholar must look beneath the surface of things and, wherever necessary and appropriate, take a stand against the bias of white scholarship. He must be biased against white bias, must be an iconoclast, rallying to the call to arms of all the black intelligentsia, to destroy obsolescent norms and values and create new ones to take their place.

. . . the defetishization of "values," "ethical judgments," and the like, the identification of the social, economic, psychic causes of their emergence, change, and disappearance, as well as the uncovering of the specific interests which they serve at any particular time, represent the greatest single contribution that an intellectual can make to the cause of human advancement.[5]

The black scholar can no longer afford to ape the allegedly "value-free" approach of white scholarship. He must reject absolutely the notion that it is "not professional" ever to become emotional, that it is somehow improper to be "bitter" as a black man, that emotion and reason are mutually exclusive. Anna Freud, in *The Ego and Its Mechanisms of Defense* suggests that it is, on the contrary, normal to be bitter in a bitter situation. If someone sticks a pin in you or a certain portion of your anatomy and you do not yell out, then there is probably something wrong with you or that portion of your anatomy. Emotion and reason may not only go together but may in fact be stimulants to each other. If one is truly cognizant of adverse circumstances, he would be expected, through the process of reason, to experience some emotional response.

To paraphrase racist Rudyard Kipling, if you can keep calm while all around you is chaos, maybe you don't fully understand the situation. If someone points a pistol at you and threatens to gun you down at the count of five (having shot your brother at the count of five, and your mother at the count of five), then gets to three and a half on you and you do not get emotional you probably are guilty of being unreasonable.

In any case, the "ideological fog" of the black scholar, which prevents his endeavors from leading to a central body of knowledge, stems in part

---

[3] C. Wright Mills, *The Sociological Imagination,* New York: Oxford University Press, 1959, *passim.* See also Pitirim A. Sorokin, *Fads and Foibles in Sociology and Related Sciences,* Chicago: Henry Regnery Company, 1965, *passim.*

[4] Karl Mannheim, *Ideology and Utopia:* An Introduction to the Sociology of Knowledge, New York; Harcourt, Brace and World, 1936, pp. xxii, xxiii.

[5] Paul M. Sweezy and Leo Huberman, eds., *Paul A. Baran: A Collective Portrait,* New York: Monthly Review Press, 1965, p. 6.

from this very aping of pseudo white scholarship camouflaged by grandiosity.

Scholarship is not realized in the individual in synthesis alone, but also in analysis. No true historical analysis is possible without the constant interpretation of meaning. In order to begin an analysis, there must already be a synthesis present in the mind. A conception of ordered coherence is an indispensable precondition even to the preliminary labor of digging and hewing.[6]

Let us look at an example of the way in which one's perspective or ideology influences interpretation. In the Moynihan Report on the black American family, where a correlation was illustrated between black unemployment and illegitimacy, ideology determines whether one concludes that it is the employment factor which must be changed in order to stabilize the family or, as Moynihan concluded, the family must be stabilized as a prerequisite to economic stability. Ideology enabled him to overlook the fact, though he had the figures showing, that there are thirty-three extra non-white females for every one hundred non-white males between the ages of 25 and 40 in New York City and that that demographic condition itself hampers family stability so long as blacks are impelled to adhere to white Western ideals (practiced only superficially) of monogamy and fidelity. Monogamous fidelity assumes a one-to-one sex ratio else the alternatives of celibacy or infidelity regardless of "moral" ideals.

Therefore, I decided to develop a Hare Report in response to the Moynihan Report. I sought to make a simple study of marital happiness with the methodological notion of planting tape recorders in the bedrooms of relatives and neighbors. A professor said in horror that that would be both unethical (ideology) and crude (methodology). He instructed me to utilize a scale of intensity under which respondents would be asked if they were very happy, somewhat happy, somewhat unhappy, or very unhappy.

I discovered that some women would say that they were very happy but, should their husbands leave the room, would switch to say that, as a matter of fact, they actually were not happy. When told of this, the professor said that I would have to be methodologically more sophisticated, that people sometimes did not know their own true feelings and also might be reluctant under certain

circumstances to tell an interviewer the truth. I must then, he said, construct an index to measure happiness by indirection. He suggested kissing as an indicator of marital happiness (as I thought of Judas), and respondents were asked how many times they kissed their spouses per day. Those who kissed their spouses five times or less a day were regarded as very unhappy; from six to 10 times a day, somewhat unhappy; from 11 to 15 a day, somewhat happy; and those who kissed their spouses 16 or more times a day were—I felt certain—very tired at the end of the day.

The black scholar must develop new and appropriate norms and values, new institutional structures, and in order to be effective in this regard, he must also develop and be guided by a new ideology. Out of this new ideology will evolve new methodology, though in some regards it will subsume and overlap existing norms of scholarly endeavor.

He must understand the social function of knowledge in general; he must re-assess the traditions, values and mores of Western European scholarship; and finally he must achieve a black perspective of all his training and experience, so that his scholarly tools can become effective instruments for black liberation.

The black scholar must not only develop a new ideology with appropriate methodology, but he must raise new and serious questions even when he cannot immediately find the answers. For "where no clear question is put, no knowledge will give response. Where the question is vague, the answer will be at least as vague."[7]

In Algiers last summer I happened to raise the question to Stokely Carmichael (as a teacher realizing that I could learn from a former student) what he thought the role of a black scholar should be. Stokely replied:

That is not an easy role, because what the black scholar must now do is to begin to find values that are anti-racist and anti-colonial. That means that the scholars must find a way to promulgate the idea of community where black people are, without actually saying that. Because that's the job of the black scholar, to give black people values very subtly because values people accept most are the most subtle values.

Black scholars must be culture carriers, recognizing that the Europeans living in America are not going to allow them to do that, are going to fight them in every way.

[6] John Huizinga, *Men and Ideas,* New York; Meridian Books, 1968 edition, p. 25.

[7] *Ibid.,* p. 26.

Which all boils down to what Paul A. Baran was speaking of when he observed that a genuine intellectual possesses at least two characteristics —the desire to tell the truth and the courage to do so.

As such he becomes the conscience of society and the spokesman of such progressive forces as it contains in any given period of history. And as such he is inevitably considered a "troublemaker" and a "nuisance" by the ruling class seeking to preserve the status quo, as well as by the intellect workers in its service who accuse the intellectual of being utopian or metaphysical at best, subversive or seditious at worst.[8]

To conclude, then, the black scholar's main task is to cleanse his mind—and the minds of his people—of the white colonial attitudes toward scholarship and people as well. This includes the icons of objectivity, amoral knowledge and its methodology, and the total demolition of the anti-social attitudes of Ivory-Towerism. Such is the challenge facing the black scholar.

[8] Sweezy and Huberman, *op. cit.,* p. 10.

Racial Spokesmen

Martin Luther King, Jr. (1929–1968)

Martin Luther King, Jr., the Christian minister who almost converted a guilt-stricken America to real and effective Christianity, was himself the grandson of a slave and hence the product of the most heinous, un-Christian system to afflict mankind. Vaulted into national prominence when he led the Montgomery bus boycott in the late 1950's, he shortly thereafter published *Stride Toward Freedom* (1958), which explains the philosophic bases of his creed of nonviolent protest against social abuse and segregation. By the beginning of the 1960's, when he was leading campaigns against segregation in Birmingham, Albany, and Atlanta, it became clear that he had fused, as a basis for forcing social action and change, some basic tenets of Judeo-Christian religion with the politics of nonviolent social protest popularized by Mahatma Gandhi in his long fight for Indian independence.

This philosophic fusion of Christian moral idealism and Indian political expediency appealed to many Americans who were trying to ease their consciences about the depressed condition of the majority of America's Black citizens. And the great saga of the early 1960's is that under this Black minister's dedicated leadership the back of legal segregation in the South was broken.

However, no nation can sustain moral idealism for long, and Northern ghetto areas such as Chicago and Cicero, Illinois, and Milwaukee, Wisconsin, proved to be peculiarly resistant to forced social change through nonviolent protest. Yet there were moments when Martin Luther King carried America with him to the mountaintop to share his dream of an integrated society and other moments when the light of his moral idealism flooded jail cells. Indeed, had it not been for the misery of the sprawling Black ghettos and the intransigence of political bosses, North and South, America might have had a religious and moral awakening never before experienced.

But such was not to be. The idealism flared, flickered, and then almost sputtered out as old hatreds revived and Black separatism, Northern style, replaced white segregation, Southern style. Then, quite predictably, the man of nonviolence was shot down, and this nation wept—not because another good man had been destroyed in a blood-riddled decade, but because, through this man's leadership, the nation had had a chance to envision its moral possibilities.

In his journey from the beginning at Montgomery to the end at Memphis, Martin Luther King, Jr., not only earned himself the coveted Nobel Peace Prize (1964) but also found time, amid a career of social activism, to write sermons and essays. His important sermons are collected in *Strength to Love* (1963), *A Martin Luther King Treasury* (1964), and *Trumpet of Conscience* (1967). Similarly, his major essays are collected in *Why We Can't Wait* (1964) and *Where Do We Go from Here: Chaos or Community?* (1967).

Inevitably, many biographers have attempted to chart the life and career of Martin Luther King, Jr. Three biographies appeared during his lifetime: Lawrence Reddick, *Crusader Without Violence* (1959); Edward T. Clayton, *Martin Luther King, Jr.: The Peaceful Warrior* (1964); and Lerone Bennett, Jr., *What Manner of Man* (1965). Following his untimely death in April, 1968, a grief-stricken world showered his memory with eulogizing tributes and several biographies. Some of the more important are Robert M. Bleiweiss, *Marching to Freedom* (1968); G. Gerasimov, *Fire Bell in the Night* (translated from the Russian in 1968); William R. Miller, *Martin Luther King, Jr.: His Life, Martyrdom, and Meaning for the World* (1968); Coretta Scott King, *My Life With Martin Luther King, Jr.* (1969); and David L. Lewis, *King: A Critical Biography* (1970).

from *Stride Toward Freedom*

IV: The Day of Days, December 5

My wife and I awoke earlier than usual on Monday morning. We were up and fully dressed by five-thirty. The day for the protest had arrived, and we were determined to see the first act of this unfolding drama. I was still saying that if we could get 60 per cent coöperation the venture would be a success.

Fortunately, a bus stop was just five feet from our house. This meant that we could observe the opening stages from our front window. The first bus was to pass around six o'clock. And so we waited through an interminable half hour. I was in the kitchen drinking my coffee when I heard Coretta cry, "Martin, Martin, come quickly!" I put down my cup and ran toward the living room. As I approached the front window Coretta pointed joyfully to a slowly moving bus: "Darling, it's empty!" I could hardly believe what I saw. I knew that the South Jackson line, which ran past our house, carried more Negro passengers than any other line in Montgomery, and that this first bus was usually filled with domestic workers going to their jobs. Would all of the other buses

follow the pattern that had been set by the first? Eagerly we waited for the next bus. In fifteen minutes it rolled down the street, and, like the first, it was empty. A third bus appeared, and it too was empty of all but two white passengers.

I jumped in my car and for almost an hour I cruised down every major street and examined every passing bus. During this hour, at the peak of the morning traffic, I saw no more than eight Negro passengers riding the buses. By this time I was jubilant. Instead of the 60 per cent coöperation we had hoped for, it was becoming apparent that we had reached almost 100 per cent. A miracle had taken place. The once dormant and quiescent Negro community was now fully awake.

All day long it continued. At the afternoon peak the buses were still as empty of Negro passengers as they had been in the morning. Students of Alabama State College, who usually kept the South Jackson bus crowded, were cheerfully walking or thumbing rides. Job holders had either found other means of transportation or made their way on foot. While some rode in cabs or private cars, others used less conventional means. Men were seen riding mules to work, and more than one horse-drawn buggy drove the streets of Montgomery that day.

During the rush hours the sidewalks were crowded with laborers and domestic workers, many of them well past middle age, trudging patiently to their jobs and home again, sometimes as much as twelve miles. They knew why they walked, and the knowledge was evident in the way they carried themselves. And as I watched them I knew that there is nothing more majestic than the determined courage of individuals willing to suffer and sacrifice for their freedom and dignity.

Many spectators had gathered at the bus stops to watch what was happening. At first they stood quietly, but as the day progressed they began to cheer the empty buses and laugh and make jokes. Noisy youngsters could be heard singing out, "No riders today." Trailing each bus through the Negro section were two policemen on motorcycles, assigned by the city commissioners, who claimed that Negro "goon squads" had been organized to keep other Negroes from riding the buses. In the course of the day the police succeeded in making one arrest. A college student who was helping an elderly woman across the street was charged with "intimidating passengers." But the "goon squads" existed only in the commission's imagination. No one was threatened or intimidated for riding the buses; the only harassment anyone faced was that of his own conscience.

Around nine-thirty in the morning I tore myself from the action of the city streets and headed for the crowded police court. Here Mrs. Parks was being tried for disobeying the city segregation ordinance. Her attorney, Fred D. Gray—the brilliant young Negro who later became the chief counsel for the protest movement—was on hand to defend her. After the judge heard the arguments, he found Mrs. Parks guilty and fined her ten dollars and court costs (a total of fourteen dollars). She appealed the case. This was one of the first clear-cut instances in which a Negro had been convicted for disobeying the segregation law. In the past, either cases like this had been dismissed or the people involved had been charged with disorderly conduct. So in a real sense the arrest and conviction of Mrs. Parks had a twofold impact: it was a precipitating factor to arouse the Negroes to positive action; and it was a test of the validity of the segregation law itself. I am sure that supporters of such prosecutions would have

acted otherwise if they had had the prescience to look beyond the moment.

Leaving Mrs. Park's trial, Ralph Abernathy, E. D. Nixon, and Rev. E. N. French—then minister of the Hilliard Chapel A.M.E. Zion Church—discussed the need for some organization to guide and direct the protest. Up to this time things had moved forward more or less spontaneously. These men were wise enough to see that the moment had now come for a clearer order and direction.

Meanwhile Roy Bennett had called several people together at three o'clock to make plans for the evening mass meeting. Everyone present was elated by the tremendous success that had already attended the protest. But beneath this feeling was the question, where do we go from here? When E. D. Nixon reported on his discussion with Abernathy and French earlier in the day, and their suggestions for an *ad hoc* organization, the group responded enthusiastically. The next job was to elect the officers for the new organization.

As soon as Bennett had opened the nominations for president, Rufus Lewis spoke from the far corner of the room: "Mr. Chairman, I would like to nominate Reverend M. L. King for president." The motion was seconded and carried, and in a matter of minutes I was unanimously elected.

The action had caught me unawares. It had happened so quickly that I did not even have time to think it through. It is probable that if I had, I would have declined the nomination. Just three weeks before, several members of the local chapter of the NAACP had urged me to run for the presidency of that organization, assuring me that I was certain of election. After my wife and I had discussed the matter, we agreed that I should not then take on any heavy community responsibilities, since I had so recently finished my thesis, and needed to give more attention to my church work. But on this occasion events had moved too fast.

The election of the remaining officers was speedily completed: Rev. L. Roy Bennett, vice-president; Rev. U. J. Fields, recording secretary; Rev. E. N. French, corresponding secretary; Mrs. Erna A. Dungee, financial secretary; Mr. E. D. Nixon, treasurer. It was then agreed that all those present would constitute the executive board of the new organization. This board would serve as the coördinating agency of the whole movement. It was a well-balanced group, including ministers of all denominations, schoolteachers, businessmen, and two lawyers.

The new organization needed a name, and several were suggested. Someone proposed the Negro Citizens Committee; but this was rejected because it resembled too closely the White Citizens Council. Other suggestions were made and dismissed until finally Ralph Abernathy offered a name that was agreeable to all—the Montgomery Improvement Association (MIA).

With these organizational matters behind us, we turned to a discussion of the evening meeting. Several people, not wanting the reporters to know our future moves, suggested that we just sing and pray; if there were specific recommendations to be made to the people, these could be mimeographed and passed out secretly during the meeting. This, they felt, would leave the reporters in the dark. Others urged that something should be done to conceal the true identity of the leaders, feeling that if no particular name was revealed it would be safer for all involved. After a rather lengthy discussion, E. D. Nixon rose impatiently:

"We are acting like little boys," he said. "Somebody's name will have to be known, and if we are afraid we might just as well fold up right now. We must also be men enough to discuss our recommendations in the open; this idea of secretly passing something around on paper is a lot of bunk. The white folks are eventually going to find it out anyway. We'd better decide now if we are going to be fearless men or scared boys."

With this forthright statement the air was cleared. Nobody would again suggest that we try to conceal our identity or avoid facing the issue head on. Nixon's courageous affirmation had given new heart to those who were about to be crippled by fear.

It was unanimously agreed that the protest should continue until certain demands were met, and that a committee under the chairmanship of Ralph Abernathy would draw up these demands in the form of a resolution and present them to the evening mass meeting for approval. We worked out the remainder of the program quickly. Bennett would preside and I would make the main address. Remarks by a few other speakers, along with Scripture reading, prayer, hymns, and collection, would round out the program.

Immediately the resolution committee set to drafting its statement. Despite our satisfaction at the success of the protest so far, we were still concerned. Would the evening meeting be well attended? Could we hope that the fortitude and enthusiasm of the Negro community would survive more than one such day of hardship? Someone suggested that perhaps we should reconsider our decision to continue the protest. "Would it not be better," said the speaker, "to call off the protest while it is still a success rather than let it go on a few more days and fizzle out? We have already proved our united strength to the white community. If we stop now we can get anything we want from the bus company, simply because they will have the feeling that we can do it again. But if we continue, and most of the people return to the buses tomorrow or the next day, the white people will laugh at us, and we will end up getting nothing." This argument was so convincing that we almost resolved to end the protest. But we finally agreed to let the mass meeting—which was only about an hour off—be our guide. If the meeting was well attended and the people were enthusiastic, we would continue; otherwise we would call off the protest that night.

I went home for the first time since seven that morning, and found Coretta relaxing from a long day of telephone calls and general excitement. After we had brought each other up to date on the day's developments, I told her, somewhat hesitantly—not knowing what her reaction would be—that I had been elected president of the new association. I need not have worried. Naturally surprised, she still saw that since the responsibility had fallen on me, I had no alternative but to accept it. She did not need to be told that we would now have even less time together, and she seemed undisturbed at the possible danger to all of us in my new position. "You know," she said quietly, "that whatever you do, you have my backing."

Reassured, I went to my study and closed the door. The minutes were passing fast. It was now six-thirty, and I had to leave no later than six-fifty to get to the meeting. This meant that I had only twenty minutes to prepare the most decisive speech of my life. As I thought of the limited time before me and the possible implications of this speech, I became possessed by fear. Each week I needed at least fifteen hours to prepare my Sunday sermon. Now I was faced with the inescapable task of preparing, in almost no time at all, a speech that was expected to give a sense of direction to a people imbued with a new and still unplumbed passion for justice. I was also conscious that reporters and television men would be there with their pencils and sound cameras poised to record my words and send them across the nation.

I was now almost overcome, obsessed by a feeling of inadequacy. In this state of anxiety, I had already wasted five minutes of the original twenty. With nothing left but faith in a power whose matchless strength stands over against the frailties and inadequacies of human nature, I turned to God in prayer. My words were brief and simple, asking God to restore my balance and to be with me in a time when I needed His guidance more than ever.

With less than fifteen minutes left, I began preparing an outline. In the midst of this, however, I faced a new and sobering dilemma: How could I make a speech that would be militant enough to keep my people aroused to positive action and yet moderate enough to keep this fervor within controllable and Christian bounds? I knew that many of the Negro people were victims of bitterness that could easily rise to flood proportions. What could I say to keep them courageous and prepared for positive action and yet devoid of hate and resentment? Could the militant and the moderate be combined in a single speech?

I decided that I had to face the challenge head on, and attempt to combine two apparent irreconcilables. I would seek to arouse the group to action by insisting that their self-respect was at stake and that if they accepted such injustices without protesting, they would betray their own sense of dignity and the eternal edicts of God Himself. But I would balance this with a strong affirmation of the Christian doctrine of love. By the time I had sketched an outline of the speech in my mind, my time was up. Without stopping to eat supper (I had not eaten since morning) I said good-by to Coretta and drove to the Holt Street Church.

Within five blocks of the church I noticed a traffic jam. Cars were lined up as far as I could see on both sides of the street. It was a moment before it occurred to me that all of these cars were headed for the mass meeting. I had to park at least four blocks from the church, and as I started walking I noticed that hundreds of people were standing outside. In the dark night, police cars circled slowly around the area, surveying the orderly, patient, and good-humored crowd. The three or four thousand people who could not

get into the church were to stand cheerfully throughout the evening listening to the proceedings on the loudspeakers that had been set up outside for their benefit. And when, near the end of the meeting, these speakers were silenced at the request of the white people in surrounding neighborhoods, the crowd would still remain quietly, content simply to be present.

It took fully fifteen minutes to push my way through to the pastor's study, where Dr. Wilson told me that the church had been packed since five o'clock. By now my doubts concerning the continued success of our venture were dispelled. The question of calling off the protest was now academic. The enthusiasm of these thousands of people swept everything along like an onrushing tidal wave.

It was some time before the remaining speakers could push their way to the rostrum through the tightly packed church. When the meeting began it was almost half an hour late. The opening hymn was the old familiar "Onward, Christian Soldiers," and when that mammoth audience stood to sing, the voices outside swelling the chorus in the church, there was a mighty ring like the glad echo of heaven itself.

Rev. W. F. Alford, minister of the Beulah Baptist Church, led the congregation in prayer, followed by a reading of the Scripture by Rev. U. J. Fields, minister of the Bell Street Baptist Church. Then the chairman introduced me. As the audience applauded, I rose and stood before the pulpit. Television cameras began to shoot from all sides. The crowd grew quiet.

Without manuscript or notes, I told the story of what had happened to Mrs. Parks. Then I reviewed the long history of abuses and insults that Negro citizens had experienced on the city buses. "But there comes a time," I said, "when people get tired. We are here this evening to say to those who have mistreated us so long that we are tired—tired of being segregated and humiliated; tired of being kicked about by the brutal feet of oppression." The congregation met this statement with fervent applause. "We had no alternative but to protest," I continued. "For many years, we have shown amazing patience. We have sometimes given our white brothers the feeling that we liked the way we were being treated. But we come here tonight to be saved from that patience that makes us patient with anything less than freedom and justice." Again the audience interrupted with applause.

Briefly I justified our actions, both morally and legally. "One of the great glories of democracy is the right to protest for right." Comparing our methods with those of the White Citizens Councils and the Ku Klux Klan, I pointed out that while "these organizations are protesting for the perpetuation of injustice in the community, we are protesting for the birth of justice in the community. Their methods lead to violence and lawlessness. But in our protest there will be no cross burnings. No white person will be taken from his home by a hooded Negro mob and brutally murdered. There will be no threats and intimidation. We will be guided by the highest principles of law and order."

With this groundwork for militant action, I moved on to words of caution. I urged the people not to force anybody to refrain from riding the buses. "Our method will be that of persuasion, not coercion. We will only say to the people, 'Let your conscience be your guide.'" Emphasizing the Christian doctrine of love, "our actions must be guided by the deepest principles of our Christian faith. Love must be our regulating ideal. Once again we must hear the words of Jesus echoing across the centuries: 'Love your enemies, bless them that curse you, and pray for them that despitefully use you.' If we fail to do this our protest will end up as a meaningless drama on the stage of history, and its memory will be shrouded with the ugly garments of shame. In spite of the mistreatment that we have confronted we must not become bitter, and end up by hating our white brothers. As Booker T. Washington said, 'Let no man pull you so low as to make you hate him.'" Once more the audience responded enthusiastically.

Then came my closing statement. "If you will protest courageously, and yet with dignity and Christian love, when the history books are written in future generations, the historians will have to pause and say, 'There lived a great people—a black people—who injected new meaning and dignity into the veins of civilization.' This is our challenge and our overwhelming responsibility." As I took my seat the people rose to their feet and applauded. I was thankful to God that the message had gotten over and that the task of combining the militant and the moderate had been at least partially accomplished. The people had been as enthusiastic when I urged them to love as they were when I urged them to protest.

As I sat listening to the continued applause I realized that this speech had evoked more response than any speech or sermon I had ever delivered, and yet it was virtually unprepared. I came to see for the first time what the older preachers meant when they said, "Open your mouth and God will speak for you." While I would not let this experience tempt me to overlook the need for continued preparation, it would always remind me that God can transform man's weakness into his glorious opportunity.

When Mrs. Parks was introduced from the rostrum by E. N. French, the audience responded by giving her a standing ovation. She was their heroine. They saw in her courageous person the symbol of their hopes and aspirations.

Now the time had come for the all-important resolution. Ralph Abernathy read the words slowly and forcefully. The main substance of the resolution called upon the Negroes not to resume riding the buses until (1) courteous treatment by the bus operators was guaranteed; (2) passengers were seated on a first-come, first-served basis—Negroes seating from the back of the bus toward the front while whites seated from the front toward the back; (3) Negro bus operators were employed on predominantly Negro routes. At the words "All in favor of the motion stand," every person to a man stood up, and those who were already standing raised their hands. Cheers began to ring out from both inside and outside. The motion was carried unanimously. The people had expressed their determination not to ride the buses until conditions were changed.

At this point I had to leave the meeting and rush to the other side of town to speak at a YMCA banquet. As I drove away my heart was full. I had never seen such enthusiasm for freedom. And yet this enthusiasm was tempered by amazing self-discipline. The unity of purpose and *esprit de corps* of these people had been indescribably moving. No historian would ever be able fully to describe this meeting and no sociologist would ever be able to interpret it adequately. One had to be a part of the experience really to understand it.

At the Ben Moore Hotel, as the elevator slowly moved up to the roof garden where the banquet was being held, I said to myself, the victory is already won, no matter how long we struggle to attain the three points of the resolution. It is a victory infinitely larger than the bus situation. The real victory was in the mass meeting, where thousands of black people stood revealed with a new sense of dignity and destiny.

Many will inevitably raise the question, why did this event take place in Montgomery, Alabama, in 1955? Some have suggested that the Supreme Court decision on school desegregation, handed down less than two years before, had given new hope of eventual justice to Negroes everywhere, and fired them with the necessary spark of encouragement to rise against their oppression. But although this might help to explain why the protest occurred when it did, it cannot explain why it happened in Montgomery.

Certainly, there is a partial explanation in the long history of injustice on the buses of Montgomery. The bus protest did not spring into being full grown as Athena sprang from the head of Zeus; it was the culmination of a slowly developing process. Mrs. Parks's arrest was the precipitating factor rather than the cause of the protest. The cause lay deep in the record of similar injustices. Almost everybody could point to an unfortunate episode that he himself had experienced or seen.

But there comes a time when people get tired of being trampled by oppression. There comes a time when people get tired of being plunged into the abyss of exploitation and nagging injustice. The story of Montgomery is the story of 50,000 such Negroes who were willing to substitute tired feet for tired souls, and walk the streets of Montgomery until the walls of segregation were finally battered by the forces of justice.

But neither is this the whole explanation. Negroes in other communities confronted conditions equally as bad, and often worse. So we cannot explain the Montgomery story merely in terms of the abuses that Negroes suffered there. Moreover, it cannot be explained by a preëxistent unity among the leaders, since we have seen that the Montgomery Negro community prior to the protest was marked by divided leadership, indifference, and complacency. Nor can it be explained by the appearance upon the scene of new leadership. The Montgomery story would have taken place if the leaders of the protest had never been born.

So every rational explanation breaks down at some point. There is something about the protest that is suprarational; it cannot be explained without a divine dimension. Some may call it a principle of concretion, with Alfred N. Whitehead; or a process of integration, with Henry N. Wieman; or Being-itself, with Paul Tillich; or a personal God. Whatever the name, some extra-human force labors to create a harmony out of the discords of the universe. There is a creative power that works to pull down mountains of evil and level hilltops of injustice. God still works through history His wonders to perform. It seems as though God had decided to use Montgomery as the proving ground for the struggle and triumph of freedom and justice in America. And what better place for it than the leading symbol of the Old South? It is one of the splendid ironies of our day that Montgomery, the Cradle of the Confederacy, is being transformed into Montgomery, the cradle of freedom and justice.

The day of days, Monday, December 5, 1955, was drawing to a close. We all prepared to go to our homes, not yet fully aware of what had happened. The deliberations of that brisk, cool night in December will not be forgotten. That night we were starting a movement that would gain national recognition; whose echoes would ring in the ears of people of every nation; a movement that would astound the oppressor, and bring new hope to the oppressed. That night was Montgomery's moment in history.

.   .   .

XI: Where Do We Go from Here?

The bus struggle in Montgomery, Alabama, is now history. As the integrated buses roll daily through the city they carry, along with their passengers, a meaning-crowded symbolism. Accord among the great majority of passengers is evidence of the basic good will of man for man and a portent of peace in the desegregated society to come. Occasional instances of discord among passengers are a reminder that in other areas of Montgomery life segregation yet obtains with all of its potential for group strife and personal conflict. Indeed, segregation is still a reality throughout the South.

Where do we go from here? Since the problem in Montgomery is merely symptomatic of the larger national problem, where do we go not only in Montgomery but all over the South and the nation? Forces maturing for years have given rise to the present crisis in race relations. What are these forces that have brought the crisis about? What will be the conclusion? Are we caught in a social and political impasse, or do we have at our disposal the creative resources to achieve the ideals of brotherhood and harmonious living?

The last half century has seen crucial changes in the life of the American Negro. The social upheavals of the two world wars, the great depression, and the spread of the automobile have made it both possible and necessary for the Negro to move away from his former isolation on the rural plantation. The decline of agriculture and the parallel growth of industry have drawn large numbers of Negroes to urban centers and brought about a gradual improvement in their economic status. New contacts have led to a broadened outlook and new possibilities for educational advance. All of these factors have conjoined to cause the Negro to take a fresh look at himself. His expanding life experiences have created within him a consciousness that he is an equal element in a larger social compound and accordingly should be given rights and privileges commensurate with his new responsibilities. Once plagued with a tragic sense of inferiority resulting from the crippling effects of slavery and segregation, the Negro has now been driven to reëvaluate himself. He has come to feel that he is somebody. His religion reveals to him that God loves all His children and that the important thing about a man is not "his specificity but his fundamentum"—not the texture of his hair or the color of his skin but his eternal worth to God.

This growing self-respect has inspired the Negro with a new determination to struggle and sacrifice until first-class citizenship becomes a reality. This is the true meaning of the Montgomery Story. One can never understand the bus protest in Montgomery without understanding that there is a new Negro in the South, with a new sense of dignity and destiny.

Along with the Negro's changing image of himself has come an awakening moral consciousness on the part of millions of white Americans concerning segregation. Ever since the signing of the Declaration of Independence, America has manifested a schizophrenic personality on the question of race. She has been torn between selves—a self in which she has proudly professed democracy and a self in which she has sadly practiced the antithesis of democracy. The reality of segregation, like slavery, has always had to confront the ideals of democracy and Christianity. Indeed, segregation and discrimination are strange paradoxes in a nation founded on the principle that all men are created equal. This contradiction has disturbed the consciences of whites both North and South, and has caused many of them to see that segregation is basically evil.

Climaxing this process was the Supreme Court's decision outlawing segregation in the public schools. For all men of good will May 17, 1954, marked a joyous end to the long night of enforced segregation. In unequivocal language the Court affirmed that "separate but equal" facilities are inherently unequal, and that to segregate a child on the basis of his race is to deny that child equal protection of the law. This decision brought hope to millions of disinherited Negroes who had formerly dared only to dream of freedom. It further enhanced the Negro's sense of dignity and gave him even greater determination to achieve justice.

This determination of Negro Americans to win freedom from all forms of oppression springs from the same deep longing that motivates oppressed peoples all over the world. The rumblings of discontent in Asia and Africa are expressions of a quest for freedom and human dignity by people who have long been the victims of colonialism and imperialism. So in a real sense the racial crisis in America is a part of the larger world crisis.

But the numerous changes which have culminated in a new sense of dignity on the part of the Negro are not of themselves responsible for the present crisis. If all men accepted these historical changes in good faith there would be no crisis. The crisis developed when the collective pressures to achieve fair goals for the Negro met with tenacious and determined resistance. Then the emerging new order, based on the principle of democratic equalitarianism, came face to face with the older order, based on the principles of paternalism and subordination. The crisis was not produced by outside agitators, NAACP'ers, Montgomery Protesters, or even the Supreme Court. The crisis developed, paradoxically, when the most sublime principles of American democracy—imperfectly realized for almost two centuries—began fulfilling themselves and met with the brutal resistance of forces seeking to contract and repress freedom's growth.

The resistance has risen at times to ominous proportions. Many states have reacted in open defiance. The legislative halls of the South still ring loud with such words as "interposition" and "nullification." Many public officials are using the power of their offices to defy the law of the land. Through their irresponsible actions, their inflammatory statements, and their dissemination of distortions and half-truths, they have succeeded in arousing abnormal fears and morbid antipathies within the minds of underprivileged and uneducated whites, leaving them in such a state of excitement and confusion that they are led to acts of meanness and violence that no normal person would commit.

This resistance to the emergence of the new order expresses itself in the resurgence of the Ku Klux Klan. Determined to preserve segregation at any cost, this organization employs methods that are crude and primitive. It draws its members from underprivileged groups who see in the Negro's rising status a political and economic threat. Although the Klan is impotent politically and openly denounced from all sides, it remains a dangerous force which thrives on racial and religious bigotry. Because of its past history, whenever the Klan moves there is fear of violence.

Then there are the White Citizens Councils. Since they occasionally recruit members from a higher social and economic level than the Klan, a halo of partial respectability hovers over them. But like the Klan they are determined to preserve segregation despite the law. Their weapons of threat, intimidation, and boycott are directed both against Negroes and against any whites who stand for justice. They demand absolute conformity from whites and abject submission from Negroes. The Citizens Councils often argue piously that they abhor violence, but their defiance of the law, their unethical methods, and their vitriolic public pronouncements inevitably create the atmosphere in which violence thrives.

As a result of the Councils' activities most white moderates in the South no longer feel free to discuss in public the issues involved in desegregation for fear of social ostracism and economic reprisals. What channels of communication had once existed between whites and Negroes have thus now been largely closed.

The present crisis in race relations has characteristics that come to the forefront in any period of social transition. The guardians of the status quo lash out with denunciation against the person or organization that they consider most responsible for the emergence of the new order. Often this denunciation rises to major proportions. In the transition from slavery to restricted emanci-

pation Abraham Lincoln was assassinated. In the present transition from segregation to desegregation the Supreme Court is castigated and the NAACP is maligned and subjected to extra-legal reprisals.

As in other social crises the defenders of the status quo in the South argue that they were gradually solving their own problems until external pressure was brought to bear upon them. The familiar complaint in the South today is that the Supreme Court's decision on education has set us back a generation in race relations, that people of different races who had long lived at peace have now been turned against one another. But this is a misinterpretation of what is taking place. When a subject people moves toward freedom, they are not creating a cleavage, but are revealing the cleavage which apologists of the old order have sought to conceal. It is not the movement for integration which is creating a cleavage in the United States today. The depth of the cleavage that existed, the true nature of which the moderates failed to see and make clear, is being revealed by the resistance to integration.

During a crisis period, a desperate attempt is made by the extremists to influence the minds of the liberal forces in the ruling majority. So, for example, in the present transition white Southerners attempt to convince Northern whites that the Negroes are inherently criminal. They seek instances of Negro crime and juvenile delinquency in Northern communities and then say: "You see, the Negroes are problems to you. They create problems wherever they go." The accusation is made without reference to the true nature of the situation. Environmental problems of delinquency are interpreted as evidence of racial criminality. Crises arising in Northern schools are interpreted as proofs that Negroes are inherently delinquent. The extremists do not recognize that these school problems are symptoms of urban dislocation, rather than expressions of racial deficiency. Criminality and delinquency are not racial; poverty and ignorance breed crime whatever the racial group may be.

In the attempt to influence the minds of Northern and Southern liberals, the segregationists are often subtle and skillful. Those who are too smart to argue for the validity of segregation and racial inferiority on the basis of the Bible set forth their arguments on cultural and sociological grounds. The Negro is not ready for integration, they say; because of academic and cultural lags on the part of the Negro, the integration of schools will pull the white race down. They are never honest enough to admit that the academic and cultural lags in the Negro community are themselves the result of segregation and discrimination. The best way to solve any problem is to remove its cause. It is both rationally unsound and sociologically untenable to use the tragic effects of segregation as an argument for its continuation.

All of these calculated patterns—the defiance of Southern legislative bodies, the activities of White Supremacy organizations, and the distortions and rationalizations of the segregationists—have mounted up to massive resistance. This resistance grows out of the desperate attempt of the white South to perpetuate a system of human values that came into being under a feudalistic plantation system and which cannot survive in a day of growing urbanization and industrial expansion. These are the rock-bottom elements of the present crisis.

The schools of the South are the present storm center. Here the forces that stand for the best in our national life have been tragically ineffectual. A year after the Supreme Court had declared school segregation unconstitutional, it handed down a decree outlining the details by which integration should proceed "with all deliberate speed." While the Court did not set a definite deadline for the termination of this process, it did set a time for the beginning. It was clear that the Court had chosen this reasonable approach with the expectation that the forces of good will would immediately get to work and prepare the communities for a smooth and peaceful transition.

But the forces of good will failed to come through. The Office of the President was appallingly silent, though just an occasional word from this powerful source, counseling the nation on the moral aspects of integration and the need for complying with the law, might have saved the South from much of its present confusion and terror. Other forces of justice also failed to act. It is true that immediately after the first decision was rendered, leading church, labor, and social welfare leaders issued statements upholding the decision, and many supporting resolutions were adopted by their organizations. But hardly a single group set forth an action program wherein their members could actively work to bring about

a peaceable transition. Neither did they develop a plan whereby individuals in Southern communities who were willing to work for desegregation could receive organization support in the face of economic reprisals and physical violence.

As a result of the failure of the moral forces of the nation to mobilize behind school integration, the forces of defeat were given the chance to organize and crystallize their opposition. While the good people stood silently and complacently by, the misguided people acted. If every church and synagogue had developed an action program; if every civic and social welfare organization, every labor union and educational institution, had worked out concrete plans for implementing their righteous resolutions; if the press, radio, and television had turned their powerful instruments in the direction of educating and elevating the people on this issue; if the President and the Congress had taken a forthright stand; if these things had happened, federal troops might not have been forced to walk the corridors of Central High School.

But it is still not too late to act. Every crisis has both its dangers and opportunities. It can spell either salvation or doom. In the present crisis America can achieve either racial justice or the ultimate social psychosis that can only lead to domestic suicide. The democratic ideal of freedom and equality will be fulfilled for all—or all human beings will share in the resulting social and spiritual doom. In short, this crisis has the potential for democracy's fulfillment or fascism's triumph; for social progress or retrogression. We can choose either to walk the high road of human brotherhood or to tread the low road of man's inhumanity to man.

History has thrust upon our generation an indescribably important destiny—to complete a process of democratization which our nation has too long developed too slowly, but which is our most powerful weapon for world respect and emulation. How we deal with this crucial situation will determine our moral health as individuals, our cultural health as a region, our political health as a nation, and our prestige as a leader of the free world. The future of America is bound up with the solution of the present crisis. The shape of the world today does not permit us the luxury of a faltering democracy. The United States cannot hope to attain the respect of the vital and growing colored nations of the world unless it remedies its racial problems at home. If America is to remain a first-class nation it cannot have a second-class citizenship.

A solution of the present crisis will not take place unless men and women work for it. Human progress is neither automatic nor inevitable. Even a superficial look at history reveals that no social advance rolls in on the wheels of inevitability. Every step toward the goal of justice requires sacrifice, suffering, and struggle; the tireless exertions and passionate concern of dedicated individuals. Without persistent effort, time itself becomes an ally of the insurgent and primitive forces of irrational emotionalism and social destruction. This is no time for apathy or complacency. This is a time for vigorous and positive action.

It is the shame of the sunshine patriots if the foregoing paragraphs have a hollow sound, like an echo of countless political speeches. These things must be repeated time and again, for men forget quickly; but once said, they must be followed with a dynamic program, or else they become a refuge for those who shy from any action. If America is to respond creatively to the present crisis, many groups and agencies must rise above the reiteration of generalities and begin to take an active part in changing the face of their nation.

First, there is need for strong and aggressive leadership from the federal government. If the executive and legislative branches were as concerned about the protection of the citizenship rights of all people as the federal courts have been, the transition from a segregated to an integrated society would be much further along than it is today. The dearth of positive leadership from Washington is not confined to one political party. Both major parties have lagged in the service of justice. Many Democrats have betrayed it by capitulating to the undemocratic practices of the Southern Dixiecrats. Many Republicans have betrayed it by capitulating to the hypocrisy of right-wing Northerners.

In spite of the crucial role of the federal judiciary in this tense period of transition, the courts cannot do the job alone. The courts can clarify constitutional principles and remove the legal basis for segregation, but they cannot write laws, appoint administrators, or enforce justice on the local level.

The states and localities have the powers if they choose to exercise them. But the Southern states have made their policy clear. States' rights, they say in effect, include the right to abrogate power when it involves distasteful responsibilities, even to the Constitution of the United States, its amendments, and its judicial interpretation. So the power and the responsibility return by default to the federal government. It is up to all branches of the central government to accept the challenge.

Government action is not the whole answer to the present crisis, but it is an important partial answer. Morals cannot be legislated, but behavior can be regulated. The law cannot make an employer love me, but it can keep him from refusing to hire me because of the color of my skin. We must depend on religion and education to alter the errors of the heart and mind; but meanwhile it is an immoral act to compel a man to accept injustice until another man's heart is set straight. As the experience of several Northern states has shown, anti-discrimination laws can provide powerful sanctions against this kind of immorality.

Moreover, the law itself is a form of education. The words of the Supreme Court, of Congress, and of the Constitution are eloquent instructors. In fact, it would be a mistake to minimize the impact upon the South of the federal court orders and legislative and executive acts already in effect. Desegregation of the armed services, for instance, has already had an immense, incalculable impact. Federal court decrees have altered transportation patterns, teachers' salaries, the use of recreational facilities, and myriad other matters. The habits if not the hearts of people have been and are being altered every day by federal action.

Another group with a vital role to play in the present crisis is the white Northern liberals. The racial issue that we confront in America is not a sectional but a national problem. The citizenship rights of Negroes cannot be flouted anywhere without impairing the rights of every other American. Injustice anywhere is a threat to justice everywhere. A breakdown of law in Alabama weakens the very foundations of lawful government in the other forty-seven states. The mere fact that we live in the United States means that we are caught in a network of inescapable mutuality. Therefore, no American can afford to be apathetic about the problem of racial justice. It is a problem that meets every man at his front door. The racial problem will be solved in America to the degree that every American considers himself personally confronted with it. Whether one lives in the heart of the Deep South or on the periphery of the North, the problem of injustice is his problem; it is his problem because it is America's problem.

There is a pressing need for a liberalism in the North which is truly liberal, a liberalism that firmly believes in integration in its own community as well as in the Deep South. It is one thing to agree that the goal of integration is morally and legally right; it is another thing to commit oneself positively and actively to the ideal of integration—the former is intellectual assent, the latter is actual belief. These are days that demand practices to match professions. This is no day to pay lip service to integration, we must pay *life* service to it.

Today in all too many Northern communities a sort of quasi-liberalism prevails, so bent on seeing all sides that it fails to become dedicated to any side. It is so objectively analytical that it is not subjectively committed. A true liberal will not be deterred by the propaganda and subtle words of those who say, "Slow up for a while; you are pushing things too fast." I am not calling for an end to sympathetic understanding and abiding patience; but neither sympathy nor patience should be used as excuses for indecisiveness. They must be guiding principles for all of our actions, rather than substitutes for action itself.

A significant role, in this tense period of transition, is assigned to the moderates of the white South. Unfortunately today, the leadership of the white South is by and large in the hands of close-minded extremists. These persons gain prominence and power by the dissemination of false ideas, and by appealing to the deepest fears and hates within the human mind. But they do not speak for the South; of that I am convinced. They speak only for a willful and vocal minority.

Even the most casual observer can see that the South has marvelous possibilities. It is rich in natural resources, blessed with the beauties of nature, and endowed with a native warmth of spirit. Yet in spite of these assets, it is retarded by a blight that debilitates not only the Negro but also the white man. Poor white men, women, and children, bearing the scars of ignorance, deprivation, and poverty, are evidence of the fact that harm to one is injury to all. Segregation has placed the whole South socially, educationally, and economically behind the rest of the nation.

Yet actually, there is no single "solid" South; there are at least three, geographically speaking. There is the South of compliance—Oklahoma, Kentucky, Kansas, Missouri, West Virginia, Delaware, and the District of Columbia. There is the wait-and-see South—Tennessee, Texas, North Carolina, Arkansas, and Florida. And there is the South of resistance—Georgia, Alabama, Mississippi, Louisiana, South Carolina, and Virginia.

Just as there are three Souths geographically, there are several Souths in terms of attitudes. A minority in each of these states would use almost any means, including physical violence, to preserve segregation. A majority, through tradition and custom, sincerely believe in segregation, but at the same time stand on the side of law and order. Hence, they are willing to comply with the law not because they feel it is sound but because it is the law. A third group, a growing minority, is working courageously and conscientiously to implement the law of the land. These people believe in the morality as well as the constitutionality of integration. Their still small voices often go unheard among the louder shouts of defiance, but they are actively in the field.

Furthermore there are in the white South millions of people of good will whose voices are yet unheard, whose course is yet unclear, and whose courageous acts are yet unseen. These persons are often silent today because of fear—fear of social, political, and economic reprisals. In the name of God, in the interest of human dignity, and for the cause of democracy these millions are called upon to gird their courage, to speak out, to offer the leadership that is needed. Still another South calls upon them: The colored South, the South of millions of Negroes whose sweat and blood has also built Dixie, who yearn for brotherhood and respect, who want to join hands with their white fellow Southerners to build a freer, happier land for all. If the moderates of the white South fail to act now, history will have to record that the greatest tragedy of this period of social transition was not the strident clamor of the bad people, but the appalling silence of the good people. Our generation will have to repent not only for the acts and words of the children of darkness but also for the fears and apathy of the children of light.

Who can best lead the South out of the social and economic quagmire? Her native sons. Those who were born and bred on her rich and fertile soil; those who love her because they were nurtured by her. Through love, patience, and understanding good will they can call their brothers to a way of noble living. This hour represents a great opportunity for the white moderates, if they will only speak the truth, obey the law, and suffer if necessary for what they know is right.

Still another agency of effective change today is the labor movement. Across the years the Negro has been a perpetual victim of economic exploitation. Prior to the Civil War the slaves worked under a system which offered neither compensation nor civil rights. Since emancipation the Negro American has continued to suffer under an essentially unreconstructed economy. He was freed without land or legal protection, and was made an outcast entitled only to the most menial jobs. Even the federal government that set him free failed to work out any long-range policy that would guarantee economic resources to a previously enslaved people—as much entitled to the land they had worked as were their former owners. The exploitation of the Negro population persisted through the Reconstruction period and continues down to the present day.

Labor unions can play a tremendous role in making economic justice a reality for the Negro. Trade unions are engaged in a struggle to advance the economic welfare of those American citizens whose wages are their livelihood. Since the American Negro is virtually nonexistent as the owner and manager of mass production industry, he must depend on the payment of wages for his economic survival.

There are in the United States 16.5 million members of approximately 150 bona fide trade unions. Of this number 142 are national and international affiliated organizations of the AFL-CIO. The unions forming the AFL-CIO include 1.3 million Negroes among their 13.5 million members. Only the combined religious institutions serving the Negro community can claim a greater membership of Negroes. The Negro then has the right to expect the resources of the American trade union movement to be used in assuring him—like all the rest of its members—of a proper place in American society. He has gained this right along with all the other workers whose mutual efforts have built this country's free and democratic trade unions.

Economic insecurity strangles the physical and cultural growth of its victims. Not only are millions deprived of formal education and proper health facilities but our most fundamental social unit—the family—is tortured, corrupted, and weakened by economic insufficiency. When a Negro man is inadequately paid, his wife must work to provide the simple necessities for the children. When a mother has to work she does violence to motherhood by depriving her children of her loving guidance and protection; often they are poorly cared for by others or by none—left to roam the streets unsupervised. It is not the Negro alone who is wronged by a disrupted society; many white families are in similar straits. The Negro mother leaves home to care for—and be a substitute mother for—white children, while the white mother works. In this strange irony lies the promise of future correction.

Both Negro and white workers are equally oppressed. For both, the living standards need to be raised to levels consistent with our national resources. Not logic but a hollow social distinction has separated the races. The economically depressed white accepts his poverty by telling himself that, if in no other respect, at least socially he is above the Negro. For this empty pride in a racial myth he has paid the crushing price of insecurity, hunger, ignorance, and hopelessness for himself and his children.

Strong ties must be made between those whites and Negroes who have problems in common. White and Negro workers have mutual aspirations for a fairer share of the products of industries and farms. Both seek job security, old-age security, health and welfare protection. The organized labor movement, which has contributed so much to the economic security and well-being of millions, must concentrate its powerful forces on bringing economic emancipation to white and Negro by organizing them together in social equality.

Certainly the labor movement has already made significant moves in this direction. Virtually every national or international union has clear policies of nondiscrimination, and the national leaders of AFL-CIO have proclaimed sincerely the ultimate objective of eliminating racial bias not only from the American labor movement but also from American society as a whole. But in spite of this stand, some unions, governed by the racist ethos, have contributed to the degraded economic status of the Negroes. Negroes have been barred from membership in certain unions, and denied apprenticeship training and vocational education. In every section of the country one can find local unions existing as a serious and vicious obstacle when the Negro seeks jobs or upgrading in employment. The AFL-CIO drive to organize the South has been virtually abandoned because of the massive resistance of a significant portion of the organized labor oligarchy, many of whom have been active in White Citizens Councils.

The existence of these conditions within the ranks of labor reveals that the job is a continuing one. The AFL-CIO must use all of the powerful forces at its command to enforce the principles it has professed. Labor leaders must continue to recognize that labor has a great stake in the struggle for civil rights, if only because the forces that are anti-Negro are usually anti-labor too. The current attacks on organized labor because of the misdeeds of a few malefactors should not blind us to labor's essential role in the present crisis.

The church too must face its historic obligation in this crisis. In the final analysis the problem of race is not a political but a moral issue. Indeed, as the Swedish economist Gunnar Myrdal has pointed out, the problem of race is America's greatest moral dilemma. This tragic dilemma presents the church with a great challenge. The broad universalism standing at the center of the gospel makes segregation morally unjustifiable. Racial segregation is a blatant denial of the unity which we have in Christ; for in Christ there is neither Jew nor Gentile, bond nor free, Negro nor white. Segregation scars the soul of both the segregator and the segregated. The segregator looks upon the segregated as a thing to be used, not a person to be respected. Segregation substitutes an "I-it" relationship for the "I-thou" relationship. Thus it is utterly opposed to the noble teachings of our Judeo-Christian tradition.

It has always been the responsibility of the church to broaden horizons, challenge the status quo, and break the mores when necessary. The task of conquering segregation is an inescapable *must* confronting the church today.

There are several specific things that the church can do. First, it should try to get to the ideational roots of race hate, something that the law cannot accomplish. All race prejudice is based upon fears, suspicions, and misunderstandings, usually groundless. The church can be of immeasurable help in giving the popular mind direction here.

Through its channels of religious education, the church can point out the irrationality of these beliefs. It can show that the idea of a superior or inferior race is a myth that has been completely refuted by anthropological evidence. It can show that Negroes are not innately inferior in academic, health, and moral standards. It can show that, when given equal opportunities, Negroes can demonstrate equal achievement.

The church can also do a great deal to reveal the true intentions of the Negro—that he is not seeking to dominate the nation, but simply wants the right to live as a first-class citizen, with all the responsibilities that good citizenship entails. The church can also help by mitigating the prevailing and irrational fears concerning intermarriage. It can say to men that marriage is an individual matter that must be decided on the merits of individual cases. Properly speaking, races do not marry; individuals marry. Marriage is a condition which requires the voluntary consent of two contracting parties, and either side can always say no. The church can reveal that the continual outcry concerning intermarriage is a distortion of the real issue. It can point out that the Negro's primary aim is to be the white man's brother, not his brother-in-law.

Another thing that the church can do to make the principle of brotherhood a reality is to keep men's minds and visions centered on God. Many of the problems America now confronts can be explained in terms of fear. There is not only the job of freeing the Negro from the bondage of segregation but also the responsibility of freeing his white brothers from the bondage of fears concerning integration. One of the best ways to rid oneself of fear is to center one's life in the will and purpose of God. "Perfect love casteth out fear."

When people think about race problems they are too often more concerned with men than with God. The question usually asked is: "What will my friends think if I am too friendly to Negroes or too liberal on the race questions?" Men forget to ask: "What will God think?" And so they live in fear because they tend to seek social approval on the horizontal plane rather than spiritual devotion on the vertical plane.

The church must remind its worshipers that man finds greater security in devoting his life to the eternal demands of the Almighty God than in giving his ultimate allegiance to the transitory demands of man. The church must continually say to Christians, "Ye are a colony of heaven." True, man has a dual citizenry. He lives both in time and in eternity; both in heaven and on earth. But he owes his ultimate allegiance to God. It is this love for God and devotion to His will that casteth out fear.

A further effort that the church can make in attempting to solve the race problem is to take the lead in social reform. It is not enough for the church to be active in the realm of ideas; it must move out into the arena of social action. First, the church must remove the yoke of segregation from its own body. Only by doing this can it be effective in its attack on outside evils. Unfortunately, most of the major denominations still practice segregation in local churches, hospitals, schools, and other church institutions. It is appalling that the most segregated hour of Christian America is eleven o'clock on Sunday morning, the same hour when many are standing to sing, "In Christ there is no East nor West." Equally appalling is the fact that the most segregated school of the week is the Sunday School. How often the church has had a high blood count of creeds and an anemia of deeds! Dean Liston Pope of the Yale Divinity School rightly says in *The Kingdom beyond Caste:* "The Church is the most segregated major institution in American society. It has lagged behind the Supreme Court as the conscience of the nation on questions of race, and it has fallen far behind trade unions, factories, schools, department stores, athletic gatherings and most other major areas of human association as far as the achievement of integration in its own life is concerned."

There has been some progress. Here and there churches are courageously making attacks on segregation, and actually integrating their congregations. The National Council of Churches has repeatedly condemned segregation and has requested its constituent denominations to do likewise. Most of the major denominations have endorsed that action. The Roman Catholic Church has declared, "Segregation is morally wrong and sinful." All this is admirable. But these stands are still far too few, and they move all too slowly down to the local churches in actual practice. The church has a schism in its own soul that it must close. It will be one of the tragedies of Christian history if a future Gibbon is able to say that at the height of the twentieth century the church proved to be one of the greatest bulwarks of segregated power.

The church must also become increasingly active in social action outside its doors. It must seek to keep channels of communication open between the Negro and white community. It must take an active stand against the injustice that Negroes confront in housing, education, police protection, and in city and state courts. It must exert its influence in the area of economic justice. As guardian of the moral and spiritual life of the community the church cannot look with indifference upon these glaring evils.

It is impossible to speak of the role of the church without referring to the ministers. Every minister of the gospel has a mandate to stand up courageously for righteousness, to proclaim the eternal verities of the gospel, and to lead men from the darkness of falsehood and fear to the light of truth and love.

In the South this mandate presents white ministers with a difficult choice. Many who believe segregation to be directly opposed to the will of God and the spirit of Christ are faced with the painful alternative of taking a vocal stand and being fired or staying quiet in order to remain in the situation and do some good. Pastors who have adopted the latter course feel that if they were forced out of their churches their successors would in all probability be segregationist, thus setting the Christian cause back. Many ministers have kept their peace not merely to save a job but because they feel that restraint is the best way to serve the cause of Christ in the South. In quiet unpublicized ways many of these ministers are making for a better day and helpfully molding the minds of young people. These men should not be criticized.

In the final analysis every white minister in the South must decide for himself which course he will follow. There is no single right strategy. The important thing is for every minister to dedicate himself to the Christian ideal of brotherhood, and be sure that he is doing something positive to implement it. He must never allow the theory that it is better to remain quiet and help the cause to become a rationalization for doing nothing. Many ministers can do much more than they are doing and still hold their congregations. There is a great deal that ministers can achieve collectively. In every Southern city there should be interracial ministerial associations in which Negro and white ministers can come together in Christian fellowship and discuss common community problems. One of the most disappointing experiences of the

Montgomery struggle was the fact that we could not get the white ministerial association to sit down with us and discuss our problem. With individual exceptions the white ministers, from whom I had naïvely expected so much, gave little.

Ministers can also collectively call for compliance with the law and a cessation of violence. This has been done by white ministers of Atlanta, Richmond, Dallas, and other cities, and not a single one has, to my knowledge, lost his job. It is difficult for a denomination to fire all of its ministers in a city. If ever the white ministers of the South decide to declare in a united voice the truth of the gospel on the question of race, the transition from a segregated to an integrated society will be infinitely smoother.

Any discussion of the role of the Christian minister today must ultimately emphasize the need for prophecy. Not every minister can be a prophet, but some must be prepared for the ordeals of this high calling and be willing to suffer courageously for righteousness. May the problem of race in America soon make hearts burn so that prophets will rise up, saying, "Thus saith the Lord," and cry out as Amos did, "... let justice roll down like waters, and righteousness like an ever-flowing stream."

Fortunately, a few in the South have already been willing to follow this prophetic way. I have nothing but praise for these ministers of the gospel of Jesus Christ and rabbis of the Jewish faith who have stood unflinchingly before threats and intimidations, inconvenience and unpopularity, even at times in physical danger, to declare the doctrine of the Fatherhood of God and the brotherhood of man. For such noble servants of God there is the consolation of the words of Jesus: "Blessed are ye, when men shall revile you, and persecute you, and shall say all manner of evil against you falsely, for my sake. Rejoice, and be exceeding glad: for great is your reward in heaven: for so persecuted they the prophets which were before you."

Here, then, is the hard challenge and the sublime opportunity: to let the spirit of Christ work toward fashioning a truly great Christian nation. If the church accepts the challenge with devotion and valor, the day will be speeded when men everywhere will recognize that they "are all one in Christ Jesus."

Finally, the Negro himself has a decisive role to play if integration is to become a reality.

Indeed, if first-class citizenship is to become a reality for the Negro he must assume the primary responsibility for making it so. Integration is not some lavish dish that the federal government or the white liberal will pass out on a silver platter while the Negro merely furnishes the appetite. One of the most damaging effects of past segregation on the personality of the Negro may well be that he has been victimized with the delusion that others should be more concerned than himself about his citizenship rights.

In this period of social change, the Negro must come to see that there is much he himself can do about his plight. He may be uneducated or poverty-stricken, but these handicaps must not prevent him from seeing that he has within his being the power to alter his fate. The Negro can take direct action against injustice without waiting for the government to act or a majority to agree with him or a court to rule in his favor.

Oppressed people deal with their oppression in three characteristic ways. One way is acquiescence: the oppressed resign themselves to their doom. They tacitly adjust themselves to oppression, and thereby become conditioned to it. In every movement toward freedom some of the oppressed prefer to remain oppressed. Almost 2800 years ago Moses set out to lead the children of Israel from the slavery of Egypt to the freedom of the promised land. He soon discovered that slaves do not always welcome their deliverers. They become accustomed to being slaves. They would rather bear those ills they have, as Shakespeare pointed out, than flee to others that they know not of. They prefer the "fleshpots of Egypt" to the ordeals of emancipation.

There is such a thing as the freedom of exhaustion. Some people are so worn down by the yoke of oppression that they give up. A few years ago in the slum areas of Atlanta, a Negro guitarist used to sing almost daily: "Ben down so long that down don't bother me." This is the type of negative freedom and resignation that often engulfs the life of the oppressed.

But this is not the way out. To accept passively an unjust system is to coöperate with that system; thereby the oppressed become as evil as the oppressor. Non-coöperation with evil is as much a moral obligation as is coöperation with good. The oppressed must never allow the conscience of the oppressor to slumber. Religion reminds every man that he is his brother's keeper. To accept injustice or segregation passively is to say to the oppressor that his actions are morally right. It is a way of allowing his conscience to fall asleep. At this moment the oppressed fails to be his brother's keeper. So acquiescence—while often the easier way—is not the moral way. It is the way of the coward. The Negro cannot win the respect of his oppressor by acquiescing; he merely increases the oppressor's arrogance and contempt. Acquiescence is interpreted as proof of the Negro's inferiority. The Negro cannot win the respect of the white people of the South or the peoples of the world if he is willing to sell the future of his children for his personal and immediate comfort and safety.

A second way that oppressed people sometimes deal with oppression is to resort to physical violence and corroding hatred. Violence often brings about momentary results. Nations have frequently won their independence in battle. But in spite of temporary victories, violence never brings permanent peace. It solves no social problem; it merely creates new and more complicated ones.

Violence as a way of achieving racial justice is both impractical and immoral. It is impractical because it is a descending spiral ending in destruction for all. The old law of an eye for an eye leaves everybody blind. It is immoral because it seeks to humiliate the opponent rather than win his understanding; it seeks to annihilate rather than to convert. Violence is immoral because it thrives on hatred rather than love. It destroys community and makes brotherhood impossible. It leaves society in monologue rather than dialogue. Violence ends by defeating itself. It creates bitterness in the survivors and brutality in destroyers. A voice echoes through time saying to every potential Peter, "Put up your sword." History is cluttered with the wreckage of nations that failed to follow this command.

If the American Negro and other victims of oppression succumb to the temptation of using violence in the struggle for freedom, future generations will be the recipients of a desolate night of bitterness, and our chief legacy to them will be an endless reign of meaningless chaos. Violence is not the way.

The third way open to oppressed people in their quest for freedom is the way of nonviolent resistance. Like the synthesis in Hegelian philosophy, the principle of nonviolent resistance seeks to reconcile the truths of two opposites—

acquiescence and violence—while avoiding the extremes and immoralities of both. The nonviolent resister agrees with the person who acquiesces that one should not be physically aggressive toward his opponent; but he balances the equation by agreeing with the person of violence that evil must be resisted. He avoids the nonresistance of the former and the violent resistance of the latter. With nonviolent resistance, no individual or group need submit to any wrong, nor need anyone resort to violence in order to right a wrong.

It seems to me that this is the method that must guide the actions of the Negro in the present crisis in race relations. Through nonviolent resistance the Negro will be able to rise to the noble height of opposing the unjust system while loving the perpetrators of the system. The Negro must work passionately and unrelentingly for full stature as a citizen, but he must not use inferior methods to gain it. He must never come to terms with falsehood, malice, hate, or destruction.

Nonviolent resistance makes it possible for the Negro to remain in the South and struggle for his rights. The Negro's problem will not be solved by running away. He cannot listen to the glib suggestion of those who would urge him to migrate en masse to other sections of the country. By grasping his great opportunity in the South he can make a lasting contribution to the moral strength of the nation and set a sublime example of courage for generations yet unborn.

By nonviolent resistance, the Negro can also enlist all men of good will in his struggle for equality. The problem is not a purely racial one, with Negroes set against whites. In the end, it is not a struggle between people at all, but a tension between justice and injustice. Nonviolent resistance is not aimed against oppressors but against oppression. Under its banner consciences, not racial groups, are enlisted.

If the Negro is to achieve the goal of integration, he must organize himself into a militant and nonviolent mass movement. All three elements are indispensable. The movement for equality and justice can only be a success if it has both a mass and militant character; the barriers to be overcome require both. Nonviolence is an imperative in order to bring about ultimate community.

A mass movement of a militant quality that is not at the same time committed to nonviolence tends to generate conflict, which in turn breeds anarchy. The support of the participants and the sympathy of the uncommitted are both inhibited by the threat that bloodshed will engulf the community. This reaction in turn encourages the opposition to threaten and resort to force. When, however, the mass movement repudiates violence while moving resolutely toward its goal, its opponents are revealed as the instigators and practitioners of violence if it occurs. Then public support is magnetically attracted to the advocates of nonviolence, while those who employ violence are literally disarmed by over-whelming sentiment against their stand.

Only through a nonviolent approach can the fears of the white community be mitigated. A guilt-ridden white minority lives in fear that if the Negro should ever attain power, he would act without restraint or pity to revenge the injustices and brutality of the years. It is something like a parent who continually mistreats a son. One day that parent raises his hand to strike the son, only to discover that the son is now as tall as he is. The parent is suddenly afraid—fearful that the son will use his new physical power to repay his parent for all the blows of the past.

The Negro, once a helpless child, has now grown up politically, culturally, and economically. Many white men fear retaliation. The job of the Negro is to show them that they have nothing to fear, that the Negro understands and forgives and is ready to forget the past. He must convince the white man that all he seeks is justice, *for both himself and the white man.* A mass movement exercising nonviolence is an object lesson in power under discipline, a demonstration to the white community that if such a movement attained a degree of strength, it would use its power creatively and not vengefully.

Nonviolence can touch men where the law cannot reach them. When the law regulates behavior it plays an indirect part in molding public sentiment. The enforcement of the law is itself a form of peaceful persuasion. But the law needs help. The courts can order desegregation of the public schools. But what can be done to mitigate the fears, to disperse the hatred, violence, and irrationality gathered around school integra-tion, to take the initiative out of the hands of racial demagogues, to release respect for the law? In the end, for laws to be obeyed, men must believe they are right.

Here nonviolence comes in as the ultimate form of persuasion. It is the method which seeks to implement the just law by appealing to the conscience of the great decent majority who through blindness, fear, pride, or irrationality have allowed their consciences to sleep.

The nonviolent resisters can summarize their message in the following simple terms: We will take direct action against injustice without waiting for other agencies to act. We will not obey unjust laws or submit to unjust practices. We will do this peacefully, openly, cheerfully because our aim is to persuade. We adopt the means of nonviolence because our end is a community at peace with itself. We will try to persuade with our words, but if our words fail, we will try to persuade with our acts. We will always be willing to talk and seek fair compromise, but we are ready to suffer when necessary and even risk our lives to become witnesses to the truth as we see it.

The way of nonviolence means a willingness to suffer and sacrifice. It may mean going to jail. If such is the case the resister must be willing to fill the jail houses of the South. It may even mean physical death. But if physical death is the price that a man must pay to free his children and his white brethren from a permanent death of the spirit, then nothing could be more redemptive.

What is the Negro's best defense against acts of violence inflicted upon him? As Dr. Kenneth Clark has said so eloquently, "His only defense is to meet every act of barbarity, illegality, cruelty and injustice toward an individual Negro with the fact that 100 more Negroes will present themselves in his place as potential victims." Every time one Negro schoolteacher is fired for believing in integration, a thousand others should be ready to take the same stand. If the oppressors bomb the home of one Negro for his protest, they must be made to realize that to press back the rising tide of the Negro's courage they will have to bomb hundreds more, and even then they will fail.

Faced with this dynamic unity, this amazing self-respect, this willingness to suffer, and this refusal to hit back, the oppressor will find, as oppressors have always found, that he is glutted with his own barbarity. Forced to stand before the world and his God splattered with the blood of his brother, he will call an end to his self-defeating massacre.

American Negroes must come to the point where they can say to their white brothers, paraphrasing the words of Gandhi: "We will match your capacity to inflict suffering with our capacity to endure suffering. We will meet your physical force with soul force. We will not hate you, but we cannot in all good conscience obey your unjust laws. Do to us what you will and we will still love you. Bomb our homes and threaten our children; send your hooded perpetrators of violence into our communities and drag us out on some wayside road, beating us and leaving us half dead, and we will still love you. But we will soon wear you down by our capacity to suffer. And in winning our freedom we will so appeal to your heart and conscience that we will win you in the process."

Realism impels me to admit that many Negroes will find it difficult to follow the path of non-violence. Some will consider it senseless; some will argue that they have neither the strength nor the courage to join in such a mass demonstration of nonviolent action. As E. Franklin Frazier points out in *Black Bourgeoisie,* many Negroes are occupied in a middle-class struggle for status and prestige. They are more concerned about "conspicuous consumption" than about the cause of justice, and are probably not prepared for the ordeals and sacrifices involved in non-violent action. Fortunately, however, the success of this method is not dependent on its unanimous acceptance. A few Negroes in every community, unswervingly committed to the nonviolent way, can persuade hundreds of others at least to use nonviolence as a technique and serve as the moral force to awaken the slumbering national conscience. Thoreau was thinking of such a creative minority when he said: "I know this well, that if one thousand, if one hundred, if ten men whom I could name—if ten honest men only—aye, if one honest man, in the state of Massachusetts, ceasing to hold slaves, were actually to withdraw from the copartnership, and be locked up in the county jail therefore, it would be the abolition of slavery in America. For it matters not how small the beginning may seem to be, what is once well done is done forever."

Mahatma Gandhi never had more than one hundred persons absolutely committed to his philosophy. But with this small group of devoted followers, he galvanized the whole of India, and through a magnificent feat of nonviolence challenged the might of the British Empire and won freedom for his people.

This method of nonviolence will not work miracles overnight. Men are not easily moved from their mental ruts, their prejudiced and irrational feelings. When the underprivileged demand freedom, the privileged first react with bitterness and resistance. Even when the demands are couched in nonviolent terms, the initial response is the same. Nehru once remarked that the British were never so angry as when the Indians resisted them with nonviolence, that he never saw eyes so full of hate as those of the British troops to whom he turned the other cheek when they beat him with lathees. But nonviolent resistance at least changed the minds and hearts of the Indians, however impervious the British may have appeared. "We cast away our fear," says Nehru. And in the end the British not only granted freedom to India but came to have a new respect for the Indians. Today a mutual friend-ship based on complete equality exists between these two peoples within the Commonwealth.

In the South too, the initial white reaction to Negro resistance has been bitter. I do not predict that a similar happy ending will come to Mont-gomery in a few months, because integration is more complicated than independence. But I know that the Negroes of Montgomery are already walking straighter because of the protest. And I expect that this generation of Negro children throughout the United States will grow up stronger and better because of the courage, the dignity, and the suffering of the nine children of Little Rock, and their counterparts in Nash-ville, Clinton, and Sturges. And I believe that the white people of this country are being affected too, that beneath the surface this nation's conscience is being stirred.

The nonviolent approach does not immediately change the heart of the oppressor. It first does something to the hearts and souls of those com-mitted to it. It gives them new self-respect; it calls up resources of strength and courage that they did not know they had. Finally it reaches the opponent and so stirs his conscience that recon-ciliation becomes a reality.

I suggest this approach because I think it is the only way to reëstablish the broken community. Court orders and federal enforcement agencies will be of inestimable value in achieving de-segregation. But desegregation is only a partial, though necessary, step toward the ultimate goal which we seek to realize. Desegregation will break down the legal barriers, and bring men together physically. But something must happen so to touch the hearts and souls of men that they will come together, not because the law says it, but because it is natural and right. In other words, our ultimate goal is integration which is genuine intergroup and interpersonal living. Only through nonviolence can this goal be attained, for the aftermath of nonviolence is reconciliation and the creation of the beloved community.

It is becoming clear that the Negro is in for a season of suffering. As victories for civil rights mount in the federal courts, angry passions and deep prejudices are further aroused. The mountain of state and local segregation laws still stands. Negro leaders continue to be arrested and harassed under city ordinances, and their homes continue to be bombed. State laws continue to be enacted to circumvent integration. I pray that, recognizing the necessity of suffering, the Negro will make of it a virtue. To suffer in a righteous cause is to grow to our humanity's full stature. If only to save himself from bitterness, the Negro needs the vision to see the ordeals of this generation as the opportunity to transfigure himself and American society. If he has to go to jail for the cause of freedom, let him enter it in the fashion Gandhi urged his countrymen, "as the bridegroom enters the bride's chamber"—that is, with a little trepidation but with a great expectation.

Nonviolence is a way of humility and self-restraint. We Negroes talk a great deal about our rights, and rightly so. We proudly proclaim that three-fourths of the people of the world are colored. We have the privilege of watching in our generation the great drama of freedom and independence as it unfolds in Asia and Africa. All of these things are in line with the work of providence. We must be sure, however, that we accept them in the right spirit. In an effort to achieve freedom in America, Asia, and Africa we must not try to leap from a position of disadvantage to one of advantage, thus subverting justice. We must seek democracy and not the substitution of one tyranny for another. Our aim must never be to defeat or humiliate the white man. We must not become victimized with a philosophy of black supremacy. God is not interested merely in the freedom of black men, and brown men, and yellow men; God is interested in the freedom of the whole human race.

The nonviolent approach provides an answer to the long debated question of gradualism versus immediacy. On the one hand it prevents one from falling into the sort of patience which is an excuse for do-nothingism and escapism, ending up in standstillism. On the other hand it saves one from the irresponsible words which estrange without reconciling and the hasty judgment which is blind to the necessities of social process. It recognizes the need for moving toward the goal of justice with wise restraint and calm reasonableness. But it also recognizes the immorality of slowing up in the move toward justice and capitulating to the guardians of an unjust status quo. It recognizes that social change cannot come overnight. But it causes one to work as if it were a possibility the next morning.

Through nonviolence we avoid the temptation of taking on the psychology of victors. Thanks largely to the noble and invaluable work of the NAACP, we have won great victories in the federal courts. But we must not be self-satisfied. We must respond to every decision with an understanding of those who have opposed us, and with acceptance of the new adjustments that the court orders pose for them. We must act in such a way that our victories will be triumphs for good will in all men, white and Negro.

Nonviolence is essentially a positive concept. Its corollary must always be growth. On the one hand nonviolence requires noncoöperation with evil; on the other hand it requires coöperation with the constructive forces of good. Without this constructive aspect noncoöperation ends where it begins. Therefore, the Negro must get to work on a program with a broad range of positive goals.

One point in the Negro's program should be a plan to improve his own economic lot. Through the establishment of credit unions, savings and loan associations, and coöperative enterprises the Negro can greatly improve his economic status. He must develop habits of thrift and techniques of wise investment. He must not wait for the end of the segregation that lies at the basis of his economic deprivation; he must act now to lift himself up by his own bootstraps.

The constructive program ahead must include a campaign to get Negroes to register and vote. Certainly they face many external barriers. All types of underhand methods are still being used in the South to prevent the Negroes from voting, and the success of these efforts is not only unjust, it is a real embarrassment to the nation we love and must protect. The advocacy of free elections in Europe by American officials is hypocrisy when free elections are not held in great sections of America.

But external resistance is not the only present barrier to Negro voting. Apathy among the Negroes themselves is also a factor. Even where the polls are open to all, Negroes have shown themselves too slow to exercise their voting privileges. There must be a concerted effort on the part of Negro leaders to arouse their people from their apathetic indifference to this obligation of citizenship. In the past, apathy was a moral failure. Today, it is a form of moral and political suicide.

The constructive program ahead must include a vigorous attempt to improve the Negro's personal standards. It must be reiterated that the standards of the Negro as a group lag behind not because of an inherent inferiority, but because of the fact that segregation does exist. The "behavior deviants" within the Negro community stem from the economic deprivation, emotional frustration, and social isolation which are the inevitable concomitants of segregation. When the white man argues that segregation should continue because of the Negro's lagging standards, he fails to see that the standards lag because of segregation.

Yet Negroes must be honest enough to admit that our standards do often fall short. One of the sure signs of maturity is the ability to rise to the point of self-criticism. Whenever we are objects of criticism from white men, even though the criticisms are maliciously directed and mixed with half-truths, we must pick out the elements of truth and make them the basis of creative reconstruction. We must not let the fact that we are the victims of injustice lull us into abrogating responsibility for our own lives.

Our crime rate is far too high. Our level of cleanliness is frequently far too low. Too often those of us who are in the middle class live above our means, spend money on nonessentials and frivolities, and fail to give to serious causes, organizations, and educational institutions that so desperately need funds. We are too often loud and boisterous, and spend far too much on drink. Even the most poverty-stricken among us can purchase a ten-cent bar of soap; even the most uneducated among us can have high morals. Through community agencies and religious institutions Negro leaders must develop a positive program through which Negro youth can become adjusted to urban living and improve their general level of behavior. Since crime often grows out of a sense of futility and despair, Negro parents must be urged to give their children the love, attention, and sense of belonging that a segregated society deprives them of. By improving our standards here and now we will go a long way toward breaking down the arguments of the segregationist.

This then must be our present program: Nonviolent resistance to all forms of racial injustice, including state and local laws and practices, even when this means going to jail; and imaginative, bold, constructive action to end the demoralization caused by the legacy of slavery and segregation, inferior schools, slums, and second-class citizenship. The nonviolent struggle, if conducted with the dignity and courage already shown by the people of Montgomery and the children of Little Rock, will in itself help end the demoralization; but a new frontal assault on the poverty, disease, and ignorance of a people too long ignored by America's conscience will make victory more certain.

In short, we must work on two fronts. On the one hand, we must continue to resist the system of segregation which is the basic cause of our lagging standards; on the other hand we must work constructively to improve the standards themselves. There must be a rhythmic alternation between attacking the causes and healing the effects.

This is a great hour for the Negro. The challenge is here. To become the instruments of a great idea is a privilege that history gives only occasionally. Arnold Toynbee says in *A Study of History* that it may be the Negro who will give the new spiritual dynamic to Western civilization that it so desperately needs to survive. I hope this is possible. The spiritual power that the Negro can radiate to the world comes from love, understanding, good will, and nonviolence. It may even be possible for the Negro, through adherence to nonviolence, so to challenge the nations of the world that they will seriously seek an alternative to war and destruction. In a day when Sputniks and Explorers dash through outer space and guided ballistic missiles are carving highways of death through the stratosphere, nobody can win a war. Today the choice is no longer between violence and nonviolence. It is either nonviolence or nonexistence. The Negro may be God's appeal to this age—an age drifting rapidly to its doom. The eternal appeal takes the form of a warning: "All who take the sword will perish by the sword."

Letter from Birmingham Jail

MARTIN LUTHER KING, JR.
Birmingham City Jail
April 16, 1963

Bishop C. C. J. CARPENTER
Bishop JOSEPH A. DURICK
Rabbi MILTON L. GRAFMAN
Bishop PAUL HARDIN
Bishop NOLAN B. HARMON
The Rev. GEORGE M. MURRAY
The Rev. EDWARD V. RAMAGE
The Rev. EARL STALLINGS

My dear Fellow Clergymen,

While confined here in the Birmingham City Jail, I came across your recent statement calling our present activities "unwise and untimely." Seldom, if ever, do I pause to answer criticism of my work and ideas. If I sought to answer all of the criticisms that cross my desk, my secretaries would be engaged in little else in the course of the day and I would have no time for constructive work. But since I feel that you are men of genuine goodwill and your criticisms are sincerely set forth, I would like to answer your statement in what I hope will be patient and reasonable terms.

I think I should give the reason for my being in Birmingham, since you have been influenced by the argument of "outsiders coming in." I have the honor of serving as president of Southern Christian Leadership Conference, an organization operating in every Southern state with headquarters in Atlanta, Georgia. We have some eighty-five affiliate organizations all across the South—one being the Alabama Christian Movement for Human Rights. Whenever necessary and possible we share staff, educational, and financial resources with our affiliates. Several months ago our local affiliate here in Birmingham invited us to be on call to engage in a nonviolent direct action program if such were deemed necessary. We readily consented and when the hour came we lived up to our promises. So I am here, along with several members of my staff, because we were invited here. I am here because I have basic organizational ties here. Beyond this, I am in Birmingham because injustice is here. Just as the eighth century prophets left their little villages and carried their "thus saith the Lord" far beyond the boundaries of their home town, and just as the Apostle Paul left his little village of Tarsus and carried the gospel of Jesus Christ to practically every hamlet and city of the Graeco-Roman world, I too am compelled to carry the gospel of freedom beyond my particular home town. Like Paul, I must constantly respond to the Macedonian call for aid.

Moreover, I am cognizant of the interrelatedness of all communities and states. I cannot sit idly by in Atlanta and not be concerned about what happens in Birmingham. Injustice anywhere is a threat to justice everywhere. We are caught in an inescapable network of mutuality tied in a single garment of destiny. Whatever affects one directly affects all indirectly. Never again can we afford to live with the narrow, provincial "outside agitator" idea. Anyone who lives inside the United States can never be considered an outsider anywhere in this country.

You deplore the demonstrations that are presently taking place in Birmingham. But I am sorry that your statement did not express a similar concern for the conditions that brought the demonstrations into being. I am sure that each of you would want to go beyond the superficial social analyst who looks merely at effects, and does not grapple with underlying causes. I would not hesitate to say that it is unfortunate that so-called demonstrations are taking place in Birmingham at this time, but I would say in more emphatic terms that it is even more unfortunate that the white power structure of this city left the Negro community with no other alternative.

In any nonviolent campaign there are four basic steps: (1) collection of the facts to determine whether injustices are alive; (2) negotiation; (3) self-purification; and (4) direct action. We have gone through all of these steps in Birmingham. There can be no gainsaying of the fact that racial injustice engulfs this community. Birmingham is probably the most thoroughly segregated city in the United States. Its ugly record of police brutality is known in every section of this country. Its unjust treatment of Negroes in the courts is a notorious reality. There have been more unsolved bombings of Negro homes and churches in Birmingham than any city in this nation. These are the hard, brutal, and unbelievable facts. On the basis of these conditions

Negro leaders sought to negotiate with the city fathers. But the political leaders consistently refused to engage in good faith negotiation.

Then came the opportunity last September to talk with some of the leaders of the economic community. In these negotiating sessions certain promises were made by the merchants—such as the promise to remove the humiliating racial signs from the stores. On the basis of these promises Rev. Shuttlesworth and the leaders of the Alabama Christian Movement for Human Rights agreed to call a moratorium on any type of demonstrations. As the weeks and months unfolded we realized that we were the victims of a broken promise. The signs remained. As in so many experiences of the past we were confronted with blasted hopes, and the dark shadow of a deep disappointment settled upon us. So we had no alternative except that of preparing for direct action, whereby we would present our very bodies as a means of laying our case before the conscience of the local and national community. We were not unmindful of the difficulties involved. So we decided to go through a process of self-purification. We started having workshops on nonviolence and repeatedly asked ourselves the questions, "Are you able to accept blows without retaliating? Are you able to endure the ordeals of jail?"

We decided to set our direct action program around the Easter season, realizing that with the exception of Christmas, this was the largest shopping period of the year. Knowing that a strong economic withdrawal program would be the by-product of direct action, we felt that this was the best time to bring pressure on the merchants for the needed changes. Then it occurred to us that the March election was ahead, and so we speedily decided to postpone action until after election day. When we discovered that Mr. Connor was in the run-off, we decided again to postpone action so that the demonstrations could not be used to cloud the issues. At this time we agreed to begin our nonviolent witness the day after the run-off.

This reveals that we did not move irresponsibly into direct action. We too wanted to see Mr. Connor defeated; so we went through postponement after postponement to aid in this community need. After this we felt that direct action could be delayed no longer.

You may well ask, "Why direct action? Why sit-ins, marches, etc.? Isn't negotiation a better path?" You are exactly right in your call for negotiation. Indeed, this is the purpose of direct action. Nonviolent direct action seeks to create such a crisis and establish such creative tension that a community that has constantly refused to negotiate is forced to confront the issue. It seeks so to dramatize the issue that it can no longer be ignored. I just referred to the creation of tension as a part of the work of the nonviolent resister. This may sound rather shocking. But I must confess that I am not afraid of the word tension. I have earnestly worked and preached against violent tension, but there is a type of constructive nonviolent tension that is necessary for growth. Just as Socrates felt that it was necessary to create a tension in the mind so that individuals could rise from the bondage of myths and half-truths to the unfettered realm of creative analysis and objective appraisal, we must see the need of having nonviolent gadflies to create the kind of tension in society that will help men rise from the dark depths of prejudice and racism to the majestic heights of understanding and brotherhood. So the purpose of the direct action is to create a situation so crisis-packed that it will inevitably open the door to negotiation. We, therefore, concur with you in your call for negotiation. Too long has our beloved Southland been bogged down in the tragic attempt to live in monologue rather than dialogue.

One of the basic points in your statement is that our acts are untimely. Some have asked, "Why didn't you give the new administration time to act?" The only answer that I can give to this inquiry is that the new administration must be prodded about as much as the outgoing one before it acts. We will be sadly mistaken if we feel that the election of Mr. Boutwell will bring the millennium to Birmingham. While Mr. Boutwell is much more articulate and gentle than Mr. Connor, they are both segregationists dedicated to the task of maintaining the status quo. The hope I see in Mr. Boutwell is that he will be reasonable enough to see the futility of massive resistance to desegregation. But he will not see this without pressure from the devotees of civil rights. My friends, I must say to you that we have not made a single gain in civil rights without determined legal and nonviolent pressure. History is the long and tragic story of the fact that privileged groups seldom give up their privileges voluntarily. Individuals may see the moral light and voluntarily give up their unjust posture; but as Reinhold Niebuhr has reminded us, groups are more immoral than individuals.

We know through painful experience that freedom is never voluntarily given by the oppressor; it must be demanded by the oppressed. Frankly I have never yet engaged in a direct action movement that was "well timed," according to the timetable of those who have not suffered unduly from the disease of segregation. For years now I have heard the word "Wait!" It rings in the ear of every Negro with a piercing familiarity. This "wait" has almost always meant "never." It has been a tranquilizing thalidomide, relieving the emotional stress for a moment, only to give birth to an ill-formed infant of frustration. We must come to see with the distinguished jurist of yesterday that "justice too long delayed is justice denied." We have waited for more than three hundred and forty years for our constitutional and God-given rights. The nations of Asia and Africa are moving with jet-like speed toward the goal of political independence, and we still creep at horse and buggy pace toward the gaining of a cup of coffee at a lunch counter.

I guess it is easy for those who have never felt the stinging darts of segregation to say wait. But when you have seen vicious mobs lynch your mothers and fathers at will and drown your sisters and brothers at whim; when you have seen hate filled policemen curse, kick, brutalize, and even kill your black brothers and sisters with impunity; when you see the vast majority of your twenty million Negro brothers smothering in an air-tight cage of poverty in the midst of an affluent society; when you suddenly find your tongue twisted and your speech stammering as you seek to explain to your six-year-old daughter why she can't go to the public amusement park that has just been advertised on television, and see tears welling up in her little eyes when she is told that Funtown is closed to colored children, and see the depressing clouds of inferiority begin to form in her little mental sky, and see her begin to distort her little personality by unconsciously developing a bitterness toward white people; when you have to concoct an answer for a five-year-old son asking in agonizing pathos: "Daddy, why do white people treat colored people so mean?"; when you take a cross country drive and find it necessary to sleep night after night in the uncomfortable corners of your automobile because no motel will accept you; when you are

humiliated day in and day out by nagging signs reading "white" men and "colored"; when your first name becomes "nigger" and your middle name becomes "boy" (however old you are) and your last name becomes "John," and when your wife and mother are never given the respected title "Mrs."; when you are harried by day and haunted by night by the fact that you are a Negro, living constantly at tip-toe stance never quite knowing what to expect next, and plagued with inner fears and outer resentments; when you are forever fighting a degenerating sense of "nobodiness";—then you will understand why we find it difficult to wait. There comes a time when the cup of endurance runs over, and men are no longer willing to be plunged into an abyss of injustice where they experience the bleakness of corroding despair. I hope, sirs, you can understand our legitimate and unavoidable impatience.

You express a great deal of anxiety over our willingness to break laws. This is certainly a legitimate concern. Since we so diligently urge people to obey the Supreme Court's decision of 1954 outlawing segregation in the public schools, it is rather strange and paradoxical to find us consciously breaking laws. One may well ask, "How can you advocate breaking some laws and obeying others?" The answer is found in the fact that there are two types of laws; There are *just* laws and there are *unjust* laws. I would be the first to advocate obeying just laws. One has not only a legal but moral responsibility to obey just laws. Conversely, one has a moral responsibility to disobey unjust laws. I would agree with Saint Augustine that "An unjust law is no law at all."

Now what is the difference between the two? How does one determine when a law is just or unjust? A just law is a man-made code that squares with the moral law or the law of God. An unjust law is a code that is out of harmony with the moral law. To put it in the terms of Saint Thomas Aquinas, an unjust law is a human law that is not rooted in eternal and natural law. Any law that uplifts human personality is just. Any law that degrades human personality is unjust. All segregation statutes are unjust because segregation distorts the soul and damages the personality. It gives the segregator a false sense of superiority and the segregated a false sense of inferiority. To use the words of Martin Buber, the great Jewish philosopher, segregation substitutes an "I-it" relationship for the "I-thou" relationship, and ends up relegating persons to the status of things. So segregation is not only politically, economically, and sociologically unsound, but it is morally wrong and sinful. Paul Tillich has said that sin is separation. Isn't segregation an existential expression of man's tragic separation, an expression of his awful estrangement, his terrible sinfulness? So I can urge men to obey the 1954 decision of the Supreme Court because it is morally right, and I can urge them to disobey segregation ordinances because they are morally wrong.

Let us turn to a more concrete example of just and unjust laws. An unjust law is a code that a majority inflicts on a minority that is not binding on itself. This is *difference* made legal. On the other hand a just law is a code that a majority compels a minority to follow that it is willing to follow itself. This is *sameness* made legal.

Let me give another explanation. An unjust law is a code inflicted upon a minority which that minority had no part in enacting or creating because they did not have the unhampered right to vote. Who can say the legislature of Alabama which set up the segregation laws was democratically elected? Throughout the state of Alabama all types of conniving methods are used to prevent Negroes from becoming registered voters and there are some counties without a single Negro registered to vote despite the fact that the Negro constitutes a majority of the population. Can any law set up in such a state be considered democratically structured?

These are just a few examples of unjust and just laws. There are some instances when a law is just on its face but unjust in its application. For instance, I was arrested Friday on a charge of parading without a permit. Now there is nothing wrong with an ordinance which requires a permit for a parade, but when the ordinance is used to preserve segregation and to deny citizens the First Amendment privilege of peaceful assembly and peaceful protest, then it becomes unjust.

I hope you can see the distinction I am trying to point out. In no sense do I advocate evading or defying the law as the rabid segregationist would do. This would lead to anarchy. One who breaks an unjust law must do it *openly, lovingly* (not hatefully as the white mothers did in New Orleans when they were seen on television screaming "nigger, nigger, nigger") and with a willingness to accept the penalty. I submit that an individual who breaks a law that conscience tells him is unjust, and willingly accepts the penalty by staying in jail to arouse the conscience of the community over its injustice, is in reality expressing the very highest respect for law.

Of course there is nothing new about this kind of civil disobedience. It was seen sublimely in the refusal of Shadrach, Meshach, and Abednego to obey the laws of Nebuchadnezzar because a higher moral law was involved. It was practiced superbly by the early Christians who were willing to face hungry lions and the excruciating pain of chopping blocks, before submitting to certain unjust laws of the Roman Empire. To a degree academic freedom is a reality today because Socrates practiced civil disobedience.

We can never forget that everything Hitler did in Germany was "legal" and everything the Hungarian freedom fighters did in Hungary was "illegal." It was "illegal" to aid and comfort a Jew in Hitler's Germany. But I am sure that, if I had lived in Germany during that time, I would have aided and comforted my Jewish brothers even though it was illegal. If I lived in a communist country today where certain principles dear to the Christian faith are suppressed, I believe I would openly advocate disobeying these anti-religious laws.

I must make two honest confessions to you, my Christian and Jewish brothers. First I must confess that over the last few years I have been gravely disappointed with the white moderate. I have almost reached the regrettable conclusion that the Negroes' great stumbling block in the stride toward freedom is not the White Citizens' "Counciler" or the Ku Klux Klanner, but the white moderate who is more devoted to "order" than to justice; who prefers a negative peace which is the absence of tension to a positive peace which is the presence of justice; who constantly says "I agree with you in the goal you seek, but I can't agree with your methods of direct action"; who paternalistically feels that he can set the time-table for another man's freedom; who lives by the myth of time and who constantly advises the Negro to wait until a "more convenient season." Shallow understanding from people of good will is more frustrating than absolute misunderstanding from people of ill will. Lukewarm acceptance is much more bewildering than outright rejection.

I had hoped that the white moderate would understand that law and order exist for the purpose of establishing justice, and that when they fail to do this they become the dangerously structured dams that block the flow of social progress. I had hoped that the white moderate would understand that the present tension in the South is merely a necessary phase of the transition from an obnoxious negative peace, where the Negro passively accepted his unjust plight, to a substance-filled positive peace, where all men will respect the dignity and worth of human personality. Actually, we who engage in nonviolent direct action are not the creators of tension. We merely bring to the surface the hidden tension that is already alive. We bring it out in the open where it can be seen and dealt with. Like a boil that can never be cured as long as it is covered up but must be opened with all its pusflowing ugliness to the natural medicines of air and light, injustice must likewise be exposed, with all of the tension its exposing creates, to the light of human conscience and the air of national opinion before it can be cured.

In your statement you asserted that our actions, even though peaceful, must be condemned because they precipitate violence. But can this assertion be logically made? Isn't this like condemning the robbed man because his possession of money precipitated the evil act of robbery? Isn't this like condemning Socrates because his unswerving commitment to truth and his philosophical delvings precipitated the misguided popular mind to make him drink the hemlock? Isn't this like condemning Jesus because His unique God consciousness and never-ceasing devotion to His will precipitated the evil act of crucifixion? We must come to see, as federal courts have consistently affirmed, that it is immoral to urge an individual to withdraw his efforts to gain his basic constitutional rights because the quest precipitates violence. Society must protect the robbed and punish the robber.

I had also hoped that the white moderate would reject the myth of time. I received a letter this morning from a white brother in Texas which said: "All Christians know that the colored people will receive equal rights eventually, but is it possible that you are in too great of a religious hurry? It has taken Christianity almost 2000 years to accomplish what it has. The teachings of Christ take time to come to earth." All that is said here grows out of a tragic misconception of time. It is the strangely irrational notion that there is something in the very flow of time that will inevitably cure all ills. Actually time is neutral. It can be used either destructively or constructively. I am coming to feel that the people of ill will have used time much more effectively than the people of good will. We will have to repent in this generation not merely for the vitriolic words and actions of the bad people, but for the appalling silence of the good people. We must come to see that human progress never rolls in on wheels of inevitability. It comes through the tireless efforts and persistent work of men willing to be co-workers with God, and without this hard work time itself becomes an ally of the forces of social stagnation.

We must use time creatively, and forever realize that the time is always ripe to do right. Now is the time to make real the promise of democracy, and transform our pending national elegy into a creative psalm of brotherhood. Now is the time to lift our national policy from the quicksand of racial injustice to the solid rock of human dignity.

You spoke of our activity in Birmingham as extreme. At first I was rather disappointed that fellow clergymen would see my nonviolent efforts as those of the extremist. I started thinking about the fact that I stand in the middle of two opposing forces in the Negro community. One is a force of complacency made up of Negroes who, as a result of long years of oppression, have been so completely drained of self-respect and a sense of "somebodiness" that they have adjusted to segregation, and of a few Negroes in the middle class who, because of a degree of academic and economic security, and because at points they profit by segregation, have unconsciously become insensitive to the problems of the masses. The other force is one of bitterness and hatred and comes perilously close to advocating violence. It is expressed in the various black nationalist groups that are springing up over the nation, the largest and best known being Elijah Muhammad's Muslim movement. This movement is nourished by the contemporary frustration over the continued existence of racial discrimination. It is made up of people who have lost faith in America, who have absolutely repudiated Christianity, and who have concluded that the white man is an incurable "devil." I have tried to stand between these two forces saying that we need not follow the "do-nothingism" of the complacent or the hatred and despair of the black nationalist. There is the more excellent way of love and non-violent protest. I'm grateful to God that, through the Negro church, the dimension of nonviolence entered our struggle. If this philosophy had not emerged I am convinced that by now many streets of the South would be flowing with floods of blood. And I am further convinced that if our white brothers dismiss us as "rabble rousers" and "outside agitators"—those of us who are working through the channels of nonviolent direct action—and refuse to support our non-violent efforts, millions of Negroes, out of frustration and despair, will seek solace and security in black nationalist ideologies, a development that will lead inevitably to a frightening racial nightmare.

Oppressed people cannot remain oppressed forever. The urge for freedom will eventually come. This is what has happened to the American Negro. Something within has reminded him of his birthright of freedom; something without has reminded him that he can gain it. Consciously and unconsciously, he has been swept in by what the Germans call the *Zeitgeist,* and with his black brothers of Africa, and his brown and yellow brothers of Asia, South America, and the Caribbean, he is moving with a sense of cosmic urgency toward the promised land of racial justice. Recognizing this vital urge that has engulfed the Negro community, one should readily understand public demonstrations. The Negro has many pent-up resentments and latent frustrations. He has to get them out. So let him march sometime; let him have his prayer pilgrimages to the city hall; understand why he must have sit-ins and freedom rides. If his repressed emotions do not come out in these nonviolent ways, they will come out in ominous expressions of violence. This is not a threat; it is a fact of history. So I have not said to my people, "Get rid of your discontent." But I have tried to say that this normal and healthy discontent can be channeled through the creative outlet of nonviolent direct action. Now this approach is being dismissed as extremist. I must admit that I was initially disappointed in being so categorized.

But as I continued to think about the matter I gradually gained a bit of satisfaction from being considered an extremist. Was not Jesus an extremist in love? "Love your enemies, bless them that curse you, pray for them that despitefully use you." Was not Amos an extremist for justice—"Let justice roll down like waters and righteousness like a mighty stream." Was not Paul an extremist for the gospel of Jesus Christ—"I bear in my body the marks of the Lord Jesus." Was

not Martin Luther an extremist—"Here I stand; I can do none other so help me God." Was not John Bunyan an extremist—"I will stay in jail to the end of my days before I make a butchery of my conscience." Was not Abraham Lincoln an extremist—"This nation cannot survive half slave and half free." Was not Thomas Jefferson an extremist—"We hold these truths to be self evident that all men are created equal." So the question is not whether we will be extremist but what kind of extremist will we be. Will we be extremists for hate or will we be extremists for love? Will we be extremists for the preservation of injustice—or will we be extremists for the cause of justice? In that dramatic scene on Calvary's hill three men were crucified. We must never forget that all three were crucified for the same crime—the crime of extremism. Two were extremists for immorality, and thus fell below their environment. The other, Jesus Christ, was an extremist for love, truth, and goodness, and thereby rose above His environment. So, after all, maybe the South, the nation, and the world are in dire need of creative extremists.

I had hoped that the white moderate would see this. Maybe I was too optimistic. Maybe I expected too much. I guess I should have realized that few members of a race that has oppressed another race can understand or appreciate the deep groans and passionate yearnings of those that have been oppressed, and still fewer have the vision to see that injustice must be rooted out by strong, persistent, and determined action. I am thankful, however, that some of our white brothers have grasped the meaning of this social revolution and committed themselves to it. They are still all too small in quantity, but they are big in quality. Some like Ralph McGill, Lillian Smith, Harry Golden, and James Dabbs have written about our struggle in eloquent, prophetic, and understanding terms. Others have marched with us down nameless streets of the South. They have languished in filthy, roach-infested jails, suffering the abuse and brutality of angry policemen who see them as "dirty nigger lovers." They, unlike so many of their moderate brothers and sisters, have recognized the urgency of the moment and sensed the need for powerful "action" antidotes to combat the disease of segregation.

Let me rush on to mention my other disappointment. I have been so greatly disappointed with the white Church and its leadership. Of course there are some notable exceptions. I am not unmindful of the fact that each of you has taken some significant stands on this issue. I commend you, Rev. Stallings, for your Christian stand on this past Sunday, in welcoming Negroes to your worship service on a non-segregated basis. I commend the Catholic leaders of this state for integrating Springhill College several years ago.

But despite these notable exceptions I must honestly reiterate that I have been disappointed with the Church. I do not say that as one of those negative critics who can always find something wrong with the Church. I say it as a minister of the gospel, who loves the Church; who was nurtured in its bosom; who has been sustained by its spiritual blessings and who will remain true to it as long as the cord of life shall lengthen.

I had the strange feeling when I was suddenly catapulted into the leadership of the bus protest in Montgomery several years ago that we would have the support of the white Church. I felt that the white ministers, priests, and rabbis of the South would be some of our strongest allies. Instead, some have been outright opponents, refusing to understand the freedom movement and misrepresenting its leaders; all too many others have been more cautious than courageous and have remained silent behind the anesthetizing security of stained glass windows.

In spite of my shattered dreams of the past, I came to Birmingham with the hope that the white religious leadership of this community would see the justice of our cause and, with deep moral concern, serve as the channel through which our just grievances could get to the power structure. I had hoped that each of you would understand. But again I have been disappointed.

I have heard numerous religious leaders of the South call upon their worshippers to comply with a desegregation decision because it is the law, but I have longed to hear white ministers say follow this decree because integration is morally right and the Negro is your brother. In the midst of blatant injustices inflicted upon the Negro, I have watched white churches stand on the sideline and merely mouth pious irrelevancies and sanctimonious trivialities. In the midst of a mighty struggle to rid our nation of racial and economic injustice, I have heard so many ministers say, "Those are social issues with which the Gospel has no real concern," and I have watched so many churches commit themselves to a completely other-worldly religion which made a strange distinction between body and soul, the sacred and the secular.

So here we are moving toward the exit of the twentieth century with a religious community largely adjusted to the status quo, standing as a tail light behind other community agencies rather than a headlight leading men to higher levels of justice.

I have travelled the length and breadth of Alabama, Mississippi, and all the other Southern states. On sweltering summer days and crisp autumn mornings I have looked at her beautiful churches with their spires pointing heavenward. I have beheld the impressive outlay of her massive religious education buildings. Over and over again I have found myself asking: "Who worships here? Who is their God? Where were their voices when the lips of Governor Barnett dripped with words of interposition and nullification? Where were they when Governor Wallace gave the clarion call for defiance and hatred? Where were their voices of support when tired, bruised, and weary Negro men and women decided to rise from the dark dungeons of complacency to the bright hills of creative protest?"

Yes, these questions are still in my mind. In deep disappointment, I have wept over the laxity of the Church. But be assured that my tears have been tears of love. There can be no deep disappointment where there is not deep love. Yes, I love the Church; I love her sacred walls. How could I do otherwise? I am in the rather unique position of being the son, the grandson, and the great grandson of preachers. Yes, I see the Church as the body of Christ. But, oh! How we have blemished and scarred that body through social neglect and fear of being nonconformist.

There was a time when the Church was very powerful. It was during that period when the early Christians rejoiced when they were deemed worthy to suffer for what they believed. In those days the Church was not merely a thermometer that recorded the ideas and principles of popular opinion; it was a thermostat that transformed the mores of society. Wherever the early Christians entered a town the power structure got disturbed and immediately sought to convict them for being "disturbers of the peace" and "outside agitators." But they went on with the conviction that they were a "colony of heaven" and had to obey God rather than man. They were small in number but big in commitment. They were too God-intoxicated to be "astronomically intimidated." They brought an end to such ancient evils as infanticide and gladiatorial contest.

Things are different now. The contemporary Church is so often a weak, ineffectual voice with an uncertain sound. It is so often the arch-supporter of the status quo. Far from being disturbed by the presence of the Church, the power structure of the average community is consoled by the Church's silent and often vocal sanction of things as they are.

But the judgment of God is upon the Church as never before. If the Church of today does not recapture the sacrificial spirit of the early Church, it will lose its authentic ring, forfeit the loyalty of millions, and be dismissed as an irrelevant social club with no meaning for the twentieth century. I am meeting young people every day whose disappointment with the Church has risen to outright disgust.

Maybe again I have been too optimistic. Is organized religion too inextricably bound to the status quo to save our nation and the world? Maybe I must turn my faith to the inner spiritual Church, the church within the Church, as the true *ecclesia* and the hope of the world. But again I am thankful to God that some noble souls from the ranks of organized religion have broken loose from the paralyzing chains of conformity and joined us as active partners in the struggle for freedom. They have left their secure congregations and walked the streets of Albany, Georgia, with us. They have gone through the highways of the South on torturous rides for freedom. Yes, they have gone to jail with us. Some have been kicked out of their churches and lost the support of their bishops and fellow ministers. But they have gone with the faith that right defeated is stronger than evil triumphant. These men have been the leaven in the lump of the race. Their witness has been the spiritual salt that has preserved the true meaning of the Gospel in these troubled times. They have carved a tunnel of hope through the dark mountain of disappointment.

I hope the Church as a whole will meet the challenge of this decisive hour. But even if the Church does not come to the aid of justice, I have no despair about the future. I have no fear about the outcome of our struggle in Birmingham, even if our motives are presently misunderstood. We will reach the goal of freedom in Birmingham and all over the nation, because the goal of America is freedom. Abused and scorned though we may be, our destiny is tied up with the destiny of America. Before the pilgrims landed at Plymouth, we were here. Before the pen of Jefferson etched across the pages of history the majestic words of the Declaration of Independence, we were here. For more than two centuries our foreparents labored in this country without wages; they made cotton "king"; and they built the homes of their masters in the midst of brutal injustice and shameful humiliation—and yet out of a bottomless vitality they continued to thrive and develop. If the inexpressible cruelties of slavery could not stop us, the opposition we now face will surely fail. We will win our freedom because the sacred heritage of our nation and the eternal will of God are embodied in our echoing demands.

I must close now. But before closing I am impelled to mention one other point in your statement that troubled me profoundly. You warmly commended the Birmingham police force for keeping "order" and "preventing violence." I don't believe you would have so warmly commended the police force if you had seen its angry violent dogs literally biting six unarmed, non-violent Negroes. I don't believe you would so quickly commend the policemen if you would observe their ugly and inhuman treatment of Negroes here in the city jail; if you would watch them push and curse old Negro women and young Negro girls; if you would see them slap and kick old Negro men and young Negro boys; if you will observe them, as they did on two occasions, refuse to give us food because we wanted to sing our grace together. I'm sorry that I can't join you in your praise for the police department.

It is true that they have been rather disciplined in their public handling of the demonstrators. In this sense they have been rather publicly "non-violent." But for what purpose? To preserve the evil system of segregation. Over the last few years I have consistently preached that nonviolence demands that the means we use must be as pure as the ends we seek. So I have tried to make it clear that it is wrong to use immoral means to attain moral ends. But now I must affirm that it is just as wrong, or even moreso, to use moral means to preserve immoral ends. Maybe Mr. Connor and his policemen have been rather publicly nonviolent, as Chief Pritchett was in

Albany, Georgia, but they have used the moral means of nonviolence to maintain the immoral end of flagrant racial injustice. T. S. Eliot has said that there is no greater treason than to do the right deed for the wrong reason.

I wish you had commended the Negro sit-inners and demonstrators of Birmingham for their sublime courage, their willingness to suffer, and their amazing discipline in the midst of the most inhuman provocation. One day the South will recognize its real heroes. They will be the James Merediths, courageously and with a majestic sense of purpose, facing jeering and hostile mobs and the agonizing loneliness that characterizes the life of the pioneer. They will be old, oppressed, battered Negro women, symbolized in a seventy-two year old woman of Montgomery, Alabama, who rose up with a sense of dignity and with her people decided not to ride the segregated buses, and responded to one who inquired about her tiredness with ungrammatical profundity: "My feets is tired, but my soul is rested." They will be young high school and college students, young ministers of the gospel and a host of the elders, courageously and nonviolently sitting in at lunch counters and willingly going to jail for conscience sake. One day the South will know that when these disinherited children of God sat down at lunch counters they were in reality standing up for the best in the American dream and the most sacred values in our Judeo-Christian heritage, and thus carrying our whole nation back to great wells of democracy which were dug deep by the founding fathers in the formulation of the Constitution and the Declaration of Independence.

Never before have I written a letter this long (or should I say a book?). I'm afraid that it is much too long to take your precious time. I can assure you that it would have been much shorter if I had been writing from a comfortable desk, but what else is there to do when you are alone for days in the dull monotony of a narrow jail cell other than write long letters, think strange thoughts, and pray long prayers?

If I have said anything in this letter that is an overstatement of the truth and is indicative of an unreasonable impatience, I beg you to forgive me. If I have said anything in this letter that is an understatement of the truth and is indicative of my having a patience that makes me patient with anything less than brotherhood, I beg God to forgive me.

I hope this letter finds you strong in the faith. I also hope that circumstances will soon make it possible for me to meet each of you, not as an integrationist or a civil rights leader, but as a fellow clergyman and a Christian brother. Let us all hope that the dark clouds of racial prejudice will soon pass away and the deep fog of misunderstanding will be lifted from our fear-drenched communities and in some not too distant tomorrow the radiant stars of love and brotherhood will shine over our great nation with all of their scintillating beauty.

Yours for the cause of
Peace and Brotherhood
MARTIN LUTHER KING, JR.

I Have a Dream

Five score years ago, a great American, in whose symbolic shadow we stand, signed the Emancipation Proclamation. This momentous decree came as a great beacon light of hope to millions of Negro slaves who had been seared in the flames of withering injustice. It came as a joyous daybreak to end the long night of captivity.

But one hundred years later, we must face the tragic fact that the Negro is still not free. One hundred years later, the life of the Negro is still sadly crippled by the manacles of segregation and the chains of discrimination. One hundred years later, the Negro lives on a lonely island of poverty in the midst of a vast ocean of material prosperity. One hundred years later the Negro is still languished in the corners of American society and finds himself an exile in his own land. So we have come here today to dramatize an appalling condition.

In a sense we have come to our nation's Capital to cash a check. When the architects of our republic wrote the magnificent words of the Constitution and the Declaration of Independence, they were signing a promissory note to which every

American was to fall heir. This note was a promise that all men would be guaranteed the unalienable rights of life, liberty, and the pursuit of happiness.

It is obvious today that America has defaulted on this promissory note insofar as her citizens of color are concerned. Instead of honoring this sacred obligation, America has given the Negro people a bad check; a check which has come back marked "insufficient funds." But we refuse to believe that the bank of justice is bankrupt. We refuse to believe that there are insufficient funds in the great vaults of opportunity of this nation. So we have come to cash this check—a check that will give us upon demand the riches of freedom and the security of justice. We have also come to this hallowed spot to remind America of the fierce urgency of *now*. This is no time to engage in the luxury of cooling off or to take the tranquilizing drug of gradualism. *Now* is the time to make real the promises of Democracy. *Now* is the time to rise from the dark and desolate valley of segregation to the sunlit path of racial justice. *Now* is the time to open the doors of opportunity to all of God's children. *Now* is the time to lift our nation from the quicksands of racial injustice to the solid rock of brotherhood.

It would be fatal for the nation to overlook the urgency of the moment and to underestimate the determination of the Negro. This sweltering summer of the Negro's legitimate discontent will not pass until there is an invigorating autumn of freedom and equality. 1963 is not an end, but a beginning. Those who hope that the Negro needed to blow off steam and will now be content will have a rude awakening if the Nation returns to business as usual. There will be neither rest nor tranquility in America until the Negro is granted his citizenship rights. The whirlwinds of revolt will continue to shake the foundations of our Nation until the bright day of justice emerges.

But there is something that I must say to my people who stand on the warm threshold which leads into the palace of justice. In the process of gaining our rightful place we must not be guilty of wrongful deeds. Let us not seek to satisfy our thirst for freedom by drinking from the cup of bitterness and hatred. We must forever conduct our struggle on the high plane of dignity and discipline. We must not allow our creative protest to degenerate into physical violence. Again and again we must rise to the majestic heights of meeting physical force with soul force. The marvellous

new militancy which has engulfed the Negro community must not lead us to a distrust of all white people, for many of our white brothers, as evidenced by their presence here today, have come to realize that their destiny is tied up with our destiny and their freedom is inextricably bound to our freedom. We cannot walk alone.

And as we walk, we must make the pledge that we shall march ahead. We cannot turn back. There are those who are asking the devotees of civil rights, "When will you be satisfied?" We can never be satisfied as long as the Negro is the victim of the unspeakable horrors of police brutality. We can never be satisfied as long as our bodies, heavy with the fatigue of travel, cannot gain lodging in the motels of the highways and the hotels of the cities. We cannot be satisfied as long as the Negro's basic mobility is from a smaller ghetto to a larger one. We can never be satisfied as long as a Negro in Mississippi cannot vote and a Negro in New York believes he has nothing for which to vote. No, no we are not satisfied, and we will not be satisfied until justice rolls down like waters and righteousness like a mighty stream.

I am not unmindful that some of you have come here out of great trials and tribulations. Some of you have come fresh from narrow jail cells. Some of you have come from areas where your quest for freedom left you battered by the storm of persecution and staggered by the winds of police brutality. You have been the veterans of creative suffering. Continue to work with the faith that unearned suffering is redemptive.

Go back to Mississippi, go back to Alabama, go back to South Carolina, go back to Georgia, go back to Louisiana, go back to the slums and ghettos of our modern cities, knowing that somehow this situation can and will be changed. Let us not wallow in the valley of despair.

I say to you today, my friends, that in spite of the difficulties and frustrations of the moment I still have a dream. It is a dream deeply rooted in the American dream.

I have a dream that one day this nation will rise up and live out the true meaning of its creed: "We hold these truths to be self-evident; that all men are created equal."

I have a dream that one day on the red hills of Georgia the sons of former slaves and the sons of former slaveowners will be able to sit down together at the table of brotherhood.

I have a dream that one day even the state of Mississippi, a desert state sweltering with the heat of injustice and oppression, will be transformed into an oasis of freedom and justice.

I have a dream that my four little children will one day live in a nation where they will not be judged by the color of their skin but by the content of their character.

I have a dream today.

I have a dream that one day the state of Alabama, whose governor's lips are presently dripping with the words of interposition and nullification, will be transformed into a situation where little black boys and black girls will be able to join hands with little white boys and white girls and walk together as sisters and brothers.

I have a dream today.

I have a dream that one day every valley shall be exalted, every hill and mountain shall be made low, the rough places will be made plains, and the crooked places will be made straight, and the glory of the Lord shall be revealed, and all flesh shall see it together.

This is our hope. This is the faith with which I return to the South. With this faith we will be able to hew out of the mountain of despair a stone of hope. With this faith we will be able to transform the jangling discords of our nation into a beautiful symphony of brotherhood. With this faith we will be able to work together, to pray together, to struggle together, to go to jail together, to stand up for freedom together, knowing that we will be free one day.

This will be the day when all of God's children will be able to sing with new meaning "My country 'tis of thee, sweet land of liberty, of thee I sing. Land where my fathers died, land of the pilgrim's pride, from every mountainside, let freedom ring."

And if America is to be a great nation this must become true. So let freedom ring from the prodigious hilltops of New Hampshire. Let freedom ring from the mighty mountains of New York. Let freedom ring from the heightening Alleghenies of Pennsylvania!

Let freedom ring from the snowcapped Rockies of Colorado!

Let freedom ring from the curvacious peaks of California!

But not only that; let freedom ring from Stone Mountain of Georgia!

Let freedom ring from Lookout Mountain of Tennessee!

Let freedom ring from every hill and mole hill of Mississippi. From every mountainside, let freedom ring.

When we let freedom ring, when we let it ring from every village and every hamlet, from every state and every city, we will be able to speed up that day when all of God's children, black men and white men, Jews and Gentiles, Protestants and Catholics, will be able to join hands and sing in the words of the old Negro spiritual, "Free at last! free at last! thank God almighty, we are free at last!"

Malcolm X (1925–1965)

Black America has honored few men in death with the intensity and emotional fervor with which it has honored Malcom X. The poets have praised him, and his memory has become almost a legend. To Sonia Sanchez "He was the sun that tagged / the western sky and / melted tiger scholars." To Gwendolyn Brooks he was full of a "sorcery devout and vertical" that "beguiled the world." To Margaret Walker he was a "Snow-white moslem head dress around a dead black face"—one whose "sand-papering words" were beautiful "against our skins." And to Etheridge Knight he was "the Sun" who came "After all the night years . . . spitting fire from his lips."

The man who became Malcolm X was born Malcolm Little in Omaha, Nebraska. His youth was filled with poverty and deprivation, illness and despair. After his father was killed under mysterious circumstances and his mother was committed to an institution for mental illness, young Malcolm, in an almost predictable sequence of events, turned to a life of crime. In 1946, aged twenty-one, he was imprisoned in the Charlestown State Prison in Massachusetts, and here his life was changed. He was converted to Black Muslimism, and when he was released from prison in 1952, he quickly captured the attention of masses of Blacks with his virulent pro-Black racism and his eloquent advocacy of racial separatism. So dynamic was his presentation of the theories of Black Muslimism that he rose to become a top man in the organization, second only to the organization's leader, Elijah Muhammad.

But Malcolm X was not only a "speaking" man; he was a thoughtful and perceptive man who could fully understand the need to review and re-evaluate and modify old programs and commitments, and he had the courage to change. As a consequence, Malcolm X moved away from the Black Muslim organization in 1964, away from its virulent Black separatism, to a philosophy stressing a broader humanism and to a point of view less determined by America's racial rigidities. Within less than a year, he was dead, assassinated in a decade riddled by assassinations.

Fortunately, he had recorded some of his story, and *The Autobiography of Malcom X* (1965), written with the assistance of Alex Haley, was published posthumously to become one of the most popular books of the decade. In addition, several of his speeches have been collected and published in the following volumes: *Malcolm X Speaks* (1965), edited by George Breitman; *The Speeches of Malcolm X at Harvard* (1968), edited by Archie Epps; and *By Any Means Necessary* (1970), edited by George Breitman. The most important assessments of this charismatic racial spokesman are George Breitman, *The Last Year of Malcom X* (1967) and *Malcolm X: The Man and His Ideas* (1970); Albert Cleage, *Myths About Malcolm X* (1968); and *Malcolm X: The Man and His Times* (1969), edited by John Henrik Clarke. Malcolm X has also been memorialized with fine poetic tributes in a volume entitled *For Malcolm* (1967), edited by Dudley Randall and Margaret Burroughs. Carol Ohmann's "*The Autobiography of Malcolm X: A* Revolutionary Use of the Franklin Tradition," *American Quarterly*, XXII (1970), 131–149, is an important essay.

from *The Autobiography of Malcolm X*

Nightmare

When my mother was pregnant with me, she told me later, a party of hooded Ku Klux Klan riders galloped up to our home in Omaha, Nebraska, one night. Surrounding the house, brandishing their shotguns and rifles, they shouted for my father to come out. My mother went to the front door and opened it. Standing where they could see her pregnant condition, she told them that she was alone with her three small children, and that my father was away, preaching, in Milwaukee. The Klansmen shouted threats and warnings at her that we had better get out of town because "the good Christian white people" were not going to stand for my father's "spreading trouble" among the "good" Negroes of Omaha with the "back to Africa" preachings of Marcus Garvey.

My father, the Reverend Earl Little, was a Baptist minister, a dedicated organizer for Marcus Aurelius Garvey's U.N.I.A. (Universal Negro Improvement Association). With the help of such disciples as my father, Garvey, from his headquarters in New York City's Harlem, was raising the banner of black-race purity and exhorting the Negro masses to return to their ancestral African homeland—a cause which had made Garvey the most controversial black man on earth.

Still shouting threats, the Klansmen finally spurred their horses and galloped around the house, shattering every window pane with their gun butts. Then they rode off into the night, their torches flaring, as suddenly as they had come.

My father was enraged when he returned. He decided to wait until I was born—which would be soon—and then the family would move. I am not sure why he made this decision, for he was not a frightened Negro, as most then were, and many still are today. My father was a big, six-foot-four, very black man. He had only one eye. How he had lost the other one I have never known. He was from Reynolds, Georgia, where he had left school after the third or maybe fourth grade. He believed, as did Marcus Garvey, that freedom, independence and self-respect could never be achieved by the Negro in America, and that therefore the Negro should leave America to the white man and return to his African land of origin. Among the reasons my father had decided to risk and dedicate his life to help disseminate this philosophy among his people was that he had seen four of his six brothers die by violence, three of them killed by white men, including one by lynching. What my father could not know then was that of the remaining three, including himself, only one, my Uncle Jim, would die in bed, of natural causes. Northern white police were later to shoot my Uncle Oscar. And my father was finally himself to die by the white man's hands.

It has always been my belief that I, too, will die by violence. I have done all that I can to be prepared. . . .

One afternoon in 1931 when Wilfred, Hilda, Philbert, and I came home, my mother and father were having one of their arguments. There had lately been a lot of tension around the house because of Black Legion threats. Anyway, my father had taken one of the rabbits which we were raising, and ordered my mother to cook it. We raised rabbits, but sold them to whites. My father had taken a rabbit from the rabbit pen. He had pulled off the rabbit's head. He was so strong, he needed no knife to behead chickens or rabbits. With one twist of his big black hands he simply twisted off the head and threw the bleeding-necked thing back at my mother's feet.

My mother was crying. She started to skin the rabbit, preparatory to cooking it. But my father was so angry he slammed on out of the front door and started walking up the road toward town.

It was then that my mother had this vision. She had always been a strange woman in this sense, and had always had a strong intuition of things about to happen. And most of her children are the same way, I think. When something is about to happen, I can feel something, sense something. I never have known something to happen that has caught me completely off guard—except once. And that was when, years later, I discovered facts I couldn't believe about a man who, up until that discovery, I would gladly have given my life for.

My father was well up the road when my mother ran screaming out onto the porch. "*Early! Early!*" She screamed his name. She clutched up her apron in one hand, and ran down across the yard and into the road. My father turned around. He saw her. For some reason, considering how angry he had been when he left, he waved at her. But he kept on going.

She told me later, my mother did, that she had a vision of my father's end. All the rest of the afternoon, she was not herself, crying and nervous and upset. She finished cooking the rabbit and put the whole thing in the warmer part of the black stove. When my father was not back home by our bedtime, my mother hugged and clutched us, and we felt strange, not knowing what to do, because she had never acted like that.

I remember waking up to the sound of my mother's screaming again. When I scrambled out, I saw the police in the living room; they were trying to calm her down. She had snatched on her clothes to go with them. And all of us children who were staring knew without anyone having to say it that something terrible had happened to our father.

My mother was taken by the police to the hospital, and to a room where a sheet was over my father in a bed, and she wouldn't look, she was afraid to look. Probably it was wise that she didn't. My father's skull, on one side, was crushed in, I was told later. Negroes in Lansing have always whispered that he was attacked, and then laid across some tracks for a streetcar to run over him. His body was cut almost in half.

He lived two and a half hours in that condition. Negroes then were stronger than they are now, especially Georgia Negroes. Negroes born in Georgia had to be strong simply to survive.

It was morning when we children at home got the word that he was dead. I was six, I can remember a vague commotion, the house filled up with people crying, saying bitterly that the white Black Legion had finally gotten him. My mother was hysterical. In the bedroom, women were holding smelling salts under her nose. She was still hysterical at the funeral.

I don't have a very clear memory of the funeral, either. Oddly, the main thing I remember is that it wasn't in a church, and that surprised me, since my father was a preacher, and I had been where he preached people's funerals in churches. But his was in a funeral home.

And I remember that during the service a big black fly came down and landed on my father's face, and Wilfred sprang up from his chair and he shooed the fly away, and he came groping back to his chair—there were folding chairs for us to sit on—and the tears were streaming down his face. When we went by the casket, I remember that I thought that it looked as if my father's strong black face had been dusted with flour, and I wished they hadn't put on such a lot of it.

Back in the big four-room house, there were many visitors for another week or so. They were good friends of the family, such as the Lyons from Mason, twelve miles away, and the Walkers, McGuires, Liscoes, the Greens, Randolphs, and the Turners, and others from Lansing, and a lot of people from other towns, whom I had seen at the Garvey meetings.

We children adjusted more easily than our mother did. We couldn't see, as clearly as she did, the trials that lay ahead. As the visitors tapered off, she became very concerned about collecting the two insurance policies that my father had always been proud he carried. He had always said that families should be protected in case of death. One policy apparently paid off without any problem—the smaller one. I don't know the amount of it. I would imagine it was not more than a thousand dollars, and maybe half of that.

But after that money came, and my mother had paid out a lot of it for the funeral and expenses, she began going into town and returning very upset. The company that had issued the bigger

policy was balking at paying off. They were claiming that my father had committed suicide. Visitors came again, and there was bitter talk about white people: how could my father bash himself in the head, then get down across the streetcar tracks to be run over?

So there we were. My mother was thirty-four years old now, with no husband, no provider or protector to take care of her eight children. But some kind of a family routine got going again. And for as long as the first insurance money lasted, we did all right.

Wilfred, who was a pretty stable fellow, began to act older than his age. I think he had the sense to see, when the rest of us didn't, what was in the wind for us. He quietly quit school and went to town in search of work. He took any kind of job he could find and he would come home, dog-tired, in the evenings, and give whatever he had made to my mother.

Hilda, who always had been quiet, too, attended to the babies. Philbert and I didn't contribute anything. We just fought all the time—each other at home, and then at school we would team up and fight white kids. Sometimes the fights would be racial in nature, but they might be about anything.

Reginald came under my wing. Since he had grown out of the toddling stage, he and I had become very close. I suppose I enjoyed the fact that he was the little one, under me, who looked up to me.

My mother began to buy on credit. My father had always been very strongly against credit. "Credit is the first step into debt and back into slavery," he had always said. And then she went to work herself. She would go into Lansing and find different jobs—in housework, or sewing—for white people. They didn't realize, usually, that she was a Negro. A lot of white people around there didn't want Negroes in their houses.

She would do fine until in some way or other it got to people who she was, whose widow she was. And then she would be let go. I remember how she used to come home crying, but trying to hide it, because she had lost a job that she needed so much.

Once when one of us—I cannot remember which—had to go for something to where she was working, and the people saw us, and realized she was actually a Negro, she was fired on the spot, and she came home crying, this time not hiding it.

When the state Welfare people began coming to

our house, we would come from school sometimes and find them talking with our mother, asking a thousand questions. They acted and looked at her, and at us, and around in our house, in a way that had about it the feeling—at least for me—that we were not people. In their eyesight we were just *things,* that was all.

My mother began to receive two checks—a Welfare check and, I believe, a widow's pension. The checks helped. But they weren't enough, as many of us as there were. When they came, about the first of the month, one always was already owed in full, if not more, to the man at the grocery store. And, after that, the other one didn't last long.

We began to go swiftly downhill. The physical downhill wasn't as quick as the psychological. My mother was, above everything else, a proud woman, and it took its toll on her that she was accepting charity. And her feelings were communicated to us.

She would speak sharply to the man at the grocery store for padding the bill, telling him that she wasn't ignorant, and he didn't like that. She would talk back sharply to the state Welfare people, telling them that she was a grown woman, able to raise her children, that it wasn't necessary for them to keep coming around so much, meddling in our lives. And they didn't like that.

But the monthly Welfare check was their pass. They acted as if they owned us, as if we were their private property. As much as my mother would have liked to, she couldn't keep them out. She would get particularly incensed when they began insisting upon drawing us older children aside, one at a time, out on the porch or somewhere, and asking us questions, or telling us things—against our mother and against each other.

We couldn't understand why, if the state was willing to give us packages of meat, sacks of potatoes and fruit, and cans of all kinds of things, our mother obviously hated to accept. We really couldn't understand. What I later understood was that my mother was making a desperate effort to preserve her pride—and ours.

Pride was just about all we had to preserve, for by 1934, we really began to suffer. This was about the worst depression year, and no one we knew had enough to eat or live on. Some old family friends visited us now and then. At first they brought food. Though it was charity, my mother took it.

Wilfred was working to help. My mother was working, when she could find any kind of job. In Lansing, there was a bakery where, for a nickel, a couple of us children would buy a tall flour sack of day-old bread and cookies, and then walk the two miles back out into the country to our house. Our mother knew, I guess, dozens of ways to cook things with bread and out of bread. Stewed tomatoes with bread, maybe that would be a meal. Something like French toast, if we had any eggs. Bread pudding, sometimes with raisins in it. If we got hold of some hamburger, it came to the table more bread than meat. The cookies that were always in the sack with the bread, we just gobbled down straight.

But there were times when there wasn't even a nickel and we would be so hungry we were dizzy. My mother would boil a big pot of dandelion greens, and we would eat that. I remember that some small-minded neighbor put it out, and children would tease us, that we ate "fried grass." Sometimes, if we were lucky, we would have oatmeal or cornmeal mush three times a day. Or mush in the morning and cornbread at night.

Philbert and I were grown up enough to quit fighting long enough to take the .22 caliber rifle that had been our father's, and shoot rabbits that some white neighbors up or down the road would buy. I know now that they just did it to help us, because they, like everyone, shot their own rabbits. Sometimes, I remember, Philbert and I would take little Reginald along with us. He wasn't very strong, but he was always so proud to be along. We would trap muskrats out in the little creek in back of our house. And we would lie quiet until unsuspecting bullfrogs appeared, and we could spear them, cut off their legs, and sell them for a nickel a pair to people who lived up and down the road. The whites seemed less restricted in their dietary tastes.

Then, about in late 1934, I would guess, something began to happen. Some kind of psychological deterioration hit our family circle and began to eat away our pride. Perhaps it was the constant tangible evidence that we were destitute. We had known other families who had gone on relief. We had known without anyone in our home ever expressing it that we had felt prouder not to be at the depot where the free food was passed out. And, now, we were among them. At school, the "on relief" finger suddenly was pointed at us, too, and sometimes it was said aloud.

It seemed that everything to eat in our house was stamped Not To Be Sold. All Welfare food bore this stamp to keep the recipients from selling it. It's a wonder we didn't come to think of Not To Be Sold as a brand name.

Sometimes, instead of going home from school, I walked the two miles up the road into Lansing. I began drifting from store to store, hanging around outside where things like apples were displayed in boxes and barrels and baskets, and I would watch my chance and steal me a treat. You know what a treat was to me? Anything!

Or I began to drop in about dinnertime at the home of some family that we knew. I knew that they knew exactly why I was there, but they never embarrassed me by letting on. They would invite me to stay for supper, and I would stuff myself.

Especially, I liked to drop in and visit at the Gohannas' home. They were nice, older people, and great churchgoers. I had watched them lead the jumping and shouting when my father preached. They had, living with them—they were raising him—a nephew whom everyone called "Big Boy," and he and I got along fine. Also living with the Gohannas was old Mrs. Adcock, who went with them to church. She was always trying to help anybody she could, visiting anyone she heard was sick, carrying them something. She was the one who, years later, would tell me something that I remembered a long time: "Malcolm, there's one thing I like about you. You're no good, but you don't try to hide it. You are not a hypocrite."

The more I began to stay away from home and visit people and steal from the stores, the more aggressive I became in my inclinations. I never wanted to wait for anything.

I was growing up fast, physically more so than mentally. As I began to be recognized more around the town, I started to become aware of the peculiar attitude of white people toward me. I sensed that it had to do with my father. It was an adult version of what several white children had said at school, in hints, or sometimes in the open, which really expressed what their parents had said —that the Black Legion or the Klan had killed my father, and the insurance company had pulled a fast one in refusing to pay my mother the policy money.

When I began to get caught stealing now and then, the state Welfare people began to focus on me when they came to our house. I can't remember how I first became aware that they were talking of taking me away. What I first remember along that line was my mother raising a storm about being able to bring up her own children. She would whip me for stealing, and I would try to alarm the neighborhood with my yelling. One thing I have always been proud of is that I never raised my hand against my mother.

In the summertime, at night, in addition to all the other things we did, some of us boys would slip out down the road, or across the pastures, and go "cooning" watermelons. White people always associated watermelons with Negroes, and they sometimes called Negroes "coons" among all the other names, and so stealing watermelons became "cooning" them. If white boys were doing it, it implied that they were only acting like Negroes. Whites have always hidden or justified all of the guilts they could by ridiculing or blaming Negroes.

One Halloween night, I remember that a bunch of us were out tipping over those old country outhouses, and one old farmer—I guess he had tipped over enough in his day—had set a trap for us. Always, you sneak up from behind the outhouse, then you gang together and push it, to tip it over. This farmer had taken his outhouse off the hole, and set it just in *front* of the hole. Well, we came sneaking up in single file, in the darkness, and the two white boys in the lead fell down into the outhouse hole neck deep. They smelled so bad it was all we could stand to get them out, and that finished us all for that Halloween. I had just missed falling in myself. The whites were so used to taking the lead, this time it had really gotten them in the hole.

Thus, in various ways, I learned various things. I picked strawberries, and though I can't recall what I got per crate for picking, I remember that after working hard all one day, I wound up with about a dollar, which was a whole lot of money in those times. I was so hungry, I didn't know what to do. I was walking away toward town with visions of buying something good to eat, and this older white boy I knew, Richard Dixon, came up and asked me if I wanted to match nickels. He had plenty of change for my dollar. In about a half hour, he had all the change back, including my dollar, and instead of going to town to buy something, I went home with nothing, and I was bitter. But that was nothing compared to what I felt when I found out later that he had cheated. There is a way that you can catch and hold the nickel and make it come up the way you want.

This was my first lesson about gambling: if you see somebody winning all the time, he isn't gambling, he's cheating. Later on in life, if I were continuously losing in any gambling situation, I would watch very closely. It's like the Negro in America seeing the white man win all the time. He's a professional gambler; he has all the cards and the odds stacked on his side, and he has always dealt to our people from the bottom of the deck.

About this time, my mother began to be visited by some Seventh Day Adventists who had moved into a house not too far down the road from us. They would talk to her for hours at a time, and leave booklets and leaflets and magazines for her to read. She read them, and Wilfred, who had started back to school after we had begun to get the relief food supplies, also read a lot. His head was forever in some book.

Before long, my mother spent much time with the Adventists. It's my belief that what influenced her was that they had even more diet restrictions than she always had taught and practiced with us. Like us, they were against eating rabbit and pork; they followed the Mosaic dietary laws. They ate nothing of the flesh without a split hoof, or that didn't chew a cud. We began to go with my mother to the Adventist meetings that were held further out in the country. For us children, I know that the major attraction was the good food they served. But we listened, too. There were a handful of Negroes, from small towns in the area, but I would say that it was ninety-nine percent white people. The Adventists felt that we were living at the end of time, that the world soon was coming to an end. But they were the friendliest white people I had ever seen. In some ways, though, we children noticed, and, when we were back at home, discussed, that they were different from us—such as the lack of enough seasoning in their food, and the different way that white people smelled.

Meanwhile, the state Welfare people kept after my mother. By now, she didn't make it any secret that she hated them, and didn't want them in her house. But they exerted their right to come, and I have many, many times reflected upon how, talking to us children, they began to plant the seeds of division in our minds. They would ask such things as who was smarter than the other. And they would ask me why I was "so different."

I think they felt that getting children into foster homes was a legitimate part of their function, and the result would be less troublesome, however they went about it.

And when my mother fought them, they went after her—first, through me. I was the first target. I stole; that implied that I wasn't being taken care of by my mother.

All of us were mischievous at some time or another, I more so than any of the rest. Philbert and I kept a battle going. And this was just one of a dozen things that kept building up the pressure on my mother.

I'm not sure just how or when the idea was first dropped by the Welfare workers that our mother was losing her mind.

But I can distinctly remember hearing "crazy" applied to her by them when they learned that the Negro farmer who was in the next house down the road from us had offered to give us some butchered pork—a whole pig, maybe even two of them—and she had refused. We all heard them call my mother "crazy" to her face for refusing good meat. It meant nothing to them even when she explained that we had never eaten pork, that it was against her religion as a Seventh Day Adventist.

They were as vicious as vultures. They had no feelings, understanding, compassion, or respect for my mother. They told us, "She's crazy for refusing food." Right then was when our home, our unity, began to disintegrate. We were having a hard time, and I wasn't helping. But we could have made it, we could have stayed together. As bad as I was, as much trouble and worry as I caused my mother, I loved her.

The state people, we found out, had interviewed the Gohannas family, and the Gohannas' had said that they would take me into their home. My mother threw a fit, though, when she heard that—and the home wreckers took cover for a while.

It was about this time that the large, dark man from Lansing began visiting. I don't remember how or where he and my mother met. It may have been through some mutual friends. I don't remember what the man's profession was. In 1935, in Lansing, Negroes didn't have anything you could call a profession. But the man, big and black, looked something like my father. I can remember his name, but there's no need to mention it. He was a single man, and my mother was a widow only thirty-six years old. The man was independent; naturally she admired that. She was having a hard time disciplining us, and a big man's presence alone would help. And if she had a man to provide, it would send the state people away forever.

We all understood without ever saying much about it. Or at least we had no objection. We took it in stride, even with some amusement among us, that when the man came, our mother would be all dressed up in the best that she had— she still was a good-looking woman—and she would act differently, lighthearted and laughing, as we hadn't seen her act in years.

It went on for about a year, I guess. And then, about 1936, or 1937, the man from Lansing jilted my mother suddenly. He just stopped coming to see her. From what I later understood, he finally backed away from taking on the responsibility of those eight mouths to feed. He was afraid of so many of us. To this day, I can see the trap that Mother was in, saddled with all of us. And I can also understand why he would shun taking on such a tremendous responsibility.

But it was a terrible shock to her. It was the beginning of the end of reality for my mother. When she began to sit around and walk around talking to herself—almost as though she was unaware that we were there—it became increasingly terrifying.

The state people saw her weakening. That was when they began the definite steps to take me away from home. They began to tell me how nice it was going to be at the Gohannas' home, where the Gohannas' and Big Boy and Mrs. Adcock had all said how much they liked me, and would like to have me live with them.

I liked all of them, too. But I didn't want to leave Wilfred. I looked up to and admired my big brother. I didn't want to leave Hilda, who was like my second mother. Or Philbert; even in our fighting, there was a feeling of brotherly union. Or Reginald, especially, who was weak with his hernia condition, and who looked up to me as his big brother who looked out for him, as I looked up to Wilfred. And I had nothing, either, against the babies, Yvonne, Wesley, and Robert.

As my mother talked to herself more and more, she gradually became less responsive to us. And less responsible. The house became less tidy. We began to be more unkempt. And usually, now, Hilda cooked.

We children watched our anchor giving way. It was something terrible that you couldn't get your hands on, yet you couldn't get away from. It was a sensing that something bad was going to happen. We younger ones leaned more and more heavily on the relative strength of Wilfred and Hilda, who were the oldest.

When finally I was sent to the Gohannas' home, at least in a surface way I was glad. I remember that when I left home with the state man, my mother said one thing: "Don't let them feed him any pig."

It was better, in a lot of ways, at the Gohannas'. Big Boy and I shared his room together, and we hit it off nicely. He just wasn't the same as my blood brothers. The Gohannas' were very religious people. Big Boy and I attended church with them. They were sanctified Holy Rollers now. The preachers and congregations jumped even higher and shouted even louder than the Baptists I had known. They sang at the top of their lungs, and swayed back and forth and cried and moaned and beat on tambourines and chanted. It was spooky, with ghosts and spirituals and "ha'nts" seeming to be in the very atmosphere when finally we all came out of the church, going back home.

The Gohannas' and Mrs. Adcock loved to go fishing, and some Saturdays Big Boy and I would go along. I had changed schools now, to Lansing's West Junior High School. It was right in the heart of the Negro community, and a few white kids were there, but Big Boy didn't mix much with any of our schoolmates, and I didn't either. And when we went fishing, neither he nor I liked the idea of just sitting and waiting for the fish to jerk the cork under the water—or make the tight line quiver, when we fished that way. I figured there should be some smarter way to get the fish—though we never discovered what it might be.

Mr. Gohannas was close cronies with some other men who, some Saturdays, would take me and Big Boy with them hunting rabbits. I had my father's .22 caliber rifle; my mother had said it was all right for me to take it with me. The old men had a set rabbit-hunting strategy that they had always used. Usually when a dog jumps a rabbit, and the rabbit gets away, that rabbit will always somehow instinctively run in a circle and return sooner or later past the very spot where he originally was jumped. Well, the old men would just sit and wait in hiding somewhere for the rabbit to come back, then get their shots at him. I got to thinking about it, and finally I thought of a plan. I would separate from them and Big Boy and I would go to a point where I figured that the rabbit, returning, would have to pass me first.

It worked like magic. I began to get three and four rabbits before they got one. The astonishing thing was that none of the old men ever figured out why. They outdid themselves exclaiming what a sure shot I was. I was about twelve, then. All I had done was to improve on their strategy, and it was the beginning of a very important lesson in life—that anytime you find someone more successful than you are, especially when you're both engaged in the same business—you know they're doing something that you aren't.

I would return home to visit fairly often. Sometimes Big Boy and one or another, or both, of the Gohannas' would go with me—sometimes not. I would be glad when some of them did go, because it made the ordeal easier.

Soon the state people were making plans to take over all of my mother's children. She talked to herself nearly all of the time now, and there was a crowd of new white people entering the picture—always asking questions. They would even visit me at the Gohannas'. They would ask me questions out on the porch, or sitting out in their cars.

Eventually my mother suffered a complete breakdown, and the court orders were finally signed. They took her to the State Mental Hospital at Kalamazoo.

It was seventy-some miles from Lansing, about an hour and a half on the bus. A Judge McClellan in Lansing had authority over me and all of my brothers and sisters. We were "state children," court wards; he had the full say-so over us. A white man in charge of a black man's children! Nothing but legal, modern slavery—however kindly intentioned.

My mother remained in the same hospital at Kalamazoo for about twenty-six years. Later, when I was still growing up in Michigan, I would go to visit her every so often. Nothing that I can imagine could have moved me as deeply as seeing her pitiful state. In 1963, we got my mother out of the hospital, and she now lives there in Lansing with Philbert and his family.

It was so much worse than if it had been a physical sickness, for which a cause might be known, medicine given, a cure effected. Every time I visited her, when finally they led her—a case, a number—back inside from where we had been sitting together, I felt worse.

My last visit, when I knew I would never come to see her again—there—was in 1952. I was twenty-seven. My brother Philbert had told me

that on his last visit, she had recognized him somewhat. "In spots," he said.

But she didn't recognize me at all.

She stared at me. She didn't know who I was.

Her mind, when I tried to talk, to reach her, was somewhere else. I asked, "Mama, do you know what day it is?"

She said, staring, "All the people have gone."

I can't describe how I felt. The woman who had brought me into the world, and nursed me, and advised me, and chastised me, and loved me, didn't know me. It was as if I was trying to walk up the side of a hill of feathers. I looked at her. I listened to her "talk." But there was nothing I could do.

I truly believe that if ever a state social agency destroyed a family, it destroyed ours. We wanted and tried to stay together. Our home didn't have to be destroyed. But the Welfare, the courts, and their doctor, gave us the one-two-three punch. And ours was not the only case of this kind.

I knew I wouldn't be back to see my mother again because it could make me a very vicious and dangerous person—knowing how they had looked at us as numbers and as a case in their book, not as human beings. And knowing that my mother in there was a statistic that didn't have to be, that existed because of a society's failure, hypocrisy, greed, and lack of mercy and compassion. Hence I have no mercy or compassion in me for a society that will crush people, and then penalize them for not being able to stand up under the weight.

I have rarely talked to anyone about my mother, for I believe that I am capable of killing a person, without hesitation, who happened to make the wrong kind of remark about my mother. So I purposely don't make any opening for some fool to step into.

Back then when our family was destroyed, in 1937, Wilfred and Hilda were old enough so that the state let them stay on their own in the big four-room house that my father had built. Philbert was placed with another family in Lansing, a Mrs. Hackett, while Reginald and Wesley went to live with a family called Williams, who were friends of my mother's. And Yvonne and Robert went to live with a West Indian family named McGuire.

Separated though we were, all of us maintained fairly close touch around Lansing—in school and out—whenever we could get together. Despite the artificially created separation and distance between us, we still remained very close in our feelings toward each other.

Eldridge Cleaver (1935–   )

Among the most formidable of the new American revolutionaries, Leroy Eldridge Cleaver was born on August 31, 1935, in Wabbaseka, Arkansas, a small town near Little Rock. His father worked at night waiting tables and playing the piano at a nightclub in Little Rock. His mother taught in a Black primary school. In the early 1940's the family moved to Phoenix, Arizona, and then two years later on to Los Angeles, where the father left the family and young Eldridge first began to have troubles with the law.

Commitment to Juvenile Hall for six months in 1947 introduced Cleaver to marijuana. After two more terms in reformatories, he was sentenced in 1954 to Soledad Prison for two and a half years for possession of "a shopping bag full of love," as he calls it in *Soul on Ice.* For almost two decades (1947–1966) he spent most of his time in reformatories and prisons on convictions for theft, possession of narcotics, rape, and assault with intent to commit murder. Here he developed a nihilistic world view; here also he turned to writing as a means of psychological self-therapy. In prison, too, he became obsessed with white women, suffered a nervous breakdown, came under the influence of a prison teacher and mystic at San Quentin, converted to the Nation of Islam but then followed Malcolm X away from Elijah Muhammad, and fell in love with his white radical lawyer Beverly Axelrod. Prison was Cleaver's world during his teens, twenties, and into his thirties, a fact that has deeply influenced his subsequent development.

As Cleaver learned to write in prison, he began to smuggle his essays out to magazines, pretending they were legal papers. In March 1962 *Negro History Bulletin* published "As Crinkly as Yours," a strong expression of Afro-American pride and self-acceptance, especially in relation to Africa. Four years later his essay on James Baldwin appeared in *Ramparts,* for which he became a staff writer early in 1967. His subsequent positions on this magazine have been assistant editor, senior editor, and, currently, international editor. Early in 1968 Cleaver published *Soul on Ice,* a collection of some of his essays and letters from prison and afterward. Altogether one of the most remarkable books of the decade, it ranges from the most intimate self-revelation to probing examinations of racial, national, and international issues: the relation of Black suppression at home to imperialistic oppression abroad, the polarization of American politics, the psychosexual consequences of racism, the failure of the penal system, boxing as symbolic cultural ritual. *Soul on Ice* reveals a brilliantly incisive mind, a literary and mythic imagination of a very high order, and a supremely lucid, firm, yet resourceful style, all brought to bear on problems of national survival as well as personal identity.

But the pressure of events has made Eldridge Cleaver as much an active revolutionary as a writer. Released on parole from Soledad Prison in December 1966, after serving nine years of a fourteen-year sentence, he chose San Francisco for his rehabilitation, wishing to avoid Los Angeles, the scene of his former criminal activity. With the playwright Ed Bullins, the poet Marvin Jackmon, and Willie Dale, he founded the Black House, a cultural center, in San Francisco, and at about the same time he became chairman of the Malcolm X Afro-American Society. Far more crucial was his encounter with the Black Panther Party in February 1967. Led by Huey P. Newton and Bobby Seale, this Oakland group was not only teaching but acting on the Maoist maxim that political power grows out of the barrel of a gun. Recognizing in Huey P. Newton "the ideological descendant, heir and successor of Malcolm X" and admiring the uncompromising courage of the Panthers, Cleaver affiliated with the party and became its Minister of Information. More than a year of political harassment, intimidation, and violence directed against the Panthers reached its climax on the evening of April 6, 1968, when, according to Cleaver's account, the Oakland police made an unprovoked attack on three carloads of Panthers. In the ensuing shoot-out, Cleaver was wounded and his friend Bobby Hutton was killed.

Only a few hours after these events, the California Adult Authority revoked Cleaver's parole, but this action was reversed and Cleaver was released from custody two months later by Superior Court Justice Raymond J. Sherwin. Sherwin's decision, in turn, was reversed by higher courts, and Cleaver was ordered to return to prison on November 27, 1968. Meanwhile, the University of California at Berkeley had arranged for Cleaver to deliver a series of ten lectures on racism, but Governor Ronald Reagan intervened to prevent him from appearing. During the dispute that followed, Cleaver traveled through the state speaking to far larger audiences than he would have otherwise reached. In the November election he ran for President of the United States as the candidate of the Peace and Freedom Party, which had formed a coalition with the Black Panther Party. As the date of November 27 grew near, he disappeared, refusing to accept the certain murder of his soul and the probable murder of his body that further incarceration would bring.

After traveling incognito to several Communist countries, Cleaver turned up in Havana, but early in June 1969 he moved to Algiers. In Algeria, where representatives of liberation groups throughout the world operate freely with government approval, Cleaver represents the Black Panther Party. Soon, he hopes, he will come home to fight and perhaps die in the violent revolutionary struggle he considers necessary to destroy the present system of "Babylon" and to replace it with a humane, socialist America.

Cleaver's second book is *Post-Prison Writings and Speeches* (1969), edited by Robert Scheer. Much material by and about Cleaver may be found in *The Black Panther,* the party newspaper that he edited for a time, and in *Ramparts* magazine beginning with the issue of June 1966. See also Cleaver's "Fire Now," *Commonweal,* LXXXVIII (June 14, 1968), 375–377;

a short story entitled "The Flashlight," *Playboy,* XVI (December 1969), 120–124, 287–290, 292, 296, 298, 301–302; and "Cleaver Speaks," *The New York Times Magazine,* November 1, 1970, pp. 31, 112.

Cleaver has been interviewed frequently, at greatest length by Lee Lockwood in *Conversation with Eldridge Cleaver—Algiers* (1970). See also "Radicals: Are They Poles Apart?" edited by W. Hedgepeth, *Look,* XXXII (January 7, 1969), 35; "Conversation with Cleaver," edited by H. E. Weinstein, *The Nation,* CCVII (January 20, 1969), 74–77; and "Eldridge Cleaver in Algiers, a Visit with Papa Rage," edited by Gordon Parks, *Life,* LXVIII (February 6, 1970), 20–23. George R. Metcalf includes a biographical sketch of Cleaver in the second edition of *Black Profiles* (1970). For critical commentary see, in addition to reviews of Cleaver's two books, Jervis Anderson, "Race, Rage & Eldridge Cleaver," *Commentary,* XLVI (December 1968), 63–69; Stanley Pacion, "Soul Still on Ice? The Talents and Troubles of Eldridge Cleaver," *Dissent,* XVI (July–August 1969), 310–316; Harvey Swados, "Old Con, Black Panther, Brilliant Writer and Quintessential American," *The New York Times Magazine,* September 7, 1969, pp. 38–39, 139, 142, 144, 147, 149, 151, 154; James Cunningham, "The Case of the Severed Lifeline," *Negro Digest,* XVIII (October 1969), 23–28; and Joyce Nower, "Cleaver's Vision of America and the New White Radical: A Legacy of Malcolm X," *Negro American Literature Forum,* IV (March 1970), 12–21. The story of the Black Panthers is told by Gene Marine in *The Black Panthers* (1969), by Earl Anthony in *Picking up the Gun* (1970), and, authoritatively, by Bobby Seale in *Seize the Time* (1970).

To All Black Women, From All Black Men

Queen–Mother–Daughter of Africa
Sister of My Soul
Black Bride of My Passion
My Eternal Love

I greet you, my Queen, not in the obsequious whine of a cringing Slave to which you have become accustomed, neither do I greet you in the new voice, the unctuous supplications of the sleek Black Bourgeoise, nor the bullying bellow of the rude Free Slave—but in my own voice do I greet you, the voice of the Black Man. And although I greet you *anew,* my greeting is not *new* but as old as the Sun, Moon, and Stars. And rather than mark a new beginning, my greeting signifies only my Return.

I have returned from the dead. I speak to you now from the Here And Now. I was dead for four hundred years. For four hundred years you have been a woman alone, bereft of her man, a manless woman. For four hundred years I was neither your man nor my own man. The white man stood between us, over us, around us. The white man was your man and my man. Do not pass lightly over this truth, my Queen, for even though the fact of it has burned into the marrow of our bones and diluted our blood, we must bring it to the surface of the mind, into the realm of knowing, glue our gaze upon it and stare at it as at a coiled serpent in a baby's playpen or the fresh flowers on a mother's grave. It is to be pondered and realized in the heart, for the heel of the white man's boot is our point of departure, our point of Resolve and Return—the blood-stained pivot of our future. (But I would ask you to recall, that before we could come up from slavery, we had to be pulled down from our throne.)

Across the naked abyss of negated masculinity,

of four hundred years minus my Balls, we face each other today, my Queen. I feel a deep, terrifying hurt, the pain of humiliation of the vanquished warrior. The shame of the fleet-footed sprinter who stumbles at the start of the race. I feel unjustified. I can't bear to look into your eyes. Don't you know (surely you must have noticed by now: four hundred years!) that for four hundred years I have been unable to look squarely into your eyes? I tremble inside each time you look at me. I can feel . . . in the ray of your eye, from a deep hiding place, a long-kept secret you harbor. That is the unadorned truth. Not that I would have felt justified, under the circumstances, in taking such liberties with you, but I want you to know that I feared to look into your eyes because I knew I would find reflected there a merciless Indictment of my impotence and a compelling challenge to redeem my conquered manhood.

My Queen, it is hard for me to tell you what is in my heart for you today—what is in the heart of all my black brothers for you and all your black sisters—and I fear I will fail unless you reach out to me, tune in on me with the antenna of your love, the sacred love in ultimate degree which you were unable to give me because I, being dead, was unworthy to receive it; that perfect, radical love of black on which our Fathers thrived. Let me drink from the river of your love at its source, let the lines of force of your love seize my soul by its core and heal the wound of my Castration, let my convex exile end its haunted Odyssey in your concave essence which receives that it may give. Flower of Africa, it is only through the liberating power of your *re*-love that my manhood can be redeemed. For it is in your eyes, before you, that my need is to be justified. Only, only, only you and only you can condemn or set me free.

Be convinced, Sable Sister, that the past is no forbidden vista upon which we dare not look, out of a phantom fear of being, as the wife of Lot, turned into pillars of salt. Rather the past is an omniscient mirror: we gaze and see reflected there ourselves and each other—what we used to be, what we are today, how we got this way, and what we are becoming. To decline to look into the Mirror of Then, my heart, is to refuse to view the face of Now.

I have died the ninth death of the cat, have seen Satan face to face and turned my back on God, *have dined in the Swine's Trough, and descended to the uttermost echelon of the Pit, have entered the Den and seized my Balls from the teeth of a roaring lion!*

Black Beauty, in impotent silence I listened, as if to a symphony of sorrows, to your screams for help, anguished pleas of terror that echo still throughout the Universe and through the mind, a million scattered screams across the painful years that merged into a single sound of pain to haunt and bleed the soul, a white-hot sound to char the brain and blow the fuse of thought, a sound of fangs and teeth sharp to eat the heart, a sound of moving fire, a sound of frozen heat, a sound of licking flames, a fiery-fiery sound, a sound of fire to burn the steel out of my Balls, a sound of Blue fire, a Bluesy sound, the sound of dying, the sound of my woman in pain, *the sound of my woman's pain,* THE SOUND OF MY WOMAN CALLING ME, ME, I HEARD HER CALL FOR HELP, I HEARD THAT MOURNFUL SOUND BUT HUNG MY HEAD AND FAILED TO HEED IT, I HEARD MY WOMAN'S CRY, I HEARD MY WOMAN'S SCREAM, I HEARD MY WOMAN BEG THE BEAST FOR MERCY, I HEARD HER BEG FOR ME, I HEARD MY WOMAN BEG THE BEAST FOR MERCY FOR ME, I HEARD MY WOMAN DIE, I HEARD THE SOUND OF HER DEATH, A SNAPPING SOUND, A BREAKING SOUND, A SOUND THAT SOUNDED FINAL, THE LAST SOUND, THE ULTIMATE SOUND, THE SOUND OF DEATH, ME, I HEARD, I HEAR IT EVERY DAY, I HEAR HER NOW . . . I HEAR YOU NOW . . . I HEAR YOU. . . . I heard you then . . . your scream came like a searing bolt of lightning that blazed a white streak down my black back. In a cowardly stupor, with a palpitating heart and quivering knees, I watched the Slaver's lash of death slash through the opposing air and bite with teeth of fire into your delicate flesh, the black and tender flesh of African Motherhood, forcing the startled Life untimely from your torn and outraged womb, the sacred womb that cradled primal man, the womb that incubated Ethiopia and populated Nubia and gave forth Pharaohs unto Egypt, the womb that painted the Congo black and mothered Zulu, the womb of Mero, the womb of the Nile, of the Niger, the womb of Songhay, of Mali, of Ghana, the womb that felt the might of Chaka before he saw the Sun, the Holy Womb, the womb that knew the future form of Jomo Kenyatta, the womb of Mau Mau, the womb of the blacks, the womb that nurtured Toussaint L'Ouverture, that warmed Nat Turner, and

Gabriel Prosser, and Denmark Vesey, the black womb that surrendered up in tears that nameless and endless chain of Africa's Cream, the Black Cream of the Earth, that nameless and endless black chain that sank in heavy groans into oblivion in the great abyss, the womb that received and nourished and held firm the seed and gave back Sojourner Truth, and Sister Tubman, and Rosa Parks, and Bird, and Richard Wright, and your other works of art who wore and wear such names as Marcus Garvey and DuBois and Kwame Nkrumah and Paul Robeson and Malcolm X and Robert Williams, and the one you bore in pain and called Elijah Muhammad, but most of all that nameless one they tore out of your womb in a flood of murdered blood that splashed upon and seeped into the mud. And Patrice Lumumba, and Emmett Till, and Mack Parker.

O, My Soul! I became a sniveling craven, a funky punk, a vile, groveling bootlicker, with my will to oppose petrified by a cosmic fear of the Slavemaster. Instead of inciting the Slaves to rebellion with eloquent oratory, I soothed their hurt and eloquently sang the Blues! Instead of hurling my life with contempt into the face of my Tormentor, *I shed your precious blood!* When Nat Turner sought to free me from my Fear, my Fear delivered him up unto the Butcher—a martyred monument to my Emasculation. My spirit was unwilling and my flesh was weak. Ah, eternal ignominy!

I, the Black Eunuch, divested of my Balls, walked the earth with my mind locked in Cold Storage. I would kill a black man or woman quicker than I'd smash a fly, while for the white man I would pick a thousand pounds of cotton a day. What profit is there in the blind, frenzied efforts of the (Guilty!) Black Eunuchs (Justifiers!) who hide their wounds and scorn the truth to mitigate their culpability through the pallid sophistry of postulating a Universal Democracy of Cowards, pointing out that in history no one can hide, that if not at one time then surely at another the iron heel of the Conqueror has ground into the mud the Balls of Everyman? Memories of yesterday will not assuage the torrents of blood that flow today from my crotch. Yes, History could pass for a scarlet text, its jot and tittle graven red in human blood. More armies than shown in the books have planted flags on foreign soil leaving Castration in their wake. But no Slave should die a natural death. There is a point where Caution ends and Cowardice begins. Give me a bullet through the brain from the gun of the beleaguered oppressor on the night of seige. Why is there dancing and singing in the Slave Quarters? A Slave who dies of natural causes cannot balance two dead flies in the Scales of Eternity. Such a one deserves rather to be pitied than mourned.

Black woman, without asking how, just say that we survived our forced march and travail through the Valley of Slavery, Suffering, and Death—there, that Valley there beneath us hidden by that drifting mist. Ah, what sights and sounds and pain lie beneath that mist! And we had thought that our hard climb out of that cruel valley led to some cool, green and peaceful, sunlit place—but it's all jungle here, a wild and savage wilderness that's overrun with ruins.

But put on your crown, my Queen, and we will build a New City on these ruins.

Folk Literature

The Blues

Young Boy Blues

I'm a real young boy, jus sixteen years ol,
I'm a real young boy, jus sixteen years ol,
I need a funky black woman to satisfy my soul.

My father was no jockey
    but he sure taught me how to ride.
I say my father was no jockey
    but he sure taught me how to ride.
He said first in the middle,
    Then you sway from side to side.

Fogyism

Why do people believe in some old sign?
Why do people believe in some old sign?
You hear a hoot owl holler, someone is sholy dyin'.

Some will break a mirror and cry, "Bad luck for seven years,"
Some will break a mirror and cry, "Bad luck for seven years,"
And if a black cat crosses them, they'll break right down in tears.

To dream of muddy water—trouble is knockin at yo do,
To dream of muddy water, trouble is knockin at yo do,
Yo man is sho to leave you an never return no mo.

When yo man comes home evil, tells you you are gettin old,
When yo man comes home evil, tells you you are gettin old,
That's a true sign he's got someone else bakin his jelly roll.

Backdoor Blues

I left my baby standin in the back door cryin',
Yes, I left my baby standin in the back door cryin',
She said, baby, you gotta home jus as long as I got mine.

887

Married Woman Blues

Well, this'll make you laugh
Though it's not funny to me,
Yes, this'll make you laugh
Though it's not funny to me.
I'm in love with a married woman,
She's in love with me.

A Big Fat Mama

I'm a big fat mama, got the meat shakin on mah bones,
I'm a big fat mama, got the meat shakin on mah bones,
And every time I shakes, some skinny girl loses huh home.

Crazy Blues

I can't sleep at night; I can't eat a bite;
Cause the man I love he didn't treat me right.

Now I got the crazy blues since my baby went away;
I ain't got no time to lose; I must find him today.

Monte Carlo Blues

My baby she found a brand new place to go,
My baby she found a brand new place to go,
She hangs across town at the Monte Carlo.

She likes my money, tells me she's goin' to the picture show,
She likes my money, tells me she's goin' to the picture show,
But that gal's been throwin my money away at the Monte Carlo.

How Long Blues

How long, how long, has that evening train bin gone?
How long, how long, baby, how long?

Had a gal lived up on the hill
If she's there, she loves me still
Baby, how long, how long, how long?

Standin at the station, watch my baby go
Feel disgusted, blue, mean an low
How long, how long, baby, how long?

Black Woman

Well, I said come here, Black Woman,
Ah-hmmm, don you hear me cryin, Lawd,
  Lawd!
I say run heah, Black Woman,
Sit on yo Black Daddy's knee, Lawd!
Mmmmm, I know yo house feel lonesome,
Ah, don you heah me whoopin, Lawd,
  Lawd,
Don yo house feel lonesome,
When yo biscuit roller gon,
Lawd, help my cryin time—
Don yo house feel lonesome, Mama,
When yo biscuit roller gon.

I say my house feel lonesome—
I know you heah me crying, oh Baby,
Ah-hmmm, ah, when I looked in my kitchen,
  Mama,
An I wen all thoo my dinin room
Ah-mmmm, when I woke up this mornin
I foun my biscuit roller done gone.

Goin to Texas, Mama,
Jus to heah the wild ox moan—
Lawd help mah cryin time—
Goin to Texas, Mama,
Jus to heah the wild ox moan,
An if they moan to suit me,
I'm goin to bring a wild ox home.
Ah-hmmm, I say I'm got to go to Texas, Black
  Mama—

I know you heah me cryin, Lawd, Lawd—
Ah-hmmm, I'm got to go to Texas, Black
  Mama,
Ahm-jus to heah the white cow, I say, moan!
Ah-hmmm, ah, if they moan to suit me, Lawd,
  Lawd,
I bleeve I'll bring a white cow back home.

Say, I feel superstitious, Mama,
'Bout my hoggin bread, Lawd help my hungry
  time,
I feel superstitious, Baby, 'bout my hoggin
  bread!
Ah-hmmm, Baby, I feel superstitious,
I say 'stitious, Black Woman!
Ah-hmmm, ah you heah me cryin
Bout I don got hungry, Lawd, Lawd
Oh, Mama, I feel superstitious
Bout my hog, Lawd Gawd, it's mah bread.

I want you to tell me, Mama,
Ah-hmmm, I heah me cryin, oh Mama!
Ah-hmmm, I want you to tell me, Black
  Woman,
O wheah did you stay las night?
I love you, Black woman,
I tell the whole worl I do.
Ah-hmmm, I love you, Black Woman,
I know you heah me whoopin, Black Baby!
Ah-hmmm, I love you Black Woman
An I'll tell yo Daddy, I do, Lawd.

Bibliography

Though not exhaustive, this bibliography is designed to serve the needs of the advanced as well as the beginning student of Afro-American literature. Together with the reading suggestions in the head-notes, it constitutes a record of the most significant scholarship in this field. For additional items before 1970 as well as for a number of minor writers not included in this anthology, the reader should consult Darwin T. Turner's *Afro-American Writers*.

RESEARCH AIDS

Adams, Russell L. *Great Negroes, Past and Present.* Chicago, 1964.

American Quarterly, annual summer supplement.

The Arthur B. Spingarn Collection of Negro Authors. Washington, D.C., 1948.

"Articles on American Literature Appearing in Current Periodicals," in each issue of *American Literature.*

Black List. New York, 1971.

Bontemps, Arna. "The James Weldon Johnson Memorial Collection of Negro Arts and Letters." *Yale University Library Gazette,* XVIII (October 1943), 19–26.

———. "Special Collections of Negroana." *Library Quarterly,* XIV (1944), 187–206.

"Books and Articles Related to Black Theatre Published from 1/1960 to 2/1968." *The Drama Review,* XII (Summer 1968), 176–180.

Brown, Warren. *Check List of Negro Newspapers in the United States, 1827–1946.* Jefferson City, Mo., 1946.

Chapman, Abraham. *The Negro in American Literature and a Bibliography of Literature by and About Negro Americans.* Stevens Point, Wis., 1966.

Corrigan, Robert A. "Afro-American Fiction: A Checklist 1853–1970." *Midcontinent American Studies Journal,* XI (Fall 1970), 114–135.

Davis, John P., ed. *The American Negro Reference Book.* Englewood Cliffs, N.J., 1966.

Deodene, Frank and William P. French. *Black American Fiction Since 1952, A Preliminary Checklist.* Chatham, 1970.

Dictionary of American Biography. New York, 1928–1937, 1946, 1958.

Dictionary Catalog of the Jesse E. Moorland Collection of Negro Life and History [at Howard University]. 9 vols. Boston, 1970.

Dictionary Catalog of the Schomburg Collection of Negro Literature & History. 11 vols. Boston, 1962, 1967.

Directory of U.S. Negro Newspapers, Magazines, and Periodicals, 1966. New York, 1966.

Dissertation Abstracts.

Drzick, Kathleen, John Murphy, and Constance Weaver. *Annotated Bibliography of Works Relating to the Negro in Literature and to Negro Dialects.* Kalamazoo, Mich., 1969.

Du Bois, W. E. B. *A Select Bibliography of the Negro American.* 3rd ed. Atlanta, 1905.

——— and Guy B. Johnson. *Encyclopedia of the Negro: Preparatory Volume.* Rev. ed. New York, 1946.

Dumond, Dwight L. *Bibliography of Antislavery in America.* Ann Arbor, Mich., 1961.

Embree, Edwin R. *American Negroes, A Handbook.* New York, 1942.

Graham, James D. "Negro Protest in America, 1900–1955: A Bibliographical Guide." *The South Atlantic Quarterly,* LXVII (1968), 94–107.

Gross, Seymour L. and John Edward Hardy, eds. *Images of the Negro in American Literature.* Chicago, 1966.

Guzman, Jessie P., ed. *Negro Year Book.* Tuskegee, Ala., 1947.

Houston, Helen R. "Contributions of the American Negro to American Culture: A Selected Checklist." *Bulletin of Bibliography,* XXVI (July–September 1969), 71–83.

Index to Periodical Articles by and About Negroes (formerly *A Guide to Negro Periodical Literature* and *Index to Selected Periodicals*).

International Library of Negro Life and History. 10 vols. Washington, D.C., 1967–1969.

Jahn, Janheinz. *A Bibliography of Neo-African Literature from Africa, America, and the Caribbean.* New York, 1965.

Johnson, Harry A. *Multimedia Materials for Afro-American Studies.* New York, 1971.

Kaiser, Ernest. "The History of Negro History." *Negro Digest,* XVII (February 1968), 10–15, 64–80.

———. "The Literature of Harlem." *Freedomways,* III (1963), 276–291.

———. "The Literature of Negro Revolt." *Freedomways,* III (1963), 26–47.

———. "Literature on the South." *Freedomways,* IV (1964), 149–167.

———. "Recent Books." *Freedomways,* in each issue.

———. "Recent Literature on Black Liberation Struggles and the Ghetto Crisis (A Bibliographical Survey)." *Science & Society,* XXXIII (1969), 168–196.

McDowell, Robert E. and George Fortenberry. "A Checklist of Books and Essays About American Negro Novelists." *Studies in the Novel,* III (1971), 219–236.

Major, Clarence. *Dictionary of Afro-American Slang.* New York, 1970.

Miller, Elizabeth W. and Mary L. Fisher. *The Negro in America: A Bibliography.* 2nd ed. Cambridge, Mass., 1970.

MLA International Bibliography.

The Negro in Print: Bibliographic Survey.

Nilon, Charles H. *Bibliography of Bibliographies in American Literature.* New York, 1970.

Penn, Joseph E. et al. *The Negro American in Paperback: A Selected List of Paperbound Books.* Washington, D.C., 1967.

Ploski, Harry A. and Roscoe C. Brown. *The Negro Almanac.* New York, 1967.

Porter, Dorothy B. "Early American Negro Writings: A Bibliographical Study." *Papers of the Bibliographical Society of America,* XXXIX (1945), 192–268.

———. *The Negro in the United States: A Selected Bibliography.* Washington, D.C., 1970.

———. *North American Negro Poets: A Bibliographical Check List of Their Writings, 1760–1944.* Hattiesburg, Miss., 1945.

———. *A Working Bibliography on the Negro in the United States.* Ann Arbor, Mich., 1968.

Reardon, William R. and Thomas D. Pawley, eds. *The Black Teacher and the Dramatic Arts.* Westport, Conn., 1970.

Roberts, Hermese E. *The Third Ear: A Black Glossary.* Chicago, 1971.

Rowell, Charles H. "A Bibliography of Bibliographies for the Study of Black American Literature and Folklore." *Black Experience, A Southern University Journal,* LV (June 1969), 95–111.

Salk, Erwin A. *A Layman's Guide to Negro History.* Rev. ed. New York, 1967.

Scally, Sister Mary Anthony. *Negro Catholic Writers 1900–1943: A Bio-Bibliography.* Detroit, 1945.

Schatz, Walter. *Directory of Afro-American Resources.* New York, 1970.

Simmons, William J. *Men of Mark: Eminent, Progressive and Rising.* Cleveland, 1887.

Smith, Jessie Carney. "Developing Collections of Black Literature." *Black World,* XX (June 1971), 18–29.

Turner, Darwin T. *Afro-American Writers.* New York, 1970.

Wayne County Intermediate School District Desegregation Advisory Project. *The Negro Freedom Movement: Past and Present: An Annotated Bibliography.* Detroit, 1967.

Welsch, Erwin K. *The Negro in the United States: A Research Guide.* Bloomington, Ind., 1965.

Whiteman, Maxwell. *A Century of Fiction by American Negroes, 1853–1952.* Philadelphia, 1955.

Woodress, James, ed. *American Literary Scholarship: An Annual.* Durham, N.C., 1965–.

Work, Monroe N. *A Bibliography of the Negro in Africa and America.* New York, 1928.

Yellin, Jean Fagan. "An Index of Literary Materials in *The Crisis,* 1910–1934: Articles, Belles-Lettres, and Book Reviews." *CLA Journal,* XIV (1971), 452–465.

PERIODICALS

Amistad
The Anglo-African
The Baltimore Afro-American
Bandung-It!
Black Academy Review
Black Creation
Black Dialogue

Black Orpheus: A Journal of African and Afro-American Literature
Black Review
The Black Scholar
Black Theatre
Black World (formerly *Negro Digest*)
Boston Guardian

Challenge and *New Challenge*
The Chicago Defender
CLA Journal
The Colored American
The Crisis: A Record of the Darker Races
Douglass' Monthly
Ebony
Essence
Fire!!
Freedom's Journal
Freedomways
Harlem
Harlem Quarterly
Harvard Journal of Afroamerican Affairs (formerly
  Harvard Journal of Negro Affairs)
The Journal of Black Poetry
The Journal of Black Studies
The Journal of Negro Education
The Journal of Negro History
The Liberator
The Messenger
The National Reformer
Negro American Literature Forum
Negro Digest (now *Black World*)
Negro History Bulletin
The Negro Quarterly

Negro Story
New York Amsterdam-News
Nkombo
Nommo
Onyx Magazine
Opportunity: A Journal of Negro Life
The Pennsylvania Freeman
People's Voice
*Phylon: The Atlanta University Review of Race and
  Culture*
Pittsburgh Courier
*Présence Africaine: Cultural Revue of the Negro
  World*
*The Quarterly Review of Higher Education Among
  Negroes*
Renaissance II
*Roots: A Journal of Critical and Creative Expres-
  sion*
Soulbook
The Southern Workman
Studies in Black Literature
Tuesday
Umbra
The Urbanite: Images of the American Negro
The Voice of the Negro
Xavier University Studies

ANTHOLOGIES

Adams, William, Peter Conn, and Barry Slepian, eds. *Afro-American Literature: Drama.* Boston, 1969; *Afro-American Literature: Fiction.* Boston, 1969; *Afro-American Literature: Non-Fiction.* Boston 1970; and *Afro-American Literature: Poetry.* Boston, 1970.

Adoff, Arnold, ed. *Black on Black: Commentaries by Negro Americans.* New York, 1968.

——, ed. *Black Out Loud: An Anthology of Modern Poems by Black Americans.* New York, 1970.

——, ed. *Brothers and Sisters: Modern Stories by Black Americans.* New York, 1970.

——, ed. *I Am the Darker Brother: An Anthology of Modern Poems by Black Americans.* New York, 1968.

Afro-Arts Anthology. Newark, 1966.

Alhamisi, Ahmed and Harun K. Wangara, eds. *Black Arts: An Anthology of Black Creations.* Detroit, 1970.

Austin, Lettie J., Lewis H. Fenderson, and Sophia P. Nelson, eds. *The Black Man and the Promise of America.* Glenview, Ill., 1970.

Baker, Houston A., Jr., ed. *Black Literature in America.* New York, 1971.

Barbour, Floyd, ed. *The Black Seventies.* New York, 1970.

Bayliss, John F., ed. *Black Slave Narratives.* New York, 1970.

BCD. *Soul Session.* Newark, 1969.

Bontemps, Arna, ed. *American Negro Poetry.* New York, 1963.

——, ed. *Great Slave Narratives.* Boston, 1969.

Brasmer, William and Dominick Consolo, eds. *Black Drama: An Anthology.* Columbus, Ohio, 1970.

Brawley, Benjamin, ed. *Early Negro American Writers.* Chapel Hill, N.C., 1935.

Brooks, Gwendolyn, ed. *A Broadside Treasury.* Detroit, 1971.

——, ed. *Jump Bad: A New Chicago Anthology.* Detroit, 1971.

Brown, Sterling A., Arthur P. Davis, and Ulysses Lee, eds. *The Negro Caravan.* New York, 1941.

Bullins, Ed, ed. *New Plays from the Black Theatre.* New York, 1969.

Cade, Toni, ed. *The Black Woman: An Anthology.* New York, 1970.

Calverton, Victor F., ed. *Anthology of American Negro Literature.* New York, 1929.

Chambers, Bradford and Rebecca Moon, eds. *Right On: Anthology of Black Literature.* New York, 1970.

Chapman, Abraham, ed. *Afro-American Slave Narratives.* New York, 1970.

——, ed. *Black Voices: An Anthology of Afro-American Literature.* New York, 1968.

——, ed. *New Black Voices.* New York, 1971.

Clarke, John Henrik, ed. *American Negro Short Stories.* New York, 1966.

———, ed. *Harlem: Voices from the Soul of Black America.* New York, 1970.

Coombs, Orde, ed. *We Speak as Liberators: Young Black Poets.* New York, 1970.

———, ed. *What We Must See: Young Black Story-tellers.* New York, 1971.

Couch, William, ed. *New Black Playwrights: An Anthology.* Baton Rouge, La., 1968.

Cromwell, Otelia, Lorenzo D. Turner, and Eva B. Dykes, eds. *Readings from Negro Authors.* New York, 1931.

Cullen, Countee, ed. *Caroling Dusk: An Anthology of Verse by Negro Poets.* New York, 1927.

Cunard, Nancy, ed. *Negro Anthology.* London, 1934.

Curry, Gladys J., ed. *Viewpoints from Black America.* Englewood Cliffs, N.J., 1970.

Davis, Arthur P. and Saunders Redding, eds. *Cavalcade: Negro American Writing from 1760 to the Present.* Boston, 1971.

Davis, Charles T. and Daniel Walden, eds. *On Being Black: Writings by Afro-Americans from Frederick Douglass to the Present.* New York, 1970.

Dent, Thomas C., Richard Schechner, and Gilbert Moses, eds. *Free Southern Theatre by the Free Southern Theatre.* Indianapolis, 1969.

Dreer, Herman, ed. *American Literature by Negro Authors.* New York, 1950.

Emanuel, James A. and Theodore Gross, eds. *Dark Symphony: Negro Literature in America.* New York, 1968.

Fabre, Michel, ed. *Les Noirs américaines.* Paris, 1967.

Ford, Nick Aaron, ed. *Black Insights: Significant Literature by Afro-Americans—1760 to the Present.* Waltham, Mass., 1971.

——— and H. L. Faggett, eds. *Best Short Stories by Afro-American Writers, 1925–1950.* Boston, 1950.

Freedman, Frances S., ed. *The Black American Experience: A New Anthology of Black Literature.* New York, 1970.

Gayle, Addison, Jr., ed. *The Black Aesthetic.* Garden City, N.Y., 1971.

———, ed. *Black Expression: Essays by and About Black Americans in the Creative Arts.* New York, 1969.

———, ed. *Bondage, Freedom, and Beyond: The Prose of Black Americans.* Garden City, N.Y., 1971.

Haslam, Gerald W., ed. *Forgotten Pages of American Literature.* Boston, 1970.

Hayden, Robert, ed. *Kaleidoscope: Poems by American Negro Poets.* New York, 1967.

———, David Burrows, and Frederick Lapides, eds. *Afro-American Literature.* New York, 1971.

Henderson, David, ed. *Umbra Blackworks Anthology 1970–1971.* New York, 1971.

Hill, Herbert, ed. *Soon, One Morning: New Writing by American Negroes, 1940–1962.* New York, 1963.

Hughes, Douglas A., ed. *From a Black Perspective: Contemporary Black Essays.* New York, 1970.

Hughes, Langston, ed. *The Best Short Stories by Negro Writers.* Boston, 1967.

———, ed. *The Book of Negro Humor.* New York, 1966.

———, ed. *New Negro Poets U.S.A.* Bloomington, Ind., 1964.

——— and Arna Bontemps, eds. *The Poetry of the Negro, 1746–1970.* Rev. ed. Garden City, N.Y., 1970.

James, Charles L., ed. *From the Roots: Short Stories by Black Americans.* New York, 1970.

Johnson, Charles S., ed. *Ebony and Topaz: A Collectanea.* New York, 1927.

Johnson, James Weldon, ed. *The Book of American Negro Poetry.* Rev. ed. New York, 1931.

———, ed. *The Book of American Negro Spirituals.* New York, 1925; *The Second Book of Negro Spirituals.* New York, 1926.

Jones, LeRoi and Larry Neal, eds. *Black Fire: An Anthology of Afro-American Writing.* New York, 1968.

Jordan, June, ed. *Soulscript: Afro-American Poetry.* Garden City, N.Y., 1970.

Katz, William Loren, ed. *Five Slave Narratives.* New York, 1969.

Kearns, Francis E., ed. *The Black Experience: An Anthology of American Literature for the 1970's.* New York, 1970.

———, ed. *Black Identity: A Thematic Reader.* New York, 1970.

Kendricks, Ralph, ed. *Afro-American Voices: 1770's–1970's.* New York, 1970.

Kerlin, Robert T., ed. *Negro Poets and Their Poems.* 2nd ed. Washington, D.C., 1935.

Knight, Etheridge, ed. *Black Voices from Prison.* New York, 1970.

Lanusse, Armand, ed. *Creole Voices: Poems in French by Free Men of Color.* Ed. Edward M. Coleman. Centennial ed. Washington, D.C., 1945.

Lester, Julius, ed. *To Be a Slave.* New York, 1968.

Locke, Alain, ed. *Four Negro Poets.* New York, 1927.

———, ed. *The New Negro: An Interpretation.* New York, 1925.

——— and Montgomery Gregory, eds. *Plays of Negro Life: A Source-Book of Native American Drama.* New York, 1927.

Lomax, Alan and Raoul Abdul, eds. *3000 Years of Black Poetry.* New York, 1970.

Major, Clarence, ed. *The New Black Poetry.* New York, 1969.

Margolies, Edward, ed. *A Native Sons Reader.* Philadelphia, 1970.

Miller, Adam David, ed. *Dices or Black Bones: Black Voices of the Seventies.* Boston, 1970.

Miller, Ruth, ed. *Blackamerican Literature 1760–Present.* Beverly Hills, Calif., 1971.

Milner, Ronald and Woodie King, eds. *Black Drama Anthology.* New York, 1971.

Moon, Bucklin, ed. *Primer for White Folks.* Garden City, N.Y., 1945.

Nelson, Alice Dunbar, ed. *Masterpieces of Negro Eloquence.* New York, 1914.

Nicholas, Xavier, ed. *Poetry of Soul.* New York, 1971.

Oliver, Clinton F. and Stephanie Sills, eds. *Contemporary Black Drama.* New York, 1971.

Osofsky, Gilbert, ed. *Puttin' on Ole Massa: The Slave Narratives of Henry Bibb, William W. Brown, and Solomon Northrup.* New York, 1969.

Patterson, Lindsay, ed. *Black Theater: A 20th Century Collection of the Work of Its Best Playwrights.* New York, 1971.

———, ed. *An Introduction to Black Literature in America from 1746 to the Present.* Washington, D.C., 1969.

Perkins, Eugene, ed. *Black Expressions: An Anthology of New Black Poets.* Chicago, 1967.

Pool, Rosey E., ed. *Beyond the Blues: New Poems by American Negroes.* Lympne, Kent, England, 1962.

Porter, Dorothy, ed. *Early Negro Writing, 1760–1837.* Boston, 1971.

Randall, Dudley, ed. *Black Poetry: A Supplement to Anthologies Which Exclude Black Poets.* Detroit, 1969.

Reardon, William R. and Thomas D. Pawley, eds. *The Black Teacher and the Dramatic Arts.* Westport, Conn., 1970.

Reed, Ishmael, ed. *19 Necromancers from Now: An Anthology of Original American Writing for the 70s.* Garden City, N.Y., 1970.

Richardson, Willis, ed. *Plays and Pageants from the Life of the Negro.* Washington, D.C., 1930.

——— and May Miller, eds. *Negro History in Thirteen Plays.* Washington, D.C., 1935.

Riley, Clayton, ed. *Black Quartet: Four New Black Plays.* New York, 1970.

Robinson, William H., ed. *Early Black American Poets.* Dubuque, Iowa, 1969.

———, ed. *Early Black American Prose.* Dubuque, Iowa, 1971.

Rodgers, Carolyn M., ed. *For Love of Our Brothers.* Chicago, 1970.

Schulberg, Budd, ed. *From the Ashes: Voices of Watts.* New York, 1967.

Shuman, R. Baird, ed. *A Galaxy of Black Writing.* Durham, N.C., 1970.

———, ed. *Nine Black Poets.* Durham, N.C., 1968.

Stanford, Barbara Dodds, ed. *I, Too, Sing America: Black Voices in American Literature.* New York, 1971.

Troupe, Quincy, ed. *Watts Poets: A Book of New Poetry and Essays.* Los Angeles, 1968.

Turner, Darwin T., ed. *Black American Literature: Essays, Poetry, Fiction, Drama.* Columbus, Ohio, 1970.

——— and Jean M. Bright, eds. *Images of the Negro in America.* Boston, 1965.

Watkins, Sylvester C., ed. *Anthology of American Negro Literature.* New York, 1944.

White, Newman I. and Walter C. Jackson, eds. *An Anthology of Verse by American Negroes.* Durham, N.C., 1924.

Wilentz, Ted and Tom Weatherly, eds. *Natural Process: An Anthology of New Black Poetry.* New York, 1971.

Williams, John A., ed. *The Angry Black.* New York, 1962.

———, ed. *Beyond the Angry Black.* New York, 1966.

Wink, Robin et al., eds. *Four Fugitive Slave Narratives.* Reading, Mass., 1969.

Woodson, Carter G., ed. *The Mind of the Negro as Reflected in Letters Written During the Crisis, 1800–1860.* Washington, D.C., 1926.

———, ed. *Negro Orators and Their Orations.* Washington, D.C., 1925.

Yetman, Norman R., ed. *Life Under the Peculiar Institution.* New York, 1970.

LITERARY HISTORY AND CRITICISM

General

Allen, Samuel. "Negritude and Its Relevance to the American Negro Writer." *The American Negro Writer and His Roots.* New York, 1960. Pp. 8–20.

Amann, Clarence A. "*Three Negro Classics*—An Estimate." *Negro American Literature Forum,* IV (1970), 113–119.

The American Negro Writer and His Roots. New York, 1960.

Anderson, Jervis. "Black Writing: The Other Side." *Dissent,* XV (1968), 233–242.

Aptheker, Herbert. "Afro-American Superiority: A Neglected Theme in the Literature." *Phylon,* XXXI (1970), 336–343.

Arnez, Nancy L. "Racial Understanding Through Literature." *English Journal,* LVIII (1969), 56–61.

Baraka, Imamu Amiri (LeRoi Jones). "The Black Aesthetic." *Negro Digest,* XVIII (September 1969), 5–6.

Barton, Rebecca C. *Witnesses for Freedom: Negro Americans in Autobiography.* New York, 1948.

Berry, Faith. "Voice for the Jazz Age, Great Migration, or Black Bourgeoisie." *Black World,* XX (November 1970), 10–16.

Bigsby, C. W. E., ed. *The Black American Writer.* 2 vols. Deland, Fla., 1969.

Bontemps, Arna. "The Black Renaissance of the Twenties." *Black World,* XX (November 1970), 5–9.

———. "Famous WPA Authors." *Negro Digest,* VIII (June 1950), 43–47.

———. "The Harlem Renaissance." *The Saturday Review of Literature,* XXX (March 22, 1947), 12–13, 44.

———. "The Negro Contribution to American Letters." *The American Negro Reference Book.* Ed. John P. Davis. Englewood Cliffs, N.J., 1966. Pp. 850–878.

———. "The New Black Renaissance." *Negro Digest,* XI (November 1961), 52–58.

Boyers, Robert. "Culture, Politics, and Negro Writers." *Salmagundi,* I, No. 1 (1965), 71–80.

Braithwaite, William Stanley. "The Negro in American Literature." *The New Negro: An Interpretation.* Ed. Alain Locke. New York, 1925. Pp. 29–44.

Brawley, Benjamin. "The Negro in American Literature." *The Bookman,* LVI (October 1922), 137–141.

———. *The Negro Genius.* New York, 1937.

———. "The Negro Literary Renaissance." *The Southern Workman,* LVI (1927), 177–180.

———. "The Promise of Negro Literature." *The Journal of Negro History,* XIX (1934), 53–59.

Bronz, Stephen H. *Roots of Negro Racial Consciousness: The 1920's: Three Harlem Renaissance Authors.* New York, 1964.

Brooks, Russell. "The Comic Spirit and the Negro's New Look." *CLA Journal,* VI (1962), 35–43.

Brown, Lloyd. "Which Way for the Negro Writer?" *Masses & Mainstream,* IV (March 1951), 53–63; IV (April 1951), 50–59.

Brown, Lloyd W. "Black Entitles: Names as Symbols in Afro-American Literature." *Studies in Black Literature,* I (Spring 1970), 16–44.

———. "The West Indian as an Ethnic Stereotype in Black American Literature." *Negro American Literature Forum,* V (1971), 8–14.

Brown, Sterling A. "The American Race Problem as Reflected in American Literature." *The Journal of Negro Education,* VIII (1939), 275–290.

———. "A Century of Negro Portraiture in American Literature." *The Massachusetts Review,* VII (Winter 1966), 73–96.

———. "The Negro Author and His Publisher." *The Quarterly Review of Higher Education Among Negroes,* IX (July 1941), 140–146.

———. "The New Negro in Literature (1925–1955)." *The New Negro Thirty Years Afterward.* Ed. Rayford W. Logan et al. Washington, D.C., 1955. Pp. 57–72.

Butcher, Margaret. *The Negro in American Culture.* New York, 1956.

Calverton, Victor F. *The Liberation of American Literature.* New York, 1932.

———. "The Negro and American Culture." *The Saturday Review of Literature,* XXII (September 21, 1940), 3–4.

Cayton, Horace R. "Ideological Forces in the Work of Negro Writers." *Anger, and Beyond: The Negro Writer in the United States.* Ed. Herbert Hill. New York, 1966. Pp. 37–50.

Chamberlain, John. "The Negro as Writer." *The Bookman,* LXX (1930), 603–611.

Chametzky, Jules and Sidney Kaplan, eds. *Black and White in American Culture: An Anthology from the Massachusetts Review.* Amherst, Mass., 1969.

Chandler, G. Lewis. "A Major Problem of Negro Authors in Their March Toward Belles-Lettres." *Phylon,* XI (1950), 383–386.

Chapman, Abraham. "The Harlem Renaissance in Literary History." *CLA Journal,* XI (1967), 38–58.

Chesnutt, Charles Waddell. "Post-Bellum, Pre-Harlem." *The Crisis,* XXXVIII (1931), 193–194.

Clarke, John Henrik. "The Neglected Dimensions of the Harlem Renaissance." *Black World,* XX (November 1970), 118–129.

———. "The Origin and Growth of Afro-American Literature." *Negro Digest,* XVII (December 1967), 54–67.

Clay, Eugene. "The Negro and American Literature." *International Literature,* No. 6 (June 1935), pp. 75–89.

———. "The Negro in Recent American Literature." *American Writers' Congress.* Ed. Henry Hart. New York, 1935. Pp. 145–153.

Conrad, Earl. "American Viewpoint: Blues School of Literature." *The Chicago Defender,* December 22, 1945, p. 11.

Cook, Mercer and Stephen Henderson. *The Militant Black Writer in Africa and the United States.* Madison, Wis., 1969.

Cullen, Countee. "The Dark Tower." *Opportunity,* monthly column, 1926–1928.

Cunningham, James. "The Case of the Severed Lifeline." *Negro Digest,* XVIII (October 1969), 23–28.

Davis, Arthur P. "Growing up in the New Negro Renaissance: 1920–1935." *Negro American Literature Forum,* II (1968), 53–59.

———. "Integration and Race Literature." *Phylon,* XVII (1956), 141–146.

———. "Trends in Negro American Literature (1940–65)." *Dark Symphony.* Ed. James A. Emanuel and Theodore Gross. New York, 1968. Pp. 519–526.

De Armond, Fred. "A Note on the Sociology of Negro Literature." *Opportunity,* III (1925), 369–371.

"The Debut of the Younger School of Negro Writers." *Opportunity,* II (1924), 143–144.

Dennison, George. "Voices of the Dispossessed." *Show,* V (May 1965), 28–33.

Dover, Cedric. "Notes on Coloured Writing." *Phylon,* VIII (1947), 213–224.

Du Bois, W. E. B. *The Gift of Black Folk: Negroes in the Making of America.* Boston, 1924.

———. "The Negro in Literature and Art." *Annals of*

the American Academy of Political and Social Science, XLIX (1913), 233–237.

————. "Postscript." *The Crisis*, monthly column, 1910–1934.

————. *The Souls of Black Folk*. Chicago, 1903.

———— and Alain Locke. "The Younger Literary Movement." *The Crisis*, XXVII (1924), 161–163.

Dumble, W. R. "A Footnote to Negro Literature." *Negro History Bulletin*, IX (1946), 82–84.

"Ebony Book Shelf." *Ebony*, monthly feature.

Eisinger, Chester E. *Fiction of the Forties*. Chicago, 1963.

Ellison, Ralph. *Shadow and Act*. New York, 1964.

Emanuel, James A. "America Before 1950: Black Writers' Views." *Negro Digest*, XVIII (August 1969), 26–34, 67–69.

————. "The Invisible Men of American Literature." *Books Abroad*, XXXVII (1963), 391–394.

Evans, Mari. "Contemporary Black Literature." *Black World*, XIX (June 1970), 4, 93–94.

————. "I'm With You." *Negro Digest*, XVII (May 1968), 31–36, 77–80.

Fabio, Sarah Webster. "A Black Paper." *Negro Digest*, XVIII (July 1969), 26–31.

Farnsworth, T. A. "The Negro in American Literature." *Contrast*, I (Summer 1960), 61–63.

Farrison, W. Edward. "Dialectology Versus Negro Dialect." *CLA Journal*, XIII (1969), 21–26.

————. "What American Negro Literature Exists and Who Should Teach It?" *CLA Journal*, XIII (1970), 374–381.

Ferguson, Blanche E. *Countee Cullen and the Harlem Renaissance*. New York, 1966.

Fiedler, Leslie A. *Waiting for the End*. New York, 1964.

Fontaine, William T. "Toward a Philosophy of the American Negro Literature." *Présence Africaine*, Nos. 24–25 (February–May 1959), pp. 165–176.

Ford, Nick Aaron. Annual "Critical Survey of Significant Belles Lettres by and About Negroes." *Phylon*, XXII (1961), 119–134; XXIII (1962), 128–138; XXIV (1963), 123–134; XXV (1964), 123–134.

————. "Black Literature and the Problem of Evaluation." *College English*, XXXII (1971), 536–547.

————. "A Blueprint for Negro Authors." *Phylon*, XI (1950), 374–377.

————. "Confessions of a Black Critic." *Black World*, XX (June 1971), 30–43.

————, Donald B. Gibson, and Charles A. Ray. "Black Literature: Problems and Opportunities." *CLA Journal*, XIII (1969), 10–20.

French, Warren. "A Montage of Minorities: Some Waspish Remarks." *Kansas English*, LV (December 1969), 6–13.

Fuller, Hoyt W. "Black Images and White Critics." *Negro Digest*, XIX (November 1969), 49–50.

————. "The Negro Writer in the United States." *Ebony*, XX (November 1964), 126–134.

————. "Of Integrity, Hope and Dead Dialogue." *The New School Bulletin*, XXIII (May 12, 1966), 1.

————. "Perspectives." *Negro Digest* and *Black World*, monthly column.

————. "Reverberations from a Writers' Conference." *African Forum*, I (1966), 11–20.

————. "The So-Called Harlem Renaissance." *Black World*, XX (November 1970), 4, 65, 130.

————, ed. "A Survey: Black Writers' Views on Literary Lions and Values." *Negro Digest*, XVII (January 1968), 10–48, 81–89.

————, ed. "The Task of the Negro Writer as Artist." *Negro Digest*, XIV (April 1965), 54–70, 72–79.

Fullinwider, S. P. *The Mind and Mood of Black America: 20th Century Thought*. Homewood, Ill., 1969.

Gale, Zona. "The Negro Sees Himself." *Survey*, LIV (1925), 300–301.

Garland, Phyl. "Skill and Maturity Mark Negro Writer of Today." *The Pittsburgh Courier*, September 17, 1960, Sec. 3, p. 4.

Gayle, Addison, Jr. "Black Literature and the White Aesthetic." *Negro Digest*, XVIII (July 1969), 32–39.

————. *The Black Situation*. New York, 1970.

————. "The Harlem Renaissance: Towards a Black Aesthetic." *Midcontinent American Studies Journal*, XI (Fall 1970), 78–87.

————, ed. *The Black Aesthetic*. Garden City, N.Y., 1971.

————, ed. *Black Expression: Essays by and About Black Americans in the Creative Arts*. New York, 1969.

Gerald, Carolyn. "The Black Writer and His Role." *Negro Digest*, XVIII (January 1969), 42–48.

————. "What Lies Ahead for Black Americans?" *Negro Digest*, XIX (November 1969), 24–29.

Gibson, Donald B., ed. *Five Black Writers: Essays on Wright, Ellison, Baldwin, Hughes, and LeRoi Jones*. New York, 1970.

Gibson, Richard. "A No to Nothing." *The Kenyon Review*, XIII (1951), 252–255.

Gilman, Richard. *The Confusion of Realms*. New York, 1969.

Glicksberg, Charles I. "The Alienation of Negro Literature." *Phylon*, XI (1950), 49–58.

————. "For Negro Literature: The Catharsis of Laughter." *Forum*, CVIII (1947), 450–456.

————. "Race and Revolution in Negro Literature." *Forum*, CVII (1947), 300–308.

Gloster, Hugh M. "The Negro Writer and the Southern Scene." *The Southern Packet*, IV (January 1948), 1–3.

————. "Race and the Negro Writer." *Phylon*, XI (1950), 369–371.

Gordon, Eugene. "Social and Political Problems of

the Negro Writer." *American Writers' Congress.* Ed. Henry Hart. New York, 1935. Pp. 141–145.

Green, Elizabeth L. *The Negro in Contemporary American Literature: An Outline for Individual and Group Study.* Chapel Hill, N.C., 1928.

Gross, Seymour L. "Stereotype to Archetype: The Negro in American Literary Criticism." *Images of the Negro in American Literature.* Ed. Seymour L. Gross and John Edward Hardy. Chicago, 1966. Pp. 1–26.

———— and John Edward Hardy, eds. *Images of the Negro in American Literature.* Chicago, 1966.

Gross, Theodore L. "The Idealism of Negro Literature in America." *Phylon,* XXX (1969), 5–10.

————. "Our Mutual Estate: The Literature of the American Negro." *The Antioch Review,* XXVIII (1968), 293–303.

Hagopian, John V. "Mau-Mauing the Literary Establishment." *Studies in the Novel,* III (1971), 135–147.

————. "Negro American Authors." *Contemporary Literature,* X (1969), 416–420.

"Harlem, Mecca of the New Negro." *Survey,* VI (March 1925), entire issue.

Haslam, Gerald W. "The Awakening of American Negro Literature 1619–1900." *The Black American Writer.* Ed. C. W. E. Bigsby. Deland, Fla., 1969. Vol. II, pp. 41–51.

————. "Two Traditions in Afro-American Literature." *Research Studies, A Quarterly Publication of Washington State University,* XXXVII (September 1969), 183–193.

Hentoff, Nat. "The Other Side of the Blues." *Anger, and Beyond: The Negro Writer in the United States.* Ed. Herbert Hill. New York, 1966. Pp. 76–85.

Hill, Herbert. "The Negro Writer and the Creative Imagination." *Arts in Society,* V (1968), 244–255.

————. "The New Directions of the Negro Writer." *The Crisis,* LXX (1963), 205–210.

————, ed. *Anger, and Beyond: The Negro Writer in the United States.* New York, 1966.

Holmes, Eugene C. "Problems Facing the Negro Writer Today." *New Challenge,* II (Fall 1937), 69–75.

Hughes, Langston. *The Big Sea.* New York, 1940.

————. *I Wonder as I Wander.* New York, 1956.

————. "The Negro Artist and the Racial Mountain." *The Nation,* CXXII (1926), 692–694.

————. "To Negro Writers." *American Writers' Congress.* Ed. Henry Hart. New York, 1935. Pp. 139–141.

————. "The Twenties: Harlem and Its Negritude." *African Forum,* I (Spring 1966), 11–20.

————. "The Writer in America." *Mainstream,* X (July 1957), 46–48.

————. "Writers: Black and White." *The American Negro Writer and His Roots.* New York, 1960. Pp. 41–45.

————, LeRoi Jones, and John A. Williams. "Prob-lems of the Negro Writer." *The Saturday Review,* XLVI (April 20, 1963), 19–21, 40.

Hurston, Zora Neale. *Dust Tracks on a Road.* Philadelphia, 1942.

————. "What White Publishers Won't Print." *Negro Digest,* V (April 1947), 85–89.

Isaacs, Harold. *The New World of Negro Americans.* New York, 1963.

Ivy, James W. "Écrits nègres aux États-Unis." *Présence Africaine,* No. 26 (June–July 1959), pp. 67–77.

Jackson, Blyden. Annual "Résumé of Negro Literature." *Phylon,* XVI (1955), 5–12; XVII (1956), 35–40.

————. "The Case for American Negro Literature." *Michigan Alumnus Quarterly Review,* LXI (1955), 161–166.

————. "An Essay in Criticism." *Phylon,* XI (1950), 338–343.

————. "Faith Without Works in Negro Literature." *Phylon,* XII (1951), 378–388.

————. "Full Circle." *Phylon,* IX (1948), 30–35.

Jackson, Esther M. "The American Negro and the Image of the Absurd." *Phylon,* XXIII (1962), 359–371.

Jackson, Miles M. "Significant Belles Lettres by and About Negroes Published in 1962." *Phylon,* XXVI (1965), 216–227.

Jacobs, George W. "Negro Authors Must Eat." *The Nation,* CXXVIII (1929), 710–711.

Jahn, Janheinz. *Neo-African Literature: A History of Black Writing.* New York, 1968.

————. "World Congress of Black Writers." *Black Orpheus: A Journal of African and Afro-American Literature,* No. 1 (September 1957), pp. 39–46.

Jeffers, Lance. "Afro-American Literature, The Conscience of Man." *The Black Scholar,* II (January 1971), 47–53.

Johnson, Charles S. "The Negro Enters Literature." *Carolina Magazine,* LVII (May 1927), 3–9, 44–48.

————. "The Negro Renaissance and Its Significance." *The New Negro Thirty Years Afterward.* Ed. Rayford W. Logan et al. Washington, D.C., 1955. Pp. 80–88.

Johnson, James Weldon. *Along This Way.* New York, 1933.

————. *Black Manhattan.* New York, 1930.

————. "The Dilemma of the Negro Author." *The American Mercury,* XV (1928), 477–481.

————. "Negro Authors and White Publishers." *The Crisis,* XXXVI (1929), 313–317.

————. "Race Prejudice and the Negro Artist." *Harper's Magazine,* CLVII (1928), 769–776.

Jones, Harry L. "Black Humor and the American Way of Life." *Satire Newsletter,* VII (1969), 1–4.

Jones, Junemary. "Teaching Afro-American Literature." *Illinois English Bulletin,* LVII (February 1970), 1–10.

Jones, LeRoi (Imamu Amiri Baraka). "Foreword." *Black Fire: An Anthology of Afro-American Writing.* Ed. LeRoi Jones and Larry Neal. New York, 1968. Pp. xvii–xviii.

———. *Home: Social Essays.* New York, 1966.

———. "Philistinism and the Negro Writer." *Anger, and Beyond: The Negro Writer in the United States.* Ed. Herbert Hill. New York, 1966. Pp. 51–61.

Kaiser, Ernest. "Recent Books." *Freedomways,* in each issue.

Keller, Joseph. "Black Writing and the White Critic." *Negro American Literature Forum,* III (1969), 103–110.

Kent, George E. *Blackness and the Adventure of Western Culture.* Chicago, 1971.

Kerlin, Robert T. *A Decade of Negro Self-Expression.* Charlottesville, Va., 1928.

———. "Singers of New Songs." *Opportunity,* IV (1926), 162–164.

———. *The Voice of the Negro.* New York, 1920.

Kessler, Sidney H. "Collectors, Scholars, and Negro Literature." *Midwest Journal,* VII (1954), 222–234.

Kilgore, James C. "The Case for Black Literature." *Negro Digest,* XVIII (July 1969), 22–25, 66–69.

Killens, John Oliver. "Another Time When Black Was Beautiful." *Black World,* XX (November 1970), 20–36.

———. *Black Man's Burden.* New York, 1965.

———. "The Black Writer and Revolution." *Arts in Society,* V (1968), 395–399.

———. "Opportunities for Development of Negro Talent." *The American Negro Writer and His Roots.* New York, 1960. Pp. 64–70.

Kinnamon, Keneth. "Afro-American Literature, the Black Revolution, and Ghetto High Schools." *English Journal,* LIX (1970), 189–194.

Kinneman, John A. "The Negro Renaissance." *Negro History Bulletin,* XXV (1962), 200, 197–199.

Lamming, George. "The Negro Writer and His World." *Présence Africaine,* Nos. 8–10 (June–November 1956), pp. 324–332.

Larson, Charles. "African–Afro-American Literary Relations: Basic Parallels." *Negro Digest,* XIX (December 1969), 35–42.

Lash, John. Annual "Critical Summary of Literature by and About Negroes." *Phylon,* XVIII (1957), 7–24; XIX (1958), 143–154, 247–257; XX (1959), 115–131; XXI (1960), 111–123.

———. "The Anthologist and the Negro Author." *Phylon,* VIII (1947), 68–76.

———. "On Negro Literature." *Phylon,* VI (1945), 240–247.

———. "The Race Consciousness of the American Negro Author: Toward a Reexamination of an Orthodox Critical Concept." *Social Forces,* XXVIII (October 1949), 24–34.

———. "The Study of Negro Literary Expression." *Negro History Bulletin,* IX (1946), 207–211.

———. "What Is 'Negro Literature'?" *College English,* IX (1947), 37–42.

Lee, Don L. "Black Critics." *Black World,* XIX (September 1970), 24–30.

———. "Directions for Black Writers." *The Black Scholar,* I (December 1969), 53–57.

Lee, Ulysses. "Criticism at Mid-Century." *Phylon,* XI (1950), 328–337.

Lester, Julius. "The Arts and the Black Revolution." *Arts in Society,* V (1968), 229.

Lewis, Theophilus. "The Frustration of Negro Art." *The Catholic World,* CLV (April 1942), 51–57.

Lieber, Todd M. and Maurice J. O'Sullivan. "'Native Sons?' Black Students on Black Literature." *Negro American Literature Forum,* V (1971), 3–7.

Liebman, Arthur. "Patterns and Themes in Afro-American Literature." *English Record,* XX (February 1970), 2–12.

Littlejohn, David. *Black on White: A Critical Survey of Writing by American Negroes.* New York, 1966.

Llorens, David. "What Contemporary Black Writers Are Saying." *Nommo,* I (Winter 1969), 24–27.

———. "Writers Converge at Fisk University." *Negro Digest,* XV (June 1966), 54–68.

Locke, Alain. "American Literary Tradition and the Negro." *The Modern Quarterly,* III (1926), 215–222.

———. Annual "Retrospective Review of the Literature of the Negro." *Opportunity,* VII (1929), 8–11; IX (1931), 48–51; X (1932), 40–44; XI (1933), 14–18; XII (1934), 8–11, 30; XIII (1935), 8–12, 46–48, 59; XIV (1936), 6–10, 42–43, 61; XV (1937), 8–13, 40–44; XVI (1938), 7–11, 27, 39–42; XVII (1939), 4–10, 36–42; XVIII (1940), 4–10, 28, 41–46, 53; XIX (1941), 4–9, 48–52; XX (1942), 36–41, 83–87; *Phylon,* VIII (1947), 17–27; IX (1948), 3–12; X (1949), 5–14, 167–172; XI (1950), 5–14, 171–175; XII (1951), 5–12, 185–190; XIII (1952), 7–18; XIV (1953), 34–44.

———. "The Negro in American Literature." *New World Writing 1.* New York, 1952. Pp. 18–33.

———. "The Negro Minority in American Literature." *English Journal,* XXXV (1946), 315–319.

———. "The Negro's Contribution to American Art and Literature." *Annals of the American Academy of Political and Social Science,* CXL (1928), 234–247.

———. "The Negro's Contribution to American Culture." *The Journal of Negro Education,* VIII (1939), 521–529.

———. "Self-Criticism: The Third Dimension in Culture." *Phylon,* XI (1950), 391–394.

———, ed. *The New Negro: An Interpretation.* New York, 1925.

Loggins, Vernon. *The Negro Author: His Development in America to 1900.* New York, 1931.

Lottman, Herbert. "'The Action Is Everywhere the Black Man Goes.'" *The New York Times Book Review,* April 21, 1968, pp. 6–7, 48–49.

Marcus, Steven. "The American Negro in Search of Identity." *Commentary,* XVI (1953), 456–463.

Margolies, Edward. "The Image of the Primitive in Black Letters." *Midcontinent American Studies Journal,* XI (Fall 1970), 67–77.

———. *Native Sons: A Critical Study of Twentieth-Century Negro American Authors.* Philadelphia, 1968.

Mayfield, Julian. "Into the Mainstream and Oblivion." *The American Negro Writer and His Roots.* New York, 1960. Pp. 29–34.

McDonnell, Thomas. "The Emergence of the Negro in Literature." *The Critic,* XX (December 1961–January 1962), 31–34.

McDowell, Robert E. "Mothers and Sons." *Prairie Schooner,* XLIV (Winter 1969–1970), 256.

Mitchell, Loften. "Harlem My Harlem." *Black World,* XX (November 1970), 91–97.

———. "The Negro Writer and His Materials." *The American Negro Writer and His Roots.* New York, 1960. Pp. 55–60.

Moore, Geoffrey. "Before Ellison and Baldwin." *Literatur und Sprache der Vereinigten Staaten: Aufsätze zu Ehren von Hans Galinsky.* Ed. Hans Helmcke et al. Heidelberg, 1969.

Morris, Lloyd. "The Negro 'Renaissance.'" *The Southern Workman,* LVIII (1930), 82–86.

Morrison, Allan. "A New Surge in Literature." *An Introduction to Black Literature in America from 1746 to the Present.* Ed. Lindsay Patterson. Washington, D.C., 1968. Pp. 221–223.

Mott, Abigail and M. S. Wood. *Narratives of Colored Americans.* New York, 1877.

Murray, Albert. *The Omni-Americans: New Perspectives on Black Experience and American Culture.* New York, 1970.

Musgrave, Marian E. "Triangles in Black and White: Interracial Sex and Hostility in Black Literature." *CLA Journal,* XIV (1971), 444–451.

Neal, Larry. "Any Day Now: Black Art and Black Liberation." *Ebony,* XXIV (August 1969), 54–58, 62.

"The Negro in Literature: The Current Scene." *Phylon,* XI (1950), 297–374.

"Negro Writing: A Literature of Protest." *American Writing Today: Its Independence and Vigor.* Ed. Allan Angoff. New York, 1957.

Nelson, John Herbert. *The Negro Character in American Literature.* Lawrence, Kan., 1926.

Nichols, Charles H., Jr. "The Forties: A Decade of Growth." *Phylon,* XI (1950), 377–380.

———. *Instructor's Guide to Accompany Cavalcade: Negro American Writing from 1760 to the Present.* Boston, 1971.

———. *Many Thousand Gone: The Ex-Slaves'*

Account of Their Bondage and Freedom. Leiden, 1963.

———. "Slave Narratives and the Plantation Legend." *Phylon,* X (1949), 201–210.

———. "Who Read the Slave Narratives?" *Phylon,* XX (1959), 149–162.

Nower, Joyce. "Foolin' Master." *Satire Newsletter,* VII (Fall 1969), 5–10.

———. "The Traditions of Negro Literature in the United States." *Negro American Literature Forum,* III (1969), 5–12.

Oden, Gloria. "Literature and Politics—The Black Investment." *The New School Bulletin,* XXIII (November 16, 1965), 1, 4.

Osofsky, Gilbert. "Symbols of the Jazz Age: The New Negro and Harlem Discovered." *American Quarterly,* XVII (1965), 229–236.

"Our Prize Winners and What They Say of Themselves." *Opportunity,* IV (1926), 188–189.

Oxley, Thomas L. G. "Survey of Negro Literature, 1760–1926." *The Messenger,* IX (February 1927), 37–39.

Palms, I (October 1926), entire issue.

Perkins, Eugene. "The Changing Status of Black Writers." *Black World,* XIX (June 1970), 18–23, 95–98.

Quantic, Diane Dufva. "Black Authors in Kansas." *Kansas English,* LV (December 1969), 14–16.

Record, Wilson. "The Negro as Creative Artist." *The Crisis,* LXXII (1965), 153–158, 193.

———. "The Negro Writer and the Communist Party." *The Black American Writer.* Ed. C. W. E. Bigsby. Deland, Fla., 1969. Vol. I, pp. 217–228.

Redding, Saunders. "American Negro Literature." *The American Scholar,* XVIII (1949), 137–148.

———. "The Black Revolution in American Studies." *American Studies: An International Newsletter,* IX (Autumn 1970), 3–9.

———. "Contradictions de la littérature négro-américaine." *Présence Africaine,* Nos. 27–28 (August–November 1959), pp. 11–15.

———. "Literature and the Negro." *Contemporary Literature,* IX (1968), 130–135.

———. "The Negro Author: His Publisher, His Public and His Purse." *Publishers Weekly,* CXLVII (March 24, 1945), 1284–1288.

———. "The Negro Writer and American Literature." *Anger, and Beyond: The Negro Writer in the United States.* Ed. Herbert Hill. New York, 1966. Pp. 1–19.

———. "The Negro Writer and His Relationship to His Roots." *The American Negro Writer and His Roots.* New York, 1960. Pp. 1–8.

———. "The Negro Writer—Shadow and Substance." *Phylon,* XI (1950), 371–373.

———. "Negro Writing in America." *The New Leader,* XLII (May 16, 1960), 8–10.

———. "The Problems of the Negro Writer." *The*

Massachusetts Review, VI (Autumn–Winter 1964–1965), 57–70.

———. "Since Richard Wright." *African Forum,* I (Spring 1966), 21–31.

———. *To Make a Poet Black.* Chapel Hill, N.C., 1939.

Reid, Ira DeA. "The Literature of the Negro: A Social Scientist's Appraisal." *Phylon,* XI (1950), 388–390.

Richardson, Jack. "The Black Arts." *The New York Review of Books,* XI (December 19, 1968), 10–13.

Rodgers, Carolyn M. "Breakforth. In Deed." *Black World,* XIX (September 1970), 13–22.

———. "The Literature of Black." *Black World,* XIX (June 1970), 5–11.

———. "Uh Nat'chal Thang—The WHOLE TRUTH —US." *Black World,* XX (September 1971), 4–14.

Rogers, J. A. "Negro Writers Have Had to Depend Upon Approval of Whites to Win Status." *The Pittsburgh Courier,* March 31, 1945, p. 7.

———. "Writers Picked up by White Publishers Fade Out Because Novelty of Product Wears Out." *The Pittsburgh Courier,* April 7, 1945, p. 7.

Rourke, Constance. "Tradition for a Negro Literature." *Roots of American Culture.* New York, 1942. Pp. 262–274.

Rousseve, Charles B. *The Negro in Louisiana: Aspects of His History and His Literature.* New Orleans, 1927.

Savage, Noël. "Black Literature: A Supplement." *The Month Ahead: Paperbound Books in Print,* XV (November 1970), 4–28.

Scally, Sister Mary Anthony. *Negro Catholic Writers 1900–1943: A Bio-Bibliography.* Detroit, 1945.

Schuyler, George S. *Black and Conservative.* New Rochelle, N.Y., 1966.

———. "The Negro Art Hokum." *The Nation,* CXXII (1926), 662–663.

———. "The Van Vechten Revolution." *Phylon,* XI (1950), 362–368.

———. "What's Wrong with Negro Authors." *Negro Digest,* VIII (May 1950), 3–7.

Scott, Nathan A., Jr. "Judgment Marked by a Cellar: The American Negro Writer and the Dialectic of Despair." *The Denver Quarterly,* II (Summer 1967), 5–35.

Shapiro, Karl. "The Decolonization of American Literature." *Wilson Library Bulletin,* XXXIX (1965), 842–853.

Shepard, Ray Anthony. "The Non-Black Teacher, Black Literature, and Black Students." *English Journal,* LIX (1970), 1071–1073.

Shih, Hsien-yung. "Impressions of American Negro Literature." *Chicago Review,* No. 4 (1966), pp. 107–112.

Singh, Raman K., ed. *Black Literature in America: A Casebook.* New York, 1970.

Smith, Arthur L. "Socio-Historical Perspectives of Black Oratory." *The Quarterly Journal of Speech,* LVI (1970), 264–269.

Smith, William Gardner. "The Negro Writer: Pitfalls and Compensations." *Phylon,* XI (1950), 297–303.

Spingarn, Arthur B. "Books by Negro Authors." *The Crisis,* 1938–1965, annual feature.

Sterling, Dorothy. "The Soul of Learning." *English Journal,* LVII (1968), 166–180.

Stimpson, Catharine R. "Black Culture/White Teacher." *Change,* II (May–June 1970), 35–40.

Swados, Harvey. "The Writer in Contemporary American Society." *Anger, and Beyond: The Negro Writer in the United States.* Ed. Herbert Hill. New York, 1966. Pp. 62–75.

Tatham, Campbell. "Double Order: The Spectrum of Black Aesthetics." *Midcontinent American Studies Journal,* XI (Fall 1970), 88–100.

Teer, Barbara Ann. "To Black Artists, With Love." *Negro Digest,* XVIII (April 1969), 4–8.

Thompson, Era Bell. "Negro Publications and the Writer." *Phylon,* XI (1950), 304–305.

Thornhill, G. C. "Negro Becomes Literary Contributor." *Poet Lore,* XXXIX (1928), 431–435.

Thurman, Wallace. "Negro Artists and the Negro." *The New Republic,* LII (August 31, 1927), 37–39.

———. "Nephews of Uncle Remus." *The Independent,* CXIX (September 24, 1927), 296–298.

Tillman, Nathaniel P. "The Theshold of Maturity." *Phylon,* XI (1950), 387–388.

Turner, Darwin T. "Afro-American Literary Critics." *Black World,* XIX (July 1970), 54–67.

———. "Literature and Society's Values." *English Journal,* LX (1971), 577–586.

———. "The Teaching of Afro-American Literature." *College English,* XXXI (1970), 666–670.

Turner, Lorenzo D. "Anti-Slavery Sentiment in American Literature Prior to 1865." *Journal of Negro History,* XIV (1929), 371–492.

Tuttleton, James W. "The Negro Writer as Spokesman." *The Black American Writer.* Ed. C. W. E. Bigsby. Deland, Fla., 1969. Vol. I, pp. 245–259.

Van Doren, Carl. "The Roving Critic." *Century,* CXI (1926), 637–639.

———. "The Younger Generation of Negro Writers." *Opportunity,* II (1924), 144–145.

Villard, Oswald Garrison. "Negro Literature." *Literary Review,* III (1923), 797–798.

Ward, Francis and Val Gray Ward. "The Black Artist—His Role in the Struggle." *The Black Scholar,* II (January 1971), 23–32.

Wessling, Joseph H. "Pressures on the Black Intellectual." *Negro American Literature Forum,* III (Winter 1970), 117–118.

Wetherill, Julie K. "The Negro as Producer of Literature." *The Chautauquan,* XV (1892), 224–225.

White, Walter. *A Man Called White.* New York, 1948.

———. "Negro Literature." *American Writers on*

American Literature. Ed. John Macy. New York, 1931. Pp. 442–451.

Wilkerson, Doxey A. "Negro Culture: Heritage and Weapon." *Masses and Mainstream,* II (August 1949), 3–24.

Williams, John A. "The Harlem Renaissance: Its Artists, Its Impact, Its Meaning." *Black World,* XX (November 1970), 17–18.

———. "Negro in Literature Today." *Ebony,* VIII (September 1963), 73–76.

Williams, Kenny J. *They Also Spoke: An Essay on Negro Literature in America, 1787–1930.* Nashville, 1970.

Woolridge, Nancy. "English Critics and the Negro Writers." *Phylon,* XV (1954), 139–146.

Wright, Richard. "Blueprint for Negro Writing." *New Challenge,* I (1937), 53–65.

———. *White Man, Listen!* Garden City, N.Y., 1957.

Yellin, Jean Fagan. *The Intricate Knot: The Negro in American Literature 1776–1863.* New York, 1971.

Zietlow, Edward Robert. "Wright to Hansberry: The Evolution of Outlook in Four Negro Writers." *Dissertation Abstracts,* XXVIII (August 1967), 701-A.

Poetry

Bailey, Leaonead. *Broadside Authors: A Biographical Directory.* Detroit, 1971.

Barksdale, Richard K. "Trends in Contemporary Poetry." *Phylon,* XIX (1958), 408–416.

———. "Urban Crisis and the Black Poetic Avant-Garde." *Negro American Literature Forum,* III (1969), 40–44.

Bennett, M. W. "Negro Poets." *Negro History Bulletin,* IX (1946), 171–172, 191.

Berger, Art. "Negroes with Pens." *Mainstream,* XVI (July 1963), 3–6.

Bland, Edward. "Racial Bias and Negro Poetry." *Poetry,* LXIII (1944), 328–333.

Bone, Robert. "American Negro Poets: A French View." *Tri-Quarterly,* No. 4 (1965), pp. 185–195.

Bontemps, Arna. "American Negro Poetry." *The Crisis,* LXX (1963), 509.

———. "Negro Poets, Then and Now." *Phylon,* XI (1950), 355–360.

Braithwaite, William Stanley. "Some Contemporary Poets of the Negro Race." *The Crisis,* XVII (1919), 275–280.

Breman, Paul. "Poetry Into the 'Sixties." *The Black American Writer.* Ed. C. W. E. Bigsby. Deland, Fla., 1969. Vol. II, pp. 99–109.

Brooks, Gwendolyn. "Poets Who Are Negro." *Phylon,* XI (1950), 312.

Brown, Sterling A. "The Blues." *Phylon,* XIII (1952), 286–292.

———. "Negro Folk Expression: Spirituals, Seculars, Ballads, and Songs." *Phylon,* XIV (1953), 45–61.

———. *Negro Poetry and Drama.* Washington, D.C., 1937.

———. *Outline for the Study of the Poetry of American Negroes.* New York, 1931.

Cartey, Wilfred. "Four Shadows of Harlem." *Negro Digest,* XVIII (August 1969), 22–25.

Chapman, Abraham. "Black Poetry Today." *Arts in Society,* V (1968), 401–408.

Charters, Samuel B. *The Poetry of the Blues.* New York, 1963.

Collier, Eugenia W. "Heritage from Harlem." *Black World,* XX (November 1970), 52–59.

———. "I Do Not Marvel, Countee Cullen." *CLA Journal,* XI (1967), 73–87.

Davis, Arthur P. "The New Poetry of Black Hate." *CLA Journal,* XIII (1970), 382–391.

Daykin, Walter I. "Race Consciousness in Negro Poetry." *Sociology and Social Research,* XX (1936), 98–105.

Echeruo, M. J. C. "American Negro Poetry." *Phylon,* XXIV (1963), 62–68.

Ellison, Martha. "Velvet Voices Feed on Bitter Fruit: A Study of American Negro Poetry." *Poet and Critic,* IV (Winter 1967–1968), 39–49.

Ely, Effie Smith. "American Negro Poetry." *The Christian Century,* XL (1923), 366–367.

Furay, Michael. "Africa in Negro American Poetry to 1929." *African Literature Today,* II (1969), 32–41.

Garrett, DeLois. "Dream Motif in Contemporary Negro Poetry." *English Journal,* LIX (1970), 767–770.

Garrett, Naomi M. "Racial Motifs in Contemporary American and French Negro Poetry." *West Virginia University Philological Papers,* XIV (1963), 80–101.

Glicksberg, Charles I. "Negro Poets and the American Tradition." *The Antioch Review,* VI (1946), 243–253.

Good, Charles Hamlin. "The First American Negro Literary Movement." *Opportunity,* X (1932), 76–79.

Heath, Phoebe Anne. "Negro Poetry as an Historical Record." *Vassar Journal of Undergraduate Studies,* III (May 1928), 34–52.

Horne, Frank S. "Black Verse." *Opportunity,* II (1924), 330–332.

Johnson, Charles S. "Jazz Poetry and Blues." *Carolina Magazine,* LVIII (May 1928), 16–20.

Johnson, James Weldon, "Preface." *The Book of American Negro Poetry.* Ed. James Weldon Johnson. New York, 1931. Pp. 3–48.

Kerlin, Robert T. "Conquest by Poetry." *The Southern Workman,* LVI (1927), 282–284.

———. *Contemporary Poetry of the Negro.* Hampton, Va., 1921.

———. "A Pair of Youthful Negro Poets." *The Southern Workman,* LIII (1924), 178–181.

———. "Present-Day Negro Poets." *The Southern Workman,* XLIX (1920), 543–548.

———. "Singers of New Songs." *Opportunity,* IV (1926), 162–164.

Kilgore, James C. "Toward the Dark Tower." *Black World,* XIX (June 1970), 14–17.

Kjersmeier, Carl. "Negroes as Poets." *The Crisis,* XXX (1925), 186–189.

Lee, Don L. "Black Poetry: Which Direction?" *Negro Digest,* XVII (September–October 1968), 27–32.

———. *Dynamite Voices: Black Poets of the 1960's.* Detroit, 1971.

Locke, Alain. "The Message of the Negro Poets." *Carolina Magazine,* LVIII (May 1928), 5–15.

Moore, Gerald. "Poetry in the Harlem Renaissance." *The Black American Writer.* Ed. C. W. E. Bigsby. Deland, Fla., 1969. Vol. II, pp. 67–76.

Morpurgo, J. E. "American Negro Poetry." *Fortnightly,* CLXVIII (July 1947), 16–24.

Morton, Lena Beatrice. *Negro Poetry in America.* Boston, 1925.

"Negro Poetry." *Encyclopedia of Poetry and Poetics.* Ed. Alex Preminger, Frank J. Warnke, and O. B. Hardison. Princeton, N.J., 1965. Pp. 558–559.

"Negro Poets, Singers in the Dawn." *The Negro History Bulletin,* II (1938), 9–10, 14–15.

Oliver, Paul. *Blues Fell This Morning: The Meaning of The Blues.* New York, 1960.

———. *Conversation with the Blues.* New York, 1965.

Pool, Rosey. "The Discovery of American Negro Poetry." *Freedomways,* III (1963), 46–51.

Ramsaran, J. A. "The 'Twice-Born' Artists' Silent Revolution." *Black World,* XX (May 1971), 58–68.

Redmond, Eugene B. "The Black American Epic: Its Roots, Its Writers." *The Black Scholar,* II (January 1971), 15–22.

Rodgers, Carolyn M. "Black Poetry—Where It's At." *Negro Digest,* XVIII (September 1969), 7–16.

Rollins, Charlemae. *Famous American Negro Poets.* New York, 1965.

Taussig, Charlotte E. "The New Negro as Revealed in His Poetry." *Opportunity,* V (1927), 108–111.

Thurman, Wallace. "Negro Poets and Their Poetry." *The Bookman,* LXVII (1928), 555–561.

"The Umbra Poets." *Mainstream,* XVI (July 1963), 7–13.

"The Undaunted Pursuit of Fury." *Time,* XCV (April 6, 1970), 98–100.

Wagner, Jean. *Les poètes nègres des États-Unis: Le sentiment racial et réligieux dans la poésie de P. L. Dunbar à L. Hughes.* Paris, 1963.

Walker, Margaret. "New Poets." *Phylon,* XI (1950), 345–354.

White, Newman I. "American Negro Poetry." *South Atlantic Quarterly,* XX (1921), 304–322.

———. "Racial Feeling in Negro Poetry." *South Atlantic Quarterly,* XXI (1922), 14–29.

Work, Monroe N. "The Spirit of Negro Poetry." *The Southern Workman,* XXXVII (1908), 73–77.

Fiction

Arden, Eugene. "The Early Harlem Novel." *Phylon,* XX (1959), 25–31.

Barcus, F. Earle and Jack Levin. "Role Distance in Negro and Majority Fiction." *Journalism Quarterly,* XLIII (1966), 709–714.

Barksdale, Richard K. "Alienation and the Anti-Hero in Recent American Fiction." *CLA Journal,* X (1966), 1–10.

Barton, Rebecca C. *Race Consciousness and the American Negro: A Study of the Correlation Between the Group Experience and the Fiction of 1900–1930.* Copenhagen, 1934.

Beja, Morris. "It Must Be Important: Negroes in Contemporary American Fiction." *The Antioch Review,* XXIV (1964), 323–336.

Blanch, Antonio, S. J. "El problema negro en la novela norteamericana." *Razón y Fe,* CLXXVIII (1968), 203–222.

Bland, Edward. "Social Forces Shaping the Negro Novel." *The Negro Quarterly,* I (1942), 241–248.

Bone, Robert A. *The Negro Novel in America.* Rev. ed. New Haven, Conn., 1965.

Brawley, Benjamin. "The Negro in American Fiction." *The Dial,* LX (1916), 445–450.

Britt, David Dobbs. "The Image of the White Man in the Fiction of Langston Hughes, Richard Wright, James Baldwin and Ralph Ellison." *Dissertation Abstracts,* XXIX (November 1968), 1532-A.

Brown, Sterling A. *The Negro in American Fiction.* Washington, D.C., 1937.

Bullock, Penelope. "The Mulatto in American Fiction." *Phylon,* VI (1945), 78–82.

Butcher, Philip. "The Younger Novelists and the Urban Negro." *CLA Journal,* IV (1961), 196–203.

Byrd, James W. "Stereotypes of White Characters in Early Negro Novels." *CLA Journal,* I (1957), 28–35.

Cary, Elisabeth L. "A New Element in Fiction." *The Book Buyer,* XXIII (1901), 26–28.

Chandler, G. Lewis. "Coming of Age: A Note on American Negro Novelists." *Phylon,* IX (1948), 25–29.

———. "A Major Problem of Negro Authors in Their March Toward Belles-Lettres." *Phylon,* XI (1950), 383–386.

Clarke, John Henrik. "Transition in the American Negro Short Story." *Phylon,* XXI (1960), 360–366.

Cooke, Michael, ed. *Modern Black Novelists: A Collection of Critical Essays.* Englewood Cliffs, N.J., 1971.

Cothran, Tilman C. "White Stereotypes in Fiction by Negroes." *Phylon,* XI (1950), 252–256.

Daykin, Walter I. "Social Thought in Negro Novels." *Sociology and Social Research,* XIX (1935), 247–252.

Ellison, Ralph. "Recent Negro Fiction." *New Masses,* XL (August 5, 1941), 22–25.

Ford, Nick Aaron. *The Contemporary Negro Novel: A Study in Race Relations.* Boston, 1936.

———. "Four Popular Negro Novelists." *Phylon,* XV (1954), 29–39.

———. "The Negro Novel as a Vehicle of Propaganda." *The Quarterly Review of Higher Education Among Negroes,* IX (1941), 135–139.

Fuller, Hoyt W. "Contemporary Negro Fiction." *Southwest Review,* L (1965), 321–335.

Gayle, Addison, Jr. "Cultural Nationalism: The Black Novel and the City." *Liberator,* IX (July 1969), 14–17.

Gérard, Albert. "Humanism and Negritude: Notes on the Contemporary Afro-American Novel." *Diogenes,* No. 37 (Spring 1962), pp. 115–133.

———. *Les tambours du néant: Le problème existentiel dans le roman américaine.* Brussels, 1969.

Glicksberg, Charles I. "Bias, Fiction, and the Negro." *Phylon,* XIII (1952), 127–135.

———. "The God of Fiction." *The Colorado Quarterly,* VII (1958), 207–220.

———. "The Negro Cult of the Primitive." *The Antioch Review,* IV (1944), 47–55.

———. "Negro Fiction in America." *The South Atlantic Quarterly,* XLV (1946), 477–488.

Gloster, Hugh M. *Negro Voices in American Fiction.* Chapel Hill, N.C., 1948.

Gordon, Eugene. "Negro Novelists and the Negro Masses." *New Masses,* VIII (July 1933), 16–20.

Grimes, Alan and Janet Owen. "Civil Rights and the Race Novel." *The Chicago Jewish Forum,* XV (1956), 12–15.

Heermance, J. Noel. "The Modern Negro Novel." *Negro Digest,* XIII (May 1964), 66–76.

Hemenway, Robert, ed. *The Black Novelist.* Columbus, Ohio, 1970.

Howe, Irving. *A World More Attractive.* New York, 1963.

Huggins, Kathryn. "Aframerican Fiction." *The Southern Literary Messenger,* III (1941), 315–320.

Hughes, Carl Milton. *The Negro Novelist: A Discussion of the Writings of American Negro Novelists, 1940–1950.* New York, 1953.

Jackson, Blyden. "A Golden Mean for the Negro Novel." *CLA Journal,* III (1959), 81–87.

———. "The Negro's Image of the Universe as Reflected in His Fiction." *CLA Journal,* IV (1960), 22–31.

———. "The Negro's Negro in Negro Literature." *Michigan Quarterly Review,* IV (1965), 290–295.

Jarrett, Thomas. "Recent Fiction by Negroes." *College English,* XVI (1954), 85–91.

———. "Toward Unfettered Creativity: A Note on the Negro Novelist's Coming of Age." *Phylon,* XI (1950), 313–317.

Kent, George E. "Ethnic Impact in American Literature: Reflections on a Course." *CLA Journal,* XI (1967), 24–37.

Knox, George. "The Negro Novelist's Sensibility and the Outsider Theme." *Western Humanities Review,* XI (1957), 137–148.

Larson, Charles R. "Three Harlem Novels of the Jazz Age." *Critique,* XI, No. 3 (1969), 66–78.

Lehan, Richard. "Existentialism in Recent American Fiction: The Demonic Quest." *Texas Studies in Literature and Language,* I (1959), 181–202.

Marcus, Steven. "The American Negro in Search of Identity." *Commentary,* XVI (1953), 456–463.

Maund, Alfred. "The Negro Novelist and the Contemporary Scene." *The Chicago Jewish Forum,* XIII (1954), 28–34.

May, John R., S.J. "Images of the Apocalypse in the Black Novel." *Renascence,* XXIII (Autumn 1970), 31–45.

Meier, August. "Some Reflections on the Negro Novel." *CLA Journal,* II (1959), 168–177.

Moon, Bucklin. "A Literature of Protest." *The Reporter,* I (December 6, 1949), 35–37.

Mulder, Arnold. "Wanted: A Negro Novelist." *The Independent,* CXII (1924), 341–342.

Muraskin, William. "An Alienated Elite: Short Stories in *The Crisis,* 1910–1950." *Journal of Black Studies,* I (1971), 282–305.

Murray, Albert. "Something Different, Something More." *Anger, and Beyond: The Negro Writer in the United States.* Ed. Herbert Hill. New York, 1966. Pp. 112–137.

Paz, Magdeleine. "Romans: La caravan noir." *Présence Africaine,* No. 4, pp. 714–718.

Peavy, Charles D. "The Black Revolutionary Novel: 1899–1969." *Studies in the Novel,* III (1971), 180–189.

Reddick, L. D. "No Kafka in the South." *Phylon,* XI (1950), 380–383.

Rideout, Walter B. *The Radical Novel in the United States, 1900–1954.* Cambridge, Mass., 1956.

Rogge, Heinz. "Die amerikanische Negerfrage im Lichte der Literatur von Richard Wright und Ralph Ellison." *Die neueren Sprachen,* No. 2 (1958), pp. 56–69; No. 3 (1958), pp. 103–117.

Starke, Catherine J. *Black Portraiture in American Fiction: Stock Characters, Archetypes, and Individuals.* New York, 1971.

Starke, Juanita. "Symbolism of the Negro College in Three Recent Novels." *Phylon,* XVII (1956), 365–373.

Thomas, Will. "Negro Writers of Pulp Fiction." *Negro Digest,* VIII (July 1950), 81–84.

Tischler, Nancy M. *Black Masks: Negro Characters in Modern Southern Fiction.* University Park, Pa., 1969.

Turner, Darwin T. "*The Negro Novel in America:* In Rebuttal." *CLA Journal,* X (1966), 122–134.

———. "The Negro Novelist and the South." *Southern Humanities Review,* I (1967), 21–29.

Turpin, Waters E. "Four Short Fiction Writers of the

Harlem Renaissance—Their Legacy of Achievement." *CLA Journal,* XI (1967), 59–72.

Ward, Theodore. "Five Negro Novelists: Revolt and Retreat." *Mainstream,* I (Winter 1947), 100–110.

Warfel, Harry R. *American Novelists of Today.* New York, 1951.

Weimer, David R. "Black Realities and White: The City and the Imagination Gap." *Southwest Review,* LIV (1969), 105–119.

Winslow, Henry. "Two Visions of Reality." *Negro Digest,* XVI (May 1967), 36–39.

Drama

Abramson, Doris E. "Negro Playwrights in America." *Columbia Forum,* XII (Spring 1969), 11–17.

———. *Negro Playwrights in the American Theatre, 1925–1959.* New York, 1969.

Alexander, Lewis M. "Plays of Negro Life, A Survey." *Carolina Magazine,* LIX (April 1929), 45–57.

Arnez, Nancy L. and Clara B. Anthony. "Contemporary Negro Humor as Social Satire." *Phylon,* XXIX (1968), 339–346.

Bailey, Peter. "Is the Negro Ensemble Company *Really* Black Theater?" *Negro Digest,* XVII (April 1968), 16–19.

——— et al. Annual "Report on Black Theater in America." *Negro Digest,* XVIII (April 1969), 20–26, 69–72; XIX (April 1970), 25–37, 42, 85, 98; *Black World,* XX (April 1971), 4–26, 95–96.

——— et al. "Talking of Black Art, Theatre, Revolution and Nationhood." *Black Theatre,* No. 5 (1971), pp. 18–37.

Baldwin, James. "Theatre: The Negro in and out." *Negro Digest,* XV (April 1966), 37–44.

Belcher, Fannin S. "Negro Drama, Stage Center." *Opportunity,* XVII (1939), 292–295.

Belcher, Fannin S., Jr. "The Negro Theatre: A Glance Backward." *Phylon,* XI (1950), 121–126.

Bessie, Alvah. "New Negro Theater." *New Masses,* XXXVII (September 24, 1940), 23.

Bigsby, C. W. E. "Black Drama in the Seventies." *Kansas Quarterly,* III (Spring 1971), 10–20.

———. "Three Black Playwrights: Loften Mitchell, Ossie Davis, Douglas Turner Ward." *The Black American Writer.* Ed. C. W. E. Bigsby. Deland, Fla., 1969. Vol. II, pp. 137–155.

"Black Playwrights Get a Break." *Sepia,* XVII (November 1968), 20–23.

Bond, Frederick W. *The Negro and the Drama: The Direct and Indirect Contribution Which the American Negro Has Made to Drama and the Legitimate Stage.* Washington, D.C., 1940.

Bradley, Gerald. "Goodbye Mr. Bones: The Emergence of Negro Themes and Character in American Drama." *Drama Critique,* VII (1964), 79–86.

Brown, Sterling A. *Negro Poetry and Drama.* Washington, D.C., 1937.

Bullins, Ed. "Black Theatre Groups: A Directory." *The Drama Review,* XII (Summer 1968), 172–175.

———. "Black Theatre Notes." *Black Theatre,* No. 1 (1968), p. 4.

———. "A Short Statement on Street Theatre." *The Drama Review,* XII (Summer 1968), 93.

———. "Theatre of Reality." *Negro Digest,* XV (April 1966), 60–66.

Butcher, Margaret. *The Negro in American Culture.* New York, 1956.

Campbell, Dick. "Is There a Conspiracy Against Black Playwrights?" *Negro Digest,* XVII (April 1968), 11–15.

Carolina Magazine, LIX (April 1929), entire issue.

Childress, Alice. "A Woman Playwright Speaks Her Mind." *Freedomways,* VI (1966), 75–80.

Coleman, Mike and Imamu Amiri Baraka. "What Is Black Theater?" *Black World,* XX (April 1971), 32–36.

Cotton, Lettie Jo. "The Negro in the American Theatre." *The Negro History Bulletin,* XXIII (1960), 172–178.

Couch, William, Jr. "The Problem of Negro Character and Dramatic Incident." *Phylon,* XI (1950), 127–133.

Davis, Ossie. "The Flight from Broadway." *Negro Digest,* XV (April 1966), 14–19.

Dixon, Melvin. "Black Theater: The Aesthetics." *Negro Digest,* XVIII (July 1969), 41–44.

Dodson, Owen. "Playwrights in Dark Glasses." *Negro Digest,* XVII (April 1968), 30–36.

Edmonds, Randolph. *Shades and Shadows.* Boston, 1930.

———. "Some Reflections on the Negro in American Drama." *Opportunity,* VIII (1930), 303–305.

Elder, Lonne. "A Negro Idea Theatre." *American Dialog,* I (July–August 1964), 30–31.

Evans, Donald T. "Bring It All Back Home." *Black World,* XX (February 1971), 41–45.

Ferdinand, Val. "The Dashiki Project Theatre, We Are the Theater." *Black Theatre,* No. 3 (1969), pp. 4–6.

———. "News from Blkartsouth." *Black Theatre,* No. 4 (1970), p. 4.

Fletcher, Tom. *The Tom Fletcher Story: 100 Years of the Negro in Show Business!* New York, 1954.

Fuller, Hoyt W. "Black Theater in America." *Negro Digest,* XVII (April 1968), 83–93.

———. "Up in Harlem: New Hope." *Negro Digest,* XIV (October 1965), 49–50.

Gaffney, Floyd. "Black Theatre: Commitment & Communication." *The Black Scholar,* I (June 1970), 10–15.

Goncalves, Joe. "The Mysterious Disappearance of Black Arts West." *Black Theatre,* No. 2 (1969), pp. 23–25.

———. "West Coast Drama." *Black Theatre,* No. 4 (1970), p. 27.

Good, Charles Hamlin. "The First American Literary Movement." *Opportunity,* X (1932), 76–79.

Greenwood, Frank. "Burn, Baby, Burn!" *Freedomways,* VII (1967), 244–247.

Gregory, Montgomery. "The Drama of Negro Life." *The New Negro: An Interpretation.* Ed. Alain Locke. New York, 1925. Pp. 153–160.

Hanau, D. "Ghetto Theatre: Vital Drama or Social Therapy?" *Community,* XXVI (April 1967), 7–10.

Harris, Henrietta. "Building a Black Theatre." *The Drama Review,* XII (Summer 1968), 157–158.

Hatch, James V. *Black Image on the American Stage.* New York, 1970.

Hilliard, Robert L. "The Drama and American Negro Life." *Southern Theatre,* X (Winter 1966), 12–13.

Holder, Geoffrey. "The Awful Afro Trend." *Show,* II (March 1962), 94–95.

Hughes, Langston and Milton Meltzer. *Black Magic: A Pictorial History of the Negro in American Entertainment.* New York, 1967.

Isaacs, Edith R. *The Negro in the American Theatre.* New York, 1947.

Jefferson, Miles M. "The Negro on Broadway." *Phylon,* 1945–1957, annual feature.

Johnson, Helen Armstead. "Playwrights, Audiences and Critics." *Negro Digest,* XIX (April 1970), 17–24.

Johnson, James Weldon. *Black Manhattan.* New York, 1930.

Jones, LeRoi (Imamu Amiri Baraka). "In Search of the Revolutionary Black Theatre." *Negro Digest,* XV (April 1966), 20–24.

———. "What the Arts Need Now." *Negro Digest,* XVI (April 1967), 5–6.

Kgositsile, K. W. "Towards Our Theatre: A Definitive Act." *Negro Digest,* XVI (April 1967), 14–16.

Killens, John Oliver. "Broadway in Black and White." *African Forum,* I (Winter 1966), 66–76.

King, Woodie, Jr. "Black Theatre: Present Condition." *The Drama Review,* XII (Summer 1968), 117–124.

———. "Black Theatre: Weapon for Change." *Negro Digest,* XVI (April 1967), 35–39.

———. "The Dilemma of a Black Theater." *Negro Digest,* XIX (April 1970), 10–15, 86–87.

"Krigwa Players' Little Negro Theatre." *The Crisis,* XXXIII (1926), 134–136.

Leonard, Claire. "Dark Drama." *Negro Digest,* II (August 1944), 81–82.

Locke, Alain. "Broadway and the Negro Drama." *Theatre Arts,* XXV (1941), 745–752.

———. "The Drama of Negro Life." *Theatre Arts,* X (1926), 701–706.

———. "The Negro and the American Theatre." *Theatre: Essays on the Arts of the Theatre.* Ed. Edith J. R. Isaacs. Boston, 1927. Pp. 290–303.

———. "Steps Toward the Negro Theatre." *The Crisis,* XXV (1922), 66–68.

Long, Richard A. "Crisis of Consciousness." *Negro Digest,* XVII (May 1968), 88–92.

Miller, Adam. "It's a Long Way to St. Louis: Notes on the Audience for Black Drama." *The Drama Review,* XII (Summer 1968), 147–150.

Miller, Adam David. "News from the San Francisco East Bay." *Black Theatre,* No. 4 (1970), p. 5.

Miller, Larry. "Spirit House." *Black Theatre,* No. 2 (1969), p. 34.

Millian, Bruce E. "Detroit Repertory Theatre." *Black Theatre,* No. 2 (1969), pp. 4–5.

Milner, Ronald. "Black Magic: Black Art." *Negro Digest,* XVI (April 1967), 8–12.

———. "Black Theater—Go Home." *Negro Digest,* XVII (April 1968), 5–10.

Mitchell, Loften. "Black Drama." *Negro Digest,* XVI (April 1967), 75–87.

———. *Black Drama: The Story of the American Negro in the Theater.* New York, 1967.

———. "The Negro Theatre and the Harlem Community." *Freedomways,* III (1963), 384–394.

———. "On the 'Emerging' Playwright." *The Black American Writer.* Ed. C. W. E. Bigsby. Deland, Fla., 1969. Vol. II, pp. 129–136.

———. "Three Writers and a Dream." *The Crisis,* LXXII (1965), 219–223.

Molette, Carlton W., II. "The First Afro-American Theater." *Negro Digest,* XIX (April 1970), 4–9.

Morrison, Allan. "A New Surge in the Arts." *Ebony,* XXII (August 1967), 134–138.

Neal, Larry. "The Black Arts Movement." *The Drama Review,* XII (Summer 1968), 28–39.

———. "Cultural Nationalism and Black Theatre." *Black Theatre,* No. 1 (1968), pp. 8–10.

———. "Toward a Relevant Black Theatre." *Black Theatre,* No. 4 (1970), pp. 14–15.

O'Neal, Frederick. "Problems and Prospects." *Negro Digest,* XV (April 1966), 4–12.

O'Neal, John. "Motion in the Ocean: Some Political Dimensions of the Free Southern Theatre." *The Drama Review,* XII (Summer 1968), 70–77.

Orman, Roscoe. "The New Lafayette Theatre." *Black Theatre,* No. 2 (1969), pp. 5–6; No. 4 (1970), p. 6; No. 5 (1971), pp. 12–13.

Patterson, Lindsay, ed. *Anthology of the American Negro in the Theater.* New York, 1969.

Peavy, Charles D. "Satire and Contemporary Black Drama." *Satire Newsletter,* VII (1969), 40–49.

Rashidd, Naima. "Black Theatre in Detroit." *Black Theatre,* No. 4 (1970), p. 3.

Reardon, William R. and Thomas D. Pawley, eds. *The Black Teacher and the Dramatic Arts.* Westport, Conn., 1970.

Riach, W. A. D. "'Telling It Like It Is': An Examination of Black Theatre as Rhetoric." *The Quarterly Journal of Speech,* LVI (1970), 179–186.

Riddell, Hugh J. "New Negro Playwrights Group Formed in Harlem." *Daily Worker,* July 27, 1940, p. 7.

Sandle, Floyd L. *The Negro in the American Educational Theatre: An Organizational Development: 1911–1964.* Ann Arbor, Mich., 1964.

Schuck, Barry. "Philadelphia's Black Drama Season '67–'68." *Black Theatre*, No. 2 (1969), pp. 34–35.

Selby, John. *Beyond Civil Rights.* Cleveland, 1966.

Taylor, Jeanne A. "On Being Black and Writing for Television." *Negro American Literature Forum*, IV (1970), 79–82.

Thompson, T. "Burst of Negro Drama." *Life*, LVI (May 29, 1964), 62A–70.

Turner, Darwin T. "The Black Playwright in the Professional Theatre of the United States of America, 1858–1949." *Black Drama: An Anthology.* Ed. William Brasmer and Dominick Consolo. Columbus, Ohio, 1970. Pp. 1–18.

———. "The Negro Dramatist's Image of the Universe." *CLA Journal*, V (1961), 106–120.

———. "Negro Playwrights and the Urban Negro." *CLA Journal*, XII (1968), 19–25.

———. "Past and Present in Negro Drama." *Negro American Literature Forum*, II (1968), 26–27.

Turner, Sherry. "An Overview of the New Black Arts." *Freedomways*, IX (1969), 156–163.

Turpin, Waters E. "The Contemporary American Negro Playwright." *CLA Journal*, IX (1965), 12–24.

Ward, Douglas Turner. "Needed: A Theater for Black Themes." *Negro Digest*, XVII (December 1967), 34–39.

Ward, Theodore. "The South Side Center of the Performing Arts, Inc." *Black Theatre*, No. 2 (1969), pp. 3–4.

"Why Not a Negro Drama for Negroes by Negroes?" *Current Opinion*, LXXII (1922), 639–640.

Williams, Jim. "The Need for a Harlem Theatre." *Freedomways*, III (1963), 307–311.

———. "Pieces on Black Theatre and the Black Theatre Worker." *Freedomways*, IX (1969), 146–155.

———. "Survey of Afro-American Playwrights." *Freedomways*, X (1970), 26–45.

X, Marvin. "The Black Ritual Theatre: An Interview with Robert Macbeth." *Black Theatre*, No. 3 (1969), pp. 20–24.

———. "An Interview with LeRoi Jones." *Black Theatre*, No. 1 (1968), pp. 16–18.

FOLKLORE

Abrahams, Roger. *Deep Down in the Jungle: Negro Narrative Folklore from the Streets of Philadelphia.* Hatboro, Pa., 1964.

———. *Positively Black.* Englewood Cliffs, N.J., 1970.

Adams, Edward C. L. *Congaree Sketches.* Chapel Hill, N.C., 1927.

Brewer, J. Mason. "American Negro Folklore." *Phylon*, VI (1945), 354–361.

———. *American Negro Folklore.* Chicago, 1968.

———. *Aunt Dicy Tales.* Austin, Texas, 1956.

———. *Dog Ghosts and Other Texas Negro Folk Tales.* Austin, Texas, 1958.

———. *Humorous Folktales of the South Carolina Negro.* Orangeburg, S.C., 1945.

———. "Negro Folklore in North America." *New Mexico Quarterly*, XVI (1946), 47–48.

———. *The Word on the Brazos.* Austin, Texas, 1953.

———. *Worser Days and Better Times: The Folklore of the North Carolina Negro.* Chicago, 1965.

Brookes, Stella Brewer. *Joel Chandler Harris, Folklorist.* Athens, Ga., 1950.

Brown, Sterling A. "The Blues." *Phylon*, XIII (1952), 286–292.

———. "Negro Folk Expression: Spirituals, Seculars, Ballads, and Songs." *Phylon*, XIV (1953), 45–61.

Byrd, James W. *J. Mason Brewer: Negro Folklorist.* Austin, Texas, 1967.

Carawan, Guy and Candie Carawan, eds. *Freedom Is a Constant Struggle: Songs of the Freedom Movement.* New York, 1968.

Carmer, Carl L. *Stars Fell on Alabama.* New York, 1934.

Clark, Kenneth. "Folklore of Negro Children in Greater Louisville Reflecting Attitudes Toward Race." *Kentucky Folklore Record*, X (1964), 1–11.

Conley, Dorothy L. "Origin of the Negro Spirituals." *The Negro History Bulletin*, XXV (1962), 179–180.

Courlander, Harold. *Negro Folk Music, U.S.A.* New York, 1963.

Crowley, Daniel J. "Negro Folklore: An Africanist's View." *Texas Quarterly*, VII (1962), 65–71.

Davis, H. C. "Negro Folklore in South Carolina." *Journal of American Folklore*, XXVII (1914), 241–254.

Dobie, J. Frank, ed. *Follow de Drinkin' Gou'd.* Austin, Texas, 1928.

Dorson, Richard M. *American Negro Folktales.* New York, 1967.

———. "The Career of John Henry." *Western Folklore*, XXIV (1965), 155–163.

———. *Negro Folktales in Michigan.* Cambridge, Mass., 1956.

———. "A Negro Storytelling Session on Tape." *Midwest Folklore*, II (1953), 201–212.

———. "Negro Tales." *Western Folklore*, XIII (1954), 77–97, 160–169.

———. "Negro Tales from Bolivar County, Mississippi." *Southern Folklore Quarterly*, XIX (1955), 104–116.

———. *Negro Tales from Pine Bluff, Arkansas, and Calvin, Michigan.* Bloomington, Ind., 1958.

————. "Negro Witch Stories on Tape." *Midwest Folklore,* II (1952), 229–241.

Ellis, A. B. "Evolution in Folklore: Some West African Prototypes of the Uncle Remus Stories." *Popular Science,* XLVIII (November 1895), 93–104.

Fauset, Arthur Huff. "American Negro Folklore." *The New Negro: An Interpretation.* Ed. Alain Locke. New York, 1925. Pp. 238–244.

Fisher, Miles Mark. *Negro Slave Songs in the United States.* New York, 1963.

Georgia Writers' Project. *Drums and Shadows: Survival Studies Among the Georgia Coastal Negroes.* Athens, Ga., 1940.

Gerber, A. J. "Uncle Remus Traced to the Old World." *Journal of American Folklore,* VI (1895), 245.

Gonzales, Ambrose E. *With Aesop Along the Black Border.* New York, 1969.

Grissom, Mary A. *The Negro Sings a New Heaven.* Chapel Hill, N.C., 1930.

Handy, W. C. and Abbe Niles, eds. *Treasury of the Blues.* New York, 1949.

Harris, Joel Chandler. *Daddy Jake the Runaway, and Short Stories Told After Dark.* New York, 1889.

————. *Nights with Uncle Remus: Myths and Legends of the Old Plantation.* Boston, 1883.

————. *Tar-Baby, and Other Rhymes of Uncle Remus.* New York, 1904.

————. *Told by Uncle Remus: New Stories of the Old Plantation.* New York, 1905.

————. *Uncle Remus and Brer Rabbit.* New York, 1906.

————. *Uncle Remus and His Friends: Old Plantation Stories, Songs and Ballads, with Sketches of Negro Character.* Boston, 1892.

————. *Uncle Remus, His Songs and His Sayings.* New York, 1880.

————. *Uncle Remus and the Little Boy.* Boston, 1910.

————. *Uncle Remus Returns.* Boston, 1918.

Heyward, DuBose and Hervey Allen. *Carolina Chansons: Legends of the Low Country.* New York, 1922.

Hughes, Langston, ed. *The Book of Negro Humor.* New York, 1966.

———— and Arna Bontemps, eds. *The Book of Negro Folklore.* New York, 1958.

Hurston, Zora N. "High John de Conjure; Negro Folklore Offers Solace to Sufferers." *American Mercury,* LVII (1943), 450–458.

————. *Mules and Men.* Philadelphia, 1935.

————. *Tell My Horse.* Philadelphia, 1938.

Jackson, Bruce, ed. *The Negro and His Folklore in Nineteenth Century Periodicals.* Austin, Texas, 1967.

Jackson, Clyde O. *The Songs of Our Years: A Study of Negro Folk Music.* New York, 1968.

Jackson, Margaret Y. "Folklore in Slave Narratives Before the Civil War." *New York Folklore Quarterly* XI (April 1955), 5–19.

Johnson, Guy Benton. *Folk Culture on St. Helena Island, South Carolina.* Chapel Hill, N.C., 1930.

————. *John Henry: Tracking Down a Negro Legend.* Chapel Hill, N.C., 1929.

Johnson, James W., ed. *The Book of American Negro Spirituals.* New York, 1925; *The Second Book of Negro Spirituals.* New York, 1926.

Jones, Harry L. "An Essay on the Blues." *CLA Journal,* XIII (1969), 62–67.

Jones, LeRoi (Imamu Amiri Baraka). *Black Music.* New York, 1967.

————. *Blues People: Negro Music in White America.* New York, 1963.

Kennedy, R. Emmett. *Black Cameos.* New York, 1924.

Krebhiel, Henry Edward. *Afro-American Folksongs: A Study in Racial and National Music.* New York, 1914.

La Crosse, Ken and Gerald Haslam. "An Inquiry Model for Black Oral Literature." *Negro American Literature Forum,* IV (1970), 127–132.

Landeck, Beatrice. *Echoes of Africa in Folk Songs of the Americas.* 2nd ed. New York, 1969.

Lester, Julius. *Black Folktales.* New York, 1969.

Lomax, Alan. "'Sinful' Songs of the Southern Negro." *Southwest Review,* XIX (1934), 105–131.

Lovell, John. "Reflections on the Origins of the Negro Spiritual." *Negro American Literature Forum,* III (1969), 91–97.

McGhee, Nancy B. "The Folk Sermon: A Facet of the Black Literary Heritage." *CLA Journal,* XIII (1969), 57–61.

Odum, Howard W. and Guy B. Johnson. *The Negro and His Songs.* Chapel Hill, N.C., 1925.

————. *Negro Workaday Songs.* Chapel Hill, N.C., 1926.

Oliver, Paul. *Blues Fell This Morning: The Meaning of the Blues.* New York, 1960.

————. *Conversation with the Blues.* New York, 1965.

Oster, Harry. "The Afro-American Folktale in Memphis: Theme and Function." *Negro American Literature Forum,* III (1969), 83–87.

————. "Negro Humor: John and Old Marster." *Journal of the Folklore Institute,* V (1968), 42–57.

Parsons, Elsie W., ed. *Folk-Lore of the Sea Islands, South Carolina.* Cambridge, Mass., 1923.

Pendleton, L. "Notes on Negro Folklore and Witchcraft in the South." *Journal of American Folklore,* III (1890), 201–207.

Puckett, Newbell Niles. *Folk Beliefs of the Southern Negro.* Chapel Hill, N.C., 1926.

Russell, Tony. *Blacks, Whites, and Blues.* New York, 1970.

Scarborough, Dorothy. *On the Trail of Negro Folk Songs.* Cambridge, Mass., 1925.

Scarborough, W. W. "Negro Folklore and Dialect." *Arena*, XVII (1897), 186–192.

Sterling, Philip. *Laughing on the Outside*. New York, 1966.

Talley, T. W. *Negro Folk Rhymes, Wise and Otherwise*. New York, 1922.

Thurman, Howard. *Deep River*. New York, 1955.

Twining, Mary Arnold. "An Anthropological Look at Afro-American Folk Narrative." *CLA Journal*, XIV (1970), 57–61.

Walton, David A. "Joel Chandler Harris as Folklorist: A Reassessment." *Kentucky Folklore Quarterly*, XI (1966), 21–26.

White, Newman I. *American Negro Folk-Songs*. Cambridge, Mass., 1928.

Work, John W. "Negro Folk Song." *Opportunity*, I (1923), 292–294.

GENERAL BACKGROUND

Adler, Mortimer J., Charles Van Doren, and George Ducas. *The Negro in American History*. 3 vols. New York, 1969.

Aptheker, Herbert. *Negro Slave Revolts in the United States, 1526–1860*. New York, 1939.

———, ed. *A Documentary History of the Negro People in the United States*. 2 vols. New York, 1951.

Bailey, Harry A., Jr., ed. *Negro Politics in America*. Columbus, Ohio, 1967.

Baker, Ray S. *Following the Color Line: American Negro Citizenship in the Progressive Era*. New York, 1908.

Barbour, Floyd, ed. *The Black Power Revolt*. Boston, 1968.

Bardolph, Richard. *The Civil Rights Record: Black Americans and the Law, 1849–1970*. New York, 1970.

———. *The Negro Vanguard*. New York, 1959.

Bell, Howard H. *A Survey of the Negro Convention Movement, 1830–1861*. New York, 1969.

———, ed. *Minutes of the Proceedings of the National Negro Conventions, 1830–1864*. New York, 1969.

Bennett, Lerone, Jr. *Before the Mayflower: A History of the Negro 1619–1962*. Chicago, 1962.

———. *The Negro Mood*. Chicago, 1965.

———. *Pioneers in Protest*. Chicago, 1968.

Bergman, Peter M. *The Chronological History of the Negro in America*. New York, 1969.

Bond, Horace Mann. *The Education of the Negro in the American Social Order*. New York, 1934.

Bontemps, Arna and Jack Conroy. *Any Place But Here*. New York, 1966.

Botkin, B. A., ed. *Lay My Burden Down: A Folk History of Slavery*. Chicago, 1945.

Bracey, John H., Jr., August Meier, and Elliott Rudwick, eds. *Black Nationalism in America*. Indianapolis, 1970.

Brawley, Benjamin. *Negro Builders and Heroes*. Chapel Hill, N.C., 1937.

———. *A Social History of the American Negro*. New York, 1921.

Brisbane, Robert H. *The Black Vanguard: Origins of the Negro Social Revolution 1900–1960*. Valley Forge, Pa., 1970.

Broderick, Francis and August Meier, eds. *Negro Protest Thought in the Twentieth Century*. Indianapolis, 1965.

Broom, Leonard and Norval D. Glenn. *Transformation of the Negro American*. New York, 1965.

Brotz, Howard, ed. *Negro Social and Political Thought, 1850–1920*. New York, 1966.

Brown, Claude. *Manchild in the Promised Land*. New York, 1965.

Buckmaster, Henrietta. *Let My People Go*. New York, 1941.

Bullock, Henry A. *A History of Negro Education in the South from 1619 to the Present*. Cambridge, Mass., 1968.

Butcher, Margaret. *The Negro in American Culture*. New York, 1956.

Carmichael, Stokely and Charles V. Hamilton. *Black Power: The Politics of Liberation*. New York, 1967.

Cash, W. J. *The Mind of the South*. New York, 1941.

Clark, Kenneth. *Dark Ghetto: Dilemmas of Social Power*. New York, 1965.

Cruse, Harold. *The Crisis of the Negro Intellectual*. New York, 1967.

———. *Rebellion or Revolution*. New York, 1968.

Dann, Martin E., ed. *The Black Press 1827–1890: The Quest for National Identity*. New York, 1971.

Davidson, Basil. *Africa in History*. New York, 1969.

Davie, Maurice. *Negroes in American Society*. New York, 1949.

Davis, Allison W. and John Dollard. *Children of Bondage*. Washington, D.C., 1940.

Davis, Allison W., Burleigh B. Gardner, and Mary R. Gardner. *Deep South: A Social Anthropological Study of Caste and Class*. Chicago, 1941.

Davis, John A., ed. *Africa Seen by American Negroes*. Paris, 1958.

Detweiler, Frederick G. *The Negro Press in the United States*. Chicago, 1922.

Dover, Cedric. *American Negro Art*. 3rd ed. New York, 1965.

Drake, St. Clair and Horace R. Cayton. *Black Metropolis; A Study of Negro Life in a Northern City*. Rev. ed. 2 vols. New York, 1962.

Drimmer, Melvin, ed. *Black History: A Reappraisal*. Garden City, N.Y., 1969.

Du Bois, W. E. B. *Black Folk: Then and Now*. New York, 1939.

———. *Black Reconstruction in America*. New York, 1935.

———. *The Gift of Black Folk: Negroes in the Making of America*. Boston, 1924.

———. *The Souls of Black Folk*. Chicago, 1903.

Dumond, Dwight Lowell. *Antislavery: The Crusade for Freedom in America*. Ann Arbor, Mich., 1961.

Elkins, Stanley M. *Slavery: A Problem in American Institutional and Intellectual Life*. 2nd ed. Chicago, 1968.

Embree, Edwin R. *13 Against the Odds*. New York, 1944.

Essien-Udom, Essien U. *Black Nationalism: A Search for an Identity in America*. Chicago, 1962.

Fabre, Michel. *Les Noirs américains*. Paris, 1967.

Fauset, Arthur Huff. *Black Gods of the Metropolis*. Philadelphia, 1944.

Fishel, Leslie H. and Benjamin Quarles, eds. *The Black American: A Documentary History*. Glenview, Ill., 1970.

Franklin, John Hope. *From Slavery to Freedom: A History of Negro Americans*. 3rd ed. New York, 1967.

———. *Reconstruction After the Civil War*. Chicago, 1961.

Frazier, E. Franklin. *Black Bourgeoisie*. Glencoe, Ill., 1957.

———. *The Negro Church in America*. New York, 1963.

———. *The Negro Family in the United States*. Rev. ed. Chicago, 1966.

———. *The Negro in the United States*. Rev. ed. New York, 1957.

Gayle, Addison, Jr. *The Black Situation*. New York, 1970.

Goldston, Robert. *The Negro Revolution*. New York, 1968.

Gossett, Thomas F. *Race: The History of an Idea in America*. Dallas, Texas, 1963.

Grant, Joanne, ed. *Black Protest: History, Documents, and Analyses 1619 to the Present*. New York, 1968.

Greene, Lorenzo J. *The Negro in Colonial New England, 1620–1776*. New York, 1942.

Grier, William H. and Price M. Cobbs. *Black Rage*. New York, 1968.

Hansberry, Lorraine. *The Movement: Documentary of a Struggle for Equality*. New York, 1964.

Hare, Nathan. *The Black Anglo-Saxons*. New York, 1965.

Hernton, Calvin C. *Sex and Racism in America*. Garden City, N.Y., 1965.

———. *White Papers for White Americans*. Garden City, N.Y., 1967.

Herskovits, Melville J. *The Myth of the Negro Past*. New York, 1941.

Higginson, Thomas Wentworth. *Army Life in a Black Regiment*. Boston, 1870.

Hughes, Langston. *Fight for Freedom: The Story of the NAACP*. New York, 1962.

——— and Milton Meltzer. *A Pictorial History of the Negro in America*. Rev. ed. New York, 1963.

Isaacs, Harold. *The New World of Negro Americans*. New York, 1963.

Johnson, Charles S. *The Negro in American Civilization*. New York, 1930.

———. *The Rise of the Negro Magazine*. Yellow Springs, Ohio, 1948.

Johnson, James Weldon. *Black Manhattan*. New York, 1930.

Jones, LeRoi (Imamu Amiri Baraka). *Blues People: Negro Music in White America*. New York, 1963.

Jordan, Winthrop D. *White Over Black: American Attitudes Toward the Negro, 1550–1812*. Chapel Hill, N.C., 1968.

Katz, William L., ed. *Eyewitness: The Negro in American History*. New York, 1967.

Killens, John Oliver. *Black Man's Burden*. New York, 1965.

Lester, Julius. *Look Out, Whitey! Black Power's Gon' Get Your Mama!* New York, 1968.

———. *Revolutionary Notes*. New York, 1969.

Lincoln, C. Eric. *The Black Muslims in America*. Boston, 1961.

Litwack, Leon F. *North of Slavery: The Negro in the Free States, 1790–1860*. Chicago, 1961.

Locke, Alain. *Negro Art: Past and Present*. Washington, D.C., 1936.

———. *The Negro in Art: A Pictorial Record of the Negro Artist and of the Negro Theme in Art*. Washington, D.C., 1940.

———. *The Negro and His Music*. Washington, D.C., 1936.

———, ed. *The New Negro: An Interpretation*. New York, 1925.

Logan, Rayford. *The Betrayal of the Negro*. New York, 1965.

———. *The Negro in the United States: A Brief Review*. Princeton, N.J., 1957.

Lomax, Louis E. *The Negro Revolt*. New York, 1962.

Marine, Gene. *The Black Panthers*. New York, 1969.

Marx, Gary T. *Protest and Prejudice: A Study of Belief in the Black Community*. New York, 1968.

Mays, Benjamin. *The Negro's God as Reflected in His Literature*. Boston, 1938.

McPherson, James M. *The Negro's Civil War: How American Negroes Felt and Acted During the War for the Union*. New York, 1965.

———. *The Struggle for Equality: Abolitionists and the Negro in the Civil War and Reconstruction*. Princeton, N.J., 1964.

Meier, August. *Negro Thought in America, 1880–1915: Racial Ideologies in the Age of Booker T. Washington*. Ann Arbor, Mich., 1963.

—— and Elliott M. Rudwick. *From Plantation to Ghetto: An Interpretive History of American Negroes.* New York, 1966.

Meltzer, Milton, ed. *In Their Own Words: A History of the American Negro.* 3 vols. New York, 1964–1967.

Moon, Bucklin, ed. *Primer for White Folks.* Garden City, N.Y., 1945.

Murray, Albert. *The Omni-Americans: New Perspectives on Black Experience and American Culture.* New York, 1970.

Muse, Benjamin. *The American Negro Revolution: From Non-Violence to Black Power, 1963–1967.* Bloomington, Ind., 1969.

Myrdal, Gunnar. *An American Dilemma.* Rev. ed. 2 vols. New York, 1963.

Nichols, Charles H., Jr. *Many Thousand Gone: The Ex-Slaves' Account of Their Bondage and Freedom.* Leiden, 1963.

Osofsky, Gilbert. *Harlem: The Making of a Ghetto: Negro New York, 1890–1930.* New York, 1966.

——, ed. *The Burden of Race: A Documentary History of Negro–White Relations in America.* New York, 1967.

Ottley, Roi. '*New World A'Coming*': *Inside Black America.* Boston, 1943.

Parsons, Talcott and Kenneth Clark, eds. *The Negro American.* Boston, 1966.

Patterson, Lindsay, ed. *The Negro in Music and Art.* 2nd ed. New York, 1969.

Pettigrew, Thomas. *A Profile of the Negro American.* Princeton, N.J., 1964.

Powdermaker, Hortense. *After Freedom: A Cultural Study in the Deep South.* New York, 1939.

Quarles, Benjamin. *Black Abolitionists.* New York, 1969.

——. *The Negro in the American Revolution.* Chapel Hill, N.C., 1961.

——. *The Negro in the Civil War.* Boston, 1953.

——. *The Negro in the Making of America.* New York, 1964.

Record, Wilson. *The Negro and the Communist Party.* Chapel Hill, N.C., 1951.

Report of the National Advisory Commission on Civil Disorders. New York, 1968.

Richardson, Ben. *Great American Negroes.* New York, 1956.

Robinson, Armstead L., Craig C. Foster, and Donald H. Ogilvie, eds. *Black Studies in the University: A Symposium.* New Haven, Conn., 1969.

Robinson, Wilhelmina S. *Historical Negro Biographies.* New York, 1969.

Rogers, Joel A. *The World's Great Men of Color, 3000 B.C. to 1946 A.D.* 2 vols. New York, 1946–1947.

Silberman, Charles E. *Crisis in Black and White.* New York, 1964.

Smith, Arthur L. *Rhetoric of Black Revolution.* Boston, 1970.

Smith, Lillian. *Killers of the Dream.* New York, 1949.

Smith, William Gardner. *Return to Black America.* Englewood Cliffs, N.J., 1970.

Spear, Allan H. *Black Chicago: The Making of a Negro Ghetto, 1890–1920.* Chicago, 1967.

Stampp, Kenneth M. *The Peculiar Institution: Slavery in the Ante-Bellum South.* New York, 1956.

Stone, Chuck. *Black Political Power in America.* Indianapolis, 1968.

Szwed, John, ed. *Black America.* New York, 1970.

Thorpe, Earl E. *The Mind of the Negro: An Intellectual History of Afro-Americans.* Baton Rouge, La., 1961.

Thurman, Howard. *Deep River.* New York, 1955.

Warren, Robert Penn. *Who Speaks for the Negro?* New York, 1965.

Washington, Booker T. *The Story of the Negro.* 2 vols. New York, 1909.

White, Walter. *Rope and Faggot: A Biography of Judge Lynch.* New York, 1929.

Williams, John A. *This Is My Country Too.* New York, 1965.

Woodson, Carter G. *The History of the Negro Church.* Washington, D.C., 1921.

——. *The Negro Professional Man and the Community.* Washington, D.C., 1934.

——, ed. *The Mind of the Negro as Reflected in Letters Written During the Crisis, 1800–1860.* Washington, D.C., 1926.

——, ed. *Negro Orators and Their Orations.* Washington, D.C., 1925.

—— and Charles H. Wesley. *The Negro in Our History.* 10th ed. Washington, D.C., 1962.

Woodward, C. Vann. *The Strange Career of Jim Crow.* Rev. ed. New York, 1966.

Wright, Richard. *12 Million Black Voices: A Folk History of the Negro in the United States.* New York, 1941.

Zinn, Howard. *SNCC: The New Abolitionists.* Boston, 1964.

Index of Authors and Titles